Oracle9*i*AS™
Portal Bible

Oracle9*i*AS™
Portal Bible

Rick Greenwald and Jim Milbery

Hungry Minds™

Best-Selling Books • Digital Downloads • e-Books • Answer Networks • e-Newsletters • Branded Web Sites • e-Learning

New York, NY ♦ Cleveland, OH ♦ Indianapolis, IN

Oracle9i AS™ Portal Bible

Published by
Hungry Minds, Inc.
909 Third Avenue
New York, NY 10022
www.hungryminds.com

Library of Congress Control Number: 2001090705

ISBN: 0-7645-4749-6

Printed in the United States of America

10 9 8 7 6 5 4 3 2 1

1B/RT/QW/QR/IN

Distributed in the United States by Hungry Minds, Inc.

Distributed by CDG Books Canada Inc. for Canada; by Transworld Publishers Limited in the United Kingdom; by IDG Norge Books for Norway; by IDG Sweden Books for Sweden; by IDG Books Australia Publishing Corporation Pty. Ltd. for Australia and New Zealand; by TransQuest Publishers Pte Ltd. for Singapore, Malaysia, Thailand, Indonesia, and Hong Kong; by Gotop Information Inc. for Taiwan; by ICG Muse, Inc. for Japan; by Intersoft for South Africa; by Eyrolles for France; by International Thomson Publishing for Germany, Austria, and Switzerland; by Distribuidora Cuspide for Argentina; by LR International for Brazil; by Galileo Libros for Chile; by Ediciones ZETA S.C.R. Ltda. for Peru; by WS Computer Publishing Corporation, Inc., for the Philippines; by Contemporanea de Ediciones for Venezuela; by Express Computer Distributors for the Caribbean and West Indies; by Micronesia Media Distributor, Inc. for Micronesia; by Chips Computadoras S.A. de C.V. for Mexico; by Editorial Norma de Panama S.A. for Panama; by American Bookshops for Finland.

For general information on Hungry Minds' products and services please contact our Customer Care department within the U.S. at 800-762-2974, outside the U.S. at 317-572-3993 or fax 317-572-4002.

For sales inquiries and reseller information, including discounts, premium and bulk quantity sales, and foreign-language translations, please contact our Customer Care department at 800-434-3422, fax 317-572-4002 or write to Hungry Minds, Inc., Attn: Customer Care Department, 10475 Crosspoint Boulevard, Indianapolis, IN 46256.

For information on licensing foreign or domestic rights, please contact our Sub-Rights Customer Care department at 212-884-5000.

For information on using Hungry Minds' products and services in the classroom or for ordering examination copies, please contact our Educational Sales department at 800-434-2086 or fax 317-572-4005.

For press review copies, author interviews, or other publicity information, please contact our Public Relations department at 317-572-3168 or fax 317-572-4168.

For authorization to photocopy items for corporate, personal, or educational use, please contact Copyright Clearance Center, 222 Rosewood Drive, Danvers, MA 01923, or fax 978-750-4470.

Credits

Acquisitions Editor
Grace Buechlein

Project Editor
Sharon Nash

Development Editor
Kezia Endsley

Technical Editor
Todd E. Vender

Copy Editor
Maarten Reilingh

Project Coordinator
Regina Snyder

Graphics and Production Specialists
Sean Decker
Laurie Stevens
Brian Torwelle

Quality Control Technician
Laura Albert
John Greenough

Senior Permissions Editor
Carmen Krikorian

Media Development Specialist
Travis Silvers

Media Development Coordinator
Marisa Pearman

Book Designer
Michelle Logan

Illustrators
Karl Brandt
John Greenough
Kelly Hardesty
Joyce Haughey
Clint Lahnen
Gabriele McCann
Ron Terry

Proofreading and Indexing
Laura Albert
John Greenough
Susan Moritz
TECHBOOKS Production Services

Cover Image
Kate Shaw

About the Authors

Rick Greenwald is a marketing manager in the server technologies group at Oracle Corporation. He has been active in the field of data processing for over 15 years, including stints with Data General, Cognos, and Gupta. He is the author of six other books on technology and dozens of articles and analyst pieces.

Jim Milbery has been involved in the software business for over 16 years and has worked for a variety of high-tech companies, including Digital Equipment Corporation, Ingres, Uniface, and Revere. He is currently a partner with the technology consulting firm Kuromaku Partners LLC, where he provides strategic consulting to a diverse group of clients. Jim lives in Easton, Pennsylvania, with his lovely wife, Renate, and two spoiled cats.

Jim Milbery — This book is dedicated to my father, Ken Milbery. Here's to you, Dad; no son loves his father more than I love you.

Rick Greenwald — For the three women in my life: LuAnn, Elinor, and Josephine Greenwald. You are the breath of love in my life.

Preface

This book is essentially the second edition of *Oracle WebDB Bible*. The product formerly known as WebDB is called Oracle9*i*AS Portal in its current incarnation, which indicates that it is both bundled with the Oracle9*i* Application Server product and that the focus of the product has been modified to encompass the fast-growing world of information portals. Consequently, the organization of this book has been enhanced and modified to fit in with the new product direction.

How This Book Is Organized

As with the previous version, the first section of this book is an introduction to Oracle9*i*AS Portal — what it is, how to install it, and the basics of the development environment you will be using.

The second section of the book jumps right into the topic of portals. Chapter 6 introduces the concept of portals, portlets, and how Oracle9*i*AS Portal handles these entities. Chapter 7 walks you through the creation of a portal page.

Part III of the book covers the creation of a variety of components. These are the same components that were supported in WebDB — reports, forms, charts, calendars, hierarchies, and dynamic HTML pages. Each of these components retains the functionality it had in WebDB, but each of them also has been enhanced in the new version of the product.

Part IV of the book covers some of the topics you will need to understand to create complete applications with Oracle9*i*AS Portal. For instance, you will almost inevitably be using lists-of-values to help your users properly utilize components, and Oracle9*i*AS Portal menus are essential for navigating through an application. Validation, the use of templates, and linking are also integral to creating complete applications, and these areas have also been changed and enhanced from their counterparts in WebDB. Finally, there will be times when you will need to use PL/SQL procedures to extend the functionality of your Oracle9*i*AS Portal components, which is also covered in this section.

In Oracle9*i*AS Portal, as in WebDB, you have the ability to create Content Areas, which were referred to as *sites* in WebDB. Part V of the book explores this area of the product, including how to deploy your content collections.

Part VI targets the administration of the Oracle9*i*AS Portal environment. Oracle9*i*AS Portal, even more than WebDB, is aimed at the enterprise. In order to operate in an enterprise environment, Oracle9*i*AS Portal has to include administration and monitoring tools, as well as a robust security model. The security model, in particular, has been dramatically changed since WebDB, so there is a great deal of new material in this section.

The last section of this book, Part VII, delves into some of the more advanced topics surrounding Oracle9*i*AS Portal. First and foremost of these topics is the ability to create your own portlets. Chapter 28 gives you a high-level view of the APIs and processes involved in creating your own custom portlets. Chapter 29 covers a variety of techniques that we felt were slightly outside of the scope of the other chapters in the book, but still of great interest to you, the potential Oracle9*i*AS Portal developer.

Contacting the Author(s)

Jim Milbery can be reached at Kuromaku Partners (`http://www.kuromaku.com`), located in Easton, Pennsylvania, or through his e-mail address at `jmilbery@kuromaku.com`.

Rick Greenwald can be reached at `greenie@interaccess.com`.

Acknowledgments

The authors would like to thank all the people at Oracle who helped them in the creation of this book, including Rob Giljum and the entire development team. In particular, we would like to thank Steven Leung, Sue Vickers, and Mohana Narayan, who provided invaluable assistance in the late-going stages. Most important, we would like to bow in reverence in the general direction of the inestimable Todd D. Vender, who provided timely advice and insight into the Oracle9iAS Portal development process.

Contents at a Glance

Preface ix
Acknowledgments xi

Part I: Introduction 1
Chapter 1: Introducing Oracle9iAS Portal 3
Chapter 2: Installing and Configuring Oracle9iAS Portal 17
Chapter 3: Introducing the Oracle9iAS Portal Environment 53
Chapter 4: Using the Navigator 79
Chapter 5: Browsing the Database 93

Part II: Building a Portal 129
Chapter 6: Introducing Portals and Portlets 131
Chapter 7: Building a Portal Page 143

Part III: Oracle9iAS Portal Components 171
Chapter 8: Building Oracle9iAS Portal Reports 173
Chapter 9: Advanced Reporting Techniques 217
Chapter 10: Building Oracle9iAS Portal Forms 251
Chapter 11: Building Forms — Part II 281
Chapter 12: Building Charts 301
Chapter 13: Building Oracle9iAS Portal Calendars 329
Chapter 14: Working with Hierarchies 361
Chapter 15: Working with HTML 379

Part IV: Building Oracle9iAS Portal Applications 409
Chapter 16: Working with Lists-of-Values (LOVs) 411
Chapter 17: Creating Oracle9iAS Portal Menus 445
Chapter 18: Building Consistency in Oracle9iAS Portal
    Web Sites and Applications 477
Chapter 19: Data Validation with Oracle9iAS Portal 513
Chapter 20: Using Links to Connect Oracle9iAS Portal Objects 559
Chapter 21: Integrating PL/SQL Logic 585

Part V: Building Oracle9*i*AS Portal Sites 615

Chapter 22: Using Content Areas 617
Chapter 23: Deploying Oracle9*i*AS Portal Sites 657
Chapter 24: Content Areas — Part II 689

Part VI: Administering Oracle9*i*AS Portal 727

Chapter 25: Administering Oracle9*i*AS Portal Components 729
Chapter 26: Oracle9*i*AS Portal Security 757
Chapter 27: Monitoring Oracle9*i*AS Portal Performance 795

Part VII: Advanced Techniques 831

Chapter 28: Creating Your Own Portlet and Provider 833
Chapter 29: Advanced Tips and Techniques 865

Appendix A: What's On the CD-ROM 897
Appendix B: Loading Portal Examples 907

Index 915
End-User License Agreement 958
CD-ROM Installation Instructions 960

Contents

• •

Preface ix

Acknowledgments xi

Part I: Introduction   1

Chapter 1: Introducing Oracle9*i*AS Portal 3

Choosing Oracle9*i*AS Portal 3
Understanding How Oracle9*i*AS Portal Is Packaged 5
Taking a Look at Oracle9*i*AS Portal Functionality 5
Understanding Oracle9*i*AS Portal Components 7
Understanding Oracle9*i*AS Portal Organization 14
    Applications 14
    Content Areas 14
    Pages 15
Creating Oracle9*i*AS Portal Components 15

Chapter 2: Installing and Configuring Oracle9*i*AS Portal 17

Obtaining a Copy of Oracle9*i*AS Portal 17
Installing Oracle9*i*AS Portal 18
    Before you begin 18
    Oracle9*i*AS Portal installation — part 1 20
    Oracle9*i*AS Portal installation — part 2 22
    Configuring network protocols 26
    Configuring Oracle9*i*AS Portal 31
Performing Post-Installation Checks 38
Creating and Using the NetU Database 44
    Installing the NetU sample data 45
    Creating an application for NetU 47
    Creating a privileged developer account 50

Chapter 3: Introducing the Oracle9*i*AS Portal Environment 53

Introducing the Oracle9*i*AS Portal Environment 53
    The banner 58
    The help system 58
    The banner properties 61

The my Links portlet 61
The my Work portlet 68
The On The Web portlet 69
The Build Tab 73
A Few Words about Wizards 74

Chapter 4: Using the Navigator 79

Introducing the Navigator 79
The Pages Tab 82
The Content Areas Tab 84
The Applications Tab 85
Using the Find Mechanism 88

Chapter 5: Browsing the Database 93

Basic Database Object Definitions 93
The Database Objects Tab of the Navigator 95
Accessing database objects with the Database Navigator 100
Working with the Database Navigator 104
Browsing Data 110
Interacting with Data 116
Updating data 116
Inserting data 119
Issues with writing data 120
Creating Database Objects 121
Creating a table 122

Part II: Building a Portal   129

Chapter 6: Introducing Portals and Portlets 131

Understanding What a Portal Is 132
Understanding What a Portlet Is 133
Supporting Portlets in Oracle9iAS Portal 136
Portlet management 136
Framework services 136
Automatic portlet generation 137
Runtime Implementation of Portals 137
Caching in Oracle9iAS Portal 138
Types of caching 139
Levels of caching 140
Caching precautions 141

Chapter 7: Building a Portal Page 143

Creating a Portal Page 143
Page layout and style 145
Customizing the banner 148

Adding Portlets 150
    Working with regions 153
    Finishing the page 155
Customizing the Page 159
Making Changes as a Page User 161
    Working with the HTML portlet 161
    Creating a personal version of a page 164
    Promoting a page 167
    Designating a default page 169

Part III: Oracle9*i*AS Portal Components   171

Chapter 8: Building Oracle9*i*AS Portal Reports 173

Building a QBE Report 173
    Defining a report 174
    Shaping your report 179
    Allowing users to shape the report 190
    Using templates and adding text to your report 192
Running Your Report 196
Creating a Report with the Query Wizard 207
Editing Your Report 214

Chapter 9: Advanced Reporting Techniques 217

Creating a Report from a SQL Statement 217
Extending Reports with SQL 222
Using the Custom Layout for Reports 227
Adding Parameters to Your Report 230
Using Multiple Tables in a Report 234
    Multiple tables for reference information 235
    Multiple tables for master-detail relationships 240
Using Reports as Portlets 243
Calling Your Reports Directly 247
More Information on Reporting 248

Chapter 10: Building Oracle9*i*AS Portal Forms 251

Understanding Forms in Oracle9*i*AS Portal 251
    Form types supported by Oracle9*i*AS Portal 253
Creating Forms Based on Tables 253
    The first part of the table-based Form Wizard 254
    Oracle9*i*AS Portal form-creation concepts 256
    Form options 259
    Button options 261
    Data field options 262
    Finishing the form 271
    Running your form 272
Adding a Form to a Portal Page 278

Chapter 11: Building Forms — Part II 281

Forms Based on Stored Procedures 281
What are stored procedures? 281
Oracle9iAS Portal and stored procedures 282
The sample stored procedure 282
Building a form based on a stored procedure 283
Master-Detail Forms 288
Building a master-detail form 289
Formatting options 290
Running your master-detail form 294

Chapter 12: Building Charts 301

Creating Charts with the Query Wizard 301
Beginning the chart-building process 302
Describing the chart 303
Display options 306
Finishing the chart 310
Running your chart 311
Creating a more complex chart 313
Creating Charts Based on a SQL Statement 316
Charts based on multiple tables 316
Formatting values and limiting rows 323
Adding a Chart as a Portlet 325

Chapter 13: Building Oracle9iAS Portal Calendars 329

Understanding Oracle Dates 330
Date arithmetic 330
Date formatting 332
Building a Simple Calendar 334
Calendar query format 336
Formatting the display 338
Specifying customization entry form
display options for the calendar 342
Text options 344
Running the Calendar 347
Adding information to a calendar 350
Linking from the calendar cells 352
Adding parameters 357
Managing calendar objects 359

Chapter 14: Working with Hierarchies 361

Understanding Hierarchies 361
Building a Simple Hierarchy 363
Navigating Through a Hierarchy 370
Enhancing Your Hierarchy 374

Chapter 15: Working with HTML **379**

　Creating Dynamic Pages 380
　　Adding additional HTML code to the page 387
　　Adding additional SQL code 390
　　Mixing HTML and SQL 393
　　Adding Parameters to Dynamic Pages 395
　Using Frame Drivers 397
　　Connecting frame drivers to components with parameters 404

Part IV: Building Oracle9*i*AS Portal Applications   409

Chapter 16: Working with Lists-of-Values (LOVs) **411**

　Defining Lists-of-Values 411
　Update versus Query List-of-Values Objects 415
　　Building a simple, static LOV object 416
　　Testing your LOV object 420
　Deploying a Static LOV Object to Another Component 422
　Creating a Dynamic LOV Object 426
　Using the Dynamic LOV to Update Records 431
　Using Multiselect Lists-of-Values 434
　Advanced Techniques for LOV Objects 437
　　Derived columns 437
　　Dynamic query lists 438
　　Multivalue tables 438
　Lists-of-Values with BIND Variables 440

Chapter 17: Creating Oracle9*i*AS Portal Menus **445**

　Understanding Universal Resource Locators 445
　Using Simple Static Pages with Portal 448
　Adding a Virtual Path to the System 452
　Building a Portal Menu 455
　　Using the Portal Menu Builder Wizard 456
　　Editing the menu 460
　　Adding menu items to menus and submenus 462
　Linking Root Menus and
　　Advanced Menu Options 467
　　Advanced menu options 467
　Using Menus as Portlets 470

Chapter 18: Building Consistency in Oracle9*i*AS Portal Web Sites and Applications 477

Content Creation versus Standards Enforcement 478
Adding Color to Your Components 479
    Video display 479
    Video color settings 481
    Defining portal colors 483
Using Fonts 488
    Adding fonts to Portal 490
    Editing fonts 492
    Deploying colors and fonts 493
Adding Images 494
    Portal image types 495
    Adding images 498
Using Templates 501
    Adding a new template 502
    Using unstructured templates 506
Deploying Templates into Your Components 511

Chapter 19: Data Validation with Oracle9*i*AS Portal 513

Data Validation Concepts 514
Using JavaScript 516
    JavaScript compatibility 517
    JavaScript form elements 519
    JavaScript elements 521
    JavaScript dates 531
Creating JavaScript Validations with Portal 532
Testing the JavaScript 538
Building More Complicated Scripts 540
Attaching Validations to Forms 545
Using Other JavaScript Events 547
    Adding JavaScript code to templates 549
Performing Cross-Field Validations 551
Performing Cross-Record Validations 555
Performing Server-Side Validations 557

Chapter 20: Using Links to Connect Oracle9*i*AS Portal Objects . . . 559

Defining Links 559
Linking from an Existing Component 560
    Linking the STUDENTS report to the CLASSES report 562
    System parameters 566
Testing a Link 567
Making a Dynamic Link 570
Using Links to Update Data 576
Using Portal Parameter Arrays 580

Chapter 21: Integrating PL/SQL Logic 585

Using Oracle HTML Packages 585
    Printing and formatting 587
    Document structure 587
    Advanced document structure procedures 589
    Additional procedures 593
    Forms 593
Using Oracle9*i*AS's PL/SQL Web Toolkit 595
    Working with OWA_COOKIE 596
Integrating HTP and PL/SQL Web Toolkit Procedures with Portal 598
    Adding database access code to PL/SQL blocks 602
    Advanced PL/SQL code 605
Debugging and Advanced Concepts 611

Part V: Building Oracle9*i*AS Portal Sites　　615

Chapter 22: Using Content Areas 617

Understanding the Content Area Architecture 617
Creating a Content Area 619
Customizing Content Areas 621
    Folders 622
Manipulating Styles with the Style Manager 629
    Setting the banners 630
    Modifying items and backgrounds 632
    Changing the folder layout 634
    Modifying the Navigation Bar 640
Adding Categories and Perspectives 647
    Adding categories 648
    Adding perspectives 650
Modifying Content Area Properties 651
    Setting basic properties 652
    Modifying Content Area quota 652
    Setting folder properties 652
    Setting Content Area logo and database access descriptors 652

Chapter 23: Deploying Oracle9*i*AS Portal Sites 657

Understanding Portal Deployment Components and Its Architecture . . . 658
    Replacing the listener 662
Modifying Database Access Descriptors 663
Understanding Application Schemas 672
Deploying Portal Applications 675
    Schema definition 676
    Staging areas 677
    Server configuration 678
    Component deployment 679

Using Direct Access URLs 680
    Pages 681
    Folders 683
    Categories and perspectives 685
    Documents 685
    Components 687

Chapter 24: Content Areas – Part II 689
Reviewing the Content Area Concept 689
Applying and Securing Content Areas 691
    Creating user accounts for Content Areas 691
    Adding users and groups to folders 695
Adding Content to Your Site 697
Adding Content with Advanced Components to the Site 707
    Application components 707
    Application components with parameters 710
    Calling PL/SQL procedures 712
    Java code 715
Using Other Accounts to Add Content 718
Considering Some Advanced Topics 721
    Item management 722
    Advanced searching 723
    Content Areas on portal pages 724

Part VI: Administering Oracle9iAS Portal   727

Chapter 25: Administering Oracle9iAS Portal Components 729
Using Oracle9iAS Portal Version Control 729
Managing Components 732
    The Develop tab 732
    The Manage tab 737
    The Access tab 741
Managing Applications 743
Exporting and Importing Components and Applications 744
    Single sign-on accounts 745
    Security data for users and groups 746
    Pages 746
    Applications 747
    Shared components 748
    Data 749
    Content Areas 749
Administering the Oracle9iAS Portal Environment 750
    Services portlet 751
    Provider portlet 754
    Node portlet 755

Chapter 26: Oracle9*i*AS Portal Security 757

Understanding Oracle Database Security 757
Creating Privileged Accounts with Portal 760
    Testing the default developer account settings 766
    Modifying account privilege settings 770
Creating Groups and Group Privileges 775
    Creating groups and assigning privileges 777
Creating Privileges on Individual Objects 781
Setting Schema Privileges 785
Using the Login Server 790

Chapter 27: Monitoring Oracle9*i*AS Portal Performance 795

Using Portal Monitoring Tools 796
    Working with the Log registry 799
    Object monitoring tools 805
    Answers to common questions — customizing the interface 813
Monitoring Database Objects 818
    Database information section 820
    Database Memory Consumption, Transactions, and
        Locks section 821
    Database objects and storage tools 825
Changing the Activity Log Settings 827

Part VII: Advanced Techniques — 831

Chapter 28: Creating Your Own Portlet and Provider 833

Using the Portal Development Kit 833
    Categories of portlets 834
Using Portlet Services 835
Creating a Portlet with PL/SQL 836
    Exposing the Oracle9*i*AS Portal APIs 836
Creating a Database Provider with PL/SQL 842
Registering Your Provider 845
Using Your Portlet 847
Customizing Your Portlet 849
    Creating user customization stores 850
    Creating a customization form 851
    Enabling customization 852
Calling a Built-in Portlet 853
Creating a Web Provider and Portlet with Java Server Pages 855
Using the URL Portlet 861

Chapter 29: Advanced Tips and Techniques **865**

Learning Tips and Tricks in PL/SQL 865
  Passing generated default values to forms 866
  Generating primary keys using sequences and/or triggers 869
Working with Cookies 873
  Cookie source code 877
Adding Custom Attributes and Types 886

Appendix A: What's On the CD-ROM **897**

Appendix B: Loading Portal Examples **907**

Index 915

End-User License Agreement 958

CD-ROM Installation Instructions 960

Introduction

◆ ◆ ◆ ◆

In This Part

Chapter 1
Introducing
Oracle9*i*AS Portal

Chapter 2
Installing and
Configuring
Oracle9*i*AS Portal

Chapter 3
Introducing the
Oracle9*i*AS Portal
Environment

Chapter 4
Using the Navigator

Chapter 5
Browsing the
Database

◆ ◆ ◆ ◆

Introducing Oracle9*i*AS Portal

◆ ◆ ◆ ◆

In This Chapter

Deciding to Use
Oracle9*i*AS Portal

Understanding How
Oracle9*i*AS Portal Is
Packaged

Taking a Look at
Oracle9*i*AS Portal
Functionality

Understanding
Oracle9*i*AS Portal
Components

Understanding
Oracle9*i*AS Portal
Organization

Creating Oracle9*i*AS
Portal Components

◆ ◆ ◆ ◆

Welcome to the Oracle9*i*AS Portal Bible. As the name
implies, this book is intended to give you everything
you need to go out and build complete application systems,
Web sites, and portals with Oracle9*i*AS Portal. This chapter
serves as an introduction to Oracle9*i*AS Portal—both the product itself and the needs the product was designed to address.

Choosing Oracle9*i*AS Portal

When the first edition of this book was published, the product
that was the subject of this book was called WebDB. At that
time, making information available over the Web was still a
relatively new undertaking, so the authors felt a need to
explain the purpose of the entire product.

Now, two years later, some of these conditions have changed,
as has the product. The current release of the product formerly known as WebDB is called Oracle9*i*AS Portal, and,
although the functionality that made up WebDB is still a part of
the product, the offering has grown to encompass a new purpose. As its new name implies, Oracle9*i*AS Portal is designed
to help you design portals—gateways to information.

In the past two years, the role of the Internet in the delivery of
information has also changed. In the recent past, the Internet
was a source of mainly static and public information. Now, the
Internet is a window on a vast world of dynamic information.
Information from the Internet may be integrated with information that is only available from your own internal colleagues,
and some of what was formerly proprietary information is
now available on the Internet. In addition, Internet protocols
and the look and feel of Web pages have become the default
interface for many intranet, internal applications.

In the light of all of these changes, Oracle9iAS Portal has become a product that can help you manage and integrate information from many different sources into a single, coherent, customizable interface — such as the one you can see in Figure 1-1.

Note

The figures in this book show Oracle9iAS Portal as accessed through Microsoft Internet Explorer (IE), Version 5.5, at this time the most popular browser on the market. You can also access the Oracle9iAS Portal development environment or any Oracle9iAS Portal application with Netscape Navigator 4.0.8 and up.

These figures are shown with the full screen option of Internet Explorer, so you will be able to see as much screen real estate as possible. If there is a need to show you some of the other toolbars, such as the address bar, those figures show the standard view of the browser.

Figure 1-1 is more than just a typical portal — it is the portal that you will build as you work through the exercises in this book.

Before introducing the different areas of Oracle9iAS Portal functionality, the chapter will briefly visit the packaging of Oracle9iAS Portal.

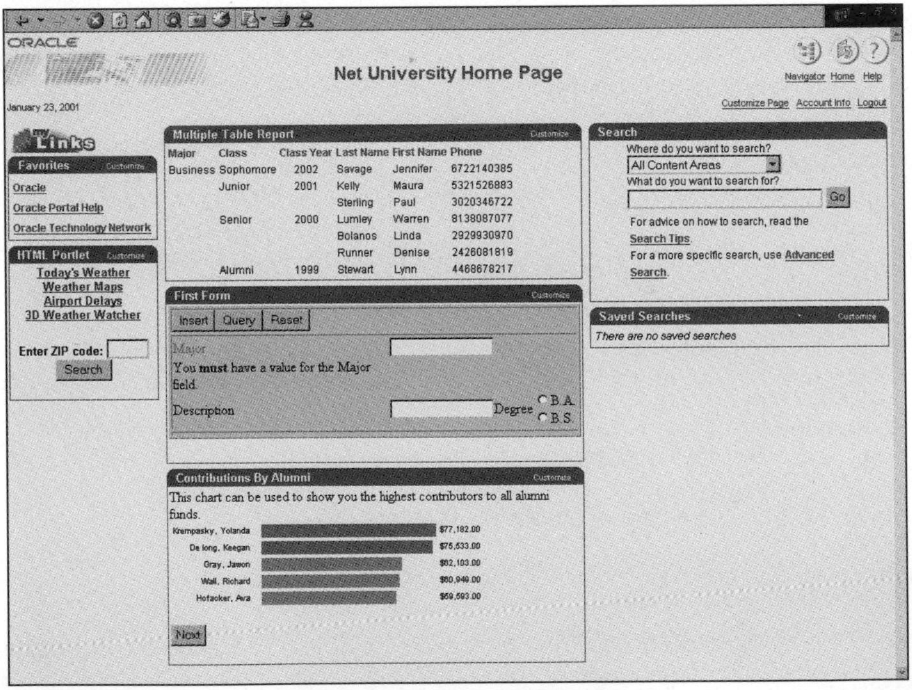

Figure 1-1: A typical report built with Oracle9iAS Portal

Understanding How Oracle9*i*AS Portal Is Packaged

When the product now known as Oracle9*i*AS Portal was first released as an official product under the name of WebDB, it was thought of as one of a number of tools that could be used with the Oracle database. The packaging and pricing for the product was a combination of two different Oracle approaches — one for the database and one for tools.

Unlike other Oracle tools, WebDB came with the Oracle8*i* database. And, like the database, most of the licensing costs associated with WebDB came from deployment licenses, rather than development licenses. With this model, a developer could create an application without spending a lot of money for licenses. However, when they deployed the application to their user community, they would have to pay for this privilege. However, WebDB was also included as one of the tools in the Oracle Developer Suite, comparable to other development tools, such as Oracle Developer or Oracle JDeveloper.

With the Oracle9*i*AS Portal release, the product is being bundled as part of a larger package called the Oracle9*i*AS Application Server. This package includes a Web server, based on the Apache server, and a number of other products, such as a Web cache and deployment servers for Oracle Developer and Reports.

Although Oracle9*i*AS Portal comes with the Oracle9*i* Application Server, you must still have an Oracle database to store the components and content generated and used by Oracle9*i*AS Portal application systems. In fact, Oracle9*i*AS Portal requires at least an Oracle8*i* database, specifically version 8.1.2 of the database, unlike WebDB, which could work on any Oracle database beyond Oracle7.3.4.

Packaging and licensing issues are beyond the scope of this book, and somewhat arbitrary as well. You should always refer to the vendor as the final authority on these issues. But the functionality of Oracle9*i*AS Portal is not so variable, so the remainder of the chapter is devoted to these topics.

Taking a Look at Oracle9*i*AS Portal Functionality

The functionality that Oracle9*i*AS Portal delivers can be broken into three basic categories: components, Content Areas, and pages.

✦ Components can interact with data stored in an Oracle database. Oracle9*i*AS Portal introduces the notion of an *application*, which is simply an organizational concept that allows you to group components together. The different types of components are described in the following section.

✦ Content Areas, formerly known as sites and folders, can access information in a variety of formats, both in an Oracle database and through standard HTML links.

✦ The use of pages is a new concept with Oracle9*i*AS Portal. A portal page can contain one or more portlets, which are regions of the real estate in a browser page. You will learn all about portlets and portal pages in Chapter 6.

Oracle9*i*AS Portal gives you the ability to define a set of global standards, such as templates and styles, which can be used by any of these categories of objects to give your work a uniform look and feel. You can also define objects such as lists-of-values (LOVs) that can be shared across many different applications.

The Oracle9*i*AS Portal development tool consists of a variety of different wizards that help you to create these types of objects. The Oracle9*i*AS Portal environment also includes a set of tools that help you to administer the Oracle9*i*AS Portal development and deployment environments. These tools help you to do things like create users, assign users to user groups or associate them with predefined roles, and designate security specifications on components, pages, and Content Areas.

New Feature   Oracle9*i*AS Portal has a new interface for exploring the contents of the Oracle9*i*AS Portal environment. This interface is referred to as a Navigator, as shown in Figure 1-2, and you can use a Navigator to view and interact with pages, applications and their components, Content Areas and the objects in your Oracle database. There is also a simplified interface to find any object within the Oracle9*i*AS Portal environment, and this find capability is also available to you as a part of your applications in the form of a portlet, which is explained further in Chapter 6.

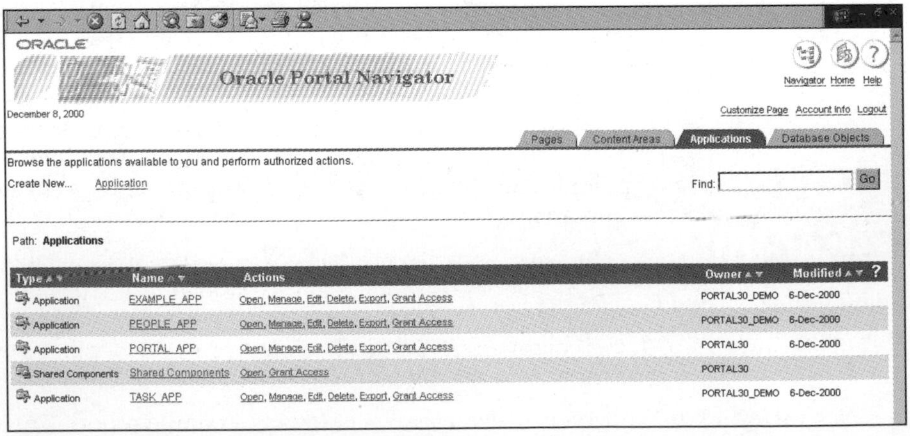

Figure 1-2: The Oracle9*i*AS Portal Navigator

Finally, Oracle9*i*AS Portal includes a wide range of monitoring tools, which allow you to check on the usage of your Oracle9*i*AS Portal application systems and the Oracle database that supports them. These monitoring tools have been enhanced since WebDB, and you will learn much more about them in Chapter 27.

As you read through this section, you may be wondering why there has been no mention of creating portals. After all, the concept of the portal page is so important that the name of the product has been changed to reflect it. The reason for this seeming omission is also one of the great strengths of Oracle9*i*AS Portal—you don't have to do anything to create the portlets that are used in a portal page. Later, in Chapter 28, this book will introduce you to the way that you can create a customized portlet by coding your own procedures, but you will not have to resort to this level of customization in the course of creating normal Oracle9*i*AS Portal application systems. All components and Content Areas can be exposed as portlets with a simple configuration option. And all portlets can be used to create portal pages. This new functionality is automatically included as part of the Oracle9*i*AS Portal environment. Chapter 6 will give you a detailed introduction to the concepts of portals and portlets, and in Chapter 7 you will build your own portal page.

This section has been intended to introduce the broad sweep of Oracle9*i*AS Portal capabilities. The rest of this book will serve to add flesh to these introductory bones.

Understanding Oracle9*i*AS Portal Components

Oracle9*i*AS Portal, like WebDB before it, allows you to create many types of components. These components, as mentioned in the previous section, give your users the ability to interact with the data in an Oracle database.

There are ten basic types of components you can create with Oracle9*i*AS Portal:

✦ **Reports:** A report is a dynamic HTML page created from a query on data in the Oracle database. A typical report is shown in Figure 1-3. You can create a report using a Query Wizard, which will create the underlying SQL needed to access the data for you, or by specifying your own SQL statement. Oracle9*i*AS Portal reports can generate output as HTML-based reports, ASCII preformatted data, and Excel spreadsheets.

Your reports can specify parameters to produce dynamic reports based on selection criteria. When you create a report with parameters, Oracle9*i*AS Portal automatically generates a customization entry form for you. There are also a number of default parameters that can be applied to every report, either by you or by your users, to control things such as sort order or break groups.

In Oracle9*i*AS Portal, you can also create a query-by-example report. This report is the same report that used to be one of the options for creating forms in WebDB. It allows a user to specify selection conditions for any of the columns in a table. Chapters 8 and 9 cover reports in much more detail.

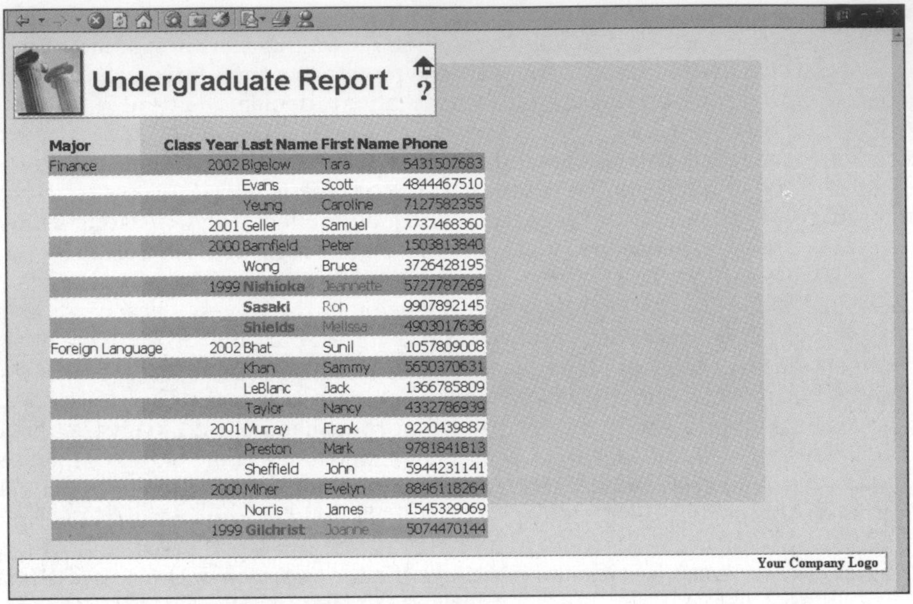

Figure 1-3: A typical Oracle9*i*AS Portal report

✦ **Forms:** You can create Oracle9*i*AS Portal forms based on tables, views, and stored procedures. A typical form is shown in Figure 1-4. You can create simple single-table forms or master-detail forms. You can format the fields in a form in many different ways, and there is a new form layout tool in Oracle9*i*AS Portal. You can add client-side validations and lists-of-values to the fields, which can be represented in a variety of ways, such as a list box or series of radio buttons in the form. Chapters 10 and 11 cover forms in much more detail.

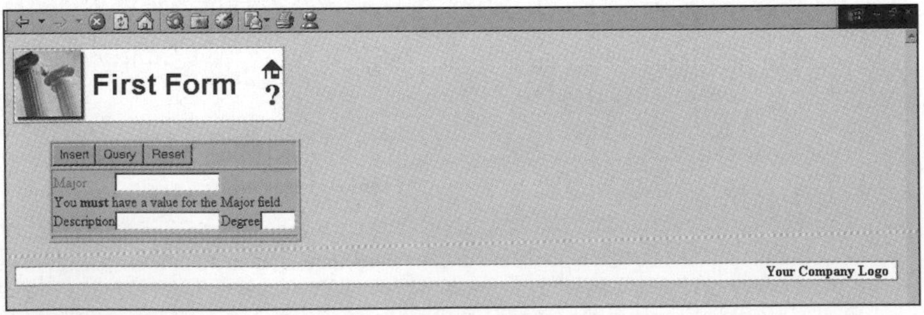

Figure 1-4: A typical Oracle9*i*AS Portal form

✦ **Charts:** Sometimes information can be more clearly understood if it is presented in the graphical format of a chart. A typical chart is shown in Figure 1-5. You can easily build charts based on data in your Oracle database with Oracle9*i*AS Portal. The charting capability of Oracle9*i*AS Portal is not intended to replace sophisticated data analysis tools, but rather to provide a quick and easy graphical display of results for database data. Oracle9*i*AS Portal's chart building capability is used throughout the systemOracle9*i*AS Portal. All of the graphs that are provided by the monitoring tools, which you will learn more about in Chapter 27, are built with this chart component. Chapter 12 covers charts in much more detail.

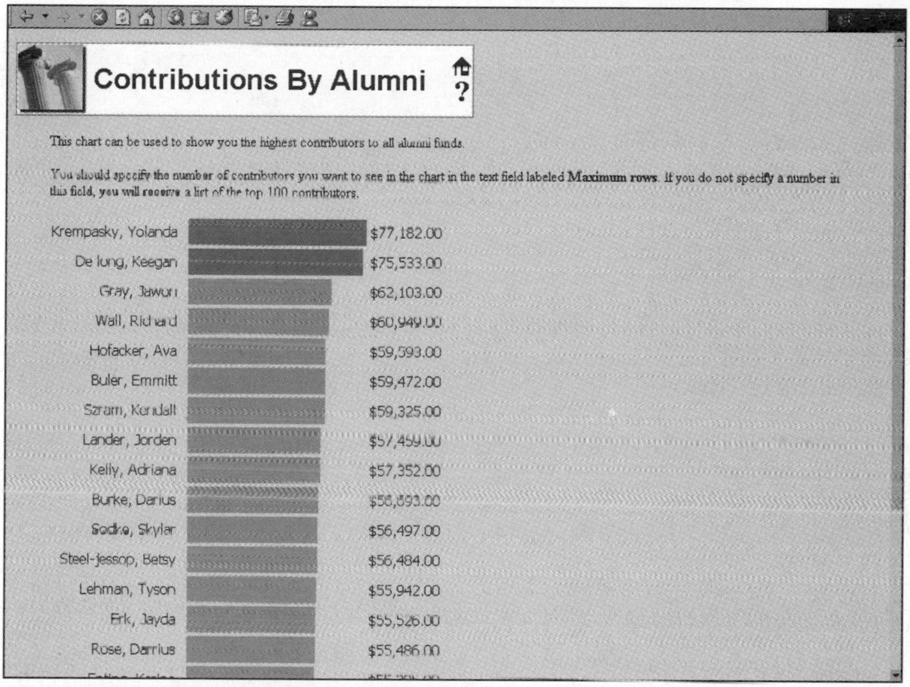

Figure 1-5: A typical Oracle9*i*AS Portal chart

✦ **Calendars:** Oracle9*i*AS Portal's calendar component is used for information that can be categorized by a calendar date. A typical calendar is shown in Figure 1-6. The calendar component is used to automatically create a calendar graphic with the relevant data inserted as links into the appropriate places in the calendar. Chapter 13 covers calendars in much more detail.

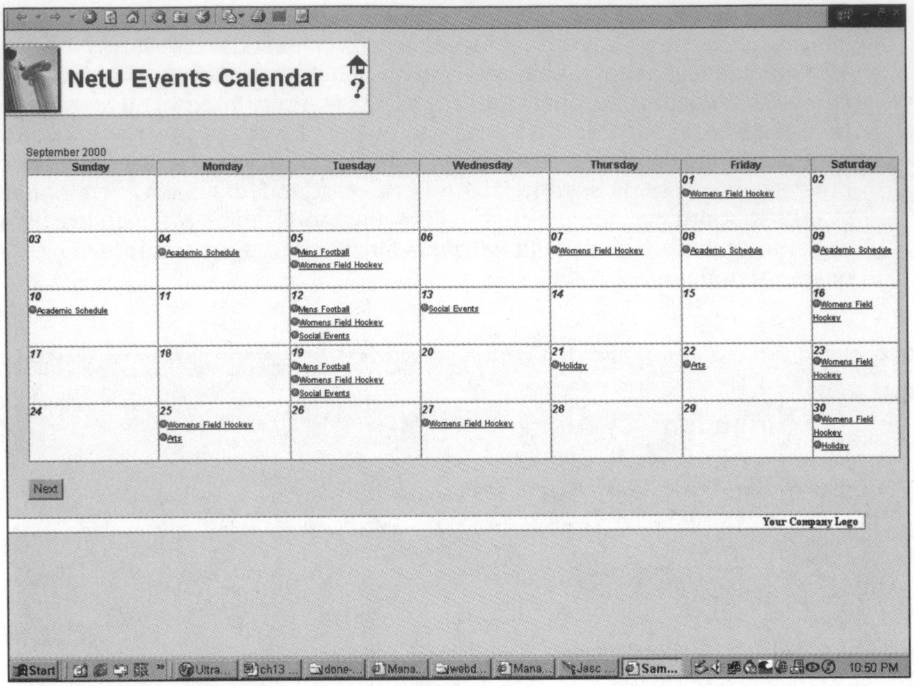

Figure 1-6: An Oracle9*i*AS Portal calendar

✦ **Hierarchies:** The Oracle9*i*AS Portal Hierarchy wizard automatically navigates through nested relationships in your database (like the classic employee/ manager hierarchy). A typical hierarchy is shown in Figure 1-7. The Hierarchy Builder makes it easy to create complex linked applications by joining different Oracle9*i*AS Portal components based on data values. Chapter 14 covers hierarchies in much more detail.

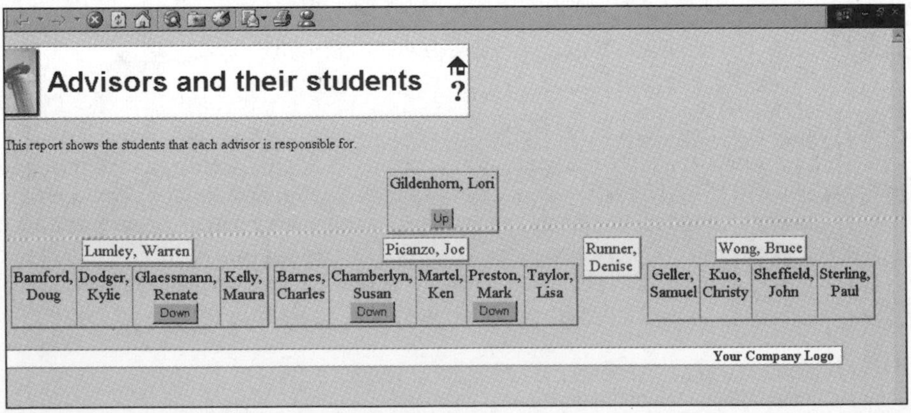

Figure 1-7: An Oracle9*i*AS Portal hierarchy

✦ **Dynamic pages:** You can create standard reports based on the data in the Oracle database with the report component as described previously. You can also create HTML pages that are more free-form and do not necessarily adhere to the more rigid structure of a report but still blend dynamic data from the Oracle database with standard HTML elements by creating dynamic page components. These dynamic HTML pages are stored in the Oracle database, just like other Oracle9*i*AS Portal components. Data is not always static. As shown in Figure 1-8, Oracle9*i*AS Portal allows you to create dynamic pages that display data as it changes. Chapter 15 covers dynamic pages in much more detail.

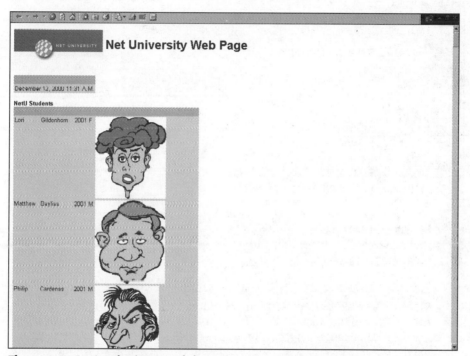

Figure 1-8: An Oracle9*i*AS Portal dynamic page component

✦ **Frame drivers:** One of the standard elements of HTML pages is the use of frames. Oracle9*i*AS Portal includes frame drivers that help you construct frames for your Oracle9*i*AS Portal site and also provides built-in frame management. A typical frame driver is shown in Figure 1-9. The frame drivers automatically trigger an action in one frame from a selection in the other frame. Frame drivers are ideal for creating simple master-detail forms, with rows from the master table driving the retrieval of rows from the detail table in the other part of the frame.

✦ However, one of the limitations of a portlet is that it does not allow the use of frames. Since the main focus of Oracle9iAS Portal is portlets and portal pages, the use of frame drivers is only included in the product for backward compatibility. Chapter 15 briefly covers frame drivers.

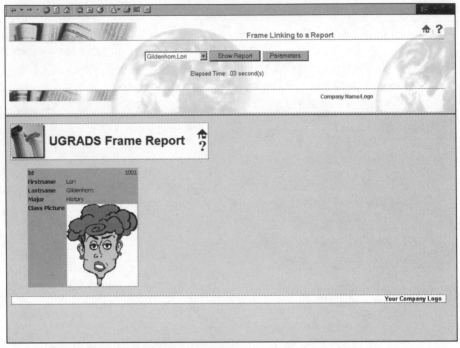

Figure 1-9: An Oracle9iAS Portal frame driver

✦ **Menus:** Oracle9iAS Portal's menu component lets you construct menus and hierarchies of menus that can access the objects you build with Oracle9iAS Portal's other tools. A typical menu is shown in Figure 1-10. Menus can also be used to create navigation paths for users. Oracle9iAS Portal's menus can link to its own components as well as to any other Web object that can be reached via a URL. Chapter 17 covers menus in much more detail.

Figure 1-10: An Oracle9*i*AS Portal menu component

✦ **Lists-of-values (LOVs):** A list-of-values is a component that makes it easy for you to limit the values used for data entry in a field. A typical list-of-values, in use, is shown in Figure 1-11. An Oracle9*i*AS Portal list-of-values is not a standard component, in that it cannot stand on its own like the components described previously, but you create lists-of-values using wizards in a manner very similar to creating the other Oracle9*i*AS Portal components. The list-of-values can be implemented in several user interface styles, such as a drop-down combo box or a pop-up window with a list-of-values. Chapter 16 covers lists-of-values in much more detail.

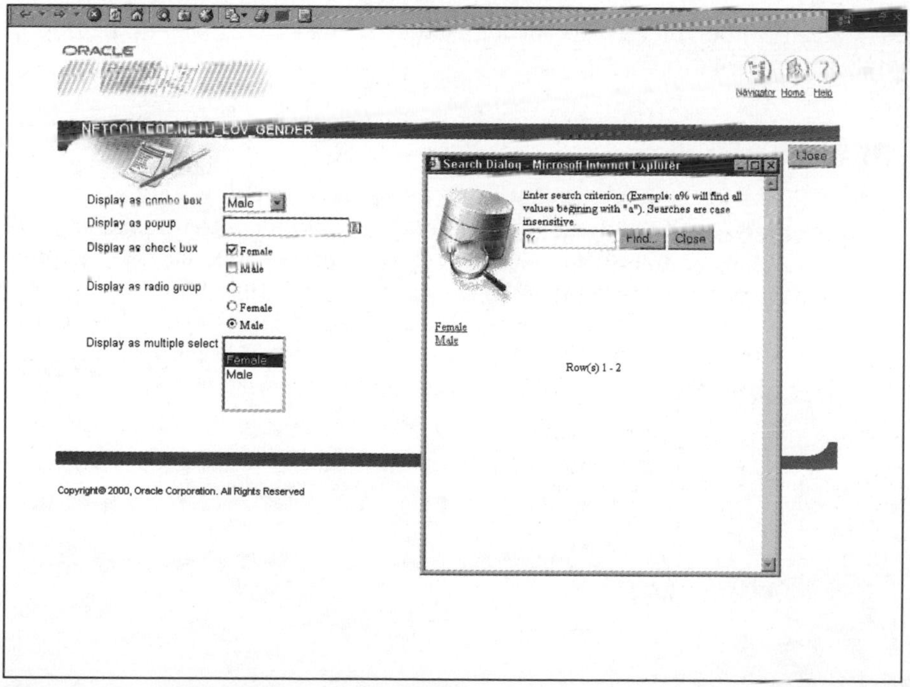

Figure 1-11: A list-of-values, hard at work

✦ **Links:** A link, as its name implies, is used to link different components together. Like a list-of-values, a link is a shared component that cannot stand on its own. A link can be used by different components because it links a value in one component to another target component. Chapter 20 covers links in much more detail.

You should note that each of the example components shown accompanying the previous descriptions is a component that you will actually be building in the course of the rest of this book.

Understanding Oracle9*i*AS Portal Organization

There are three organizational units that you can use in Oracle9*i*AS Portal — the application, the Content Area, and the page.

Applications

The application is a logical organizational unit for components. Each component you create belongs to one, and only one, application. An application is associated with a single schema inside of an Oracle database but unlike with WebDB, a single schema can contain more than one application. You can back up and restore individual applications.

Content Areas

The Content Area is a logical organization of related content. A Content Area can contain content items or folders, which can also contain content items or additional subfolders. A Content Area also provides a specific look and feel, as shown in Figure 1-12.

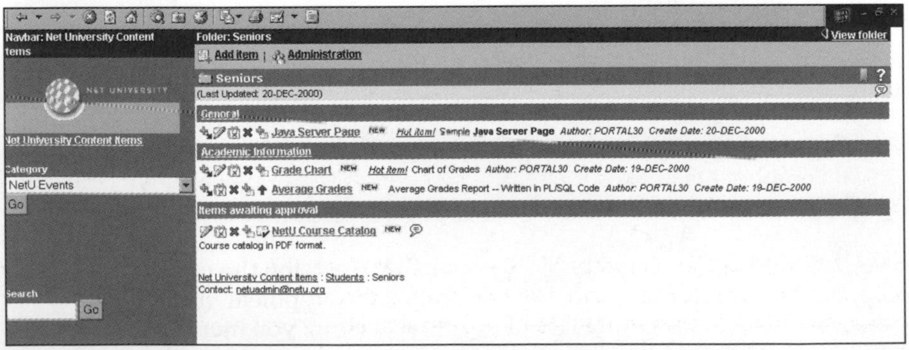

Figure 1-12: A Content Area

The specific layout of the Content Area page shows a header at the top, items and folders in the main area of the page, and navigation aids on the left. The standard user interface for a Content Area also includes the ability to search for individual content items and the ability to organize the contents by perspectives and categories.

The items in a Content Area can be content stored in the Oracle9*i*AS Portal database or links to other destinations. These links can be any standard URL, which means they can point to other locations on the Internet or on your intranet or to an Oracle9*i*AS Portal component.

Pages

A page is a way to organize the user interface to the various other items that are a part of an Oracle9*i*AS Portal system. A page can support the display of many different portlets. In fact, a page is essentially a container that supports the display of portlets.

As mentioned previously, both Oracle9*i*AS Portal components and Content Areas can be automatically displayed as portlets. (Individual folders can also be displayed as portlets.) Oracle9*i*AS Portal includes some pre-built portlets you can quickly add to your application, such as the Favorites portlet. Other external portlets, such as portlets that give you access to the news services of Excite, are available as part of the Portal Development Kit. The Portal Development Kit is a set of examples and documentation available for no charge from Oracle Technology Network (OTN), which you can reach through the URL `http://otn.oracle.com`, or through the main Oracle home page, `http://www.oracle.com`.

Note

Oracle plans to encourage the development of additional third-party portlets. At this time, there are hundreds of third-party portlets available. Periodically, you should check out Oracle Technology Network (OTN) to learn about the latest portlets and how to publish your own portlets.

Creating Oracle9*i*AS Portal Components

At this point, you might be feeling a little worried about the potential complexity of the task ahead of you. All these different components to keep track of and you haven't even touched on the code you have to write to create these components.

Fear not. Oracle9*i*AS Portal, with its emphasis on centralized storage and management of components, makes it easy to track the different pieces of an Oracle9*i*AS Portal application. And don't worry about learning code—there normally isn't any.

As you will see in the chapters of this book that describe the creation and use of components, Oracle9*i*AS Portal is a *declarative* development environment. This means that instead of writing lots of procedural code, you merely have to supply a set of values that describe the functionality of your Oracle9*i*AS Portal component. Each Oracle9*i*AS Portal component uses a wizard that prompts you for the appropriate parameters and can supply online help about the parameters. After you supply these parameters, Oracle9*i*AS Portal generates the underlying PL/SQL code that actually builds the HTML pages of your application.

There is no need to know much about PL/SQL to create applications with Oracle9*i*AS Portal. If you want to change an application, you merely edit the values you originally supplied to the wizards.

Note You can, however, use JavaScript on the client, and use PL/SQL procedures or Java servlets on the server to extend the functionality inherent in your Oracle9*i*AS Portal application system. Because of this, you can do almost anything you want with Oracle9*i*AS Portal, within the limitations of the static nature of HTML.

You will read a relatively detailed discussion of the use of PL/SQL or Java code in Chapter 28, one of the final chapters of this book, when you read about creating your own Oracle9*i*AS Portal portlets. But this type of customized development is normally not needed in the creation of a site with Oracle9*i*AS Portal.

In certain sections of this book, you will learn about the underlying code that Oracle9*i*AS Portal generates and how to extend it, if necessary. But aside from the special cases used in these chapters, you will not write logical code to create the application system used in this book.

Summary

This chapter has given you a basic understanding of Oracle9*i*AS Portal, the various types of objects you can create with Oracle9*i*AS Portal, and the basic structure of Oracle9*i*AS Portal and Oracle9*i*AS Portal components.

You have also learned why this version of the product is different from previous versions, and gotten a high level overview of the major new area of the product, the use of portal pages and portlets.

This chapter has only provided the briefest of introductions to Oracle9*i*AS Portal. The rest of this book simply expands on the principals you acquired in this chapter.

Onward into Oracle9*i*AS Portal — biblically speaking.

✦   ✦   ✦

Installing and Configuring Oracle9*i*AS Portal

In This Chapter

Obtaining a Copy of
Oracle9*i*AS Portal

Installing Oracle9*i*AS
Portal

Performing Post-
installation Checks

Creating the NETU
Sample Database

Although you are probably chomping at the bit to start using Portal, you have to install it first. This chapter walks you through the installation process for the Portal product itself, including setting up the Portal listener and configuring data access to Portal.

In addition to setting up the basic product environment, you also have to set up the sample database and create a Portal developer account. The sample database is based on the information needs of a fictional university. This chapter explains the structure of the database and gives you complete instructions for Oracle9*i*AS Portal and the NetU database schema.

Obtaining a Copy of Oracle9*i*AS Portal

The previous release of Oracle9*i*AS Portal (formerly called WebDB 2.2) was available as a separate product from Oracle. Oracle has bundled Oracle Portal into Oracle 9*i*AS — which is available from the Oracle Technology Network (OTN) Web site at:

```
http://technet.oracle.com
```

The installation kit for Oracle 9*i*AS clocks in at approximately one gigabyte of disk space — which translates to lots of download time if you are not on a fast Internet connection. The nice folks at Oracle have added the ability to order a free CD copy of the software at the download area on OTN.

You can locate the CD request forms by following the download links for the Internet Application Server product on the OTN site. In order to gain access to downloads and CD request forms, you will need to be registered on OTN — but registration is free.

Oracle made significant incremental changes to the previous version of Oracle9*i*AS Portal throughout the first year of WebDB's release. Within the space of 11 months, they released 2.0, 2.1, and 2.2. Each of these releases used a different format for the portal dictionary, which caused existing import/export scripts to break. While we expect Oracle9*i*AS Portal to be a stable release of the product, Oracle has plans to update the software incrementally over the life of this book. Oracle prefers that you work with the most recent versions of their software whenever possible and that you download the most recent versions from OTN (or order the CD). Thus, we have elected not to include a copy of the software within the book.

Caution   If you have not already done so, you will need to download a copy of both Oracle Database (Oracle 8i or Oracle 9i) from OTN and Oracle 9*i*AS in order to continue.

Installing Oracle9*i*AS Portal

The product installation described in this chapter is for the NT version of Portal, because that is the most common platform used by developers. All Oracle software makes use of the Oracle Universal Installer program (a Java-based installation utility) and you will find that the installation process on Solaris, LINUX, HP-UX, and other platforms will closely follow that of the Windows NT release.

Before you begin

Before you get started on the installation you will need to take care of some prerequisites. Oracle9*i*AS Portal works with Oracle 8i release 2 (8.1.6.2); Oracle9*i*AS includes a copy of Oracle 8.1.7 Standard Edition. During the beta-testing process, many developers experienced problems with Portal running on the Oracle 8.1.6 database. Since that time, Oracle has added a number of patches to the 8.1.6 release that improve its compatibility with Oracle9*i*AS Portal. We encourage you to log on to the OTN site to get the latest news about database compatibility.

There are three actions that you need to undertake before attempting to install Oracle9*i*AS Portal:

✦ Disable the existing Oracle Apache server.

✦ Verify that you have sufficient disk space for the installation.

✦ Change several Oracle database initialization parameters.

Working with Other Oracle Versions

Oracle 8.1.6 and 8.1.7 databases can connect to older versions of Oracle (i.e., 8.1.5, 7.3, etc.) However, Oracle9iAS Portal relies on some database services that are not included in these older releases. If you have production databases that are built with these older releases, it's best to install Portal into an 8.1.7 database and then link to these older databases as needed.

Oracle 8i Release 3 (8.1.7) also includes a copy of the Apache server. We recommend that you disable this version of the Apache Listener before you attempt to install Oracle 9iAS. The Apache HTTP server that is installed with the database does not include some of the advanced functions that are available with the Oracle 9i application server.

Oracle 9iAS takes approximately 500MB of disk space. Inside of the database Portal requires 150MB of storage in the SYSTEM tablespace and 150MB of storage in the USERS tablespace upon installation. You will want to verify that you have sufficient disk space on your fileserver as well as enough free tablespace storage for the various tables, packages, and other database objects.

Previous versions of Oracle9iAS Portal relied solely upon PL/SQL in order to run — but Oracle 9iAS makes use of Java Services in the Oracle Database. In order to safely load the Java classes and Java stored procedures, you will need to change several initialization parameters.

1. Select the instance of the database that you wish to install Oracle9iAS Portal into and get the password for the SYS account (and the INTERNAL password as well).

2. Locate the init.ora file for the selected instance (in the `%oracle_home%` path) (`%oracle_home%/admin/<instance-name>/pfile/init.ora`).

3. Locate and change the following parameters to the values as shown here:
```
large_pool_size = 25728640
java_pool_size = 30971520
```

Note   Oracle's Database JVM uses these parameters internally to manage Java classes in the database. The default values for these parameters are too small, causing certain Java classes to abort during the installation process. If the values for these two parameters on your server are larger than the values shown here, then leave them unchanged.

4. Stop and restart the database server.

Oracle9*i*AS Portal installation – part 1

You will need to either unpack the ZIP archive or insert the trial CD from OTN in order to install the software.

Note

The download from OTN comes in two archive files. The first file should be extracted into the hierarchy "disk1" – i.e. d:\disk1\... The second archive is "disk2", and it should be extracted into a *separate* directory at the same root level as disk1 (i.e., d:\disk2...).

Once you have extracted the archive kits, the next step is to locate and run the setup.exe program to begin the installation of Oracle 9*i*AS and Oracle9*i*AS Portal.

1. Run the setup.exe file (from the installation CD, or in the disk1 directory from the Oracle9iAS download). This brings up the initial screen shown in Figure 2-1.

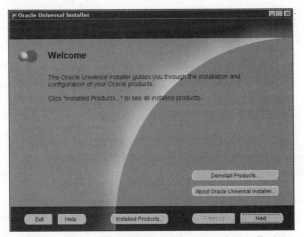

Figure 2-1: The first screen of the Portal installation process

2. Press the Next button to continue with the panel as shown in Figure 2-2.

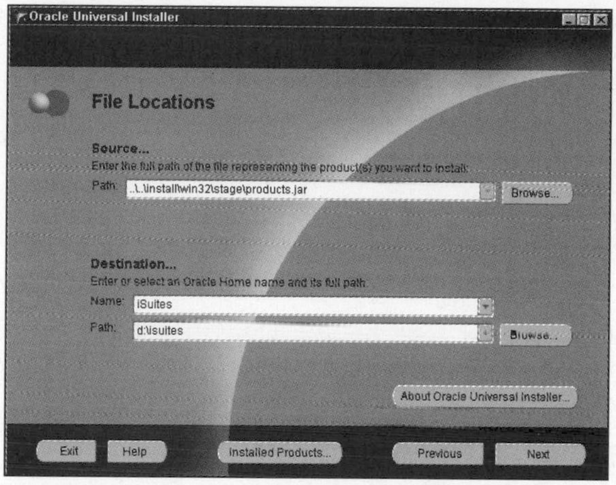

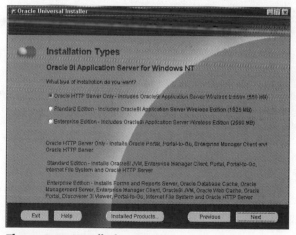

Figure 2-2: File Locations

The Oracle 9*i* Application Server should be installed into a separate Oracle home. By default, the installer will choose the name iSuites.

3. Accept the default name and enter a file system directory for the Path field as shown in Figure 2-2.

4. Press the Next button to display the panel as shown in Figure 2-3.

Figure 2-3: Installation Types

There are three possible installation choices. The simplest installation is the Oracle HTTP server installation, which includes Oracle9*i*AS Portal.

Note   You may choose to install the complete Oracle9*i*AS product at this point. However, the order of the panels as shown in this chapter follows the Oracle HTTP Server Only installation.

> **5.** Choose the Oracle HTTP Server Only option and press the Next button to continue.

The installation program will run for a few minutes, and then it will signal for a reboot (only under Windows), as shown in Figure 2-4.

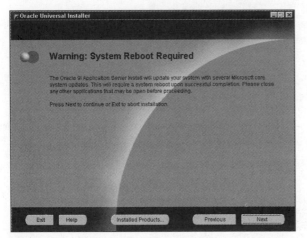

Figure 2-4: System reboot

Caution   The server should automatically reboot — but it does not always appear to under Windows 2000. If the installation program should simply terminate, then you will need to manually reboot. The installation will not continue properly unless you reboot.

> **6.** Press the Next button to continue — remember to reboot your server if it does not automatically do so.

Oracle9*i*AS Portal installation — part 2

Once the server comes back up, you must manually restart the installation program.

> **1.** Rerun the setup.exe program. Oracle9*i*AS Portal will continue to run as shown in Figure 2-5.

Figure 2-5: Installation of files

Once the installation program has loaded all of the program files onto your hard disk, the installation program will continue as shown in Figure 2-6.

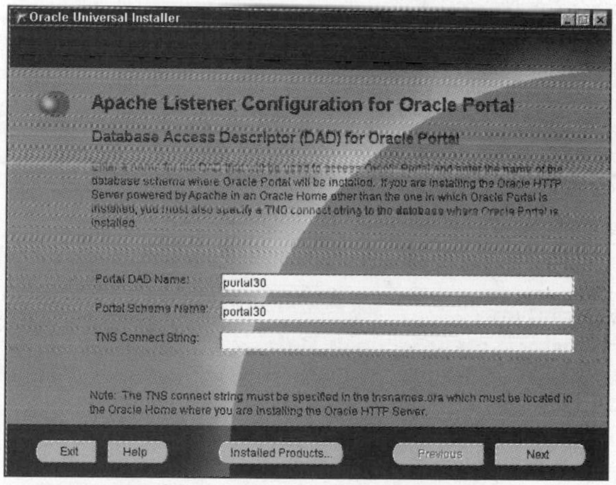

Figure 2-6: Apache Listener configuration

The next step is to configure the Apache Listener, Portal, and the Portal-to-Go product. The first selection that you need to make is the schema into which Oracle9*i*AS Portal should be installed. There is no need to change the default value of "portal30" for either the DAD or the Schema name. The TNSNAMES string should be filled in with the address of the database into which Portal will be installed. The TNSNAMES entry can be added to the TNSNAMES during the Net8 installation later on.

Note   As long are you are installing Portal into the same instance as the Apache Listener, you should be able to leave the TNS Connect String field blank. However, we have noticed that the installer occasionally has problems. If you leave this field blank and the installer program opens a SQL*Plus window and prompts you for a logon, enter the SYS user name, password, and TNS connect string for your database in the form: `sys/password@myserver-tns-name`.

2. Accept the default values on Database Access Descriptor Panel.

3. The next three panels as shown in Figures 2-7, 2-8, and 2-9 are specific to the Portal-to-Go product. Leave them blank.

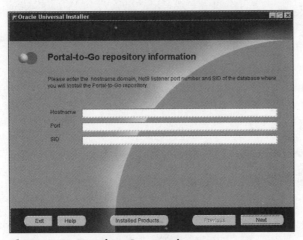

Figure 2-7: Portal-to-Go repository

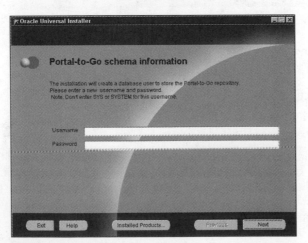

Figure 2-8: Portal-to-Go schema

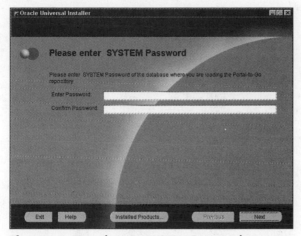

Figure 2-9: Portal-to-Go SYSTEM Password

Once you have completed entering the various parameters, you will see the panel as shown in Figure 2-10. At this point, you can use the Previous button to navigate back and correct any mistakes that you made.

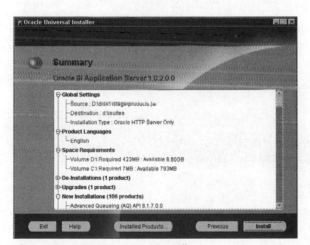

Figure 2-10: Summary of install

4. Press the Install button to continue.

The installer will process some additional files as shown in Figure 2-11.

Figure 2-11: Copying files

Configuring network protocols

The installation program recommends that you install the Application Server into a separate Oracle Home. You are, however, expected to connect Portal to a database server that is running in a different Oracle Home. In order to make this work you will need to install and configure a new installation of Net8 — Oracle's networking protocol. Once the installer has finished copying files to the system, it will invoke the Net8 Configuration Assistant as shown in Figure 2-12.

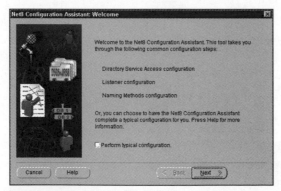

Figure 2-12: Net8 Configuration
Assistant — Welcome

The Net8 Configuration Assistant will guide you through the process of configuring the necessary network protocols so that the Oracle9i Application Server and Oracle9*i*AS Portal can communicate with your Oracle Database.

1. Press the Next button to display the panel as shown in Figure 2-13.

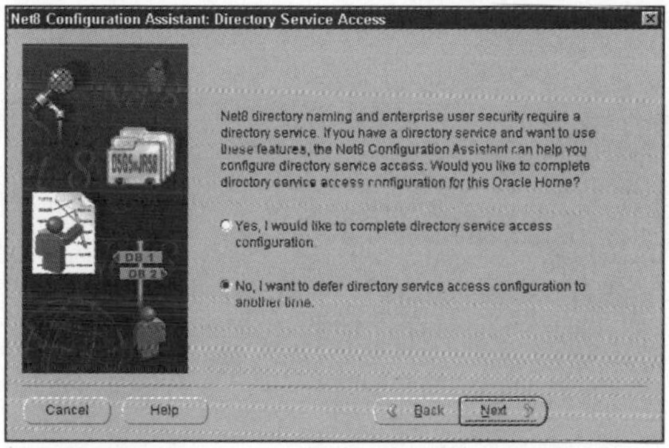

Figure 2-13: Net8 – Directory Service Access

Oracle's Net8 software can work with directory services (such as Oracle's LDAP server). This allows the database and application server to authenticate users against a company-wide directory of services (including print servers, file servers, etc.).

2. Accept the No option and press the Next button to display the panel as shown in Figure 2-14.

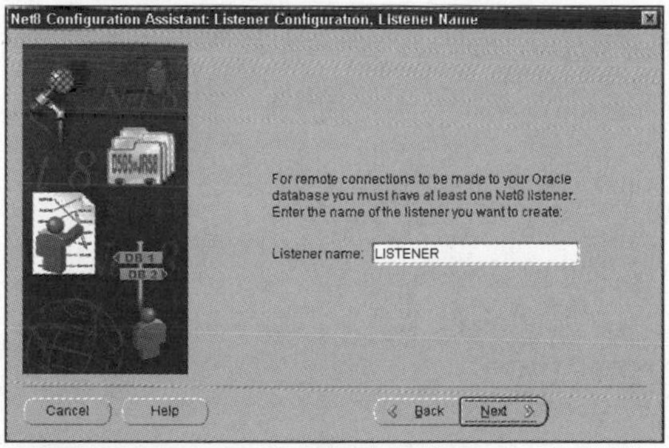

Figure 2-14: Net8 – Listener Name

Each Net8 installation has a listener, which is responsible for watching for connection requests. If you are installing Oracle9*i*AS Portal and the Apache Listener on the same server as your Oracle database, then you might want to give this process a new name (something like **PORTAL-LISTENER**). This will help you differentiate between the two processes at the operating system level.

   3. Enter a listener name (or accept the default) and press the Next button to display the panel as shown in Figure 2-15.

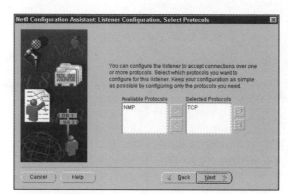

Figure 2-15: Net8 — Select Protocols

The Net8 software layer can work with multiple kinds of networking protocols, such as Named Pipes (NMP) and Transmission Control Protocol (TCP). In most cases you will choose the TCP protocol for the transport layer as shown in Figure 2-15.

   4. If the TCP protocol is not in the right-side list box by default, select the TCP protocol by clicking on it from the list box using the arrow button to move it over to the right-side list box. Press the Next button to display the panel as shown in Figure 2-16.

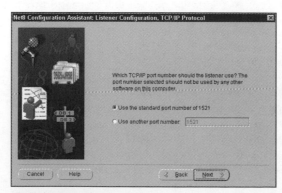

Figure 2-16: Net8 — Port

Each network listener is set to "listen" on a specified port. The default port for Oracle's networking product is 1521. If you are installing Oracle9*i*AS Portal on an existing database server node, you might choose another port number for this listener so that it does not conflict with your existing Net8 Listener.

5. Accept the default value or enter a specific port number and press the Next button to display the panel as shown in Figure 2-17.

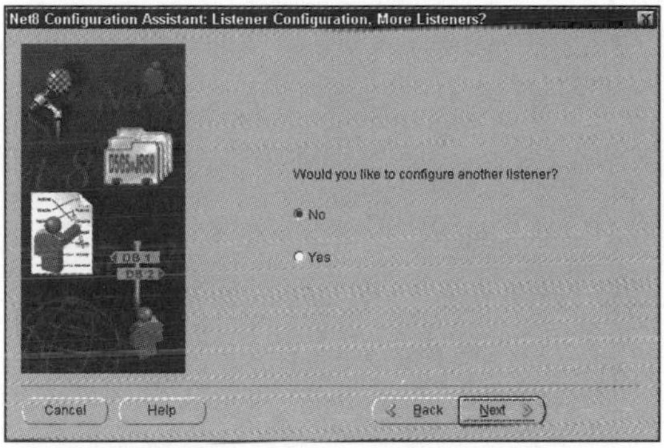

Figure 2-17: Net8 — More Listeners?

The Net8 wizard permits you to install multiple listeners, but you only need the one listener for the purposes here.

6. Select No and then press the Next button to continue.

Note   You may receive a warning that the listener that you just created conflicts with a previously installed and running Net8 Listener as shown in Figure 2-18. Oracle9*i*AS Portal can work around this problem — so you can choose the Yes option to continue. Technically speaking, you only need this new listener for inbound requests to the application server. When you connect to the database you will be using a TNSNAMES file in the new Net8 directory — but you will be connecting to an existing listener.

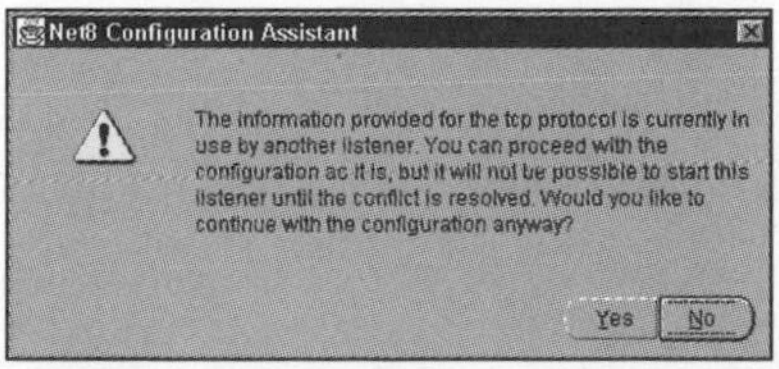

Figure 2-18: Listener currently in use

7. Press the Next button to complete the Listener installation as shown in Figure 2-19.

Figure 2-19: Net8 — Listener Complete

The next section of the Net8 configuration is the Net Service Name. These are the names by which Oracle client programs can locate particular database servers. The default naming method is to use a local network configuration file that is called the TNSNAMES.ORA. The TNSNAMES string that you enter on this panel should match the string that you entered on the "Apache Listener Configuration for Oracle Portal" (see Figure 2-6).

8. Accept the default naming method as shown in Figure 2-20 and press the Next button to continue.

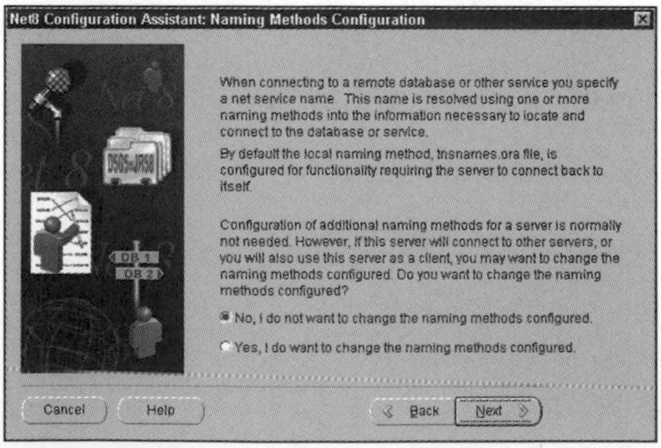

Figure 2-20: Net8 — Naming Methods

Note   You might wish to check with your local Oracle Systems Administrator to see whether your organization is using a different naming method. However, there is no harm in accepting the default value — as it can always be changed later.

9. Press the Finish button to complete the Net8 installation as shown in Figure 2-21.

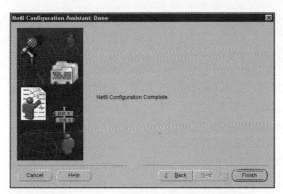

Figure 2-21: Net8 — Configuration Complete

Configuring Oracle9iAS Portal

Once you have successfully configured your Net8 installation, the Oracle Installer program will display the panel shown in Figure 2-22. (You might also see this panel briefly before the Net8 installation begins.)

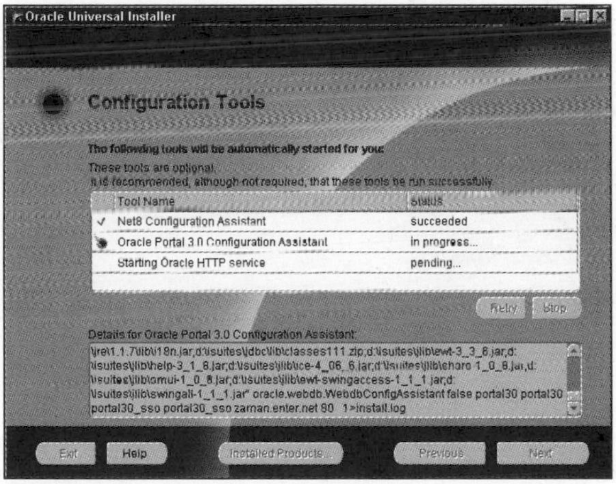

Figure 2-22: Configuration Tools

The installation icon next to the Oracle Portal 3.0 Configuration Assistant line item tells you that the installer is beginning the portal-specific portion of the installation. There are six panels in the Oracle Portal Configuration Assistant. The first panel that will appear is shown in Figure 2-23.

Figure 2-23: Step 1 — Installation Options

Your first option is to either install or uninstall the Oracle9*i*AS Portal.

1. Choose the Install radio button and press the Next button to display the panel shown in Figure 2-24.

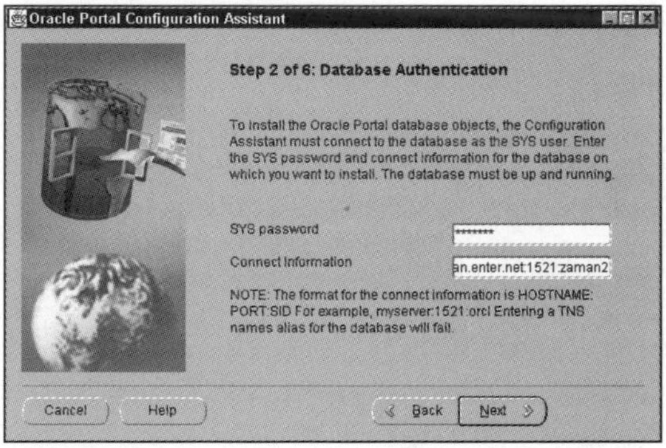

Figure 2-24: Step 2 — Database Authentication

Oracle9*i*AS Portal relies upon an Oracle database to host all of its tables, records, and stored procedures. During the installation process, you will need to give the installer privileged access to the target database. You must specify the password for the SYS user, because the installer will need to create schemas and grant privilege roles to these new schemas. You also need to supply the network address of the database and the database instance information to the installer. Although the production installation of Oracle9*i*AS Portal uses Net8's TNSNAMES.ORA configuration file — *the installation program does not.* You *must* specify the database connection information using a special format as follows:

```
server:port#:instancename
```

The *server* field points to the network name of the server itself. You need to include all the parts of the name (including the top-level domain and the second level domain). The second field (*port#*) is the port number of the Listener for the database and the last field is the instance name. Each field is separated from the others by use of the colon (:) character. This information can be found in the TNSNAMES.ORA file in the following path:

```
%oracle_home%\network\admin\tnsnames.ora
```

You will find the information for the database connection in the TNSNAMES file in the following format:

```
ZAMAN2.ENTER.NET =
  (DESCRIPTION =
    (ADDRESS_LIST =
     (ADDRESS = (PROTOCOL = TCP)(HOST = zaman)(PORT = 1521))
    )
    (CONNECT_DATA =
      (SERVICE_NAME = zaman2.enter.net)
    )
  )
```

Tip   If you want to install Oracle9*i*AS Portal onto a remote database—here is where you elect to do so. All that you need to do is to enter the servername, port, and instance name of a remote machine.

The three fields are in bold and can be read from top to bottom. The values in the TNSNAMES entry as shown previously would translate into the following Connect Information string on the panel as shown in Figure 2-24.

```
zaman.enter.net;1521:zaman2.enter.net
```

   2. Enter your SYS password and the connect information for your database and then press the Next button to continue.

The installation program will create a number of Oracle schemas including one for Portal and one for the Single Sign-on Server as shown in Figures 2-25 and 2-26. Each schema has two values, the schema itself and the schema Database Access Descriptor (DAD). The schema name translates into the name that the installer will use when it creates the schema in the database. The DAD entry is the logical name by which Oracle9*i*AS Portal will refer to this schema within the Portal environment.

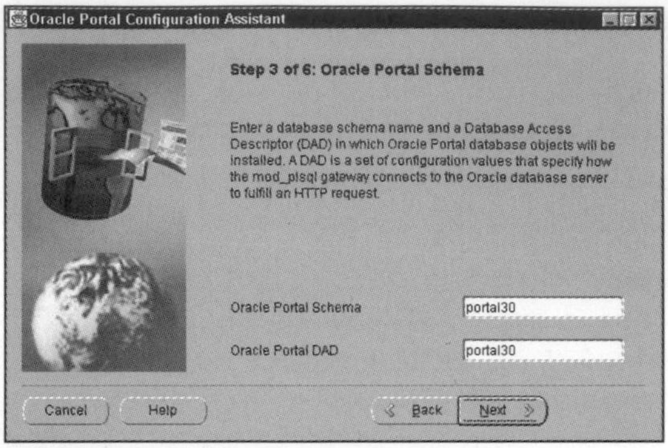

Figure 2-25: Step 3 — Portal Schema

Figure 2-26: Step 4 — Single Sign-On Schema

3. Accept the default values for the Portal and Single Sign-On Schemas by using the Next button.

The next panel to appear is the Tablespace Options panel as shown in Figure 2-27.

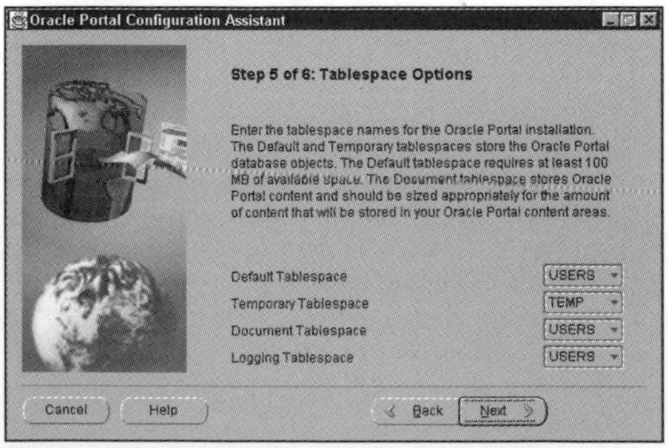

Figure 2-27: Step 5 — Tablespace Options

The Typical Installation Process

All information stored in an Oracle database is stored in a *tablespace*. A tablespace is nothing more than one or more physical files that hold data. The typical Portal install seeks out an appropriate tablespace by starting with the name TOOLS, followed by USERS, USER_DATA, USR, and others. Typically, one of these tablespaces is available for the installation process.

The SYSTEM tablespace must have at least 150MB available and the USERS tablespace must have 150MB in order to load Portal. If you are unsure if the target tablespace has enough space, check with your database administrator.

You can create your own tablespace for Portal, but it is just as easy to store the portal objects inside of an existing tablespace.

   4. Select tablespaces for each of the four object types and press the Next button to continue.

At this point in the installation process, you may see a warning dialog box that tells you that a copy of the PL/SQL Web Toolkit Packages was found on your server (as shown in Figure 2-28). These packages are a standard set of PL/SQL procedures that are used to create HTML from within the database. The packages come with a number of different Oracle products, including the Oracle Database itself, so they may already exist as part of your Oracle environment. We recommend replacing them with the new version of the packages that comes with Portal — but you should check with your DBA to make sure this will not affect other applications running against the database server.

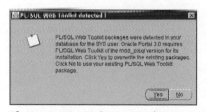

Figure 2-28: PL/SQL warning

The installation process automatically creates a user named PORTAL30 (or whatever name you chose on Step 3 of the Configuration wizard) and installs all the Portal packages under that user name. We refer to the owner of the PORTAL packages as PORTAL30 throughout the rest of the book, so we recommend you use that user name to avoid confusion.

The installation of the Portal packages takes a while—usually over half an hour. The installer will display progress messages along the way as shown in Figure 2-29, so that you can keep track of the progress.

Figure 2-29: Step 6—Installing Oracle9*i*AS Portal

The installation process for Portal creates a Data Access Definition that automatically logs a developer on to Portal with the user name that you installed Portal under, which should be PORTAL30 for the purposes of this book.

When the package installations are complete, the installer program will display the panel as shown in Figure 2-30.

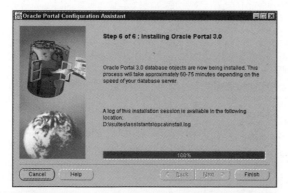

Figure 2-30: Step 6—Portal installation complete

5. Press the Finish button to complete the installation of the Portal Packages and display the panel as shown in Figure 2-31.

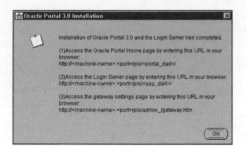

Figure 2-31: Installation Complete

The status panel shows you the URL information that you can use to connect to Oracle9*i*AS Portal. However, you will want to make sure that the Apache HTTP server is running before you attempt to connect to Oracle9*i*AS Portal.

6. Press the OK button to acknowledge that the Portal installation has completed.

The installer will start the Apache Listener and display the End of Installation panel as shown in Figure 2-32.

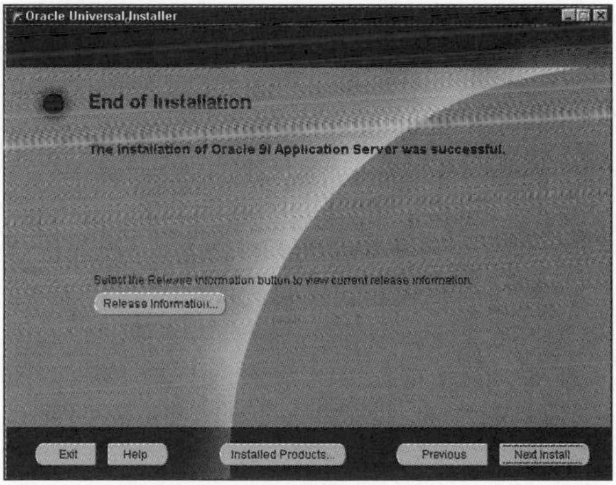

Figure 2-32: End of Installation

7. Use the Exit button to exit the installer.

Tip   Technically speaking, you should be able to use Oracle9*i*AS Portal immediately — but we recommend that you reboot your server first. We have had some problems with the Apache Listener and the configuration program that can be resolved simply by rebooting. If you installed Oracle9*i*AS Portal into a remote database, you need not reboot the database server. Just restart the server on which Oracle9*i*AS and the portal are running.

   8. Reboot your portal server.

Performing Post-Installation Checks

Once the installation process completes, you might have a few problems with the installation. In most cases, these can be cleared up with a few manual steps as outlined in the following steps.

   1. Open a browser session and navigate to the Apache Listener for the Oracle Application server that you just installed. (Normally, this will be as simple as entering the URL — `http://servername` — i.e., `http://zaman.enter.net`.)

The Apache Listener should display the page shown in Figure 2-33.

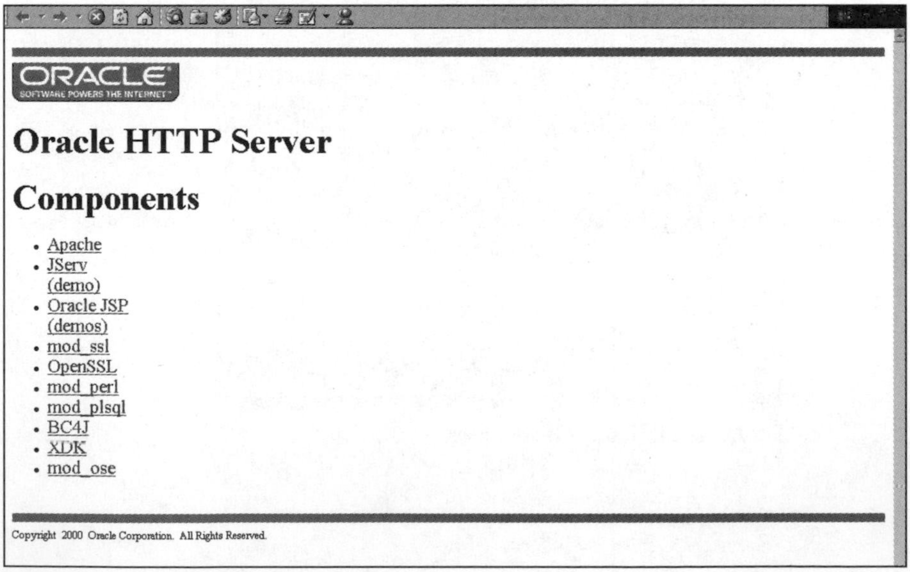

```
ORACLE
SOFTWARE POWERS THE INTERNET™

Oracle HTTP Server

Components

• Apache
• JServ
  (demo)
• Oracle JSP
  (demos)
• mod_ssl
• OpenSSL
• mod_perl
• mod_plsql
• BC4J
• XDK
• mod_ose

Copyright 2000 Oracle Corporation. All Rights Reserved.
```

Figure 2-33: Oracle9*i*AS Home Page

Note

If the home page does not appear as shown in Figure 2-33, then the Apache HTTP listener has failed to install correctly. Contact Oracle Technical Support for assistance.

2. Use the mod_PLSQL link to display the panel as shown in Figure 2-34.

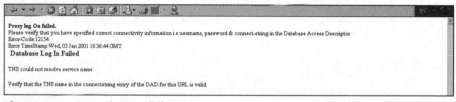

Figure 2-34: Gateway Configuration Menu

The Gateway Configuration Menu connects the Apache Listener to the mod_plsql gateway. From this menu you can test the gateway and you can also adjust some of the gateway settings.

3. Use the Home link in the upper-right corner of the page to test the gateway connection.

If you fail to connect to the gateway, you will see an error much like the one shown in Figure 2-35.

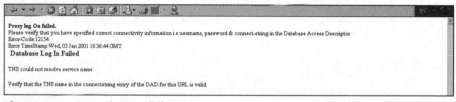

Figure 2-35: Proxy log on failure

Typically, this failure is caused by one of two problems. Either the TNSNAMES entry that the gateway is using is incorrect, or the TNSNAMES entry itself does not exist.

4. Navigate back to the previous page and use the Gateway Database Access Descriptor Settings link to display the panel as shown in Figure 2-36.

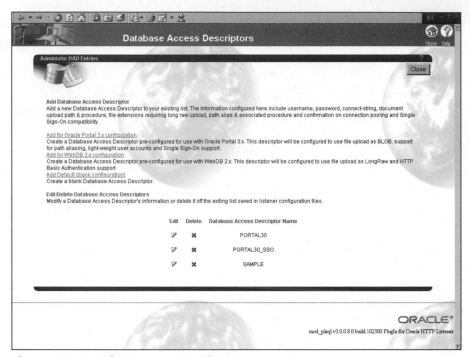

Figure 2-36: Database Access Descriptors

Cross-Reference   We'll be talking more about Database Access Descriptors in Chapter 23. At the moment, all that you need to do is to get the default DADs configured properly.

5. Click on the Edit link (the pencil) next to the PORTAL30 record. (Note: The record name PORTAL30 will match the name of the schema that you provided in Step 3 of the Configuration wizard.)

The critical entry will appear on the panel as shown in Figure 2-37 (zaman2.enter.net).

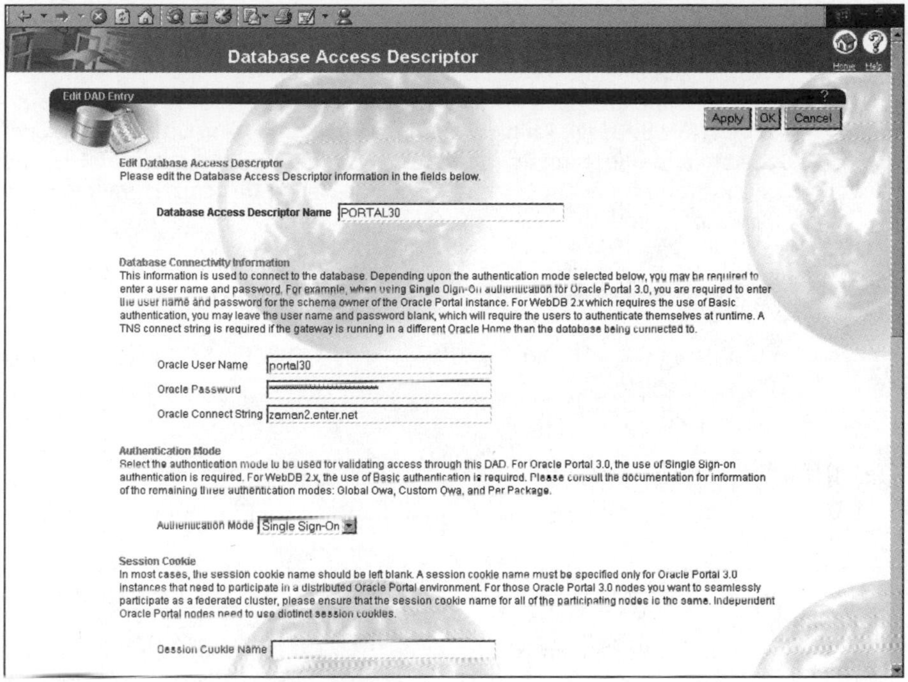

Figure 2-37: Oracle Connect String

The value for the Oracle Connect String field must match an entry in the TNSNAMES.ORA file in the directory tree into which Oracle9*i*AS Portal was installed. If this field is empty or incorrect, then the Apache server will be unable to connect to the mod_plsql gateway.

6. Use a text editor and open up the TNSNAMES.ORA file:

```
%oracle_ias_home%/network/admin/tnsnames.ora
```

where %oracle_ias_home% is the root directory into which you installed Oracle9*i*AS Portal.

There should be an entry in the TNSNAMES file that matches the value for the Oracle Connection String as follows:

```
ZAMAN2.ENTER.NET =
  (DESCRIPTION =
    (ADDRESS_LIST =
      (ADDRESS = (PROTOCOL = TCP)(HOST = zaman)(PORT = 1521))
    )
    (CONNECT_DATA =
      (SERVICE_NAME = zaman2.enter.net)
    )
  )
```

The instance name is shown in bold. There may be multiple entries in this file; choose the one that connects to the Oracle database into which you installed Oracle9*i*AS Portal.

Note

If the TNSNAMES.ORA file does not have an entry for your database server you will need to add one using the Net8 Configuration Assistant. Alternatively, you can simply add one manually, provided that you have the correct values for the server name, port, and instance name.

7. Verify, add, or modify the entry in the TNSNAMES.ORA file and save the changes.

8. Enter the instance name in the Oracle Connect String field as shown in Figure 2-37.

9. Use the OK button to save the modified DAD record.

10. Press the Close button to return to the Gateway menu.

11. Press the Home link again to display the panel as shown in Figure 2-38.

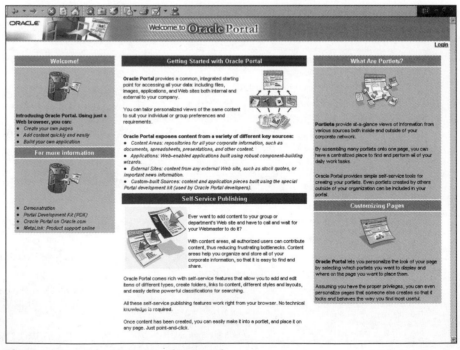

Figure 2-38: Welcome to Oracle9 Portal

At this point, you should be able to authenticate yourself to Oracle9*i*AS Portal as the portal30 user.

12. Use the portal30/portal30 account to authenticated to the Portal as shown in Figure 2-39.

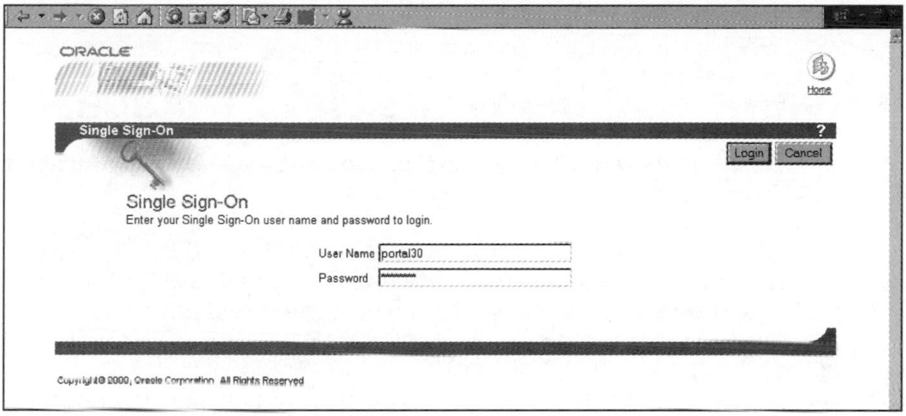

Figure 2-39: Sign on to Oracle Portal

After you have logged onto Oracle9*i*AS Portal, you should see the panel as shown in Figure 2-40.

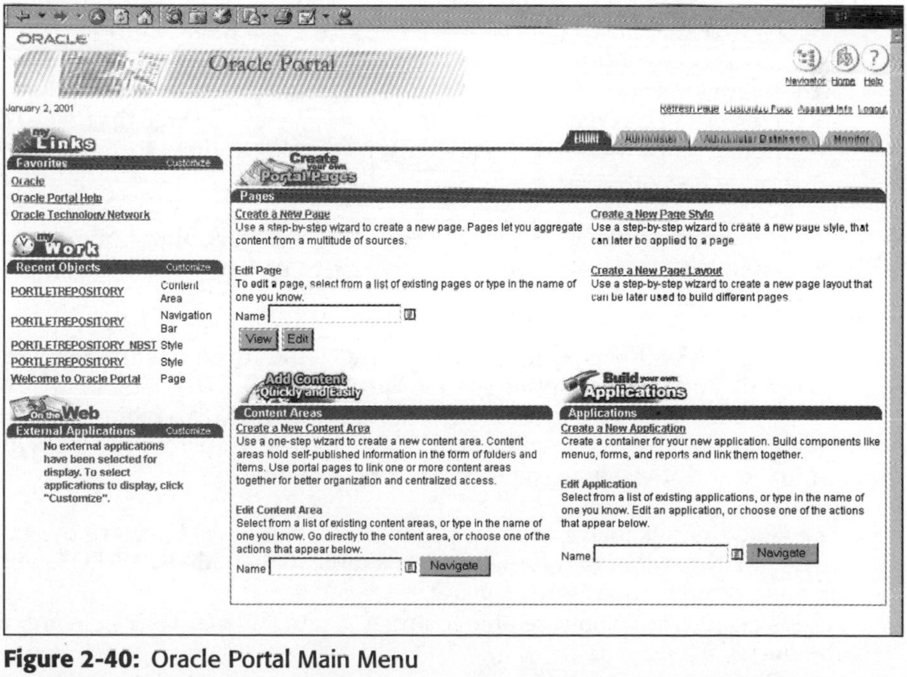

Figure 2-40: Oracle Portal Main Menu

13. Keep this authenticated session open.

Note   If you do not see the Oracle Portal Welcome page, or you cannot log on to Portal you will need to contact Oracle Technical Support for assistance.

Creating and Using the NetU Database

All the modules you will create in this book are based on a mythical university called Net University.

All the scripts you need to load the data structures and data into your Oracle database are included in a self-extracting ZIP file called netuniversity#.exe. This file also includes some documentation on the structure of the database, which is explained in this section.

Note   The exact name of the executable will vary according to the release of the demo data. The file name includes a character string "#" that represents the release number. Larger numbers mean more recent releases of the demo data.

Copy the netuniversity#.exe file from the Data directory on the CD-ROM that accompanies this book to its own directory on your hard drive. Run the file to extract the scripts and documentation.

Because these files are used by SQL*Plus, you may want to install them on the machine with your Oracle database because it will have SQL*Plus installed.

There are approximately 16 tables in the sample database. Eight of the tables are interrelated in one data complex, four in another, and three in another, with the relationships between the tables in each complex defined through a series of primary and foreign keys.

The core of the schema is the UGRADS table, which contains information about the individual students enrolled at Net University, known to its students and alumni as good old NetU.

The UGRADS table is connected to the two tables used to enforce referential integrity and for descriptive values. The first is the STATES table, which translates state codes into state names. The second is the CLASSES table, which translates a code for the year that represents the specific class, such as the class of 2001, to a more descriptive name, such as "Seniors" or "Juniors."

Each student can have a major, so the UGRADS table is linked to the MAJORS table. The MAJORS table is in turn linked to a table named MAJOR_REQS, which describes the required courses for the major.

Students are required to take classes at NetU, so the UGRADS table is linked to a TRANSCRIPT table that registers the courses that the student has taken. Grades are stored in the TRANSCRIPT table using numbers and the TRANSCRIPT table is linked to a GRADES table that translates these numbers into letter grades. The COURSE_CATALOG table serves as a master reference for all courses, so both the TRANSCRIPT and MAJOR_REQS tables use it to verify that a course exists and to get additional information about the course.

There is a second group of tables called ALUMNI, PLEDGES, DONATIONS, and RESTRICT_CODES that are used to track alumni and contributions to the NetU endowment.

These tables are included to provide some large tables full of numeric information, which are very useful for creating charts. If you examine the columns in the ALUMNI table, you can see that it is similar to the UGRADS table. There is also a stored procedure you will use that automatically adds a row to either the UGRADS table or the ALUMNI table from the same Portal form component.

The last group of tables is built around the events at NetU. The EVENTS table is linked to two other tables in the schema. The first is the BUILDINGS table, which contains maps of the campus that provide detailed information for event locations, and the second is the TICKETS table, which tracks the tickets purchased for an event through a Portal interface. These three tables are not directly related to the other tables in the schema, but they are included so that the examples in this book can work with date-type data.

Finally, the REVISION_HISTORY table tracks the changes to this schema as it was developed. You do not need to use it in the rest of the book — it is present strictly for documentation purposes. The Web site http://www.oracleportalbible.com has a separate folder that contains periodic updates to the NetU database schema.

Installing the NetU sample data

We have included a script that automatically loads all the sample data into your Oracle database. All you need is your trusty companion, SQL*Plus. The authors of this book, being longtime Oracle users, tend to rely on SQL*Plus. Although it has a somewhat ugly character interface, it gets the job done.

Because the installation script calls a lot of other scripts, and because you can have those scripts anywhere that you want, you have to change the working directory of SQL*Plus to the directory that contains the installation script. The simplest way to handle this is to use the command line interface for SQL*Plus.

1. Open a command window and set your default to the directory into which you extracted the NETU files like the one shown in Figure 2-41.

```
C:\WINNT\System32\command.com                              _ □ X
12/10/00  06:47p                 514  classes.sql
03/22/99  03:04p               8,169  college.sql
10/08/98  02:58p              13,691  course_catalog.sql
02/04/00  09:54a             535,265  donations.sql
11/04/00  03:27p              27,121  events.sql
10/08/98  02:58p                 682  grades.sql
12/10/00  07:01p               3,729  license.txt
10/08/98  02:58p               7,586  major_reqs.sql
10/08/98  02:59p               1,117  majors.sql
12/10/00  06:51p             176,105  netu.LST
12/10/00  06:40p               1,349  netu_install.sql
12/10/00  07:01p               2,314  readme.txt
11/16/99  11:54a               2,970  restrict_codes.sql
12/10/00  06:40p               2,461  revision_history.sql
03/22/99  06:58a               2,647  states.sql
12/07/99  08:44a               1,272  synonyms.sql
12/10/00  06:48p                 647  SYS_netu.LST
12/10/00  06:56p             121,754  transcript.sql
12/10/00  06:27p              15,017  ugrads.sql
12/10/00  06:39p                  20  version.txt
04/27/99  11:40a               4,290  views.sql
              26  File(s)       1,254,564  bytes
                           807,763,968  bytes free

C:\NETU>_
```

Figure 2-41: Command window

2. Start SQL*Plus and log on with the user name and password of a user that has DBA privileges (SYS).

Note

If you do not have access to a user with DBA privileges, you can ask your support group to create the tablespace for you. If you are not the normal DBA of the target database, make sure you check with the normal DBA before creating these tablespaces.

3. When SQL*Plus starts, enter the following code at the prompt:

```
CREATE TABLESPACE NETU_SPACE
        DATAFILE 'filename' SIZE 30M
        DEFAULT STORAGE (
               INITIAL 100K
               NEXT 100K
               MINEXTENTS 2
               MAXEXTENTS 50);
```

Replace *filename* with the complete pathname of the actual physical file for the tablespace.

Alternatively, you can use an existing tablespace for the NETU database.

Tip

You can simply press the Enter key while entering a command in SQL*Plus to go to the next line. A command is not executed until you enter that all-important semi-colon (;) at the end of the line.

The SIZE keyword indicates the overall size of the tablespace you are creating. The rest of the keywords shape the way that the Oracle database initially allocates disk space for the tablespace and how it grabs more disk space when needed. If you would like more information on creating tablespaces, please refer to the Oracle documentation.

You also need to specify a temporary tablespace for the user schema you are about to create. A temporary tablespace, as the name implies, is used for transitory data, such as the tables used internally for sorting results. Most Oracle databases already have a temporary tablespace set up with a descriptive name like TEMPORARY_DATA, which you can use for temporary table space.

Now that you have your tablespaces all ready, you can install the NETU data.

4. Enter the following line of code as shown in Figure 2-42.

```
@netu_install netu tablespace temp_tablespace tnsnames-entry;
```

For example:

```
@netu_install netu users temp zaman2.enter.net
```

The first parameter for the netu_install procedure (netu) is the name of the schema that will hold the NetU data. This has to be a user name that does not currently exist. The user is created with a password that is the same as the user name. You do not have to use NETU as the user name, but we refer to the NETU user for the rest of the book, so it makes sense to use that name for the sake of conformance. Here, <TABLESPACE> and <TEMP_TABLESPACE> are the names of the tablespace you created earlier in this section and of the temporary tablespace, respectively. The <TNSNAMES-ENTRY> value should be replaced by the TNSNAMES entry of the database into which you want the NetU schema installed.

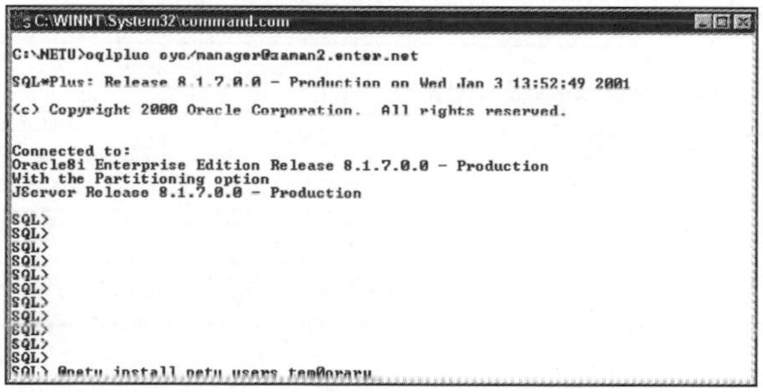

Figure 2-42: Installing NetU from SQL*Plus

5. When the script completes, enter the following command:

```
exit
```

Then press Enter to leave SQL*Plus.

Creating an application for NetU

Portal application components such as portal pages, forms, and reports are all stored within an application. Applications, in turn, are stored inside of schemas. In most cases, you will create applications separately from your other database data. Portal components will be stored in one schema and all of your relational data that is used by these components will be stored in a separate schema (or multiple schemas). For example, if you were to create an employee portal you would most likely create pages and components that access your existing Human Resources data. This data will already exist somewhere in an Oracle schema, so it is just a matter of pointing to this schema from within Oracle9*i*AS Portal. However, for the purposes of the sample NETU database, we are going to store the Portal components right alongside the demo data.

1. Return to your authenticated browser session and choose the Administer Database tab.

2. Enter the name **netu** into the name field in the schema section as shown in Figure 2-43 and press the Edit button to continue.

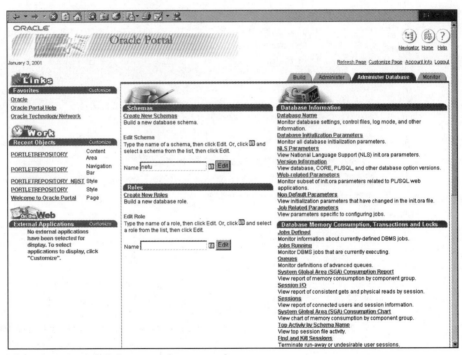

Figure 2-43: Administer Database panel

3. Click the check box next to the Application Schema field as shown in Figure 2-44.

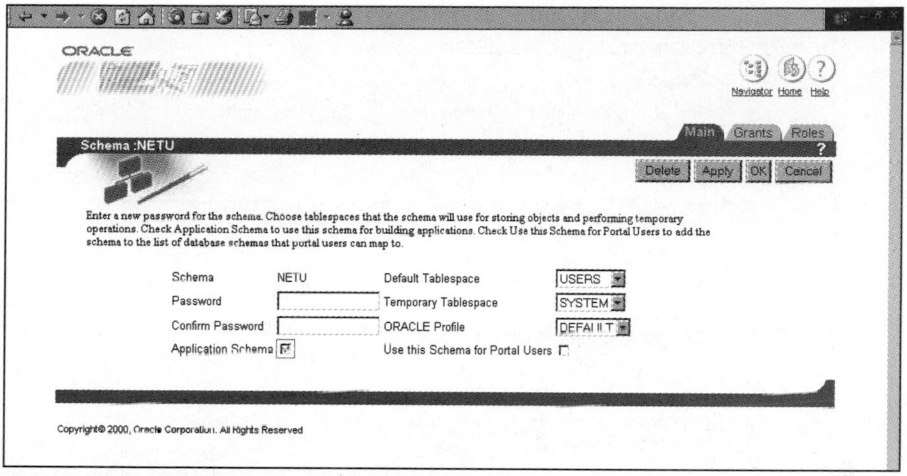

Figure 2-44: Modifying the NetU schema

4. Press the OK button to save the change.

5. Click back to the Build panel and click on the Create a New Application link as shown in Figure 2-45.

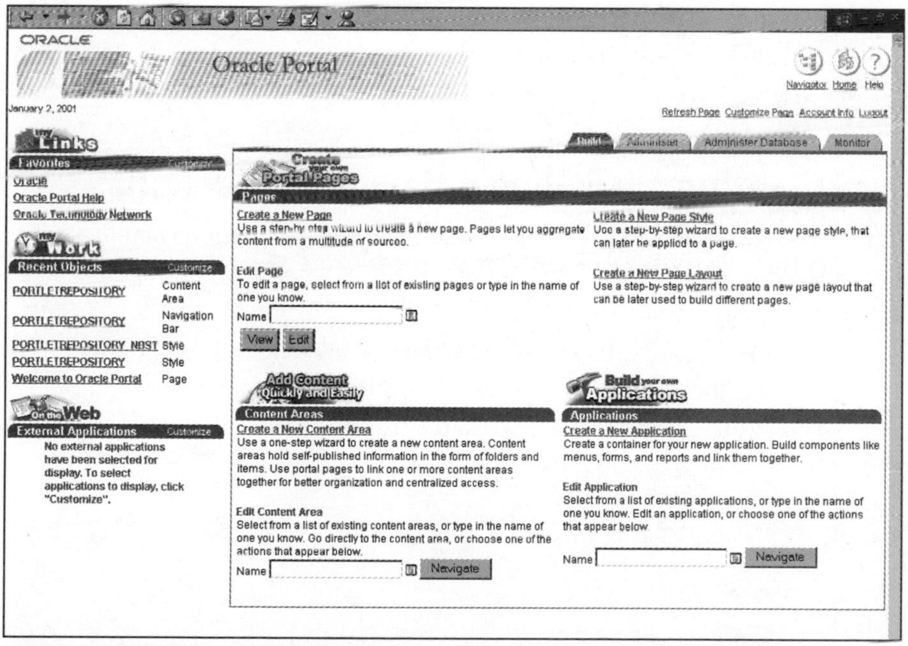

Figure 2-45: Create a New Application

6. Enter or select the following information into the fields on the resulting form as shown in Figure 2-46.

```
Application Name—netcollege
Display Name—Net University Application
Schema—NETU
```

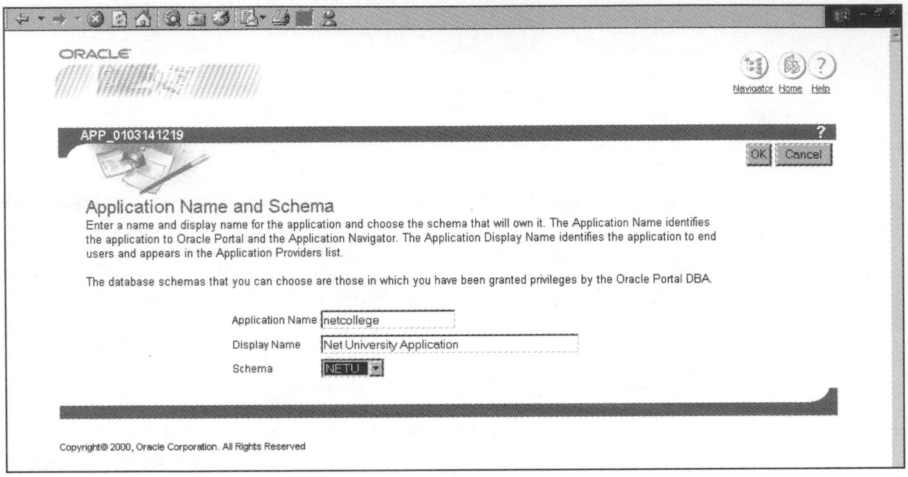

Figure 2-46: Creating the NETCOLLEGE application

7. Press the OK button and then the Close button to complete the process.

8. Keep your browser session open.

Creating a privileged developer account

Although you can use the Portal administrator account to build all of the examples in this book, we recommend that you create a developer account called NETUDEV — NetU developer.

1. Navigate to the Administer Tab and click on the Create New Users link to display the panel as shown in Figure 2-47.

2. Enter the following parameters for the new account as shown in Figure 2-48.

```
User Name—netudev
Password—netudev
Confirm Password—netudev
```

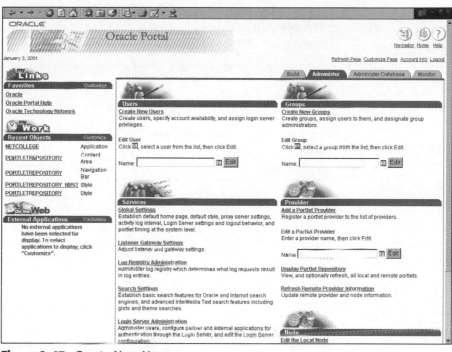

Figure 2-47: Create New Users

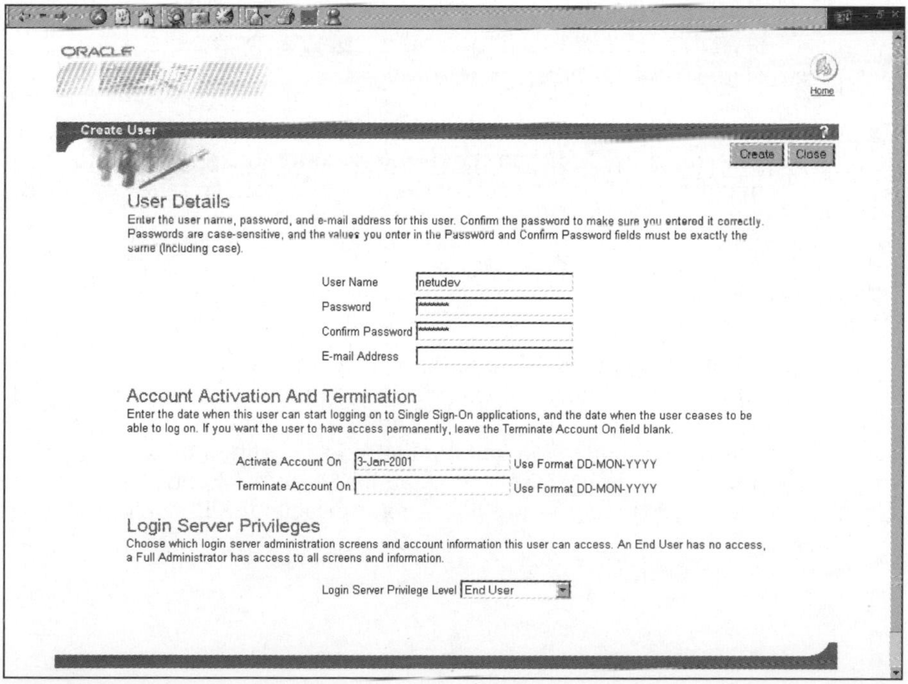

Figure 2-48: NETUDEV User

3. Press the Create button to create the new developer account. Use the `NETUDEV` link on the resulting page to edit the new account as shown in Figure 2-49.

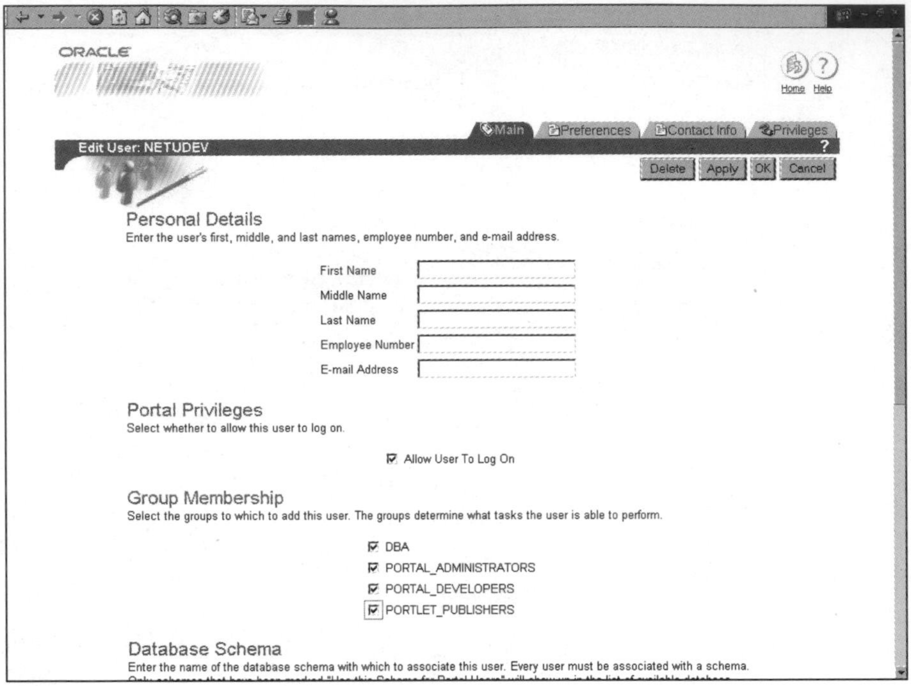

Figure 2-49: `NETUDEV` group privileges

4. Use the check boxes in the Group Membership section to make `NETUDEV` a member of all groups and press the OK button to save your changes.

Summary

This chapter walked you through the installation of Portal and the sample database you will use for the rest of this book. In the following chapters you will learn how to use the various component builders and page development tools. Once you have Oracle9*i*AS Portal installed and configured as outlined in this chapter, the rest is easy. You are ready to start getting familiar with the Portal development environment. In the next chapter, we'll introduce Oracle9*i*AS Portal's working environment.

✦   ✦   ✦

Introducing the Oracle9*i*AS Portal Environment

◆ ◆ ◆ ◆

In This Chapter

Becoming Comfortable with the Oracle9*i*AS Portal Environment

Learning to use the Build Tab

Using Wizards Effectively

◆ ◆ ◆ ◆

Now that you have installed Oracle9*i*AS Portal, you are ready to start exploring the Oracle9*i*AS Portal environment. This chapter introduces you to all the basics you need to start using Oracle9*i*AS Portal.

If you are familiar with WebDB, most of the functionality you used to have in the environment is still around. In fact, most of this functionality has been enhanced, either with additional options, a better user interface, or both.

This chapter will get you familiar with most of the areas and options that are a part of your environment. It will also touch briefly on the concept and use of wizards in Oracle9*i*AS Portal.

Introducing the Oracle9*i*AS Portal Environment

You have installed Oracle9*i*AS Portal, and you've brought up several Oracle9*i*AS Portal HTML pages in Chapter 2. Before you go any farther into the product, it's worth taking a few minutes to look at the browser environment that Oracle9*i*AS Portal lives in.

Oracle9*i*AS Portal lives utterly and completely in a browser. Oracle9*i*AS Portal has been tested, with Microsoft's Internet Explorer 4.0.1 with Service Pack 1 installed, and with Netscape Navigator 4.0.8. The Oracle9*i*AS Portal startup page in each of these popular browsers is shown in Figures 3-1 and 3-2, respectively.

Because Internet Explorer is the most popular browser in today's environment, all upcoming figures in the book use Internet Explorer as the browser environment. However, as you can see from Figures 3-1 and 3-2, there is very little difference in the appearance of Oracle9iAS Portal between the two browsers.

Note However, you should always test your completed application with all the potential target browsers, because there may be differences in how fast pages are rendered on Netscape Navigator and Internet Explorer.

In addition, you should make sure that any clients running Internet Explorer Version 5 and above set their caching option to "Check for newer versions of stored pages: On Every Visit to the Page". Any other setting could lead to pages that are not properly refreshed. For Internet Explorer 5.5, you can set this option by going to the Internet Options selection in the Tools menu, selecting the General tab, and clicking on the Settings button in the portion of the page labeled Temporary Internet files.

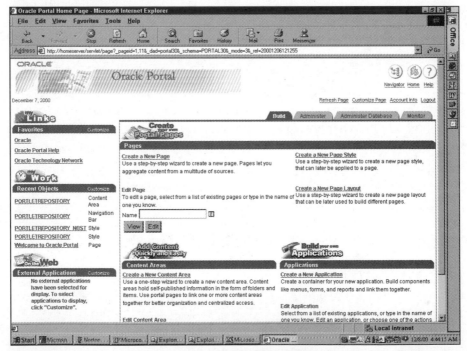

Figure 3-1: Oracle9iAS Portal running inside Microsoft Internet Explorer 5.5

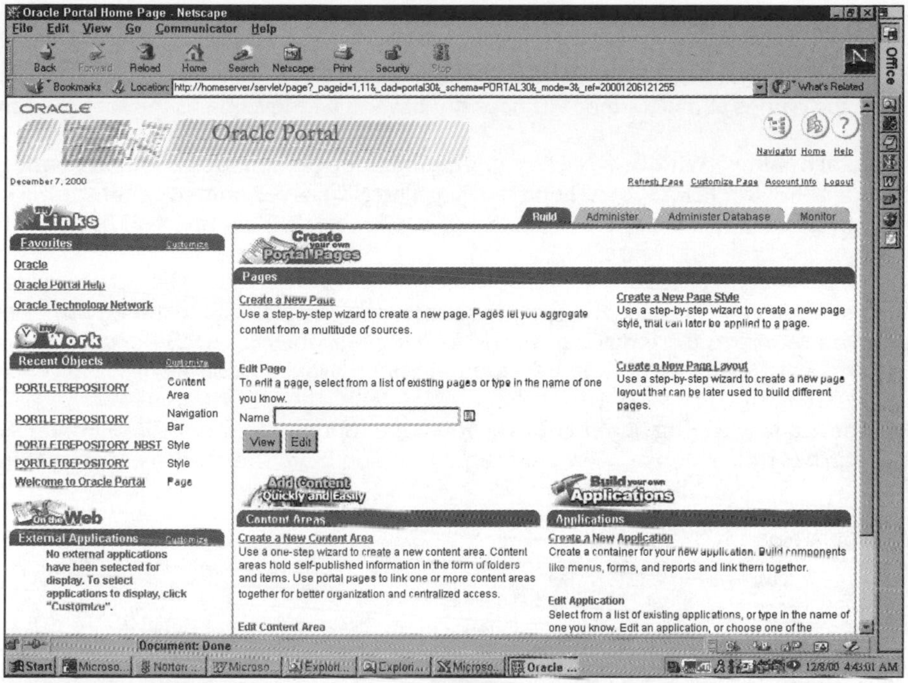

Figure 3-2: Oracle9iAS Portal running inside Netscape Navigator 4.5

You can change the look of the Oracle9iAS Portal environment through the standard settings on your browser. Most of the text displayed in Oracle9iAS Portal is standard HTML text, and most browsers give you the ability to change the color and font of displayed HTML text.

All the standard browser features work while you are using Oracle9iAS Portal. This means that you can use the navigation features of the browser, such as bookmarks or a favorites list and the Forward and Back buttons of the browser. And, as you will see in the rest of this chapter, Oracle9iAS Portal itself has given you lots of additional navigation options.

Because the Oracle9iAS Portal environment is itself built with Oracle9iAS Portal, you will be able to customize the look and feel of the environment, as you could with any portal page. You will learn a lot more about customizing portal pages later in this book.

The standard URL to get to the Oracle9iAS Portal environment is
servername:*portno*/pls/*portal_DAD* where *servername* is the name of the server with Oracle9iAS Portal installed, *portno* is the port number of the Oracle9iAS Portal listener, and *portal_DAD* is the name of the DAD you used to install Oracle9iAS Portal.

Note

For the examples in this book, the DAD is the same name as the schema the DAD accesses — PORTAL30. However, although this practice is the default way of assigning names to a DAD, the DAD does not have to be the same as the schema name.

If you are using a Windows NT server, the default port number is 80, so connecting to a default Oracle9*i*AS Portal start page on an NT server named homeserver would use the URL `http://homeserver:80/pls/portal30`. This URL will bring up the start page shown in Figure 3-3.

This start page is shown when you first enter the Oracle9*i*AS Portal environment, and you return to this start page when you log out of Oracle9*i*AS Portal. The page is generic, with some marketing information about Oracle9*i*AS Portal.

In order to start doing any real work, you have to log in to Oracle9*i*AS Portal. For the start of this exercise, we will assume that you have the start page shown in Figure 3-3 in your browser.

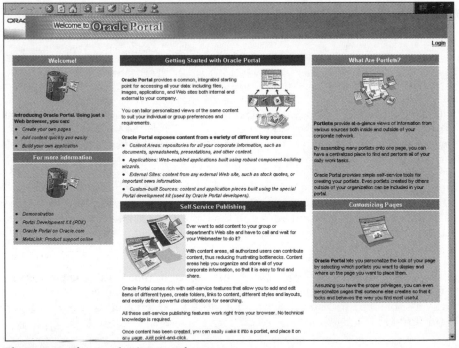

Figure 3-3: The Oracle9*i*AS Portal start page

1. Click on the Login link in the upper-right portion of the page. The Login page, as shown in Figure 3-4, will appear.

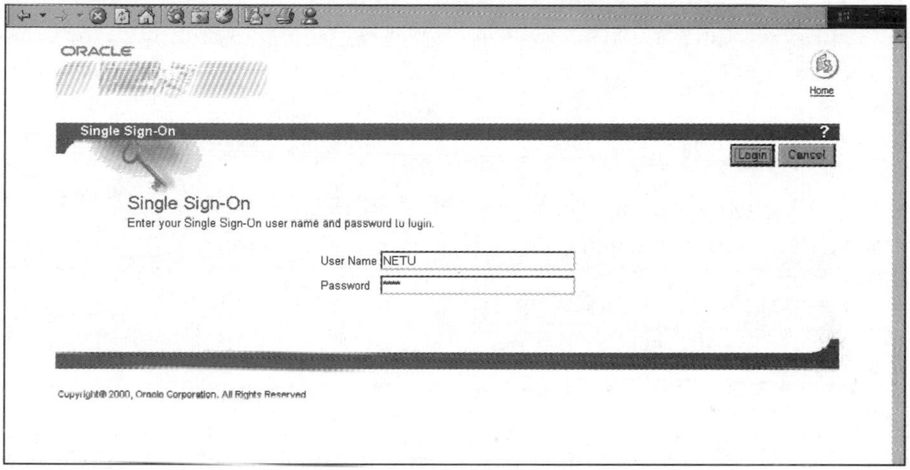

Figure 3-4: The Login page

Note   You can get to this page through the direct URL of `servername:portno/pls/portal_DAD`, which works the same way as the direct path to the start page, mentioned previously, except that the `portal_schema_sso` will be replaced by the DAD in which you installed the Login Server.

This page will let you use the Login Server to establish a user identity to Oracle9*i*AS Portal. Keep in mind that you are logging into Oracle9*i*AS Portal, not the database, so you have to use one of the user names you created in the previous chapter.

2. Enter `NETU`, the user name and password you created in the previous chapter, for both the User Name and the Password, and click on the Login button.

The Oracle9*i*AS Portal home page, as illustrated in Figure 3-1, will appear.

If you have been using WebDB, you can immediately see that the home page for Oracle9*i*AS Portal is significantly different.

There are six main areas in this portal page:

✦ The banner
✦ The banner properties, which are menu items in the banner
✦ The my Links portlet
✦ The my Work portlet
✦ The On The Web portlet

✦ The main portion of the page, which is referred to as the Build tab, since it is where most of the building processes originate

With the proper privileges, you can change the layout of this home page, moving some of these areas around or even dropping some of them and adding new ones. However, the rest of this section discusses and explores each of the areas as they appear by default.

The banner

At the top of the Oracle9*i*AS Portal home page is a banner, as shown in Figure 3-5.

Figure 3-5: The banner of the Oracle9*i*AS Portal home page

You can see that there are three icons on the right of the banner. These icons take you, from left to right, to the Navigator, which will be explored in the next chapter, the home page, or the Oracle9*i*AS Portal help system.

Your own home page is determined by a hierarchy. If you have designated a home page for yourself, clicking on the Home icon will take you there. If you do not have a home page specified, but are a member of a group that does have a home page specified, clicking on the icon will take you there. If you do not meet either of these criteria, you will be taken to the default home page for Oracle9*i*AS Portal. The portal administrator can alter this system-wide home page.

Cross-Reference You will learn more about using pages in Chapters 6 and 7.

The help system

The best way to understand the help system is to use it.

3. Click on the Help icon in the Oracle9*i*AS Portal banner. This action will bring up the Oracle9*i*AS Portal help system in a separate browser window, as shown in Figure 3-6.

The Oracle9*i*AS Portal help system is a standard Oracle9*i*AS Portal Content Area. There are a couple of links to content pieces in the top part of the main area and several manuals listed in the main part of the page.

On the left is a navigation bar. The navigation bar includes a link to an index of help topics, as shown in Figure 3-7, a data entry box that allows you to search for one or more words in all the content in the help system, and links to the documents shown in the main part of the page.

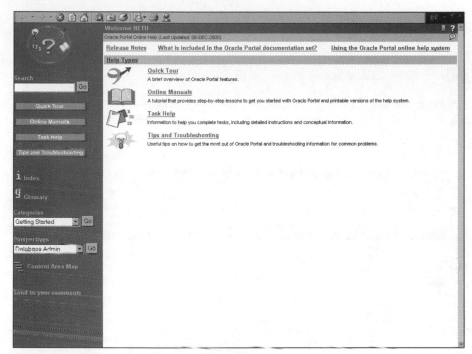

Figure 3-6: The Oracle9*i*AS Portal help system

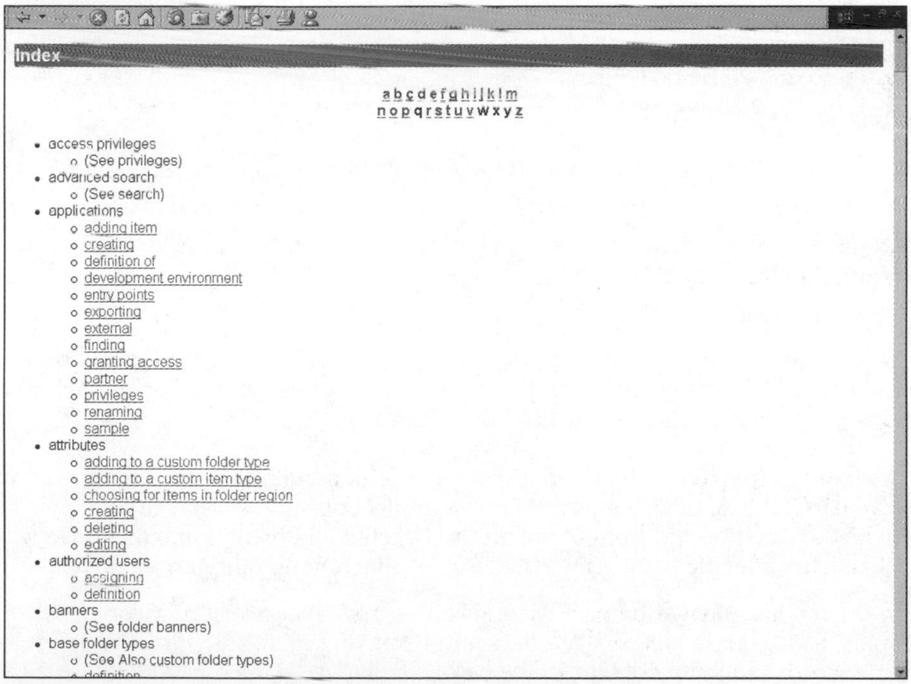

Figure 3-7: An index of Oracle9*i*AS Portal help topics

You can select a category or perspective, which are ways to select and display the information in the Content Area.

Cross-Reference   You will learn a lot more about these concepts in the chapters on Content Area: Chapters 22 and 24.

Finally, there are links to a hierarchical map of the Content Area, shown in Figure 3-8, a glossary of terms, and a way to send feedback to the authors of the help documents themselves.

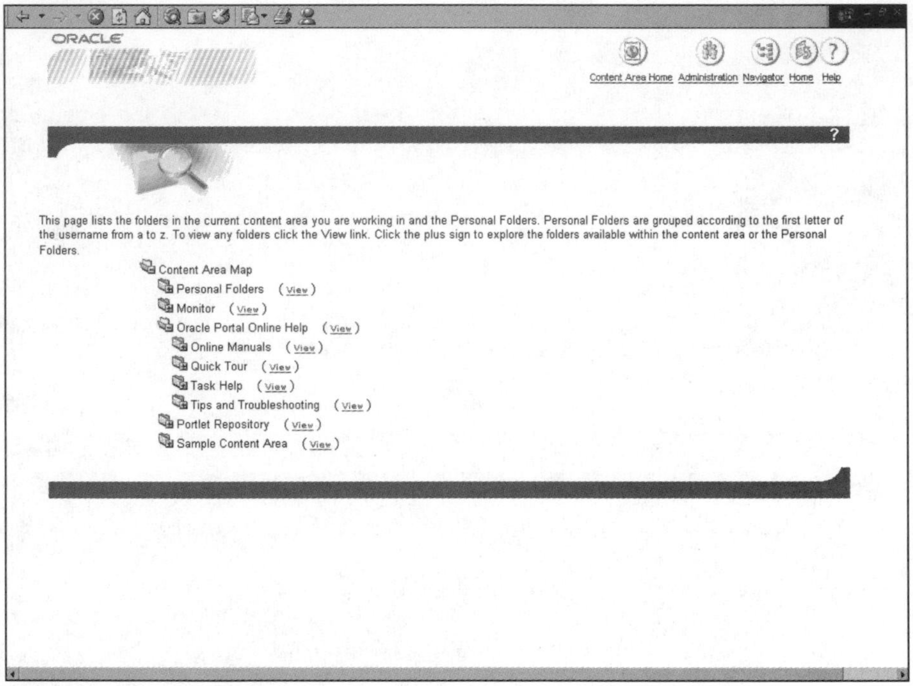

Figure 3-8: The map of help Content Areas

There is one more link in the Oracle9iAS Portal banner, although it is slightly hidden. Clicking on the graphic on the far left of the banner will take you back to the home page, just as clicking on the Home icon will.

The icons displayed in the banner can change, depending on the specific area in the Oracle9iAS Portal environment. As an example, you can see that the banner icons in Figure 3-8 are different from those on the Oracle9iAS Portal home page. We will discuss the specific icons as we discuss specific functionality areas throughout this book.

The banner properties

At the top of each page in the Oracle9*i*AS Portal environment, just below the banner, are a number of links, which are part of the banner and are called banner properties. As with the icons in the banner, these links can change, depending on the particular Oracle9*i*AS Portal page.

4. Switch back to the main Oracle9*i*AS Portal window by clicking on the browser window that contains it, by using the key combination for your client machine that switches between windows, or by simply closing the browser with the help system.

On the home page, there are four banner properties:

✦ Refresh Page forces the parallel page server to explicitly recreate a page. This choice is meaningful only when you understand caching, which is explained in Chapter 6.

✦ Account info takes you to a page where you can enter or edit the user information for the user you are currently logged in as. You can use this link to change your password.

✦ Logout logs you out of the Oracle9*i*AS Portal environment and puts you back at the starting page, as shown in Figure 3-3.

If you were logged in as a user with more privileges, such as the NETUDEV user, you would see one more banner property:

✦ Customize Page allows you to actually change the look and feel of the Oracle9*i*AS Portal home page. The process of customizing pages is explained in Chapter 7.

The rest of the Oracle9*i*AS Portal home page is composed of four areas on the page. Each of those four areas is discussed in the following sections.

The my Links portlet

In the upper-left corner of the main Oracle9*i*AS Portal home page is a portlet titled my Links, as shown in Figure 3-9.

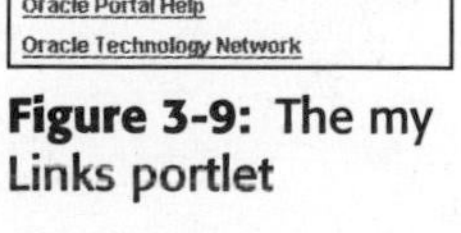

Figure 3-9: The my Links portlet

This portlet is very much like the favorites or bookmarks listing supported by your browser. You can assign a page to this list, and a link to the page will be displayed in the portlet.

This portlet has a special link in the banner at the top of the list labeled Customize. You will be seeing this link a lot when working with Oracle9*i*AS Portal.

1. Click on the Customize link in the banner of the my Links portlet, which will bring up the Edit Favorites Portlet Settings page shown in Figure 3-10.

This page allows you to customize the look and feel and information shown in the portlet. You can see that you have three different areas you can customize for this portlet:

✦ You can change the text in the banner. The default text is Favorites.

✦ You can change the manner in which your favorite links are displayed, as either a hierarchy or a flat listing that ignores the defined hierarchy structure.

✦ You can specify whether you want all the links shown, or you can limit the number displayed to a fixed number.

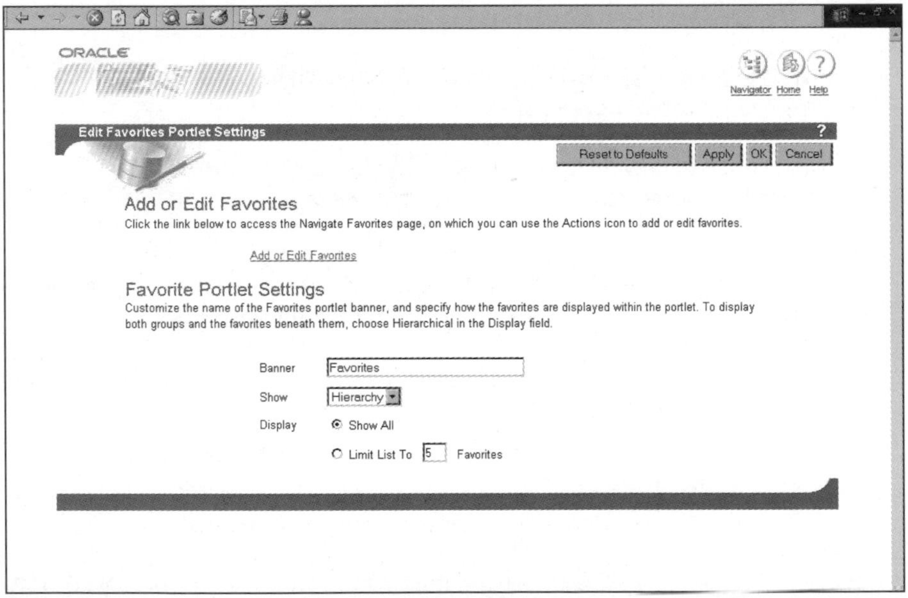

Figure 3-10: The Edit Favorites Portlet Settings page

Normally, the links are displayed in a hierarchical manner. The links displayed in the Figure 3-9 are displayed as a hierarchy, although from looking at them, you might not think so. This is because the default list of favorites does not contain any groups, which could in turn contain other favorites.

The easiest way to understand how to use groups of favorites is to create a group of your own.

2. Click on the Add or Edit Favorites link at the top of the Edit Favorites Portlet Settings page to bring up the Navigate Favorites page shown in Figure 3-11.

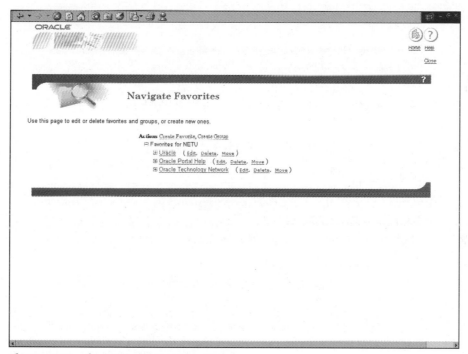

Figure 3-11: The Navigate Favorites page

As you can see, this page gives you the ability to navigate through a list of favorites, as well as to add either a group of favorites or individual ones.

3. Click on the Create Group action link, which will bring up the page shown in Figure 3-12.

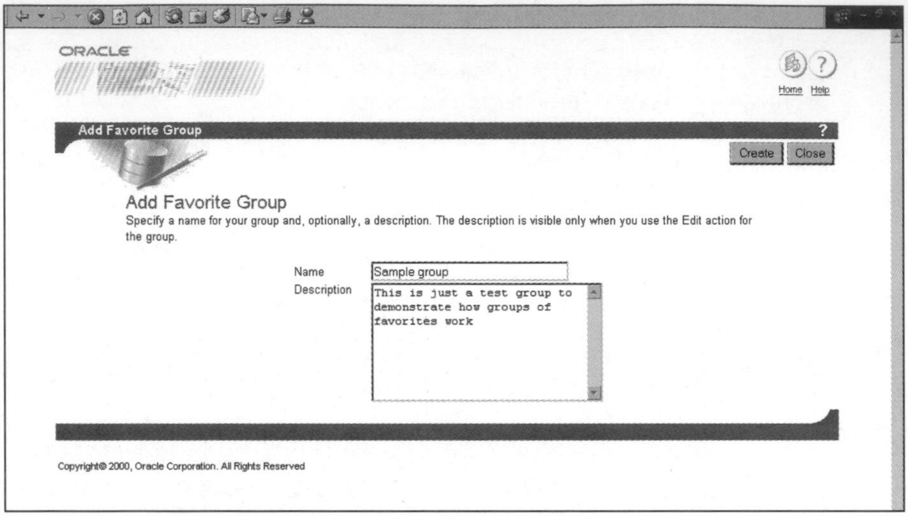

Figure 3-12: The Add Favorite Group page, completed

On this page, you provide the group a name and a description. The name of the group is displayed in the my Links portlet; the description is only used for documentation of the Favorite.

4. Give the group the name **Sample group** and some type of description.

5. Click on the Create button at the top of the page to create the group, and then click on the Close button on the next page to return to the Navigate Favorites page.

The new listing in the Customize page includes the group you just created.

You can see that the links to the right of the newly created group give you some additional choices: Create Favorite, which will add a link to the Sample group, and Create Group, which will add a subgroup under the Sample group.

6. Click on the Create Favorite link, which will bring up the Add Favorite page shown in Figure 3-13.

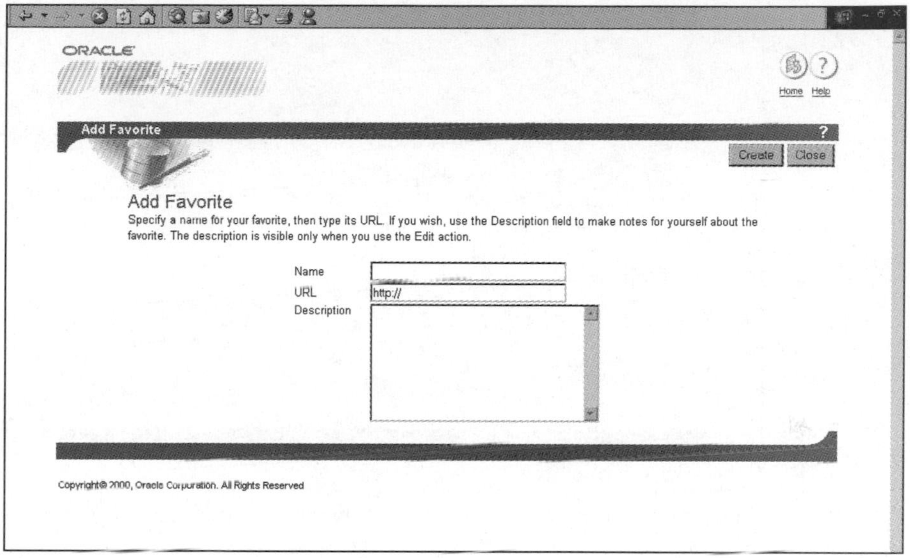

Figure 3-13: The Add Favorite page

On this page, you simply add a name for the favorite, which will be displayed in the portlet, a URL for the favorite, and a description, which, again, is only used for documentation.

7. Give the favorite a name, such as **Favorite 1**, and fill in a URL for the favorite. Click on the Create button to add the favorite. Of course, if you were adding an actual link, you would probably give it a more descriptive name.

8. Create two more favorites in the same manner as you did above. When you have done this, click on the Close button to return to the Navigate Favorites page.

9. Click on the plus sign to the left of the Sample group, which will bring up the page shown in Figure 3-14.

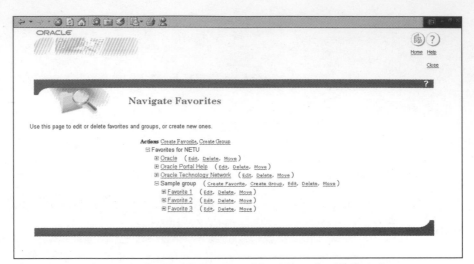

Figure 3-14: The Navigate Favorites page, with a hierarchy displayed

Once you have a group defined, you can see that the Navigate Favorites page lets you expand and contract the favorites hierarchy. Now that you have a few favorites, you can see how the other preferences in this page work.

10. Click on the Close link to close the Navigate Favorites page, and then click the OK button to return to the Oracle9*i*AS Portal environment.

You may have noticed that there are actually four buttons at the top of the Edit Favorites Portlet Settings page:

✦ The OK button applies the changes you have made and returns you to the Oracle9*i*AS Portal environment.

✦ The Apply button applies the changes you have made and leaves you on the Edit Favorites Portlet Settings page.

✦ The Cancel button discards the changes you have made and sends you back to the Oracle9*i*AS Portal environment.

✦ The Reset to Defaults button resets the values for the Edit Favorites Portlet Settings page to the defaults specified for the portlet.

You can see that your hierarchy of favorites is displayed, as shown in Figure 3-15.

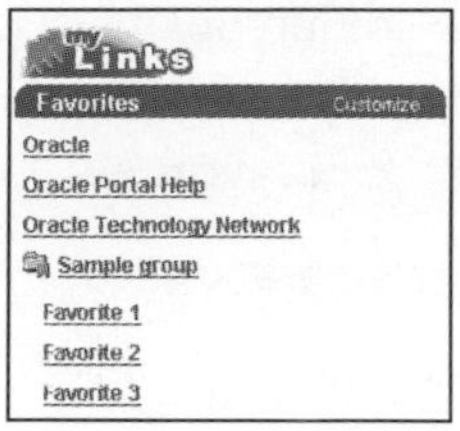

Figure 3-15: The my Links portlet
with a hierarchy displayed

Now that you have a hierarchy and a few more favorites displayed, you can see
more about how this portlet works.

> **11.** Click on link for the Sample group in the my Link portlets. The listing in the
> portlet changes to look like Figure 3-16.

Figure 3-16: Drilling down
in the favorites hierarchy

The new display shows only the favorites listed in the selected group of favorites.
In this view, you can either navigate up one level, with the link on the left, or to the
top of the entire hierarchy, with the link on the right.

> **12.** Click on the Up link to return to the top level of the hierarchy.
>
> **13.** Click the Customize link for the my Links portlet.
>
> **14.** Change the selection in the Show combo box to **Flat list**.
>
> **15.** Click on the OK button to return to the Oracle9*i*AS Portal environment.

The favorites are now displayed in a simple one-level list, as shown in Figure 3-17.

Figure 3-17: Favorites
shown in a flat list

16. Click on the Customize link and change the Show combo box back to **Hierarchy**.

17. Under the Display choice, limit the list to showing four favorites.

18. Click on the OK button.

You can now see the list of favorites as shown in Figure 3-18.

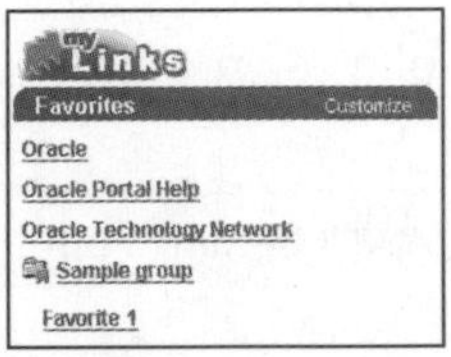

Figure 3-18: Only displaying four favorites

Notice that the list only shows four favorites, and has no indicator that there are any more. On one hand, this is a bit misleading. There is no way for a user to know if there are more favorites than are listed here.

But you can easily get to the complete list of favorites by clicking on the Favorites title in the banner for the portlet. And, even more importantly, the list of favorites displayed in this portlet is *your* list of favorites. The automatic customization features of Oracle9*i*AS Portal mean that there is a separate list of favorites for every individual user. So the only person seeing this list should be you — and you should know that there are more favorites.

Before moving on to the next portlet, you should remove the favorites group you added for demonstration purposes only.

19. Click on the Favorites link in the banner for the my Links portlet.

20. Click on the Delete action link for the favorites group you just added.

21. When you are prompted on the next page to confirm the deletion, click on the Yes button.

22. Click on the Home link in the banner of the Navigate Favorites page to return to the Oracle9*i*AS Portal environment.

The my Work portlet

The second portlet displayed on the Oracle9*i*AS Portal environment's home page is the my Work portlet. If you look at Figure 3-1 or 3-2, you can see that this portlet only displays the title "(None available)".

The my Work portlet displays the last Oracle9*i*AS Portal objects you have worked on. Because the earlier figures were taken before the NETU user had worked on any objects, the listing for my Work was empty.

Just like the listing of the last documents shown at the bottom of the File menu in Microsoft Word, the my Work portlet can act as a shortcut to those objects you were most recently working on.

You can customize the display for the my Work portlet. When you click on the Customize link, you see the Recent Objects Portlet Settings page shown in Figure 3-19.

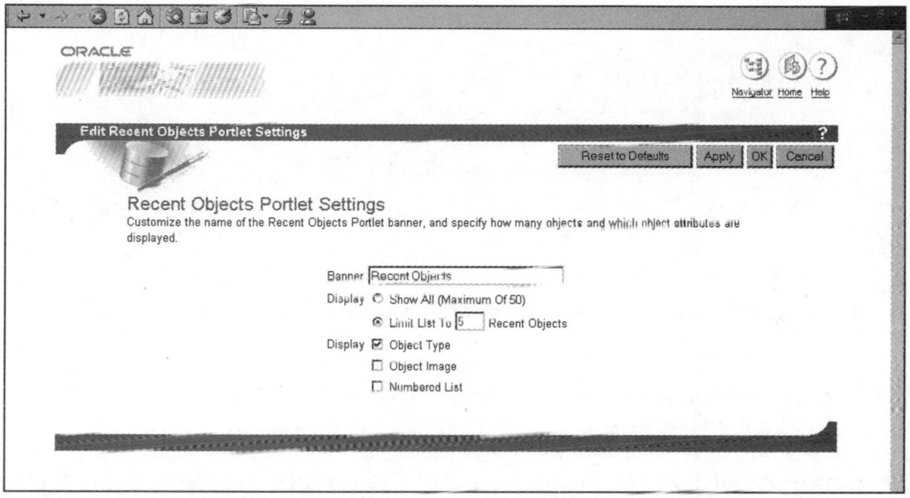

Figure 3-19: Customization for the my Work portlet

With this page, you can change the text in the banner for the portlet, limit the number of recent objects to display, or cause the portlet to display a name or an icon for the object type, or to number the list of recent objects. This customization page also contains the same four buttons that were seen on the Edit Favorites Portlet Settings page.

The On The Web portlet

The third portlet displayed on the left side of the Oracle9*i*AS Portal environment home page is labeled On The Web. This portlet can provide a direct link to different Web-based applications. The applications that come with Oracle9*i*AS Portal are Hotmail and OracleMobile, but administrators can add other applications to this portlet. Again, the best way to understand this functionality is to try it.

1. Click on the Customize link for the On The Web portlet, which will bring up the Edit External Applications Portlet Settings page shown in Figure 3-20.

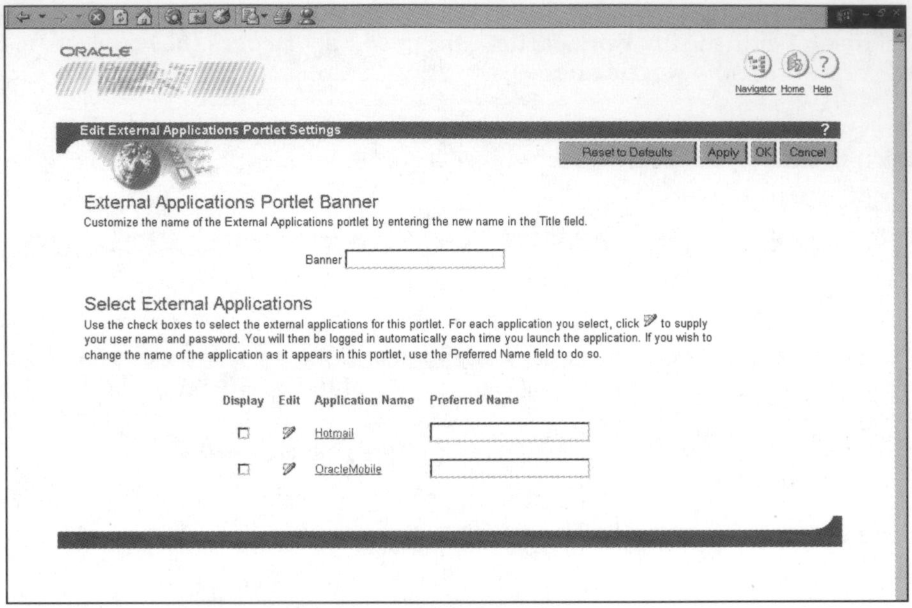

Figure 3-20: Customizing the On The Web portlet

As with the other portlets, you can customize the name displayed in the banner. Unlike the other portlets, though, you can use the check boxes in the Display column in the Select External Applications section to display links to these external applications, edit the characteristics of these applications, or go directly to the applications themselves by clicking on the name of the application.

For now, you should just assign an application to be displayed.

2. Select the Display check box for the OracleMobile entry and click on the OK button to return to the Oracle9*i*AS Portal environment.

3. Click on the OracleMobile link in the On The Web portlet. This action will bring up another browser window that prompts you for a user name and password for the OracleMobile application, as shown in Figure 3-21.

This link would be much better if you could automatically assign a user name and password to log into the OracleMobile application. You will do this in the next set of steps.

Caution   When you clicked on this external link, did you get the page shown in Figure 3-21, or did you get a page that looks more like Figure 3-22? Remember that the link to this external application is essentially a URL for a Web site. If you are using Oracle9*i*AS Portal on an intranet that does not include a connection to the Internet, you will be unable to reach any of these remote locations.

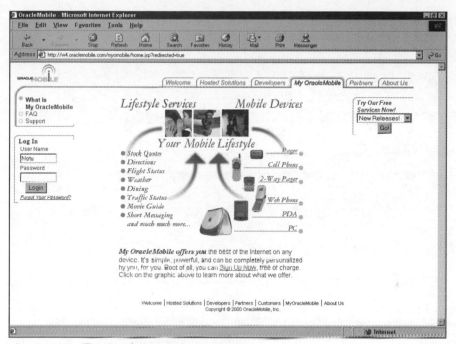

Figure 3-21: The OracleMobile home page

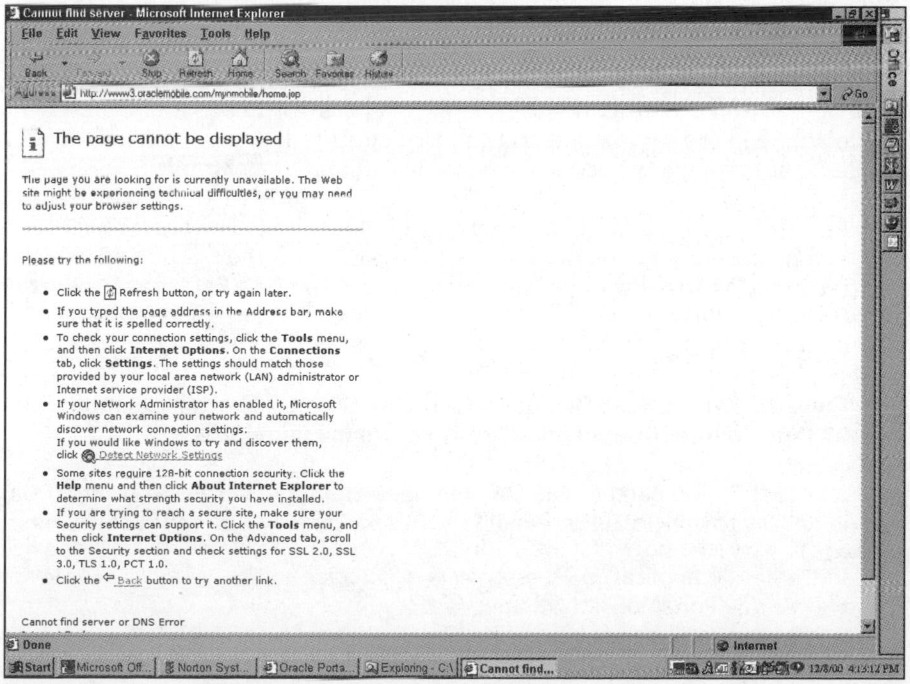

Figure 3-22: No Internet connection, no OracleMobile

4. Close the browser window with the log in page.

5. Click on the Customize link for the On The Web portlet.

6. Click on the Edit link for the OracleMobile application, which will bring up the page shown in Figure 3-23.

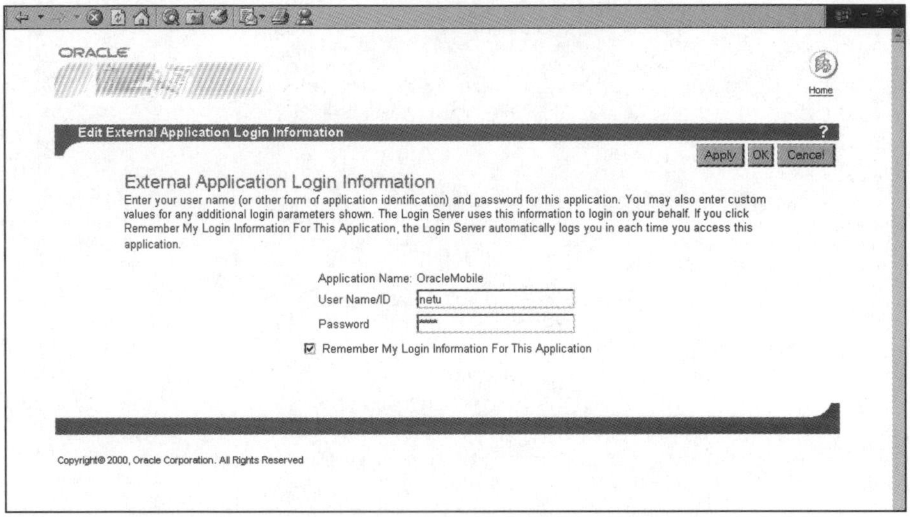

Figure 3-23: Customizing the login for OracleMobile

The page shown in Figure 3-23 is actually an interface to the Oracle9*i*AS Portal Login Server. You can store the user name and password used for accessing OracleMobile in the server, and you can also specify that this login information should be automatically used whenever you call up OracleMobile.

7. Enter Netu for the User Name/ID and 1234 for the Password. (This user name has been set up for readers of this book.) Click on the OK button, which will close the browser window and return you to the Edit External Applications Portlet Settings page.

8. Click on the OK button to return to the Oracle9*i*AS Portal environment.

9. Click on the OracleMobile link again. This action will bring up another instance of the browser window, as shown in Figure 3-24.

You can see that you can use the Oracle9*i*AS Portal login server to provide single sign-on access to applications, even if they use a slightly different user name and password.

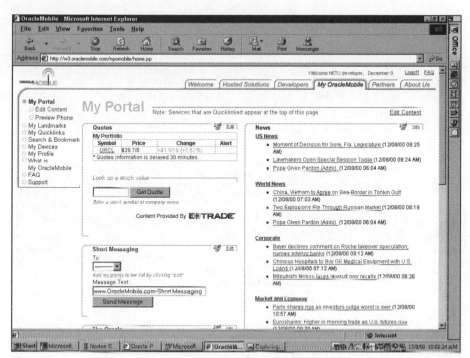

Figure 3-24: OracleMobile, using the stored user name and password

The Build Tab

You've explored all the supporting portlets on the Oracle9iAS Portal environment home page. We won't be discussing these subsidiary portlets much in the rest of this book. But you will be spending quite a bit of time using the main portlet region as a switching ground for your development activities.

If you look back at Figure 3-1 or 3-2, you can see that about 75 percent of the right side of the page is taken up with a region that contains three portlets. These portlets act as a gateway for working with the three main areas of development in Oracle9iAS Portal — pages, Content Areas, and applications.

If you look at the portlets, you see that you can edit any one of these objects, but you can only create a new page. Why is this?

The answer lies in the security built into Oracle9iAS Portal. You may remember that you created the NETU user as a simple user, whereas the NETUDEV user was given full administration privileges. The Oracle9iAS Portal environment looks different for these two users, given their different levels of security. To see how things look to the NETUDEV user, follow these steps:

1. Close the OracleMobile browser window and return to the Oracle9iAS Portal environment.

2. Click on the Logout link on the far right side of the banner at the top of the page.

3. After returning to the Oracle9iAS Portal start page, click on the Login link just below the banner and log in as the NETUDEV user.

The Oracle9iAS Portal environment now looks a little different, as shown in Figure 3-25.

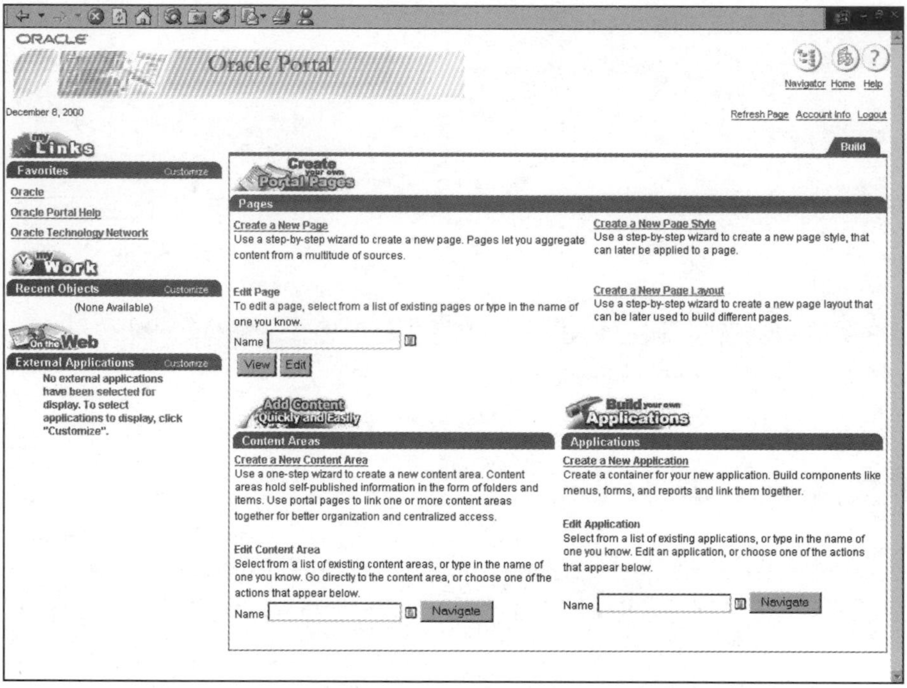

Figure 3-25: The Oracle9iAS Portal environment for the NETUDEV user

You now have the ability to create Content Areas and applications — because the NETUDEV user was given the privileges to do these tasks.

4. Close your browser to leave the Oracle9iAS Portal environment.

A Few Words about Wizards

Much of this book is devoted to building components, Content Areas, and pages with Oracle9iAS Portal. Oracle9iAS Portal uses a *wizard* to help you create each of these objects.

You are probably familiar with wizards from other software products. A wizard contains a series of forms that prompt you for information that it uses to create something for you. In many other products, wizards are used to gather information and generate code for you, which you subsequently have to understand and maintain. Oracle9*i*AS Portal's wizards do generate code under the covers, but you never have to see or understand the code it generates.

Oracle9*i*AS Portal is what is called a *declarative* environment. This means that the process of development is no more than the process of declaring the values for a series of parameters. You don't have to write code. Even more importantly, you don't have to debug and maintain code. If you want to change the way an Oracle9*i*AS Portal component operates, simply change the declared parameters.

After you summon it, there may be some pages that appear before you enter the actual Oracle9*i*AS Portal wizard, but you can always tell when you are in a wizard by a few common user interface conventions, as displayed in Figure 3-26.

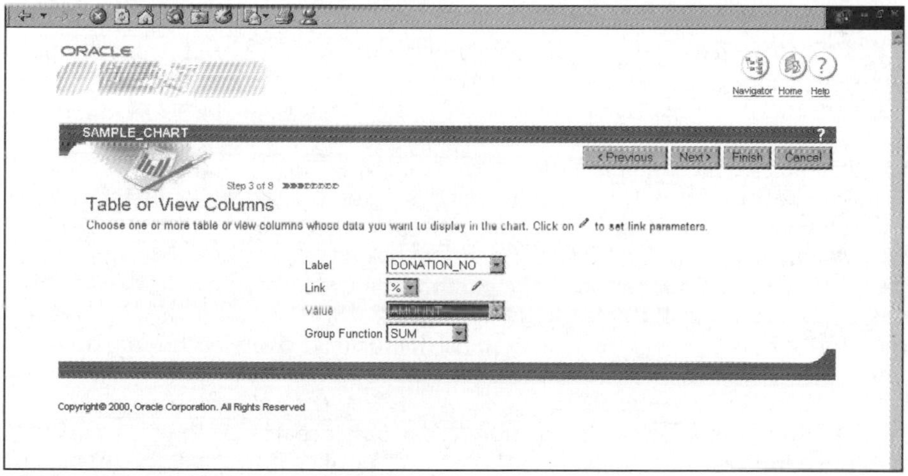

Figure 3-26: A typical wizard panel

Each page in a wizard contains a panel, which has a banner at the top, like other pages in the Oracle9*i*AS Portal environment. At the top of the wizard panel is a small group of arrows. These arrows indicate how many steps, or pages, are involved in using the wizard.

In the upper-right corner of the panel is a small Help icon. When you click this Help icon, it brings up a help page that corresponds to the current wizard page.

Just below the Help icon are the Previous or the Next buttons, or both, depending on where you are. These buttons walk you through the wizard. The Next button takes you to the next page of the wizard, and the Previous button takes you to the previous page of the wizard. There is only a Next button on the first page of each wizard, because there is nowhere to go back to from the first page. Correspondingly, the last page of each wizard only contains Previous button.

To the left of these two buttons are the Finish and the Cancel buttons. If you click on the Finish button, Oracle9*i*AS Portal will complete the creation of your object, using the default values for any item that was not seen. You can use this button to quickly finish the creation of an object, and later return to the object to edit those default values that you wish to change. All the parameters on all the forms have default values, and any parameters that can only accept a particular set of values have value lists associated with them.

Note   Not all pages in the wizard have a Finish button. The Finish button only starts appearing on the wizard pages after the wizard has collected all required information for the creation of the object.

The Cancel button will end the creation of the object, discarding any values already entered.

Located below the wizard panel, in most wizard pages is a brief description of the purpose of that page's entries. In the interest of conserving screen real estate, this description is not present on some wizard pages that contain lots of entries.

The designers of Oracle9*i*AS Portal have tried to arrange the wizards so they prompt you for information, page by page, in a logical order. For instance, the wizard for creating a form component prompts you, in the following order, for a schema and name for the form, the name of the table or view the form is based on, the formatting and validation of the columns on the form, basic options for the display and running of the form, the buttons that will be displayed on the form, the descriptive text that will be displayed on the form, and any additional procedural code you would like to add to the form.

Keep in mind, though, that the component is only created once you have clicked on the Finish button on some page of the wizard. Until that time, all the information you have entered for the component is held in a waiting area in the Oracle database. It is best if you do not use any of the navigation options in the browser itself to leave a wizard until you have completed the process of creating the component. You will spend a lot more time with the wizards in the rest of this book, but you know enough about their general structure for now.

Summary

In this chapter, you got your feet wet while learning the basics of Oracle9*i*AS Portal operation. You learned your way around the Oracle9*i*AS Portal home page, and explored some of the functionality on that page that relates to using the product in general. This knowledge is a necessary precursor to using Oracle9*i*AS Portal to create application systems.

There are a few more broad areas to investigate before you start creating portals with Oracle9*i*AS Portal.

In the next two chapters, you will look at the Oracle9*i*AS Portal Navigator. The Navigator is new to Oracle9*i*AS Portal, and you can use it to examine the pages available to you, the applications and components that you have created with Oracle9*i*AS Portal, and the database objects you can use as the source of data for your Oracle9*i*AS Portal systems.

✦   ✦   ✦

Using the Navigator

◆   ◆   ◆   ◆

In This Chapter

Introducing the
Navigator

Using the Pages Tab

Using the Content
Areas Tab

Using the
Applications Tab

Using Find

◆   ◆   ◆   ◆

One of the most visible changes in Oracle9iAS Portal
from WebDB is the introduction of the Navigator. As its
name implies, the Navigator helps you get from one place to
another within the Oracle9iAS Portal environment. But, in
another sense, the Navigator serves the same function for the
Oracle9iAS Portal environment that your complete portal
application will serve for its users. The Navigator acts as a
connection point for accessing all the objects involved in your
Oracle9iAS Portal system, so you will find yourself using it
again and again.

Introducing the Navigator

You have already been introduced to the Navigator in Chapter
3, where you saw the icon for the Navigator in the banner at
the top of the Oracle9iAS Portal development environment.
Because the Navigator is so central to your activities with
Oracle9iAS Portal, the Navigator icon is one of the three icons
to achieve such a prominent location. To see these three
icons, follow these steps.

1. Log in to the Oracle9iAS Portal environment using the
   user name and password of NETUDEV.

2. Click on the Navigator icon in the banner at the top of
   the page. This action will bring up the page shown in
   Figure 4-1.

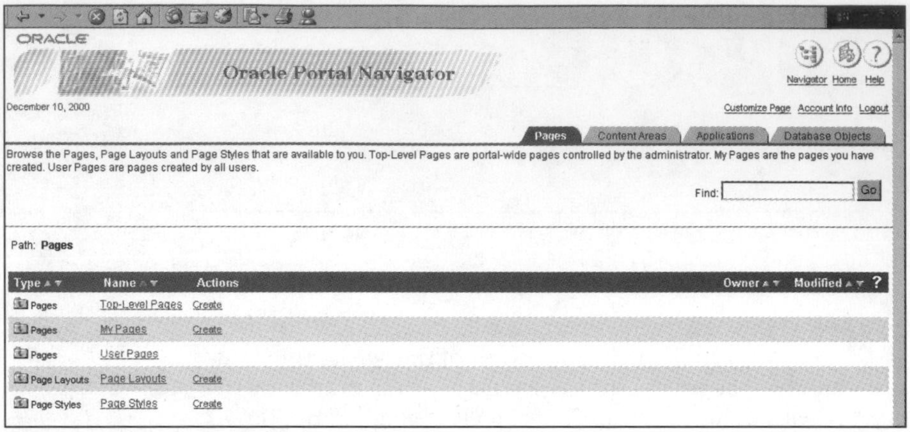

Figure 4-1: The Navigator

There are only a few basic features in the Navigator, and it is easy to quickly grasp the meaning of each of them.

At the very top of the page are three links: Customize Page, Account Info, and Logout. Each of these links performs the same function as they do in the Oracle9*i*AS Portal development environment home page.

Beneath the links are a series of four tabs: Pages, Content Areas, Applications, and Database Objects. The first three of these tabs will be discussed in the next section, and the Database portion of the Navigator will be discussed in the next chapter.

Just below these tabs is a brief explanation of the tab that is displayed and just below that explanation is a Find field. As you might guess, you can search for Oracle9*i*AS Portal objects using the Find field, but because the Find functionality will make more sense after you learn about the rest of the Navigator, we will discuss that later in the chapter.

The substance of the Navigator's capabilities begins below the horizontal line under the Find field. In Figure 4-1, you can see the title, Path, followed by Pages, in bold. This title looks merely informational at this point, but the Navigator moves through a hierarchy of objects in Oracle9*i*AS Portal. The Path line allows you to switch between different levels in this hierarchy.

   3. Click on the Top-Level Pages link on the Pages tab of the Navigator to bring up the page shown in Figure 4-2.

You can now see that the Path includes a hot link back to the previous level in the Pages hierarchy. With this single line, the Navigator gives you shortcuts to navigate back up a chain of objects.

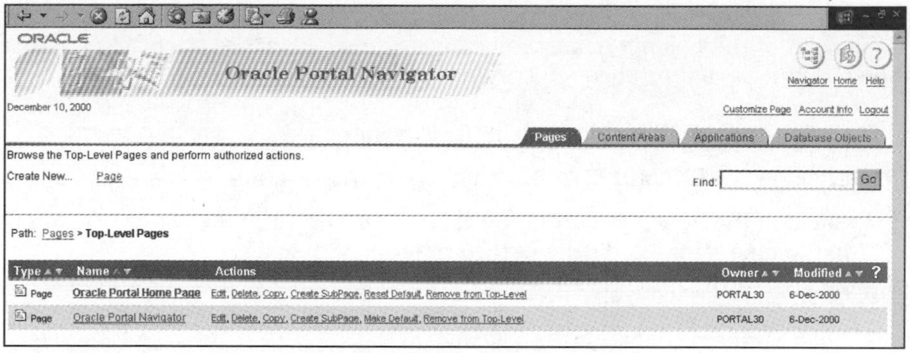

Figure 4-2: The Top-Level Pages displayed in the Navigator

4. Click on the Pages link to return to the top level of the Navigator.

The lowest level in the Navigator is the listing of the actual objects for that tab and place in the hierarchy. This section of the Navigator has its own mini-banner, which contains column headings and a help link. The columns are described in Table 4-1.

	Table 4-1
	Columns in the Navigator
Name of Column	**Function**
Type	This column will contain an icon representing the type of object. If the object is a container object, it will display a folder icon, as shown in Figure 4-1.
Name	The name of the object. This name also acts as a hot link. For container objects, the link will drill down to a listing of the objects in the container. For base level objects, such as pages or application components, the hot link will take you to the most commonly used action for the object.
Actions	This column contains a list of the actions you can take for each item shown in the hierarchy. The Actions list is explained for each area of the Navigator later in this chapter. Notice in Figure 4-1 that the User Pages item does not allow any actions. Because this item is simply a listing, there are no allowable actions for the item.
	The available actions for an object are also based on the user's privileges. If a user is not allowed to perform certain actions on an object, those actions will not appear in the list.
Owner	The Oracle9*i*AS Portal user name of the user who created the object.
Modified	The time and date that the object was last modified.

All of the columns, with the exception of the Actions column, also have little arrows to the right of the column name. You can use these arrows to sort the entries shown in the Navigator page. To sort your entries, follow these steps:

5. Click on the Applications tab in the Navigator.

6. Click on the EXAMPLE_APP hot link in the Name column.

7. Click on the downward-pointing arrow to the right of the Name column heading to change the ordering of the contents of the page.

8. Click on the Pages tab.

9. Click on the Applications tab again.

When you return to the Applications tab, you can see that the context of that tab has been preserved — the Navigator is still on the EXAMPLE_APP level of the Applications hierarchy and the components are still sorted in the same way. The Navigator retains the context of each tab separately for the duration of your Oracle9iAS Portal session. This feature is mighty handy because you will typically be working with one particular page type, Content Area, or application for some time.

As with other parts of Oracle9iAS Portal, the Navigator can appear differently for different users, depending on the user's security privileges. For instance, if you were to log on as the NETU user, who does not have the same level of privileges as the NETUDEV user, you would not see a Customize option as a link at the top of the page or the Create option for the Top-Level Pages entry on the Page tab. Normally, all users with access to the Oracle9iAS Portal development environment can get to the Navigator, but a user without privileges can only use the Navigator to navigate between objects that are visible to everyone.

The Pages Tab

Now that you've explored the most basic functionality of the Navigator, it's time to look at each of the first three tabs. First, click on the Pages tab at the top of the Navigator page.

Because you are logged on as NETUDEV, and thus have a broad range of privileges, you will see the page in Figure 4-3. Because the Pages tab is Navigator's default tab, Figure 4-3 is identical to Figure 4-1.

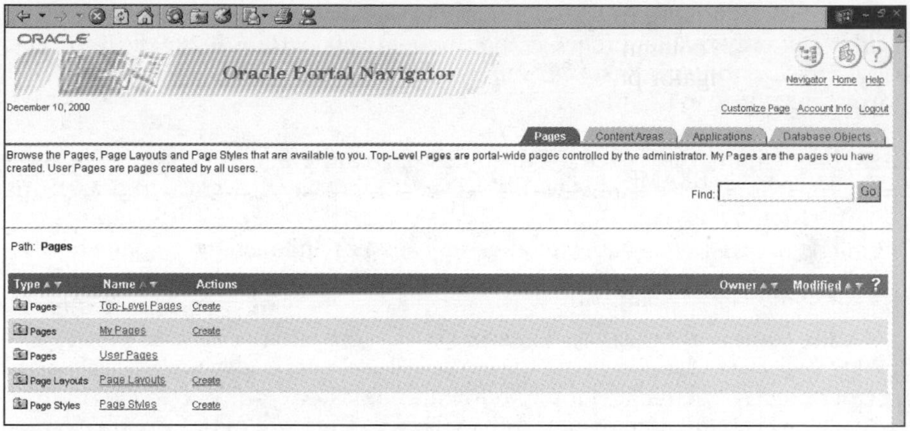

Figure 4-3: The Pages tab in the Navigator

There are five containers listed on the Pages tab:

✦ **Top-Level Pages:** Contains pages that have been designated as top-level pages.

✦ **My Pages:** Contains pages created by the current user.

✦ **User Pages:** Contains a listing of all of the pages available to the user. These pages are alphabetically grouped by the user who created them. If you create either a standard page or a top-level page, it will also be listed in the User Pages container.

✦ **Page Layouts:** Contains look-and-feel layouts that can be used for pages.

✦ **Page Styles:** Defines a set of standards for features like fonts and colors that you can use for pages.

You will learn a lot more about pages in Chapter 7. There are a few more things to learn about this area of the Navigator, though.

You can see that there is only one action listed for the containers on this page — the Create option. (There is no Create option for the User Pages container, because this container is simply a listing of the available pages.) To see more actions listed, you have to go to another level in the Navigator.

1. Click on the Top-Level Pages hot link, which will bring up the page shown in Figure 4-2.

This page looks familiar—which illustrates one of the virtues of the Navigator's design. The only real difference is that there are six actions listed: Edit, Delete, Copy, Create Sub-Page, Reset Default, and Remove from Top-Level. You will learn more about these in Chapter 7.

There is one more difference between this page and the main Pages page in the Navigator. You can see a label with the text "Create New ..." at the top of the page.

There is a Create New ... label, followed by a list of links, on every page in the Navigator—at least every page that you have the privilege to create an object of that type. You can use this title to create base level objects. The Create link always works the same—it brings up a floating menu with a list of all of the types of objects you can create on that page. For the Top-Level Pages page, there is only one type of object—the Page. But to maintain a consistent look and feel to the Navigator, this individual choice still appears to the right of the Create New ... label.

The Content Areas Tab

The next area of the Navigator to examine is the Content Areas tab. To access it,

1. Click on its tab at the top of the Navigator page; this will bring up the page shown in Figure 4-4.

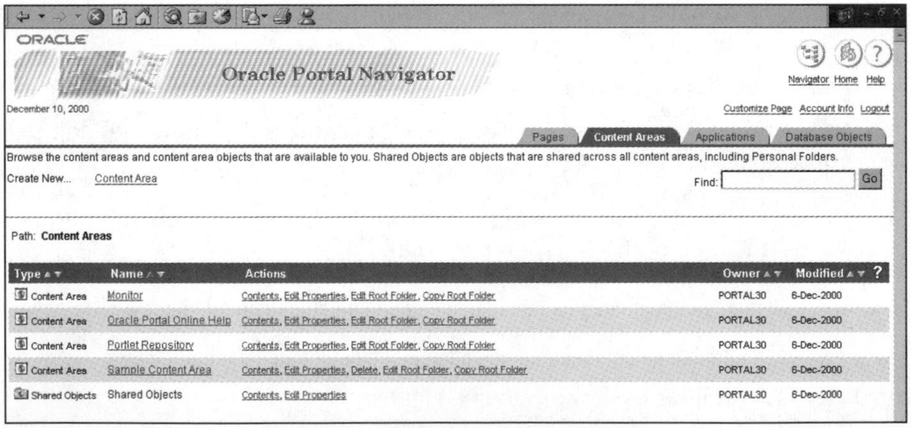

Figure 4-4: The main Content Areas page in the Navigator

There are a couple of new things you can see in this page. First, you can see a mixture of base-level objects—the first four Content Areas listed—and below them, a container—the Shared Objects container. No problem here, because containers and base level objects can be intermixed, as the next few steps will show you.

2. Click on the Contents action for the Oracle9*i*AS Portal Online Help item, which will bring up the page shown in Figure 4-5.

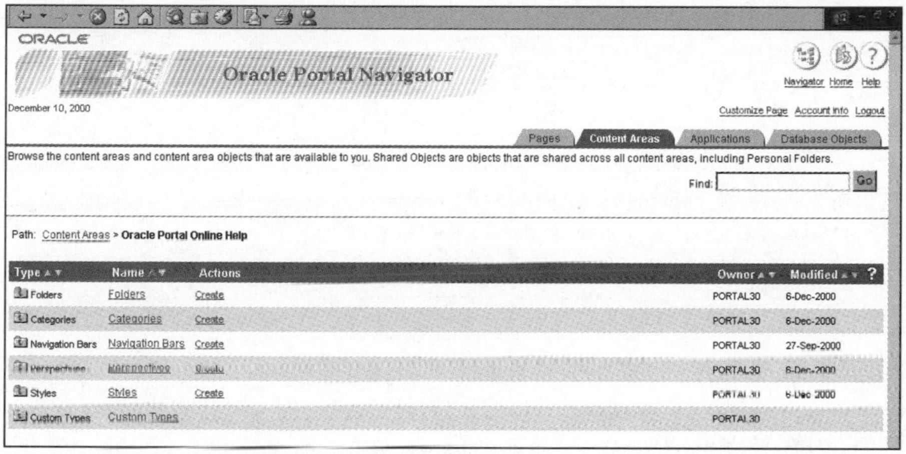

Figure 4-5: The contents of the Oracle9*i*AS Portal Online Help Content Area

You can see that you can even have containers as children of individual items.

3. Return to the start of the Content Area by clicking on the link in the Path listing.

The other thing to notice about the Content Areas is that there are three sets of actions. The Monitor, Oracle9*i*AS Portal Online Help, and the Portlet Repository listings have four actions: Contents, Edit Properties, Edit Root Folder, and Copy Root Folder. The Sample Content Area listing also has a Delete action, because the NETUDEV user has been granted Administer privileges for the folder. The Shared Objects Content Area is a special area owned by Oracle9*i*AS Portal, so you have extremely limited privileges on it.

As with the Pages listing, you will learn a lot more about the use of these choices in Chapter 22.

The Applications Tab

A lot of the work that you will be doing in this book revolves around the different components you can use to build an application, so the Applications tab will be one of your most frequent stops. To view it,

1. Click on the Applications tab at the top of the Navigator page.

Because this tab still shows the contents of the EXAMPLE_APP, click on the Applications tab in the Navigator, which will bring up the page shown in Figure 4-6.

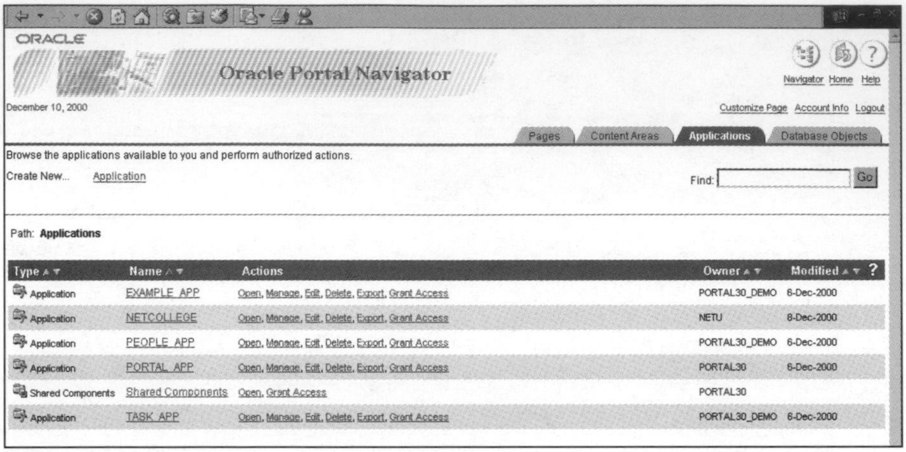

Figure 4-6: The Applications tab in the Navigator

Again, there are a few small differences with this page in the Navigator. There is a different set of actions for the listings: Open, Manage, Edit, Delete, Export, and Grant Access. For the Shared Components container, there are only two actions listed, based on the access rights granted to this internal Oracle9*i*AS Portal container.

The other difference is how the link works for the listings.

> **2.** Click on the hot link for the EXAMPLE_APP application, which will bring up the page shown in Figure 4-7.

This time, the hot link takes you to a listing of the components in the application container. This action is taken from the hot link because it is the most commonly used action for an application.

> **3.** Click on the hot link for the EXAMPLE_CAL component in the EXAMPLE_APP listing in the Navigator, which will bring up the page shown in Figure 4-8.

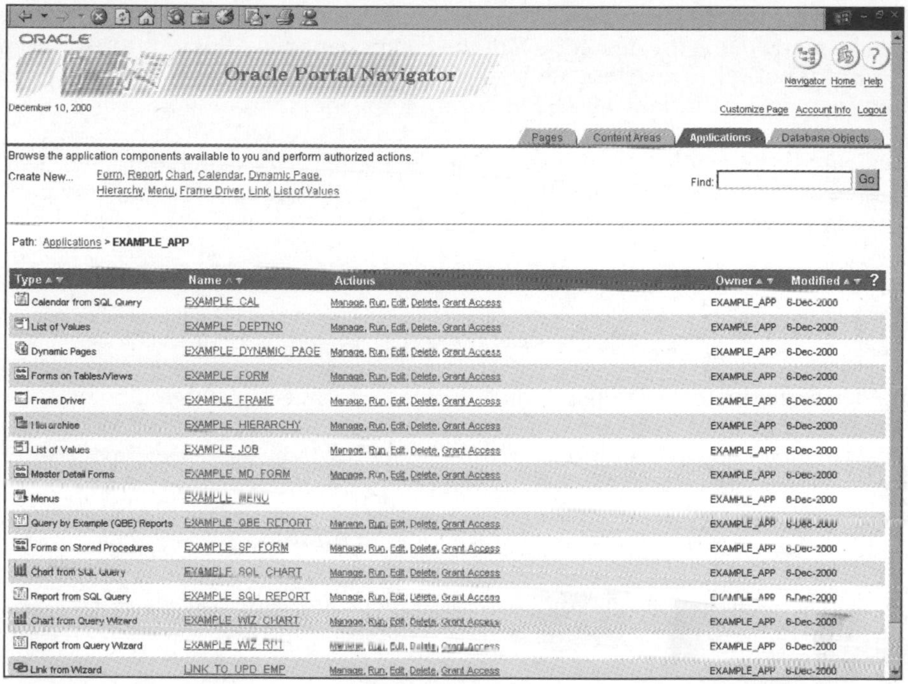

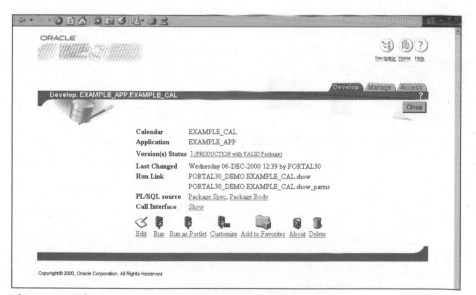

Figure 4-7: The listing for the EXAMPLE_APP application in the Navigator

Figure 4-8: The Manage Component page for EXAMPLE_CAL

The Manage Component action is the most commonly used action for a specific component, so it is the destination of the component's hot link. Although this practice is not entirely consistent across the Navigator, it saves time in working with the many aspects of the Oracle9iAS Portal development environment.

You will learn a whole lot more about building applications and components in Sections III and IV in this book. Before leaving this introduction to the Navigator, you will have to check out one final feature—Find.

Using the Find Mechanism

In WebDB, the Find mechanism was one of the primary ways of finding objects in the development environment. In Oracle9iAS Portal, there is still a Find operation, but many users have found that they use it much less because the Navigator is such an easy and clear way to get to objects. To use Find, follow these steps:

1. Click on the Navigator link in the banner of the Manage Component page.

You will see that you came right back to the same spot you were in when you left the Navigator—a handy feature, because you will usually be working in a specific area for a while.

2. Enter P% in the Find field at the top of the page and click on the Go button to the right of the field. This action will bring up the page shown in Figure 4-9.

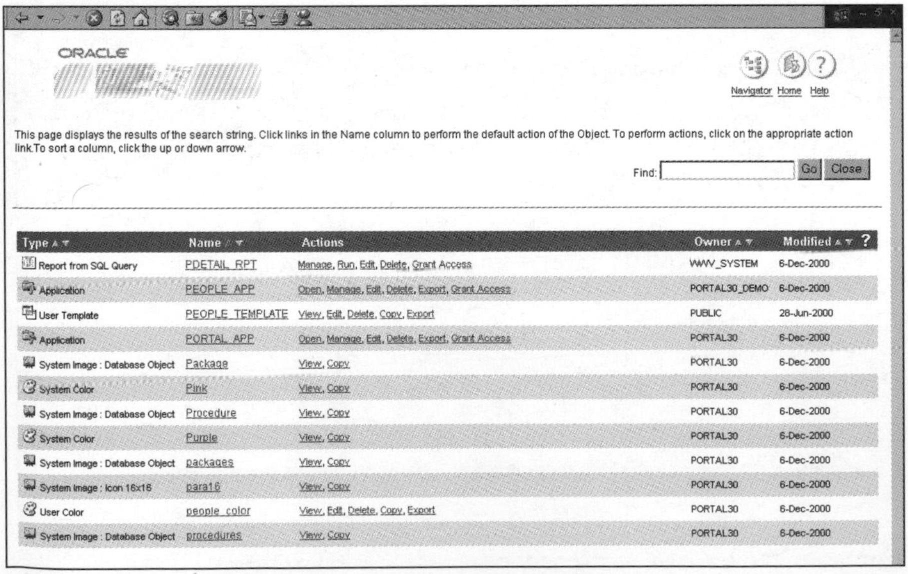

Figure 4-9: The results of a Find in the Applications tab

The listing in Figure 4-9 includes all the components in all applications that begin with the letter P because you specified a wildcard following the letter.

Note

> You can use a wildcard at any place in the Find field. If you use the % wildcard at the beginning of an entry that allows any number of characters, your Find will typically bring back a load of results. Because the purpose of this field is to find an object, it is a good practice to enter as much of the object name as possible to reduce the objects returned. Of course, it is also a good practice to implement a naming scheme for all of your objects to make this possible.

The available wildcards for use in the Find box are the same as the wildcards used in searching for character data in an Oracle database. They are listed in Table 4-2.

Table 4-2 Oracle Wildcards Used with Find	
Wildcard	**Meaning**
_	Represents any one character.
%	Represents one or more characters.

A Find operation only returns the matching objects that are available for that particular tab in the Navigator.

3. Click on the Close button at the top of the Find Results page.

4. Click on the Content Areas tab at the top of the Navigator page.

5. Enter P% in the Find field and click on the Go button; this will bring up the page shown in Figure 4-10.

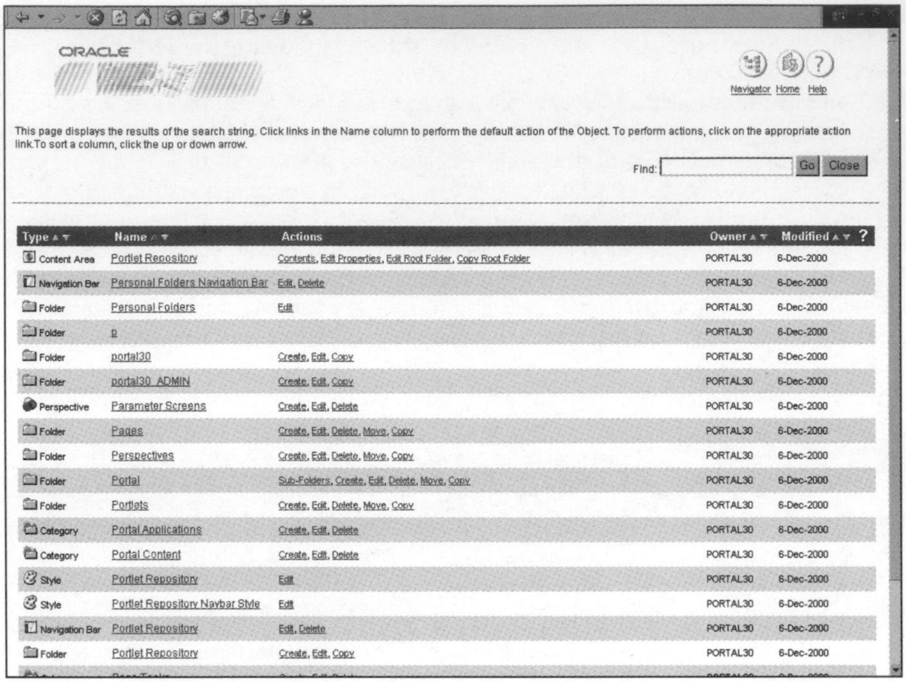

Figure 4-10: The results of a Find in the Content Areas tab of the Navigator

As you can see, this set of results is different from the results listed for the identical operation in the Applications tab.

Summary

This chapter has been rather brief, which is a sign that the user interface provided by the Navigator is clear and concise—a good thing for such a central piece of the product.

The Navigator is essentially an internal utility built into the Oracle9*i*AS Portal environment, but this new feature will have a significant positive affect on your development process. The Navigator acts as a common jumping-off point for most of your development activities, and will become the area that you visit the most.

In this way, the Navigator acts as the doorway and welcome mat for the entire Oracle9*i*AS Portal product. The authors of this book have discovered this first hand, and, after working with Oracle9*i*AS Portal for a while, we have grown to love and cherish the Navigator. It is integrated and straightforward and simple — just the thing for this type of common switching area. We are confident you will come to know and love the Navigator too.

But your tour of the Navigator is not quite over. The Navigator acts as a single point of entry to both the objects you will build with Oracle9*i*AS Portal and the database that underlies those objects. Because most of these objects will be discussed in more detail later, this chapter doesn't spend much time discussing their detailed functionality.

The Navigator also provides a lot of supplemental functionality for interacting with the database, which is the topic of the next chapter.

✦   ✦   ✦

Browsing the Database

✦ ✦ ✦ ✦

In This Chapter

Understanding Basic
Database Object
Definitions

Accessing Database
Objects with the
Database Objects
Tab of the Navigator

Working with the
Database Objects
Tab of the Navigator

Browsing Data

Interacting with Data

Creating Database
Objects

✦ ✦ ✦ ✦

Oracle9iAS Portal, as you have already been told, is built on an Oracle database. The Oracle database provides a number of functions for your Oracle9iAS Portal application — a secure storage mechanism, an engine that you can use to implement your application logic, and a way to help implement security. But, for most of you, your Oracle database's primary purpose is to store your organization's data. You have probably been using your Oracle database for this purpose long before you even thought of getting involved with Oracle9iAS Portal.

This chapter covers using Oracle9iAS Portal to interact with the data structures and data in your database. In a way, this is an overly simplistic statement. After all, almost everything you build with Oracle9iAS Portal is used to interact with your data in one way or another. This chapter focuses on using the Database Objects portion of the Oracle9iAS Portal Navigator, and subsequent chapters cover building components that interact with your data in more specific and customizable ways.

Basic Database Object Definitions

Before you jump right into interacting with your data through the Oracle9iAS Portal Database Navigator, you might want to get a basic understanding of the different types of data objects that can be stored in an Oracle database. If you are already familiar with standard relational database object types, you can skip this section.

The Oracle database can store a wide variety of database objects. All of these objects can be accessed with Oracle9iAS Portal. Table 5-1 gives you a brief description of the most important database objects that you encounter when you create applications with Oracle9iAS Portal.

Table 5-1
Database Objects

Object	Purpose
Table	A table is the basic unit of storage for data in a relational database. A table contains columns, which hold the individual pieces of data. A table is made up of rows, which represent the complete set of columns for the table. If you are familiar with file-based database systems, the equivalent entities for a table, column, and row are a file, field, and record.
View	A view, as the name implies, is another way to look at the data in a table. A view can represent a subset of the columns in a table or a combination of columns from one or more tables. A view is also sometimes used to enforce security on the data in the underlying table by limiting the rows a particular user can see. A view is the product of an SQL statement, and, as such, does not directly store data. Instead, it gives access to the data in the underlying tables the view is based upon.
Index	An index is a database object that is related to a particular table. An index is made up of one or more columns in a table, and provides faster access to rows in the table. Indexes can also improve performance by returning rows from the database sorted by the values in the index.
Procedure	A procedure is a piece of logic that is stored and executed in an Oracle database. Traditionally, Oracle procedures have been written in a language called PL/SQL. With Oracle8i, procedures can be written in either PL/SQL or Java, although, technically, the code for Java is stored in classes or objects. A procedure is a set of logical steps that can be called up and that return one or more values. All of the functionality you use in your Oracle9iAS Portal modules is implemented with Oracle procedures; although, because Oracle9iAS Portal is a declarative environment, you do not have to write any PL/SQL or Java code.
Package	A package is a group of procedures. A package contains a package header, which describes the interfaces to the procedures in the package, and a package body, which contains the actual code used in the procedures.
Function	A function is a piece of logic that returns a single value. A function can be written in either PL/SQL or Java, although once again the naming convention is different for Java. A function can be used in an SQL statement.

Object	Purpose
Trigger	A trigger is a specific piece of logic that is called when a particular database event occurs. Triggers are attached to tables, and you can specify that a trigger be executed when a database event, such as adding or deleting a row in a table, takes place. Triggers use the same syntax as procedures to implement their logic.
Sequence	A sequence is a special type of database object that has only one purpose: it supplies the next number in a sequence of numbers. Sequences are often used to assign unique identifiers to rows in a database table.
Synonym	A synonym is an alias for a database object. Creating a synonym for a database object can make it easier to reference the object.

Many other database objects can be contained in an Oracle database, including snapshots, packages, clusters, and functions. If you are new to Oracle, you will probably not have to deal with these types of database objects as you create Oracle9*i*AS Portal application systems. If you are familiar with Oracle and its database objects, you no doubt already understand them. Thus, no more explanation is necessary here.

The rest of this chapter concentrates on explaining how Oracle9*i*AS Portal enables you to interact with the main types of database objects listed in Table 5-1.

The Database Objects Tab of the Navigator

Oracle9*i*AS Portal introduces a whole new way to look at database objects in your Oracle database — the Database Objects tab of the Navigator.

The designers of Oracle9*i*AS Portal figured that database objects were just another component in your portal environment, so you can explore database objects the same way you can explore sites or applications.

Figure 5-1 shows the first page of the Database Objects tab for the NETU schemes used in this book.

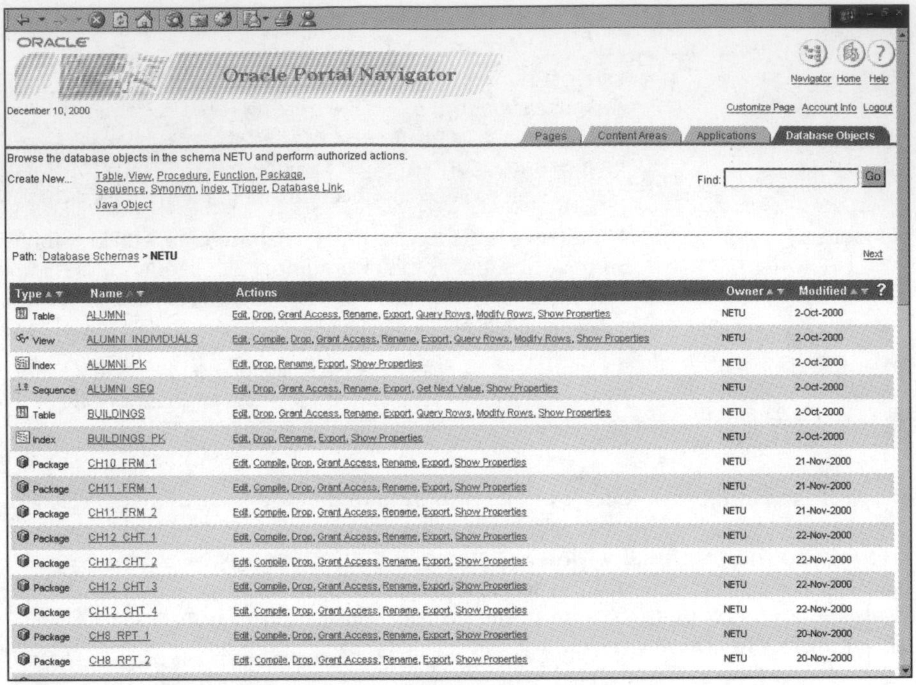

Figure 5-1: The Database Objects tab of the Navigator

You can see that there are five columns for each database object — Type, Name, Actions, Owner, and Modified — just as there were for other objects in the Navigator. You can sort the list of database objects by the values of all of the columns except the Actions column. In the default view of database objects, they are sorted by object type, and then by object name within type. As with the other areas of the Navigator, each sortable column heading has two arrows to the left of the heading — an upward pointing arrow, which you can click on to sort the objects in ascending order for that column value, and a downward pointing arrow, which you can click on to sort the objects in descending order for that column value.

The Name column contains the name of the object, which is also a hyperlink to the most frequently used action page. The Actions column contains the possible actions for each type of object. Depending on the type of object, there are slightly different sets of actions.

All of the objects can have three actions, based on privilege level of the user:

✦ Edit takes you to a page where you can edit the object definition.

✦ Drop drops the object from the database, after prompting you to confirm the deletion.

✦ Show takes you to a page where the extended properties of the object are shown.

Table 5-2 lists the unique actions for each type of database object and the destination of the Name link for the object type.

Table 5-2		
Database Objects Tab of the Navigator Object Attributes		
Object	*Unique Actions*	*Linked Action from Name*
Table	Grant Access allows you to assign access privileges for the object to users and groups.	Query Rows
	Rename allows you to rename the object.	
	Query Rows takes you to a Query-By-Example (QBE) page, where you can specify conditions to limit the rows returned.	
	Modify Rows takes you to a QBE page, where you can specify conditions to limit the rows returned or insert new rows. Once the rows are returned, you can edit or delete existing rows.	
	Export exports the table to a file, which can be used to transfer the object to another database.	
View	Compile allows you to compile the view and returns the resultant status of the view.	Query Rows
	Grant Access allows you to assign access privileges for the object to users and groups.	
	Rename allows you to rename the object.	
	Query Rows takes you to a QBE page, where you can specify conditions to limit the rows returned.	
	Modify Rows takes you to a QBE page, where you can specify conditions to limit the rows returned or insert new rows. Once the rows are returned, you can edit or delete existing rows.	
	Export exports the view to a file, which can be used to transfer the object to another database.	

Continued

Table 5-2 *(continued)*

Object	Unique Actions	Linked Action from Name
Index	Rename allows you to rename the object. Export exports the index to a file, which can be used to transfer the object to another database.	Show Properties
Procedure	Compile allows you to compile the object. Grant Access allows you to assign access privileges for the object to users and groups. Rename allows you to rename the object. Execute executes the procedure and returns any result generated by the procedure. Export exports the procedure to a file, which can be used to transfer the object to another database.	Edit
Package	Compile allows you to compile the object. Grant Access allows you to assign access privileges for the object to user and groups. Rename allows you to rename the object. Export exports the package to a file, which can be used to transfer the object to another database.	Edit

Note: You will only be allowed to edit packages that have less than 30K of text.

Object	Unique Actions	Linked Action from Name
Function	Compile allows you to compile the object. Grant Access allows you to assign access privileges for the object to users and groups. Rename allows you to rename the object. Execute executes the procedure and returns any result generated by the procedure. Export exports the function to a file, which can be used to transfer the object to another database.	Edit
Trigger	Rename allows you to rename the object. Export exports the trigger to a file, which can be used to transfer the object to another database.	Show Properties
Sequence	Grant Access allows you to assign access privileges for the object to users and groups. Rename allows you to rename the object. Get Next Value retrieves the next value from the sequence. Export exports the sequence to a file, which can be used to transfer the object to another database.	Show Properties
Synonym	Grant Access allows you to assign access privileges for the object to users and groups. Rename allows you to rename the object. Export exports the synonym to a file, which can be used to transfer the object to another database.	Show Properties

There are actually several more database objects that can be shown in the Database Navigator: Database Links, Java Classes, Java Sources and Java Resources. Because these objects are not used in this book, we have not described them in detail, but they follow the same pattern for interaction as the other objects described in the table above.

The Database Objects tab of the Navigator also gives you the ability to create new objects for any of these types, with the same Create New... methodology used for the other tabs of the Navigator. A closeup of this option is shown in Figure 5-2.

Create New...	Table, View, Procedure, Function, Package, Sequence, Synonym, Index, Trigger, Database Link, Java Object

Figure 5-2: The Create New... area in the Database Objects tab of the Navigator

Clicking on the object type will take you directly to the creation wizard for that type of object. You will learn more about creating database objects in the final section of this chapter.

You will be working with the Database Objects tab of the Navigator for the rest of this chapter. In fact, because the Database Objects tab of the Navigator is readily available from any browser, you may find that this Navigator is a quick and easy way to interact directly with your Oracle database.

Accessing database objects with the Database Navigator

You are probably ready to start exploring with the Database Navigator, so let's jump in:

1. Open the Oracle9iAS Portal home page in your browser by entering the URL `http://servername:portno/pls/schema_DAD` in your browser's address field, where `servername` is the name of the server hosting Oracle9iAS Portal, `portno` is the port number of the port assigned to Oracle9iAS Portal (optional if you used the default port for a Windows NT installation), and `schema_DAD` is the name of the schema in which you installed Oracle9iAS Portal, which defaults to `portal30`.

2. Click on the Login link at the upper-right corner of the page.

3. Log in as the `NETUDEV` user you created in Chapter 2.

4. Click on the Navigator link on the right side of the Oracle9iAS Portal title area.

5. Click on the Database Objects tab at the top of the Navigator page. You will get the page shown in Figure 5-3.

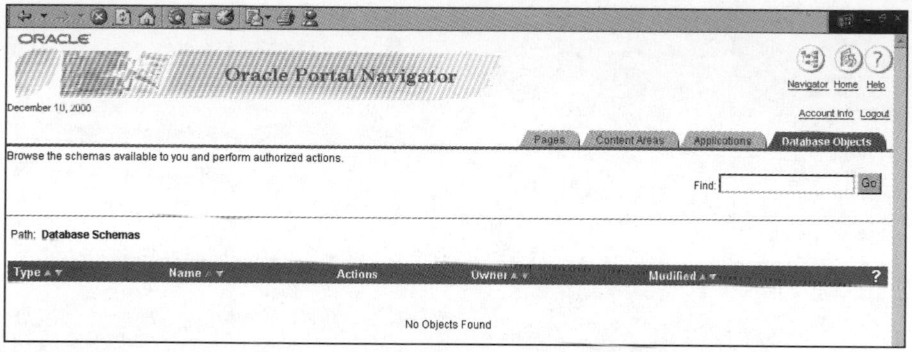

Figure 5-3: Your first attempt at accessing the Database Navigator

You can see a whole host of schemas in your Database Navigator view. You see them all because the user, NETUDEV, was made a part of the DBA group when you created it in Chapter 2. Being part of the DBA group is a powerful privilege — one that you might not want to give out lightly. What if you only wanted to give a user access to a single database?

The new version of Oracle9iAS Portal has a significant difference from earlier versions. In Oracle9iAS Portal, all security is enforced by Oracle9iAS Portal. This new feature means that a user must be given the capability to access data with administration privileges through Oracle9iAS Portal, regardless of the database privileges assigned to the database schema the user is assigned to.

The only user who can grant the required privilege by default is the owner of the Oracle9iAS Portal installation. This user is the owner of the schema you installed Oracle9iAS Portal into, which, by default, is Oracle9iAS Portal. To grant the NETUDEV user access to the NETU schema, follow these steps:

6. Click on the Logout link in the upper-right corner of the page.

7. Click on the Login link in the upper-right corner of the page.

8. Log in as the owner of the Oracle9iAS Portal installation. The owner of the installation is the user you defined when you installed Oracle9iAS Portal in Chapter 2. If you did a default installation, the user name and password are Oracle9iAS Portal.

9. When the home page of Oracle9iAS Portal appears, click on the Navigator link in the Oracle9iAS Portal title bar. Click on the Database Objects tab at the top of the page to bring up the Database Objects tab of the Navigator for the Oracle9iAS Portal owner, as shown in Figure 5-4.

You can see that the owner of the Oracle9iAS Portal environment can view all of the different schemas that can be used with Oracle9iAS Portal. You will want to grant the NETUDEV user access to the NETU schema, which is where your data lies.

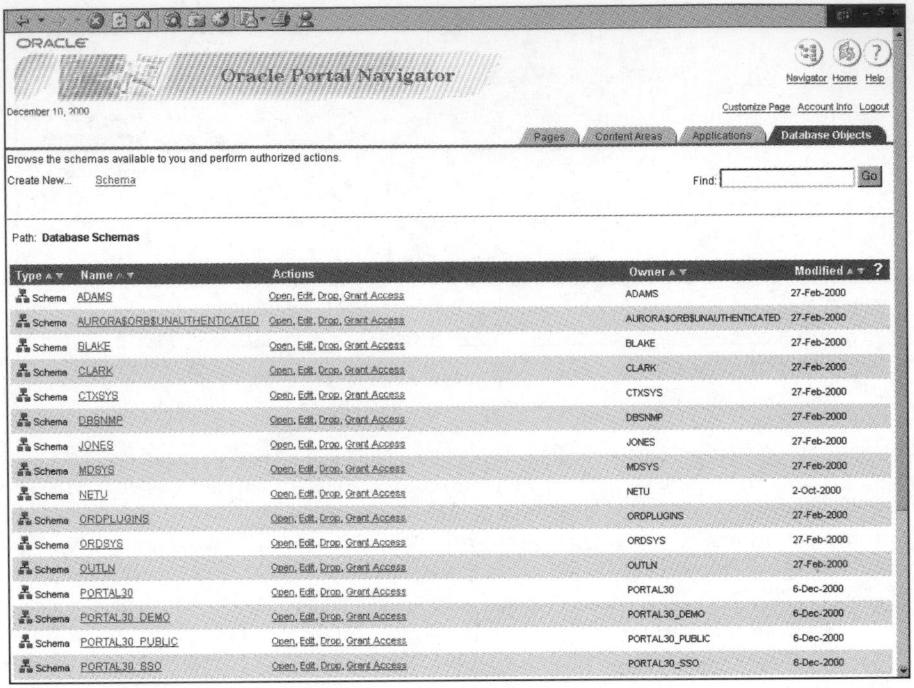

Figure 5-4: The Database Navigator for the Oracle9*i*AS Portal owner

10. Click on the Grant Access link in the list of actions for the NETU schema. The page shown in Figure 5-5 will appear.

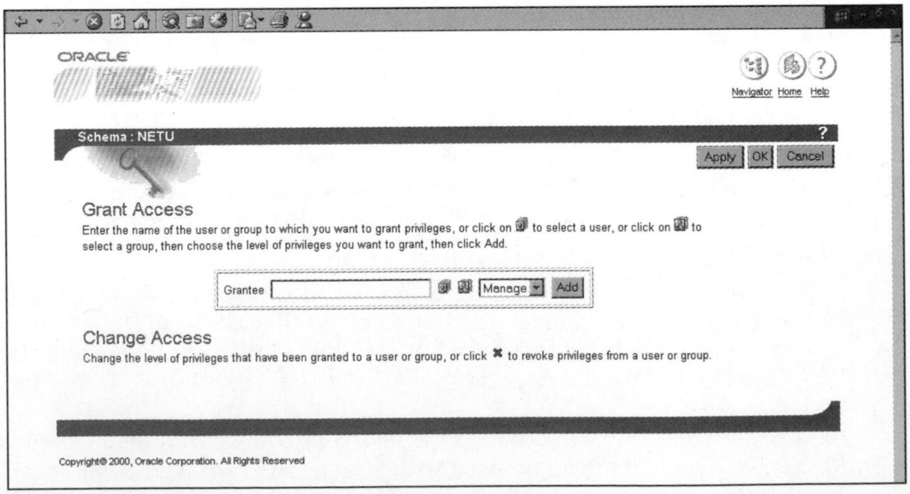

Figure 5-5: Granting access to a schema

11. Enter NETUDEV as the Grantee, leave the Manage privilege as shown in the drop-down list box to the right of the Grantee field, and click on the Add to List button, which grants the privilege.

12. Click on the OK button to close the dialog.

13. Log out as the Oracle9*i*AS Portal owner and log back in as user NETUDEV.

14. Click on the Navigator link in the banner and on the Database Objects tab in the Navigator.

15. Click on the NETU schema name.

You would now see the Database Objects tab of the Navigator in all its glory, as shown in Figure 5-6.

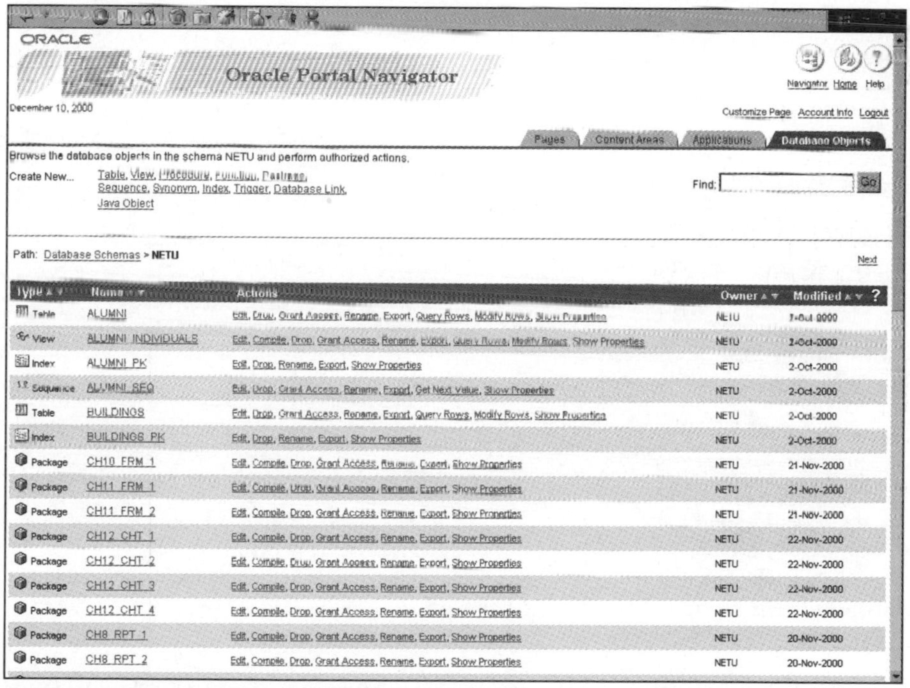

Figure 5-6: The Database Navigator, showing the NETU schema

Now that your user has access to database objects through the Database Objects tab of the Navigator, you can start to explore its capabilities.

Working with the Database Navigator

The purpose of this section is not to give you a complete tour of all the actions on the Database Navigator. Instead, the section concentrates on showing you a representative set of actions for some of the object types.

Working with indexes

1. Scroll down to the GRADES_PK object and click on its Show Properties action link. The page shown in Figure 5-7 will appear.

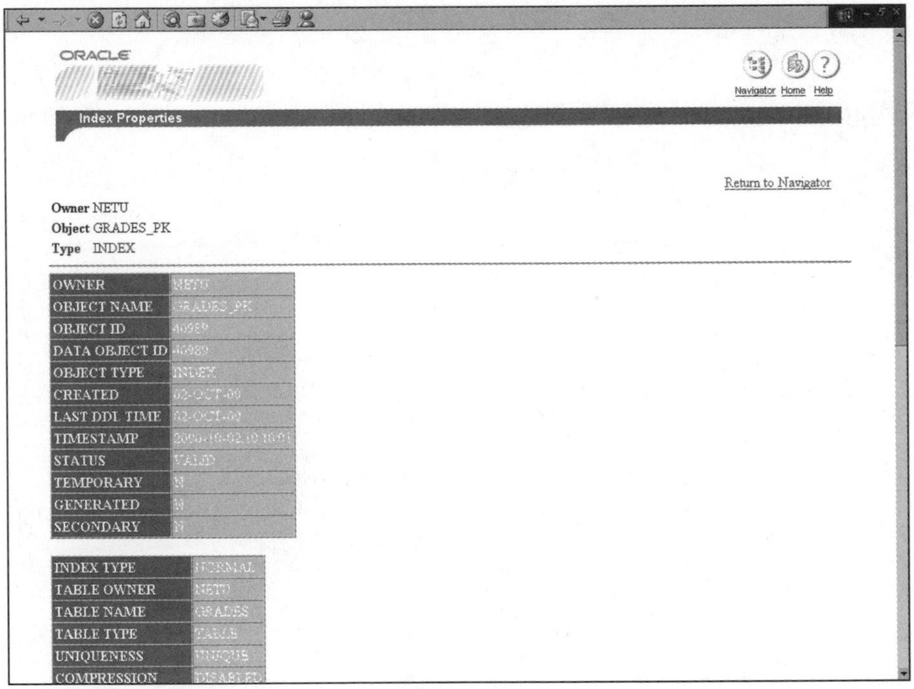

Figure 5-7: Browsing the Index Properties page

You can see that there is an exhaustive list of properties for this index. If you are familiar with Oracle database objects, you will recognize the properties as attributes assigned to an index. If you are not familiar with Oracle database objects, you may be a bit mystified by some of the property names, such MAXTRANS or INITIAL EXTENT. These attributes are important to database administrators, but it is not necessary for you to understand them to use the data in the database.

2. Scroll to the bottom of the page. You will see a table with the heading of Indexed Columns, as shown in Figure 5-8.

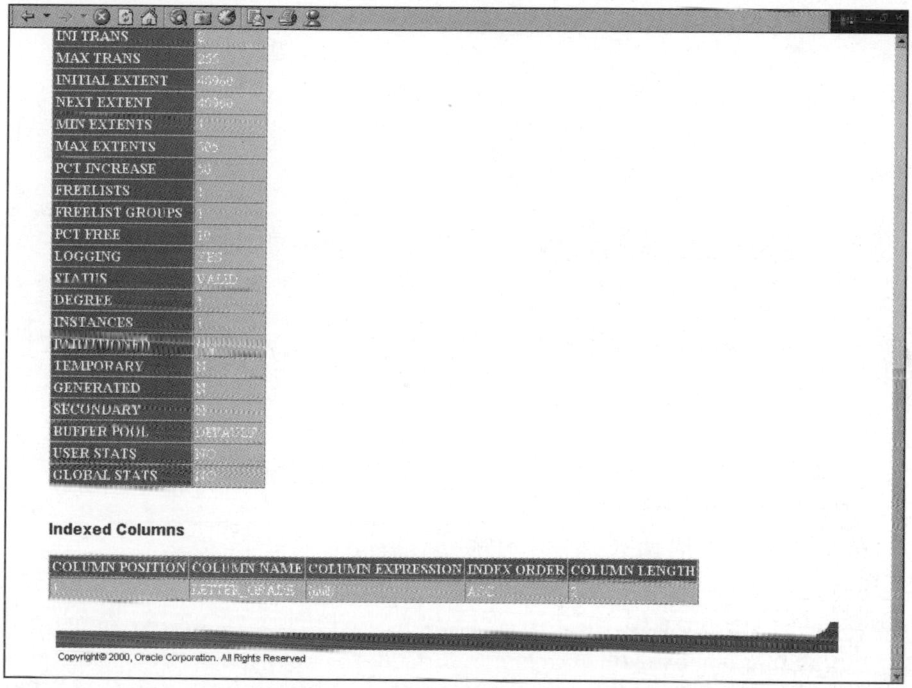

Figure 5-8: The Indexed Columns table in the Index Properties page

This Indexed Columns table is created with information gathered from a different part of the Oracle database system catalog.

Working with procedures

3. Scroll to the top of the page and click on the Return to Navigator link. Click on the Edit action link for the NEW_CLASS_YEAR procedure.

The page shown in Figure 5-9 will appear.

```
ORACLE

NETU.NEW_CLASS_YEAR                                              ?
                                                          OK  Cancel

Procedure Body

        Create or Replace PROCEDURE NETU.NEW_CLASS_YEAR

as
        current_max_year number(4);
begin
        select max(classyr) into current_max_year from
classes;
        update classes set classcode = 'Sophomore' where
classyr = current_max_year;
        update classes set classcode = 'Junior' where
classyr = current_max_year-1;
        update classes set classcode = 'Senior' where
classyr = current_max_year-2;
        update classes set classcode = 'Alumni' where
classyr = current_max_year-3;
        insert into classes values
(current_max_year+1, 'Freshman');
end;

Copyright© 2000, Oracle Corporation. All Rights Reserved
```

Figure 5-9: Editing the NEW_CLASS_YEAR procedure

The NEW_CLASS_YEAR procedure comes as a part of the standard installation of the sample database for this book. The procedure is written in the PL/SQL language, and you can probably understand that the procedure is used to set the values of the CLASSCODE column, based on the class year.

You could edit the procedure directly in this page, but at this time you should leave it alone and just return to the main page of the Database Objects tab of the Navigator. Simply click on the Cancel button to return to the main Database Objects tab of the Navigator page.

On the CD-ROM

The only capabilities you have in editing a procedure through this page in the Database Navigator are those of a simple text editor. It's much better to use another tool to create and edit procedures. In fact, you'll find a shareware version of a popular PL/SQL editor, PL/SQL Developer, on the CD that accompanies this book.

When you edit a procedure and click on the OK button, the procedure is automatically recompiled. There are some times, though, when you might want to use this interface to recompile a procedure that had not properly compiled previously. Follow these steps to do so:

1. Click on the Compile action link for the NEW_CLASS_YEAR procedure.

Oracle9*i*AS Portal will return a page that tells you the procedure was successfully compiled and has been given a status of VALID, as shown in Figure 5-10.

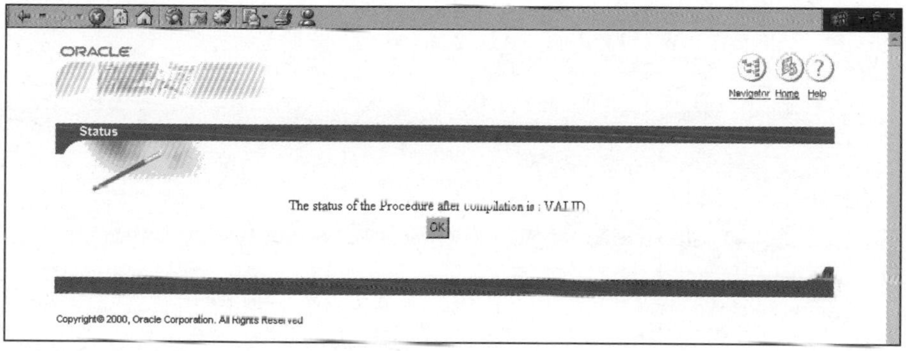

Figure 5-10: A successful compilation of a procedure

2. Click on the OK button to return to the main Database Objects tab of the Navigator page.

3. Click on the Execute action link to run the NEW_CLASS_YEAR procedure.

The page shown in Figure 5-11 will appear.

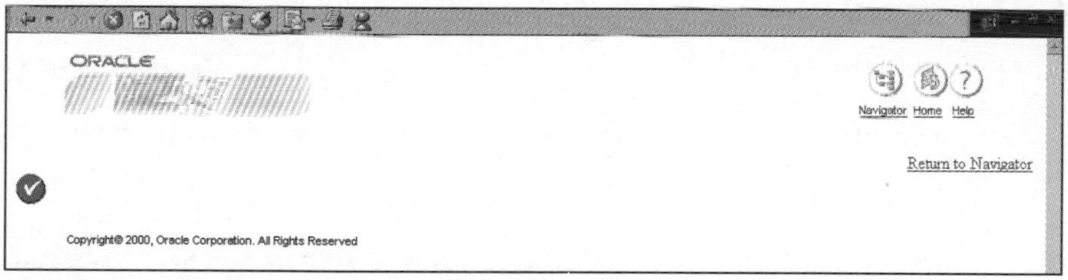

Figure 5-11: The result of executing a procedure

You can see the green check mark, which indicates that the procedure ran successfully. If the procedure returned a result, the result would also be shown on this page.

Note If the procedure you were executing allowed any parameters, you would be presented with a page that prompted you for those parameters before the procedure executed.

You have seen enough of the capabilities of the Database Navigator for procedures; it's time to move on to working with tables.

Working with tables

4. Click on the Return to Navigator link at the top of the page.

5. Click on the Grant Access action link for the ALUMNI table. You will see the page shown in Figure 5-12.

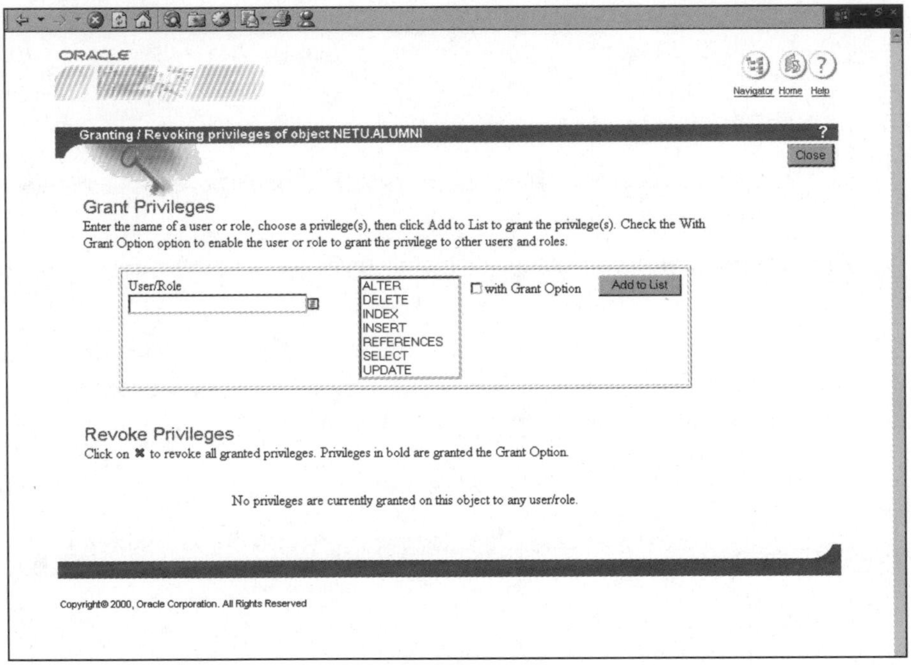

Figure 5-12: Granting access to a table

On this page, you can see a text field, where you can specify the user or role to grant access, and a list box with a list of actions for the table. Be aware that the users and roles used in this page are *database* users and roles. If you were to look at a list of the available users, you would see the NETU user, but no user listing for NETUDEV. The reason for this is that both the NETU and NETUDEV user (in Oracle9*i*AS Portal) are associated with the NETU schema and user of the host database.

To the right is the with Grant Option check box. A user or role given the with Grant Option for a type of access has the ability to grant that type of access to other users. To the far right is the Add to List button.

To add a new access privilege, you would specify the user or role in the text field, select the privileges that you want to assign, and click on the Add to List button. Once you have granted privileges to a user or role, that user or role will appear at the bottom of the page, with a red X to the left of their name that will allow you to revoke their privileges.

Note
All of the privileges for each user are listed on a single line. You can only revoke all privileges for a user. If you wanted to delete a single privilege, you would have to revoke all of a user's privileges and then re-grant the privileges you wanted the user to keep.

6. Click on the Close button to return to the main Database Navigator page.

Working with sequences

7. Scroll down to the TICKETS_SEQ sequence and click on the Get Next Value action link. You will see the page shown in Figure 5-13.

Figure 5-13: Retrieving a sequence number

The number returned as the next sequence number for the TICKETS_SEQ is 1, because no tickets have been assigned yet. Try this experiment to see how the sequencer works:

8. Click on the OK button to return to the main Database Navigator page.

9. Click on the Get Next Value action link for the TICKETS_SEQ again.

This time, you can see that the value returned for the sequence is 2. Calling the Get Next Value action for a sequence incrementally increases the value in the sequence object.

10. Click on the OK button to return to the main Database Objects tab of the Navigator page.

At this point, you have played around with most of the standard actions available to you in the Database Navigator. It's time to jump into the biggest functional area in the Database Objects tab of the Navigator, the ability to browse and modify the actual data in your database tables.

Browsing Data

Not only can you work with database objects and their properties with the Database Navigator, you can also work directly with the data in your views and tables.

The Navigator interface to your data has a lot more flexibility than the actions you have already examined. The best way to understand the way this interface works is to plunge right in and use it.

1. Click on the Name of the EVENTS table, which will have the same effect as clicking on the Query Rows link. You will see the page shown in Figure 5-14.

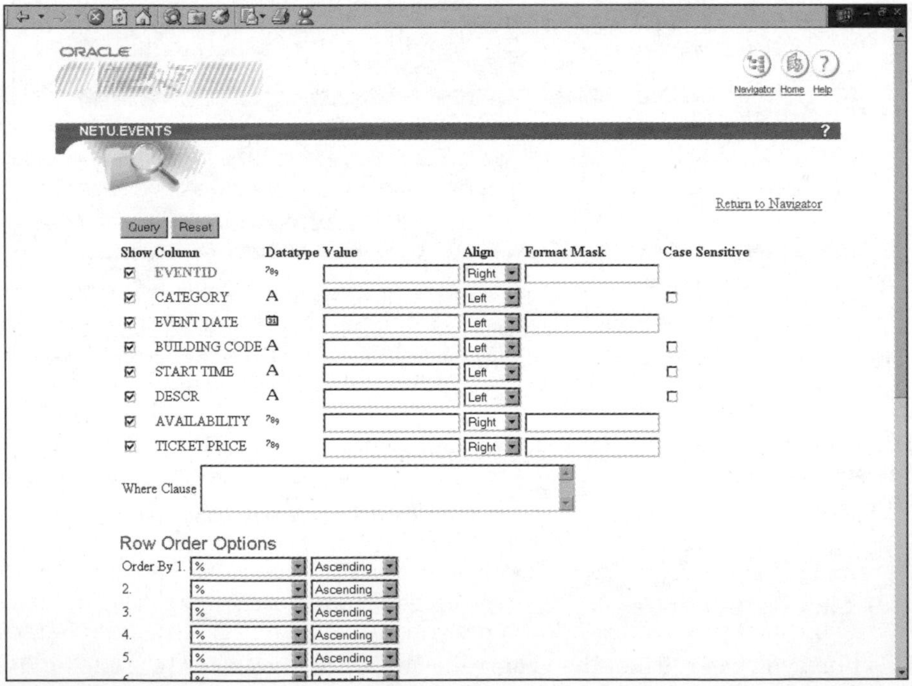

Figure 5-14: The main page for querying rows in the Database Objects tab of the Navigator

The page shown in Figure 5-14 is used to enter selection criteria for the data that will be returned from the table. It can also be used to insert data into the table, as you will see later.

The basic areas of the query and insert page are as follows:

✦ **Column Information:** The selection page includes a line for each column in the table. The line for each column includes the name of the column, an icon to the right of the column name that indicates the datatype, such as a character, a number or a date, and a check box to the left of the column name. If the check box is checked, it indicates that the corresponding column is returned for browsing as part of the results for the query on the table. By default, all of the check boxes are initially checked. If the name of the column is in bold red text, it means that the column is part of the primary key of the table.

The next text field for each column is the Value data entry box; this is where you add selection criteria, which are described in the next bullet point.

After the Value text entry box, there is a combo box that enables you to specify how you want to align the data returned from the query. The data returned from your query is displayed in an HTML table object, and you have the option of aligning a column's data to the right, left, or center within the column. If a column in the database table is a character or date column, the default alignment for the data is left-justified. All other column types have a default alignment of right-justified.

If a column in the database table does not contain character data, you see another text entry box, called Format Mask, to the right of the alignment combo box. The Format Mask text box enables you to specify the formatting for the column data.

If the data for a column is character data, there is a Case Sensitive check box at the far right of the line of column information. If you check this box, the selection criteria for the column are imposed with case sensitivity on. If the box is not checked, which is the default, the selection criteria are imposed without regard for case.

✦ **Column Selection Criteria:** Each column also includes a text entry field to the right of the datatype icon called Value. You can add selection criteria in these fields. The selection criteria could be a specific value that you want all returned data to match, or a relational expression, such as > or < (greater or lesser than signs) followed by a value. You can use the % (percent sign) or _ (underscore) wildcards as part of the selection criteria for character fields. You can have selection criteria indicated for columns that are not checked, and therefore not returned as part of the results of the query. You can only have a single selection criterion for each column using the fields on the column lines. If you have selection criteria indicated for more than one column, the returned rows must match all criteria. If you want to use more complex selection criteria, you can enter them in the data field for the WHERE clause, which is described next.

✦ **WHERE Clause:** The WHERE clause is a standard part of the SQL language. The WHERE clause implements the selection criteria in an SQL statement. You can enter any valid WHERE clause in the Where Clause text field. But whereas a normal SQL statement would require that you include the WHERE keyword, use of the WHERE keyword is optional here. A WHERE clause can include any combination of logical criteria, including multiple specifications joined by the keywords AND and OR. You can enclose sets of conditions within parentheses to specify that they should be evaluated before the entire clause is evaluated. If you are using string values in the WHERE clause, you have to enclose the strings in single quotes. If you specify an invalid WHERE clause in the Where Clause field, Oracle9*i*AS Portal returns an error when you attempt to browse the data. The WHERE clause can be implemented in a sophisticated manner that is beyond the scope of this small introduction. If you are familiar with SQL, you already know that. If you want more information on the various ways you can use the WHERE clause, please refer to the standard Oracle SQL documentation.

✦ **Row Order Options:** There are six combo boxes that enable you to specify the columns Oracle9*i*AS Portal uses to order the rows returned from your query. Each combo box contains a list of all of the columns in the table. You can specify that each ordering column is used to sort the data in either ascending order, which is the default, or descending order. If you specify more than one column for ordering the data, the column specified in the topmost Order By box is the primary sort column, the next column is the secondary sort column, and so on. In other words, if you specified that you wanted the rows returned in the EVENTS table ordered by CATEGORY and then LOCATION, the rows would be returned sorted by category, with the rows within each CATEGORY group sorted by location. Just as with selection criteria, you can sort the rows returned from the database based on the value of a column that is not included in the display of the query.

✦ **Output Format:** You can choose to have the output from your browsing of the table displayed three ways: as HTML-based text; as straight, unformatted ASCII text within a single HTML table column; or in Microsoft Excel data format. These options make it easy to transfer data taken from your Oracle database to personal productivity tools. If you choose to save the data in Excel format, you are prompted for a filename that is used to store the data.

Note   The Output Format, and the rest of the options on this page, are not shown in Figure 5-14 due to space limitations.

✦ **Maximum Rows:** This field enables you to specify the maximum number of rows returned from a query, and it can have a dramatic effect on the performance of the return of rows from the query. The maximum number of rows returned indicates the maximum number of rows returned from a query on a single page, not the total maximum number of rows returned. If there are additional rows in a table that match the selection criteria, the page has, by default, a Next button at the bottom of the page that enables you to retrieve the next set of rows. The value for the maximum number of rows directly affects the overall size of the page, which correspondingly affects the amount of time it takes to retrieve the rows over your network. The default value for this field is 20. If you have a large number of rows of data, a slow connection to the database server, or a combination of these factors, you get a better response time by limiting the number of rows returned on each results page.

✦ **Show Null As:** You can use this data field to enter a value that is displayed in place of null values in the database. The default value for this field is (null).

✦ **Query Options:** The Query Options box gives you several choices for the way that you want the data to appear. You can choose one or more options in the list box with the standard key combinations for your platform — holding down the Ctrl key while you click an option in the Windows environment, for instance.

Table 5-3 describes each of the options available for Query Options.

Table 5-3	
Query Options Values	
Query Option	**Meaning**
Show SQL	If you choose this option, Oracle9iAS Portal shows you the SQL statement it constructs to get your data before it retrieves the data. If you are familiar with the SQL language, you can check it with this option to make sure you have made the right choices on the query selection page. If you are not familiar with SQL, you might be able to learn about the language by examining the SQL that results from the choices you have made.
Display Results in Table with Borders	This option causes the data to be returned with borders surrounding the table.
Show Total Row Count	Selecting this option causes Oracle9iAS Portal to display the total number of rows at the end of the returned data.
Count Rows Only	This option will cause the result of the query to be limited to a single piece of data — the total number of rows that will be returned to satisfy the query. The suppression of other data will be carried out whenever this choice is selected, regardless of the other Query Options selected.

Continued

Table 5-3 (continued)	
Query Option	**Meaning**
Show Paging Buttons	By default, Oracle9*i*AS Portal returns data a page at a time and displays one or two buttons at the bottom of the page that enable you to move to the next or previous set of rows, as appropriate. If this option is not selected, Oracle9*i*AS Portal does not display these paging buttons at the bottom of the page. Instead, Oracle9*i*AS Portal returns the number of rows specified in the Maximum Rows field. If this option is not selected, it can reduce the amount of data that is sent from the database server, but it can also give a misleading impression of the amount of data that satisfies the selection criteria. You do not know whether the amount of data returned is the complete set of data or just the maximum number of rows. In addition, you can avoid much of the overhead of additional data by simply choosing not to request additional pages of data. Because of this, the Show Paging Buttons option is selected by default.
Show HR Between Rows	This option inserts a horizontal rule (HR) between each row returned. This can be useful if your rows contain a lot of data and stretch over several rows in the browser.
Replace ASCII new lines	This option replaces the ASCII new line characters with the with HTML breaks character when a new row of data begins.

The only Query Option that is selected by default is Show Paging Buttons. If you want to Show Paging Buttons and still select other choices, you have to remember to hold down the Control key (in Windows) to maintain the selection of the default choice.

To demonstrate querying the EVENTS database, assume that you want to find out the road games of old NetU's basketball teams, since you might want to catch a game in your travels. Follow these steps:

2. Enter `%Basket%` into the Value box for the CATEGORY column.

3. Enter `at%` in the DESCR Value box.

4. Uncheck the Show check box for the BUILDING CODE column and the TICKET PRICE column, because the building code is irrelevant for away games and money is no object.

5. Holding down the Control key (for Windows, or another key for another platform), select the Show SQL and the Display Results in Table with Borders query options choices.

6. Click on the Query button to retrieve your data, as shown in Figure 5-15.

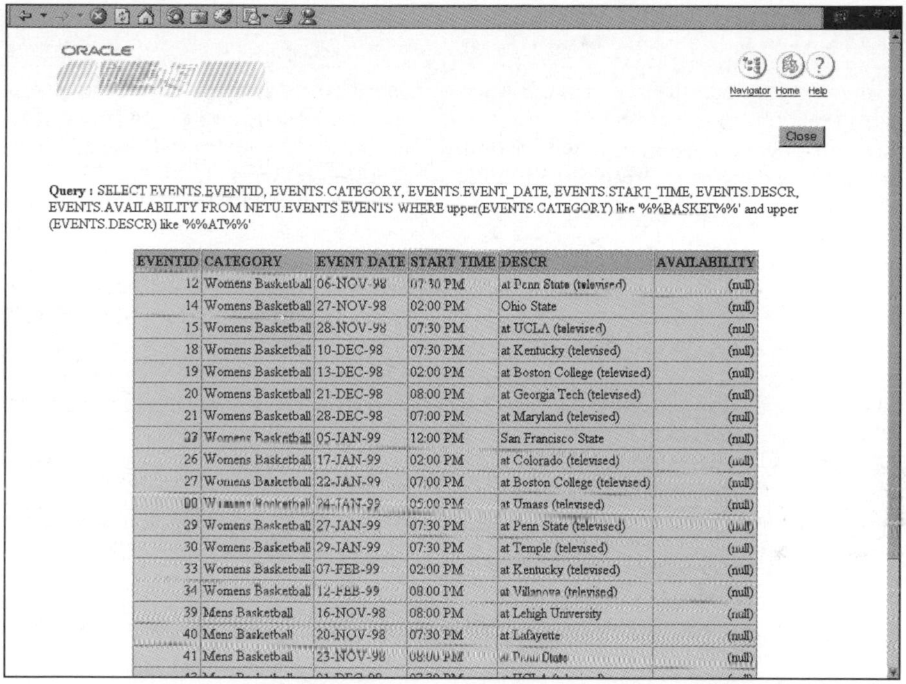

Figure 5-15: Data returned from a query launched from the Navigator

You can see the first page of data displayed in Figure 5-15. The SQL statement at the top of the page includes the use of the upper() function, because the selection criteria are not supposed to be case-insensitive.

The data is not displayed in the most attractive manner, but at least you can get to it. For end users, you would probably create a simple report, rather than have them use this browsing capability.

The Query interface of the Database Objects tab of the Navigator also has a Reset button to the right of the Query button. The Reset button resets the values in the page to the defaults — no selection criteria and only the Show Paging Buttons Query Option selected.

For now, you can simply go back to the Database Objects tab of the Navigator to see how you can use it to add data to a table:

7. Click on the Close button at the top of the report page.

8. Click on the Return to Navigator link at the top of the query page.

Interacting with Data

In the previous version of Oracle9*i*AS Portal, you could use the same page to query or insert data. In Oracle9*i*AS Portal, these two functions are accessed by entirely different pages. This change was primarily implemented to allow different levels of data access to users with different levels of privileges.

Updating data

To get to the portion of the Database Objects tab of the Navigator that allows you to modify data, you select a different action link.

1. Select the Modify Rows action link for the EVENTS table. The page shown in Figure 5-16 will appear.

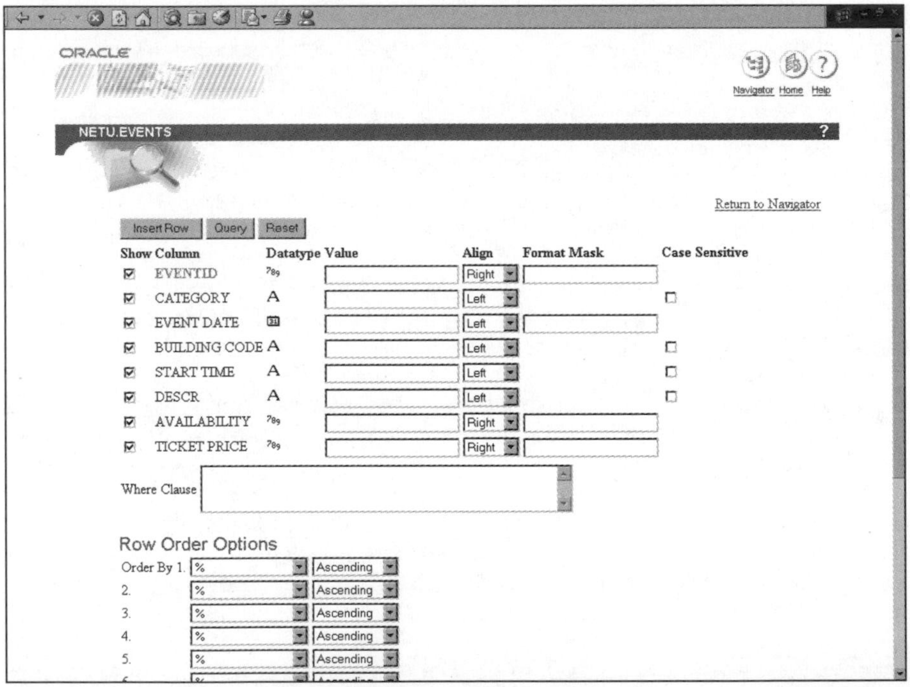

Figure 5-16: The Query and Modify page in the Database Objects tab of the Navigator

This page looks very similar to the page you used to query rows in the table. There are only two differences.

One difference is that there is no combo box at the bottom of the page to specify the output type. Because you specifically use this action to interact with data, you cannot choose to have it returned as ASCII text or in Excel format.

The other difference is in the buttons in the upper-left corner of the working area of the page. There is a new button, labeled Insert New Rows, to the left of the Query button, which appears only if the user has the privilege to add data to the table. You will see how this button works in a moment. But first, you can see how the Query button has a slightly different effect in this page than it does in the Query page:

2. Uncheck the Show check box for the BUILDING CODE and DESC columns.
3. Click on the Query button. The page shown in Figure 5-17 will be returned to your browser.

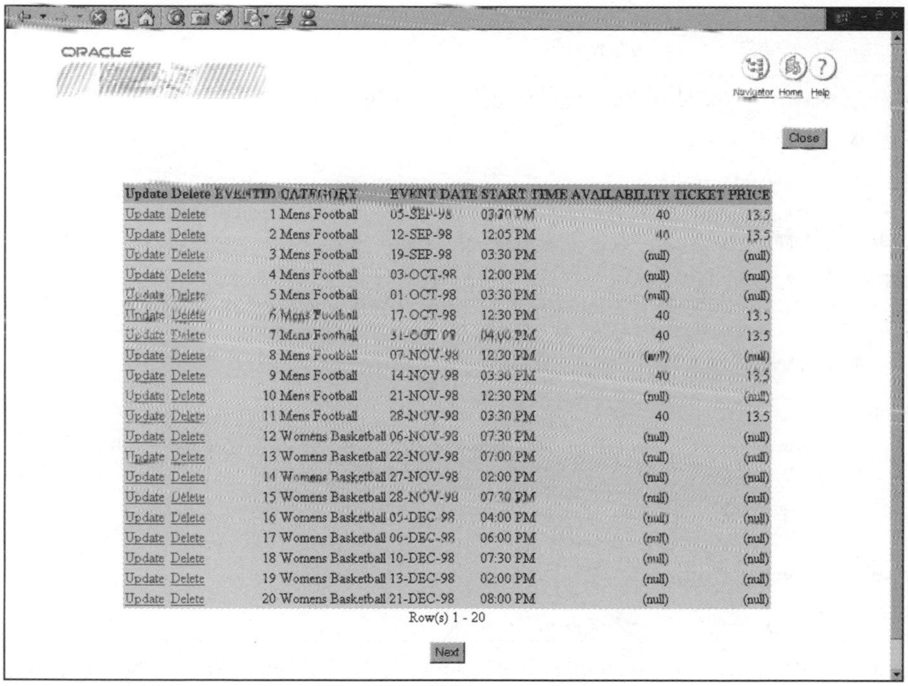

Update	Delete	EVENTID	CATEGORY	EVENT DATE	START TIME	AVAILABILITY	TICKET PRICE
Update	Delete	1	Mens Football	05-SEP-98	03:30 PM	40	13.5
Update	Delete	2	Mens Football	12-SEP-98	12:05 PM	40	13.5
Update	Delete	3	Mens Football	19-SEP-98	03:30 PM	(null)	(null)
Update	Delete	4	Mens Football	03-OCT-98	12:00 PM	(null)	(null)
Update	Delete	5	Mens Football	01-OCT-98	03:30 PM	(null)	(null)
Update	Delete	6	Mens Football	17-OCT-98	12:30 PM	40	13.5
Update	Delete	7	Mens Football	31-OCT-98	04:00 PM	40	13.5
Update	Delete	8	Mens Football	07-NOV-98	12:30 PM	(null)	(null)
Update	Delete	9	Mens Football	14-NOV-98	03:30 PM	40	13.5
Update	Delete	10	Mens Football	21-NOV-98	12:30 PM	(null)	(null)
Update	Delete	11	Mens Football	28-NOV-98	03:30 PM	40	13.5
Update	Delete	12	Womens Basketball	06-NOV-98	07:30 PM	(null)	(null)
Update	Delete	13	Womens Basketball	22-NOV-98	07:00 PM	(null)	(null)
Update	Delete	14	Womens Basketball	27-NOV-98	02:00 PM	(null)	(null)
Update	Delete	15	Womens Basketball	28-NOV-98	07:30 PM	(null)	(null)
Update	Delete	16	Womens Basketball	05-DEC-98	04:00 PM	(null)	(null)
Update	Delete	17	Womens Basketball	06-DEC-98	06:00 PM	(null)	(null)
Update	Delete	18	Womens Basketball	10-DEC-98	07:30 PM	(null)	(null)
Update	Delete	19	Womens Basketball	13-DEC-98	02:00 PM	(null)	(null)
Update	Delete	20	Womens Basketball	21-DEC-98	08:00 PM	(null)	(null)

Figure 5-17: The Update and Delete page for a data row

The page looks a lot like the default page returned for the Query Rows action, except that there is a link for Update and Delete for each row to the left of the first column.

4. Click on the Update link for the first row in the table. You will see the page shown in Figure 5-18.

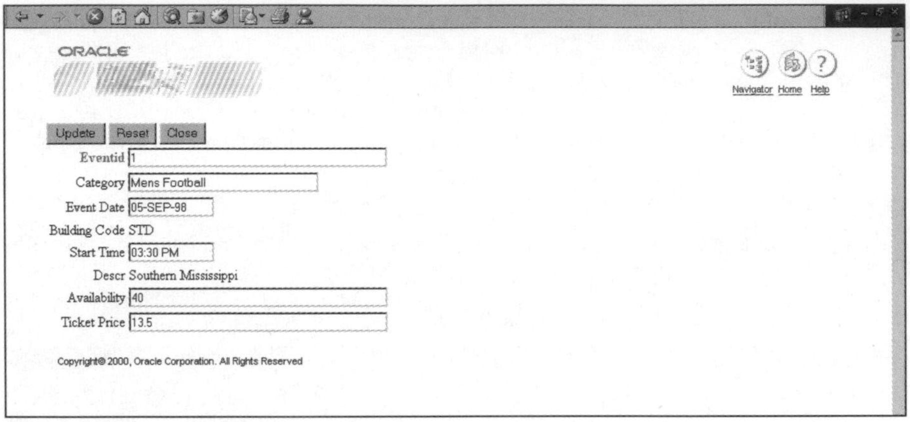

Figure 5-18: Updating a row through the Database Objects tab of the Navigator

The page shown in Figure 5-18 will allow you to change any of the values for any of the columns selected in the original page. As you can see, the values for the columns you unchecked are still shown, but as read-only values.

5. Change the value for the Availability column to 30 and the value for the Ticket Price column to 13.

6. Click on the Update button. You will see the page shown in Figure 5-19.

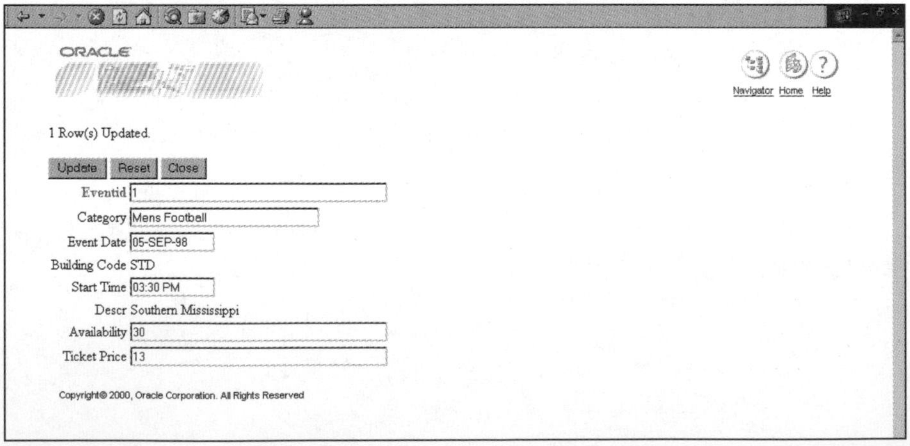

Figure 5-19: A successful update through the Database Objects tab of the Navigator

The indications that your update was successful comes through the little message at the top of the page and as the changed values shown on the page.

7. You can also delete rows through this interface. Click on the Navigator link in the banner for the page.

8. Click on the Modify Rows action link for the EVENTS table again.

9. Click on the Query button to return some rows.

10. This time, click on the Delete link for the first row in the database. You will be prompted as to whether you really want to delete the row.

11. Click on the No button to return to the listing of the rows for the EVENTS table.

You can also use the Modify Rows action to add new data into a particular table or view.

Inserting data

To insert a new row of data into a database table, you use the same page that you use for specifying query conditions for the Modify Rows action. Instead of entering selection criteria, you enter the values that you want to insert into the database and click the Insert Rows button.

If you insert data into a table by clicking the Insert Rows button, you get a similar message returned at the top of the cleared page that is returned, as shown in Figure 5-20.

If you have inserted data that is appropriate for the columns and the table, you get a success message page as shown in Figure 5-20 in the top part of the page. But sometimes it doesn't quite work out that way.

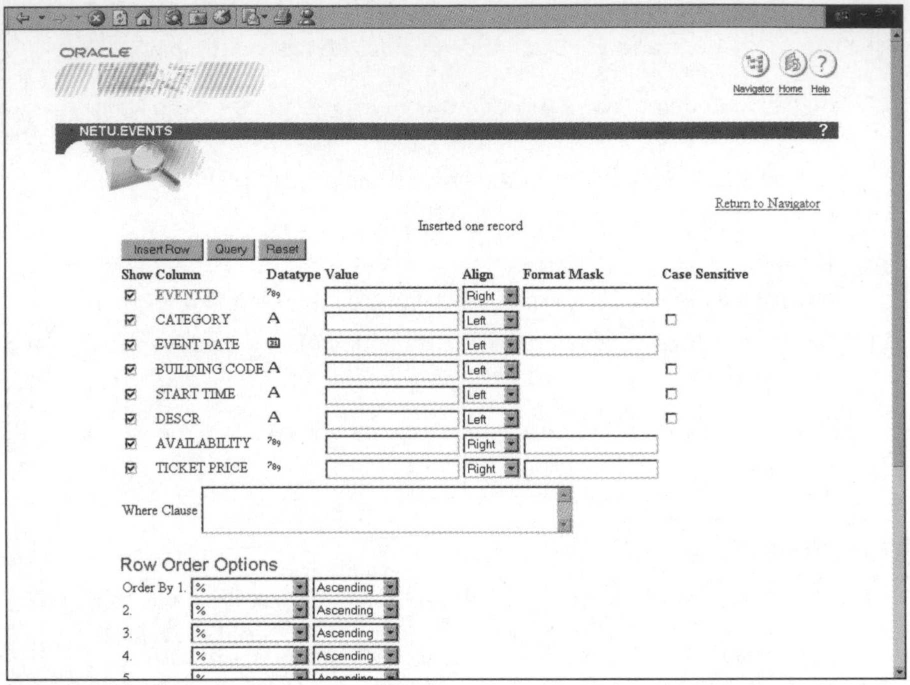

Figure 5-20: The result of a successful data row insert

Issues with writing data

Oracle9*i*AS Portal does give you an easy way to insert and update data in the database through the Browse interface; however, the Database Objects tab of the Navigator interface is not smart enough to make sure that the data you are entering is valid. When you define a database table, you usually specify some sort of integrity rules for the data. These rules can require that a value for a particular column already exist in a different column in a different table.

For instance, you must add an event with a unique value for the EVENTID. This limitation certainly makes sense, but its existence is not indicated in the interface provided by the Navigator.

If you should try to add an event with an EVENTID that already exists, the database returns an error if the new values for the data violate any of these rules, as shown in Figure 5-21.

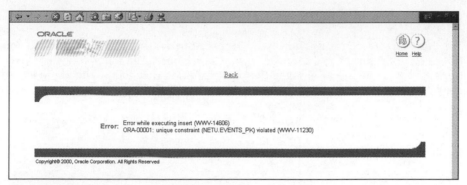

Figure 5-21: The result of a forbidden insert

There might be other limitations described in the database, such as a limited set of values that were accepted for a particular column, which would create similar problems.

The Database Navigator interface to your data is very useful, but it is not designed to replace any custom application system you might build with Oracle9iAS Portal. Just as the browsing capability of Oracle9iAS Portal does not replace the report components, the same capability does not replace the need to create customized forms for entering data. If you want to allow users to modify data in the database, you should design a form for them that enforces all the integrity constraints necessary to avoid this type of error message.

Creating Database Objects

Besides browsing different database objects, you can also use the Database Objects tab of the Navigator to create new database objects.

In the previous release of Oracle9iAS Portal, you created database objects using a totally separate interface than the one you used for browsing database objects. As you have already seen, you can create any of the supported database objects using the same Database Navigator page, which lets you interact with existing objects.

You can use the links following the Create New... label at the top of the Database Objects tab to create new database objects.

Oracle9iAS Portal gives you a wizard-driven interface to create database objects. As an example, the following section walks you through the creation of a table.

Creating a table

You can start by exploring the wizard for creating database tables. Because you do not need to perform any actions in this section, there aren't any specific instructions, but you can follow along with the explanation by clicking the Table icon on the main Build Database Objects page.

The first page, as shown in Figure 5-22, is similar for all of the database object creation wizards.

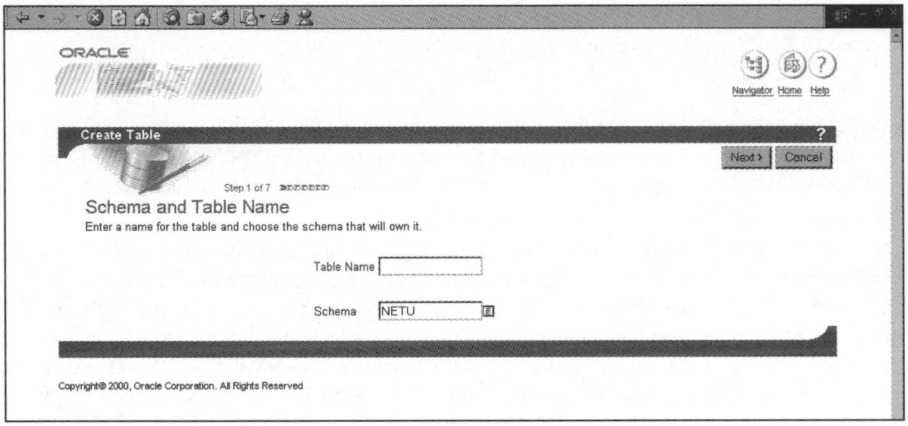

Figure 5-22: The first page of the table creation wizard

Your first step is to enter a name for the table that the wizard will create. Each table must have a unique name within its own schema. If you enter a name for an object that already exists in the schema, Oracle9*i*AS Portal notifies you of this conflict with an error message as soon as you leave the first page. You must then return to the page and give the table a different name.

You must enter a schema name in the second text box. As you can see, there is an icon to the right of the text box that will allow you to select a schema from a list of all schemas you have access to.

All the types of database objects have a slightly different set of pages for most of the rest of the wizard operations. The purpose of all but the final page in the wizards is to prompt you for the information needed to create the database object. For a database table, the next page in the wizard (shown in Figure 5-23) enables you to enter the columns that make up the table. The page has spaces to enter information for five columns in the table. If you need to define a table that has more than five columns, you can click the Add More button at the bottom of the panel.

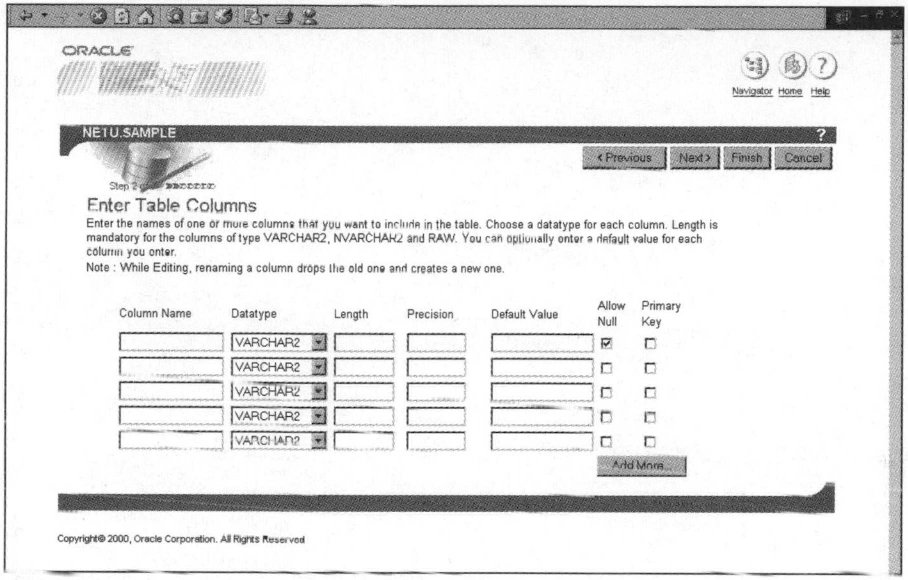

Figure 5-23: The Enter Table Columns page of the table creation wizard

For each column, you have to enter a column name, a datatype for the column, a length for the column, and, if the column is a numeric column, a precision for the column. You can also enter a default value for the column if you want. If a user is inserting a row into this table and does not supply a value for the column, the default value is used.

Note: It makes sense to supply a default value mainly if you allow nulls on the column.

Each column has a check box that enables you to specify whether null values are allowed for the column, and whether the column is a primary key for the table.

When you try to move to the next page in the table creation wizard, Oracle9iAS Portal does some rudimentary error checking for the values you entered for the columns. For instance, if you entered a value for the Precision data field for a column that you defined as a character, Oracle9iAS Portal brings up an error page and directs you back to the previous page of the table creation wizard.

The next page of the table creation wizard, shown in Figure 5-24, allows you to add one or more UNIQUE constraints onto your table. As its name implies, a UNIQUE constraint requires that each value in a table have a unique value.

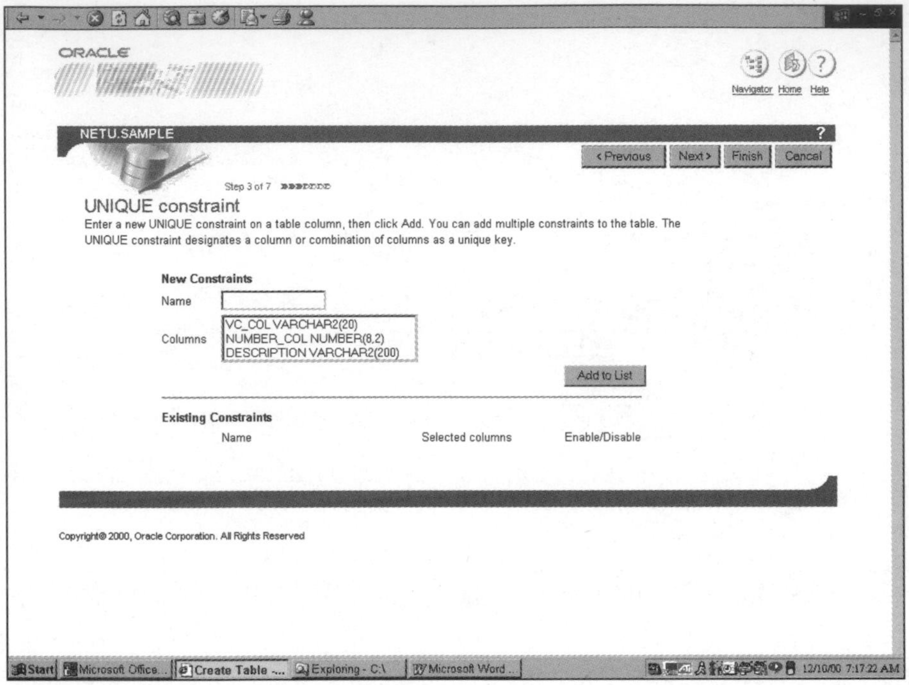

Figure 5-24: Adding a UNIQUE constraint

> **Note**
>
> Even if you have designated a column with a UNIQUE constraint, if you allow nulls in the column, more than one row in the table can contain a null value. The reason for this lies in the definition of a null. Since a null represents no value at all, multiple nulls do not have the same value.

You can define a UNIQUE constraint on a group of columns. You simply use the multiple-select method to choose multiple column names in the Columns list box — holding down the Control key on a Windows machine, for instance.

> **Note**
>
> If you are unfamiliar with basic relational concepts like constraints, or other terms in this section, we recommend you explore these important concepts in a book about relational databases in general, or Oracle specifically. The Oracle9*i* documentation contains explanations of these constraints and their uses.

Once you add a constraint, you click on the Add to List button to add the constraint to the list of constraints. Once you have added a constraint, this page also gives you the ability to delete or disable a constraint you have added.

The next page of the table creation wizard, shown in Figure 5-25, allows you to add one or more CHECK constraints to your table, in the same way that you could add a UNIQUE constraint in the previous page of the wizard.

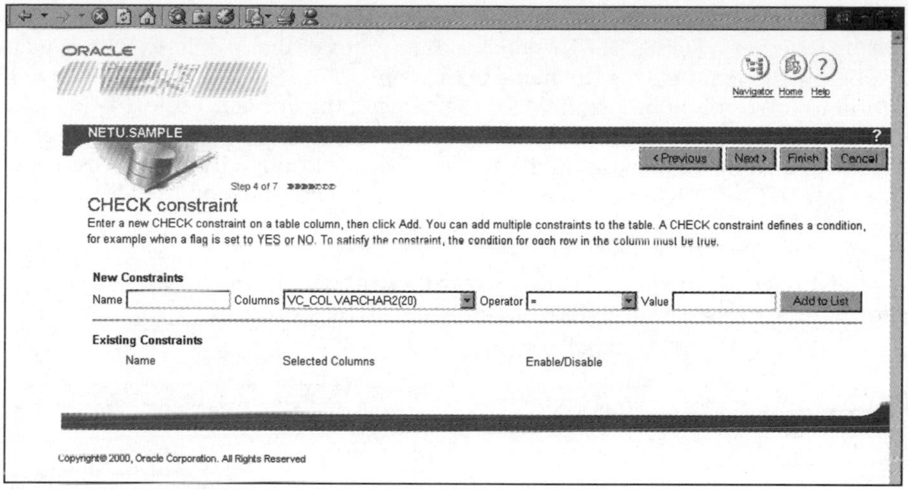

Figure 5-25: Adding a CHECK constraint

The next page of the table creation wizard, shown in Figure 5-26, gives you the ability to add a FOREIGN KEY constraint to your table.

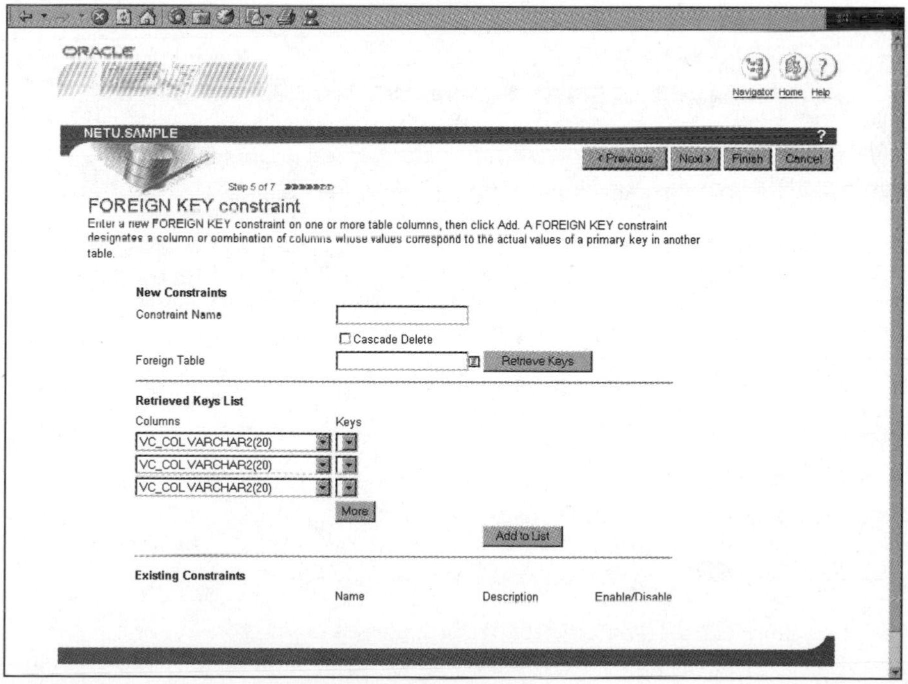

Figure 5-26: Adding a FOREIGN KEY constraint

This page in the wizard is a little more complex than the previous two pages. You can specify whether a FOREIGN KEY constraint requires cascade deletes with the check box below the text field for the name of the constraint. There is also a Retrieve Keys button to the right of the text field for the name of the Foreign Table. Clicking on this button will populate the combo boxes in the lower, Retrieved Keys, section of the page with a list of all the keys in the Foreign Table. Although there are three lines for entering FOREIGN KEY constraints in this page, you can click on the More button to add reveal FOREIGN KEY constraints to a table.

The next page of the table creation wizard, as shown in Figure 5-27, prompts you for information about how the data in the table will be stored.

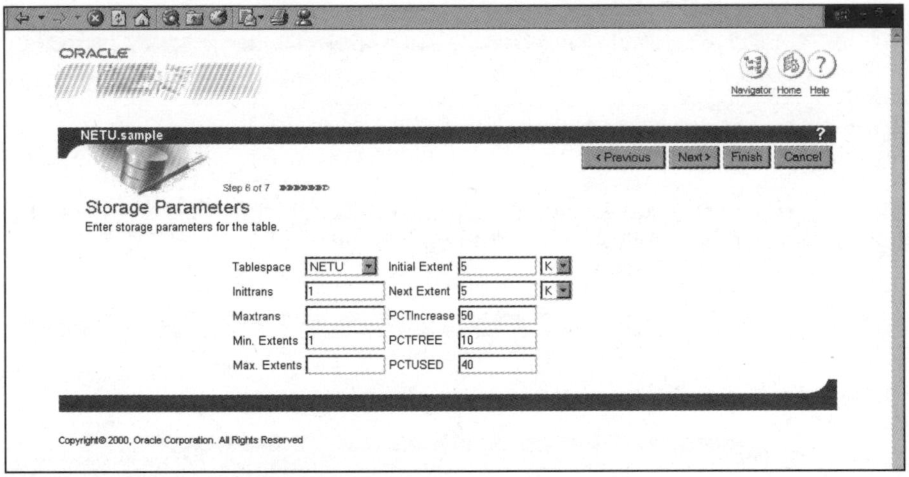

Figure 5-27: Specifying storage parameters for a table

You have to specify the tablespace for the table, which defaults to the tablespace specified for the schema that owns the table. This page gives you the ability to enter nine other storage attributes for your table:

✦ Initial Extent

✦ Next Extent

✦ Min. Extent

✦ Max. Extent

✦ PCTIncrease

✦ PCTFREE

✦ PCTUSED

✦ Inittrans

✦ Maxtrans

When you specify the size of the initial and next extents, you can select the letter K, for kilobytes, or M, for megabytes, from the list box to the right of the extent size text boxes.

A complete description of the purpose of each of these storage parameters is beyond the scope of this book, but you do not have to specify any values on this page, because the storage parameters for tablespace and basic extent attributes will default to values specified for the schema.

Tip   For a concise description of the purpose of these storage parameters and a lot of other important information about your Oracle database, try *Oracle Essentials* by Rick Greenwald, Robert Stackowiak, and Jonathan Stern.

The final page of the table creation wizard gives you the ability to enter comments about your table. Comments have no formal purpose, but they can be a handy way to store some documentation about a table in the actual data dictionary.

Once you have gone past the first page of the wizard, where you enter a unique table name, you can click on either the Finish button, to create the table, or the Cancel button, to cancel the creation process, in the upper right corner of the working area of the page. However, if you were to click on the Finish button before you had defined any columns for the table, you would get an error page.

The database object creation wizard is a handy tool, and in this version of the product, it allows you to create database objects with a much more complete set of options. If you are a professional DBA, you will already be using another Oracle utility, such as the Oracle Enterprise Manager or SQL*Plus, to create your database objects. The various database object creation wizards included with Oracle9*i*AS Portal are not meant to replace any of these tools, but it is handy to be able to quickly add database objects while working in the Oracle9*i*AS Portal development environment. There may be other times when you cannot get to another utility or tool from the machine that you are running, but you can use Oracle9*i*AS Portal because it requires only a browser environment.

Summary

Although many of the capabilities present in the Database Navigator were available in earlier versions of Oracle9*i*AS Portal, the Database Objects tab of the Navigator is a very nice new way to explore and interact with the database objects and data in your database.

The Database Navigator not only allows you to explore the sources of the data objects you will be working with in your Oracle9*i*AS Portal environment, but also lets you create and modify those objects, if you have the appropriate privileges.

The ability to insert and modify data through the Database Objects tab of the Navigator is a handy tool, but it is not really designed to be used for anything other than basic maintenance functions.

The new portal capabilities of Oracle9*i*AS Portal are so important, and so cool, that you will start to explore them in the next chapter.

✦　　✦　　✦

Building a Portal

P A R T

In This Part

Chapter 6
Introducing Portals
and Portlets

Chapter 7
Building a Portal Page

Introducing Portals and Portlets

✦ ✦ ✦ ✦

In This Chapter

Learning What a
Portal Is

Learning What a
Portlet Is

Supporting Portlets in
Oracle9*i*AS Portal

Understanding
Runtime
Implementation of
Portlets

Caching with
Oracle9*i*AS Portal

✦ ✦ ✦ ✦

por·tal (pôrtl, pr-) n.
1. A doorway, an entrance, or a gate, especially one that is large and imposing.
2. An entrance or a means of entrance: the local library, a portal of knowledge.

As this definition makes clear, a portal is an opening through which items can pass. In the case of the modern world of information technology, a portal is a gateway that allows users to gain access to information. More specifically, a portal helps a user access information that is accessed through the Internet, or using Internet protocols.

In terms of the subject of this book, to paraphrase that other great technical author, W. Shakespeare, the portal's the thing. As its name implies, Oracle9*i*AS Portal provides all the capabilities you need to create enterprise information portals.

Although this is version 3.0 of this product, the product has always been oriented towards providing information to browsers. The first iteration of this product was an internal release known as WebView and another internal release known as SiteBuilder. The purpose of the product was to give users a way to view the data in an Oracle database over the Web. The second version of the product, which was publicly released as WebDB, was, as its name implies, focused towards providing Web access to data in a database. WebDB really emphasized the capability of building a site, which was a repository of information and pointers to information, organized in a hierarchical manner.

This version of the product has been renamed Oracle9*i*AS Portal — and the scope of its gateway capabilities has been correspondingly enlarged. This chapter is devoted to providing you with an understanding of these new capabilities. In the next chapter, you will build your first portal page. Later in this book, in Chapter 28, you get an introduction on how to drill down and create your own portlet providers.

Understanding What a Portal Is

It is obvious from the history of name changes described in the previous section that Oracle9*i*AS Portal is a tool designed to create portals. But what, exactly, is an Oracle9*i*AS Portal?

A *portal* fulfills several different needs, all of which relate to the ability of a user to gain access to information through the Web. First, a portal acts as an easy-to-use guide to pertinent information. The information environment is much more like a tangled, overgrown jungle of information, rather than a well-behaved, cultivated field. A portal can help guide users to the information and services that are most important to them, without having to waste time discovering the data themselves. A well-designed portal helps to increase user productivity by reducing the time it takes users to accomplish their tasks. In this way, portal developers improve the overall operations of their businesses.

A portal also helps to control access to information. By offering easy-to-use paths to get information, the portal reduces the need to search for information in an ad hoc manner. For instance, if your portal contains a Content Area that represents the latest marketing documents for your organization, users are much less likely to go searching for the most recent version of these documents themselves, and are correspondingly less likely to mistakenly find and distribute the wrong version.

From a developer's point of view, a portal provides a couple of key advantages. First of all, a portal framework, as delivered by Oracle9*i*AS Portal, gives developers a common set of services that they can use to create portals, such as user identification, security, the ability to store and retrieve individual user customizations, and the ability to maintain state information over multiple stateless HTTP requests. A portal can also automatically coordinate user requests with other services that can be used to monitor and enhance the performance characteristics of a particular site.

Finally, and, in a way most importantly, a portal provides server-based capabilities for Web clients. All of the management of the individual applications and Content Areas that make up a portal take place on the server. By making these operations server-centric, a portal is easier to manage than a collection of user-based bookmarks, or some other client-side organizational practice, because a single server-based portal can uniformly server hundreds of clients.

Understanding What a Portlet Is

The core of the portal services offered by Oracle9iAS Portal is found in the entity known as a *portlet*. The portlet is a way to overcome the tyranny of the HTML page.

The Web has provided an immense amount of good for the world of electronic information, with its creation of universal standards for communications protocols, resource addresses, and the markup language used for display (HTML). But the Web and its protocols are designed around the concept of a page — a single static piece of information, delivered to a browser. The page is delivered to the browser, a complete and unchanging entity. To view other information, a user has to call another page.

At this point in time, efforts to surmount this limitation have revolved around either the extensive use of code, such as JavaScript, to react to client actions; or the implementation of nonstandard variants of Internet standards, such as the various flavors of Dynamic HTML.

The portlet is one way to surmount the "all-or-none" nature of the HTML page. A portlet is an area on an HTML page that can contain its own information. A portal page is composed of one or more portlets, combined into a single page delivered to the browser. Oracle9iAS Portal creates portal pages from the portlets you assign to the portal page.

You have already been working with portal pages — both the Oracle9iAS Portal home page and the Navigator are portal pages. To learn more about the underpinnings of these portal pages, you have to log into Oracle9iAS Portal as a user with the privilege to modify these pages, as these steps describe:

1. Log into Oracle9iAS Portal as the owner of the portal environment. If you loaded the product with the defaults for the owner, the owner name and password will be PORTAL30.

When you come into the Oracle9iAS Portal environment, you will see that there is an extra link on the right, just below the main portion of the banner. This is the Customize link.

2. Click on the Customize link in the banner, which will bring up the page shown in Figure 6-1.

> **Note** Please proceed through this section of the chapter with great care. You are looking into the main page for the Oracle9iAS Portal environment, as a user with the ability to change the page. We strongly advise that you simply look, as we instruct, and not touch, to avoid doing harm to the environment.

You can see that the portlets you explored in Chapter 3, such as the my Links portlet, are shown on the left side of the page. On the right, you can see the Build tab and the other tabs that are shown in the main region of the home page.

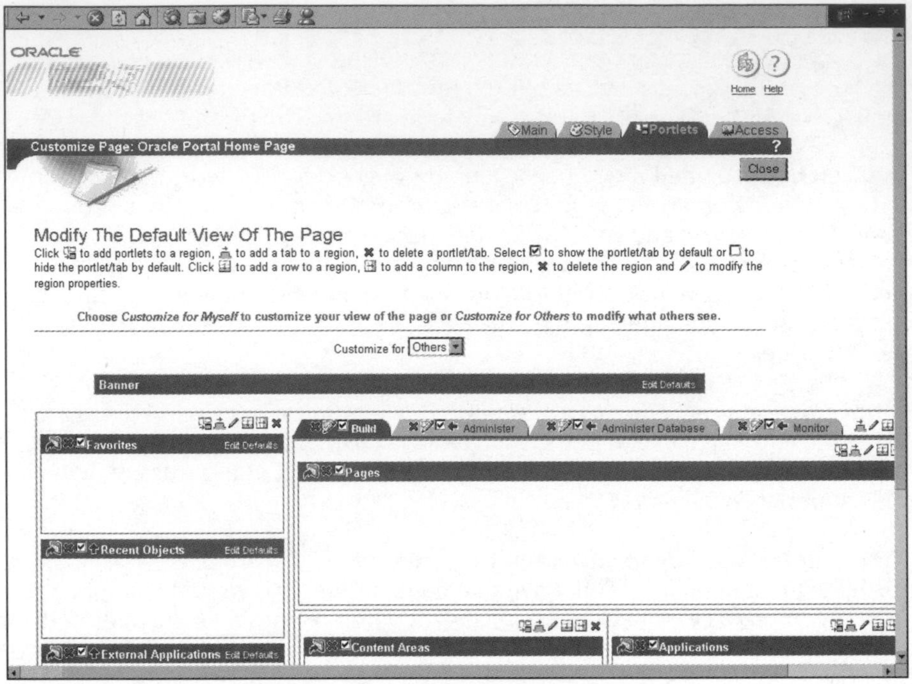

Figure 6-1: Customizing the Oracle9*i*AS Portal home page

The view presented to you in Figure 6-1 may seem a bit overwhelming. The main reason for the proliferation of information on this page is that you are looking at the layout of a fairly sophisticated, complete portal page. You will walk through the creation of your own portal page in the next chapter, where all the capabilities of this page will be introduced in a more orderly fashion.

But there is one thing to notice while you have this Customize page in view. If you remember from Chapter 3, only the NETUDEV user could see the last three tabs in the main portion of the Oracle9*i*AS Portal home page. You can see why by drilling down into the attributes of those tabs.

3. Click on the little pencil icon on the Administer tab of the main region of the page.

4. Click on the Advanced Options tab at the top of the Edit tab for the Administer page, which will bring up the page shown in Figure 6-2.

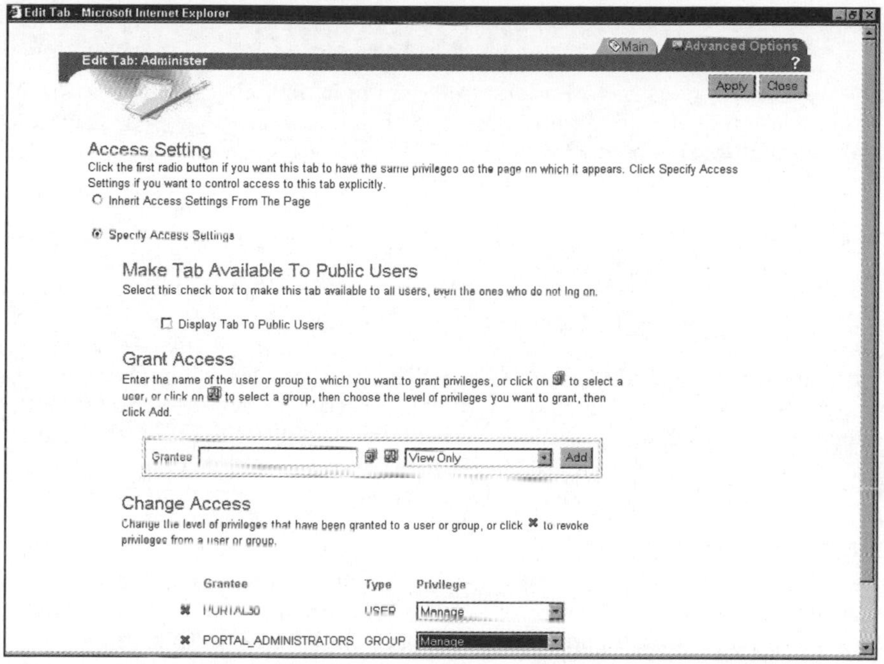

Figure 6-2: The Advanced Options page for the a region of a portal page

You can see that only the PORTAL30 user or members of the
PORTAL_ADMINISTRATORS group have any type of access to this tab. Because the
NETU user was not a member of the PORTAL_ADMINISTRATORS group, that user
could not even see the tab, while the NETUDEV user could.

Because changing the attributes or layout of the Oracle9*i*AS Portal home page
would disrupt the rest of this book, you should leave it alone for now.

5. Click on the Close button on the Administer page.

6. Click on the Close button in the Customize page.

Between working with the home page and the Navigator, you already know enough
about portals and portlets from a user perspective. But before you move on to creating a portal page, you should understand how Oracle9*i*AS Portal actually assembles and uses pages.

Supporting Portlets in Oracle9*i*AS Portal

You now should have a basic understanding of how portlets can be used to build a rich information environment for Web users. But what, exactly, does Oracle9*i*AS Portal do to support portlets?

Portlet management

Oracle9*i*AS Portal automatically manages the retrieval of information for a portlet and the display of that information on a portal page.

When you design a portal page, you lay out the portlets that will make up the page. Laying out portlets on a page is very much like creating the cells in an HTML table. You describe each portlet as if it were an individual cell in the table, and you can create one or more columns in the table by dividing the overall page into two columns, and then separating each of these columns into additional columns, if necessary.

Once you lay out a portal page, the runtime environment of Oracle9*i*AS Portal assembles the information provided by the individual portlets into a portal page. The actual steps taken to assemble the page are described in more detail in the section entitled "Runtime Implementation of Portals," later in this chapter.

Oracle9*i*AS Portal makes it easy for users to customize their own view of the information in a portal page or a portlet, and also makes it easy to provide help for each portlet. If you are familiar with components that could be built with WebDB, you will realize that the same customization and help features that were automatically created for these components are also available through the portlet interface of Oracle9*i*AS Portal. And if you are not familiar with these built-in services, you will learn much more about them in Sections III and IV of this book.

Oracle9*i*AS Portal also makes any proxy calls necessary for retrieval of information from other Internet or intranet sites. The Oracle9*i*AS Portal server acts as a redirector for these proxy requests.

Framework services

In addition to managing the portlets on a portal page, Oracle9*i*AS Portal also gives developers access to a host of services used by the portlets. These services are known as *framework services*, and they are accessible through the portlet application program interface (API).

For instance, a portlet developer can access the personal privileges stored by users when they customize their own pages; or the developer can access the security system used by Oracle9*i*AS Portal to identify users. You will learn a lot more about the framework services and the portlet API in Chapter 28, which covers creating your own portlets.

Automatic portlet generation

Oracle9*i*AS Portal provides portlet management at runtime, as well as access to portlet services for developers. In addition to these services, Oracle9*i*AS Portal also gives you the ability to generate Oracle9*i*AS Portal components and Content Areas as portlets. For much of this book, you will be creating these components and Content Areas.

Oracle9*i*AS Portal does not include any third-party portlets with the standard product, but some third-party portlets, such as portlets that let you access information services from Excite, are included in the Portal Development Kit, or PDK. You can get this kit, which is a set of documentation and examples, through the Oracle Technology Network (OTN) site. OTN also includes a list of available third-party portlets.

 To join OTN, simply go to `http://technet.oracle.com` and sign up. It's free, and there is an abundance of useful technical information available there.

Runtime Implementation of Portals

Oracle9*i*AS Portal is used to manage the way that portlets interact when requested by a user. The runtime implementation of portlets is one of the key ways that Oracle9*i*AS Portal makes it easy for you to develop portals.

The most visible capabilities of the runtime implementations of portals is in the way that Oracle9*i*AS Portal manages individual portlets. When a user requests a portal page, Oracle9*i*AS Portal makes calls to the *portlet providers,* which supply the basic information for the portlets. The runtime Oracle9*i*AS Portal environment can also massage the data that is returned by the portlet providers.

The portlet providers also prepare the information for each individual user, based on customization information indicated for that individual user.

Once all the portlet information has been returned, the Oracle9*i*AS Portal runtime environment arranges the individual portlets into a single HTML page, and returns that page to the user who requested it. The process flow is shown in Figure 6-3.

The runtime environment also handles larger user issues, such as identifying individual users and implementing security for these users. All of the capabilities of the runtime environment are available to portlet developers, because they create their own portlet providers and the API that is used by the Oracle9*i*AS Portal runtime environment to interact with the portlet provider.

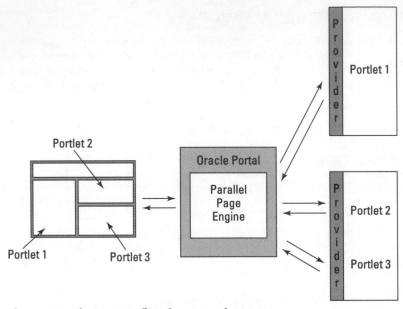

Figure 6-3: The process flow for a portal page

The architecture of the portlet provider interface allows a single portlet provider to support multiple portlet programs. For instance, most Oracle9iAS Portal components created with the wizards in the product are delivered by a single portlet provider.

Caching in Oracle9iAS Portal

The diagram shown in Figure 6-3 is really not the complete story of how Oracle9iAS Portal assembles portlets. Oracle9iAS Portal uses a technique called *caching* to improve the performance of portal pages, as well as the ability of a portal to scale to address the needs of many users. Caching, in a nutshell, provides a rapid way to deliver frequently accessed data.

One of the key facets of creating a Web-based solution is the ability to handle large numbers of users. In the old world of internal networks, not only could you limit the number of users who accessed a certain type of information, but also the number of total users was fairly manageable. You would never see the number of people accessing a particular report or piece of data grow by an order of magnitude overnight. But this type of increased usage is possible on a public Web site. And users would still expect to see a rapid response from the site. They don't really care how many other users are making requests at the same time.

One of the ways to handle this type of performance demand is through the use of *caching*. A cache is a way to make information readily available. The Oracle database uses a memory cache, where frequently or recently requested data is stored in memory, rather than requiring time-consuming disk I/O operations to retrieve it. Oracle9*i*AS Portal also uses a cache to store frequently used information in a disk file in the middle tier. When a user requests this information, Oracle9*i*AS Portal can simply retrieve it from the cache, rather than having to make relatively long and expensive calls to the Oracle9*i* database.

Types of caching

If you are unfamiliar with caching, you might, at this point, see it as something that has only positive ramifications. After all, caching is a way to improve performance without having to do anything in your application or components. Pure magic!

But there is a dark side to caching. Remember, caching serves static versions of objects, because it provides stored, not fresh, data. The information those objects are based on might have changed, which means that Oracle9*i*AS Portal returns invalid data to the users, without the unsuspecting user even knowing it.

Because of this potential hazard, a caching mechanism must always have a way to invalidate the cached objects — to cause the page repository, which holds the cached versions of the pages, to create a new version of the object. There are two types of caching rules in Oracle9*i*AS Portal: time-based caching, which is also called expiry-based caching, and validation-based caching.

Time-based caching, as its name implies, uses a specific timestamp to invalidate an object at a certain time. You can tell Oracle9*i*AS Portal that a particular page or component should only be cached for a certain length of time. If a user requests the object before the time has expired, Oracle9*i*AS Portal serves up the version from the cache without checking the database. Validation-based caching tries to determine whether the *meta-data* for an object has changed since the object was cached. This meta-data includes the specifications for the object and any personalization that has been applied to the object by the user. This type of caching sends a message (pings) the database to check for potential changes every time a user requests a page. As someone who is creating objects, you cannot specify validation-based caching — the rules and the way they are enacted are built into the portlet provider.

In fact, Oracle9*i*AS Portal always does validation caching for all cached objects. Even if you specify time-based caching on an object built with the Oracle9*i*AS Portal wizards, the parallel page engine still makes sure the meta-data for the object has not changed since the object was cached. The designers of Oracle9*i*AS Portal figured that a page whose meta-data has changed should never be displayed, so a validation check is always required. If an object with time-based caching returns successfully from a validation check, it is then served up from the disk file.

Using time-based caching, though, can eliminate the need for Oracle9iAS Portal to do validation checking. If you have specified an expiry time for an object, and that time has been exceeded, the parallel page engine will not even bother to do a validation check—it will simply refresh the page.

Note If you are building your own portlet provider, you can include your own validation rules. When you use validation-based caching, the portlet is returned to the parallel page engine with an identifying key. When a user requests the object again, the key is returned to the portlet provider, which is responsible for determining whether the cached object is still valid. Because the portlet provider is responsible for making this determination, the validation rules could implement almost any type of checking.

All caching is done on a per-user basis, and on a per page basis, as you will learn in the next section.

Note Well, almost all. If an object is available to the universal Public user, the object is cached for the entire system, because all users see the same object.

Objects in the cache are maintained for each user. (The caching mechanism is continually being improved, though, so more sophisticated caching schemes will be introduced into subsequent releases for Oracle9iAS Portal.)

If you write your own provider, you can specify that a particular portlet be cached for the entire system. This type of global caching makes it possible for Oracle9iAS Portal to address an extremely large number of users, because common pages can be rapidly served up from the cache.

Levels of caching

With Oracle9iAS Portal, you can specify caching at both the page and the portlet level. You will learn more about how to specify the caching as you build a page (in Chapter 7) and your first component (in Chapter 8).

For pages, you can specify that the meta-data is cached, that the meta-data and the content is cached for a specific length of time, or that there is no caching done for the object. If only the meta-data is cached, the portal page engine will use validation-based caching for the page, checking to see whether the object definition or the personalization options associated with the object have changed since the object was cached. If you choose to cache content and definitions, the parallel page engine will use time-based caching.

Even if you choose not to cache the content for a page, the parallel page engine might still retrieve a cached copy of the portlet, if the portlet itself had caching set. But by specifying that a page and its contents are both cached, you are automatically retrieving a cached version of the portlets on the page. Oracle9iAS Portal will not do any validation checks on the portlets.

Keep in mind that there is a separate instance of a portlet for each page it belongs to, so caching the portlets for one page would not affect the caching of the portlet on another page.

This type of caching can provide a tremendous performance boost — imagine simply serving up a static page rather than retrieving data from many portlets and then assembling it into a page and returning it. But, as intimated previously, there is a danger associated with expiry-based caching.

Caching precautions

When an object is cached, based on time, Oracle9iAS Portal doesn't question the decision — it simply serves up a stored copy of the page, as long as the meta-data is still valid. The data the page or its portlets is based on may have changed, making the displayed information incorrect. You should not specify expiry caching without considering the potential harm that could result from showing a page whose information is no longer correct.

You can look at two ends of the spectrum of pages to understand your caching choices better. At one end of that spectrum is a page that is primarily static. The home page for a site might only have links to other pages, which only change on a daily basis, so there would be no need to refresh that page more than once a day.

At the other end of the spectrum would be a page that included some "real-time" data, like a stock quote. During business hours, you would not ever want the portlets on this page to be cached, since the data is frequently changing. The designers of Oracle9iAS Portal actually gave the users a way around the problems created by time-based caching. If you specify expiry caching for a page, or for the components in the page, the Refresh Page link appears on the right side of the page, just below the banner. If the user clicks on this link, the Oracle9iAS Portal engine will create a fresh copy of the page from scratch. The new page will be tagged with the expiration information for the page. Users can always use this link to get the most current information for a page.

It's a great thing that the Oracle9iAS Portal designers have done with this clever little link. But users still have to know how to use it, and use it at the right times, to be sure of getting valid information in a page. Don't let the existence of this cool workaround blind you to the need to carefully consider the effects of expiry-based caching. Whenever you set expiry caching for a page or a component, you should always assume the worst-case scenario to avoid the potentially serious problems that can be caused by stale data.

Summary

This chapter has given you a taste of the power of portals. You now have an understanding of the concepts of portlets and portal pages, and how the Oracle9*i*AS Portal parallel page engine assembles pages. You have also learned, at a fairly high level, how caching works in the Oracle9*i*AS Portal environment. You are no doubt raring to start building your own portal page.

In the next chapter, you will learn how to create your own portal page — and you just might be surprised at how easy it is.

✦   ✦   ✦

Building a Portal Page

◆ ◆ ◆ ◆

In This Chapter

Creating and Styling
Portal Pages

Adding Portlets to
Pages

Customizing Your
Pages

◆ ◆ ◆ ◆

In the last chapter, we introduced you to the whole idea of a portal page and portlets. The ability to create portal pages is the biggest new feature in the release of Oracle9iAS Portal — so big that Oracle named the product to reflect this capability.

Whether you are an experienced user of WebDB or new to Oracle9iAS Portal, you are probably quite anxious to learn more about this new functionality. In this chapter, you will jump right in and build your first portal page.

Creating a Portal Page

Let's get right to your task of creating a portal page.

1. Log in to the Oracle9iAS Portal development environment as the NETUDEV user you created when you installed the product in Chapter 2.

2. Click on the Create A New Page link in the Page area at the top of the main portlet.

The page that appears is shown in Figure 7-1.

Note   This book was written using Version 3.0.7 of Oracle9iAS Portal. The next release, 3.0.8, included the capability to assign templates for pages, as well as certain other organizational aspects of page management that might cause your individual pages in this wizard to look slightly differently than those displayed in this chapter.

You create pages in Oracle9iAS Portal like you create all other objects — through the use of a wizard. As you can see by the arrows on top of the page in Figure 7-1, this wizard has four steps.

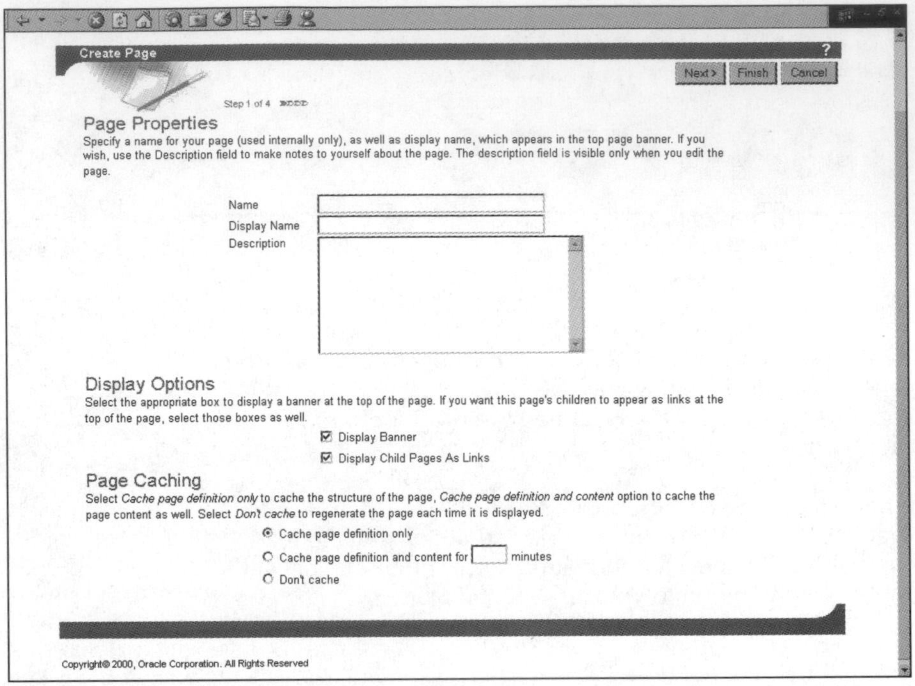

Figure 7-1: The first page of the Page wizard

This first page of the wizard has three main sections—Page Properties, Display Options, and Page Caching. The top section, Page Properties, gives you the ability to enter information used to identify the page. The Name field requires a unique name for the page that will be used to identify the page. This name should not include spaces or any other special characters and cannot be more than 40 characters. The Display Name is the name that will be shown in the banner for the page, as well as shown in the Navigator, and this name can include spaces. Finally, the Description field is simply a supplemental text area where you can add information about the page that will only be seen when the page is being edited. This field is ideal for entering notes about the functionality of the page or other information you want to document for the benefit of you and other developers. The Description field is optional, whereas the other two fields are not.

   3. Enter **NETUPAGE** in the Name field and **Net University Home Page** in the Display Name field. Enter relevant text for the Description field.

The next section of this first page in the wizard includes two check boxes. These check boxes are used to indicate whether you want to display a banner for the page and whether you want to include links for child pages just under the banner on the right side of the page. If you do not have a banner for the page, all the information normally shown in the banner, such as the page logo, the page title, links to other pages, and the functionality supplied by the banner will not be available for the page. You will be introduced to the concept of child pages on the next page of the wizard.

For this page, you might as well leave both of these check boxes checked.

The final section of the page is related to page caching. You were introduced to the topic of caching in Chapter 6. For a page, you have three caching options:

✦ You can cache the page definition only. This definition is the meta-data that the Oracle9*i*AS Portal page engine uses to assemble the page. If you cache only the page definition, you will avoid having to retrieve this information every time the page is requested. Because your pages may not change that often, caching the page definition can improve the performance of page delivery.

✦ You can cache the entire page and its content. This type of caching will deliver even greater performance gains, because you will not have to fetch either the page definitions or the meta-data. However, if you choose to cache the page and its contents, you run the risk of displaying old, invalid data on a page. Caching both the page and its contents is done for a specific length of time — a time-based type of caching. There is nothing wrong with this type of caching, but due to the potential repercussions caused by invalid data, using time-based caching is something you should do only after careful consideration.

✦ You can also choose to decline caching for the page.

 Note   For a more complete description of caching, please refer to Chapter 6, if you have not already read it.

Once again, you should just leave the default selected — cache page definition only.

Page layout and style

4. Click on the Next button at the top of the page. This action will bring up the page shown in Figure 7-2.

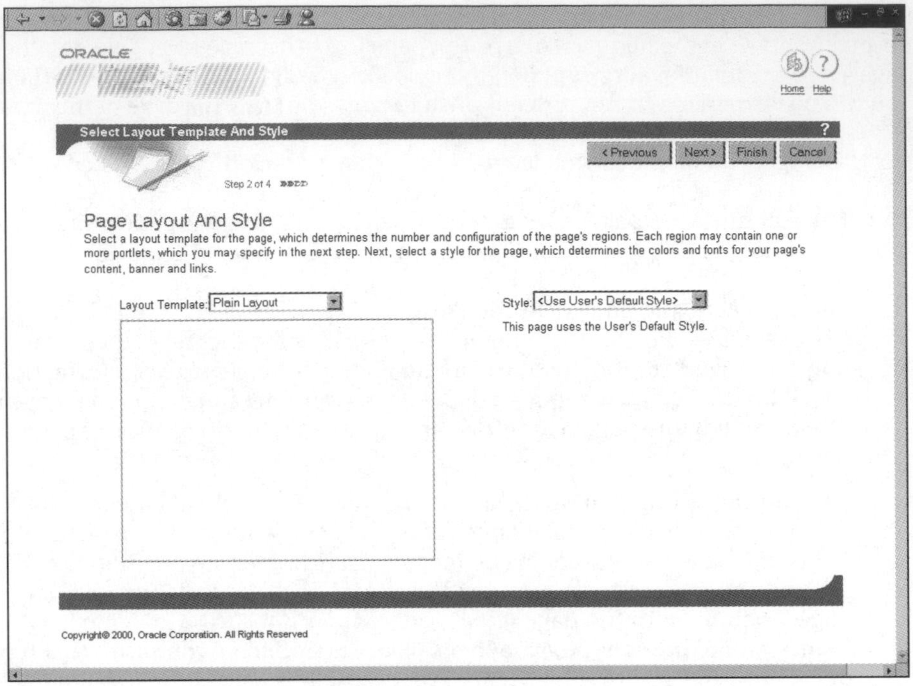

Figure 7-2: The second page of the Page wizard

This second page of the Page wizard allows you to select a page layout template and style for your page. On the left side of the page, you have the option to select a page layout template from the Layout Template: combo box. A layout template is nothing more than a preliminary definition of regions for a page. There are three layout templates that come with Oracle9iAS Portal — a one-, two-, and three-column layout — or you can define your own templates.

> **Tip** If you define your own regions, the layout template will show the value "Your layout for *pagename*," where *pagename* is the display name of your page, when you return to this page in the wizard.

You can choose to use a layout template or you can simply define your regions manually in the next page. Typically, you would use a layout template as a way to save a little development time or as a way to provide the same layout for many different types of pages.

Beware, though — the page layout is used only when you select it from the combo box. Oracle9iAS Portal does not update the layout of a page when changes are made to the layout template. Any subsequent changes in the layout template are not automatically applied to any of the pages that used the template in their creation. If you change a layout template and want to apply the changes to your page, you will have to go back into this design mode and reselect the layout from the combo box.

On the right side of the page is the Style: combo box.

5. To understand exactly what a style is, select Main Page Style from the Style: combo box. This action will change the display of this page of the wizard to look like Figure 7-3.

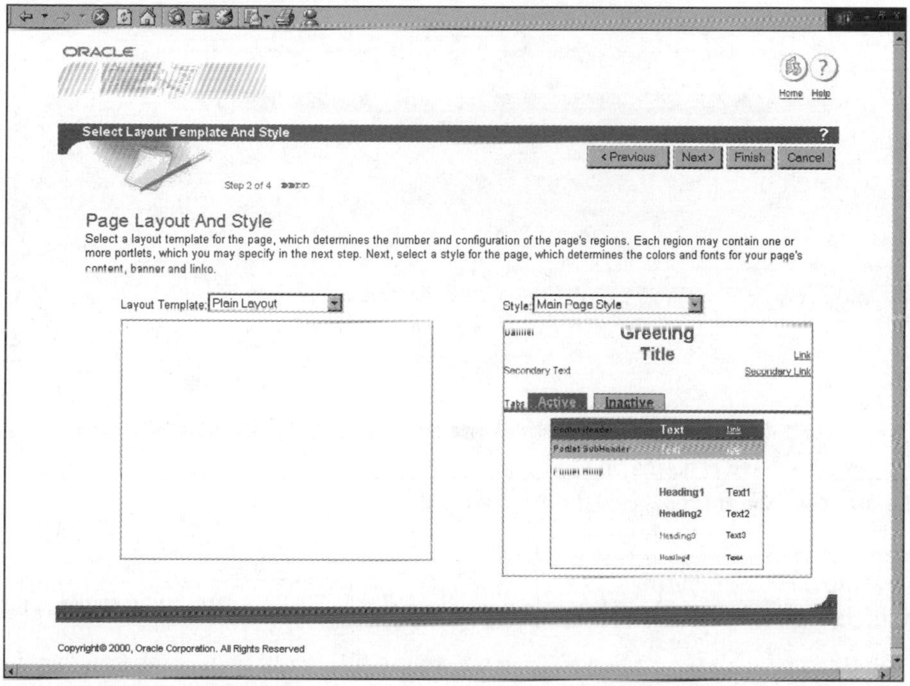

Figure 7-3: The second page of the Page wizard displaying a style

As you can see, a style defines the look and feel of a page, including the color of various components and the fonts used to display text in different areas of the page. The style for a page is very much like the display schemes used in Windows 9x operating systems.

You can also define your own styles for use in the Oracle9iAS Portal development environment.

Cross-Reference You will learn how to define layouts and styles in Chapter 18.

For now, you can use the Main Page Style for your page.

6. Click on the Next button at the top of the page. This action will bring up the page shown in Figure 7-4.

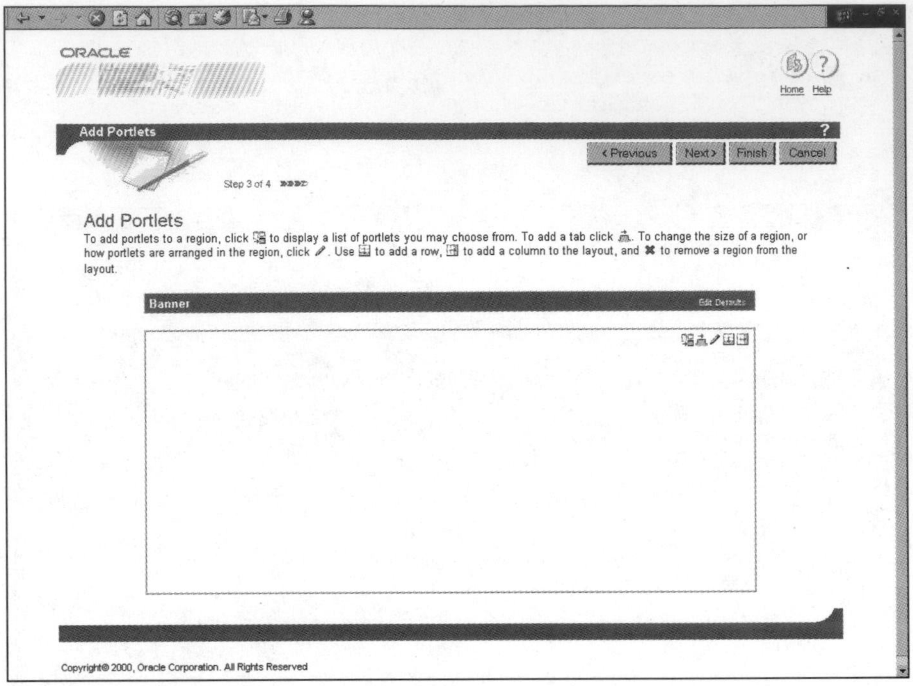

Figure 7-4: The third page of the Page wizard

Customizing the banner

The third page of the Page wizard is where the fun really begins. As you can see in Figure 7-4, this is the page where you can start to add regions and portlets to your page. But before adding anything to the page, you should take a look at the options you have for customizing the banner of the page.

   7. Click on the Edit Defaults link on the right side of the banner. This action will
       bring up the page shown in Figure 7-5.

The banner in a page is not only a way to give a consistent look to your page, but also can provide some top-level information and navigational aids.

The top section of the page is labeled Banner Greeting and Date Settings. In this section you can specify a greeting for the page, which will replace the display name you defined for the page, or a Greeting Image, which will replace both the display name and any greeting you have defined for the page.

Note   Yes, these three choices (and the Image field in the next section) seem a bit
         redundant, but this is one of the places where the designers of Oracle9*i*AS Portal
         decided to simply give you a set of check boxes for some commonly desired
         actions, seeking ease-of-use over brevity.

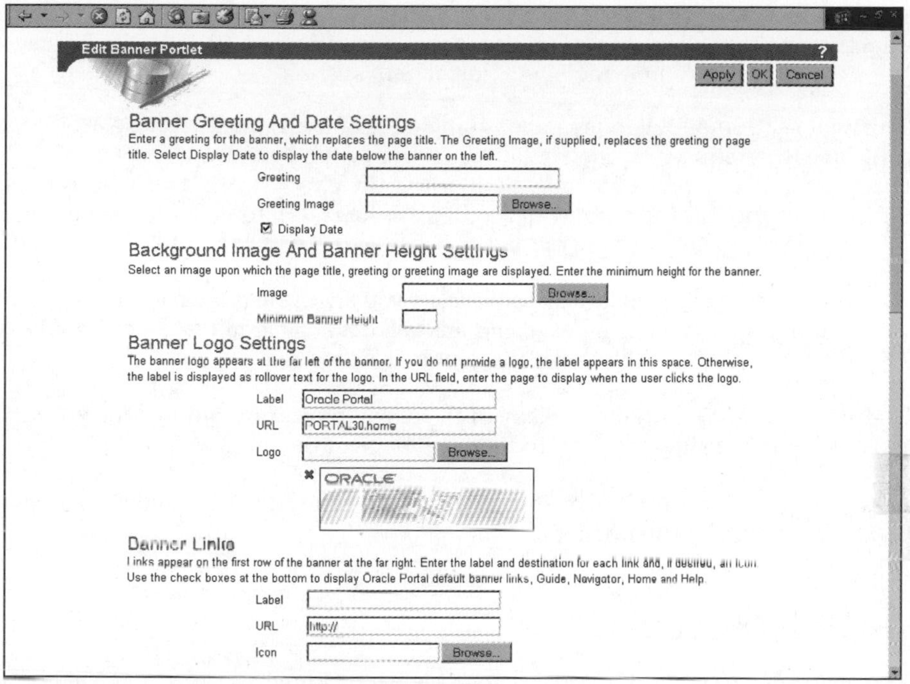

Figure 7-5: Customizing the banner

The Display Date check box gives you the ability to display the date on the left side of the banner

The next section of the page, labeled Background Image And Banner Height Settings, gives you some formatting options for the banner. The Image field lets you indicate an image that will be shown instead of the display name, greeting, or greeting image for the page. The Minimum Banner Height field lets you set an absolute minimum height for the banner. The banner is normally displayed as a percentage of the overall page area available. If your banner includes a graphic that is, say, 200 pixels high, you should indicate that the minimum height for the banner also be 200 to ensure that the graphic is properly displayed.

The Banner Logo Settings section reveals another piece of functionality in the banner. In Chapter 4, which introduced you to the Oracle9iAS Portal development environment, you discovered that the logo on the left side of the banner also acts as a hot link to another page. In this section, you have the ability to set the destination of that link, as well as the logo that is displayed and the text that is shown when a user's pointer passes over the logo.

You can only see the first choice of the Banner Links section of this page in the wizard in Figure 7-5. Once again, you have already seen those banner links at work. The logos and text that are displayed on the right side of the banner, such as those that take you to the Navigator or the Oracle9iAS Portal home page, are described in this section. You can add your own links in this section. At the bottom of the page are check boxes that allow you to suppress the default banner links to the Navigator, the Home page, and the Oracle9*i*AS Portal help system.

The final section on this busy page is labeled Secondary Links. These are the text-only links that appear on the far right, just below the banner on the same line as the date. You can add your own links here or use the check boxes at the bottom of the section to suppress the display of the Refresh Page, Customize Page, Account Information, and Login or Logout links.

Note   The Refresh Page link is only applicable if you are caching the page. If you have no caching specified for the page, this link will not appear on the page, regardless of whether you leave the check box for this link checked.

There is no real need to change any of these customization options for your first page, so you can simply return to the third page of the Page wizard.

8. Click on either the OK or Cancel button to return to the main wizard page. It's time to add those portlets.

Adding Portlets

You are about to add substance to your page by adding portlets to it. This process is really very easy.

9. Click on the Add portlet icon on the left of the line of icons in the page. This action will bring up the Add Portlets page, as shown in Figure 7-6.

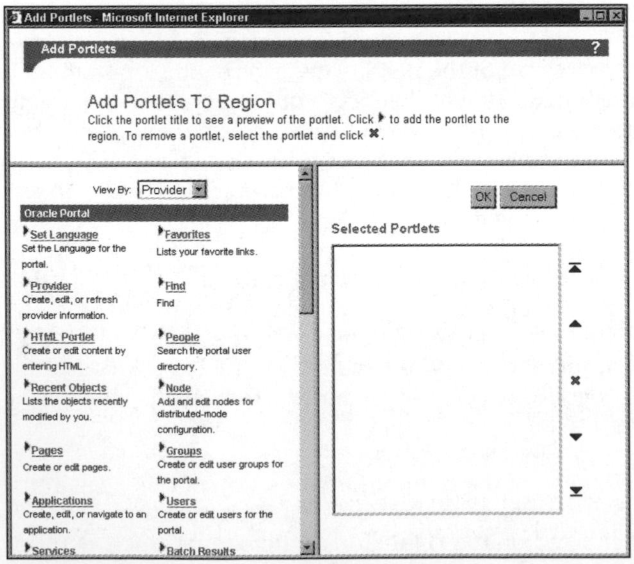

Figure 7-6: The Add Portlets page

This page has a pretty clean look and feel to it. The frame on the left of the page gives you a view of all of the available portlets. You can view the portlets grouped by portlet provider or by a category assigned to the portlet.

In the right frame is a list box where the portlets you select are shown. You can move the portlets around in the list with the arrows on the right of the frame, or delete a portlet from the list with the red X. The order that the portlets are listed in the Selected Portlets box is the order that the portlets will be shown in the portal page.

You will build your first portlet page using the default portlets that come with Oracle9iAS Portal:

10. Click on the Favorites portlet under the Oracle9iAS Portal portlets at the top of the portlet listing. This action will bring up the page shown in Figure 7-7.

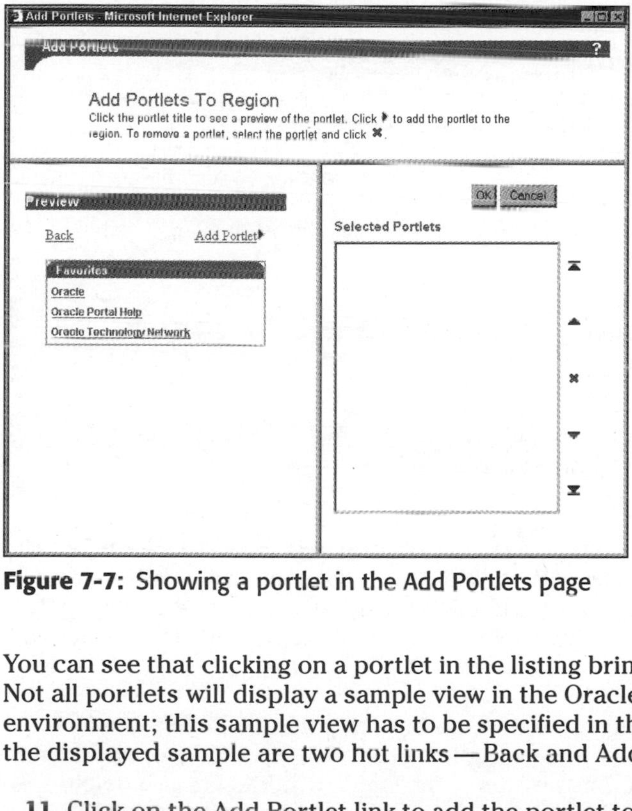

Figure 7-7: Showing a portlet in the Add Portlets page

You can see that clicking on a portlet in the listing brings up a view of the portlet. Not all portlets will display a sample view in the Oracle9iAS Portal development environment; this sample view has to be specified in the portlet code. At the top of the displayed sample are two hot links—Back and Add Portlet.

11. Click on the Add Portlet link to add the portlet to the current page.

12. Click on the Back link to return to the portlet selection page.

13. Following the same steps you used for the previous portlet, add the HTML portlet and the People portlet from the Oracle9iAS Portal portlets to your page.

The HTML portlet is a special type of portlet that you will explore when you finish building your portal page. The People portlet is a portlet that lets you search the Login Server for users.

14. Click on the OK button in the Add Portlets page to close the page and return to the Page wizard, which should now look like Figure 7-8.

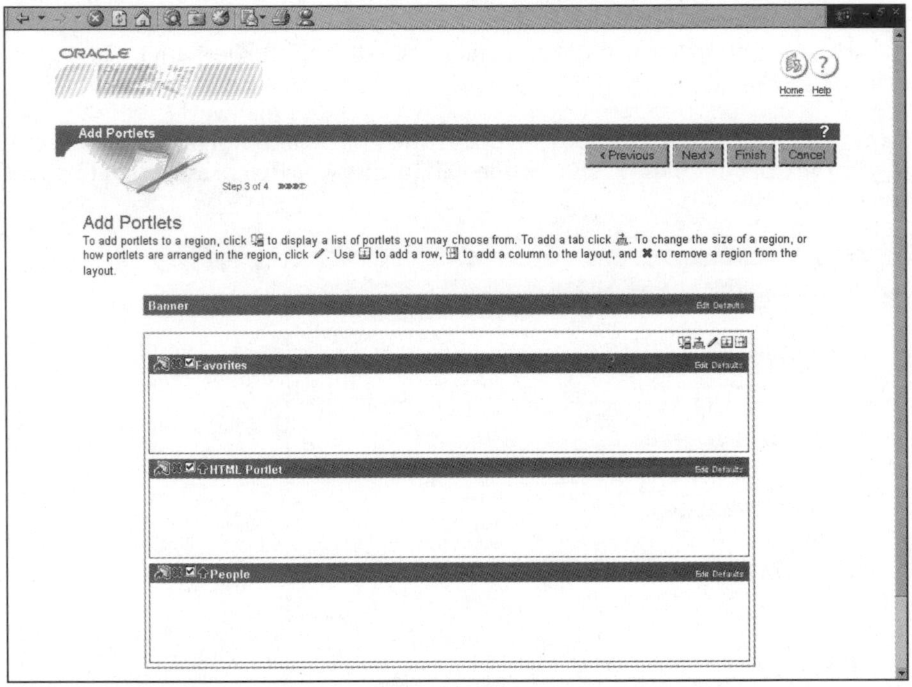

Figure 7-8: The page with a few portlets added

You may be a little disappointed with the way the page looks in Figure 7-8. The layout used here is not exactly WYSIWYG — it is more of a schematic layout. To see how the page will look with its portlets displayed, you will have to display the actual page. You will do that when you have completed your first complete pass through the Page wizard.

You can also see that there are four icons in each portlet. The left-most icon, which is a folder with an arrow pointing to it, lets you move a portlet from its current region to another region. The next icon, the familiar red X, lets you delete a portlet. The next icon, a check box, gives you the ability to hide the portlet on the page.

Note   Why not just delete the portlet, instead of hiding it? You might want to have it around later, or you might not have the privilege to delete portlets for the page, but still don't want to see it.

The final icon is an upward-pointing arrow. This arrow will move the portlet up in the display of portlets for the region. The top portlet in the region doesn't have this icon for obvious reasons. Of course, you could always go to the Add Portlets page and use the arrows along side the Selected Portlets list box to accomplish the same thing.

Finally, you can see that some of the portlets have an Edit Defaults hot link. This link will take you to another page that allows you to set the default values for the customization attributes of the portlet. Not all portlets have this link, because this capability has to be explicitly included in the portlet code—it is not required.

Keep in mind that you, as an owner of the page, will see the Edit Default links, which allows you to assign global settings. If an individual who is not the page owner brings up this page, they would see the same link labeled as Customization, where they could change their own values, but not assign defaults for the page in general.

> **Cross-Reference** You will learn how to use the Edit Defaults section of an HTML portlet later in this chapter, and the basics of coding your own portlet in Chapter 28.

But you have a lot more flexibility in working with pages than simply adding portlets. You will explore some of that flexibility in the next section.

Working with regions

A portal page in Oracle9iAS Portal is divided into areas that are called *regions*. You have already seen some regions in the Oracle9iAS Portal home page, or if you explored the different layout styles earlier in this wizard.

A region is an area of a portal page that you can use to display portlets. While you may think that you have been working with a portal page up until now, in fact you have been working with a region within a portal page, which itself only has one region.

You can create additional regions by using the two icons at the far right of the portal page region. The icon with an arrow pointing to a blue region on the bottom adds a new region at the bottom of the current region. The icon with an arrow pointing to a blue region on the right adds a region to the right of the current region. This description may sound a little cryptic, but you can easily see the effect of these actions by trying them yourself.

15. Click on the Add Column icon on the far right of the icon line in the page. This action will bring up the new version of the Add Portlets page, as shown in Figure 7-9.

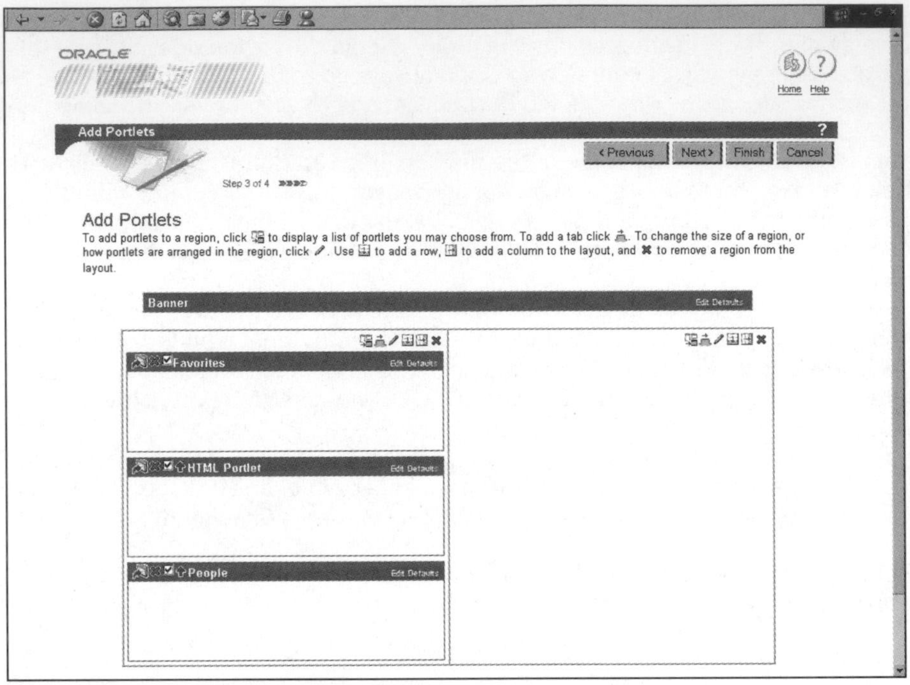

Figure 7-9: Your page with two regions

There is no real theoretical limit to the number of regions you can create, but you may find yourself running out of screen real estate after creating more than six or eight regions. The region acts as a formatting device, much like the cells in an HTML table operate. Each region will expand as necessary to display all of its portlets.

For this particular page, you will want to add one more column, and then add a few portlets to this column.

16. Click on the Add Column icon in the rightmost column of the portal page.

Note   Now that you have two columns in your page, the icon to the far right is that red X, which can be used to delete the region.

17. Click on the Add Portlets icon in the right-most column.

18. Using the techniques described previously, add the Search portlet, from the Portal Content Area section of the portlet list and the Saved Searches portlet from the same section to the region.

19. Click on the OK button to return to the main wizard page, which should now look like Figure 7-10.

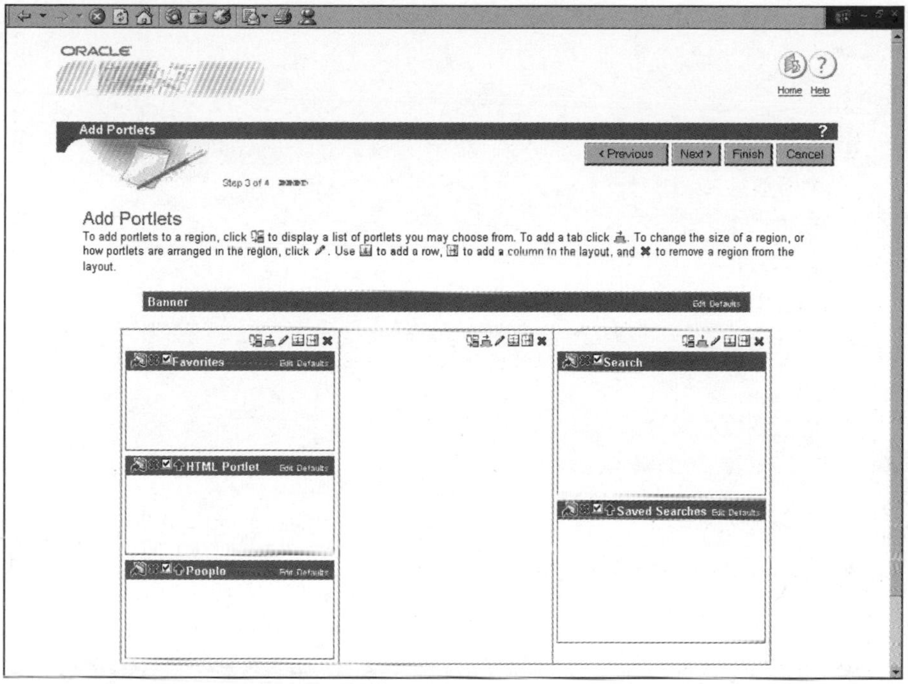

Figure 7-10: Your portal page with three regions

You have added enough portlets for your portal page, at least at this point. That big empty region in the middle is where you will put components that you will develop later.

At this point, you might be starting to see some of the beauty and power of the portlet capabilities of Oracle9iAS Portal. You can create a single portlet and use it in many different locations and on many different pages. Later in this chapter, you will see how each user of your page can also be given the right to customize parts or all of the page. The portlet capabilities added to the product known as WebDB really do take the offering to another level of functionality.

Finishing the page

There is one more page of the wizard to look at before you complete the creation of your first portal page.

20. Click on the Next button at the top of the page. This action will bring up the page shown in Figure 7-11.

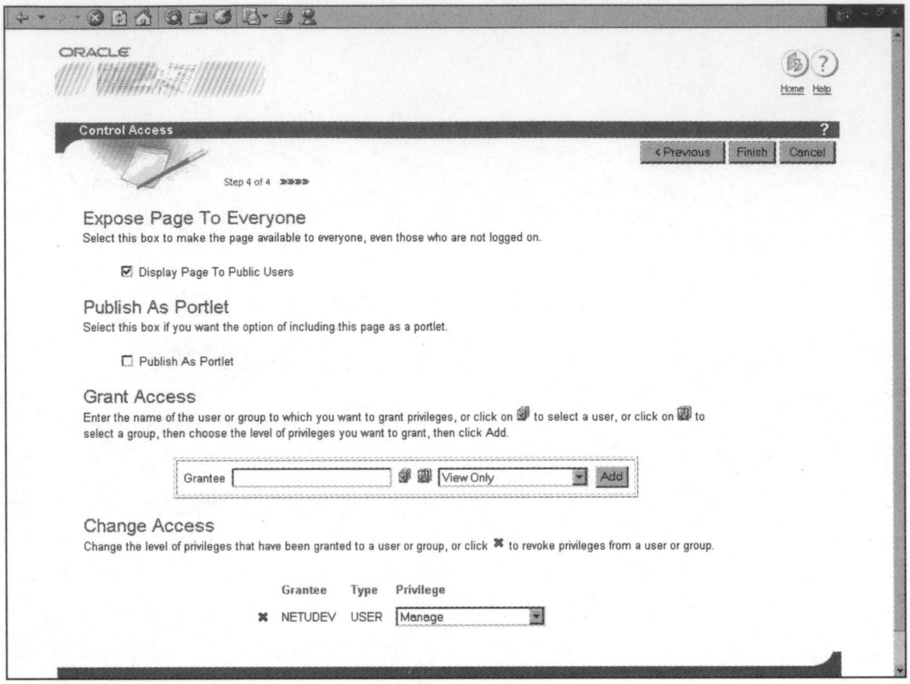

Figure 7-11: The fourth page of the Page wizard

This last page in the Page wizard revolves around the type of access you will grant to your new portlet page. The first heading for the page is labeled Expose Page To Everyone, and contains a check box that will do just that.

> **Note**   This selection will do exactly the same thing as adding the View privilege for the PUBLIC user group. The check box is another one of those shortcuts mentioned earlier in this chapter.

The next section of this page is the Publish As Portlet wizard. This simple phrase opens up a whole new world. Any of the components you develop with Oracle9*i*AS Portal — components, Content Areas, or pages — can be exposed as portlets. Oracle9*i*AS Portal is the portlet provider and each object can be a portlet. This simple fact has vast implications, such as the portlet page that you are now creating can be a portlet on another page.

Normally, this course would not make sense, due to the ever-diminishing amounts of screen real estate that a page exposed as a portlet could use. But you could use a page-as-portlet as a way to group logical or functional collections of other portlets. When you modified the page-as-portlet, the modifications would not affect the parent page.

The next two sections on this page of the wizard have to do with how the rest of the world can access and interact with this portal page. There are six levels of privilege you can grant, as shown in Table 7-1.

Table 7-1	
Privilege Levels for Portal Pages	
Privilege	*Access Granted*
Manage	Users can make any changes to a page, including adding and deleting regions, setting defaults for the page, and deleting the entire page.
Edit Contents	Users can add or delete portlets or tabs for the public or private versions of the page.
Manage Style	Users can change the style for a page.
Customization (Full)	Users can hide or show portlets on the page or add their own portlets to their own personal version of the page.
Customization (Add-only)	Users can only add portlets or delete portlets that they have placed on their personal version of the page.
View-Only	The lowest level of privilege. Users can only view the portal page. A user could also set the page as a default.

The privileges are listed in Table 7-1 in decreasing order of access. Every privilege also contains all the capabilities listed for all lower levels of privilege.

You can also assign privileges for an individual user or for a group of users. In fact, there are two lookup icons to the right of the Grantee field in Figure 7-11 — one to look up individual users and one to look up groups. If a user is assigned different levels of privilege by belonging to different groups, that user will assume the highest level of privilege.

For this page, you will want to grant some access to the NETU user.

21. Enter NETU in the Grantee field and select Customization (Add-only) from the combo box to the right of the field.

22. Click on the Add button, which will cause the page to look like Figure 7-12.

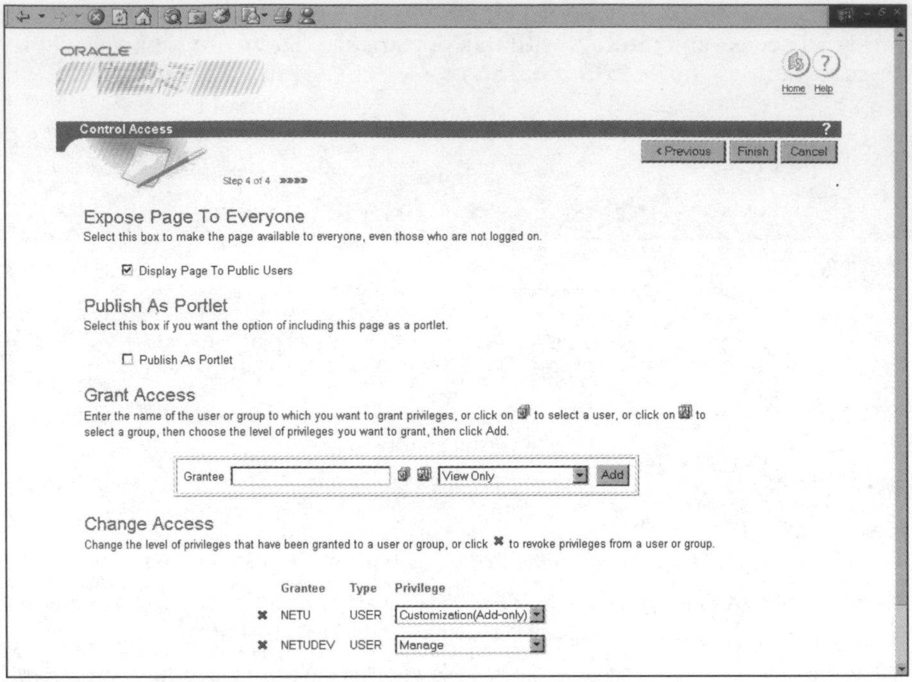

Figure 7-12: Access for the `NETU` user

If you have the Manage privilege for a portal page, you can change the access levels or delete all privileges for a user or group by clicking on the red X to the left of the Grantee column at the bottom of the page.

23. Click on the Finish button to complete the page. This action will bring up the completed portal page, as shown in Figure 7-13.

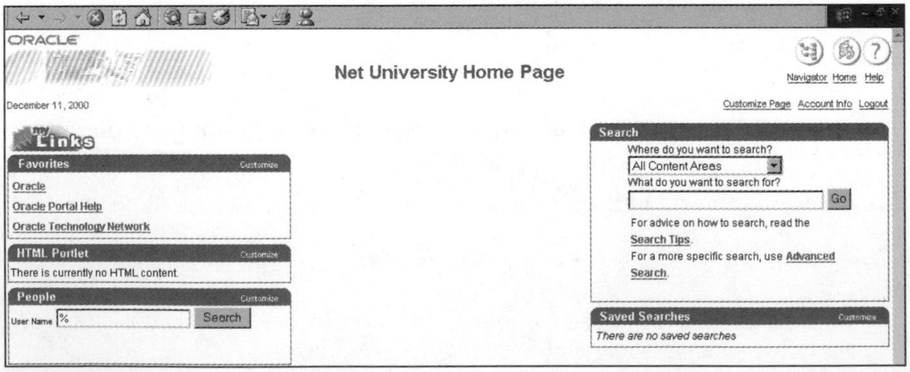

Figure 7-13: Your first portal page

Your portal page should look like the page shown in Figure 7-13. Pretty cool, huh?

It is fairly exciting to see the attractive display of your first portal page, but you could probably improve the way it looks. The final section of this chapter will lead you through the various ways you can customize the look and feel of a portal page.

Customizing the Page

One of the first things that you might have noticed about the portal page as it currently displays is that each region is the same width. Once you add the components to the currently blank middle region, you will probably want that region to be larger than the other two.

You can easily fix this problem by editing the attributes of the page. You can edit these attributes by either returning to the Oracle9iAS Portal environment and editing the page, or, more simply, by using the Customize Page link at the top of the portal page, which is available to you as the page owner.

1. Click on the Customize Page link in the banner of the Net University Home Page.

2. Go to the top of the leftmost region and click on the Edit Region icon, which looks like a pencil. This action will bring up a browser window with the page shown in Figure 7-14.

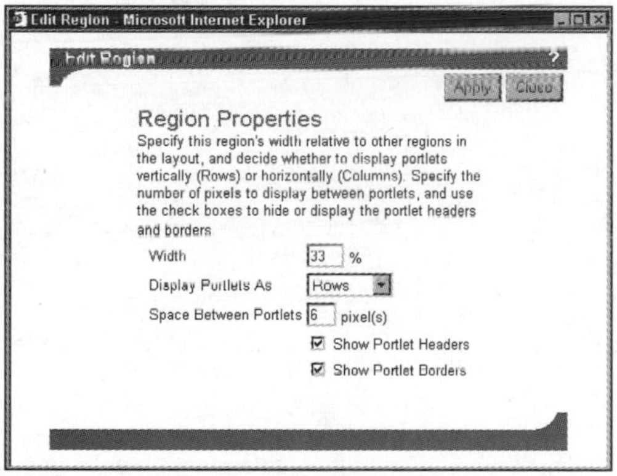

Figure 7-14: Editing the attributes of a region

There are only a few things you can change about a region, as follows:

✦ You can change the width of the region, which is represented by a percentage of the overall width available to display the page.

✦ You can choose to show the portlets in the region as rows within the region (the default), or as columns.

✦ You can specify the number of pixels between the portlets in the page.

✦ You can suppress the display of the portlet headers or borders, which are indicated by check boxes, and shown by default.

For this particular portal page, you will merely have to change the width of each of the regions:

3. Change the width of the region to 20.

4. Click on the Close button.

5. Click on the Edit Region icon for the right most region in the portal page layout.

6. Change the width of the region to 20 and click on the Close button.

   You don't have to change the width of the middle region. Not only will this region simply take up the remaining space, but the value of the Width parameter will automatically be changed by Oracle9iAS Portal.

7. Click on the Close button on the Customize Page page, which will bring up the modified portal page, as shown in Figure 7-15.

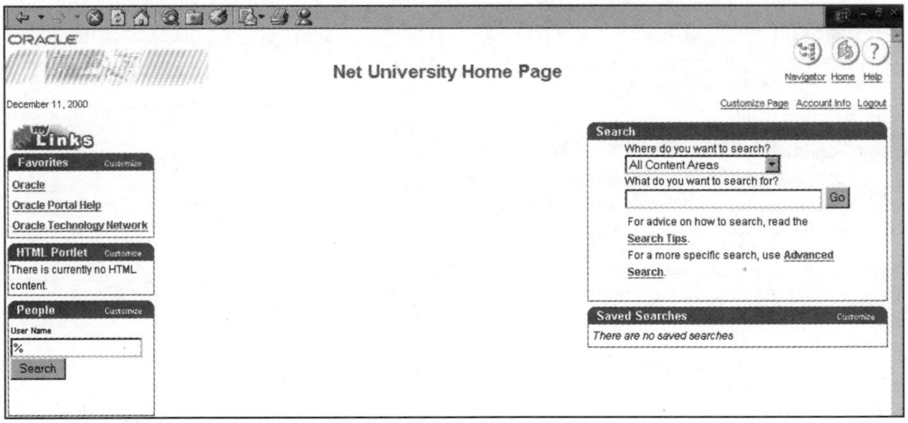

Figure 7-15: The modified portal page

The Net University Home Page looks pretty good now. But before you leave this chapter, you should take a look at how each individual can modify the look and feel of their own individual versions of the page.

Making Changes as a Page User

You are the page owner for this page, but you are also a user of the page. By looking at the sort of changes you can make as an individual user of a page, you can start to understand and appreciate the personalization features of Oracle9*i*AS Portal.

Working with the HTML portlet

You have probably noticed by now that the HTML portlet you added to your page looks a little lonely. It is just sitting there, telling you that it has nothing to give with the message "There is currently no HTML content." Your next step in this chapter is to give that little old portlet something to say.

1. Click on the Customize link for the HTML portlet, which will bring up the page shown in Figure 7-16.

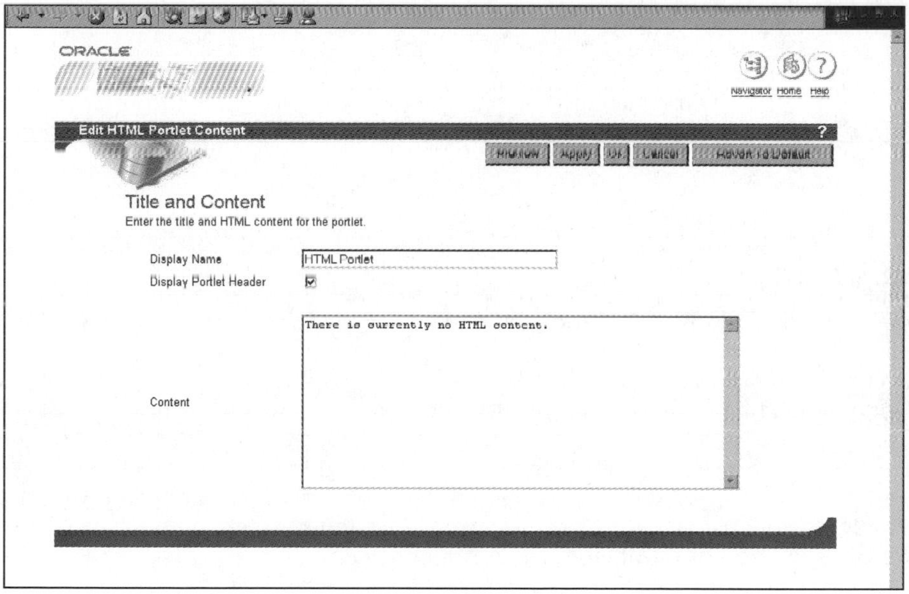

Figure 7-16: Customizing the HTML portlet

In this page, you can see that you can change the display name, uncheck a check box to suppress the display of the portlet header, and add in your own HTML code.

2. Add this text in the Content text box: **This is your\<i\>very\</i\> \<b\>first\</b\> portlet customization.**

3. Click on the Preview button to see the HTML portlet displayed, as it is in Figure 7-17.

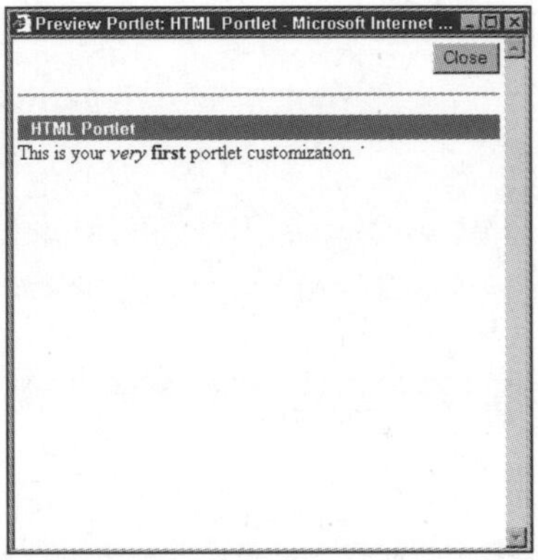

Figure 7-17: Your first HTML portlet

4. Click on the Close button to return to the Edit HTML Portlet Content page.

This first pass at adding HTML is not the most exciting message, but it is a (small) step above "Hello World." (And a bit of a mistaken claim, since you did customize some of the portlets in Chapter 4.)

If this type of functionality was all you could look forward to with the HTML portlet, you might not find it so great. However, the very name of the portlet is a bit mis-leading, because you can add more than just straight HTML to the HTML portlet. You can also use JavaScript to include other types of functionality in the portlet. The HTML portlet is like a blank area that you can use to create your own portlet pages with straight HTML and JavaScript code.

To see how this works, you can add some JavaScript that comes straight from a customized portlet. The Excite portlets, which come with the Portal Development Kit, generate JavaScript code that is used to access information from the Excite online services. The code fragment used in the next steps comes directly from one of these portlets.

5. Delete the previous HTML code in the Content window and add the following code:

```
<FORM>
<TABLE WIDTH=100% CELLSPACING=0 CELLPADDING=0 BORDER=0>
<TR><TD ALIGN=CENTER><FONT FACE=geneva,arial SIZE=-1 ><B>
<A TARGET=_top
HREF=http://affiliates.excite.com/relocate/co=afl_718841+sect
ion=weather;http://www.excite.com/weather/>Today's
Weather</A><BR>
<A TARGET=_top
HREF=http://affiliates.excite.com/relocate/co=afl_718841+sect
ion=weather;http://www.excite.com/weather/weather_maps/?wea_m
ap=USA>Weather Maps</A><BR>
<A TARGET=_top
HREF=http://affiliates.excite.com/relocate/co=afl_718841+sect
ion=weather;http://www.excite.com/weather/airport_delays/>Air
port Delays</A><BR>
<A TARGET=_top
HREF=http://affiliates.excite.com/relocate/co=afl_718841+sect
ion=weather;http://www.excite.com/weather/java_forecast/srch_
index.dcg>3D Weather Watcher</A><BR>
<P>
Enter ZIP code: </FONT><INPUT NAME=forecast_search SIZE=5
MAXLENGTH=5><BR></B>
<INPUT type=submit value=Search>
</TD></TR></TABLE></FORM>
```

This code is available on the CD-ROM in the *excitenews.htm* file.

Even though they may not appear that way here, due to margin constraints, you should make sure that the URLs specified as HREFs are all contained on a single line, so that they can be properly understood and referenced.

6. Click on the Preview button again to bring up the preview window shown in Figure 7-18.

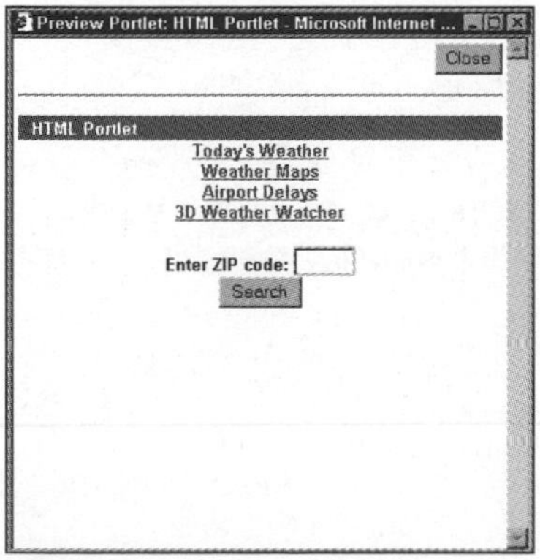

Figure 7-18: Accessing the Excite weather service

Of course, this is just the tip of the iceberg. You can use the HTML portlet to accomplish an enormously wide range of functionality. But there is one caution to be aware of.

If a user has customization privileges for this portlet, they can go in and modify the actual HTML code — typically not the greatest idea. If you want to use the HTML portlet, it is usually a good practice to deny users the ability to customize the resulting portlet by assigning a level of privilege below Customization (Full). If you want to use some of the functionality you can deliver in an HTML page and give users the ability to modify some of the ways it works, you might have to create your own portlet and customization page, as described in Chapter 27.

7. Click on the Close button in the preview window, and then click the OK button in the customize window to return to the view of the page.

Creating a personal version of a page

One of the powerful features of portal pages is the ability for individual users to customize their own personal version of the page.

You may have noticed a little combo box at the top of the portal page layout where you define the portlets in your page. The combo box has a "Customize for" label that offers Myself and Others as choices. As you might gather from these choices, Oracle9*i*AS Portal gives you the ability to change the view of a page for yourself or for others, depending on the level of privileges you have for this portlet.

To see this capability at work, you will have to become someone else:

1. Click on the Logout link in the banner. This action will take you back to the Oracle9*i*AS Portal home page.

2. Log in as the NETU user you defined in Chapter 2.

3. Go to the Navigator by clicking on the icon in the banner.

4. Click on the User Pages container, and then the letter N, then the user NETUDEV to get to the Net University Home Page that you created as NETUDEV in the previous section.

Cross-Reference If this seems a bit unwieldy, understand that there could be many users, with many pages. You will see a quicker way to make this page available to others in the next section.

5. Click on the Net University Home Page to bring up the page.

6. Click on the Customize Page link to bring up the page shown in Figure 7-19.

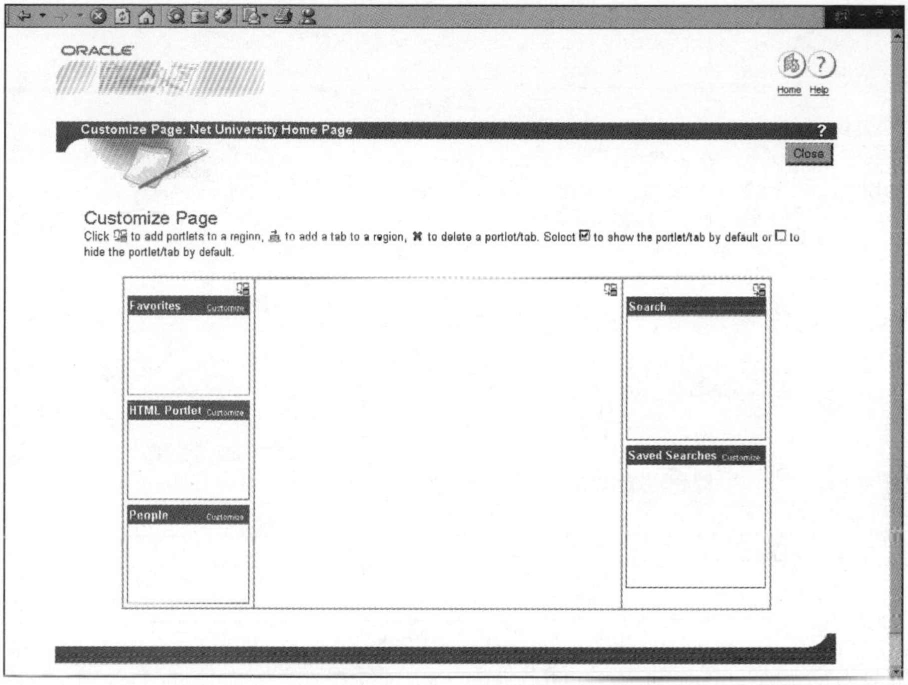

Figure 7-19: Customizing a page for a user with the Add-on customization privilege

If you remember, you gave the user NETU the ability to customize a page only by adding on portlets. So the customization page does not allow this user to change the existing portlets — only to add new portlets to the page.

7. Add the Find portlet from the list of Oracle9iAS Portal portlets using the Add Portlets routine you used earlier in this chapter. Click on the OK button to return to the customization page, which will now look like Figure 7-20.

You can see that you have the ability to delete the portlet that you just added for yourself, but not the other portlets. The last step in exploring this capability is to see what happens for this user when the page owner changes something.

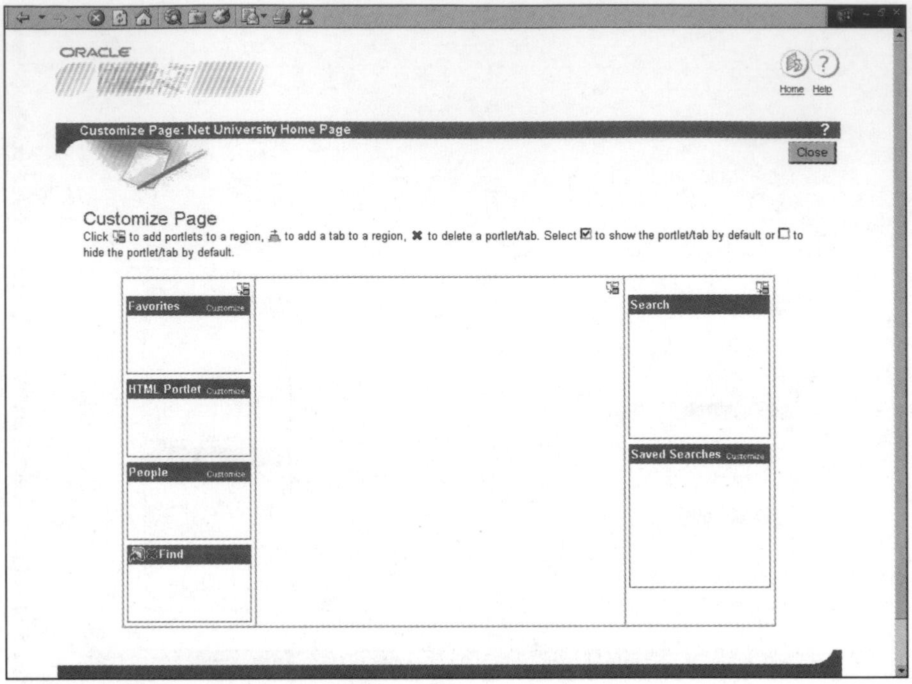

Figure 7-20: The newly customized page

8. Click on the Close button to return to the NetU home page.

9. Click on the Logout button.

10. Log in as the NETUDEV user.

11. Use the "my Work" portlet to quickly access the Net University Home Page for editing.

12. Click on the Portlets tab.

13. Delete the People portlet from the leftmost region. By default, this customization applies to other users' view of the page.

14. Click on the Close button to leave the customization area.

15. Log out from Oracle9iAS Portal, and log back in as the NETU user.

16. Click on the Net University Home Page in the my Work portlet to bring up the page shown in Figure 7-21.

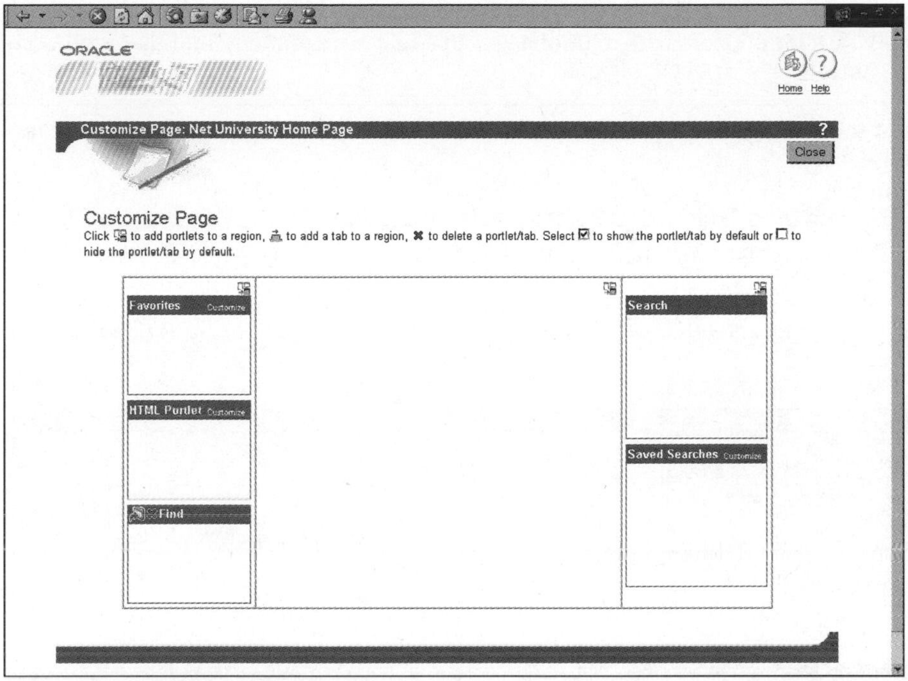

Figure 7-21: The modified page

You can see that the portlet that was dropped is missing, while your portlet is still there. When a user can only customize a page by adding portlets, they have no control over the areas of the page that were designed by the owner of the page—just over their own portlets. This type of partial control can be used to implement a deployment strategy that empowers users to customize their own versions of a page, but not to disrupt the parts of the page that are considered mandatory for all users.

The next brief topic to cover is how to make pages more available in the Navigator.

17. Click on the Close button to leave the customization page, and log out of Oracle9iAS Portal.

Promoting a page

You learned earlier that it can be somewhat cumbersome to have to click on the user pages container, then the first letter of a user's name, and then the user's name to get to a particular page.

The reason for this type of navigation, as mentioned above, is straightforward—there may be a lot of users with a lot of pages in a real environment, and this method of organization is, at least, logical.

But there is another type of page designation that raises a page to a higher level—the top-level page.

1. Log in to Oracle9*i*AS Portal as the user NETUDEV.
2. Click on the Navigator icon in the banner.
3. Click on the My Pages container in the Navigator to bring up the page shown in Figure 7-22.

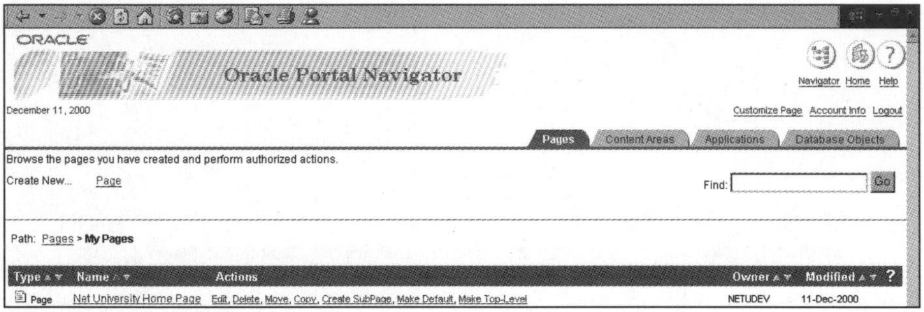

Figure 7-22: The My Pages listing

You can see the action at the end of the Actions list is Make Top-Level. If you click on this action, the page will be "promoted" to a top-level page.

4. Click on the Make Top-Level action for the page.
5. Click on the Pages link in the Path list.
6. Click on the Top-Level Pages container to bring up the page shown in Figure 7-23.

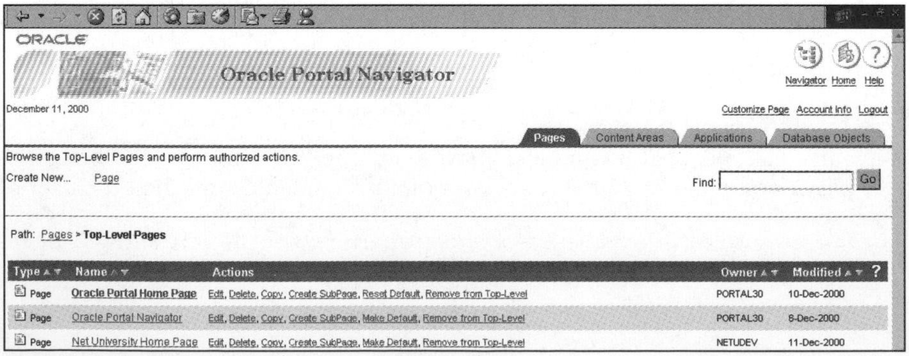

Figure 7-23: The new listing of Top-Level Pages

The Net University Home Page is now a top-level page, which means that any user can find it in this container, without all that clicking. Promoting a page to the top level really has no other effect — top-level pages are just like any other page.

There is one other thing you can specify for a page, which you will see in the next, and last, section of this chapter.

Designating a default page

Make Default is a choice in the list of actions for the pages shown in Figure 7-23. Using this choice will assign a particular page as the default page for the Oracle9iAS Portal environment for the current user. Once again, the best way to understand this capability is to use it:

7. Click on the Make Default action for the Net University Home page.

   The only real change you can see at this time is that the name of this page is now shown in bold, indicating that it is the default page. To see the more dramatic effect of this change, you will have to leave Oracle9iAS Portal and come back again.

8. Click on the Logout link to log out of the Oracle9iAS Portal environment.

9. Log back into Oracle9iAS Portal as the user NETUDEV.

This time, when you come into the Oracle9iAS Portal environment, you go straight to the Net University Home Page. The ability to set a default home page for the environment is a feature that each user can customize.

You still have access to the Navigator in the banner, so you had best go back and reset the default to the Oracle9iAS Portal home page for the rest of the lessons:

10. Click on the Navigator.

11. Go to the Top-Level Pages container.

12. Click on the Reset Default action for the Net University Home Page.

This action will reset the default home page to the original default, the Oracle9iAS Portal Home Page. This concludes your exploration of the wonderful world of portal pages.

Summary

You've learned a lot about the latest and greatest feature of Oracle9iAS Portal in this chapter — portals. In fact, everything that you dealt with in this chapter is new to this release of the product.

But there is a lot more that you can do with Oracle9*i*AS Portal — such as building your own components and Content Areas. In the next few chapters, you will explore these other capabilities of Oracle9*i*AS Portal, occasionally stepping back to add a newly created object to this original portal page.

You will return to the topic of portals later, in Chapter 28, when you learn what you have to do to create your own portlet provider. You will also be adding a few of the objects you will be building in the rest of the book to this page. In the next two sections of this book, you will delve into building components, one of the main types of object you can create with Oracle9*i*AS Portal.

✦   ✦   ✦

Oracle9*i*AS Portal Components

In This Part

Chapter 8
Building Oracle9*i*AS
Portal Reports

Chapter 9
Advanced Reporting
Techniques

Chapter 10
Building Oracle9*i*AS
Portal Forms

Chapter 11
Building Forms —
Part II

Chapter 12
Building Charts

Chapter 13
Building Oracle9*i*AS
Portal Calendars

Chapter 14
Working with
Hierarchies

Chapter 15
Working with HTML

◆ ◆ ◆ ◆

Building Oracle9*i*AS Portal Reports

CHAPTER

8

✦ ✦ ✦ ✦

In This Chapter

Building a QBE
Report

Running a Report

Building a Simple
Report with the
Query Wizard

Editing a Report
Component

Building a Simple
Report with a SQL
Query

✦ ✦ ✦ ✦

U sing a computer is, at its most basic level, a matter of working with data. Most data is read much more often than it is written. Reporting is the process of reading data and presenting it in a meaningful and understandable format, so building a report is a good place to start learning about Oracle9*i*AS Portal components.

Because many of you have probably come to Oracle9*i*AS Portal in part to make data from your Oracle database widely available over the Internet or an intranet, you will be creating and using a lot of reports with Oracle9*i*AS Portal.

Much of the functionality in the component building areas of Oracle9*i*AS Portal is the same as the corresponding areas of the previous release, which was known as WebDB. However, with Oracle9*i*AS Portal, the emphasis is on building components that will be used as portlets, rather than complete pages. Fortunately, you gain this ability with virtually no work on your part, as you will see later in this chapter.

Building a QBE Report

You can build a report component either by using the Query Wizard or by writing an SQL statement that supplies data to the report. The first page of the Report wizard is the same for both methods, and is followed by two slightly different sets of pages, and then concluded with the same set of pages for both methods.

Defining a report

You use the first page of the Report wizard to identify the report you are building.

1. Log into Oracle9iAS Portal as the NETUDEV user.
2. Enter the name of the application you are building, **NETCOLLEGE**, into the Name field in the Applications portlet on the home page.
3. Click the Navigate button to the right of the Name field.
4. Click on the Report link to the right of the Create New ... label at the top of the page, which will bring up the page shown in Figure 8-1.

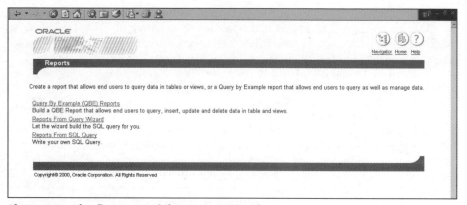

Figure 8-1: The first page of the Report Wizard

The first page you come to, as shown in Figure 8-1, has a similar look and feel to the first page of the form-definition process, which you will explore in Chapters 10 and 11. At the top of the page, there are three basic options for creating a report:

✦ By defining a Query-By-Example report, which allows the user to enter different selection parameters for the report

New Feature In WebDB, implementing QBE functionality was included in the Form Wizard, rather than the Report Wizard.

✦ With the Query Wizard, which walks you through a series of pages that help you define the data you want in the report
✦ By writing your own SQL statement

The first report you will create will be a simple QBE report. The QBE is a fairly specialized report. You can give the user a lot of options for specifying search conditions. You can even automatically give the user the ability to update or delete data with links from this report.

5. Click on the Query By Example (QBE) Reports link. The first page used to build a QBE report, which is labeled QBE Report Name and Application and is shown in Figure 8-2, is just like the first page on all of the other wizards.

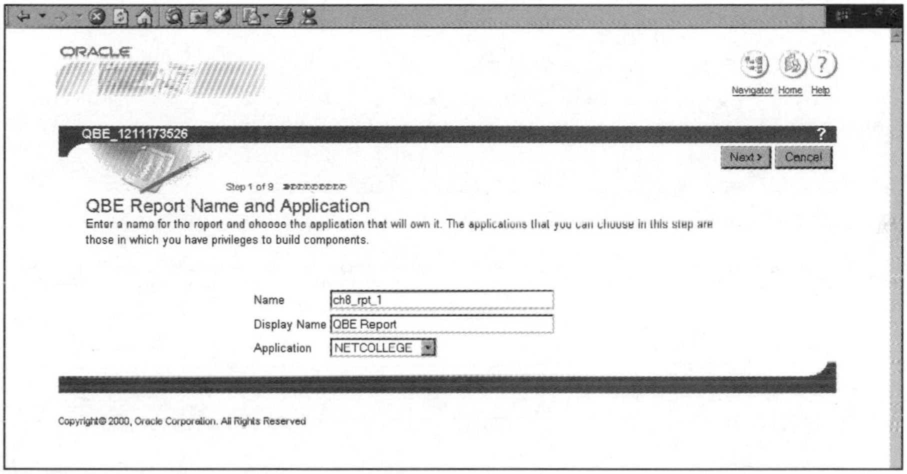

Figure 8-2: The QBE Report Name and Application page, with values filled in

The first data field asks for a name for the report, which is actually the name of the procedure stored in the Oracle9*i*AS Portal repository that creates the report at run time. You can enter any report name that is unique in its own schema. Of course, you should use some naming convention for all of your Oracle9*i*AS Portal components to make it easier to find them later in the development process. Because the purpose of this report is to be a part of the example application system you are building for this book, the naming convention here is the chapter number followed by a descriptive identifier followed by a number.

The second field on the page asks you for the Display Name of the report. This value will be displayed at the top of the report.

The combo box below the second field asks you for the name of the application that will contain the report you are creating. Because you chose the NETCOLLEGE application in the Builder portlet, NETCOLLEGE is the default choice in the Application combo box.

This page also contains a little series of arrows at the top of the page. There is an arrow, and a page, for each step in the Wizard. The set of arrows is simply a visual indicator of the progress you have made in the Wizard. As each step is displayed, its arrow gets filled in with a light blue color.

6. Enter **ch8_rpt_1** as the Name of the report.

7. Enter **QBE report** as the Display Name of the report.

8. Leave the NETCOLLEGE application as the choice in the Application combo box.

9. Click on the Next button.

The next page in the Report Wizard, labeled Table or View and shown in Figure 8-3, allows you to specify the table or view for this QBE report.

Tip   For QBE reports, you can only select a single table or view.

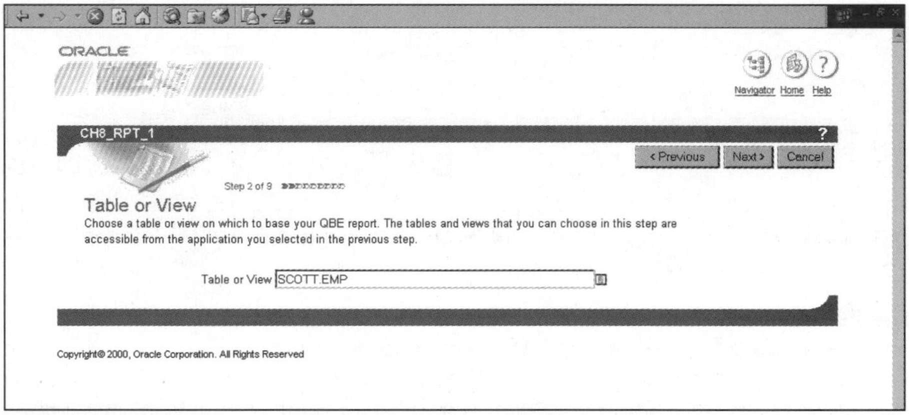

Figure 8-3: The Table or View page in the QBE Report Wizard

You can enter the schema and table name into the Table or View entry field. You can also click on the little page icon to the right of the entry field. This action will bring up the Search dialog box, as shown in Figure 8-4.

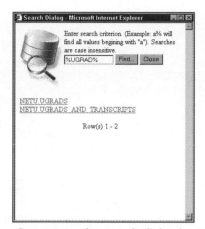

Figure 8-4: The Search dialog box

The Search dialog box is a generic dialog box that gives you the ability to search the database for a value. You can enter any combination of characters and wildcards. Typically, you will use the % wildcard at either the beginning, the end, or both sides of a character string. For instance, if you wanted to find all the tables and views in the NETU schema, you would enter **NETU.%** in the data field in the Search dialog box. If you wanted to try and locate all the tables that had the characters UGRAD in their names, regardless of schema, you would enter **%UGRAD%** in the data field — as was done in the example shown in Figure 8-4. To add a value retrieved in the Search dialog box to a data field in the Wizard, simply click on the value. The dialog box will close and the value will be placed in the appropriate field.

10. Enter NETU.UGRADS into the Table or View data field.

11. Click on the Next button.

The next page in the QBE Report Wizard, labeled Table or View Columns, is shown in Figure 8-5. This page has two list boxes. The Columns list box, on the left, contains all unselected columns in the table or view that the QBE report will be based on, while the list box on the right contains the columns that have been selected for display in the report. To select a column, you simply select the column name and click on the right-pointing arrow in between the two list boxes. Once a column is selected, it moves to the Selected Columns list box, on the right, and is removed from the left list box.

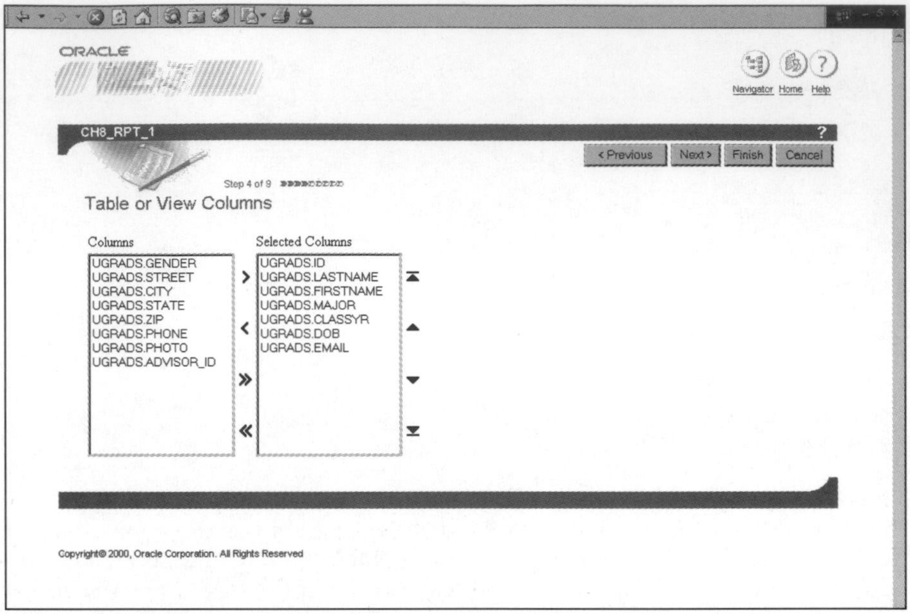

Figure 8-5: The Table or View Columns page in the QBE Report Wizard

You can select multiple columns for movement by using the appropriate key for multiple selections, such as the Ctrl key in Windows.

You can select all the columns in the left box by clicking on the double right arrows in between the two list boxes. To deselect a column, you select it in the right list box and click on the left pointing arrow in between the two list boxes. You use the double right arrows to deselect all of the columns in the right list box.

The columns you select are added to the Selected Columns list box in the order you select them. The columns are displayed in the subsequent QBE parameter page in the order they are listed in the Selected Columns list box. The arrows to the right of the Selected Columns list box can be used, from top to bottom, to move the position of a column to the top of the list, up one place in the list, down one place in the list, or to the bottom of the list.

   12. Move the ID, LASTNAME, FIRSTNAME, MAJOR, CLASSYR, DOB, and EMAIL columns, in that order, to the Selected Columns list box.

   13. Click on the Next button.

You have finished defining the data that will be used in your first report. Your next step is to shape how the report appears to the users.

Shaping your report

The rest of the pages in the QBE Report Wizard are used to adjust how your report will appear when it is run. The next page in the QBE Report Wizard, labeled Column Formatting, is shown in Figure 8-6.

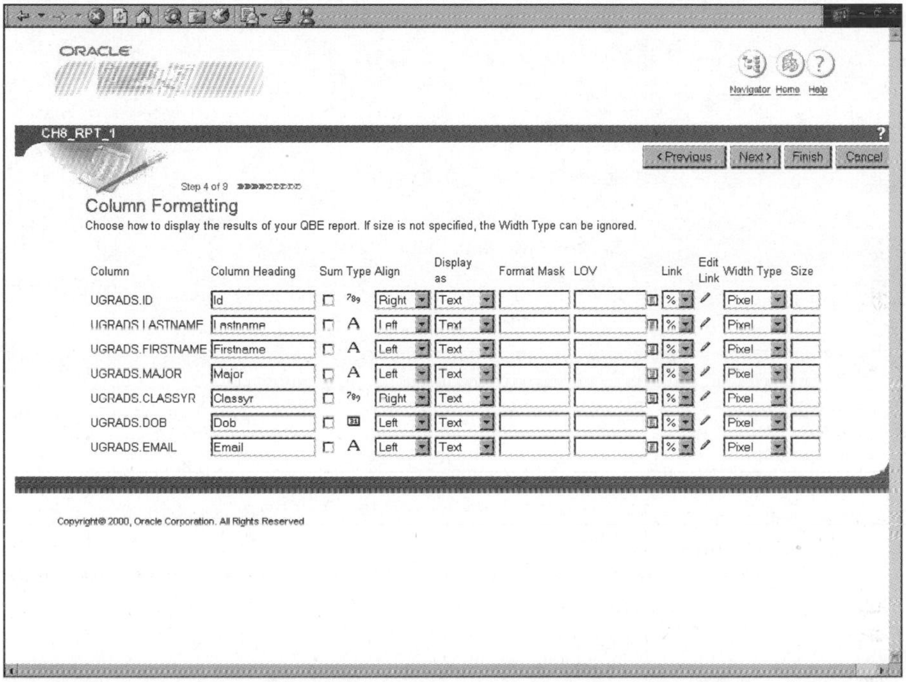

Figure 8-6: The Column Formatting page in the QBE Report Wizard

As the name implies, this page gives you the opportunity to format the columns in your QBE report. There are eleven columns of information or options on this page, which are described in Table 8-1.

<table>
<tr><td colspan="2" align="center">Table 8-1
Column Formatting</td></tr>
<tr><td>*Column*</td><td>*Purpose*</td></tr>
<tr><td>Column</td><td>The name of the column that will be in the finished report.</td></tr>
<tr><td>Column Heading</td><td>The heading that will appear in the report for the column, By default, Oracle9*i*AS Portal takes the name of the column, substitutes spaces for underscores, and capitalizes the first letter of each word.</td></tr>
</table>

Continued

Table 8-1 *(continued)*

Column	Purpose
Sum	This check box specifies that the column will have a sum displayed with it.
	If you just check the Sum box, your report will have sums at the end of each page for the page and for the total report up to that time. If you want to sum a value after a particular value in a column in the report changes, you have to order the report according to that column and break the report on the column. You will learn how to do this later in this chapter.
	There is a Sum check box for each column, even though it doesn't make sense to sum character or date fields.
Type	This column contains an icon that represents the datatype of the column in the report.
Align	You can align the data and the column heading for a column to the left, the right, or center it. By default, numeric columns are aligned on the right and all other datatypes are aligned on the left.
Display As	The Display As combo box gives you three choices:
	Text — Displays the value for the column as straight text. If there are any formatting tags in the value, they will be displayed.
	HTML — Uses any valid HTML formatting tags to format the value displayed.
	Hidden — Causes the value to not be displayed.
Format Mask	This column allows you to format the value in the data column. You can use standard Oracle formatting for numeric or date values. Basically, this means you can specify the separators and the decimal symbol for a number and the display format for a date. If you have a column that you wanted to display as a monetary value in the United States, you would type $999,999,999.99 into the formatting field, with the 9s representing the digits in the column value and the dollar sign, the commas, and the decimal point added for clarity. Leading zeros are automatically suppressed. If you enter an invalid format mask into this field, the resulting report has the value displayed as a string of # signs.
	You can use any format mask that you can use with the Oracle function TO_CHAR, to be specific. Basically, this means currency symbols, commas, decimal points and a variety of date formats.

Column	Purpose
LOV	An LOV is a *List-Of-Values,* which you can use to limit the data entry choices of the report user. The LOV is only valid if you are allowing a user to use this QBE to update data. LOVs are explained in depth in Chapter 16.
Link	This column allows you to specify a link for the column. Links are one of the primary ways that you can build complete application systems with Oracle9iAS Portal. The Edit Link icon allows you to edit the parameters used for a link. You will learn more about links in Chapter 20.
Width Type	The Width Type is a combo box where you can choose Pixel, Char, or Percent. The type you select will be used, in conjunction with the Size field, to determine the size of the column in the report.
Size	The Size column accepts an integer. This is the number of pixels, characters, or percent of the table that will determine the width of the table.

For this first report, you will accept the defaults for most of the fields in this page. The only things you will really change are the column headings for a few of the columns:

14. Change the text in the Column Heading column as follows: change Id to **ID**, LASTNAME to **Last Name**, FIRSTNAME to **First Name**, CLASSYR to **Class Year**, DOB to **Date of Birth**, and EMAIL to **E-mail**.

15. Click the Next button.

The next page in the QBE Report Wizard, labeled Formatting Conditions, is shown in Figure 8-7.

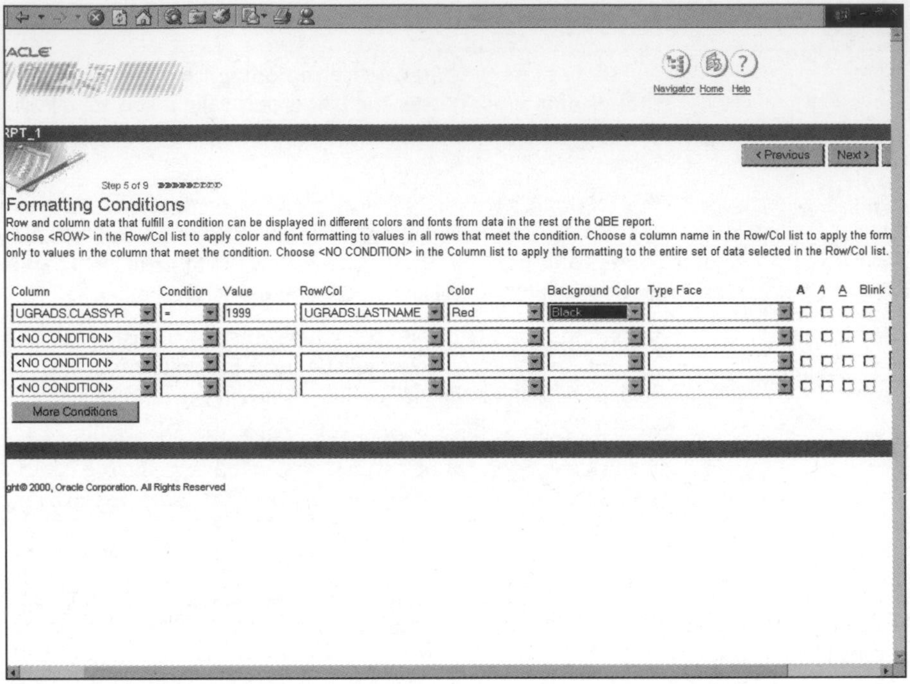

Figure 8-7: The Formatting Conditions page in the QBE Report Wizard

On this page, you can specify formatting conditions that will affect the look of the data retrieved for this report. The conditions you impose here will work invisibly — the user of the report will not be able to remove or change these conditions.

The Formatting Conditions page has space for four conditions, but if you want to add more, you can fill the available rows and then click on the More Conditions button at the bottom-left side of the page.

As you will see, users can impose their own selection conditions through use of the Query-By-Example form that is generated for this report. However, you can also use this page to specify different types of formatting for different values in the report.

New Feature The ability to highlight individual cells in a report, based on value, is a new feature in Oracle9*i*AS Portal.

Because seniors are special people at old NetU, you will want to show off their names.

16. In the first row on the Formatting Conditions page, select CLASSYR from the Column combo box, and = from the Condition combo box.

17. Enter **2001** in the Value data field.

18. Select LASTNAME from the Row/Col combo box.

19. Select Red from the Color combo box.

20. Select Black from the Background Color combo box.

You can also specify a different typeface, or make the data bold, italic, or underlined, respectively, in the three check boxes. The last column on this page, Seq, allows you to specify the sequence that the formatting conditions you impose on this page are applied in a specific order.

Tip If you want to format a column in a particular way, regardless of the values in its row, you can specify NO CONDITION in the Column combo box.

21. Click on the Next button.

The next page in the QBE Report Wizard, labeled Display Options, is shown in Figures 8-8 and 8-9.

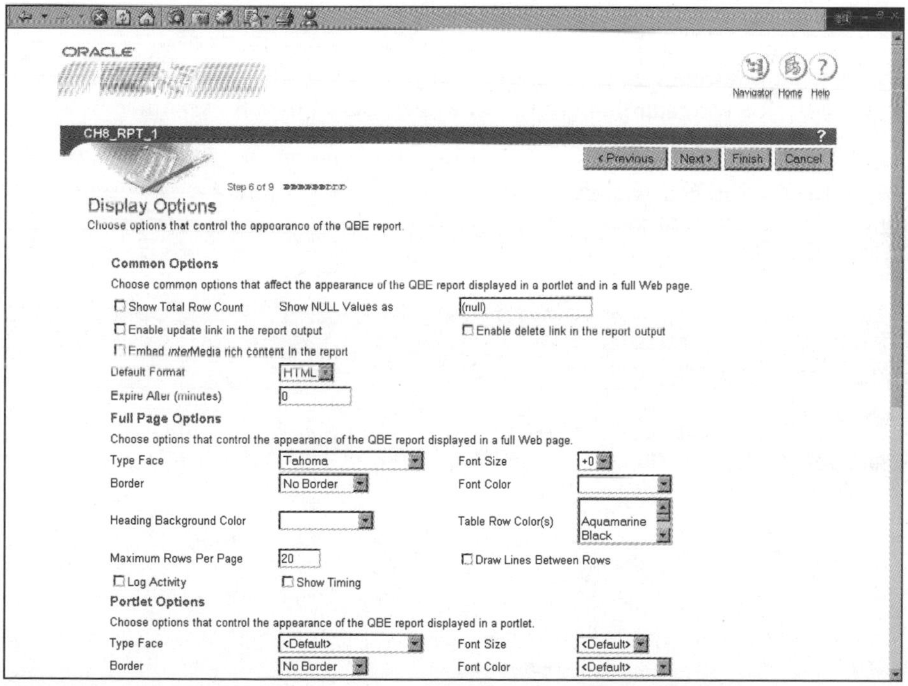

Figure 8-8: The upper portion of the Display Options page in the QBE Report Wizard

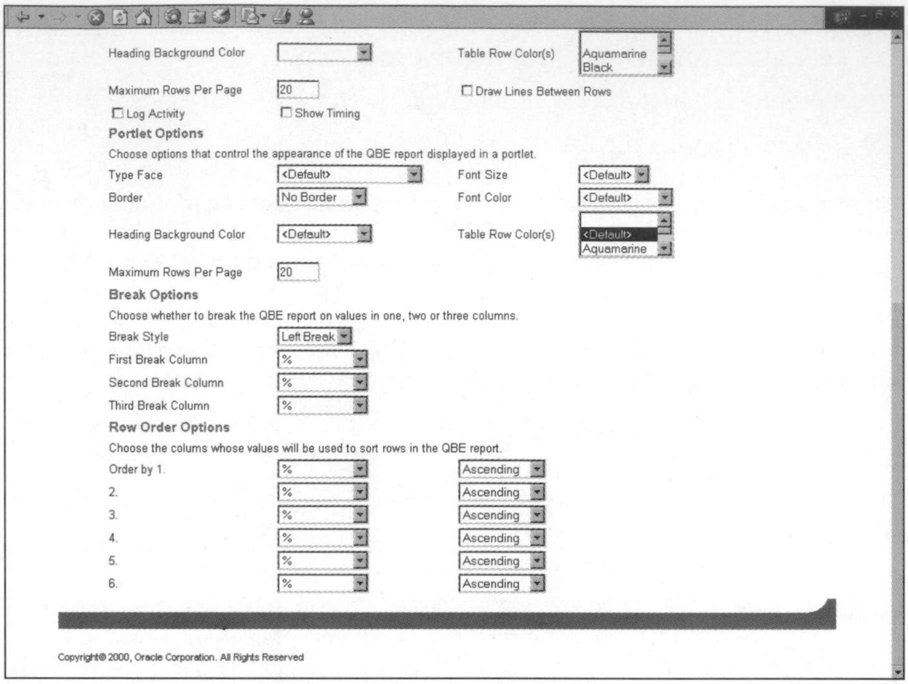

Figure 8-9: The lower portion of the Display Options page in the QBE Report Wizard

There are five types of display options, and several options for each type of display. All of the options are described in Table 8-2.

Table 8-2 Display Options		
Display Type	**Option**	**Usage**
Common Options		These options are applied to all QBE reports.
	Show Total Row Count	This check box will cause a line to appear at the bottom of each report page that tells the numbers of rows on the page, such as "Rows 1-20", "Rows 21-40", and so on.

Display Type	Option	Usage
	Show NULL Values as	This field allows you to specify a text string that will be displayed in place of a NULL value.
		If you want to suppress the display of any value for NULLs in the database, you can leave this space blank. The authors do not recommend this approach, because Oracle9*i*AS Portal automatically suppresses the display of repeating values for a break field, and having blanks for NULLs might cause some confusion.
	Enable update link in the report output	This check box will place an Update link for each row, which will take the user to an update page for the row. The update page will display all the data in the row, but only allow the user to update the data specified in the QBE report.
	Enable delete link in the report output	This check box will place a Delete link for each row, which will allow the user to delete the row. This link will take the user to a page that will ask the user to confirm the deletion.
	Embed *inter*Media rich content in the report	This check box will embed images that are supported by the Oracle *inter*Media option to be displayed in the report.
	Default format	There are three choices for formatting:
		HTML — The default format, which causes the report to be shown as an HTML format.
		Excel — Outputs the data from the report as an Excel-compatible file. This option is ideal if you are extracting data from your Oracle database for use in a spreadsheet or other data format that can import Excel files.
		ASCII — ASCII text. ASCII formatting means that the report is presented in a fixed-width standard ASCII format. In HTML terms, this means the report is presented between <PRE>, or preformatted, tags. You may want to use this option if the eventual purpose of the report is to take the straight text and put it into another text document that does not support HTML.

Continued

Table 8-2 *(continued)*

Display Type	Option	Usage
	Expire After (minutes)	For frequently used reports, you can specify that the report should remain in a cache for a certain amount of time, which can be specified here. If a report is cached, a new request for the report will simply read the complete report from the cache, rather than recreate it by accessing the data. For more information on this type of caching, refer to Chapter 6, which discussed caching for Oracle9*i*AS Portal.
		The default value for the field is 0, which indicates that the report should not be cached.
Full Page Options		These display options are used when the report is being displayed as a full page.
	Type Face	HTML gives you the option of using different typefaces, and this combo box gives you a choice of the potential typefaces for your browser. If a user accesses your report with a browser that does not support the typeface you have chosen, the report is displayed in a default font. Fonts are detailed in depth in Chapter 18.
	Font Size	There are eight values for this option — +1 through +4; −1 through −3; and 0, the default choice. Any value other than the default causes the font to be either larger or smaller than the default font. The font size controls the size of the font in the body of the report, but does not affect the size of the heading of the report.
		Note that in the 3.0.8 version of Oracle9*i*AS Portal, these relative sizes are replaced with point sizes.
	Border	There are three choices in this combo box: No Border, Thin Border, and Thick Border, whose names are self-explanatory.

Display Type	Option	Usage
	Font Color	This combo box enables you to select the color for the report font from a list of font colors that are available on your browser. The default value, which is blank, causes the font to use the default color for the template or browser you use for the report. Templates are explained in Chapter 18. The default for the Font Color is blank, which means it will use the default color for the font for the page.
	Heading Background Color	This combo box enables you to select the color for the background of the heading of the report. The default value, which is blank, causes the heading to use the default color for the template or browser you use for the report.
	Table Row Color(s)	All the data in a Oracle9*i*AS Portal report is returned in an HTML table if you choose HTML as the display option. As the name implies, this combo box enables you to choose the color or colors for the rows in the report. You can also select more than one color in this box to vary the colors between each row. The default color scheme for a report is to alternate gray and white rows for readability. Keep in mind that this background color is only for the cells of the table, so selecting a color here that contrasts with the default background color for the template you choose in a subsequent page can result in a truly ugly report.

Continued

Table 8-2 *(continued)*

Display Type	Option	Usage
	Maximum Rows Per Page	The Maximum Rows option enables you to specify how many rows are returned on each page of your report. The more rows that are returned per page, the more data per page, and the longer the page takes to be sent back to the client browser from the server. If there are more rows in your report than can fit on a single page, a Next button appears at the bottom of the page. If the user has moved to a page beyond the first page of the report, a Previous button also appears at the bottom of the page. If you want to have the entire report delivered as a single page, set the Maximum Rows value to a number at least equal to the number of rows you expect to be returned from the query. This is especially important if you plan to direct the output to an Excel file and want to make sure that all the data is included in the spreadsheet. The default value for Maximum Rows is 20.
	Draw Lines Between Rows	This check box causes a horizontal line to be inserted between each row in the report. By default, this option is not checked.
	Log Activity	Oracle9*i*AS Portal gives you the option of logging all Oracle9*i*AS Portal activity for later review. By default, this option is checked.
	Show Timing	Your report can show the amount of time the server took to assemble the page returned to the browser if this option is checked. By default, this option is checked.
Portlet Options		These options are used when the report is being displayed as a portlet. The options have the same meaning as their counterparts under Full Page Options, with one important difference.

Display Type	Option	Usage
		The default choice for all of the Portlet options except Border and Maximum Rows Per Page is <Default>. This choice means that the portlet will inherit the values for these properties from the page that the portlet sits on—a choice that allows the portlet to fit into a variety of pages.
Break Options		These options control how the data in the report is broken up.
	Break Style	There is only one style of break, which is Left Break. This break indents the report rows as the value in the break column changes.
	Break Columns	There are three combo boxes for break columns. The first combo box you select is the primary break column, the second is the next break column, and the third is the final break column.
		The first break column is always the first column in each row, followed by the second and third break columns, if specified. After the break columns have been displayed, Oracle9*i*AS Portal sequences the remainder of the columns in the order they were listed in the Selected Columns list box.
		Selecting a column for a break column does not necessarily cause the rows in the report to be sorted on that column value—it only suppresses the display of repeating values for the row. In other words, if you specified MAJOR as the first break column and CLASSYR as the second break column, and specified these as the first and second Order By column, your report would look like Figure 8-10.
Row Order Options		These options specify how the data rows in the report are sorted.

The Row Order Options section of the Display Options page consists of six lines of two combo boxes. The first combo box enables you to select the column value to use for the top-level sort of your report from a list of columns in your report. The default value for the first combo box is a blank space, which means that the report is not sorted. The second combo box enables you to choose to sort the rows in either ascending order, which is the default, or descending order. This first line of the Row Order Options section is where you choose the primary sorting column — the column that is used to sort the report into major groupings.

The second line in the Row Order Options section of this page has the same fields as the first line in the section. The difference between the two lines is that the choices you make in this section are used to implement the secondary sort order — the way that the rows are sorted within the primary sort groups defined by the previous line's entries.

You can sort on up to six columns in your Oracle9*i*AS Portal report.

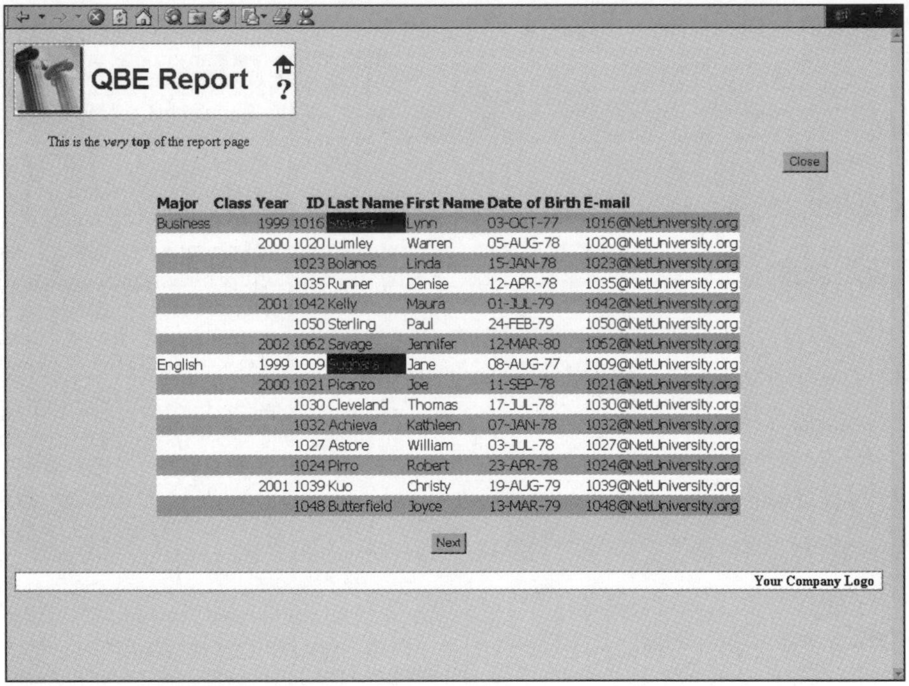

Figure 8-10: Break columns in a report

Many of the options listed in Table 8-2 include a <Default> choice. This choice will cause the option to inherit its value from the value specified for the page.

Allowing users to shape the report

The Display Options give you a lot of choices, but for the purposes of your first report, you will accept the default values for all of them. In the next section, when you run your report, you will see how the Row Order and Break options affect the display of the report.

22. Click on the Next button.

The next page in the QBE Report Wizard, labeled Customization Form Display Options, is shown in Figure 8-11.

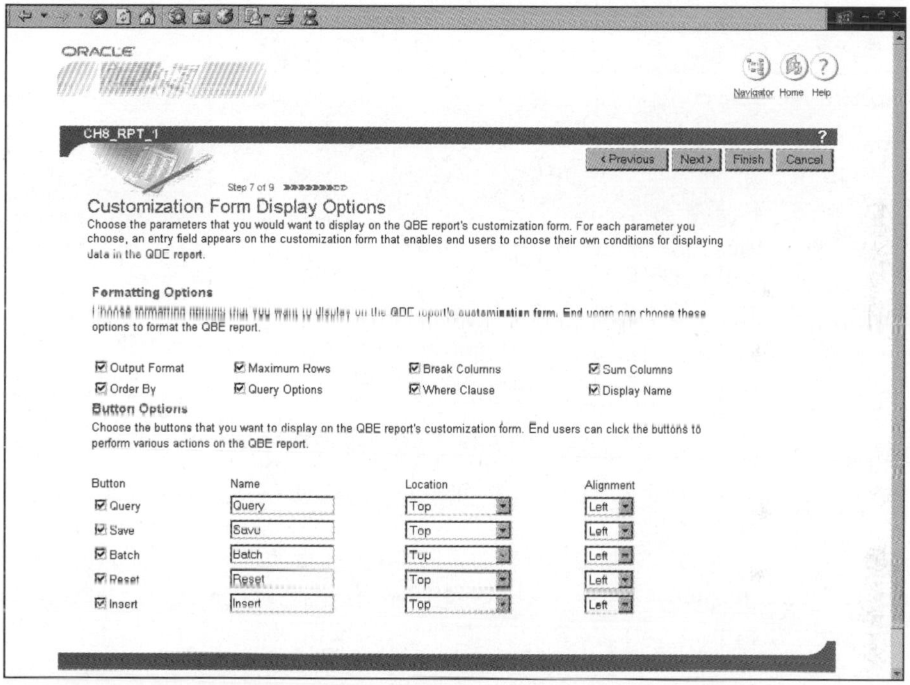

Figure 8-11: The Customization Form Display Options page in the QBE Report Wizard

Although you cannot specify parameters for a QBE report, as you can for other reports you will learn about later, the report can still be customized by the users. Oracle9*i*AS Portal will generate a customization form for the report. This form will include the ability to define a selection criterion for each of the columns in the report, just as if they had been defined as parameters, as well as having two other features, which are common to all types of customization forms for all Oracle9*i*AS Portal components.

You can allow your users to set their own values for some of the Formatting Options you specified in the Display Options page. There are check boxes on the Customization Form Display Options page for Output Format, Maximum Rows, Break Columns, Sum Columns, Order By (columns), Query Options, Where Clause, and Display Name options. If any of these are checked, the parameter form will give the users the ability to set their own values for these options. The values that you selected for these options will become the defaults. The default is for all the Formatting Options check boxes to be checked.

The Customization Form Display page also includes a number of buttons, which each call a particular function. The button choices for a QBE Report are described in Table 8-3.

	Table 8-3 Button Options
Button	**Function**
Query	Causes the query to run and the report to be generated, using the values entered into the QBE fields as selection criteria.
Save	Saves the current values in all of the parameter and option fields as the default values for this user. Every time the user returns to this report, the saved values will reappear.
Batch	Causes the report to be submitted into a batch queue. Using the batch queue will reduce the real-time overhead on the target database. There is a single batch queue for each Oracle9*i*AS Portal server. Once a report is submitted in batch, the user can check the batch status page to see if the report has been executed and, if it has completed, to view the report.
Reset	Resets all fields to their default values, as defined by you, the developer, or as saved by the user.
Insert	Inserts a row into the underlying table or view with the values specified in the QBE form. Oracle9*i*AS Portal does not do any checking on the values in the form, so it is very possible for errors to occur if users enter invalid values for a column or neglect to enter a value for a required column.

Each button has a check box, which, if checked, causes the button to be displayed. If a button is not displayed, the users will not have access to the functionality of the button.

You can specify a name for each button. You can also choose an alignment for each button, which will cause the buttons to be displayed at the top of each page, at the bottom of each page, or in both locations. Finally, you can specify whether a button is to be aligned on the left of the page or the right of the page.

Using templates and adding text to your report

Once again, for this first report, you can accept the defaults.

23. Click on the Next button.

The next page in the QBE Report Wizard is the QBE Report and Customization Form Text page, shown in Figure 8-12.

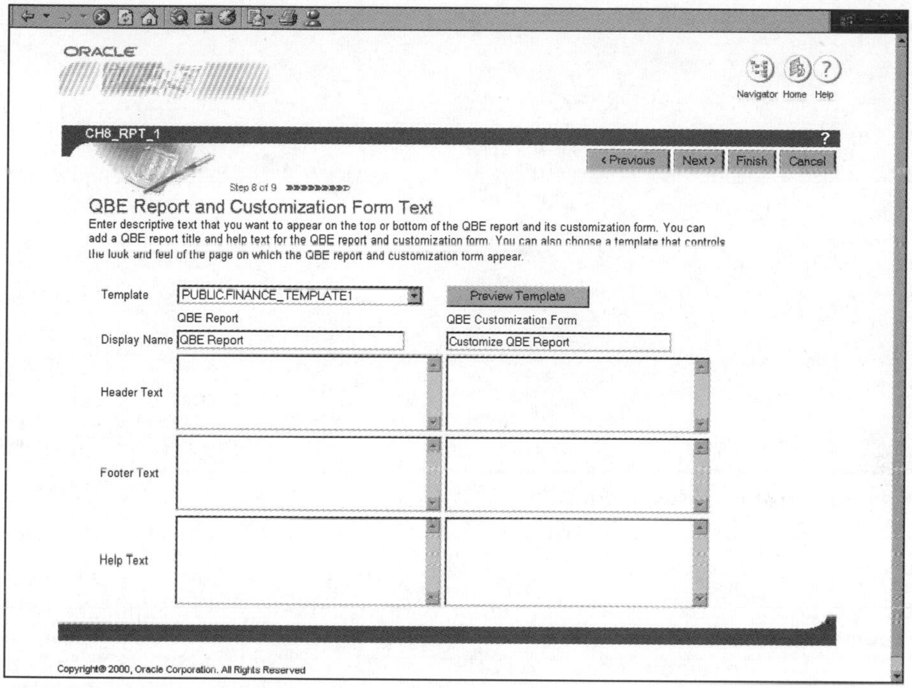

Figure 8-12: The QBE Report and Customization Form Text page in the QBE Report Wizard

This page in the QBE Report wizard gives you a lot of control in shaping the overall appearance of your report.

The Template combo box, the first entry on this page presents one of the most powerful choices you can make in the QBE Report Wizard. Oracle9*i*AS Portal supports an object known as a template. A template provides the default layout for all of the entities in a Oracle9*i*AS Portal application system — reports, forms, charts, calendars, and all the other Oracle9*i*AS Portal objects.

Oracle9*i*AS Portal comes with a number of default templates. The template you choose gives a standardized look and feel to your report, the parameter form for your report, and the help pages for the report and the parameter forms.

In Chapter 18, you will learn how to create your own templates, but right now you can see the power of templates by selecting one of them for your report:

24. Select the PUBLIC.TEMPLATE_6 in the Template combo box.

25. Click on the Preview Template button.

You will see a preview of the template open up in a separate window, as shown in Figure 8-13.

Figure 8-13: Previewing a template

If you look at the template for PUBLIC.TEMPLATE_6, you can see that it is more than just another pretty face. The public template allows you to specify a company name or graphic as part of the display for all pages that use the template. More importantly, the template has two hotlinks on it. One link looks like a little house, which always takes the user back to a home page you specify, and the other link looks like a question mark, which brings up a help page for the associated page, whether it is a report page or a parameter form.

The rest of the fields on the Add Text page help you shape your report by adding text to the report. You can add the following four types of text:

Display Name	Displayed at the top of the first page of the report and the parameter and help pages, and is also used as the identifying title in the title bar of the browser
Header Text	Displayed at the top of each report page or parameter form, just below the title on the first page of the report
Footer Text	Displayed at the bottom of every page of the report or the parameter form
Help Text	Displayed in a separate page for the report and parameter forms

You can specify this text separately for either the report pages or the parameter forms. Oracle9*i*AS Portal treats this text as straight HTML, so you can include HTML formatting tags in the text you enter for any of these areas.

26. Leave the title "QBE Report" for the report and change the title for the QQBE Customization Form to **QBE Report Customization**.

27. Enter **This is the <I>very</I> <B>top</B> of the report page** for the Header Text for the report.

28. Enter **Please complete the customization entries.** for the Header Text for the parameter entry form.

29. Enter **<CENTER>You can save your choices as defaults by clicking on the
<B><I>Save</I></B>
 button.</CENTER>** as the Footer Text for the customization entry form.

30. Enter **There is no help available for this basic report.** for the Help text for the report.

31. Click on the Next button.

The next page of the Report Builder wizard gives you the opportunity to add PL/SQL code that executes before or after the display of the page or the header for the page. You can learn about using this feature of Oracle9*i*AS Portal in Chapter 21.

Because you are on the last step in defining a QBE report, you can simply click the Finish button to generate your component.

Tip You can click on the Finish button at any point in any Oracle9*i*AS Portal wizard. Oracle9*i*AS Portal will simply use the default values for any fields on any pages you haven't visited.

It is important to understand exactly what happens when you press the Finish button. Up until this point in the development process, you have been giving values for the parameters that Oracle9*i*AS Portal uses for your report. These parameters have been stored in Oracle9*i*AS Portal's internal data tables. But these parameters are not used in the actual production of your report. Oracle9*i*AS Portal uses the parameters you have entered to create a PL/SQL procedure. When your application system calls this Oracle9*i*AS Portal report, it is actually calling the PL/SQL procedure that runs and creates the report as output.

Oracle9*i*AS Portal creates this all-important procedure when you click the Finish button on the final page of the Report Builder Wizard.

32. Click on the Finish button.

You did it! You have successfully generated your first Oracle9*i*AS Portal component!

You have landed at the Manage Component page, from which you can launch your new report. The next section will explore the options you have for running your report.

Running Your Report

So far, all you have is a procedure that supposedly produces a report for you. You are probably dying to see the results of your work.

Once you have successfully created the procedure for your report, Oracle9*i*AS Portal immediately does two things for you. One of these things is internal — the status for the report changes from EDIT to PRODUCTION. When a component has a status of PRODUCTION, the values of the parameters that control the generation of the component procedure have not changed since the procedure was generated. In other words, the component has not been changed since the procedure for the component was generated. If you were to leave a creation wizard before reaching the final page and clicking the OK button, the component would have a status of EDIT. The same status would be set if you were to leave an editing session without clicking the Finish button, which you will learn about shortly.

The other thing that Oracle9*i*AS Portal does for you is to bring up a page that enables you to run and manage your QBE report object, as shown in Figure 8-14.

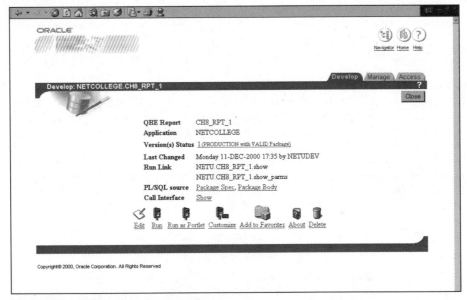

Figure 8-14: Managing your report

There is some basic information about the component at the top of the page. The information about the component includes the name of the component, a list of all of the versions of the component, the time the component was last changed, and three links that allow you to see the PL/SQL package spec and body for the component, listed beside the label PL/SQL source, and the interface you can use to call the generated PL/SQL packages, listed beside the Call Interface label.

Cross-Reference   You will learn more about how to understand and use this PL/SQL when you build your own portlet in Chapter 28.

Each time you edit and regenerate a component, Oracle9*i*AS Portal saves the previous version of the component and the values for its parameters in an archive version. The archived versions of a component are numbered in increments of 1 (starting with 1), and given the status of ARCHIVE. You will learn more about Oracle9*i*AS Portal's version control in Chapter 25.

There are seven links at the bottom of the page. The purpose of these links will be described when you need to use them in this and later chapters. Right now, you are ready to run your first report:

1. Click the Run link at the bottom of the panel. This action will bring up your report in a separate browser window.

The first page of your first report should look like Figure 8-15.

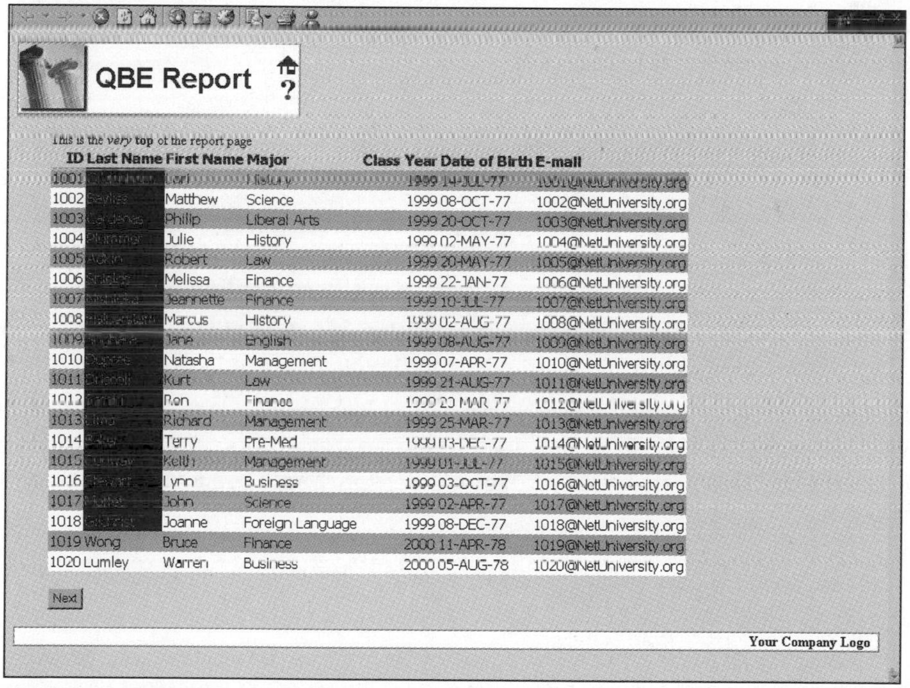

Figure 8-15: The first page of your first report

There are a few things you may immediately notice about this report. First, the design template you specified for the report gives it a nice look and feel, regardless of the fact that the data in the report could be arranged in a more meaningful fashion.

Second, the report title and heading you specified appear in their appropriate places. There is also a Next button, which has been placed at the bottom of the page.

You can also see that the highlighting option you specified to make the seniors stand out seems to be working appropriately.

Before leaving this page, you might want to check out the help page for the report.

2. Click the Help (question mark) icon in the top-right corner of the report page banner.

The help page that appears looks like Figure 8-16.

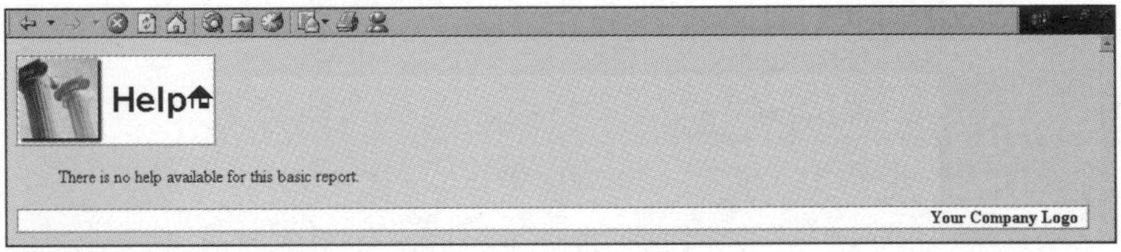

Figure 8-16: Your first help page

The help page has the same look and feel as your report, thanks to the uniform use of the template by Oracle9*i*AS Portal.

Because this is your first report, you will no doubt want to see all of it.

3. Click the Back button of the browser to return to the first report page.

4. Click the Next button at the bottom of the report page to go to the next page of the report. Click the Next button until you arrive at the last page of the report—the page that only contains a Previous button.

You can also see that the intermediate pages of the report have both a Next and Previous button and that the last page of the report only has a Previous button, as you would expect.

5. Close the report browser window and return to the Manage Component page of Oracle9*i*AS Portal.

New Feature

With WebDB, you would have to use the Back button on your browser to return to the development environment. By firing off the report in a different browser window, Oracle9*i*AS Portal has made a significant improvement in the usability of the development environment.

It was a little thrilling to see your first report, but it seems as though there was something missing. This type of report is called a Query-By-Example report, but there doesn't seem to be any way to add the selection criteria that a QBE would use.

In addition, it would have been nicer to see the information in the report sorted, perhaps by major and then by class year.

The way to address both of these issues is through another link in the Manage Component page: the Customize link.

New Feature In WebDB, this page was called the Parameters page.

Whenever you generate a QBE report, Oracle9/AS Portal automatically generates a form that can be used to set parameters for customizing the report. These parameters are the columns you specified when building the report, as well as the display options that were enabled by default.

To see how this customization page can be used, you have to simply click on the Customize link in the Manage Component page.

6. Click on the Customize link at the bottom of the Manage Components page, which is located to the right of the Run As Portlet link.

The Customize page for your first QBE report is shown in Figures 8-17 and 8-18.

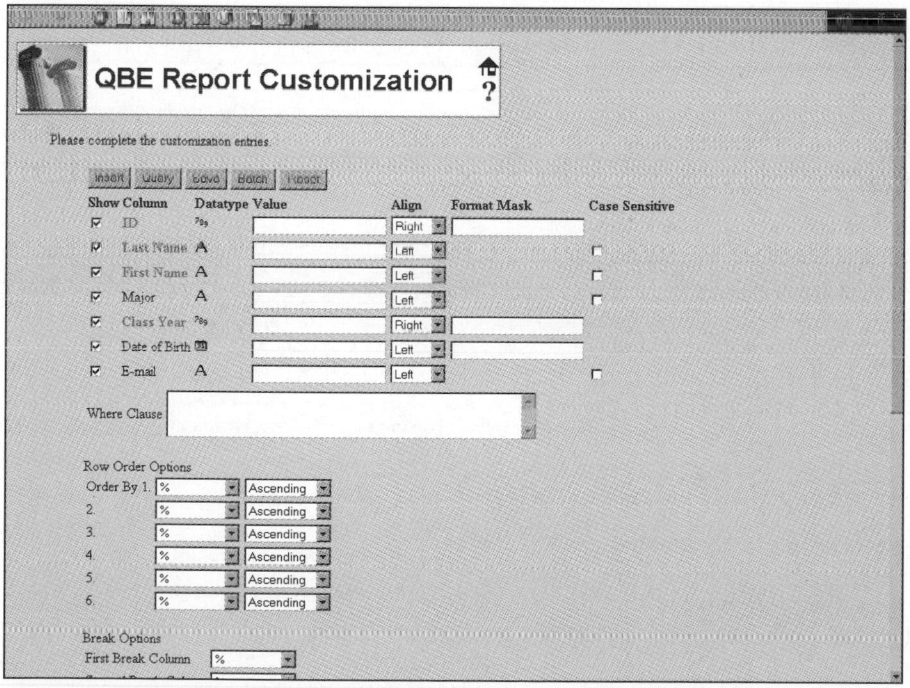

Figure 8-17: The upper part of the Customize page for your QBE report

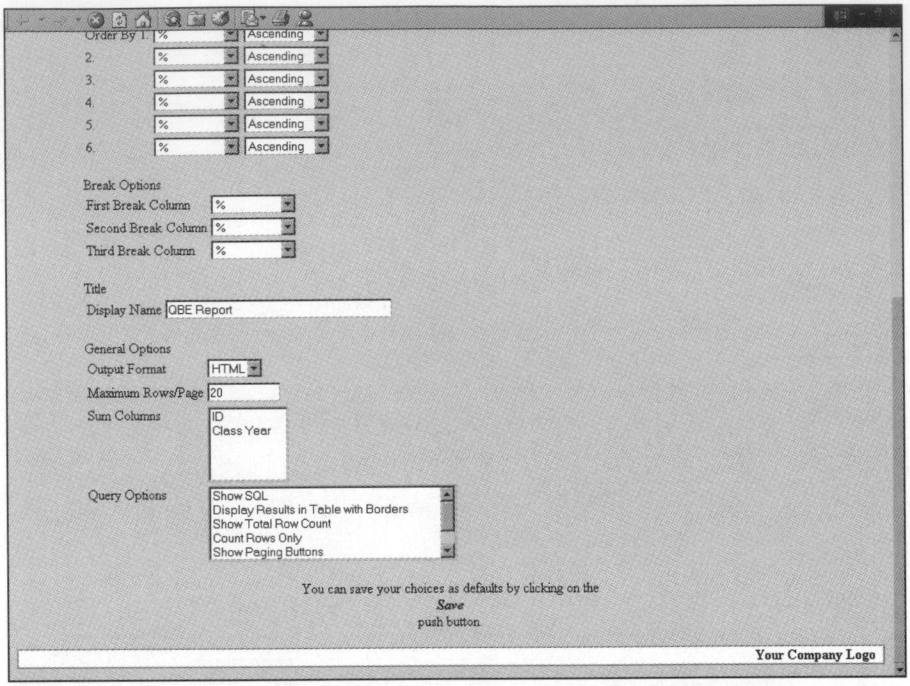

Figure 8-18: The lower part of the Customize page for your QBE report

As you might expect, you can see each of the columns you selected for this report displayed at the top of the page. Each column has a number of options, as described in Table 8-4.

Table 8-4
QBE Column Parameter Options

Column Name	Usage
Show	This check box controls whether the column is shown in the resulting report.
Column	The name displayed in this column is the same as the column heading specified in the QBE Report Wizard. The names displayed in red indicate that the column requires a value, which is important if a user tries to insert data with this form.
	You learned about the potential dangers of inserting data with a QBE Report Customize form when you learned about adding data with the default data management forms.

Continued

Column Name	Usage
Datatype	This column contains a graphic that represents the datatype of the column.
Value	The value placed in this field is used to create a selection criteria. For numeric and date columns, you can use either an exact match, such as "1010" for the ID column, or a relational operator combined with a value, such as "> 1010".
	For a character column, Oracle9*i*AS Portal will search for an occurrence for the entered value in the corresponding column.
	You will see this at work later in this section.
Align	As with the alignment option in the QBE Report Wizard, this align option defaults to Right align for numeric columns and Left align for all other datatypes. The user can also choose to center the data.
Format Mask	The Format Mask is only displayed for numeric fields, and serves the same purpose as the format mask described as part of the QBE Report Wizard.
Case Sensitive	This check box only appears for character columns. If it is checked, the selection criterion is treated as a case sensitive string. If it is not checked, which is the default, the selection criteria is not case sensitive.

There is also a text box that allows you to enter a WHERE clause for the query in this portion of the customization form. If you are familiar with SQL, you no doubt understand that the WHERE clause can be used to implement virtually any type of selection criteria.

The best way to understand how to use the QBE criteria is to try them out:

7. Enter **1010** into the Value field for ID and click on the Query button.

The report returned is short and pictured in Figure 8-19.

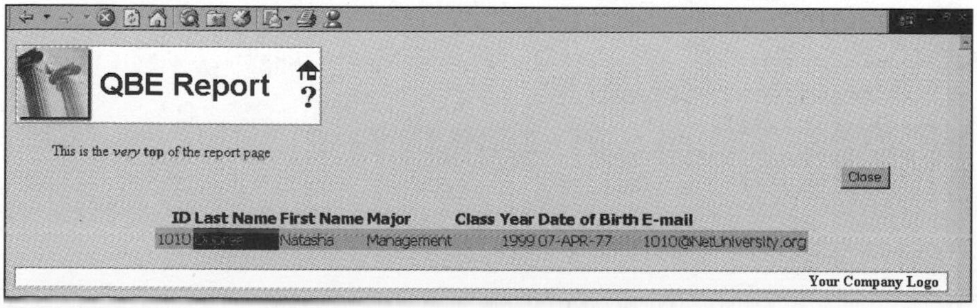

Figure 8-19: Your first QBE report driven by a parameter

You may also notice that there is something else new in this version of the report. There is a Close button at the top of the report, which will take you back to the Customization form.

To get a little larger report, make the selection criterion a little broader.

8. Use the Close button at the top of the report page to return to the Customize page.

9. Enter **> 1010** into the Value field for ID and click on the Query button.

This report, as shown in Figure 8-20, includes much more data.

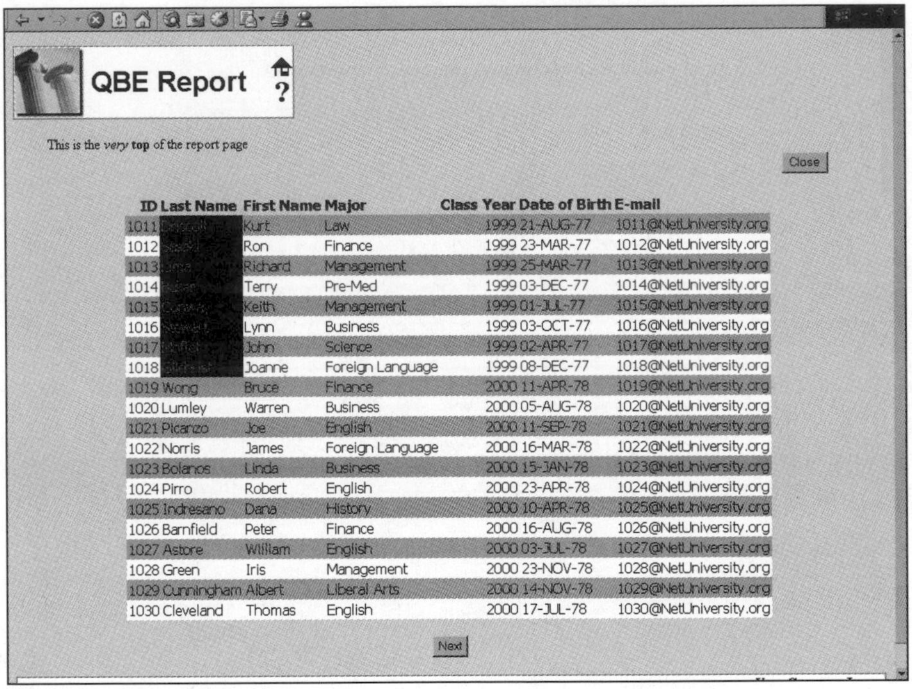

Figure 8-20: Your first QBE report driven by a different parameter

Before moving on to the other areas of the Customize page, you might want to see how to use character criteria.

10. Use the Close button in the report page to return to the Customize page.

You can see that the values for the columns are cleared when you return to the QBE Customization form.

11. Enter the letter **H** into the Value field for the Major column and click on the Query button.

The result is shown in Figure 8-21, but it might not be exactly what you were expecting. The report includes History majors, as you would have thought, but also includes English majors.

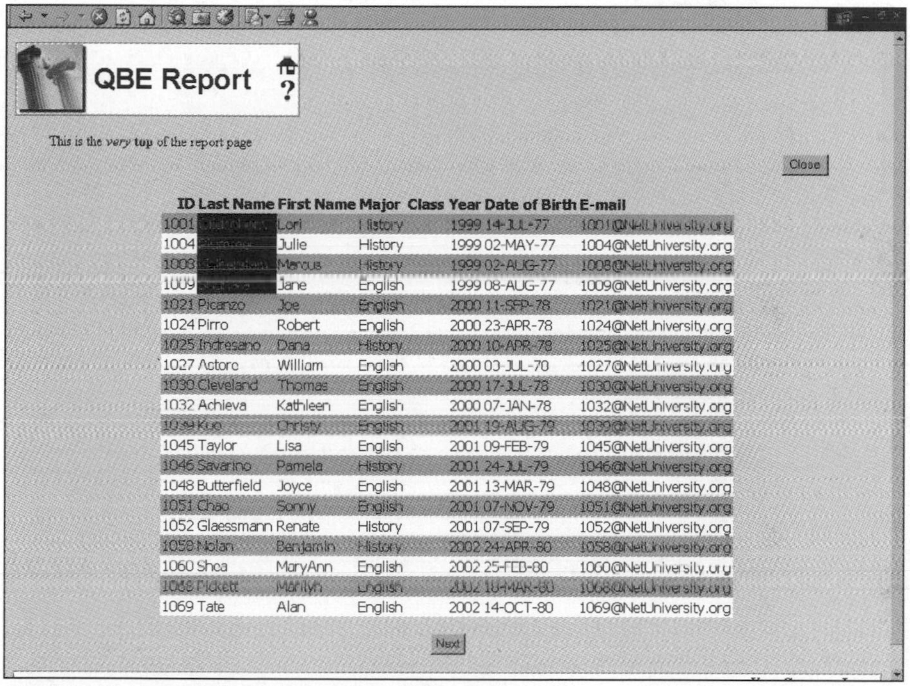

Figure 8-21: The QBE report with all "H" majors

The reason for this goes back to that little Case Sensitive check box. Remember that the search criterion for character strings searches for the string anywhere in the target column. Because you did not check the Case Sensitive check box, the QBE Report found the lower case "h" in "English."

12. Use the Close button to return to the Customize page.

13. Enter **H** into the Value field for the Major column again, and also check the Case Sensitive check box for the Major column and click on the Query button.

The results, as shown in Figure 8-22, now look as expected.

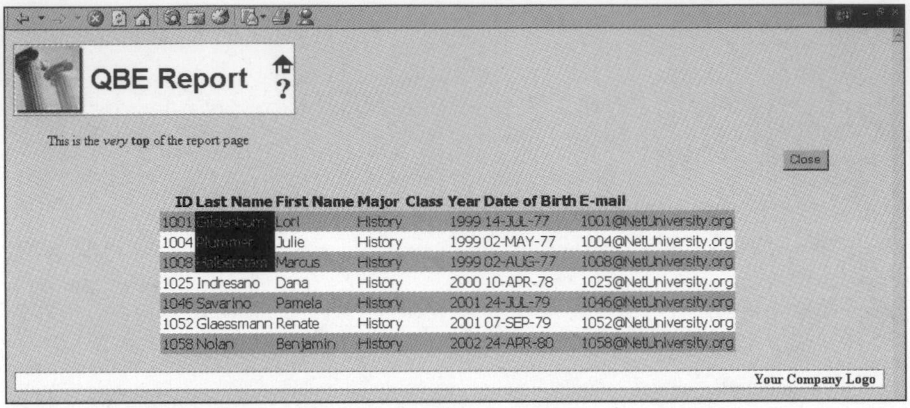

Figure 8-22: The QBE report with only History majors

Before leaving this QBE report, you should explore some of the other formatting options that are available to your users. If you scroll down in the Customization page, you will find that the user can specify up to six columns in the Row Order Options part of the form. The data in the report would look much better if it were a little bit more organized:

14. Use the Close button to return to the Customize page.

15. Select Major from the first Order By combo box.

16. Select Class Year from the second Order By combo box, and select Descending from the second combo box.

You want to have the class years in descending order, so that freshman will be listed before sophomores, and so on.

Also notice that the names in the Order By combo box are the same as the column headings, while in the Order By combo on the Display Options page in the Wizard contained the column names. Oracle9*i*AS Portal assumes, correctly, that users will want to see the more user friendly column names you have assigned, while the rough and tough developer will want to see the actual name of the column.

17. Select Last Name from the third Order By box and click on the Query button.

The results, shown in Figure 8-23, are starting to look better.

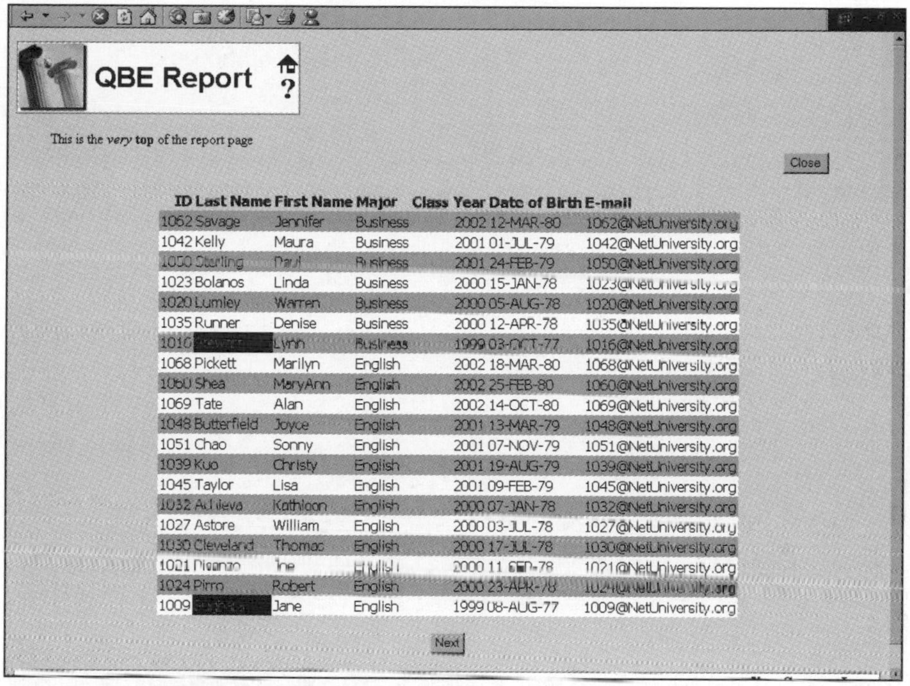

Figure 8-23: The QBE report, nicely sorted

The final step for you to take to improve the appearance of your report is to add some break columns to suppress the display of redundant information.

18. Use the Close button to return to the Customize page.

19. To reset the previous Order By conditions, reselect Major, Class Year, and Last Name as the Order By columns, and set the Class Year to a Descending order.

20. Scroll to Break Options section of the page.

After you go below the Order By columns, you can see that the user has the option to select columns for sums, although, unlike the similar check boxes in the QBE Report Wizard, the list box labeled Sum Columns only includes numeric columns.

You also have the opportunity to change the output format of the report or the maximum number of rows per page. But for this report, you simply want to use the Break Columns combo boxes.

21. Select Major from the first Break Column combo box.

22. Select Class Year from the second Break Column combo box.

23. Click on the Query button.

Now, that is more like it. This set of formatting options presents the data in a fairly pleasing method, as shown in Figure 8-24.

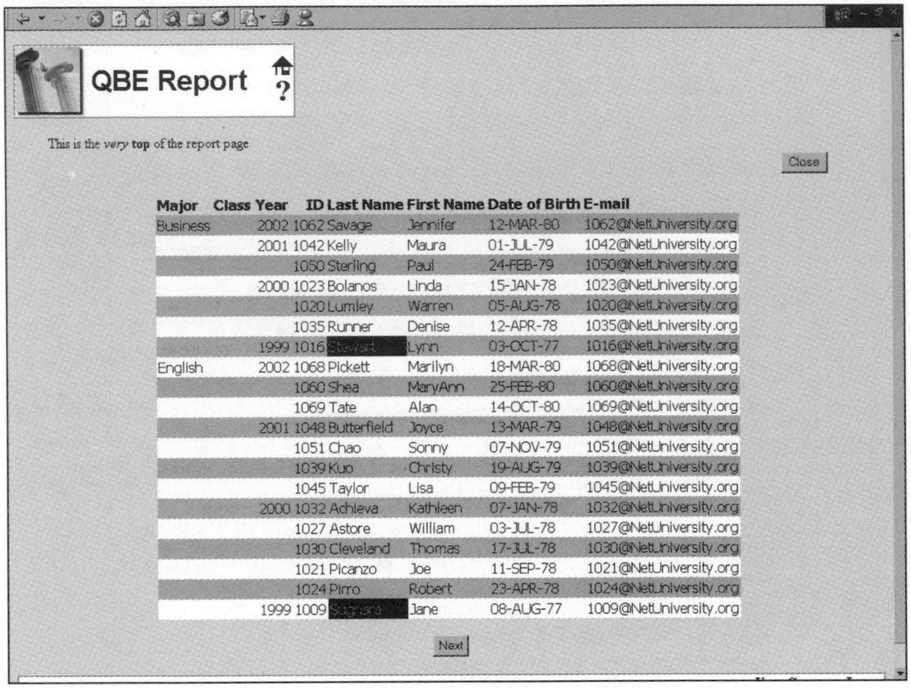

Figure 8-24: The QBE report, sorted and with break columns

If, as a user, you want these formatting options to act as your new defaults, all you have to do is to save them.

24. Use the Back button of your browser to return to the Customize page.

25. Click on the Save button to save the current set of parameters.

26. Enter some characters in some of the Value fields, and set each of the Order By boxes back to their default values of %.

27. Click on the Reset button.

You can see that the action of the Reset button now returns the values of all of the parameters to the values you saved.

Note   Once you save your preferences, those preferences are used for the report, even if you run it without first going to the Customize form.

Cross-Reference   There is one final set of customization options that a user can set on the customization page. These options include the Display Name and four types of General Options: Output Format, Maximum Rows/Page, Sum Columns, which were explained earlier in this chapter, and a list of Query Options, which were discussed in Chapter 5.

You are done running your QBE report. Before leaving this chapter, you should build a couple of simple examples of the two other reports.

Creating a Report with the Query Wizard

The QBE Report you just created is powerful, but it seems to be a little constrained. You can only choose one table, and the customization page presented a welter of choices. For many production reports, you want to have a little more control.

You will develop most of your report components with the other two Report Wizard options. The Query Wizard is a way to specify the data for your report without having to know anything about the SQL language. The Query Wizard walks you through the definition of the columns you use as the basis for your report, and also enables you to indicate selection criteria to be passed to the report.

To build a report with the Query Wizard, you have to come back to the Oracle9*i*AS Portal environment.

1. Close the report window and return to the Oracle9*i*AS Portal development environment.

2. Click on the Navigator link at the top of the page to return to the Navigator.

3. Click on the Report link to the right of the Create New ... title.

4. Click on the Reports From Query Wizard link in the first page of the Report Wizard.

5. Give your new report the Name of **ch8_rpt_2** and the Display Name of **Query Wizard Report**.

6. Click on the Next button.

The first page of the Report Wizard with the Query Wizard is shown in Figure 8-25. This page looks like the Table or View page from the Report Wizard for the QBE report. There is a data entry field, and an icon to call up the Search dialog box.

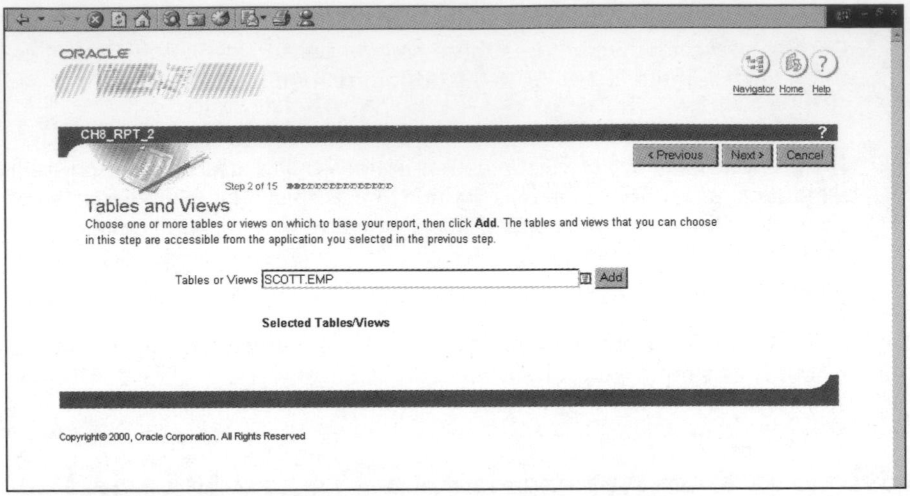

Figure 8-25: The Tables and Views page in the Report Wizard

There is a difference, though. The labels on this page and its entry field refer to plurals — tables, views — which indicates that you can you more than one table or view in the report. Once you select a table or view, it is listed in the area below the data entry field, with a red X to the left of the listing, as shown in Figure 8-26. You can click on the red X to delete the table or view from the list of selected tables or views.

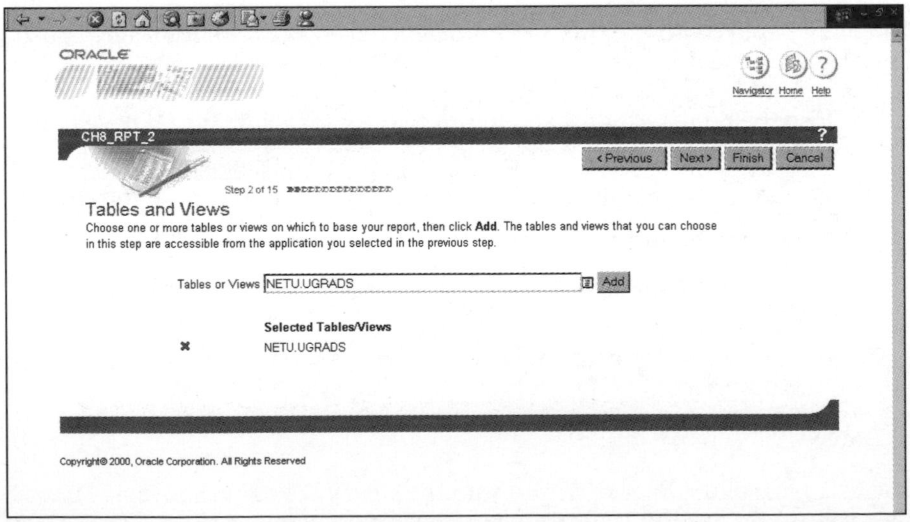

Figure 8-26: Listing selections in the Tables and Views page in the Report Wizard

Note   There are differences between tables and views in the Oracle database—you are not allowed to update data in all views. But since a report only reads data, the two objects are interchangeable for a report component. For the remainder of this chapter and the next, the term *table* refers to both data structures.

You will learn about working with multiple tables in Chapter 9. For now, selecting a single table will be enough.

7. Enter **NETU.UGRADS** as the table.

8. Click on the Add button to add the table to the report.

9. Click the Next button.

The next page of the Report Wizard using the Query Wizard looks familiar. The Table or View Columns page contains two list boxes that allow you to select the columns that will be used in this report. These two list boxes are exactly like the same two list boxes on the same page in the QBE Wizard, so you can just use them to select the columns you want in the report.

10. Move the UGRADS.MAJOR, UGRADS.CLASSYR, UGRADS.LASTNAME, UGRADS.FIRSTNAME, and UGRADS.PHONE columns to the Selected Columns list box. Make sure they are listed in the order named.

11. Click on the Next button.

The next page that comes up as part of the Query Wizard section of the Report Wizard, the Column Conditions page, is shown in Figure 8-27.

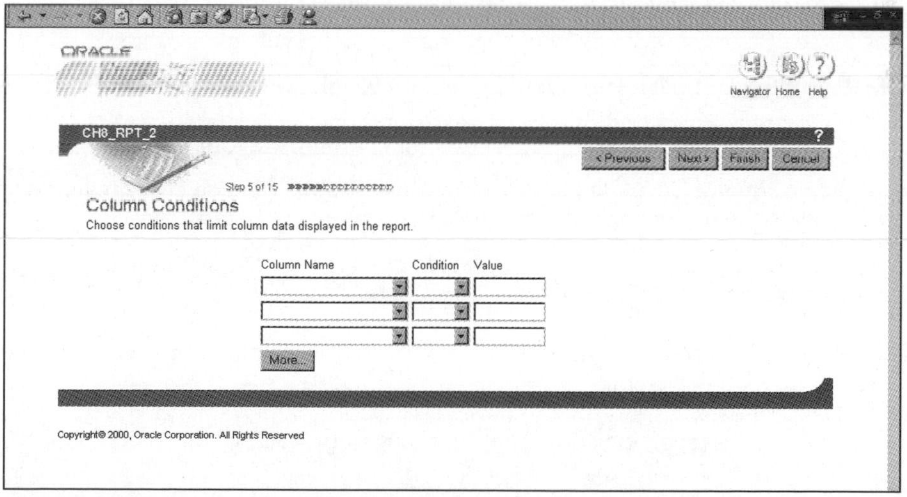

Figure 8-27: The Column Conditions page in the Report Wizard

This page enables you to define conditions used to limit the data shown in the report. As in the QBE Wizard, the conditions you described on this page are transparently applied to the report selection criteria. For this report, you will not need to use them.

12. Click on the Next button on the Column Conditions page.

The next page, the Report Layout page, is shown in Figure 8-28.

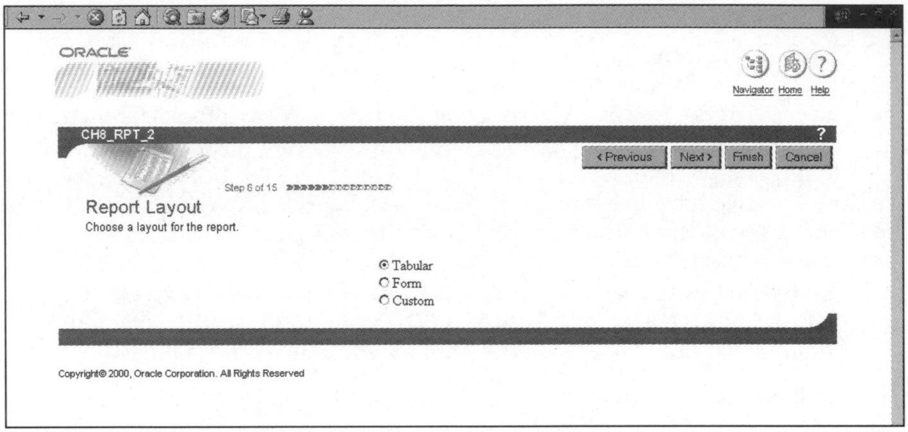

Figure 8-28: The Report Layout page in the Report Wizard

New Feature   The choice of report layouts is new in Oracle9*i*AS Portal.

The Report Layout page gives you three choices for the basic layout of your report:

✦ **Tabular layout:** the traditional rows and columns layout of a report

✦ **Form layout:** a type of layout where the columns of each row are listed vertically, with a blank line in between each row

✦ **Custom layout:** where you can design any type of layout that can be implemented with an HTML table

For this, your first report with the Query Wizard, you should stick with the default, which is the Tabular layout.

Caution   This overall Report Layout cannot be changed by editing your report, which you will learn about later in this chapter.

13. Click on the Next button in the Report Layout page.

The next page in the Report Wizard looks familiar. The Columns Formatting page is the same page that you encountered in the QBE Wizard. Since you are dealing with many of the same columns, you should make the same changes to the column headings that you did in your first report.

14. Change the Column Heading for the CLASSYR column to **Class Year**, the Column Heading for LASTNAME to **Last Name**, and the Column Heading for FIRST NAME to **First Name**.

15. Click on the Next button in the Columns Formatting page.

The next page, the Formatting Conditions page, is also identical to the corresponding page in the QBE Wizard. This time, you can try a slightly different formatting option for seniors.

16. In the first row of the page, select the CLASSYR column from the Column combo box, the = from the Condition combo box, and enter **2001** as the Value.

17. Select the UGRADS.LASTNAME column from the Row/Col combo box and Green from the Color combo box, and click on the check box in the Bold column, which is indicated by a column heading that looks like the letter A in bold.

18. Set the same Column, Conditions, and Value in the second row of the Formatting Conditions page.

19. Select the UGRADS.FIRSTNAME column from the Row/Col combo box and Green from the Color combo box.

The completed Formatting Conditions page should look like Figure 8-29.

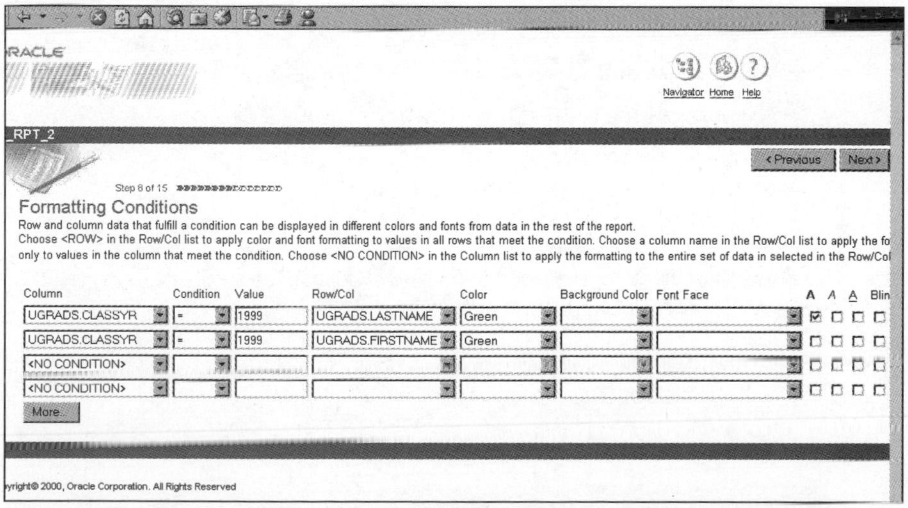

Figure 8-29: The completed Formatting Conditions page in the Report Wizard

20. Click on the Next button in the Formatting Conditions page.

The rest of the pages in the Report Wizard are virtually the same as their corresponding pages in the QBE Wizard, so you can move quickly through them until you get to the appropriate page to assign a template to the report.

21. Click on the Next button on the Display Options page.

22. Click on the Next button on the Customization Form Display Options page.

23. On the Report and Customization Form Text page, select the PUBLIC. TEMPLATE_6 template from the list of templates.

24. Enter **Undergraduate Report** as the Title of the report and **Undergraduate Report Customization** for the Title of the Customization Form.

25. Click on the Finish button to generate your report.

You should always run your report immediately—both for the joy of accomplishment and to make sure the report looks the way you anticipated.

26. Click on the Customize link in the Manage Component page.

You can see that the Customize page for your latest report, as shown in Figure 8-30, is a bit different from the corresponding page for your QBE report.

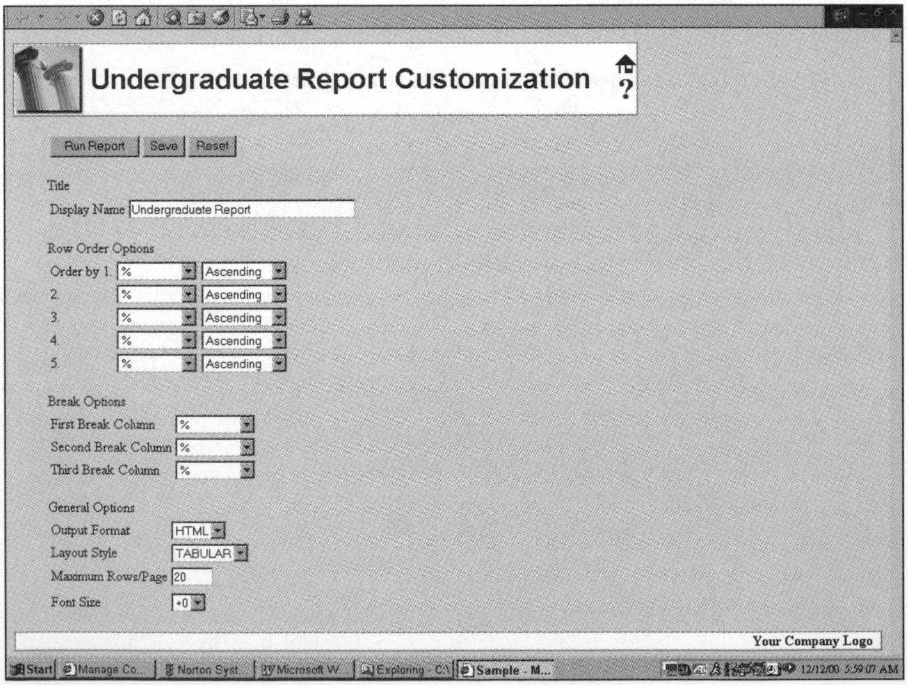

Figure 8-30: The Customization form for your latest report

By default, there are no selection parameters for a standard report. You can specify selection parameters — and you will in the next chapter. For now, you can just add Order By and Break conditions.

27. Set the first Order By combo box to Major.

28. Set the second Order By combo box to Class Year and set the second combo box to Descending.

29. Set the third Order By combo box to Last Name.

30. Set the First Break Column combo box to Major and the Second Break Column combo box to Class Year.

31. Click on the Run Report button.

This report, as shown in Figure 8-31, looks pretty good.

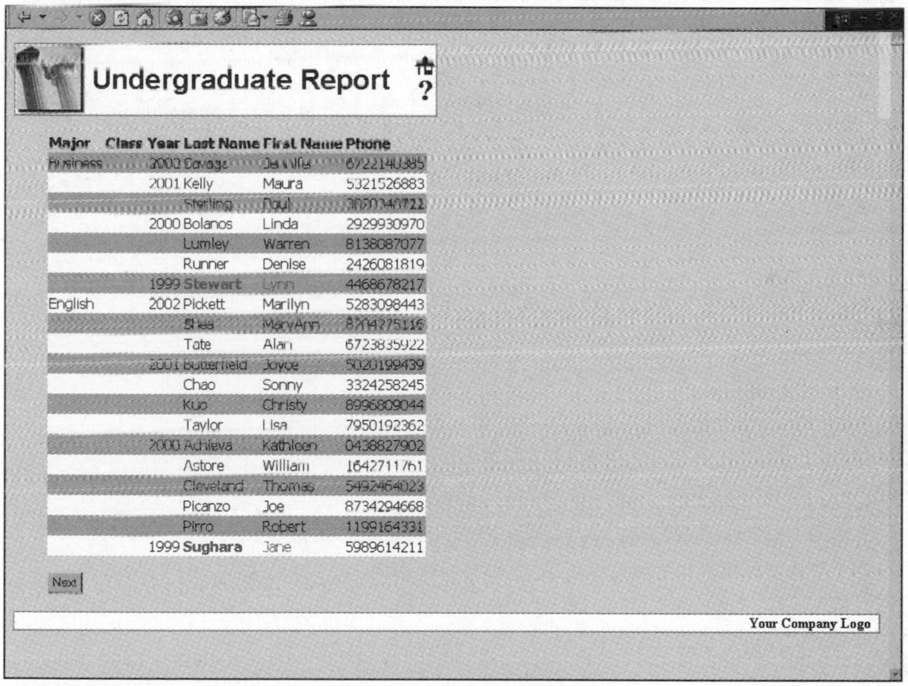

Figure 8-31: The actual report from the Report Wizard

In fact, it looks so good that you would probably like to make the row ordering and break specification permanent without having to force your users to set these parameters and save them. In fact, you probably want to prevent your users from changing these defaults themselves. You can reach both of these goals by editing your report.

Editing Your Report

Although you may find that you can easily define many of your reports properly with a single pass through the Report Wizard, you will invariably discover that you have to make changes to reports that you have already created with the wizard.

To edit a report, you simply choose a different link in the Manage Component page.

1. Close the report browser window and return to the Oracle9*i*AS Portal development environment.

2. Click on the Edit link at the bottom of the Manage Component page.

The Edit environment for a report created with the Query Wizard looks like Figure 8-32.

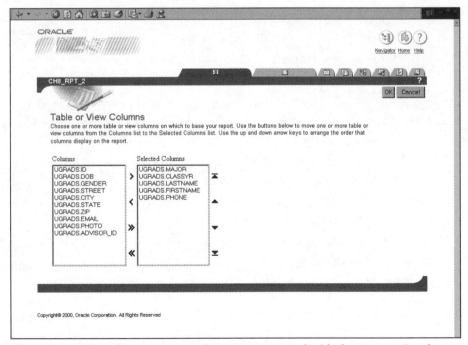

Figure 8-32: The Edit environment for a report created with the Query Wizard.

The Edit environment for reports created with the Query Wizard is a little bit different than the Edit environment for reports created with one of the two other methods. This version of the environment uses the same interface as the Query Wizard to allow you to change the data on which the report is based.

There are eight tabs at the top of the Edit page. These eight tabs correspond to the eight pages of the Report Wizard that you encountered while initially creating your report. In fact, each of the tabbed pages looks exactly like the corresponding page in the Wizard.

You can see the title of each tab as you hold your cursor over the tab. You will want to change two things about this report. First, you will want to assign Order By columns and Break columns.

3. Click on the Display Options tab, which is the fifth tab from the left.

4. Scroll to the bottom of the page and select UGRADS.MAJOR for the First Break Column and UGRADS.CLASSYR for the Second Break Column.

5. Select UGRADS.MAJOR for the first Order By combo box.

6. Select UGRADS.CLASSYR for the second Order By combo box, and select Descending in the second combo box.

7. Select UGRADS.LASTNAME in the third Order By combo box.

You have set up the appropriate ordering and breaking conditions for the report. The second thing you want to do is to prevent a user from modifying these conditions.

8. Click on the Customization Form Display Options tab, which is the sixth tab from the left and the third tab from the right.

9. Under the Formatting Options section in the middle of the page, uncheck the check boxes for Break Columns and Order By.

10. Click on the OK button at the top of the form.

Clicking on the OK button tells Oracle9*i*AS Portal to recreate the PL/SQL packages that generate the report. When you return to the Manage Component page, you can see that you now have a version of the report labeled ARCHIVE as well as one labeled PRODUCTION. The ARCHIVE version of the report contains the values used to generate the previous version of the component.

11. Click on the Customize link at the bottom of the Manage Component page.

As you can see in Figure 8-33, the Order By and Break Columns options are no longer on the customization page.

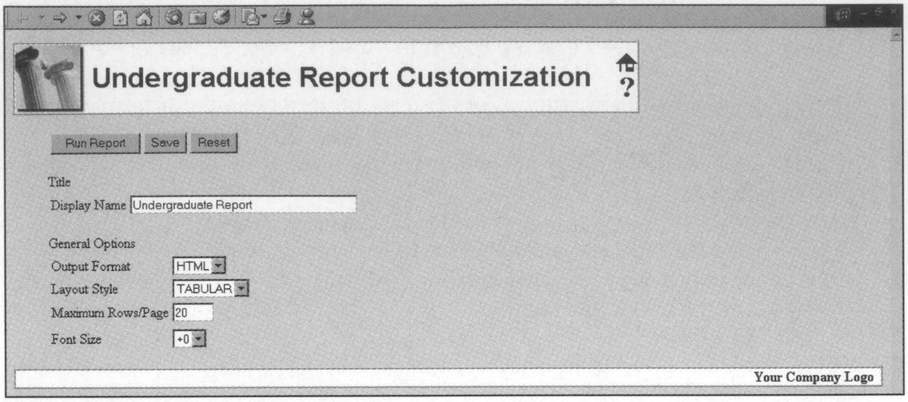

Figure 8-33: The new Parameter page

12. Click on the Run Report button.

The report that is created has the sort order and break groups that you specified when you edited the component.

Summary

You have covered a lot of ground in this chapter. But keep in mind that the common interface used in Oracle9*i*AS Portal means that a lot of the things you learned in this chapter apply to any component that you create.

You have created reports using two of the three Wizards: a QBE report, which, although limited in flexibility, allows you to retrieve as well as insert, update, and delete data, and a standard report created with the Query Wizard.

Through the use of wizards, Oracle9*i*AS Portal makes it easy for you to create reports, yet still gives you the ability to shape your reports in many ways. In fact, you may want to play around with some of the other options in Oracle9*i*AS Portal to get an even better idea of the range of reports you can create.

Oracle9*i*AS Portal gives you wizards to walk you through the creation of reports, but it also allows you to edit the parameters that control the creation of a report.

In the next chapter, you will learn how to create a report using SQL to describe the data used for the report as well as a number of other more advanced techniques for creating reports in Oracle9*i*AS Portal.

✦   ✦   ✦

Advanced Reporting Techniques

◆ ◆ ◆ ◆

In This Chapter

Creating a Report
from a SQL Statement

Using SQL Statements
for Extended
Functionality

Creating Custom
Report Layouts

Adding Parameters to
a Report

Adding Multiple
Tables in Reports

Using Reports as
Portlets

Calling Your Reports
Directly

◆ ◆ ◆ ◆

In the previous chapter, you learned the basics of reporting data with Oracle9*i*AS Portal. The reports you can create with the techniques you already know will answer many of your informational needs.

But there is even more to creating a report with Oracle9*i*AS Portal. This chapter takes you further into the power of Oracle9*i*AS Portal reporting. You will be introduced to using SQL statements to create reports, and learn how to call one of the report components you are creating directly with a URL. You will learn how to limit the data in a standard report through the use of parameters and combine data from multiple tables in your report. You will get a glimpse of how you can use your own SQL statements to go beyond the limitations of the Oracle9*i*AS Portal Report Wizard. And you will find some pointers to other areas in this book that can give you even more information on using Oracle9*i*AS Portal reports.

Creating a Report from a SQL Statement

In the previous chapter, you learn how to create a QBE report or a report using the Query Wizard, which allows you to avoid using SQL statements to specify the data you want in your report. You can also use a SQL statement as the data specification for a report.

A good introduction to using SQL to specify the data in a report would be to recreate the report you made in the last chapter with the Query Wizard.

1. Start by going to the Oracle9*i*AS Portal home page and using the Navigator to go to the NETUCOLLEGE application.

2. Click on the Report link to the right of the Create New ... label.

3. On the Reports Menu page, click on the Reports from SQL Query link.

4. Give the report a Name of **ch9_rpt_1** and a Display Name of **SQL-based Report** and click on the Next button.

The next page in the wizard, as shown in Figure 9-1, contains a large text box where you can enter your SQL statement.

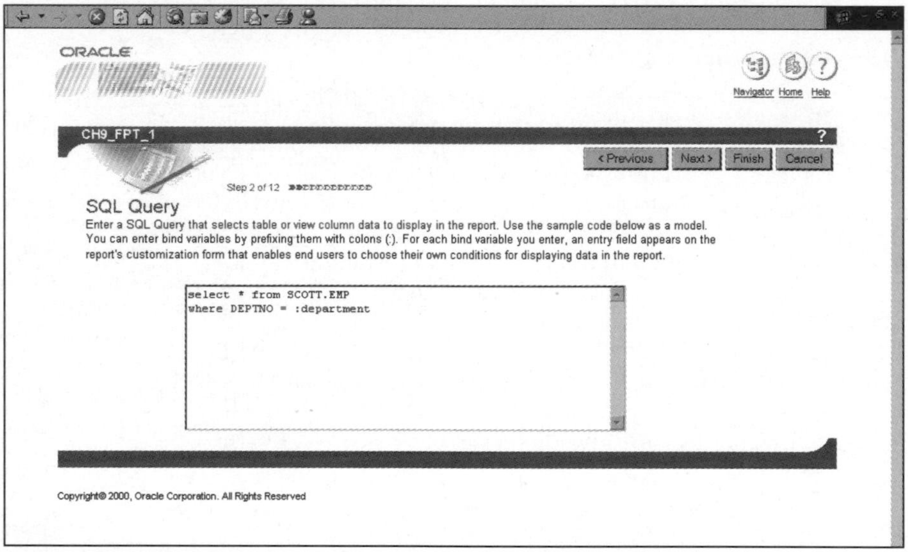

Figure 9-1: The SQL Query page in the Report Wizard for a SQL Query

The text box has a default SQL query, which you will replace with your own SQL statement.

5. Select the entire SQL query in the text box and delete it.

6. Enter the following query into the text window in the SQL Statement page of the Report Builder Wizard:

```
SELECT MAJOR, CLASSYR, LASTNAME, FIRSTNAME, PHONE FROM UGRADS
```

Using Correct SQL

If you typed in the SQL query correctly, you won't have any problems moving to the next page in the Report Wizard. However, if you made an error when entering the SQL, you'll receive an error, as shown in the following figure.

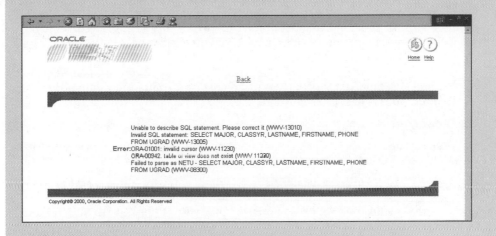

An error in defining a report with SQL

The error message you get is not the most helpful error message in the world. You do get the standard SQL error statement, but these statements sometimes are direct in pointing to the source of the problem. And, when you receive an error like this, it would be great if you could quickly try different changes to correct the statement. For this reason, it's best to use a standard Oracle utility, such as good old SQL*Plus, to create your SQL statements, and then you can simply cut and paste them into the text box on the SQL Query page.

The SQL statement you have just entered gives you the same data for your report that the steps you took in the Query Wizard in Chapter 8 did.

7. Click the Next arrow on the SQL Query page.

The next page that comes up in the Report Wizard looks very familiar. This page prompts you for the basic report layout for your report. In fact, the rest of steps of the wizard are the same as the steps you encountered when using the Query Wizard.

Note The pages in the wizard that allow you to specify your table and column names are not necessary with a SQL-based report, since you have done this in your SQL statement.

To make this pass through the Report Wizard a little different, you should set the layout for this report to the Form Layout option. To do so:

8. Select the Form Layout radio button in the Report Layout page.

9. Click on the Next button.

The next page of the Report Wizard is also the same as its corresponding page in the Query Wizard. You can use most of the options for formatting and display of this report, even though you have used SQL to define the report source.

10. Change the Column Heading Text for the CLASSYR column to **Class Year**, the Column Heading Text for LASTNAME to **Last Name**, and the Column Heading Text for FIRSTNAME to **First Name**.

11. Click on the Next button.

12. Click on the Next button on the Formatting Conditions page, since you don't have to reproduce the conditions from your previous report in this report.

13. On the Display Options page, select the blank entry for Table Row Color(s).

When you see the finished report in Form Layout, you will be able to understand why having alternating colors for the rows of the report would not look very good.

14. Scroll to the bottom of the Display Options form. Set the first Order By to UGRADS.MAJOR, the second Order By combo box to UGRADS.CLASSYR and the second combo box in that row to Descending and the third Order By combo box to UGRADS.LASTNAME.

You don't have to set the Order By columns, since, if you wanted them, you could have already included an ORDER BY clause in your SQL statement. Notice that you do not have the option to specify Break Columns. The lack of Break Columns is due to the Form Layout option you chose, as you will see in a moment.

15. Click on the Next button.

16. Click on the Next button on the Customization Entry Form Display Options page.

17. Select PUBLIC.TEMPLATE_6 from the Template combo box. You can give this report and its parameter form an appropriate title.

18. Click on the Finish button to complete the report.

19. Click on the Run button.

The generated report is shown in Figure 9-2.

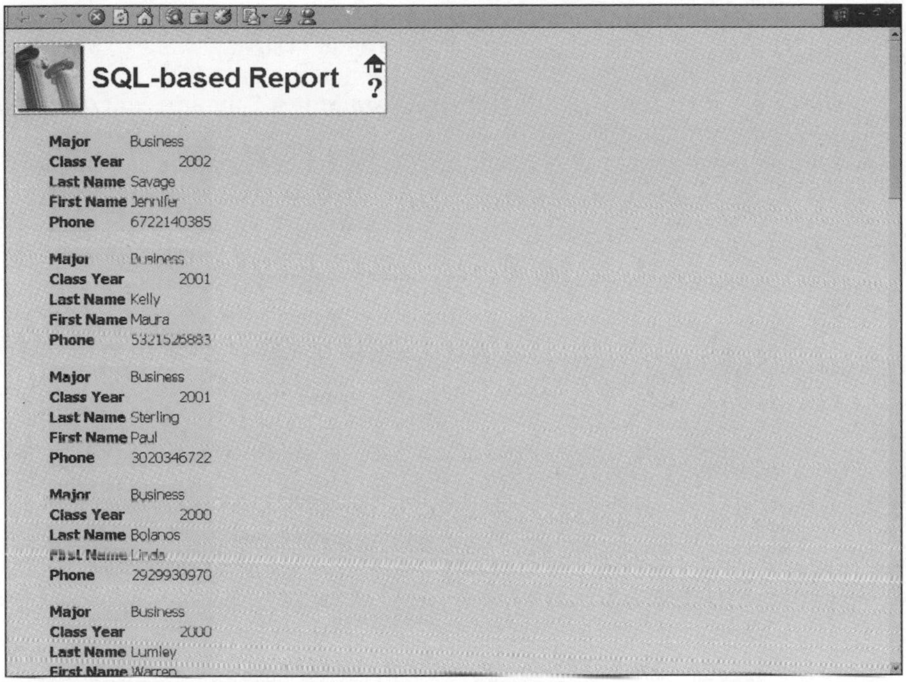

Figure 9-2: The completed report from a SQL statement

The report looks different, but this is only because of the Form Layout. The Form Layout option causes each row of the report to be displayed with each column on a separate line vertically, with a blank line between each row. On seeing the layout, you can understand why it wouldn't make sense to have break columns in this report.

The process of creating this report showed you that there is very little difference between specifying the query with the Query Wizard and using your own SQL. So when do you use a SQL statement and when do you use the Query Wizard? There are three basic reasons for using a SQL statement to define your data source:

✦ **You are already familiar with SQL.** If you are experienced with SQL, you may find the process of entering a SQL query faster and more straightforward than using the Query Wizard.

✦ **You already have reports that are based on existing SQL statements.** You can directly lift SQL statements from existing reports and paste them into the SQL statement text window. Reusing existing SQL statements ensures the use of a correct SQL statement and is faster than trying to re-create the statement with the Query Wizard.

✦ **You want to specify data in a way that goes beyond the capabilities of the Query Wizard.** This can cover a lot of ground. You may want to use a SQL construct that you cannot implement through the easy graphical interface of the Query Wizard, such as a UNION or a subquery. Similarly, you may want to add some parameters to your report that the Query Wizard does not allow, such as using comparison operators (BETWEEN, for example), or implementing a compound condition. You might also want to use some of the power of SQL functions or formatting to shape the data before it goes to the report. As an example, if you wanted to combine the data in the LASTNAME and FIRSTNAME fields into a single value separated by a comma, you could use the following SQL statement:

```
SELECT MAJOR, CLASSYR, (LASTNAME || ', ' || FIRSTNAME) AS
Name, PHONE FROM UGRADS
```

Note   Note that when you create a column in a SQL statement, you *must* give it a name, with the AS keyword, so that Oracle9*i*AS Portal can properly handle the created value.

In the next section, you will use SQL to give you functionality that is not available through the other Query Wizards in Oracle9*i*AS Portal.

Extending Reports with SQL

In this section, you will explore one of the reasons why you use SQL for creating a report — to extend the functionality of your reports.

As you may have noticed, Oracle9*i*AS Portal only gives you the opportunity to use one *aggregate function*. An aggregate function is a function that acts on groups, or aggregations, of rows. In Oracle9*i*AS Portal, the only aggregate function that you can use through the standard Report Builder interface is SUM, which adds a group of numeric values.

There are other aggregate functions that you may want to use in your report. For instance, you might want to know how many students are in each different major at Net University. You can use the aggregate function COUNT to deliver this information.

1. Close the browser window with the report and return to the Oracle9*i*AS Portal development environment.

2. Return to the Navigator page for Oracle9*i*AS Portal by clicking on the Navigator icon at the top of the Manage Component page.

3. Click on the Report link to the right of the Create New ... label.

4. Select the Report from SQL Query link.

5. Give the new report a Name of **ch9_rep_2** and a Display Name of **Aggregate SQL Report**.

6. Click the Next arrow on the Report Name and Schema page.

7. Delete the default SQL query from the text window in the SQL Statement page. Enter the following query exactly as shown:

```
SELECT MAJORS.MAJOR, MAJORS.MAJOR_DESC, COUNT(*) AS Students
FROM UGRADS, MAJORS
WHERE UGRADS.MAJOR = MAJORS.MAJOR
GROUP BY MAJORS.MAJOR, MAJORS.MAJOR_DESC
```

This query is included on the CD-ROM accompanying this book. Look in the ch9 directory of the Examples directory, which is under the portal30 directory, under the name ch9_sql1.txt.

When you are using an aggregate function, such as COUNT, you must include all columns that are not aggregate functions as part of the GROUP BY clause. Because you want to see the name of the major and some descriptive information about the major in the report, you have to have both columns listed in the GROUP BY clause.

8. Click the Next arrow on the SQL Query page.

9. Click on the Next arrow on the Report Layout page to accept the default Tabular layout.

10. Change the Column Heading Text for the MAJOR_DESC column to **Description**. Enter **Number of Students** for the Column Heading Text for the COUNT function, which is shown with the column name of Students.

All the functionality you need is encapsulated in the SQL statement you have just defined as the source of your report. You don't need to specify a row order or a break clause.

11. Click the Next arrow on each page until you reach the Text Options page. Set the Template for the report to PUBLIC.TEMPLATE_6.

You could also simply click on the Finish button and then go into the component and edit the template.

12. Click the Finish button to complete your report.

13. Click on the Run link to run the report.

The report that comes back should look like the one in Figure 9-3.

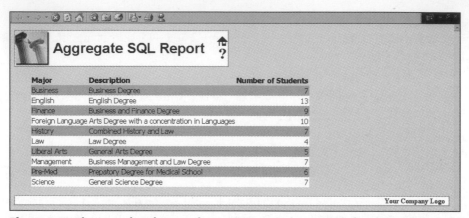

Figure 9-3: The completed report from a SQL statement using the `COUNT` function

You will create one more report using SQL that uses another aggregate function, `AVG`, to calculate the grade point average for each student, sorted by major.

1. Close the browser with the report to return to the Oracle9*i*AS Portal development environment.

2. Return to the Navigator page for Oracle9*i*AS Portal by clicking on the Navigator icon at the top of the Manage Component page.

3. Click on the Report link to the right of the Create New ... label.

4. Select the Report from SQL Query link.

5. Give the new report a Name of **ch9_ rep_3** and a Display Name of **Average Report**.

6. Click the Next button.

7. Delete the default SQL query from the text window in the SQL statement page. Enter the following query exactly as shown:

```
SELECT UGRADS.MAJOR, UGRADS.LASTNAME, UGRADS.FIRSTNAME,
 AVG(GRADES.NUMERIC_GRADE) AS Average
FROM UGRADS, TRANSCRIPT, GRADES
WHERE UGRADS.ID = TRANSCRIPT.ID AND TRANSCRIPT.GRADE =
GRADES.LETTER_GRADE
GROUP BY UGRADS.MAJOR, UGRADS.LASTNAME, UGRADS.FIRSTNAME
```

You can find this query on the CD-ROM accompanying this book in the ch9_sql2.txt file in the ch9 directory under the Examples directory under the portal30 directory.

Note You can see that this report uses multiple tables joined together. Later in this chapter, you will learn how to use multiple tables in reports that you create with the Query Wizard.

You need to use the GRADES table to get the numeric value for the letter grade that is listed in the TRANSCRIPT table. The AVG function automatically takes the sum of the values in the NUMERIC_GRADE column and divides it by the count of rows in the particular break group.

Because you are using an aggregate function, you have to specify all the nonaggregate function columns in the GROUP BY clause.

8. Click the Next button on the SQL Query page.

9. Click on the Next button on the Report Layout page.

10. On the Columns Formatting page, change the Column Heading Text for the LASTNAME, FIRSTNAME, and AVG columns to **Last Name**, **First Name**, and **Grade Point Average** respectively.

11. Enter a format mask of **9.99** for the AVG column.

12. Click the Next button on the Columns Formatting page.

13. Click on the Next button on the Formatting Conditions page.

14. Select the MAJOR choice for the first combo box in the Break Options section on the Display Options page.

You have to specify a break on the MAJOR column because there is more than one student per major and you would like to suppress the display of the repetitive value of the MAJOR column.

15. Click the Next buttons on each page until you reach the Text Options page. Set the Template for the report to PUBLIC.TEMPLATE_6.

16. Click the Finish button to generate your report.

17. On the Manage Component page, click the Run link.

The report you get back from Oracle9iAS Portal should look like Figure 9-4.

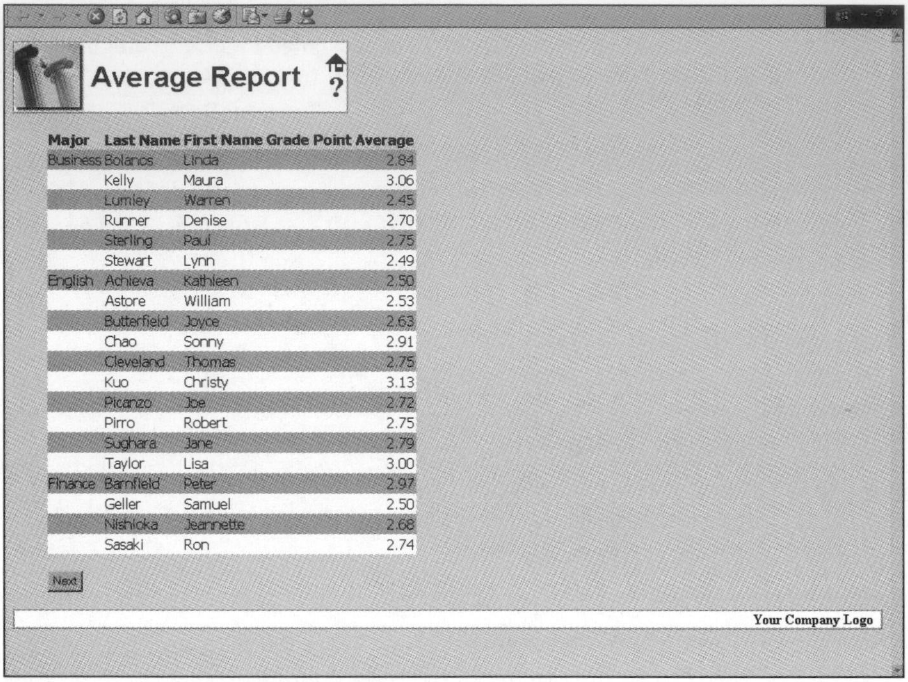
Average Report

Major	Last Name	First Name	Grade Point Average
Business	Bolanos	Linda	2.84
	Kelly	Maura	3.06
	Lumley	Warren	2.45
	Runner	Denise	2.70
	Sterling	Paul	2.75
	Stewart	Lynn	2.49
English	Achieva	Kathleen	2.50
	Astore	William	2.53
	Butterfield	Joyce	2.63
	Chao	Sonny	2.91
	Cleveland	Thomas	2.75
	Kuo	Christy	3.13
	Picanzo	Joe	2.72
	Pirro	Robert	2.75
	Sughara	Jane	2.79
	Taylor	Lisa	3.00
Finance	Barnfield	Peter	2.97
	Geller	Samuel	2.50
	Nishioka	Jeannette	2.68
	Sasaki	Ron	2.74

Next

Your Company Logo

Figure 9-4: Using the AVG function in a report

Although the Query Wizard used with Report Builder imposes some limits on the data that can be retrieved, you can use standard SQL to get around many of these limitations.

In Chapter 20, you will learn techniques you could use to link these individual reports together to give a more complete picture of the data. You could call the report that provides a count of the students in each major and create a link from the field containing the major to the report that lists the students for each major and their grade point average. You could link from the student field in this report to a detailed listing of each student's classes and their grades in the classes, which would be a modified version of the report you created at the start of this section.

In the next section, you will get a brief taste of using the Custom Layout for a report.

Using the Custom Layout for Reports

The third layout option for reports is the Custom Layout. As its name implies, the Custom Layout option gives you the ability to specify virtually any layout for your report. You are only limited by the capabilities of an HTML table.

For generic HTML, the table is one of the most powerful formatting options. You can define a table with different rows and columns indicating different display areas. Oracle9iAS Portal uses the HTML table to provide the overall formatting characteristics for a report — indeed, for most Oracle9iAS Portal components.

When you choose the Custom Layout option, you are allowed to go in and create your own specifications for the underlying HTML table. Since it is very easy to make mistakes while entering HTML code, you will not have to walk through the process of creating this report. Instead, you will see the default code and results for a Custom Layout and the completely modified code and layout for the same report.

This report is based on this SQL statement:

```
SELECT LASTNAME || ', ' || FIRSTNAME AS NAME,
PHONE, EMAIL, MAJOR,
CLASSYR, DOB FROM NETU.UGRADS
```

You can see that the SQL statement includes some formatting SQL functions to create a combined Name column.

When you select the Custom Layout option, you will come to the Report Layout Editor page. There are three text boxes on the page, one each for the headings, body, and footer for the report page. The default for the body of the report is shown here:

```
<TR BGCOLOR=#DEFAULT#><TD ALIGN="LEFT"><#NAME.FIELD#></TD>
<TD ALIGN="LEFT"><#PHONE.FIELD#></TD>
<TD ALIGN="LEFT"><#EMAIL.FIELD#></TD>
<TD ALIGN="LEFT"><#MAJOR.FIELD#></TD>
<TD ALIGN="LEFT"><#CLASSYR.FIELD#></TD>
<TD ALIGN="LEFT"><#DOB.FIELD#></TD>
</TR>
```

The report that this code generates is shown in Figure 9-5.

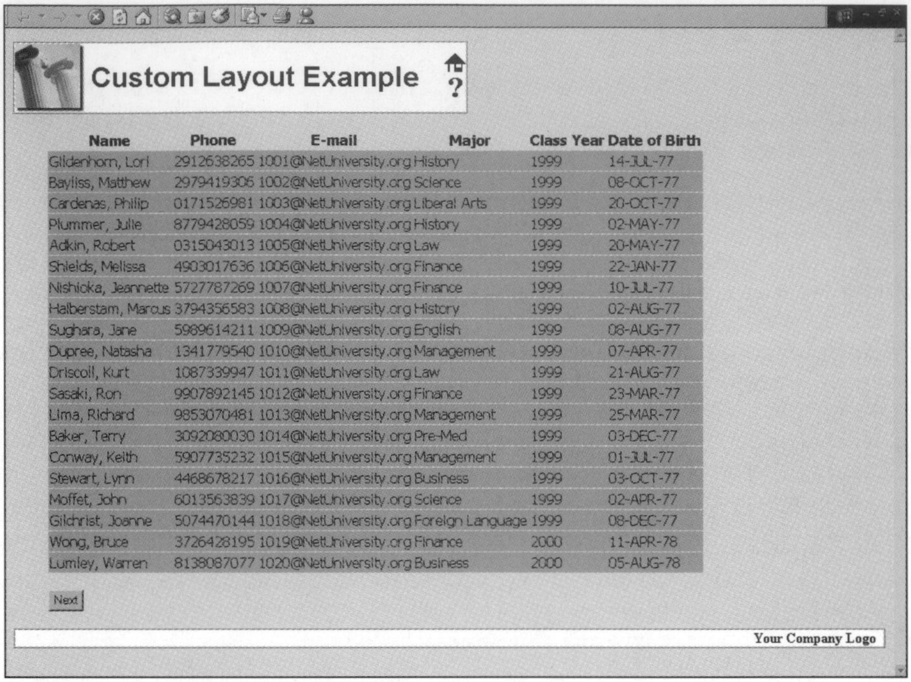

Name	Phone	E-mail	Major	Class Year	Date of Birth
Gildenhorn, Lori	2912638265	1001@NetUniversity.org	History	1999	14-JUL-77
Bayliss, Matthew	2979419306	1002@NetUniversity.org	Science	1999	08-OCT-77
Cardenas, Philip	0171526981	1003@NetUniversity.org	Liberal Arts	1999	20-OCT-77
Plummer, Julie	8779428059	1004@NetUniversity.org	History	1999	02-MAY-77
Adkin, Robert	0315043013	1005@NetUniversity.org	Law	1999	20-MAY-77
Shields, Melissa	4903017636	1006@NetUniversity.org	Finance	1999	22-JAN-77
Nishioka, Jeannette	5727787269	1007@NetUniversity.org	Finance	1999	10-JUL-77
Halberstam, Marcus	3794356583	1008@NetUniversity.org	History	1999	02-AUG-77
Sughara, Jane	5989614211	1009@NetUniversity.org	English	1999	08-AUG-77
Dupree, Natasha	1341779540	1010@NetUniversity.org	Management	1999	07-APR-77
Driscoll, Kurt	1087339947	1011@NetUniversity.org	Law	1999	21-AUG-77
Sasaki, Ron	9907892145	1012@NetUniversity.org	Finance	1999	23-MAR-77
Lima, Richard	9853070481	1013@NetUniversity.org	Management	1999	25-MAR-77
Baker, Terry	3092080030	1014@NetUniversity.org	Pre-Med	1999	03-DEC-77
Conway, Keith	5907735232	1015@NetUniversity.org	Management	1999	01-JUL-77
Stewart, Lynn	4468678217	1016@NetUniversity.org	Business	1999	03-OCT-77
Moffet, John	6013563839	1017@NetUniversity.org	Science	1999	02-APR-77
Gilchrist, Joanne	5074470144	1018@NetUniversity.org	Foreign Language	1999	08-DEC-77
Wong, Bruce	3726428195	1019@NetUniversity.org	Finance	2000	11-APR-78
Lumley, Warren	8138087077	1020@NetUniversity.org	Business	2000	05-AUG-78

Figure 9-5: A report with a default Custom Layout

If you are familiar with HTML, you will see that some parts of the code shown above look familiar. There are tags to denote table rows (<TR> and </TR>) and columns with the rows (<TD> and </TD>).

Note If you are not familiar with HTML, this section will include some potentially confusing code.

But there are also some unfamiliar parts of this code. It appears that each data column specified for the report is listed in a tag that begins and ends with the # symbol. This tag is a placeholder for the dynamically generated code that Oracle9*i*AS Portal will create, based on the data returned from the SQL query.

You must leave these tags as is, if you want to include the data in the report, but you can change the rest of the tags to modify the appearance of the report. In the following example each data row has been split over three lines in the report by adding more table row tags. Each line in the report is five columns wide, so that you can format a triangle shaped report, with a single column in the first line, two values in the next line, and three values in the third line, and the first line of the report spans all five columns. A few of the alignment specifications were changed to make the report a little more attractive. Finally, some break tags (<BR>) were inserted to add spacing to the report.

The completed code for the new layout is shown here, with all the new code highlighted in bold:

```
<TR> <TD ALIGN="CENTER" COLSPAN=5>
<BR><BR><#NAME.FIELD#></TD></TR>
<TR>
<TD></TD>
<TD ALIGN="LEFT"><#PHONE.FIELD#></TD>
<TD></TD>
<TD ALIGN="RIGHT"><#EMAIL.FIELD#></TD>
<TD></TD>
</TR>
<TR>
<TD ALIGN="LEFT"><#MAJOR.FIELD#></TD>
<TD></TD>
<TD ALIGN="CENTER"><#CLASSYR.FIELD#></TD>
<TD></TD>
<TD ALIGN="LEFT"><#DOB.FIELD#></TD>
</TR>
```

Note

Note that the assignment of the BGCOLOR has been removed from the <TR> tag, and the row color option is set to blank, to display the report more attractively.

This code results in the report shown in Figure 9-6.

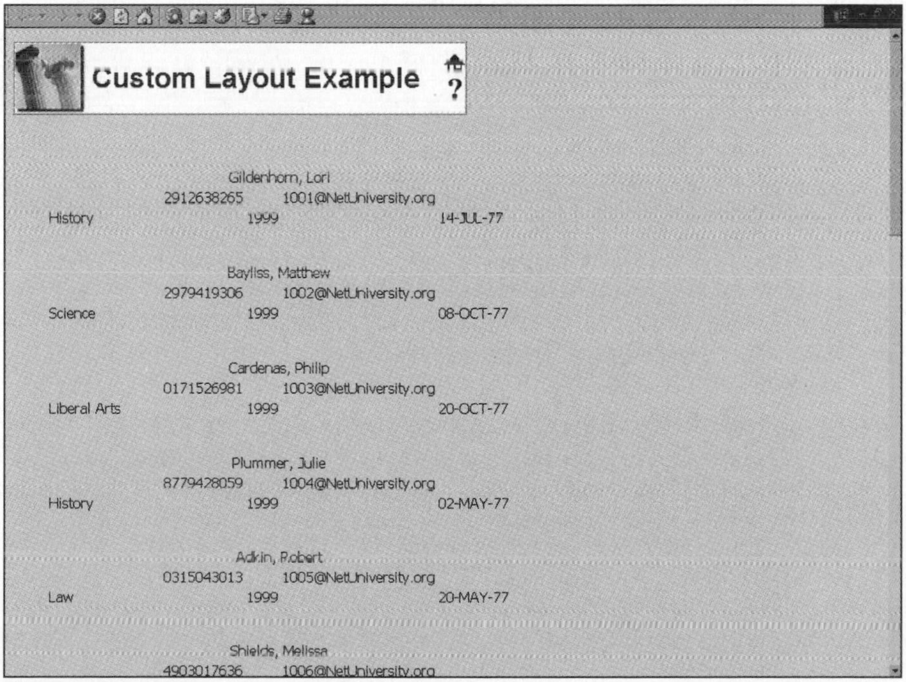

Figure 9-6: Report using custom formatting

In order to create this report, the header code was deleted.

Although you may or may not find the report shown in Figure 9-6 aesthetically pleasing, the idea is that it shows you the flexibility offered by the Custom Layout option.

On the CD-ROM   The completed report is included on the CD in the Chapter 9 directory as an export file called custom_rep.sql. Appendix A describes how to import the examples included in the CD-ROM.

Adding Parameters to Your Report

You have already seen the use of parameters in the QBE report that you created in Chapter 8. You have also probably already noticed that Oracle9*i*AS Portal's Report Wizard gives you the ability to add parameters to your reports. These parameters are added to the customization form that is automatically generated for you by Oracle9*i*AS Portal as part of the report package.

One of the chief uses for parameters is to enable your users to specify selection criteria at run time for a report. You can create a single report component that can be used for a wide variety of information, depending on the values of the criteria.

For instance, the report you created in the last chapter displayed data in a meaningful way, but perhaps it displayed too much data. Maybe a typical user of this report is not interested in all the students in all the majors, but only in all the students in one particular major.

1. Close the browser window with the report to return to the Oracle9*i*AS Portal development environment.

2. Return to the Home Page by clicking on the Home icon in the banner.

3. Select the report you created in the last chapter, ch8_rep_2, from the Recent Objects portlet.

Note   If this report is not visible as one of the recent objects, you can use the Navigator, as explained in Chapter 4, to locate it.

4. Click the Edit link at the bottom of the Manage Component page.

5. Click the Customization Entry Form Display Options tab, which is the sixth tab from the left or the third tab from the right.

You see a page that looks like Figure 9-7.

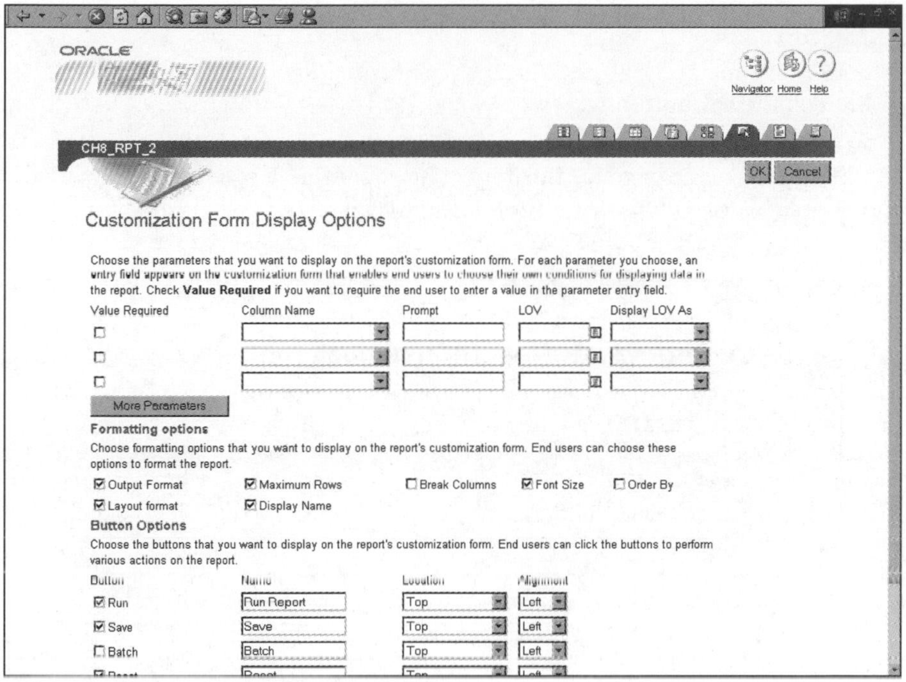

Figure 9-7: Adding a parameter to a report

Because you are in the Oracle9*i*AS Portal development environment, you are presented with a list of table and column names, as Oracle9*i*AS Portal assumes you understand the underlying data structures for the report. You do not have to specify anything else for the parameter, because the user is given a choice of 11 selection conditions on the parameter page at run time.

> **6.** Go to the Column Name combo box on the first line of the Customize page and select the UGRADS.MAJOR column.
>
> **7.** You should change the prompt for the condition. Enter **Major:** in the Prompt field for the new condition.

The data entry fields for LOV and Display LOV are used for List-of-Values objects, which are covered in Chapter 16. You can leave them blank for now.

You also should not select the check box labeled Value Required on the far left side of the column conditions line. When you check this choice, you force the user to select a condition before running the report. This option is useful if you are using a condition to prevent the return of large amounts of data in a report. Because you are just trying to give the user some options with this parameter, you should leave it unchecked.

8. Click the OK button.

9. When you return to the Manage Component page, click the Customize link. The parameter page for this report now features a prompt and data field for the MAJORS column, as shown in Figure 9-8.

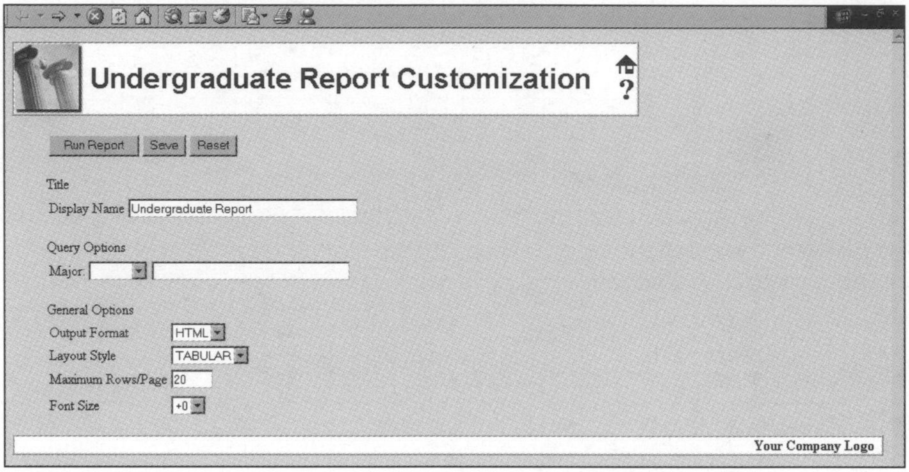

Figure 9-8: The Customization Entry Form, with the MAJOR parameter

10. Click the Run Report button without entering a value in the Major field.

If a user does not enter a value for a selection criterion, the Oracle9*i*AS Portal report package understands it to mean that the selection criterion should not be applied to the report.

11. Return to the customization page by clicking the Back button in your browser.

12. Select the = conditionin the combo box in the first Query Options line, enter **Finance** into the text field following it, and click the Run Report button.

The report returned this time only shows you the information for Finance majors, as shown in Figure 9-9.

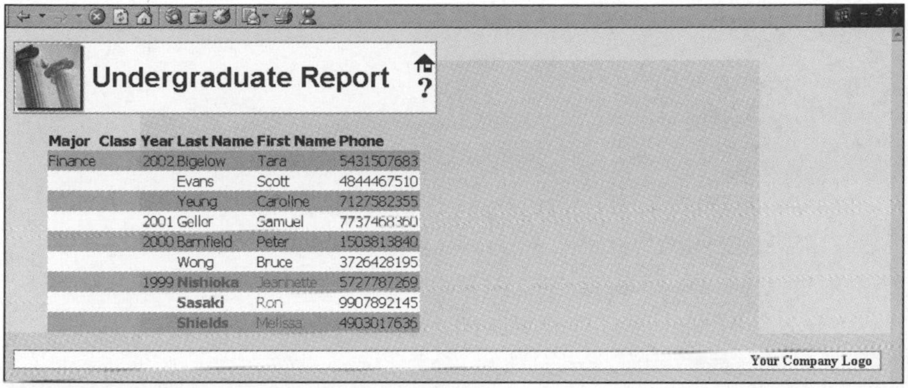

Figure 9-9: The report for Finance majors

When you use this parameter, you can see that the condition combo box gives a user more choices than the combo box for the QBE form. However, these parameters do not allow you to specify that the query is not case-sensitive, and a user will have to know to add the appropriate wildcards and use the *like condition* to search a column for a specified value.

13. Return to the customization page by clicking the Back button in your browser.

14. Enter **F%** into the Major field and click the Run Report button.

You can see that the report does not contain any data. If you are familiar with the concept of wildcards, you may be confused. After all, doesn't the % wildcard mean that entering a value such as F% should at least return the Finance majors? However, remember that you selected = as the relational operator for this condition.

15. Return to the customization page by clicking the Back button in your browser.

16. Change the value in the combo box for the first Query Options line to "like" and click the Run Report button.

This time, you can see that the wildcard worked the way you wanted, as shown in Figure 9-10.

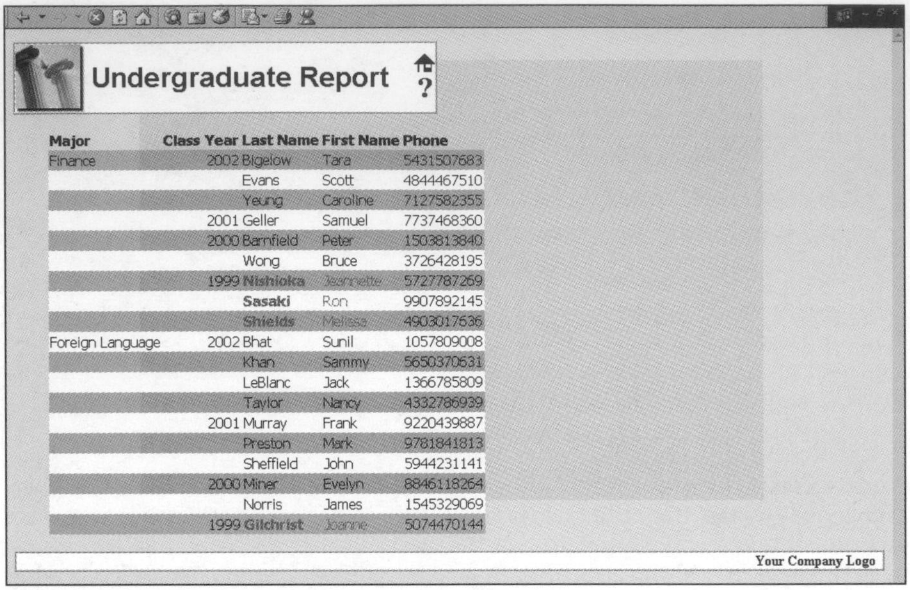

Major	Class Year	Last Name	First Name	Phone
Finance	2002	Bigelow	Tara	5431507683
		Evans	Scott	4844467510
		Yeung	Caroline	7127582355
	2001	Geller	Samuel	7737468360
	2000	Barnfield	Peter	1503813840
		Wong	Bruce	3726428195
	1999	**Nishioka**	Jeannette	5727787269
		Sasaki	Ron	9907892145
		Shields	Melissa	4903017636
Foreign Language	2002	Bhat	Sunil	1057809008
		Khan	Sammy	5650370631
		LeBlanc	Jack	1366785809
		Taylor	Nancy	4332786939
	2001	Murray	Frank	9220439887
		Preston	Mark	9781841813
		Sheffield	John	5944231141
	2000	Miner	Evelyn	8846118264
		Norris	James	1545329069
	1999	**Gilchrist**	Joanne	5074470144

Figure 9-10: The report for all majors that begin with F.

You can enable your users to select criteria, but you cannot guarantee that the selection criteria makes sense — at least not with the default parameter page. You can use JavaScript to validate entries on a form, and you can create your own form with validation and link the form to a report. But the automatic generation of a parameter form certainly gives you a great deal of flexibility with very little work, and you can always include instructions on using the parameters in the header, footer, or help text for the form.

The next step toward enlarging the scope of your Oracle9*i*AS Portal reports is to learn how to create reports that use data from more than one table.

Using Multiple Tables in a Report

One of the great benefits of a relational database like Oracle is its ability to normalize your data. The process of normalization lets you divide your data into multiple tables and simply join the smaller tables together when you need information that is not included in any one table.

The database that is being used for the application in this book has gone through a process of normalization. Some of the tables in the database act as reference tables to a main table. These tables perform functions like supplying more descriptive names for codes used within the database. Some of the tables in the database have a master-detail relationship — a row in one table shares a common attribute with one or more rows in another table. In this section, you will create multitable reports for both of these types of relationships.

You have already seen the use of multiple tables in a SQL statement. In this section, you will learn how to specify multiple tables using the Query Wizard.

Multiple tables for reference information

The first report you create with multiple tables will use a second table that acts as a reference to a code in the UGRADS table. You have to create a new report from scratch because Oracle9iAS Portal does not enable you to add another table to an existing report.

1. Return to Oracle9iAS Portal development by closing the browser window of the previous report.
2. Click on the Navigator icon in the banner.
3. Click on the Report link to the right of the Create New ... label.
4. Click on the Reports from Query Wizard link.
5. Enter **ch9_rep_4** as the Name and **Multiple Table Report** as the Display Name.
6. Click the Next button on the Report Name and Application page.
7. Enter **NETU.UGRADS** in the Tables or Views entry box. Click on the Add button.
8. Enter **NETU.CLASSES** in the Tables or Views entry box and click on the Add button.

The Tables and Views page will look like Figure 9-11.

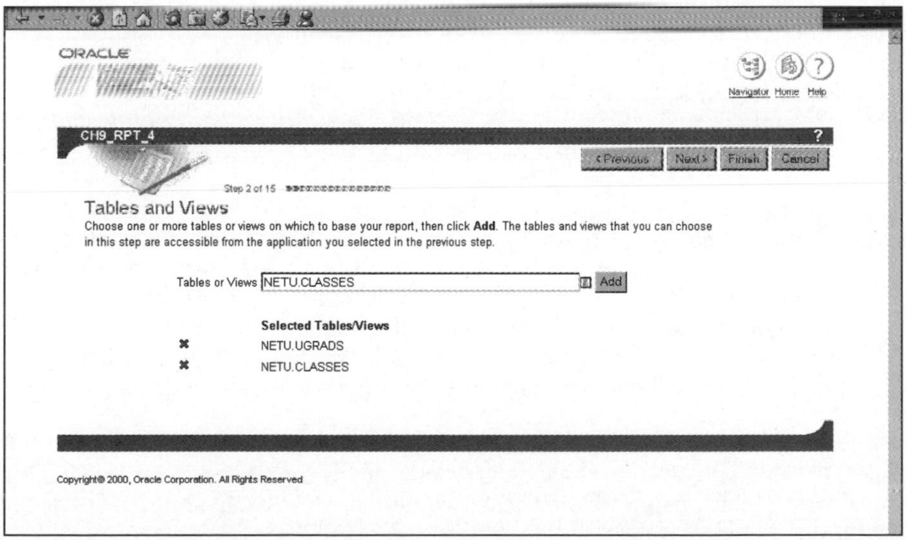

Figure 9-11: The Tables and Views page with multiple tables selected

You are joining the CLASSES table into this report so that you can view the easier-to-read CLASSCODE column in the report.

9. Click the Next button on the Tables and Views page.

Because you have selected two tables for this report, the next page in the Query Wizard looks like Figure 9-12.

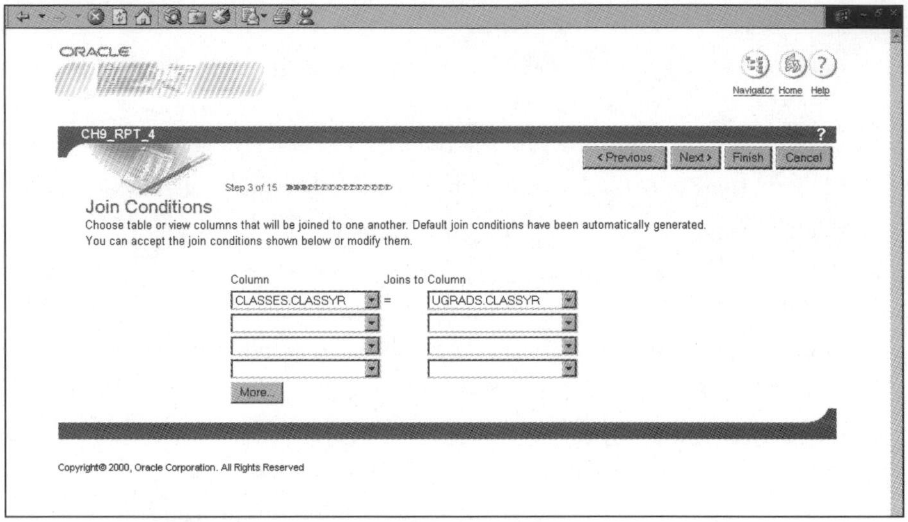

Figure 9-12: The Join Conditions page in the Query Wizard

The Join Conditions page has a simple purpose: It enables you to indicate the columns in the two different tables that act as a link between rows in the two tables. Oracle9*i*AS Portal looks through the two tables to see if there is a relationship between the two tables, such as a *primary key-foreign key relationship*, or two columns that have the same name in both tables.

Note   A primary key-foreign key relationship is a common way to associate two tables in a relational database. The value for the foreign key in one table refers to the value for the primary key in another table. This type of relationship is also used to enforce data integrity in the database. If anyone tries to enter a value into the CLASSYR column in the UGRADS table that does not already exist in one of the rows of the CLASSES table's CLASSYR column, the change is rejected by the database. You will learn more about enforcing data integrity in Chapters 14 and 17.

You can see that Oracle9*i*AS Portal has discovered that the CLASSYR column in the UGRADS table is related to the CLASSYR column in the CLASSES table. This is the appropriate relationship to join these two tables, so you can simply accept the join condition.

10. Click the Next arrow on the Join Conditions page. You are basically trying to reproduce the report that you created in the previous chapter, so you should add similar selection parameters on the next page of the Report Builder Wizard.

Because the whole purpose of this report is to display the easier-to-understand CLASSCODE column, you should use that as your parameter, rather than the CLASSYR column.

11. Select the UGRADS.MAJOR, CLASSES.CLASSCODE, CLASSES.CLASSYR, UGRADS.LASTNAME, UGRADS.FIRSTNAME, and UGRADS.PHONE columns in that order.

12. Click the Next button in the Table or View Columns page.

13. Click the Next button on the Column Conditions page.

14. Accept the Tabular Format for this report by clicking on the Next button on the Report Layout page.

15. Change the Column Heading Text for the CLASSCODE column to **Class**. Change the Column Heading Text for the CLASSYR column to **Class Year**. Change the Column Heading Text for the LASTNAME column to **Last Name**. Change the Column Heading Text for the FIRSTNAME column to **First Name**.

16. Change the Align for CLASSYR by selecting Center.

17. Click the Next button on the Columns Formatting page.

18. Click on the Next button on the Formatting Conditions page.

19. Select the UGRADS.MAJOR, CLASSES.CLASSCODE, and CLASSES.CLASSYR entries in the Break Options combo boxes.

20. Select the UGRADS.MAJOR column in the first line of the Row Order Options area of the Display Options page. Select the CLASSES.CLASSYR column and the Sort Order of Descending in the second combo box of the second row.

21. Click the Next button on the Display Options page.

Why did you select the CLASSYR column and not the CLASSCODE column for sorting? You have to use the CLASSYR for sorting the report because you want to show the class of 2001, then the class of 2002, and so on. If you were to select the CLASSCODE column for sorting, the entries would be sorted in alphabetical order, such as Freshman, Junior, Senior, and Sophomore.

Notice that the columns you selected for breaks are different from the columns you selected for sorting. There is nothing wrong with this. A break column controls how the Oracle9iAS Portal report suppresses redundant data and creates totals, whereas the order by columns controls the order that the rows of data in the report are sorted. In this case, you didn't have to explicitly sort on the CLASSYR column, because the CLASSYR and CLASSCODE columns are always linked. You want to break on the three columns named in the Break Options section because you want to suppress the display of the redundant CLASSCODE and CLASSYR values.

In order to give your users the ability to limit the rows retrieved, you should add some parameters:

22. Select UGRADS.MAJOR in the first line of the Customization Entry Form Display Options page. Set the prompt to "Major:". Check the Value Required check box.

23. Select the CLASSES.CLASSCODE for the second line of the page. Set the prompt to "Class:".

You can accept the default button choices for the report and move on to define some header and footer text for your report.

24. Click the Next button on the Customization Entry Form Display Options page.

25. Select PUBLIC_TEMPLATE_6 as the template for the new report.

26. Give the report and the parameter entry page a suitable title.

27. Enter **The <b>Major</b> parameter is required. The <b>Class</b> parameter accepts the name of the class, such as <I>Freshman</I>, <I>Sophomore</I>, <I>Junior</I> or <I>Senior</I>.** for the Customization Entry Form's Header Text.

28. Click the Finish button to complete the report.

You're ready to try out your new report. Because you have already seen how parameters work in your previous report, you can just run this report directly.

29. Click the Run link at the bottom of the Manage Component page.

Oops! Trying to run the report directly brings up an error page, as shown in Figure 9-13.

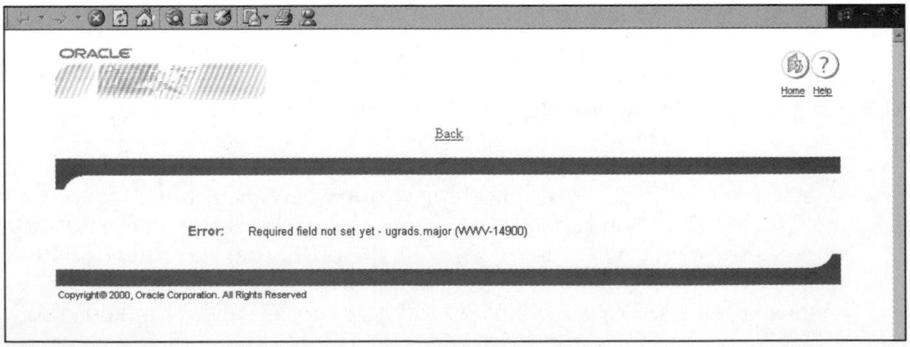

Figure 9-13: Error caused by missing required parameter

Remember—you indicated that the Major parameter required a value. This time, call the customization form.

30. Close the report browser window and return to the Manage Component page.

31. Click the Customize link at the bottom of the Manage Component page. The parameter page should look like Figure 9-14.

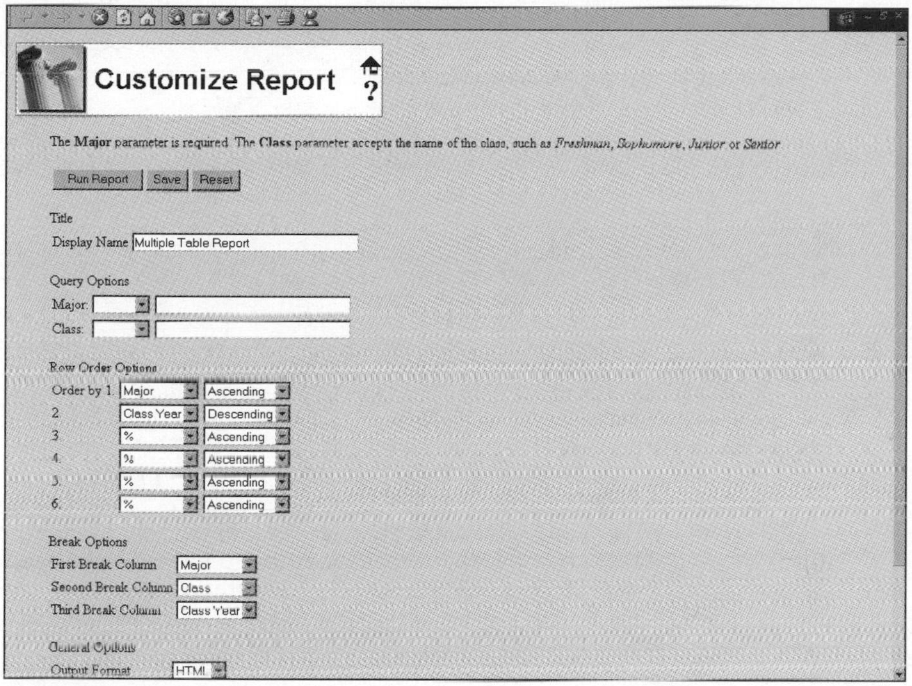

Figure 9-14: The parameter form for your report

32. Select = for the condition and enter **Finance** for the value for the Major parameter.

33. Click the Run Report button.

The report that appears should look like the one shown in Figure 9-15.

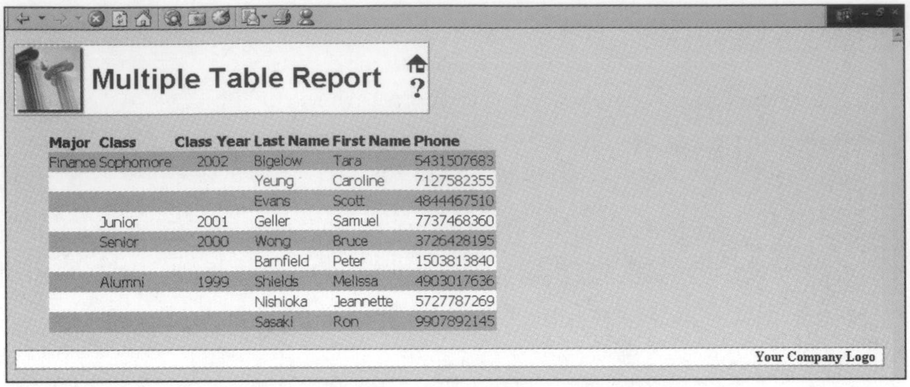

Major	Class	Class Year	Last Name	First Name	Phone
Finance	Sophomore	2002	Bigelow	Tara	5431507683
			Yeung	Caroline	7127582355
			Evans	Scott	4844467510
	Junior	2001	Geller	Samuel	7737468360
	Senior	2000	Wong	Bruce	3726428195
			Barnfield	Peter	1503813840
	Alumni	1999	Shields	Melissa	4903017636
			Nishioka	Jeannette	5727787269
			Sasaki	Ron	9907892145

Figure 9-15: Your report with data from UGRADS and CLASSES

You can see that everything worked as planned — the data is correctly sorted and the redundant values for MAJOR have been properly suppressed.

Multiple tables for master-detail relationships

One of the classic uses for linked tables in a relational database is to establish a master-detail relationship. A *master-detail* relationship is one where a single master row in one table is related to multiple detail rows in another table.

In the Net University sample database you can see a master-detail relationship between the UGRADS table, which contains information about individual students, and the TRANSCRIPT table, which holds data about the courses each student has taken. These two tables can be linked together through the value in the ID column, which is used to uniquely identify a student.

1. Return to Oracle9*i*AS Portal development environment by closing the report browser window.
2. Click on the Navigator icon in the banner.
3. Click on the Report link to the right of the Create New ... label.
4. Select the Report from Query Wizard link.
5. Give the new report a Name of **ch9_rpt_5** and a Display Name of **Master-detail Report**.
6. Click the Next arrow on the Report Name and Application page.
7. Enter **NETU.COURSE_CATALOG** into the Table or View data field and click on the Add button.
8. Enter **NETU.TRANSCRIPT** into the Table or View data field and click on the Add button.

9. Enter **NETU.UGRADS** into the Table or View data field and click the Add button.

10. Click on the Next button.

You will want to establish a master-detail relationship between the UGRADS table and the TRANSCRIPT table and a referential relationship between the TRANSCRIPT table and the COURSE_CATALOG table. Oracle9*i*AS Portal has found one set of correct columns to use for the table joins — CAT_NUM — but you will have to add the link for the ID columns in the TRANSCRIPT and UGRADS table.

11. In the second line of combo boxes, set the first box to TRANSCRIPT.ID and the second box to UGRADS.ID.

12. Click on the Next arrow on the Join Conditions page.

13. Move the UGRADS.LASTNAME, UGRADS.FIRSTNAME, TRANSCRIPT.YEAR, TRANSCRIPT.SEMESTER, and the COURSE_CATALOG.COURSE_NAME columns to the Selected Columns list box, in that order.

14. Click the Next button on the Table or View Columns page.

15. Click the Next button on the Column Conditions page.

16. Accept the Tabular Format in the Report Layout page and click on the Next button.

You gathered information from all three tables as you needed it in your report. Notice that you did not need to display the ID column used for linking in the report. The ID column is not really meaningful information in this database; instead, it is just used as a unique identifier to establish relationships between tables.

17. Change the Column Heading Text for the LASTNAME column to **Last Name** and the Column Heading Text for the FIRSTNAME column to **First Name**.

18. Click the Next button on the Columns Formatting page.

19. Click on the Next button on the Formatting Conditions page.

20. Select the UGRADS.LASTNAME, UGRADS.FIRSTNAME, and TRANSCRIPT.YEAR columns in the Break Options section of the page and select UGRADS.LASTNAME, TRANSCRIPT.YEAR, and TRANSCRIPT.SEMESTER as the Row Order Options.

21. Click on the Next button on the Display Option page and the Customization Entry Form page.

You are hoping to be able to use a trick by breaking on the UGRADS.FIRSTNAME column but not sorting on it. This works as long as there are no two people with the same last name, which happens to be true in the sample database. However, in the real world, you would not depend on this likelihood and you would correspondingly lose the ability to sort on the SEMESTER column in a report based on the

Query Wizard. When you enter your own SQL statements, you can, of course, increase the number of columns you use for sorting.

22. You should select the PUBLIC.TEMPLATE_6 template on the Add Text page to keep a consistent look and feel on your reports. You can add other text on this page, if you like.

23. Click the Finish button to finish the report.

24. Click the Run link at the bottom of the Manage Component page to run the report.

The report should look like Figure 9-16.

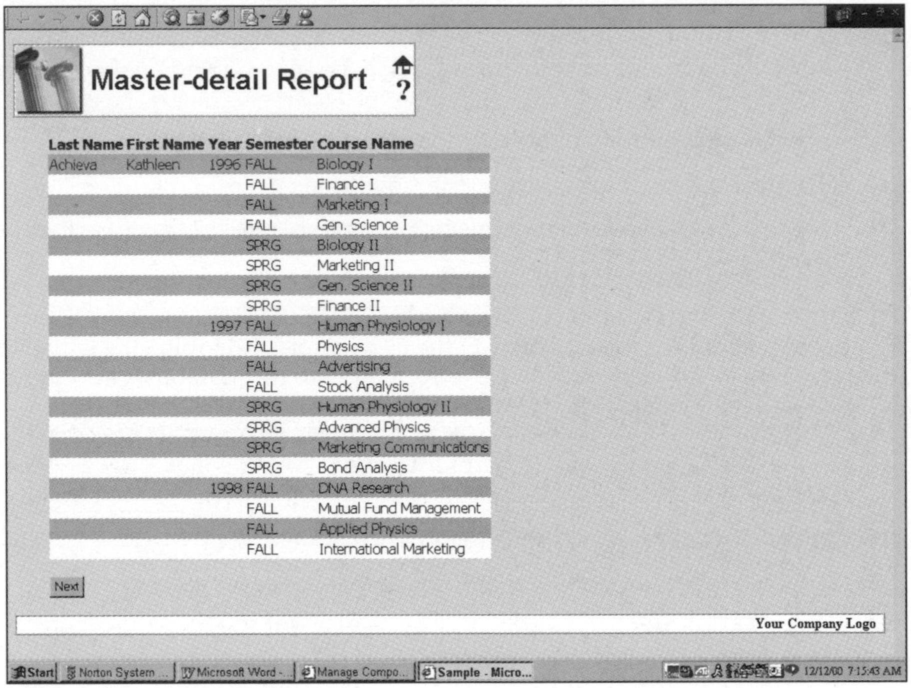

Figure 9-16: Your transcript report

You have created quite a few reports in these last two chapters, and explored some, but not all, of the options available to you for building reports. But the chapter has not yet covered one important aspect of using reports — using them as a portlet in your portal page.

Using Reports as Portlets

What, did we forget all about portlets after making such a big deal about them a few short chapters ago? Not at all. But one of the virtues of portlets in Oracle9*i*AS Portal is that using a component as a portlet is almost exactly the same as using the report as a full page report — almost.

1. Go to the Navigator and select the ch9_rpt_4 report to edit.

2. In the Manage Components page, click on the Access tab, which will bring up the page shown in Figure 9-17.

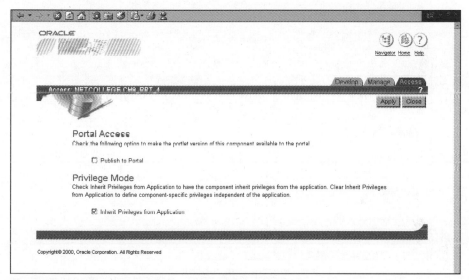

Figure 9-17: The Access tab for a report component

3. Click on the check box labeled Publish to Portal at the top of the page. Note that this check box will only appear if you have the Publish to Portal privilege and this application has been exposed as a provider.

4. Click on the Close button to return to the Navigator.

5. Click on the Pages tab of the Navigator.

6. Click on the Top-Level Pages entry.

7. Click on Edit for the Net University Home Page.

8. Click on the Add Portlets button for the center region of the page.

Cross-Reference   The concepts behind creating pages were discussed in Chapter 7.

9. Scroll to the bottom of the portlet list on the left side of the Add Portlets browser window. You can now see the ch9_rpt_4 report listed by its name, Multiple Table Report.

10. Click on the name of the report to bring up the portlet in the window. You will get the unexpected page shown in Figure 9-18.

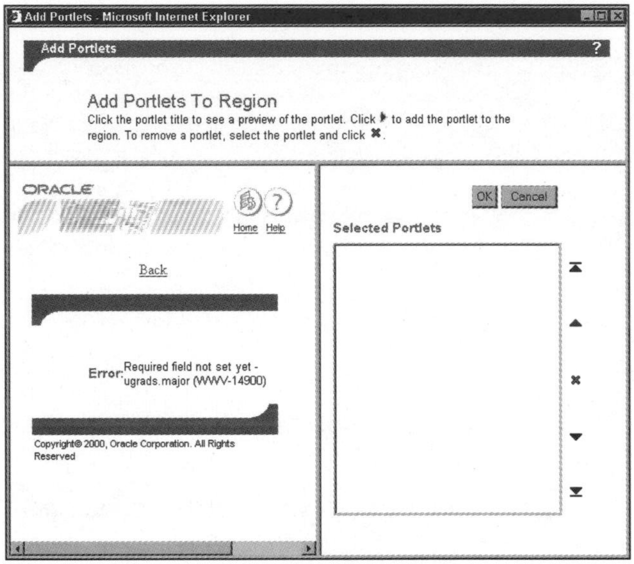

Figure 9-18: Your first view of the report portlet

The view shown on the left in Figure 9-18 is not what you were expecting. What happened?

If you remember, you indicated that the value for the Major parameter was required. This indication made sense at the time — you had not planned on anyone accessing this report without first going through the customization page. But when you add the report as a portlet, the portlet page engine in Oracle9*i*AS Portal did, in fact, call the report directly.

Tip   You would have gotten the same result by clicking on the Run As Portlet link in the Manage Component page. If you are planning to deploy a component as a portlet, it always makes sense to take a look at it as a portlet before leaving the development area.

This situation is an example of one of the design considerations you have to think about when you are designating a component for delivery as a portlet. Fortunately, this situation is easy to correct.

11. Close the Add Portlets browser window to return to the main Oracle9iAS Portal page.

12. Click on the Close button to return to the Navigator and click on the Applications tab.

13. Click on the Edit link for the ch8_rpt_4 report.

14. Go to the Customization Form Display Options tab in the Edit window, the seventh tab from the left or the third from the right.

15. Uncheck the Value Required check box for the UGRADS.MAJOR check box.

Note   This is one solution for this issue. Another potential solution would be for the page owner to specify defaults for this customization—which you will do later in this section.

16. Click on the OK button to return to the Manage Component page, and then on the Navigator link.

17. Click on the Pages tab, the Top-Level Pages link, and the Edit link for the Net University Home Page.

18. Click on the Add Portlets icon again, scroll to the bottom of the portlets list and click on the Multiple Table Report portlet again. This time, you get the view shown in Figure 9-19.

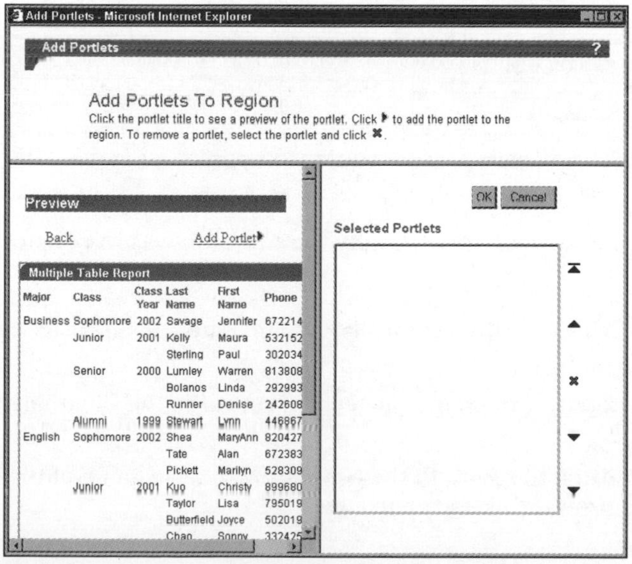

Figure 9-19: The new view of the report portlet

This view is more like it. There are too many listings to make the portlet compact enough to fit in the region nicely, but you will get to that soon enough.

19. Click on the Add Portlet link and the OK button to add the portlet to the region.

20. When you return to the Customize Page browser page, click on the Edit Defaults link for the report you just added to the center region, which will bring up the page shown in Figure 9-20.

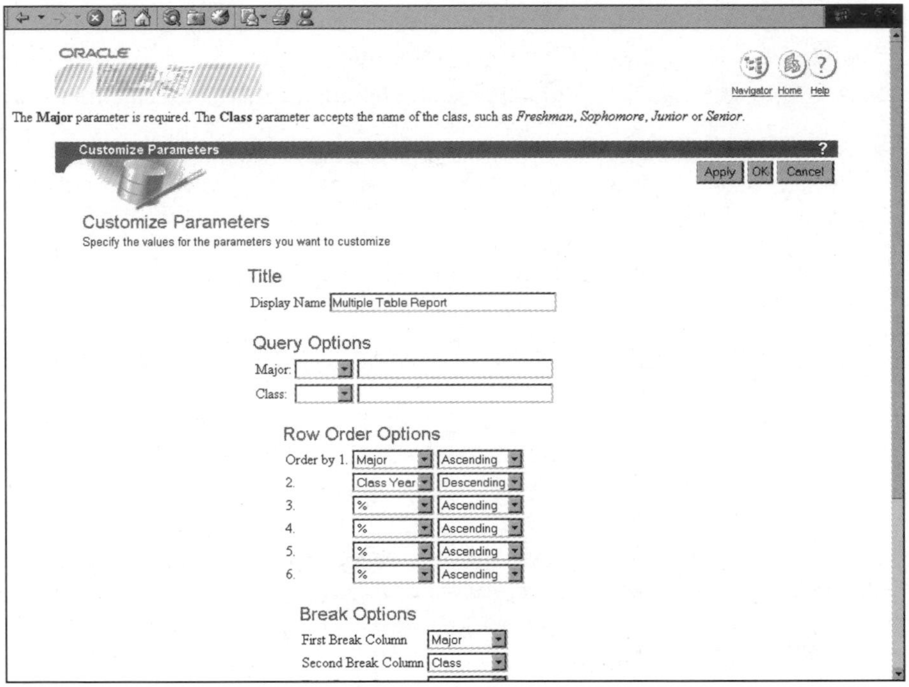

Figure 9-20: The Customize Parameters page for your report portlet

This page looks very familiar. In fact, it is virtually the same page as the Customize page for the report.

21. Select the = sign from Query Options for Major:, and enter Business as the value.

22. Click on the OK button to save your changes and return to the Customize page.

23. Click on the Close button to return to the Navigator, and the name of the page to bring it up in the browser, as shown in Figure 9-21.

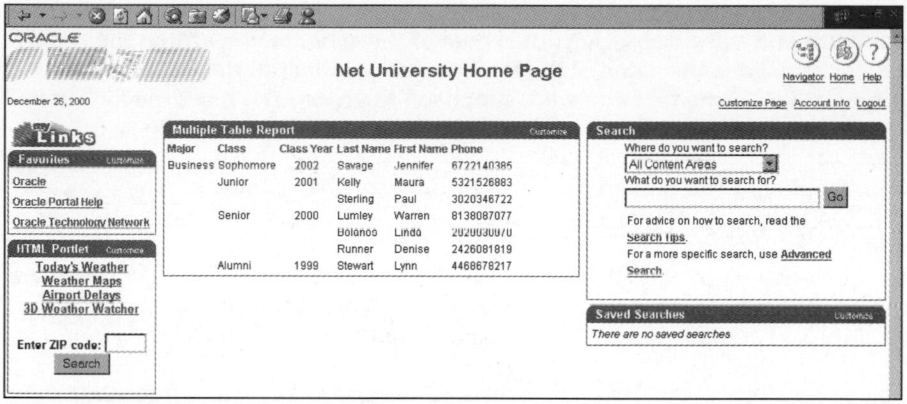

Figure 9-21: The new version of your portal page

Pretty slick, eh? Your report is there in the portal page. By adding a default value for the Major parameter, you limited the length of the report as it is initially displayed. Each user can still customize the report to show the list of the students that they want to see using the Customize Page link in the portlet.

The final topic for this chapter gives you another way to access your reports — by calling them directly from a browser.

Calling Your Reports Directly

Up to this point, you have been calling your report from within the Oracle9*i*AS Portal development environment. You can also call your report directly from your browser, which means that the default values for the parameters are used, or you can use the parameter form to call your report.

You accomplish this by specifying a URL to call the PL/SQL procedures that were generated to produce the report. There are two procedures in the report package that was generated — one that calls the report (the show procedure), and one that calls the show_params procedure.

> **Note**
>
> Of course, you will still need the appropriate access privileges on these components, as defined in the Oracle9*i*AS Portal security system.

1. Enter the following text into the navigation window of your browser:

```
http://servername:port/pls/portal30/netu.ch9_rep_5.show
```

In this URL, *servername* and *port* are replaced with the appropriate values for your site and *netu* represents the name of the schema you stored the report in. The *portal30* is the name of the DAD you used to install the Oracle9*i*AS Portal product. The name that you were supposed to give to the most recent report is ch9_rep_5.

You should see the same report in your browser that appeared when you clicked the Run link in the Manage Component page of Oracle9*i*AS Portal. Oracle9*i*AS Portal addresses all components with the same form of URL: the server for Oracle9*i*AS Portal, followed by the virtual directory for the Oracle9*i*AS Portal components, followed by a three-part locator made up of the schema name, module (or, more technically, package) name, and the procedure name you use to call the component.

To see how to use different procedures to call the same basic Oracle9*i*AS Portal component, you can try a couple more URLs in your browser.

 2. Enter the following text into the navigation window of your browser:

    http://*servername:port*/pls/*portal30*/*netu*.ch9_rep_5.show_parms

The only difference in this URL is that the show_parms procedure is called, rather than the show procedure as in the previous example. This URL should bring up the parameter entry page in the browser.

 3. Enter the following text into the navigation window of your browser:

    http://*servername:port*/pls/*portal30*/*netu*.ch9_rep_5.help

This URL should bring up the customized help page for the report you just created. There will probably not be very many times when you want to directly access the help page from an Oracle9*i*AS Portal application, but seeing the results of this URL reinforces the way that Oracle9*i*AS Portal components are stored and recalled.

More Information on Reporting

In the past two chapters, you learned a lot about using Oracle9*i*AS Portal to create reports. Hopefully, what you discovered will address most of your reporting needs.

Two more topics covered later in this book will help you extend the capabilities of your reports even more. The first topic is the use of PL/SQL to implement logic at specific places in your reports. You have already seen the page in the Report Wizard that gives you the ability to add PL/SQL code to your report. Chapter 21 covers using PL/SQL with Oracle9*i*AS Portal components. The use of PL/SQL is a vast topic, and there are many excellent books on the subject. Consequently, Chapter 21 is not a complete tutorial on PL/SQL. The chapter will help you understand how PL/SQL interacts with Oracle9*i*AS Portal components, which should be enough to guide an experienced PL/SQL developer in using the language with Oracle9*i*AS Portal.

There is also a terrific feature of Oracle9*i*AS Portal called *batch reporting*. You have also seen evidence of this feature already—the Batch button displayed on the report parameter page. When you click that button, your report is sent to a queue to await execution. Using batch reports can help improve the throughput of your Oracle9*i*AS Portal applications by using the Oracle database's internal queuing technology. You can learn more about batch reporting in the Oracle9*i*AS Portal documentation.

Summary

In this chapter, you delved more deeply into the creation of reports with Oracle9*i*AS Portal. You learned how to use SQL to specify the data source for a report. You were introduced to the custom layout feature of Oracle9*i*AS Portal. You also learned how to add parameters to reports and how to create reports from multiple tables. And finally, you learned how to call a report, its parameter entry page, or its help page directly from your browser.

Reporting is a read-only process. Data comes to you, but you can't insert or update data in the database. The next two chapters introduce you to creating forms that can interact with the data in the database.

✦   ✦   ✦

Building Oracle9*i*AS Portal Forms

✦ ✦ ✦ ✦

In This Chapter

Understanding Forms
in Oracle9*i*AS Portal

Creating Forms
Based on Tables

Adding Forms to
Portal Pages

✦ ✦ ✦ ✦

Forms are the basic building blocks of interactive applications. Most of your application systems require you to create a significant number of forms. This chapter is your introduction to building forms with Oracle9*i*AS Portal.

As you can imagine, Oracle9*i*AS Portal gives you a lot of flexibility in creating forms to match your specific needs — far too much flexibility and power to cover in a single chapter. By the end of this chapter, you will be able to create a basic form and understand the wide range of formatting and functionality you can add to these forms. The next chapter will extend your form-building ability to cover more complex forms, such as master-detail forms and forms based on stored procedures.

Understanding Forms in Oracle9*i*AS Portal

We all know what a form is. In a physical sense, a form is a preformatted piece of paper with headings to identify the information that is required on the form and blank spaces where you can enter that information.

The physical form translates into an electronic form pretty directly. The headings on an electronic form are static labels, while the blanks on the form are typically text fields where users can enter data. In the graphical world that Oracle9*i*AS Portal lives in, user input can also be presented as a series of choices such as radio buttons or check boxes, or a list-of-values to choose from, such as a list box or a combo box.

But you have already created Oracle9*i*AS Portal components that had these types of objects. The customization forms that were automatically generated for the reports you designed in the previous chapter had objects for user input. And the QBE report you created in Chapter 8 included a QBE form that could also be used to insert data into a table, as well as a customization form.

But the key difference in Oracle9*i*AS Portal between a form and a report centers on the way that these two components interact with the Oracle database. A report reads data from the Oracle database. The user input that is accepted in customization form is simply used to configure the data and the report that are returned to the user.

The many different types of forms that you can create with Oracle9*i*AS Portal allow users to write data back to the Oracle database. This has a dramatic impact on the way you design and implement Oracle9*i*AS Portal forms. The most important asset of any information system is its data. The value of the system lies in its capability to store and return large amounts of data. In a report, the user is never allowed to add new data to the database, so this important asset is always safe. You still may need to add security to reports because you are concerned about unauthorized people reading your data, but no one is able to damage the integrity, or correctness, of your data through a report.

A form, however, is different. Users can write data to the database and, if you are not careful, they can write logically incorrect data to the database, thus compromising the value of the data and any and all decisions that are based on it. Because of this, you have to think about ways to protect the integrity of your data as you create Oracle9*i*AS Portal forms.

Furthermore, most forms have a single primary purpose: entering data into the database. Consequently, the way you design your forms is somewhat different from the way you might design your reports. When a user is working in a form, they are typically dealing with a single row at a time. This is in direct contrast to reports, which almost always involve many rows of data for a single report or page in a report.

In the end, it is easy to determine when you want to create an Oracle9*i*AS Portal form as opposed to an Oracle9*i*AS Portal report. If the user has to write data to the database, a form is the appropriate component.

Form types supported by Oracle9*i*AS Portal

Oracle9*i*AS Portal lets you build three types of forms. These types of forms are the following, in order of increasing complexity:

✦ **Forms based on tables or views:** The table- or view-based form is the most common type of form. These types of forms are based on a single table or view, and can be used to insert or update data in the corresponding table or view.

✦ **Forms based on stored procedures:** An Oracle stored procedure can accept any number of parameters. These parameters act like the columns in a normal Oracle table. When you create a form based on a stored procedure, the process of writing data sends the values entered to the parameters of the stored procedure, just as it would send the values to the columns of the underlying table. You may sometimes create a stored procedure to handle more sophisticated processing logic, and Oracle9*i*AS Portal enables you to easily integrate that logic into Oracle9*i*AS Portal components. Forms based on stored procedures are covered in the next chapter.

✦ **Master-detail forms:** Master-detail forms enable you to enter the values for a master row and more than one associated detail rows. Master and detail rows are normally linked by a common column or key relationship. Oracle9*i*AS Portal's master-detail forms automatically handle all the integrity issues that come when you are writing to more than one table. Master-detail forms are covered in the next chapter.

The most basic type of form you can create is a form based on a table. This gives you a lot more flexibility in determining how the user interacts with the form while writing data to the database.

Creating Forms Based on Tables

If you are developing an Oracle9*i*AS Portal application whose primary purpose is to enter data in the database, you will create a lot of form components that are based on tables or views.

1. Log into Oracle9*i*AS Portal as the NETUDEV user.

2. Go to the Navigator and select the NETCOLLEGE application.

3. Click on the Form link to the right of the Create New ... label at the top of the Navigator.

4. Select the "Form based on table or view" link in the main Forms page.

The first part of the table-based Form Wizard

The first page of the Form Wizard for a form based on a table or view looks just like the first page of the Report Wizard. You use this page to enter a name for your form.

5. Enter **ch10_frm_1** as the Name and **First Form** as the Display Name.

6. You can accept NETUCOLLEGE as the application. Click the Next button on the Form Name and Application page.

The second page of the Form Wizard for a form based on a table or view also looks just like the corresponding page for a report. In order to reduce the complexity of your first form, you should pick a table that does not have very many columns.

7. Enter **NETU.MAJORS** in the table in the Table or View data field.

8. Click the Next button on the Table or View page.

In the next page of the Form Wizard, you have to choose the type of layout you will be using for the form. You already learned about the Custom Layout as it relates to reports in Chapter 7. The Custom Layout option for forms is very similar to the option for reports, since both of them use an HTML table as the basic formatting structure.

You should leave the default layout option for this, your first form.

9. Click on the Next button on the Form Layout page.

The next page of the Form Wizard, the Formatting and Validation Options page, is shown in Figure 10-1.

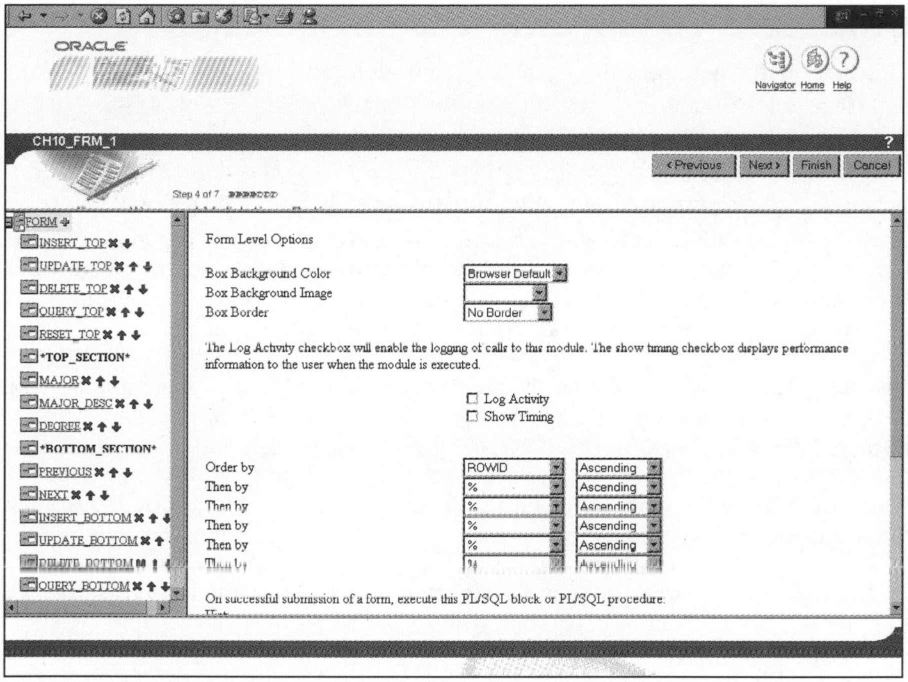

Figure 10-1: The Formatting and Validation Options page in the Form Wizard

This page is by far the most important and complicated page in the entire process of defining a form.

> **New Feature**
>
> This page, the core of building forms, has a completely new look and feel in Oracle9*i*AS Portal.

Before you actually begin to use this Formatting and Validation Options page to set the options for your first form, you have to understand a few concepts behind Oracle9*i*AS Portal forms.

Oracle9*i*AS Portal form-creation concepts

There are three general topics you should understand before you can comfortably use the Formatting and Validation Options page: navigation on the page, the areas of a form, and basic layout concepts.

Navigating the Formatting and Validation Options page

The first thing to understand about the very powerful Formatting and Validations Option page is how to use it. On the left side of the page is a Form Navigator. This Navigator is used to select different entities in the form. As you select an entity, the properties for that entity appear in the right side of the form.

There are four icons used in the Navigator. To the left of the Form name at the top of the list of entities is a little minus sign. If you click on the minus sign, the list of objects below the Form heading will disappear — they are contracted into the Form entity. The icon to the left of the Form entry will change to a plus sign. Since you will usually want to be working with objects in the form, this option is not tremendously useful.

To the right of the Form entry is a little green cross. If you click on this cross, a dialog box will appear that will prompt you for the name of a new item for the form, as shown in Figure 10-2.

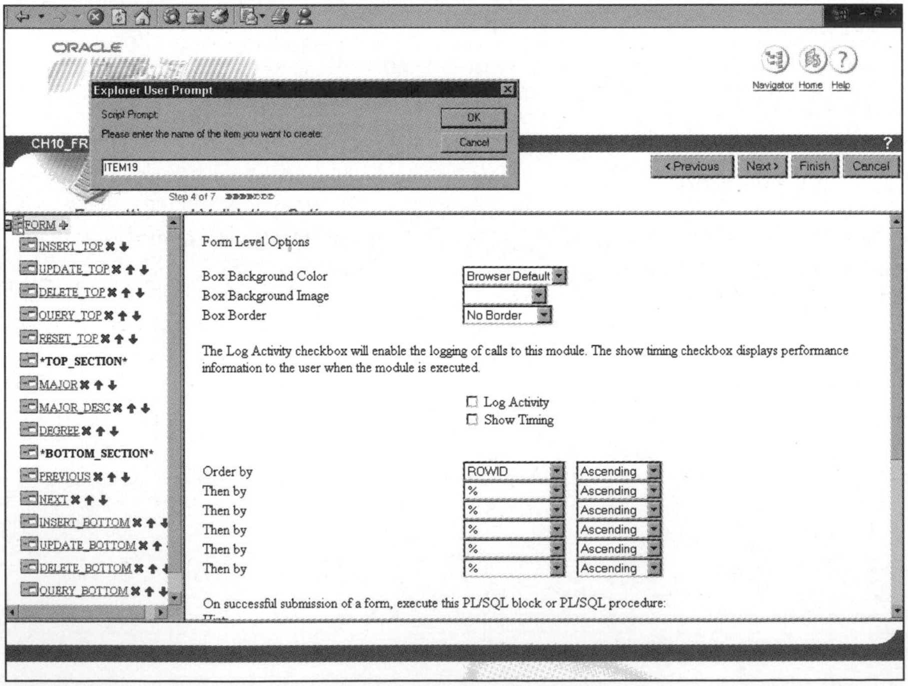

Figure 10-2: Adding a new item in the Form Wizard

Why Add a New Field?

You may be wondering why you would want to add a new field to a form. Each field is directly associated with a column in an underlying table, and Oracle9*i*AS Portal handles the interaction between the field and the column. Since you cannot add a new column to the database from the Form Builder, why would you ever create a new field for the form?

There are a number of reasons why you might find yourself wanting to add a new field to a form. You might want to add a visual element, such as a label or a horizontal rule, or use a blank field to implement a certain visual layout. You might add a field that could accept data that would be handled by a JavaScript validation function and then passed in to the table in a different form.

Once you enter a name for the item and click on the OK button, the new field will be placed at the bottom of the list of entities.

To move the field to a different location, you can use the little blue arrows that appear to the right of each of the entities in a form. As you might expect, the upward arrow moves an entity up one line, while the downward arrow moves the entity down one line.

The little red X to the direct right of each object in the Form Navigator will delete the object from the form. You will be prompted to confirm each object deletion after clicking on the red X.

Understanding the areas of the form

When you look at the lineup of entities in the Form Navigator, you can see that there are three groups of objects in the form. Both the Top Section and the Bottom Section of the form contain five buttons, with the buttons in the top of the form having their names ending in _TOP and the buttons in the bottom of the form having their names ending with _BOTTOM to distinguish them. The Insert, Update, and Delete buttons control the interaction of the data in the form with the table in the database. The Query button launches a query of the database, while the Reset button resets the values in the form to the original values. This action causes any changes you have made in the data in the form to be discarded and the original values in the row to be restored.

The corresponding buttons in the Top and Bottom sections implement the same functionality. You may want to only have one button for each operation, so you would delete the other.

The Bottom section of the form also contains a Previous and Next button, which control the navigation through the data that is retrieved by the form. You will see all of these buttons in action when you complete your first form.

In between the Top and Bottom Sections of the form is the area where the data fields reside. You have to keep all the data fields in the middle section of the form, although you can add objects to any section of the form.

Understanding the layout of the form

In order to understand how an Oracle9*i*AS Portal form is laid out, you have to understand a little bit about HTML tables.

Each data field in an Oracle9*i*AS Portal form is actually made up of two parts: a label and some type of data entry object. Each of these parts is implemented as a cell in an HTML table.

In the discussion of custom layouts in Chapter 9, you learned that the HTML table provided the basic layout structure for an Oracle9*i*AS Portal report. The HTML table also controls the basic layout of an Oracle9*i*AS Portal table.

Three important concepts determine the layout options in the Formatting and Validation Options page. The first concept is that every row in an HTML table has a fixed number of columns. The number of columns in each row is equal to the maximum number of columns in any row of the table.

Each data field in an Oracle9*i*AS Portal form generates two columns for the underlying HTML table. If you decide that you want two data fields on one line in your Oracle9*i*AS Portal form, you will end up with four columns in every row in the underlying HTML table, because one of the rows has four columns — one for each label and data entry object, as shown in Figure 10-3.

Label	Column1	Label	Column2
Label	Column3	Label	Column4
Label	Column5		

Figure 10-3: HTML table layout for five data fields, with two on one line

The second concept about HTML tables is that any individual cell can span more than one column in the table. You can cause this to happen by setting the Column Span of a column. In Figure 10-4, the first row of the table has a column with a column span of 3—causing it to span three columns and, in effect, limiting that row of the table to a single label and data entry object.

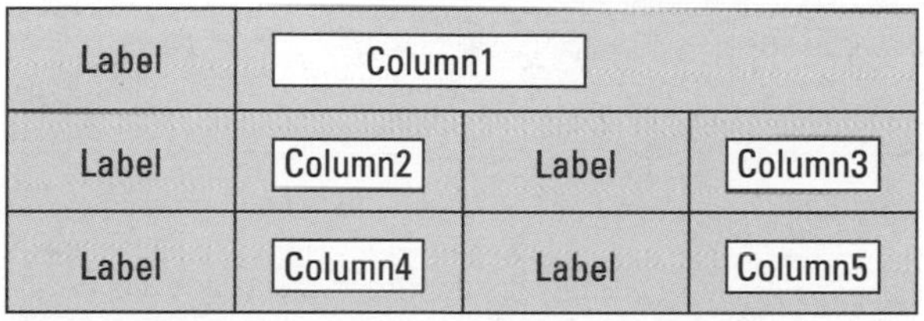

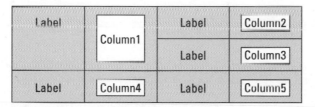

Figure 10-4: HTML table layout for five data fields, with one with a Column Span of 3

The third concept about HTML tables is that any individual cell can span more than one row. In Figure 10-5, the first data field has a Row Span of 2. This means that the label and the data entry object both take up two rows. The second data field is not on a new line, so it goes after the first data field. The third data field is on a new line, but it has to start in the third column in the table, since the first two columns are taken up with the row-spanning first data field.

Figure 10-5: HTML table layout for five data fields, with one with a Row Span of 2

With your understanding of the way the Formatting and Validation Options page works, you are ready to examine the particulars of assigning these options.

Form options

The first set of options to examine on this page are the options that apply only to the form.

10. Click on the Form entry in the Form Navigator. The form options come up on the right. The upper part of the available form options were shown in Figure 10-2, while Figure 10-6 shows the lower portion of the form options.

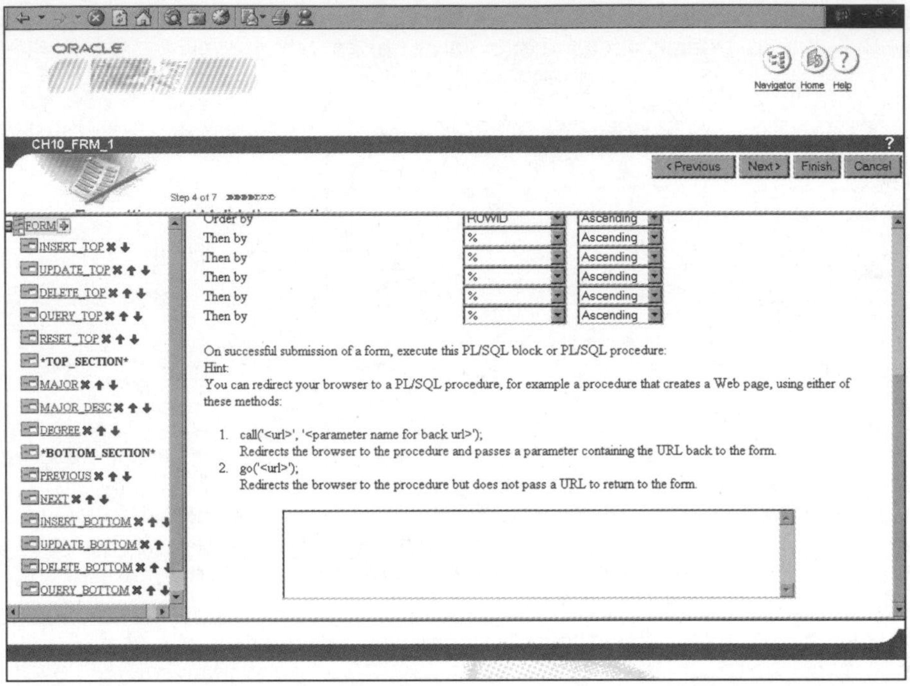

Figure 10-6: Lower portion of the Form options in the Formatting and Validation Options page of the Form Wizard

At the top of the page, there are three options that control the formatting of the overall form, which is contained within a box. You can set the Background Color for the box, or a Background Image for the box. You can also specify a Thin Border, a Thick Border, or No Border, the default, for the box.

Below these formatting options are two check boxes, which allow you to select whether the activity of this component gets logged and whether the time it takes the PL/SQL procedure that handles this box is displayed to the user. The logging activity does consume some resources, but it probably won't be noticeable in terms of run-time performance. Because each log entry does take up a row in a table in the database, it makes sense to turn this option off unless you want to specifically monitor the activity of this form for a particular reason.

Below these two check boxes are a series of combo boxes that allow you to order the results returned from a query with the form with the values for up to six columns. You can specify that each of the columns of data is sorted in ascending or descending order. By default, the rows are sorted by ROWID, an internal row identifier that is assigned as a row is added to the database.

At the bottom of this set of form options, there is a text box where you can enter a PL/SQL procedure that is executed whenever the form is successfully submitted by a click on a button. If the form gets sent to the server, this PL/SQL code executes. Typically, the PL/SQL code you enter here performs an action on the data, such as inserting it into a new row, and then creates an HTML page to return to the user.

You can alter some of the form options to see their effect on the form.

11. Change the Box Background Color for the form to "Blue, Light".

12. Change the Box Border to "Thin Border".

Button options

The buttons on your Oracle9*i*AS Portal forms have their own sets of options.

13. Click on the INSERT_TOP button in the Form Navigator.

The options for buttons come up on the right side of the page, as shown in Figure 10-7.

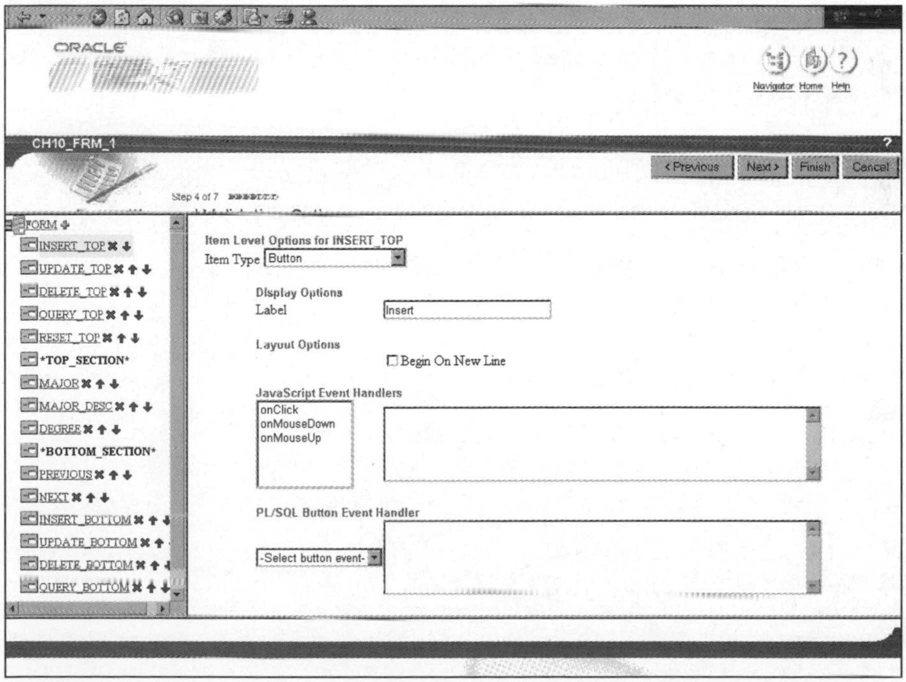

Figure 10-7: Button options in the Formatting and Validation Options page of the Form Wizard

There are five basic types of options for one of the buttons. The first option on the page is a combo box that allows you to choose the Item Type for the object. This option is more appropriate for the objects you will have in the main portion of the form, so it will be explained with those objects in the next section.

The next section of options is labeled Display and only contains one option. You can change the Label that appears on the button.

The Layout section of options is next. In this section, you can implement the table-based layout options described earlier in this chapter. This section contains a Begin on New Line check box. This check box, as you might guess, forces the object onto a new line (really, a new row in the layout table) when checked.

The last two sections give you the ability to associate either JavaScript or PL/SQL event handlers with this object. These topics will be covered at length in Chapters 19 and 21, which cover JavaScript, PL/SQL, and the new event model for Oracle9*i*AS Portal, respectively. For now, all you really need to know about these validation options is that each of these predefined buttons calls a specific PL/SQL event handler.

You can modify the appearance and layout options for one of the generated buttons, but it is easier to see the effects of these type of changes with the objects in the central portion of the form, which you will learn about next.

Data field options

The last, and most inclusive, set of options to understand on this page are the options that apply to the objects in the middle of the form. This is the area where the data fields associated with the columns in the underlying table are placed.

14. Click on the MAJOR object in the Form Navigator. The options for buttons come up on the right side of the page, as shown in Figure 10-8.

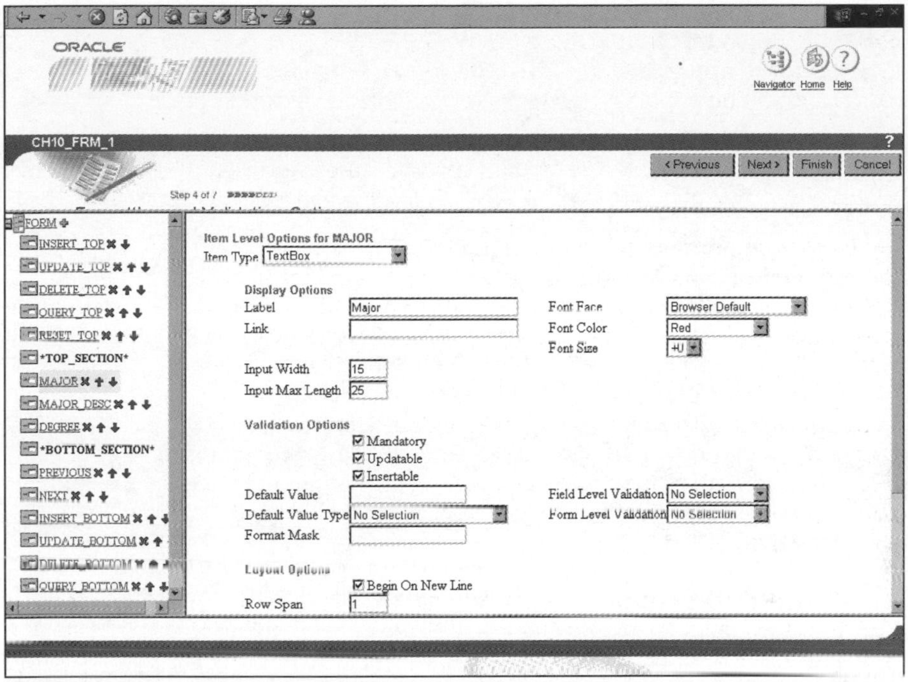

Figure 10-8: Data field options in the Formatting and Validation Options page of the Form Wizard

The first option for these data field objects is the combo box for Item Type. There are 15 item types you can use, which are explained in Table 10-1.

Table 10-1
Button Item Types

Item Type	Function
Blank	This item type causes a blank space to be inserted into the two columns in the form table created for the form by Oracle9*i*AS Portal. The Blank option, when applied to a field based on a database column, prevents both the label or the data from being present in the table.
Button	This item type displays an item as a button on the form. The only appropriate reason to use this item type is to call an event handler.
CheckBox	The CheckBox HTML object creates one or more check boxes for data entry in the form table. It makes sense to use a CheckBox object if you only have two possible values for a column.
ComboBox	The ComboBox HTML object creates a combo box that contains all of the valid values for an object in the table form. This option is appropriate only if you specify a List-of-Values object for the column.
File Upload (Binary) File Upload (*inter*Media)	There are two File Upload item types. Both of them have similar characteristics — they will cause three objects to be placed in your form — a label, a text box to enter the path name of the file you want to upload, and a Browse button, which will bring up a window that lets you browse and select a file from your file system. When the form is used to insert or update rows, the file will be properly uploaded to the designated field.
	The difference between the two types of items is how they are treated at their destinations. If you use the Binary type, the item is treated as a standard binary object — it is simply stored in the database. If you use the *inter*Media upload, the file type must be one of the types recognized by *inter*Media, such as a .jpg file; and the advanced options available to you with *inter*Media, such as sophisticated manipulation and searching, will be available for use on the object.

Item Type	Function
Hidden	This option suppresses the display of the data for a column in the table, but the data is still present in the appropriate column in the table. You might want to use this option if you don't want the data to be seen in the browser but you do want it to be used as part of a logical routine that was a part of the page.
	Although the information in a hidden field is not visible on the page in the browser, the data is a part of the ACSII HTML code returned to the browser. If users choose to view the source code of the page, they are able to see the data.
Horizontal Rule	This option replaces the label portion of a column with a Horizontal Rule HTML object. When you use this option, the Width value in the Column Formatting and Validation page is used to indicate the width of the horizontal rule, and the Height value is used to indicate the thickness of the rule.
	Keep in mind that, by default, the horizontal rule only occupies the column of the form table for the label, not for the data entry object. If you want a horizontal rule that crosses the entire browser page, you have to increase the column span, as described in the next section.
Image	An Image HTML object is necessary if the column contains image data. An Image object cannot be edited. You might also want to use an Image object if you are going to use images to improve the appearance of your form.
Label Only	This choice causes a blank space to be inserted into the column in the form table reserved for the data entry portion of the object. The Label Only option prevents the data from being present in the table.
Password	A Password item is just like a text box object, except that all characters are shown as asterisks when retrieved or entered.

Continued

Table 10-1 *(continued)*

Item Type	Function
Popup	The Popup option puts a little pop-up icon to the right of a text entry box. If the user clicks the icon, Oracle9iAS Portal brings up the standard Find dialog box so the user can search a large group of possible values and select one for the value of the text box. A Popup object, because it includes a text object, also enables a user to directly enter a value into the text box, so you may have to add some additional validation logic for the column. This option is appropriate only if you specify a List-of-Values object for the column.
RadioGroup	The RadioGroup HTML item type creates a group of radio buttons for the acceptable values for the column. This option is appropriate only if you specify a List-of-Values object for the column.
TextArea	The TextArea HTML object is a text entry box. The Height value lower on the page determines the number of rows in the box, while the Width value determines the width of the box. The TextArea box automatically performs word wrap.
TextBox	The TextBox is the default HTML object for data entry. If you specify a Max Length value that is greater than the Width value, the data in the TextBox scrolls as a user enters or scrolls through it.

As you might imagine, each one of these item types has a slightly different set of options available for modification. In Table 10-2, each of these options is listed and examined, including the options that apply to more than one item type.

Table 10-2
Button Item Type Options

Item Type	Option	Description
Common options		These common options apply to most of the item types.
	Label	The Label option allows you to specify the label for an object.
		You can include HTML formatting tags in a Label.

Item Type	Option	Description
	Link	The Link option allows you to specify that the Label field contains a URL that links to another Oracle9*i*AS Portal object, location on the Web, or HTML page.
	Font Face	The Font Face option allows you to choose a font from a combo box containing a list of fonts.
	Font Color	The Font Color option allows you to choose a font color from a combo box containing a list of font colors. By default, the Font Color for a mandatory field in the database is red.
	Font Size	The Font Size option allows you to choose a font size from a combo box.
	Layout options	Most item types have the same set of three layout options that were described for the buttons in the previous section.
	Event handlers	Most item types have JavaScript event handlers, as described in the previous section.
Blank		The Blank item type does not contain any options.
Button		The Button item type does not contain any of the Font options.
	Event handlers	This item type contains both JavaScript and PL/SQL event handler options.
CheckBox		The CheckBox item type only contains the common options.
ComboBox		The ComboBox item type contains all of the common options.
	Input height	The Input height option allows you to specify the height of the combo box item.
	Input width	The Input width option allows you to specify the width of the combo box item.

Continued

Table 10-2 *(continued)*		
Item Type	*Option*	*Description*
	LOV	The LOV option lets you specify a List-Of-Values (LOVs) object that will be used to retrieve the values placed in the combo box. There is a Search button to the right of this option that you can use to search for available LOVs.
		Chapter 16 covers LOVs in depth.
	Default value	A default value is a value that is automatically assigned if the user does not enter a value for the column. You can use a default value in order to automatically display a selection, for items with lists-of-values, or to assign a value to a column that is not shown on the page.
	Default value type	There are three basic choices for the default value type:
		✦ No Selection, which is applicable if you do not specify a default value. This is the default value.
		✦ Constant, which is applicable if you have a constant for a default value.
		✦ Either a function, expression, or SQL statement that will return a character value, a number value, or a date value.
		For the last type of default value, you would enter a function, an expression, or a SQL statement in the Default value field. You have to specify which of these types of calculations you are using for Oracle9iAS Portal to create the appropriate code in your form. You also have to specify the data type of the value returned in order for the value to be properly converted for display.
		For more information on using functions, expressions, and SQL statements for generating default values, refer to the Oracle9iAS Portal documentation.
Hidden		The only common option used by the Hidden item type is the Label option.

Item Type	Option	Description
	Default value Default value type	The Hidden item type is not displayed to the user, so it should contain a default value if the form is going to be used to insert new data.
Horizontal Rule		The `Horizontal Rule` item type does not contain any options.
Image		The `Image` item type only contains the common layout options.
	Image	The `Image` entry field lets you specify a particular image. There is a Search button to the right of this option that will give you a list of the images that are available in Oracle9*i*AS Portal.
Label Only		The `Label Only` item type only contains the common appearance and layout options.
Password		The `Password` item type contains all of the common options.
	Input length	This option specifies the length of the entry field that will be used on the form.
	Input max length	This option specifies the length of the data that can be contained in the entry field for the form. A user is not allowed to enter more characters than specified in this option.

If this value is greater than the `Input length` value, the data will scroll horizontally, when necessary. |
| | Mandatory | This check box signifies that this data field must have a value. If the user clicks on the Insert or Update buttons without a value in a field specified as mandatory, they will receive a JavaScript-generated error.

By default, this check box is checked if the associated data column is marked as `NOT NULL`. |
| | Updateable | If this check box is not checked, Oracle9*i*AS Portal will display the data value as a label, rather than an entry field.

By default, this check box is checked. |

Continued

Table 10-2 *(continued)*

Item Type	Option	Description
	Insertable	If this check box is not checked, Oracle9*i*AS Portal will not allow a value to be inserted for this field when a new row is added to the database.
		By default, this check box is checked.
	Field level validation	This option allows you to specify a JavaScript validation routine that is executed each time a user modifies the data in the field and leaves the field. The option uses a combo box that lists all the available JavaScript procedures in Oracle9*i*AS Portal. You can define your own JavaScript procedures, as described in Chapter 19.
		The Field level validation procedure will give immediate feedback to the user, as opposed to the Form level validation procedure. However, some types of validations are based on the interaction between data in two fields, so they would be more suitable for Form level validation.
	Form level validation	This option allows you to specify a JavaScript validation routine that is executed each time a user clicks on the Insert or Update buttons. As with the Field level validation, this option uses a combo box to list available JavaScript procedures.
Popup		The Popup item type contains the common options, as well as the Input height, Input width, and LOV options, which were described for the ComboBox item type.
Radio Group		The RadioGroup HTML item type creates a group of radio buttons for the acceptable values for the column. This option is appropriate only if you specify a List-of-Values object for the column.

Item Type	Option	Description
TextArea		The TextArea item type contains all of the options listed for the Password item type, except that the Input length and the Input max length are replaced by the Input height and Input width options, as described for the combo box.
		The TextArea also contains an option for Default Value, like the Hidden item type.
TextBox		The TextBox item type contains the options described for the Password item type.
		The TextBox also contains an option for Default Value, like the Hidden item type.

Tables 10-1 and 10-2 provide a lot of information about the various options available to you. Now it's time to modify some of the options for your first form.

15. Click the MAJOR_DESC column in the Columns list box. Change the Text for the label to **Description**. You will modify some of the other characteristics of your form later, after you see how the default options affect the operation of the form.

Finishing the form

Although most of the important definitions for your form are contained on the Formatting and Validation Options page, there are still a few more pages to see in the Form Wizard.

16. Click on the Next button on the Formatting and Validation Options page.

17. Select the PUBLIC.TEMPLATE_6 choice from the Template combo box.

You can see that the name of the form is set to the value you entered as the Display Name at the beginning of the wizard.

Since the last page of the Form Wizard simply allows you to add PL/SQL logic to the form, you can finish your form now.

18. Click on the Next button.

At first glance, the page for entering additional PL/SQL code looks just like its corresponding page in the Report Wizard. But if you scroll down to the bottom of the page, you can see that there are two more options for entering PL/SQL code: before and after processing the form. Since the functionality of a form, which allows you to insert, update, and delete data, is more complex than the functionality of a report, which only allows you to read data, these additional events have been added to the Oracle9*i*AS Portal form. There will not be a big use for them right now, but in the last section of the book, where you learn additional tips and techniques, you will be using these events extensively to check the validity of incoming data.

19. Click on the Finish button.

The next step is to see exactly what your newly created form does.

Running your form

You are ready to start to use your first table-based form.

1. Click the Run button on the Manage Component page.

And here is your form, as shown in Figure 10-9.

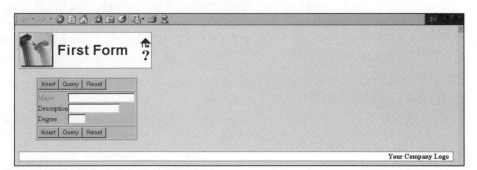

Figure 10-9: Your table-based form

You can see that your form has a lot of buttons, implying a lot of different functionality.

New Feature Some of the default buttons for a form, most notably the Query button, are new with Oracle9*i*AS Portal.

One of the new features of this default, general-purpose form is the Query button. The best way to understand how it works is to make it work.

2. Click on the Query button.

A New Type of Default Form

If you have grown used to using WebDB, you probably resigned yourself to the fact that a default form could be used to either insert data or update/delete data. There were good reasons for implementing this type of automatic functionality in a default form, but, unfortunately, this functionality was not easy for beginning users to find or use.

The new default forms are much more functional and easier to understand.

The page that is returned looks like Figure 10-10.

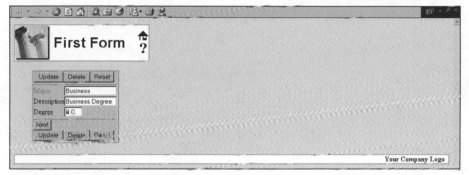

Figure 10-10: The result of clicking the Query button

When data has been retrieved from the database into the form, the Next button appears to allow you to go to the following row.

3. Click on the Next button.

You can see that the Query button acts like the corresponding button on a QBE report — clicking on it without any entries in the data fields retrieves all the rows in the table.

4. Click on the Reset button.

You can see the selection capabilities of the form by clearing out the fields and starting again.

5. Enter **F%** into the Major field and click on the Query button.

Since you have some data in the form, why not try to update it?

6. Change the value in the Major field to **Finance and Business**.

7. Click on the Update button.

Oops! It looks like you got some kind of error from your Oracle database, as shown in Figure 10-11.

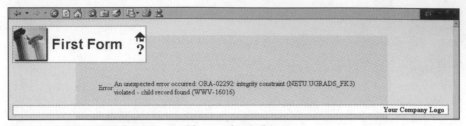

Error An unexpected error occurred: ORA-02292: integrity constraint (NETU.UGRADS_FK3) violated - child record found (WWV-16016)

Figure 10-11: An update error with your basic form.

> **Note**
> The actual error refers to the fact that the MAJORS table is a parent in a foreign key relationship, and a constraint put on the database means you cannot change the value of the primary key in the table as long as there are child rows associated with the parent row. If you are not familiar with database constraints, don't worry too much about the actual source of the error. At least this error message is more informative than the error messages in WebDB!

It doesn't really matter why you can't update the page, although you should note that the error came from the database. This error source means that the data was sent to the database and this page was returned, as opposed to a JavaScript error, which you will see later in this section.

You can prevent this error from coming up again by modifying your form.

8. Close the browser window that contains the form to return to the Manage Component page.

9. Click on the Edit link in the Manage Component page.

10. Select the MAJOR field in the Form Navigator.

11. Uncheck the Updateable check box in the Validation section of the form.

12. Click on the OK button.

13. Click on the Run link in the Manage Component page.

14. Click on the Query button in your form.

You can now see that the value for the Major field is displayed as a title, rather than a data field, as shown in Figure 10-12.

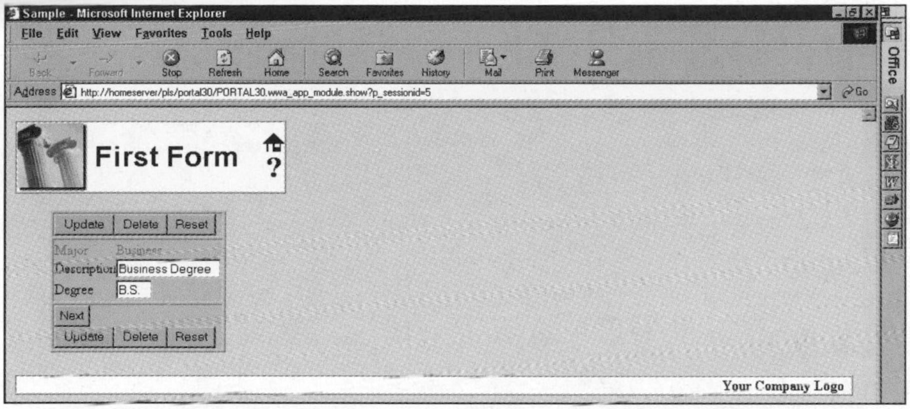

Figure 10-12: The result of clicking the Query button with a nonupdateable field

15. Click on Reset button to clear the form.

16. Click on the Insert button.

You have not entered a value for a mandatory field, the Major field. Because of this, you have received an error, as shown in Figure 10-13.

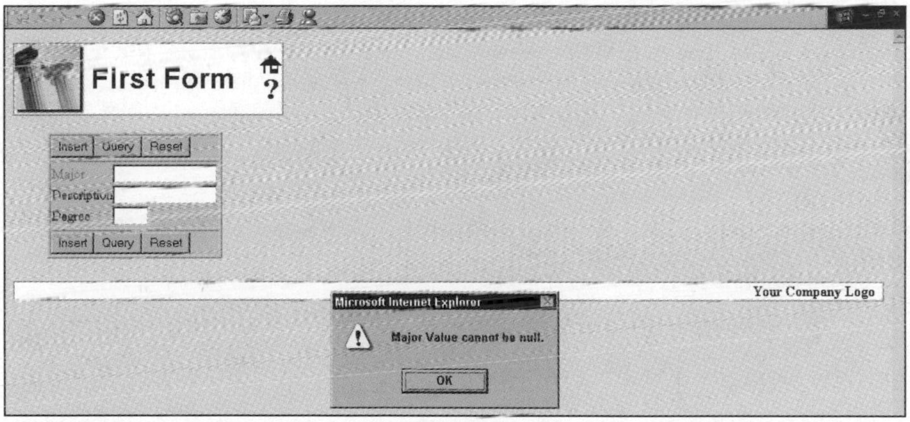

Figure 10-13: The result of inserting with a NULL value for a mandatory field

Notice how this error pops up in a little message box, instead of on its own page. The reason for this is that you have indicated the Major field is mandatory, which causes a JavaScript validation routine to be run — in the browser — before the form is submitted.

This automatic functionality is great, but the form might be more effective if you added some text to alert the user to the required nature of the Major field.

17. Click on the button in the message box.

18. Close the browser window that contains the form to return to the Manage Component page.

19. Click on Edit in the Manage Component page.

20. Click on the green plus sign to the right of the Form entry in the Form Navigator.

21. When the dialog box comes up, enter **RequiredMajor** for the name of the new item.

The item will appear at the bottom of the list of items in the Form navigator.

22. Use the Up arrows to the right of the RequiredMajor item to move it up to just below the Major field.

23. Change the Item type for the Required Major item to Label only.

24. Enter **You must have a value for the Major field.** for the label of the item.

25. Enter a Column Span of **4** for the item.

Why enter a Column Span of 4? If you didn't, the entire label for this item would be displayed in the first column of the underlying HTML table. Since the width of a column is expanded to include the largest text string in the column in any row of the table, this long label would mess up the formatting of the overall form. By using all four columns in the resultant table (remember, there are two labels and two text boxes on the second line), you ensure a nicer formatting.

While you are editing the form, it might be a good idea to get rid of the redundant buttons at the bottom of the form.

26. Delete the INSERT_BOTTOM, UPDATE_BOTTOM, DELETE_BOTTOM, QUERY_BOTTOM, and RESET_BOTTOM buttons from the form by clicking on the red X to the right of each item.

Finally, it might improve the overall appearance of the form to place the DEGREE data field on the same line as the Description data field.

27. Select the DEGREE data field in the Form Navigator.

28. Uncheck the check box labeled Begin on New Line in the Layout area of the page.

29. Click on the OK button to regenerate your form.

30. Click on the Run link to run the new version of the form.

The new version of the form is shown in Figure 10-14.

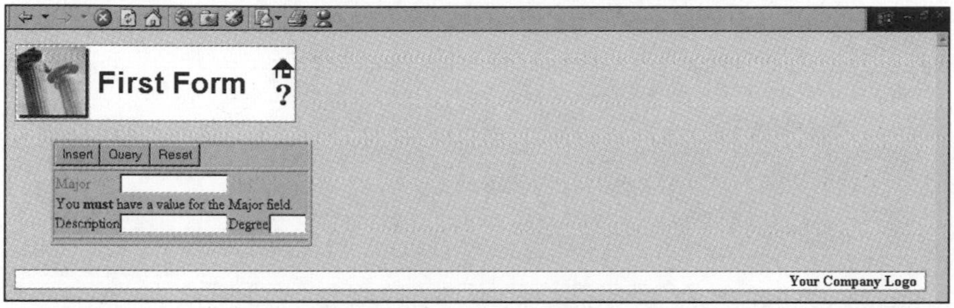
First Form
Insert
Query
Reset
Major
You must have a value for the Major field.
Description
Degree
Your Company Logo

Figure 10-14: A more attractive version of the form

This version of the form looks easier to use, but there is still one little problem. The DEGREE data field can accept any type of degree, when, in reality (well, the reality of this book), good old NetU only gives out B.A. and B.S. degrees.

Your users may not be aware of this, or they might be prone to inputting the wrong value for the field. To complete your form, you will want to make it so that the users cannot make these mistakes.

31. Click on the Back button in the browser to return to the Manage Component page.
32. Click on Edit in the Manage Component page.
33. Select the DEGREE item in the Form Navigator.
34. Change the Item type to Radio Group.
35. Select DEGREELOV from the LOV combo box in the Appearance area of the options.

On the CD-ROM

If you followed the complete installation instructions in Chapter 2, DEGREELOV should have been loaded and available. If you did not, refer to Appendix A for instructions on installing individual prebuilt components.

36. Click on the OK button to regenerate the component.
37. Click on the Run link to see the new form.
38. Click on the Query button to see how the radio buttons are automatically set by the retrieved data.

As you can see in Figure 10-15, the buttons in the radio group are properly set, according to the values in the data.

Figure 10-15: An even more attractive and useful version of the form

By providing a radio group for the DEGREE column, which has a limited set of values, you have not only improved the visual appearance of the form, but also made it so that users cannot enter invalid data for that column.

Adding a Form to a Portal Page

You can add this form to your portal page, just as you did for the report.

1. Close the form browser window to return to the Manage Component page for your form.

2. Click on the Access tab for the form.

3. Check the check box labeled Publish to Portal. Click on the Close button to return to the Navigator.

4. Click on the Pages tab of the Navigator, and the Top-Level Pages entry.

5. Click on the Edit link for the Net University Home Page page.

6. Click on the Add Portlets icon in the middle region of the page.

7. Scroll to the bottom of the portlets list to find the Net University Application section. Click on the form you just published as a portlet.

8. On the Preview page, click on the Add Portlet link to add the form portlet to the portlet region.

9. Click on the OK button to close the Add Portlet browser page.

10. Click on the Close button in the Customize Page page to return to the Navigator, and click on the name of the Net University Home Page to bring up the new version of the portal page, shown in Figure 10-16.

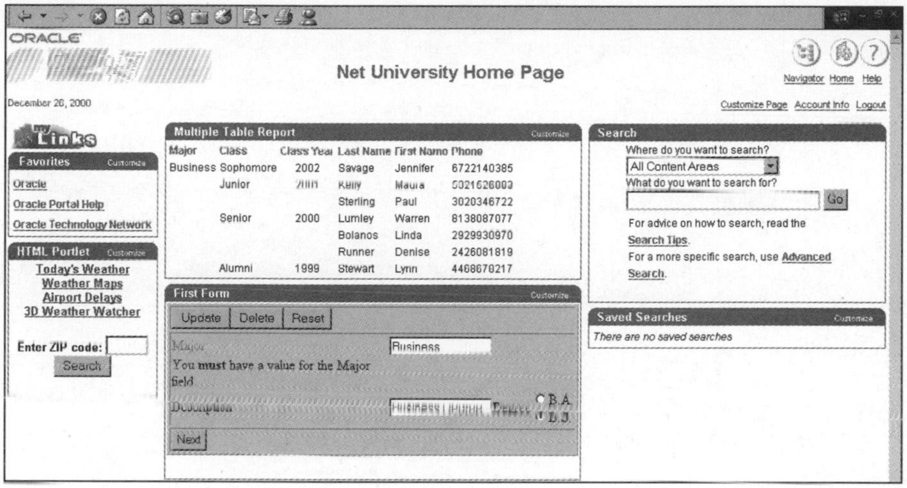

Figure 10-16: The portal page with a form portlet

The form fits in pretty well as a portlet. Before leaving this brief section, you might want to play around with the form as a portlet, just to verify that all the functionality you included in the form is still present in its new life as a portlet.

Summary

So far, so good.

You have created a form based on a table that you can use to enter data into your database. You even learned some basic methods you can use to preserve the integrity of your data and prevent user entry errors.

In the next chapter, you will learn how to create a form based on an Oracle stored procedure, which will allow you to take advantage of the sort of sophisticated interaction with the database you can build into stored procedures. You will learn how to create a form that is based on a master-detail relationship between two tables. As you may not like the way the form you created allows users to do everything with the data — insert, update, and delete any piece of data — in the next chapter, you will see how to shape the behavior of your form so that it can only be used to update or delete a particular row.

✦   ✦   ✦

CHAPTER

11

♦ ♦ ♦ ♦

In This Chapter

Creating a Form
Based on a Stored
Procedure

Building Master-
Detail Forms

♦ ♦ ♦ ♦

Building Forms – Part II

In the last chapter, you learned how to create basic forms. The forms you created gave you the ability to write data to your Oracle database, and they were certainly easy to build. This chapter introduces you to the two other types of forms you can build — forms based on stored procedures and master-detail forms — and helps you understand how to use the forms you have created to update or delete existing data in your database.

Forms Based on Stored Procedures

If you are new to the Oracle database, or to relational databases in general, it is probably worth spending a little time discussing the purpose and structure of stored procedures before moving on to building forms based on these stored procedures.

What are stored procedures?

Structured Query Language (SQL) was popularized in the 1970s and added an important dimension to the world of data processing. SQL gives developers a more-or-less standard language and interface to use to interact with data in a wide variety of relational databases. Oracle rose to prominence as the leading relational database in the world, in part because of its adherence to the SQL standard.

Note This book assumes that you have a basic working knowledge of SQL, as you have already seen in the chapters on reporting. Although you do not need to understand SQL to use Oracle9iAS Portal, you can broaden the range and functionality of Oracle9iAS Portal with timely use of SQL, so it's a good idea to learn the basics of the language to complement your knowledge of Oracle9iAS Portal.

SQL combines simplicity and power, but it mainly revolves around the actions needed to read and write data. There are times when developers or a database administrators want to supplement SQL with their own unique, procedural logic. Stored procedures get their name from two simple facets of their existence: they can be used to create virtually any type of logical procedure, and they are stored and executed in the database. Stored procedures were the precursor to today's server-based applications, such as those you are building with Oracle9*i*AS Portal.

The Oracle database uses a procedural language called PL/SQL for its own stored procedures. If you get some understanding of the capabilities of PL/SQL, all you have to do is to look at Oracle9*i*AS Portal itself. All the Oracle9*i*AS Portal components you create are actually groups of PL/SQL stored procedures, called packages, which are generated by Oracle9*i*AS Portal and stored and executed in the Oracle database. In fact, Oracle9*i*AS Portal itself is written as a collection of PL/SQL procedures, and when you install Oracle9*i*AS Portal, you are actually installing those PL/SQL procedures.

Oracle9*i*AS Portal and stored procedures

Many of you are probably already experienced Oracle users and pretty familiar with PL/SQL. If you have been using Oracle for a while, you probably have existing PL/SQL routines that you use to interact with the data in your Oracle database. Oracle9*i*AS Portal enables you to create forms easily that are based on your PL/SQL procedures.

Stored procedures can include parameters that are passed to the procedure as part of the procedure call. Oracle9*i*AS Portal treats these parameters just like it treats the columns in a table. When you select a stored procedure as the foundation for a form, Oracle9*i*AS Portal queries the stored procedure to discover the number and type of parameters the procedure expects to receive, just as it does for a table or view.

At this time, the forms you build with Oracle9*i*AS Portal can only send data to a PL/SQL procedure. Some PL/SQL procedures create their own internal cursors that can be used to scroll through a set of data in the same way that you would use a standard SQL cursor to scroll through the result set from an SQL query. You cannot take advantage of this capability of stored procedures in Oracle9*i*AS Portal.

You can also use a PL/SQL function, which returns a single result, as a part of a standard SQL statement in Oracle9*i*AS Portal when you are creating reports or charts.

The sample stored procedure

The sample `NETU` database includes a stored procedure that you can use to insert data into the database based on a simple logical criterion.

The NETU database is used for more than just tracking students and their courses. The database also includes information about NetU alumni and their contributions to their alma mater. Alumni can either send in checks as donations, or send in pledges to donate, and follow them with checks later.

The only difference between these two actions is whether or not a check is included. If a check is present, the contribution is a donation; if there is no check, the contribution is a pledge.

The stored procedure netu_add_donation accepts data about a donation and automatically inserts it into the appropriate table, depending on the presence or absence of a check number.

The netu_add_donation **stored procedure is as follows:**

```
procedure netu_add_donation (p_id number, p_fund
varchar2, p_restriction varchar2,
      p_amount number, p_gift_date date, p_checkno number)
   as
   begin
      if p_checkno is null then
   —
   —No check, this must be a pledge
   —
         insert into pledges (donation_no, id, fund,
            pledge_amount, pledge_date, pledge_no)
         values (null, p_id, p_fund, p_amount, p_gift_date,
            pledges_seq.nextval);
      else
   —
   —Check number means that this is a donation receipt
   —
         insert into donations (donation_no, id, fund,
            restriction, amount, gift_date, check_number)
         values (donations_seq.nextval, p_id, p_fund,
            p_restriction, p_amount, p_gift_date, p_checkno);
         end if;
   end netu_add_donation;
```

Building a form based on a stored procedure

Building a form based on a stored procedure is very much like building a form based on a table or view.

1. Return to the Oracle9iAS Portal Navigator and navigate to the NETCOLLEGE application.

2. Click on the Form link to the right of the Create New ... label.

3. Click on the "Form based on procedure" link.

The first page of this wizard looks just like the first page of the other component builder wizards. You are prompted for a storage location for the form you are building and the name of the form.

4. Enter **ch11_frm_1** as the Name of the form and **Stored Procedure Form** as the Display Name. The NETCOLLEGE application is already selected for you.

5. Click the Next button on the Form name and Application page.

The next page in the wizard prompts you to select an existing PL/SQL procedure for the form. When you click on the Search button, the resulting dialog will show you a whole bunch of available procedures, as shown in Figure 11-1.

Where did the procedures come from? They were created for you by Oracle9*i*AS Portal, just as you created the sample reports and forms in earlier chapters. All the procedures created by Oracle9*i*AS Portal are used to accept parameters and then return an HTML page the browser, so they would not really be suitable as the basis for a form you would build with this wizard.

Note   It's a good development practice to keep your components in a separate schema to avoid this type of issue.

6. Enter **%ADD_DONA%** into the Find box at the top of the search dialog.

7. Select the NETU.NETPACKAGE.NETU_ADD_DONATION procedure in the Procedure combo box.

8. Click the Next button on the Procedure page.

Note   The extended name for the procedure includes the name of the owner schema (netu), followed by a period and the name of the package (netpackage) that contains the procedure, followed by a period and the name of the procedure.

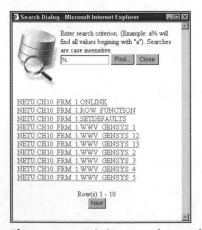

Figure 11-1: Existing stored procedures

The next page in the Form Wizard asks you whether you want to use the tabular or custom layout option. In order to concentrate on the differences in building a form based on a stored procedure, you should leave the tabular choice selected.

9. Click on the Next button on the Form Layout page.

The next page in the Form Wizard for procedures looks very familiar. In fact, aside from a different title at the top of the panel, this page is identical to the corresponding page for formatting columns in the other form wizards.

There are only four differences:

✦ The first difference is that all the names of the parameters begin with the characters "P_". The P, as you could probably guess, stands for "Parameter," and giving the parameters for stored procedure names that begin with "P_" is a standard practice for Oracle stored procedures. You will probably want to change the labels for the parameters in your form.

✦ The second difference is that all the parameters have a width of 30 and a maximum length of 2000. Oracle9*i*AS Portal assigns all parameters these same values, so you will probably have to change these values too.

✦ The third difference is that all the labels for these parameters have a color of red, by default, since they are all required.

✦ The last difference is that all the parameters are marked as mandatory and updateable.

These are good guesses by Oracle9*i*AS Portal, because most stored procedures are expecting to receive values for all their parameters. But you will still want to adjust the labels and lengths of the parameters for this particular PL/SQL function.

10. Select the P_ID column in the Form Navigator. Change the Text in the Label section to **Alumni ID**. Change the Max Length and the Width to **6**.

The P_ID parameter must have a value that already exists as the ID of a person in the ALUMNI table. That makes the P_ID field ideal for using a list-of-values pop-up. In following the Oracle9*i*AS Portal standard, you will leave the mandatory fields red.

11. Set the Display As combo box to Popup and select ALUMNILOV for the LOV field.

12. Select the P_FUND column in the Form Navigator. Change the text in the Label section to **Fund**. Change the Display As to Radio Group. Set the LOV to FUNDLOV, which will create radio buttons based on the values in the FUNDLOV, thus making sure that users don't enter an invalid fund.

On the CD-ROM

If you have not loaded the samples for the book, you have to load the list-of-values for the FUND types by importing the fundlov.sql script, the list-of-values for the ALMUNI by importing the alumnilov.sql script, and the list-of-values for the RESTRICTION by importing the restrictlov.sql script. Please see Appendix A for instructions on how to import objects.

Because there are only two valid values for the FUND parameter, it makes sense to use a simple list-of-values that are displayed as a group of radio buttons. You will learn much more about lists-of-values later in Chapter 14.

13. Select the P_RESTRICTION column in the Form Navigator. Change the text in the Label section to Donation Restriction. Set Display As to Popup. Set the LOV to RESTRICTLOV. Uncheck the check box for "Begin on new line" so that this field appears on the same line as the previous field.

14. Select the P_AMOUNT column in the Form Navigator. Change the text in the Label section to **Amount**. Change the Max Length and Width to **15**. Set the Format Mask to **$999,999,999.99**, because the fundraisers are very hopeful that one of their alumni will hit the big time and remember dear old NetU.

15. Select the P_GIFT_DATE column in the Form Navigator. Change the text in the Label section to Gift Date. Change the Max Length and Width to 11.

Note

The Oracle database only accepts date values in the format of DD-MON-YYYY—two numbers for the day, three letters for the month, and four numbers for the year. You should note this format limitation in the help for this form.

16. Select the P_CHECK_NUMBER column in the Form Navigator. Change the text in the Label section to Check Number. Change the Color to Black and uncheck the Mandatory check box, because this field is not mandatory. Set the default value as (null) and the default value type as Constant. Change the Max Length and Width to 10.

If there is no check number, the stored procedure knows to enter the data as a pledge rather than a donation. Unfortunately, if the user does not enter a value for the check number, Oracle9*i*AS Portal does not include the P_CHECK_NUMBER parameter in the call to the stored procedure and the procedure does not execute properly. In order to avoid this, a missing check number must be listed as the value null, which sends the parameter with a null value to the procedure. Of course, you might want to create a JavaScript validation, which you will learn about in Chapter 19, to check for a numeric value or the text of null.

Before moving on, you will also have to change the title of one of the buttons. The SUBMIT_TOP button will do a submit function for the form, but, to the users, all they will be doing is inserting the donation, so it makes sense to change the label on the button so as to not confuse end users.

17. Select the SUBMIT_TOP item in the Form Navigator. Change the Label to **Insert**.

18. Click the Next button on the Formatting and Validation page.

The final two pages are identical to the final two pages of the other form components. You can specify text options that enable you to add text to the header and footer of the page displayed to users, associate help text with the page, and give the page a standard look and feel with a template. To make this component look like the other components you have created, you should assign a template.

19. Select the PUBLIC.TEMPLATE_6 choice from the Template combo box.

20. Give the form a header text of **Alumni Donations**.

21. Click on the Next button on the Form Text page.

You might wonder why the Advanced PL/SQL code page exists for a form based on a stored procedure. After all, why would you add more PL/SQL code to a stored procedure written in PL/SQL code? The purpose of this page is to enable you to add PL/SQL code that executes at some specific points in the creation of the page that is presented to the user as the interface for this component.

If you have been using Oracle for a while, you probably have some stored procedures that you want to use in your Oracle9iAS Portal application. These stored procedures were not necessarily designed with an appropriate user interface, so the need to add customized logic to surround a form based on a stored procedure is the same as the corresponding need for other components.

22. Click the Finish button on the last page of the Form Builder Wizard.

It's time to see the form at work:

23. Select the Run link at the bottom of the Manage Component page for the form you have just created. The form looks like Figure 11-2.

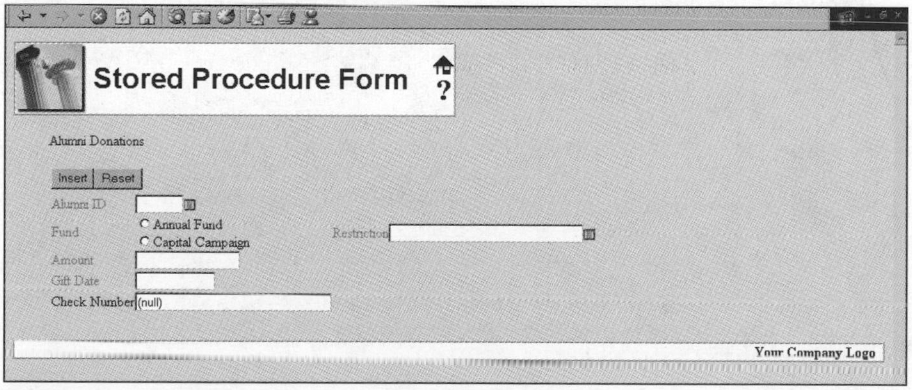

Figure 11-2: The form based on a stored procedure

24. Enter your own information into the fields on the page. Click the Insert button.

The ability to build forms to pass parameters to a PL/SQL procedure helps you to leverage work you may have already done to add logical procedures to your Oracle environment. The last type of form to explore is the master-detail form.

Master-Detail Forms

Up until this point, you have been dealing with individual forms based on individual tables or stored procedures. Many of the forms you create in any application system are based on individual tables in the database. Due to the connectionless nature of the HTTP communications between a browser and a server, this makes a lot of sense. You want to deal with tables as atomic units for updating and inserting data. If two tables are somehow related, you can simply build separate forms for each table and implement the relationship by building an Oracle9*i*AS Portal link.

But Oracle9*i*AS Portal gives you the ability to build forms based on two tables that are part of one of the most common types of relationship, the master-detail

Master-Detail Relationships and Arrays

One of the significant ways that relational databases changed the design of databases was to introduce the concept of related multiple tables that reduce the storage of redundant data. Master-detail relationships are the result of this advance. Rather than store, for instance, lots of student information with each record in a student transcript, the rows in the TRANSCRIPT table contain a value in their ID column that matches the value in the ID column of the UGRADS table. The ID column in the UGRADS table is the primary key of the table, and the primary key of the TRANSCIPT table points back to the primary key of its master table.

If you have been used to designing a nonrelational system, you may have used an array to implement the same type of relationship. A master-detail relationship has several advantages over an array. For instance, the rows in both the UGRADS table and the TRANSCRIPT table are smaller than a single row containing all of the data, which makes retrieval faster if someone just wants to see the student information or calculate on values in the TRANSCRIPT. More importantly, a master-detail relationship is dynamic. A student can take a single class or a thousand classes and the relationship doesn't change. With an array, you have to predefine the maximum number of details that can be assigned to a single master.

Relational databases are designed to join related tables very rapidly, so there is no real performance penalty to using master-detail relationships between tables rather than an array. In fact, the rules for good relational database design forbid the use of arrays.

relationship. In a master-detail relationship, a single row from the master table is related to one or more rows in a detail table and linked by a common value that exists in both tables.

You will see that creating a master-detail form gives you a single form that can be used to implement a host of actions for the form.

Building a master-detail form

There are a number of master-detail relationships in the NETU sample database. But, as with previous examples, you will build your first master-detail form based on two of the smaller tables in the database. This way, you can focus on the process of building the form, rather than on tracking and formatting a table with a lot of different columns.

Beginning the building process

You start out building a master-detail form in the same way that you began to build the other form components.

1. Return to the Oracle9iAS Portal environment by closing the browser window with the previous form.

2. Go to the Navigator page, which should still show the NETCOLLEGE application tion.

3. Click on the Form link to the right of the Create New ... label.

4. On the main Forms page, click on the Master Detail Form link

As with the other component builders, the first page of the Master-Detail Form Wizard requires you to indicate which schema in the database will own the resulting form. You also must give the form a name.

5. Give the form the Name of **ch11_frm_2** and a Display Name of **Master-detail form**. Click the Next button on the Master Detail Form Name and Application page.

The next page of the wizard prompts you for the master and detail tables that will be used in the form, as shown in Figure 11-3.

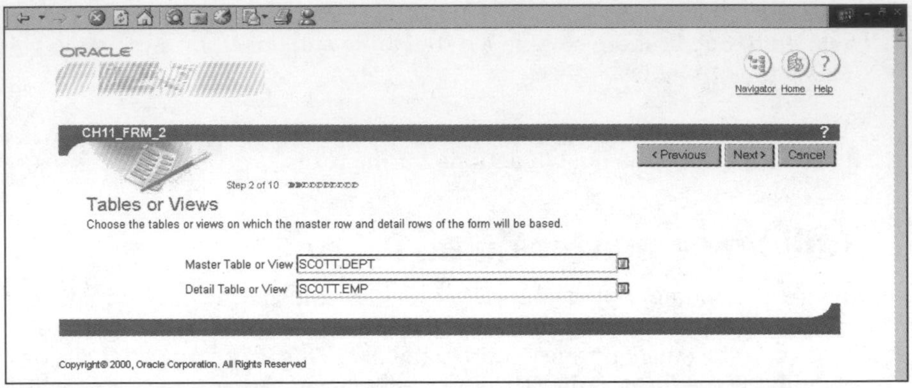

Figure 11-3: Specifying master and detail tables for a master-detail form

6. Select the NETU.MAJORS table in the Master Table or View combo box and the NETU.MAJOR_REQS table in the Detail Table or View combo box. Click the Next button on the Tables or Views page.

The next page of the Master-Detail Form Builder Wizard is used to specify the join between the master and detail tables. Oracle9*i*AS Portal uses some intelligence in proposing candidates for the link, including checking if there is a foreign key relationship between the two tables or, failing that, if there are matching column names in the two tables.

7. Accept the proposed join condition between the MAJOR column in both tables by clicking the Next button on the Join Conditions page.

Formatting options

The next page of the Master-Detail Form Wizard asks you to indicate whether you want the overall layout to be tabular or custom. As with the earlier forms, you should accept the default of a tabular layout.

8. Click on the Next button in the Form Layout page.

The next page in the Master-Detail Form Wizard, shown in Figure 11-4, looks like another page you have seen.

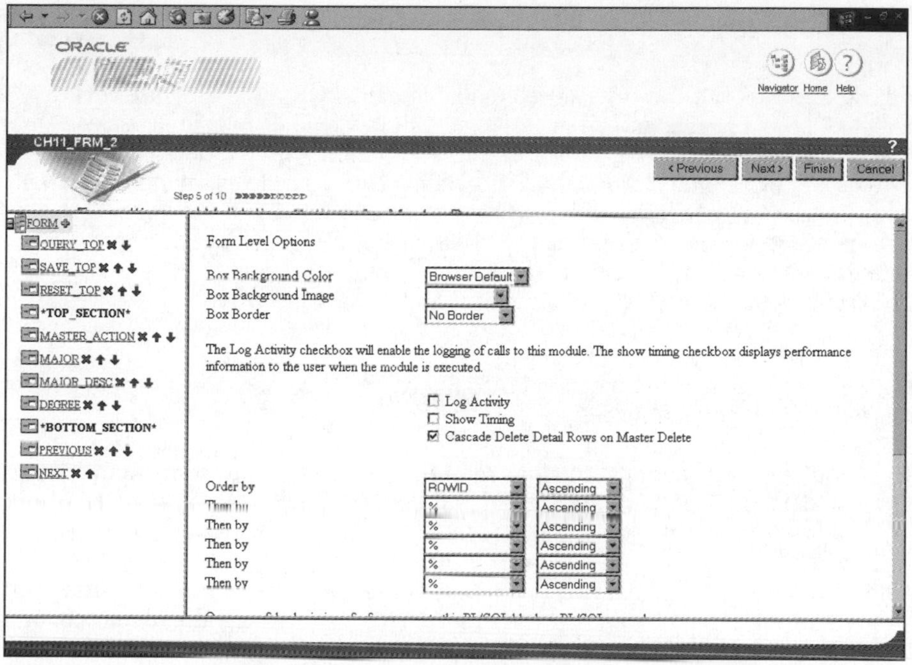

Figure 11-4: Formatting and Validation Options for Master Row

However, there are a number of key differences. The first main difference is in the name of the page. The page is called Formatting and Validation Options, like the similar page in the other versions of the Form Wizard, but the name includes the specification that these options are for the Master Row. As you will see later, the master-detail form is, in effect, two separate forms linked together, so this page is for the top form, which handles the master row.

When you look at the form properties, you can see that there is one additional check box, labeled Cascade Delete Detail Rows on Master Delete. By default, this box is checked, which means that when a user deletes the master row, all associated detail rows will also be deleted.

When you look at the items in the master part of the form, you can see that there is no INSERT_TOP, UPDATE_TOP, or DELETE_TOP buttons. You can also see that there

Don't Create Orphans!

If you are familiar with the rules of referential integrity, you will recognize this rule and understand its purpose. If you are not familiar with this type of rule, imagine what would happen if you deleted the master row and did not delete the associated child rows. The child rows would be orphans, and the logical integrity of your data would be disturbed. In this particular case, when you delete a major, you would delete the rows that list the requirements for the major — which only makes sense. If the major is gone, there is no need to clutter the database with requirements for the nonexistent parent.

is a new, unknown column called MASTER_ACTION. These two differences are related, as you will soon see.

New Feature   The missing buttons in the master portion of the form and the new MASTER_ACTION item are the result of the new design of master-details forms in Oracle9*i*AS Portal.

Aside from these few differences, the rest of this page is the same as the Formatting and Validation Options page for the other forms. You can go ahead and clean up the formatting for the fields on the page.

9. Select MAJOR in the first Order By combo box under the options for the Form.

10. Click on the MAJOR_DESC item in the Form Navigator. Change the label for the item to **Description**.

11. Click on the DEGREE item in the Form Navigator. Change the Item type to Radio Group and set the LOV to the DEGREELOV. Uncheck the "Begin on new line" check box.

On the CD-ROM   If you have not already loaded the preexisting LOV objects into the Oracle9*i*AS Portal database, you should import the object called courselov.sql into your database. (If you did not load the degreelov.sql LOV in the previous chapter, you should import that object also.) For information on how to import objects, please refer to Appendix A.

12. Click on the Next button in the Formatting and Validation Options for Master Row page.

The next page is the Formatting and Validation Options for Detail row, as shown in Figure 11-5.

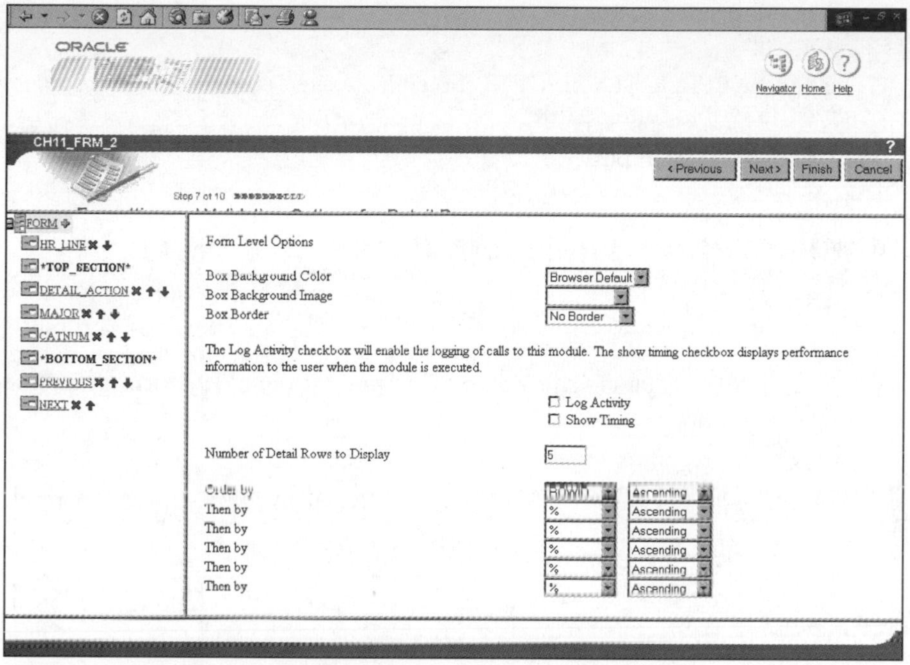

Figure 11-5: Formatting and Validation Options for Detail Row

Once again, this page looks like a standard formatting and validation options page. But on this page, you can see a new form option labeled Number of Detail Rows to display. In a master-detail form, Oracle9iAS Portal will show a single master row in the top part of the form, and a number of detail rows in the bottom part of the form. You can leave the default of 5 for the number of detail rows.

You can also see that there is a DETAIL_ACTIONS item in the Form Navigator, which is similar to the MASTER_ACTIONS item in the previous page. In addition, there is an item called HR_LIINE, which is simply a horizontal line separating the master portion of the form from the detail portion of the form. There are no other buttons in this part of the form, which you will understand when you see the form at work.

As with the master part of the form, you will want to clean up this section of the form a bit.

13. Select CATNUM for the first Order By combo box.

14. Select the CATNUM item in the Form Navigator.

15. Change the Description for the item to **Catalog Number**.

16. Click on the Next button in the Formatting and Validation Options for Detail Row page.

17. Select the PUBLIC.TEMPLATE_6 choice from the Template combo box, and give the form a suitable title.

18. Click on the Finish button.

Running your master-detail form

At this point, you are probably suspecting that there might be quite of bit of functionality in the completed form, so you might as well jump right in and run it.

1. Click on the Run link in the Manage Component page. The form that shows up looks like Figure 11-6.

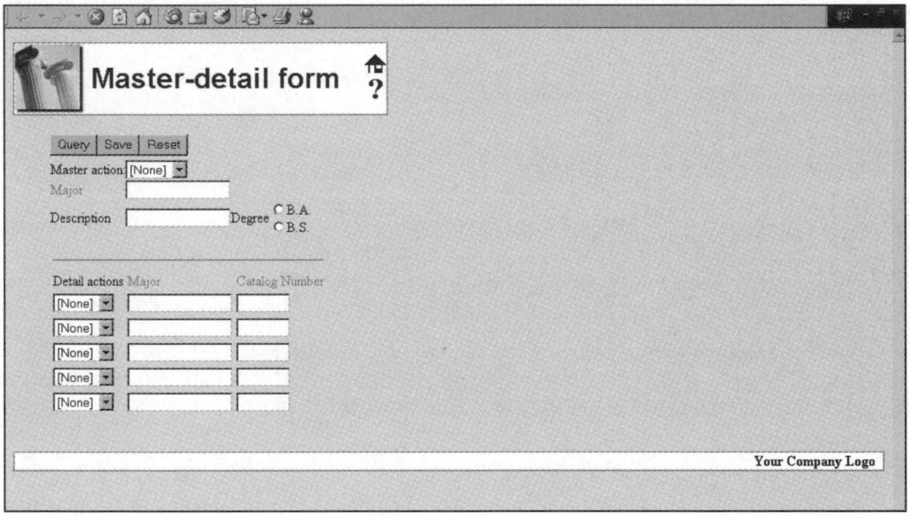

Figure 11-6: The first look at your master-detail form

New Feature In Oracle9*i*AS Portal, the single form shown in Figure 11-6 replaces the complex of forms that were created in WebDB.

You can see that the master part of the form is at the top, while the detail part of the form, with its repeating rows, is in the bottom of the form under a horizontal rule.

You can also see the previously mysterious Master and Detail action items. These items show up as combo boxes with four choices: [None], Insert, Update, and

Delete. As you can probably guess, these action items give you the ability to perform different actions on the master row and each individual detail row — pretty slick.

You can start exploring the functionality of your master-detail form by retrieving some master rows.

2. Click on the Query button. Once you have queried for master and detail rows, the master-detail form looks like Figure 11-7.

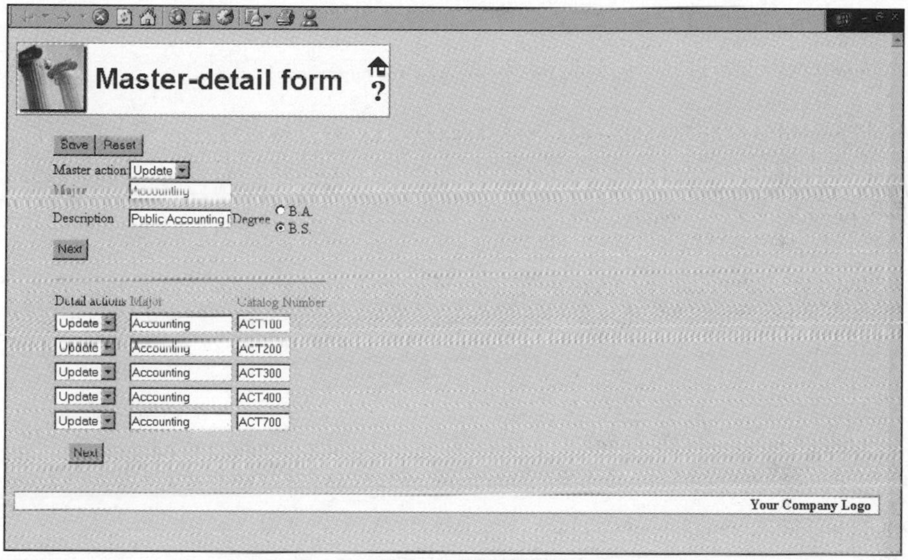

Figure 11-7: Data retrieved for the master-detail form

This form looks ready to use, but you can tell by simply thinking about its operations that it leaves something to be desired in its current form.

There are two apparent problems with the detail portion of the form. First of all, the Major data field is editable in the detail section of the form. Remember that this is the column value used to link the detail row to the master row, so you should not allow users to modify this value.

In addition, the value should be, in essence, the default for new rows, so you should turn off the update capability for this form. You should also make the default value for the MAJOR column in the detail table the same value as the one shown in the master table.

Note

This is one solution to these problems. This solution, however, has a problem of its own. What if a user is entering a new major? There will not be a value for Major column in the detail table, so the user will have to first insert a major and then retrieve it and add required courses. This seems a little kludgey, but, in this particular scenario, a user will be adding and deleting required courses, besides adding brand new majors. The inconvenience of taking these two steps is outweighed by the possibility that the user could accidentally or mistakenly change the Major for an existing required course.

In Version 3.0.8 of the product, this situation has been remedied. The developers have added some code that automatically makes the value for the master row the default value for the new detail row. By the time you read this book, Version 3.0.8 should be out.

Also, you can see that the user will be required to enter a catalog number. It would be much nicer if you could provide some type of lookup capability, so the user could identify the course based on the more understandable course name or the course title.

Finally, since this form operates in a slightly different way than the other forms you have seen, you should add some text to the help for the form.

3. Close the form to return to the Oracle9*i*AS Portal environment.

4. Click on the Edit link.

5. Select the CATNUM item in the Form Navigator. Change the Item type to Popup, the Description to **Course** and the LOV to COURSELOV.

6. Click on the Form Text tab, which is the third tab from the left.

7. Enter the following code for the Help Text:

```
To use this form, you start by clicking on the Query button,
which will retrieve one or more Majors and their
corresponding required courses.
<blockquote>You can enter selection criteria to retrieve a
selection of rows into the fields for Master before you click
on the Query button.</blockquote>
Once you retrieve your rows, you can add, delete, or modify
the associated required courses in the lower part of the
form. The Detail Actions combo box gives you a choice of
these three actions.
<p>
When you have made your changes to the data in the form,
click on the Save button at the top of the form to save all
of your changes.
<p>
```

You can also use this form to insert a new Major and its required courses by clicking on the Reset button, entering the information for the Major, and clicking the Save button. After entering the Major, you can retrieve it and enter the required courses.

8. Click on the OK button to complete these revisions.

9. Click on the Run link in the Manage Components page.

10. Click on the Query button to retrieve the values for the Accounting major.

11. Click on the Next button at the bottom of the detail portion of the page to bring up the next set of required courses.

12. Go to the first blank line in the new details portion of the page. Enter Accounting for the Major.

13. Click on the Popup button to the right of the Course data entry field. Select the English I — ENG100 entry.

14. Change the Detail actions for the new row to Insert. The page will now look like Figure 11-8.

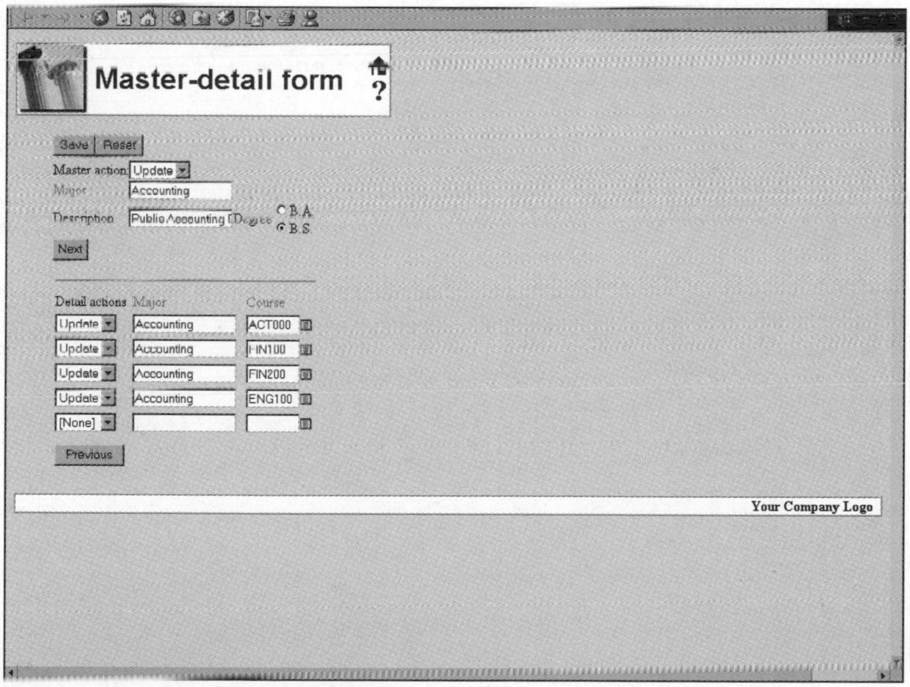

Figure 11-8: Inserting a new course

15. Click on the Save button.

You can see that the results of the Save action are shown at the top of the form. Since the default action for retrieved rows is Update, you can see that the form updated the master row and the three existing detail rows, and inserted the new row.

16. Click on the Query button again. Once the first set of requirements has been returned, click on the Next button in the detail portion of the form, which will bring up the page shown in Figure 11-9.

As shown in Figure 11-9, the new course requirement has been added. You should delete it before leaving the master-detail form.

17. Select Delete from the Detail actions combo box for the new course requirement of ENG100.

18. Click on the Save button.

19. Click on the Query button to review the effects of your actions.

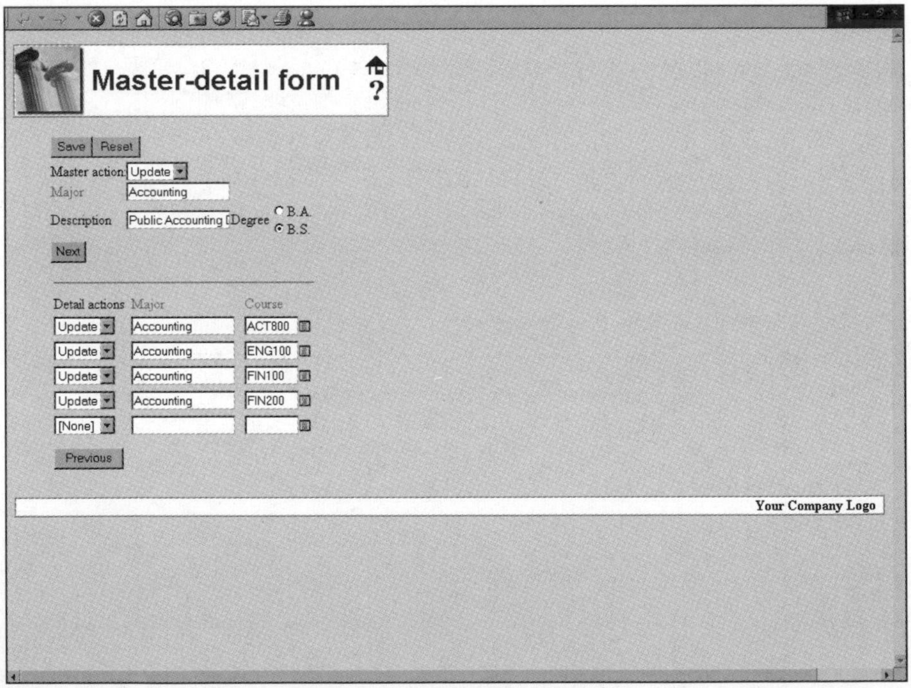

Figure 11-9: Data inserted with the master-detail form

As you can see, the new detail actions combo box allows you to perform multiple actions on the detail and master rows in a master-detail form. In fact, you could perform different actions on different detail rows in the same page.

The functionality of the master-detail form is quite rich, although, in its current form, presents some potential issues with regards to data integrity.

Summary

In this chapter, you completed examining some of the more complex features in Oracle9iAS Portal form components, including building forms based on stored procedures and creating master-detail form components through a single process.

This is far from the end of using forms in your Oracle9iAS Portal application system. You will use other forms as you learn about the rest of the functionality in Oracle9iAS Portal. And, as was stated at the beginning of the previous chapter, you will build many forms as you create your applications with Oracle9iAS Portal. However, in order to cover the breadth of the features delivered with Oracle9iAS Portal, you have to move on to building other components.

✦   ✦   ✦

Building Charts

Since the dawn of flow charts, people have found it easier to comprehend large amounts of information when it is presented in a graphical format. Computers, which are used for storing and processing larger amounts of data than a normal person can easily absorb, can create reports based on summaries of this data. However, the most convenient way to quickly spot trends and to understand the big picture is through a chart.

Oracle9iAS Portal charts, like all other Oracle9iAS Portal components, have their strengths and weaknesses. Although Oracle9iAS Portal charts may not offer the broadest range of options and flexibility, they are certainly quick and easy to build. And, like all other Oracle9iAS Portal components, they offer a significant amount of user interaction and they are available to anyone who has access to a browser.

New Feature Generally, creating charts with Oracle9iAS Portal follows the same process as creating charts with WebDB.

In This Chapter

Building Charts with the Query Wizard

Building Charts Based on SQL Statements

Adding a Chart as a Portlet

Creating Charts with the Query Wizard

A chart is essentially a type of report. Both the chart and the report have a single purpose: to present data to the users to read. So you will find that pages of the Chart Wizard closely resemble those of the Report Wizard. However, because a chart is a very particular type of report, the process of building it is a bit more concise than the process of creating a general report.

Beginning the chart-building process

You start the process of building a chart component in much the same way that you start the process of building other components.

1. Enter the Oracle9*i*AS Portal development environment as the NETUDEV developer.

Cross-Reference If you have not yet loaded the sample NETU database, refer to Chapter 2 for instructions on how to install the sample data and create the necessary users. If you are unfamiliar with how to use the Navigator, refer to Chapter 5.

2. Use the Navigator to go to the NETCOLLEGE application.

3. Click on the Chart link to the right of the Create New ... label at the top of the page.

The first page of the Charts Wizard looks just like the first page of the other wizards, as shown in Figure 12-1.

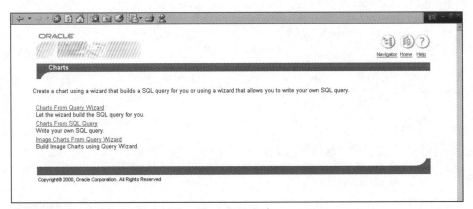

Figure 12-1: The first page of the Charts Wizard

You have two basic choices on this main page. You can build a chart using the Query Wizard or using your own SQL statement.

You should use the Query Wizard to build your first chart.

4. Select the Charts From Query Wizard link.

The actual Chart Wizard starts on the next page. The first page of the Wizard looks exactly like the first page of the other Wizards you have encountered so far. You have to indicate which application the chart belongs to and give the chart a unique name.

5. Enter **ch12_cht_1** as the Name of the component and **First Chart** as the Display Name.

6. Leave the NETCOLLEGE choice in the Application combo box.

7. Click the Next button on the Chart Name and Application page.

The next page of the Chart Wizard prompts you to identify the name of the table or view that you want to base the chart on. In the sample database included with this book, there is a table, DONATIONS, that is ideal for chart building. The DONATIONS table contains a record of donations made by all the alumni to the two basic charitable funds. You can sort the data in this table based on the identity of the alumni, the fund the donation was intended for, or any restrictions on the use of the funds. Because there are a lot of rows in the table, and because contribution levels are exactly the sort of thing that administrators at old Net University want to see quickly summarized, use the DONATIONS table as the main source table for all the charts you build in this chapter.

8. Enter the NETU.DONATIONS table in the Table or View field.

Note   You could also use the search box, which can be called with the little pop-up icon to the right of the Tables/Views data entry field, to find and select a table.

9. Click the Next button on the Table or View page.

Describing the chart

The next page of the Chart Wizard, shown in Figure 12-2, is the most important page in the wizard.

This page is where you specify the data that will be used to create the chart. In some ways, this is the cleanest high-level page in any of the wizards in Oracle9*i*AS Portal. By selecting and entering values in just a few fields, you tell Oracle9*i*AS Portal about the relationships that it will use to build the resulting chart.

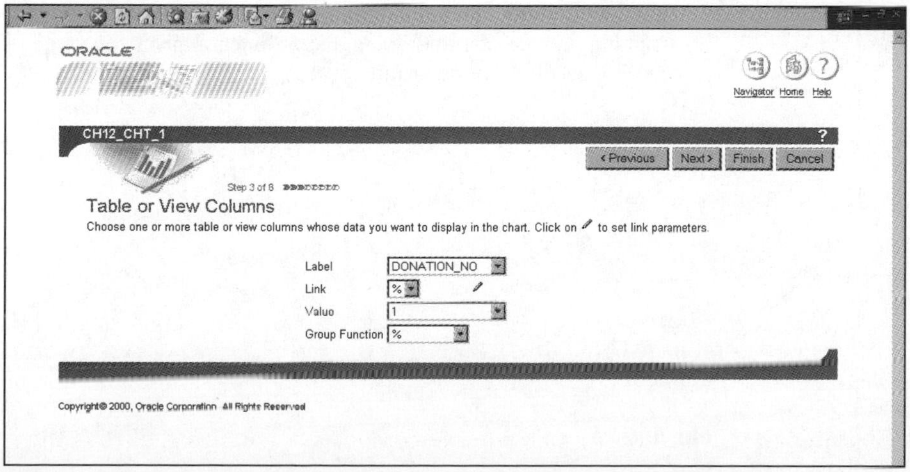

Figure 12-2: The Table or View Columns page in the Chart Wizard

Table 12-1 describes the four data entry elements listed on this page and the way to use them.

Table 12-1 Data Entry Elements for Formatting Chart Columns	
Element	*Use*
Label	The Label combo box gives you a choice of the columns in the table you have selected. The column you indicate in this combo box is used as the grouping value for the resultant chart component.
	The Group Function is applied to all the rows on the basis of the value of the Label column. For instance, if you choose FUND as the Label, the values in the chart are presented based on the different values for the FUND column. The column chosen as the label also, as the name implies, provides a value for the label in the chart.
Link	As with all Oracle9*i*AS Portal components, you can associate a Link object with the chart. The Link object must be previously defined, and the combo box displays all the Link objects in the application. Links are commonly used with chart components, because a chart typically gives a high-level view of the data and users frequently want to drill down for a more detailed report based on the different categories presented in the chart.
	There is a pencil icon to the right of the combo box for the Link that can be used to edit the data binding for this usage of the link.
Value	The Value field is where you specify the column that provides the values that are used as the basis for the chart. You can see that this is a combo box that brings up a list of the numeric columns in the selected table. The default value for the Value field is 1. Use this default value if you are planning on selecting a Group Function that is not dependent on the values in a table row — such as the Count function. In fact, assigning a Value of 1 and doing a Sum function gives the same results as doing a Count on the group.

Element	Use
Group Function	The Group Function combo box lists the functions you can use to summarize the data in each of the groups of the chart. There are seven aggregate functions available to you:
	AVG gives you the average for each group in the chart.
	COUNT gives you a count of the number of rows for each group in the chart.
	MAX gives you the maximum value for any single row for each group in the chart.
	MIN gives you the minimum value for any single row for each group in the chart.
	STDDEV gives you the standard deviation for each group in the chart.
	SUM, the most commonly used group function, gives you a sum of the values for the column listed as the Value column for each group in the chart.
	VARIANCE is mainly used for computing standard deviations. There is more documentation on this function in the standard Oracle documentation, but if you don't know what a standard deviation is, you probably will never use this function.
	The default value for the Group Function combo box is the percent sign (%) wildcard. If you leave the wildcard selected, there is no group function applied to the groupings in the chart. You may want to use this function if the chart data is already in the summarized format you want, but you want to present it in a graphical manner.

Your first chart component is pretty straightforward. You simply want to see the total amount of donations for each of the two alumni funds.

10. Select FUND in the Label combo box.

11. Select the AMOUNT column from the Value combo box.

12. Select SUM as the Group Function.

13. Click the Next button on the Table or View Columns page.

The next page of the Chart Wizard enables you to specify selection criteria columns for your chart. Although you can only use two columns in your chart — one for the grouping and one for the value — you can include any number of columns as part of the selection criteria used to shape the data for the chart. You don't need any selection criteria for this simple chart.

14. Click the Next button on the Column Conditions page.

Display options

The next page of the Chart Wizard, as shown in Figure 12-3, is similar to the page you can use to indicate display options for reports and other Oracle9*i*AS Portal components.

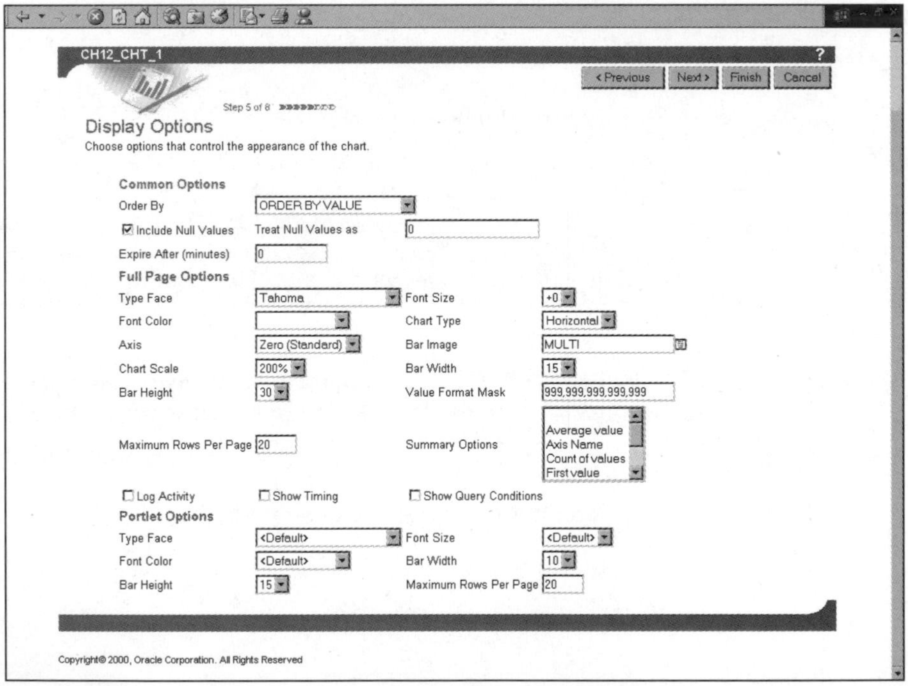

Figure 12-3: The Display Options page in the Chart Wizard

Many of the selections available to you are exactly the same as the selections that were described when reports were first discussed in Chapter 8. The Maximum Rows, Log Activity, Show Timing, and Show Query Conditions elements in the Run Options section of the page perform the same functions as they do for a report. The Type Face, Font Size, and Font Color elements in the Full Page Options section of the page also perform the same functions as their counterparts in the report. For more information on any of these options, refer to Chapter 8.

You can also see that you have the ability to specify how long a copy of this chart should be cached with the Expire by field. Using caching for a chart is the same as using caching for reports or other Oracle9iAS Portal components.

Cross-Reference   For a detailed explanation of the use of caching in Oracle9iAS Portal, refer to Chapter 6.

There are three types of display options shown on this page — Common Options, which apply to both charts deployed as full pages and portlets; Full Page Options, which only apply when a chart is being displayed as a full page chart; and Portlet Options, which only apply when a chart is being displayed as a portlet. All of the Portlet Options are the same as their counterparts in the Full Display Options area of the page, so they will not be described separately.

Table 12-2 describes the options unique to the chart object on the Display Options page.

Table 12-2	
Display Options Unique to Charts	
Common Options	**Use**
Order By	The Order By combo box gives you a limited number of choices as to how you want to order the data presented in your chart.
	Remember that you really only have two values in your chart: the label and the value based on each group in the chart. Because of this, your only choices for the Order By combo box are ORDER BY LABEL, ORDER BY LABEL DESC, ORDER BY VALUE, and ORDER BY VALUE DESC. The DESC stands for descending, while the other selections are in ascending order.

Continued

Table 12-2 *(continued)*	
Common Options	**Use**
NULLs	A NULL value indicates the absence of a value. You have the option of including NULL values in your chart or ignoring them altogether. To skip the rows with NULL values in the Value field, you can uncheck the Include Null Values checkbox, which, by default, is checked. You would want to take this course of action if you were performing calculations, such as deriving the average donation, where a NULL value might mean something other than a donation of $0.00. Therefore, you have to tell your chart component what value to use for NULLs that it finds in the data. Typically, this value is represented 0, which is the default. If you are displaying NULL values, you can specify what you want them displayed as in the text box labeled Treat Null Values As. Although the default for displaying NULLs is the digit 0, you can specify any character string in this box.
Full Page Options	**Use**
Chart type	There are only two types available to you for your charts: a horizontal bar chart (the default) or a vertical bar chart.
Axis	The Axis combo box enables you to specify where you want to place the main perpendicular axis of the chart. The default value of Zero (Standard) uses zero as the left axis in a horizontal chart and as the bottom axis in a vertical chart. The Average Value choice uses the average value as the center axis for the chart. Those bars in the chart with smaller values appear to the left of the axis in a horizontal chart and below the axis in a vertical chart. The First Value and Last Value choices use the first and last values on the page respectively as the axis, and the values for each bar are grouped around them as they are for the Average Value axis. The Minimum Value and Maximum Value choices cause a similar effect, although these axes are always to one side of the chart because they represent the extremes of the values presented in the chart. The value for the axis can be listed as one of the summary options at the bottom of the chart page. If you are using any axis other than the default zero-based axis, you should include the value for the axis.

Full Page Options	Use
Bar image	The Bar Image text box enables you to specify the basic image you use for the bars in your chart. There is a pop-up icon to the right of the text field that enables you to select the bar image from a list of the available bar styles. There are seven color choices and a multiple colors choice (MULTI, the default) listed in the pop-up list. If you choose any of the single color choices, your chart appears as a series of bars in that color. If you choose the Multiple colors option, your chart appears in a number of different colors.
Chart scale	The Chart Scale combo box enables you to choose a scale percentage for the chart. The percentage relates to the overall size of the page, but all you really need to know is the bigger the percentage, the larger the chart appears in relation to the page.
Bar Width	The Bar Width combo box enables you to select the size (in pixels) of each bar on the page of a vertical chart.
Bar Height	The Bar Height combo box enables you to select the size (in pixels) of each bar on the page of a horizontal chart.
Value Format Mask	The Value Format Mask enables you to specify the formatting for the Mask display of values for the bars in the chart.
Summary Options	The Summary Options list box contains a list of information that may be displayed at the bottom of each page of the chart. By selecting a summary option in this multiselect list box, you cause the summary information to be selected by default. If the chart is run directly by calling the RUN procedure, only those summary options you have selected are displayed. If a user accesses the chart through the parameter form, the summary options you choose are selected by default in the Summary Options list box presented on the parameter form.
	Most of the summary options are aggregate functions. These functions include Average Value, Count of Values, Maximum Value, and Sum of Values, which are user-friendly names for the same aggregate functions available in the Chart Builder Wizard. The other summary options—Axis Name, First Value, and Last Value—simply display some of the information available in the chart in the summary at the bottom of the page.
	If you select a summary option, the aggregate calculation is derived from all of the information shown on the page. For instance, if you select First Value, the summary displays the first value for the page, not for the overall chart.
	You can select more than one summary option (by using the standard keyboard technique, such as holding down the Control key and clicking on multiple values) or suppress the display of all summary information by selecting the blank row in the list box.

You can leave all the display options with their default values for your first chart. In some of the charts you will create later, you will want to shape the options.

15. Click the Next button on the Display Options page.

Finishing the chart

The rest of the pages in the Chart Wizard are very similar or exactly the same as the corresponding pages in the Report Wizard.

If you are unfamiliar with these pages and their implications, refer to Chapters 8 and 9 on reports, where they are explained in detail.

The Customization Entry Form Display Options page is very similar to the same page for a report. The only difference is in the center section of the page, where the Customization Entry Form options are slightly different.

As with a report component, the Formatting Options are displayed as a series of check boxes that allow you to specify which parameter options elements are exposed to the users in the parameter form for the report. The Axis option displays the value used for the axis at the bottom of the page. The Include NULLs, Maximum Rows/Page, and Type options perform the same functions as their counterparts on the Display Options and Table or View Columns pages. These parameters display the default values you select for them in the Chart Wizard, but the users can override your defaults if the parameters are displayed. The Summary parameter option, if selected, gives the users a list box with all of the summary options that were discussed in the previous section. The Type check box gives the users the option to change the type of chart at run time.

The button options are the same as the button options for report components, so you can just accept the defaults.

16. Click the Next button on the Customization Form Display Options page.

You have to assign the same template to your chart as you have to all the other components you have created.

17. Select the PUBLIC.TEMPLATE_6 choice in the Template combo box.

18. Enter **Total Revenue By Fund** as the Title of the Chart.

19. Enter **Total Revenue Chart Customization** as the title of the Customization Entry Form.

20. Click the Finish button on the Text Options page to complete the generation of the chart module.

Running your chart

You can see the results of your work by running your chart. Because you want to see how the parameters affect the latest generation of the chart, you should start the chart from the parameter form page, even though you are going to accept all the default values for the parameters.

1. Click the Customize link at the bottom of the Component Manager page.

Figure 12-4 shows the parameter page for a chart.

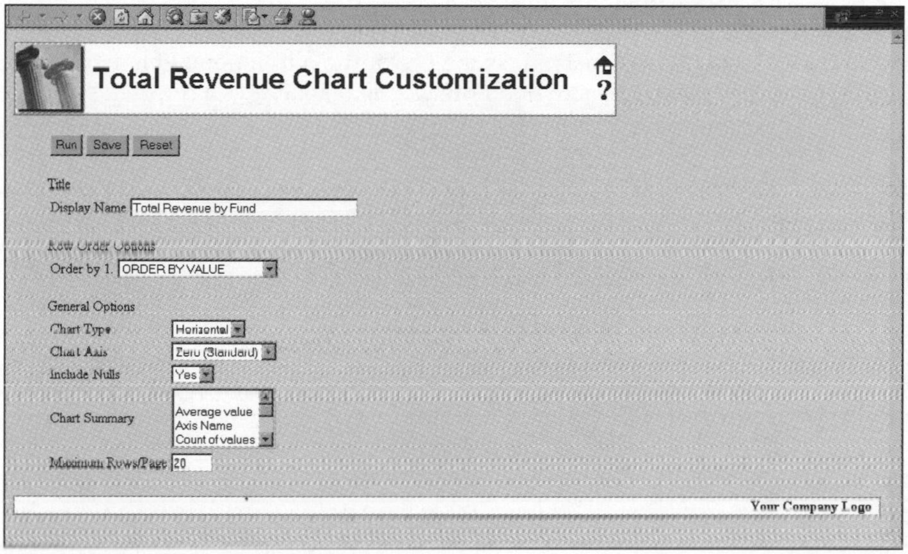

Figure 12-4: The parameter page for a chart

You can see the familiar buttons at the top of the page, and the familiar text field for the Maximum Rows/Page. The Order by combo box also looks familiar, but, as in the Chart Wizard, there are only four options available. The Chart Type, Chart Axis, and Include Nulls? combo boxes contain the same choices and defaults that you specified in the Chart Wizard.

As with a report, you could have included the Batch button on the page for a user, although it is not shown by default.

The Chart Summary is a list box with none of the options selected. In order to see their effect, you should select all of the options before running the report.

2. Select all of the Chart Summary options by selecting the first option (Average value) and, while holding down your multiselect key (on Windows, the Shift key), select the last option (Sum of Values).

3. Click the Run button.

Your first chart appears, as shown in Figure 12-5.

Not the most exciting chart, but it does get across some valuable information. You can see at a glance that the Annual Fund has received more revenue than the Capital Campaign, although not that much more in relative terms. You can also see that all of the summary information for the chart page is included at the bottom of the page. The information includes the average value for the two bars in the chart, the fact that the axis of the chart is at 0, the number of entries in the chart (Count), the first and last values displayed on the chart, the minimum and maximum values for the chart page, and the sum of all the values displayed on the chart page.

4. Move the cursor over one of the bars in the chart. You can see the label and value for the bar displayed.

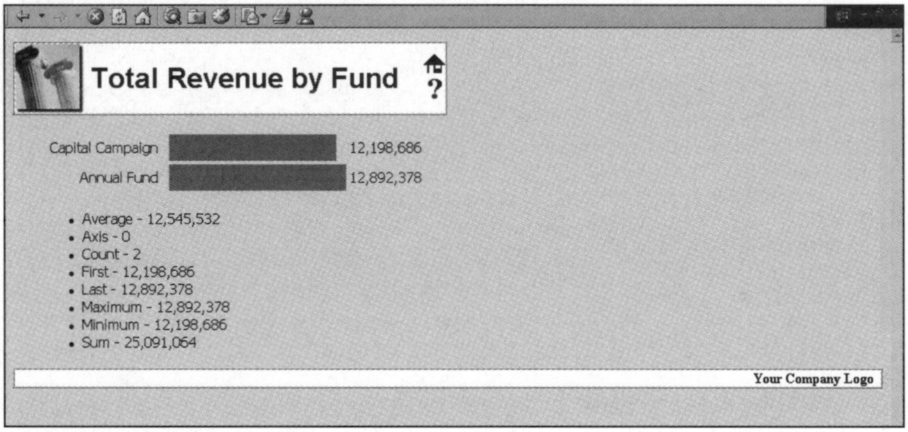

Figure 12-5: Your first chart

Of course, for this particular chart, the Axis, Count, First, Last, Maximum, and Minimum values are pretty meaningless, so the chart would probably be more to the point if you eliminated these lines from the chart page.

5. Return to the parameter page for the chart by clicking the Back button in your browser.

6. Click the Average Value choice in the Chart Summary list box. Notice that all the other choices are deselected when you select another choice.

7. Hold down the Ctrl key (in Windows) and click the Sum of Values choice in the Chart Summary list box.

8. Click the Run Chart button on the parameter page for the chart.

The new version of this chart page is much less cluttered with useless information. You have gotten pretty much all you can get out of this simple but useful chart. Your next basic chart will present even more information in a simple-to-understand format.

Creating a more complex chart

Now that you are familiar with the basics of creating a chart, you can create a chart that displays many more values. You can also limit the parameters that are available to users at run time to suit the needs of the chart.

1. Return to the Oracle9*i*AS Portal development environment by closing the browser window with the chart.

2. Go to the Navigator and click on the Chart link to the right of the Create New ... label.

3. Click on the Chart from Query Wizard link.

4. Enter **ch12_cht_2** for the Name and **Funds By Restrictions** for the Display Name.

5. Click the Next button on the Chart Name and Application page.

6. Enter **NETU.DONATIONS** for the table and click the Next button on the Table or View page.

The next page, the Table or View Columns page, is where the main attributes of the chart are specified, so you will do most of your work here.

7. Select RESTRICTION as the Label, AMOUNT as the Value, and SUM as the Group Function.

8. Click the Next button on the Table or View Columns page.

9. Click the Next button on the Column Conditions page.

10. Deselect the Include Null Values check box, since you will not want nulls to be included in this summary report.

11. Change the Value Format Mask to $999,999,999,999.99.

12. Select the Average value, Count of values, Maximum value, Minimum value, and Sum of values choices in the Summary Options list box to show these values in the chart.

13. Click the Next button on the Display Options page.

14. Deselect the Include Nulls choice in the center of the Customization Entry Form Display Options page.

As mentioned previously, to avoid confusion over the average contribution you don't want the null values to be included in the chart. This chart is being designed for use by your fund-raising staff, who are not that technically savvy. Also, you don't want to give them the ability to include null values in the chart, because they don't really understand the concept of nulls and averages. By removing the parameter from the parameter form, you can avoid the run-time errors and the confusion this might cause.

15. Click the Next button on the Customization Entry Form Display Options page.

16. Select the PUBLIC.TEMPLATE_6 template.

17. Change the Title of the Chart Parameters form to **Funds by Restrictions Chart Customization**.

18. Enter **This chart displays contributions made to all funds grouped by fund restriction.** as the Header Text.

19. Click the Finish button on the Text Options page to build the chart component.

This chart is a little bit more complex, because it displays many more values than your first chart.

20. Click the Customize link at the bottom of the Manage Component page.

You can see that this parameter page is just a little bit different from your previous parameter page. The Include Nulls check box is gone, and there are some choices selected in the Chart Summary list box. But the options for this chart are set to appropriate defaults, so you can simply run the chart.

21. Click the Run Chart button.

Figure 12-6 shows the generated chart.

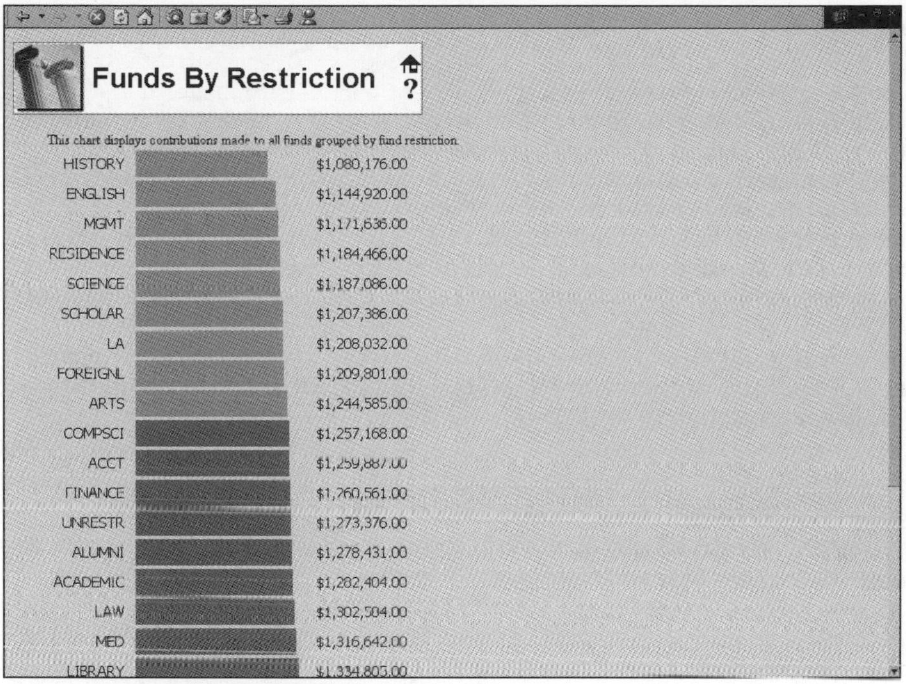

Figure 12-6: Your second chart

When you look at the chart a little more closely, you can see that the values in the RESTRICTION column are not as useful as they could be. These values are codes, and some of these codes are not really names. Because this chart might be used by people who are not intimately familiar with the meaning of these codes, it would be nice to show more descriptive names. There are more descriptive names available for the restriction codes, but they are in a separate table. In order to use them, you have to create your own SQL statement, as the Query Wizard only allows you to use a single table in your chart. You will learn how to do this in the next section.

Creating Charts Based on a SQL Statement

The Query Wizard that comes as part of the Chart Wizard makes it easy to quickly build basic charts. But, you may find yourself trying to access data that is outside the capabilities of the Query Wizard. You have already experienced one of those situations in the last chart you created to show the donations for a fund based on restrictions placed on the donations, but the only descriptive information available for a restriction was a cryptic code. Having a code for a restriction makes a lot of sense for a normal database structure, but it is not very helpful to end users reading charts based on a single table.

By using the ability to describe the data source for a chart with your own SQL statement, you can easily surmount this difficulty and still provide run-time flexibility to the users through the use of chart parameters.

Charts based on multiple tables

The first chart you base on a SQL statement is essentially an enhancement of the chart you made in the previous section.

1. Return to the Oracle9*i*AS Portal development environment by closing the browser window with the chart.

2. Go to the Navigator and click on the Chart link to the right of the Create New ... label.

3. Click on the Chart from SQL Query link.

4. Enter **ch12_cht_3** as the Name of the chart and **Funds By Restriction** as the Display Name.

5. Click the Next button on the Chart Name and Application page.

The next page of the Chart Builder Wizard, as shown in Figure 12-7, looks a little bit different from what you might have expected.

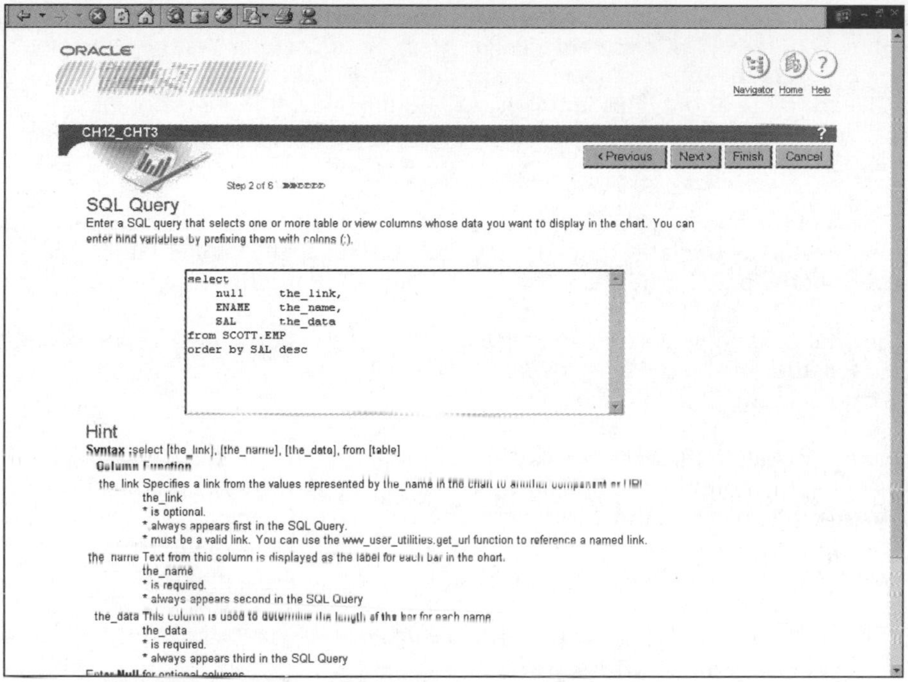

Figure 12-7: Entering a SQL statement as the basis for a chart

There is a text area there that enables you to specify your own SQL statement, but the sample SQL statement is not what you may have expected. There are only three columns in the statement, and each column has an alias listed for it.

To understand this statement, it is important to understand that Oracle9iAS Portal is more than just a way of passing data from a database to a browser. The SQL statements that you specify, either with the assistance of the Query Wizard or by entering your own statement, act as a conduit to get a set of data back from the database. Oracle9iAS Portal then uses this data to construct the HTML pages that you and your users see on the browser.

Any SQL statement you use as the basis for a chart must have three and only three columns in the SELECT statement. The first column, which has the alias of the_link, is the internal name for any link that is associated with the chart. You will learn more about links in Chapter 20 of this book. If there is no link for a chart, this column should be given the value of null, which means there is no value for the column.

The second column, which has the alias of the_name, represents the same column you selected as the label in the Query Wizard. This is the value that is used for the names of the bars in the chart and is also used to group the data in the chart.

The final column, which has the alias of the_data, is the same column you specified for the value in the Query Wizard. This column supplies the value that is used to calculate the bars in the resultant chart.

You can't change the basic way a chart is constructed by Oracle9iAS Portal by changing the number of columns. In fact, if you include more columns in the SQL statement, you get an error when you try to move to the next page in the wizard. You can supplement the way the data is sorted and grouped and the number of tables involved in the chart, as the SQL statement you enter shows.

6. Enter the following text into the text area on this page:

```
SELECT NULL the_link,
       RESTRICT_NAME the_name,
       SUM(AMOUNT) the_data
FROM DONATIONS, RESTRICT_CODES
WHERE DONATIONS.RESTRICTION = RESTRICT_CODES.RESTRICT_CODE
GROUP BY FUND, RESTRICT_NAME
```

As with the SQL statements in earlier chapters, this statement is included in the Chapter 12 Examples directory on the accompanying CD-ROM under the name ch12_sql1.txt.

With this SQL statement, you add a second table to the chart and use a descriptive name from that second table, RESTRICT_NAME, for the labels on the chart. You can also see that you have added a GROUP BY clause to the statement that groups the donations by fund and then by the name for a restriction. This grouping has the effect of creating two bars for each restriction category — one for each fund.

In order to see this at work, you should quickly finish the definition of the chart.

7. Click the Next button on the SQL Query page.

The next page is the Display Options page, which is very similar to the corresponding page for the Query Wizard.

You can see that there is no place for you to specify how you want to order the results, or how to specify NULL values. If you define your own SQL query, you will have to handle the ordering in the SQL statement. You will also have to include selection criteria to eliminate NULL values from the result set if you want this result.

8. Change the Value Format Mask to $999,999,999,999.99.

9. Click the Next button on the Display Options page.

10. Click the Next button on the Customization Entry Form Display Options page.

11. Select PUBLIC.TEMPLATE_6 in the Template combo box and give the chart and its parameter form an appropriate title and header. Click the Finish button to generate the chart component.

12. Click the Run link at the bottom of the Manage Component page.

Your new chart is shown in Figure 12-8.

You can immediately see that the names of the restrictions used as labels in this chart make the data in the chart more understandable to the common user.

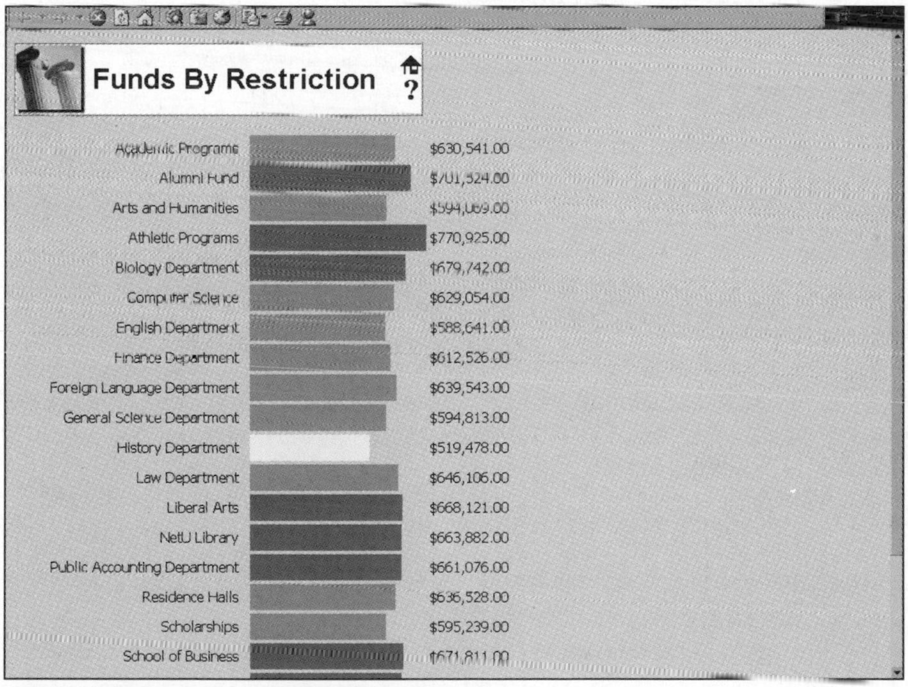

Funds By Restriction

Academic Programs	$630,541.00
Alumni Fund	$701,324.00
Arts and Humanities	$594,069.00
Athletic Programs	$770,925.00
Biology Department	$679,742.00
Computer Science	$629,054.00
English Department	$588,641.00
Finance Department	$612,526.00
Foreign Language Department	$639,543.00
General Science Department	$594,813.00
History Department	$519,478.00
Law Department	$646,106.00
Liberal Arts	$668,121.00
NetU Library	$663,882.00
Public Accounting Department	$661,076.00
Residence Halls	$636,528.00
Scholarships	$595,239.00
School of Business	$671,811.00

Figure 12-8: Your first chart from a SQL query

Trickery?

You may be wondering, "Why don't they just leave the report as it is, since each page of the report displays the fund totals for exactly one fund?" Because the maximum number of rows for a page and the actual number of fund restrictions are the same, you could just take the user parameter for the maximum number of rows off the parameter form.

This is a bad idea for two reasons. The first reason is that there is always a chance that the number of fund restrictions could change, which would require you to change this chart and other components that depend on there being a specific number of fund restrictions. Building a data dependency like that into an application is always an invitation for increased maintenance overhead.

The second reason is practical. Users cannot easily tell which page of the chart applies to which fund. You could add some header text that would explain this, or some PL/SQL code to somehow indicate the particular fund for the page, but it is probably easier just to give users an option as to which fund they want to see.

Because browsers only display a single page at a time, you may have to change your design philosophy a little bit to accommodate, and take advantage of, this fact. If users want to see a chart for each of the two funds, all they have to do is to run one chart, use the Back button to return to the parameter form, and then run the other chart. They can use the list of recently visited pages to quickly flip back and forth between the two charts.

But there is no way for users to know this, so you should go back and modify the basis of the chart.

However, there is a little problem with this chart. If you scroll to the bottom of the page, you can see that there are more bars for this chart.

13. Click the Next button at the bottom of the first chart page.

The second page of the chart looks suspiciously like the first page. The reason for this is that you specified that the donations were to be first grouped by fund and then by restriction. This means that all the bars on the first page of the chart represent contributions to the Annual Fund, and all the bars on the second page of the chart represent contributions to the Capital Campaign.

1. Return to the Oracle9*i*AS Portal development environment by closing the browser window that contains your chart.

2. Click on the Edit link at the bottom of the Manage Components page for the chart.

3. Change the text of the SQL query to read as follows:

```
SELECT NULL the_link,
RESTRICT_NAME the_name,
```

```
SUM(AMOUNT) the_data
FROM DONATIONS, RESTRICT_CODES
WHERE DONATIONS.RESTRICTION = RESTRICT_CODES.RESTRICT_CODE
AND FUND = :fund
GROUP BY FUND, RESTRICT_NAME
```

by adding the line AND FUND = :fund just before the GROUP BY clause.

4. Click the Customization Form Display Options tab, which is the center tab.

You can see that the BIND variable you indicated in your SQL statement by preceding it with a colon (:) is recognized by Oracle9*i*AS Portal as a parameter.

5. Click the OK button to generate the new chart.

6. Click the Customize link at the bottom of the Manage Component page.

7. Enter **Capital Campaign** into the Fund text field.

8. Click the Run Chart button.

This time, you can see that the chart only returns 20 bars — if you click on the Next button, no more rows appear. The value you entered in the Fund text field is listed at the bottom of the chart, so this chart is more easily understood by a non-technical user.

Tip
It would be a good idea to put some text into the chart header that pointed the users to the Fund identifier at the bottom of the chart, because they may not be able to see the identifier when the top of the chart is in the browser.

But there is still a problem with this iteration of the chart. Users would have to know the exact name of a particular fund in order to select it. Because there are only a limited number of funds, you should be able to provide a list of values for the parameter form and you should clean up the parameter form by eliminating the parameters that you wouldn't want a user to change.

9. Return to the Manage Component page in the Oracle9*i*AS Portal environment by closing the Report browser window.

10. Click on the Edit link at the bottom of the Manage Components page for the chart.

11. Go to the Display Options tab (the second from the left) and select the Average value, Minimum value and Maximum value from the Summary Options list box.

12. Go to the Customization Entry Form Display Options tab and enter **NETU.FUNDLOV** for the LOV, **Capital Campaign** for the Default, and **Radio group** as the LOV type.

On the CD-ROM If you haven't loaded the sample application, you have to explicitly import this LOV by importing the fundlov.sql file that came with the samples on the CD-ROM accompanying this book. For information on importing files, please refer to Appendix A.

By eliminating the Summary list box from the parameter form, you are ensuring that only those summaries that you selected are shown at the bottom of the chart.

13. Click the OK button.

14. Click the Customize link in the Manage Component page to see the new customization form.

You can see the effect that your parameter changes had on the new look of the parameter form in Figure 12-9. The form looks cleaner and the values for the fund parameter are clearly indicated.

```
┌─────────────────────────────────────────────────────────────────┐
│ ← → ◎ 🖹 🏠 │ 🔍 📑 🎃 │ 🗐 🖨 🖋 ⚙        │               🖨 – 🔧 │
├─────────────────────────────────────────────────────────────────┤
│  🏌️  Customize Chart  🔼                                          │
│                         ?                                         │
│                                                                   │
│  ┌─────────┐ ┌────┐ ┌─────┐                                       │
│  │Run Chart│ │Save│ │Reset│                                       │
│  └─────────┘ └────┘ └─────┘                                       │
│  Title                                                            │
│  Display Name │Funds By Restriction          │                    │
│                                                                   │
│  Query Options                                                    │
│         ○ Annual Fund                                             │
│  Fund   ◉ Capital Campaign                                        │
│                                                                   │
│  General Options                                                  │
│  Chart Type      │Horizontal ▼│                                   │
│  Chart Axis      │Zero (Standard) ▼│                              │
│                  ┌──────────────┐▲                                │
│  Chart Summary   │Average value │                                 │
│                  │Axis Name     │                                 │
│                  │Count of values│▼                               │
│  Maximum Rows/Page │20 │                                          │
│                                                                   │
│  ┌─────────────────────────────────────────────────────────────┐│
│  │                                          Your Company Logo   ││
│  └─────────────────────────────────────────────────────────────┘│
└─────────────────────────────────────────────────────────────────┘
```

Figure 12-9: The new look of the customization form for your first SQL-based chart

15. Select one of the values in the Fund radio button group and click the Run Chart button.

The new version of the chart is delivering just the right amount of information in an easy-to-comprehend manner, even for users who are not familiar with the structure of the underlying data. For your last chart, you will use a SQL statement to help you create values that are not in the underlying data.

Formatting values and limiting rows

Of course, the SQL language offers you some formatting options you can leverage when you are using a SQL query as the basis of your chart.

For this last chart, you will use formatting options, and shape the way users can interact with the parameters of the chart to deliver some nice capabilities to your chart.

1. Return to the Oracle9*i*AS Portal environment by closing the chart browser window.

2. Go to the Navigator and click on the Chart link to the right of the Create New ... label.

3. Click on the Chart from SQL Query link.

4. Give the chart the name of **ch12_cht_4** and **Contributions By Alumni** as the Display Name. Click the Next button on the Chart Name and Application page.

5. Enter the following code into the text area in the SQL Query page.

```
SELECT
        NULL the_link,
        LASTNAME || ', ' || FIRSTNAME the_name,
        SUM(AMOUNT) the_data
FROM DONATIONS, ALUMNI
WHERE DONATIONS.ID = ALUMNI.ID
GROUP BY LASTNAME, FIRSTNAME

ORDER BY 3 DESC
```

On the CD-ROM

This query is included in the examples for the book under the name chap12_sql2.txt.

This query assigns a concatenation of two columns and a character string to the column with the alias of the_name and an aggregate function to the column with an alias of the_data. Because of the aggregate function, you have to include a GROUP BY clause in the SQL statement listing all the columns that are not the subject of an aggregate function. The GROUP BY clause for this statement has to include the LASTNAME and FIRSTNAME columns.

The ORDER BY clause in this SQL statement indicates that you want the rows to return to a descending order from the top value in the third column in the statement, the value returned from the SUM function on the AMOUNT column.

6. Click the Next button on the SQL Query page.

7. Enter **100** in the Maximum Rows Per Page field. This value will be used as the default, which will create a chart with the top 100 contributors.

8. Enter **$999,999,999,999.99** as the Value Format Mask.

9. Select the Average value, Count of Values, First value, and Last value choices in the Summary Options list box.

10. Click the Next button on the Display Options page.

11. Deselect the Show Axis check box in the middle of the page.

12. Click the Next button on the Customization Display Options page.

13. Select the PUBLIC.TEMPLATE_6 choice in the Template combo box.

14. Add the following text as the Header Text for the Customization Entry Form:

```
This chart can be used to show you the highest contributors
to all alumni funds.
<P>
You should specify the number of contributors you want to see
in the chart in the text field labeled <b>Maximum rows</b>.
If you do not specify a number in this field, you will
receive a list of the top 100 contributors.
</P>
```

This simple text, complete with HTML formatting for highlights, helps users understand how to use the default capabilities of Oracle9*i*AS Portal charts to produce the type of information they are interested in seeing.

As long as you are adding text, you might as well give the chart and the parameter form titles.

15. Add an appropriate title for the Customization form.

16. Click the Finish button on the Text Options page to generate the chart.

You are getting to be an old pro at this, so you might as well jump in and see the chart you just created.

17. Click the Customize link on the Manage Component page.

18. Click the Run Chart button on the parameter form.

The chart that is returned to you should look like the one shown in Figure 12-10.

There they are, the top alumni contributors to old Net U. With the simple extensions available in standard SQL, you were able to create a fairly useful chart with Oracle9*i*AS Portal.

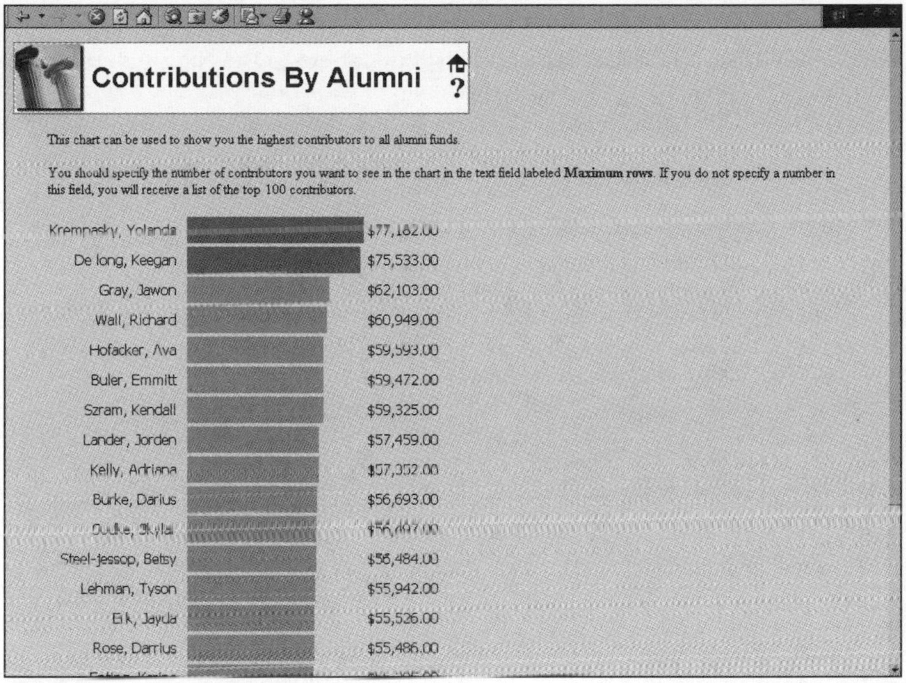

Contributions By Alumni

This chart can be used to show you the highest contributors to all alumni funds.

You should specify the number of contributors you want to see in the chart in the text field labeled **Maximum rows**. If you do not specify a number in this field, you will receive a list of the top 100 contributors.

Krempasky, Yolanda	$77,182.00
De long, Keegan	$75,533.00
Gray, Jawon	$62,103.00
Wall, Richard	$60,949.00
Hofacker, Ava	$59,593.00
Buler, Emmitt	$59,472.00
Szram, Kendall	$59,325.00
Lander, Jorden	$57,459.00
Kelly, Adriana	$57,352.00
Burke, Darius	$56,693.00
Duuke, Skylar	$56,497.00
Steel-Jessop, Betsy	$56,484.00
Lehman, Tyson	$55,942.00
Elk, Jayda	$55,526.00
Rose, Darrius	$55,486.00

Figure 12-10: Top contributors chart

Adding a Chart as a Portlet

Your last chart looks pretty good. You will no doubt want to add it to your portal page as a portlet.

1. Close the chart browser window to return to the Manage Component page.

2. Click on the Access tab and check the check box labeled Publish as Portlet.

3. Click on the OK button.

4. Return to the Navigator, click on the Pages tab and then the Top-Level Pages link.

5. Click on the Edit link for the Net University Home Page.

6. Click on the Add Portlets icon in the middle region.

7. Scroll down to the bottom of the list of portlets to the Net University Application area and click on the name of the chart you just published as a portlet. This action will bring up a preview of the portlet in the left frame, as shown in Figure 12-11.

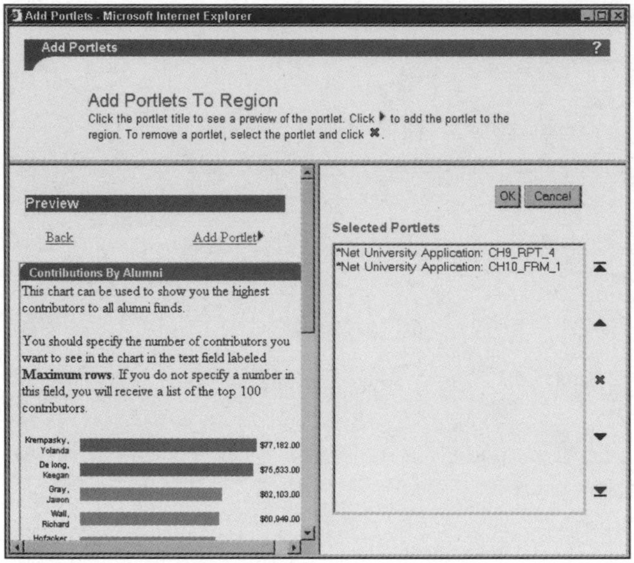

Figure 12-11: Your first look at your chart portlet

Hmm, this chart doesn't really look right. First of all, there are way too many lines in the chart by default. If you add this as a portlet, the real estate of your portal page will stretch down for several pages. You will be able to easily fix this problem by limiting the number of rows that show in the chart when the chart is shown as a portlet.

The other problem is that there seems to be a lot of text at the top of the chart. Although this seemed like useful documentation when you had a whole page to work with, it now takes up too much space. You can fix this problem.

8. Close the Add Portlets browser window.

9. Close the Customize Page page by clicking on the OK button.

10. Go to the Applications tab of the Navigator and click on the Edit link for the ch12_cht_4 chart.

11. Click on the Display Options tab, which is the second tab from the left.

12. Change the Maximum Rows Per Page value in the Portlet Display Options section to 5.

13. Click on the Chart and Customization Form Text tab, which is the second from the right.

14. Cut out the second paragraph of Header Text, including the paragraph tag.

Eliminating the second paragraph may not be the optimal approach, since it eliminates some of the instructional information you included, but keeping this text in a portlet would take up too much room.

15. Click on the OK button to return to the Manage Component page.

16. Click on the Navigator, go to the Pages tab, and click on the Edit link for the Net University Home Page.

17. Click on the Add Portlets button and select the chart you just modified in the left frame.

18. Click on the Add Portlet link and the OK button to add the portlet to your portal page.

19. Click on the Close button to close the Customize Page page, and then click on the name of the page in the Navigator to bring up the new version of the portal page, as shown in Figure 12-12.

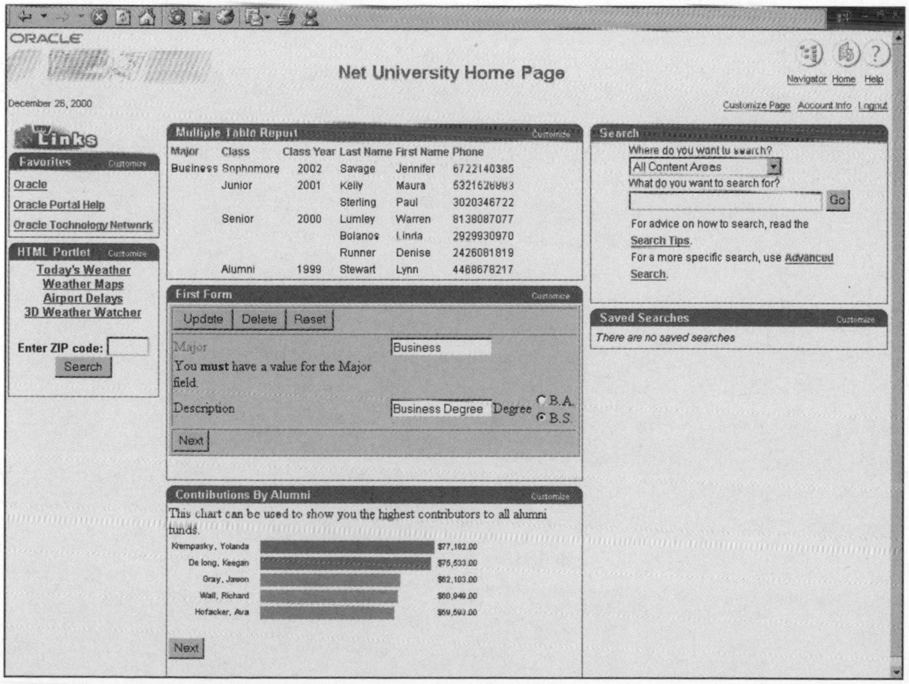

Figure 12-12: The latest version of the portal page

The chart has added a nice visual representation of your top alumni contributors to your portal page.

Summary

Charts have long been one of the most popular ways of displaying data, because they can transmit an overview of the general meaning of large amounts of data in a visual way. Although Oracle9*i*AS Portal's charts do not necessarily provide you with all the functionality of some mature graphics products, they are fairly easy to create and, like all Oracle9*i*AS Portal components, they run in a simple browser environment and can be automatically used as a portlet.

In the next chapter, you will learn about creating a specialized type of component, the calendar.

✦   ✦   ✦

Building Oracle9*i*AS Portal Calendars

✦ ✦ ✦ ✦

In This Chapter

Working with Oracle
Date Fields

Building Simple
Calendars

Implementing
Advanced Calendar
Formatting and Date
Manipulation

Linking Calendars to
other Portal
Components

✦ ✦ ✦ ✦

In previous chapters you worked with forms, reports, and charts to create structured content from data in your database. Portal's forms and reports enable you to build output formats that match the row- and column-style displays found in typical enterprise reports and Web pages. As you saw in Chapter 12, the Chart Wizard offers you a different view of your data by formatting the output according to numeric values stored within your database. The Calendar Wizard is designed to give you the same type of display freedom for your date fields that the Chart Wizard provides for your numeric fields.

Most databases are filled with date fields, and dates are an important component for many different types of records. For example, inventory systems make extensive use of date fields to value inventory items, control shipping, and determine product reorder points. Although you can display dates as standard text fields on reports and forms, there is an advantage to working with your date data in a different manner. You can often get a much clearer picture of your data when you visualize it in a new fashion — just as you did with a chart based on numeric data. The perfect way in which to visualize your date-based data is with a calendar. After all, if you are trying to visualize reorder points for an inventory, laying them out on a calendar can help you to get a clearer view of the big picture.

Portal's Calendar Wizard is all about formatting your database data using date fields and a calendar display format. In this chapter, you will work with date-based fields to create sophisticated calendar views.

Understanding Oracle Dates

Almost every database that you work with includes some date fields. For example, even the simplest employee table has a field to store the date of birth. After all, how can the company know when it is time for you to retire if they are not keeping track of your birthday?

All time-sensitive information must be stored in a date/time field somewhere within the data. You can store date and time values in string fields, but you lose access to certain automatic date-handling features of the database if you do so. The Oracle database offers a special DATE datatype, which has its own unique data storage properties and features. No matter which date format you use, Oracle always stores the data in a special internal format that includes the month, day, and year along with the hour, minute, and second. Despite the fact that the datatype is called DATE, the field can actually be used to store time data as well.

Date arithmetic

The Oracle database recognizes the date format for a given field and understands that the functions you use on the field should use date arithmetic. For example, if you create a numeric database column and add one to it, Oracle performs an arithmetic add operation on the data. If you create the same field as a date field and add one, then Oracle increments the field by a single day, as shown in Listing 13-1.

Listing 13-1: **Standard date arithmetic**

```
create table test_date(mydate date)
/
insert into test_date values ('01-sep-2000')
/
commit
/
update test_date set mydate = mydate + 1
/
select * from test_date
```

The final SELECT statement in this code returns a value of 02-sep-2000.

Standard mathematical functions can be applied to dates, and Oracle automatically handles the conversion for you. The base of any arithmetic operation on dates is days. When you add an integer increment to a date, Oracle assumes that the integer refers to the number of days, and when you subtract dates from each other, Oracle returns the result as an integer of a number of days. In addition to the basic mathematical operations, Oracle offers a number of date-specific mathematical functions, as shown in Table 13-1.

Table 13-1
Oracle Date Functions

Date Function	Description	Example
Add_months (*date,count*)	Adds a specified number of months to a given date value.	add_months(to_date ('01 sep 2000'),5) = '01-sep-2000'
Greatest (*date1, date2,...*)	Selects the most recent date from a list of dates in a single row.	greatest(to_date ('01-sep-2000'),to_date ('01-sep-2001')) = '01-sep-2001'
Max(*date_field*)	Selects the most recent date from a specified date field in a set of records.	select max(mydate) from mytable
Least(*date1, date2,...*)	Selects the oldest date from a list of dates in a single row.	least(to_date('01 sep-2000'),to_date ('01-sep-2001')) = '01-sep-2000'
Min(*date_field*)	Selects the oldest date from a specified date field in a set of records.	select min(mydate) from mytable
Last_day (*date*)	Selects the last day of the month for the month value of the specified date.	select last_day(to_date ('01-sep-2000')) = '03 sep 2000')
Months_between (*date2,date1*)	Calculates the difference, in months, between two dates. The result can be a floating point value or an integer depending on whether the comparison starts on the same day of the month.	months_between ('01-nov-2001', '01-sep-2000') = 14
Newtime (*date,current_ time_zone, new_time_zone*)	Calculates the specified date and time for the new_time_zone given the current_time_zone value.	select newtime (mydate,'EST','PST') = converts mydate from eastern standard time to pacific standard time.
Next_day (*date,'day'*)	Calculates the date of the next specified day following a given date.	Select next_day ('01-sep-2000',) = '08-sep-2000'. (The first Friday after the September 1, date).

Continued

Table 13-1 *(continued)*		
Date Function	**Description**	**Example**
Round(*date*) Round(*date,format*)	Rounds the date to the closest day based upon the time value entered. If the time associated with the date is before 12 noon, the day remains the same. If the time is after 12 noon, the date rounds up to the next day.	select round(mydate) from mytable
Trunc(*date*) Trunc(*date,format*)	Sets the time of a specified date field to 12 a.m., in effect, truncating the time value from the date.	select trunc(mydate) from mytable

Date formatting

The Oracle database provides an additional set of features for converting between character fields and date fields. Because Oracle stores dates internally in a specialized format, you cannot simply enter dates as strings and have them behave as dates. Portal automatically formats date fields for you in forms, reports, charts, and calendars, but you need to convert dates explicitly from strings when you handcraft SQL queries inside the Calendar Builder. Oracle supports two basic data-conversion routines for dates: TO_CHAR and TO_DATE. TO_CHAR converts date fields to strings and TO_DATE converts strings to date fields. Both functions accept a format parameter as follows:

```
to_char(date, format_string)
to_date(string, format_string)
```

The format string is an optional character string that defines a format to be used when the string or date is converted. Portal uses this same format string for all of the date format masks in the other wizards. If you have formatted date fields using masks in any of the other content wizards, then you already know to use the format string with TO_CHAR and TO_DATE. Table 13-2 provides a list of some of the format strings available for dates and times.

Table 13-2
Selected Date and Time Format Mask Elements

Format Element	Description
DD	Day displayed as a number
DY	Day displayed as a three-letter abbreviation (MON)
DAY	Day displayed as a complete name (MONDAY)
MM	Month displayed as a number (9)
MON	Month displayed as a three-letter abbreviation (SEP)
MONTH	Month displayed as a fully-spelled string (SEPTEMBER)
YY	Year displayed as a two-digit number (00)
YYYY	Year displayed as a four-digit number (2000)
RRYY	Year displayed as a four-digit number relative to the current century (99 = 1999, 01 = 2001)
YEA	Year displayed as a text string (NINETEEN-NINETY-NINE)
HH	Hour displayed in a two-digit format (08:)
HH24	Hour displayed in a 24-hour format (20:)
MI	Minutes display of time (:56)
SS	Seconds display of time (:43)
AM	Displays a.m. or p.m. along with string as indicated (00:00 AM)

Within a date string, Oracle disregards any character other than the standard date format characters in the formatting of the output. If you include additional characters, Oracle simply includes them in the display. This is a useful feature that enables you to include punctuation (; - / : > =) within a format string.

The TO_CHAR function is used to format dates as strings for display purposes and the TO_DATE function is used to translate strings into dates using a specified format. The TO_DATE function is primarily used for inputting dates into the database from a SQL statement. Portal automatically formats dates for you, so you do not normally need to use the TO_DATE function from within Portal. The TO_CHAR function handles the conversion of a date to a specific display format. You will find more uses for this function within Portal, especially when you are working with Dynamic Pages and calendars. The format string is easy to create and use, as shown in Listing 13-2.

Listing 13-2: Sample format query for TO_CHAR

```
select to_char(event_date, 'DAY - Month dd, yyyy')
as EventDate from events

EVENTDATE
----------------
SATURDAY   - November  21, 2000
MONDAY     - November  23, 2000
TUESDAY    - December  01, 2000
SATURDAY   - December  05, 2000
MONDAY     - December  07, 2000
THURSDAY   - December  10, 2000
SATURDAY   - December  12, 2000
FRIDAY     - November  20, 2000
```

You can test the preceding query on the EVENTS table using SQL*Plus (or using the trial copy of PL/SQL Developer on the CD-ROM).

Notice that Oracle replicates the spaces and "-" characters exactly as you entered them into the format mask. You can use this identical mask within Portal to format any date field. In fact, Portal actually executes a TO_CHAR function for dates wherever you see a format mask for a date field.

Note   Oracle automatically converts date expressions in WHERE clauses when the format is the standard DD-MON-YYYY format. If you use any other format in your query, you have to convert the string to a date using TO_DATE. (The default date for your installation might be different if your DBA has set the NLS_DATE parameter for your database instance.)

Building a Simple Calendar

The Calendar Wizard behaves much like any other Portal content creation wizard. It appears as the Calendar Link on the applications panel in the Oracle Portal Navigator.

1. Navigate to the NETCOLLEGE application and click the Calendar link to create a new calendar object as shown in Figure 13-1.

2. Type **netu_cal_event**, the name of your new calendar, in the Calendar Name field, and type **NetU Events Calendar**, in the Display Name field.

3. Set the application of the new calendar to NETCOLLEGE (which should be the default).

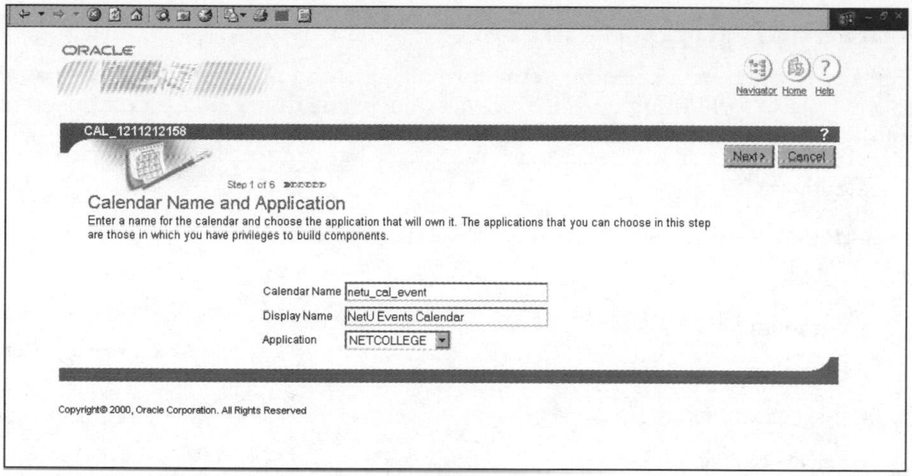

Figure 13-1: First page of the Calendar Wizard

The initial content panel of the Calendar Wizard is less structured than in some of the other builders, such as the form or report builder wizards. The Calendar Wizard works off a standard SQL query as shown in Figure 13-2.

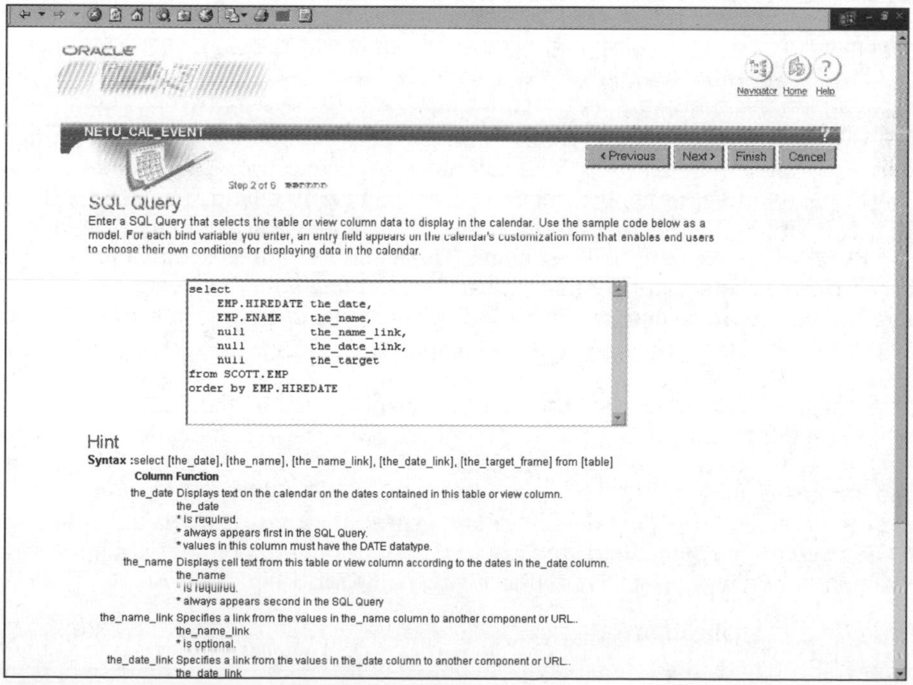

Figure 13-2: Building a calendar from a SQL query

Calendar query format

The key to building a calendar is the formatting of the SQL query, which is similar to the type of formatting used for a chart query. The query text is composed of the following nine basic sections:

✦ SELECT

✦ date

✦ name

✦ name link

✦ date link

✦ target frame

✦ FROM clause

✦ WHERE clause

✦ ORDER BY clause

The first part of the query is the SELECT keyword. In effect, you are entering a normal SQL SELECT statement, so the keyword SELECT is a requirement. In the end, the query that you enter here could just as well be entered into SQL*Plus as a simple SELECT statement. The difference is how Portal interprets the SELECT statement.

The date field is the first item in the body of the SQL statement. The date field is the data item that the Calendar Wizard uses to generate the calendar display format. You will have an opportunity to determine the actual display of the calendar later, but the data in this field determines how the data is deployed to the resulting calendar. The date can be either a valid database DATE column, a derived date using the TO_DATE function, or an arithmetic operation on a date field. The date is the value that appears in the day box on the calendar. You are going to build a calendar on the EVENTS table in the NETU schema. The EVENTS table contains information on the various events that take place at NetU, including sporting events, social events, and the academic calendar. The EVENT_DATE is the date field in the EVENTS table that you will use for the date field in the query.

The Calendar Wizard creates the calendar display and the date field determines where on the display that a particular record appears. The name is the data object that appears on the face of the calendar in the box supplied by the date, along with the date field. In the EVENTS table example, the CATEGORY field is a good choice for the name column. Portal enables any expression that resolves down to a string to be used as the name field. You are free to use concatenation characters and string functions to create a complex string value for the name field.

The name link is a Portal link to another Portal component that is attached to the name field. The calendar display is an active object as opposed to a static report. If you include a name link, then Portal attaches the link to the display of the name on the calendar. The end user is able to select the link on the face of the calendar; and

Portal navigates to that component at run time. While dates and names are required to build calendars, links are optional. If you do not want to specify a name link, you must pass the NULL value as a placeholder for the name link.

The date link is the second link from the calendar to a second Portal component. While the name link connects from the value in the calendar to an object, the date link connects from the date itself. While you might use the name link to show details for a particular entry on a calendar, you can use the date link to show additional details for all entries on a particular day. The date link is also optional. If you do not want to specify a date link, you must pass the NULL value as a placeholder. Typically, you use the date link to connect to a second component object that provides information that is specific to the particular date. For example, you might link a report that lists all of the pay dates from any single pay date on a calendar.

The target frame is the URL of a frame in which you want the optional link objects to be displayed. When you are viewing a calendar, it is often convenient to be able to see the big picture alongside the details. You can use a frame to display the details of either of the link fields next to the calendar. This can simplify the navigation of your calendar for the end user. Target frames are also optional, and you must pass a NULL placeholder if you choose not to use a frame.

The FROM clause is part of a standard SQL query. It is used to specify the table from which you are extracting the date and name fields. You can use a public synonym for your table name, or you can specify the table name preceded by the Oracle USERID of the owner of the table. The default behavior for the Calendar Wizard is to select data from a single table, but you are free to make use of multiple tables in the name and link fields to create a table join. If you join tables, you must specify the tables in the FROM clause.

The next section of the query is the WHERE clause, which is not shown by default in the Calendar Wizard. As with any SQL SELECT statement, you are free to add a condition to the query using a WHERE clause. In the EVENTS table example, you may want to build a calendar based on a specific category of events. You could add a WHERE clause to restrict the calendar to build a football schedule by adding the following text to the query:

```
where category = 'Mens Football'
```

Alternatively, you can make your calendar a more general-purpose object by using a BIND variable within the WHERE clause. Portal prompts for a value for the BIND variable when you run the parameterized version of the calendar. BIND variables are specified by using a colon (:) and a variable name to the right of the operator in the WHERE clause as follows:

```
where category = :enter_a_category
```

Although Portal does not display a WHERE clause in the default display, you can add one as necessary.

The last item in the query is the ORDER BY clause, which determines the sort order of the calendar. You should always sort the calendar by the date field in order to present the calendar in a logical format. However, you may want to add the name field to the ORDER BY clause if you are likely to have many entries for a given date.

You will find it easier to build calendars incrementally. Initially, you should work to get the date and name portions of the query set before you attempt to add links or frames.

4. Enter the following query to build a simple calendar on the EVENTS table, substituting the USERID of your sample account for NETU if you used a different account:

```
select event_date, category, null, null, null from
netu.events order by event_date
```

5. Click the Next arrow on the SQL Query page.

Formatting the display

The Display Options panel is the next step in the Calendar Wizard. As with the other content builders, the Display Options panel is divided into three sections as shown in Figure 13-3. The first section of the panel (Common Options) controls the options that apply for the calendar when shown as either a full page or a portlet. The middle section contains the Full Page Options for the calendar, and the bottom panel (Porlet Options) controls a similar set of options for deploying the calendar as a portlet.

The Common Options section is composed of three items:

✦ Show Monday-Friday only

✦ Expire After (Minutes)

✦ Link Icon

The Show Monday-Friday Only option is used to limit your calendar to a classic, business week calendar. If you select this option, Portal does not display entries for Saturday and Sunday and it eliminates any data in the calendar that falls on a Saturday or a Sunday from the calendar display. Since the data for a calendar object may not change frequently, you can also set data caching options using the Expire After (Minutes) field. The value that you enter into this field is an integer that corresponds to the number of minutes that you to want to cache. Once the calendar has been run for one user, Portal will use the cached version for each subsequent request until the number of minutes has passed. However, if the calendar object is called using different parameters or the calendar is regenerated, Oracle Portal will throw out the cached version and use the updated one. This option is particularly useful with the NetU calendar object — as events are not entered into the system on an ongoing basis.

Should you choose to link data in the calendar to another component, Portal can provide a graphical link as shown in the Link Icon field. This allows the calendar to conserve real estate by using a small GIF file for the URL link. (You'll be using this later on with this calendar).

The Full Page Options panel is composed of the following items:

✦ Maximum Months Per Page

✦ Page Width

✦ Show Query Conditions

✦ Log Activity

✦ Show Timing

✦ Font Sizes and Colors

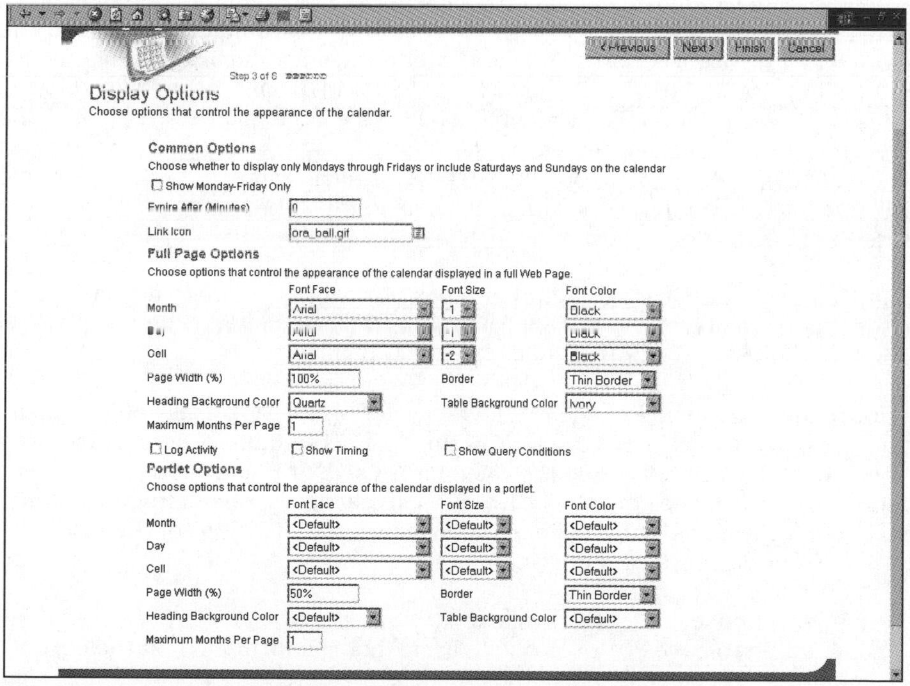

Figure 13-3: Customization Form Display Options page

Maximum Months Per Page is used to specify the maximum number of months you wish to display for your calendar on each HTML page of output.

New Feature   Previous releases of Portal used the Maximum Months option to control the *total* number of months that the calendar could display. This option has been changed to limit the number of months that will be displayed on a per page basis. The total number of months displayed in the calendar is determined by the range of dates in the SQL query that is used to construct the calendar.

Normally you will want to specify a value for the Maximum Months Per Page that will create the best visual display for your data. Portal stops outputting data once it hits the maximum number of months for any given page. Specifying a large value for this parameter can cause delays in the display of the data to the browser. If you have specified an ORDER BY clause, Portal completes the sort before it outputs the first page, and so large sorts on unindexed fields will cause performance delays at the browser client.

Calendars can eat up screen real estate if you have lots of data appearing on each date entry. Portal provides you with the Page Width parameter to help you squeeze more data into a smaller area. You can enter a smaller value for the Page Width to reduce the size of the calendar relative to the HTML page. The value you enter is an integer between 1 and 100, although Portal does enable you to enter values that are greater than 100. Entering a value larger than 100 causes Portal to default to its normal calendar size. (If you show the calendar within a frame, the width percentage will apply to the frame area in which the calendar displays and not the entire browser page.)

Enabling the Show Query Conditions check box causes Portal to display the parameters that were used to create the calendar as well as the time at which the calendar was created at the bottom of the calendar display.

Choose the Log Activity check box if you want Portal to log usage of the calendar into the performance monitor log. You should elect to monitor your calendar object if you want to track how often the calendar is used, or if your users have been reporting performance problems. If you are dynamically calculating lots of the information in the body of the calendar, then you will want to monitor the calendar to be sure it is performing fast enough.

Even if you choose not to log the calendar's activity, you can choose the Show Timing option to have Portal calculate basic timing information on the output of the calendar itself. Portal calculates the timing as the difference between the time that the component was called and the time the HTML is sent on to the browser.

The Look and Feel Options for the calendar object are similar to those that are provided in the form and report builder wizards, except that you have control over the typeface, font, and color of different logical sections of the calendar. The options that you set here control the look and feel of the calendar as opposed to the data in the calendar, and each setting specifies a font, a font size, or a color value. Table 13-3 lists the various options and their associated values.

Table 13-3 Look and Feel Display Options	
Option	**Description**
Month Font Face	Font name to be used to render the name of the month and the year at the top of each block of calendar cells.
Month Font Size	The Month Font Size is a relative setting used to determine the size of the font in which the month is displayed. The base font size is the font of the text that is displayed in each cell. The default value of +2 renders the month name in a font size that is two sizes larger than the text in the cells.
Month Font Color	The Font Color is the Portal color setting that is used to color the month name.
Day Font Face	Each calendar is displayed as a series of months followed by a table of the day names and day numbers for each of the days in the given month. The Day Font Face is the font name used to render the day of the week and the day number.
Day Font Size	Size of the font used to render the day of the week and day number measured in "points" The default value is a point size of one (one size larger than the text of the cells and one size smaller than the month and year.)
Day Font Color	Color of the font used to render the day of the week and the day number.
Cell Font Face	The cell of the calendar maps to the name value that you specified in the SQL query. The cell value contains the data elements that appear on the face of the calendar, and the Cell Font Face is the font that is used to render the text within each cell.
Cell Font Size	The Cell Font Size setting determines the font size relative to the default text font size that is set by your browser. Selecting a larger value causes the body of your calendar to use more real estate. You may choose to use a smaller setting if the text data on your calendar is overly dense.
Cell Font Color	The Cell Font Color sets the color of the text that is displayed inside each box on your calendar. Cell font colors are determined by the color settings in the Shared Component Library.
Page Width	The Page Width controls the size of the calendar relative to the web page on which it appears. Choosing 100% displays a full-size calendar. Smaller percentages display smaller sized calendars.

Continued

Option	Description
	Table 13-3 *(continued)*
Border	The border combo box allows you to set the thickness of the border that will be used to display each cell. You can set a "thick" border, a "thin" border, or you can choose to eliminate borders around each cell altogether.
Heading Background Color	The Heading Background Color sets the color that shows behind the days of the week on the calendar pages at the top of each calendar block. The color you select here displays on top of the template and background color that you set for the calendar itself.
Table Background Color	Sets the background color for the individual cells. As with the Heading Background Color, this color is used in addition to any background colors and images that you use.

When you display a calendar object within a portlet interface you may wish to select a different set of display options. The bottom portion of the panel allows you to select a second set of options for the portlet interface that match those listed in Table 13-3 (and shown in Figure 13-3).

   6. To continue, accept the default options for your calendar and click the Next arrow.

Specifying customization entry form display options for the calendar

The next panel in the Calendar Wizard should be very familiar to you as it appears in all of the other content wizards in some fashion or another. The Customization Entry Form Display Options panel enables you to choose the type and location of the run-time buttons for the customization form, as well as the parameters for the calendar, as shown in Figure 13-4.

The top portion of the form enables you to specify values for any parameters that you included as part of the query definition. You can specify values for BIND variables or connect BIND variables to lists-of-values just as with reports or forms. Because you have yet to specify any parameters for the netu_cal_events calendar, this top panel appears empty.

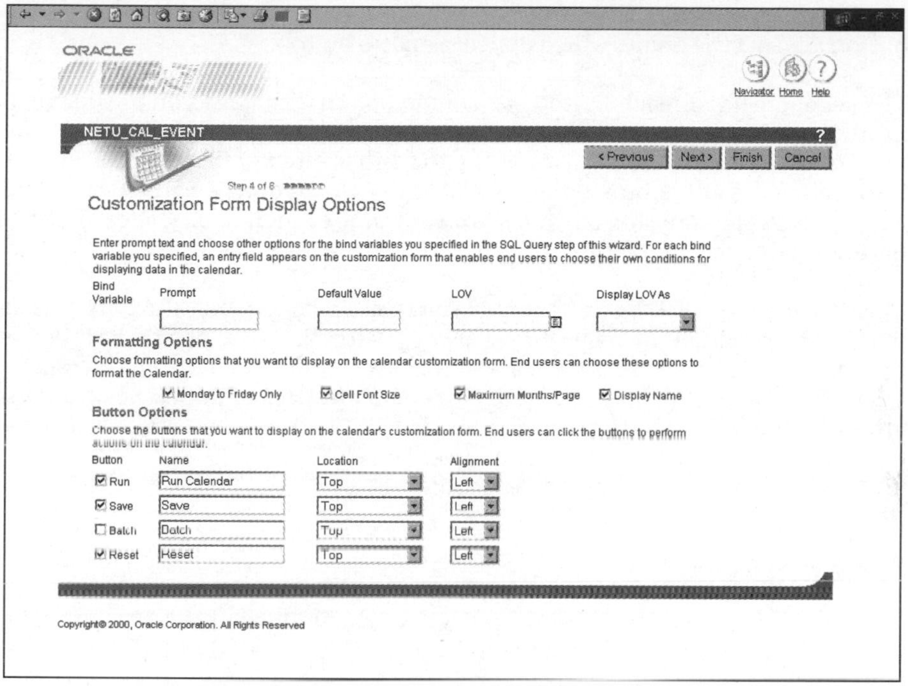

Figure 13-4: Customization Entry Form Display Options for the calendar object

The Calendar Wizard permits you to enable your end users to control three display options for the calendar: Monday-Friday Only, Cell Font Size, and Maximum Months/Page. The default setting for these three values enables the end user to control these settings from the customization form. (The Monday-Friday Only and the Cell Font Size, and the Maximum Months Per Page settings were displayed and discussed in the preceding section.) There are four button choices just like the choices for reports and calendars:

✦ **Run:** This button causes the procedure that produces the report to be run and the results of the procedure to be returned to the browser.

✦ **Save:** This button saves the options chosen in parameters. Once a user saves his or her choices, these choices appear as the defaults every subsequent time he or she runs the report.

✦ **Batch:** This button submits the report job to a batch queue. There is a single batch queue for each Portal server. Once a report is submitted in batch, the user can check the batch status page to see if the report has been executed and, if it has completed, to view the report.

✦ **Reset:** This button resets the choices in the parameter page to the default choices.

You can specify three attributes for each of these buttons. The first field for each button accepts the name, which appears on the button.

The second field for each button is a combo box that enables you to specify the location of the button. Each button can appear at the top of the customize page, the bottom of the customize page, or at the top and bottom of the customize page. Deselecting the check box to the right of any of the options disables that option altogether at run time. If a button is not shown, the functionality offered by that button is not available to the user of the report.

The final field for each button enables you to indicate whether the button is aligned to the left or right of the page. Portal always determines the position of the buttons by going through a simple process. Portal goes through the button list from the top to the bottom to form button groups, based on location, and then positions each group justified either to the left or to the right.

> **7.** To continue, click the Next arrow on the Button Options page.

Text options

The next panel in the Calendar Wizard is the Text Options panel. This panel enables you to add HTML and text to the body of your calendar as shown in Figure 13-5.

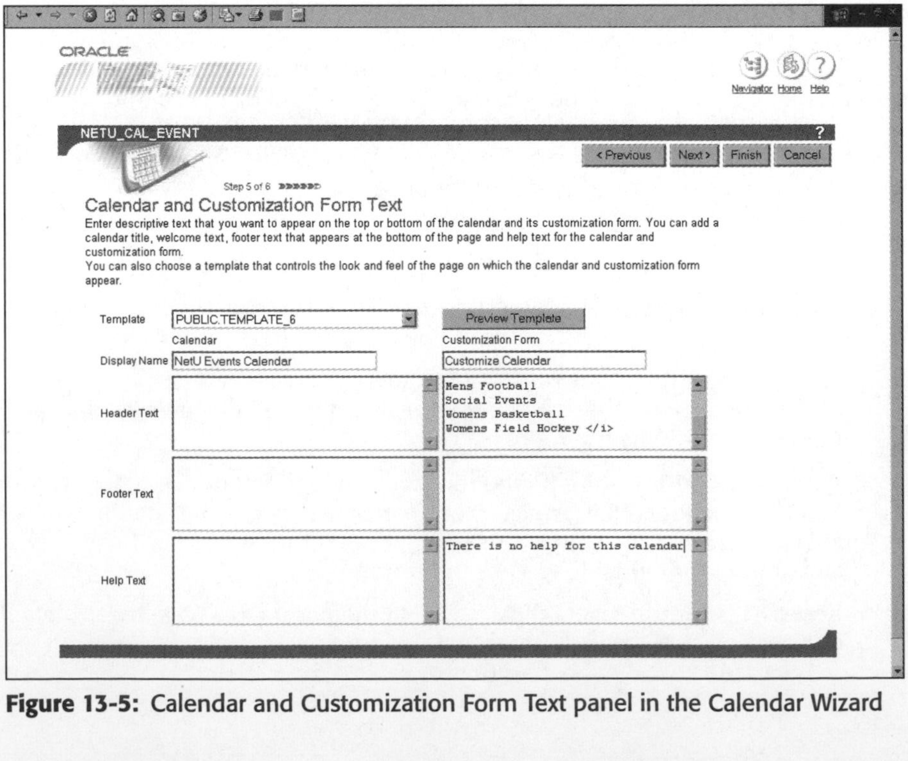

Figure 13-5: Calendar and Customization Form Text panel in the Calendar Wizard

This page is exactly like the text options page for the other components. The first field on this page enables you to specify a template, which you can use to give a standard look and feel to all of your Portal components.

Later in this book, you will learn how to create your own templates, but right now you can see the power of templates by selecting one of them for your report.

8. Click the drop-down arrow for the Template combo box and select PUBLIC.TEMPLATE_6.

9. Click the Preview Template button to see the basic template design.

When you choose to preview a template, Portal opens a little window in your browser to show you the template. If you return to the browser, select another template, and click the Preview button, the newly selected template appears in the template window. Figure 13-6 shows the template design for PUBLIC. TEMPLATE_6.

10. Close the Preview window.

The rest of the fields on the Add Text page help you shape your report by adding text to the calendar. You can add four types of text:

Title	Displayed at the top of the first page of the calendar and the customize and help pages. Portal will use the title that you entered on the first panel as the default title for the text options page — but you are free to override the title on this page.
Header Text	Displayed at the top of each calendar page or customize page, just below the title on the first page of the calendar.
Footer Text	Displayed at the bottom of every page of the calendar or the customize page.
Help Text	Displayed in a separate page for the calendar and customize pages.

Figure 13-6: Previewing a template

You can specify this text separately for either the report pages or the customize pages. Portal treats this text as straight HTML, so you can include HTML formatting tags in the text you enter for any of these areas.

11. Change the title of the customize form to the string **NetU Calendar Options**.

12. Enter the following block of text and HTML tags into the Header Text for the parameter entry column:

```
<b>Categories:</b>
<i>Academic Schedule
Arts
Holiday
Lectures
Mens Basketball
Mens Football
Social Events
Womens Basketball
Womens Field Hockey </i>
```

13. Enter **There is no help for this calendar** as the Help Text for the calendar.

14. Reselect the PUBLIC.TEMPLATE_6 template for the calendar.

15. Click the Next arrow on the text options page.

The next page of the Calendar Builder Wizard gives you the opportunity to add PL/SQL code that executes before or after the display of the page or the header for the page. You will learn more about using this panel in Chapter 21, which covers advanced PL/SQL programming with Portal. The Additional PL/SQL panels give you the opportunity to select additional information from the database and format the data during the run of your calendar. For now, you can just move past it.

16. Click the Finish button on the Additional PL/SQL code panel shown in Figure 13-7 to create your new calendar.

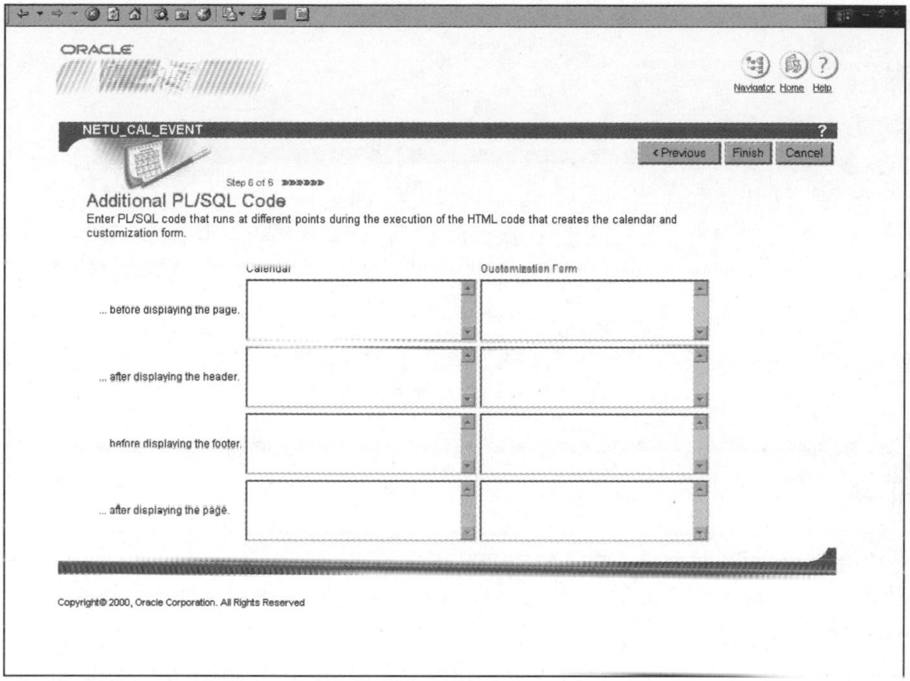

Figure 13-7: The Additional PL/SQL Code panel

You have created your first Portal calendar component. The next section helps you explore some of the functionality of this simple calendar.

Running the Calendar

Once you have successfully created the procedure for your calendar, Portal immediately does the same two things that it does when you create any form, report, chart, Dynamic Page, hierarchy, or calendar.

First, it changes the status of the calendar from EDIT to PRODUCTION. When a component has a status of PRODUCTION, the values of the parameters that control the generation of the procedure that run a component have not changed since the procedure was last generated. In other words, the component has not been modified since the procedure for the component was generated. If you leave a creation wizard before reaching the final page and clicking the Finish button, the component has a status of EDIT. The second thing that Portal does for you is to bring up a page that enables you to run and manage your calendar object, as shown in Figure 13-8.

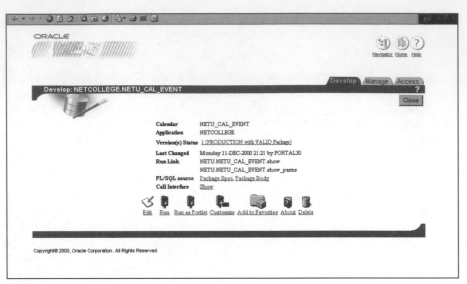

Figure 13-8: Managing a calendar component

There is some basic information about the component at the top of the panel and seven linked options in the bottom part of the panel. The information about the component includes the name of the component, all of the versions of the component, the time the component was last changed, and the existing ways to call the component. You should be familiar with this panel from the other major content wizards, as the Develop, Manage, and Access tabs (in the top-right corner) are the same for all of the major components.

Each time you edit and regenerate a component, Portal saves the previous version of the component and the values for its parameters in an archive version. The archived versions of a component are numbered, starting with 1 in increments of 1, and given the status of ARCHIVE.

The links at the bottom of the page should all be enabled. This is the standard situation for a component that has been successfully created. If you had left the Calendar Builder Wizard before you had generated the procedure for the report, the Run and Parameter links would not be enabled on this page.

1. Select the Run Link to execute your new calendar.

You created the calendar with the default option of displaying multiple months on a single HTML output page, the top of which is shown in Figure 13-9.

You can see the various components of the calendar in Figure 13-9. The title bar is in the same format as the title bar in any other Portal component. If you click the question mark icon in the header, Portal navigates to the help text that you defined on the text options panel. The color scheme and font for the title in the heading are determined by the template that you chose for the calendar.

The body of the page comprises a series of month-sized blocks with dates, days of the week, and data. At the top of each block is a title, which consists of the month name and the year. The interval size for the calendar object is months, and that is the smallest unit of output that the Calendar Wizard uses to format data. Even if the EVENTS table has only a single record in it, the calendar still shows a minimum of one month. It works much the same way that your wall calendar at home works. Even if you write in only one box of your wall calendar, the calendar itself still shows one whole month at a time.

Portal calculates the first month of the calendar by sorting the data on the date that you defined in the SQL query. If you chose to sort the calendar on the name field, then the calendar is created in the order of the name field. In this case, you almost always get a complete month for each record, because there has to be a calendar object for each sort group in the returned data. Normally you sort your data on the date field in order to maximize the value of the calendar display. If you need to sort the data according to the name field, then you might be better off using a report or form.

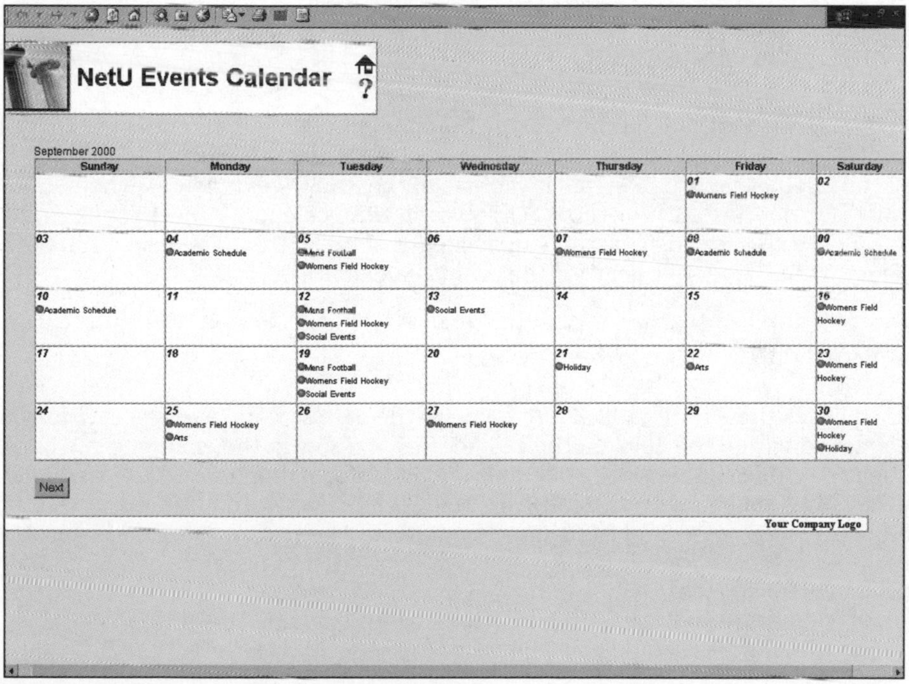

Figure 13-9: Top portion of the calendar page

One alternative to sorting the data on the name field is to link the calendar to another content object that displays the detail data in a different way. If you look at the calendar in Figure 13-9, you can see that the first entry is on September 1, 2000. The entry for that date is "Womens Field Hockey." There is no indication of who the Lady TabbyCats are playing, what time the game starts, or even where the game is being played. All of this information is stored in the EVENTS table, but it hasn't been made available to the calendar. If you scroll down through the calendar output, you find that the data gets even more difficult to dissect when there are multiple events on the same date. On September 4, 2000 there is an entry for the "Academic Schedule," but we have no idea what the details of this item are.

The solution to the problem is to add some new functionality to the calendar that displays additional information and provides some links from the calendar to other detail objects.

  2. Return to the Portal development environment by closing the calendar browser window.

Adding information to a calendar

The Calendar Wizard provides you with options for making your calendar more useful. You can either add information to the body of the calendar, or you can link from the calendar to other Portal objects.

  1. Use the Edit link on the Manage Component page to edit your calendar object.

Portal enables you to take full advantage of the PL/SQL extensions when you create your SQL queries. Although the SQL query for the calendar object requires that you use a very specific format, you can make use of PL/SQL extensions within the SQL query itself. The SQL query for the events calendar is as follows:

```
select event_date, category ,null,null,null
from netu.events order by event_date
```

Portal uses the event_date field to create the date stream, and the category field is displayed within the cells on the calendar as you saw in the example run. In and of itself the category field does not offer enough information about the particular event. You can augment the category field with more information by concatenating any other character field to the category string. The key to string concatenation is the double-bar character. Table 13-4 shows you a list of possible combinations for the EVENTS calendar.

Table 13-4
String Concatenation

Concatenation String	Description
category||':'||descr	Combines the *category* field with a colon character and the description of the event. (Oracle uses the double pipe string || to concatenate fields and single quot350es ' ' to denote string literals.)
to_char(eventid)||'-'|| category||'@'|| start time	The *eventid* field value is converted to a string followed by a hyphen, the category of the event, an at sign @, and the starting time of the event. (It is not necessary to convert the start time, because it is already a string.)
Upper(category)||'-'||descr	Converts the category field to all uppercase characters followed by a hyphen and the description.

You are free to use any combination of functions and concatenation characters as long as the result is a string. The other requirement that you must follow is to name the resulting string using the AS clause as shown in the following snippet of code:

```
category||'-'|| descr as name
```

Portal attempts to build a label for the string that you create and it greatly simplifies the process if you use the AS clause. It is possible that the string you create does not require the AS clause, but it is safer to get in the habit of specifying it whenever you use string concatenation. Portal enforces a limit of 32 characters on the name that it can derive for your concatenated column. If you do not provide a name, or the string is longer than 32 characters, you get a parsing error within the wizard.

2. Edit the calendar and change the SQL statement to the following value:

```
select event_date, upper(category)||'-'||descr as
name,null,null,null from netu.events order by event_date
```

3. Use the OK button to save the changes and then rerun the calendar.

The resulting calendar looks like the one shown in Figure 13-10.

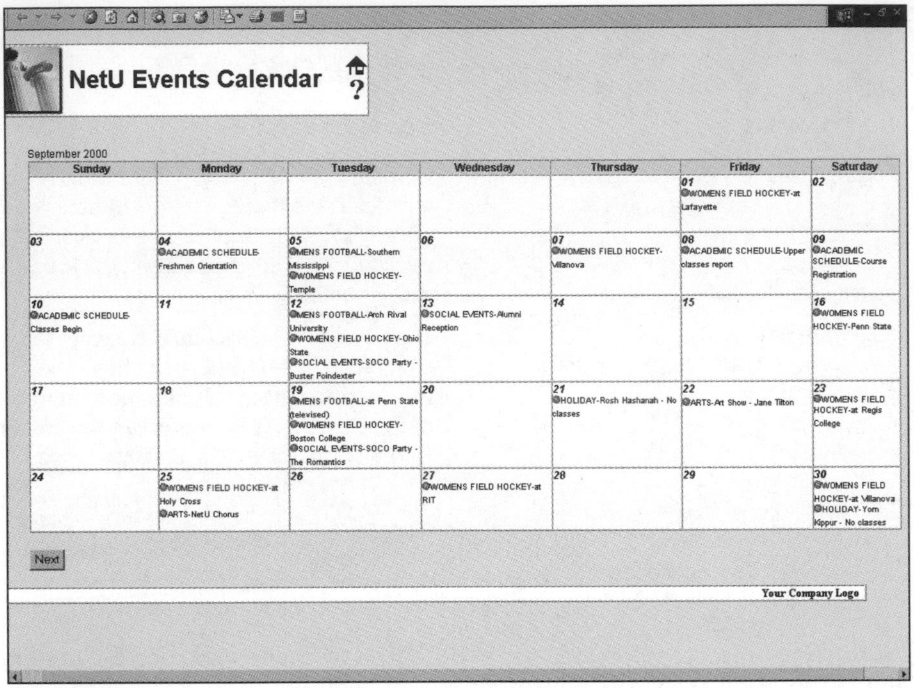

Figure 13-10: Calendar output using concatenated strings

The calendar now shows the category of the event followed by the description of the event. Each cell is easier to read, but the calendar itself is very unbalanced because some months have lots of events with lengthy descriptions, while other months appear narrow. Using records with uneven field lengths has this effect on the calendar. In cases where you need to provide lengthy descriptions that are uneven in length, you have several simple choices:

✦ Use the Display Options panel to force each month onto its own page. This has the effect of separating the displays for each month.

✦ Truncate the string to a consistent length that matches the shortest record length. You can use the MIN and LENGTH functions to determine the length of the shortest string.

A better alternative is to remove the details from the cells of the calendar and link to them by using a second component.

Linking from the calendar cells

Rather than adding extra information to the body of the calendar, you can use the link fields within the SQL query to connect from the calendar cells to any other Portal component. You will learn about Portal links in detail in Part III of this book, but you can work with them in the calendar without understanding all the ins and outs.

1. Import the following two reports: rpt_cal_event and rpt_cal_sched.

2. Copy the map images (MAP_*.GIF) to the /netu/ virtual directory path.

Cross-Reference

If you are unfamiliar with how to import Portal components, please see Appendix B. In previous releases of Oracle Portal, virtual directories were defined within the listener environment. With the release of Portal 3.x, the file system tasks are managed by the Apache listener. Chapter 2 provides details on creating virtual directories.

3. Return to the Portal development environment by closing the display browser window.

4. Click the Edit link in the Manage Component page for the calendar.

So far you have made use of the first two columns in the SQL statement, but the remaining columns have been left null. The third and fourth columns can be used to link the information within the cell to another component.

The third column is the name link, which creates a connection between the text of the display field and a URL that you specify as the name_link. You can add a second link, the date_link, which is connected to the day number and can link to a second component. Portal enables you to use any valid link for either of the link columns. Normally you use the name_link to connect to data that is relevant to the cell data, and you use the date_link to connect to data that is relevant to the date itself.

You can also specify a frame URL as the fifth column, in which case Portal displays the two links that you specified for the name and the date inside of a frame when the user uses either of the links. You need to be familiar with using Portal's frame links in order to use them with the calendar object. Frames are an advanced topic and are examined in greater detail in the third part of this book. For the time being, you can leave the frame link null, but keep in mind that it is an option for displaying your calendar.

The form of the link text that you use for the name_link and the date_link is a specialized string based upon the standard procedure calling syntax of Portal. Once again, you will have an easier time working with a link text if you have some experience with Portal's Link Wizard. However, you do not need to use the Link Wizard to create links within the Calendar Wizard. The key to creating link text is to remember that each Portal component is a self-contained PL/SQL procedure of its own. You can use the procedure name as the URL link from the calendar, and you can use the link to pass parameters.

Note

Most of the other Portal builders provide you with a structured field display panel that you can use to directly link from a field to an object. The calendar object does not provide this field option window, and your only recourse is to build the link directly in the SQL query. You are better off working with links and menus in detail before you attempt to make extensive use of links with the calendar object.

The link text itself is a stored procedure call that includes a parameter to be passed as shown in the following code snippet:

```
select event_date, category,
'NETU.rpt_cal_sched.show?p_arg_names=my_date&p_arg_values='||
event_date as name_link, null, null as frame from netu.events
order by event_date
```

The key piece of information is highlighted in bold text in the code snippet, and it represents a call to a Portal stored procedure. Every stored procedure call that you make using a manual link is composed of the following three parts:

✦ Package name

✦ Procedure parameter

✦ Parameter value

The package name is a concatenation of the Oracle Portal Application USERID that owns the Portal object, the name of the object, and the procedure name. In almost every case, the procedure name is a fixed value called ".show". (The SHOW procedure is what Portal uses to run a procedure that it creates, and you can find additional information about this all-important procedure in Chapter 20) The procedure name is followed by a question mark.

Note   Oracle provides a set of utilities within the procedure WWV_USER_UTILITIES for managing URLs with SQL code. We found these utilities to be somewhat unstable during the development phase, but they may be stable by the time that you are using this book. You may want to investigate using this alternative format on Oracle's Technology Network (OTN) Web site.

The second part of the procedure is a series of calls to the P_ARG_NAMES and P_ARG_VALUES array values. Once again, this will be clearer once you have completed the chapter on links, but for the time being all you need to understand is that this a parameter that is passed to the procedure. The last portion of the stored procedure call is the database value that you are passing as a parameter to the link.

In effect, you are creating a call to another Portal component and passing a value to that component. The goal of doing all of this work is to link the text of the calendar to another detail object. In the spirit of the NetU example, you are going to provide detailed information about individual calendar entries by using two additional components.

The real value of the calendar object is twofold. First, you can use the calendar as a tool for getting a visual image of the big picture. In this chapter's example, the NetU calendar shows what the academic year looks like in terms of events. Second, the calendar serves as a menu for navigating to other content, which is the real value of a calendar. If you think about the calendar that you hang on your refrigerator as an example, you can see that it serves much the same purpose. While you use the calendar to make notes of key events, you probably do not write all the details about each event on the calendar page itself. For example, you probably write down the directions and the location of a certain event on another piece of paper, which you take with you as a reference. The calendar is used to remind you of the event and the date; it is not necessarily the storage space for all the relevant information.

The Portal calendar works much the same way. Currently, the NetU calendar shows a minimal amount of information about individual events on the face of the calendar. You can use a second report or form to provide details about the event.

5. Edit the calendar object and change the SQL query to the following text:

```
select event_date, category,
'NETU.rpt_cal_sched.show?p_arg_names=my_date&p_arg_values='||
event_date as name_link, null, null as frame from netu.events
order by event_date
```

6. Save the changes by clicking the OK button.

When you rerun the calendar, the output should look similar to Figure 13-11.

Notice that the category text is now underlined within the cells. Portal has linked the text to another component, and the browser acknowledges that a link exists by underlining the text.

1. Click "Mens Football" link for Tuesday, September 5, 2000 to see the output as shown in Figure 13-12.

Caution   In order to complete the example in this section you will need to have the /netu/ virtual directory configured with the Apache server, as outlined in Chapter 2.

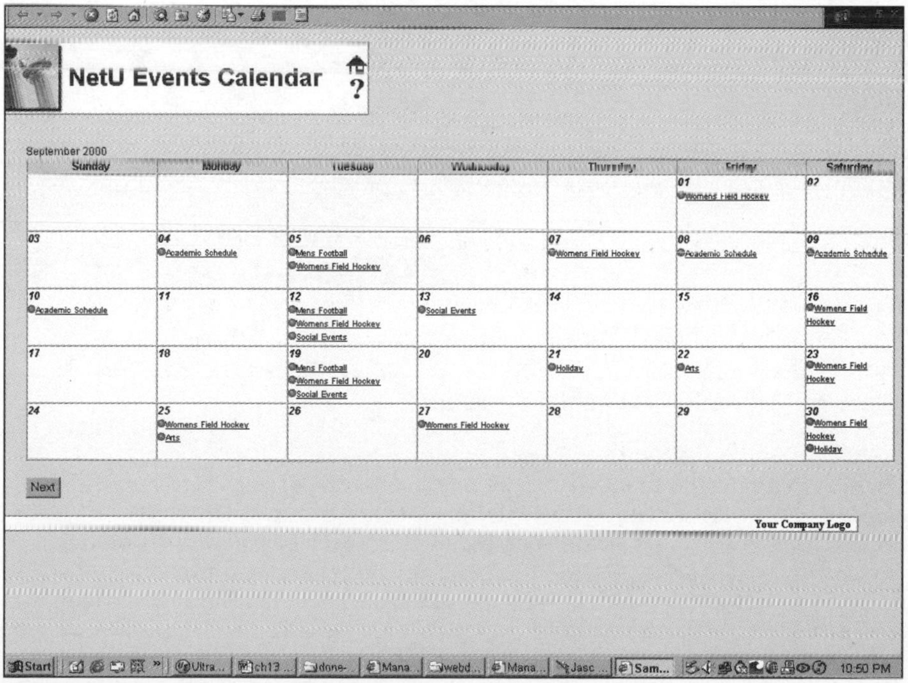

Figure 13-11: Calendar object with links

Figure 13-12: Link from the calendar to a report

The report object accepts a date parameter that is passed from the calendar, which in turn generates a report showing the details for all of the events for the selected date. You can see that this format gives you more room to display additional detailed information about the events. Portal does not limit you to just this one level of integration, however. Notice that the EVENTID field displays as a link as well.

2. Click the link for EVENTID 1 to see the data shown in Figure 13-13.

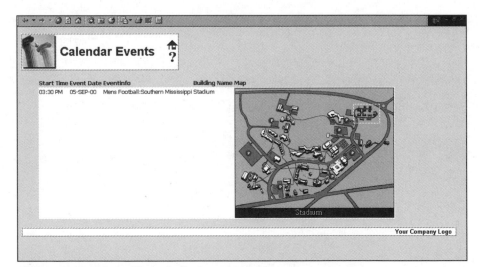

Figure 13-13: Nested links from the calendar

The EVENTID link connects from the day's schedule of events to a more detailed display of the selected event. The details include a map of the NetU campus with the location of the football stadium highlighted with a large white square.

Note   If you navigate around through the various events, you find that some events do not have detail records. This is because certain events are taking place off-campus and there is not a location record for the join operation.

This concept of nested linking is one of the keys of Portal. End users have become accustomed to making use of the drill-through concept when they use Web applications, and Portal has been designed to leverage this phenomenon. While you could load up the calendar with lots of detailed data, it is better to use the calendar as a navigation tool.

Portal provides two opportunities for linking content on the body of a calendar. If you look back at Figure 13-11, you notice that the name link is connected to the text inside the cell. If you had used the link with the date link instead of the name link, the day number within the cell would be connected to the linked report. You are actually permitted to use both links on the face of the calendar at the same time. Portal provides the date link as a link to other date-specific information and the name link as a link to content details. For example, you might create a report that details all the events that occur on a particular date in every month, such as payroll dates. You could connect this report to the date link and a second report detailing the current date to the name link. One link drills across the data and the other link drills into the data.

There is one additional piece of functionality you can add to this calendar that gives the users the ability to specify exactly what data they want in their calendar through the use of a parameter prompt.

Adding parameters

Calendar objects support the use of parameter values and BIND variables just like any other Portal object.

1. Return to the Portal development environment by closing the browser display window.

2. Click the Edit link on the Manage Component page for the calendar object and navigate to the SQL Query page.

3. Change the text of the SQL query to the following:

```
select event_date, category,
'NETU.rpt_cal_schedule.show?p_arg_names=my_date&p_arg_values=
'||event_date as name_link, null, null as frame from
netu.events where category like :my_category order by
event_date
```

The additional text of the query is shown in the code snippet in bold text. Calendars use BIND variables to supply parameters just like forms, reports, charts, and hierarchies. You can add a complete WHERE clause to the SQL query, which builds the calendar, and you can add parameters to the WHERE clause as shown in the previous code snippet. In the case of the calendar, you are adding a prompt that enables the user to select categories of events such as "Womens Basketball" or "Social Events."

4. Navigate to the Customization Entry Form Display Options tab.

Once you add a BIND variable to the calendar, Portal adds the entry to the list of parameters for the calendar as shown in Figure 13-14.

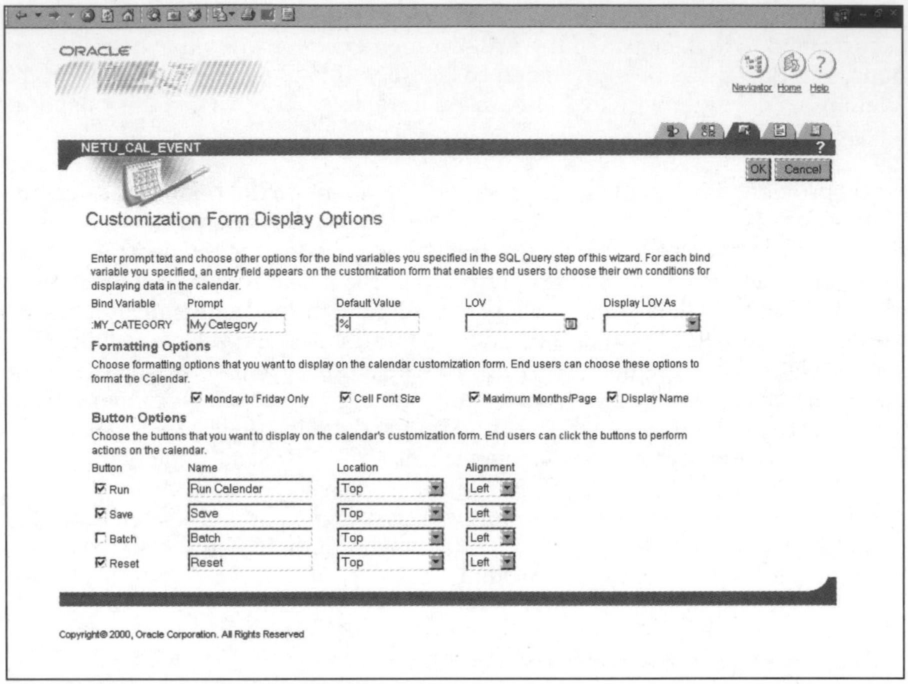

Figure 13-14: Calendar parameters

You can provide a default value for the parameter as shown in Figure 13-14, or you can also use a List-of-Values object just like with any of the other content wizards. You will learn more about using LOV objects in Chapter 16, and you can leave the LOV fields blank for the time being.

> **5.** Enter the percent character (%) in the Default Value field. This causes the calendar to select all of the events if the customization form is not used.

> **6.** Save the changes and then use the Customize link from the Manage Component page to run the calendar.

> **7.** Enter the value %Mens Football% as the My Category value and change the Monday-Friday Only value to No as shown in Figure 13-15.

Earlier in this chapter, you added some text to the customization form. You can see the results of your handiwork in Figure 13-15. At the top of the page is a list of categories that the user can reference when he or she makes a selection for the My Category field. As you saw in previous chapters, you can attach a drop-down list box of values to the My Category field, and you will learn how to build your own list-of-values in the fourth section of this book. However, adding the list to the body of the form as text is a viable alternative for the time being, especially if you want to add detailed descriptions of the choices on the customize page itself.

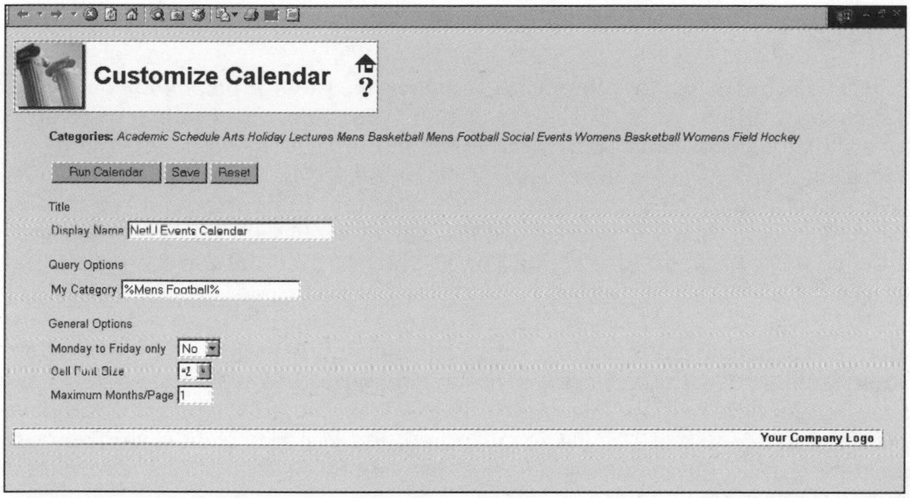

Figure 13-15: Customize page for calendar object

When you test the calendar using the Run Calendar button, you notice two interesting things about the calendar. First, the default behavior is to run the query for all days of the week unless you have changed the default on the customization form. Second, when you choose a link on the face of the calendar, you still see a list of all of the events for the chosen day, not just the events that match your My Category parameter. The parameter is only used by the calendar to select data, and the link within the cell uses the date rather than the category to formulate its query. This is something to keep in mind when you plan out the drill-downs for your application.

1. Test the parameter version of the calendar using an entry for the My Category parameter.

2. Return to the Portal development environment by clicking the Back button in your browser.

Managing calendar objects

The Manage Component interface for Calendar Objects works exactly the same as the form and report versions. Portal automatically tracks versions of calendars and you can export calendars, assign privileges, delete older versions, and monitor the use of calendars. Portal uses the same underlying panel for implementing the management interface. You can find more details about using advanced management techniques for components in Chapter 25.

Summary

Portal's Calendar Wizard offers you an innovative tool for displaying date-sensitive data in an intuitive format. Calendars can be used as an alternative menu structure for navigating from dates to detailed content. They can also be used to give end users a better view as to how their data is organized by date. The Calendar Wizard offers a set of options that match the other content builders, but it requires more detailed coding than you may be used to. Once you have become familiar with creating your own SQL queries within Portal, you will find that the calendar is easier to use.

Many of the advanced linking options you can include within calendars require some familiarity with the workings of the Link Wizard. You should stick to building simple calendars without links until you have completed Chapter 20. You have plenty of things to work on in the meantime, and you may want to concentrate on mastering date conversions and formatting with PL/SQL functions before moving on to links later in this book.

✦   ✦   ✦

Working with Hierarchies

In This Chapter

Understanding
Hierarchies

Building a Simple
Hierarchy

Navigating Through
a Hierarchy

Enhancing Your
Hierarchies

In the last three chapters, you learned how to create specific Oracle9*i*AS Portal components for specific tasks. A master-detail form is used to link together two tables with a specific type of relationship, a chart is used primarily to display summary information, and a calendar is used to create HTML pages that revolve around dates. Each of the wizards you used is very powerful, enabling you to create a complex function that was automatically generated for you. In addition, each of these complex objects required a certain type of data relationship to exist in the data used for the object.

The hierarchy is another one of these types of complex Oracle9*i*AS Portal objects. You can only use it for one specific type of data relationship. But the data relationship that a hierarchy is based on is quite common, and the Oracle9*i*AS Portal component that is created to deal with a hierarchy is quite cool.

Understanding Hierarchies

In the dictionary, a hierarchy is defined as "an order of persons or things ranked in grades." This definition also applies to the hierarchy object in Oracle9*i*AS Portal. The essence of a hierarchy is the concept that a group of data is ranked, with each rank linked in some fashion to a lower rank.

The other key feature of an Oracle9*i*AS Portal hierarchy component is the recursive nature of the relationships between the ranks. A recursive relationship is a relationship that is implemented between two instances of the same type of object. In practical terms, this means that an Oracle9*i*AS Portal hierarchy is based on a relationship between two different columns in the same table.

The classic example of a hierarchical relationship is a parts explosion, as shown in Figure 14-1. A parts explosion enables you to see a master component at the top of the hierarchy, the components that make up the master component on the next level, the components that make up those child components on the next level, and so forth.

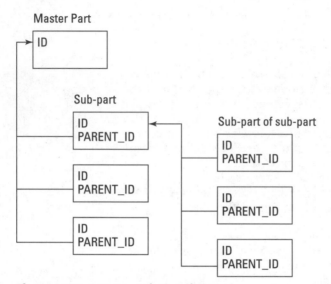

Figure 14-1: A parts explosion diagram

The parts explosion in Figure 14-1 is based on an ID column and a PARENT_ID column. If a part is part of a larger component, the PARENT_ID column contains a valid ID number for the parent part.

A similar situation exists in the infamous organizational chart. The relationship between the levels of the hierarchy is implemented through the use of an ID number for an employee and a MANAGER column that contains the ID value of an employee's manager. The hierarchy you build from the sample Net University data in this chapter is very similar to this classic organizational chart.

There is one more important attribute of an Oracle9*i*AS Portal hierarchy component. As you have already seen from building a master-detail form in Chapter 11, it is fairly easy to design and implement a master-detail relationship. This type of relationship is called a *one-to-many* relationship because one master row relates to one or more detail rows.

It is much more difficult to implement a *many-to-many relationship*, where each member of either side of the relationship can have multiple related partners. So difficult, in fact, that most systems try and break down a many-to-many relationship to a collection of one-to-many relationships. Oracle9iAS Portal hierarchies are implemented as a series of one-to-many relationships. This means that, in effect, an Oracle9iAS Portal hierarchy looks like a pyramid, with one piece (a master piece) of data at the top of the hierarchy and multiple levels of details below. Oracle9iAS Portal provides lots of really nice functionality within the pyramid of a hierarchy, which you will see throughout the rest of this chapter.

Building a Simple Hierarchy

The Oracle9iAS Portal wizard for building a hierarchy is similar in many ways to the wizard you used for building a chart object. Like a chart, a hierarchy component provides some very powerful functionality within a fairly specific environment. And, like the Chart Wizard, you do not need to enter very many parameters into the pages of the Hierarchy Wizard to create a complete Oracle9iAS Portal hierarchy object.

1. Log on to Oracle9iAS Portal as user NETDEV; use the Navigator to reach the NETCOLLEGE application.

2. Click on the Hierarchy link to the right of the Create New ... label at the top of the page.

The first page of the Hierarchy Wizard is exactly like the first page of the other user interface wizards. You are prompted for a name for the hierarchy and an application for the resulting object.

3. Give the hierarchy a name of **ch14_hie_1** and a Display Name of **Advisors and their students**.

4. Click the Next button on the Hierarchy Name and Application page.

The next page prompts you for the name of the table that contains the columns needed to implement the recursive, hierarchical relationship. The combo box for the table and view names contains the names of all the tables that the schema containing the application can access, but, of course, there are a limited number of tables that contain columns that can be used to build a hierarchy.

5. Enter the **NETU.UGRADS** table in the Table or View field and click the Next button on the Table or View page.

You have now reached the page where all the magic happens, as shown in Figure 14-2.

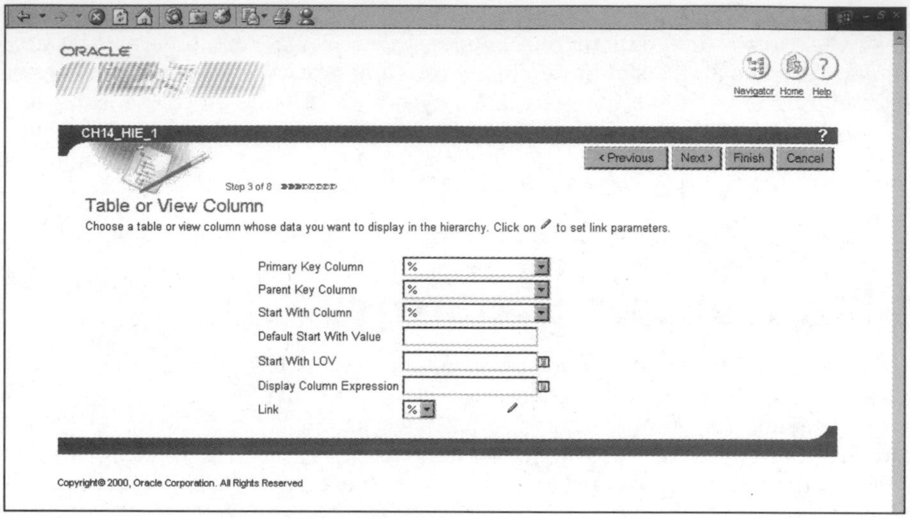

Figure 14-2: The Table or View Column page

With just a few entries, you will now define the relationships and data that form the content of the resulting hierarchy.

   6. Select the UGRADS.ID column as the Primary Key Column.

   7. Select UGRADS.ADVISOR_ID from the Parent Key Column combo box.

The two columns listed in the Primary Key Column and the Parent Key Column combo boxes define the relationship that the hierarchy is built on. The value in the Parent Key Column should match a value that is in the Primary Key Column of another row of the same table. In the case of the UGRADS table, each student may have an advisor, whose ID is the value in the ADVISOR_ID column of their row in the table.

The Start with Column combo box is used to indicate the column that begins building the hierarchy. Oracle9iAS Portal starts to build a hierarchy by looking in the ID column for a value indicated as the Start with Value. Then Oracle9iAS Portal looks in the Parent Key Column for a matching value, and finally looks into the Primary Key Column for another matching value for the child. As you will see shortly, Oracle9iAS Portal hierarchies can contain multiple levels of parents and children.

You need to explicitly define the value you want to begin the display of the hierarchy.

   8. Select UGRADS.ADVISOR_ID as the Start With Column.

   9. Enter **1001** as the Default Start With Value.

You could also specify a List-of-Values (LOV) that can be used to select the starting value.

You can also specify a link for the values in the hierarchy or, with the little pencil icon, edit the values for the link. For this, your first hierarchy in Oracle9*i*AS Portal, all you will need to do is indicate the data that you want displayed in the hierarchy.

10. Enter **LASTNAME** into the Display Column Expression field.

11. Click the Next button on the Table or View Columns page.

You do not need to have any conditions in your hierarchy, so you can skip the Column Conditions page.

12. Click the Next button on the Column Conditions page.

The next page is the Display Options page, shown in Figure 14-3. This page may look familiar from Chapter 13, with three sets of Options — Common Options, which apply to all pages built with this component; Full Page Options, which only apply to full pages built with this component, and Portlet Options, which only apply when the component is displayed as a portlet.

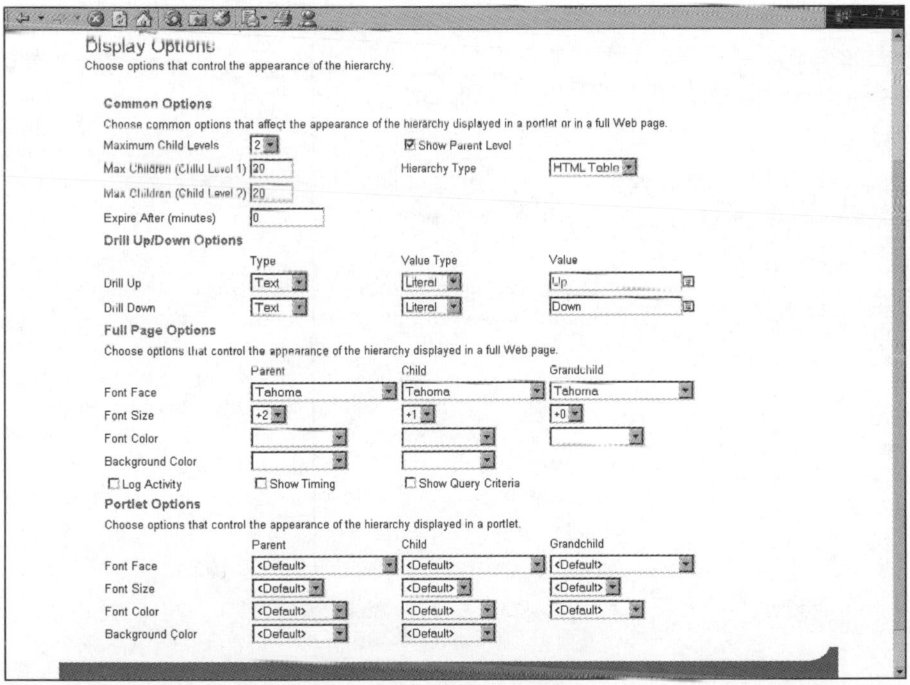

Figure 14-3: The Display Options page for a hierarchy

The only choices that you haven't encountered in other components, such as reports and charts, are the Common Options. Table 14-1 describes the Common Options available for hierarchies.

Table 14-1	
Display Options for an Oracle9*i*AS Portal Hierarchy	
Option	*Description*
Maximum Child Levels	The Maximum Child Levels combo box enables you to specify how many child levels in the hierarchy are displayed on a single page of the hierarchy. You can indicate that you want either one level, which will show a single child from the current level, or two, which will also include the grandchild level.
	Keep in mind that the maximum levels you specify in this combo box limits the number of levels displayed on a single page, not in the overall hierarchy. You will see this at work in the next section.
Show Parent Level	The Show Parent Level check box indicates whether you want to also show a parent level in the hierarchy. This level is shown above the current level, which gives the hierarchy the ability to display up to four levels — three total (one parent, the current, and the child) or four (an additional grandchild level).
Max Children (Child Level 1)	The Max Children field for Child Level 1 enables you to specify the maximum number of entries you want displayed for the current parent at the child level. Because the child level rows are displayed horizontally across the page, there may be times when you want to limit the number of child rows for formatting reasons. However, Oracle9*i*AS Portal gives the user no indication as to whether there are additional child rows for a particular parent, so you should include some type of explanation for the user if you intend to limit the number of child rows.
	The default value for this field is 100.
Max Children (Child Level 2)	The Max Children field for Child Level 2 enables you to specify the maximum number of entries you want displayed for each parent at the grandchild level. Because the grandchild level rows are displayed vertically below the child row that is their parent, there is less of a reason to limit the number of grandchild rows.
	The default value for this field is 100.

Option	Description
Hierarchy Type	You can specify a hierarchy as either an HTML table or as a Break Down report. In an HTML table, each level of the hierarchy is displayed as a horizontal row, with successive levels as horizontal rows underneath the parent, as shown in Figure 14-4. The Break Down option displays each successive level of the report with a different indentation, as shown in Figure 14-5.
Expire After (minutes)	This field allows you to set a expiry time for a cached version of the page. For more information on caching, refer to Chapter 6.

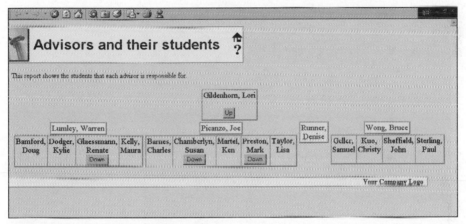

Figure 14-4: An HTML table hierarchy

You also have the option to specify how you want to display the drill down and drill up indicators on the hierarchy. You can use text, a button, or an image for these indicators, which you select in the Type combo. The Value Type combo box indicates whether these values come from a literal value or a column, and the Value allows you to indicate the actual column, value, or pathname to the image. These options are, of course, unique to hierarchies.

New Feature   The ability to define the drill down and up indicators is new in Oracle9*i*AS Portal.

The rest of the display options on this page have the same effect as they do in other components. You can specify the Font Face, Font Size, and Font Color for each of the three levels in the chart, as well as the Background Color for the Parent and Child levels of the chart.

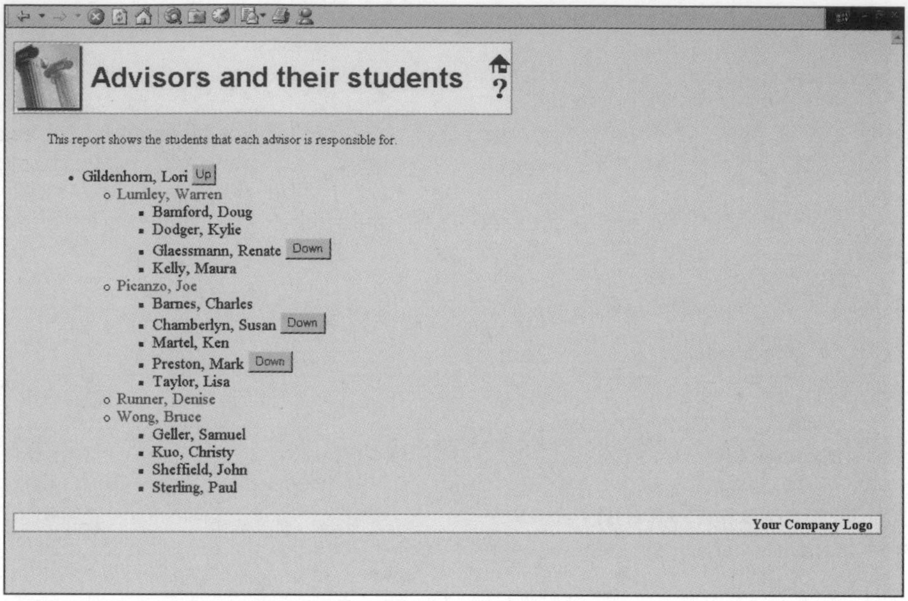

Figure 14-5: A Break Down hierarchy

You can also specify to log the activity of this component, show the timing of the execution of this component, or show the query criteria for the component on the full page version of the hierarchy.

Now that you've reviewed the basic and new choices available on the Display Options page, it is time to begin creating the format for your hierarchy.

13. Set the Maximum Child Levels parameter to 1.

14. Select the Times New Roman entry for the Type Face for the parent.

15. Select +1 for the Font Size, Blue for the Font Color, and Yellow for the Box BG Color for the parent.

Note   Version 3.0.8 of Oracle9*i*AS Portal uses absolute font sizing.

By selecting a different typeface, font size, and background color for the parent row in the hierarchy, you give the chart, in theory at least, a more pleasing appearance.

16. Select Helvetica for the Type Face and leave +1, the default, for the Font Size for the Child.

17. Select Courier for the Type Face for the child.

At this point, you will not have to worry about setting the Portlet display options.

  18. Click the Next button on the Display Options page.

The next page is the Customization Entry Form Display Options page, which also looks very familiar. Here you can indicate the customization options that the end user is offered to limit the retrieval of data for the hierarchy. You can limit the options that are shown on the customization page, and you can set the buttons that appear on the page.

You can define parameters to limit the retrieval of values, just as you can for a report.

The customization options for hierarchies enables you to specify which options appear on the standard customization form for the object. The Hierarchy Style, Start With Value, Maximum Level, Max Children (Child Level 1), Max Children (Child Level 2), Show Parent Level, and Display Name check boxes enable the user of a hierarchy to override the values you have specified for the seven Display Options specified on earlier pages in the wizard.

A user can change the default values by using the Save button on the hierarchy parameter entry page.

The button options look very much like the button options for a report that were described in detail in Chapter 8. The only real difference is that you don't have a Batch button option for a hierarchy. Once you see how a hierarchy works, this makes perfect sense. A user can, and inevitably does, directly interact with an Oracle9iAS Portal hierarchy component, so it doesn't make sense to submit a hierarchy as a batch job.

  19. Click the Next button on the Customization Entry Form Display Options page.

  20. Select PUBLIC.TEMPLATE_6 in the Template combo box.

  21. Enter **This report shows the students that each advisor is responsible for.** into the Header Text for the hierarchy.

  22. Click the Finish button to generate the hierarchy component.

Oracle9iAS Portal now generates the PL/SQL package that creates the component at run time and takes you to the Manage Component page for the recently created object.

You have built your first hierarchy. The next section shows you how to not only run an Oracle9iAS Portal hierarchy component, but also, more importantly, how you can interact with this highly responsive component.

Navigating Through a Hierarchy

Many of the other components you have created so far have a passive life in the run-time environment. For instance, when you run a report you have the option of shaping the data the report retrieves and the way the report is formatted through a customization form, but the data returned from the report is totally static. In contrast, a hierarchy component provides much more interaction with the user, so you should spend more time than usual looking at the way the hierarchy operates at run time.

You start a hierarchy component in the same way that you start any other Oracle9*i*AS Portal component from the Oracle9*i*AS Portal development environment.

23. Click the Customize link on the Manage Component page for your hierarchy component. You see the standard Hierarchy Customization form, as shown in Figure 14-6.

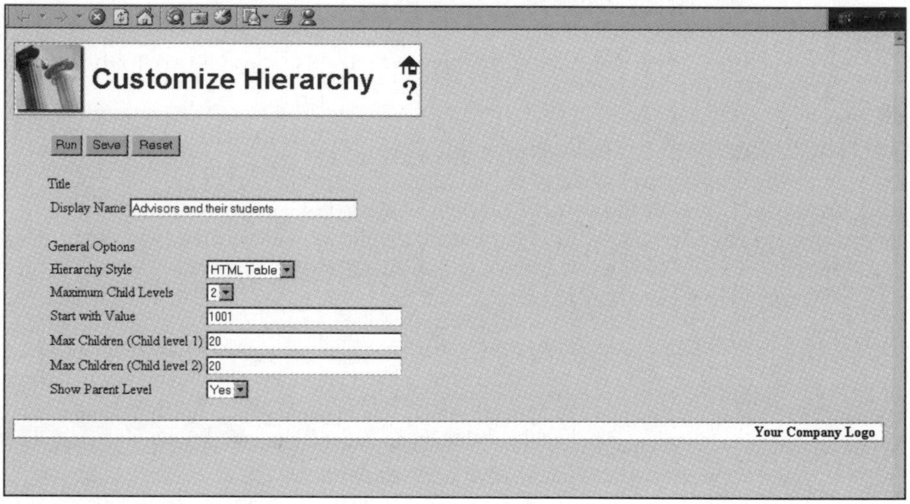

Figure 14-6: The standard hierarchy customization page

24. Click the Run button at the top of the page.

The Oracle9*i*AS Portal component returns a valid hierarchy description, as shown in Figure 14-7. Not the most attractive display in this book, but a valid hierarchy nonetheless.

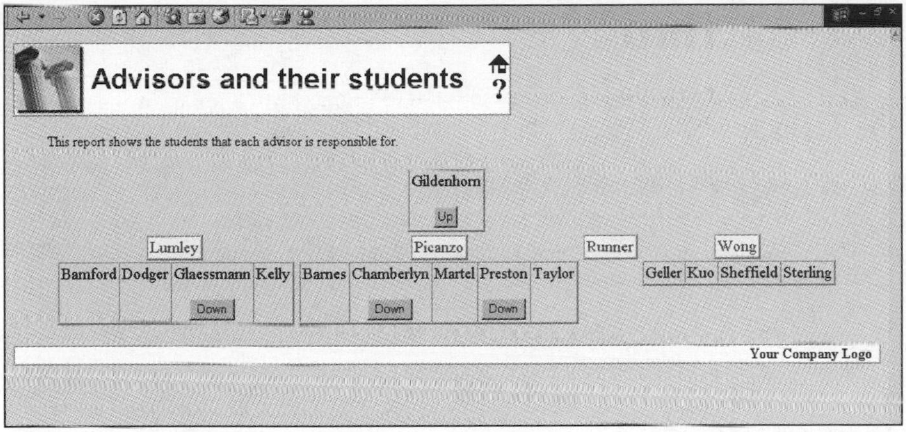

Figure 14-7: A valid one-level hierarchy with parent

You can see that there are two levels displayed in the hierarchy. The top-level value, which is the employee with the ID that you entered into the Start with Value text field, is centered in the page and enclosed in a frame. The entries in the next level of the hierarchy are also enclosed in their own frames. Three of the values have buttons with the label Down on them, which indicates that the entry shown in this hierarchy can be a parent to other values in the hierarchy.

To graphically see how to use this hierarchy, you can use the buttons on the page.

25. Click the Down button under the Glaessmann entry at the bottom level of the hierarchy, which will send the hierarchy display down a level.

Figure 14-8 shows the page that appears as a result of this action.

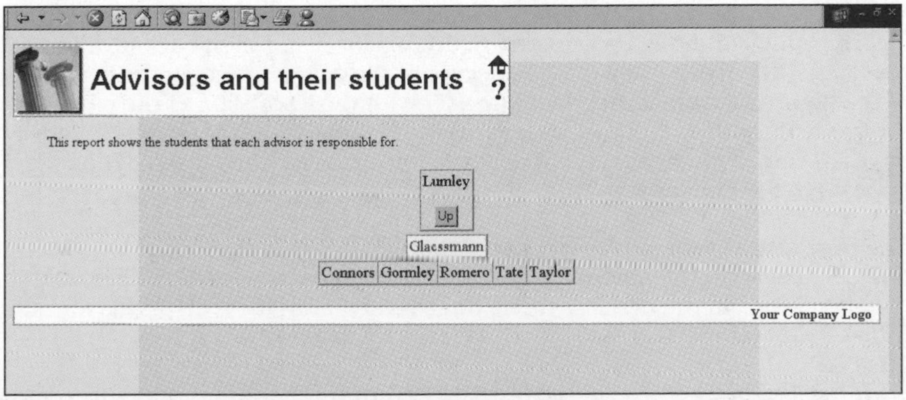

Figure 14-8: Moving down in a two-level hierarchy

You can see that this hierarchy display looks very much like the previous hierarchy display. The top-level value, which is Lumley in this display, is centered on the page and has its own frame, and the values in the next level in the hierarchy also have their own frames. The hierarchy also makes it clear that Glaessmann's children have no children of their own.

The one difference is the button in the Lumley entry at the top of the hierarchy. This button is labeled Up, which means, as you might guess, that there are levels in the hierarchy above this entry. In other words, Lumley is not only at the top of this hierarchy display, but is also a child in another hierarchy display.

26. Click the Up button at the top of the hierarchy, which will return the page shown in Figure 14-9.

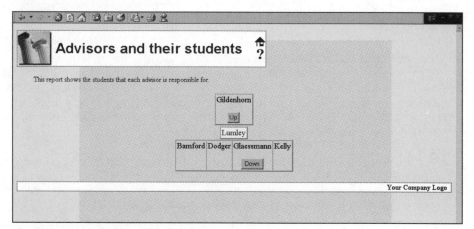

Figure 14-9: A slightly different view of the hierarchy

The image shown in Figure 14-9 is not exactly the same as the image shown in Figure 14-7, even though you just went down a level and then back up a level. The reason for this has to do with the concept of the current item. In the initial display of the hierarchy, you started with the user with the ID of 1001 as the parent. All of the students who had this user as an advisor appeared in the current row. Now, you have specifically indicated that Lumley is the current student, so only Lumley appears in the current row.

The page that is returned as a result of this action is the same page that was initially displayed in the hierarchy. The displays you have been looking at contain only two levels in the hierarchy. The three-level hierarchical display is formatted a little bit differently than the two-level hierarchy display.

27. Use the Back button in the browser to return to the Hierarchy Customization form.

28. Set a level of 2 in the Maximum Child Levels combo box. Leave the value 1001 in the Start with Value text box.

29. Click the Run button at the top of the page.

This time, the hierarchy display looks like Figure 14-10.

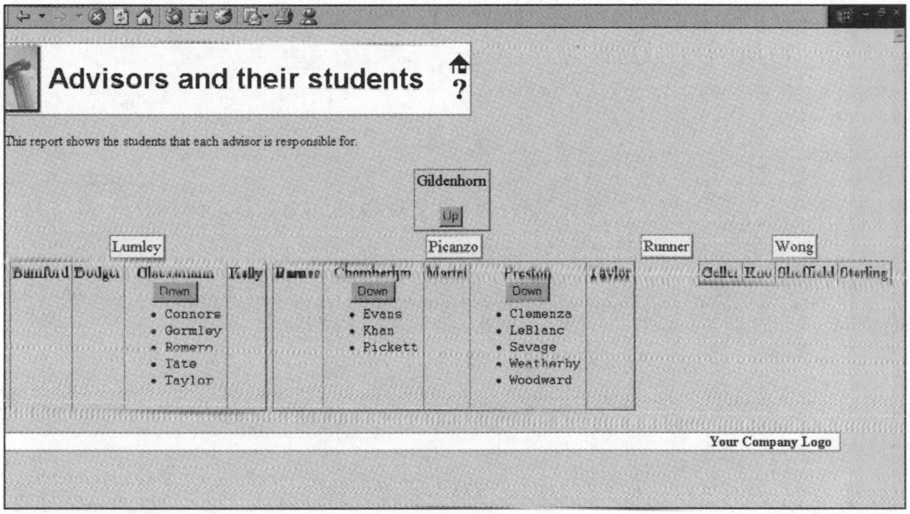

Figure 14-10: A three-level hierarchy, with parent

The same information is displayed in the three-level hierarchy as in the two-level hierarchy: the single parent, the framed displays, and the Down buttons. This hierarchy display also contains a third level in the hierarchy — the values preceded by a bullet. In the last display, you knew that there were at least three levels of hierarchy by the existence of down buttons in three of the four child entries; you just didn't know the values of that third level in the hierarchy. In this display, you can see the last names of the students whose advisor is advised by the student named Gildenhorn.

You can see that only the child level entries that have children contain a Down button. Let's see what happens when you try to drill down on the entries under Glaessmann as you did with the two-level display.

30. Click the Down button under the Glaessmann entry in the child level of the hierarchy.

Figure 14-11 displays the result

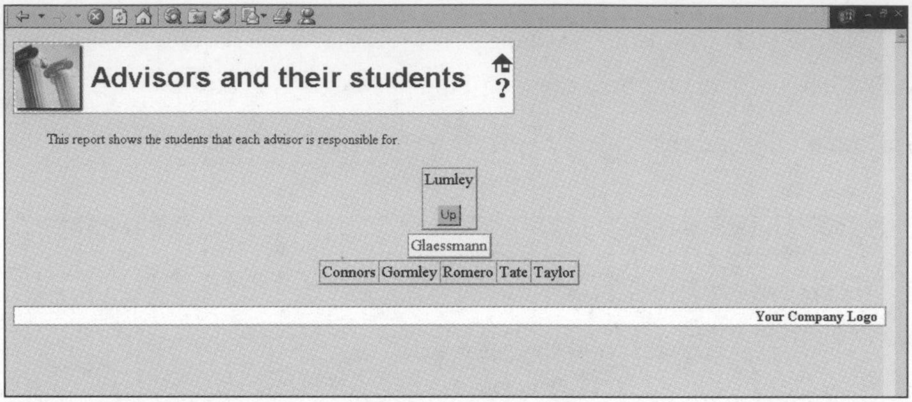

Figure 14-11: Drilling down in a three-level hierarchy

As expected, you can see the students whose advisor is Lumley in the child level of the hierarchy. You can also see, as with the two-level hierarchy, that the student named Glaessmann is also an advisor to other students, who are listed in bulleted display in the same frame.

You may be a bit surprised by the display, as shown in Figure 14-11.

This display only has three levels — the current item, one parent and only once child. But remember, the customization that was different was called Maximum Child Levels. This means that the Oracle9*i*AS Portal hierarchy component shows up to two levels of children, if there are two levels present. All the Down button for Glaessmann indicated was that Glaessmann was a parent in the same hierarchical relationship that produced the display. Oracle9*i*AS Portal has no way of knowing that the children in that relationship were already displayed in the three-level hierarchy.

Before leaving this chapter, you should spend some time making the hierarchy component display more useful information.

Enhancing Your Hierarchy

You have probably already spotted some ways that you could improve the hierarchy you just created. One way is to help prevent user errors by giving the all-important Start with Value parameter a default value, so at least a user accepting the defaults does not run into the same problem that you did the first time you ran the hierarchy.

1. Close the hierarchy window to return to the Manage Component page in the Oracle9*i*AS Portal development environment.

2. Click the Edit link.

You can increase the amount of information delivered in the hierarchy. As you can tell by the label, the Display Column Expression can accept more than just a simple column name, even though the pop-up list only gives you a choice of individual columns. Be careful to enter the concatenation character, which is two vertical bars, and the single quotes properly. Oracle9iAS Portal accepts the expression you enter into this field without any error checking, so if you make a mistake, you will only find out once you run the hierarchy.

  3. Change the Display Column Expression to **LASTNAME** | | ', ' | | **FIRSTNAME**.

  4. Click the OK button.

  5. Click the Run link.

This time, the hierarchy looks better, because each student and advisor is readily identifiable through their first and last names, as shown in Figure 14-12.

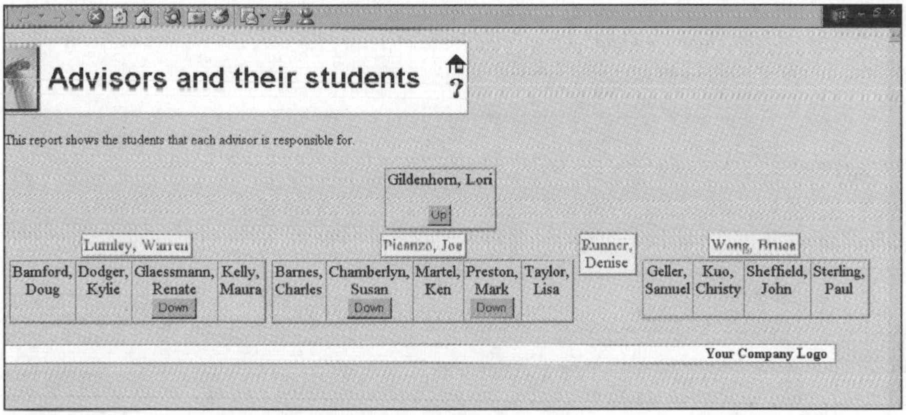

Figure 14-12: Second version of the hierarchy

By changing the Display Column Expression, you changed the way the data is displayed for all levels of the hierarchy.

There is one more modification that might improve the ease of use for the existing hierarchy. There is a kind of disconnect between the customization page and the display pages for the hierarchy. The display pages use an easily understood expression to list the advisors and their students, while the customization form currently requires an ID number for the starting point for the hierarchy, which is more difficult to remember and understand. You can fix this situation by using a List-of-Values for the starting value.

  6. Use the Back button in the browser to return to the Manage Component page in the Oracle9iAS Portal development environment.

  7. Click the Edit link and then click the Table or View Column tab.

8. Click the pop-up icon to the right of the Start with LOV entry field. Click the ADVISORLOV choice.

If the ADVISORLOV choice does not show up in the pop-up list, you have to load the advisorlov.sql script from the samples included on the CD-ROM for this book, as well as the studentlov.sql script which you will use shortly. Refer to Appendix A for instructions on how to import objects by loading SQL scripts.

9. Click the OK button.

10. Click the Customize link at the bottom of the Manage Component page.

You can immediately see the difference on the Customization page, as shown in Figure 14-13.

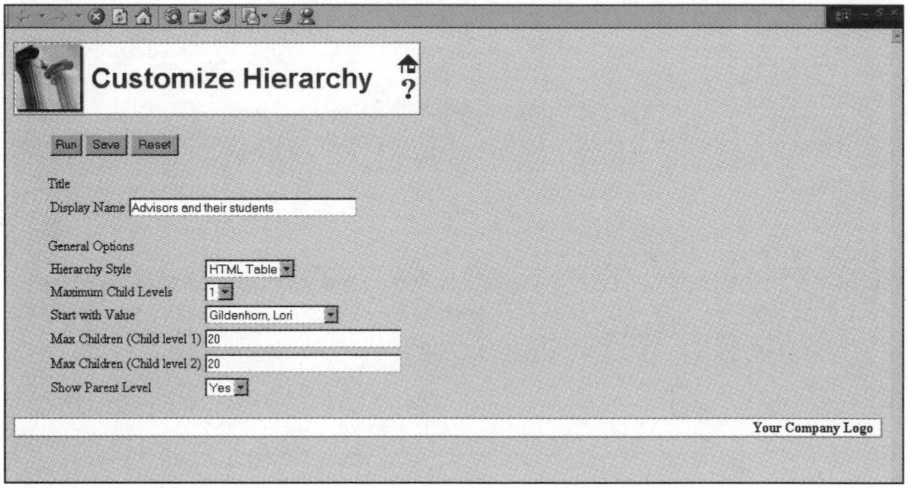

Customize Hierarchy

| Run | Save | Reset |

Title
Display Name Advisors and their students

General Options
Hierarchy Style   HTML Table
Maximum Child Levels   1
Start with Value   Gildenhorn, Lori
Max Children (Child level 1) 20
Max Children (Child level 2) 20
Show Parent Level   Yes

Your Company Logo

Figure 14-13: The Hierarchy customization page with a list-of-values

You can see that the text box for Start with Value has been replaced with a combo box, which is the only way that a list-of-values object for the Start with Value parameter is displayed on a parameter page. Notice that the value you entered in the development environment for the Default Start with Value is still having an effect — the advisor with the number you entered for that value (1001) is still the default choice in the list-of-values (Gildenhorn, Lori).

11. Click the Run button at the top of the page to explore the hierarchy.

As you look around the hierarchy, you can see that it still operates just like the previous version of the hierarchy. The ADVISORLOV is a list-of-values that displays only those students who are at the top level of advisors: seniors who are advisors to underclass students, but who have no advisors themselves.

This limits the display of the hierarchy to the same format every time. The pyramid of the hierarchy always begins at the top level. However, it is not necessary to always start at the top with a hierarchy. You can change the list-of-values for the Start with Value for this hierarchy to see this principle at work.

12. Close the hierarchy browser window to return to the Manage Component page in the Oracle9*i*AS Portal development environment.

13. Click the Edit link.

14. Change the Start with LOV entry to STUDENTLOV.

15. Click the OK button.

16. Click the Customize button.

17. Select the Lumley, Warren entry from the Start with Value combo box.

Because this list-of-values has a lot of values, you can quickly get to the approximate location for Lumley, Warren by entering the letter *l* in the combo box. This scrolls the display to the people whose last names start with an *l*.

18. Click the Run button at the top of the page.

The hierarchy looks a little bit different this time, as shown in Figure 14-14.

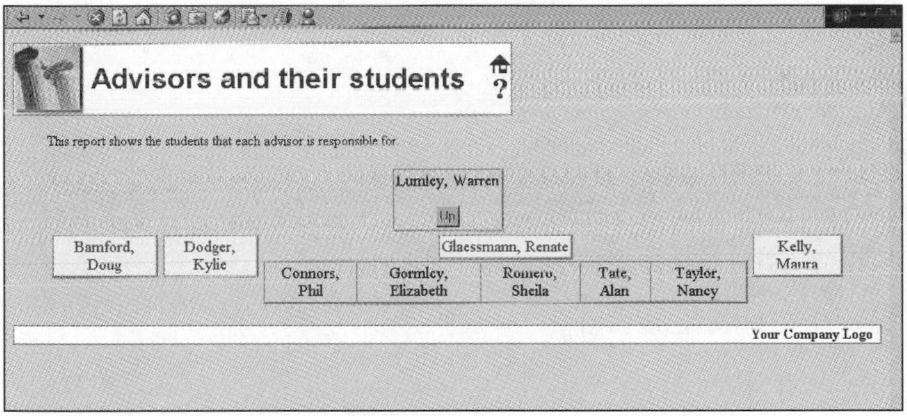

Figure 14-14: Starting a hierarchy in the middle

The hierarchy still works in the same way, but instead of starting at the top of the hierarchy, you have chosen a starting value that is in the middle of a hierarchy. Notice that this view of the hierarchy is different from the one shown in Figure 14-11, because even Lumley is the parent in the hierarchy, so this display shows all of the students with Lumley as an advisor as the current level.

You can use this final version of the hierarchy in different ways than the previous version of the hierarchy because it applies to any student, rather than just looking at advisors from the top down. This illustrates the last point you should take away from this chapter. An Oracle9*i*AS Portal hierarchy component is a way to display a specific type of data relationship through the use of a particular type of display. But that is the only limitation on this component. You can start a hierarchy anywhere that you want, and the Oracle9*i*AS Portal component builds the appropriate levels for you, both above and below the selected starting value.

And, of course, a hierarchy can be used as a portlet, just like all the other Oracle9*i*AS Portal components.

Summary

The hierarchy object provides quite a bit of powerful functionality with very little work on your part. With just a few simple parameters, Oracle9*i*AS Portal creates a powerful interactive component that can be used to view a specific type of data-based relationship. Although use of the component is limited to a specific type of data relationship, Oracle9*i*AS Portal nonetheless endows it with a great deal of functionality.

In the next chapter, you will learn how you can create components that are made up of straight HTML code, which gives you even more flexibility in the appearance of your component.

✦　　✦　　✦

Working with HTML

In This Chapter

Using Dynamic Pages

Adding Your Own
HTML Code

Using Multiple SQL
Statements

Using Frame Drivers

Integrating Frames
and Other
Components

In previous chapters, you had the chance to work with Portal's wizards to produce structured components. Although the eventual output of these components is HTML code, you do not need to concern yourself with the details of writing the HTML code itself, because the Portal components generate the HTML for you. There are opportunities for entering a certain amount of handcrafted HTML code directly, such as when you add text to the headers and footers of pages. However, there may be times when you wish to have a finer grain of control over the HTML that is used to render a page. Portal provides two additional components, Dynamic Pages and frame drivers, that are less formally structured and offer you more formatting opportunities than the other content creation wizards.

The Dynamic Pages Wizard enables you to create your own SQL code directly and then mix this code with your own custom HTML. Dynamic pages enable you to build reports using multiple SQL statements and blocks of PL/SQL code. You can also add extra HTML text alongside this code and create very complex HTML pages that rival handcrafted code.

The Frame Driver Wizard helps you link the SQL code that you write in other components, such as forms and reports, into an HTML framed page. These two wizards provide you with a finer grain of control over generated HTML code than is possible with the component builders you have used thus far. You control the complete HTML formatting of the objects that you create with Dynamic Pages and Frames and you are free to insert custom HTML syntax (such as tables) directly into the code. Some of the techniques that you will learn in this chapter can be applied to the Portal Form Builder's unstructured forms option as well.

Creating Dynamic Pages

Portal's Dynamic Pages Wizard is the most free-form tool that you will work with inside of the Portal environment.

Part of the power of Portal is that much of the low-level HTML coding is automatically handled for you. The downside of this approach is that you are required to live within the confines of the HTML code that Portal knows how to generate. While there are certain exceptions to this rule, such as the ability to place custom HTML in headers and footers, you are still basically working within the confines of the Portal structure. With the Dynamic Pages Wizard, you are free to build your own HTML code and Portal will manage this code for you. This enables you to closely mimic some of your existing static HTML code and enhance it with dynamic data. The price of this freedom is reduced productivity, because the Dynamic Pages Wizard requires you to take complete control of the HTML code, while the other wizards take care of most of the detail work for you. For example, Portal reports automatically create the HTML tables that display the data. If you display the same data with Dynamic Pages you will be responsible for creating the HTML table code. However, you are then free to make the display much more sophisticated (i.e. using nested tables). Yet, conceptually, the Dynamic Pages Wizard is simple, in that it enables you to mix SQL statements and handcrafted HTML code together in one manageable component.

1. Be sure that you are logged on as the NETUDEV developer. Navigate to the NETCOLLEGE application off the main panel and select the Dynamic Page Link to display the initial page of the wizard as shown in Figure 15-1.

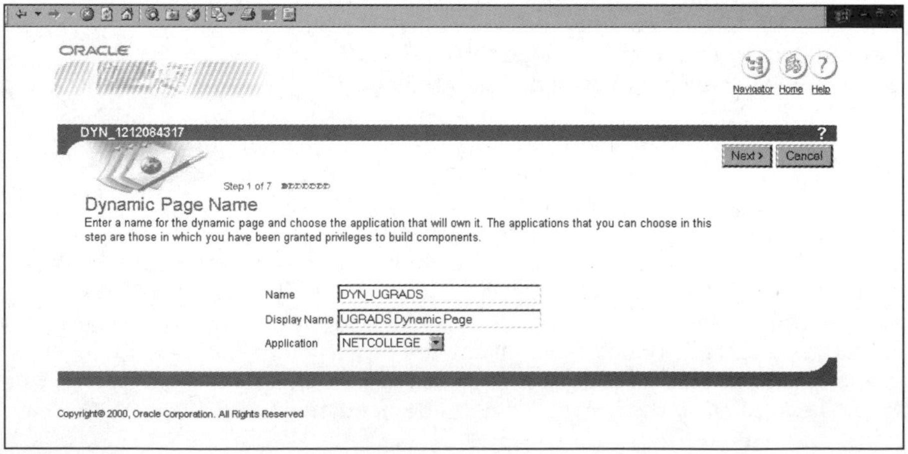

Figure 15-1: Dynamic Page Name panel

The initial page of the Dynamic Page builder looks the same as any of the other component wizards. The primary page is composed of three separate fields: a top field for naming new Dynamic Pages, a middle field for adding a title, and a bottom combo box that displays the available applications that can be used as the host environment for the Dynamic Page. Portal automatically generates a unique component name for you, but as with the other component builders, we recommend that you use a more structured naming convention.

2. Enter the string **dyn_ugrads** as the name of the Dynamic Page to be created, and set the display name to UGRADS Dynamic Page.

The application name field behaves the same as in the other wizards — it provides a list of applications that you have been given permission to build in.

3. Select the NETCOLLEGE application as the host application for the new Dynamic Page.

4. Click the Next arrow to continue.

The most important panel in the Dynamic Pages Wizard is the Dynamic Page Content panel as shown in Figure 15-2.

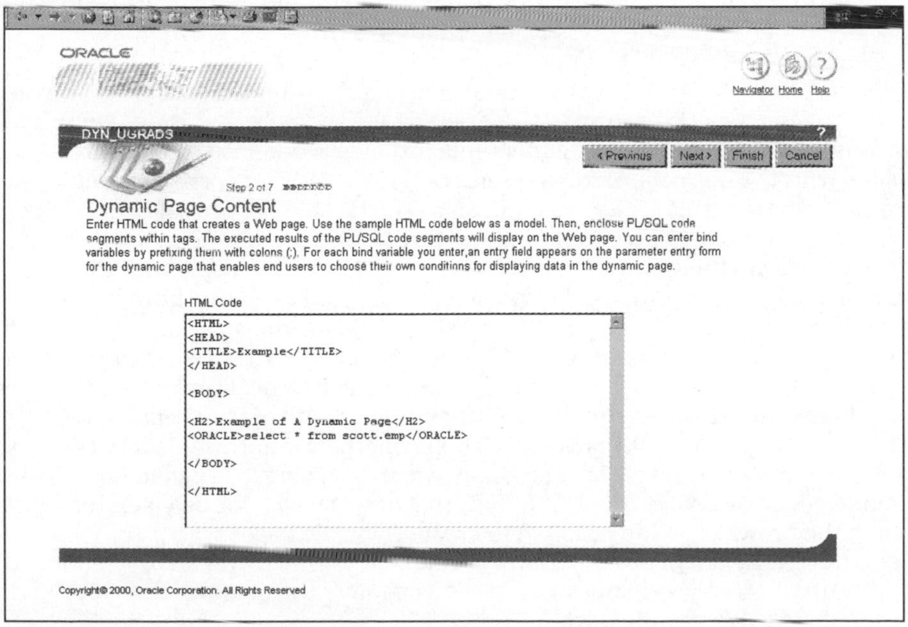

Figure 15-2: Dynamic Page Content panel

The complete functionality of the Dynamic Pages Wizard is contained in this single page. The page itself is nothing more than a single large HTML text box in which you can enter code. Initially this text box is filled with a sample SQL statement as shown in Listing 15-1.

> ### Listing 15-1: **Standard Dynamic Page SQL statement**
>
> ```
> <HTML>
> <HEAD>
> <TITLE>Example</TITLE>
> </HEAD>
> <BODY>
> <H2>Example of A Dynamic Page</H2>
> <ORACLE>select * from scott.emp</ORACLE>
> </BODY>
> </HTML>
> ```

The key to using the Dynamic Pages Wizard is to understand the format of the code that you enter into this single text area. Although the text area is essentially a free-form text area field, Portal attempts to derive the format of the page by looking at the structure of the code that you enter into this field.

There are essentially two types of code you can enter into this field. First, you can enter any block of text such as the phrase `Example of A Dynamic Page`, as shown in Listing 15-1. Portal renders this text as entered into the text area in accordance with the normal processing rules of HTML. You can enhance any block of text by enclosing it within a pair of HTML tags. The HTML tags provide Portal with the necessary clues as to how to format the text that you enter. Actually, Portal itself does not do anything with either the text you enter or the tags other than passing the results on to the browser. In the preceding example listing, both of the text strings, `Example` and `Example of A Dynamic Page`, are surrounded by HTML tags to indicate that the first string is a title and the second string is a heading. You are free to use any HTML tag set that the browser can handle. Portal does not attempt to validate the HTML tags that you enter into the body of the Dynamic Page. Therefore, you do not have to worry about whether or not Oracle9*i*AS Portal supports the most current HTML standards when designing a Dynamic Page. This is a double-edged sword, as any HTML tags that you use will not be validated until they reach the browser. So it's possible to create Dynamic Pages with advanced HTML code that work fine in the browser environment in which you are developing the application—and yet do not work in the version of the browser that your end users are running to access the portal.

Thus, you would be wise to be careful as to the amount of raw HTML that you code into Dynamic Pages. In addition to enhancing and adding text strings, you are free to load images and links in the text areas as long as they are enclosed in the appropriate HTML tags.

The remaining types of code that you can enter into this field are Oracle SQL and PL/SQL statements enclosed within the Oracle-specific custom HTML tags <ORACLE> and </ORACLE>. Unlike the standard HTML tags, Portal will search for these tags and then format the remainder of the Dynamic Pages Wizard using them.

By default, Portal fills the text area with a sample block of text that includes both types of code. You are free to modify this code and add or remove any of the elements as necessary to build the page layout that you desire. The Dynamic Pages Wizard features only a small number of panels and it is easy to use a build, test, and modify development strategy when designing your pages.

5. Edit the text between the <ORACLE> </ORACLE> tags to include the following SQL query:

```
select sysdate from dual
```

6. Click the Next arrow to continue.

Portal processes the text that is entered into the form and searches for the <ORACLE> tags. Portal isolates the SQL code you enter between the tags and then builds a panel that enables you to further customize the code as shown in Figure 15-3.

Initially, you may find that this particular panel is not overly useful, as its sole function is to isolate your PL/SQL code and provide you with an opportunity to modify the code. The power of this panel becomes obvious only when you build multiple SQL statements into the same panel. For the time being, you can ignore this panel.

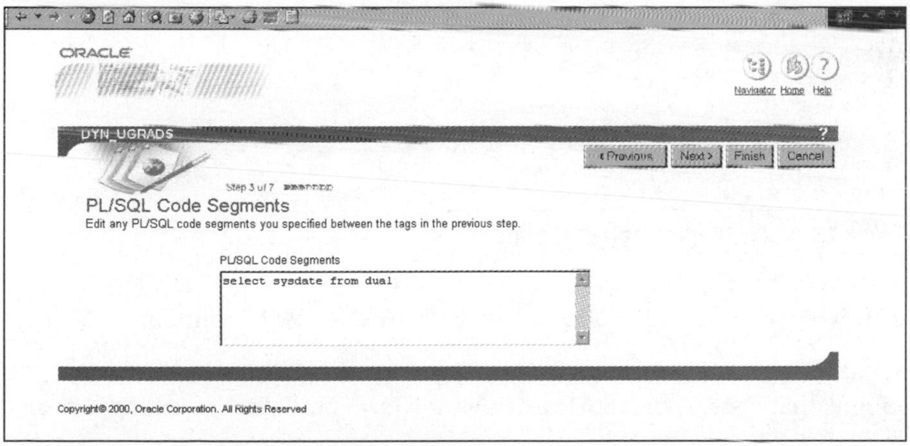

Figure 15-3: PL/SQL Code Segments panel

7. Press the Next arrow to continue to display the page as shown in Figure 15-4.

The next panel allows you to decide whether you want Portal to log usage statistics against the Dynamic Page that you are creating. By selecting this checkbox (which is the default) you cause Portal to write usage statistics into the activity log tables. You can monitor user activity and performance statistics in these log files through Oracle9iAS Portal's administrative interface. While you will almost always elect to do so for the formal reports and forms that you create with Portal, you may chose not to do so with certain Dynamic Page objects. However, if you plan on deploying a Dynamic Page into a production portal site we would encourage you to turn on logging, at least initially. Because Dynamic Pages allow you to embed lots of custom SQL code into a single object, it is more likely that the resulting object will become overly complex. You will want to be sure that such objects perform reasonably well when they are deployed to users.

Keep in mind that Portal does not paginate Dynamic Pages as it does other components, and you may find that the performance of Dynamic Pages appears to lag behind that of other objects because of this fact. As with the other components you also have the choice on this panel to set the default caching option for your Dynamic Page. If the underlying data for the Dynamic Page is likely to change frequently, then you will want to set the value for this field to a smaller number. By accepting the default value of 0, Portal will rerun this page every time that it is called by a browser session.

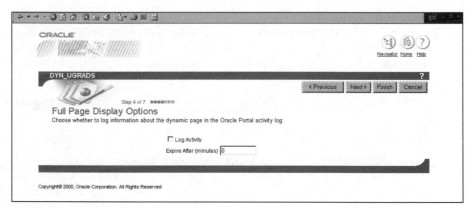

Figure 15-4: Full Page Display Options panel

   8. Select the logging option and click the Next arrow to continue.

The next panel in the wizard allows you to specify Customization Form Display Options that control the BIND variables and form buttons that will appear on the Dynamic Page.

New Feature   BIND variables for Dynamic Pages are new with Portal 3.0, and we will take a more detailed look at this feature later on in this chapter.

9. Skip over the Display Options Panel by pressing the Next button to continue.

The next panel in the Dynamic Pages Wizard is the Customization Entry Form text panel. If you create a Dynamic Page that accepts parameter values, you can use this panel to control the look and feel of the customization page. You can also select a template that will be used when the customization form for the Dynamic Page is displayed. By using a template for your customization page you will be able to make this object blend in with the other Portal components that you create. By default Dynamic Pages lack the basic header and footer banners that are present in reports and forms. You can use a template to add these banners to your Dynamic Pages, but the template will only appear on the customize page for the Dynamic Page. If you wish to add template information to the page itself, you will have to cut and paste the raw HTML directly into the Dynamic Page on the first panel of the wizard.

10. Select the PUBLIC.TEMPLATE_6 template for the Dynamic Page as shown in Figure 15-5 and then press the Next button to continue.

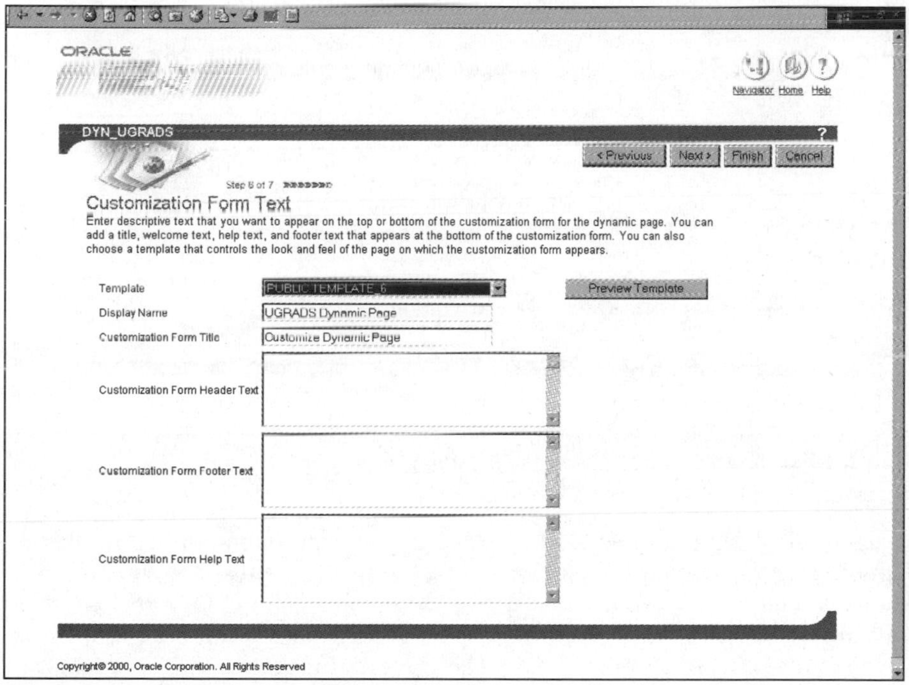

Figure 15-5: Customization Form Text panel

The final panel in the wizard is the Additional PL/SQL Code panel. This is a very important panel for custom development with the other wizards such as reports and forms. With reports and forms you have limited flexibility in the user interface; and the PL/SQL code panel provides you with the ability to insert custom code into the generated object. Although Portal provides these same panels in the Dynamic Pages Wizard they are not as critical there: Because you are free to add your own PL/SQL anywhere within the Dynamic Page, there is little need to have a custom panel for entering this code. In fact the sole reason for including these panels here is to allow you to add custom PL/SQL to the Customization Entry Form.

11. Skip over the Additional PL/SQL Code panel by using the Finish button to create the Dynamic Page object and display the Manage Component panel as shown in Figure 15-6.

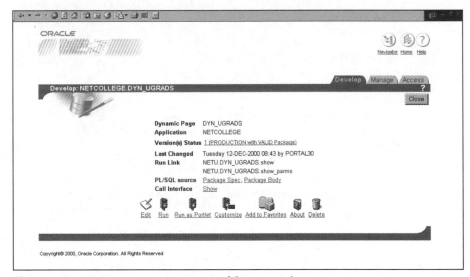

Figure 15-6: Manage Component panel for Dynamic Pages

Dynamic pages behave just like any other Portal component and you will find the familiar set of image buttons for executing them at the bottom of the panel as shown in Figure 15-6. We will take a look at the management options in more detail later on in this chapter.

The resulting HTML page is relatively simple, as you can see from Figure 15-7.

You will remember from the HTML code that there are only three objects in the source code: a page title, a heading, and the Oracle SQL code. During the wizard process you were not given the opportunity to set many of the formatting and processing options that you may have used within the other wizards, and this is reflected in the output of the page. For example, the page in Figure 15-7 does not make use of any templates and there are no provisions for setting the color scheme of the page, such as foreground or background colors. Portal offers the Dynamic Page builder as a way for you to roll your own HTML, and therefore it does not provide many of the features you have relied upon in the other wizards.

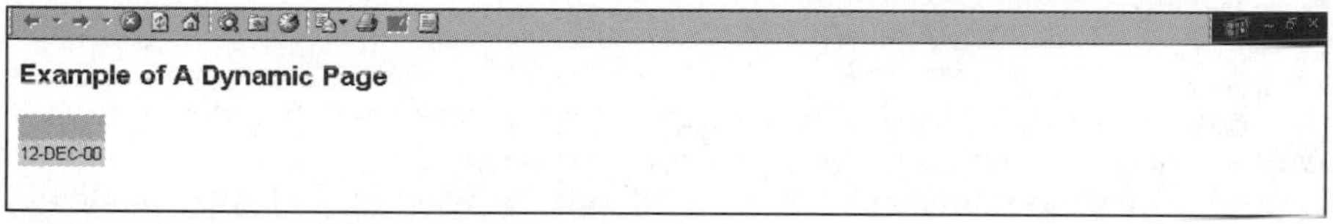

Figure 15-7: Example Dynamic Page

As you will learn shortly, you are still able to control many of these settings. The real difference is that you are required to enter the code by hand. The designers of Portal purposefully left out some of the advanced settings pages in the Dynamic Pages Wizard so as not to interfere with the custom HTML that you might enter into your dynamic HTML pages. For example, if you were to provide a background color setting on your page in your own HTML code, as well as setting it on a display options panel, Portal would not be sure of which setting to use. In order to avoid any such confusion, the templates and display options panels simply do not exist in the Dynamic Pages Wizard.

> **Note**
>
> You can still perform all of the formatting functions, however, by editing your own HTML directly inside of the page itself. For example, the background color for your page can be set by using the BG HTML parameter in the <BODY> tag. The exception to this rule is when you run a Dynamic Page as a portlet. Then, Oracle9iAS Portal will add the appropriate colors, headers, and fonts. If you have added your own headers using HTML in the body of the Dynamic Page, then both sets of headers will appear in the page when it is run as a portlet. Bear this in mind when you design your Dynamic Pages.

Adding additional HTML code to the page

The Dynamic Pages Wizard is designed to provide flexibility for the HTML gurus within your organization. Although Portal can easily reference existing static HTML pages by using virtual directories, these static pages cannot be dynamically generated from data in your database. On the other hand, there may be times when you want to combine some of your existing HTML code with data from your database, and this is where the flexibility of the Dynamic Pages Wizard comes in.

The real power of the Dynamic Pages Wizard is in the flexibility it offers you. Initially, the HTML text displayed in the main panel, as shown in Figure 15-2, is relatively simple. However, you are free to add your own HTML code into this window and replace the existing HTML code that Portal suggests. If you are an HTML guru, you can simply start typing over the HTML code that exists in the edit frame in Figure 15-2. If, on the other hand, you are not an HTML guru, you are free to use any visual HTML authoring tool, such as Symantec's Visual Page or Macromedia's DreamWeaver, to create your HTML. Importing this code into Portal is as simple as cutting and pasting the HTML source into the Dynamic Page Content panel.

Note   Before continuing with this section, make sure that you have copied the NetU images to a directory accessible to Portal, and that you have created a virtual directory for these images, as instructed in Chapter 2.

The Dynamic Pages Wizard is designed to move quickly between development and testing modes. You will find it easy to add new HTML code in blocks and then test the code quickly before making any additional changes. Although Dynamic Pages do not provide for the use of templates, you can use your own blocks of HTML code to add headings as desired. For example, you can replace the default heading with a more descriptive heading using standard HTML.

In addition to making changes to the HTML, you can also make changes to the SQL code that is contained within the Oracle tags. You are free to use any valid SQL statement, PL/SQL statement, or function call just as if you were entering the code into SQL*Plus. You are, however, limited to entering a single SQL statement within each pair of <ORACLE> </ORACLE> tags, but Portal enables you to enter multiple sets of tags, as you will see in the next section. For example, the default date selection on the example page does not provide much in the way of details, but it is easy to add some additional formatting using standard Oracle data functions.

1. Return to the Manage Component page for Dynamic Pages and edit the page you just created.

2. Select `<H2>Example of A Dynamic Page</H2>` in the text area and replace it with the code segment found in ch15_dynamic1.htm.

3. Replace the line:

   ```
   <ORACLE>select sysdate from dual</ORACLE>
   ```

   with the following code:

   ```
   <ORACLE>select to_char(sysdate, 'Month DD, YYYY HH:MI A.M.')
   from dual</ORACLE>
   ```

The net result of the changes to the page should be the code shown in Listing 15-2.

Listing 15-2: Modified HTML code

```
<HTML>
<HEAD>
<TITLE>Example</TITLE>
</HEAD>

<BODY>
```

```
<H2><P><IMG SRC="/netu/netu_logo.jpg" ALIGN="MIDDLE"
BORDER="0"> <B><FONT SIZE="6">Net
University Web Page</FONT></B></P>

<P><B><FONT SIZE="6"></FONT></B></H2>
<ORACLE>select to_char(sysdate, 'Month DD, YYYY HH:MI A.M.')
from dual</ORACLE>

</BODY>

</HTML>
```

Note It is possible to duplicate the functionality of any Portal template in your own code simply by viewing the source for the template within the browser and copying the source into your Dynamic Page object. You have to selectively cut and paste the sections of the HTML code that reference the template, but this is not overly difficult. In fact, you can duplicate the functionality of almost any static HTML page by following this same technique.

The structure of the HTML code must still conform to the basic rules of HTML coding. However, you are free to add any parameters to the HTML tags, such as adding document information to the <HTML> tag. Typically, you would add document-indexing information into the HTML code via the <META> tag, but this information is not as useful in the Portal environment. Documents can only be indexed by a search engine when the HTML page is stored externally to the database. Because Dynamic Pages are stored inside the database, they are not indexed or accessible to standard Web search engines. They can however, be indexed by Oracle's interMediaText database cartridge.

Caution Portal does not attempt to validate the HTML code you enter into a Dynamic Page, and the only indication that there is a problem with the code comes when you attempt to use the page at run time. HTML code that is copied from within a word-processor document will often cause problems within Portal. Be sure to copy HTML code from a Text editor before pasting it into Oracle9iAS Portal Pages.

If you add images or links to other objects into the HTML code you use, you must be sure to make the links and paths accessible to Portal. In Listing 15-2, you will note that the image name (netu_logo.jpg) is preceded by a virtual directory path that is known to Portal via the Apache Listener (/netu/). All links must be made relative to Portal or point to a fully qualified URL in order for them to work within Portal.

Note If you are importing code into Portal from other visual HTML tools, you almost always need to check the images and links to be sure they are accessible from within Portal. Oracle plans to provide a substitution tag called #BASE# that will automatically get the base URL for your Portal site. This feature should be available in release 3.0.8 and later.

4. Click the OK button to save your changes and then use the Run link to test out the modified page, as shown in Figure 15-8.

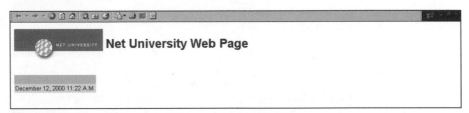

Figure 15-8: Dynamic page with custom HTML code

The modified page includes the banner graphic, a more descriptive block of title text, and a modified display for the date and time. The result is a customized HTML page that is much more flexible than the other Portal components. Of course, the price for this increased flexibility is a lower level of productivity as you are responsible for manually formatting the HTML code. You will find that expert HTML programmers will be the most frequent users of Dynamic Pages, because they offer the ability to leverage HTML expertise directly.

Note   You might also want to try running the page as a portlet. When the Dynamic Page uses the portlet interface, it inherits your custom banner and the portlet banner. This is a unique feature of the Dynamic Page object.

Adding additional SQL code

When you built your initial Dynamic Page object, you noticed that the SQL code was surrounded by the Oracle tags <ORACLE> and </ORACLE>. Although the default page uses only one set of these tags, you are free to add as many pairs of these tags as you wish. This enables you to build pages that have multiple, separate SQL queries, which are separated by custom HTML code. This can offer incredible opportunities for customization, because the various SQL statements need not have any direct relationship to one another.

1. Return to the Manage Component page for the Dynamic Page.

2. Edit the Dynamic Page using the Edit link.

3. Insert an additional set of tags and a new SQL statement, as shown in Listing 15-3.

Listing 15-3: Dynamic page with multiple SQL statements

```
<HTML>
<HEAD>
<TITLE>Example</TITLE>
</HEAD>

<BODY>

<H2><P><IMG SRC="/netu/netu_logo.jpg" ALIGN="MIDDLE"
BORDER="0"> <B><FONT SIZE="6">Net
University Web Page</FONT></B></P>

<P><B><FONT SIZE="6"></FONT></B></H2>
<ORACLE>select to_char(sysdate, 'Month DD, YYYY HH:MI A.M.')
from dual</ORACLE>
<hr>
<b>NetU Students</b>
<ORACLE>select firstname, lastname, classyr, gender, photo from
netu.ugrads order by classyr</ORACLE>

</BODY>

</HTML>
```

The new code is shown in boldface text in Listing 15-3. The first change is the addition of a block of bold text that displays a title for the date SELECT statement. Next, an HTML break has been added after the date selection and a bold string of text has been entered after the break. Most importantly, an additional block of SQL code has been inserted that selects student records grouped by class year.

4. Enter the code as shown in Listing 15-3, remembering to preface the UGRADS select statement with the schema owner if you did not install the Net University database in the NETU schema as recommended.

5. Click the PL/SQL Code Segments Tab to save your changes and display the PL/SQL code segments as shown in Figure 15-9.

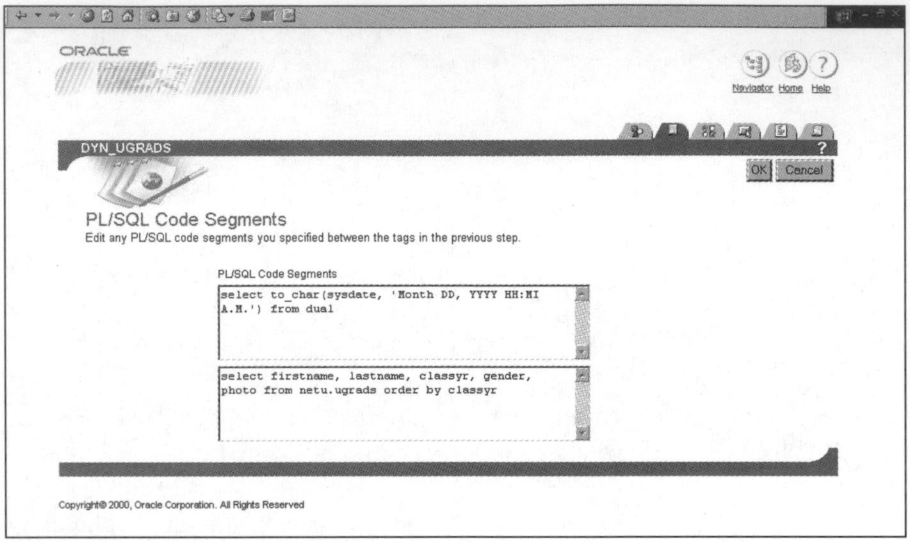

Figure 15-9: PL/SQL code segments

Notice that Portal has built two text areas, one for each of the SQL queries that you entered using the pair of <ORACLE> </ORACLE> tags. Portal extracts the text just as you entered it between the tags and it ignores any of the extraneous HTML code that may surround the tags. This gives you the opportunity to refine the SQL code without having your view obstructed by any HTML text.

When the page is executed, Portal executes the code in the order that it was entered into the page, as shown on the panel in Figure 15-9. In this example, you are selecting the current date and time followed by a list of students in the Net University database. If necessary, you could insert new records into the database in one query and then select these records in a second query. You can also use this technique to populate a temporary table with one query and then display the results with a second query on the same page. Portal displays the results in the order that they are executed, so UPDATE or INSERT queries are transparent to the end user.

Caution   You can enter almost any combination of SQL statements into the <ORACLE> tags, including INSERTS and DELETES, but you are not permitted to make *explicit* use of DDL statements such as CREATE TABLE within the <ORACLE> tags. (It is possible to access DDL statements by using the built-in PL/SQL procedures.)

6. Save the changes to this page by clicking the OK button and then use the Run link to test the modified version as shown in Figure 15-10.

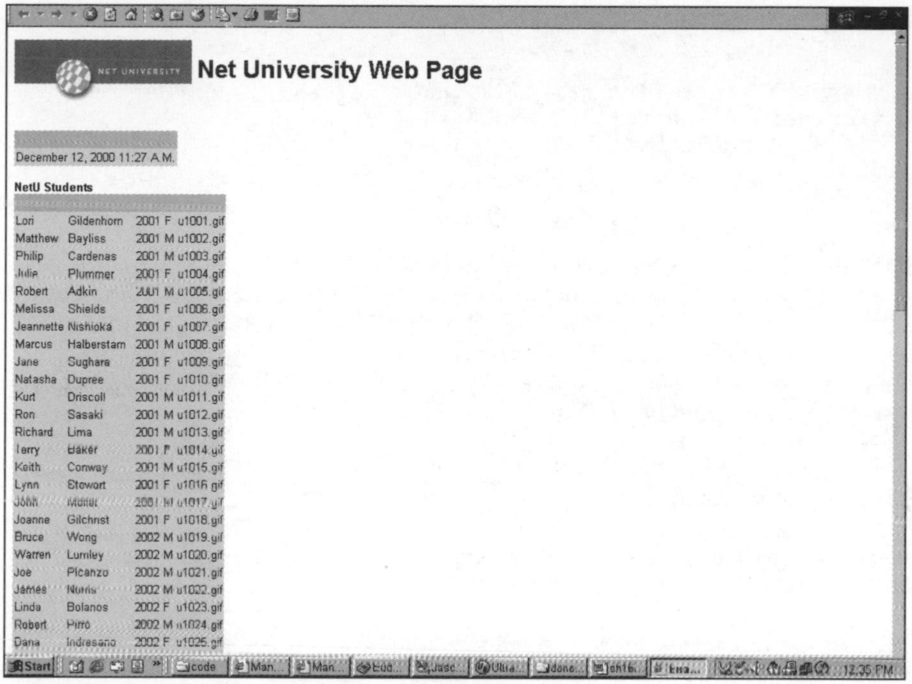

Figure 15-10: Dynamic page with two queries

The resulting page shown in Figure 15-10 is built using your exact specifications. Notice that the SQL query for the UGRADS records even lacks titles for the various columns. If you wanted titles for the columns, you would be forced to build the titles by hand, using HTML. You can easily see that the increased flexibility comes at a price in terms of productivity. However, this flexibility can also be an important asset. Notice that the last field in the UGRADS list is a filename. This filename maps to a photo image of the student that is accessible to Portal. Instead of pointing to the filename, you can actually mix HTML code with your SQL and get Portal to render the image for you at run time.

Mixing HTML and SQL

Portal enables you to combine HTML command syntax with SQL when you are building queries. This feature enables you to provide some extra display formatting for your data that blends nicely with standard HTML formatting.

1. Return to the Manage Component page and edit your Dynamic Page one more time.

2. Modify the second SQL statement to use the code shown in Listing 15-4.

Listing 15-4: **Mixing SQL and HTML code**

```
<ORACLE>select firstname, lastname, classyr, gender,'<IMG
src=/netu/'||photo||'>' photo from netu.ugrads order by
classyr</ORACLE>
```

The critical change is highlighted in bold text. Instead of selecting just the filename as a text string, you are building an HTML IMAGE tag using some HTML code along with the value of the PHOTO field. Each UGRADS student has a pointer to a picture file that is stored within the database as a text field. The actual file is stored outside the database, but it could just as easily be stored inside the database. For each record, you are building an IMAGE tag that looks like the following snippet of HTML code:

```
<IMG SRC=/netu/u1001.gif>
```

When the browser processes this string, it generates an image link instead of the text.

Note Oracle provides a set of prebuilt functions that can generate complicated HTML syntax for you quickly and easily. Chapter 18 provides a detailed look at these utilities, which can be used inside Dynamic Pages.

3. Save the change by clicking the OK button in the edit session and then run the modified query using the Run link to display results, which are shown in Figure 15-11.

This time when the query executes, the filename string is converted into the HTML IMAGE tag format and the browser displays the actual photo file for each student instead of displaying just plain text. Part of the power of using Dynamic Pages is that you are free to build HTML code around your SQL statements and produce very powerful, dynamic HTML code in the process.

On the CD-ROM In order to see the image files, you will need to copy the class pictures to the /netu/ virtual directory as outlined in Chapter 2.

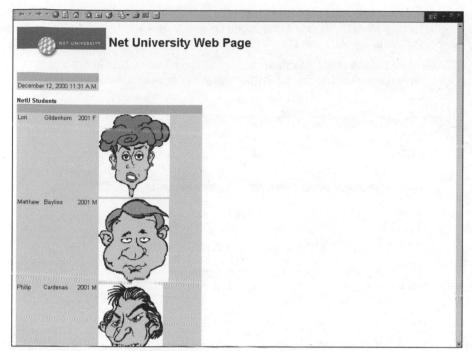

Figure 15-11: SQL output with advanced formatting

Adding Parameters to Dynamic Pages

Previous versions of Portal did not allow you to add parameters to Dynamic Pages — but this restriction has been lifted with release 3.0. You can now create Dynamic Pages that include BIND variables just as you can with every other Portal component.

1. Return to the Manage Component panel and edit the Dynamic Page object dyn_ugrads.

2. Edit the second query as shown in Listing 15-5.

Listing 15-5: **Dynamic queries with BIND variables**

```
<ORACLE>select firstname, lastname, classyr, gender,'<IMG
src=/netu/'||photo||'>' photo from netu.ugrads where classyr =
:myclassyr order by classyr</ORACLE>
```

The change to the SQL query is shown in boldface in Listing 15-5. Instead of selecting all of the ugrads records, the query now fetches data from specific class years based upon the classyr field and a new BIND variable.

3. Use the Button Options tab at the top of the panel to navigate to the Customization Entry Form Display Options panel as shown in Figure 15-12.

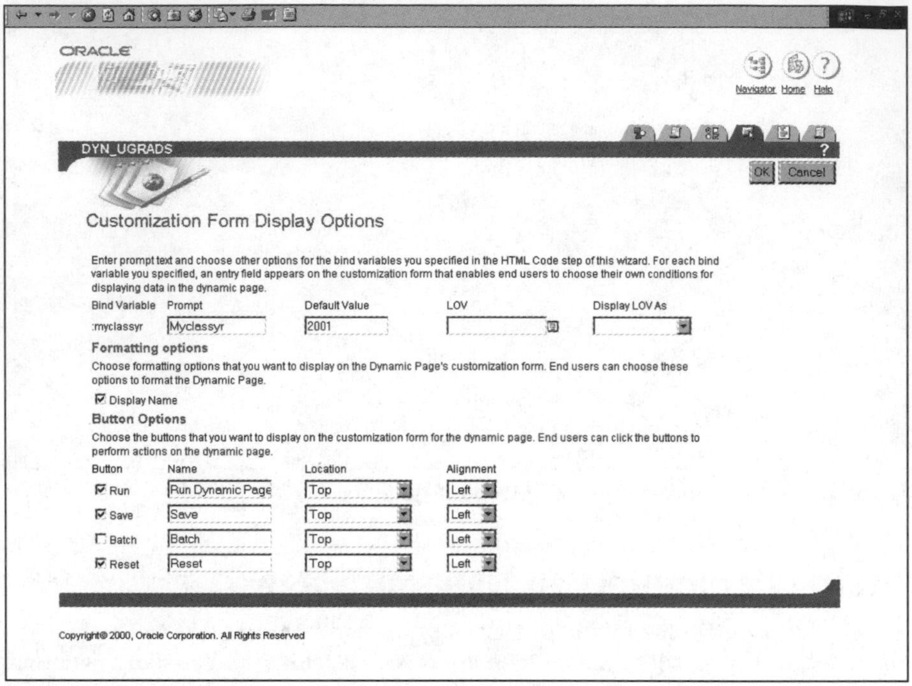

Figure 15-12: Dynamic Pages Customization Entry Form Options

Any BIND variables that you enter within the <ORACLE> </ORACLE> tags on the first panel will be displayed in the top part of this panel. In this example case the myclassyr variable appears as the first and only entry. As with parameters that are used with reports and forms, you are allowed to enter a default value for each BIND variable and you can map the BIND variable to an LOV object.

4. Enter the default value of **2001** for the myclassyr BIND variable and press the OK button to save the changes to your Dynamic Page.

5. Use the Customize link to run the modified page and display the panel as shown in Figure 15-13.

Figure 15-13: Customization Form Run-time Panel for Dynamic Pages

You will notice that the parameters panel makes use of the template that you specified when you first created this Dynamic Page. Although the template is not used with the Dynamic Page itself, you could cut and paste the template code from the parameters page into the body of the Dynamic Page to achieve the same effect. Portal does not apply the template format to the page automatically because there is no way for Portal to know if the generated template code interferes with the hand-crafted HTML code that you may have added to the page.

6. Enter a `classyr` string (or accept the default value) and run the modified page.

Portal applies the value of the parameter to the Dynamic Page and restricts the records to those UGRADS that match the value of the `classyr` that you entered on the parameter form.

Despite this additional flexibility, Dynamic Pages behave in as consistent a fashion as the other content wizards in all other regards. Portal provides a Manage Component panel for Dynamic Pages and you can set security, manage versions, and import and export pages just as you can with any other component. You can also use the familiar access panel to publish the Dynamic Page to the portal.

Using Frame Drivers

Portal provides an additional component builder that enables you to work more closely with HTML in the form of the frame driver. The frame driver enables you to create dual-paned windows based on the HTML frames extension that was pioneered by Netscape. Frames provide you with finer a level of control over the display of your components. Frames can be built using new components that are created along with the frame objects themselves, or they can be used to manipulate existing objects in a new way.

Note The general trend in the industry has been to move away from frames for building Web sites. (Users have found frames to be difficult to work with and this has been the main cause of their demise.) In most cases you can use HTML tables to achieve the same effects as frames. However, Portal's Frame Drive Driver is still quite useful as a component-building tool.

1. Use the Frame Drivers link in the Oracle Navigator for the NETCOLLEGE application to access the Frame Driver Wizard as shown in Figure 15-14.

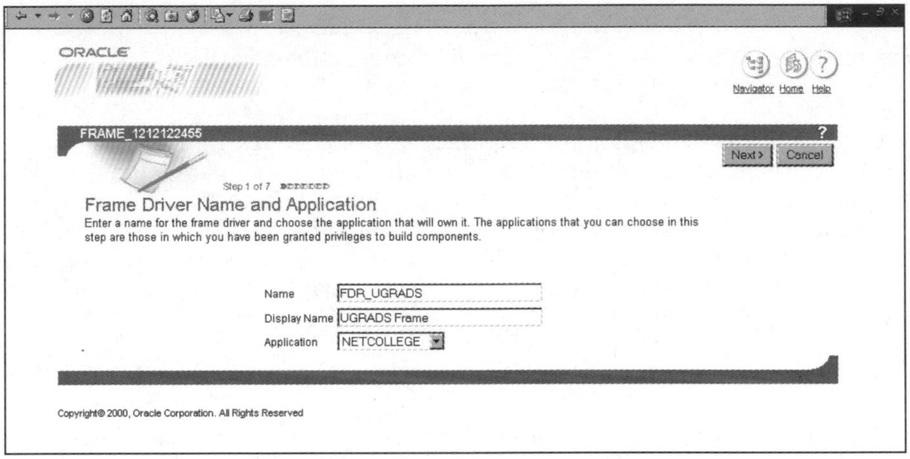

ORACLE

Navigator Home Help

FRAME_1212122455   ?

Next > Cancel

Step 1 of 7 ▓▓▓▓▓▓▓
Frame Driver Name and Application
Enter a name for the frame driver and choose the application that will own it. The applications that you can choose in this
step are those in which you have been granted privileges to build components.

Name   FDR_UGRADS
Display Name UGRADS Frame
Application   NETCOLLEGE ▼

Copyright© 2000, Oracle Corporation. All Rights Reserved

Figure 15-14: Frame Driver Wizard page

The main Frame Driver Wizard page offers three entry fields just like any of the other component builders. The top field enables you to name the frame, the middle field is the display name and the bottom combo box allows you to associate the frame with an application.

2. Enter **FDR_UGRADS** as the name of the new frame and set the display name to **UGRADS Frame**.

3. Select NETCOLLEGE as the application.

4. Click the Next arrow to continue.

The main task in designing a frame is to build a SQL query that serves as the driving force for the frame. You may be familiar with building static HTML pages using frames. This is typically a fairly detailed but static process. You design a frame set and then you load pages into the frames. The frame driver is designed to automate this process by driving detailed frames from database data contained in the master frame. Figure 15-15 shows the basic components of the SQL Query panel used to construct the frame set.

The key to the frame object is a formatted query that is entered into the main text area. The SQL query is built using two columns that must be coded in a specialized format. Portal frames are designed to be two-panel frames, and the SQL query columns map one to one with the two frames. From Portal's perspective, the first frame in the frame set is considered to be the driving frame, and it maps to the first column in the SQL query. The column values in this frame drive the results in the second frame.

The second frame in the set is the result frame, and the data that is displayed in the result frame is built by the data in the second column. You can think of this combination as a type of master-detail display with values in the master controlling the display of data in the detail frame. If you have previously used a Portal report or form object to link to a second report or form, then you have the basic idea of what the frame driver is designed to do. The difference is that with the frame driver, both the parent and the child can be displayed in a single window. Consider the SQL query in Listing 15-6.

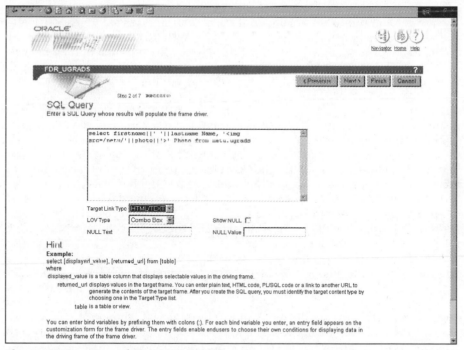

Figure 15-15: Frame driver query panel

Listing 15-6: **Frame driver query format**

```
select firstname||' '||lastname Name, '<img
src=/netu/'||photo||'>' Photo from netu.ugrads
```

In this example, the first column is a concatenation of the FIRSTNAME and LAST-NAME fields of the UGRADS table. The frame driver specifies that only two columns can be selected, but these columns can be coerced using any combination of fields, functions, and concatenation characters that are allowed by Oracle at the SQL level.

As with any long string of concatenation, Portal requires that you provide a pseudo-column title for any string that exceeds 32 characters. The Name string literal is used as the column title for the combination of FIRSTNAME and LASTNAME in the first part of the query. For the result column, notice that the string is identical to the one used to display student photos in the example of the Dynamic Page object in the preceding section. As with the first column, the image string is given a pseudo-column title. The remainder of the SQL string uses standard SQL syntax; and you are free to make use of FROM clauses, WHERE clauses, and ORDER BY qualifiers in formulating your query. Typically, the first column in the query is based upon standard database data. The second column, however, can take three formats as shown in the Target link type drop-down list box.

The result frame can be HTML/Text, a URL, or a block of PL/SQL code. The simplest result frame format is the HTML/Text display. If the second column of data returns textual data or data that is mixed with HTML syntax, then the frame is considered to be of the type HTML/Text. The query shown in Listing 15-6 returns an HTML tag that builds an image link, and is thus considered to be of the format HTML/Text. If the second column points to another object via a URL, then the format of the query is considered to be of the type URL. You may find you need to build a list of addresses that a user can choose from for navigational purposes. In this case, the first column would be the list of addresses and the target column would be a URL that connects to the first column.

You can control the manner in which the first column is displayed by using the LOV Type field. The driver column can take one of three formats: a Combo Box, a Radio Group, or a List format. If you have a large number of choices, the List format is the best choice as it presents the most data in the smallest amount of screen real estate. Combo boxes are appropriate for up to about 50 entries and radio groups are only appropriate for a small number of choices.

The last type of result frame is the PL/SQL format. This format is used to connect to existing PL/SQL blocks that return HTML data, such as procedures that were built using the mod_PL/SQL cartridge in the Oracle Internet Application Server (iAS). Chapter 21 of this book is dedicated to advanced PL/SQL topics and there are several examples of using handcrafted HTP procedures with PL/SQL.

The remaining three fields on this panel all control the manner in which the frame handles NULL values in the database. By default, Portal does not show null values in the target frame unless you select the Show NULL check box. If you elect to display NULL values, you can enter a constant value in either the NULL text or NULL value field. This text is displayed in place of the missing data whenever the frame encounters a database null value. The NULL text field literal is displayed for null values in the first column and the NULL value literal is displayed for null target column values.

5. Enter the SQL statement shown in Listing 15-6 as the SQL query for the new frame.

6. Select HTML/Text from the Target link type list box, and choose the Combo Box format for the LOV type.

7. Click the Next arrow to continue until you reach the initial page panel shown in Figure 15-16.

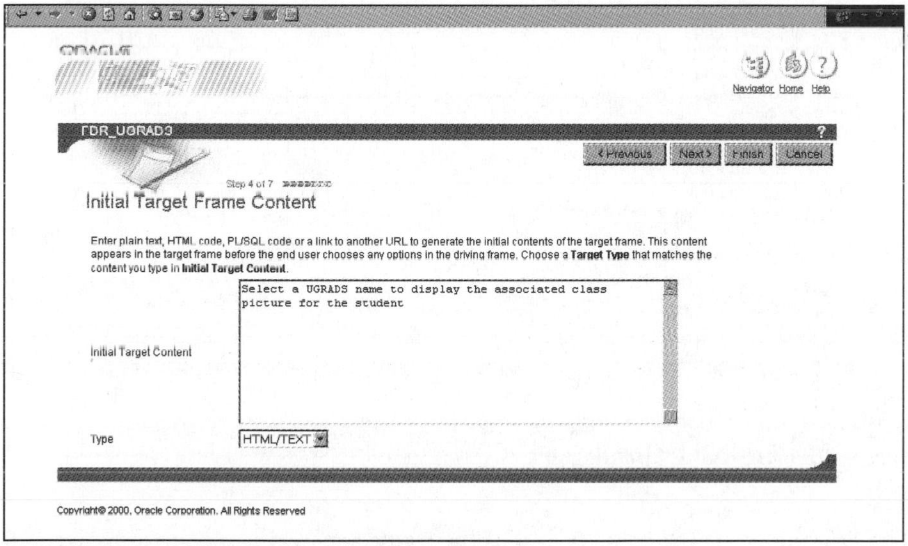

Figure 15-16: Initial target frame content panel

While the frames themselves can be dynamic, the initial display is static and you are permitted to specify a literal string of text, a PL/SQL procedure name, or a URL. Once you have entered the string into the text area, you need to select the Type for the string in the combo box just below the text area. Portal has no way of determining whether the string you enter into the text area is HTML, PL/SQL code, or a URL.

The value you select determines how Portal processes the string of text in the text area. If you choose to enter text, you are free to make use of HTML tags to improve the formatting of this text.

Caution   You must be sure that the Type value matches the text in the text area. Portal has no way of determining on its own what the value that you entered into the text area is meant to be.

8. Enter **Select a UGRADS name to display the associated class picture for the student** into the text area.

9. Select the HTML/Text option as the frame type.

10. Click the Next arrow to continue.

The next page in the Frame Driver Wizard controls the Display Options for the frame driver. The Display Options panel for frames serves the same purpose as with the Display Options panel in the other component wizards, but the choices are different, as shown in Figure 15-17.

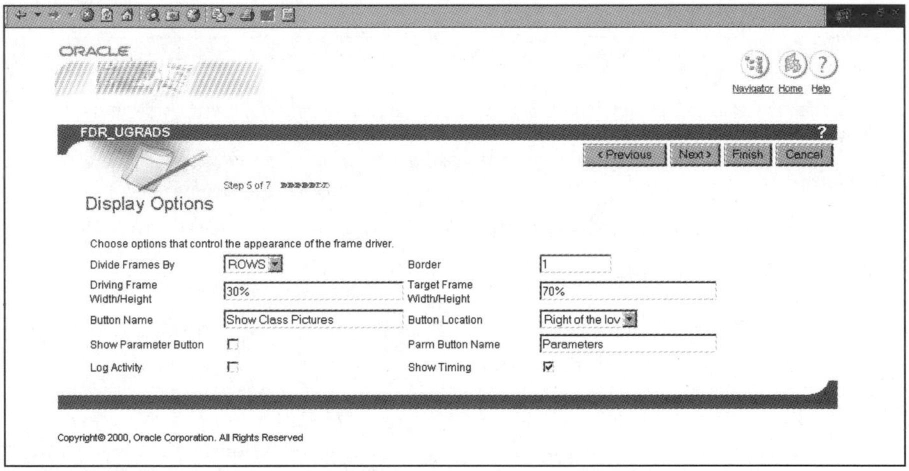

Figure 15-17: Display Options panel

The first choice is the basic layout of the frame set. You can choose between ROWS and COLS. Frames that are row-oriented show the driving frame on top and the result frame on bottom. Frames that are divided as COLS display the driving frame to the left as a column and the results frame to the right. You can set the width of the border between the two frames by entering larger integer values for the Border field. Portal expects that most of the data will actually appear in the target frame, and it allocates a larger amount of screen real estate to the target frame. You can change the default weighting by entering a specific value as a percentage. Percentages must range from 1 to 99 and must be followed by the percent (%) character. If the frames are aligned as rows, then the setting determines the height of the frame. If the frames are displayed as columns, then the setting determines the width of the respective columns.

When the frame loads, Portal selects the data in the first column and fills the combo box, list, or radio group with values. In order to display the data in the target frame, the end user is required to select a value in the driving frame. In order to minimize unnecessary processing, Portal does not build the target when the user selects a value. Rather, the user is required to select a value and then press a submit button. Portal enables you to set the label for the button using the Button Name field. You can set the position of the button using the Button Location combo box.

The SQL query you use to build the driving frame can include BIND variables. If you choose to make use of BIND variables, Portal provides an additional button that displays a parameter form for entering values for the BIND variables at run time. Portal makes this an optional choice, because you can pass the values for BIND variables as link arguments. If you wish to display the parameter button, you must select the Show parameter button check box, and you can enter a custom label for the parameter button as well.

Note If you do not use BIND variables in your query, we recommend that you choose *not* to display the parameter button, because the use of the parameter button results in a blank page.

11. Divide the frame using ROWS and change the height percentages to **30%** and **70%** for the source and target.

12. Change the label of the button name to **Show Class Pictures**.

13. Deselect the Show parameter button check box.

14. Click the Next arrow to continue.

Text options within frame drivers only apply to the driving frame. You can choose a template, and set titles, headers, footers, and help text for the driving frame. The Template list box is populated by the templates that have been created within the Shared Component Application. Portal renders the template only in the driving frame and you may find that your existing templates do not fit in the area that has been assigned to the driving frame. In such cases, you may wish to create a smaller version of the template that will fit in the reduced area. The remaining text fields can be filled with plain text and HTML tags as with the other component builders.

15. Enter a title for the driving frame, select the PUBLIC.TEMPLATE_6 template and click the Next arrow to continue.

Frame drivers support the use of additional PL/SQL procedures that run at various points during the process of program execution. As with the text options panel, these settings only apply to the driving frame. If you wish to make use of PL/SQL blocks in the target frame, then you have to code them into the components that are called by the driving frame.

16. Skip over the PL/SQL Options panel by clicking the Finish arrow to complete the frame.

17. Test the frame driver by clicking the Run link.

Portal displays the frame driver, as shown in Figure 15-18. Initially the bottom frame is filled with the data that was set by the Initial Target Frame Content panel. In the example case, the bottom frame consists of a simple text message that tells the user to select a student name in order to display the associated image.

Note   The bottom frame will generally load faster than the top frame, since the top frame is being built from data in the database.

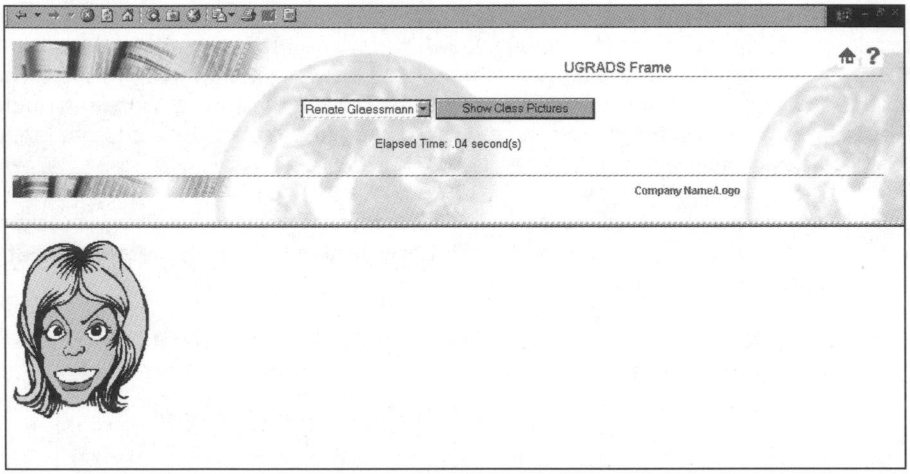

UGRADS Frame

Renate Glaessmann   Show Class Pictures

Elapsed Time: .04 second(s)

Company Name/Logo

Figure 15-18: Executing the example frame

18. Select a student name and click the Show Picture button to display the bottom frame.

The bottom frame fills with the student picture to match the student name, similar to the way that the image was shown in the Dynamic Page object. The difference with the frame driver is that the user is able to individually select records as needed rather than displaying all of the data in one SELECT statement. Alternatively, you could build similar functionality using a QBE form with a Customization Entry Form. You can also link an existing report, form, calendar, chart, or hierarchy to a frame by passing parameters from the driving frame to the linked component.

Connecting frame drivers to components with parameters

You can add parameters to the driving frame itself, and you can also link the driving frame to parameters in a component that displays in the target frame.

1. Load the ch15_rpt_ugrads report from the companion CD-ROM into Portal. Return to the Manage Component page and edit the NETCOLLEGE application once again.

2. Create a new frame, **fdr_ugrads2** under the NETCOLLEGE application.

Note

It's best to read Chapter 20 to fully understand the specialized structure of Portal's link text. You do not need to know all the particulars about links to complete the examples in this chapter — but you will want to understand links fully before embarking on building your own link-based components with frames.

The link text is composed of three pieces: the component procedure name, the parameters list, and the values list. The component procedure name is the schema owner followed by the object name and the procedure name. Every Portal procedure, with the exception of Dynamic Pages, has a set of built-in parameters along with parameters for any BIND variables that have been defined. Parameter names are passed to the URL by entering the P_ARG_NAMES literally followed by an equals sign, the parameter name, and an ampersand for each parameter. In a similar fashion, argument values for the parameters are passed to the URL by entering the literal P_ARG_VALUES followed by an equals sign, the value of the parameter, and an ampersand for each value. You do not need to supply trailing ampersands, but the number of parameters and values must match. In addition, each pair of values must be sent in order: first an argument name, then an argument value.

The format of the target link type must match the format of the query. If you change the query to link to a component, then you must change the target link type to the URL setting. The drop-down list box setting for the link type must match the actual link. For example, if the page links to an external URL, then the target link type must be set to URL. Although you would think that the format would be the PL/SQL setting for a Portal component, the call to the procedure is actually a URL. The PL/SQL setting is only used if you are calling a block of PL/SQL code, such as procedures that were created with the PL/SQL cartridge in the Oracle Application Server. Links to other Portal components are considered to be URLs.

An Alternative Approach to Links

Oracle has included a new set of utilities with the release of Oracle9*i*AS Portal 3.0 that can help you with the formatting of HTML links inside of queries. In particular, the built-in function "WWV_USER_UTILITIES.GET_URL" will format string text and parameter values as HTML links when it is used inside of a SQL statement. Using this format, the SQL statement as shown in Listing 15-7 could be re-written as:

```
select lastname||' '||firstname,
portal30.wwv_user_utilities.get_url('NECOLLEGE.ch15_rpt_ugrads','
id',id) from netu.ugrads where classyr = :classyr
```

Although Oracle suggests that you use this function for embedding links within your queries, we discovered some inconsistencies with it during testing. We recommend that you review the Oracle9*i*AS Portal 3.0 documentation for the latest information on these utilities.

3. Enter the code for your frame to match the code in Listing 15-7 and change the target link type to the URL setting.

4. Choose the Customization Form Display Options tab. Figure 15-19 shows the Customization Form Display Options panel.

Listing 15-7: **URL query format**

```
select lastname||','||firstname,
'netu.ch15_rpt_ugrads.show?p_arg_names=id&p_arg_values='||id
url from netu.ugrads where classyr = :classyr
```

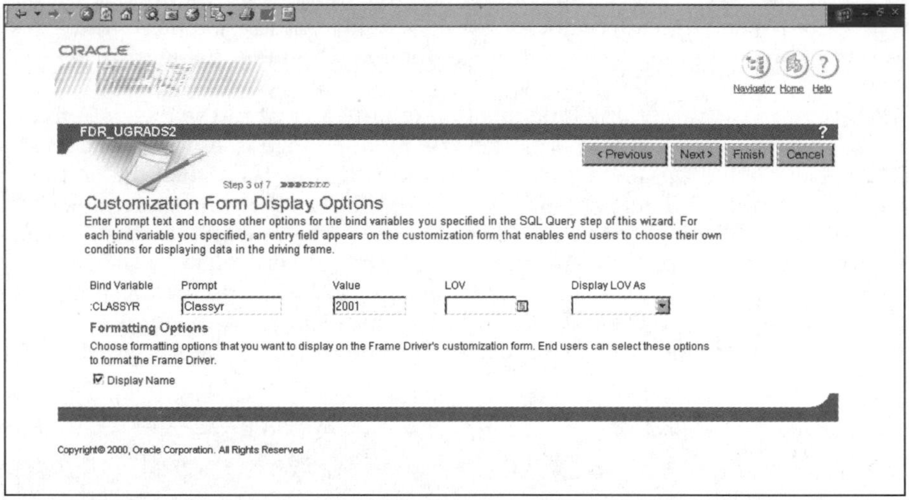

Figure 15-19: Customization Form Display Options panel

If you add BIND variables to the query, such as the CLASSYR variable used in the code as shown in Listing 15-7, Portal enables you to format the BIND variable just as with any of the other Portal components. If you have created lists-of-values, these can be bound to the variable as well, or you can specify a fixed value as a default value. The BIND variable is applied to the driving frame and it affects the records that are shown as the source. In the example case, the classyr variable restricts the student records to matching the classyr value before building the combo box.

5. Enter **2001** as the value for the classyr BIND variable and then navigate to the Display Options panel.

6. If you have not already done so, enable the Show Parameter Button check box in order to display the Customization Entry Form for the BIND variable and change the text for the parameter button to Enter Class Year.

7. Navigate to the Frame Driver and Customization Form Text panel and select the PUBLIC.TEMPLATE_6 template from the drop-down list box.

8. Save your changes by clicking the Finish button and execute the new frame by clicking the Run link on the Manage Component page to display the page as shown in Figure 15-20.

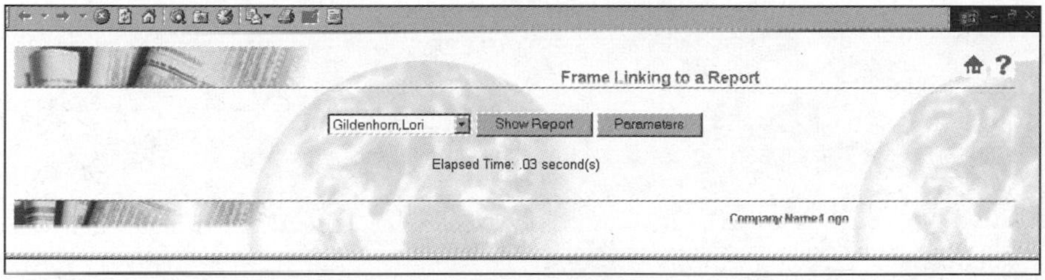

Figure 15-20: Example frame with links and BIND variables

When you execute the new frame object you will notice two differences. First, the combo box initially shows only NetU Seniors and the target frame is blank. In order to fill in the combo box with other data, you must select the parameter button and enter a valid class year value for the BIND variable.

1. Choose the Enter Class Year button and enter a valid class year to fill the list box: 2001, 2002, 2003, or 2004. Use the Run button to fill the combo box with data.

2. Select a student name from the recently populated drop-down list box and then click the Submit button, as shown in Figure 15-21.

Upon selecting a student name, the frame driver passes the ID number of the student to the report that runs in the target frame. The report accepts a single parameter that uniquely identifies a record and displays some basic background information about the student along with the same class picture. Although this example report only selects a single row from the database, you are free to build objects that accept multiple parameters as well as objects that retrieve multiple rows from the database.

3. Navigate back to the Manage Component page.

Portal frames support the standard suite of manage component options, and you can import and export frames, set security options, and monitor the performance of them.

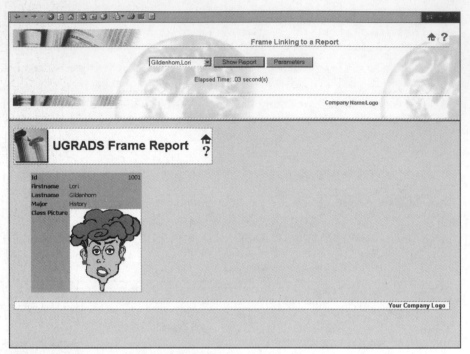

Figure 15-21: Frame with detailed report

Summary

Dynamic pages and frame drivers offer a lower level of control than the other component builders you have worked with in previous chapters. Dynamic pages provide you with a tool for leveraging your existing investment in HTML code while working in the Portal environment. You can use them to render complex documents that include complex HTML formatting and dynamic database data.

You can use frame drivers to link your existing components together in a parent/child format and allow your users to have an easier time accessing data. In Part III, you will learn about a suite of tools in the Shared Component Application that can be used to link various components together into a cohesive unit. These shared components will assist you in the process of building consistency into your applications, which makes your applications easier to use.

✦   ✦   ✦

Building Oracle9*i*AS Portal Applications

♦   ♦   ♦   ♦

In This Part

Chapter 16
Working with Lists-of-Values (LOVs)

Chapter 17
Creating Oracle9*i*AS Portal Menus

Chapter 18
Building Consistency in Oracle9*i*AS Portal Web Sites and Applications

Chapter 19
Data Validation with Oracle9*i*AS Portal

Chapter 20
Using Links to Connect Oracle9*i*AS Portal Objects

Chapter 21
Integrating PL/SQL Logic

♦   ♦   ♦   ♦

Working with Lists-of-Values (LOVs)

♦ ♦ ♦ ♦

In This Chapter

Understanding the
List-of-Values Object

Understanding
Update versus Query
List-of-Values Objects

Building LOV Objects
from Static and
Dynamic Data

Deploying a Static
LOV Object to
Another Component

Creating a Dynamic
LOV Object

Employing Advanced
Techniques for LOV
Objects

♦ ♦ ♦ ♦

Portal applications offer you the opportunity to use information from your Oracle database both for reporting and for entering data into forms. In the days of client/server computing, user applications offered simplified data entry through drop down combo boxes and list boxes. These objects provided a standardized interface for querying data by prompting the user with a simple list of possible values. When the user was given the opportunity to update data in the database, these objects served as the first line of defense in the endless struggle for data integrity. The usefulness of these objects carried them over from client/server computing into the realm of thin-client computing and HTML pages. Portal provides a powerful List-of-Values wizard that enables you to create reusable lists-of-values that augment your reports, forms, and graphs.

Defining Lists-of-Values

The list-of-values concept has been around since the earliest days of dumb terminal applications. Originally, lists-of-values were displayed by use of an overlaying, or pop-up, window in terminal-based applications. You can use lists-of-values both to limit user choices for data entry and to make it easier for users to understand codes stored in the database. A list-of-values displays a descriptive name on the screen, but inserts a code for that name into the database. The simplest example of list-of-values objects is the ubiquitous table of state codes and state names. An application could offer a simple listing of state codes, but it might be more helpful to offer a list of state names and then have the list-of-values object translate the state name into the state code when the value is added to the database. Almost every application that stores address information for North America offers a look-up list or list-of-values display that shows some combination of state code and state name. HTML supports the <OPTION> tag for just this purpose.

In general, list-of-values objects consist of two separate data elements: a code and a description. You often see list-of-values objects referred to as code and description lists. The code is the data value that is used to link one table to another, and the description is the full-fledged name for the code. For example, in most data entry operations you select the value PA for the state of Pennsylvania. The application stores the value PA in the record, but the display shows you the full name, Pennsylvania, when you view the record. Figure 16-1 shows a typical relationship between a code and description table and a data table.

The STATES table joins to the UGRADS by means of the STATE_CODE and STATE fields. For consistency's sake, most applications use the same field name for the code in both the description table and the join table, but this is not mandatory. In many cases, list-of-values (LOV) objects can be used to hide the fact that the join table uses a different name for the code column than the associated code and description table. In relational parlance, the code and description table acts as a master table to the join table, which is referred to as the detail table. This makes sense when you think about it, because there may be *many* undergraduate students for *each* state in the STATES table. In most cases, your list-of-values source table acts as a master table for database join operations.

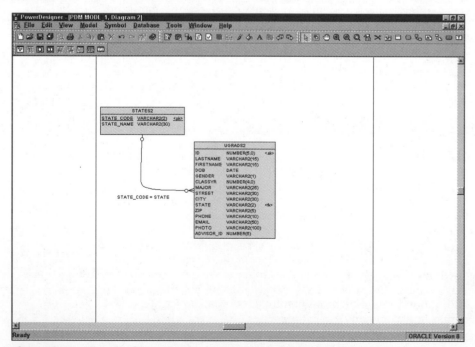

Figure 16-1: List-of-values sample data model from the NetU database

From a strictly database perspective, you can use lists-of-values as part of a standard SQL join as shown in the query in Listing 16-1, which uses the example NetU database.

Listing 16-1: **Sample join query for NetU database**

```
select firstname, lastname, state_name from netu.ugrads,
netu.states where ugrads.state = states.state_code
```

Caution
Remember that you may need to preface each table name with the Oracle owner for that table (as shown previously) if you did not use public SYNONYMS for the NetU database. If you connect to Oracle as owner of the NetU database, you need not worry about providing a preface or using a SYNONYM.

You may choose to run the preceding query using the Dynamic Pages capability of Portal or with SQL*Plus or the PL/SQL Developer. As discussed in Chapter 15, you may choose to create a general-purpose Dynamic Page object for SQL testing purposes. In this case, you can simply replace the current SQL text of your Dynamic Page object each time you wish to test a new SQL statement.

It is not a strict requirement that the source for an LOV object come from a master table, and there are cases where you can derive a list-of-values from data directly out of a detail table. For example, if you look at the COURSE_CATALOG table by using the Database Navigator or a Dynamic Page, you see the data shown in Figure 16-2.

Notice that that CATNUM column has a combination of both letters and numbers as part of the catalog number. In this case, the alphanumeric field contains some additional information about the individual course record. The first three characters of the CATNUM column are also a code for the department that is offering the course. Run the query in Listing 16-2 to see the subpattern in the CATNUM field.

Listing 16-2: **Finding the subpattern in the CATNUM field**

```
select distinct substr(catnum,1,3) Department
from netu.course_catalog
order by Department
```

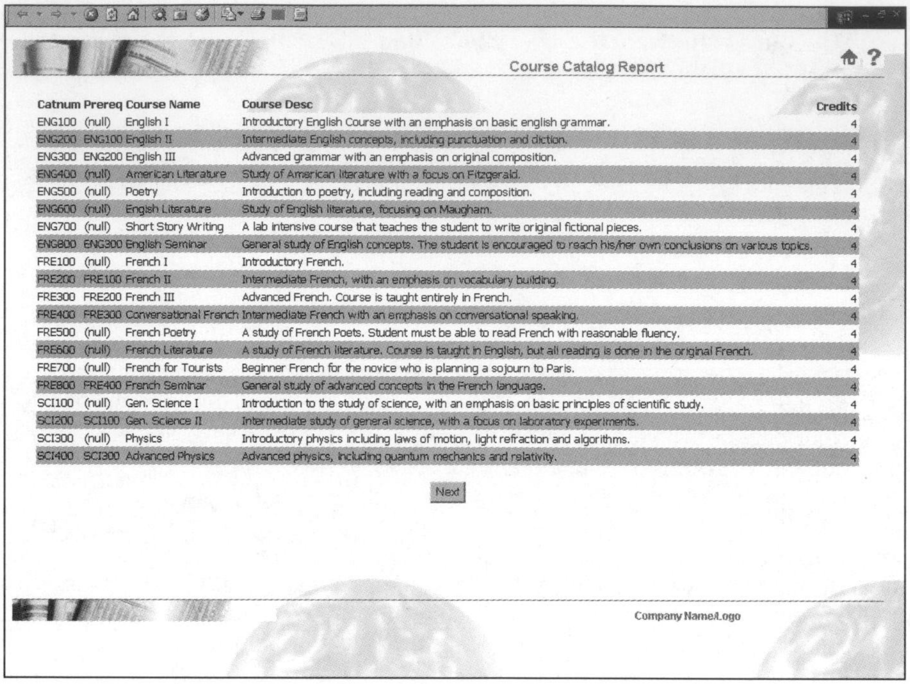

Catnum	Prereq	Course Name	Course Desc	Credits
ENG100	(null)	English I	Introductory English Course with an emphasis on basic english grammar.	4
ENG200	ENG100	English II	Intermediate English concepts, including punctuation and diction.	4
ENG300	ENG200	English III	Advanced grammar with an emphasis on original composition.	4
ENG400	(null)	American Literature	Study of American literature with a focus on Fitzgerald.	4
ENG500	(null)	Poetry	Introduction to poetry, including reading and composition.	4
ENG600	(null)	English Literature	Study of English literature, focusing on Maugham.	4
ENG700	(null)	Short Story Writing	A lab intensive course that teaches the student to write original fictional pieces.	4
ENG800	ENG300	English Seminar	General study of English concepts. The student is encouraged to reach his/her own conclusions on various topics.	4
FRE100	(null)	French I	Introductory French.	4
FRE200	FRE100	French II	Intermediate French, with an emphasis on vocabulary building.	4
FRE300	FRE200	French III	Advanced French. Course is taught entirely in French.	4
FRE400	FRE300	Conversational French	Intermediate French with an emphasis on conversational speaking.	4
FRE500	(null)	French Poetry	A study of French Poets. Student must be able to read French with reasonable fluency.	4
FRE600	(null)	French Literature	A study of French literature. Course is taught in English, but all reading is done in the original French.	4
FRE700	(null)	French for Tourists	Beginner French for the novice who is planning a sojourn to Paris.	4
FRE800	FRE400	French Seminar	General study of advanced concepts in the French language.	4
SCI100	(null)	Gen. Science I	Introduction to the study of science, with an emphasis on basic principles of scientific study.	4
SCI200	SCI100	Gen. Science II	Intermediate study of general science, with a focus on laboratory experiments.	4
SCI300	(null)	Physics	Introductory physics including laws of motion, light refraction and algorithms.	4
SCI400	SCI300	Advanced Physics	Advanced physics, including quantum mechanics and relativity.	4

Figure 16-2: Sample data from the COURSE_CATALOG table

The `substr` function extracts a substring from the column named in the first parameter ("`catnum`") from the starting position indicated in the second parameter ("`1`") for the length indicated by the third parameter ("`3`"). The keyword following the `substr` function, `Department`, is the name used as the column heading in the returned results. This query yields the following results when it runs from SQL*Plus:

```
DEP
---
ACT
ART
BIO
BUS
CHM
COM
ENG
FIN
FRE
GER
HIS
ITA
LAT
LAW
MKT
SCI
SPA
```

This may not be an optimal technique for providing department information for COURSE_CATALOG records, but you may find this technique already in use in some of your existing Oracle databases.

Because one of the strengths of Portal is its capability to leverage these existing databases on the Web, you may find that you wish to display some of these hidden codes on your portal pages. Later in this chapter, you will make use of these hidden codes in a list-of-values object.

Update versus Query List-of-Values Objects

List-of-values objects come in two types: the first type (update) provides data integrity and the second type (query) simplifies querying the database. You use update LOV objects during the data entry process to ensure that a user only enters a valid value for a given field. The LOV object in this case typically matches a database integrity rule on the server side. For instance, in the NetU database, each UGRADS record includes address information, and the address information includes a field to indicate which state the student hails from. When you allow a user to enter new UGRADS records, you should prevent the user from adding a new record with a state value that does not appear in the STATES table. An LOV object can be attached to the data entry form in order to prevent the user from entering a value for a column that does not appear in the LOV attached to that column. The LOV object does not protect the data's integrity from non-Portal applications, but it does prevent the user from entering a value that does not appear in the LOV within the Portal environment.

The second type of LOV object (the query type) is more widely used throughout Portal applications and serves as a means to make it easier for users to submit queries to the database through Portal. In this case, you can use the LOV object to simplify the query process by providing a quick menu for query-by-example. For example, if you build a query or report against the UGRADS table, you may wish to enable the user to select records by state. By providing a LOV object for states and attaching it to the customization form, the user could quickly select UGRADS records by state. There are several examples of LOV objects within the NetU data model, and you will make use of them as you move ahead in this chapter.

The only difference between an update LOV and a query LOV is where the LOV object is used. You can use a single LOV object both for validation and for query purposes, and no distinction is necessary when you create a list-of-values object. However, in most cases, you will use the query LOV object to simplify the task of entering parameters for queries and reports. Table 16-1 shows you where LOV objects can be used within a Portal application.

Table 16-1
Using LOV Objects with Portal's Component Builders

Builder	Validation	Parameter Entry
Forms	X	X
Dynamic Pages		X
Reports		X
Charts		X
Calendars		X
Hierarchies		X

Building a simple, static LOV object

You can build list-of-values objects directly off your data model, or you can build them by explicitly adding the values to a LOV object. If you choose to build a static LOV object, the display does not change when data in the database changes. The values change only if you manually edit the LOV object.

In previous versions of Oracle9iAS Portal, LOVs were part of the Shared Components Library. Lists-of-values are associated with applications in this release of Oracle9iAS Portal.

Portal enables you to create either a dynamic LOV object or a static LOV object. Static LOV objects have a hard-coded list of values that must be manually edited by the LOV developer. Dynamic LOV objects derive their values from data in the database and are automatically changed when the data in the database tables changes. The main panel for the LOV Wizard provides two links, one for each type of LOV object, as shown in Figure 16-3. The simpler of the two types is the static LOV object, which you will create as your first list-of-values object.

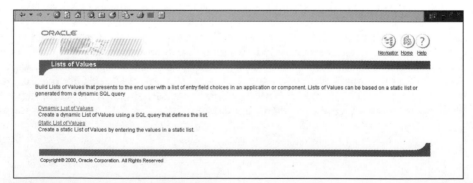

Figure 16-3: Main list-of-values panel

1. Navigate to the NETCOLLEGE application and use the Create->List of Values Link.

2. Select the Static List of Values link to create your first LOV object.

Portal presents you with a simple panel that you will use to create all the elements for your static LOV object. As Figure 16-4 shows, the top portion of the panel enables you to specify critical information for the LOV that you are about to create.

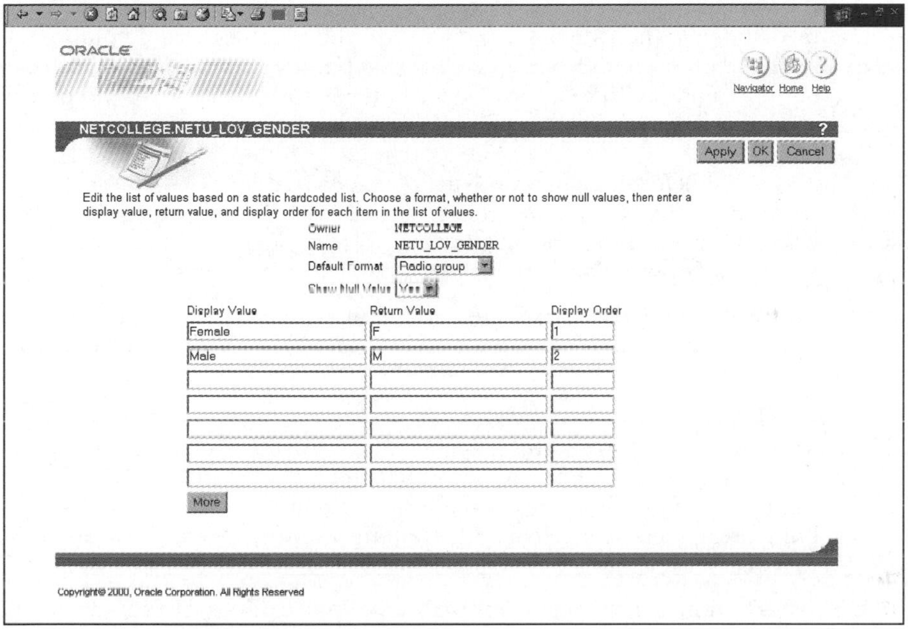

Figure 16-4: Static LOV creation panel

3. Select NETCOLLEGE as the application owner for the LOV.

Note

In general, you want to organize your applications by using a common Portal application owner for all the objects that are part of a single, logical application. There are occasions when you may use a single LOV object across a group of applications. For example, say you are going to build an LOV object to provide the user with a choice of gender values: M for male and F for female. It is quite possible to use this list-of-values object across several applications, as it has widespread applicability for all applications that track gender information. In previous releases of Portal, it was possible to share the same LOV object across logical applications by using a common, public owner. With the release of 3.0, Oracle has implemented the application "owner" that acts as a container for all application objects.

You now need to fill in the name of the new LOV object. Although Portal tracks objects by type for your user name automatically, we recommend using a standard scheme for naming your objects in order to make applications easier to manage.

> 4. Enter **netu_lov_gender** as the name for your LOV object.

Note   You needn't worry about mixing upper- and lowercase letters in the name, because Portal converts all names to uppercase when it stores the object.

After you have named your new LOV object, the next task is to decide on a default format for displaying the values for the list. Use the Default Format combo box to make one of five choices for your default at this point: check box, combo box, pop-up, radio group, and multiple select. These choices roughly correspond to their equivalent display types from the days of client/server:

✦ The check box format causes the list-of-values to display as a series of labels with an associated check box next to each label. The user can select a value by clicking the check box. This display format is typically reserved for situations where you can select multiple values, and the list of choices is relatively short.

✦ The next choice is the combo box option, which displays as a drop-down list box. Combo boxes are most often used to display a long list-of-values, such as a table of states.

✦ If the list of data items you wish to display is extremely long, then you may wish to use the pop-up format, which causes Portal to display the data in a pop-up window. When you choose this format, Portal automatically provides a Find function, which enables you to quickly search a long list for a specific value. Portal itself makes use of the pop-up window extensively for all of its object-search screens.

✦ The next choice on the list is radio group. Radio groups are similar to check boxes, but the graphic display features a circle instead of a box. Radio groups are typically used to denote either/or-type choices, and are perfect for options such as on/off, true/false, and yes/no/maybe.

✦ The final format is the multiple select choice, which is similar to a list box style of display. One distinguishing characteristic of the multiple select format is that it enables you to select multiple choices from the list at once. This makes the multiple select format the ideal choice for query by example panels. For example, consider the course catalog list at the beginning of this chapter. If you wish to enable your users to select multiple departments at the same time for a query, you can display the parameter list of departments using a multiple select format.

Caution   Multiple select LOVs can only be used for querying data. Portal does not directly support the use of multiple select LOVs for data entry or data updates.

Radio groups and check boxes are appropriate only for limited lists-of-values, because they use up lots of page real estate with an object for every individual choice. Conversely, the combo box and pop-up options are best for longer lists-of-values. Multiple select boxes are reserved solely for situations in which the end user is permitted to select multiple values for a single field. However, you do not need to spend too much time choosing how to display your LOV at this point, because Portal gives you the opportunity to change the display every time you deploy the list-of-values object. It is convenient to enter a value here in order to enforce consistency, but you will have the chance to override this choice later.

For the example object you are about to create, the radio group is the most appropriate choice for the gender field, because there a small number of choices (two) and you can only be one or the other, not both.

5. Select the radio group choice for your first list-of-values object.

The last decision you need to make on this portion of the panel is whether you wish to display NULL values. From a database perspective, NULL values are used to indicate that the data value for a given field is missing. For example, if you did not know the gender of a UGRAD when you entered them into the system, the gender field would be NULL. When you build a list-of-values, Portal optionally displays an entry to indicate null or missing data. If you wish to allow users to enter new UGRADS records without entering a value for the gender field, change the Show Null Value option to Yes.

The bottom portion of the current panel offers you the ability to enter static values for your LOV object. The structure you use to enter these values is quite simple. For each row of the LOV, you are asked to provide three values. First, in the text box on the extreme left-hand side, enter the display value as shown in Figure 16-4. The display value is the text the end users see when they use the LOV object. In the case of our GENDER example, the text that users see is either "Female" or "Male." The display value is often considered the *friendly value* for a list, because it is the portion that is shown on the screen when the user interacts with the data.

The return value is the actual data value passed along to the database as the data value for the column when the data is written or the table is queried against. In this example, the database itself stores the values (F and M) in the database for the column gender, so F and M become the return values for Female and Male. Figure 16-4 shows the display value and return value for GENDER.

In addition to the display and return values, Portal gives you the opportunity to choose the order in which the display values are shown. The default is the order in which the data values are entered. Notice that the user interface for adding and inserting new display/return values does not provide a way to insert values in the middle of a current list. This is due to the fact that Portal uses straight HTML for its interface, which limits some user interface flexibility that you may have been used to in other development tools. The solution to this is to make sure that you always insert a display order value as shown in Figure 16-4. As long as Portal has a display order value, the order in which you entered the display/return values does not matter.

You can see that initially Portal only provides ten display/return text field combinations for you to work with. This makes it impossible to use the static LOV object if you have more than ten display/return combinations. However, you can fill in all the available slots and then save the LOV by using the Apply button. Once you have save the LOV using Apply, you can use the More button to refresh the page with additional empty rows.

While this may initially appear to be a limitation, it is actually a conscious design decision on the part of Portal's developers. If you have more than ten LOV entries, you should probably store them in a database table as a dynamic LOV object. Later in this chapter, you'll see how to use a single table to store multiple LOV lists. You can do this in situations where you may not feel that you need to create a dynamic LOV.

6. Enter the following values for the static list-of-values shown in Figure 16-4:

```
Display Value - Female
Return Value - F
Display Order - 1

Display Value - Male
Return Value - M
Display Order - 2
```

7. Click the OK button to complete the list-of-values object and return to the Manage Component LOV page.

Portal provides the familiar set of development links at the bottom of the main panel. The Run link causes Portal to display a panel that allows you to test your LOV object using all five display formats.

Testing your LOV object

1. Use the Run link to display the test panel as shown in Figure 16-5.

The top object of Figure 16-5 shows the NETU_LOV_GENDER object as a combo box. As you can see from the graphic, the combo box features a drop-down arrow for showing the display values, and the values themselves appear in a multiline text box. The combo box is an ideal format for an LOV object that has between 3 and 50 possible values, and it only allows the user to select a single value.

The second object on the panel shows the NETU_LOV_GENDER list-of-values object displayed in the pop-up format. Pop-up is short for pop-up window, and Portal itself uses this format for most of its search screens. The display is simple enough to begin with, as it is just a text box with a small icon to the right. If you click the icon, Portal displays the search panel as shown in the overlay for Figure 16-5.

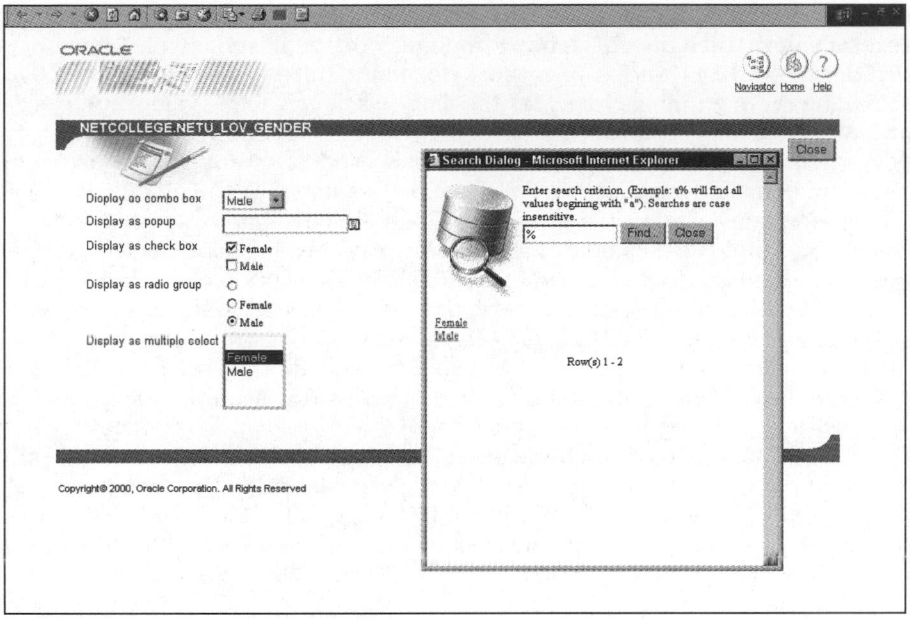

Figure 16-5: LOV Wizard test panel

Initially, the body of the panel is filled with up to ten rows of data. However, if you enter search criteria and press the Find button, Portal displays the complete list of display values that match your search criteria. Entering the % wildcard as search criterion by itself returns the entire list. You can select a given entry simply by clicking the link displayed as part of the value. The pop-up format is ideal for long lists-of-values that are generated from data in the database, because you can easily restrict the list to only the values that you are interested in. Because the NETU_LOV_GENDER LOV only has two values, the pop-up format is overkill for this particular LOV object.

> **Note**
>
> Pop-ups operate as nonmodal windows and Portal does not automatically close the window when the user navigates back to the main window. (However, Portal will close the window automatically if the user selects one of the links on the search page.)

The middle object of Figure 16-5 shows NETU_LOV_GENDER as a radio group and check box. The radio group is traditionally used to distinguish among several mutually exclusive choices. Radio groups are suitable for both data entry and query entry and they give the user a fast visual cue as to the range of values for a given field. Unlike the combo box and multiple select box display formats, but similar to the check box format, you can see all the values of a radio group when you print the HTML page. This is a plus if the user is planning on printing a page for note taking before entering data into the system.

If you have a limited number of choices, but you want the user to be able to select several values, then the check box format may be the best choice. You can see NETU_LOV_GENDER shown as a check box in the third position in Figure 16-5. While the radio group only enables the user to select a single value, such as Female or Male, the check box format enables the user to select both values. This format is best when a data field has a default value of No and you want to give the user the choice of turning the option on. For example, assume that you change the UGRADS table to include a field called PUBLISH_GRADES. The default value at the database level is N, or null, for this field. You could display this field as a single-value check box. If the field is checked, the value of PUBLISH_GRADES is changed to Y, which causes a copy of the student's next report card to be sent to his or her parents.

The last object shows the same LOV displayed as a multiple select box. The multiple select box is shown as a multiline text box; and Portal automatically adds a vertical scroll bar to the right-hand side if there are more than four entries for the LOV. One feature unique to the multiple select box and check box formats is the ability to select multiple entries from the list. You can select several entries by pressing the Ctrl or Shift key and clicking your mouse at the same time. This makes the multiple select display format type ideal when you are using your LOV object to send parameters to a query or a report.

Caution   As mentioned previously, multiselects are ideal for allowing users to select multiple values for query panels. In the case of data entry, however, it is the wrong format to use, because the database is only going to allow you to store one value in the field.

2. Use the objects on the Test List of Values page to test the NETU_LOV_GENDER LOV. Return to the management component panel when you are finished testing your new static LOV.

Caution   The LOV Wizard does not attempt to validate any of the data that you enter into the display/return fields. The only indication that you have entered incorrect data comes when you attempt to use the LOV object to query or store data. For this reason, it is important to test your LOV lists carefully with other Portal components before deploying them to production portal pages.

Deploying a Static LOV Object to Another Component

The default behavior for the LOV Wizard is to take you back to the Manage Component page when you have finished building or modifying an LOV object. As you saw in the preceding section, you can test the visual display for your new LOV object directly from this page as well. However, the real test of whether you have designed your LOV properly is to use the LOV object with a container Portal object such as a form or report.

Remember that you can use LOV objects for both updating data and submitting queries to the database. The simplest technique for making use of your new LOV object is to attach it to a report or form.

On the CD-ROM

If you have completed Chapter 5, you may wish to modify the UGRADS report from that chapter. Otherwise, you can load the sample report rpt_lov_1 from the CD-ROM.

1. Load the sample report ch16_rpt_lov using the Portal account and SQL*Plus and then use the Find panel on the main page within Portal to locate the ch16_rpt_lov report as shown in Figure 16-6.

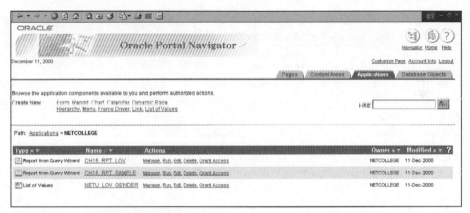

Figure 16-6: Find results panel

2. Select the ch16_rpt_lov Edit link from the panel as shown in Figure 16-6.

3. Navigate to the Customization Form Display Options panel, as shown in Figure 16-7.

Portal shows you a familiar panel that enables you to provide a query prompt for any field in the current report. The sample report already has an entry for the GENDER field, but the details of the prompt have not been entered.

4. Click the icon to the right of the LOV text field.

This action causes Portal to display a familiar search panel that enables you to search for matching objects (as shown in the overlay in Figure 16-7). You can enter the name of your static LOV object directly, or you can use the Find button to locate the object NETU_LOV_GENDER.

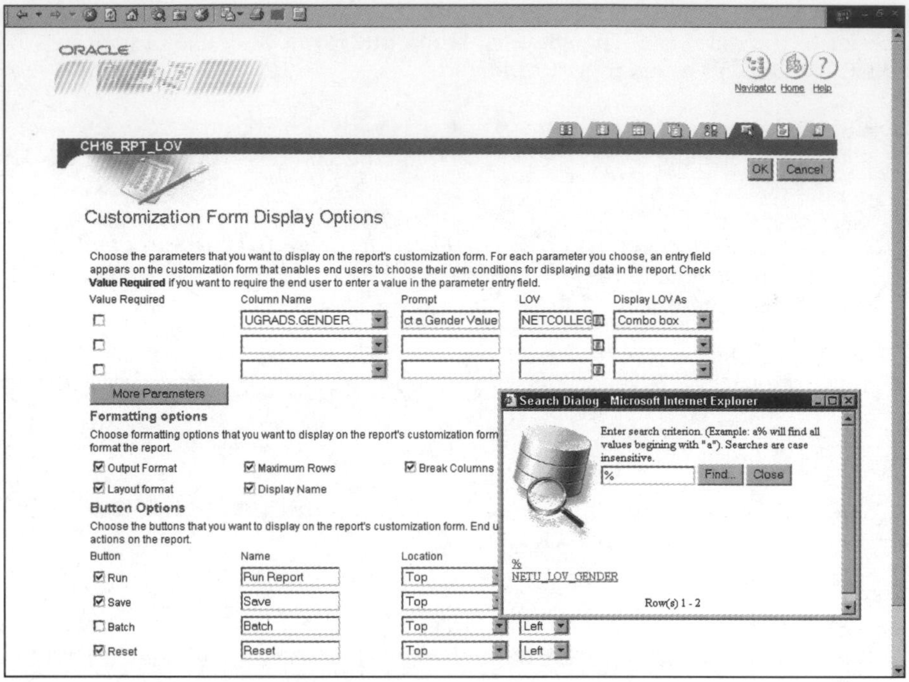

Figure 16-7: Customization Form Display Options panel

5. Click the name of the NETU_LOV_GENDER object.

Portal has now attached your LOV object to the GENDER prompt in this sample report. Although you chose a display format when you created your static LOV object, you can override this formatting decision directly in this panel. The drop-down combo box to the right of the LOV field enables you to select a new format for this display.

6. Select the combo box format for the LOV type combo box. The panel should now look like the panel shown in Figure 16-7.

There is no need to view any of the remaining panels, because you are only concerned with modifying the report to use NETU_LOV_GENDER.

7. Click the OK button to save your changes to this report.

8. Click the Customize link and Portal displays a parameter panel, as shown in Figure 16-8.

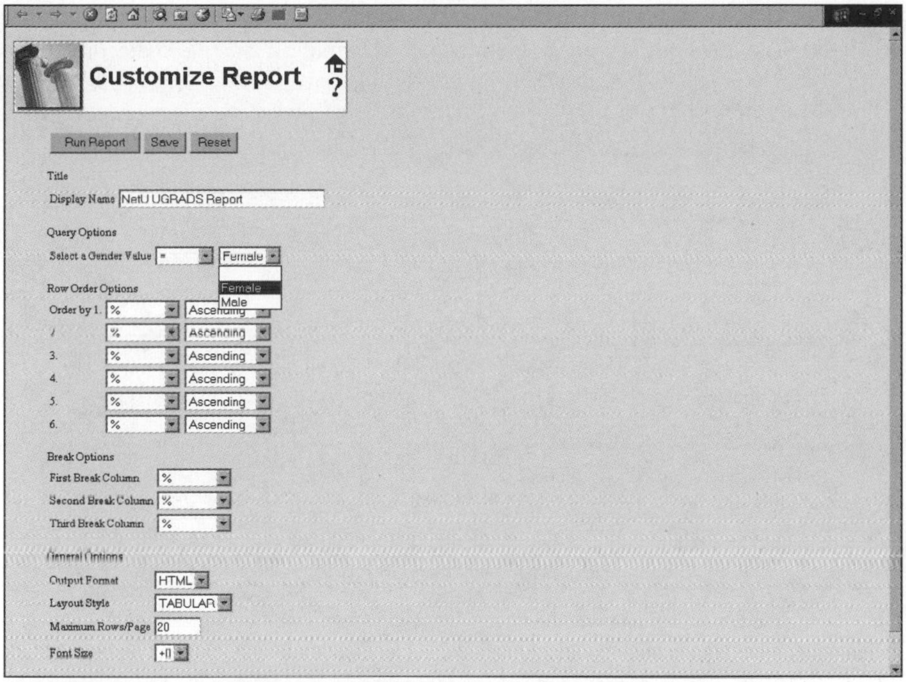

Figure 16-0: Customize entry form with NETU_LOV_GENDER LOV

Notice that Portal automatically uses the LOV object that you attached to the GENDER parameter field. All the end user needs to do is select either Female or Male by clicking one of the combo box options next to the Gender field (along with a Boolean value). You will notice that Portal adds a third wildcard (%) value to the list. This value allows the user to select all of the parameters (male and female in this case). Portal automatically adds the wildcard option to LOV objects that are used on parameter forms. If you allowed the user to enter NULL values, Portal would also add a blank line for NULL values for this LOV object. Once the end user selects an option, he or she can click the Run Report button to execute the query and review the results, as shown in Figure 16-9.

9. Select the option for Female along with the = operator and then use the Run Report link to display the results of the query.

10. Navigate back to the Main Component panel when you are finished testing the GENDER query.

The Gender database column contains the values F and M, and Portal's radio group automatically translates the user's selection into one of those two values for the query. The alternative to using an LOV object is to display the GENDER prompt as a text box. This may not make it clear to users just which values they are supposed to enter for the report. As you can see, the LOV object makes it much clearer to users just what the choices are for the GENDER prompt.

Note

Portal enables you to provide additional information on the customize page to assist the user with formatting and selecting data. These topics are covered in detail in the Chapters 8 and 9.

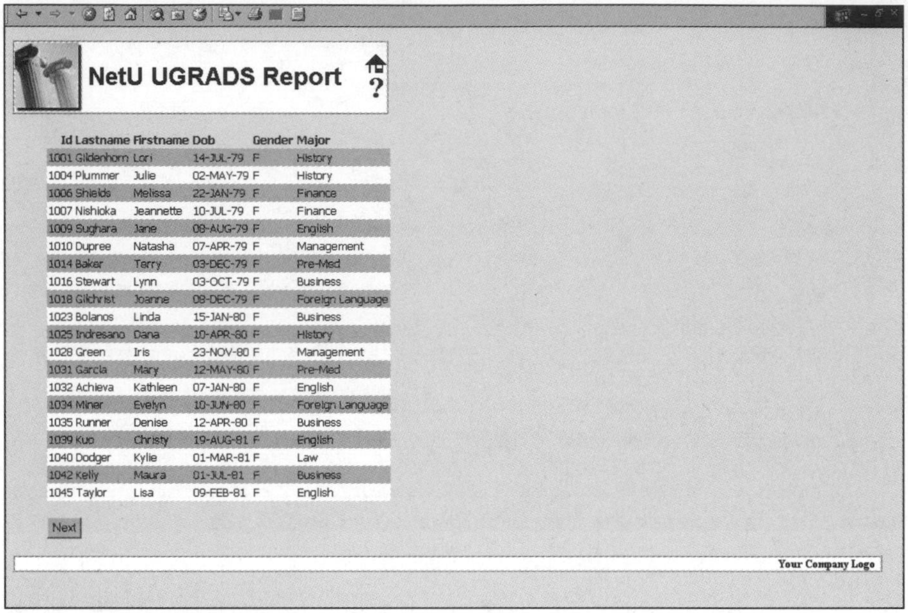
NetU UGRADS Report
Id Lastname Firstname Dob Gender Major
1001 Gildenhorn Lori 14-JUL-79 F History
1004 Plummer Julie 02-MAY-79 F History
1006 Shields Melissa 22-JAN-79 F Finance
1007 Nishioka Jeannette 10-JUL-79 F Finance
1009 Sughara Jane 08-AUG-79 F English
1010 Dupree Natasha 07-APR-79 F Management
1014 Baker Terry 03-DEC-79 F Pre-Med
1016 Stewart Lynn 03-OCT-79 F Business
1018 Gilchrist Joanne 08-DEC-79 F Foreign Language
1023 Bolanos Linda 15-JAN-80 F Business
1025 Indresano Dana 10-APR-80 F History
1028 Green Iris 23-NOV-80 F Management
1031 Garcia Mary 12-MAY-80 F Pre-Med
1032 Achieva Kathleen 07-JAN-80 F English
1034 Miner Evelyn 10-JUN-80 F Foreign Language
1035 Runner Denise 12-APR-80 F Business
1039 Kuo Christy 19-AUG-81 F English
1040 Dodger Kylie 01-MAR-81 F Law
1042 Kelly Maura 01-JUL-81 F Business
1045 Taylor Lisa 09-FEB-81 F English
Next
Your Company Logo

Figure 16-9: Gender query results

Creating a Dynamic LOV Object

While static LOV objects provide you with a tool for making your applications more consistent, they do have one major drawback. In order to change the values that are either displayed or stored, you must change the LOV code within Portal. In the case of the NETU_LOV_GENDER object, this is not really a concern, because it is unlikely that you will need to add a new gender value to your system. However, there are many cases when your list-of-values is more dynamic and you need to add and change data in the list more frequently. For example, in the Net University system, each student record has a MAJOR field, which contains that student's chosen field of study. The value in the MAJOR field joins to the table MAJORS. This table contains the master list of majors for Net University students. To see a list of the possible majors currently in the database, enter the query in Listing 16-3 in a SQL*Plus session (or with a Portal report).

Listing 16-3: **Displaying a list of majors**

```
select major, major_desc from netu.majors
```

You should get the results shown in Figure 16-10.

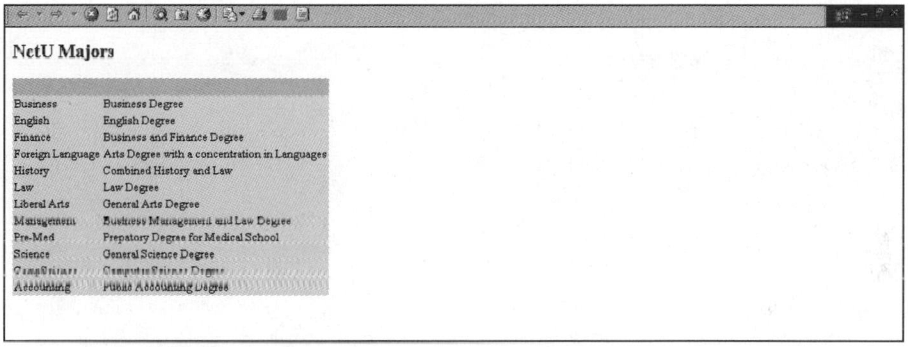

Figure 16-10: List of NetU majors

It is likely that NetU will need to add, delete, or modify majors over the life of your Portal application. In light of this, it does not make sense to hard-code these values into a static LOV object that you will then have to modify by hand *each* time the list of majors changes. A simpler solution is to build the LOV dynamically from the data in the database. Portal offers you the dynamic LOV Wizard to help you create such an object.

1. Navigate to the NETCOLLEGE application.

2. Use the List of Values Link to create a new LOV.

3. Select the Dynamic LOV Link.

Portal displays a panel similar to the one you used to create the static list-of-values object, as shown in Figure 16-11. The top part of the panel is identical to the one you used for the static LOV and provides you with the opportunity to name your object and select a display format.

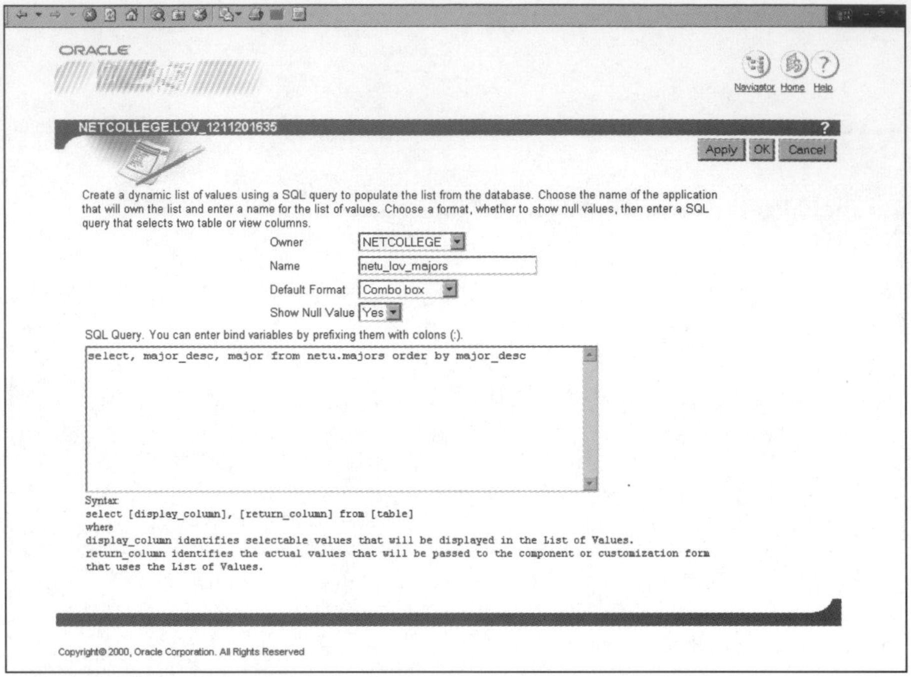

Figure 16-11: Dynamic LOV object panel

4. Enter the following information into the top portion of the panel:

```
Owner Application- NETCOLLEGE
Name - NETU_LOV_MAJORS
Default Format - Combo
Show Null Value - No
```

The main difference between the static wizard interface and the dynamic wizard interface is the bottom portion of the panel. Whereas the static LOV object required you to input specific values into text boxes, the dynamic LOV object uses a SQL statement to create the data. The good news is that Portal provides you with a simple multiline text box in which you can enter your SQL statement. The bad news is that you need to have a basic understanding of SQL SELECT statements in order to build your list-of-values. Portal provides you with a sample SELECT statement so that you can see the format Portal is looking for.

Portal displays the default query structure in two formats. Within the query text box you see a sample query using the default Oracle EMP table. Just below the query text box, Portal shows the same query statement in a default syntax format. In order to build a dynamic LOV object, you have to pattern your SQL SELECT statement after the default query Portal provides. The key to building your LOV SELECT statement is to understand the three portions of the SELECT statement:

✦ The first element to be aware of is the display_column. The display_column is the database column you wish to display in the LOV to the user. It correlates to the display column text box of the static LOV Wizard.

✦ The second element is the value_column, which is the value you wish to pass along to the database as part of the query or as part of the insert/update operation. The value column corresponds to the Value Column text box in the static LOV Wizard. For example, if you build an LOV against the STATES table, the STATE_CODE (AL, AK, and so on) is the value column and the STATE_NAME (Alabama, Alaska, and so on) is the display column.

✦ The final element of the query is the table_name, which corresponds to the name of the table on which you are basing this query.

Caution   While the table_name may initially appear to be the simplest portion of the query, you must enter your table name cautiously. If you have created a public synonym for the table name within your Oracle database, then you can simply enter the table name directly in the LOV query. However, if you have not created a public synonym, you need to preface the table_name column with the Oracle USERID that owns the table. Entering a USERID as part of the table_name affects the portability of your application, and you need to remember this if you attempt to move any object you create in this manner between systems or users.

Listing 16-4 shows the query that you should enter for the NETU_LOV_MAJORS LOV.

Listing 16-4: Query text for NETU_LOV_MAJORS

```
select major_desc, major
from netu.majors
order by major_desc
```

Note the addition of a clause that Portal did not offer to you in the sample SELECT statement in the form of an ORDER BY clause. When you created your static LOV object, you were able to input a display order value along with the display and value entries. If you do not specify an ORDER BY clause for your SQL query, the Oracle database returns the data in an order of its own choosing, which may not be the order you were hoping for. In general, the Oracle database follows some basic rules for selecting data; and you will find that code and description tables are likely to be queried by default in code order. However, it is always best to build consistency into your objects, so you should always add the ORDER BY clause in your dynamic SQL statements.

Note   If you wish to sort your data in a custom format (nonalphabetic), you may need to add your own display order field to your data table. You could then enter custom values in the display order field and sort your data based on these values, much as the static LOV automatically sorts on the numeric values in the display order field.

Although it does not initially appear as though you have much flexibility in the format of your SQL statement, this is a bit of a misconception. In actuality, you can enter any valid Oracle SQL statement that returns a unique set of rows in the `display_column, value_column` format.

For example, if you only wanted to include values in your NETU_LOV_MAJORS list that actually matched preexisting NetU student records, you could enter the query shown in Listing 16-5.

Listing 16-5: Query text for NETU_LOV_MAJORS

```
select major_desc, major
from netu.majors where major in (select major from netu.ugrads)
order by major
```

Enter the query in Listing 16-4 (or Listing 16-5) and then click the OK button to save the new LOV.

Once you have stored the object, you can test the display using the same links at the bottom of the panel that you used to test the static LOV. Figure 16-12 shows the NETU_LOV_MAJORS list-of-values as a pop-up window.

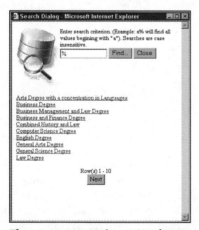

Figure 16-12: Majors LOV shown as a pop-up window

The value of building this list dynamically is that it is derived from the data in the database, so it changes as the data in the database changes. Once you have a system in production, you will likely provide your users with a set of forms for adding new majors to the MAJORS table. In this manner, the LOV object is self-maintaining, because each time it is executed it derives its data from the database. This saves you the trouble of having to edit the LOV manually each time your end users need to make a change to the data. The pop-up format allows you to search through long lists of data, which is ideal for dynamic LOV objects. Users can enter text into the text box and use the Search button to locate matching strings of data. Each returned value is displayed as a link, which you can click to return the value to the calling form.

For the sake of simplicity, you can test this theory easily without having to use a data entry form for the MAJORS table.

1. Connect to your NETU USERID using SQL*Plus (or PL/SQL Developer) and enter the commands shown in Listing 16-6.

Listing 16-6: **Inserting a new record in the majors table**

```
insert into majors values ('ArtHistory', 'Combined Art and
History Degree','B.A.');
commit;
```

2. Retest the NETU_LOV_MAJORS object.

You can see that the new major shows up in the list automatically as the fifth entry. You may wonder why the entry did not show up with the As in the list, but remember that you chose to sort this list by MAJOR_DESC and not MAJOR.

Using the Dynamic LOV to Update Records

In the previous sections, you used your LOV object to simplify the process of inputting query parameters to a report. You can also use lists-of-values to improve the process of inserting or updating data in the database. The UGRADS table is the center point for the application, so you will use this table to test the NETU_LOV_MAJORS object.

1. Open SQL*Plus, log in as Portal, and import the component ch16_frm_ugrads into the NETCOLLEGE application.

2. Locate the ch16_frm_ugrads object that you just imported. Click the Run link to execute the form.

You should see a page similar to the one shown in Figure 16-13.

Figure 16-13: UGRADS form for modifying data

By default, this sample form does not include an association with the dynamic LOV you just created or the static LOV that you created earlier, so neither the MAJORS LOV nor the GENDER LOV appears in the form.

You can correct the problem easily by editing the ch16_frm_ugrads form object.

1. Use your browser's back button to return to the Oracle9*i*AS Portal Navigator and select the Edit option. The panel you need to adjust is the first panel Portal displays for you, as shown in Figure 16-14.

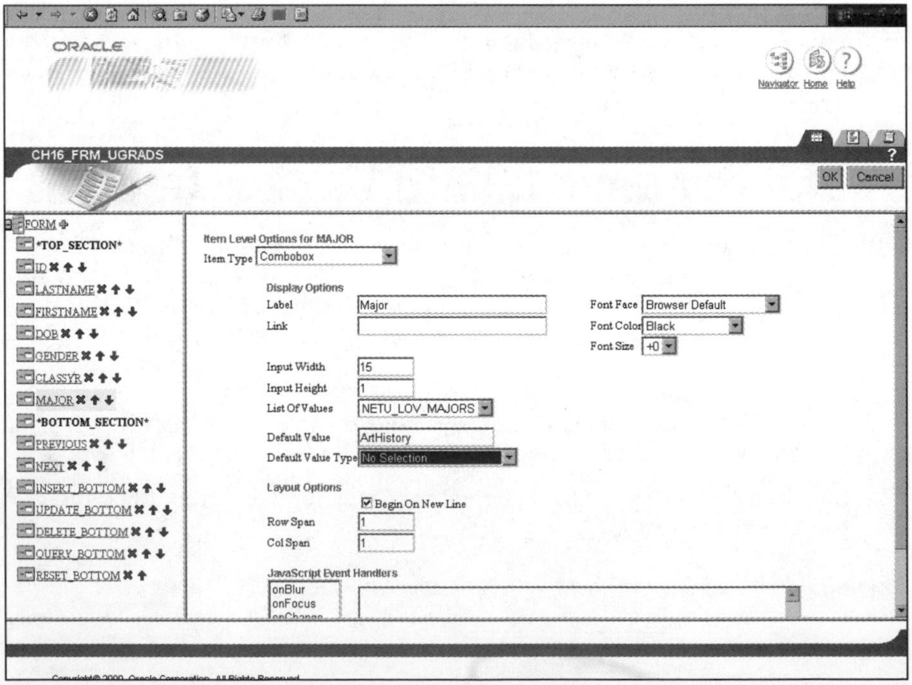

Figure 16-14: Column formatting and validation panel

2. Use the vertical text box on the left side of the panel to select the MAJOR column as shown in Figure 16-14.

3. Select the combo box entry from the Item Type box to set this particular form to a combo box format.

4. With the cursor in the left-hand panel still highlighting the Major field, navigate down to the list-of-values combo box and select the NETU_LOV_MAJORS object as shown in Figure 16-14.

Note

It is also possible to select a default value for your LOV object at this point in the editing process. The "Default Value" field on the form is used for this purpose. However, with LOV objects you must remember to use the CODE value and not the DESCRIPTION value for the default. For example, you would use "ArtHistory" instead of "Combined Art and History Major" as the entry in the default value field.

5. Click the OK button at the top of the page to save your changes, compile the form, and return to the Manage Component page.

6. Click the Run option to test your form.

7. You can see that the MAJOR field is displayed as a combo box as shown in Figure 16-15.

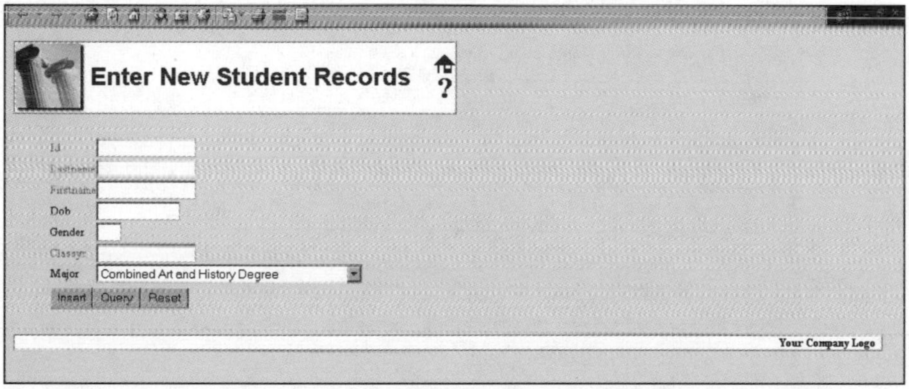

Figure 16-15: MAJOR displayed as a combo box on the student record form

Tip

Check boxes, radio groups, combo boxes and multi select boxes all display the description field (the first field in the LOV) on the form. Pop-up window LOVs will show the *description* field on the search panel, but they will display the *value* field on the hosting form once the user has selected an entry.

Using Multiselect Lists-of-Values

So far, you have used LOV objects to select and modify records. In all cases, you have used a single value. Often, you will create reports or queries that enable your users to search for several values at the same time. For example, your users may want to create a report on UGRADS that selects students based on their current major, and your users may want to select several majors at the same time. Fortunately, you can use the LOV object to help users to enter query parameters for such a report.

1. Return to the Navigator and edit the report ch16_rpt_lov.

2. Click the Customization Form Display Options tab to display the panel, as shown in Figure 16-16.

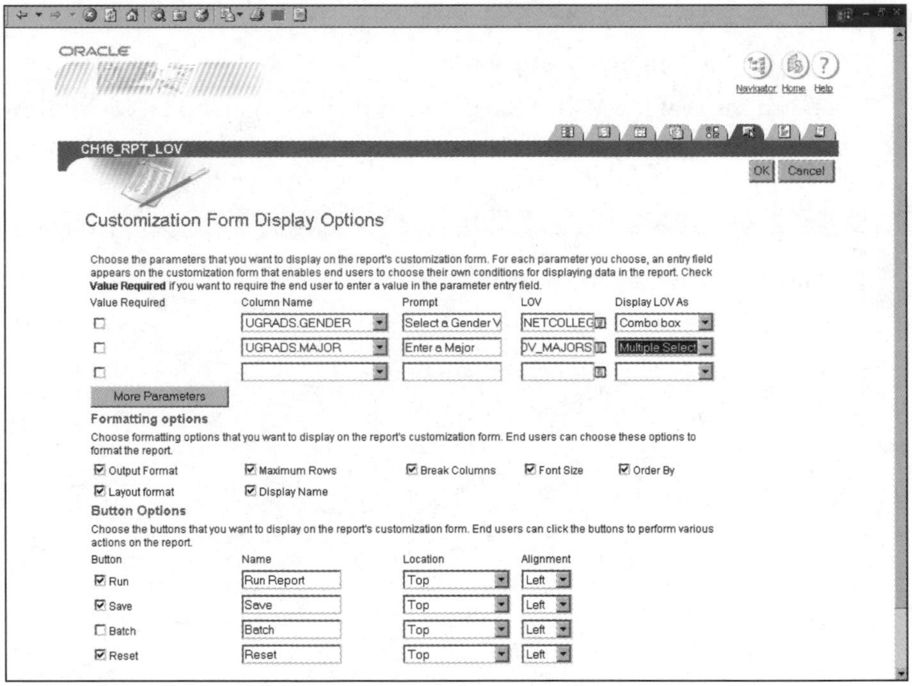

Figure 16-16: Parameter prompt for MAJOR

You will remember from the chapter on building reports that you can enter a variety of search conditions for a given field prompt. This particular form is identical to the first report that you used with the GENDER field.

3. Add the MAJORS field to the selection list. Then click the list icon in the LOV column to locate the NETU_LOV_MAJORS list box, and use the multiple select display option for this field.

The parameter engine for Portal automatically associates this prompt with a value condition on the parameters form at run time. This enables users to select *groups* of UGRADS by their MAJOR. The use of the multiple select format enables end users to select multiple MAJOR codes for a single query.

4. Click the OK button to save this report.

5. Execute this report by clicking the Customize option, which shows you the page in Figure 16-17.

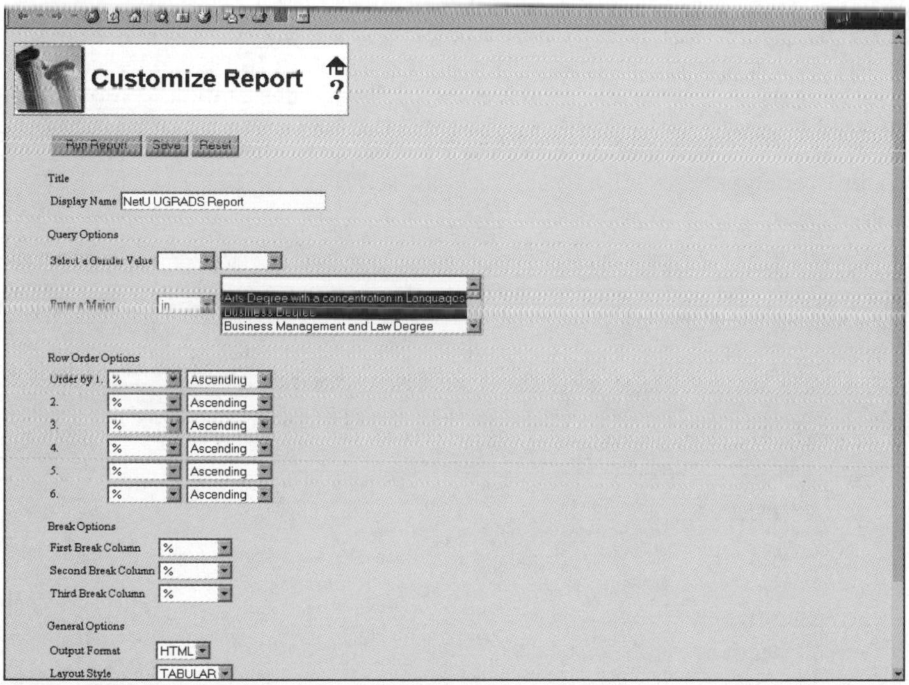

Figure 16-17: Entering multiple parameters

Notice that you can select multiple query parameters by using either Shift+click (Macintosh users) or Ctrl+click (for Windows users) within the "Enter a Major" multiple select box. To instruct Portal to use multiple values in the query, you also have to set the Enter Values string to "in." Portal uses the multiselected values and the "in" clause to create a dynamic query.

6. Select the "Business Degree" and "Arts Degree..." majors as shown in Figure 16-17 and click the Run Report button to execute your query. Figure 16-18 displays the results.

Note

You may note that the values that appear in the report as the majors text do not match the displayed values on the customization panel. The customization panel LOV object displays the description value from the LOV, while the report displays the code value. You will often find this type of mismatch in your own databases. Oracle9*i*AS Portal does not automatically display the description value for dynamic LOV objects in reports, calendars and hierarchies. In order to display the description, you must edit the report and display the description column manually (via a SQL join operation).

Portal uses your selections to build a multiple select query against the data in the report. Notice that the customize form shown in Figure 16-18 enables you to specify a sorting option. When you give users the option to select multiple values for a query, it makes sense to enable them to sort the data as well. Typically, you will want to have the returned results sorted by the multiselect field to make the data easier to analyze.

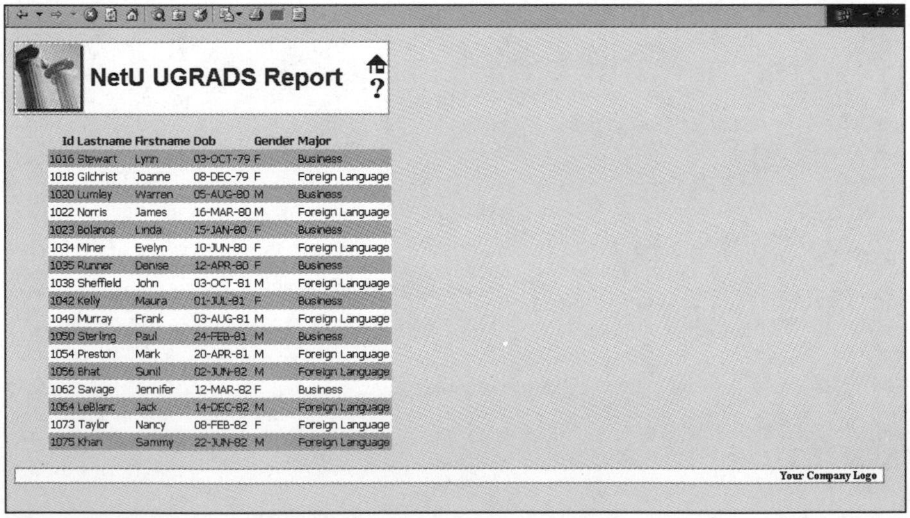

Id	Lastname	Firstname	Dob	Gender	Major
1016	Stewart	Lynn	03-OCT-79	F	Business
1018	Gilchrist	Joanne	08-DEC-79	F	Foreign Language
1020	Lumley	Warren	05-AUG-80	M	Business
1022	Norris	James	16-MAR-80	M	Foreign Language
1023	Bolanos	Linda	15-JAN-80	F	Business
1034	Miner	Evelyn	10-JUN-80	F	Foreign Language
1035	Runner	Denise	12-APR-80	F	Business
1038	Sheffield	John	03-OCT-81	M	Foreign Language
1042	Kelly	Maura	01-JUL-81	F	Business
1049	Murray	Frank	03-AUG-81	M	Foreign Language
1050	Sterling	Paul	24-FEB-81	M	Business
1054	Preston	Mark	20-APR-81	M	Foreign Language
1056	Bhat	Sunil	02-JUN-82	M	Foreign Language
1062	Savage	Jennifer	12-MAR-82	F	Business
1064	LeBlanc	Jack	14-DEC-82	M	Foreign Language
1073	Taylor	Nancy	08-FEB-82	F	Foreign Language
1075	Khan	Sammy	22-JUN-82	M	Foreign Language

Figure 16-18: Multiple values for a query

Note

In order for Portal to properly associate a multiselect LOV with a BIND variable, the BIND variable must be compared using the "in" clause as part of the evaluation expression. Ch16_rpt_lov as defined by Oracle9*i*AS Portal automatically includes the correct format of an "in" clause for the MAJORS query and is shown in Listing 16-7. You might also notice that the majors as shown in the report do not necessarily match the *display* values in the LOV. This is because the report shows the code value, while the LOV shows the description value. You will want to bear this in mind when creating reports for users.

Listing 16-7: LOV Query using the "in" clause

```
select major, classyr, firstname, lastname, phone from
netu.ugrads where major in :my_majors
```

Advanced Techniques for LOV Objects

In addition to the simple data structures discussed in the preceding sections, there are often some additional LOV objects hiding within existing tables in your database. You can often use these lists to improve your data query process.

The three common techniques for deriving additional dynamic lists from your database are as follows:

✦ Derived columns

✦ Dynamic query lists

✦ Multivalue tables

Derived columns

Derived columns are probably less common than other formats, but they are very useful in building complex applications. Database columns often have useful information hiding within the single value stored inside a column. For example, in the PHONE field in the UGRADS table, the first three characters represent the area code of a student's phone number. That may be useful information to have if you are planning a local fundraising event for the college and you are attempting to group people by a common area smaller than a state and larger than a city or town.

You have already seen another example of a derived value earlier in this chapter. You discovered that the department heading is the first three characters of the catalog number for each course. So, if you were writing a report or query and you wanted to select courses by department, you could build a dynamic LOV object using the preceding query as part of the parameter form. In general, it would be better programming practice to store the department number as a separate field. However, you will often find that you are building Portal applications on preexisting data structures that you cannot change, and you may need to use derived columns in order to build your queries.

There are also cases where you can find this hidden data in a nonunique column. For example, while there is no table in the NETU database that can give us a list of student advisors, you can derive the list from the UGRADS table as follows:

```
select distinct advisor_id from netu.ugrads
```

Derived LOV objects can often improve the flexibility of the applications you write with Portal.

Dynamic query lists

Dynamic query lists are the least common LOV you are likely to come across, but they are very powerful and worth knowing about.

A dynamic query is similar to a dynamic list-of-values object, but it uses data from the detail table to restrict the query. For instance, suppose you wanted to use your MAJORS LOV, but you wanted to make sure every major on the list was actually being used. From a query perspective, you may not want to show a long list-of-values to the user if most of the values will not return any valid records. You could use a query such as the following to restrict the LOV to MAJORS that students are currently using:

```
select major_desc, major, from netu.majors where major in
(select major from netu.ugrads)
```

While this query incurs some additional overhead to build because it has to join to the UGRADS table each time it is executed, it guarantees that all values on the list return at least one UGRADS record. You should generally use dynamic query lists for queries and reports, not for data integrity purposes. This makes sense when you think about it. For example, if you only show lists of majors currently associated with students, you will never be able to select a new major for a student, because that major will not show up on the LOV unless it is already in use.

Multivalue tables

Multivalue tables offer a solution to one of the problems associated with static LOV objects. If you have a lot of short LOV lists, you may not want to incur the management overhead of creating tables in your database to store these values. At the same time, if these values turn out to be more dynamic than you thought, you may find yourself having to change them constantly within Portal. A solution to this problem is to combine these lists into a single list that can be stored within a database. You do this by adding a third column that is the name of the list itself. Figure 16-19 shows a sample design and some sample entries for such a table.

```
                                                                              _ □ ×
Oracle SOL*Plus
File  Edit  Search  Options  Help
SQL> desc multilov
 Name                              Null?    Type
 ---------------------------------- -------- ----
 CODE_VAL                                   VARCHAR2(10)
 DISPLAY_VAL                                VARCHAR2(15)
 MULTI_NAME                                 VARCHAR2(15)

SQL> select * from multilov order by multi_name
  2  /

CODE_VAL   DISPLAY_VAL     MULTI_NAME
---------- --------------- ---------------
BLUE       Blue Eyes       EYECOLOR
GREEN      Green Eyes      EYECOLOR
BROWN      Brown Eyes      EYECOLOR
F          Female          Gender
M          Male            Gender
Y          Yes             YesNo
N          No              YesNo

7 rows selected.

SQL> |
```

Figure 16-19: Code and description of a multivalue table

Each set of code and description values is tied together via the MULTI_NAME field. When you create your individual LOV objects as shown in Table 16-2, you use the MULTI_NAME column to organize each list.

Table 16-2
Multivalue LOV Objects

LOV Object	Query
NETU_LOV_GENDER	select display_val, code_val from multilov where multi_name = 'Gender'
NETU_LOV_YESNO	select display_val, code_val from multilov where multi_name = 'YesNo'
NETU_LOV_EYES	select display_val, code_val from multilov where multi_name = 'EYECOLOR'

This technique can save you time if you have lots of small code and description tables. The downside to using this approach from the database perspective is that you cannot automatically make use of declarative database integrity constraints. This is because the addition of the third column prevents the primary key from joining directly with the foreign key. However, you can get around this problem by using database triggers to enforce these requirements. In the end, you need to decide whether these code and description tables will be dynamic enough to warrant storing them as values in the database.

Lists-of-Values with BIND Variables

One of the main deficiencies with lists-of-values in prior releases of Oracle9*i*AS Portal was their inability to support *BIND variables*. BIND variables allow a component to dynamically select data based upon user-supplied values. Without support for BIND variables, it was impossible to make the contents of one LOV dependent upon values in a second LOV. When users are entering data into forms it is quite common to restrict the entries for one field based on a value selected in a prior field. Take the NETU data model for instance. Each UGRADS record contains a CLASSYR field and an ADVISORID field. The CLASSYR determines whether the student is a freshman, sophomore, junior, or senior — and the ADVISORID is a foreign key that contains the ID number of the student that has been assigned as the "Student Advisor." Common sense tells us that advisors must be more senior than the students that they are advising. For example, a Freshman has no business being an advisor to a Junior.

Portal 3.0 allows you to reflect this requirement in LOVs for data entry using BIND variables within LOV objects.

1. Load the objects CH16_LOV_MULTI, CH16_LOV_MULTI2 and CH16_FRM_DYNAMICLOV into Oracle9*i*AS Portal using the Portal account and SQL*Plus.

Listing 16-8 shows the query that is used for the class year LOV, which is a simple query based upon a single table.

Listing 16-8: **Class year LOV (CH16_LOV_MULTI2)**

```
select classcode, classyr from netu.classes
```

Listing 16-9 shows the query for the advisor LOV, which is a complex query based on several tables.

Listing 16-9: **Advisor LOV (CH16_LOV_MULTI)**

```
select classcode||' -- '||lastname||','||firstname, id from
netu.ugrads, netu.classes where ugrads.classyr =
classes.classyr and ugrads.classyr < :classyr
```

In the first part of the advisor query, we concatenate the `classcode` value from the `classes` table to the `lastname` and `firstname` of the student record. This gives you a description field in the following format:

```
Senior - Doe, Jane
```

The description quickly displays the grade year of the student along with the student's name. So, you can see that Jane Doe is a Senior, just by looking at this string. In the second part of the query, the `id` field is used as the code field. Since the `advisorid` field must match a valid student ID, you must use the `id` field as the basis for the code value. The `classcode` value that is used in the description comes from the classes table, so the two tables must be joined on a common field — the `classyr`. Finally, the query is restricted based on the BIND variable `classyr`. If you were to run this LOV object in test mode, Portal would prompt you for a value for the `classyr` field. However, it is more interesting to use this LOV in combination with the first LOV within a data entry form.

2. Use the Navigator to locate and edit the form object CH16_FRM_DYNAMICLOV.

3. Navigate to the `advisor` field.

4. The `advisorid` field settings should look like those shown in Figure 16-20.

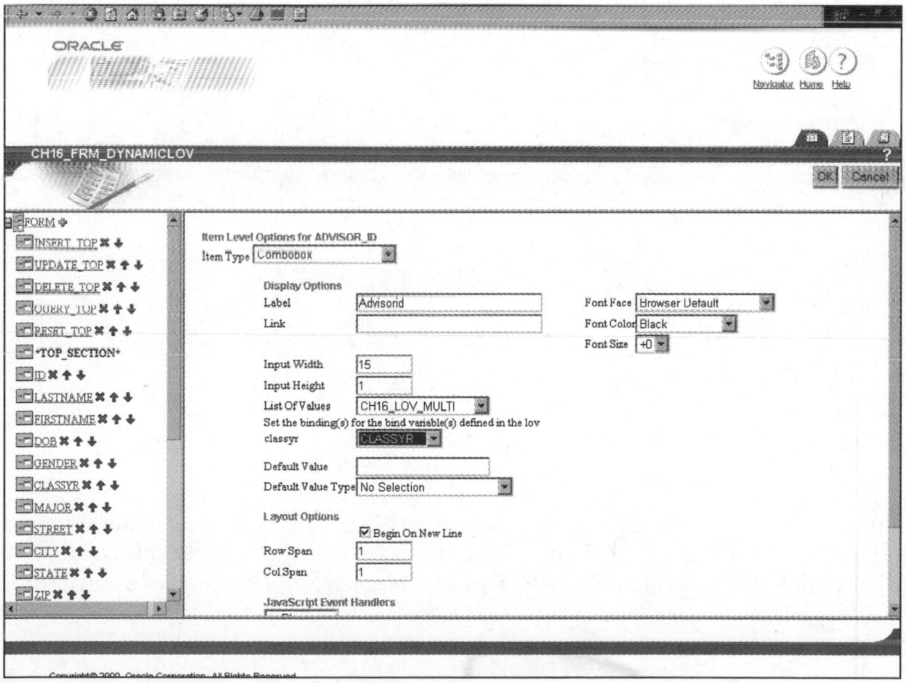

Figure 16-20: Mapping the Advisor ID to the `classyr`

The `advisorid` field has been set to display as a combo box and the LOV object CH16_LOV_MULTI has been attached to it. This is no different than any of the other LOVs that you have used in this chapter thus far. The difference is the field that is just below the List of Values setting, which is referenced by the string "Set the binding(s) for the BIND variable(s) defined in the lov." Portal detects the BIND variable within the LOV and creates a variable on the form to match the BIND variable name. (In this case, the BIND variable is `classyr`.) To the right of the `classyr` field is a combo box that lists all of the fields that are on the form. In effect, Portal is asking you to choose which field on the form to use as the constraint for the BIND variable. In the example form, you are using the classyr field, which is itself mapped to an LOV (CH16_LOV_MULTI2).

5. Use the Cancel button to discard any changes that you may have made.

6. Use the Run link to run the form CH16_FRM_DYNAMICLOV as shown in Figure 16-21.

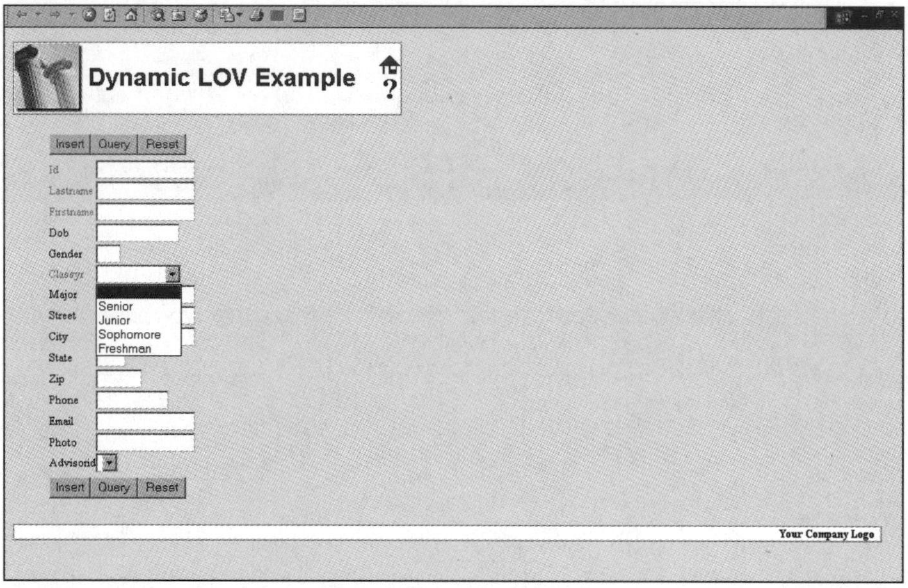

Figure 16-21: Setting the BIND variable for an LOV

When the form is initially executed, the Classyr field combo box is filled in with data, but the Advisorid field contains a blank LOV. Upon selecting a value for the Classyr field, Portal reloads the form with values for both LOVs as shown in Figure 16-22.

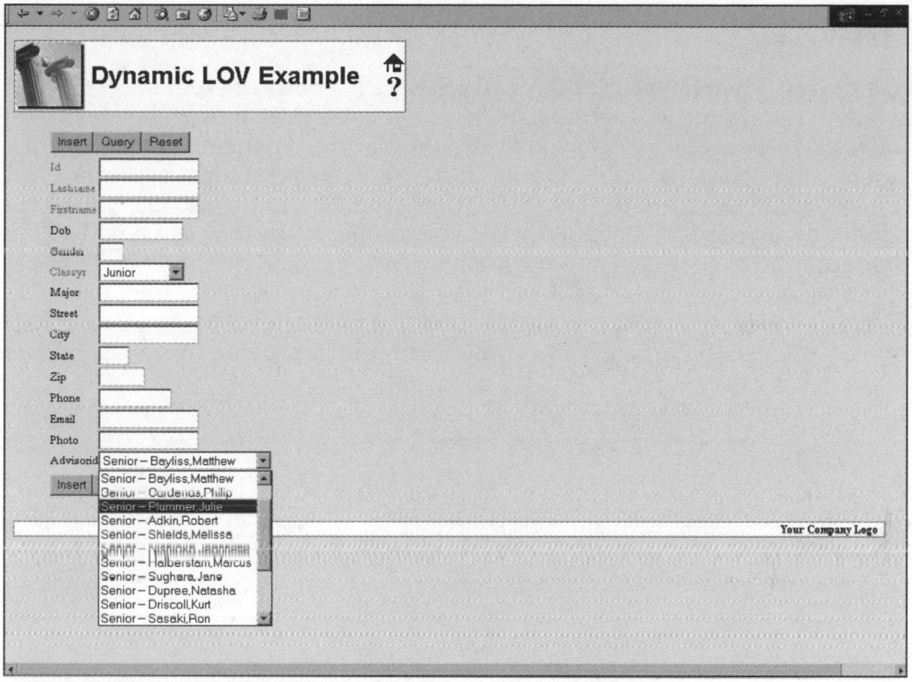

Figure 16-22: Advisorid LOV with parameterized values

The original query specified that advisors were to be greater than the selected classyr. By choosing the value of "Junior" for the classyr, you restrict the list of advisors to seniors. By prepending the class code to the student name, you can easily see that the resulting list is composed only of upperclassmen. (Although it is not necessary to do so from a functionality perspective.) The use of BIND variables within the LOV query allows you to create dynamic LOVs that respond to user selections that are made elsewhere on the form.

Caution   Portal only provides support for BIND variables on LOVs that are used within forms. You cannot use these same LOVs for customization pages within reports, calendars, hierarchies, and charts. They are only provided for use within data entry applications.

Portal allows you to map any field on the form to the LOV BIND variable. You could just as easily use a simple text box for the Classyr field and enter the numeric classyr value manually.

Summary

Portal's Lists-of-Values Wizard provides you with a powerful tool for building parameter entry forms, look-up lists, and client-side data integrity checks. You will find they are most valuable if you create them at the beginning of the project in order to have them available as you create your reports, forms, calendars, and hierarchies. Static LOVs are the simplest objects to build, but we advise you to consider storing your lists as data in a database table. In the long run, you will find that your applications are easier to maintain if your code and description data is stored within the database and is easily accessible from outside of program code. LOV Objects connect data to forms and reports and in the next chapter, you'll take a look at Oracle9*i*AS Portal's Menu Component, which provides for a logical grouping of forms and reports.

✦　　✦　　✦

Creating Oracle9*i*AS Portal Menus

✦   ✦   ✦   ✦

In This Chapter

Understanding
Universal Resource
Locators (URLs) and
Menus

Using Simple Static
Pages with Portal

Building a Portal
Menu

Building a Menu from
Scratch

Linking Root Menus

Managing the Menu

✦   ✦   ✦   ✦

Portal applications are composed of different Portal components. Initially, you may use Portal to create content objects that can be used on their own, without relating them to other components. Portal provides shared components for fonts, colors, and images to give all the objects in a Portal application a standardized look and feel. While these elements help you make Portal's HTML pages consistent in appearance, they do not necessarily assist you in the process of providing consistent navigation through a logical grouping of content objects. Portal gives you a way to add a standard navigation interface to your application systems with the menu component. Menus provide you with a tool for building navigational flow into your Portal applications — you can use menus to navigate between Portal components, portal pages, content folders, and external pages. This chapter covers the creation and use of menus.

Understanding Universal Resource Locators

Basic Portal applications are built around three basic elements: Hypertext Transport Protocol (HTTP), Hypertext Markup Language (HTML), and Universal Resource Locators (URLs). HTTP is the protocol used to get content from the server to your browser. HTML is the system of tags that enable your browser to interpret the graphical display of content returned from the server as a page. URLs are the addresses used to get a particular HTML page from the server to your desktop. Initially, most Web applications were built around static, preexisting HTML pages, which made the URL a relatively simple object to understand. The basic format of a URL is as follows:

```
protocol://servername:port/path
```

Each section of the URL represents a different portion of the location of the HTML page, just like each portion of your telephone number represents a specific portion of the telephone routing system. The first portion of the address is the protocol, which indicates to the browser the transmission technology that should be used for the address. Table 17-1 shows possible values for the protocol section.

Table 17-1
Protocol Values for URLs

Protocol Name	Protocol Description
HTTP	Hypertext Transport Protocol is the standard communications mechanism for Web applications.
HTTPS	Secure Sockets version of HTTP for encrypted data communications.
FILE	File access protocol that opens files from the operating system in your browser.
FTP	File Transfer Protocol transfers files from a remote system to your desktop.
NNTP	Protocol that connects your browser to shared bulletin board data.
MAILTO	Connects your browser to a user via an electronic mail address.
GOPHER	Makes a link to a GOPHER server.
TELNET	Provides a Telnet session to the specified server. A Telnet session is a terminal-based interface, typically to a UNIX server or mainframe computer.

In general, you will use the HTTP protocol type most often, because it is the standard communications protocol for communicating between your browser and the Portal database. You may find that you need to use the other protocols on occasion, and you will find some examples of these other protocols later in this chapter. The :// characters are required literal characters that separate the protocol name from the server address.

The second portion of the URL is the *servername*, which corresponds to the name of the machine the unique page is located on. When you are accessing pages in a Portal application, the *servername* is the name of the server the Portal listener is located on. The exact name of your server may not be readily apparent, so you may need to look in your local hosts file, which is located in the /system32/drivers/etc subdirectory under your Windows NT root directory. On most UNIX systems, the hosts file can be found in the /etc directory.

You may not even be able to find your host name on your local server machine. In many cases, your Portal server uses a secondary server called a DNS (Domain Name Server) machine that resolves addresses for your server machine. In this case, you may need to contact your systems administrator in order to get the full name for your server machine. Table 17-2 shows the forms the machine name may take.

Note Your portal server will need to have a static IP address in order for your users to reach the server. For development purposes, it is possible to use "localhost" on a local server or desktop workstation — but you cannot use this configuration for production portal servers.

Table 17-2
Common Server Names

Server Name Style	Description
pumpkin	Simple machine name that is usually found within an intranet.
www.pumpkin.com	Commercial Web server application. Typically, official Web sites use this format.
fred.server1.pumpkin.com	Once you register a domain name such as pumpkin.com, you are technically free to add any number of "names" to the left of the domain name. Companies often use this format for secondary servers, especially if they have very large Web sites.
ftp.pumpkin.com	File transfer services are typically offered on separate server machines from the standard World Wide Web server.

Note Recently, ICANN (The Internet Corporation for Assigned Names and Numbers) has been working on a formal process to approve some additional extensions, such as .biz, .web, and .shop.

The next section of the URL address is the port number (:port), which refers to the specific TCP/IP port on which the Portal server listens. Most standard protocols such as HTTP are set to listen on a standard port number. In this case, you do not need to specify the port number explicitly. However, any links that you create from other Web applications to Portal applications typically require you to specify the listener port number. (For a review of the listener's port configuration, refer to Chapter 2).

Common Server Extensions

In addition to the standard .com extension, you will find a number of standard server extensions such as .org, .edu, .net, .mil, and, .gov. Each country also has its own server extension specific to that country.

The final portion of the URL address is the /path, which refers to the specific object sent from the server to the client browser. The path portion of the address can be as simple as a singular HTML page or as complicated as a call to a Portal procedure with parameter values. Later in this chapter you will see just how sophisticated the path portion of the address can become. For the time being, consider the path section of the URL to be the name of the specific Portal procedure you wish to run.

In general, you will find that the standard path of the links you build with Portal are calls to other Portal components. However, when you link to preexisting Web components or other applications, you will encounter more complicated path definitions.

Cross-Reference

Oracle Portal 3.0 makes use of the Apache HTTP listener as its standard "Web" interface. Through the Apache httpd.conf file it is possible to add virtual path settings that mask portions of the URL as it is used by the portal server. Chapter 2 explains this process in more detail.

Using Simple Static Pages with Portal

Portal's link builder technology is based upon the standard linking capabilities of browser-based applications. Traditional HTML applications link pages through URLs embedded within the HTML text. For the most part, you will find that Portal manages the URLs it needs automatically. This is an extremely powerful feature of Portal and you will find that it makes developing applications much easier than building URLs by hand. This functionality is especially useful when you need to pass parameters between HTML pages, as you will see later in this chapter.

Portal was designed to enable you to create completely self-contained application systems. Despite this fact, you are likely to find that you need to link to other Web sites, servers, and applications at times in order to take advantage of the wealth of information available on the Web and on various intranets. Your organization may already have Web applications in place, and you may need to integrate your Portal site and components into these preexisting Web applications. The most common type of page you may need to link across applications is a static HTML page.

Listing 17-1: **A simple, static HTML page**

```
<!DOCTYPE HTML PUBLIC "-//W3C//DTD HTML 3.2//EN">
<HTML>
<HEAD>
<META HTTP-EQUIV="Content-Type" CONTENT="text/html;CHARSET=iso-
8859-1">
<META NAME="GENERATOR" Content="Visual Page 2.0 for Windows">
<TITLE>NetU Home Page</TITLF>
</HEAD>
<BODY BGCOLOR="white">
<P><BR>
</P>
<P ALIGN="CENTER"><I><B><FONT SIZE="6">Home Page
for:</FONT></B></I></P>
<P ALIGN="CENTER"><A HREF="netu_about.htm"><IMG
SRC="netu_logo.jpg" ALIGN="BOTTOM" BORDER="0"></A>
</BODY>
</HTML>
```

Listing 17-1 shows a simple Web page in HTML source format. You could enter this text into a text editor and save the file with an HTML extension, or you could retrieve it directly from the directory where you loaded the course examples by its name — netu_home.htm.

1. Copy the HTML files from the ch17 directory to a working directory on your local hard drive.

2. Open the file netu_home.htm directly from your browser using the Open menu. The page that appears in your browser looks like Figure 17-1.

Figure 17-1: Simple, static HTML text as displayed by Internet Explorer running on Windows

This particular HTML page contains very little information of value to an application; it is nothing more than a simple home page for Net University. However, you can still use this page format to illustrate how to create a simple link. The page is composed of a heading along with an image that displays the label of a URL link. If you allow your mouse to linger over the Net University logo, you see that the browser's message line displays a block of text much like the following string:

```
file:///E:/portal30/ch17/code/netu_about.htm
```

The URL link would look quite different if you copied the example file to a path that is accessible to the Apache listener and referenced the same HTML page as a URL using HTTP. The example HTML pages both use relative links, as shown in bold text in Listing 17-1. The Web browser will automatically look for the included reference along the same path as the source page, which in this example case is a file path. If you had placed the netu_home.htm page in the Apache listener's default page path, the link would have looked like the code shown here:

```
http://zaman.enter.net/netu_about.htm
```

In either case, this line of text is the URL, or address, of the link associated with the text on the page. If you click on the text link, the browser automatically retrieves the associated HTML page for you. The browser assumes that the page exists and is located in the same directory path as the first page. The browser will be unable to locate the page unless they are both stored in the same physical file directory. Listing 17-2 shows the HTML source for the second, linked page.

Listing 17-2: **Linked static page source**

```
<!DOCTYPE HTML PUBLIC "-//W3C//DTD HTML 3.2//EN">
<HTML>
<HEAD>
<META NAME="GENERATOR" Content="Visual Page 1.0 for Windows">
    <META HTTP-EQUIV="Content-Type"
CONTENT="text/html;CHARSET=iso-8859-1">
<TITLE>Net University - About Page</TITLE>
</HEAD>

<BODY BGCOLOR="#FFFFFF">

<P><IMG SRC="netu_logo.jpg" ALIGN="MIDDLE" BORDER="0"> <FONT
SIZE="4"><B>Net University
A Progressive College for Higher Education</B></FONT></P>
<P>
<TABLE BORDER="0" WIDTH="100%">
    <TR>
        <TD WIDTH="49%" VALIGN="TOP">
            <P><B><I>Net University is a leading edge
University offering degree programs in science and liberal
arts. Students at Net University are encouraged to pursue
academic study using computer technology</I></B></P>
```

```
            <P><B>Contact Information:</B></P>
            <PRE>Admissions - 1-800-867-5309</PRE>
            <PRE>Hotline - 1-900-555-1212</PRE>
            <PRE>http://www.netu-university.com</PRE>
                <P>
                <ADDRESS><FONT SIZE="1">Net University<BR>
                <BR>
                1313-7 Ave of the Americas<BR>
                <BR>
                New York, NY 60609</FONT>
        </TD>
        <TD WIDTH="51%">
                <P><IMG SRC="netu_tabbycat.gif" WIDTH="3//"
HEIGHT="336" ALIGN="BOTTOM" BORDER="0"></P>
                <P ALIGN="CENTER"><B><I>Net University TabbyCats
- Go Cats Go !</I></B>
        </TD>
    </TR>
</TABLE>
</BODY>
</HTML>
```

3. Click the link from the page in the browser and the second HTML page appears, as shown in Figure 17-2.

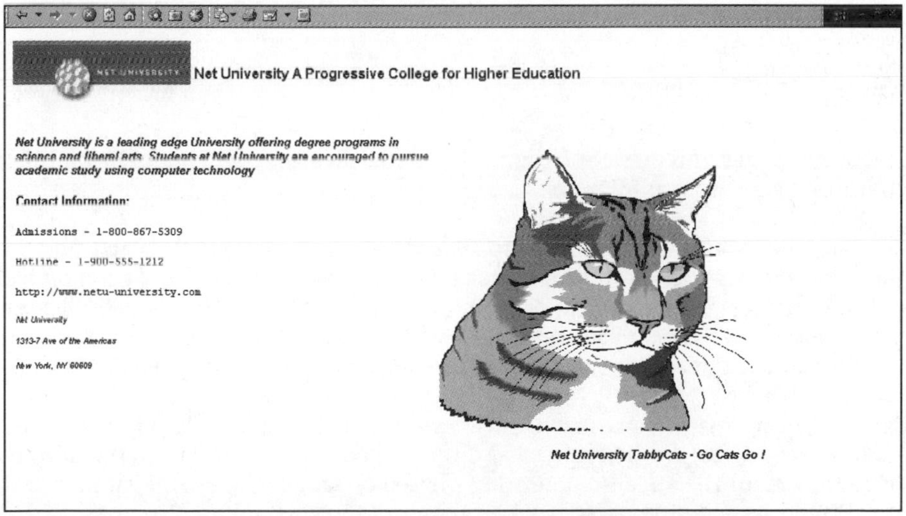

Figure 17-2: Linked page as displayed by Internet Explorer on Windows

The default behavior for your browser is to assume that a linked page can be found along the path of the calling page. You can override this behavior by specifying a complete URL for the link instead of specifying a simple page name as shown in Listing 17-1. While using the complete pathname as a URL makes it easy for you to view your Web pages, it is not the best way to deploy these pages to your users because it requires you to know the file structure on the machine where the files are stored. A better solution is to deploy these files to your Web server. The *optimal* solution is to generate these files dynamically using Portal components on demand. However, there may be times when you need to reference data or other Web pages from outside of Portal, and Portal enables you to use links to accomplish this task. You can easily take the two HTML files you created and deploy them to the Portal server via the Apache HTTP Server.

Adding a Virtual Path to the System

The first step in adding a simple, static HTML link from Portal is to build a directory in which to store your external content.

You added the virtual directory /netu/ to Portal when you installed the product in Chapter 2. In order to complete the examples in this section you will need to locate the physical server directory that matches the virtual directory.

1. Copy the following files to the directory that matches the /netu/ virtual directory.

```
netu_home.htm
netu_about.htm
netu_logo.gif
netu_tabbycat.gif
```

The static pages you just copied into the /netu/ directory will be integrated into your Portal example application.

In order to make external directories and files available to both Oracle Portal and the Apache listener, you must make changes to the Apache configuration files — this process is explained in detail in Chapter 2. Before continuing with this example be sure that you have read the installation section in Chapter 2 that discusses the process of adding virtual paths and directories to the Apache HTTP Server.

Each directory mapping consists of two pieces of information: a physical directory and a virtual directory. The physical directory component refers to the actual file system path for the specific operating system on which the Portal listener is running. The physical directory matches an operating system file directory, and all components must be valid, including the drive and the file directory. Any security settings on this path must enable the Portal listener to have at least read access to the directory path and to the files within the directory.

Cross-Reference   As you will recall from Chapter 2, you can provide additional security controls for the individual directory paths by editing the code between the <DIRECTORY> tags that appear below the virtual directory paths.

The virtual directory is the shorthand notation by which the physical directory path is known to the rest of Portal. The Apache HTTP Server automatically translates the virtual directory into the corresponding physical directory for all other Portal components, including the menu builder and the Link Editor. The value of using this virtual directory is that you can easily move the physical directory and its contents at any time. The only change you need to make is to map the virtual directory back to the physical directory. This insulates your applications from changes to physical file locations, and using virtual directories can save you lots of time when you move applications from development into production. You will note that the string format for virtual directories is very similar to actual file system directory paths, with the exception that the slash marks appear to be backward (at least for Windows NT developers).

You will typically create a number of such entries as a means of organizing your external content. If you had a number of different groups of content, it makes sense to locate them in different physical directories and provide each with its own virtual directory name. In fact, you might want to create separate include files for each logical application and its associated virtual directories, as we have done with the Net University application.

However, we advise you not to use a virtual directory as a standard way to store external data for Portal. Portal's Content Area tools provide you with routines to move external content from the file system into the Portal repository, and they should be your first choice for working with external content. You should use virtual directories when you are getting content from another source (or department) that may not be able or willing to have content stored within Portal. For example, you may have a group within your organization using an automated system to refresh a set of HTML pages on an hourly basis. Further, they are creating this content primarily to serve a different constituency. It may not be possible for this group to use the Portal repository to store their pages or modify their preexisting publishing strategy to push content into Portal. In this case, it may make sense to reference the material from within Portal using virtual directories.

One additional situation may call for the use of virtual directories. Portal has a built-in facility for indexing content based upon Oracle8i's *inter*Media searching and indexing technology. Oracle8i *inter*Media automatically indexes content stored within the database for you, and access to *inter*Media's search engine is built into Portal. While this makes your searches for specific content fast and easy, it does have one significant drawback. Content stored within the database cannot be automatically searched and indexed by *external* search engines such as Yahoo!, AltaVista, Lycos, and Excite. Web crawlers work by indexing URLs, but they cannot index documents that are stored within a database. This may make it difficult for external users to find your content if they are not already on your portal. This is true even if you are deploying your application on an intranet, where groups of users may be linking from their site to your portal application.

One solution to this problem is to create a series of external pages to use as entry points into your portal. These pages can be stored externally and accessed by Portal by means of a virtual directory. This way, an external search engine can index the external pages and these external pages can serve as entry points into your Portal application.

Once you have created your virtual directory entry and copied HTML source files to this new directory, Portal has all the information it needs to use the content. Accessing this new content is as simple as providing your browser and Portal with the proper URL. The following snippet of code shows a typical URL that might be used with Oracle Portal.

```
http://zaman.enter.net:80/netu/netu_home.htm
```

The left side of the URL is the server path portion of the complete URL address. The URL address has a content-type indicator (`http://`), a server name (`zaman.enter.net`), and an optional port number (`:80`). The server name and port number may be different on your Portal server machine, and you may have a number of server name and port number combinations for a larger site.

Chapter 20 provides a much more detailed reference on the different URL formats that you may use with Oracle Portal. Portal itself can accept many parameter formats for referencing components and pages, and URLs may include these optional parameters as necessary. For the purposes of the examples in this chapter, it is not necessary to understand all of these additional options.

In the first URL, the remaining text is composed of two parts — a virtual directory `/netu/`, followed by the name of an HTML page `netu_home.htm`. This is the simplest form of URL that you will find with Oracle Portal — and it does not actually touch Oracle Portal directly. Virtual directories are managed by the Apache HTTP Server, which handles requests for external files without passing the request onto the Portal engine. This technique is essentially one that is used by all HTTP servers. All of the images that are used within the Portal Component Builders make use of small external GIF images. Portal finds these images by using the virtual path `/images/` and the name of the external GIF file. However, the real power of Oracle Portal is the way in which it makes use of dynamic strings that can be included as part of a URL (as shown in the following code sample):

```
http://zaman.enter.net/pls/portal30/NETU.CH15_REP_UGRADS.show
```

This URL is more complex, in that it includes several additional directives. The first of these directives is another virtual directory `/pls/`, which is used by the Apache listener to map requests for the modPLSQL interface from the Apache Server to the PL/SQL engine. Next up is the Data Access Descriptor `/portal30/` and the application owner and procedure name `NETU.CH15_REP_UGRADS.SHOW`. The owner name corresponds to the Oracle USERID that owns the particular application, which controls the application that "owns" the component. The rightmost portion of the content object, the object name, is the most complicated portion of the Portal address and it varies widely by content type. The object name is itself a compound object that includes an Oracle package name, an Oracle procedure name, and an optional list of parameters.

Note We'll talk more about these additional URL strings later in this chapter.

The key portion of the address to understand in order to use your recently created virtual directory is the server name. External virtual directories are connected with the Portal listener, and are therefore associated with the server. If you choose to create multiple Portal installations, they can all share a single listener and a common set of virtual directories.

2. Test using Portal to access to the static external pages by entering the following URL in your browser's address window (substitute your server name and port number for `zaman.enter.net`).

    `http://zaman.enter.net/netu/netu_home.htm`

If you have connected the virtual directory properly and moved the content to the associated physical directory, Portal returns the page shown in Figure 17-3.

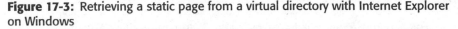

Home Page for:

Figure 17-3: Retrieving a static page from a virtual directory with Internet Explorer on Windows

Your browser automatically associates the linked page to the same path, so choosing the Net University Logo link produces the correct page as well. If you choose to move the linked page to another location, simply edit the link as you would any other HTML page link.

Building a Portal Menu

Up until this point, we have not discussed building an actual menu with Portal. The key to understanding Portal's menus is to have a thorough understanding of URLs, because the Portal menu builder is entirely based upon URLs. You can even deploy Portal's menus to a Content Area just like any other Portal component. However, you do not need to create a Web site in order to use Portal's menus. In fact, the simplest strategy for building and deploying a Portal application is to start by building content and menus without creating an entire site. In many cases, you will already have some type of Web application in place, even if this application is nothing more than a series of static Web pages. You can easily create some new, dynamic content and deploy this content to your existing environment by using Portal's Menu Builder Wizard.

Using the Portal Menu Builder Wizard

The Portal Menu Builder Wizard can be a breeze to work with even if you are starting from ground zero without any menu structure in place.

1. Navigate to the familiar NETCOLLEGE application and use the Menu link to display the panel as shown in Figure 17-4.

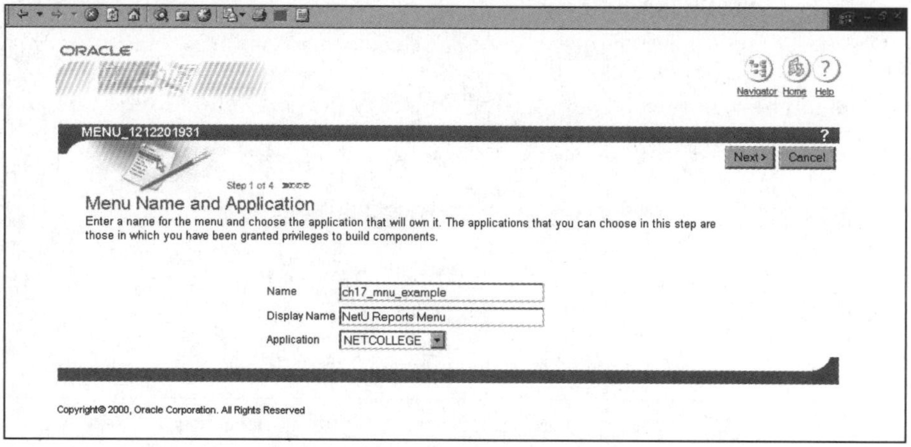

Figure 17-4: Menu Builder Wizard Menu Name and Application panel

The first panel in the menu builder requires the same three parameters that are used by all of the other component builders — a name, a display name, and an application owner.

2. Enter the name of the menu **ch17_mnu_example**, followed by a display name **NetU Reports Menu** and the application owner **NETCOLLEGE** as shown in Figure 17-4.

3. Use the Next button to continue.

The next panel that displays is the main functional panel in the Menu Wizard. All of the settings that you will wish to make to menus can be made from this single panel. The left side of this panel is the menu navigator, which allows you add, edit, and delete menu items and submenus. The right side of the panel controls the settings for the menu item that is selected in the right panel. By default, Oracle Portal selects the top-level menu item whenever you create a new menu. The options that appear in the right panel will vary slightly depending on the menu object and any of the menu items that it contains.

4. Start working with the Menu Items and Submenus panel by changing the main options for the menu as shown in Figure 17-5.

All menus, menu items, and submenus will have a name as indicated by the first field on the right side of the panel as shown in Figure 17-5. The name field for the menu will appear as the title line when the menu is displayed. The next field in the list is the familiar template field. You can select a template that will control the logo, colors, and fonts for the menu. Keep in mind that any template settings that you choose on this panel will be overridden by Portal's run-time system if the menu is displayed as a portlet. Reports, Forms, Chart, Calendars, Hierarchies, and Dynamic Pages allow you to input help text directly into the body of the object. However, menus do not support the familiar text panels for entering text. You can add help text to a menu by creating an external object such as an HTML page or even a Dynamic Page; and you can link the object to the menu by using the Help Link field.

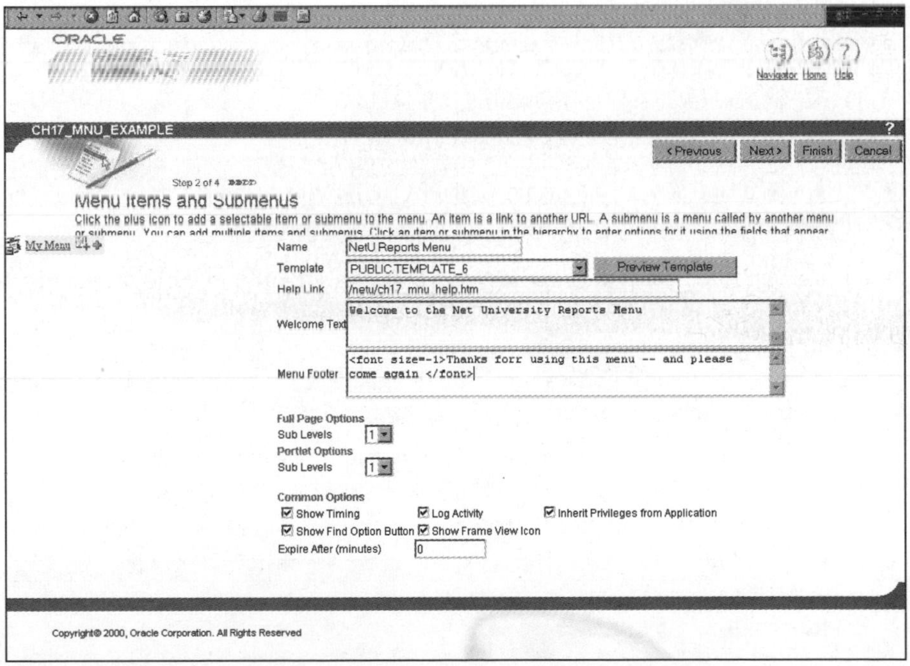

Figure 17-5: Menu Items and Submenus Panel of the Menu Wizard

5. Copy the file ch17_menu_help.htm to the /netu/ directory that you used in the first part of this chapter.

The format of the Help Link is a standard URL, but you can also use a partial URL entry and allow Portal to reference the link in the context of the current Portal Site. Consider the two formats for the help link as shown here:

```
http://zaman.enter.net/netu/ch17_mnu_help.htm
```

and

```
/netu/ch17_mnu_help.htm
```

In the first case, the link is a complete URL link that points to the server and the content. If the portal site were moved to a different server (or if you needed to change the port number), then this first URL would not longer work. The second case uses a relative URL reference, and the browser will use the current context of the browser state to resolve the reference. You will want to make use of relative references whenever possible to ensure that the content can be moved about as necessary.

Cross-Reference Earlier in this chapter, we used this same principle with static HTML files. Remember that the reference to the graphic images in the NetU home page and NetU about page were also *relative* references.

The next two entries are the header and footer text for the menu. The information that you enter in these fields will be displayed above and below the menu items and submenus when the menu is displayed. These two fields work the same as the header and footer text fields for reports, forms, charts, hierarchies, calendars, and Dynamic Pages. You can enter simple text as well as HTML tags directly into these fields. The remaining options on the current panel will make more sense once you have added some menu items to this menu.

6. Enter a name, **NetU Reports Menu**, for the menu in the Name field and choose a template to display with the menu as shown in Figure 17-5.

7. Add the **/netu/ch17_mnu_help.htm** URL to the Help Link field and then add your own Welcome and Menu Footer text. (Feel free to mix in some custom HTML into these fields as well.)

8. Use the Finish button to skip over the remaining menu choices and save the menu. Use the Run Link to display the menu as shown in Figure 17-6.

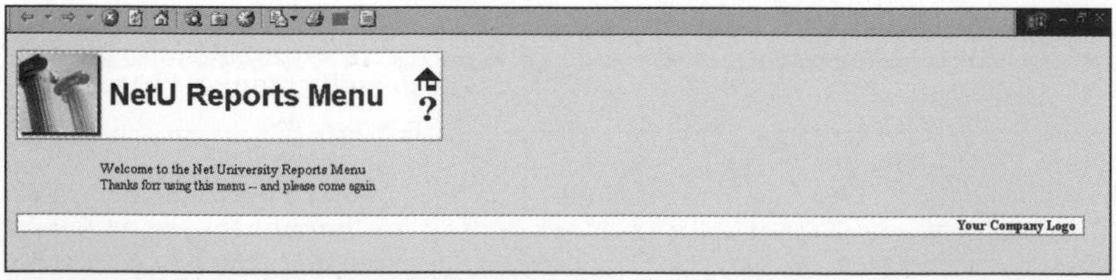

Figure 17-6: NetU Reports Menu

The resulting menu is overly simple, because you do not yet have any menu choices or submenus.

Portal menus work very much like any other Portal-formatted page. The template used to create the page determines the graphic display of the menu. Both the header and footer of the page can include different color schemes and fonts depending upon how extensively you have edited the template. Changing the template changes all the menus without requiring you to change the menu itself. This makes it very easy to customize the menus without having to agonize over items such as color schemes when you create the initial menu. The core menu area in the middle of the panel is divided into four sections:

- ✦ Header
- ✦ Menu body
- ✦ Search function
- ✦ Footer

The *header* is the text area at the top of the page just below the title bar. The header is a block of HTML text that Portal formats for you as the introductory text for the menu. As with most other blocks of text within Portal, you can include any combination of text and HTML tags to construct the header.

Just below the header is the *menu body*, which is the actual link text that creates the menu itself. This body is entirely composed of menu choices in the form of text, links, and images. (Since our menu does not yet have any submenus or menu items, this area is blank.) In the next section, you will modify this menu to include menu items and submenus as well as some additional text and images.

Just below the menu body is a text box and a button, which together provide a search option for the menu. Typically, a Portal menu is a hierarchy of options, and the *search function* provides you with a tool to search for menu options for all submenus below the current menu. This feature makes it very easy to provide a deep hierarchy of menus you can quickly search for matching menu options. While deep menus appeal to the novice application user, the search function enables the more experienced user to jump to a lower-level menu without having to remember the exact menu hierarchy. This feature is also ideal for situations where a developer has moved a menu hierarchy from one area to another, as a user can find the new location by executing a search from the upper menu. You can use the Find Menu Options search by entering any text string in the text box and then clicking the button. The search uses a LIKE comparison, so you do not need to worry either about capitalization or surrounding your search string with wildcard characters. (You cannot perform compound searches, as the search command uses an implied LIKE comparison.)

The last section of the panel is the *footer* text. Footer text offers the identical functionality for the bottom of the form that the header offers for the top of the form. You can embed text, HTML tags, Oracle PL/SQL commands, and graphics within the footer to provide additional information on a menu.

9. Use the question mark link in the NetU Reports Menu (see Figure 17-6) to display the help text.

Upon selecting the help button you will notice that Portal displays the help HTML file that you associated with the menu. In a production portal site, you might choose to make use of some advanced audio or video in your help files for menus or subsystems that are especially complex.

10. Close the Menu window.

Editing the menu

Menu items and submenus appear in the outline tree on the left side of the edit panel. The green plus button to the right of the menu name permits you to add items to your menu.

1. Edit the menu using the Edit link on the Develop tab.

2. Click on the "Add submenu" image (the green plus button) to the right of the Menu Name in the left panel as shown in Figure 17-7.

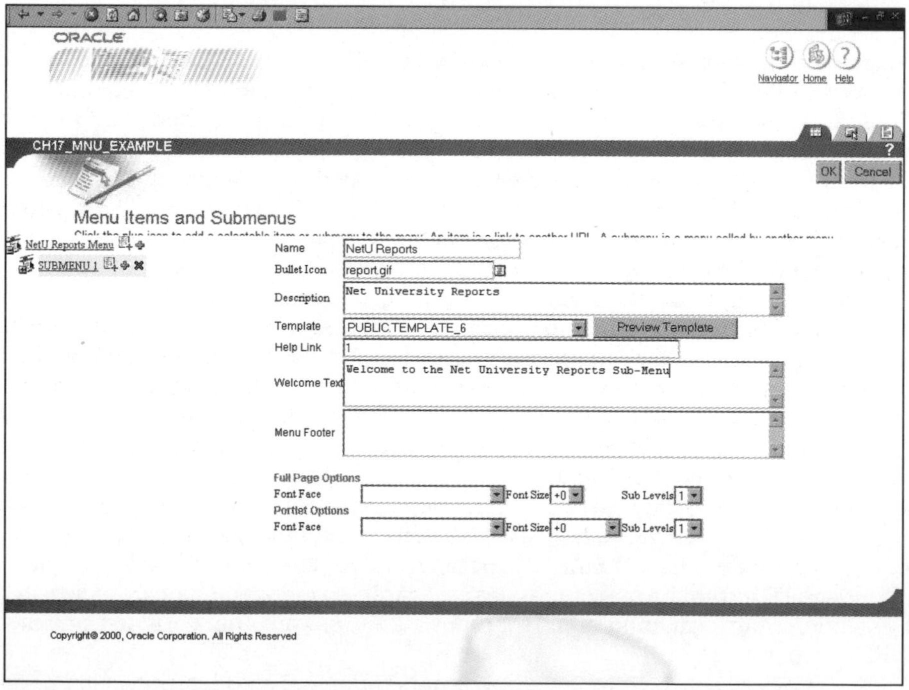

Figure 17-7: Menu Items and Submenus panel

When you read a Portal menu tree, you read it from the top down. Portal indents the outline tree to display the hierarchy of menus and submenus. The right-most items correspond to a URL, static page, or component object, such as a Dynamic Page, report, form, chart, hierarchy, or calendar. All items to the left of the menu items are either menus or submenus. Once you create the submenu, Portal automatically selects the new submenu as the *current* item and changes the right side of the panel to reflect the appropriate display options.

The configuration options for a submenu are very similar to those for the menu itself, but there are some subtle differences. The main link for a submenu will appear in the body of the master menu, and the name that you give to the submenu will be used as the link on the body of the menu page. You can make this link more visually appealing by adding a graphic image to the text of the link. Oracle Portal provides the Bullet Icon field for just this purpose. The search button to the right of the field will display a pop-up list of known images in the miscellaneous category.

Chapter 18 shows you how to manage images with Oracle Portal and provides examples of adding your own custom graphics to Portal sites.

3. Enter the name **NetU Reports** for your submenu, and then locate the report.gif icon for the bullet icon field.

4. Enter a description for the submenu, and then add some welcome text as shown in Figure 17-7.

Just below the Menu Footer area are the Font Face and the Font Size combo boxes. Font sizes are displayed as a range of positive integers and correspond to the <FONT SIZE=#> HTML tag. Selecting any of the positive values causes your menu's title to be displayed in the specified point size. The Portal developers limited the range of values you can enter in this field to match HTML best practices. In general, take the default value for this field unless you have a particularly dense menu page, in which case you may want to use a smaller font size.

Note

If you are generally not going to increase the font size, then you may ask why Portal gives you the option to do so. One of the advanced menu options you can take advantage of is the ability to attach a graphic image to the menu choice (as we discussed in the preceding section). You may find that the image overpowers your menu text, and increasing the font size helps to balance the two visually.

As with the other component builders you have the option to set different font faces and sizes when the menu is displayed as a portlet.

The Shared Components area manages the list of fonts. Chapter 18 shows you how to add custom fonts and sizes to your Portal and other components.

You will notice that the submenu that you just created also features a green plus button (and an associated red delete button as well). This button is used to add menu items and submenus to the currently selected submenu. Oracle Portal allows you to nest submenus to a very detailed level. While deeply nested menus can be used to organize your menu items, they can make the menu display appear cluttered. Portal provides the Sublevels button on menus and submenus as a means of controlling how Portal displays deeply nested menu items. The integer value for the sublevel combo box controls the precise number of submenus that Portal will display at any one time. The default value of 1 indicates that Portal will only show the current menu. This means that the user will have to click through to the submenu in order to see any of the nested menu items or submenus.

5. Repeat Step 2 to add one more submenu to the NetU Reports Menu for calendars and charts. Name this new menu **NetU Calendars and Charts**. Select a bullet icon for this new submenu, and provide a description and welcome text.

6. Press the OK button to save the modified menu, and then use the Run link to display the menu as shown in Figure 17-8.

Figure 17-8: NetU Reports Menu with submenu items

You will notice that the two submenus appear as links with bullet icons between the welcome header and the menu footer. The submenu names appear as link text, and the descriptions that you provided are shown below the links. Portal will automatically format the description text beneath the menu links, but you are free to add your own HTML code to the text to provide a custom look and feel.

Adding menu items to menus and submenus

Menus and submenus provide the means to organize your components into logical groups, but it is the menu items themselves that form the bulk of this component.

1. Load the following three components into the NETCOLLEGE application: ch17_cht_grades, ch17_rpt_courses, and ch17_rpt_ugrads.

Cross-Reference If you are unsure about loading components into your Portal you can review this process in Chapter 2.

2. Use the Navigator to locate and edit the menu once again.

3. Use the green plus option to add a new menu item to the NetU Reports submenu as shown in Figure 17-9.

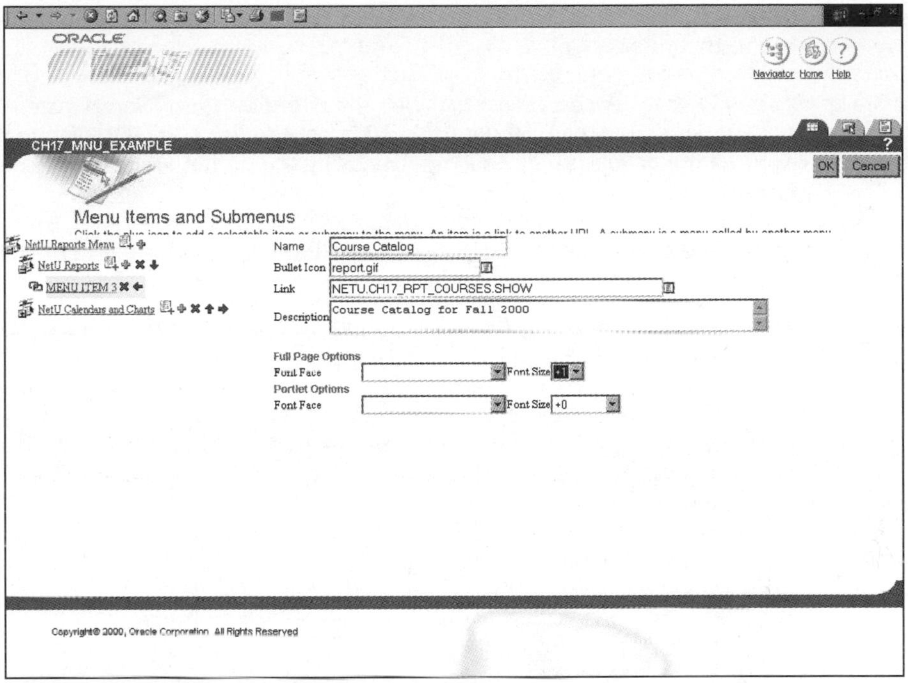

Figure 17-9: Adding menu items to a submenu

Menu items can be attached to the main menu or any one of the submenus — and you are free to move menu items around within the wizard interface using the blue arrows on the tree outline. Once you create a menu item, you will need to provide a name, optional bullet icon, and a description. However, the focal point for menu items is the link that is used as the menu item itself. The link that is entered in the link text box is nothing more than a standard URL. Thus, a menu item could easily connect a user to an external Web site or address. However, the main purpose of a menu item is to connect a menu choice to another Portal component, such as a report, form, chart, hierarchy, calendar, or Dynamic Page. In fact, the search button to the right of the link text box will search the current application for all components that are available as link objects.

> **Caution**
> Although it is possible to manually enter the URL for an object in a different application, this is not good programming practice with Oracle Portal. Portal "applications" are meant to be the container objects for subcomponents and links to components within menus should not normally cross these "application boundaries."

When Portal serves up a menu with an external link (such as http://www.oracle.com), it is merely passing the address within the HTML page as part of the link. The Portal server is not processing this link when you use the menu; your browser is processing the link. This gives you lots of flexibility to link to other content from your Portal menu. Your server does not need to have authorization and access to connect to external sites — only the browser needs authorization. This is particularly powerful when you have stored your Portal server behind a firewall and plan on limiting its access to the outside world.

Note   Should you wish to connect to external Web sites from the Portal Server *instead* of the browser, you can either call out to the external site using PL/SQL Web toolkit packages via the database — or build the link using the portlet API as discussed in Chapter 28.

4. Use the link search button to find the CH17_RPT_COURSES object and select this component for the link text as shown in Figure 17-9.

5. Add a name, bullet icon, and descriptive text for this submenu item as shown in Figure 17-9.

Oracle Portal automatically uses relative link references, so there is no server, port or virtual directory information included in the link text that is returned to the link field. The result is a very simple link, but you can override this default link text with your own code at any point in time.

6. Add another menu item under the NetU Reports Menu link.

7. Enter the following information for this new menu item as shown in Figure 17-10:

```
Name = Senior Class List
Bullet icon = report.gif
Link =
NETU.CH17_RPT_UGRADS.SHOW?p_arg_names=ugrads.classyr&p_arg_
values=2001
Description = Senior Class List - Dynamically Generated
```

Note   Link text corresponds to a URL and so it must be entered on a single line, without spaces. Note that some of the lines here may wrap into two lines due to book size constraints.

The link text for this second menu item includes some parameter values that are passed to the report. This report accepts a single parameter value for the Class Year, and then it selects only those students in the specified class. Portal components can accept parameters via the customize option, and they can also be passed parameters on the URL command line.

Cross-Reference   The use of "links" within Oracle Portal is a complex topic and it is discussed in detail in Chapter 18. For the moment, all that you need to know about component links is to copy the URL as shown into the link text field.

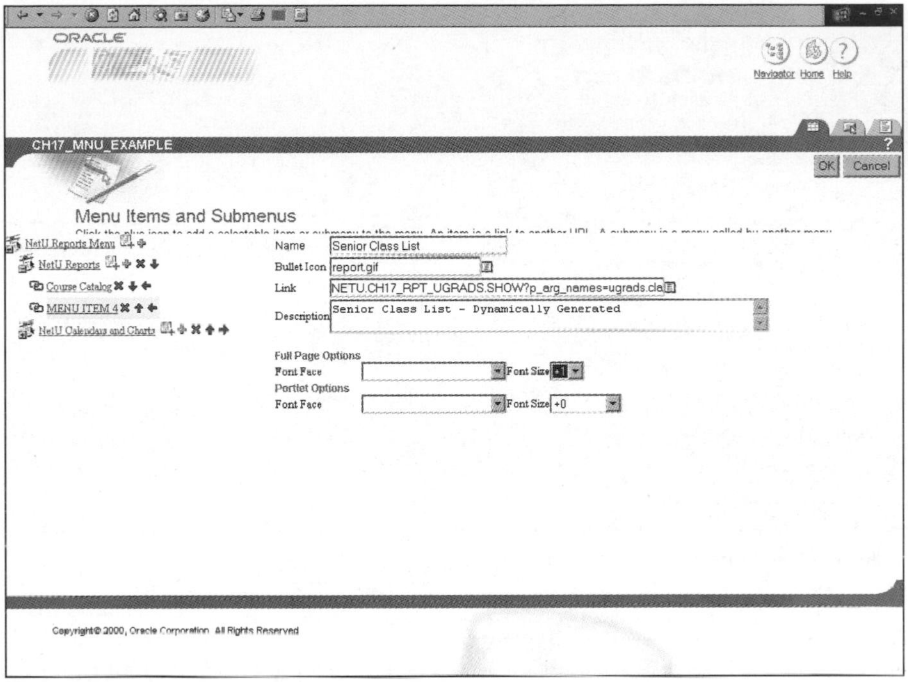

Figure 17-10: Menu item with parameters

8. Save the modified menu using the OK button and then use the Run link to test the menu. Click on the NetU Reports link on the menu to display the submenu.

9. Test the Senior Class List Report Link.

When you select the NetU Reports link from the main menu, you will be presented with the submenu as shown in Figure 17-11. Each of the items on the submenu links to a separate report component. The first link simply calls the entire course catalog report without any parameters, but the second report uses the Class Year to select the data for the body of the report as shown in Figure 17-12.

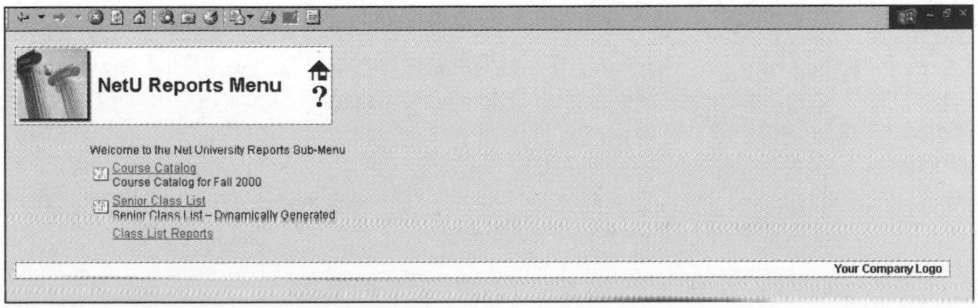

Figure 17-11: NetU Reports submenu

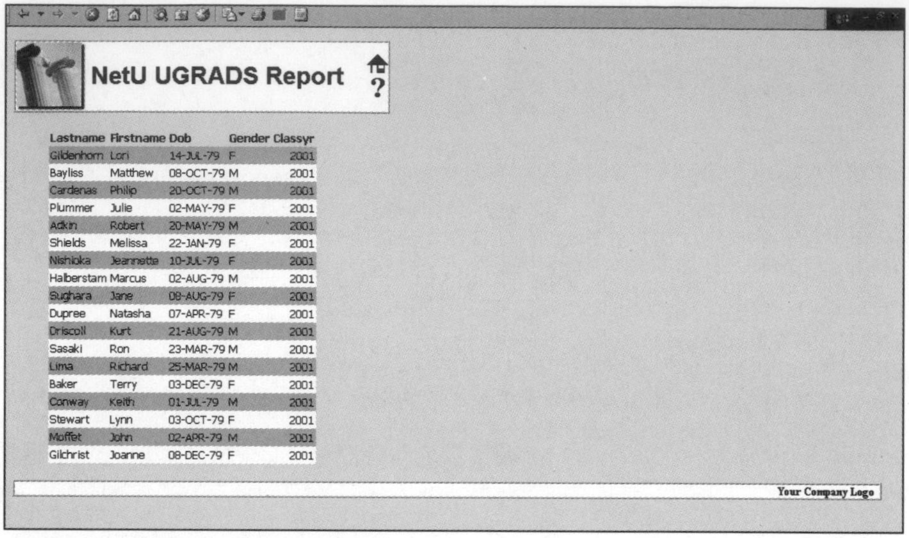

Figure 17-12: Senior Class List Report

You could easily add some additional menu items to this submenu that would show the class list for each of the four class years. In each case, the main body of the link text would remain the same, but the parameter value would change as shown here in boldface text:

```
Seniors
NETU.CH17_RPT_UGRADS.SHOW?p_arg_names=ugrads.classyr&p_arg_
values=2001
Juniors
NETU.CH17_RPT_UGRADS.SHOW?p_arg_names=ugrads.classyr&p_arg_
values=2002
Sophomores
NETU.CH17_RPT_UGRADS.SHOW?p_arg_names=ugrads.classyr&p_arg_
values=2003
Freshmen
NETU.CH17_RPT_UGRADS.SHOW?p_arg_names=ugrads.classyr&p_arg_
values=2004
```

The menu object hides this complexity from the end user of your portal. Once you have created a menu using the preceding links it could be published as a portlet. End users would then be free to add this menu to their own version of the portal site without having to understand Portal parameters or Portal's customization options.

   10. Return to the Manage Component menu.

Linking Root Menus and Advanced Menu Options

The last major task remaining is to link two root menus and set some advanced menu options. Although Portal does not allow you to separate submenus, it does allow you to link from one root menu to another. To take advantage of this capability, it makes sense to organize your menus into groups of menu choices that exist as linked root menus. You will be able to modify the structure of each of the root menus easily and still be able to link them.

> **Note**
>
> Try to strike a balance between too many and too few root menus when you design your menu structure. If you create too many root menus, you could have trouble keeping track of all of them. And if you create too few menus, you may encounter locking problems if there are a lot of developers working on the menu system simultaneously.

1. Import the menu component ch17_mnu_linked.

2. Edit the menu ch17_mnu_example1 once again and create a new menu item called **Class List Reports** under the NetU Reports submenu.

3. Change the Name on the new child menu to **Class List Reports**, and change the link text to **NETU.CH17_MNU_LINKED.SHOW**. (This links your new menu back to the first menu you created earlier.)

4. Click the OK button to save the menu changes.

5. Test the root menu again using the Run link.

If you choose the NetU Reports Menu link, you are connected to the menu that you imported in the first part of this chapter. Because you are calling another root menu, any root menu settings you may have modified for the initial menu apply when the menu is run. For example, if you choose to use different templates for the two menus, they display with their specified template, even when the menus are nested. This is because the menus are considered separate objects and they are only linked through a URL link.

Advanced menu options

Portal menus have some additional display options that you can use to customize the look and feel of the menu.

1. Edit the ch17_mnu_example menu at the Menu Items and Submenus panel (Figure 17-7) once again and scroll to the bottom of the right panel.

If you wish to display multiple levels of menu items and submenus within a single panel, you can use the Sub Levels combo boxes to the display value for the menu. The default value of one causes Portal to show only one level of menus. By setting the Sub

Levels to a higher value, you will increase the display density of each menu page. Portal gives you the choice to set this value for the menu itself as well as for the menu when it appears as a portlet. While you may wish to increase the number of sublevels for a full-page display, you normally do not want to do so for a portlet-based menu. End users will normally use a portlet within a section of a portal page — and menus that display lots of submenus will eat up too much screen real estate.

2. Set the sublevel to 2 for the Full Page Options value.

Just below the Sublevel options are six additional options as listed here:

- ✦ Show Timing
- ✦ Log Activity
- ✦ Inherit Privileges from Application
- ✦ Show Find Option Button
- ✦ Show Frame View Icon
- ✦ Expire After (minutes)

The first three options are shared by all of Portal's other component wizards. The Show Timing check box controls whether or not Portal displays the amount of elapsed time to the end user when the component is run. The Log Activity check box determines whether Portal logs access and the elapsed time values to Portal's activity logs. In most cases, it does not make sense to display the elapsed time for menus unless you are having performance problems with your application. By default, Oracle Portal ties menu privileges to the application privileges. However, you can override this value by deselecting the Inherit Privileges from Application check box. Doing so will cause Portal to display a list of users and roles in a multis-elect list box at the top of the page. This allows you to limit access to the menu to specific groups of users.

Caution   Portal does not currently cascade user and group security settings to submenus and individual menu items. Thus, it is possible for an end user to "see" a menu choice without being able to access the actual component that the menu item is connected to. However, Oracle is addressing this issue in a forthcoming maintenance release of Portal.

Oracle Portal provides two custom display options that apply only to menus. The default behavior for Portal is to display a Find Menu Option text box and button on all menus. An end user of the menu can type search criteria into the text box and click the button to search for text in any menus that are linked from the menu containing the button. Clicking a search result navigates to the menu containing the text. You can also elect to allow end users to display menus using HTML frames. The Show Frame and Show Find check boxes are used to either enable or disable these two options.

Menus are not generated from data within your database, and they normally do not change on a minute-by-minute basis. Therefore, it makes sense to keep them cached within a user's browser cache to improve performance. The default behavior is to cache menus indefinitely. However, if you are actively changing menu options on a production menu, you can use the "Expire After (minutes)" field to manually expire a Portal menu on a shorter interval.

Normally your users will not need to customize a menu as they might a form, report, chart, calendar, hierarchy, or Dynamic Page. By default, Oracle Portal permits users to change most of the display options as shown in Figures 17-13 and 17-14.

These options will appear when an end user elects to customize the menu when it is displayed as a portlet. There are fewer choices on the Display Options panel for a menu component as compared to the same page in the form builder or report builder wizards. You can choose a template for the menu and set the typeface and font size for the menu choices. You had these same choices when you were editing a preexisting menu in the preceding section. You can also select whether to log activity to the activity logs and whether to show the menu timing on the face of the menu. In addition to these familiar choices, you can elect to allow users to display the Find Menu Options button on the face of the new menu. If you accept the default value and enable this setting, Portal enables users to search for submenu strings from the main menu panel. This Find Menu button is a powerful feature for your users, especially if you have deeply nested menus.

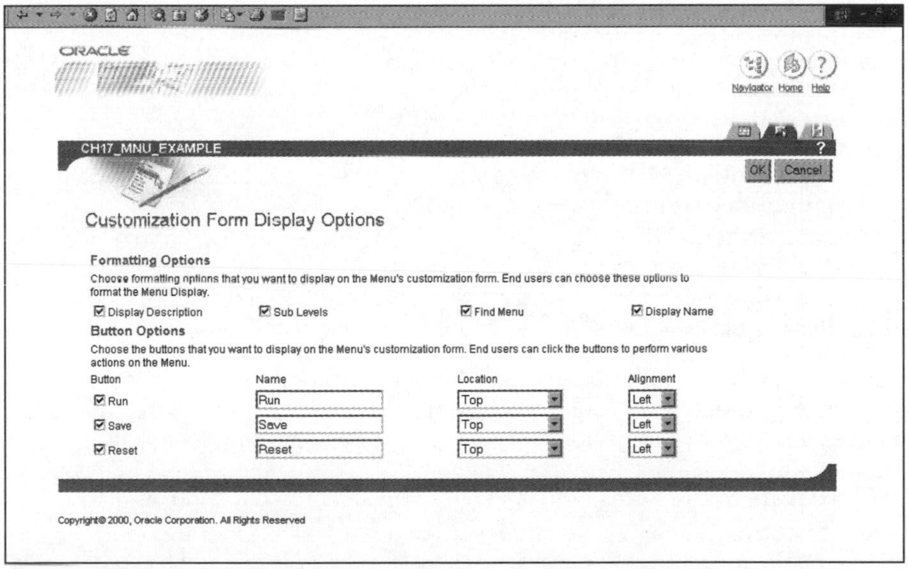

Figure 17-13: Customization Form Display Options for menus

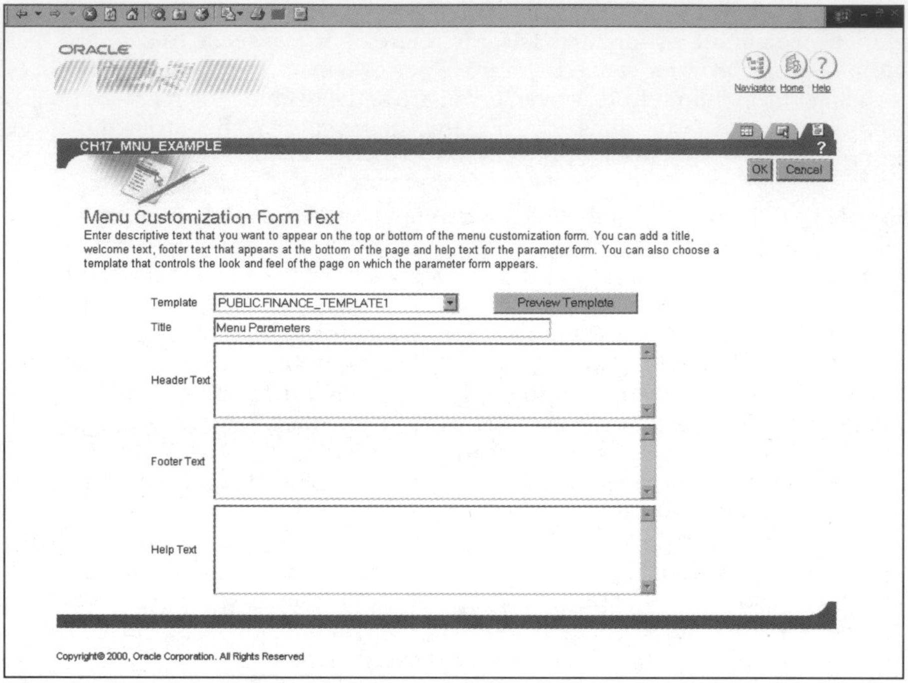

Figure 17-14: Menu Customization Form Text

3. Use the OK button to save your changes, and then run the modified version of the menu.

Note You will notice that Portal now displays your submenus as indented items on a single menu panel. This modified view comes as a result of entering a larger value for the Sub Levels setting.

Using Menus as Portlets

Portal provides you with the standard Manage Component option for menus so that you perform routine tasks such as copying, renaming, and exporting menus. You can also set access permissions for your menu by using the Access tab.

1. Navigate to the Access tab for your menu as shown in Figure 17-15.

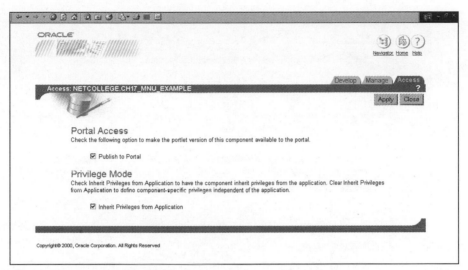

Figure 17-15: Access panel for menus

The security option on the access panel is identical for those of reports, forms, charts, calendars, hierarchies, and Dynamic Pages. You have the choice to set the security access for your menu to default to that of the application (which you can also do from inside the menu editor as discussed in the preceding section). You can also elect to publish the menu as a portlet.

2. Set the access privileges as shown in Figure 17-15 and the set the Publish to Portlet option.

Cross-Reference   In order to complete the following portion of this chapter you will need to have worked through the examples in Chapter 6 and created the Net University Main Page.

3. Add the menu component to the Portlet repository as discussed in Chapter 6.

4. Navigate to the Pages panel and edit the Net University Main Page as shown in Figure 17-16.

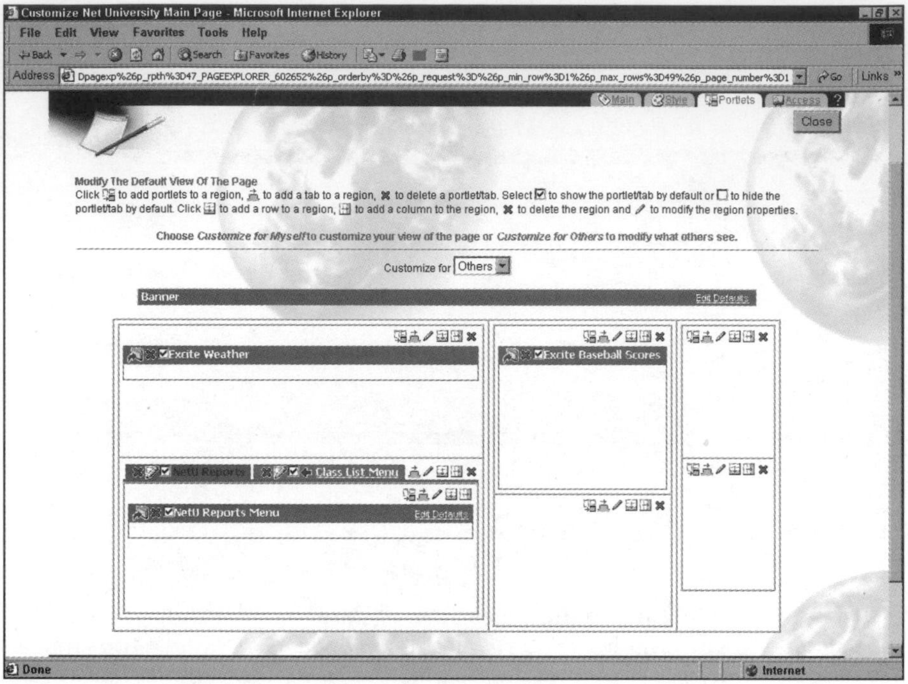

Figure 17-16: Net University main page panel — Edit mode

5. Choose the edit link for the first tab and set the title for the tabbed page to **NetU Reports** as shown in Figure 17-16.

6. Add the **NetU Reports Menu** portlet to the current panel as shown in Figure 17-17.

7. Edit the second tab and set the title for the tabbed page to **Class List Menu**.

8. Add the **Ch17 Linked Menu** portlet by using the Add Portlet Link.

9. Save the modified page and then view the page as shown in Figure 17-18.

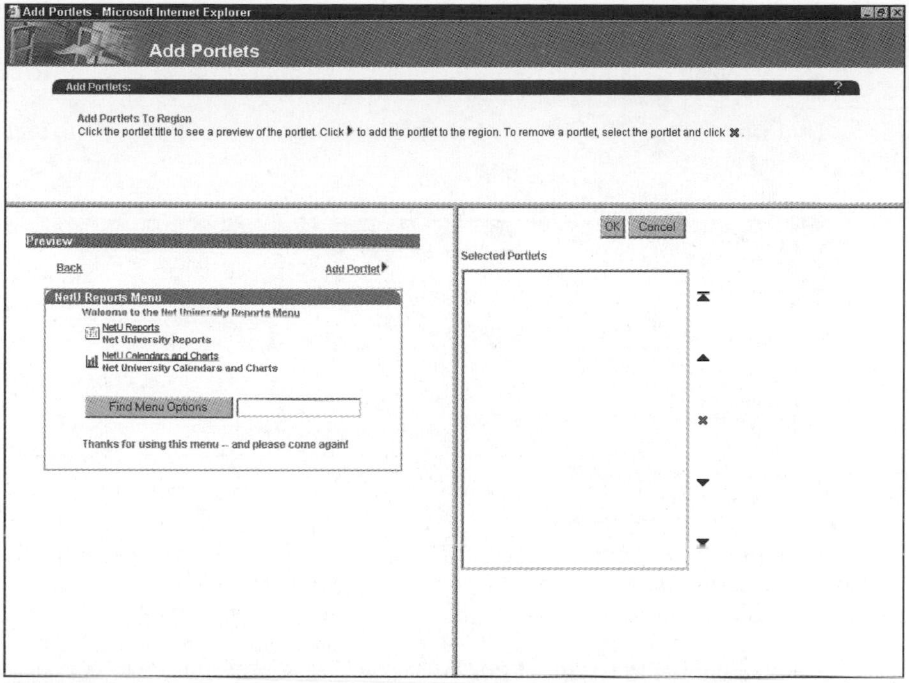

Figure 17-17: Adding the NetU portlet to the Net University main page

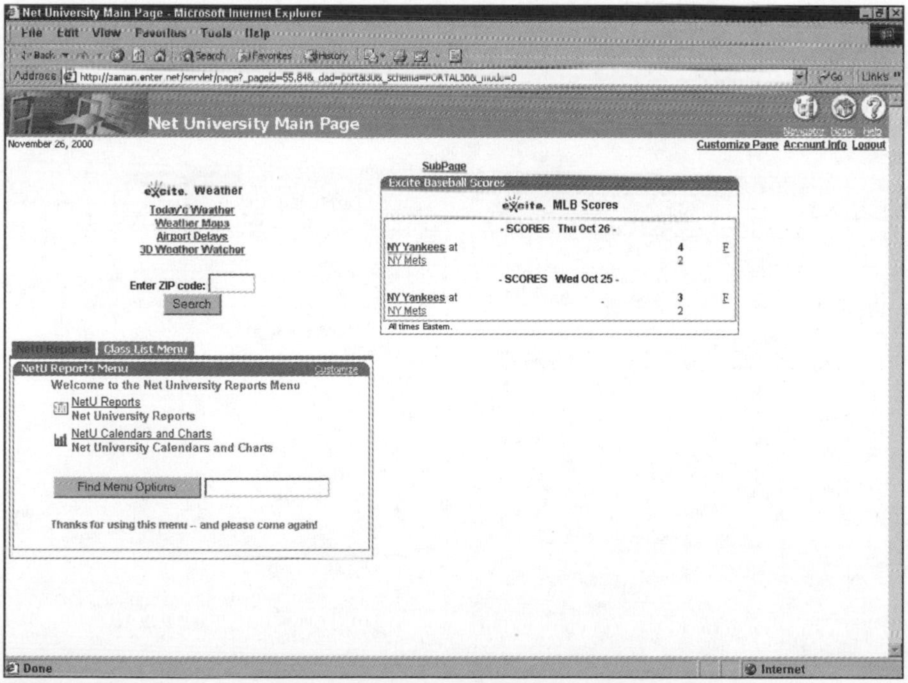

Figure 17-18: Menu components deployed into portal pages

Oracle Portal automatically handles the formatting of the menu into the defined portal area as shown in Figure 17-18. Portal automatically overrides any template settings that you may have applied to the menu with the appropriate portal page settings.

10. Choose the NetU Reports link within the first tab to display the page as shown in Figure 17-19.

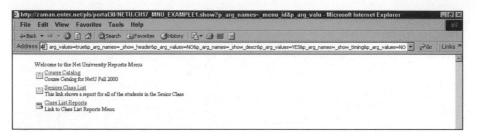

Figure 17-19: Ch17 linked menu

Although Oracle Portal displays the first menu as a portlet, it displays the linked menu as a full component without its associated template. The portlet interface only applies to the initial panel of the menu, so it does not get applied to the linked menu. However, if you accessed the very same menu directly, it would appear as a portlet as shown in Figure 17-20.

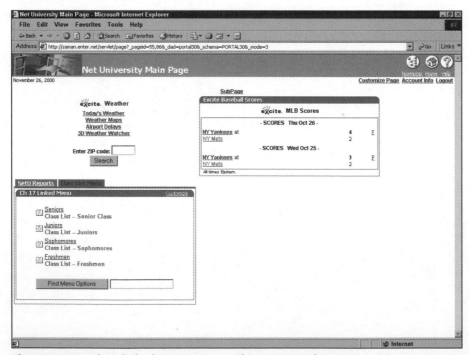

Figure 17-20: Ch17 linked menu as a portlet on a portal page

In order to preserve the standard portal page look and feel we recommend that you limit the number of linked menus and submenus. If you have lots of menu items you can distribute them over a series of separate menus and then deploy each of these menus individually to tabs on portal pages.

Summary

Portal works in conjunction with existing Web technology and HTML standards to help you create Web applications. You can use the menu objects in Portal to provide the basic navigational path through your application system with standard links and URLs. Portal itself communicates between all of its own components using URLs. Portal's Menu Builder Wizard offers a very powerful interface for rapidly creating and modifying menus. You can easily incorporate external HTML pages and Web sites by embedding links into Portal's menus. Menus allow you to build some consistency into the display of forms and reports by displaying them from a single panel. In the next chapter we'll take a look at using templates and images to provide additional display consistency between components.

✦   ✦   ✦

Building Consistency in Oracle9*i*AS Portal Web Sites and Applications

◆ ◆ ◆ ◆

In This Chapter

Considering Content
Creation and
Standards
Enforcement

Creating
Standardized Colors
and Fonts

Adding and
Modifying Fonts,
Images, and
Templates

Importing Custom
Images into Portal

Building User
Interface Templates

◆ ◆ ◆ ◆

In Part III of this book, you learned about the various build wizards Portal offers for creating content objects for your Web sites. Each of the wizards for creating components is designed to ensure some consistency between objects. The Report Wizard, for example, provides the same customization options for every report you create in order to ensure that groups of related reports look and behave in a similar fashion. Furthermore, many of the options for a single wizard are shared among the other tools. For example, you will find the same page for adding PL/SQL code in many of the various builders. This feature helps you share a common set of features and functions across objects.

If you survey a number of public Web sites and portals across the Internet, you will find that the most useful and well-organized Web sites offer a basic consistency in their design and appearance. When you build consistency into groups of related pages, you deliver two advantages to your site. First, you make the site easier to navigate by offering a consistent set of options and functionality. Second, you create a type of informal brand recognition by making the content for a logically related group of objects appear in a similar format. Portal provides an additional set of tools for building an enhanced level of consistency into your objects in the form of colors, fonts, images, and user interface templates. The content wizards use these components to create a consistent, visual theme for your applications.

Content Creation versus Standards Enforcement

Portal provides a set of tools that are called Shared Components for building standards and consistency into your applications. Portal's Shared Components consist of a set of utilities and wizards that create objects, which are then used by the other content builders within Portal. You were exposed to the Shared Components indirectly when you used templates for reports and forms. The utilities within the Shared Components are divided into two categories: those that produce content and those that enforce visual standards. The main menu for the Shared Components appears in Figure 18-1.

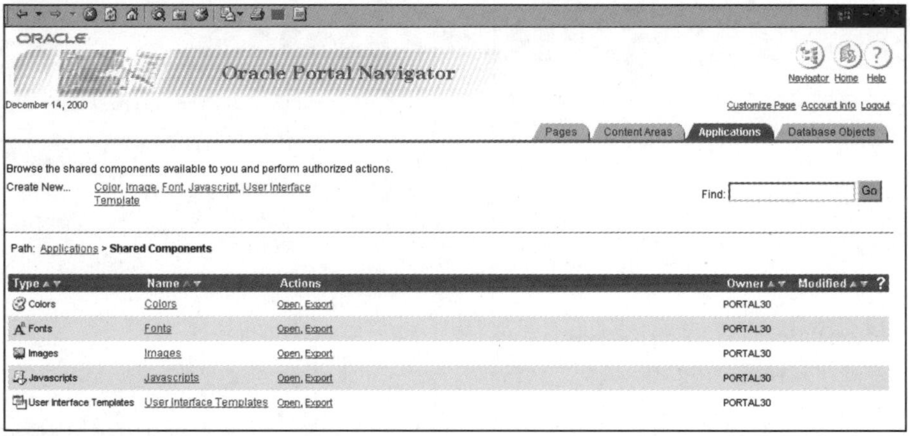

Figure 18-1: Main branch for the Shared Components within the Navigator

> **Note**   Oracle Portal stored these objects in a different manner in prior releases of the product. Version 3.0 of Portal uses a specialized application as the storage container for Shared Components. This application is available to all of the applications that you create within the portal environment.

All of the utilities within the Shared Components area are used to enforce some type of consistency. Colors, Fonts, Images, and User Interface Templates are used to provide visual consistency, while the JavaScript wizard is used to build data consistency into your applications. While the former are relatively similar in design and function, the latter is much more complicated and sophisticated. Thus, although JavaScript is part of the Shared Components area of Portal—we deal with in separately in Chapter 19.

The remaining tools in the Shared Components are geared toward creating visual consistency within your Portal applications. These utilities also build objects used by the other wizards, but generally, they are not used to interact with data directly. The following utilities fall into this category:

✦ Colors

✦ Fonts

✦ Images

✦ User Interface Templates

You use each of these utilities to enforce visual standards for your Portal applications in some way. Images are the exception to the rule, because they are actually content in and of themselves. Within the Shared Component Library, you should consider images to be part of the tools for building consistency into your applications. Image files that provide data for your application should be either stored in the database or referenced from entries in database tables.

Adding Color to Your Components

Colors can have a profound impact on the way your data is displayed within a browser. In many cases, the use and abuse of color determines the level of user satisfaction of your site. Since the dawn of the client/server age, color monitors have been a standard for users. End users expect color screens for their applications, and single-color sites are unacceptable. However, there are countless examples of Web sites that are difficult to use solely because the designers went overboard with color to the detriment of the overall site. Users do not want screens that read like a black-and-white newspaper and they do not want screens that remind them of a psychedelic trip back to the sixties.

Portal enables you to make frequent use of colors throughout the various wizards. In most cases, you can provide a color value for many of the visual settings for each of the builders. If you are familiar with the way in which colors are used within a Web browser, then you will find Portal's Color Editor easy to work with. The Portal color palette is based upon the colors typically found in Netscape Navigator and Microsoft Internet Explorer.

Video display

The colors displayed by your computer are based upon the video card installed in the machine and the video display driver that controls the interface between the computer and the video card. On most Windows PC desktops, the standard video card is either a Video Graphics Adapter (VGA) or Super Video Graphics Adapter (SVGA) compatible card.

The particular video card installed in a given desktop computer has an effect on two aspects of the way in which your Portal applications are displayed. The first attribute is the resolution of the display, which controls the amount of information on a single screen. The decision of level of resolution to use is a critical one and it can have a dramatic effect on the usability of your applications. Because Portal cannot automatically convert content from one level of resolution to another, it does not provide you with any tools for changing the screen resolution. In general, most computer desktops support 800 by 600 pixel resolution, and this setting is typical for desktop applications. Portal itself was designed with this resolution in mind, and you will find that most of Portal's pages fit nicely onto a screen of this size. If you choose to develop using a higher level of resolution, you may find that your pages are too large to view comfortably at the lower settings. Figures 18-2 and 18-3 show the Shared Components page at two different levels of resolution.

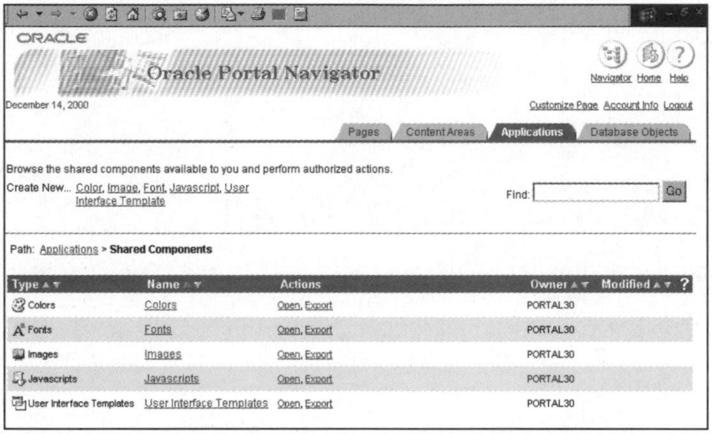

Figure 18-2: Portal home page at 800 by 600 resolution

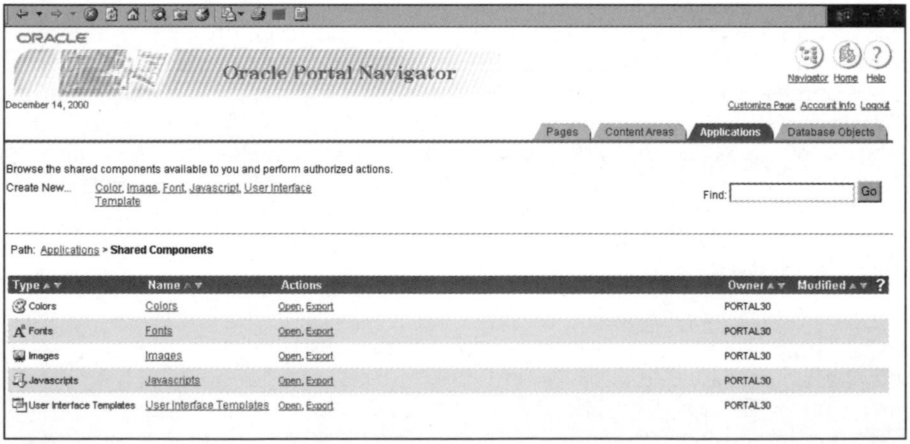

Figure 18-3: Portal home page at 1024 by 1768 resolution

The Portal home page comfortably fits in the 800 by 600 window, but it shows off more of the page at the higher resolution. Extra large display monitors can display higher resolution output in a readable format, but very few users have such large monitors because they are prohibitively expensive. In general, your Portal applications should be designed to fit on 800 by 600 screens unless you are sure that your user base is able to support the higher resolution.

Note   We have used the higher resolution setting for all of the screen captures in this book to minimize the number of separate pages that you need to view.

The higher resolution displays enable you to show more information on a single page, and some applications may require this level of resolution. Portal automatically uses the additional screen real estate at application run time. On Windows desktops, the control panel sets the resolution of the display, and the user can change it from his or her desktop. The examples for resolution settings in this chapter are taken from Windows, but the same principles apply to other desktop operating systems. If the user changes to a higher resolution, the objects you create with Portal automatically use the additional space. The Portal development environment itself will *not* necessarily use this additional real estate, however, because most of the wizards have been designed to show a fixed amount of information.

Video color settings

The video display adapter also controls the color settings for the desktop. Although Portal does not specifically provide tools for managing the display resolution, Figure 18-4 shows the control panel's Display Properties screen for a Windows desktop.

Figure 18-4: Display settings for video adapter

The Desktop Area setting controls the resolution of the display as discussed in the previous section. To the right of the Desktop Area is the Color Palette, which controls the color settings for the computer's display. The setting for the Color Palette is typically a number between 256 and 16 million, and it refers to the number of unique colors the video adapter can display. Older video cards may not support the higher settings, and the valid range of values appears in the list shown on the Display Properties page. The desktop operating system attempts to compensate for missing colors when running an application that uses more colors than the computer can handle. Although applications run them, the colors and images displayed are often very hard to read and ugly.

Portal leaves the rendering of colors to the browser and operating system, and it works well with 256 colors. However, there is a "browser-safe" palette that is used by Internet Explorer and Netscape Navigator, which may be different than your desktop. Furthermore, out of a possible 256 colors, only 216 of them are consistent between Windows and Macintosh computers. Browser-safe means that the color will appear consistently in Internet Explorer and Netscape Navigator on both Windows PCs and Macintosh computers. If you set your display adapter to a higher Color Palette setting, you are able to add many more colors and variations to your applications. However, if you build applications using these additional colors, your applications will not necessarily look the same when they are deployed to an end-user's browser with a lower resolution.

The operating system compensates for you by attempting to simulate the missing colors, but the display itself appears fuzzy. The safest solution from a consistency perspective is to stick to the 216 browser-safe colors. Lynda Weinman is one of the foremost authorities on Web-safe colors and images for the Web. Figure 18-5 shows Lynda's list of browser-safe colors ordered by hue.

Note   We have also included this image in the code directory for this chapter so that you can view the colors directly on your screen.

Colors are determined by a particular combination of the three primary colors: red, green, and blue. The amount of each of the primary colors contained in any one combination determines the final color. At a lower resolution you may not be able to see the color as it will be rendered at a higher resolution. Using Lynda's browser-safe palette solves this problem.

As mentioned earlier, Portal itself uses 256 colors as the basis for all of its wizards — but the browser-safe palette is limited to 216 colors. You can set your display resolution for a higher number of colors and Portal still displays just fine. However, if you build Web sites while running at a higher color resolution setting or with a color outside of the browser-safe 216 colors, you are likely to end up with colors and images that may not show consistently across browsers and platforms.

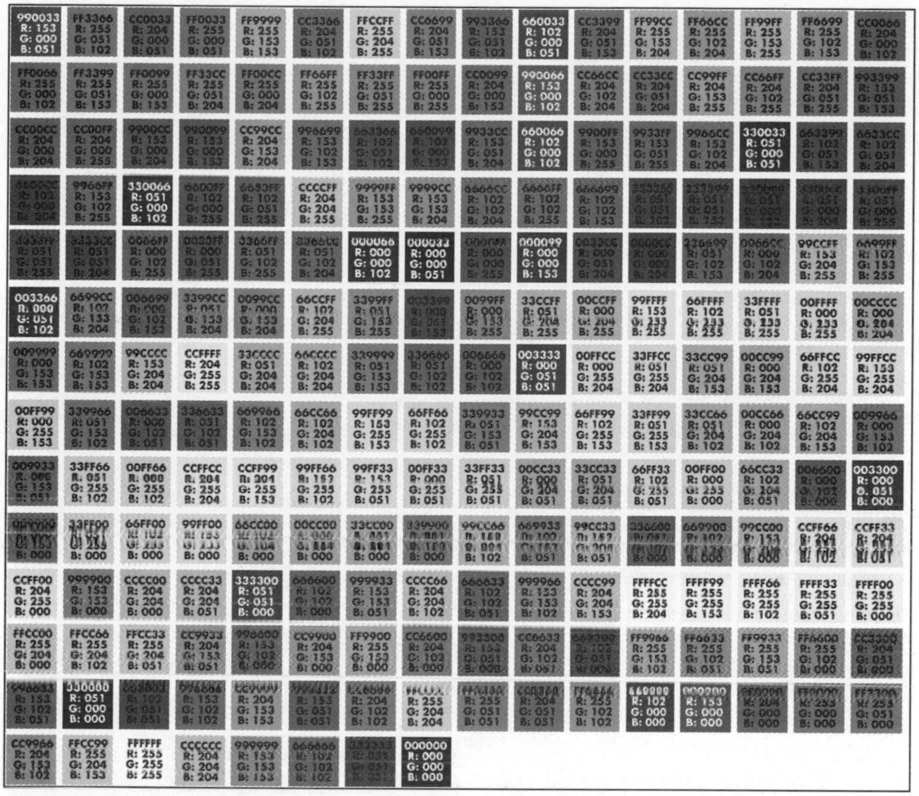

Figure 18-5: Lynda Weinman's browser-safe color palette

Defining portal colors

Because the use of color has such a significant impact on the visuals of your applications, Portal provides a wizard to assist you in the process of defining colors. As mentioned earlier in this chapter, the Color Wizard is part of the Shared Components.

1. To start the Color Wizard, edit the NETCOLLEGE application and select the Applications Link to display the Shared Components as shown in Figure 18-1.

 Note In order to have access to Shared Components you must be assigned to the Portal Developer Role.

2. Click on the Colors Link to display the Colors panel as shown in Figure 18-6.

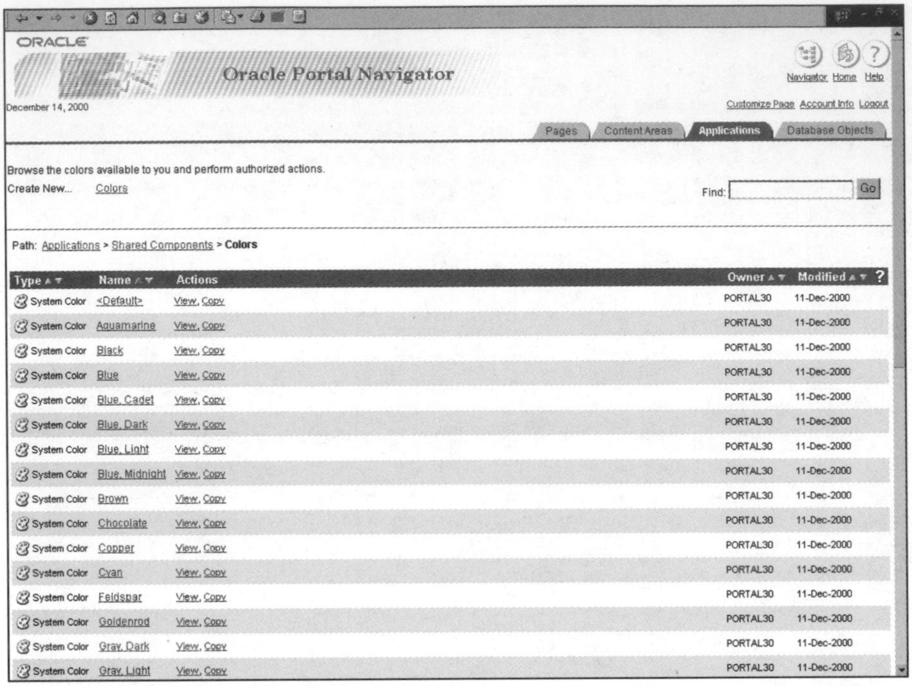

Figure 18-6: Shared Components Color panel

The color values are sorted alphabetically by color name and they are divided into two basic categories—System colors and User colors. System colors are those that are defined by Oracle Portal itself and you are free to copy and view them, but you are not allowed to edit them. User colors can be viewed and copied as well, but you are also free to edit them, delete them, and export them. Since you cannot edit system colors, the simplest way to create a new color is to copy a system color.

3. Use the Create New ... Colors link to display the new color panel as shown in Figure 18-7.

The edit panel is composed of three pieces of information: the color name, the color value, and a Preview button for testing the color display. The color name is the user-friendly name for the color combination, and it is the name by which you refer to the color from within any of Portal's other wizards. The color value field is where you provide the RGB value of the color in format string. The format string is a seven-character string starting with a hexadecimal code indicator followed by three two-character fields for each of the three primary colors, as shown in Figure 18-8.

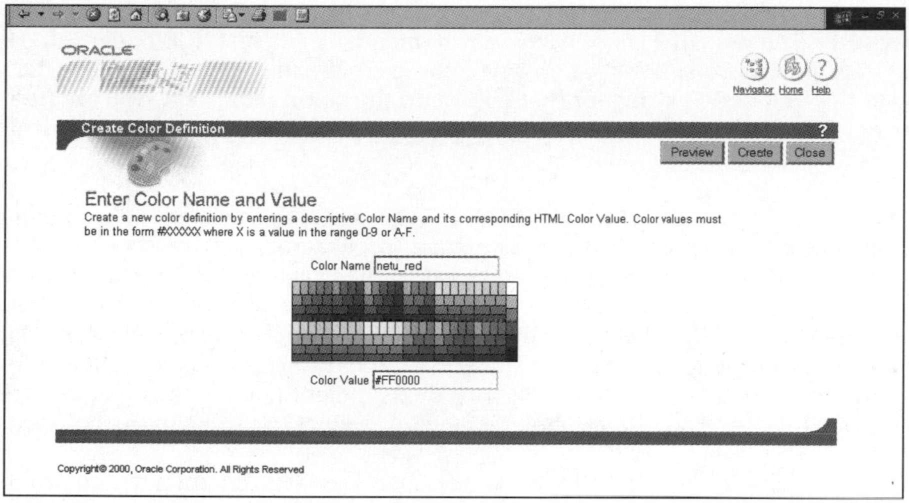

Figure 18-7: Create Color Definition panel

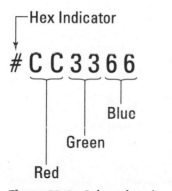

Figure 18-8: Color values in encoded format

The developers of the HTML standard decided to use hexadecimal (HEX) values to represent colors. If you are not familiar with HEX, all you really need to know is that it is a number system based on powers of 16. You need not be familiar with HEX in order to define color settings as this is the only place in which HEX is used, and you only need to convert small numbers between 0 and 255.

A random tour of almost any corporate home page will show that the vast majority of color settings are made using this HEX format. If you are familiar with HEX values from other applications, you may be surprised to note that the color format lacks the leading 0X HEX indicator. The designers of HTML replaced the standard hexadecimal identifier with the number (#) character.

The color field in the middle of the panel provides you with an interactive interface for setting colors, so it is not necessary to manually convert RGB codes into HEX strings. When you single-click on any colored square in the color table, Portal will load the HEX-coded string for that color into the color value field. You are free to select a value using this point and click approach or you can enter a HEX string directly in the color value field.

One of the keys in the definition of colors is to create a consistent color naming convention for your applications. There are three factors you need to consider when you define your colors: the color value, the usage of the color, and the color setting for the color. It is easy to see what a color looks like when you are using the color definition panel, but the other wizards do not show colors, only the color names. If you use a color name that does not accurately reflect the actual color value, you may find that the rest of your development team is selecting incorrect colors. Thus, the color name should somehow reflect the value of the color.

The exception to this rule is to assign the color name based upon the color usage. For example, Net University has its own "college colors" that are used to enforce branding on their Web site. The standard color scheme for NetU is light cream with red highlights. It makes sense to use a cream background for most components in light of this fact. Rather than creating a color called cream, it might be better to define a color named netu_standard_bg to indicate that the color is the standard background color for NetU. In this case, the name of the color indicates usage rather than color value.

The colors that you create are stored externally to the applications that use them. So, it's also a good idea to include the name of the application (or a shorthand name) in the definition for the color. This allows your developers to quickly locate all of the colors for a given application within the other wizards.

Note   We recommend that you create two types of colors schemes: one set based upon the color value and one set based upon usage. This gives your developers guidance as to which colors to use directly within the name of the color.

Caution   Color names are case sensitive, and "Netu_red" is considered a different color than "netu_red" in this release of Oracle Portal.

Once you have decided on a color name scheme, the only remaining step for creating colors is to calculate the color value code or select it from the visual color table. As mentioned earlier, the color value is a HEX string in the format shown in Figure 18-8.

On the CD-ROM   We have provided a utility for converting color numbers on the CD-ROM. Ch18_tohex.htm is an HTML page for converting colors on-screen.

Before you create the HEX color code, you should decide on the mix of red, green, and blue you want to use for the color. Once you have selected the values for the color you wish to create, the HEX conversion is relatively straightforward.

1. Open the ch18_to_hex.htm file in your browser as shown in Figure 18-9.

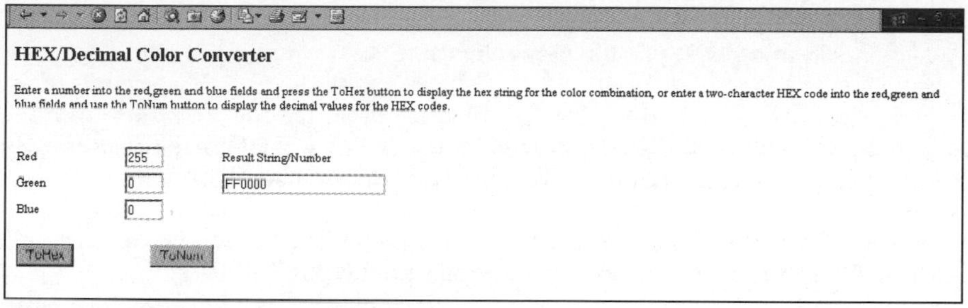

Figure 18-9: HEX conversion HTML page

You can enter any numbers between 0 and 255 in the fields labeled red, green, and blue. Once you have entered the values into the page, you can use the ToHex button to convert the numbers to a HEX string. Conversely, entering uppercase two-character HEX codes into the red, green, and blue fields and using the ToNum button converts the HEX codes to a string of comma-delimited RGB values.

You are going to create a header background color for the NetU application. The color will be the standard red color.

2. Use the conversion page to create the HEX string (#FF0000), or select the red color from the visual palette.

3. Enter a new color for the NetU application by using the name netu_red as the Color Name as shown in Figure 18-7.

4. Enter the value for the new color by entering a number character (#) followed by the six HEX characters for the color name as indicated from the HEX conversion HTML page.

5. Use the Preview button to view the color setting, and then use the Create button to store the new color.

Once you have created a new color, it appears in the Colors panel, and you can modify the color by clicking its edit link. Portal enables you to create duplicate color values with different names, but the color name itself must be unique. You can also use the Colors panel to delete any colors you create. A color that appears in the Colors panel also appears in all of the other wizards wherever you are allowed to enter colors. Later in this chapter, you will use a set of custom colors as part of building a template.

6. Add three additional colors for NetU through the Manage Colors panel by recursively entering the name/value pairs as follows:

```
netu_black / #000000
netu_cream / #FFFFCC
netu_dk_cream / #FFCC99
```

7. Use the Close button to return to the Colors panel.

Caution   Portal does not automatically cascade color changes throughout your application. If you change the color value for a given color, you have to regenerate your objects manually in order to use the new color value.

Once you return to the main colors panel you will notice that the four colors that you created are all sorted at the bottom of the panel. Portal sorts the colors alphabetically; and lowercase color names sort after uppercase color names.

Once you have defined a color it will appear in all of the combo boxes as a valid color in all of the other component tools and portal page editors.

Using Fonts

Fonts are managed in an identical fashion to colors within Portal, and you will find the interface for working with fonts to be a familiar one. Fonts control the manner in which text is rendered on the HTML pages, and they can have a dramatic impact on the way data is displayed. The simple choice of a particular font can transform an HTML page from a conservative look into a bold, lighthearted look, or vice versa. Portal provides you with many opportunities to use specialized fonts within all of the content wizards.

Fonts are also part of Shared Components and they should be universally defined for your application in the same way you define colors. Like colors, fonts are supplied to the browser by the operating system, and it is possible to define fonts within Portal that are not found on the end user's desktop. Web browsers automatically substitute a missing font with a replacement font available on the desktop for the user, but the results of this automatic substitution may not be aesthetically pleasing. It is best to choose a range of fonts that are generally available to your end users when you create your Portal fonts. Although you need to access the operating system to determine your machine's color settings, the browser automatically prepares a list of fonts available to you. The font settings are usually found in the Preferences section of the browser in the same general area as the color setting, as shown in Figure 18-10.

Your browser uses two types of fonts to render HTML pages: variable width fonts and fixed width fonts. *Variable width fonts* — also known as *proportional fonts* — use characters that vary in dimension. Each letter is not guaranteed to use a fixed amount of display real estate. Proportional fonts are the standard for displaying text on HTML pages and within most desktop office tools such as Microsoft Word and PowerPoint.

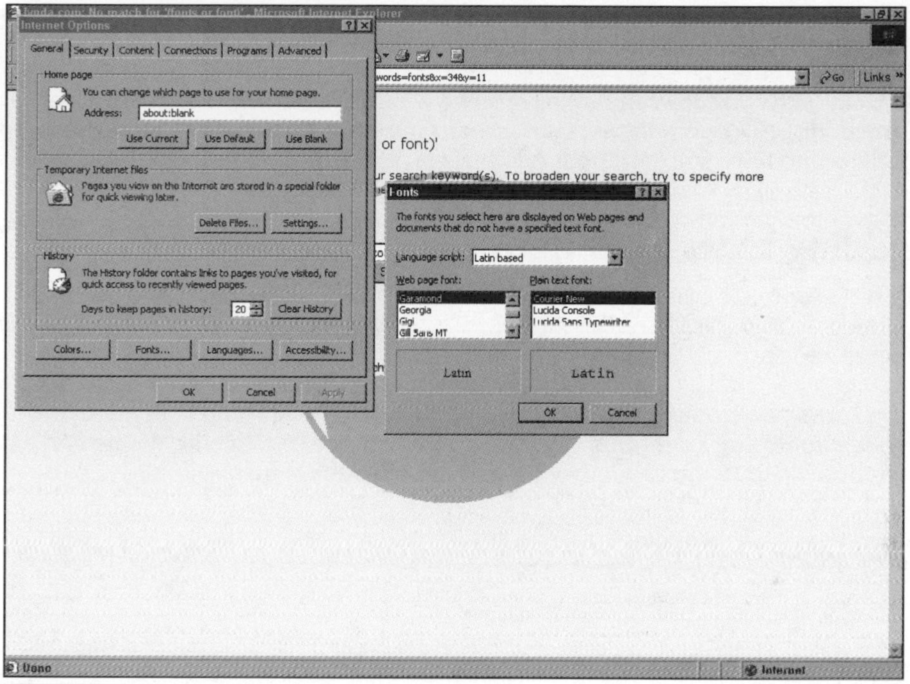

Figure 18-10: Font settings for Internet Explorer

Fixed width fonts display all letters and characters using a consistent amount of real estate. Data entry fields on HTML pages, such as text boxes and text areas, are typically displayed using fixed width fonts. Data entry fields are usually tied back to database fields that have a fixed size within the database. However, using a proportional font for the data entry box for these fields does not allow a user to enter more data into the form than can be stored within the database. A fixed width display font for a data entry field enables the user to see all of the characters that have been entered up to the maximum number of characters allowed. Most HTML tools prevent you from using proportional fonts for input fields, and Portal honors this standard.

The Web browser provides combo boxes for both variable width and fixed width fonts, as shown in Figure 18-10. The browser builds the list of available fonts from the operating system each time the browser starts. If the font appears in the combo box, the system has the font available for display. Of course, you cannot be sure that every user's machine has this same set of font files. If a user does not have access to a specified font, the browser makes a substitution automatically. However, the substitute font may not display your data as you intended. Fonts are organized into families of fonts and the browser attempts to substitute for a missing font using a font from the same family. The fonts themselves are typically broken down into two broad classifications, TrueType and PostScript. TrueType fonts are the standard format supported by the Windows operating system, while PostScript is the more common format for UNIX operating systems. When your browser is running under Windows, you need to have software from Adobe if you plan on using PostScript fonts.

Adding fonts to Portal

Portal's font management facility is part of Shared Components. Selecting the Fonts link from the Shared Components panel displays the Fonts page shown in Figure 18-11.

The Fonts page looks almost identical to the Colors page, and is divided into System fonts and User fonts. As with colors, you are free to edit, delete and export user fonts — but you can only view and copy system fonts.

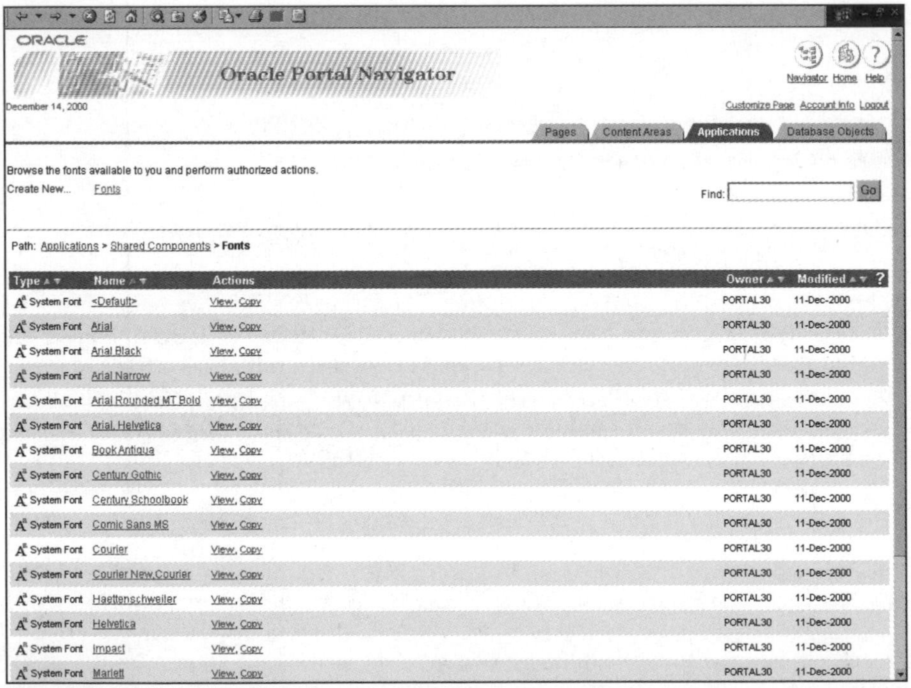

Figure 18-11: Fonts Panel

Portal's font names must map *exactly* to the name of the physical font. In order to add a new font to the system, you need to obtain the actual font name from the browser. The fastest way to do this is to use the browser preferences, as shown in Figure 18-10. Font definitions require a font name and a font value; and the naming conventions that you use should follow the same recommendations as with color names.

1. Click the Create New ... Fonts link choice.

2. Use the name **netu_text** as the font name, and **Verdana** as the font value (as shown in Figure 18-12).

3. Use the Create button to save the new font. Use the Close button to return to the Navigator.

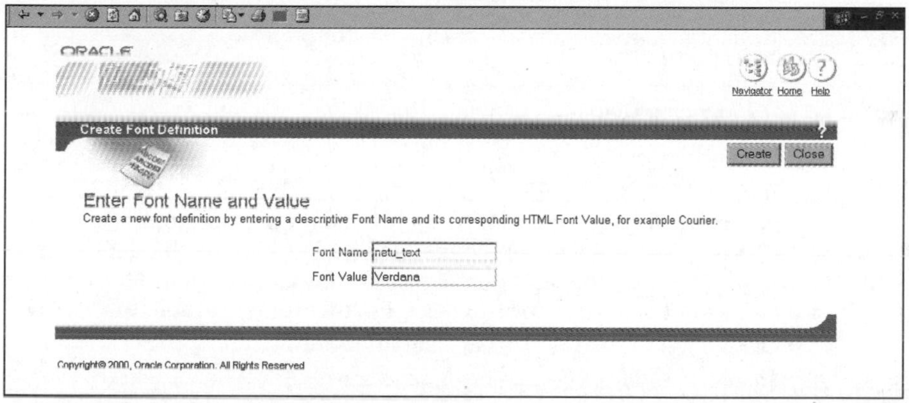

Figure 18-12: Create Font Definition panel

Note

Portal does not attempt to validate the font when you enter the value. If you enter an invalid font, the Web browser simply displays a default font value for the invalid font name.

The Fonts panel does not provide an interface for viewing the font. The only way to see the font that you created is to use the View link in the action column.

4. Scroll down to the netu_text entry on the Fonts page and use the View link to display the panel as shown in Figure 18-13.

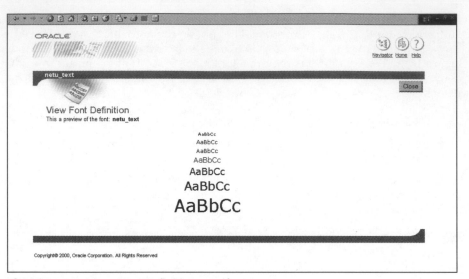

Figure 18-13: View Font Definition panel — netu_text

The view panel shows you the selected font as it will appear on a Web page. Oracle Portal automatically displays the font using the most common font sizes — ranging from one to seven. This will give you some idea how the font will look when it is deployed to your components and portal pages. You can verify the font face and the sizes by viewing the source for the page. Portal creates a table to display the font sample as shown in the following fragment of code:

```
<TABLE  ALIGN="CENTER">
<TR ALIGN="CENTER">
<TD>
<FONT FACE="Verdana" SIZE="1">
AaBbCc</FONT>
</TD>
</TR>
<TR ALIGN="CENTER">
<TD>
<FONT FACE="Verdana" SIZE="2">
AaBbCc</FONT>
</TD>
</TR>
```

Editing fonts

Editing font definitions is easy because the only edits you can make are to delete the font or change the font definition. You can edit the font using the edit link, which will cause an edit Font panel to appear. Click on the Delete link to cause

Portal to display a confirmation panel and then delete the font definition. In effect, the only changes you can make are either to add fonts or to delete fonts. The following list shows all the standard fonts preinstalled by Portal.

✦ Arial

✦ Arial Black

✦ Arial Narrow

✦ Arial Rounded MT Bold

✦ Arial, Helvetica

✦ Book Antiqua

✦ Century Gothic

✦ Century Schoolbook

✦ Comic Sans MS

✦ Courier

✦ Courier New, Courier

✦ Haettenschweiler

✦ Helvetica

✦ Impact

✦ Marlett

✦ Monotype Sorts

✦ Tahoma

✦ Times New Roman, Times

✦ Verdana

Most of the fonts you add to the system will be variable width fonts. Portal uses the fixed width font defined by the browser to display text data entry fields. You cannot set the fixed width font from within Portal. If you need to change the fixed width font, you need to use the browser Preferences page shown in Figure 18-10.

Deploying colors and fonts

Once you have created colors and fonts you are free to use them within any of the other component wizards — forms, reports, charts, calendars, and hierarchies. Figure 18-14 shows both fonts and colors as they appear in the formatting conditions panel for a report. You will notice that Oracle Portal sorts the fonts and colors by name, so the lowercase fonts and colors that you created in this section appear at the bottom of the list.

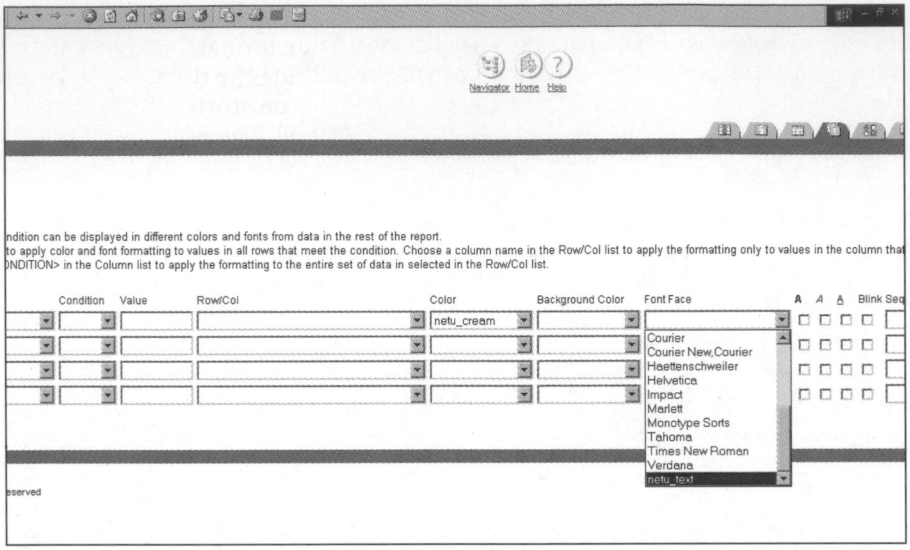

Figure 18-14: Colors and fonts in a report

Adding Images

Most Web sites are composed of a mixture of HTML text and images. HTML in and of itself often does not offer a fine grain of display for formatting certain types of information. It is often impossible to even display certain text formatting due to the limitations of how HTML formats text. Many popular Web sites, including Oracle's home page, use a mix of HTML and images in order to display data in the desired format. Portal offers advanced formatting options for display, but the final output is always in HTML format and is subject to the same display limitations as static HTML text. Graphic images, on the other hand, are displayed as rendered by the browser, and they can offer you a much higher resolution of display when compared to standard HTML text. The downside of images is that, unlike HTML-rendered text, a graphic is static — you cannot easily change it on the fly.

Web images are typically stored in one of two formats: GIF or JPEG. Graphics Interchange Format, or GIF, is one of the most popular Web graphics formats. Joint Photographic Expedition Graphics, or JPEG, is the other common type of Web graphics file. JPEG files are considered to be vector graphics files, and can be enlarged easily without losing the crispness of the image. GIF files are typically used as simple images on a form, and JPEG files are typically used to display photographs and wallpaper backgrounds. Portal itself makes use of both types of image file formats.

Caution   Images are subject to the same color reduction problems that affect text colors. If you create images that use a large number of colors, you may have problems viewing these images at lower color settings.

The Oracle database can store images directly within the database itself, and you can build SQL queries that retrieve the data in graphic format from the database. However, Portal itself stores its standard images outside the database in the file system of the host machine. Initially, you should plan on storing the images you create for use with Portal in a file system directory as well. The exception to this rule is the Content Area of Portal, which has been designed to help you store content (including images) directly in the database.

Note

Chapter 2 discusses the process of adding file system directories so that Portal can use objects in them. Before you proceed with the examples in the following sections, you need to create these file system directories and be familiar with Portal's /images/ directory hierarchy. Techniques for storing images in the database via Content Areas are covered in Chapter 22.

Portal image types

Portal images are normally stored as either a GIF or JPEG file. (Technically speaking, you can use other formats such as TIFF, but you will have to be sure that your end users have the capability of display these non-native types in their browsers.) Portal organizes its images in a series of *logical* image categories and this distinction is made only inside Portal. You can find the Images panel for Portal under the Shared Components panel, as shown in Figure 18-15.

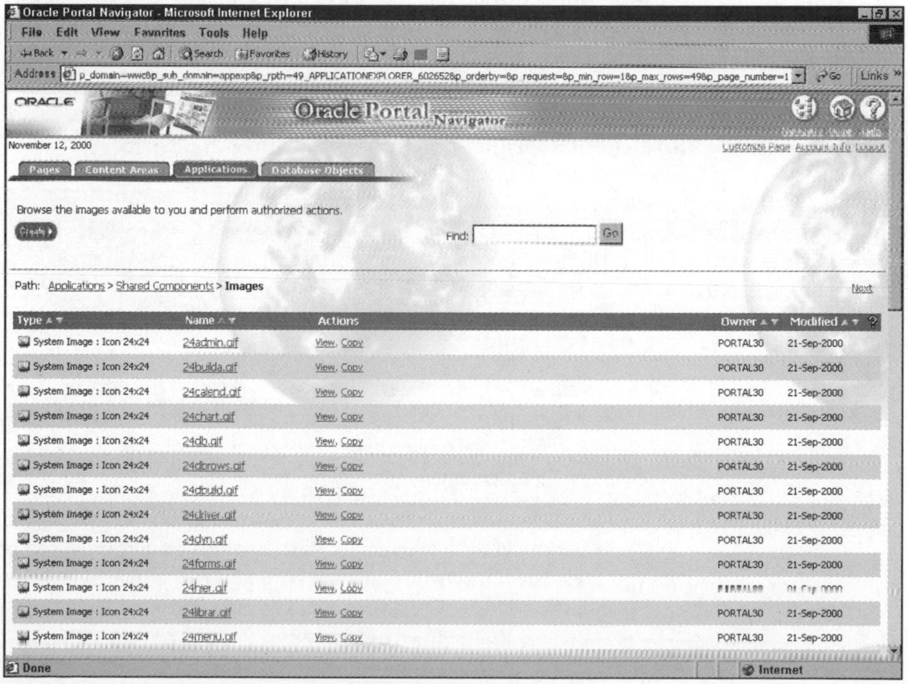

Figure 18-15: Portal Navigator Images panel

Images are divided into two categories, System images and User images, just like colors and fonts are. Images are comprised of the following three pieces of information:

✦ Image name

✦ File name

✦ Image type

The image name is the logical name that developers use to refer to the image from within Portal's content wizards. Image names work the same way as color names — they are a logical association between a particular graphic image and a reference name. In most cases, Portal's own images use the filename as the image name, but this is not a requirement. As with colors and fonts, consistent use of logical names can make your images much easier to find and remember. The filename is the *physical operating system* filename for the image. Portal stores image files in operating system directories and needs to have access to the actual physical filename in order to load the associated image. If you store all of your application images within Portal's standard images file system directory, then the filename is nothing more than the name and a file extension. If you locate your own graphic files in a separate directory tree, then the filename must include a virtual path definition as part of the filename.

> **Note**   Virtual paths are not managed inside of Portal itself, they are controlled by the Apache HTTP Server in the httpd.conf file. Chapter 2 provides a description of creating virtual file paths in the httpd.conf file. Although you are free to use virtual paths when loading images through PL/SQL code, you cannot use virtual paths for images that you create within the Portal environment.

Within Portal, images are organized by a usage indicator, which is referred to as the image type. Table 18-1 lists the various image types defined by Portal.

Table 18-1 Portal Image Types	
Image Type	*Description*
Arrows	Arrows are the directional arrows displayed at the top of the panel within the wizards. Portal supplies these images and you are free to use them, but you will typically not create new images under this heading.
Backgrounds	Background images are designed to replace a color as the backdrop for a Web page. Portal comes equipped with some sample background images, and you can add your own backgrounds. The pale gray database and magnifying glass picture that appear behind all of Portal's pages is an example of a background.

Image Type	Description
Database Browsing	These are images used by the database browsing tool. Portal supplies these images and you are free to use them, but you will typically not create new images under this heading.
Database Objects	Portal associates these images with the various database objects (tables, views, triggers, and so on) within the database browser. Portal supplies these images and you are free to use them, but you will typically not create new images under this heading.
Heading Icons	Heading icon images appear in the top-line header of the page within the various templates. The Oracle logo and globe picture shown on Portal's panels is an example of a heading icon, as are the Home and Help images.
Icons 24X24	Icons are used throughout Portal as menu choices and as links. The menu bar at the bottom of Portal is built using icons. Portal itself uses three different size icons, 16-pixel, 24-pixel, and 32-pixel. The 24X24 size is the middle size, and all the images in this category are 24 pixels by 24 pixels square, as implied by the name. You may add your own icons to this category, and you can use these icons in your own applications as menu choices within the menu builder.
Icons 32X32	This is the largest icon size and it is used for the same purpose as the 24X24 size icons. The larger size is more appropriate for less densely populated menus and forms.
Logos	Logo images are designed for storing company logos and trademark images. Oracle's standard red and white trademark is stored as a logo image. Although you may use the company logo within other images, the standard logo is meant to be stored in this category.
Miscellaneous	This artwork does not specifically fit into other categories and can be stored here. Portal's miniature "new" image is stored in this category.
Public Template Art	Templates provide a complete structure for displaying content in a standard and consistent format. Templates are composed of colors, fonts, and images. Graphics to be used in the building of templates are stored in this category.
Icons 16X16	Icons 16X16 are the 16 by 16 pixel graphics that Portal uses on panels within the wizards to provide visual cues. These are the smallest graphic objects used by Portal.
Wizard Images	Wizard images are the purple and gray styled images shown at the top left on each wizard panel within a wizard page. These images are specific to Portal, and you will not need to add images to this category.

Portal uses the image type categories to limit searches when you are creating templates and using graphics. If you wish to add a background image to a template, for example, Portal only shows you background images when you perform an image search.

Adding images

Adding images to the Portal system is a simple two-part process. The first part of the process is to locate the GIF or JPEG image files you plan to use and copy them to a virtual path that is accessible by Portal. Portal can store images within its own images subdirectory in the file system. (The Apache Listener configuration file sets the physical path for the default virtual file location.) As with colors and fonts, images that are associated with a particular application should have some indication of this fact in the image file name so that these files can be easily identified at the operating system level. The Net University application uses a number of standardized images, as shown in Table 18-2.

<table>
<tr><td colspan="3" align="center">Table 18-2
NetU Images</td></tr>
<tr><td>*Image Name*</td><td>*Image Type*</td><td>*Description*</td></tr>
<tr><td>netu_bg</td><td>Background</td><td>Stucco background for use as a backdrop for report pages</td></tr>
<tr><td>netu_campus</td><td>Miscellaneous</td><td>GIF image of the NetU campus buildings</td></tr>
<tr><td>netu_heading</td><td>Heading Icon</td><td>University image for upper-left corner of page (built with SWiSH)</td></tr>
<tr><td>netu_help</td><td>Heading Icon</td><td>Graphic image of a question mark for use with templates</td></tr>
<tr><td>netu_home</td><td>Heading Icon</td><td>Home image for navigation back to the NetU home page within templates</td></tr>
<tr><td>netu_internal_use</td><td>Background</td><td>Small background image with light gray text for use as a backdrop on sensitive report pages</td></tr>
<tr><td>netu_logo</td><td>Logo</td><td>Net University corporate logo</td></tr>
<tr><td>netu_tabbycat</td><td>Miscellaneous</td><td>Picture of the NetU mascot, the Tabby Cat</td></tr>
</table>

Each of the images in Table 18-2 includes "netu" within the name of the graphic file. This helps keep the images grouped together when you transfer the files or edit the images.

1. Go to a file manager that can access the directory structure on the machine that is hosting the Apache HTTP Listener for Portal.

2. Copy the image files listed in Table 18-2 to your /images/ directory. You may need the assistance of your system administrator to gain permission to write to this directory. The images must be located in a directory mapped to the Oracle Portal virtual directory /images/.

Note

Portal supports the use of animated image files. You can copy animated images into Portal's image directory just like any other image. Portal displays the animation at run time for you. (Self-contained animation formats, such as GIF, will display automatically. The image file netu_heading.swf is an animated Flash-compatible image. You will need to add HTML code to view this image.)

Once you have moved the files to a location Portal has access to, the rest of the image creation process is simple.

3. Use the Create button on the Image panel to create a new image as shown in Figure 18-16.

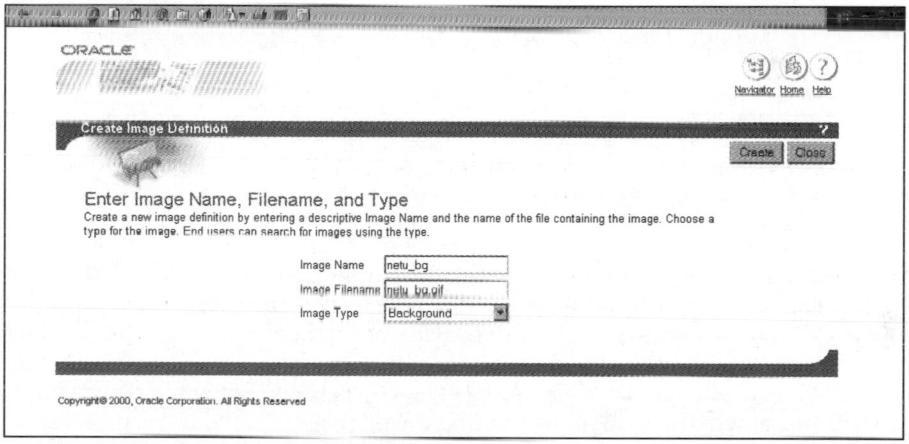
ORACLE
Navigator
Home
Help
Create Image Definition
Create
Close
Enter Image Name, Filename, and Type
Create a new image definition by entering a descriptive Image Name and the name of the file containing the image. Choose a type for the image. End users can search for images using the type.
Image Name
netu_bg
Image Filename
netu_bg.gif
Image Type
Background
Copyright© 2000, Oracle Corporation. All Rights Reserved

Figure 18-16: Create Image Definition panel

The Image Name is the name you wish to use to refer to the graphic from inside Portal, and the Image Filename is the physical name of the image file, including the file extension. You cannot use virtual directory paths for image files that you create with the image wizard. Portal does not verify that the physical file name you enter is correct, or that the image *exists* when you add the entry. Portal verifies that the file exists only when you attempt to display the image.

Cross-Reference

External images in virtual directory paths can be used with Oracle Portal by referencing the virtual path within your PL/SQL query. Chapter 15 provides you with detailed instructions on how to do this with Dynamic Pages.

4. Enter the information shown in Figure 18-16 for the first NetU image. The Image Name is netu_bg, the Image Filename is netu_bg.gif and the Image Type is Backgrounds. Use the Close button to return to the Navigator.

Once the image has been added to the system, Portal includes the image in the Find panel and the list of images. However, there are so many system images it is unlikely that you will see the image that you just created in the first page of entries. You can either search for images using the Find text box, or you can use the down arrow button in the title bar over the TYPE field to re-sort the list to show the user images first.

5. Locate the netu_bg image and use the View link to display the image as shown in Figure 18-17.

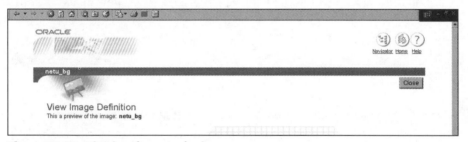

Figure 18-17: Viewing the netu_bg image

The view panel shows you the image as it will appear on a Web page within Oracle Portal. The only images that will not appear exactly as displayed are those images that are marked as backgrounds. Portal will automatically tile background images that are smaller than the actual page size when the image is displayed. So, the netu_bg image will appear as its actual size when shown in Figure 18-17, but it *may* tile this image when you include it within a Web page.

Cross-Reference
We will use this image in the last part of this chapter as a background image, so you'll be able to see how the tiling feature works.

The actual image files are stored outside Portal and you can only edit the image itself from outside Portal. If the image is changed, Portal does not give you any indication that the image has been modified on the edit panel. Portal does not attempt to verify the contents of the image and it does not track file system dates on images.

6. Add the remaining images for Net University using Table 18-2 as your guide. Upload the netu_heading.swf file — but do not add an image entry for it.

Using Templates

Templates are the organizers for your colors, fonts, and images. Templates provide a complete structure for your content objects and ensure that your reports, forms, charts, menus, calendars, and hierarchies look and behave consistently. The template object is comprised solely of the three object types that you have worked with thus far in this chapter. In effect, templates are used to mix and match colors, fonts, and images to produce a particular look for your applications.

You can build a single application entirely on a single template, and one template can be used by many applications. Applications are more likely to be built using several templates, unless the application is targeted at a single class of user. For example, divide the contents of the NetU Web site into the following three categories: students, faculty, and alumni. You could create a separate template for each of the three different groups and use it when building a component for the associated group. In this manner, every piece of content for each group looks and behaves consistently.

1. You can call the User Interface Templates page from the Shared Components Navigation page, as shown in Figure 18-18.

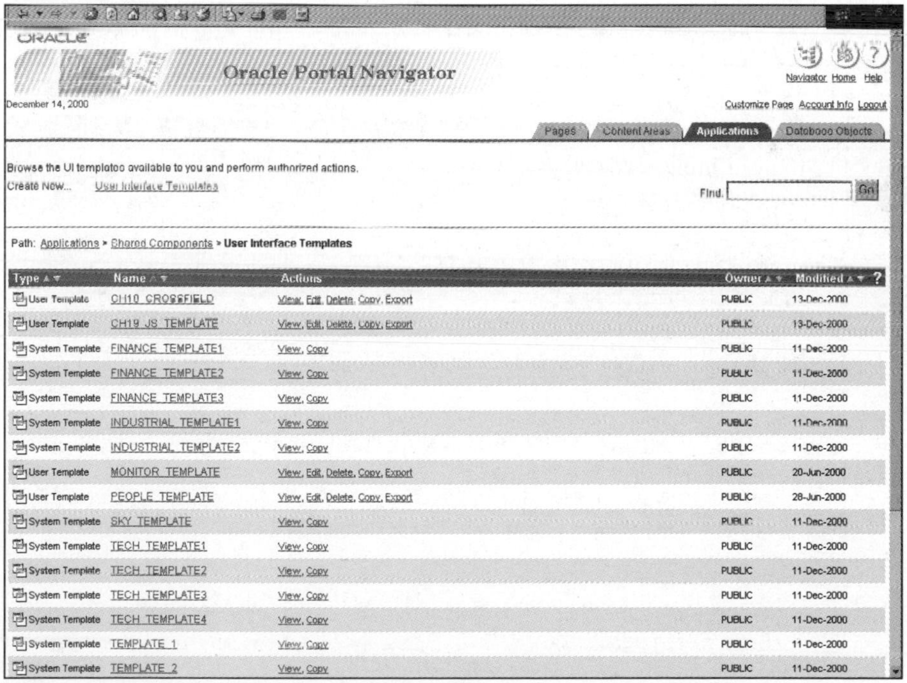

Figure 18-18: User Interface Templates page

Adding a new template

The User Interface Templates panel is divided into System and User templates, just the same as colors, fonts, and images. While the fonts, colors, and images that are controlled by the system will appear frequently within the portal environment, this same rule does not apply with templates. Template entries that are marked as "system" entries are display-only. (It can be useful to use the view button to look at these templates before you create your own.) The template builder is closer to a true wizard than the equivalent builder for colors, fonts, and images.

Templates come in two basic types: structured and unstructured. Structured templates use a fixed format for positioning content, loading images, and setting colors and fonts. They are simple to build, and the structure ensures that you use all of the capabilities of the template skeleton. Unstructured templates are based upon HTML and enable you to have a much finer level of control over the layout and behavior of your templates. Unstructured templates assume a firm knowledge of how structured templates are meant to work, and you should avoid using unstructured templates until you have sufficient experience with the structured version.

1. Use the Create New... User Interface Templates link to display the first page of the wizard as shown in Figure 18-19.

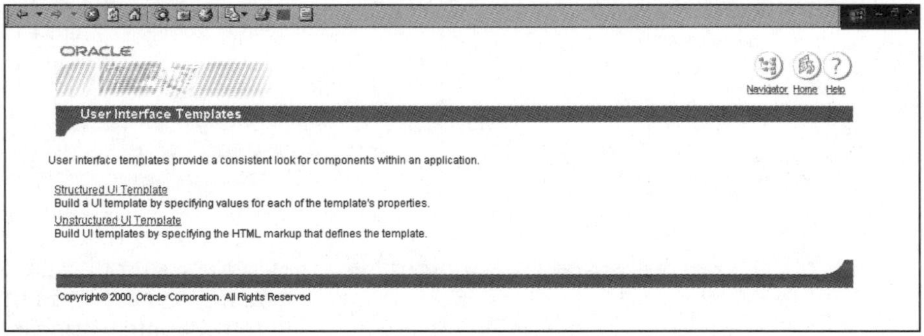

Figure 18-19: Structured and unstructured templates

2. Choose the Structured UI Template Link to display the page as shown in Figure 18-20.

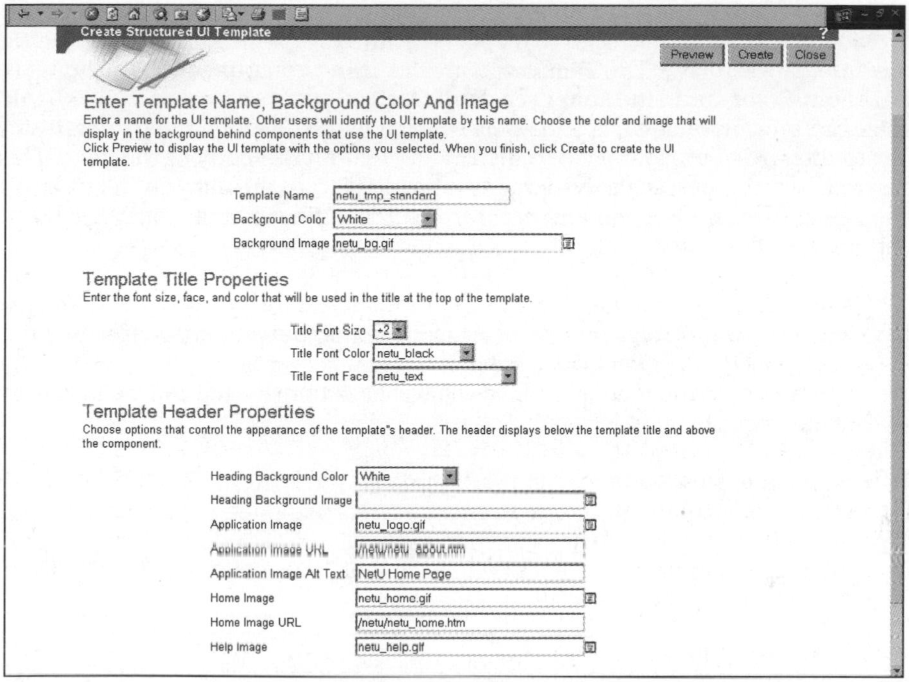

Figure 18-20: Creating a user interface template

The various parts of the template editor frame are divided into sections using bold text. The top section is the Template Name, Background Color, and Image. You will want to use a consistent method for naming templates, just as with any other content object — and the name follows the same rules as those for colors, fonts, and images. The background color is the color that will be used as the background for the HTML page that is constructed from the template. The list of available colors is built from the list of system and user colors that you defined earlier in this chapter. You will notice that the new colors that you added to the system appear in the combo box that appears next to the Background Color field. Alternatively, you use an image as the background for your template. Oracle Portal will automatically tile background images that you select so that the image fills the entire background area of the page.

3. Use the name **netu_tmp_standard** as the name of the new template, and select White. Choose the netu_bg.gif image as the background.

The next section shown in Figure 18-20 is the Template Title. The information you provide in this section is used to display the title text, which appears to the right of the application image. The Template Title has three components: Title Font Size, Title Font Color, and Title Font Face. Font Size is a point setting and you should select an integer value (1, 2, and so on). Portal uses the number as a relative number to the size of the font used to display the text on the body of the page. This ensures that the title is always larger (or smaller) than the data on the page. You can select the font face and font color from combo boxes built from your Portal font and color tables.

> **Caution**   Portal uses the color name to search for colors and the image name to search for images, but it always copies the actual color number and image filename to the calling field. If you later change the color definition or image, the change will not be carried into your template, and you will have to make the change to your template manually.

Title Font Face is the last entry in the Template Title section, and it determines the font used to display the title text. The text itself is provided inside component objects such as forms, reports, and charts. Portal extracts the title from these components at run time and renders it in the font, size, color, and location you specify in the template.

   4. Enter the following information for the Template Title:

```
Font Size: +2
Font Color: netu_black
Font Face: netu_text
```

The final section of the structured template page is the Template Header Properties. The first two entries in this section control the background color for the heading of the template. Oracle Portal displays the title for each page in a separate ribbon area of color at the top of the page. As with the page itself you have the choice to set a background color or to use a separate background image that will be tiled within the heading area of the page. By using a contrasting color or image for the header you can provide a nice visual separation between the body of the page and the header and title.

   5. Use the combo box next to the Heading Background Color label to locate the White color and select this color as the background for the heading of your new template.

The application image appears in the upper left-hand corner of the template. It can be used to provide a URL link for your applications. For example, you might use the application image as a button to connect your users back to the home page for your portal. You are able to specify three attributes for the application image. First, you can specify a application image to be displayed. You can use the icon to the right of the image name field to search for a particular image by name, but Portal only displays images that have been entered as heading images as results of this search.

Just below the image field is the link field, which enables you to specify a link to be followed when the end user clicks the image. You are permitted to enter any valid URL into this field, including links to other Portal components. Because this link is shown everywhere the template is used, this link is typically used to connect the end user to a standard information page. Within Portal itself, this link is used to display the Connection Information page. You are not required to provide an application image in the template, but if you provide a URL link, then you must provide an image for the link. The Application Image Alt Text entry field is used for entering text that is displayed when the user hovers over the application image with their mouse, or for those browsers that cannot display images

6. Enter the following information into the Application Image section:

```
Name: netu_logo.gif
Link: /netu/netu_about.htm
ALT Tag: Net University Information Page
```

The next to last set of fields in the bottom part of the panel is the Home Link, as shown in Figure 18-20. The Home Link section defines whether an image exists on the upper-right corner of the page. Portal uses the miniature house image as its Home Link. The Home Link is composed of two pieces of data: the URL and the Image. The URL points to a valid Web address in either a full or relative format. In many cases, the home page for your application will be served up by the Oracle 9iAS Apache HTTP Server. You can link to this server by entering a URL in this field. If the link is a relative link, then the browser uses the Portal listener to locate the page. You can also search for an image to represent the link by using the search button in the Home Link section. Only images that were filed in the headings category can be used. It is possible to circumvent this check by entering a filename directly, but we recommend against doing so, as Portal is liable to enforce this check in the future.

7. Enter the following information into the Home Image URL section.

```
Home Image URL: /netu/netu_home.htm
Home Image: netu_home.gif
```

Below the Home Link section is the Help Image section, which is also shown in Figure 18-20. Much like the Home Link section, it enables you to select an image to be displayed next to the home link in the upper-right corner of the page. The help image does not have an associated URL link because Portal determines the link at template execution time. If the run-time object has help associated with it, Portal links to that help dynamically from this image.

8. Enter the following information into the Help Image section:

```
Help Image: netu_help.gif
```

9. Use the Preview button at the top of the page. The Test function causes Portal to render the template as shown in Figure 18-21.

Figure 18-21: Previewing a template

Portal implements the template specifications that you entered in the top portion of the page. Portal displays icons for the application image, home page, and help as indicated and sets the background color for the heading. You can achieve different background effects by using different types of images as a background. There is an additional background included in the sample application that you can test — netu_internal_use. The internal use image displays a white background with faded gray text showing the phrase "internal use only." (This image is smaller and Portal will tile the image automatically).

10. Close the preview window and change the background image to **netu_internal_use**.

11. Preview the template again to view the tiled image.

12. Close the preview window and reset the background image to **netu_bg.gif**.

13. Use the Create button and the Close button to save the template and exit the wizard.

Using unstructured templates

While structured templates provide you with the ability to add advanced formatting to your Portal components, you are limited in the type of interface you can build. If you are an advanced HTML author and you find that you need to provide additional flexibility for your applications, Portal offers the unstructured template format.

1. Create a new template from the User Interface Templates Menu.

2. Click the Unstructured User Interface link to create an unstructured template as shown in Figure 18-22.

The Unstructured U/I Template page lacks the individual fields and sections found in the structured template builder. An unstructured template is nothing more than a block of HTML in a certain format. Underneath the covers, the structured template format is actually nothing more than a block of HTML text as well.

Portal implements the heading block using HTML tables. This enables you to align the application image, title text, Home icon, and Help icon along the same line. As you can see in Figure 18-22, the equivalent HTML source in the unstructured format is much smaller than that of the structured template, because you are expected to add your own HTML. This gives you lots of flexibility, but you must be well versed in the set of HTML tags in order to take advantage of this free-format template.

The secret to building an unstructured template is a series of keywords provided by Portal. The Portal run-time system replaces the keywords with generated data when the template is used. Table 18-3 lists the keywords and their usage.

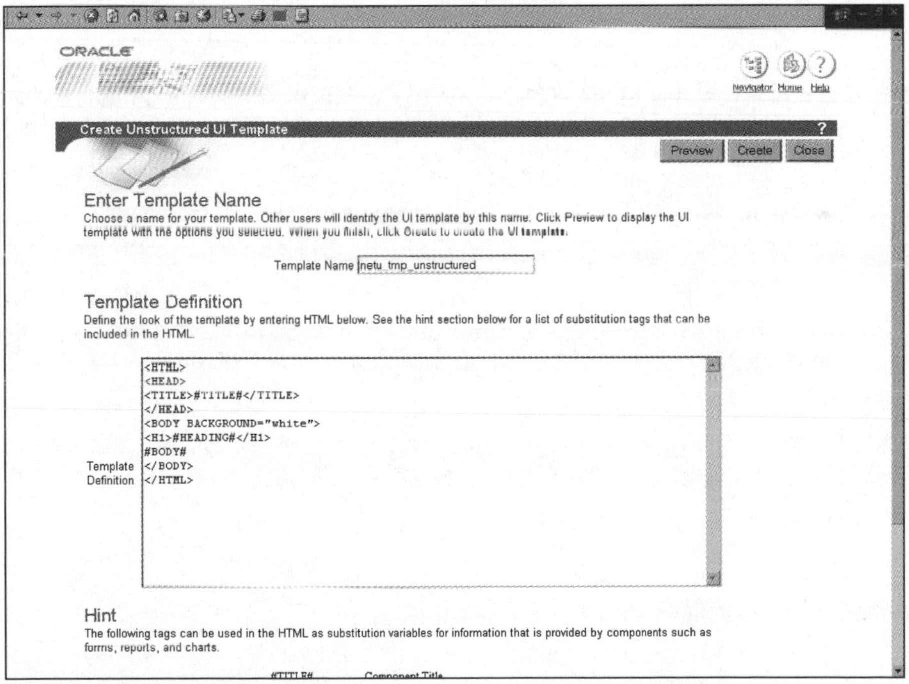

Figure 18-22: Unstructured template

Table 18-3
Sample Template Keywords

Keyword	Use
#TITLE#	The title is the text that appears at the top of the browser and is transmitted by the component object to the template at run time. When you create a Portal report, form, chart, calendar, and so on, you include title text on the Add Text panel. Portal replaces the string #TITLE# with this text.
#HEADING#	The heading text is supplied on the same panel as the title, and it appears just below the title text.
#FRAMELINK#	Frame links are used exclusively by menus and serve as a target for menu navigation.
#BODY#	The body of the template is replaced with the data generated by the Portal component when it is executed.
#IMAGE_PREFIX#	Normally, Portal looks for images in a standard image directory, but you can replace the path by using the image prefix keyword.

You can add any of your own HTML code to the HTML shown by default for the unstructured template by simply choosing to edit the HTML code that is contained within the Template Definition field.

3. Set the name of the new template to **netu_tmp_unstructured**.

4. Copy the netu_heading.swf file to the /images/ virtual directory if you have not already done so.

5. Delete the HTML from the text box and replace it with the code found in the file ch18_unstructured.htm using cut and paste (see Listing 18-1).

New Keywords

Oracle has plans to make templates available for use with pages in release 3.0.8 of Oracle Portal. In order to support this new functionality, they will be adding over 40 new keywords that can be embedded within templates. Be sure to check the on-line documentation for Oracle Portal to view the current list of keywords.

Listing 18-1: **Unstructured HTML Code**

```
<html>
<title>#TITLE#</title>
<body bgcolor=white>
<h1><i>#HEADING#</i></H1>
#BODY#
</body>
<TABLE  width="100%" height="40" cellpadding=0 cellspacing=0
border=0 bgcolor="#FFFFCC" >
<TR>
<TD width="20%" align="LEFT"><A
HREF="/netu/netu_about.htm"><OBJECT classid="clsid:D27CDB6E-
AE6D-11cf-96B8-444553540000"

codebase="http://active.macromedia.com/flash2/cabs/swflash.cab#
version=4,0,0,0"
        ID=netu)logo WIDTH=100 HEIGHT=60>
        <PARAM NAME=movie VALUE="/images/netu_logo.swf">
        <PARAM NAME=quality VALUE=high>
        <PARAM NAME=bgcolor VALUE=#FFFFCC>
        <EMBED src="/netu/netu_logo.swf" quality=high
bgcolor=#FFFFCC
                WIDTH=100 HEIGHT=60 TYPE="application/x-
shockwave flash"

PLUGINSPAGE="http://www.macromedia.com/shockwave/download/index
.cgi?P1_Prod_Version=ShockwaveFlash">
        </EMBED>
</OBJECT></A></TD>
<TD width="80%" align="LEFT"><FONT COLOR="#FFCC99"
FACE="Garamond" SIZE="+2"><B> </B></FONT></TD>
<!----- frame_link =  ----->
<TD ALIGN="right" width="1%"><A HREF="#HOMELINK#"
target-"_top"><IMG SRC="/images/netu_home.gif" valign=top
ALT="Application Home" border=" 0"></A></TD>
<TD ALIGN="right"><A HREF="#HELPLINK#"><IMG
SRC="/images/netu_help.gif" valign=top ALT="Help"
border="0"></A></TD>
</TR>
</TABLE>
</html>
```

Listing 18-1 shows the results of importing the customized HTML code. The main changes to the code are the italics around the page header and the heading line is displayed below the body of the document. The critical keywords to include within the template are the TITLE, HEADING, and BODY. Oracle Portal will replace these macro tags with content when the template is deployed to an object such as a report, form, or calendar.

The other major change that we have made is to reference an external object through the file /netu/netu_heading.swf. This external object is a Macromedia Flash-compatible object from SWiSHzone. This particular object provides an advanced dynamic logo for the template, but you could just as easily make use of other object types such as ActiveX controls.

On the CD-ROM   SWiSHzone's SWiSH product allows you to create Flash-compatible graphics in a fraction of the time that it would take with Macromedia's Flash Product. We have included a trial copy of SWiSH on the CD so that you can make your own animated graphics for use with Oracle Portal.

Unstructured templates offer more advanced capabilities than the simpler, structured templates. If you have existing static HTML code, you can often use it to supplement your Portal applications using unstructured templates. Initially, it is easier to begin working with structured templates. As you become more familiar with the capabilities of templates, you can begin to branch out into using the unstructured variety.

6. Use the Preview button to test your unstructured template as shown in Figure 18-23.

7. Use the Close button to exit the preview window, and then use the Create and Close buttons to exit the template builder interface.

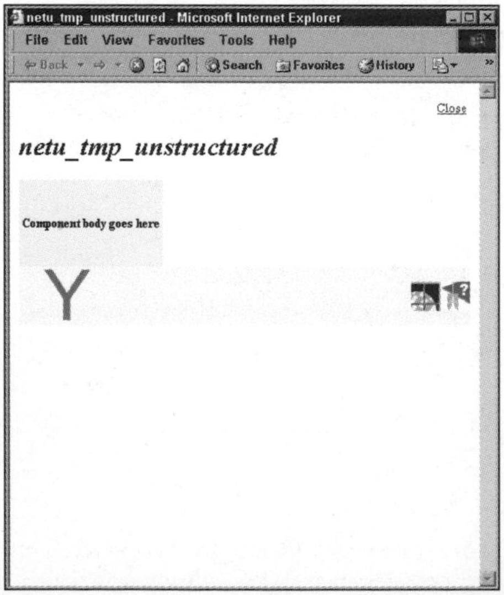

Figure 18-23: Testing the unstructured display template

Deploying Templates into Your Components

The power of templates becomes apparent when you deploy them to your applications. Deploying templates is as simple as making a combo box selection within any one of the builders.

Cross-Reference   Please refer to Appendix A for information on importing components.

1. Choose any report, chart, form, calendar, hierarchy, or menu you have already built, or import the file ch18_rpt_catalog.sql.

2. Edit the report (or any other object you choose) and select the Customization Form Tex tab within the wizard.

3. Select the netu_tmp_standard template from the Template combo box.

4. Save the changes and run the report.

Figure 18-24 shows a simple report for the course catalog table with your structured template applied to the report. You can click the application image, the home image, and the help image, and Portal displays the linked objects automatically.

5. Navigate through the report and test the remaining template features.

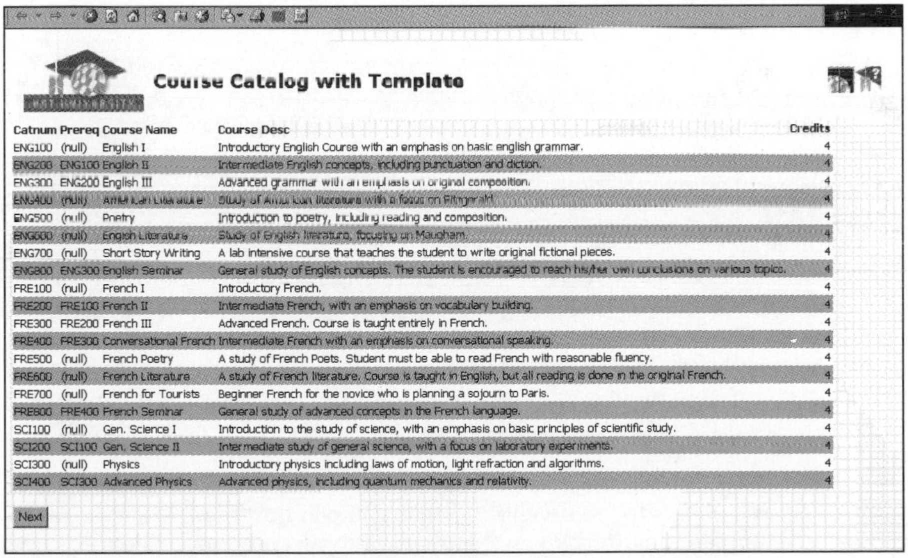

Course Catalog with Template

Catnum	Prereq	Course Name	Course Desc	Credits
ENG100	(null)	English I	Introductory English Course with an emphasis on basic english grammar.	4
ENG200	ENG100	English II	Intermediate English concepts, including punctuation and diction.	4
ENG300	ENG200	English III	Advanced grammar with an emphasis on original composition.	4
ENG400	(null)	American Literature	Study of American literature with a focus on Fitzgerald	4
ENG500	(null)	Poetry	Introduction to poetry, including reading and composition.	4
ENG600	(null)	English Literature	Study of English literature, focusing on Maugham.	4
ENG700	(null)	Short Story Writing	A lab intensive course that teaches the student to write original fictional pieces.	4
ENG800	ENG300	English Seminar	General study of English concepts. The student is encouraged to reach his/her own conclusions on various topics.	4
FRE100	(null)	French I	Introductory French.	4
FRE200	FRE100	French II	Intermediate French, with an emphasis on vocabulary building.	4
FRE300	FRE200	French III	Advanced French. Course is taught entirely in French.	4
FRE400	FRE300	Conversational French	Intermediate French with an emphasis on conversational speaking.	4
FRE500	(null)	French Poetry	A study of French Poets. Student must be able to read French with reasonable fluency.	4
FRE600	(null)	French Literature	A study of French literature. Course is taught in English, but all reading is done in the original French.	4
FRE700	(null)	French for Tourists	Beginner French for the novice who is planning a sojourn to Paris.	4
FRE800	FRE400	French Seminar	General study of advanced concepts in the French language.	4
SCI100	(null)	Gen. Science I	Introduction to the study of science, with an emphasis on basic principles of scientific study.	4
SCI200	SCI100	Gen. Science II	Intermediate study of general science, with a focus on laboratory experiments.	4
SCI300	(null)	Physics	Introductory physics including laws of motion, light refraction and algorithms.	4
SCI400	SCI300	Advanced Physics	Advanced physics, including quantum mechanics and relativity.	4

Next

Figure 18-24: Report deployed with a template

A talented designer can use templates, fonts, colors, and images to create some spectacular formatting for Oracle Portal Pages. Figure 18-25 shows a portal page with custom colors, images, and an imagemap. Portal automatically reformats components using templates each time a component is run, so it is easy to start simple and add custom formatting as you go along.

Note   A local artist named Anna DeAugustine designed all of the graphics for this chapter (along with the customized form shown in Figure 18-25). Anna creates custom graphics for Web sites, paints, designs brochures, letterheads, and business cards — she can create almost anything. She was kind enough to provide some simple pieces for this chapter — which the authors are grateful for. Anna can be reached via her email address at annadea@yahoo.com.

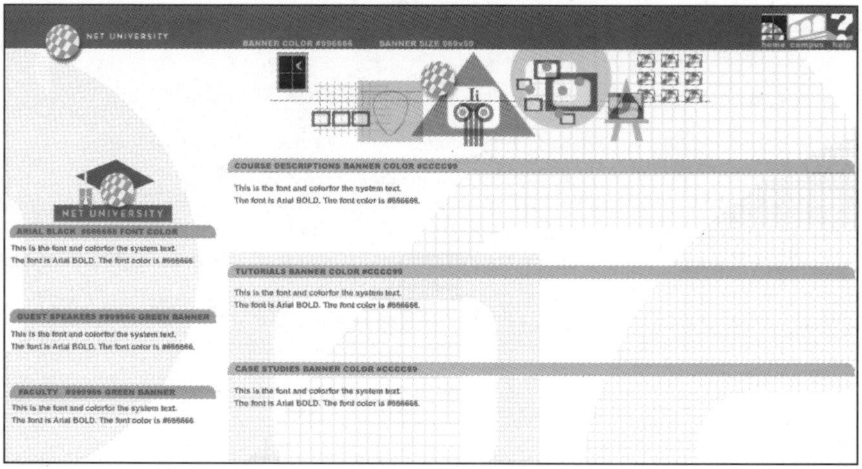

Figure 18-25: Fully-customized form

Summary

Portal's shared objects provide you with a suite of tools for building consistency into your applications. A single application likely has several templates to match the different classes of users and component types. Certain objects may require additional formatting, which templates can provide. Consistent use of colors, fonts, and images can help build commonality into your applications and make them easier to use. Training costs will decrease as users find that individual objects look and behave the same way.

Templates are so easy to create and use that you will find them indispensable when you are creating applications. Even if individual reports, charts, calendars, menus, forms, hierarchies, and pages are built inconsistently, you can use templates to tie them together at run time. In this next chapter we'll be taking a look at adding data validation logic to Oracle Portal forms. You can embed data validation code inside of templates to improve the usability of your forms and reports.

✦   ✦   ✦

Data Validation with Oracle9*i*AS Portal

CHAPTER

19

In This Chapter

Understanding Data Validation Concepts

Creating JavaScript Validations with Portal

Testing the JavaScript

Building More Complicated Scripts

Attaching Validations to Forms

Using Other JavaScript Events

Performing Cross-Field Validations

Performing Server-Side Validations

In the days of mainframe computing, the user was often forced to wait until a screen was filled completely before the system provided any feedback on the data the user entered. One of the keys to the success of client/server applications was the capability to provide the user with rapid feedback on the validity of data that was input to the system. By using the computing power of the desktop, it was possible to validate data entry values directly from the client workstation, giving the user immediate feedback on the data.

As client/server systems spread, developers quickly realized there was a problem with this solution. They found that different developers working on separate projects that accessed the same data were often using different validation rules. On one screen, the user was allowed to enter one value and on another screen, a different value was permitted for the same column. The solution to this problem was to embed rules in the database that would verify the correctness of the data before it was stored in the database. These rules acted as a last line of defense against improper values being written to the database. Application developers made use of both types of rules: client-side validation for making forms easier to use, and server-side rules for ensuring that data entered into the database was valid and logical. Browser-based applications have continued this tradition by using the same two technologies for data validation, albeit with a slightly different implementation. Web browsers use JavaScript to validate data entry on the client side, and they rely on the same database constraints and triggers from the days of client/server computing to validate data on the server side. In this chapter, we'll be talking about using client-side validation with JavaScript.

Data Validation Concepts

Data values must be validated against a set of rules before data is stored within a database in order to ensure the consistency of the resulting information. Some database columns do not require validation, such as comment fields or notes fields. However, the vast majority of database columns require some sort of basic validation in order to be sure they contain values consistent with the needs of the organization. Data validations fall into a set of six basic categories as follows:

✦ NULL/Not NULL

✦ Exact match

✦ Referential integrity

✦ Ranges

✦ Pattern matching

✦ Cross-field validation

The simplest form of validation is the NULL/Not NULL validation. If your applications require that a user enter a value for a given column, the field is considered to have a Not NULL validation. On the other hand, if the user is not required to enter a value for the field, the column is considered nullable, and a column that lacks a value for a record is considered NULL. In the NetU database, the LASTNAME and FIRSTNAME fields in the UGRADS table must be filled in, so they have been given the Not NULL validation. You would not want to create a student record if you did not have a first name and last name for the student. On the other hand, you can leave the gender field blank, or NULL. You would certainly want to know the gender of the student, but it is not a requirement for entering a record into the system. Values that are critical to a given record should be given a Not NULL validation test, and values that are optional can accept NULL values.

Cross-Reference The choice of whether or not to require the user to enter a certain value for a given field within a browser client is a serious design decision. Many portal sites permit users to "enter" records with NULL data values by validating the data at the server level. The server-side code can then make the decision whether to send back a response page that requires the user to enter a value for a field.

In the case of the gender field, it is permissible that the value for this field be left as NULL. However, if the user supplies a value for this field, you will want to be sure the value entered is consistent across records. The gender field is a single-character field and the intent is for the user to enter either an F for female or an M for male into this field. This type of validation is an exact match requirement. Users can leave the gender field blank, but if they enter a value, it can only be the letters F or M. Exact match validations are typically case sensitive because you do not want to permit your users to enter both uppercase and lowercase letters for the same intended value. Doing so makes querying the database much more difficult, because you are forced to check for the presence of both case values (F/f, M/m) every time you execute a query.

If the exact match validation value for a field is stored in a column in another table, the validation is considered to be a foreign key or referential integrity validation. The value in the column matches a primary key value in another table, and, in relational jargon, this is called a foreign key. Within the UGRADS table, the CLASSYR field requires a foreign key validation that matches the CLASSYR field of the CLASSES table. You cannot enter a value for the CLASSYR field in the UGRADS tables that does not already exist in the CLASSES table. After all, you do not want to associate a student with a graduation year that does not exist. Using a foreign key validation ensures that your user only enters student records with valid class years. You may also wish to enforce uniqueness using references to keys across tables, and this type of validation falls under the broad category of referential integrity as well. Typically, you perform these validations at the server level as well as the client level to ensure that bad data does not find its way into the database. Although this may seem like a duplication of work, the two sets of validations serve different purposes. Server-side validations, which are typically written in PL/SQL, protect the data across applications. Client-side referential integrity constraints make it easier for the user to work with the data on the form — within a single application. So, if you have several different applications accessing your data, it makes sense to protect the integrity of the data using server-side integrities such as database triggers.

Some fields within your database allow for a large number of values that do not match fields within a parent in a table. Nevertheless, these same fields may only permit a limited number of values. The most common column format for this type of validation is dates. While you will often allow your users free rein to add a date value, you should still validate the value entered in some way. For example, within the UGRADS table, the user is allowed to enter a date of birth for each student in the DOB field. NetU does not discriminate on the basis of age, and you are free to add students of any age, within reason, to the system. Range validations determine what "within reason" means for a given column. For example, you would not want to enter a student into the system who was less than 17 years old. Furthermore, the birth date you enter should be a valid birth date — you cannot be born on September 41, for example. These are both examples of range validations; the value for the day of the month ranges from 1 to 31 and the value for the range of years should correspond with students being at least 17 years old. The width of the range is based upon the type of data that you are capturing.

If you were storing the daily temperature in Fahrenheit into a column in a table, then the logical range of values might be from −100 to +200. On the other hand, if you were storing the date of a gift record in the DONATIONS table, then the AMOUNT field would range from one dollar to one million dollars. One of the most common forms of range validations is the datatype validation. Datatype validations ensure that character data is not entered into numeric fields and vice versa.

Sometimes the validation you need to enforce upon a field does not follow a set of values, but rather it follows a set of rules. Postal codes in most foreign countries are a mix of a certain number of letters and numbers, and the particular mix is usually a pattern. In this case, the data validation for the column is a pattern matching validation. The data for the field contains a fixed combination of numbers and characters. Pattern matches are common for fields in which the individual characters within a field have their own particular meaning. The CATNUM field in the COURSE_CATALOG table is an example of one such field in the NetU database. The catalog number is composed of three letters indicating the department followed by three numbers indicating the course number for the department. The pattern is three uppercase characters followed by three numbers.

The last category of data validation is the most complicated. Cross-field validations check the value of one column against a value in a subsequent column. For example, in an order entry system, the value you enter for the tax rate may be based upon the state from which the customer is ordering. In this case, the valid value for the tax field cannot be determined without checking the ship-to-state field. Sometimes you enforce a cross-field validation by looking at a range of records. For example, the valid discount percentage may require that you add up the amount the customer has spent.

Each validation type can be performed at either the client side or the server side, and in most cases, it is performed at both levels. Portal enables you to easily handle all of the preceding types of validations at both the client side and the server side. Only cross-field validations prove more difficult to enforce at the client side. If the cross-field validation requires you to access database values that are not part of the current page, you are not able to enforce the validation at the client side. However, you are still able to enforce the restriction at the database server level. Client-side validations are made with JavaScript; and server-side validations are enforced with Oracle constraints and triggers written in either PL/SQL or Java.

Normally you build database validations from the server out to the client. This means that you create your database constraints and triggers first, and then you create the client-side validations to match these constraints later. With Portal, you may find that you can skip over the server-level validations if you have a preexisting database, because the database is likely to already have these validations in place.

Using JavaScript

JavaScript is a client-side scripting language for your browser created by Netscape Communications Corporation. JavaScript was originally named LiveScript. The language's name was changed to JavaScript in 1995 after Netscape entered into a marketing agreement with Sun Microsystems to sublicense the Java prefix. JavaScript is often erroneously thought to be a version of the Java language for your browser. While it is true that both JavaScript and the Java programming language share some common syntax and style, they are not equivalent. JavaScript was intended to be a programming language for working with HTML documents, while Java is a full-fledged object-oriented programming language.

The two languages require a completely separate processing engine within the browser, and they are more different than they are the same. Programmers have attempted to draw the distinction that Java is primarily for the server and JavaScript is primarily for the client. As it turns out, both assertions are false. The Java programming language is equally good at building client-side applications and server applications, but it is not integrated into the user interface of Oracle Portal. From the Portal perspective, JavaScript is a scripting language for working with HTML on the client side. Portal uses JavaScript scripts to enforce data validation logic at the browser level.

JavaScript compatibility

Netscape Navigator and Microsoft Internet Explorer both support a version of JavaScript, although Microsoft has historically lagged behind in its support for JavaScript. Technically speaking, the correct name for JavaScript is ECMAScript, but the common convention is to refer to the language as JavaScript. As of this writing, the current production release of the JavaScript language is version 1.5 (ECMA-262 Revision 3) and both Netscape Navigator 3 and higher and Microsoft Internet Explorer 4.01 and higher support the 1.2 version. Microsoft has run into licensing issues with Sun Microsystems over the Java language and with Netscape over the name JavaScript. The result is that Microsoft calls their version of JavaScript, JScript, but it is basically compatible with JavaScript 1.2. Microsoft offers a client-side scripting language called VBScript, which is based upon Microsoft's Visual Basic Language. Although JavaScript is not derived from Java, VBScript is derived directly from Visual Basic. The designers of Portal specifically chose to use JavaScript as the client-side data validation tool for Portal because JavaScript is supported by a wider variety of browsers (and platforms) than VBScript. While it may be *possible* to use VBScript with Portal, we discourage you from doing so because it limits your users to running Internet Explorer as their browser.

JavaScript is a much simpler language to learn than Java, but that does not mean that JavaScript is limited in functionality. In fact, you can build some very complex and sophisticated user interfaces if you make use of all of JavaScript's capabilities.

In order to make applications easier to develop, both Netscape and Microsoft have created a hierarchy of objects within their browsers. This hierarchy determines the names, addresses, and attributes of the objects within an HTML page. This hierarchy is commonly known as the *document object model* for the browser. If you were developing HTML applications from scratch with raw HTML text, you would find that a complete understanding of the document object model might be necessary. However, because Portal is managing and creating most of the HTML that you generate, it is not necessary for you to understand all the ins and outs of the document object model in order to use JavaScript within Portal applications. Table 19-1 shows you the four key elements of the document object model you may use within Portal.

JavaScript Notes

JavaScript has become an international standard, ECMA-262, but it still suffers from some immaturity as a true language. ECMA is an international industry association, founded in 1961, that is dedicated to the standardization of information and communication systems. ECMAScript is the name used for JavaScript as standardized by the TC39 committee of the ECMA standards organization. It is suitable for use as a client-side language within a browser, but you would need Java itself to build truly robust client applications that are independent of a browser. Version 2.0 of JavaScript is currently under discussion and updated information on the status of the JavaScript standard can be found at `http://www.mozilla.org/js/language/`.

Table 19-1
Document Object Model Elements

Element	Description
Window	The top of the document object model hierarchy is the Window object, and it represents the browser in which the application is running. Generally, you will work with a single window unless you make extensive use of frames, in which case you need to work with multiple windows because each frame is displayed within its own window.
Document	Each HTML page created and loaded into your browser by Portal is a document. It is very rare to work with multiple windows, but it is possible that you will work with multiple documents. Documents are also the container object for any of the form elements you create.
Form Object	HTML forms are created by using the <FORM> and </FORM> tags within an HTML page. It is possible to create more than one form within a document, and thus forms are one level below documents in the hierarchy. The Form Object is a container for all the display fields that are shown on a data entry page.
Form Elements	Form Elements are the individual form fields that appear on an HTML page (for example, text boxes, check boxes, and radio groups). By and large, you will find the JavaScript validations you build for Portal concern themselves with Form Elements, which are described in more detail in the next section.

JavaScript form elements

Form elements have a number of associated events you are probably familiar with if you have programmed in JavaScript before. JavaScript *scripts* define what to do and *events* define when to do it. For example, you want to make sure the date of birth for a student is at least 17 years ago. The event determines when you enforce this validation. Do you want to enforce this when the user tabs out of the field? How about when the mouse passes over the date of birth field? The document object model provides many opportunities for firing off this validation.

Portal uses the List-of-Values Wizard to create validations based upon data values in the database, as you learned in Chapter 16. Lists-of-values can take many different display formats. Oracle Portal supports a number of JavaScript events for fields, including specialized events for LOV objects. Oracle Portal supports a variety of field display types:

 ✦ Blank

 ✦ Button

 ✦ Check box

 ✦ ComboBox

 ✦ File UpLoad (Binary)

 ✦ File UpLoad (*inter*Media)

 ✦ Hidden

 ✦ Horizontal Rule

 ✦ Image

 ✦ Label

 ✦ Password

 ✦ Popup

 ✦ Radio Group

 ✦ Text Area

 ✦ Text Box

The document object model allows for the following field-level events as listed in Table 19-2.

Table 19-2 **JavaScript Field Events Supported by Oracle Portal**	
Event Name	*Description*
onBlur	Signaled when the user leaves the field either using the keyboard or the mouse.
onChange	Fired when the user begins to change a value within a form field.
onFocus	Called when the user enters the field either using the keyboard or the mouse.
onSelect	Fired when the user uses the mouse to select a block of text within the field as in a copy operation.
onKeyDown	Signaled when the user presses a key on the keyboard within the field. This event fires for each keystroke within a given field.
onKeyUp	Signaled when the user releases a key that was previously pressed on the keyboard. This event fires for each keystroke within a given field.
onKeyPress	Signaled when the user presses a function key on the keyboard.
onClick	Signaled when the user clicks on a button with a mouse.
onMouseDown	Signaled when the user presses down with either mouse button.
onMouseUp	Signaled when the user releases a previously pushed mouse button.

The browser permits you to attach a block of JavaScript code to each of the events listed in Table 19-2. This enables you to have an incredible amount of control over the data validation within form elements, because you can add code for *each* event. However, as far as Oracle Portal is concerned each event applies only to certain fields, as listed in Table 19-3.

Table 19-3 **Portal Field Types and Events**	
Field Type	*Supported Events*
Blank	N/A
Button	onClick, onMouseDown, onMouseUp
CheckBox	onClick, onMouseDown, onMouseUp
ComboBox	onBlur, onFocus, onChange

Field Type	Supported Events
File UpLoad (Binary and *inter*Media)	onClick, onMouseDown, onMouseUp
Hidden	N/A
Horizontal Rule	N/A
Image	N/A
Label Only	N/A
Password	onBlur, onFocus, onChange, onSelect, onKeyDown, onKeyPress, onKeyUp
Popup	onBlur, onFocus, onChange
Radio Group	onClick, onMouseDown, onMouseUp
TextArea	onBlur, onFocus, onChange, onSelect, onKeyDown, onKeyPress, onKeyUp
TextBox	onBlur, onFocus, onChange, onSelect, onKeyDown, onKeyPress, onKeyUp

The document object model and the event model for JavaScript are much more complicated than portrayed in this chapter. However, because Portal hides most of this complexity from you, it is unnecessary for you to dive into the details of the event model in order to use JavaScript with Portal for data validation purposes.

Cross-Reference   Initially, almost all of the data validations that you will build with JavaScript will be based on the onBlur event. A more detailed discussion of the other events is included at the end of this chapter.

If you are not familiar with building JavaScript validations, you are probably slightly confused, because you are not even sure what a JavaScript script looks like, never mind how to attach one to a form. Never fear, you will be introduced the basic elements of JavaScript later in this chapter.

JavaScript elements

While you can build sophisticated programs in JavaScript, the basic script type for performing data validation is a function. Functions are composed of a series of JavaScript syntax statements, as shown in Listing 19-1.

Listing 19-1: **Simple JavaScript function**

```
//
// Comment Text
//
function netu_showvalue (theElement)
{
var my_variable = 5
if (theElement.value > 10) {
    alert("The value is greater than 10")
} else {
    alert("The value is less than 10")
}
return true
}
```

The preceding block of code is fairly simple, but it shows off the basic components of a JavaScript function. JavaScript scripts are much like any other program and they have a number of parts, as follows:

✦ Comment text

✦ Function declarations

✦ Names

✦ Parameter lists

✦ Variable declarations

✦ Control structures

✦ Methods

✦ Return values

The key to any complex system is proper documentation. JavaScript supports a comment indicator using the double slash character (//). Although it is not a requirement of JavaScript itself, it is a good idea for you to start all of your scripts with some comment information. Doing so makes the task of maintaining these scripts much easier for the programmer who has to support your code later. The function shown in Listing 19-1 includes three lines of comment text to identify the function.

The first requirement for a JavaScript program unit is the function statement. The job of the `function` keyword is to name the following block of code as a JavaScript program unit. The function statement starts with the keyword `function` and includes the name and the parameter list for the function.

Note

JavaScript blocks that are defined without a function statement are used to declare global variables and code blocks, and we'll talk about this type of JavaScript later in this chapter.

The name of the JavaScript function follows the `function` keyword. The name is a string of up to 32 characters that must start with a letter and may not contain any punctuation characters other than the underscore character (_). Portal adds a further restriction (for data validation purposes) that the function name must match the name that you use to identify the script to Portal, as you will see later on in this chapter.

Note

JavaScript passes the element handle by default and you must use method calls within the function to extract the information you need from the element. JavaScript offers a great deal of flexibility in this area, but you do not need to concern yourself with most of the details in order to build data validation routines into Portal.

The next item is the parameter list, which is a list of elements passed to the function when it is called. The parameter you pass from your page to the JavaScript is a type of pointer to the field on the page. Portal handles the transformation of the parameter for you and gives you access to the various parts of the parameter through a series of standard method calls. These method calls are a series of keywords appended to the name of the parameter.

For the most part, you will use a single method in your Portal JavaScript functions — the VALUE method, which refers to the value of the parameter. You could also get access to the number of characters stored in the parameter by using the LENGTH method.

JavaScript uses dot-based notation to separate object names and methods. For instance, if you pass an element called MY_PARM to a function, you can derive the value of MY_PARM by making a method call within the function as follows:

```
var my_variable
my_variable = MY_PARM.value
```

Parameters can be a very complex topic, but Portal simplifies the process by controlling the manner in which the function is called at run time. Portal only allows you to pass a single parameter to the function, and Portal always translates the field name that calls the script into the element name that you use. In other words, the only parameter you can pass into a JavaScript is a pointer to the calling field. For the moment, you do not need to worry about the specifics of the parameter name, only that you can pass a parameter to the script.

The next item in the function is the declaration of variables. Just like any other programming language, JavaScript supports the declaration of variables. Unlike most other languages, it automatically converts data between one datatype and another. Variables can be declared anywhere within the body of a JavaScript function. Table 19-4 lists the base datatypes that JavaScript supports.

Table 19-4
JavaScript Datatypes

Datatype	Description	Sample
String	Any series of characters surrounded by double quotes	"Joe", "Joe Smith"
Number	Any set of numbers and punctuation separators not surrounded by quotes	10, 4.5
Boolean	A logical true or false	true, false

You must declare variables by using the `var` keyword, and the names of your variables must follow the same restrictions as the name of functions. In addition, you must be careful to avoid using JavaScript keywords in the names of variables. It is often a good idea to use mixed case variable names and underscore characters in order to avoid the likelihood of running into keywords inadvertently. Notice that there is no declaration of the datatype for a variable, because the variable type is set whenever you use the variable in an expression. Expressions are composed of variables and operators, and JavaScript supports a standard set of operators, as shown in Table 19-5.

Table 19-5
JavaScript Operators

Operator	Name	Type	Works On
=	Set Equal to	Value	Numbers, Strings
+	Plus	Value	Numbers, Strings
-	Minus	Value	Numbers
*	Multiply	Value	Numbers
/	Divide	Value	Numbers
%	Modulo	Value	Numbers
++	Increment	Value	Numbers
—	Decrement	Value	Numbers
= =	Equality	Comparison	Numbers, Strings
!=	Not Equal	Comparison	Numbers, Strings
>	Greater Than	Comparison	Numbers, Strings
>=	Greater Than or Equal to	Comparison	Numbers, Strings

Operator	Name	Type	Works On
<	Less Than	Comparison	Numbers, Strings
<=	Less Than or Equal to	Comparison	Numbers, Strings
&&	And	Boolean	Numbers, Strings
||	Or	Boolean	Numbers, Strings

The top portion of Table 19-5 holds the value operators that are used to set the value for a variable or expression. The bottom half of the table contains the comparison operators and Boolean operators, which are used for the purpose of decision making. In addition to the standard operators, JavaScript provides the additional NULL keyword used to set the value of a variable to an empty state, much like a database NULL value. JavaScript automatically converts variables between types, as the following lines of code demonstrate:

```
"Joe " + "Smith" // result  = "Joe Smith"
9 + 9            // result  = 18
"9" + 9          // result  = "99"
"9" - 1          // result  = invalid, "9" is not a number
```

The comparison operators are primarily used in control structures, which are the sixth element of a JavaScript function. Control structures provide you with decision-making processes for your JavaScript functions. JavaScript offers a very powerful set of control structures, including commands to step through the properties of an object at run time. JavaScript provides five types of control structures that you will find useful in working with Portal:

✦ `if-else`

✦ `switch`

✦ `for` loop

✦ `while` loop

✦ `do...while` loop

The `if-else` control structure is a standard set of syntax for basic decision making and it is structured as follows:

```
if (condition) {
    code if true
} else {
    code if false
}
```

The condition is an operator-based expression that evaluates to a true/false condition and it can contain any number of variables, value operators, and comparison operators. You are free to nest `if-else` statements and you can have any number of lines of code within the curly braces as shown in the following code sample:

```
var var_a = 10
var var_b = 20
if (a > b) {
    alert("a is larger than b")
} else {
    alert("b is larger than a")
    a = a + b
}
```

Caution   You must use the *equality comparison* operator (= =) for comparisons in expressions; the *set equals* operator (=) causes the comparison value to be set to the comparison value.

JavaScript enables you to nest multiple levels of if-else statements, but you will want to avoid excessively deep hierarchies of if-else loops because they are harder to read and maintain. JavaScript provides the switch statement as an alternative for lengthy if-else statements. The switch statement uses the following syntax structure:

```
switch (expression) {
    case label1:
            code
            [break]
    case label2:
            code
            [break]
      ...
    default:
            code
}
```

The expression can be any valid variable or combination of operators that evaluates to a value. The case/label: structure gives you a place to list a value for comparison, and the code below the value gets executed only if the expression evaluates to a value that matches the label. In the following example code fragment, the switch statement is used to test for a specific value of class year:

```
var some_year = "2002"
var my_class = null
switch (some_year) {
    case "2001":
            my_class = "Senior"
            break
    case "2002":
            my_class = "Junior"
    case "2003":
            my_class = "Sophomore"
    default:
            my_class = "Freshman"
}
```

In the preceding example, the switch statement falls through to the default value because it does not match any of the strings beside the other case statements. JavaScript provides a break command to enable you to break out of a switch statement once a match has been found. By default, switch statements continue to process even after a match has been found, enabling you to modify the value of the expression in the body of the switch statement. Adding a break statement after a command statement, as shown previously for the "2002" example, causes the switch statement to end once a match has been found. You must add the break statement to each case substatement you wish to break out of.

If you need to cycle through a fixed number of expressions several times, the for loop is probably a better choice. For loops follow a fixed number of cycles through a set of code and they work much like for loops in C, Java, and PL/SQL.

```
for (initial expression; condition; update expression) {
    code
}
```

The loop proceeds until the conditional expression becomes false, and the loop starts with a value for the initial expression as set by you in the for statement. Each complete cycle results in the update expression being executed, and the value for the expression can be used in the body of the loop as follows:

```
for (var i= 1; i< 10; i++) {
    alert ("The Value of i is :" +String(i))
}
```

The for loop is ideal for parsing through a string searching for a set of characters or for enforcing a pattern.

Tip   String indexes start with the zero (0) position in JavaScript, and you need to keep this in mind if you use for loops to parse strings of values. The first character position of a string is always zero.

JavaScript permits you to embed functions within for loops, and you can combine conditions with the Boolean and/or operators (&& and ||) to produce compound expressions with for loops. For example, the comparison operation can itself be a function call to another procedure or built-in method, which itself may return a Boolean result. You can use this feature to build a loop that is equal to the length of a string field as follows:

```
string my_var = "abcdefgh"
for (var i= 1; i< my_var.length; i++) {
    alert ("The Value of i is :" +String(i))
}
```

If you need to build a more general-purpose looping routine, JavaScript offers the `while` loop and the `do...while` loop. Both of these control structures loop indefinitely until a given condition becomes false. `While` loops check the condition at the beginning of the loop, and `do...while` loops check the condition at the end of the loop. `Do...while` loops always execute at least once, and `while` loops may or may not execute at least once depending upon the condition. The format for the two structures is as follows:

```
// While Loop
while(condition){
    code
}

// Do Loop
do {
     code
} while (condition)
```

The `while` loop evaluates the condition before cycling through its code. In the following example, the body of the loop never gets executed because the expression is false to begin with:

```
while (1<0) {
    alert("Did you know one is less than zero?")
}
```

If you changed the `while` loop to a `do...while` loop, the code within the loop executes at least once:

```
do {
    alert("One is less than zero for one time only!")
} while (1<0)
```

Because of this, you use a `do...while` loop when you want to guarantee that a given block of code is executed at least once, and a `while` loop when you only want to execute a block of code when a condition is true.

> **Tip** There are many subtleties to JavaScript's control structures and you will want to have a copy of a more detailed text on JavaScript if you plan on building very complex JavaScript procedures. Hungry Minds offers Danny Goodman's *JavaScript Bible* (0-7645-3342-8) for those of you who want to learn more about JavaScript in detail.

The Sun/AOL/Netscape Alliance has added a great deal of built-in functionality to JavaScript in the form of methods and functions that are included directly within the language. These methods can be invaluable in helping you build more complex functions and programs. You have seen fragments of some of these methods in the previous sample code blocks and Table 19-6 shows a partial table of these functions.

Table 19-6
JavaScript Methods and Functions

Method	Description	Example
`alert(string)`	Alert displays a message to the user. The `alert` method is part of theWindow object, but you can use the method all by itself without prepending the window keyword,because the window is the highestpart of the document hierarchy.	`alert("Hello World!")_`

`confirm(string)`	`Confirm` is an advanced form of the `alert` method. The syntax is almost identical, but the confirm method gives the user two response choices: ok and cancel. The confirm statement evaluates to true or false depending on the user's interaction with the confirm box. You typically wrap a confirm method call in an `if-else` statement to test for a response.	```if (confirm("Are you ok?"))
		  {
		          // Yes_
		  }
		    else_
		          // No
		  }```

`prompt` `(string,default)`	The `prompt` method is related to alert and confirm and is the most powerful of the three message structures. `Prompt` opens a text box and enables you to insert a manual value. You can also pass a default value for the text prompt, and prompt also offers the user the same pair of ok and cancel options as the confirm method. If the user chooses the ok button, then the variable contains the value in the text box. If the user clicks the cancel button, the reply variable is NULL.	`var my_reply - prompt` `("Are you ok?","Yes")`
`focus( )`	Sets the focus on the HTML page to the specified FORM object.	`my_textfield.focus()`

Continued

	Table 19-6 *(continued)*	
Method	**Description**	**Example**
select( )	Selects the text entered into the field on the form.	`my_textfield.select()`

indexOf(string)	Finds the starting position of a substring within a string.	`var string_x = "ABCDEF"`
		`var num_y =`
		`string_x.indexOf("B")`
		`// result = 1`

charAt(position)	The charAt method returns the single character at the specified numeric position within a string. JavaScript strings all start at position zero (0). The charAt function is part of the string object and it is called by appending it to the string name.	`var my_string = "ABCDEF"`
		`my_string.CharAt(1)`
		`// result = "B"`

Number	Number converts a string of numeric characters to a number. The Number method is part of the window structure and it can be called directly.	`var my_value = "123"`
		`Number(my_value)* 10`
		`// result = 1230`

String	String converts a number to a string value. The String method is part of the window hierarchy and it can be called directly.	`var my_value = 123`
		`String(my_value) +`
		`"Oak St."`
		`// result = "123 Oak St."`

Caution   JavaScript functions and methods are case sensitive. Take note of the mixed case characters when you attempt to use any of the preceding methods in your own code.

JavaScript has literally hundreds of prebuilt methods for browser windows and HTML pages you can use to accomplish a variety of tasks. You only need to know the basics in order to perform validations with Portal, but we recommend that you get a copy of *JavaScript Bible* if you plan on doing any complex JavaScript coding. In many cases, JavaScript already has a method or function that handles the complex problem you are trying to solve by writing your own routine. One such example is the Date object, which offers well over a dozen functions, as you will see in the next section.

JavaScript dates

You are likely to want to manipulate dates on the client side frequently. After all, you can perform simple checks such as making sure the product shipment date is later than the order date on the client side. This type of validation makes your applications easier to use and it saves your browser from having to make unnecessary trips back to the database server to validate "bad" data. JavaScript implements dates as objects within the page, and you need to reserve a variable and create a date using the new keyword in order to work with dates.

```
var my_date - new Date( )
```

If you create a date without passing it any parameters, JavaScript uses the current date and time from the browser as the value for your date. Most of the methods associated with dates are used to either extract values or to set values as shown in Table 19-7.

Table 19-7
JavaScript Date Methods

Method	Description
GetTime( )	Milliseconds since 1/1/70 00:00:00 in GMT.
GetYear( )	Year minus 1900.
GetMonth( )	Month within the year as a number starting with month number zero (0).
getDate( )	Day number within the month, starting with 1.
getDay( )	Day of the week starting with Sunday as the first day. As with months, days of the week start numbering at zero (0).
GetHours( )	The hour of the day in 24-hour time starting at hour zero (0).
GetMinutes( )	The minute of the hour starting with minute zero (0).
GetSeconds( )	The seconds within the minute starting with second zero (0).

Each of the get methods has an associated set method that enables you to change the value of the specified unit of the date and time. JavaScript provides a shorthand method for setting the date and time, so you only need to use the set methods if you want to change a value that you have already set.

```
var my_date = new Date("September 25, 2000")
my_date.setYear(2001)
```

The preceding block of code sets the initial value of date to September 25, 2000 and then changes the value of the year to 2001. Dates can be one of the more complicated types of validation you need to perform, and JavaScript's date functions come in handy for performing date validations with Portal.

Creating JavaScript Validations with Portal

Portal uses JavaScript functions to validate data on the client side of the application. JavaScript scripts are part of the Shared Components Application shown in Figure 19-1.

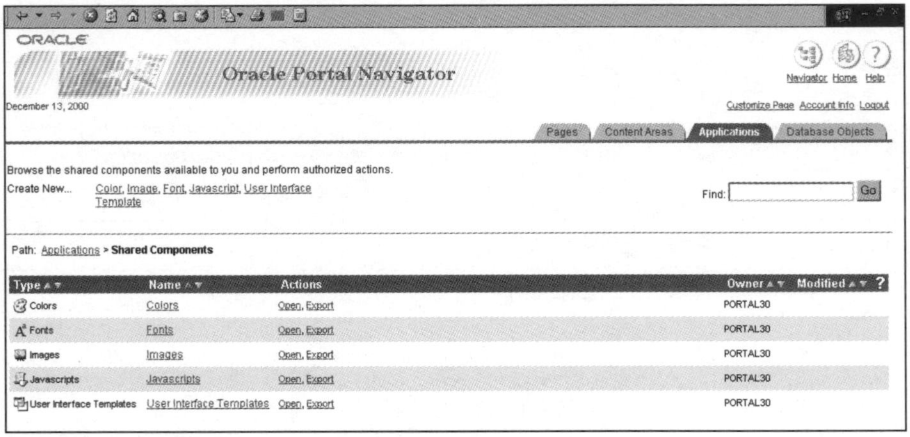

Figure 19-1: Shared Components Application

Both JavaScript scripts and lists-of-values can be used for validating data at the browser level. JavaScript scripts are used to validate the data that users have entered into fields, while Lists-of-values limit the choices a user has when they enter data into a field — and they can be combined with JavaScript scripts as well. List-of-values objects are covered in detail in Chapter 16 of this book, but it is important to understand a little about them when you are deciding which technique to use when validating data at the browser level. LOVs build lists of acceptable data values based upon records in your database and they require some communication with the database. JavaScript scripts, on the other hand, do not require any communication with the user but they do not provide the user with any visible clue as to the valid values for a given field.

1. Select the JavaScripts link from the Shared Components Application page to begin creating a JavaScript validation. Use the Create New ... JavaScripts link to create a new JavaScript.

The Portal wizard for creating JavaScript validations is one of the simplest interfaces that Portal provides. The developers of Portal have not attempted to guide you through the process of writing JavaScript code with the JavaScript Wizard. If you are building JavaScript validations, Portal assumes that you have a working knowledge of JavaScript. The initial panel for constructing JavaScript validations appears in Figure 19-2.

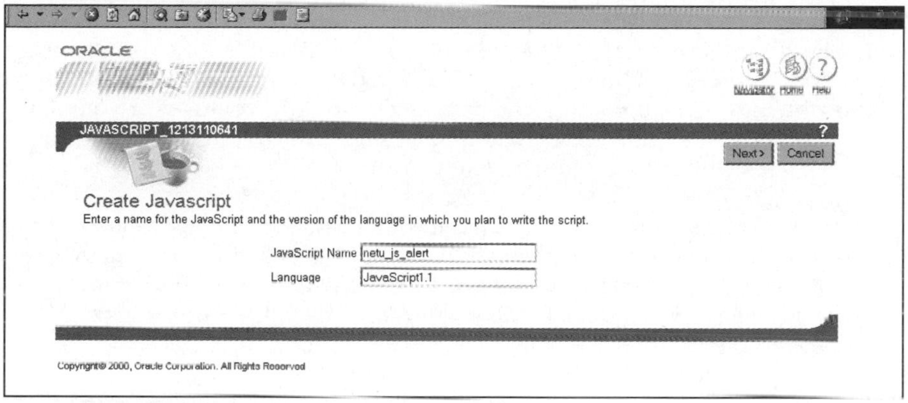

Figure 19-2: Create JavaScript panel

The Create JavaScript panel is very similar to that of the other Shared Components Application objects. You can create a new JavaScript by entering a name in the top field as shown in Figure 19-2.

> **Note**
>
> Client browsers make use of scripting by embedding the script code within HTML, and there are two popular scripting languages that are used to provide scripting for Web pages — JavaScript and VBScript. Oracle Portal only supports JavaScript1.1, but there is the potential to support other scripting languages and versions in future releases. Thus, Portal provides a language textbox that can be used to enter a different script language tag. Portal does not validate the data that you enter into the Language field, and it is possible to change the language setting to VBScript. Although this *may* work, Portal does not support changing the language setting, and VBScript will only work with Microsoft Internet Explorer. Technically, it is possible to change the language setting to VBScript and then code your script using VBScript code instead of JavaScript. This is not supported, however, and we do not advise you to change the language setting for this release of Portal.

The JavaScript Name is the name you use to refer to the component, and it follows the same naming convention and requirements as any other Portal component. However, the JavaScript Name serves one additional function in that it is also used as the name for the function within the code itself. Portal will automatically embed the name of the JavaScript on this panel into the body of the code itself — as shown on the next panel in Figure 19-3.

A single JavaScript validation may be used throughout many applications, or it may apply to a single field in a single table. The name you give to your JavaScript should reflect your planned usage of the validation. You may want to consider creating a common set of routines for general validation, which you can then augment with some additional application-specific validations. JavaScript enables you to call functions from functions, so it is theoretically possible to build general-purpose routines that you can refer to from field-specific validations. Portal, however, only transfers the code for individual validations within a Web page. This prevents you from calling out of one function into another. Furthermore, it is not possible to attach multiple *validations* to a single field. The net result is that you are likely to create specific-field validations just like you would create specific database constraints: on individual columns. The naming convention you use for your JavaScript scripts should reflect this policy, and it makes it easier to find the validation you are looking for when you build data entry forms.

> **Note**   You can attach multiple JavaScript scripts to a field for different form events — but only a single JavaScript script is considered the "validation" script. You can also call out to other JavaScript scripts from validations and events by embedding the called functions into your HTML page using templates. We will look at both of these techniques in more detail later in this chapter.

JavaScript itself has gone through several iterations of development, and this is reflected in the Language field. The current revision of JavaScript is JavaScript 1.3, but many older browsers do not support this version of the code. Portal defaults to using JavaScript 1.1, and that is the value that you see loaded into the Language field by default. When Portal renders your HTML pages, it loads your JavaScript validations into the page using the <SCRIPT> and </SCRIPT> tags. One of the parameters of the <SCRIPT> tag enables you to set the client-side language, and Portal uses the Language value on this page to set this parameter at run time. The browser reads the language tag before it executes the script, making it possible to use different scripting languages for validation routines. At the current time, Portal only supports JavaScript 1.1 as its validation language for the browser, but the presence of the Language identifier allows Portal to support other languages and versions in the future. For this release of Portal, you should leave the Language setting to the default value as provided by Portal.

    2. Enter the name **netu_js_alert** as the JavaScript Name for your new script and press the Next button to display the panel as shown in Figure 19-3.

The only item on this page is the script code field, which is a large text area used for entering the actual JavaScript validation code. The script code field is not a full-functioned editor, and you may find that as you use JavaScript more often, you will want to create your code in a more powerful desktop editor and paste it into this window. You are certainly free to do so, as Portal does not provide any help in building the JavaScript procedure itself. You must enter your JavaScript code into the script code text area as a complete JavaScript function, including the function declaration, function name, and body as shown in Listing 19-2.

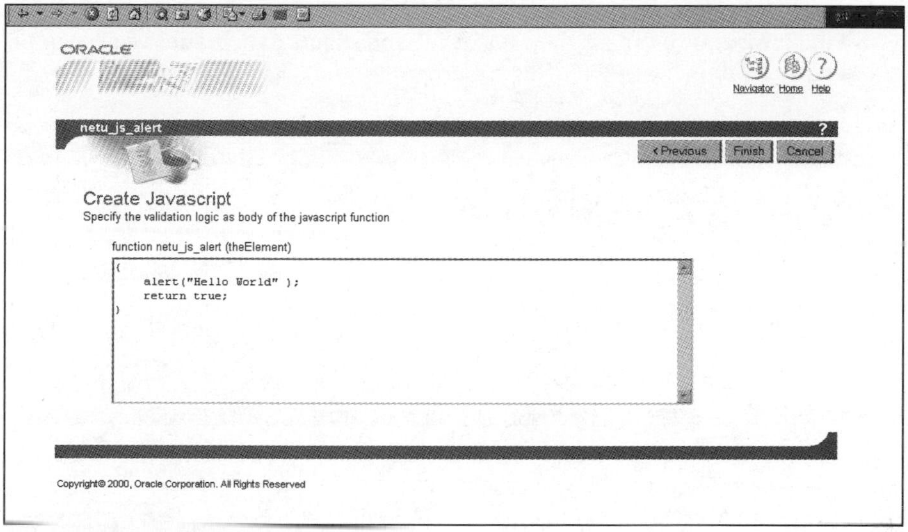

Figure 19-3: Entering JavaScript code

Listing 19-2: **Sample JavaScript function**

```
function netu_js_alert(theElement){
    alert( "Hello World" );
    return true;
}
```

Oracle Portal uses the name that you entered as the definition for the JavaScript function and It automatically creates a single parameter value for the function. As a developer, you are only responsible for providing the code elements within the function. Although this particular sample block of code is artificially simple, it includes all the basic components you must include in the JavaScript code that you enter in the script code text field.

The parameters for the function you create are shown between the two parentheses. If you are familiar with JavaScript from building previous applications, you know that the name you use for the parameter is typically specific to the script. In this case, Portal automatically creates the parameter value—which will contain the value of the field that calls the JavaScript at program execution time. Portal's scripts use the mixed case name theElement as the parameter value name.

3. Accept the default code for the JavaScript as shown in Figure 19-3 and use the Finish button to create the JavaScript and display the panel as shown in Figure 19-4.

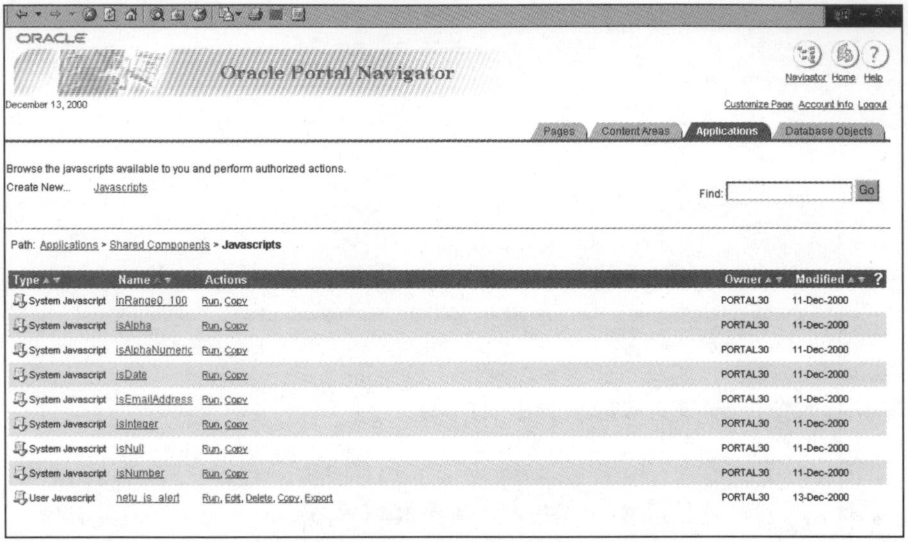

Figure 19-4: Navigator display panel for JavaScript scripts

The JavaScripts management panel provides a test link so that you can see your JavaScript scripts in action before you deploy them into applications. However, Portal does not provide you with any tools for verifying that an *individual* line of JavaScript is working properly. Both Internet Explorer and Netscape Navigator provide workarounds for this problem.

4. Use the File/Open Page menu choice on the pull-down menu bar for Navigator and enter the string **javascript:** as the URL and press the Open button.

Navigator opens up a two-pane window that enables you to enter single lines of JavaScript and test them immediately within the browser as shown in Figure 19-5. Although this is a far cry from the interactive debug windows provided with other integrated development environments, it does provide a basic test capability for your JavaScript functions.

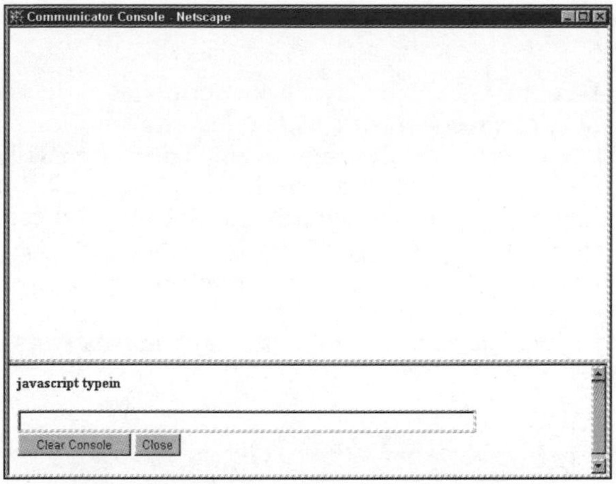

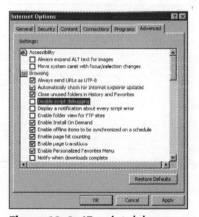

Figure 19-5: Navigator JavaScript test window

5. Internet Explorer provides a built-in script debugger, which can be enabled by using the Tools->Internet Options menu choice and deselecting the Disable Script Debugging check box, as shown in Figure 19-6.

Figure 19-6: IE script debugger settings panel

Tip

There are several good interactive JavaScript programming tools on the market, such as NetObject's ScriptBuilder. If you plan on building large or complex JavaScript functions, you will probably want to invest in one of these sophisticated JavaScript Interactive Development Environments.

Testing the JavaScript

Portal provides a management and test panel for JavaScript scripts as shown in Figure 19-7. The JavaScript panel provides you with six familiar choices. You can choose the Name link (or the Edit link) to edit the component. The Copy link allows you to replicate a script, and the Delete link will remove the script from the Shared Components Application. The Export link creates a PL/SQL script that you can use to move the JavaScript between different instances of Oracle Portal. Last, but certainly not least, is the Run link, which is used to test the JavaScript code.

1. Choose the Run link for the netu_js_alert script to display the panel as shown in Figure 19-7.

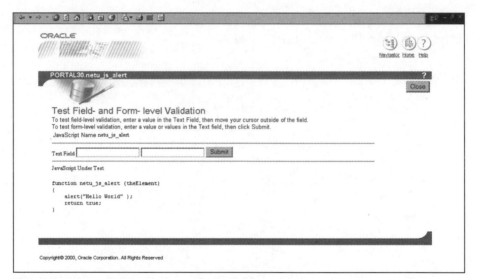

Figure 19-7: Testing JavaScript code for fields and forms

You can attach JavaScript scripts to many events on a form field within an HTML page. For data validation purposes, Portal currently restricts you to using only two of the possible events within the HTML pages it generates. The first event is the onBlur event, which is fired when the user leaves a field on a form. The second event is the onClick event for the form, which is fired when the form is sent back to the server. Although there is certainly value in being able to use the other events, you only really need these two events to validate data in a form.

Cross-Reference

Oracle Portal allows you to make use of other JavaScript events, as listed in Table 19-3. We'll be looking at these additional events later in this chapter.

If the item you are trying to validate is a single field, then you can use the `onBlur` event to enforce your restriction. On the other hand, if the value you are trying to enforce is based upon a value in another field, then the form's `onClick` event is the better event to use. You would not want to attempt to validate cross-field data until all of the required fields are filled in, and the `onClick` event determines the moment when the data entry fields are expected to be complete. Portal provides you with the two links on the edit panel so that you can test a single JavaScript with either the `onBlur` event or with the `onClick` event. Portal presents you with two text boxes, a Submit button, and the source code for your JavaScript on the generated test page.

2. Enter some text into the Text Field text box and tab to the next field in the test form to display the panel as shown in Figure 19-8.

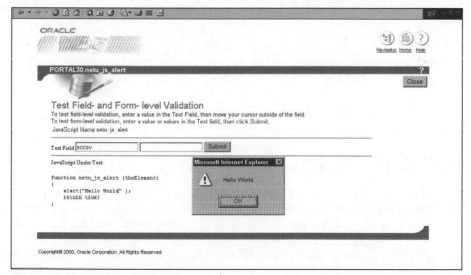

Figure 19-8: Alert message box

Portal associates the JavaScript code with the first text box within the HTML that it generates for the test page. If you were to look at the source HTML for the test page, you would see the following fragment of code embedded within the <FORM> and </FORM> blocks:

```
<HR>
Text Field
<INPUT TYPE="text" NAME="TextField" onBlur="netu_js_alert(this,
'TextField')">
<INPUT TYPE="text" NAME="TextField2">
```

```
<INPUT TYPE="submit" VALUE="Submit" onClick="return
netu_js_alert(TextField, 'TextField' )">
<BR>
<HR>
```

Notice that Portal ties the JavaScript to the `onBlur` event of the first text box. The parameter value is passed to the function by using an advanced feature of the JavaScript language. JavaScript enables you to use a shorthand name for any object using the keyword `this`. Portal uses the field name and the `this` keyword to pass a handle to the text box object to the function. In this manner, the function has access to all of the properties of the original object, which is how you are able to access the data within the field while running your JavaScript functions. You may also notice that Portal has tied the same procedure to the Submit button that it has generated for you so you can test the function at the form level as well as the field level from this one test page. Through the handle to the `theElement` value you gain access to all of JavaScript's built-in methods for fields such as:

```
theElement.name - name of the field
theElement.value - value of the field (contents)
theElement.length - length of the text entered into the field
theElement.focus() - position the cursor in the field
```

3. Return to the Oracle Portal Navigator for JavaScripts.

Building More Complicated Scripts

The JavaScript scripts you create for field validations are based upon the needs of the forms you create and the tables and columns you use. You will find it easier to create and manage JavaScript scripts by driving them from the data in your applications. In Chapter 8 of this book, you built a data entry form based upon a stored procedure, and that particular form makes an excellent case on which to build some validations.

 Cross-Reference If you are not familiar with how to import scripts to Portal, please see Chapter 2.

1. Import the scripts lov_alumni.sql, lov_fund.sql, and lov_restrict_codes.sql.

2. Import the script ch19_frm_donations.sql to create a copy of the donations form from Chapter 8.

3. Test the form to display the page shown in Figure 19-9.

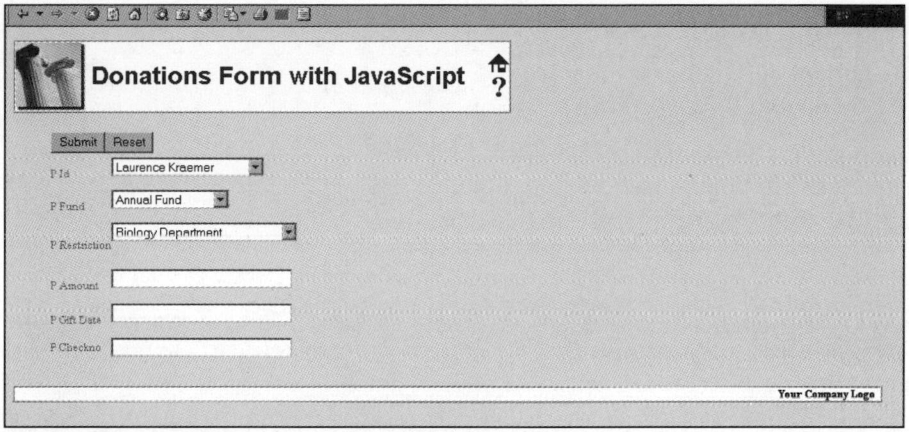

Figure 19-9: Reviewing the Donations Form

Although this form is quite simple, it can be difficult for the user to work with at run time. The form is based upon a stored procedure and the procedure is particular about the number and format of the data that is passed to it at execution time. A few client-side validation routines can make this form much easier to work with. Before you start building these JavaScript validations, take a close look at the existing data on the form. Notice how the fields ID, FUND, and RESTRICTION all have list-of-values objects associated with them. Essentially the data that you enter into these fields is already "validated," because the range of permissible values has been set by the list-of-values object. You can still attach JavaScript code to these fields — but such code is not considered to be "validations" by Oracle Portal.

Pure JavaScript validations are better suited to cases where the data cannot be presented to the user as a list. For example, the fields AMOUNT, GIFT DATE, and CHECK NUMBER are all free-form fields. It would be all but impossible to build a list-of-values object that would cover *all* of the possible values for these fields. JavaScript validations are the better choice for these fields.

    4. Return to the Shared Components Application.

The import script creates four JavaScript validations for use with the Donations form. Each script shows you a different type of validation and illustrates a different technique for working with data, as shown in Listing 19-3.

Listing 19-3: **Replace missing data with NULL**

```
function netu_js_makenull (theElement){
//
// Replace blanks with null
//
if (theElement.value == null || theElement.value == "") {
    theElement.value = "null"
    }
return true
}
```

Listing 19-3 shows you several ways to work with NULL or missing data. The Value method is used to extract the value that has been passed from the data entry field to the parameter of the script. The script checks to see if the value is NULL, or if it has been deleted. If the user never enters the field, it will be NULL, but if the user enters a value and then uses the Delete key, then the field is technically not NULL according to JavaScript. To circumvent this problem, the routine checks for both situations. Normally, you could simply leave a NULL value as NULL, but in the example case, the stored procedure requires you to pass the NULL value as a keyword string to the procedure. The JavaScript routine converts missing data into the string NULL. You can just as easily strip characters out of the field entry as you can check for NULL, as Listing 19-4 demonstrates.

Listing 19-4: **Range check**

```
function netu_js_range_1_to_50000(theElement){
var num_x = 0
//
// Check for blank or zero
//
if (theElement.value == null || theElement.value == "" ||
theElement.value == "0") {
    alert("Field " + theElement.name + " must be > 0 and
<50001");
    theElement.focus()
    return false
    }
//
// Not blank or zero, eliminate character values
//
var string_y = theElement.value
var string_z = ""
for (var i = 0; i<string_y.length; i++) {
    var single_char = string_y.charAt(i)
    if (single_char < "0" || single_char > "9"){
        continue
    } else {
```

```
            string_z = string_z + single_char
        }
    }
    // Check value range
    //
    num_x = Number(string_z)
    theElement.value = num_x
    if (num_x < 1 || num_x > 50000) {
        alert("Value is out of range (1-50000)")
        theElement.focus()
        return false
    } else {
        return true
    }
}
```

In this case, the routine performs three different types of validation. First, it checks to be sure that the field is not either blank, zero, or NULL. Next, it uses a for loop to step through the individual characters using the charAt() function to eliminate any nonnumeric characters. This part of the JavaScript function is where you cross over the line from simply validating data to improving the usability of the application. You could simply look for nonnumeric values and then signal an error when you find them. However, it is better to search for a light than to curse the darkness, and it is correspondingly better to attempt to eliminate common user errors and make the form easier to use. The JavaScript function is meant to search for numeric values out of range, and it makes sense to strip out any nonnumeric characters. If a user should inadvertently enter punctuation into the field, this routine quietly removes the errors. The final task for this validation is to check that the remaining numeric data is within the range of valid values. Notice that the function actually changes the value of the field with the code:

```
theElement = num_x,
```

If the resulting value is out of range, the cursor is returned to the field, and the user is given the "clean" version of the field to work with. In some cases, you may find it is too complex to repair the data a user entered into a field. For example, Listing 19-5 shows a simple date-checking script.

Listing 19-5: **Simple date check**

```
function netu_js_currentyear(theElement){
    //
    // Check date. Assumes input date of dd-mmm-yyyy
    //
```

Continued

Listing 19-5 *(continued)*

```
var string_x = theElement.value
//
// Check the length first
//
if (string_x.length != 11) {
     alert("Date does not appear to be in the correct dd-mmm-
yyyy format")
     theElement.focus()
     return false
}
// Check the year
//
var thisYear = (new Date()).getYear()
var year_y = Number(string_x.charAt(7) +
string_x.charAt(8)+string_x.charAt(9) + string_x.charAt(10))
if (year_y != Number(thisYear)) {
     alert("Date year must match current year")
     theElement.focus()
     theElement.select()
     return false
} else {
     return true
}
}
```

You could write a complete routine to check for a valid date value, and attempt to repair the data if the user entered it incorrectly. However, it may be enough just to show the user the correct format for the date and perform a rudimentary check of the data.

This function first checks to see if the length of the date field is 11, which is the correct length for a date in the Oracle dd-mmm-yyyy format. Next, the script finds the year of the current date by using the Date function and then compares it to the last two characters of the date entered by the user. If the two numbers match, then the date entered by the user is in the current year, otherwise the date is invalid. The Select function causes the browser to lasso the date field when the user is returned to the page. This makes it easier for the user to change the value of the field.

5. Use the JavaScript Wizard to create three functions for each of the Listings 19-3, 19-4, and 19-5. Be sure to match the name of the function to the Portal name for the function.

The JavaScript source code is included as part of the book's examples on the CD-ROM and can be opened, cut, and pasted into Portal.

Once you have created the three sample functions, the next step is to attach them to fields on a data entry form.

Attaching Validations to Forms

Once you have created your JavaScript validations, you can easily attach them to any Portal form.

1. Use the applications page in the NETCOLLEGE application to edit the ch19_frm_donations form.

2. Select the P_AMOUNT field as shown Figure 19-10.

You should be familiar with this panel from building forms in previous chapters of this book. The column selector on the left side of the form enables you to click a field name and display the formatting options for the form. The two combo boxes at the bottom of the page labeled Field Level Validation and Form Level Validation are the places where you attach your JavaScript validations to your fields. Portal loads all of the validations into each of the combo boxes and you can select the script you wish to use from the list of available validations. If you attach a JavaScript validation to the Field Level Validation item, Portal associates the JavaScript with the onBlur event. If you associate a script with the Form Level Validation combo box, Portal associates the validation with the onClick event for the Insert/Update buttons added to the form on the Button Options page.

3. Select the netu_js_1_to_50000 validation for the P_AMOUNT field as a field validation.

4. Select the netu_js_currentyear validation for the P_GIFT_DATE field as a field validation.

5. Select the netu_js_makenull validation for the P_CHECKNO field as a field validation.

6. Click the OK button to store your changes.

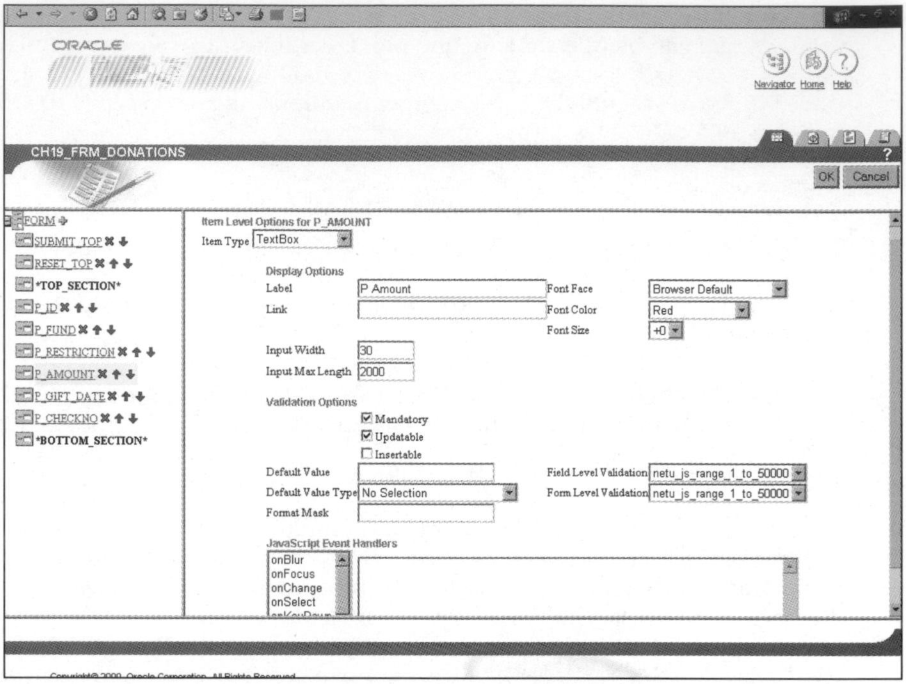

Figure 19-10: Formatting and validation options panel

7. Use the Run link to test the modified version of your form. Portal renders the form and adds the specified validations to yield a new copy of the form.

The modified form does not look different from the previous version of the form, but you will see that it behaves differently. If users try to enter invalid information into the Amount, Gift Date, or Check Number fields — the browser displays alert boxes.

> **Caution**
>
> It is possible to get yourself into an endless loop with validation scripts, even if it appears that the validation code is properly designed. We recommend that you provide acceptable default values for form fields if you plan on attaching validation scripts to these fields. This ensures that the users do not get caught in an error loop from which they cannot escape.

8. Enter improper values into the AMOUNT and GIFT DATE fields to see how the validations operate.

Although all of the fields are protected in some way on this form — either through JavaScript validations or list-of-values entries — you can still do more to this form. There will be cases where you want to warn your users about an improper value, but still allow them to proceed with the transaction. There are also cases where the validation for one field is dependent upon the values in a subsequent field. Portal enables you to add JavaScript code that can handle both of these problems.

Using Other JavaScript Events

Oracle Portal provides the Field Level Validation and Form Level Validation settings for validating the data that is entered into a field. You can make use of additional JavaScript events to control other actions on a form, and these additional JavaScript events can assist you in the process of building advanced data integrity checks such as cross-field validations. Table 19-3 lists the various field types and their associated JavaScript events, and Table 19-2 describes each of the JavaScript events in more detail. You will find it easier to understand just how each of these events work by seeing them in action.

1. Load the template file ch19_js_template.sql, the list-of-values file ch19_lov.sql, and the form ch19_frm_javascript.sql.

2. Run the form ch19_frm_javascript to display the form as shown in Figure 19-11.

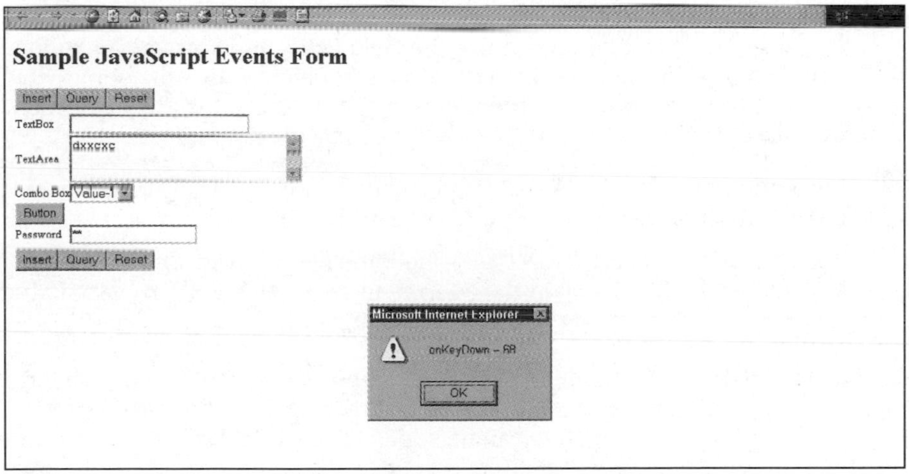

Figure 19-11: Sample JavaScript Events Form

Each of the fields that appears on the form ch19_javascript has a number of JavaScript events associated with it, as listed in Table 19-8.

| | Table 19-8 |
| | JavaScript Events on the Example Form |

Field	Events
Textbox	onBlur, onFocus, onChange, onSelect
TextArea	OnSelect
Combo Box	onBlur, onFocus, onChange
Button	onClick, onMouseDown, onMouseUp
Password	onKeyDown, onKeyPress, onKeyUp

All of the examples use the alert function to display a message that contains the name of the event that has been fired along with the value of the field at the time of that the event is signaled.

3. Test the various events on the form as listed in Table 19-8 and shown in Figure 19-11.

The additional JavaScript events allow you to have a much finer grain of control over user-interaction on your forms. These additional events can also be used for the purposes of data validation just like the Field Level and Form Level Validations. In fact, the major difference between the two techniques is the manner in which you reference the JavaScript and the way that the JavaScript is physically stored within Oracle Portal.

4. Close the ch19_frm_javascript form and navigate to the forms editor for ch19_frm_javascript.

5. Edit the ch19_javascript form and select the FIELD1 field. Scroll down to the bottom of the right panel in the editor and select the onBlur event in the JavaScript Event Handler as shown in Figure 19-12.

Each display field type provides a scrolling combo box of supported JavaScript events. The specific events that are supported by each field type are listed in Table 19-3. JavaScript event code can be added to each field by selecting a single event in the JavaScript Event Handlers combo box and then entering a function call to a JavaScript function in the text area to the right of the combo box as shown in Figure 19-12. Once you have entered code into a JavaScript Event Handler, Oracle Portal marks the event with an asterisk suffix that indicates that a JavaScript call exists for the selected event and the selected field.

Portal does not allow you to enter multiple lines of JavaScript code into each event handler. As Figure 19-12 clearly shows, you are only permitted to enter a call to a JavaScript event along with function parameters. Thus, the example code for FIELD1's onBlur event is a simple function call as follows:

```
ch19_onblur(this)
```

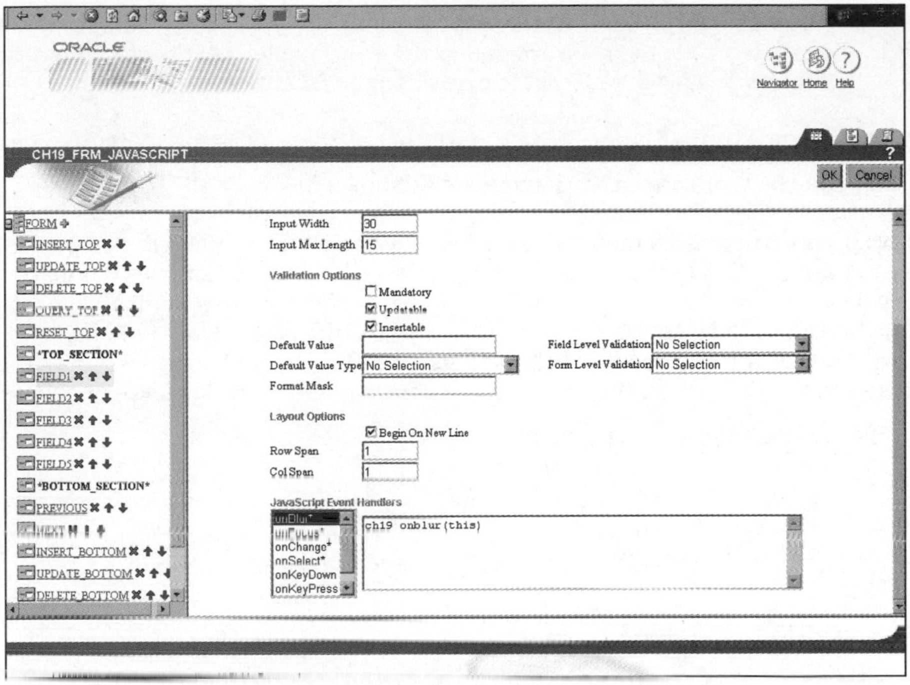

Figure 19-12: JavaScript events in the forms editor

When the field loses focus (just like the Field Level Validation event), Oracle Portal will cause the function `ch19_onblur` to fire. The function call takes advantage of a built-in capability of JavaScript and the document object model by using the `this` keyword — which is a pointer to the field in which the event occurs. Within the function `ch19_onblur`, the `this` object pointer allows you to gain access to data in the field by using the implicit field methods such as `value` and `length`.

Thus, the process of using events with fields is as simple as selecting a JavaScript event and then calling a function when the event is triggered. The only remaining hurdle is to attach the body of the JavaScript function to the form. The fastest way to do so is to embed the code within an unstructured template.

6. Exit the current form.

Adding JavaScript code to templates

There are two ways in which you can add custom JavaScript code to a form. You can embed the JavaScript code within a PL/SQL package, or you can add the JavaScript code directly to a template.

Cross-Reference The remainder of this section uses templates for embedding JavaScript code. Portal's template tools are covered in detail in Chapter 18. Chapter 29 provides examples of adding JavaScript to pages using PL/SQL blocks.

1. Navigate to the Templates folder within the Shared Components Application.

2. Edit the template ch19_js_template as shown in Figure 19-13.

Portal's unstructured templates provide you with the opportunity to add your own custom HTML to a template file. Portal's run-time engine intersperses database results and generated HTML with your template code to create a finished HTML document. Figure 19-13 shows the edit panel for the ch19_js_template object that is used with the form ch19_javascript. The JavaScript code is loaded using <SCRIPT> tags between the <HEAD> and <BODY> tags as shown in the following snippet of code:

```
<SCRIPT LANGUAGE="JavaScript1.1">
<!--
function ch19_onblur(theElement)
{
alert("onBlur -- " + theElement.value);
}
//-->
</SCRIPT>
```

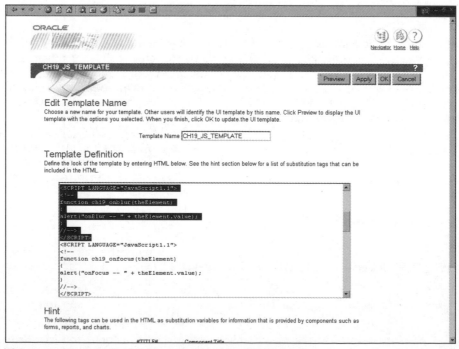

Figure 19-13: Template with embedded JavaScript code

The <SCRIPT> tags identify the block of text as script code to the browser, and the <!--and //--> comment tags ensure that the code will be ignored by older browsers that do not support JavaScript.

Caution Portal itself makes extensive use of JavaScript within generated Portal pages. Thus, almost all pre-JavaScript browsers will have trouble using Oracle Portal pages — even if you have not made use of custom JavaScript code. This makes the use of the comment tags somewhat irrelevant, but it is still good programming practice to place them within your scripts.

The function name ch19_onblur matches the name of the function as it is called by the onBlur event within the form as shown in Figure 19-12. We use the Oracle Portal convention and use the name theElement as the parameter value for the function. Portal will pass the context of the current field to the theElement parameter when the function is called. Within the body of the function, the alert function displays a message to the user that describes the event that was called and the value of the field at the time that the event was triggered. While this function is overly simple, you could add any amount of JavaScript code to the function. In fact, the ch19_onkeypress function captures the user's keystrokes as they enter data into the field.

```
<SCRIPT LANGUAGE="JavaScript1.1">
<!--
function ch19_onkeypress(theElement)
{
alert("onKeyPress -- " + window.event.srcElement.keyCode);
}
//-->
</SCRIPT>
```

In fact, any of the examples that were used to perform field validation as described in the preceding section could also be used within these custom event handlers. The combination of the Field Level Validations, Form Level Validations, and JavaScript Event Handlers give you the tools to create very powerful client-side programs. In this next section, you'll combine both types of JavaScript to build cross-field validations.

Performing Cross-Field Validations

Cross-field validations are those validations that compare the data in one field to the data within a second field. The secret to working with cross-field validations is to understand how Portal works with JavaScript events and the browser's document object model.

 Tip Portal does not provide direct access to field names and methods, but you can use JavaScript events to transfer data between fields on a form. You can also use JavaScript code to identify fields on a form.

In the example Donations form there is the additional need to check for large pledge records. The form itself uses a stored procedure to write data into the database as either a DONATIONS record or as a PLEDGE record. Donations that have a NULL value for the check number are assumed to be pledges. Although the form enables users to add gifts up the amount of $50,000, it is unlikely that you would have pledges over $10,000. You can use a form-based JavaScript to check for large gifts that have a NULL check number by using the following code in Listing 19-6.

Listing 19-6: Cross-field validation

```
<SCRIPT LANGUAGE="JavaScript1.1">
<!--
var v_amount
//-->
</SCRIPT>
<SCRIPT LANGUAGE="JavaScript1.1">
<!--
function amount_onblur(theElement)
{
v_amount = theElement.value
}
//-->
</SCRIPT>

<SCRIPT LANGUAGE="JavaScript1.1">
<!--
function netu_js_donation(theElement){
//
// Get value of amount and check number
//

if (v_amount> 10000 && (theElement.value == "NULL" ||
theElement.value == "")) {
 if (confirm("This looks like a large pledge, are you sure?")){
        return true
    } else {
        theElement.focus();
        return false
    }
}
return true
}
//-->
</SCRIPT>
```

In Listing 19-6, there are three separate <SCRIPT> routines. The first block of code does nothing more than declare a variable called v_amount without any function declaration. JavaScript considers such fields to be global variables and they are accessible to any of the other functions that are included within the same HTML page. By declaring variables in this fashion, you are able to *pass* values between fields. The second block of code (`amount_onblur`) copies the *value* of a passed parameter into the global variable `v_amount`. The final block of code (`netu_js_donation`) compares the value of the variable to the value of the parameter that is passed into the function.

The actual validation is simple: If the amount of the gift is over $10,000 and the check number is NULL, then the user is asked to confirm the entry. Instead of preventing the user from storing the data, the use of the CONFIRM method of the window object enables the user to accept the item or reject the entry. After all, it is possible that a donor will make such a large pledge to the university, even if it is unlikely.

If you enter a gift amount over $10,000 and leave the check number as NULL, the script prompts you to accept or reject the data with a dialog box. The user can accept the change with the OK button, or reject the data with the Cancel button. If the user elects to cancel the operation, the cursor returns to the current field. You can change this behavior simply by adding some custom code to the else block of the if then code. You will find that end users often prefer this type of validation because it gives them some additional control over the process. Large, complex data entry forms can be frustrating for users if they are continually forced to reenter data that is rejected based upon unclear data entry requirements.

Form-level validations that ask the user for confirmation of questionable data can make the user more comfortable with your applications, while also ensuring that your data remains consistent. The downside to building this type of validation is the need to build and test your JavaScript scripts directly against each data entry form.

Note   Portal dynamically loads the JavaScript code into the form when you run it, so it is not necessary to recompile your forms each time you change your script code. Once you have attached the JavaScript to a field, you can simply edit the script and retest the form without recompiling it.

The most complex part of using this code is attaching it to the appropriate fields.

1. Load the ch19_crossfield.sql template script into Oracle Portal.

2. Edit the ch19_frm_donations form and navigate to the CHECK_NUMBER Field.

3. Choose the `onBlur` event in the JavaScript Event Handler Field Combo Box and then enter `netu_js_donation(this)` as the JavaScript routine to be called. (See Figure 19-14.)

4. Edit the AMOUNT field, select the `onBlur` event and add the function `amount_onblur(this)` as the JavaScript Event Handler.

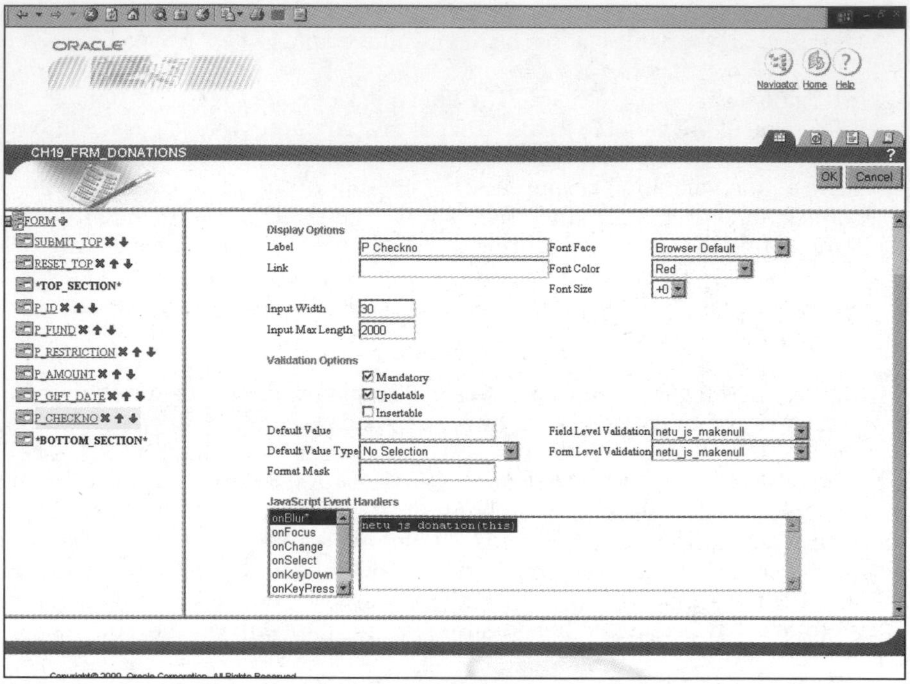

Figure 19-14: Adding a cross-field validation to a form

5. Navigate to the Text panel in the form ch19_form_donations and attach the ch19_crossfield template to the form.

6. Save your changes, compile the form, and then test it.

By attaching the `amount_onblur` validation to the AMOUNT field the function is able to pass a pointer to the AMOUNT field into the validation routine. The function sets the value of the `v_amount` global variable to the value of the AMOUNT field when the user exits the AMOUNT field. When the user leaves the CHECK_NUMBER field, the `netu_js_donations` function compares the value of the CHECK_NUMBER field and the value of the `v_amount` variable within an `if-else` block. If the CHECK_NUMBER field is either blank or NULL and the AMOUNT field is greater than 10,000, the function prompts the user for a response.

7. Test the new JavaScript functions on the ch19_donations form.

8. Exit the form when you are finished testing the JavaScript code.

Global variables are not necessarily the most efficient means of comparing data on a form. However, since the designers of Oracle Portal do not provide explicit access to fields on a form it may seem like the only solution. An alternative design is to make use of the browser's document object model. Through JavaScript code, you can interrogate your HTML pages at run-time—and this is an especially good technique for handling cross-record validations.

Performing Cross-Record Validations

When you create master-detail forms with Portal, you are allowed to enter multiple detail records for each client record. If you have designed your primary and foreign key relationships properly the database rejects duplicate child records for a given parent record automatically. However, the browser does not validate the data against the database until you attempt to save your changes. This enables the user to unknowingly enter duplicate records into the browser page that will cause errors when the page is stored to the database.

The solution is a simple JavaScript function as shown in Listing 19-7.

Listing 19-7: **Looping through fields on a page**

```
function ch19_frm_loop(theElement){
var form = document.forms[0]
for (i = 0; i <form.elements length; i++){
    if ((theElement.value == form.elements[i].value) &&
(theElement.name != form.elements[i].name)){
    alert('Field Name: "'+ form.elements[i].name + '" has a
duplicate value')
    break
}
}
}
```

This function makes use of the built-in capabilities of JavaScript and the document object model. JavaScript routines have access to the internal properties of every window, frame, page, and field. Thus, you can interrogate the fields and values on a page by using a simple JavaScript routine. Listing 19-7 offers one such solution. This short function loops through each field on a form by using the document.forms[0] attribute — which translates to the current form object on the current HTML page. The function loops through all of the elements of the form using a simple comparison. If the value of the current field (passed into the function using theElement) matches the value of any field in the elements array and the name of the current field does not match the name of the array field (that is, they are two different fields in two different records) — then an alert message is displayed to the form.

1. Load the JavaScript component ch19_js_loop.sql and the form ch19_frm_md.sql into Portal.

2. Run the form ch19_frm_md

3. Enter the value **2001** for the Classyr field in the Master Record and press Query to display data in the form as shown in Figure 19-15

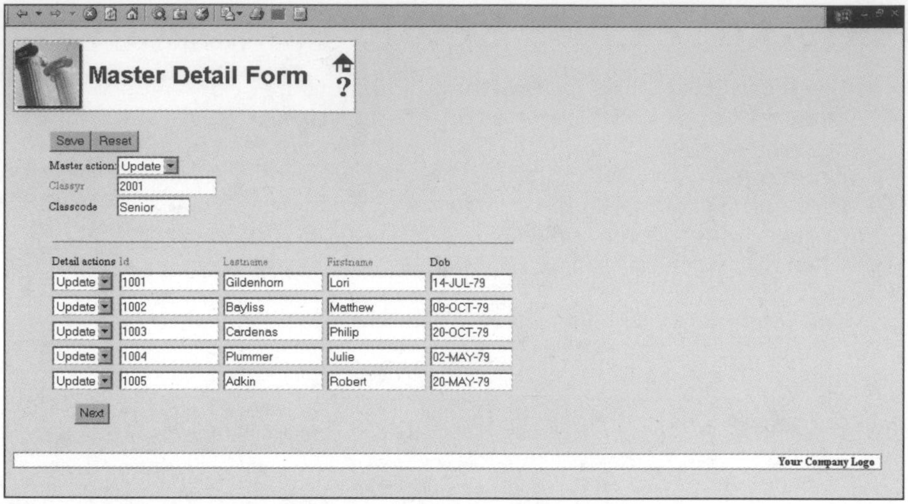

Figure 19-15: Master Detail Form for classes and students

4. Tab to the ID field in the detail record for first student record. Change the ID value to a value that matches any of the other student records and then tab out of the field to display the panel as shown in Figure 19-16.

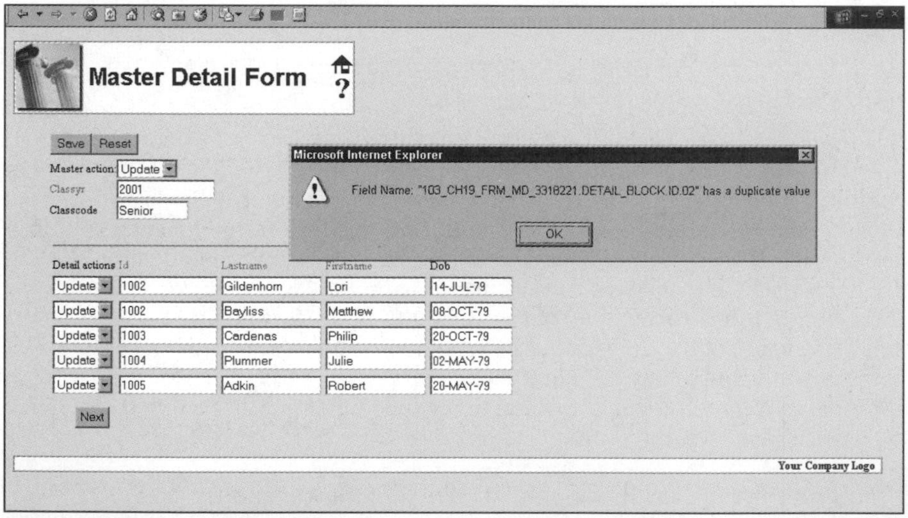

Figure 19-16: Duplicate value error

The JavaScript function loops through the detail records and catches the duplicate value. The error message includes the name of the field with the duplicate value surrounded by quotes. You will notice that Oracle Portal uses a very long and complex string as the name for each field. However, the document.form[0] attribute hides this complexity from you. The `ch19_frm_loop` function is attached as a Field Level Validation to the ID field in the detail record. So, it fires every time that a user enters and exits the ID field. This is a simple and elegant solution to a complex problem.

Cross-Reference

Oracle Portal does not automatically fetch all of the detail records for a given master record on master/detail forms. Thus, the `ch19_frm_loop` function will only detect duplicate records that are *currently* displayed on the page. There may be duplicate records in the database that have not been fetched and displayed on the form — and the JavaScript function will not catch these duplicate values. Triggers and PL/SQL procedures are meant to handle this type of problem.

Performing Server-Side Validations

You will find that users are much more satisfied with your applications if you provide them with clean, user-friendly data validation within the browser. However, the primary line of defense for your data is the constraints and triggers provided inside the Oracle database. Oracle permits you to define simple rules called *constraints* that are associated with fields and tables within your database. There are three types of constraints found in the typical database:

✦ Primary key constraints

✦ Foreign key constraints

✦ Check constraints

Primary key constraints define the primary key for a table and are typically used to enforce uniqueness on a table's key field. Within the NetU database schema, every table has a designated primary key constraint that ensures uniqueness.

Foreign key constraints are the server-side equivalent of lists-of-values and they associate a field in one table with the primary key of a second table. A foreign key constraint prevents you from entering data into a field on one table that does not match preexisting data in a field on a second table. For example, you cannot add or modify a UGRADS record with a value for the CLASSYR field that does not match a CLASSYR value in the CLASSES table. This prevents you from entering students for a class year that does not yet exist. In most cases, you will want to provide a list-of-values object for foreign key field validations within Portal forms.

Oracle's Check constraints provide a more general-purpose tool for limiting the allowable data values for a field. Check constraints enable you to set a range of values for a field at the server level. Within the NetU database, the FUND field in the DONATIONS table has a check constraint that limits the allowable entries in the FUND field to either "Annual Fund" or "Capital Campaign." Check constraints are used when a foreign key table does not exist, or wherever a range of values is to be permitted.

Check constraints are limited to comparing data within a single table. If you need to compare the value of one field to a value in another table, then Oracle provides an additional tool in the form of database triggers. Oracle triggers are blocks of PL/SQL code that are processed whenever a change to a table — such as inserts, updates, or deletes — is performed. You can use triggers to make silent modifications to your data or to stop completion of the changes you make. For example, you could create a trigger on the ALUMNI table that would prevent any record from being deleted if the alumni had given more than $10,000 to the university. You can also use triggers to massage your data, such as converting the first letter of every last name to an uppercase value when the record is either updated or inserted.

Cross-Reference

Some in-depth understanding of PL/SQL is needed to work with database triggers. Chapter 21 provides a more detailed discussion of PL/SQL.

If you are building a Portal application on top of an existing Oracle database, you are likely to find that the database already has constraints and triggers in place. Be sure to create a client-side JavaScript data validation for these existing database rules within Portal. This ensures that the data entered into your forms satisfies the database requirements when it is passed from the browser to the database.

Summary

Data validations can make your applications much easier to use and improve the quality of the information stored within your database. You will find that typical applications are a mix of list-of-values objects and JavaScript validations and that each object serves a distinct purpose. End users will be more comfortable with applications that attempt to solve data entry problems rather than applications that merely point out the inconsistencies. Keep this in mind as you build your JavaScript validation functions, and consider making an extra effort to simplify the overall process for your users. If you find that you need to build larger JavaScript validations, we recommend that you invest in a more complete guide to the JavaScript language, such as Hungry Minds' *JavaScript Bible*. In the next chapter we'll work with Oracle Portal links, which connect reports and forms together using data from the database.

✦   ✦   ✦

Using Links to Connect Oracle9*i*AS Portal Objects

✦ ✦ ✦ ✦

In This Chapter

Defining Links

Linking from an
Existing Component

Testing a Link

Making a Dynamic
Link

Using Links to Update
Data

Using Portal
Parameter Arrays

✦ ✦ ✦ ✦

In Chapter 17, you learned how to use menus to create complete application systems using Portal's component objects. One of the problems you may have encountered when building your menus is the difficulty in determining just which Portal component should be used to connect to a menu choice. Portal provides a second utility in the form of the Link Builder that can help you create reusable connections between Portal components. In this chapter, you will learn how to build links based on Portal components and how to use these links to provide parameter passing for your applications.

Defining Links

In its simplest form, a link is nothing more than a standard URL string, as discussed in Chapter 17. Links are the backbone of navigation for Web applications, and the Portal Link Builder is designed to assist you in the process of creating custom URL links for your Portal content. As you also saw in Chapter 17, Portal enables you to link to components from menu items, so at first it may seem as if a separate link builder is not necessary. The Link Builder provides you with access to links in places where Portal does not allow you to directly connect to other components or menu items, but this is not the most important reason for using links.

A Portal link provides you with the capability to drill up or drill down to other Portal components containing related data. Browser users have learned to make use of links in static Web pages as means of navigating through content. Portal links provide a similar experience for dynamic, database data. For example, a user who is looking at high-level summary data may wish to have the capability to drill down to more detailed transactional data. You can use links to determine which specific summary data the user is viewing and then connect that data to the appropriate, detailed transactional data. Conversely, a user who is looking at transactional data may also wish to jump up to a higher level of abstraction, and Portal links can address this requirement as well.

The Link Builder is specifically designed to enable you to link a Portal component such as a report, form, chart, calendar, or hierarchy to an individual target component. The presence of a link on a database column enables a Portal application user to click through from one component to another automatically.

Linking from an Existing Component

Links are easy to understand once you see them in action. As of Oracle Portal 3.0.8 there are ten user interface components can be linked directly to another Portal component using links. In fact, you can link any Portal component to any other URL-based application using links. The simplest way to create a link is to attach a target component to a specific column in a source component.

1. Load the view script view_netu_class_totals.sql into the NETU account via SQL*Plus.

2. Load the sample reports ch20_rpt_students and ch20_rpt_classes using SQL*Plus into the Portal account.

The sample report creates a list of UGRADS students that is organized by class year and last name, and it shows off the various majors for each of the students.

3. After you have loaded the report into the database, navigate to the Reports menu, select the ch20_rpt_students, and execute it.

Figure 20-1 shows the results of running this simple report. This body of this report shows student records organized by class year and includes the major for each student.

4. Exit the ch20_rpt_students report.

5. Run the ch20_rpt_classes report, as shown in Figure 20-2.

The Student Report shows a summary of class information from the UGRADS table and the CLASSES table. This report counts the number of students per class year and prints the total along with the class year and associated class code.

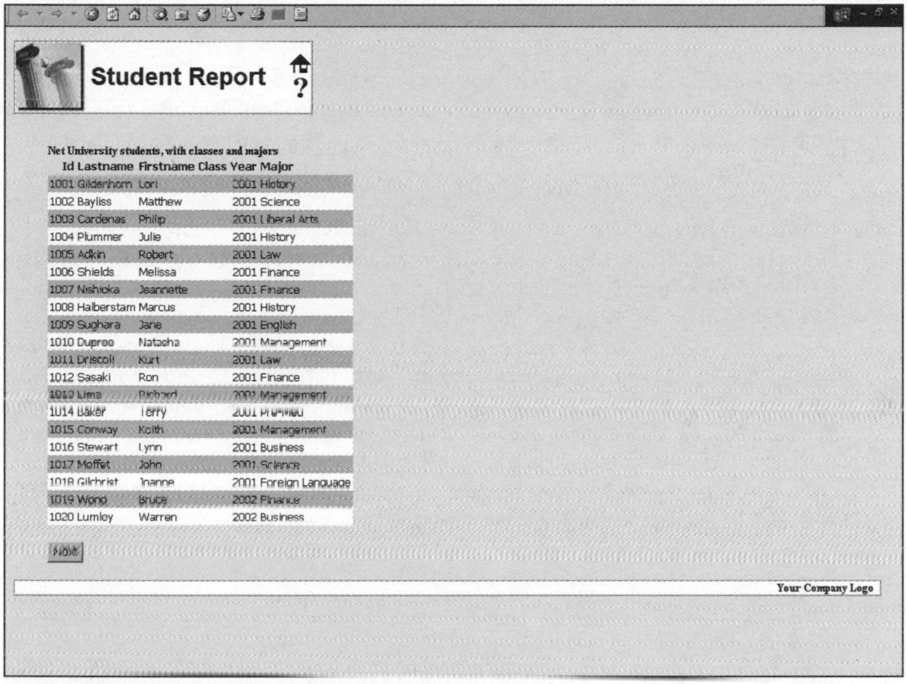

Figure 20-1: Student Report sorted by class year

Figure 20-2: Class Years Report showing class totals

Linking the STUDENTS report to the CLASSES report

It would be useful to automatically associate the UGRADS report with the CLASSES report so users can automatically drill up from the Class Years column to a summary of the class years at Net University (or vice versa). The Link Wizard is the tool that Portal provides to make such a connection.

1. Navigate to the NETCOLLEGE application and select the Create New ... Links link to display the panel shown in Figure 20-3. Portal displays the familiar create panel that allows you to name the component and associate it with an application.

Links are owned by applications just like most other Portal components, and you should create links in the same application as the link targets (forms, reports, etc.). It is possible to link together objects from separate applications using handcrafted URLs, but it is more common to link objects using the Link Builder.

Note The decision to group components by an "application" with Oracle Portal 3.0 was made to improve the ergonomics of the user interface for developers and tighten up the security. While links and LOVs can cross applications, you may consider keeping all of the objects for a single logical application within the same portal application. This greatly simplifies the display of list-of-values boxes for LOVs and links within the development environment.

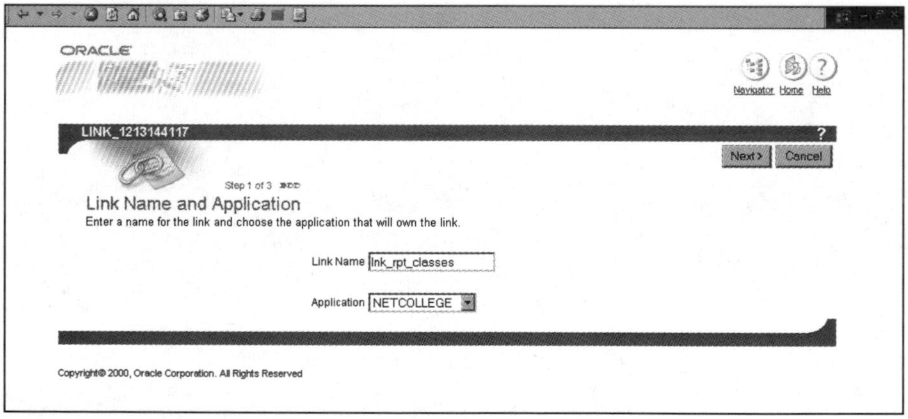

Figure 20-3: Naming a link and setting the owner

Links follow the same naming conventions as any other Portal component, and you are free to name links using any scheme you choose. You may find it more difficult to adequately name link objects, because a descriptive name should include a reference to both the calling component and the linked component.

2. Select the NETCOLLEGE application as the owner of your new link and enter **lnk_rpt_classes** as the name of the link.

3. Click the Next arrow to display the page shown in Figure 20-4.

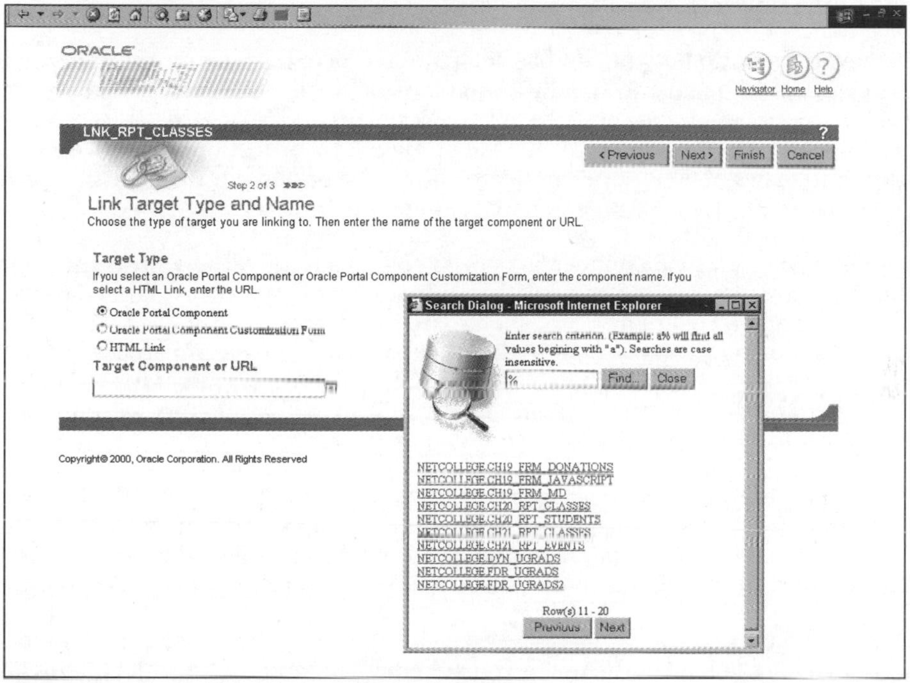

Figure 20-4: Link Target Type and Name page

Links are designed in reverse order: the *target* link is selected first followed by the *source* link. Although this may seem illogical to begin with, it actually makes the overall process much easier. In fact, the source link can be dynamically determined when the link is actually used, as we will see later on in this chapter. The key to building a link is the passing of parameters between the source and target component.

By selecting the target component first, Portal can interrogate the target component and build a list of possible parameters for you. There are three possible link types as defined by the Link Wizard:

✦ Portal Component

✦ Portal Component Customization Form

✦ HTML Link

Portal components are the most common type of link and they include any of the other Portal component objects such as forms, reports, charts, menus, calendars, hierarchies, and Dynamic Pages. In effect, by selecting the Portal Component type, you are connecting to a procedure of the target component (normally the SHOW procedure). It makes no difference at this point whether you are passing parameters to the target or not.

However, if you do not plan on passing parameters to a target object, but you want the end user to be able to specify parameters manually, then you would select the Portal Component Customization Form link type. This causes Portal to call the SHOW_PARAMETER procedure instead of the SHOW procedure for a given component. End users of your application are shown the parameter form for the target component and they are able to enter parameters interactively.

In most cases, you will connect links from columns to the SHOW procedure. One of the most common intents of a link is to provide a drill up or a drill down from a column to a detailed user interface object. Therefore, you are more likely to create these links using parameter values in order to invoke the SHOW procedure with appropriate data. Because links are most often used to drill down or drill up through data, the SHOW procedure, which can accept parameters without user intervention, is the most likely destination of a link.

Portal links can also connect to external components using the HTML Link type. You can link external Web sites and applications as the target component with URLs within the Link Wizard using HTML links. For example, you might want to link a Net University sports calendar to the NCAA Web site using the HTML Link type.

Once you have chosen the link type, you can specify the name of the component to which you are linking in the text box just below the radio buttons. If you are linking to either a Portal Component or a Portal Component Parameter Form, you can use the Find button to search for a listing of components, as shown in the overlay on Figure 20-4.

The Search panel displays a list of Portal components sorted by Application USERID and component name. You can enter a partial search string such as **netu.ch20%** to search for components that are specific to a certain schema or application name. The Search panel lists only those packages that have been built with Portal. If you have created other packages within Oracle, they will not appear in the Search panel even though they are valid packages from the database's perspective. If you need to link to an *external* PL/SQL package (such as one built for 9*i*AS outside of Portal), you must do using the HTML Link type.

Cross-Reference   Chapter 21 contains a detailed look at using PL/SQL packages with Portal.

The text box should be filled with the name of the external URL link or external PL/SQL package name for the HTML Link type. For example, if you wanted to connect the UGRADS report to the virtual Web campus at college.com, you would enter http://www.college.com in the name text box. You are free to add parameters to any external URL that you enter as additional strings on the command line.

4. In the Link Target Type and Name page, select the Oracle Portal Component radio button for your new link.

5. Use the search icon to locate the report NETU.CH20_RPT_CLASSES as the target component name.

6. Click the Next arrow to display the panel shown in Figure 20-5.

The Link Target Inputs panel is constructed by interrogating the component procedure and building a list of *possible* parameters. Notice that there are two groups of fields: *user parameters* and *system parameters*. Both groups of fields are actually parameters, but those marked as user parameters are the formal parameters that have been created as part of the component. For example, assume that the Class Total Report included a BIND variable that allowed the user to select a class year as a parameter for the report. In such a case, the Link Wizard would display that BIND variable as a user parameter option on the link panel. In this particular example, because there are no BIND variables as part of the Class Total Report, the parameters group does not contain any values. Any values that are selected at this point can be overridden when the link is used with a component.

Note The user parameter option is discussed in more detail in the next section of this chapter.

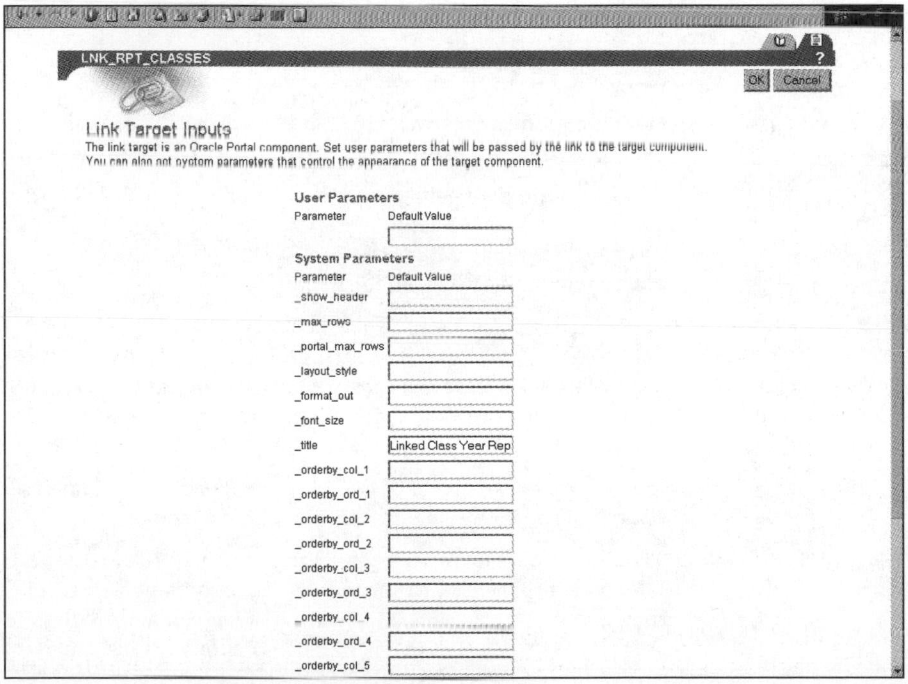

Figure 20-5: Link Target Inputs panel

System parameters

The second group of parameters is the system parameters group. This group represents display parameters you can use to affect the execution of the component in some way. The specific list of parameters is somewhat consistent between all of the various user interface objects: forms, reports, Dynamic Pages, calendars, and hierarchies. The parameters themselves are taken from the Display Options page in each wizard. Table 20-1 lists the most common parameters along with their functions.

Table 20-1
Common Display Parameter Names and Functions

Parameter Name	Description	Submit Values
_show_header	Indicates whether the component should display the header section of the report (including the title).	YES, NO
_font_size	Font size for output data. Determines the size of the font used to render the body of the report, form, chart, calendar, or hierarchy.	1,2,3...
_format_out	Determines how the data is displayed. There are three possible formats: HTML, ASCII, and Excel spreadsheet.	HTML, EXCEL, ASCII
_max_rows	Maximum number of rows that should be displayed on a single page.	Positive integer value
_orderby_col_1 _orderby_col_2 _orderby_col_3	Three separate parameters used to indicate the sort order for the report. You must use these parameters in order — you are not allowed to supply a value for col_2 without first supplying a value for col_1.	Tablename. Column-name (for example: UGRADS.CLASSYR
_orderby_ord_1 _orderby_ord_2 _orderby_ord_3	Sort order for selected columns.	ASC (Ascending A-Z), DSC (Descending Z-A)
_break_cols	Literal value for the name of the column on which the report should break.	Tablename.Column-name (for example: UGRADS.CLASSYR)
_title	Title to be displayed by the linked component.	Component Name (for example: Linked Class Total Report)

The specific display options parameters that appear depend on the type of component you are linking to and the specific built-in features of the component. For example, although _break_cols is a standard parameter for reports, it will not appear if you have not specified break columns in the report to which you are linking. (In particular, the Chart Wizard features a number of additional parameters that are specific to *only* the chart object.)

Generally, every Portal system parameter begins with the underscore (_) character to distinguish the name from other types of data within a procedure. While you never have to look at the detailed PL/SQL source for your procedures, the internal parameter names of these procedures appear in the header. Portal uses the procedure declarations to create the pick lists for the Link Builder and the result is that you are presented with parameter names that begin with the _ character.

7. In the Link Target Inputs panel, add the string **Linked Class Year Report** for the _title System Parameter.

8. Click the OK button to save and compile the new link.

Testing a Link

Once you have saved the new link, Portal returns you to the main link page. You can view the link by using the Run link in the bottom panel on the Manage Links page.

1. Use the Run link for lnk_rpt_classes as shown in Figure 20-6.

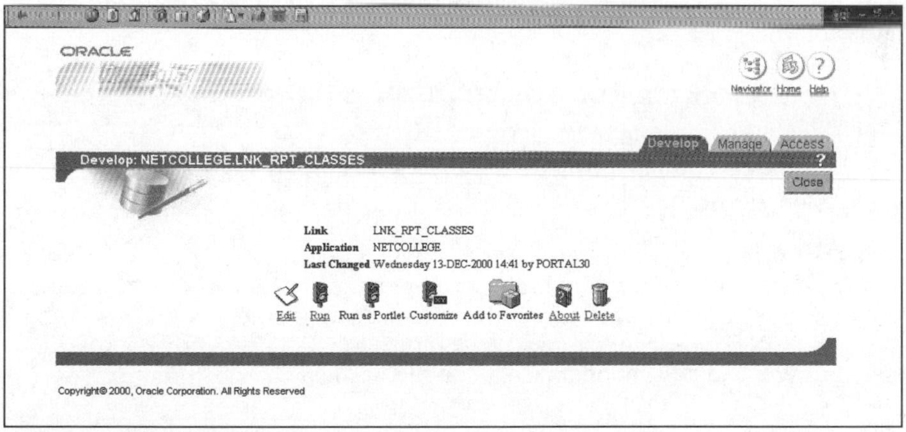

Figure 20-6: Run Link page

If all goes as planned, the result of testing the link is the Class Totals Report, the same as the one that is shown in Figure 20-2. The one difference that you will notice is that the title for the report has been changed to "Linked Class Year Report." You changed the title when you entered a value for the _title system parameter. Because of this change, Oracle Portal generates a URL in a specialized format:

```
http://whiskeysoda/pls/portal30/NETU.CH20_RPT_CLASSES.SHOW?p_ar
g_names=_title&p_arg_values=Linked+Class+Year+Report
```

The first part of the URL is the server name, port, virtual directory and data-access-descriptor for your portal site. The string NETU is the owner of the NETCOLLEGE application, and CH20_RPT_CLASSES.SHOW is the procedure call for the report.

The system parameter _title is passed to the report using an array of name/value pairs called p_arg_names and p_arg_values. Every Oracle Portal component includes these name/value pairs in their procedure declaration. Oracle Portal uses these name/value pairs to pass values to parameters. The two strings are always passed in pairs, the name first, followed by the value for the name. The name/value pairs are separated from the procedure call by the ? character, and name/value pairs are separated from one another by use of the & character.

> **Note**   Certain characters, such as the space character, cannot be safely transmitted in a URL over HTTP. Oracle Portal automatically provides a substitute for these problem characters on the client side — and then converts them back to their original values at the server side. You will often see the + character in place of the space character when you pass character strings to system parameters.

The use of parameter name/value pairs will become clearer when you link components together. We'll start by connecting the new link to the preexisting STUDENTS report.

2. Navigate back to the main Report Wizard and select the ch20_rpt_students report.

3. Edit the report and navigate to the Column Formatting panel, as shown in Figure 20-7.

Links are normally connected to columns unless you are using a link with a menu item. When you connect a column to a component, Portal can pass the value of the column to the component as a user parameter. This is where you can see the real power of links. The example Class Years report does not take any user parameters itself, but you can still connect it to a column in the STUDENTS report.

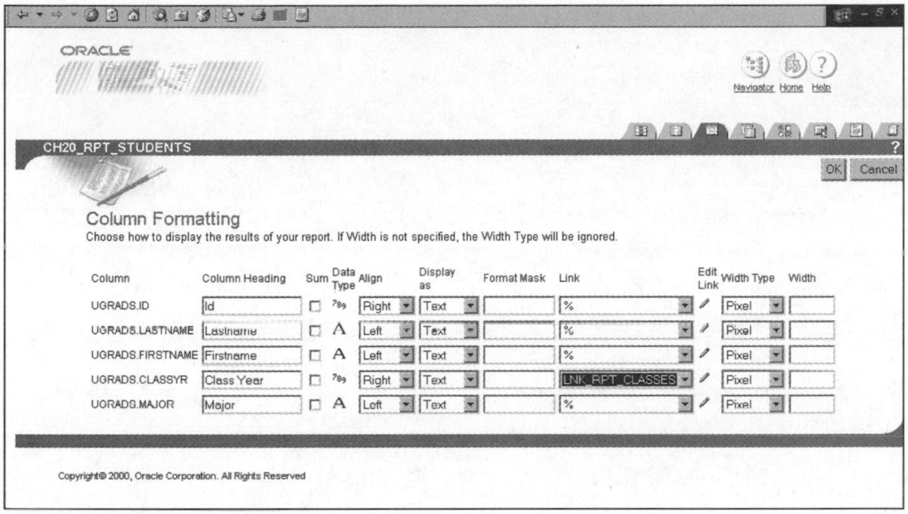

Figure 20-7: Adding a link to a report

4. Find the CLASSYR column and select the lnk_rpt_classes link in the link combo box, as shown in Figure 20-7.

5. Use the OK button to save this change and compile the modified report.

6. Choose the Run link to display the page shown in Figure 20-8.

This time when you run the UGRADS report, the classyr field appears as an HTML link. From the HTML perspective, the field is a link, and the link is built by Portal when the page is rendered using the link object you created with the Link Wizard.

7. Click the classyr field in any row to display the total, as shown in Figure 20-8.

When you use the link on the classyr field, you connect to the CLASSES report. No matter which row you click through, however, you are always taken to the same report because the link itself is a fixed link. Although the link is dynamically created by Portal for you, the destination point is fixed to a single location — the netu.ch20_rpt_classes.show procedure.

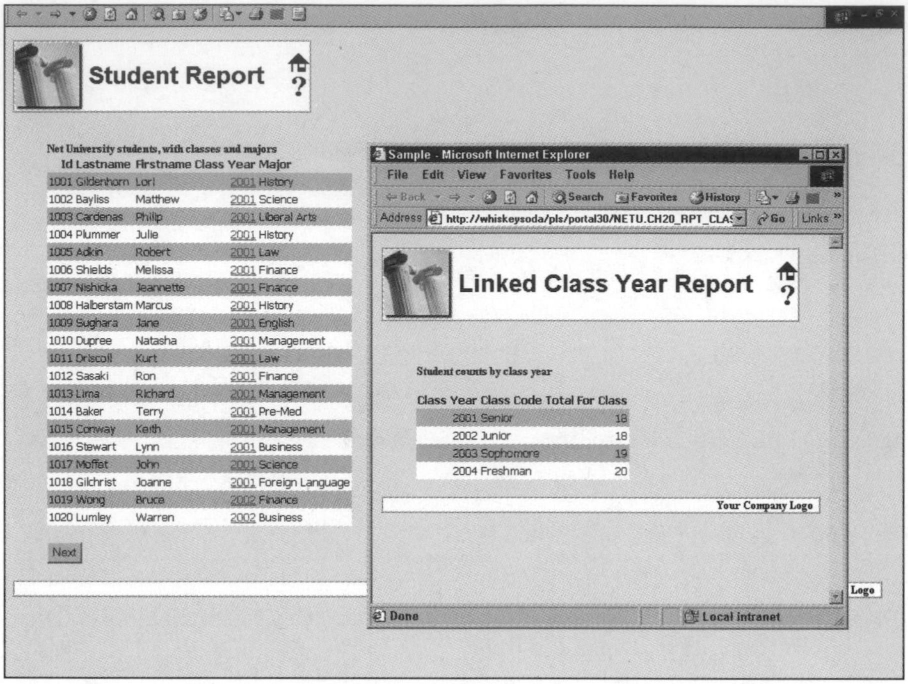

Figure 20-8: UGRADS report with links on the `classyr` field

No matter which record you choose, you will see HTML output similar to the data shown in Figure 20-8, because there are no user parameters being passed to the linked component. Ideally, the link would select only the student records for the class year that you chose from the UGRADS report. At the moment, your report has no way in which to divine this intention, but it does provide you with the ability to customize the link and your repot in order to achieve the desired result. In the next section, you will learn how to use parameters to limit the rows shown in a linked report.

Making a Dynamic Link

The difference between a fixed link and a dynamic link is as simple as the use of parameters. Every Portal component can potentially accept values through the use of parameters. The SHOW procedure for Portal objects expects to be passed parameters, but it executes with default values if the parameters are not supplied. When Portal creates the SHOW procedure, it includes sufficient information within the body of the procedure for it to run by itself, without using any parameters. A placeholder exists for parameters created as part of a component (the name/value pairs), and the Link Builder automatically finds them and displays them for you as necessary.

1. Load the ch20_cht_gender chart file into the Portal account using SQL*Plus.

The chart you loaded compares the number of males and females for a given class year, and accepts the class year as a parameter. Each parameter has three settings: the condition, the value type, and the value. The condition field is the comparison operator for the parameter and it is displayed as a combo box. The setting that you make for the condition determines how Portal manages the comparison of the parameter and the list of comparison operators matches the standard Oracle PL/SQL comparison operators. For example, if you want to make an exact match, select the equality (=) operator. On the other hand, if you want to locate all records greater than a certain value, select the greater than (>) operator, and so on.

2. Return to the Manage Links menu and create a new link called lnk_cht_gender in the NETCOLLEGE application.

3. Select the Portal Component radio button as the link type.

4. Locate the netu.ch20_cht_gender chart as the component name.

5. Click the Next arrow to display the page shown in Figure 20-9.

The only difference between the fixed link you created previously and a dynamic link is the use of user parameters. Portal displays all of the parameter fields for the selected component at the top part of the form. The list of parameters is constructed by interrogating the Portal component that you selected on the preceding panel in the wizard. (If you select the HTML radio button, the wizard will not even display the panel as shown in Figure 20-9.)

The Link Target Inputs panel shows a single user parameter that matches the parameter value in the chart — classyr. The Link Wizard detects the classyr parameter and includes it as a user parameter on the panel as shown Figure 20-9. Each custom parameter that appears in a target form, report, chart, hierarchy, calendar, menu, or Dynamic Page will appear as a user parameter in the Link Target panel.

In this example, Portal passes the user parameter value to the chart object. Initially the user parameter for classyr is left blank — which means that Portal will complete the parameter substitution at run-time. However, you can enter a default value directly into the user parameter field on the Link Targets panel. If you do, Oracle Portal will use the default value only if it encounters an empty parameter value at run-time. For example, if you were to enter the value **2001** into the classyr field at this point, the chart object would show gender comparisons for seniors. The ch20_cht_gender report already accepts the classyr as a parameter, so all that you need to do is pass the *current* class year value to the classyr field at run time. You can accomplish this task by leaving the classyr field blank on the Link Target Inputs panel.

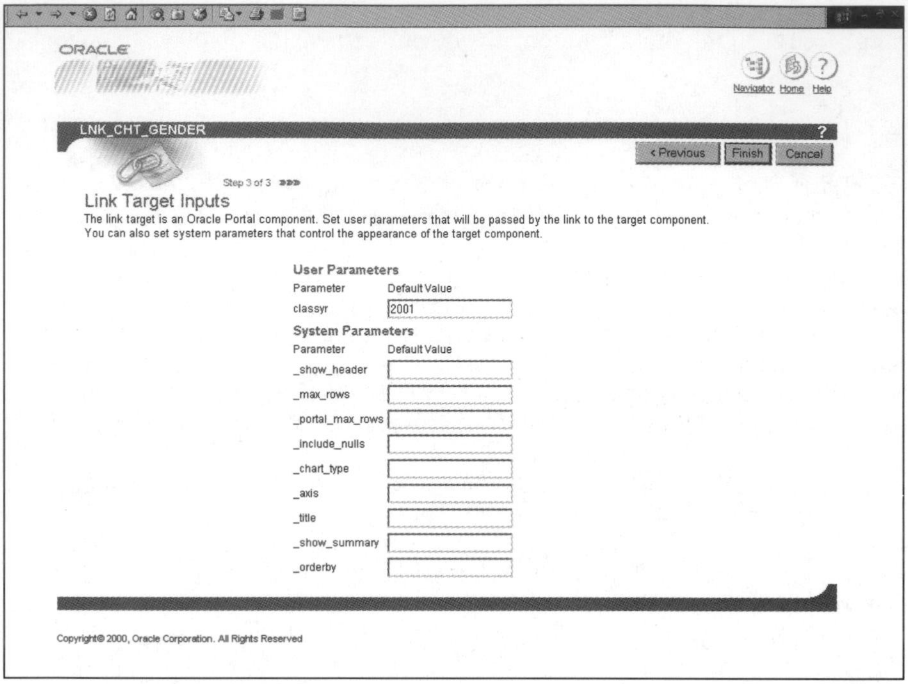

Figure 20-9: Link parameters

In order for this link to work, you have to be sure to connect the link to a component that passes the correct values for the CLASSYR column.

6. Enter the default value **2001** for the `classyr` field and **New Chart Title** for the `_title` parameter and press the Finish button to save the new link.

Note If you were to test this new link at this point you would see a chart that only displayed gender comparisons for seniors — because the chart has a default value of 2001.

The process of linking the variable to the link parameter is very simple. All you need to do is locate the `classyr` field on the report and select the proper link.

7. Edit the ch20_rpt_classes report and navigate to the column-formatting panel, as shown in Figure 20-10.

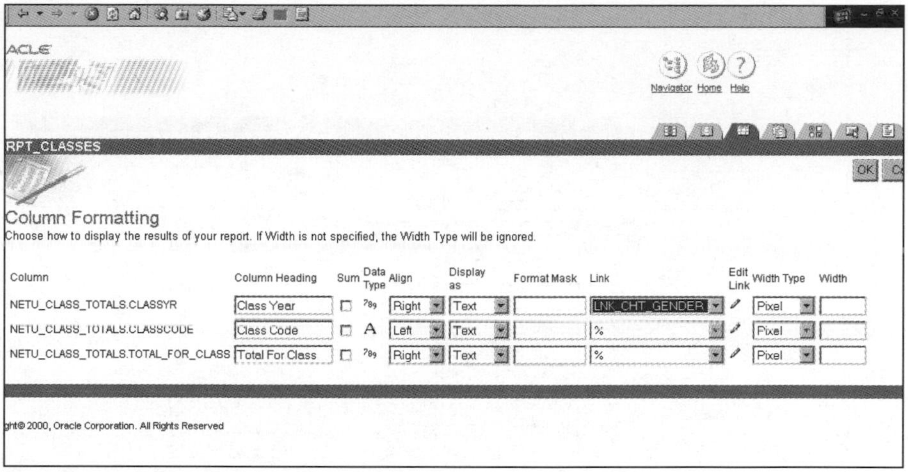

Figure 20-10: Passing column parameters

8. Navigate to the `classyr` field and select the entry lnk_cht_gender link.

In order to pass a value to a link you must connect the link to a column and then edit the properties of the link.

9. Click on the Edit Link button (the pencil) that appears to the right of the link combo box to display the form as shown in Figure 20-11.

In the first column Oracle portal displays a list of parameters for the current object (form, report, chart, hierarchy, calendar, chart or Dynamic Page). This list includes both user parameters and system parameters from the *linked object*. Portal generates this list of parameters by reading the source of the link that you entered on the preceding panel. Oracle Portal uses an underscore as the first character for the name of all system parameters, and this allows you to quickly separate user parameters from system parameters on the link edit panel. (Portal displays the user parameters at the top of the Parameter column as well).

The Condition combo box on the current panel provides you with a tool to specify a Boolean operator to be used with your user parameters. (System parameters cannot handle Boolean operators — so Oracle Portal will only display the condition combo box for user parameters.) When you are matching a value from one component to another you will generally use the equality operator (=) as the condition value. However, Portal allows you to choose from a number of Boolean operators in order to make your links more powerful. For example, you could choose to link from a `classyr` value to a chart that shows the gender breakdown for all of the class years "equal to or less than" the selected value by using the <= condition.

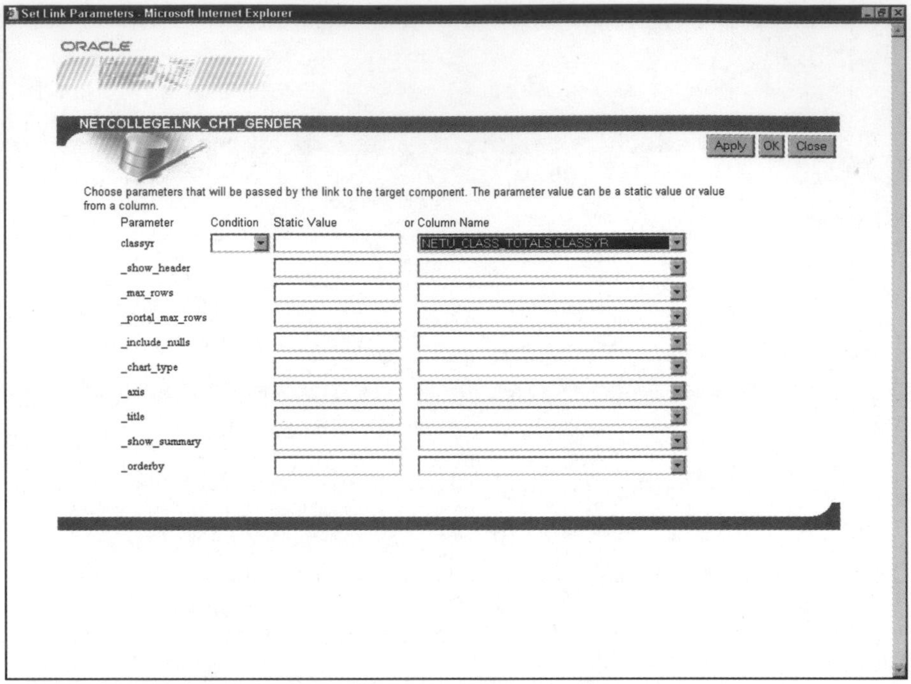

Figure 20-11: Editing link properties

Values that you provide within the Link Wizard override the values that are specified in the referenced component. When you set the new value for the title of the class year report in the Link Wizard it automatically replaced the title that was embedded in the report. This may not be the default behavior that you want. Portal provides the Static Value column so that you can force a value for any user or system parameter within the referenced component. The value that you enter on this panel will override the parameter value that is listed in the Link Wizard.

10. Locate the `_title` system parameter and change the Static Value to "Title Override — Gender Chart" in order to override the "New Chart Title" that you used within the lnk_cht_gender link.

While you can also specify static values for user parameters on this current panel as well, you will most often want to make use of dynamic values for user parameters. Each user parameter will display a matching combo box that contains the list of columns that appear in the linked component. In this example case, the editor displays the CLASSYR, CLASSCODE, and TOTAL_FOR_CLASS columns. Portal will automatically pass the value of the column that you specify to the link parameter at run-time (along with the column's COMPARISON operator). Selecting = and NET_CLASS_TOTALS.CLASSYR for the `classyr` parameter will cause Portal to pass the selected class year to the link when the link is called.

11. Select = and NET_CLASS_TOTALS.CLASSYR for the `classyr` parameter and press the OK button to save the change.

12. Press the OK button to close the report.

13. Use the Run link to execute the modified report.

14. Click on the CLASSYR link for the various class years, 2001, 2002, 2003, and 2004.

Figure 20-12 shows the results of testing the form and using several of the links. Portal automatically maps the value of the CLASSYR column to the `classyr` parameter in the gender chart. The Class Year Report becomes a drill-through to detailed information about the selected class year.

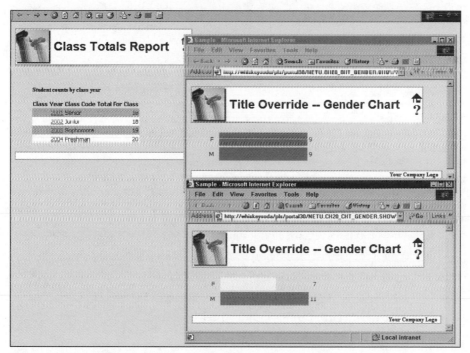

Figure 20-12: Class Totals Report with Gender Chart Overlays

> **Note**
>
> The `classyr` value is passed via the link as part of a URL as a string — so you normally do not have to worry about converting numbers to strings and vice versa.

The real power of links is the ability to chain them together and allow your users to drill through your Web applications. Although you connected the chart object to the CLASSES report, you can get to the chart object by starting with the very first UGRADS report and drilling through to the chart.

15. Locate the ch20_rpt_students report and use the Run link to test it.

16. Click any `classyr` field to display the ch20_rpt_classes report. Notice that the `classyr` field on the report is now displayed as a link itself.

17. Click any `classyr` field to display the chart as shown in Figure 20-12.

Using Links to Update Data

Portal's Link Wizard provides one additional piece of functionality that is critical in building interactive applications. In Part III of this book, you learned how to build reports to display data, and forms to both read and write data. Portal uses the link object to drive data entry forms by passing key values to form objects. When you build a data edit form, Portal does not display any data in the form, nor does it provide update buttons unless the form object is passed key values when it is executed.

1. Load the form ch20_frm_students using SQL*Plus.

2. Run ch20_frm_students to display the page shown in Figure 20-13.

Notice that the form does not appear with any data loaded into it and the only options are INSERT, QUERY, and RESET. Internally, the procedure that renders the form looks for parameter values to be passed to a procedure as record selection keys. If it finds these parameters, then Portal uses the parameter values to load data into the form and display additional buttons. By default, none of these values are passed to the procedure and you must pass them to the procedure yourself either manually or by using links.

3. Return to the Link Wizard and create a new link owned by the NETU account called **lnk_frm_students**.

4. Choose the Portal Component radio button.

5. Load **netu.ch20_frm_students** as the component name.

6. Navigate to the Link Target Inputs panel.

All of the fields for the form are available as parameters, so it is possible to restrict the display of the form by entering query parameters directly. Because you can edit these parameters when you use the link with a component there is no need to enter any values on this panel.

7. Use the Finish button to save the new link.

8. Edit the form ch20_rpt_students and navigate to the Column Formatting panel.

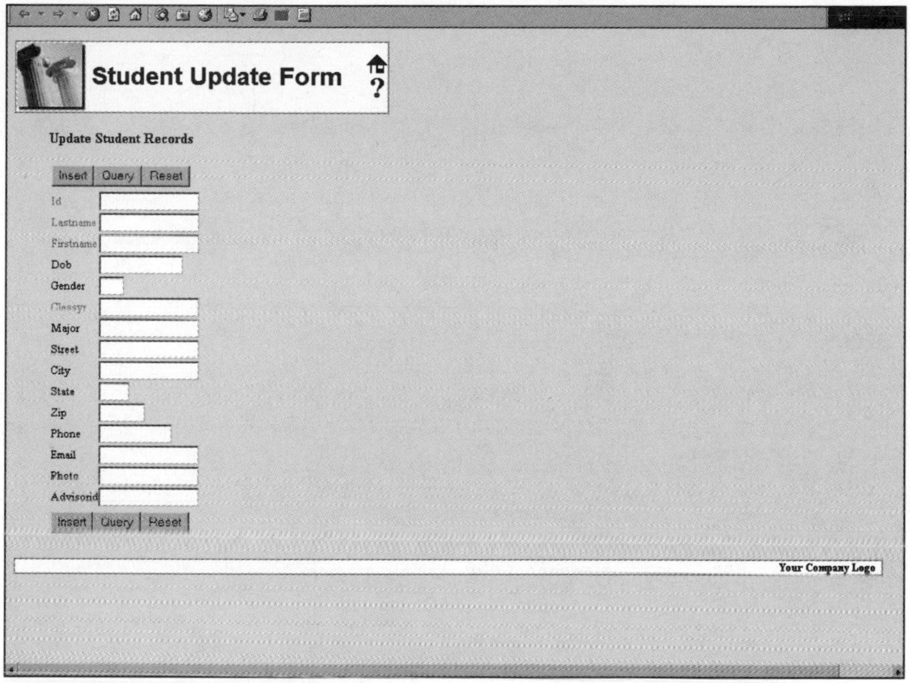

Figure 20-13: Update UGRADS form

9. Add lnk_frm_students to the ID column as shown in Figure 20-14.

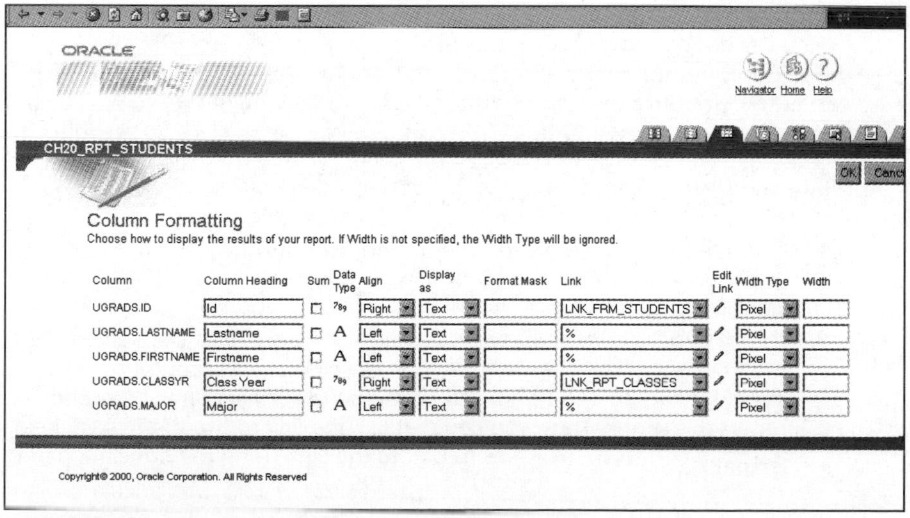

Figure 20-14: Column Formatting for the ID column

10. Use the Edit Link button (the pencil) to edit the link parameters as shown in Figure 20-15.

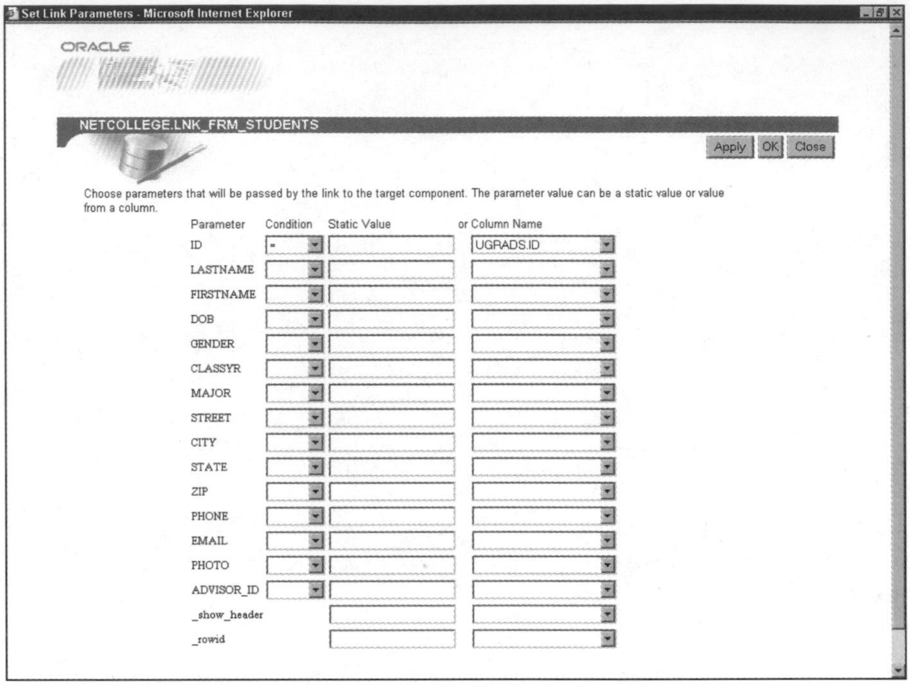

Figure 20-15: Edit Link Parameters for ID field

Portal needs to load a record into the browser in order to allow users to edit the data. The Edit Link panel allows you to pass this parameter to the called form. You can either pass the required primary key values or pass the ROWID to the form. Figure 20-15 shows the ID field (the primary key for the UGRADS table) being passed to the link. The ch20_frm_students form will receive the ID parameter and it will know enough to fetch the record and fill the form with the correct data.

11. Choose the equality comparison operator and the UGRADS.ID as the Column Name parameter for the ID user parameter.

Tip If you do not want the ID to display on the report — but you still want to pass it to the form — you can choose Hidden in the Display As combo box on the preceding panel (Figure 20-14). Portal will allow you to connect any one of the fields on the report to the link. Thus, you could attach the link to the LASTNAME field, but then pass the correct ID/UGRADS.ID pair to the Link using the Edit Link panel.

12. Use the OK button to save the link and then use the OK button again to save the modified report. Use the Run link to test the report and then click on the ID for the first record when the report displays to show the panel in Figure 20-16.

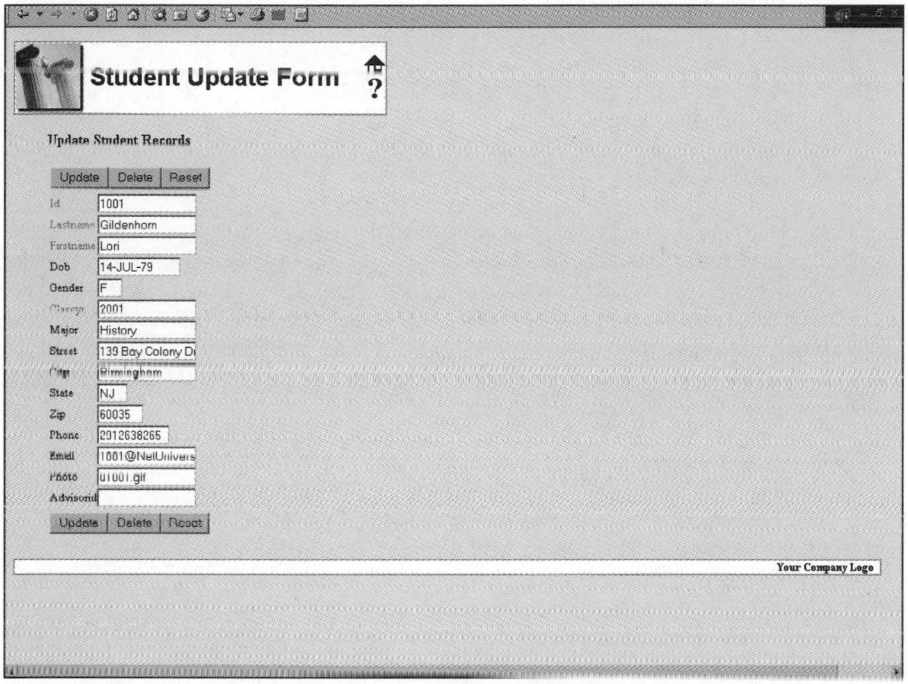

Figure 20-16: Ch20_frm_students form filled with data

> **Note** If the Update and Delete buttons have been deselected in the form object, they will not appear even if the primary key parameters have been properly passed.

When the form appears this time, it is filled with data as shown in Figure 20-16. The procedure that renders the form has been passed the proper parameters and it therefore displays the data and additional form buttons for Update and Delete.

13. Make some changes to the displayed record and then use the Update button to save the changes.

Using Portal Parameter Arrays

You might notice that when you select a particular link, Portal builds a URL based on the data value you selected.

Click the link for ID 1001 in the CH20_RPT_STUDENTS report and then view the link that appears in the location bar in your browser:

```
http://whiskeysoda/pls/portal30/PORTAL30.wwa_app_module.link?p_
arg_names=_moduleid&p_arg_values=1213459820&p_arg_names=_sessio
nid&p_arg_values=&p_arg_names=ID&p_arg_values=1001&p_arg_names=
_id_cond&p_arg_values=%3D
```

All parameters are passed to Portal components using the p_arg_names and p_arg_values pairs. Any Portal component that accepts parameters (including display options parameters) can accept a formatted parameter string as a URL. Portal uses the question mark (?) character to indicate the end of the procedure name and the start of the parameter list, and the ampersand (&) character to separate parameters from one another. Each parameter is passed using a fixed structure as follows:

```
p_arg_names=name&p_arg_values=value
```

The p_arg_names= portion of the string is a fixed required value and it denotes that the next value Portal finds should be read as a parameter name. The name portion of the string is read as the name for the parameter. Next up is the & character, which separates the name of the parameter from the value of the parameter. The p_arg_values= string tells Portal that the next value Portal finds should be read as the value for a parameter. The value itself is matched up with the parameter name that was passed just ahead of the value. So, in plain English, the substring tells Portal that the next parameter is the name of the parameter and the value for this parameter is value.

The result is an incredibly powerful and elegant means of allowing procedures to accept a dynamic array of parameters. Portal displays the complete list of parameters for any component as part of the Manage Component menu.

1. Navigate to the Manage Component panel for the ch20_cht_gender chart.

2. Click the Show Call Interface link to display the page shown in Figure 20-17.

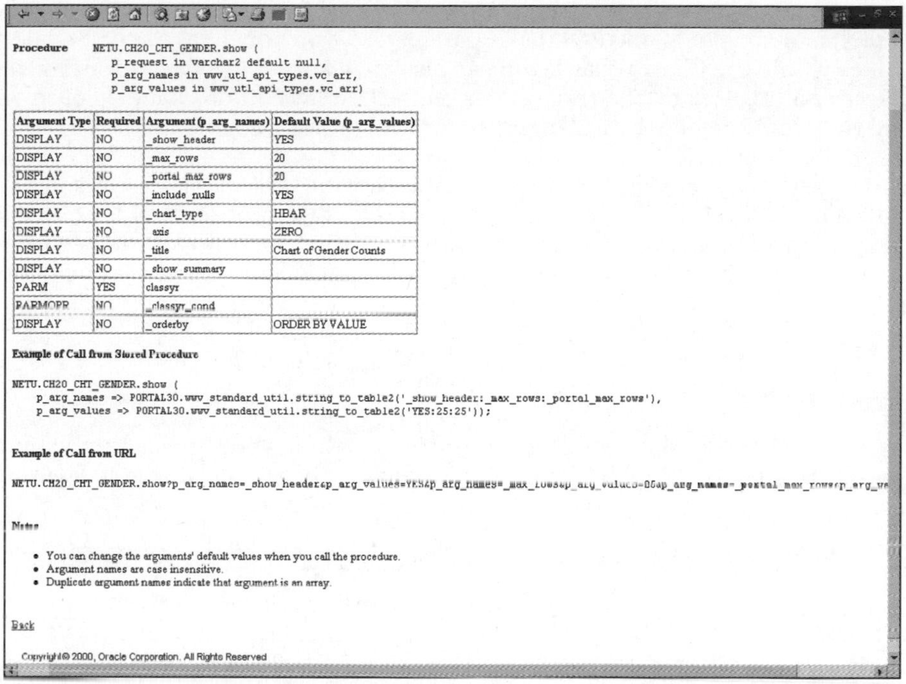

Procedure

```
NETU.CH20_CHT_GENDER.show (
    p_request in varchar2 default null,
    p_arg_names in wwv_utl_api_types.vc_arr,
    p_arg_values in wwv_utl_api_types.vc_arr)
```

Argument Type	Required	Argument (p_arg_names)	Default Value (p_arg_values)
DISPLAY	NO	_show_header	YES
DISPLAY	NO	_max_rows	20
DISPLAY	NO	_portal_max_rows	20
DISPLAY	NO	_include_nulls	YES
DISPLAY	NO	_chart_type	HBAR
DISPLAY	NO	_axis	ZERO
DISPLAY	NO	_title	Chart of Gender Counts
DISPLAY	NO	_show_summary	
PARM	YES	classyr	
PARMOPR	NO	_classyr_cond	
DISPLAY	NO	_orderby	ORDER BY VALUE

Example of Call from Stored Procedure

```
NETU.CH20_CHT_GENDER.show (
    p_arg_names => PORTAL30.wwv_standard_util.string_to_table2('_show_header:_max_rows:_portal_max_rows'),
    p_arg_values => PORTAL30.wwv_standard_util.string_to_table2('YES:25:25'));
```

Example of Call from URL

```
NETU.CH20_CHT_GENDER.show?p_arg_names=_show_header&p_arg_values=YES&p_arg_names=_max_rows&p_arg_values=25&p_arg_names=_portal_max_rows&p_arg_va
```

Notes

- You can change the arguments' default values when you call the procedure.
- Argument names are case insensitive.
- Duplicate argument names indicate that argument is an array.

Back

Copyright© 2000, Oracle Corporation. All Rights Reserved

Figure 20-17: Component Call Interface panel

The top part of the panel shows a table with all of the valid parameters for a given component organized according to four values: argument type, required indicator, argument name, and default value. Display argument types control things such as the header and font size. (The specific list of display options varies by component object type.) Argument types marked as PARM elements indicate that the parameter is a user parameter. In the case of the GENDER chart, the `classyr` field in the UGRADS table is used a query parameter, and it is marked as a PARM value. Portal creates a matching parameter for each PARM type called the PARMOPR, which is short for Parameter Operator. Portal enables you to pass the comparison operator as a parameter to the component using the PARMOPR string.

So, although the example GENDER chart accepts a `classyr` parameter using an equality comparison, you can override the equality operator (=) and use the greater than operator (>) if you wish.

The Required column indicates whether any particular parameter is required to execute the component, and you will find that most BIND variables are required parameters. The final two columns show the `p_arg_names` and the default `p_arg_values` for each parameter. Although the GENDER chart does not provide defaults for the PARM and PARMOPR parameters, you could have specified default values within the Chart Wizard. You can also view alternative values for any of the display parameters by changing values on the Display Options panel in each wizard and then redisplaying the call interface for the resulting component.

Portal displays a sample call interface just below the table of parameters in two formats. First, Portal shows the call interface as a PL/SQL procedure call, so that you can embed the component inside of another PL/SQL procedure. Portal also shows the same procedure as a URL string, which you can use to embed the component as a manual link within any Web page. For example, take the following URL string:

```
http://whiskeysoda/pls/portal30/NETU.CH20_CHT_GENDER.SHOW?p_arg
_names=classyr&p_arg_values=2001
```

If you were to enter this string into the location field of your browser (substituting your server, port, and DAD entries) you would get the results shown in Figure 20-18.

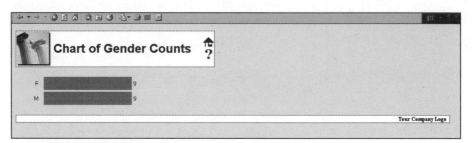

Figure 20-18: Gender chart using a manual URL entry

Portal renders the chart by using the `classyr` parameter that you passed as a Web URL address. You can even change the chart entirely by passing in a different comparison operator as follows:

```
http://whiskeysoda/pls/portal30/NETU.CH20_CHT_GENDER.SHOW?p_arg
_names=classyr&p_arg_values=2001&p_arg_names=_classyr_cond&p_ar
g_values=>
```

In this case, the `classyr` parameter of 2001 was used as a *greater-than* comparison to yield the output shown in Figure 20-19.

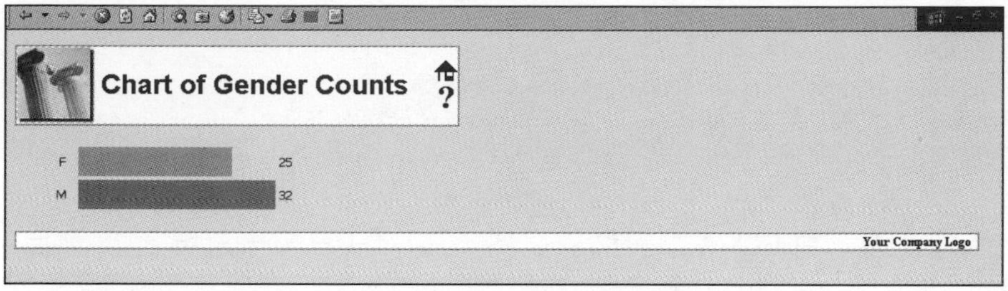

Figure 20-19: Gender chart with a greater-than operator

You are free to pass parameters in any order, but they must always be passed using the same format, with the `p_arg_names` string first and the `p_arg_values` string second. Conditions can be passed ahead of comparison operators and display options can be mixed in with PARM parameters as long as you follow the required format.

You can use these URL strings wherever URL values are permitted, and you will find them especially useful for menus. For example, you could build a Portal menu with four options for the GENDER chart, one for each class year. The link text for each menu item would be a URL string with the proper parameter for the class year as shown in the preceding URLs.

Summary

Portal's Link Builder is a useful tool for providing drill-up and drill-down access for your dynamic database data. Consistent use of links can make your data much easier to navigate through and can help your users make information out of raw data. Parameters enable the links to respond appropriately to specific end user requests, which can make your Web application much more intuitive. Parameters also have the effect of making the data on your site appear fresher and more up to date, as each new interaction by a user may take him or her down a new path. It's best to add links to your application after you have built most of your user interface objects, because they are derived from these objects. When used in conjunction with menus, you can quickly bundle blocks of database content together into a cohesive application in record time.

✦   ✦   ✦

Integrating PL/SQL Logic

◆ ◆ ◆ ◆

In This Chapter

Using Oracle's
PL/SQL Web Toolkit

Integrating HTP and
PL/SQL Web Toolkit
Procedures with
Portal

Debugging and
Advanced Concepts

◆ ◆ ◆ ◆

The precursor to Oracle's Portal product was a set of PL/SQL packages that enabled you to output Oracle data in HTML format. These packages were combined with the PL/SQL cartridge within the Oracle9iAS to provide a solution for building dynamic HTML applications from Oracle data. The original PL/SQL packages were known as the HTF/HTP packages, and they offered a very low-level interface to both the database and HTML. Coding the creation of HTML pages at this level is not as productive as working with Portal, but the packages do enable you to control the data in a fashion that is not possible with Portal alone.

You can take advantage of the power of these packages, as well as the more generalized ability of PL/SQL to implement logic, when you build components in the Portal environment. In this chapter, we look at building some of these advanced features, as well as investigating techniques for handling errors within procedures and debugging custom PL/SQL procedures.

Using Oracle HTML Packages

As part of the Oracle9iAS architecture, Oracle created a series of procedures that enable you to embed HTML code within PL/SQL procedures. There are a large number of procedures, which in turn are organized into three to four separate Oracle packages: with the HTML routines being grouped into the HTP (or hypertext procedure) package and the HTF (or hypertext function) package.

The HTF and HTP packages are almost identical in functionality and design. Each of the major HTML tags is represented by a procedure within the HTP package. The various procedures within the HTP package output HTML tags along with custom data and send the results back to the current output stream. The HTF procedures shadow the HTP procedures and are used solely for nesting functions. In most cases, you will use the HTP procedures, because HTF calls are not passed back to the PL/SQL gateway. They are only used to format results within a call to an HTP procedure. For example, to print a string of bold text into the standard output stream, you could use the following fragment of code:

```
htp.bold('Hello World!');
```

However, if you wish to print this string with strong emphasis, you need to wrap the bold command within the strong command as follows:

```
htp.bold((htf.strong('Hello World!'));
```

The HTF package is designed solely for handling this type of contingency, and you will find that every HTP procedure has an associated HTF procedure. Unless you are nesting functions frequently, however, you will usually use the HTP version of each procedure.

Each HTP/HTF procedure is designed to support one of the HTML tags, and Oracle continues to add new procedures to these two packages. The Oracle9*i*AS and Oracle Database generally come equipped with these packages by default, but Portal automatically installs them if they are not already in place.

Note
Oracle 9*i*AS Portal and Portal 3.0 require a special set of these packages that are designed to work specifically with the mod_PLSQL Apache interface. When you install Oracle Portal, it will ask permission to overwrite your existing PL/SQL Web Toolkit Packages.

In addition to inserting HTML tags, you may have the need to handle some specialized Web processing such as reading and writing cookies. Oracle provides the PL/SQL Web Toolkit to address this requirement. The PL/SQL Web Toolkit is built on the same HTF/HTP foundation as Portal. We introduce the nine separate PL/SQL Web Toolkit packages in the next section of this chapter.

The HTML procedures in the HTF and HTP packages can be grouped into the following logical units:

✦ Printing and Formatting

✦ Document Structure

✦ Document Body

✦ Frames

✦ Lists

✦ Tables

✦ Form Objects

Because you use these procedures as you add PL/SQL code to expand the reach of the HTML pages created for you by Portal, you should understand what they do for you.

Printing and formatting

The printing and formatting procedures send a string of text into the standard output stream. They are the main mechanism for creating and formatting text output. You will find most of these procedures familiar if you are experienced in the use of the basic HTML tags. Table 21-1 lists the major printing and formatting procedures, and most of these tags support both the HTF and HTP versions.

Note

We have only included those procedures that are normally used within Portal. The actual list of procedures is quite extensive, but many of these additional procedures will either be ignored by Portal or will interfere with the processing of Portal if explicitly used.

Table 21-1
Printing and Formatting Procedures

Procedure	Description
htp.print (*string*)	Sends a standard string of text to the output stream of the PL/SQL gateway.
htp.emphasis (*string*)	Formats the enclosed string with emphasis tags.
htp.keyboard (*string*)	Formats the output string in monospace formatting suitable for showing code or user input instructions.
htp.teletype (*string*)	Formats the text in typewriter style — similar to the keyboard procedure.
htp.strong (*string*)	Formats the enclosed string with strong HTML tags.
htp.bold (*string*)	Formats the string in boldface text.
htp.italic (*string*)	Formats the string in italics text.
htp.br	Inserts a new line into the output stream.
htp.line	Inserts a horizontal line in the output stream.

Document structure

Portal automatically creates document objects for you in the process of building your Dynamic Pages. However, Oracle9iAS developers that use the HTP/HTF packages directly are responsible for building the complete HTML page from start to finish. To address this requirement, the HTF/HTP packages come equipped with procedures that you can use to design the required HTML document structures in addition to the HTML data. Using these particular tags within Portal components typically has little or no effect, because Portal has already specified them. You must make use of them, however, if you are creating your own complete components. Table 21-2 lists the major HTP functions that control HTML document formatting.

Table 21-2
Document Structure Procedures

Procedure	Description
htp.htmlOpen	Creates the required <HTML> tag within a document. Using this procedure can cause problems within Portal, as Portal normally opens and closes pages for you.
htp.htmlClose	Generates the closing tag </HTML> used with htmlOpen.
htp.headOpen	Defines the HTML document head by inserting the <HEAD> tag.
htp.headClose	Generates the closing tag for the document head </HEAD>.
htp.bodyOpen	Inserts the <BODY> tag into the HTML document.
htp.bodyClose	Generates the closing tag for the document body.
htp.title (*string*)	Inserts a title into your document that is bracketed by the <TITLE> and </TITLE> tags.
htp.meta (*description string, name, content*)	Generates document information for use by the browser. Typically, you would use the meta tag to provide information for search engines. This does not apply when working with Portal, because the pages are dynamically generated. However, you can also use this tag to refresh or redirect Web pages. For example, htp.meta('Refresh',NULL,5); causes the page to refresh every five seconds.

The meta procedure is powerful enough that it warrants some extra discussion. Within the HTML world, you are probably familiar with using the <META> tag for providing search indexes with page information. For example, using the following code as the standard <META> tag of your page enables Web search programs to index this page as being related to information about Portal:

```
<META NAME="description", CONTENT="Portal, oracle, html,
programming">
```

However, with Portal, the pages are generated dynamically for you from the database and Web search engines may not have access to these pages to begin with, which invalidates the use of the <META> tag for this particular purpose in some cases. Typically, Web crawlers can traverse through URLs dynamically, even those that are generated by an application server. All that they really need is a starting point that is stored outside of the database. Oracle9*i*AS uses the Apache server as its Web server and you can easily store index HTML pages on the file system for the Apache server. Web crawlers can read these pages and then traverse through the remaining, Dynamic Pages as required.

Note This technique will only work with public portal pages, because Web crawlers cannot automatically log on to private Web pages.

You can use the <META> tag to set other attributes that Portal will not override. For example, you can use the <META> tag to cause a page to refresh according to a set interval as shown in the following fragment:

```
<META HTTP-EQUIV="Refresh" CONTENT="5">
```

In this example case, the browser automatically refreshes the page every five seconds. You could also add additional parameters to the CONTENT parameter to redirect users to a new page, or ensure that the browser fetches a new copy and not a cached copy of the page. The `htp.meta` procedure can be used to send this type of information into the Portal HTTP streams as shown in the following line of code:

```
htp.meta('Refresh',NULL,'5;http://my_server/someotherpage.htm');
```

The first parameter is the `meta` type and the second parameter is the name or description of the tag. The second parameter is generally left as NULL for refreshes and redirects. The final parameter is a string value that gets mapped to the CONTENT parameter and you are free to supply any valid content values to this string.

Advanced document structure procedures

Oracle does not differentiate between the capabilities of various HTF/HTP procedures within the documentation, but from an ease-of-use perspective it helps to break the more complicated routines into their own category. So far, you have looked at routines that are mostly simple procedural calls. The procedures in this section require some additional explanation because they each accept a number of run-time parameters that can have a dramatic effect on the output. Each of these procedures maps to a standard HTML tag, but you need to work with them carefully to understand how the tags are generated from the values you load into the procedures. Oracle supports a long list of these objects, but Portal-compatible routines are as follows:

✦ Anchor

✦ Comments

✦ FontOpen/FontClose

✦ Header

✦ Img

✦ Mailto

✦ PreOpen/PreClose

Anchor

The `htp.anchor` procedure is one of the most powerful procedures in that it enables you to build links to other objects from within PL/SQL procedures. Within the Portal environment, you can explicitly embed anchors in your documents within any of the text blocks. The `htp.anchor` procedure gives you the tools to build dynamic links inside Portal components. Calls to the `htp.anchor` procedure take the following format:

```
htp.anchor(URL string, Text/image string, Name, Attributes)
```

The first parameter is the URL link that is called when the user attempts to access the link at run time, and the second parameter is the string of text or image that connects to the link. You can also name the link by using the `Name` parameter and pass along any additional HTML attributes supported by the `anchor` tag in the attributes parameter position. For example, to link a string of text to another page you might use the following code:

```
htp.anchor('http://my_server/mypage.html', htf.bold('Link to
this page'),null,null);
```

In the preceding snippet of code, notice the use of the HTF version of the bold procedure. This was necessary in order to nest the bolding of the text within the call to the anchor procedure. If you wish, you can add some parameters to the `anchor` tag, such as `TARGET=new_window`, to cause the link to open into a new browser. Within static HTML pages, you are likely to use anchors with `name` values to enable users to jump from one section of the page to another. This is less common within Portal, because Portal automatically paginates output for you.

Comments

The `htp.comment` procedure is used to embed developer comments into the source for a Web page. By default, your users do not see these comments displayed on the page, but they become visible if users look at the source for the page. You can use the comments procedure to embed system documentation into your output files that can be effective in debugging problems at run time. The comments procedure accepts a single string of text as shown in the following example:

```
htp.comment('PAGE=ALUMNI1, AUTH=JFM, VERSION=1.8');
```

You can use PL/SQL code to dynamically build the comment string and pass it to the comments procedure or you can hard-code the string. In the preceding code block, the comment string includes some author information along with a version indicator. Should a user have trouble with the application, your support desk could instruct them to view the source and search for this string. You would then be able to track the version of the component that caused the problem.

fontOpen and fontClose

The htp.fontOpen and htp.fontClose procedures are always used in pairs to set the font characteristics for a given block of text. The htp.fontOpen procedure accepts four parameters as follows:

```
htp.fontOpen(color, fontface, size, attributes)
```

The color parameter is passed as a string using the hex color format (#C0C0C0), and the fontface is a string that matches a font known to the browser. The size parameter is an integer value and refers to the relative size of the text. Positive integers are used to increase the size, and negative values can be passed to shrink the associated text. The call to this procedure should preface the generation of your text and a call to htp.fontClose is required to end the font setting as shown in the following code:

```
htp.fontOpen('#C0C0C0',null, -2,null);
htp.print('Hello World!');
htp.fontClose;
```

Most HTML tags support a number of custom extensions commonly referred to as attributes. You can pass values for these attributes by using the attributes parameter for any HTP procedure that supports them.

Header

The htp.header procedure is used to input document headings and levels within your HTML pages. Although Portal automatically includes such information in the pages that it builds on your behalf, you can combine the htp.header procedure with dynamic database data to provide an additional layer of customization. The htp.header procedure accepts four parameters as shown in the following code segment:

```
htp.header(level number, text string, alignment, wrap-
indicator);
```

The level number is an integer value that sets the heading level for the associated string and the text string is the value displayed as the header. The last two parameters are optional and are used to set the alignment (with the values of left, right, and center) and whether or not the text string should wrap around (with the values of wrap and nowrap). The following block of code shows the htp.header procedure in action:

```
htp.header(1, 'This is a level one heading',null,null);
```

Img

The `htp.img` or image procedure is used to load a graphic image onto a page. Oracle enables you to load simple images as well as images along with image maps. Dynamic images are particularly useful if you are planning to add your own menu bar to the body of a form. The format of the `htp.img` procedure is as follows:

```
htp.img(url, alignment, alternate, ismap, attributes);
```

The only required parameter for this procedure is the `url`, which is a string that points to the location of the image. You are free to pass a string value for the alignment parameter to justify the image, and you can pass an alternative value to be displayed in the event that the browser does not support images. Oracle provides an additional set of procedures to create image maps, and the fourth parameter (`ismap`) passes the name of the associated map file. As with any of the other extended HTML tags, you are free to pass strings of other attributes, such as horizontal and vertical positioning, using the `attributes` parameter. The following block of code loads the logo image from a virtual directory into a fixed size on a page:

```
htp.img('/netu/netu_logo.gif',null,null,null,'HEIGHT=20,
WIDTH=30');
```

Calls to the `htp.img` procedure can include references to Portal virtual directories as shown in the preceding example. Oracle provides a second version of this procedure, `htp.img2`, which is used for handling images with client-side image maps.

Mailto

The `htp.mailto` procedure creates an HTML HREF tag that points to the text and electronic mail address specified in the call to the procedure. The format of the `htp.mailto` procedure accepts four parameters as follows:

```
htp.mailto(emaddr, text, name, attributes);
```

The `emaddr` and `text` fields are associated with the e-mail address string and text description that displays on the page. You can provide a link name for the mailto link as well as passing the usual string of extended attributes as shown in the following example:

```
htp.mailto('joe_smith@net.com', 'webmaster@Netu',null,null);
```

preOpen and preClose

There are cases in which you do not want the browser to format your text, but rather to display the text directly as it was entered into the source file. Oracle provides a pair of procedures that initiate a preformatted section and then terminate a preformatted section with the `htp.preOpen` and `htp.preClose` routines. Although `htp.preOpen` accepts some parameters, it is usually executed without parameters. While your browser normally ignores things such as tabs, spaces, and carriage returns, it displays all text between the <PRE> and </PRE> tags exactly as entered. As the following example shows, you can use these two procedures to output text in a specific format:

```
htp.preOpen;
htp.print('                        Alumni Donations Report');
htp.print('                            Summary Data');
htp.preClose;
```

Additional procedures

Oracle provides additional procedures that enable you to create objects such as HTML Lists, Tables, and Frames. Because Portal creates most of these objects for you, it is not likely that you need to use these procedures directly within Portal. Each new release of Oracle9iAS and Portal includes new procedures provided to support enhancements to the HTML standard. You can review the procedures in the OAS_PUBLIC USERID using the database navigator capability of Portal to look for new procedures and additional procedures such as list, table, and frames.

Forms

Additional sets of procedures that have some relevance to your work with Portal are the form-building procedures. Portal, of course, provides an advanced form generation capability all on its own, but you may find the need to create some additional subforms in order to support specialized processing within one of your component objects. For example, you may wish to add some additional buttons to a form to add new functionality not provided through the Portal run options. (Separate forms require separate Submit buttons, however, which can lead to unintended results.) By embedding a form object into the page, you can add your own navigational and data entry fields. Table 21-3 lists the various form procedures and their example usage.

Table 21-3
Sample Form Procedures

Procedure	Description	Example
htp.formOpen(url, method,target, encryption type, attributes)	Creates a form object that can host subform items such as buttons and text fields.	htp.formOpen ('Netu.myproc.show', 'POST');
htp.formClose	Closes a previously opened form. Embeds a </FORM> tag into the output stream.	htp.formClose;

Continued

	Table 21-3 *(continued)*	
Procedure	**Description**	**Example**
`htp.formSubmit(name, value, attributes)`	Creates a submit button within a form area.	`htp.formSubmit (NULL,'Push Me!');`
`htp.formText(name,size, maxlength,value, attributes)`	Creates a text field of the specified length (`size`) that will accept a specified number of characters of input (`maxlength`).	`htp.formText ('lastname',20,30);`
`htp.formPassword(name, size,maxlength,value, attributes)`	Creates a text field that masks the input characters as they are typed.	`htp.formPassword ('Password',10,20);`
`htp.formHidden(name, value,attributes)`	Creates a text field that is not displayed on the form — useful for storing embedded information within a Web page.	`htp.formHidden ('secretfield');`
`htp.formCheckbox(name, value,checked, attributes)`	Generates a check box field within a form. Values are separated by the underscore character.	`htp.formCheckbox ('yesno','Yes_No');`

Oracle provides HTP procedure calls for all of the common form objects, and you are free to use them within Portal components. Because Portal uses form objects, you might be tempted to use the individual form items by themselves without using the surrounding `htp.formOpen` and `htp.formClose` routines. We advise against doing so, because the structure of the output does not always guarantee that your fields are embedded between valid form tags.

It is safer to create your form objects inside explicitly created form tags as shown in the following example:

```
htp.formOpen('/netu/mycgi');
htp.print('Username ');
htp.formText('v_username',10,20);
htp.br;
htp.print('Password');
htp.formPassword('v_password',10,20);
htp.br;
htp.formClose;
```

This example code segment creates a simple form that displays a user name and password field for the user. The use of specialized form items within a page can provide you with additional flexibility you can use to supplement your Portal components. In the third section of this chapter, we show you how to apply these routines to the PL/SQL code entry points within the various wizards. However, before you begin experimenting with the HTF and HTP procedures, it is important to look at one additional set of functionality.

Using Oracle9*i*AS's PL/SQL Web Toolkit

In order to improve the interaction between the database and the Web browser, Oracle provides an additional set of procedures called the PL/SQL Web Toolkits, which were created for the original Oracle Web Application Server. Oracle has since renamed the Oracle Web Application Server to Oracle9*i*AS, but the utilities themselves still carry the legacy of the Web Toolkit name.

The PL/SQL Web Toolkits provide some functionality above and beyond the basic HTF/HTP utilities, and you may need some of this functionality within Portal. Portal itself uses the PL/SQL Web Toolkits, so they are part of the Portal installation, even if you are not using the Oracle9*i*AS. Table 21-4 lists the various PL/SQL Web Toolkits along with a basic description of their capabilities.

<table>
<tr><td colspan="2">Table 21-4
PL/SQL Web Toolkit Utility Packages</td></tr>
<tr><td>Package</td><td>Description</td></tr>
<tr><td>OWA_COOKIE</td><td>This package sends cookies to and from your client browser to the server. Cookies are helpful in storing information across sessions, and the OWA_COOKIE package simplifies the process of working with cookies. Portal itself uses this package to maintain login information between the client browser and the listener.</td></tr>
<tr><td>OWA_IMAGE</td><td>This package enables you to handle image maps by providing a set of procedures to determine the X and Y coordinates of a mouse click within an image map.</td></tr>
<tr><td>OWA_INIT</td><td>The OWA_INIT package provides a series of constant values used to help you convert cookie settings between time zone variations when the client and server are located within different time zones.</td></tr>
<tr><td>OWA_PATTERN</td><td>This package contains a set of procedures used for string manipulation and search mapping. The three functions within this procedure offer you three different techniques for performing pattern matching between strings of data.</td></tr>
<tr><td>OWA_OPT_LOCK</td><td>This procedure implements a general-purpose optimistic locking scheme used by Portal to verify modified records before they are written back to the database.</td></tr>
</table>

Continued

Table 21-4 *(continued)*	
Package	**Description**
OWA_PARMS	The parameters procedure fetches and sets data in PL/SQL arrays, and it is used by Portal to perform updates against tables.
OWA_TEXT	The text utility package provides a high-level interface for manipulating strings of data and formatting the resulting output on HTML pages.
OWA_SEC	This package implements a security mechanism for users and procedures used by both Oracle9*i*AS and Portal.
OWA_UTIL	This package provides a set of information utilities that report on the status of the PL/SQL environment. Portal uses this package internally to display the listener settings and path configuration.

Each of these packages provides a number of features that warrant a detailed discussion outside the Portal environment. Programmers who are building applications for the Oracle9*i*AS using the mod_PLSQL cartridge work with each of these procedures extensively. However, within the Portal environment, there is less need to work with these procedures directly because the wizards handle most of the complex coding for you. The OWA_COOKIE package is worth investigating in more detail, though, because you may need to work with cookies directly.

Working with OWA_COOKIE

If you wish to carry information over from one session of your browser to subsequent sessions, you need to store the information in some format. The commonly used Web slang for this information is *cookies,* and cookies are generally stored somewhere on your desktop by the browser. Cookies enable your Web applications to store useful information about you and use that information in subsequent sessions. For example, if you wish to acknowledge the return of an existing user to an application, you might record their previous visit within a cookie file. When the user returns to your application, the system can search for a matching cookie and respond accordingly.

Cookies can be defined as being *transient*, which means that they can be set to expire after a certain date. Browser users do not have to accept cookies and most browsers allow the user to turn off cookies or at least to receive a message when a cookie is sent to them.

 Note   Portal applications *require* browser-side cookies to maintain connection and state information even if you do not explicitly plan to make use of cookies in your code.

The OWA_COOKIE package contains four procedures:

✦ OWA_COOKIE.GET

✦ OWA_COOKIE.GET_ALL

✦ OWA_COOKIE.REMOVE

✦ OWA_COOKIE.SEND

Oracle PL/SQL packages can handle complex datatypes, and the OWA utilities have been designed to leverage this capability. Within the OWA_COOKIE utility, Oracle has created a compound datatype called COOKIE to describe the format of a cookie record. This compound object takes the following format:

```
type cookie is RECORD
{
   name varchar2(4096),
   vals vc_arr,
   num_vals integer
}
```

When you attempt to get the value for a given cookie or set of cookies, Oracle returns the data to you in the cookie record format. To obtain the value for a specified cookie, use the OWA_COOKIE.GET procedure as shown in the following example fragment:

```
owa_cookie.get('ITEM1');
```

The OWA_COOKIE.GET utility searches your cookie file for the item called ITEM1 and returns the compound datatype cookie to the calling program. Within the cookie record are three fields: name, vals, and num_vals. The name field is the item name, which you passed in as a parameter; the vals field holds the value for the item; and num_vals field returns an integer that displays the number of values. In the case of the OWA_COOKIE.GET procedure, the num_vals variable always returns 1 or 0. If you wanted to get all of the currently defined cookies, you would use the OWA_COOKIE.GET_ALL procedure, which takes no input parameters but returns an array of type cookie with name and value pairs. In this case, the num_vals variable contains the number of name/value pairs that were found. Within a block of PL/SQL code, you can select all the cookies and then loop through the result set to find the name/value pairs you are interested in.

You can remove any cookie entries you find by using the OWA_COOKIE.REMOVE procedure, which takes the following format:

```
owa_cookie.remove(name, value, path)
```

The name and value parameters are varchar2 strings, and they must match a name/value pair. The path of the cookie can be used to remove a name/value pair that is not unique to a single application, and it defaults to NULL. The

`OWA_COOKIE.REMOVE` procedure must be called within the header of the HTTP stream before the document is opened. Portal provides an entry field that matches this requirement, and you will see this in the next section.

Oracle also permits you to create cookie file entries by using the `OWA_COOKIE.SEND` procedure, which generates a cookie file entry within the user's browser environment. This procedure is the most complicated, and it takes six parameters as shown in the following code fragment:

```
owa_cookie.send(name, value, expires, path, domain, secure);
```

The only required values are the first two, which are the *name* and *value* pair for the cookie. The third parameter is a date field used to hold an expiration date for a cookie. The path, domain, and secure settings allow for a lower level of control over the cookie and are unlikely to be used directly within the Portal environment. All three of these parameters default to NULL. Setting the cookie can be as simple as setting the name value pair as follows:

```
owa_cookie.send('COLOR','Blue');
```

Both the `remove` and `send` procedures output a string of text to the output stream that acknowledges the completion of the action.

Cross-Reference   You can also use JavaScript to work directly with cookies from within your browser. Chapter 29 provides you with several examples of JavaScript and PL/SQL code that work with cookies.

Integrating HTP and PL/SQL Web Toolkit Procedures with Portal

Using the HTP and PL/SQL Web Toolkit requires you to have a working knowledge of PL/SQL procedural syntax. Portal is built with both PL/SQL packages and Java code, but, so far, you have been completely insulated from the lower-level PL/SQL CODE. The HTP and OWA procedure calls can only be called in the context of a PL/SQL procedural block.

1. Import the report file ch21_rpt_classes.sql component.

Most of the Portal wizards provide a panel you can use for entering specialized PL/SQL code. The entry point for this code is the Add advanced PL/SQL code page, and it is provided as the final page within the following wizards:

✦ Forms

✦ Reports

✦ Calendars

✦ Charts

✦ Hierarchies

Portal provides four entry points for entering PL/SQL procedures, and they are all contained on the single panel. Despite the simplicity of this mechanism, it provides a great deal of power for customizing the generated HTML pages.

2. Open the ch21_rpt_classes report and navigate to the Additional PL/SQL Code page, as shown in Figure 21-1.

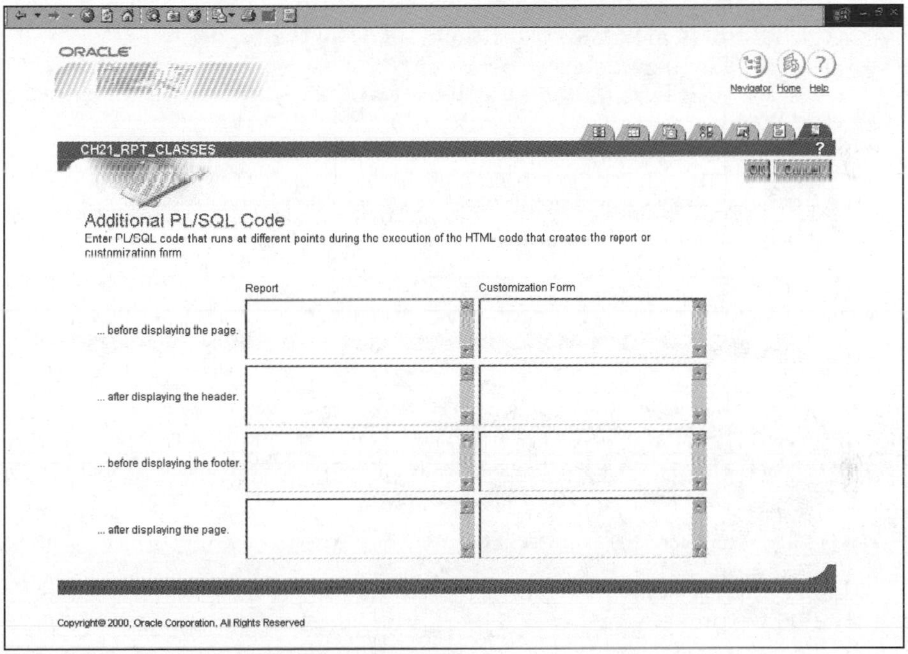

Figure 21-1: Additional PL/SQL Code page

The four entry points appear in pairs of two. The four text boxes on the left side of the page apply to the resulting component object and the four text boxes on the right apply to the parameter form for the object if one exists. Each of the four entry points applies to a certain area of the HTML output page, and this is easier to understand by entering sample code into each window.

3. Enter the following PL/SQL commands into the four text boxes in the left panel from top to bottom. Be sure to enter the semicolon to end each line as shown in the code.

Enter this code into the "... before displaying the page" box:

```
htp.print('Before Page');
```

Enter this code into the "...after displaying the header" box:

```
htp.print('Before Header');
```

Enter this code into the "... before displaying the footer" box:

```
htp.print('Before Footer');
```

Enter this code into the "... after displaying the page" box.

```
htp.print('After Page');
```

4. The Add advanced PL/SQL code page should look like the page shown in Figure 21-2. Once you have entered the procedures as shown, use the Finish button to save the changes and then run the report.

Tip   The HTP.PRINT procedure outputs text directly into an HTML format within the page.

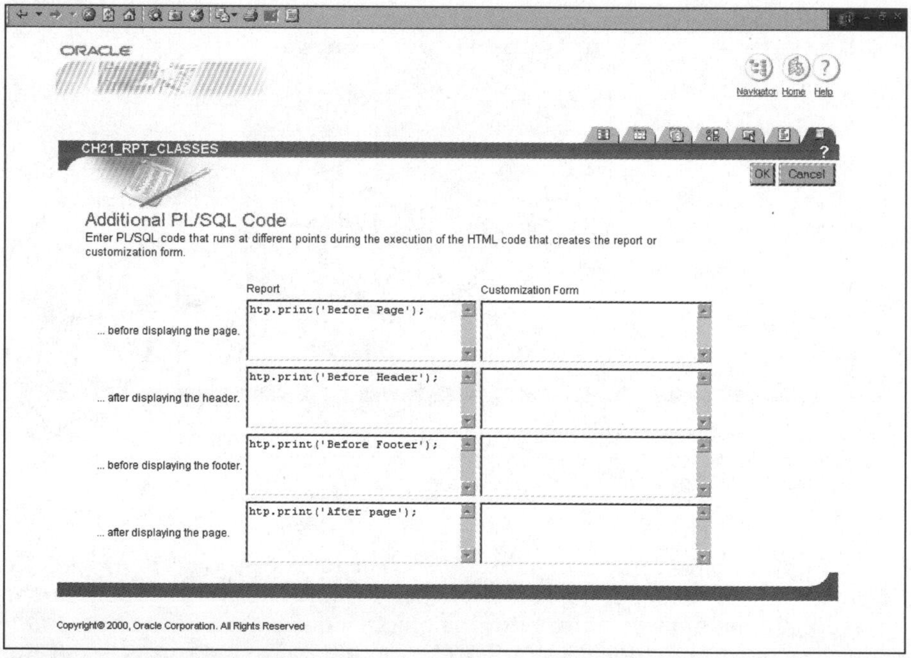

Figure 21-2: PL/SQL entries

Notice that the calls to the HTP procedures cause a block of text to be written to each segment of the HTML output, as shown in Figure 21-3. The first text item shows the string "Before Page" and it appears before any other output in the page. Portal invokes the procedure as part of the HTTP header that follows the data in the output stream. If you were to view the source code for this page, you would find that the "Before page" string appears ahead of the <HTML> tag in the output.

Under most conditions, there is little value in having any code appear before the start of the HTML document. The exception to this rule is the `OWA_COOKIE.REMOVE` and `OWA_COOKIE.SEND` procedures, which must be called within the header. By invoking the code in this procedure block within the header, you are free to make use of these two routines to set and remove cookie values. Remember that on the Display Options panel, which precedes the Additional PL/SQL code panel, you have the ability to add straight HTML text as header and footer text. The entry fields on the PL/SQL code panel provide the opportunity to mix HTML and code using the HTP and OWA procedures.

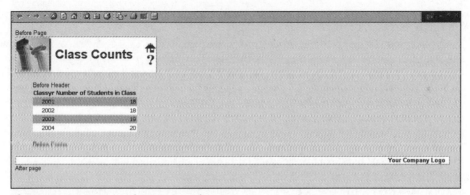

Figure 21-3: Output of HTP procedures

The second block of custom code that appears is the string Before Header and it is executed before Portal inserts the <FORM> tag into the document. The title "Before Header" references to the Portal Header element and not the HTML <HEAD> tag. Portal keeps track of the current state of most output pages by using hidden fields within the document and this requires that <FORM> and </FORM> tags be inserted into the resulting document. Portal invokes the second PL/SQL code window just ahead of creating the FORM tags in the output. In our example case, the executed code is a simple print statement, but you are free to use any of the HTF/HTP and OWA procedures within this code block. In fact, if you wish to add your own form field items, you are free to create your own form elements by using the `htp.formOpen` and `htp.formClose` procedures within this code block.

> **Tip**
> Form tags must be completely enclosed and we recommend that you create separate form objects if you wish to add form items to multiple sections of the HTML page. This ensures that your custom inserts do not interfere with the form tags generated by Portal. For example, if you want to add form objects within each of the PL/SQL entry points, make sure that you wrap each section in its own set of <FORM> and </FORM> tags. Be advised, however, that the use of multiple forms requires multiple Submit buttons, and this can lead to problems with the user's interaction on your pages.

The third block of text appears before the Portal footer. The footer contains any of the display options settings selected, such as timing information and USERID — and it appears just after the </FORM> tag. You can see the text string "Before Footer" as it appears in Figure 21-3. If you plan to display information before the footer area it is a good idea to use the Display Options panel to remove any of the information that Portal loads into the footer in order to save valuable screen real estate.

The final text string appears at the very bottom of the document and, if you were to view the source for this document within your browser, you would see that it actually appears outside the <HTML> and </HTML> tags. Although the text appears on the page, the browser does not consider this text to be part of the HTML document itself.

Adding database access code to PL/SQL blocks

Portal surrounds the code that you enter into the four PL/SQL entry windows with the required begin/end delimiters. Although you do not see them in the code window, they are inserted into the generated PL/SQL code for you automatically. Oracle calls these unnamed blocks of code anonymous PL/SQL blocks, and they are one of the main structural components for the PL/SQL language. (Technically, these procedures are not anonymous blocks because Portal embeds them within a named procedure behind the scenes.) Normally you provide your procedures and packages with a name, but Oracle does not require you to do so. This is very important for a product such as Portal, because it could become very cumbersome if you were forced to provide a specific, unique name for every little snippet of code. The entries you make into the four PL/SQL code windows on the Additional PL/SQL Code panel are implemented as anonymous blocks of code that are then inserted in the named procedure when it is created.

In the example you worked with in the preceding section, the entire procedure was a simple call to one of the HTP print routines. However, you can input any valid block of PL/SQL code into these windows, and that is the real power of the PL/SQL entry windows. The output shown in Figure 21-3 could just as easily have been created with the Add Text panel used for inputting title text for the form. The power of the PL/SQL code windows is their ability to add additional SQL code into these panels and have this code processed as part of the procedure.

Consider the PL/SQL procedure that is shown in Listing 21-1.

Listing 21-1: **Before_page procedure**

```
create or replace procedure before_page(my_variable varchar2) is
begin
   htp.print('Parameter Value --> '||my_variable);
end before_page;
```

The `htp.print` function is embedded in a named procedure called `before_page` that is owned by the `NETU` schema. The procedure accepts a single string parameter, which it uses as part of the output that the `htp.print` function produces. Essentially, this routine is no more complex than the format that you already used in the preceding example. In the example case the following PL/SQL call was used in the `'Before Page'` block:

```
htp.print('Before Page');
```

You could replace this function call with the procedure as shown in Listing 21-1 by surrounding the code with begin/end PL/SQL blocks as follows:

```
begin
netu.before_page('Hello World!');
end;
```

The modified procedure would create the output as shown in Figure 21-4.

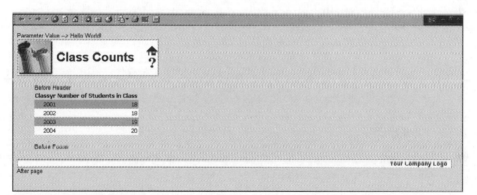

Figure 21-4: PL/SQL Procedure Call

The text that appears at the top of the page includes both the fixed text and the "Hello World!" string that was passed to the procedure. The advantage of using this alternative PL/SQL code approach is that the procedure code is managed outside of the portal environment. You can customize the procedure code without recompiling the ch21_rpt_classes report. Editing and compiling large blocks of PL/SQL code on the Additional PL/SQL Code panel is a cumbersome and error-prone process. External procedures can be edited with a more powerful PL/SQL development tool, such as the PL/SQL Developer.

Caution   We recommend that you carefully review the specifics of PL/SQL if you are not familiar with PL/SQL programming before you attempt any complicated programming with the code windows. The Portal interface assumes that you are familiar with the particulars of PL/SQL and it does not provide you with any assistance or meaningful error messages for PL/SQL problems within the wizard interface.

1. Edit the ch21_rpt_classes report and navigate to the Additional PL/SQL Code panel.

2. Replace the text in the "... before displaying the page" PL/SQL window with the code in Listing 21-2.

Listing 21-2: PL/SQL code block to select date

```
declare
v_curdate varchar2(40);
begin
select to_char(sysdate, ' Day, Month DD YYYY HH:MI')
into v_curdate from dual;
htp.bold('Page displayed on: '||v_curdate);
end;
```

Portal enables you to add any valid block of PL/SQL code as part of the form, but you must follow some careful formatting rules. Notice that in Listing 21-2 the code includes a pair of begin/end identifiers, even though Portal is required to enter them for you automatically. The need for the additional begin/end keywords is a result of using local variables within the scope of the procedure. PL/SQL requires you to indicate your plans to use local variables through the declare keyword, which itself requires a set of begin/end braces. These are provided for you automatically by Portal, but you must then add your own set of begin and end tags for any procedural PL/SQL code inserted after the declare keyword.

3. The code in Listing 21-2 is quite simple — the routine declares a local variable, selects the current date and time into the variable, and finally prints the value into the HTML document. Notice how each line of PL/SQL code (with the exception of the begin and declare keywords) is terminated by the use of the semicolon character as required by PL/SQL. Save this change to the procedure using the Finish button and rerun the report to produce the screen shown in Figure 21-5.

Figure 21-5: PL/SQL code with SQL

Notice the formatting of the date and time string at the top of the page. Because this block of code is included as part of the page header, it is refreshed for each page if the report were to output multiple pages of data. Although this particular example is quite simple, you can see the potential power of this interface. The PL/SQL blocks can be used to implement a complete read/write interface, as you will see in the next section.

Advanced PL/SQL code

The code windows for entering PL/SQL statements on the Additional PL/SQL Code panels are relatively small. If you have any experience in working with PL/SQL code, you have no doubt reached the conclusion that these panels are not sufficient for working with long or complicated procedures. However, because the entry panels are themselves PL/SQL code windows, you are free to call out to any existing PL/SQL procedure. As mentioned in the preceding section—if you plan to build large or complicated procedures, it is simpler and easier to build your PL/SQL code *outside* of Portal. A more comprehensive example can show you the full power of the PL/SQL code windows.

1. Load the report file ch21_rpt_events.sql into the Portal schema.

2. Load the following two PL/SQL scripts into the Net University account using SQL*Plus with the user name and password for the NETU user.

   ```
   ch21_plsql_buy_tickets.sql
   ch21_plsql_show_ticket_form.sql
   ```

Note   Normally, you use the Portal account to load in your components. However, the two PL/SQL scripts shown previously must be loaded into the NETU account, just as you installed the original sample database tables.

Listing 21-3: **Buy_tickets PL/SQL procedure**

```
-
-Listing 21-3
-
-Buy_tickets procedure
-
create or replace procedure buy_tickets (p_id number,
p_eventid number, p_no_of_tickets number,p_cc_type varchar2,
p_cc_number number)
as
   v_ticket_price number(5,2);
   v_extended_price number(8,2);
begin
-
-Select the ticket price for the event
-
```

Continued

Listing 21-3 *(continued)*

```
select ticket_price into v_ticket_price from events
where eventid=p_eventid;
—
—If the ticket_price is blank, print default
—message
—
if v_ticket_price is null then
  htp.htmlOpen;
        htp.headOpen;
        htp.header(1,'Tickets are not required for this
event');
        htp.headClose;
        htp.bodyOpen;
        htp.print('EventID not found for selection');
        htp.bodyClose;
        htp.htmlClose;
        return;
end if;
—
—Found valid event, insert ticket purchase into
—tickets table
—
insert into tickets (id, eventid, no_of_tickets, cc_type,
cc_number, trans_date) values (p_id, p_eventid,
p_no_of_tickets, p_cc_type, p_cc_number, sysdate);
—
—Update events availability to record the
—number of tickets purchased
—
update events set availability = availability - p_no_of_tickets
where eventid = p_eventid;
v_extended_price := v_ticket_price * p_no_of_tickets;
—
—Output a result message
—
htp.htmlOpen;
htp.headOpen;
htp.header(1, 'Ticket Sale Completed');
htp.headClose;
htp.bodyOpen;
htp.print('$'||to_char(v_extended_price)||
'was charged to your card number:'||to_char(p_cc_number));
htp.bodyClose;
htp.htmlClose;
end buy_tickets;
```

Listing 21-3, although a bit complex, is a PL/SQL procedure that accepts a number of parameters and inserts a record into the tickets database table. The procedure outputs status messages in HTML format by using the HTF/HTP packages.

This procedure has been simplified for the purposes of example, and you will notice that it does not include any PL/SQL error-handling code. Furthermore, the procedure outputs all messages in HTML format, which forces the procedure to be used only within a Web environment. Ideally, you would separate the output routines into a second procedure to provide an extra level of insulation. The code as shown ignores these conventions in order to make the listing easier to read and understand.

The first part of the procedure accepts a number of parameters and then validates the EVENTID field by selecting the TICKET_PRICE from the EVENTS table. If the TICKET_PRICE is NULL, a message is printed informing the user of this fact, and the procedure terminates. If the TICKET_PRICE is valid, the routine inserts a record into the TICKETS table that records the necessary information. Once a record has been inserted into the TICKETS table, the procedure updates the EVENTS table to reduce the availability field by the number of tickets that were sold. Finally, the procedure prints the completion of the process as an HTML message.

Caution We have made this procedure overly simple to keep the focus on HTML processing. In a production environment, you would want to take additional precautions in the procedure, such as error handling for each INSERT and UPDATE statement. All of the parameter values should be validated for correctness against database columns, including those parameters that do not join to other tables.

3. Run the report ch21_rep_events to display the form shown in Figure 21-6.

Figure 21-6: Events report

The Events report shown in Figure 21-6 displays a single record from the EVENTS table on each page. You can use the Next and Previous buttons to navigate your way through the data in this report. For this sample application, it would be useful if students could buy tickets for these events directly from this Web page. It is certainly possible to build a link into this report that would call a Portal form object to perform this task. However, you can also use the HTP procedures and the BUY_TICKETS stored procedure to provide this service directly from the existing report page. Consider Listing 21-4.

Listing 21-4: **Creating a form with HTP procedural code**

```
—
—Listing 21-4
—
—Display ticket form in HTML
—
create or replace procedure show_ticket_form as
begin
  htp.print(htf.bold('Fill in field values and use the push
button to buy ticket'));
  htp.br;
  htp.formOpen('netu.buy_tickets');
  htp.teletype('Student Id___:');
  htp.formText('p_id',5,5);
  htp.br;
  htp.teletype('Event Id_____:');
  htp.formText('p_eventid',5,5);
  htp.br;
  htp.teletype('# of Tickets_:');
  htp.formText('p_no_of_tickets',5,5);
  htp.br;
  htp.teletype('Credit Card');
  htp.br;
  htp.teletype('AMEX,MC,VISA_:');
  htp.formText('p_cc_type',5,5);
  htp.br;
  htp.teletype('Card #_____:');
  htp.formText('p_cc_number',10,10);
  htp.br;
  htp.formSubmit(NULL,'Buy Ticket');
  htp.formClose;
end;
```

This procedure creates an HTML form by using the HTF/HTP procedures to build the required components. Two special aspects to this code may not be immediately obvious, even to an advanced PL/SQL programmer. The htp.formOpen procedure is called with a single parameter value of netu.buy_tickets, which is the name of the insert procedure you created earlier concatenated with the USERID that owns the procedure. The formOpen procedure uses this parameter as the value for the ACTION item with the <FORM> tag of the generated HTML. This means that when the form is submitted, the procedure netu.buy_tickets will be called. Portal automatically binds each of the fields within the form and their associated values and passes them along as part of the FORM GET process.

If you look carefully, you will notice that the names of the HTML FORM fields match the names of the parameters in the BUY_TICKETS procedure. The exception to this is the Submit button, which is not given a name value, but is left NULL instead. This is one of the very powerful features of Portal and HTML, as any form fields not explicitly named are not passed as part of the FORM submission process. This enables you to add any number of extra fields to the form that can be used for informational purposes.

Tip

As mentioned earlier in this chapter, we recommend that you do not enter long PL/SQL scripts directly into the PL/SQL code windows within Portal. A better solution is to create your code as a series of named procedures (as in Listing 21-4) that can then be called from the code windows. You need to store these procedures in the same USERID as the container Portal Application (NETCOLLEGE/NETU) in order to keep the two objects together, but this should not be difficult to remember. As you can see from the preceding instructions, this makes the PL/SQL entry window within Portal easier to read. You will also find that the process of creating large PL/SQL procedures is much easier to manage if you use the Oracle Procedure Builder.

4. Edit the report ch21_rpt_events and add the following snippet of code to the ". . . before displaying the footer" code window:

```
netu.show_ticket_form;
```

5. Save the changes and run the report to produce the page shown in Figure 21-7.

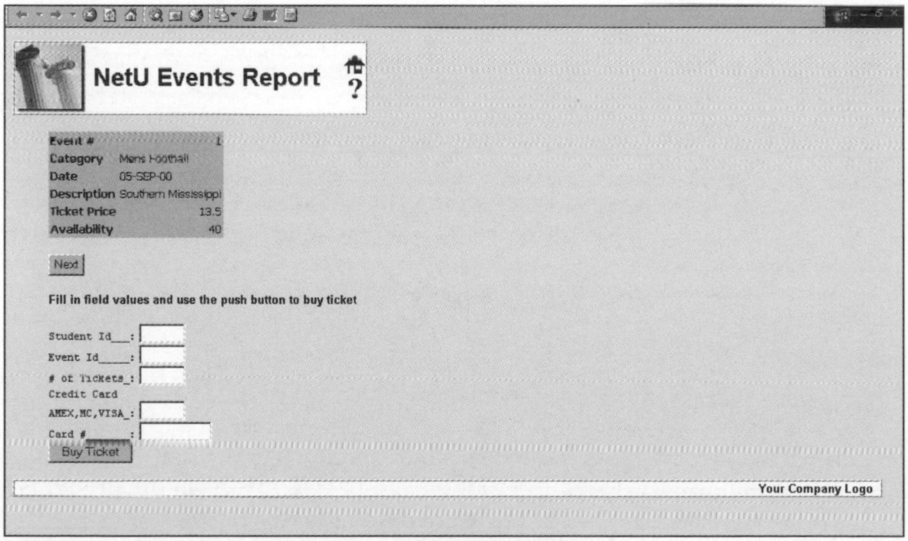

Figure 21-7: Events report with ticketing HTML code

Portal calls the SHOW_TICKET_FORM procedure after the footer display to produce an HTML form as shown in Figure 21-7. The form itself is quite simple, but it would be a small matter to add colors, fonts, and images to give the routine a more professional look.

6. Enter the following values into the form fields and click the Buy Ticket button to update the database:

```
Student Id: 1001
Event Id: 1
# of Tickets: 3
Credit Card: AMEX
Card #: 123456789
```

Figure 21-8 shows the updated database.

Ticket Sale Completed

$40.5was charged to your card number:123456789

Figure 21-8: Return status message from procedure

As you can see from Figure 21-8, the procedure executes and outputs an HTML status message informing you that the data was entered successfully. This is not exactly true, because there is no error-handling code in the program. However, it would be a simple matter to modify the procedure to add error handling for the INSERT statement as shown in the following code fragment:

```
—
—Found valid event, insert ticket purchase into
—tickets table
—
begin
        insert into tickets (id, eventid, no_of_tickets,
cc_type,
        cc_number, trans_date) values (p_id, p_eventid,
        p_no_of_tickets, p_cc_type, p_cc_number, sysdate);
exception
        when others then
                htp.print('SQL Error Message:'||substr(SQLERRM,
1, 200));

end;
```

You can surround your individual PL/SQL statements with their own begin/end blocks and use the exception statement to trap errors. In the previous sample code, the error message is displayed to the browser using the htp.print procedure along with the first 200 characters of the error message text.

7. Navigate back with your browser and use the Reload button in the browser menu to refresh the page, as shown in Figure 21-9.

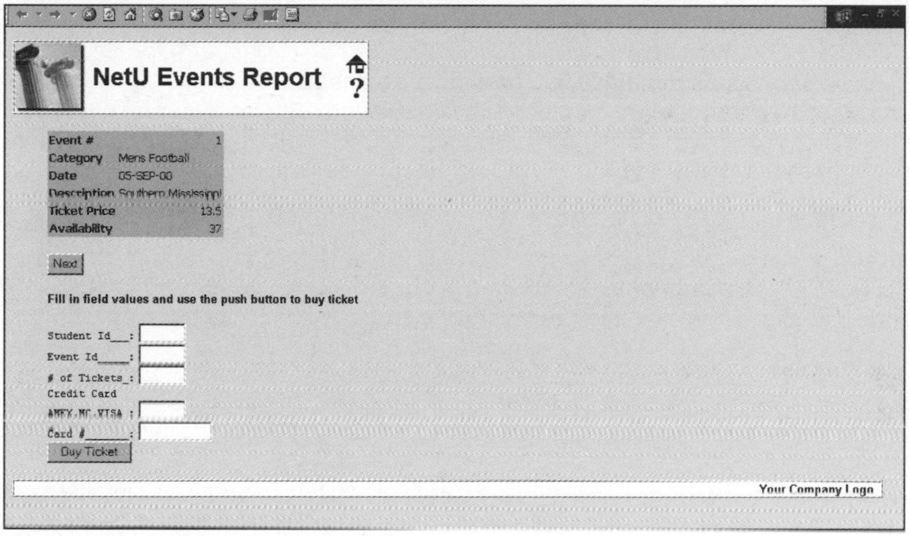

Figure 21-9: Updated Events table

> **Note**
>
> In a production application, you could easily add a link to the report that would call the custom procedure directly. This enables you to create a shopping cart–style application using the standard Portal components. The difference with a Portal application is that the data is securely written to the database (not to a local cookie file), so if the user is disconnected from the network, the data is safely stored in the database. It would be a simple matter to set a status value in the TICKETS table and enable a user to return to the system at a later point (with a valid USERID and PASSWORD) to make changes to the stored data before completing the purchasing process.

Portal performs a database fetch to load the data into the page. You can see that the Availability field drops to 37 from 40 once the first block of tickets has been ordered.

Debugging and Advanced Concepts

The link between PL/SQL procedures and Portal is very powerful. Once you have mastered the basic techniques, you can build some powerful applications by integrating PL/SQL code into your applications. Although Portal only provides a single panel for each wizard in which to enter PL/SQL code, you are free to call procedures directly as links anywhere Portal links are used. Even existing static HTML pages can insert records into the database simply by mapping the ACTION parameter to a PL/SQL procedural call. (You can also embed PL/SQL code in Dynamic Pages, as discussed in Chapter 15.)

PL/SQL is a procedural language, providing access to if-then-else logic and looping functions in additional to simple database-manipulation statements. We recommend that you spend some time reviewing the capabilities of PL/SQL in order to maximize your investment in Portal. If you are new to PL/SQL, you have probably found it is difficult to detect problems in your code through the Portal environment.

Although Portal provides the Show/Hide SQL Query Info function on the Manage Component panel, there is really no way to adequately search for PL/SQL errors within Portal. The designers of Portal are responsible for making sure that the generated Portal procedures work correctly, so it is rare that you need to view PL/SQL debug information within Portal. The exception to this rule is those PL/SQL procedures that you build yourself, and there is no easy way to debug these procedures or edit them within Portal.

There are two solutions for building external PL/SQL procedures. The simplest solution is to make use of your favorite text editor to create and manipulate your code. Once you are ready to install and test the code, you can simply use SQL*Plus as the host environment. Through SQL*Plus, you can cut and paste your code into the edit window, or you can use the at (@) command to load a script file into the workspace. Within SQL*Plus, you can show the errors in any procedure by creating the procedure and using the Show Errors command.

The Show Errors command displays a table that shows each line of code along with the associated error message from the PL/SQL compiler. This is not a perfect solution, because a simple error such as a forgotten semicolon can sometimes result in pages of errors. However, it is light-years ahead of the Portal environment, which does not even show you an error message.

A better solution is to invest in a PL/SQL Interactive Development Environment (IDE) such as Oracle's Procedure Builder or All Around Automation's PL/SQL Developer. PL/SQL Developer is a custom edit and run-time environment for developing PL/SQL code, and it features an advanced debugger as well as code-editing utilities. Figure 21-10 shows PL/SQL Developer with the source for the SHOW_TICKET_FORM procedure open in the debug and edit windows.

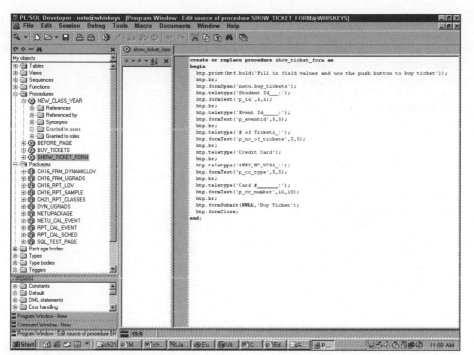

Figure 21-10: PL/SQL Developer

On the CD-ROM

A detailed examination of the many features of PL/SQL Developer is beyond the scope of this book, but we have included a trial copy of the software on the CD-ROM for you to work with.

Summary

The PL/SQL language has long been a cornerstone of the Oracle database and development environments. Portal itself is built with PL/SQL, and Oracle has taken great pains to provide access to HTML directly from PL/SQL procedures. The designers of Portal built the product with productivity in mind, and this sometimes causes a lack of flexibility. In this chapter, you have seen how you can overcome these limitations by building your own custom PL/SQL procedures and combining them with Portal.

Despite this power, you should resist the temptation to drop down into PL/SQL coding until you have exhausted the native capabilities of Portal. Relying too heavily on PL/SQL code can make your applications difficult to maintain for subsequent developers who may not be familiar with the specifics of PL/SQL coding. Chapter 22 introduces Oracle Portal's most important feature — Content Areas. All of the components that you have created in previous chapters can be loaded into Portal's Content Areas.

✦   ✦   ✦

Building Oracle9*i*AS Portal Sites

In This Part

Chapter 22
Using Content Areas

Chapter 23
Deploying
Oracle9iAS Portal
Sites

Chapter 24
Content Areas —
Part II

Using Content Areas

In This Chapter

Understanding the
Content Area
Architecture

Creating Content
Areas

Customizing Content
Areas

Manipulating Styles

Adding Perspectives
and Categories

Modifying Content
Area Properties

Portal provides a component for generating portal storage areas that are directly addressable by end users. Content Areas provide a complete content-management solution for portal sites. Many document-management vendors have provided similar types of repositories in the past — but Oracle is one of the first vendors to combine portal technology and content management. Developers can deploy structured components to your users through the various Portal component wizards — but Content Areas allow authorized users to self-publish documents to your portal site. Content Areas are often the glue that holds your portal site together. They are an integral part of Portal, but you can leverage the power of Content Areas without using any of the other component wizards. In this chapter, we will introduce you to Content Areas and walk you through the process of building and modifying a site.

Understanding the Content Area Architecture

Portal Content Areas have two main components: the Content Area environment and the Administration Interface. Content Areas are created using a simple wizard interface — which represents a very small part of the content management process. Content Areas contain numerous additional utilities for modifying both the structure and the user interface of your portal folders. The key to understanding how Content Areas work is by understanding the three mechanisms that Portal uses for organizing content:

+ Folders
+ Categories
+ Perspectives

A *folder* represents a distinct organizational area of a portal site. Each folder has one or more owners who define the components and content that appears in the folder. A Content Area is nothing more than a collection of folders, where the folders are arranged within a hierarchy.

A folder owner can assign security on a folder to individual users or groups of users. The security assigned to a folder cascades to the items contained within the folder. Through the folder security settings, you can determine whether an individual user can view, modify, delete, or create items within a folder. With the use of folder security, a single Content Area folder can serve the needs of a wide variety of users. Folder access is implemented through Oracle Portal security just as it is for Portal component objects and pages. For the Net University Portal, you might create a Content Area for the college with folders for each of the main constituents of the portal: Faculty, Alumni, and Undergraduates.

The *content* in a Content Area is classified in two basic ways: as a member of a category or as a perspective. A *category* is a way to classify items. For example, in the Net University database, the categories might include such items as academics and sports. Categories are classifications applied to content within folders. All folders in a given Content *can* have the same set of categories — but it's not a requirement. For example, you might create a Tickets category that applies to the sports teams, campus lectures, and entertainment folders. Yet, you would not want Tickets to be part of the Course Catalog folder. (Students don't have to buy tickets to view the course catalog!) *Items* within a folder are associated with a *single* category.

Perspectives provide another way to classify items in a folder. For example, you might create perspectives that are specific to each undergraduate class (Seniors, Juniors, etc.) or that identify "hot" topics. A perspective can span multiple categories and a single item can have *multiple* perspectives. By default, items are assigned to one and only one category and *zero or more perspectives*. Perspectives, as well as categories, can be used as search criteria.

Folders use categories and perspectives to organize their contents. The use of these powerful organizing classifications, coupled with the ability to define users and user roles, makes it easy to create portals that automatically deliver a customized view of the information available in your Portal site. Most of the work you do in setting up a Content Area is creating the folders, categories, and perspectives, and assigning attributes, ownership, and styles to each of these objects. Once these structures are in place, the portal continues to organize itself automatically as new information is added to the site according to the folders, categories, and perspectives that you created during the configuration process. You can add new folders, categories, and perspectives to production portals as the need arises.

Creating a Content Area

The Portal Creation wizards that you have worked with up to this point have all guided you from start to finish using a series of panels. The Content Area Create wizard consists of a single, simple panel. When you use a component builder wizard, the edit panels mirror the create panels. There are no options on the edit panels that were not presented to you during the creation process. With the Content Area Create Wizard this is not true, because *many* additional options *only* appear during the edit phase. In fact, so many options are available within the Content Area that displaying them within the build wizard would make the entire "create" process unproductive.

The simplest way to get a handle on Content Areas is to create one.

1. Navigate to the Main Panel of Oracle Portal as shown in Figure 22-1.

2. Click on the Create a New Content Area link to display the panel as shown in Figure 22-2.

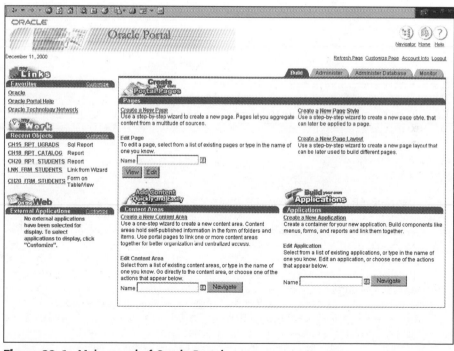

Figure 22-1: Main panel of Oracle Portal

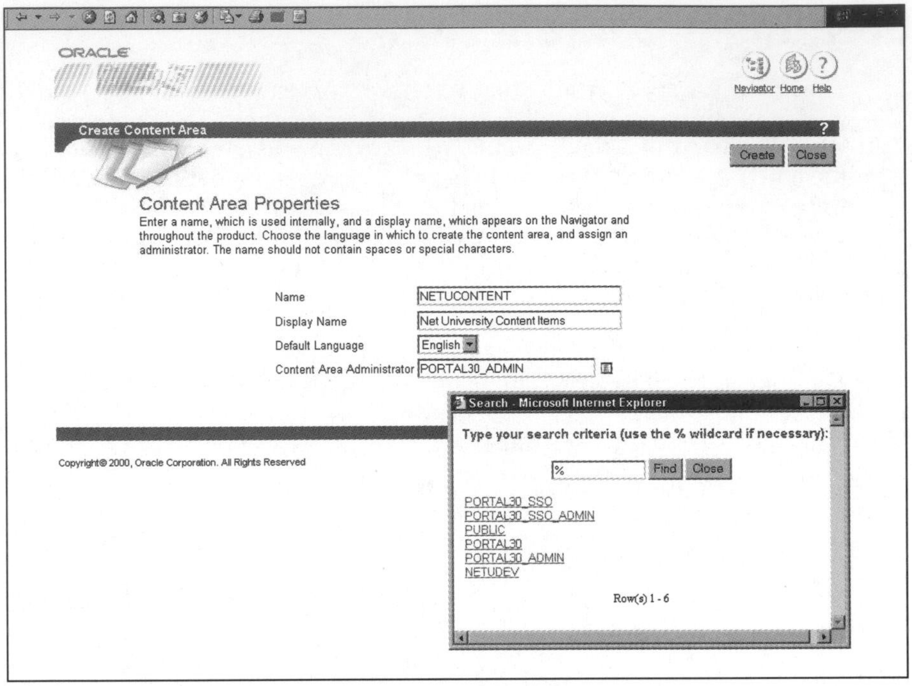

Figure 22-2: Create Content Area panel

There are four elements to creating a Content Area:

✦ Name

✦ Display Name

✦ Default Language

✦ Content Area Administrator

Portal uses the Name element to manage the Content Area internally. Since you can create an unlimited number of Content Areas within a single site, Oracle Portal uses the name as the *primary key* for the Content Area. The Display Name is the user-friendly name for your Content Area that will appear in the various edit and display panels. The language code sets the default language for your Content Area, but you are free to add content in different languages. The language code that you provide at this level simply applies to the *standard display and error messages* that are displayed within the Content Area portion of Oracle Portal — this becomes the default language for content that is created within the Content Area.

Content administrators manage Content Areas, and administrators can either be an individual or a group of users. The overlay window in Figure 22-2 shows both individual users such as NETUDEV and groups such as PORTAL30_ADMIN. When you assign a *group* as the administrator for a Content Area you enable all members of that group to act as administrators.

3. Enter the name **NETUCONTENT** as the name of the new Content Area.

4. Set the display name to **Net University Content Items**.

5. Accept the default language code of English.

6. Assign the group **PORTAL30_ADMIN** as the administrator for the Content Area as shown in Figure 22-2.

7. Return to the main page of Oracle Portal.

It's as simple as that — you've just created your first Content Area.

Customizing Content Areas

Oracle Portal uses the familiar navigator interface to manage the elements of a Content Area. If you are familiar with the various component tools, then you already have a head start working with Content Areas.

In the Main panel, enter the name **NETUCONTENT** in Edit Content Area text box (Figure 22-1) and use the Navigate button to display the panel as shown in Figure 22-3.

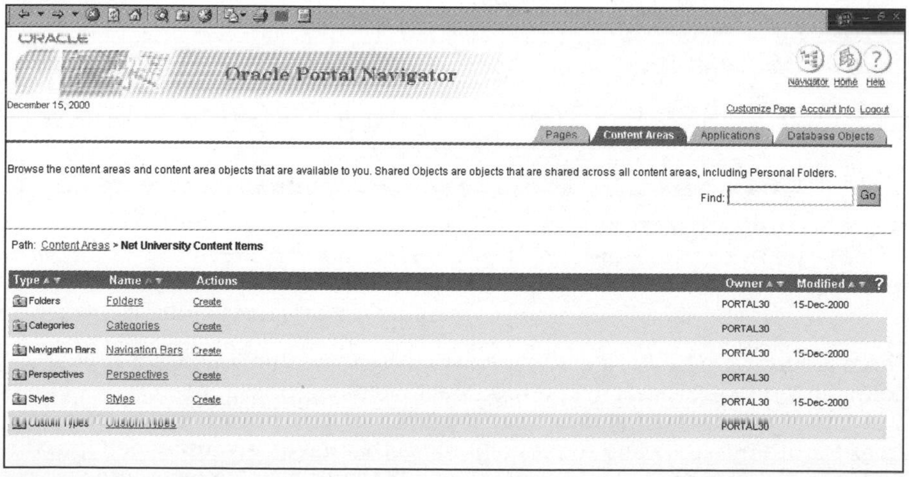

Figure 22-3: Editing a Content Area

Five basic elements make up the Content Area framework:

✦ Folders

✦ Styles

✦ Categories

✦ Perspectives

✦ Custom Types

Folders

Portal content objects are called items, and items are stored within folders or sub-folders in a Content Area. Folders provide the organization, but items are the *leaf* objects within a Content Area. (A Content Area is a tree, the folders are the branches, and the items within folders are the leaves.) At this point, it is only important to understand that items are content objects (documents, files, URLs) that are stored in the Content Area. When you create a new Content Area the next task that you will likely undertake is to create some folders for the new Content Area.

1. Use the Create link next to the Folders item in the Navigator for the NETU-CONTENT Content Area to display the panel as shown in Figure 22-4.

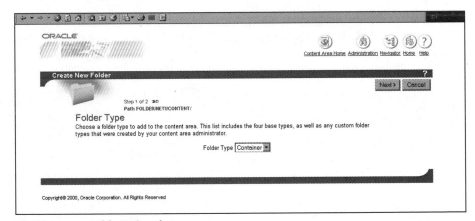

Figure 22-4: Folder Wizard

There are four types of folders that you can create within a Content Area—Containers, PL/SQL, Search, and URL. Containers are the simplest type of folder and they have been part of Portal since the earliest releases. Containers are storage areas for other folders and for content items that have been uploaded into the database. Folders can contain content, and they can also act as pointers to content items. Should you wish to connect a folder to a custom block of code you would use the PL/SQL block. You can use the Search folder type as a placeholder for saved searches. You will sometimes find it necessary to locate content items in other Content Areas as well. The URL folder connects a folder definition to a URL string that can connect you directly to a separate Content Area, portal page, or even to another Web site.

In most cases, you will start out by creating a series of container folders.

> **2.** Choose the Container folder type and click on the Next button to display the panel shown in Figure 22-5.

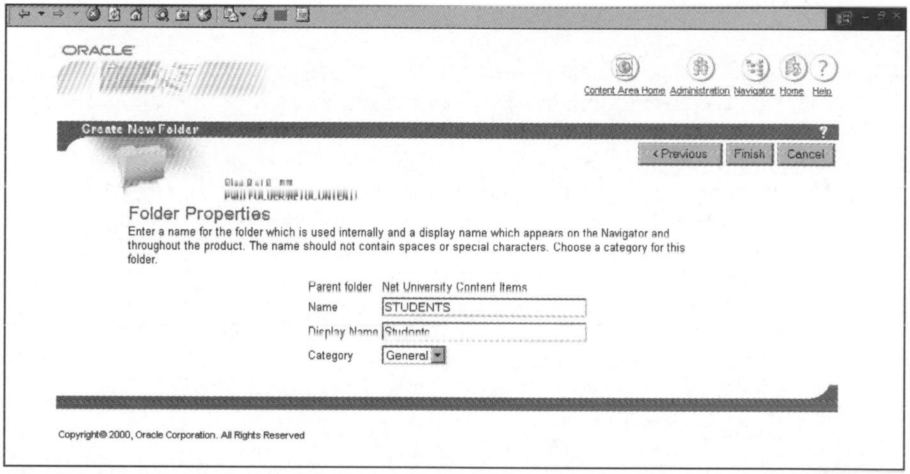

Figure 22-5: Folder Properties

Folders are just like any other Portal component — they have a unique name and an associated display name. They are also assigned to a category. Categories provide the superstructure for folders, which we mentioned in the first part of this chapter. Oracle Portal provides a single category when you create a new Content Area — the General category.

> **3.** Enter **STUDENTS** as the name for your first folder and then enter **Students** in the Display Name field. Use the Finish button to save the new folder and display the panel as shown in Figure 22-6.

Once you create a folder you are free to edit the properties of the folder, enter content items, or even create subfolders. In this example, you will create four subfolders for the Students folder — one for each class year.

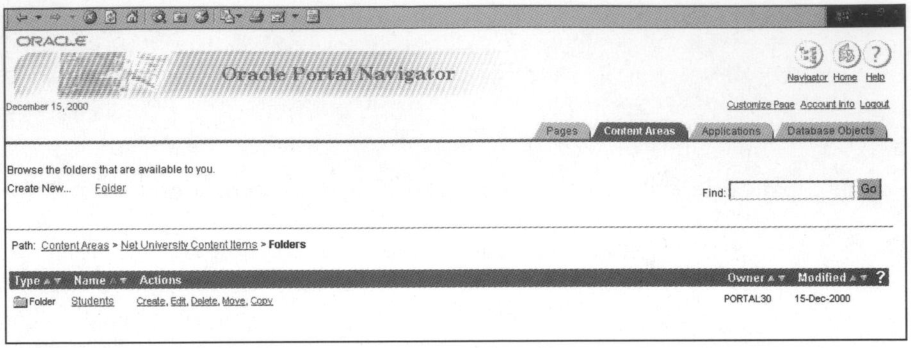

Figure 22-6: Students folder

4. Use the Create link in the Students folder area of the Navigator to create four container subfolders under the STUDENTS folder, as follows:

```
Name—seniors
Display Name—Seniors

Name—juniors
Display Name—Juniors

Name—sophomores
Display Name—Sophomores

Name—freshmen
Display Name—Freshmen
```

5. When you have finished creating the four subfolders, use the Students link in the folder area to display the folder hierarchy as shown in Figure 22-7.

The display as shown in Figure 22-7 contains all of the elements of a Content Area (with the exception of items). You first will notice that the left side of the form contains a rudimentary menu that is known as the Navigation Bar. The Navigation Bar includes links for administering the Content Area and searching and logging on and off from the portal site. The right side of the panel is the Content Area and it displays the hierarchy of folders that you have created. The colors, fonts, and background images of the folders and the Navigation Bar are all controlled by the style that is associated with the folders. Portal *automatically* applies a default style to folders when they are created—but you have the opportunity to override these defaults with your own custom styles. You are also free to change the layout of both the Content Area and the Navigation Bar when you customize the style. By default, Oracle Portal displays a background image in the Navigation Bar so that you can see the contrast between the Content Area and the Navigation Bar. At this point you could actually begin adding content items to your folders by using the Edit folder link in the upper-right corner of the page. However, it makes sense to make some additional customizations to the folders before turning them over to your portal users.

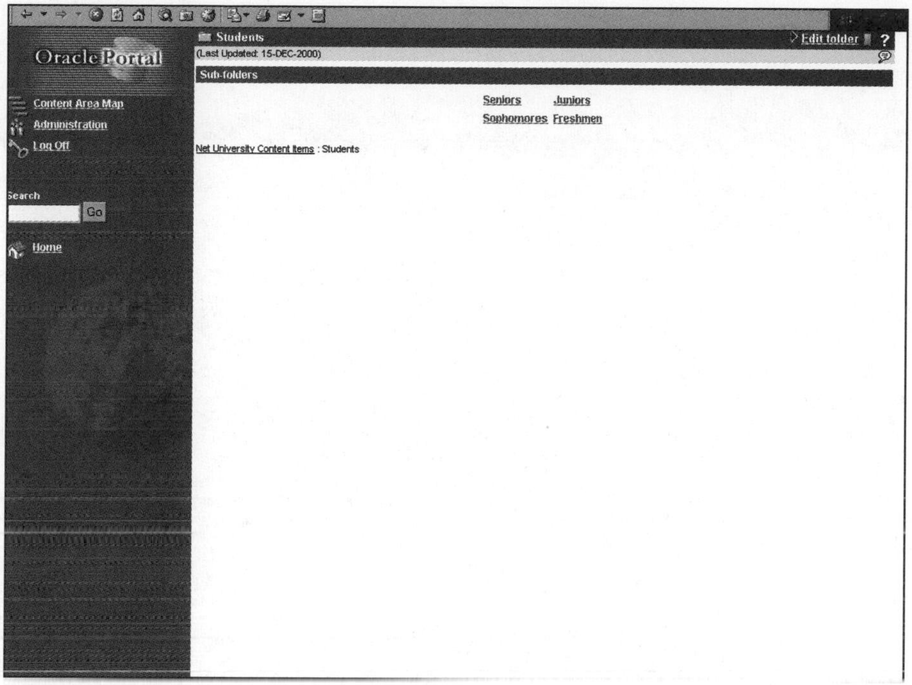

Figure 22-7: Students folder and subfolders

6. Use the Back button on your browser to return to the Navigator Interface.

7. Choose the Edit link to display the panel as shown in Figure 22-8.

There are six categories of edits that you can make to a folder, but the two most important changes are the required items and security access. When you create a folder, you are forced to select a name, a display name, and a category. Once the folder has been created you can add a description for it and set some additional deployment options. We have added a short description of the Students folder as shown in Figure 22-8. Portal will display this description in a sub-banner for portal users when they view the folder. Although we displayed the Students folder as a complete page in Figure 22-7, we can also choose to display the folder as part of a portal page. By selecting the Publish As Portlet check box you enable Portal to deploy the folder hierarchy as part of a page. When Portal displays the folder it will use the colors, fonts, and backgrounds that have been defined as part of the style for the folder — but you can override this behavior by selecting the Use Page Style check box as shown in Figure 22-8.

Cross-Reference   Folder styles are sophisticated objects in their own right and we'll look at them in detail in the next section.

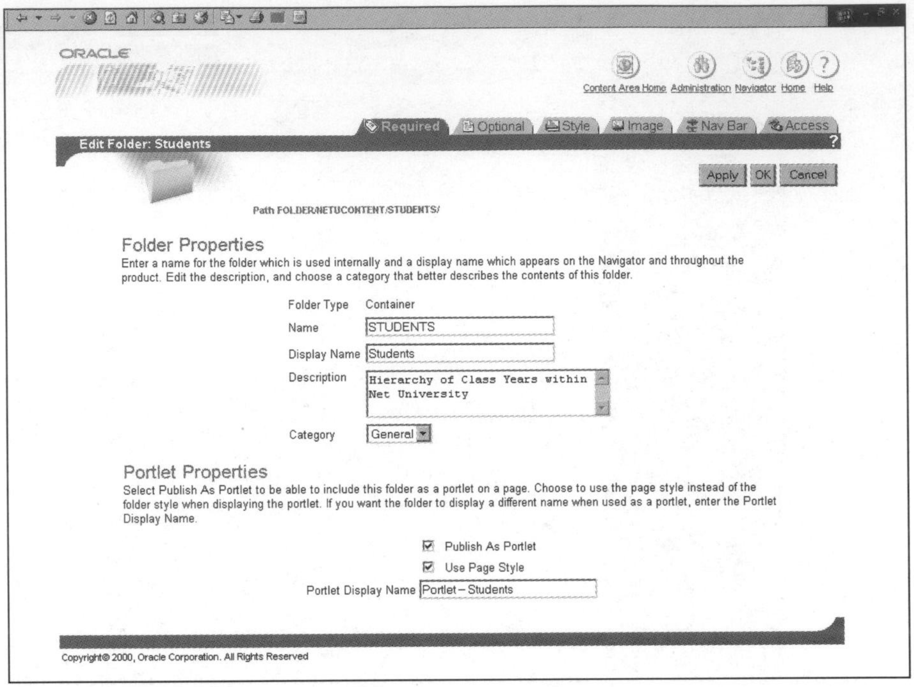

Figure 22-8: Edit Folder — Required items

8. Add a description for the Students Folder and enable the Publish As Portlet and Use Page Style check boxes. Click on the Apply button to save your changes.

9. Choose the Access Tab to display the panel as shown in Figure 22-9.

Folder security is integrated tightly into the Oracle Portal security layer — but there are several security settings that are unique to Content Areas. Folders have four sets of security parameters available to them:

✦ Access Settings

✦ Cascade Privileges

✦ Grant Access

✦ Change Access

First, you can elect to bypass any detailed user security settings by making the folder available to the public, as shown in Figure 22-9. Portal users will not be able to *add* content to public folders but they will be able to see the contents of the folder automatically. If you plan on including some sensitive materials in a public folder you can elect to add security settings to individual items within a folder through the Enable Item Level Security check box.

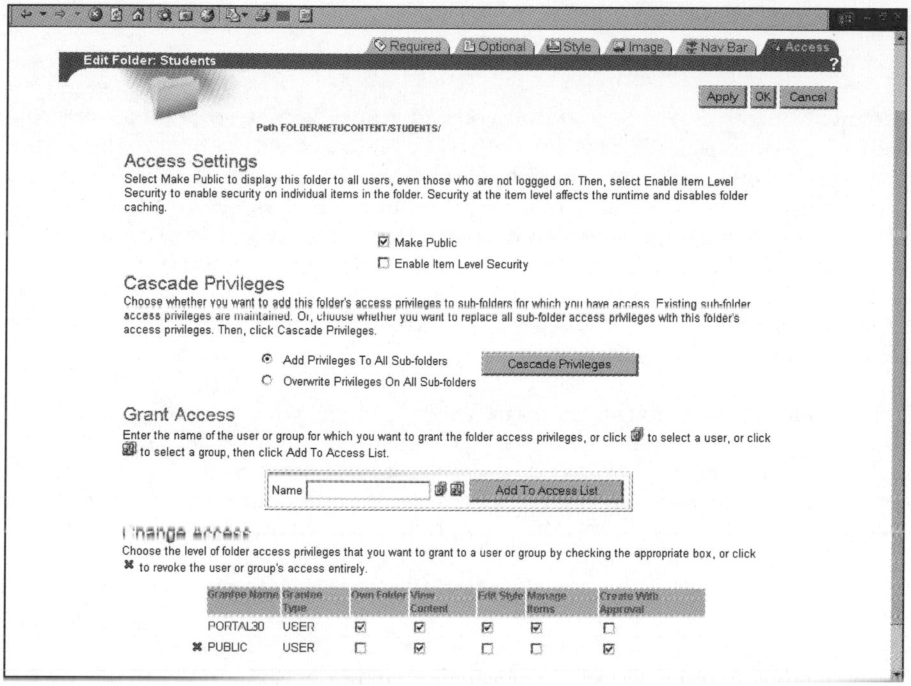

Figure 22-9: Folder Access Settings

Tip
In the case of Net University, we might elect to create a public folder for Student information such as the course catalog and holiday schedule. In order to prevent all students from viewing sensitive documents (such as exam scores), we could choose to enable item-level security on this folder.

Folders are designed to work in hierarchies and you can elect to control security for all subfolders at the root folder level. Once you have made your changes on the root folder you can use the Cascade button to cascade your security settings to all subfolders or to overwrite the existing subfolder privileges. For the Students example, it might make sense to keep the security settings separate across all of the four subfolders — Seniors, Juniors, Sophomores, and Freshmen. In this way, we can add specialized content for each class year that can only be viewed by students in the selected class year. If you elect to allow your end users to add content to your folders, you can use the Grant and Change Access options to grant specific privileges to users or groups of users.

Each folder and subfolder inside a Content Area has five possible permissions you can set for user accounts that access the site, as shown in the following list:

✦ Own

✦ View

✦ Edit style

✦ Manage items

✦ Create with approval

The most powerful permission that you can grant to any user account or group is the Own permission. When you create a Content Area within Portal, the administration account owns all the folders that you create by default. At first glance, you might assume that ownership of a folder is limited to a single user account. In fact, multiple users and/or groups can be granted ownership of a folder. The Own privilege grants the holder the ability to manage the folder completely, including the ability to add, delete, and update any items that might be contained within the site. Granting the own privilege to a user account effectively makes that user a system administrator for that folder.

The second privilege in the list is the View privilege, which is the least powerful of all the permissions on this panel. A user account must have the View privilege set in order to view both the folder and any items contained within that folder (unless the folder is set as a public folder). Users cannot add content to the site, however, unless they have been granted the "Create with approval" privilege.

Once the user or group has been granted the "Create with approval" privilege they are able to add new content to the specified folder in any of the supported content formats. When a user adds a new item to a folder, Portal marks the item as "pending." The only users who are able to see the pending item are the user who input the new item and any user who has the Own privileges for that folder.

Users can be granted the authority to edit items and move them around within folders through the Manage items privilege.

The final permission you can grant is the ability to change the style of the folder. Once a style has been set for a folder, all the content within that folder appears in a consistent manner. You might grant a user the authority to approve content without allowing that user the ability to change the look and feel of the folder itself.

The permissions on this panel are independent of one another, which gives you the flexibility to tailor the capabilities for any given user or group. Functionally, the panel works like any of the other add panels. You select a user account with the Find icon and then you add the user to the access list by using the Add To Access List button. Once the user has been added to the list, you can enable permissions by selecting the appropriate check boxes and using the Apply button.

10. From the Folder Access Settings panel, check the Make Public check box.

11. An alternative to step 1 is to find the PUBLIC group and add it to the access list.

12. Grant the following permissions to the PUBLIC user: View and Create with approval.

13. Save these changes using the Apply button.

You can apply the same permissions to groups of users as well as individual accounts. Normally you will assign *individual permissions* to the *managers* of folders and *group permissions* to *end users*. However, there are exceptions to this rule. For example, you may decide that none of your end users should have the ability to add items to your site. Over time you might find the need to delegate the "Create with approval" privilege to some of your more responsible users. You can still keep these users as part of the end-user group, but you can also add them to the individual user list for a folder and grant them "Create with approval" privileges.

Tip	One final piece of advice is critical to managing the security of your folders. Any folder-specific security settings you make to a folder are not applied to the subfolders contained with that folder. If you want users to have access to specific subfolders, you must explicitly provide them with subfolder privilege settings using the Cascade Privileges button.

The remaining tabs on the current page allow you to adjust the appearance of the folder and items within the folder. You will likely find it easier to apply these additional settings after you have created some styles at the root level of the Content Area. The next section will walk you through the process of managing styles.

Manipulating Styles with the Style Manager

The Navigator panel provides control over the inner workings of the Content Area, but it does not enable you to adjust the look and feel of the Content Area. Oracle Portal provides a utility called the Style Manager that provides you with the editing tools for making user interface changes.

1. Use the Styles link on the navigator panel of the Net University Content Items area to display the panel shown in Figure 22-10.

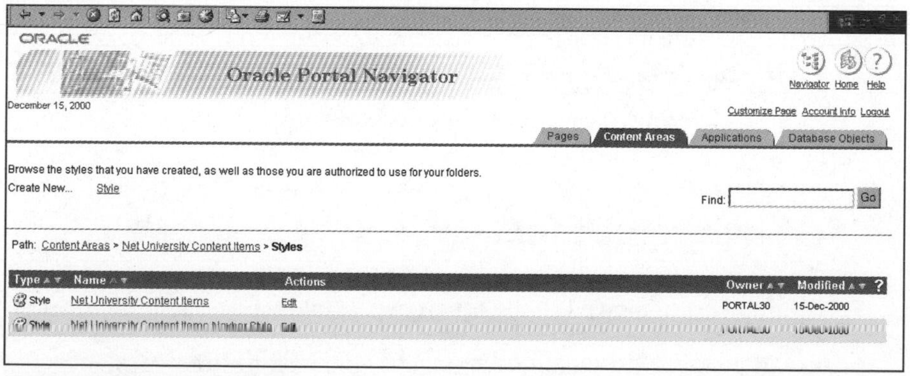

Figure 22-10: Style Manager

Oracle Portal automatically creates two styles for you when you create a new Content Area. The first style is for the items that you upload into the Content Area and the second style is for the Navigation Bar. Items are the bread and butter for Content Areas. All of the components that you have built in the previous chapters qualify as content items, and external elements such as word processing documents, presentations, and spreadsheets are also classified as items. Oracle Portal uses styles to make items appear in a consistent and well-organized fashion within your Content Areas.

2. Use the Edit link for the Net University Content Items Style to display the panel as shown in Figure 22-11.

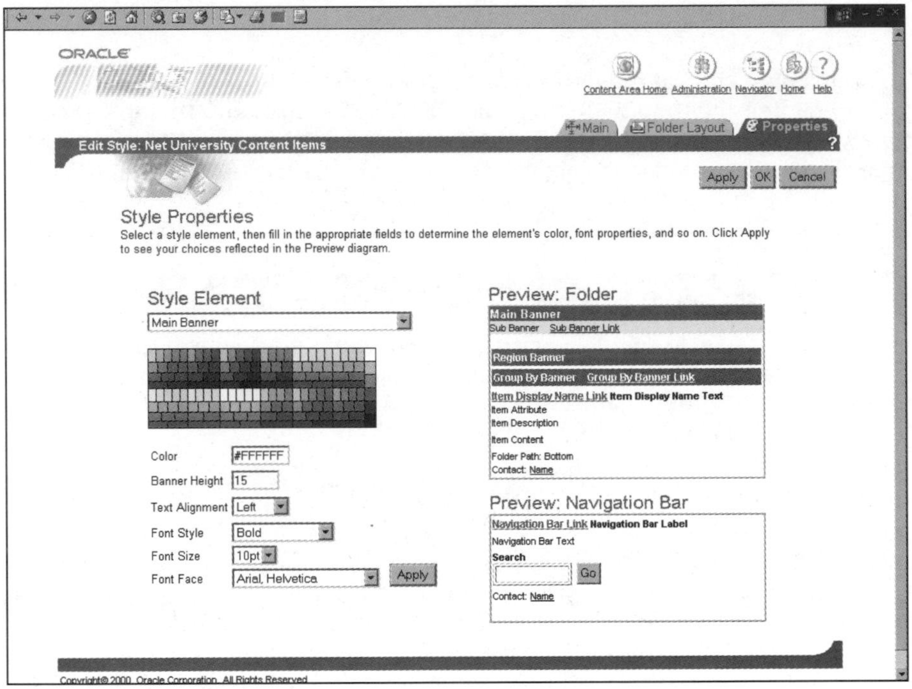

Figure 22-11: Edit Style: Net University Content Item

Setting the banners

The banner is the first major object in the Style Editor. Banners are the ribbons of color and text displayed at the top of pages, folders, and subfolders. Portal labels the various sections of a page using these banners and they form the borders that separate content within categories and folders from subfolders.

The Style Properties panel is divided into two sections. The left side of the panel allows you to select from a list of style elements using the Style Element combo box. Once you have selected a style you can then edit the style using the individual fields that appear below the color matrix. The specific entries that appear below the color chart will vary according to the selection that you make in the combo box.

The right side of the panel shows the two main types of style objects — the Content Area and the Navigation Bar. Portal displays a miniaturized version of both objects so that you can visualize the layout of folders and the Navigation Bar as you make your selections. There are two main categories of folder style elements — banners and items. Folders, subfolders, and categories are separated with strips of color that are called banners. Banners contain descriptive text about the folder to which they apply and this text appears in the body of each banner. (You can also associate images with banners should you wish to do so.)

By default the Style Editor starts by displaying the Main Banner — which appears at the top of each folder and each folder hierarchy. Each banner is composed of two entries in the Style Element combo box — one for the background of the banner (Banner Color) and one for the text that appears on the banner. Banner color selections only allow you to set a single color value for the background, but Banner entries allow you to set four display attributes:

✦ Color

✦ Height (in pixels)

✦ Text alignment

✦ Font (font face, size, and style)

You will use the Banner and Banner Color entries for each banner area to set the background color and then the text color. The banner areas themselves stretch from left to right and the Height pixel setting determines how much real estate the panel takes in the vertical dimension. For the most part, you need not change the pixel height unless you wish to use an extra-large font face for the banner text. The exceptions to this rule are the Main and Sub Banners, which display together at the top of the page. You will often wish to set the Main Banner *slightly* larger and the Sub Banner *slightly* smaller in order to emphasize the title and subtitle nature of these two ribbons. By default, Portal left-justifies the text in the banners, but you can change this to right justification or center justification as desired using the Text Alignment combo box. Portal will automatically display the Main Banner item when you begin to edit the style as shown in Figure 22-11.

3. Change the Font Style to Bold, Set the Font Size to 10pt, and select the Verdana font face for the Main Banner.

Cross-
Reference

You should see the font face NETU_TEXT appear in the list of fonts for the banners. (You created the NETU_TEXT font in Chapter 18.) The hex value format for banner colors is described in detail in Chapter 18 as well.

4. Select the Main Color item by clicking on a color and then changing the color setting field to the color code **#996665**. Use the Apply button to save the two changes.

You will notice that Oracle Portal automatically modifies the preview panel to display the font and color changes that you make. As you select and modify each element of the Folder area, Portal will adjust the preview display — making it easy for you experiment with different fonts and color schemes.

5. Change the remaining banner backgrounds to the match the modified Main Banner setting.

Modifying items and backgrounds

Banners represent one major category of style element — items are the other. Items are the leaf nodes on your content tree. Folders organize content and banners provide the visual cues that separate folder areas. Items include the documents, links, and application components that appear in the body of the folders. Five elements appear as part of each item:

✦ Item Display Name Text

✦ Item Display Name Link

✦ Item Attribute

✦ Item Description

✦ Item Content

Each of the item elements supports a color value and font settings just like the banner areas. When a portal user navigates into the body of a folder, they will see the item elements appear. The Item Display Name Link connects the label for the item to the actual content. In HTML parlance, it is the anchor tag <A> for the item. Items that are uploaded into folders can have a customized set of attributes associated with them such as document size, create date, and a whole host of user-defined attributes. These attributes appear just below the item link.

Oracle Portal allows you to choose which attributes appear with which items. Chapter 24 provides a detailed description and several examples of using customized attributes with items. We'll also display some of the built-in attributes later in this chapter.

An extended text-base description can appear as part of every item and it is the last element that is associated with all items. (Portal provides one additional element, called Item Content, which is used only to display items that are of the built-in Text type.)

6. Still in the edit panel (Figure 22-11), locate Item Attribute in the Style Element combo box and change the Font Style to Italic.

Oracle Portal allows you to select a background color for the Content Area, but you can also select an image to display in the background.

7. Choose Background Image in the Style Element combo box.

8. Locate the netu_bg.jpg image in the examples folder for Chapter 22 and use the Browse/Apply buttons to load the image as a background for the Content Area as shown in Figure 22-12.

Note

We have removed the background image from the remaining screen shots in this chapter in order to make them easier to view.

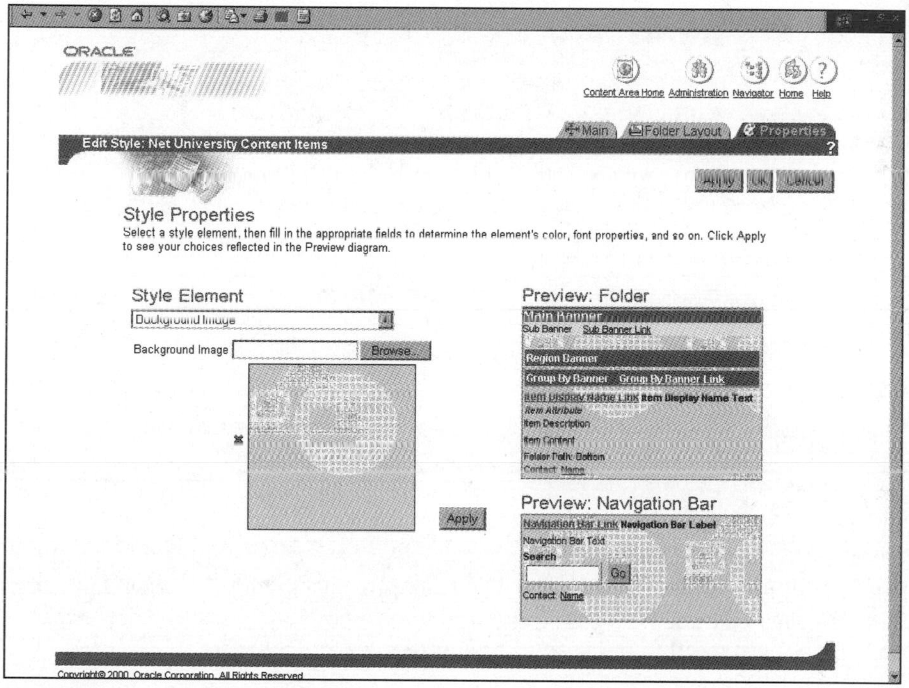

Figure 22-12: Background image

Portal tiles the image in the background area behind the text and the banners. Background images allow you to provide a more complex background for your items than you could achieve with a simple color setting.

Tip

You can also create background images with faded text for internal use only items—or to include copyright information as part of the display of all items—as shown in Chapter 18.

Changing the folder layout

Use the Folder Layout Tab within the Style Editor to display the panel as shown in Figure 22-13.

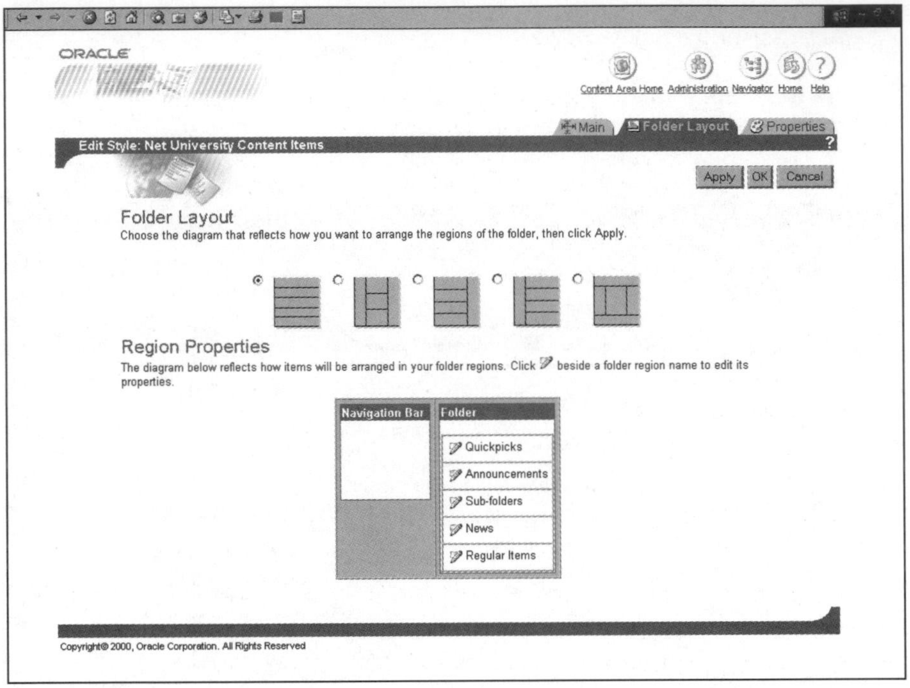

Figure 22-13: Folder Layout

Folders within Content Areas follow a certain physical layout as shown in Figure 22-13. Every Folder has one Navigation Bar and five regions — Quick Picks, News, Announcements, Subfolders, and Regular Items.

Quick Picks

Quick Picks are URL links that are embedded in the reserved space just below the banner. These links can vary on a folder-by-folder basis and are used as menu choices specific to a given menu. Normally they appear at the top of each folder. Their main purpose is to provide a visible and fast mechanism for reaching popular items that may be folder-specific, but are not necessarily associated with any of the categories within that folder.

News and Announcements

Portal reserves a special area of the page for news and announcement items. News items are pieces of time-sensitive information stored within a special section in the folders on your site. News items are generally short messages that have a specified shelf life. Announcements provide a similar service, but Portal gives them a higher profile by placing them below the Quick Picks items at the top of the screen.

Subfolders

Folders are nested in hierarchies as shown in Figure 22-7. When a portal user is viewing a container folder, you can control how the subfolder list appears within the body of the container folder.

Regular Items

Regular Items are the bread and butter of your Content Area. Documents, presentations, files, links to applications — these are the objects that are loaded into your Content Area, and you can control how Portal displays these items within your folders.

Folder Layouts

There are five possible Folder Layouts that you can use as part of a style. Portal rearranges the various elements in the layout area based upon the layout that you select. The default layout for folder regions is the same for Portal 2.2 and Portal 3.0, and it the layout as shown in Figure 22-13.

Click the radio button next to the right-most layout style and then use the Apply button to visualize the change as shown in Figure 22-14.

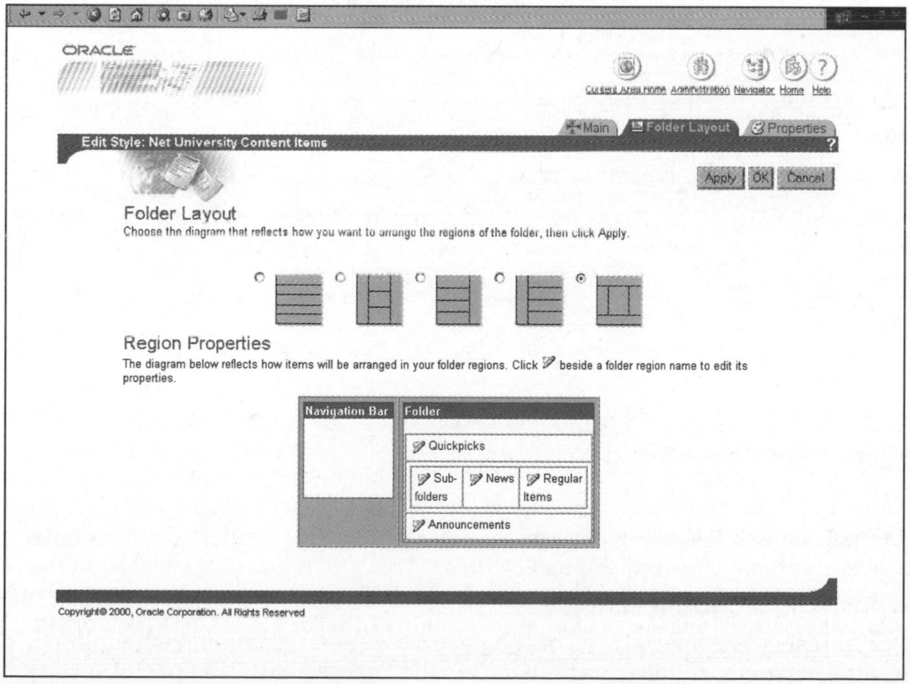

Figure 22-14: Modified Layout

The modified layout in Figure 22-14 shows the Quick Picks at the top and the Announcements on the bottom. Portal automatically applies the layout that you select to the folder regions each time the folders are displayed. A simple change on this panel will cascade throughout your folders and subfolders immediately after you make the change. This is part of the elegance of folders and Content Areas. The user interface and style are kept separate from the data so that you can quickly make wholesale changes to the look and feel of your portal as desired.

You can freely experiment with the layout of the various regions, and you can also set a variety of properties *within* each of the regions.

Specifying Region Properties

Click on the edit link (the pencil) next to the Regular Items region to display the panel as shown in Figure 22-15.

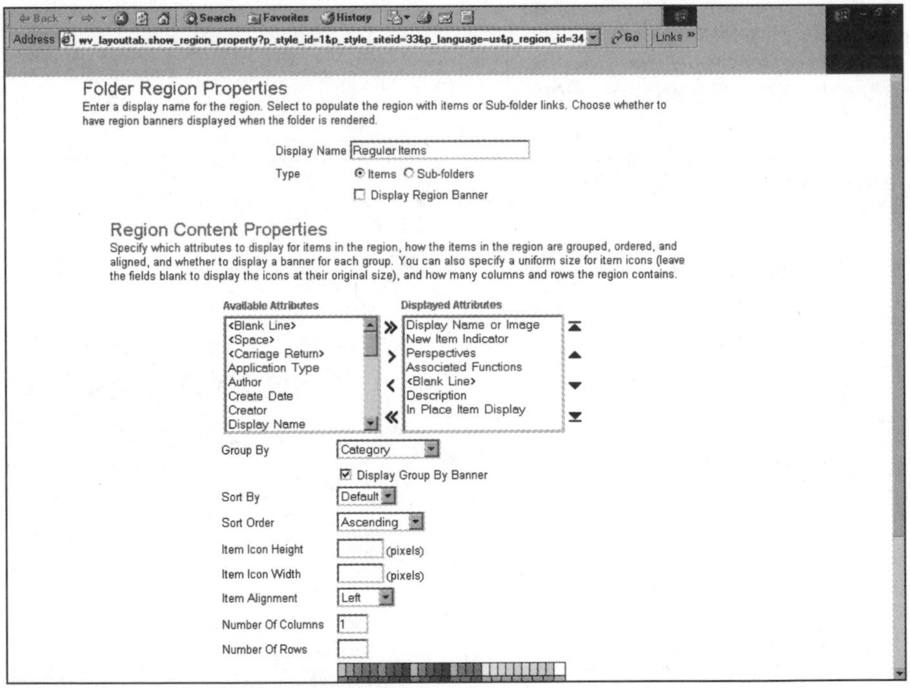

Figure 22-15: Folder Region Properties

Each of the five folder regions has an associated set of properties that control both the content and the look-and-feel of the region. The focus of this panel is the Region Content Properties, which appears in the middle of the panel. The starting point for this panel is the long list of available attributes that are stored as part of each item (or region). For content items, Oracle Portal stores a number of data attributes along with the actual item:

- ✦ <Blank Line>
- ✦ <Space>
- ✦ <Carriage Return>
- ✦ ApplicationType
- ✦ Author
- ✦ CreateDate
- ✦ Creator
- ✦ DisplayName
- ✦ DocumentSize
- ✦ ExpireDate
- ✦ Gist
- ✦ HelpURL
- ✦ Image
- ✦ ImageURL
- ✦ InitialPageName
- ✦ JarFile
- ✦ Keywords
- ✦ PortletId
- ✦ PropertySheet
- ✦ ProviderId
- ✦ ProviderName
- ✦ SiteId
- ✦ Themes
- ✦ Translations
- ✦ UpdatedItemIndicator
- ✦ Versions
- ✦ ViewasHTML

The first three items are formatting attributes used to assemble the layout of the region. The remaining attributes are data fields that are associated with the region type. Items are stored in a database table and they have the longest list of available attributes. Attributes are the descriptive elements of your items, such as author, document size, and item creation data. The actual list of attributes will vary by the *type* of item and by the *type* of region. For example, when you upload a document as an item into the portal, Oracle will track the size of the physical file. However, you can also upload URL *links* into a folder and it makes no sense to store the document size of a link — does it? The ability to display custom attributes with content items is a major benefit of using Oracle Portal.

There are two list boxes displayed on this panel, one called Available Attributes and the other, Displayed Attributes. The Available Attributes list matches the previous bulleted list. These are the elements that the Portal engine is capturing for the various item types and they are available for display as part of the *style* that you are working on. The Displayed Attributes are those items from the "available" list that have been selected as attributes for display within the items region for the current style. By default, Portal exposes a subset of attributes for each region (Quick Picks, News, Announcements, Subfolders, and Regular Items). Portal provides the directional arrows (>, >>, <, <<) so that you can move individual attributes between the two boxes. (The up/down arrows change the order of the items.)

There are three special attributes — <Blank Line>, <Space>, and <Carriage Return> — that allow you to create special output formats within the display region. Consider the display list shown in Listing 22-1.

Listing 22-1: **Sample Display List for Regular Items**

```
Display Name or Image
New Item Indicator
Perspectives
<Carriage Return>
Description
<Carriage Return>
In place Item Display
<Carriage Return>
Author
<Space>
Create Date
```

Oracle Portal will display the elements in the order in which they are presented. The name of the item appears first, followed by a graphic that indicates whether the item has been added in the past seven days (both the time interval and graphic can be changed by the administrator). Any perspective that you create (which you will do later on this chapter) appears next to the name on the same line. Portal inserts a carriage return to start the remaining content on a new line, followed by the description of the item and another carriage return. If the item is a text item, it will display the actual content below the description (In place Item Display), followed by another carriage return. On the last line you will see the Author's name and the date that the item was created.

The text formatting of these last items is controlled by the folder display options, which was discussed in the preceding section. You will remember that we elected to display attributes using *italics* — so the author name and create date will appear in italic text on the HTML page.

Change the region content for the Regular Items region to match the code as shown in Listing 22-1.

Here are other settings that you can change on the region panel that will affect the display of the output.

Group By

Portal will group similar elements together when items are displayed in a folder. The nature of the grouping will depend up the type of region. By default, Portal will display items by category. (Remember that each item belongs to a single category.) Alternatively, you can choose to group the items by Author, Date, Item Type (Document, File, Application Component, etc.), or the Provider (for portlets).

Sort By

The default behavior for items is to sort them by the "first-in-first-out" rule within categories. This makes the most recent entries appear at the top of the list within categories. However, you can also sort items by item size and title. In either case, the sorting will be applied within the grouping. For example if you group by Date and sort by Title the entries will appear in date order, sorted by title within the date.

Icon Height/Width

You are permitted to attach icons to items when they are uploaded into Portal. These icons are standard GIFs or JPEGs and they can be quite large. If you specify a height and width value for icons on this panel, Portal will crop the images to fit in the allotted space.

Number of Columns/Rows

These two fields determine the layout of items within the region. By default Portal will display items in a single column, but you can change this behavior by specifying values for the columns and rows fields. For example, setting both fields to **2** causes Portal to display items in two columns of two rows (like a grid).

1. Accept the default values for the remaining fields on the region panel and use the Apply button to save your changes. Use the Close button to exit from the region layout panel.

2. Use the OK button to complete the changes to the style of the Content Items.

Each of the other regional areas — Quick Picks, Announcements, News, and Subfolders — has a similar set of layout options. The Regular Item layout is the most comprehensive of the layouts because items are the primary display element within Content Areas, and they have the largest number of attributes.

Modifying the Navigation Bar

The Navigation Bar is the menu for a Content Area and appears by default on the left side of the page. The Navigation Bar provides two types of links: administration tasks and navigation. Users can log on to the portal and adjust administrative information, such as passwords and user information, from links on the Navigation Bar.

> **Note** You can create complete portal sites using just Content Areas. Portal allows you to place logon/logoff buttons on the Navigation Bar for this purpose.

You can also include navigation options such as folder links, category links, and perspective links within the Navigation Bar. Custom Styles can be applied to the navigation menu as well. Figure 22-7 shows how the Navigation Bar will appear in the NETUCONTENT Content Area by default.

1. Navigate back to the main content panel for the Net University Content Items area and click on the Navigation Bars link to display the panel as shown in Figure 22-16.

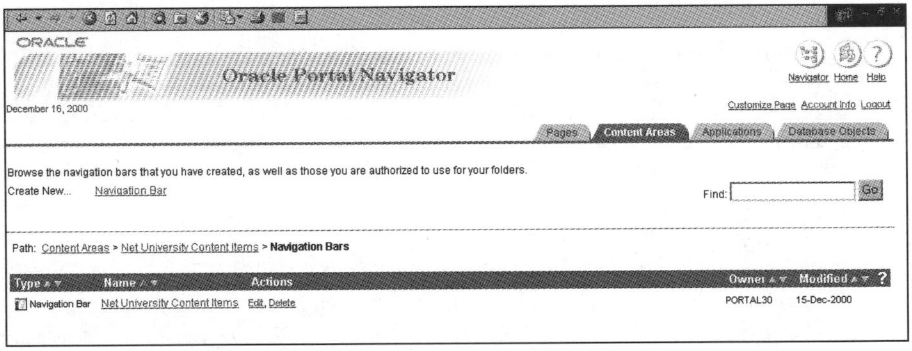

Figure 22-16: Navigation Bar folder

2. Use the Edit link to display the panel as shown in Figure 22-17.

The Navigation Bar acts as a menu for the Content Area and you can set a number of display properties for it.

Navigation Bar Properties

Navigation Bars are just like any other application component within the Oracle Portal environment. You can supply an internal name and display name for the object. Portal provides default values for both of these fields. You are also able to set the justification to left, right, or center. This controls how the Navigation Bar will align the items that you display on its face.

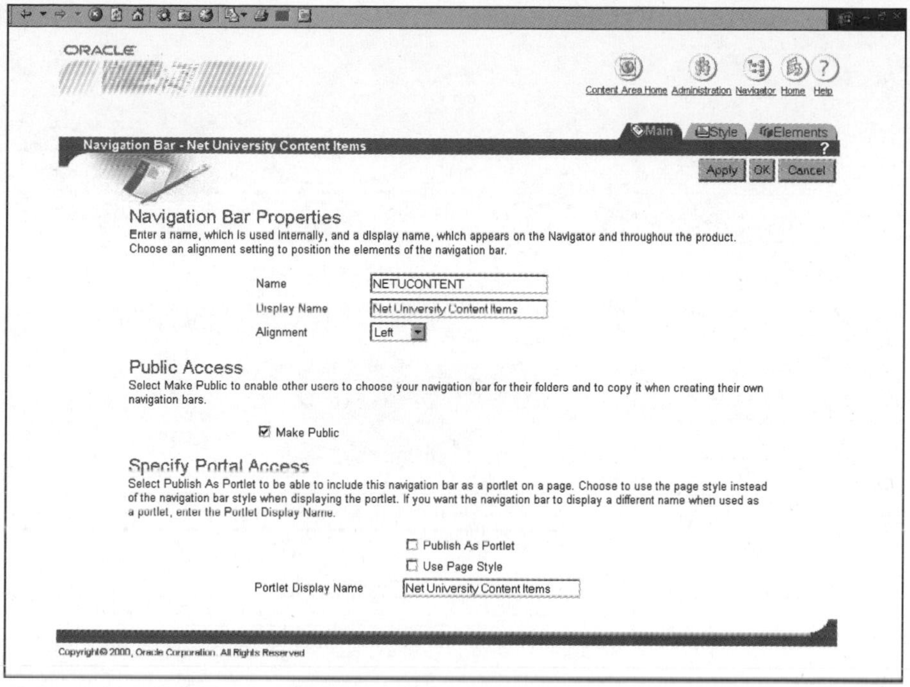

Figure 22-17: Editing the NetU Navigation Bar

Public Access

Use the Make Public check box to allow any user to include this Navigation Bar in their folders or copy it when creating their own Navigation Bars. If you do not select this option, only the Navigation Bar creator and Content Area administrators will be able to use this Navigation Bar.

Specify Portal Access

Navigation Bars are treated as separate objects from the portal perspective. If you wish, you can elect to display the Navigation Bar itself as a portlet. Navigation Bars contain links to folders and items, so publishing them to portal pages is a legitimate menuing technique for portal pages. If you elect to publish a Navigation Bar as a portlet you can choose to have the Navigation Bar inherit the style of the portal page.

3. Select the Publish as Portlet check box and the Use Page Style check box. Click on the Apply button to save the changes.

4. Click on the Style tab to display the panel as shown in Figure 22-18.

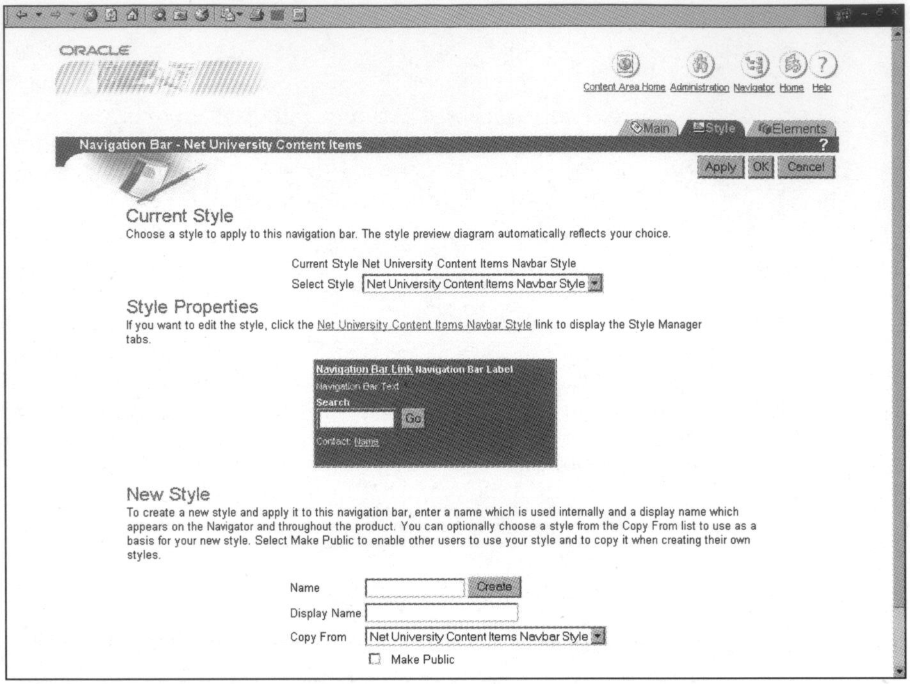

Figure 22-18: Navigation Bar style

 Navigation Bars have their own set of style elements — colors, fonts, and background images. Some of these elements are controlled by the Style Properties panel, which is cross-linked to the current page.

5. Choose the Net University Content Items Navbar Style link on the current panel to display the panel as shown in Figure 22-19.

The panel that is shown in Figure 22-19 looks exactly like the panel shown in Figure 22-11. You will notice, however, that the changes that you made on this panel in the previous sections are no longer shown. This is because the Navigation Bar has its own style record associated with it. The panel is the same, but the *style* that you are editing is a different style. (If you wished, you could set the Content Area and the Navigation Bar area to use the same style.)

There are six style elements that can be set for the Navigation Bar from the Style panel.

✦ Navigation Bar Link

✦ Navigation Bar Label

✦ Navigation Bar Text

✦ Background Image

✦ Navigation Bar Width

✦ Navigation Bar Search Field Width

The first four elements are shared in common with item elements on the folder area. Normally you will use the Navigation Bar to provide links to items — so it makes sense to use the same settings for the labels, links, and text for these items. However, since you are free to use a separate Style for the Navigation Bar, you do not have to make them the same. Portal gives you the opportunity to set the background for the Navigation Bar to an image as well as to a specified color. The default background for the Navigation Bar includes a blue globe shown in the background of the Navigation Bar, but you can replace this with your own image using the Background Image in the Style Element combo box. You are free to use either a GIF image or a JPEG image, and Portal automatically tiles the image to fit the available space in the Navigation Bar. The last two settings are unique to the Navigation Bar and they control the width of the Navigation Bar and the Search Field Width. Both settings affect how much page real estate the Navigation Bar will consume at deployment time.

6. Remove the Background Image for the Navigation Bar using the Background Image setting.

7. Change the Background color to **#996665**.

8. Select the Navigation Bar Width (Pixels) item in the Style Element combo box to display the panel as shown in Figure 22-20.

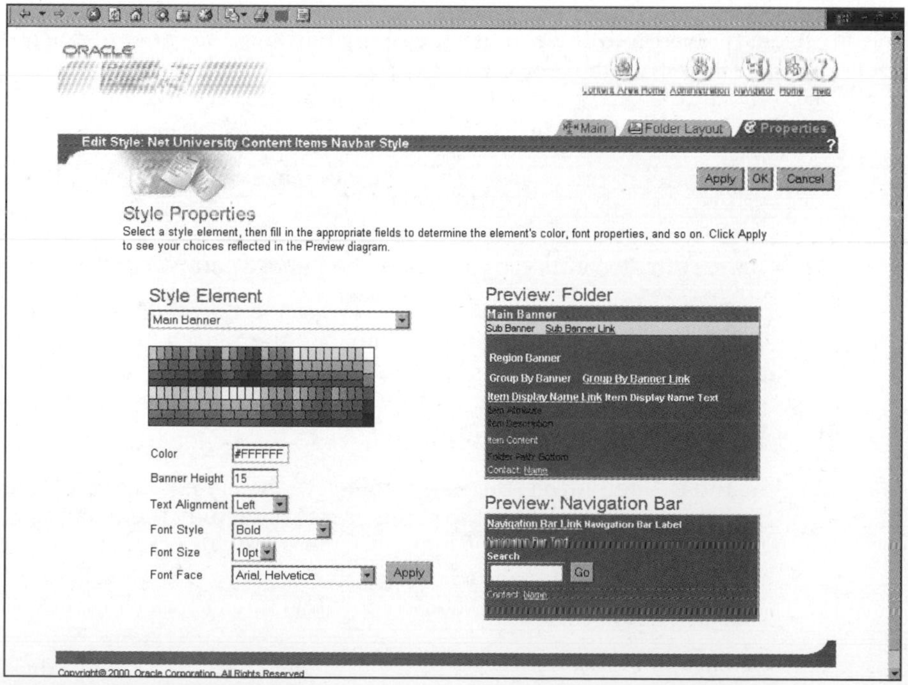

Figure 22-19: Style Properties

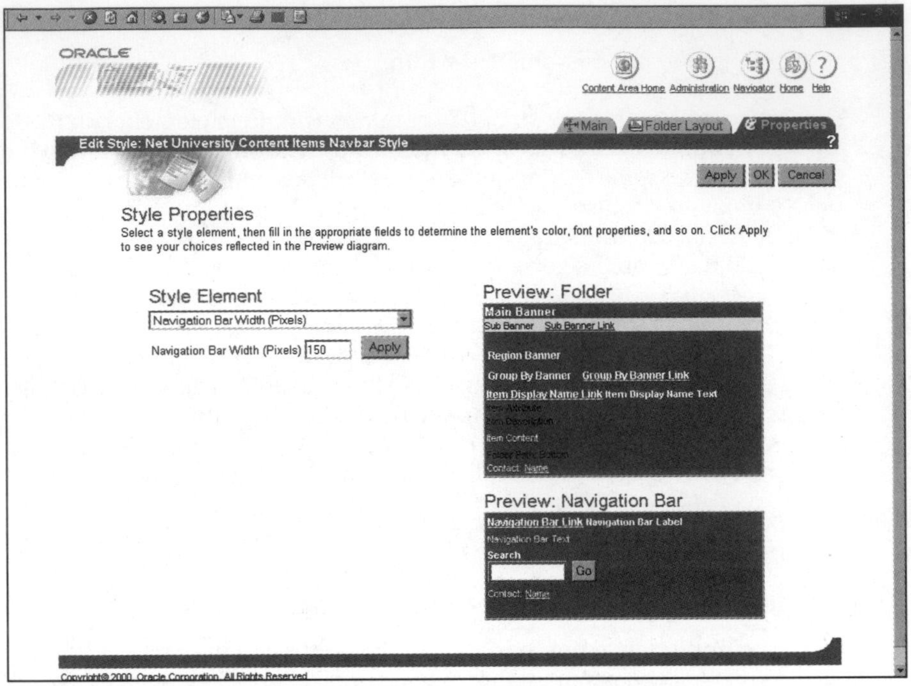

Figure 22-20: Navigation Bar Width

9. Set the width to 150 and use the Apply button to save the changes. Choose the OK button to close the current form.

Navigation Bar elements

The vast majority of the changes that you can make to a Navigation Bar are made using the Elements tab.

10. Choose the Elements tab to display the panel as shown in Figure 22-21.

Four standard elements appear on every Navigation Bar: the Log On Prompt, the Administration icon, the Content Area Map, and the Search field. You can position these items by choosing to edit the elements using the pencil icon. Portal includes a logo within the Navigation Bar by default, but you can change this logo along with any of the default elements.

11. Use the Delete button (the red X) to delete the elements of the Navigation Bar, then use the Add button (the green cross) to display the panel as shown in Figure 22-22.

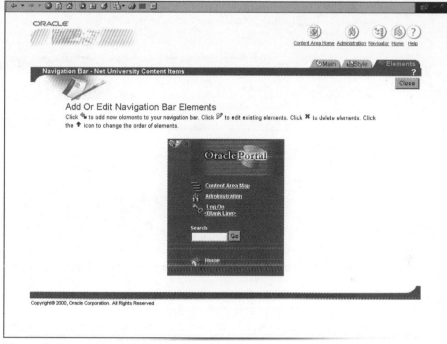

Figure 22-21: Add or Edit Navigation Bar Elements

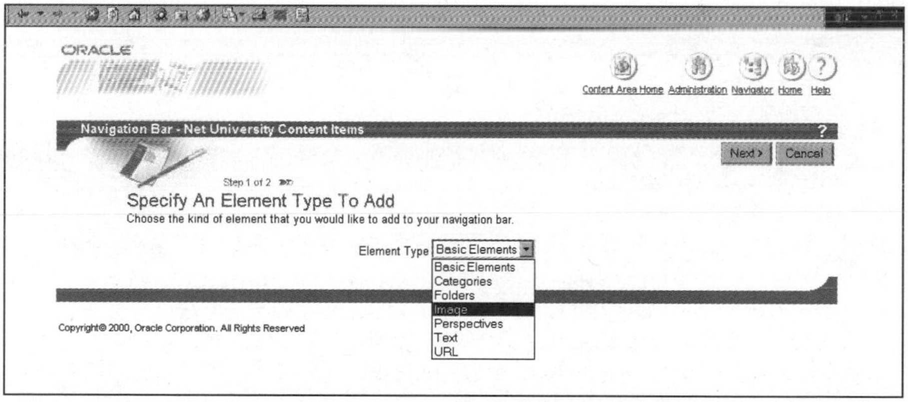

Figure 22-22: Specifying Navigation Bar elements

12. Select the Image Element Type and choose the Next button to add a new logo.

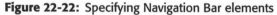

You are free to add plain images or image maps as the logo for your Navigation Bar. Chapter 24 provides an example of using an image map with Content Areas.

13. Select the image netu_logo.gif as the new logo for the Navigation Bar and choose the Finish button to display the panel as shown in Figure 22-23.

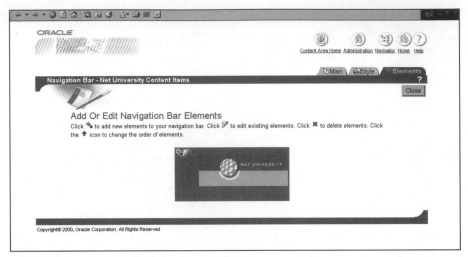

Figure 22-23: Modified Navigation Bar logo

14. Use the Plus icon to add "Basic Elements" to the Navigation Bar as shown in Figure 22-24.

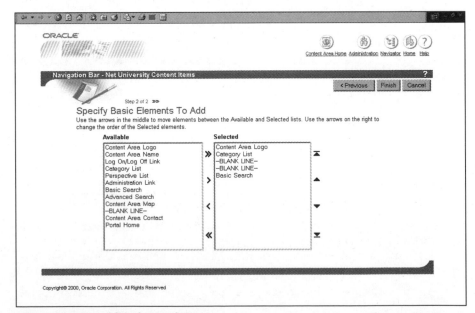

Figure 22-24: Adding basic elements

Portal provides a pair of list boxes that work exactly like the Available/Display list boxes for attributes. Most of the elements that appear in the available list are navigational elements. For example, the Perspective List element displays a list of the perspectives that have been added to your Content Area. Portal users can locate all content items that match a particular perspective by selecting the perspective using this link.

15. Add the following basic elements to the Modified Navigation Bar and use the Finish button to save your changes:

```
Content Area Logo
Category List
--BLANK LINE--
--BLANK LINE--
Basic Search
```

16. Close the Add or Edit Navigation Bar Elements panel and navigate back to the Net University Content Items panel as shown in Figure 22-25.

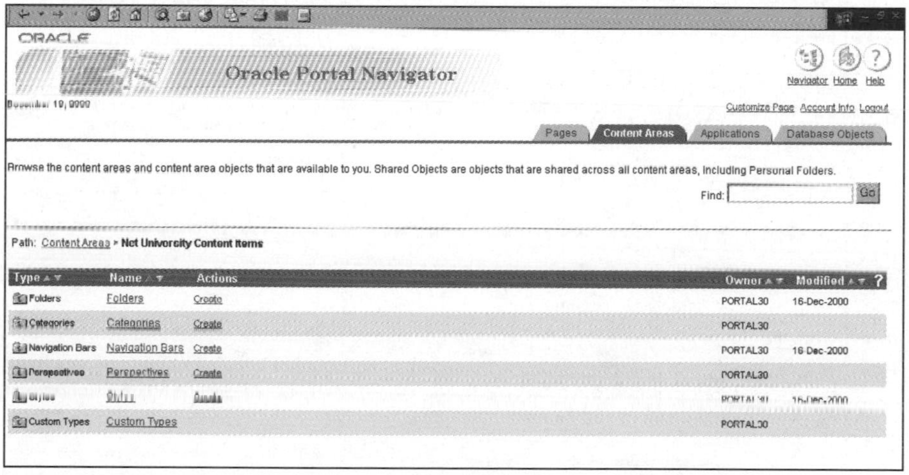

Figure 22-25: Net University Content Items as shown in the Navigator

Adding Categories and Perspectives

Once you have created your folders, you can further organize them by adding categories and perspectives. Categories and perspectives provide a cross-reference for items that are stored in folders. Categories are sections that appear in folders.

Adding categories

Portal displays content items by loading them into categories, and users can elect to view content by category instead of just by folder. In effect, categories serve as a type of cross-reference for folders. When you create categories for a portal site, they *can* appear in every folder contained in that site. You are not required to add content for every category in each folder — and you can limit the categories that appear in any given folder.

In the example case for Net University, four basic categories have been identified: General Information, Academics, Events, and Athletics. Oracle Portal builds the general category when the site is created to deal with the restriction that all content must be loaded into a category.

Note News items are the one exception to this rule, as news content is in effect a category all its own. However, Portal does not list news as a separate category. We advise against creating your own category called "news," and instead recommend that you use the built-in news interface to add content of this type.

1. Use the Categories Create link to display the page shown in Figure 22-26.

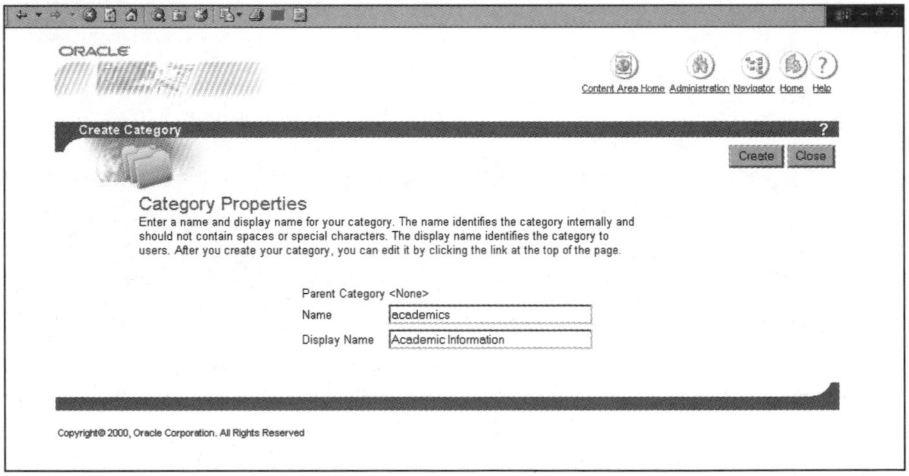

Figure 22-26: Create Category panel

The Create Category panel is even simpler than the Create Folders panel. The only function the interface supports is the ability to enter a new category name and display name and save them using the Create button. If you inadvertently enter a duplicate value, Portal displays an error message. You can use the same panel to repetitively create multiple categories.

2. Add three categories for Net University as follows:

```
Name—academics
Display Name—Academic Information

Name—events
Display Name—NetU Events

Name—Athletics
Display Name—Athletics
```

Once you have added a category, you can use the Edit button on this panel (which appears after the category is created) to display a page that enables you to add images for the category. Portal displays a banner for each category within a folder, but you may to choose to add an image to better identify each category. You can also publish Categories as portlets.

In some cases, you will want to nest categories into subcategories. If you use the Create link from the Navigator within a category, Portal will assign the new category as a subcategory as shown in Figure 22-27.

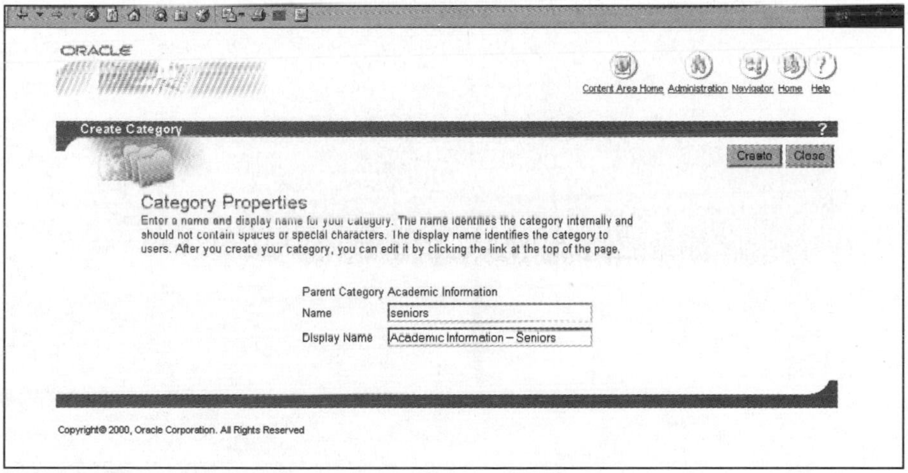

Figure 22-27: Nested academic information for seniors

Note

Remember, it is not necessary to fill in all of the options (such as images and rollover images) for each category or perspective up front. You can always work with the Content Area for a bit and then go back and add in these extra settings once you have a better idea of how your portal will be used.

3. Navigate back to the Net University Content Items panel when you are finished.

Adding perspectives

Perspectives are the third and final mechanism for organizing content (along with folders and categories) in your Content Area. Perspectives are associated with individual content items, but unlike categories, you can assign *multiple* perspectives to a single item. An item also does not need to be associated with any perspective, while every item must be associated with one and only one category. Portal users can even search your site for items that have been assigned to a particular perspective.

The Net University example has two perspectives: one to mark a particularly hot topic and one to indicate that the particular event requires *advance* ticketing. You can add perspectives any time, and you may find that your end users are the best source for generating suggestions as to which perspectives to add. Although you can add search criteria for any object, perspectives provide a type of organized search. When folder managers add content to your site, they may choose to index entries based upon keywords or phrases that may be inconsistent. Perspectives are defined centrally, and can serve as a more consistent high-level indexing scheme.

1. Use the Perspectives Create link to navigate to the panel shown in Figure 22-28.

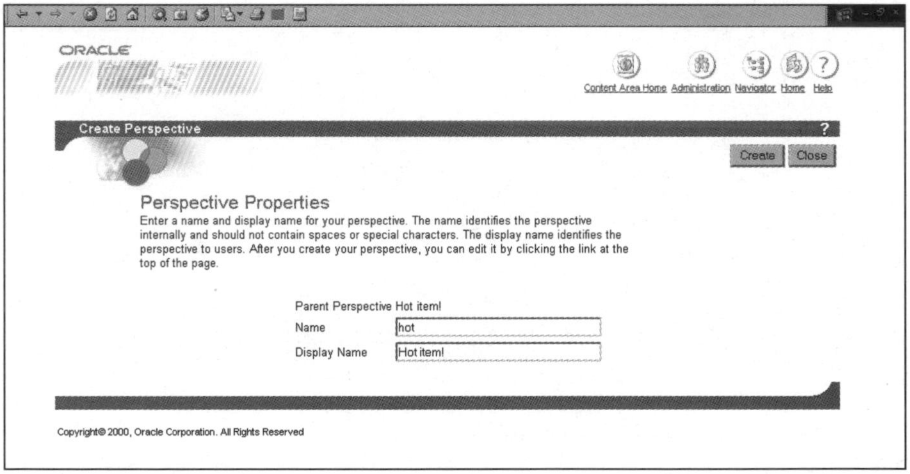

Figure 22-28: Create Perspective panel

2. The Create Perspective panel works in an identical fashion to the Category panel. Add two new perspectives as follows:

```
hot/Hot Item
tickets/Tickets Required
```

Although you may choose not to display icons with categories, you usually choose to do so for perspectives. You can add icons for each perspective by using the browse function to load an image file. Images used with perspectives should be of a consistent size so that they appear evenly when multiple perspectives are added for a single item of content. Because perspectives serve as indexes, you may choose to create certain perspectives without an associated image. Users are able to search for matching items using this perspective, but there is not a visual cue that the perspective is associated with a content item on the page.

3. Navigate back to the main administration panel for Content Areas.

Modifying Content Area Properties

There are a number of properties that you can set that affect the entire Content Area.

1. Choose the Edit Properties Link for NETUCONTENT to display the panel as shown in Figure 22-29.

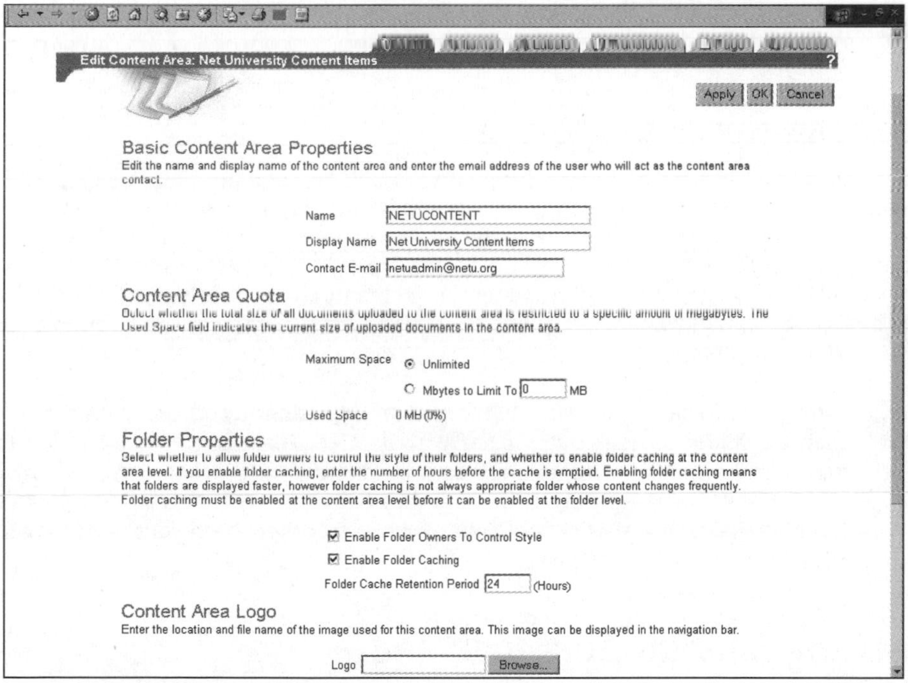

Figure 22-29: NETUCONTENT Properties

The main panel of content properties controls most of the common settings that you will make for a Content Area.

Setting basic properties

When you create a Content Area you can provide both a name and a display name for it. Portal permits you to change both of these values on the main panel. You can also supply an e-mail address for the Content Area Administrator. Portal will optionally display this address as a MAILTO HTML link within the Content Area.

Modifying Content Area quota

As you will see in Chapter 24, Content Areas can store complex documents and items for portal users — and users themselves can add content to a site. Theoretically, it is possible for your users to use up all of your database space by adding lots of oversize items. In order to prevent this from happening you can set a disk storage amount in megabytes for the Content Area.

 Tip We would highly recommend that you enable this setting for production Content Areas to ensure that portal users do not clutter your database with large MPGs or AVIs.

Setting folder properties

Each folder within your Content Area can have its own custom style assigned to it. While this feature provides lots of flexibility, it can lead to a very inconsistent look-and-feel across your folders. Normally, folder owners have the ability to make style changes to folders that they own. Clear this check box to allow only Content Area and style administrators to choose which styles to apply to folders. Folder contents can also be cached to improve performance — and you can set the cache window for folders on this panel as well.

Note If the style for a folder is changed or items are added/modified within a folder then the folder cache is *automatically* invalidated. There is no chance that a user will miss content due to cache intervals — therefore it makes sense to enable caching. We would only recommend that you disable caching on a folder-by-folder basis for those folders that are very dynamic in order to prevent wasting cache resources.

Setting Content Area logo and database access descriptors

Last, but not least, you can change the logo for your Content Area and modify the Data Access Descriptor that links the database to the Content Area.

2. Use the red X link to delete the site logo.

3. Choose the Labels tab to display the panel as shown in Figure 22-30.

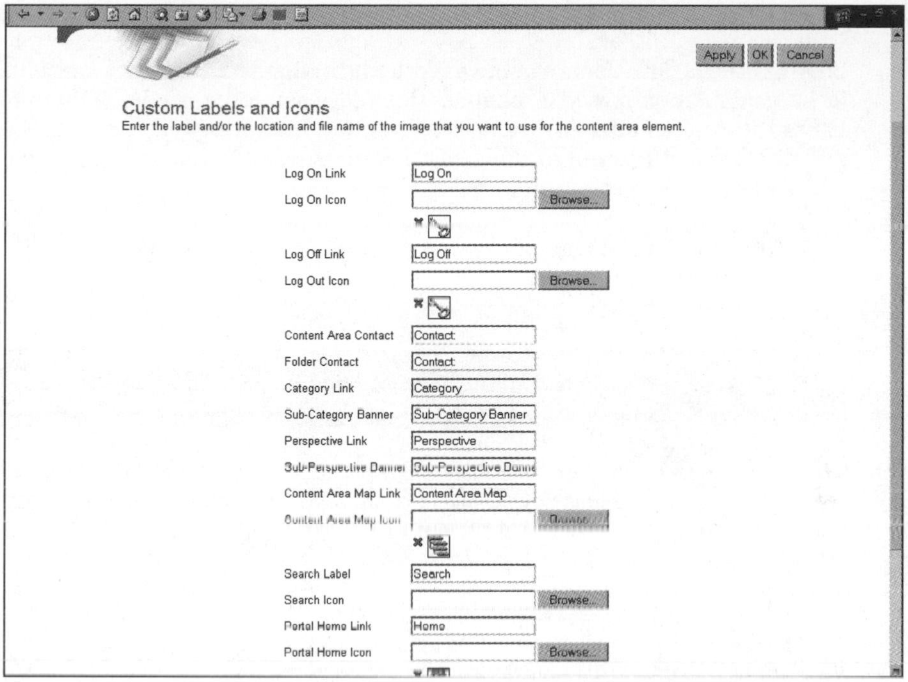

Figure 22-30: Custom Labels and Icons

Portal includes seven basic links in all Content Area sites regardless of the number of folders, categories, perspectives, or items. Four of these links — news, folders, categories, and perspectives — point to content. The remaining three links display a map of the site and enable users to either log on or log off the system. Portal provides default text for each of these links, but you can change this text on the Custom Text panel. Notice that you cannot change the color or font for these links on this panel, but you can change these items within the Style menu.

Cross-Reference These items were discussed in the preceding sections in conjunction with the Navigation Bar.

4. Change the Log On Link text to LogOn.

5. Change the Log Off Link text to LogOff.

6. Click the OK button to save your changes and exit the form.

Changes that you make on the individual panels are stored in the database when you click the Apply button. When you are finished using the Site Manager, click the Finish button to return to the main administration menu.

At this point, the site has all of the features required for deployment to end users with the exception of some security settings. However, you will likely make some changes to the site once you have worked through the process of adding content to it. In particular, you will probably assign responsibility for your folders to power users within your site. For example, in the Net University system, it makes sense to give the class officers of each of the undergraduate classes some control over the items in the class year subfolders.

7. Click on the Net University Content Items link to display the modified site as shown in Figure 22-31.

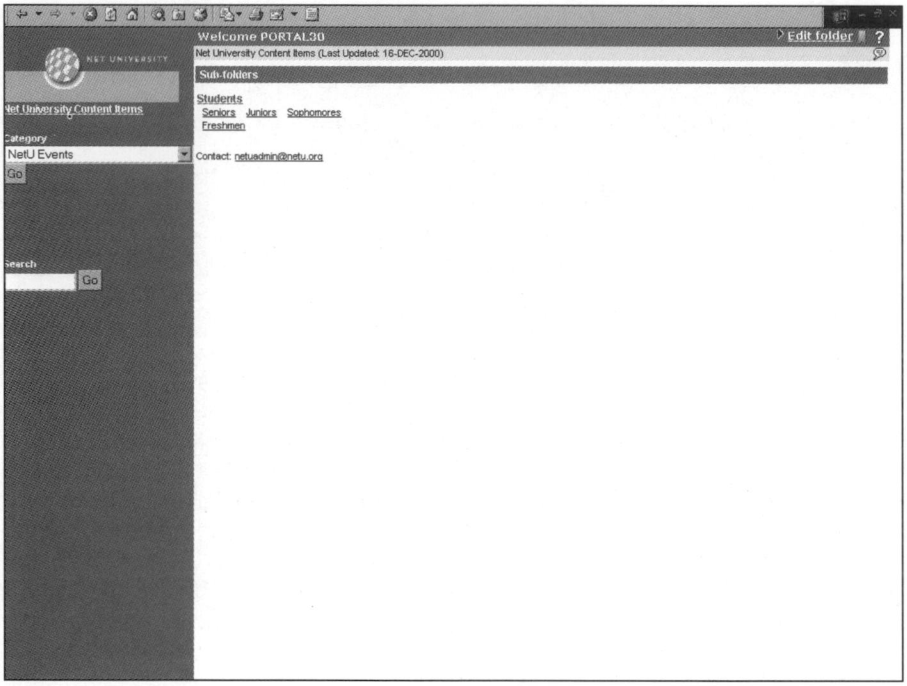

Figure 22-31: Net University Content Items site

You will notice that all of your changes — colors, logos, fonts, categories and the Navigation Bar have been deployed to the Content Area.

Summary

This chapter covered the basics of building a Content Area with Oracle Portal and how the various content editors work. You are no doubt a bit confused at this point because your site does not actually contain any content. The only thing you have managed to accomplish is to create the structure for your site and adjust some of the look and feel of the site.

Before you tackle the next phase of Content Areas, it is important that you understand the Portal security and deployment mechanisms covered in Chapters 26 and 23. You must create the security scheme for your site before you can turn access to your site over to your users. In the next chapters of this book, we introduce you to the administration tools of Portal. In the final part of this book, you will return for a second look at Content Areas, and begin deploying content and assigning folder privileges to users. We'll also be looking at some of the advanced customizations that are available within folders.

✦   ✦   ✦

Deploying Oracle9*i*AS Portal Sites

✦ ✦ ✦ ✦

In This Chapter

Understanding Portal
Deployment
Components and
Architecture

Using Database
Access Descriptors

Considering
Application Schemas

Deploying Portal
Sites

Using Direct Access
URLs

✦ ✦ ✦ ✦

Four major tasks are involved in the development of portal sites: design, development, testing, and deployment. The previous chapters in this book introduced you to Portal's methodology for developing portal components. Part of Portal's value proposition is the reduced amount of design and development time it takes to deliver a portal application. Of course, this is partly due to the capabilities of the product itself. Portals by their very nature are "developed" on an ongoing basis. While traditional applications are thoroughly designed, documented, and tested before they are deployed — portal sites are less rigorously designed. You will often sketch out the basic layout of your portal and then build on this design even after the portal site has been deployed to your end users. The Portal component wizards provide you with fast methods to develop individual portal items, but the wizards do leave you on your own to deploy those items.

Application deployment is more art than science with Portal, because the tool itself does not contain any *specific* deployment tools. Unlike some other application development environments, the components in Portal are in place and ready to go when you are finished creating them with the wizard interface. The architects of Oracle Portal built the product to be easy to work with and highly productive, and no one would argue that this is not a good thing. However, the downside to this design is that Portal lacks a layer of insulation between the design phase and the deployment phase. Although this is normal practice for portal sites, traditional application developers this will probably need some time to get familiar with this system. This also places an additional burden on you as the developer to implement a deployment strategy that makes sense for your organization. In this chapter, we will introduce you to the various components of Portal's deployment architecture, and you will learn how you can use these different components to implement a variety of run-time configurations.

Understanding Portal Deployment Components and Its Architecture

The designers of Portal concentrated on integrating the product tightly with the Oracle database and making the wizards easy to use. While we believe they have succeeded with both of these design goals, one questionable result of their efforts is the fact that no *separate run-time environment exists for Portal*. You are probably familiar with other application development environments that provide separate sets of tools for developing and then deploying an application. Part of Portal's elegance is the fact that there is no separate development environment outside of the browser. This makes it conceptually simple to install and use. However, the normal separation between development and deployment is not present in Portal. Because of this, the process of deploying applications requires you to have a firm understanding of the components of the Portal architecture. Once you understand the various parts of this architecture, you can then decide how to best deploy those parts to your users.

Logically, it is possible to divide the Portal product into individual components and then consider how these pieces are used for development and deployment. The net result of this analysis is that the deployment process with Portal is more an issue of strategy than it is a specific set of tools and utilities. Following is a list of components that constitute the overall Portal environment:

✦ Oracle database server

✦ HTP/HTF packages and utilities (PL/SQL Web Toolkit)

✦ Portal procedures

✦ Portal Schema (Database tables)

✦ Oracle 9*i*AS Application Server (and Logon Server)

✦ Apache HTTP Server

✦ Mod_PLSQL Apache Plug-in

✦ Portlets

✦ External images

✦ Tables and data upon which the application is built

The starting point for any Portal application is the Oracle database. Portal is built with the services provided by the Oracle database, and you cannot deploy a Portal application without the database. Portal applications are also designed to be data-driven, and the Oracle database is the foundation for both the development environment and for your deployed portal site. If you are building portal sites that are nothing more than a series of static pages, Portal is probably not the right solution. Portal applications are dynamic. With Portal, the root element for an application is the Oracle database server itself. Portal can even take advantage of advanced features within the Oracle database such as XML and *inter*Media.

Layered within the database are sets of PL/SQL packages used by Oracle to render HTML output. These packages are commonly referred to as the PL/SQL Web Toolkit. Portal is built on top of these procedures, which were designed as part of the database interface for Oracle's previous application server product, which was called Oracle Application Server. Oracle provides some additional procedures, called the OAS utility procedures, which are specific to the Application Server. These utilities provide some additional services for managing Web objects such as cookies, and are part of the HTF/HTP installation. Oracle 9*i*AS automatically installs all of these foundation packages during the application server installation process, and they appear as a set of PL/SQL packages in a separate schema.

Portal itself requires an additional set of procedures built on top of the HTF/HTP packages. These packages are added to the Portal Database Schema (PORTAL30) created when you install Portal. From a development perspective, these packages implement all of Portal's functionality (portal pages and the various build wizards) and you are probably familiar with them from using the development environment. Some additional "hidden" packages and procedures are used to implement much of the lower level functionality of Portal. For example, individual shared objects, such as JavaScripts, are not converted into database procedures by the JavaScript wizard. The JavaScript objects are written to a series of database tables, and an internal Portal procedure handles all of the display of such elements at run time.

In addition to these procedures, a number of database tables are used internally by Portal. Some of these tables store the source definitions for the objects that you build, and some are used by Portal itself. When you create an object with the component wizards, the source for the object is stored within these tables. However, the actual object is implemented as a PL/SQL package of its own. Many of the shared components, on the other hand, are stored as records within a table, and there is no one-to-one mapping with a stored procedure. As with the internal Portal procedures, Oracle has not publicly documented the functionality of individual tables within the Portal account, so there is no way for you to tell which tables are needed for deployment. *The safest and most accurate assumption for you to make is that all the Portal procedures and tables are required for both development and deployment.*

Note   Oracle may elect to provide a set of utilities in the future for deployment. However, since most portal applications are modified on an ongoing basis, the need for specific deployment tools is somewhat unnecessary. This is especially true in light of the fact that individual portal users can add their own content to the portal. How practical do you think that it would be to have deployment tools when portal users are constantly adding items to the production site?

The Oracle9*i* Application Server and Apache HTTP Listener are the next components of the architecture, and together they are one of the most important pieces of the deployment puzzle. The listener is paired with the Mod_PLSQL gateway. The listener itself is a full Apache HTTP Server, which acts as the process for managing HTTP-style requests. The Mod_PLSQL gateway is responsible for shuttling data to and from the database, and it works in conjunction with the Apache Listener. The Mod_PLSQL gateway contains all of the necessary information for communicating with the SQL*NET and Net8 libraries. Oracle installs both the Apache HTTP Server and the Mod_PLSQL gateway as part of the Oracle 9*i*AS installation.

Note In previous releases of Oracle Portal, the listener layer communicated to the database *solely* through the PL/SQL layer. With the release of Portal 3.0, Oracle handles some of the communication between the database server and the listener through a Java Servlets interface as shown in Figure 23-1.

Portal provides access to third-party components through the portlets architecture. Portlets are "served up" to the portal middle tier either through the database layer, the Servlets interface, or the Mod_PLSQL interface. (Chapter 28 discusses the portlets architecture in more detail.)

The last component of the portal architecture is the graphic images used by Portal. These images are stored in two formats: Graphic Interchange Format (GIF) files and Joint Photographic Expedition Graphics (JPEG) files. Both formats are browser-compatible, and most browsers automatically handle images in these formats. Portal stores these images outside the database, and the Apache Server manages them and displays them on behalf of Oracle Portal.

The final element of your portal application is the tables, structured database objects, and content items that comprise the data for your portal. Although these elements are not specifically a part of the portal architecture, you cannot deploy a portal without content.

A Portal application requires all nine of these base objects in order to function, and they are required whether you are building portals or deploying portals. The deployment architecture of Portal is depicted in Figure 23-1.

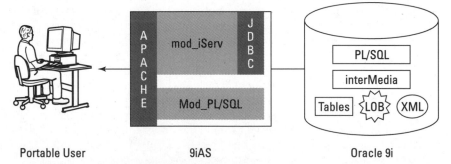

Figure 23-1: Portal architecture components

The simplest possible deployment architecture from a system's perspective is an intranet on a single server as shown in Figure 23-1. All of the components in this model are deployed on a single server machine, with the Apache HTTP Server and Application Server working on the same machine as the database. From this viewpoint, it is not necessary to delve into the specifics of how the Oracle database itself is laid out. It does not matter how many USERIDs you have, nor does it matter where the data and procedures are stored within the database server. You may have several Oracle servers running on different machines and you can run a copy of Portal on each of them, as shown in Figure 23-2.

The Apache HTTP Listener is associated with a particular server machine and port number. Users can navigate to both machines through the browser as shown in Figure 23-2 and gain access to a Portal application on either machine, provided they have the necessary permissions and logon information. Because Portal itself does not mark individual components as being part of any particular application, you could have several logical applications stored within a single Oracle instance. Figure 23-2 shows a single browser user connecting to Oracle Portal installations on two separate servers—Whiskeysoda and Pumpkin. A single browser page cannot be pulled from multiple servers, but a single browser session can be connected to multiple Oracle Portal installations.

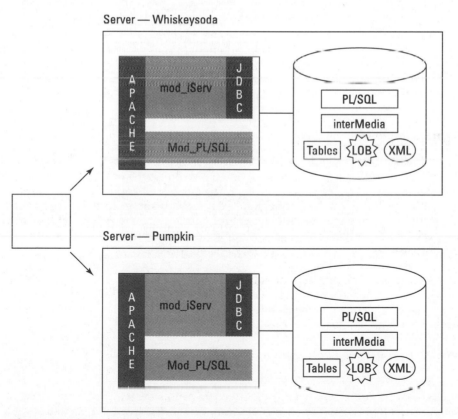

Figure 23-2: Deploying multiple copies of Portal

An installation of the nine Portal components constitutes both the *development* architecture as well as the *deployment* architecture. Furthermore, you cannot build applications or deploy applications without including all nine components. However, it is possible to separate your portal application across multiple servers. For example, the application server (Apache Listener, Mod_PLSQL interface, and JServlets) can run on one server — while the database runs on a separate machine. However, any deployment strategy that you use for your Portal applications must account for these nine components in one way or another. Normally you will deploy the various components in three distinct groups:

✦ Application Server (and Logon Server)

✦ Portal Database

✦ User Database(s)

Most of the components of the Oracle 9*i* Application Server are installed as a group — and they are normally deployed on a *single* machine. The exception to this rule is the Portal Repository. When you install the application server's portal data, known as the Portal Repository, it will be stored in an Oracle database (which need not reside on the same server machine as the Apache HTTP Server, Logon Server and Oracle9*i* Application Server). *Application* data that you display within your portal does not have to reside within the Portal database. These user databases can be any Oracle database (local or remote). Such databases can even access external data in non-Oracle databases through Oracle's Gateway products.

Replacing the listener

One of the options available to you is to replace the listener with a third-party Web server. Chances are good that you already have some type of Web server in your organization, and you may want to integrate your Portal applications with the existing Web server. You can easily link your existing Web server to the Portal application simply by embedding a URL link pointing to the Apache HTTP Listener within any page on your existing Web server application. The connection is not made from server to server, but rather from browser client to server.

For example, assume that you already have a Web server running on port 80 on machine A. Further, assume that you have the Oracle Apache HTTP Listener running on port 4000 on machine B. Adding a link such as the following in any page on Web server A connects the user to the Portal application:

```
http://serverb:4000/pls/portal30/portal30.home
```

Using Other Web Servers

Although it is possible to use a third-party Web server to "front" Oracle Portal applications — you must use the Apache Listener as the HTTP server for Oracle Portal. Oracle has standardized on the Apache product for their entire application server product line. As of the production release of Oracle Portal there is no server-to-server interface between Oracle's version of the Apache Server and either Microsoft's IIS product or the iPlanet Enterprise Web Server.

In the previous code, *serverb* is the name of the server that contains the Portal environment (serverb:4000/pls), the string /portal30 is the name of the Data Access Descriptor, and portal30.home is the default home page for Oracle Portal.

Because it is so simple to connect the Apache HTTP Listener to your existing Web server by using links, you may simply choose to add links from your existing Web pages to the Portal components.

Modifying Database Access Descriptors

One of the major innovations of the Portal Mod_PLSQL gateway is the Database Access Descriptors (DADs). DADs are the mechanism by which users are connected to the database via the Mod_PLSQL gateway. DADs can be used to provide a logical grouping of users and applications for your Portal components.

The Database Access Descriptor settings are found in the Administration tab under the Services section. The Listener Gateway Settings link takes you to the main settings page, as shown in Figure 23-3. And each Database Access Descriptor is composed of a number of individual settings, which are described in Table 23-1.

1. Navigate to the Administration panel and select the Listener Gateway Settings link.

2. Click the Gateway Database Access Descriptor link to display the panel as shown in Figure 23-3.

3. Click on the Edit link next to the PORTAL30 entry to display the panel as shown in Figures 23-4 and 23-5.

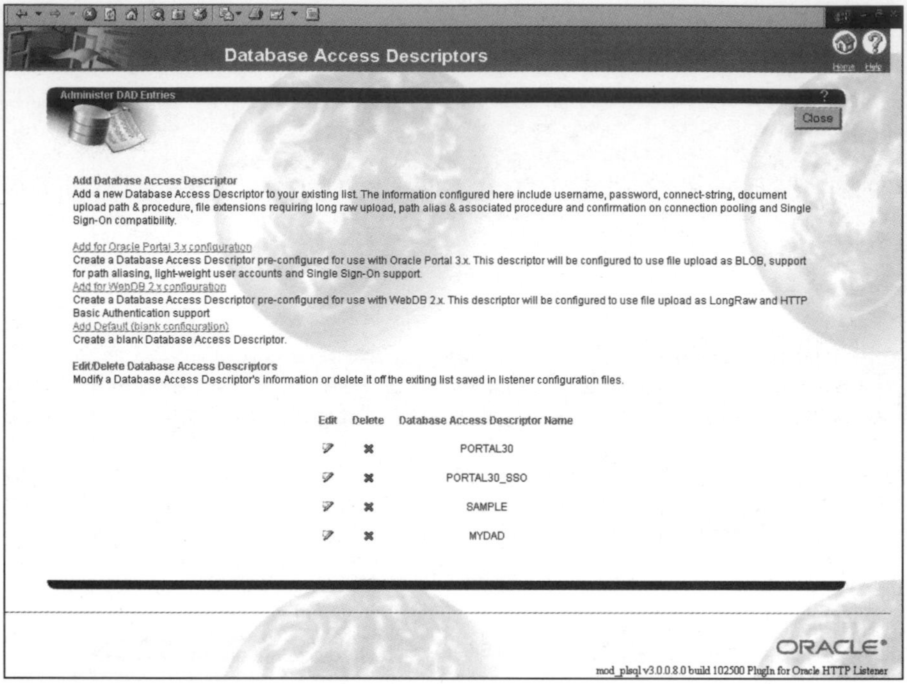

Figure 23-3: Database Access Descriptors

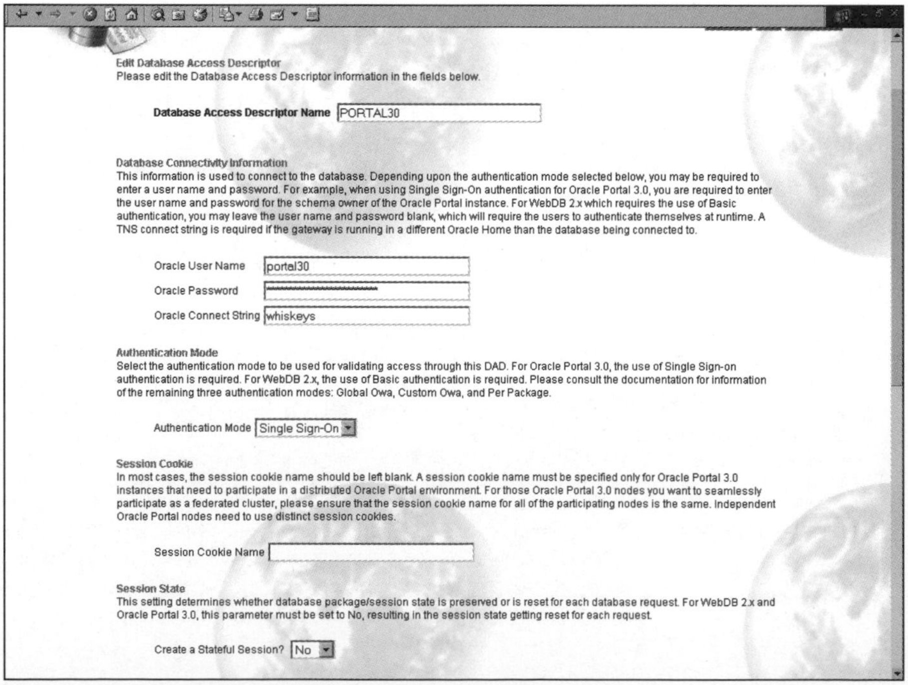

Figure 23-4: PORTAL30 Database Access Descriptor — part 1

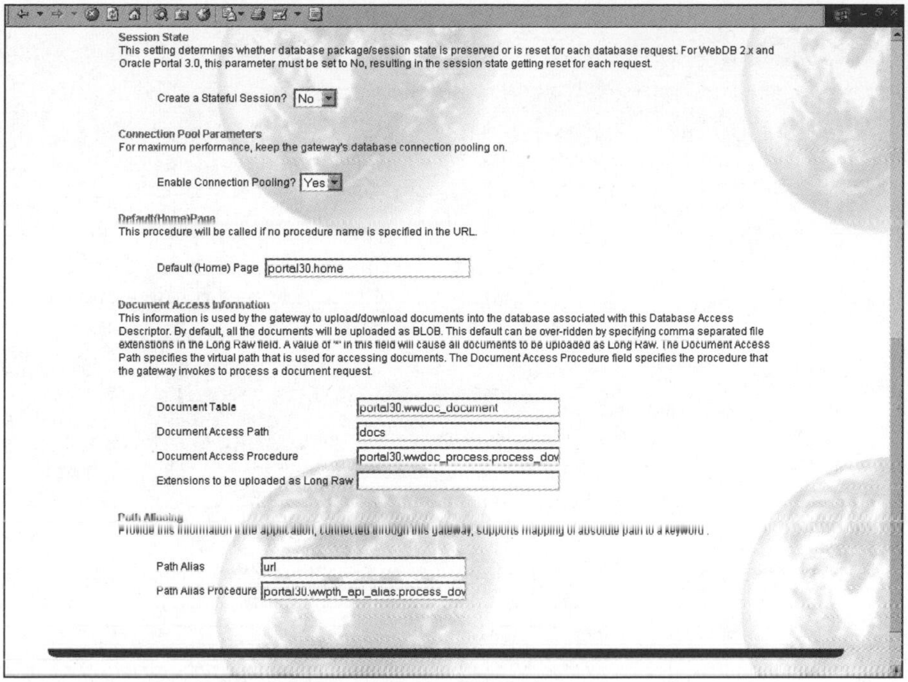

Figure 23-5: PORTAL30 Database Access Descriptor — part 2

Table 23-1
Database Access Descriptor Fields

Field	Description
Database Access Descriptor Name	The Descriptor Name field identifies the entry in the DAD table and is used as part of the URL.
Oracle User Name	Portal 3.0 relies upon Single Sign On with the Login Server. The user name specified in this field is used to specify which Oracle database account the portal schema is currently installed in. Note: In prior releases of Oracle Portal (WebDB 2.X) the user name and password were used to log the user onto the portal.
Oracle Password	Displays the password for the Oracle Schema in which Portal is installed.
Oracle Connect String	This field contains the TNS names alias, also referred to as a net service name, defined for the database. This value must already exist in the TNS service files ($ORACLE_HOME/network/admin on UNIX and ORACLE_HOME\network\admin on Windows).

Continued

Table 23-1 *(continued)*

Field	Description
Authentication Mode	The Apache Server supports multiple types of authentication with the Oracle database. Portal 3.0 requires the use of the "Single Sign-On" methodology.
Session Cookie Name	Oracle Portal can connect to remote Portal servers on other machines. In order to keep track of session authentication across machines you are permitted to specify a cookie-name that will apply to the current server.
Session State	The Apache Server can maintain state across database requests — but Oracle Portal requires you to drop state for each database call.
Connection Pool Parameters	Oracle Portal improves the performance of database access by keeping database sessions open between user requests. Portal handles this transparently for you, and it automatically cleans up database sessions as required.
Default Home Page	This entry determines the procedure that runs if no parameters are supplied for a given URL. In effect, this is the default home page for the DAD entry. (The Apache Server can have its own home page as well.)
Document Table	Identifies the table that will be used to store uploaded and downloaded files.
Document Access Path	Identifies the URL setting for files that have been uploaded into Portal. Portal uses this value as the virtual directory for Content Items.
Document Access Procedure	Contains the name of the procedure that will be used to upload and download documents. The default value in this entry field is based on the name of the schema in which the application is installed. The format of this string is `<schema>.wwdoc_ process.process_download`, where `<schema>` matches the Oracle user name that you supplied in the previous field.
Extensions to be Uploaded as Long Raw	Contains the file name extension(s) for documents you want to upload and download as a Long Raw datatype. These are typically large files containing content such as graphic images, video clips, and sound waveforms. For example, you could enter these extensions: * .avi, * .mpg. Note: If you leave this field blank, all documents will be uploaded and downloaded as Binary Large Objects (BLOBs). Oracle stores Long Raw fields differently than BLOB fields within the database.

Field	Description
Path Alias	The Path Alias works like a virtual directory. The string that you enter here will act as a substitute for the database stored procedure that Portal uses to connect to the database from the Mod_PLSQL layer. By default, this value is set to `url`.
Path Alias Procedure	The default procedure the Mod_PLSQL layer uses to connect to the database. The default value is `<schema>.wwpth_api_alias.` `process_download`, where the string `<schema>` points to the Oracle Database Schema in which Portal is installed.

This group of 15 settings provides the flexibility to tune your deployment strategy as necessary. Logically, these parameters can be divided into two distinct groups according to how they are used. The first group—made up of the Descriptor Name, Oracle User Name, Oracle Password, Oracle Connect String, and Default (Home) Page settings—controls the connection information. The second group controls settings used primarily for Content Items, and includes the Document Table, the Document Access Path, the Document Access Procedure, and LONGRAW Extensions. Normally you will not need to adjust any of the other settings on this form.

Note

Oracle will continue to add new settings to the DAD area of Portal with each subsequent release (and especially with release 3.0.8). Be sure to check the on-line documentation within the Portal environment for information on these new settings as they appear.

The connection field group is the main tool for logically linking a group of users together into a single application. The Descriptor Name becomes the physical name by which you refer to the group of users who are identified by the name. The Descriptor Name is used as part of the URL string that feeds the content to the browser. Within the development environment of Portal, you have used a URL similar to the following string to connect to the Portal build interface:

```
http://whiskeysoda/pls/portal30/portal30.home
```

The string `portal30` within the URL matches a Descriptor Name that has been defined as part of the PL/SQL gateway. When you installed Portal, the default Descriptor Name `portal30` is automatically created. Even if you have allowed multiple developers to work with Portal using separate Portal Developer Accounts, you have most likely used the same DAD entry. After all, the Descriptor Name is nothing more than a logical connection. The physical connection is made using the secondary fields: Oracle User Name and Oracle Password. Portal uses these values to log on to the database as the Portal Schema user. Within the URL string, the information to the left of the Descriptor Name refers to the server. The information to the right of the DAD name refers to the component being called. When a browser sends a URL to the portal server, the gateway checks its client-side cookies to determine if there is valid logon information for the DAD name from the individual TCP/IP client. If the gateway does not contain valid logon credentials for the session, it then uses the DAD entry information to redirect the user to the logon server.

Consider the following two URL strings:

```
http://whiskeysoda/pls/portal30/portal30.home
http://whiskeysoda/pls/mydad/portal30.home
```

The two strings are identical except for the DAD names in the center of the strings. In order for Portal to use these URLs, the strings `portal30` and `mydad` must match DAD entries in the Database Access Descriptors panel. If the string does not match an existing entry, then Portal returns a "No DAD Configuration Found" error message to the browser. However, if the DAD entry is valid, Portal attempts to use the entry to connect to the database on your behalf.

> **Note**
>
> In addition to the user name and password, you are free to specify a connection to a remote Oracle database server by entering a value in the Oracle connect string field. The value string you enter must match an existing Net8 alias as set by the Oracle Nameserver or TNSNAMES.ORA file. However, the schema that you specify *must* be configured as a Portal Schema and include all of the necessary portal objects. It is possible to manually install a portal schema, but it is better practice to use the Oracle 9*i*AS installation program to do so.

1. Return to the Administer DAD Entries panel as shown in Figure 23-3.

2. Click the "Add for Oracle Portal 3.x configuration" link to add a new DAD entry with the following values (as shown in Figures 23-6 and 23-7).

```
Database Access Descriptor Name—mydad
Schema Name—<portal30>
Oracle User Name—<portal30>
Oracle Password - <portal30 password>
Oracle Connect String - <portal30 connect string>
```

The values for the user name, password, and connect string must match the values as entered for the PORTAL30 DAD on your installation. Portal will automatically use the SCHEMA NAME field to fill in the values for the remaining DAD fields on the form.

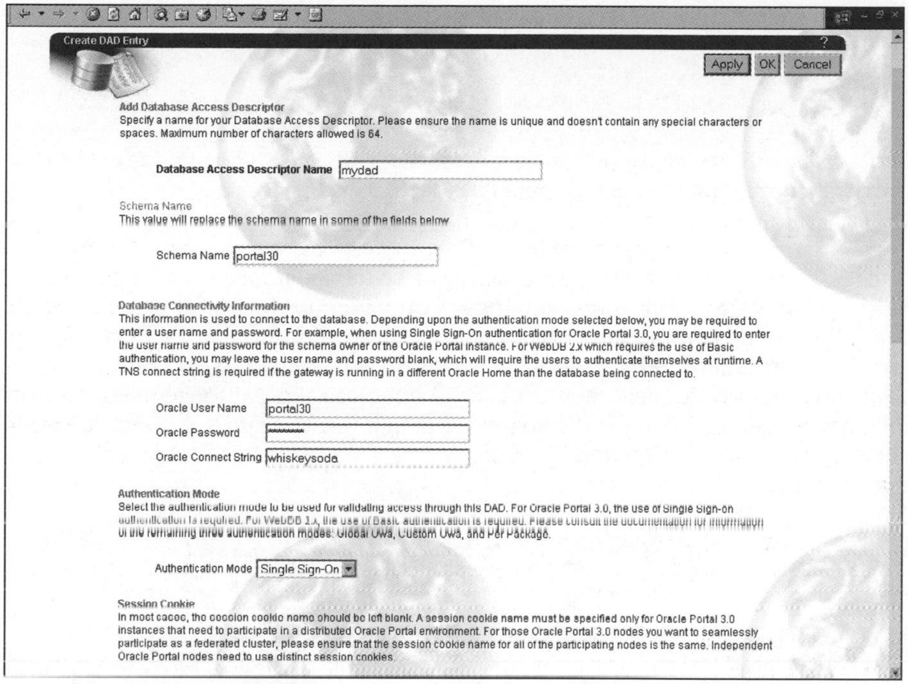

Figure 23-6: "mydad" — part 1

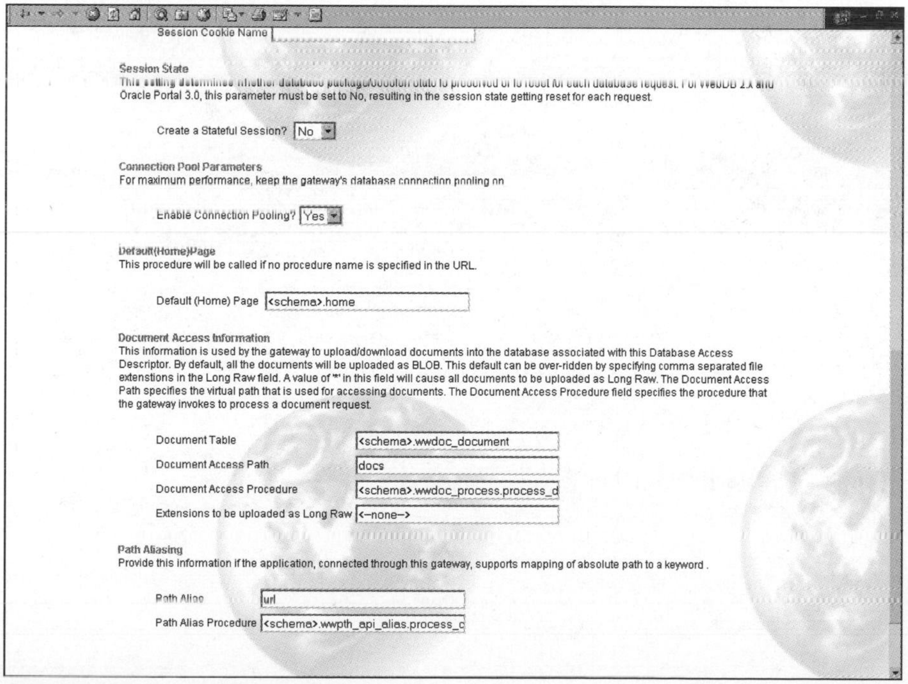

Figure 23-7: "mydad" — part 2

3. Click the OK button to save your changes.

4. Enter the following URL into your browser location field:

```
http://whiskeysoda/pls/mydad/portal30.home
```

Replace the server name (`whiskeysoda`) with values for your local server (and port if you are not using the default port 80).

Portal proceeds to display the Oracle Portal home page as shown in Figure 23-8. Although you have already logged on to the database in order to change the Mod_PLSQL gateway settings, you logged on using the DAD entry `portal30`. By using the `mydad` DAD you are considered to be a different user by Portal. From the portal development perspective, there is little value in using different DADs for your developers, because they are able to log on to the database using different USERIDs within the same DAD. The value is in using the DADs to separate logical groups of content during deployment.

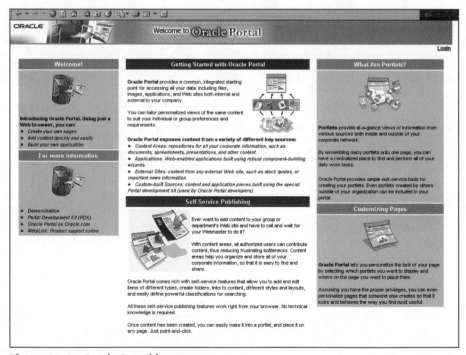

Figure 23-8: Oracle Portal home page

From a security perspective, there are two types of application components within the Portal environment: unauthenticated (public) and authenticated (private). Public components are those objects to be made available to your entire user community, whether through an intranet or over the entire Internet. Although Portal always requires a valid logon to the Oracle Portal, you are free to use the public user. Doing so causes Login Server to authenticate automatically, and the connection is transparent to the user.

Private components are those objects restricted to the use by authenticated users. You will typically want to require an interactive logon for these components.

For example, in the Net University site, the events calendar and sports schedule are examples of public components. Although you store the source data for these objects in the database, you do not want to require the user community at large to have a user name and password in order to view this data. You want the public to be able to access these pages easily, and the public includes people that you may not be familiar with in advance.

One solution to this problem is to use static pages for public data, because the Apache HTTP Listener never requires logon information for static pages. However, the benefit to using Portal is to drive your HTML pages from data in your database. As the Net University schedule changes, you do not want to manually update static schedule pages. If the pages are stored in the database, a Portal component can automatically display the updated schedule as requested, without any manual intervention — using the "portal30_public" user.

Conversely, you may want to require that your users have a valid, individual logon before they can access certain data items. For example, in the Net University application, there is place for NetU alumni to review their biographical information and keep track of one another. In the interest of privacy, you would not want members of the more general public to have access to this information. You can protect this data by limiting access to these forms and reports to a specified DAD record that prompts for a valid user name and password. The connection between the DAD record and the component object is made at run time, which enables you to build components without having to worry about how they are later deployed. Every component can be serviced by any Database Access Descriptor, and any DAD can work with multiple components. For each DAD record, you are also free to specify a home component through the Default Home Page entry.

The second group of fields in the DAD record is made up of the Document Table, the Document Access Path, and the Document Access Procedure. These fields are used for accessing and storing files for Content Areas. Notice that for the new DAD record you entered, these values were simply copied from the Portal DAD entry.

When you install Portal, the installer automatically populates these fields. The Document Table item is a concatenation of the schema owner and a table name (wwv_document). Portal uses this entry to store information uploaded by a portal user into a Content Area. You can change this value in order to accommodate the situation in which you wish to have multiple DAD records pointing to the same Content Area. For the purposes of Portal components, this item is not used, and you can copy the value for this field from the PORTAL DAD entry when you create a new DAD record.

The Document Access Path is a virtual directory Portal uses to locate files that have been uploaded into Content Areas. The string entered into this field becomes a shorthand technique for extracting files directly. For example, assume that you have uploaded a file called sample.htm into a Content Area with the DAD of mydad and a document access path of docs. You can view the sample.htm file using a built-in link within Portal, or you can pass a URL such as the following directly through the browser interface:

```
http://whiskeysoda/pls/mydad/docs/FOLDER/NETUCONTENT/STUDENTS/
SENIORS/SAMPLE.HTM
```

The last field in this group is the Document Access Procedure, and contains the schema owner and procedure name for a procedure used to download a file to the browser. The default value for this field is the Portal schema owner and the literal string portal30.wwdoc_process.process_download. Normally, you take the default for this field as well, but there are cases where you may wish to change this value. For example, you could elect to store uploaded content items in a *different* schema from the core portal installation.

Oracle Portal considers each DAD entry to be a separate logon. If the same portal user navigates to the same relative URL through portal with two *different* DAD entries, then Portal will redirect the call to the Logon Server. Thus, the following two URL strings will be treated as different users:

```
http://whiskeysoda/pls/portal30/portal30.home
http://whiskeysoda/pls/mydad/portal30.home
```

In fact, the same user can log on using two different portal USERIDs within the same browser session. Thus, it is possible to use DAD entries to separate portal content items within the same portal instance.

Understanding Application Schemas

Oracle organizes all database content by the USERID (or schema) that owns the individual objects. Within a database, there are any number of USERIDs that own content along with a number of USERIDs that are used for connecting to the data in other schemas. The Oracle database does not differentiate between a USERID created for storing objects and a USERID created as a storage area for tables, views, and procedures. Portal, however, notes that there is a logical difference between the two types of accounts.

1. Log on to the Portal as the Portal Administrator and navigate to the Administer Database panel.

2. Edit the NETU schema as shown in Figure 23-9.

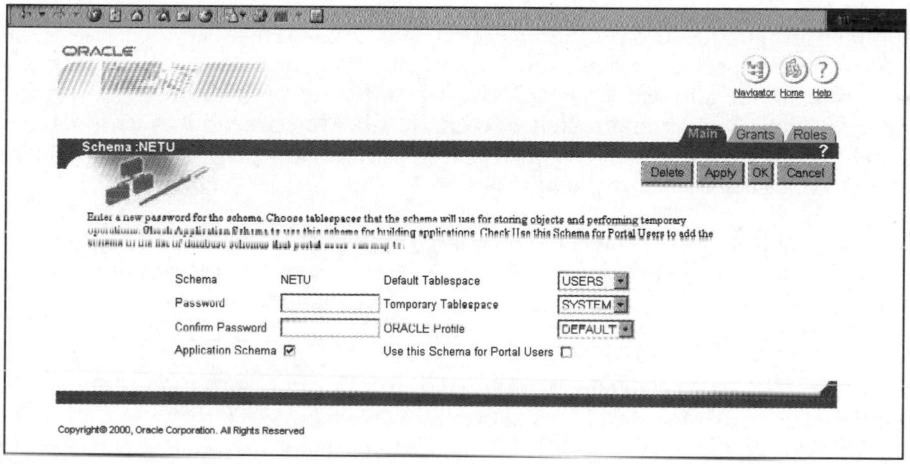

Figure 23-9: NETU Application Schema

Portal provides the Application Schema check box to indicate whether the Oracle USERID is used for storing portal components. If the check box is selected, Portal considers the account to be an *application schema*. This means that Portal assumes users will not be logging on to the account directly, but rather that the account is to be used as a container for tables, views, and procedures used by Portal. Your application data need not be stored in the application schema, but this schema will be used to store the generated database packages for any Portal component that you create within the application that is associated with this schema. When the check box is not selected, Portal assumes that the USERID is a normal Oracle account.

Remember, the Oracle database does not distinguish between the two. Only Portal makes this distinction, but it is an important distinction from the application building perspective. Portal applications should be stored within their own, unique schemas. There are several reasons for doing so. From an organizational standpoint, it is much easier to keep track of an application if all of the parts are kept in one place. This makes everything from import and export to backup and recovery much easier to manage. The second reason for doing so is to simplify your security framework. Users and roles can be given permission to use database procedures, but procedures themselves only see privileges that have been granted to the *schema* explicitly. Procedures take their privileges from the Oracle USERID that *owns* the procedure. Keeping all of your Portal components for an application (which are database procedures) in a single schema makes it much easier to manage the privileges.

For example, assume that Net University is a long-time Oracle database user and all of its existing data is stored inside an Oracle schema called NETU_DB. Net University decides to create a Portal application called NETU_ALUMNI to provide access to interesting alumni data to the NetU alumni community through a portal application. The NETU_DB schema contains all of the tables, views, indexes, and custom stored procedures used by the portal application. Because Portal deploys all *portal components* as stored procedures, and stored procedures inherit the privileges of their owner, it makes sense to create all of the procedures within a single Oracle schema. Doing so guarantees that table and view privileges only need to be granted to one schema for the purposes of Portal.

To continue the example, assume that the developers at Net University create a second Portal application, called NETU_UGRADS, targeted at the undergraduate students. If the objects between the two applications do not have much in common, it makes sense to create this new application in a third Oracle schema.

Three Oracle USERIDs are used for storing content. The NETU_DB schema is the Oracle USERID that holds the tables and views for the application. The NETU_ALUMNI schema holds the Portal stored procedures that access the alumni data in the NETU_DB, and the NETU_UGRADS schema holds the Portal components that access the undergraduate data in the NETU_DB schema. Each developer who works on the NETU_ALUMNI application uses their own individual portal account to log on to the portal, but all Portal components are created in the database user account NETU_ALUMNI. The NETU_ALUMNI account is given the necessary permissions to access the individual tables, views, and procedures in the NETU_DB account.

When it comes time to deploy the NETU_ALUMNI application, you can then provide access to the Portal procedures in the NETU_ALUMNI *application* to individual portal accounts (or groups). (The same rules apply to the NETU_UGRADS application.) This greatly simplifies your deployment task because you only have to assign *database* table and view security to a *single database account* for each application. Oracle automatically applies the *schema* privileges to the Portal procedures at run time.

Note   If you do not plan to allow your end users to have "browse" privileges in the database with the Portal Navigator, then this technique is even more powerful. You do not need to grant access to the NETU_DB objects to your end-user accounts at all. Portal uses database procedures as the access mechanism for all of its objects, and the end users are only able to get to the underlying data through the specified Portal procedures within the application.

In its simplest incarnation, you can build the Portal objects in the same *application* schema as the database objects as we have done with the examples in this book. (The NETCOLLEGE application is stored in the NETU database schema, where the tables and views are also held.) However, best practices dictate that you create separate Portal *application* schemas for each of your Portal applications. If you allow your developers to create Portal components inside of multiple portal "applications" against the same set of database tables, you will be forced to grant access from each application schema.

Deploying Portal Applications

Deploying Portal applications requires you to consider two aspects of the application. First, you need to consider the application components themselves, such as the files, servers, and security. Then you need to consider how to package your applications logically and deliver them to your users. The previous sections of this chapter have covered the deployment components in detail, and this last section of the chapter concerns itself with the logical packaging of these applications.

One of the most important concepts to remember with Portal is that there is no separate deployment model, such as you would find with other development tools. Although we stated this repeatedly in the first portion of this chapter, it is worth repeating in the context of logical application deployment. In order to deploy applications built with Portal, you must make the entire Portal *environment* available to your users. This does not mean that you have to allow your users to have access all of the pages, forms, reports, and so on. What it means is that the portal environment must be made available to your user community. (There simply is not any way to install a subset of the portal.)

Portal applications are delivered as procedures, but certain objects, such as shared components, use database tables in the Portal schema. Even if you build all of the components for your application inside an application schema, you still need access to certain Portal schema objects at run time. The designers of Portal have not included a run-time environment with this release of the software, so there is no documentation as to exactly which Portal objects (tables, components) are required for supporting your run-time applications. Consequently, you must consider four factors when making a decision to deploy your portal application:

✦ Schema definition

✦ Staging areas

✦ Server configuration

✦ Component deployment

The combination of each of these elements determines how you handle the process of developing and deploying Portal applications within your organization.

Schema definition

Portal schema definition is a combination of the application schema technique and the use of Database Access Descriptors. We recommend that you create a schema for each portal "application" that you build and store all of the Portal components for that application within this single schema. This makes the maintenance and deployment of your application much easier. You only need to assign object privileges to one Oracle schema and you are able to use Oracle's Import and Export utilities to manage the compiled objects. Under this design scheme, a single target database schema can be accessed by multiple logical Portal applications.

For example:

- ✦ **Data_schema:** Contains all of the data for your application (UGRADS, ALUMNI, etc.)
- ✦ **Application_schema(s):** Contains the logical portal application(s) and all of the associated stored procedures
- ✦ **Portal_schema:** Contains the central portal objects and the Content Areas

Remember, Oracle Portal stores the source code for all of the procedures within the PORTAL schema (portal30). The compiled PL/SQL procedures for each logical application are stored in the application schema that is associated with the portal application as shown in Figure 23-10.

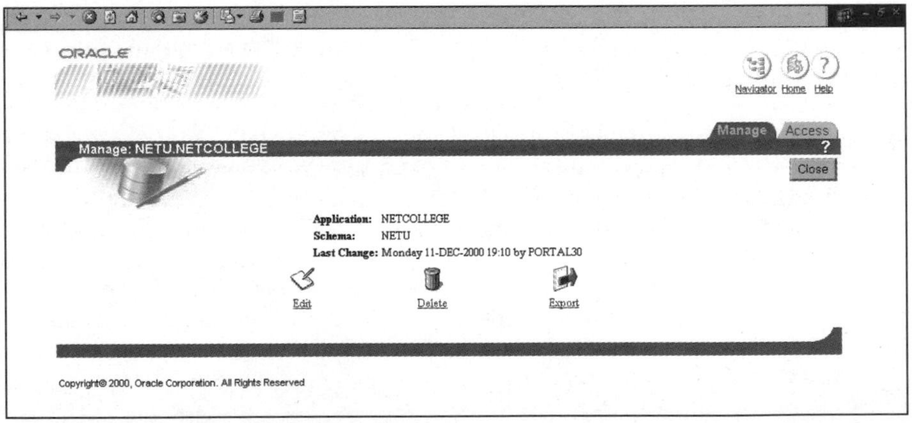

Figure 23-10: NETCOLLEGE application

The logical portal application NETCOLLEGE stores all of its generated code (i.e., stored procedures) in the application_schema (netu). The data that is accessed by the application can be stored in any number of other Oracle data_schemas. Any single Portal application can work with multiple data_schemas and more than one Portal application can work with a single data_schema.

Under this architecture, the Portal_schema itself is still used by the deployed application to handle such tasks as templates, JavaScripts, Content Areas, and the source code for components. If you have developers working in the Portal_schema at the same time as end users are running applications, there is the possibility of the two groups colliding and causing problems. This is especially true if your developers are performing bulk loads and unloads of components. As long as your developers are not working on the same components that your end users are trying to run, this should not be a major problem. However, if this is likely to occur, you may need to implement a staging area.

Staging areas

Most professional application developers separate their development data from the production data. This is normally true for both the data as well as the actual applications code. For example, if you were to design and build an Oracle JDeveloper application for Net University, you would probably make a copy of the core database and set up a separate instance for doing the development work. You would also create an area on the file system where the completed programs would be stored, and you would point end users to this finished program area for running the application.

Note
: The difference, of course, between a JDeveloper application and a Portal application is that the end users of a portal also participate directly in its development. End users normally would not write JDeveloper code (Java code), but they do contribute content to the portal site on a continual basis. In a sense, the portal is "always under development."

It is possible to stage Portal sites, although it takes a little more planning to do so — and it may not be worth the effort. You can run multiple copies of both the Oracle server, as well as the Apache HTTP Listener and Oracle9*i* Application Server, on separate servers (or as separate instances). Periodically you can then export from the development site and import into the production site. You will need to import and export the following schemas:

✦ Portal30 schema

✦ Each Application schema

The secret to making this approach work is to use the same object names in both instances. When a developer has finished building a component (or an application), the various objects can be exported from the development instance and imported into the production instance. Keep in mind that a logical component might be composed of several physical components. For example, a Portal report might have several shared components such as a list-of-values or template built into it. Portal does not automatically export these referenced objects when you export the report; you need to export these other objects yourself. Furthermore, you still need to set security for the components in the production environment, and you may need to copy external image files to the proper directories on the production server. However, you will have successfully created a layer of insulation between your developers and your end users.

Note   In most cases, you will find that this separation of development from deployment is too complex for portal sites. The real value of a portal is to allow your end users to add their own content—and there is no easy way to separate development from production under this model. In the future, Oracle will be adding some additional workflow capabilities to Oracle Portal that will allow you to separate development and production within the *same* portal environment. For the time being, our advice is to run development and production within the same site.

Server configuration

The server configuration is a relatively simple issue because only one configuration option is available: the Oracle 9*i* Application Server. Oracle9*i*AS is itself composed of three parts, the Oracle9*i*AS server (which is part of the Apache Server), the Apache HTTP Server, and the Logon Server.

If you are deploying your Portal application within an intranet or extranet where security is provided for you at the network layer, the Apache HTTP Listener is a good choice. The listener is lightweight, it can cache connections across user requests, and it is tightly integrated with the Mod_PLSQL gateway. Furthermore, nothing prevents you from embedding links to another Web server if you want to connect your Portal applications to an existing Web application that uses a different Web server. This is a perfectly acceptable solution within an intranet environment, and the cross-server connections are transparent to your users.

If you need to connect outside of your intranet, then Oracle Portal allows you to configure the server to work with a *proxy server* as shown in Figure 23-11.

Proxy servers act as firewalls to prevent unauthorized traffic through your portal site. Oracle portal allows you to use a proxy server at the portal server layer. All requests that are made by the portal server will pass through the proxy. Normally, proxy servers are configured just like HTTP servers. The panel as shown in Figure 23-11 allows you to reference the URL and port for a proxy server.

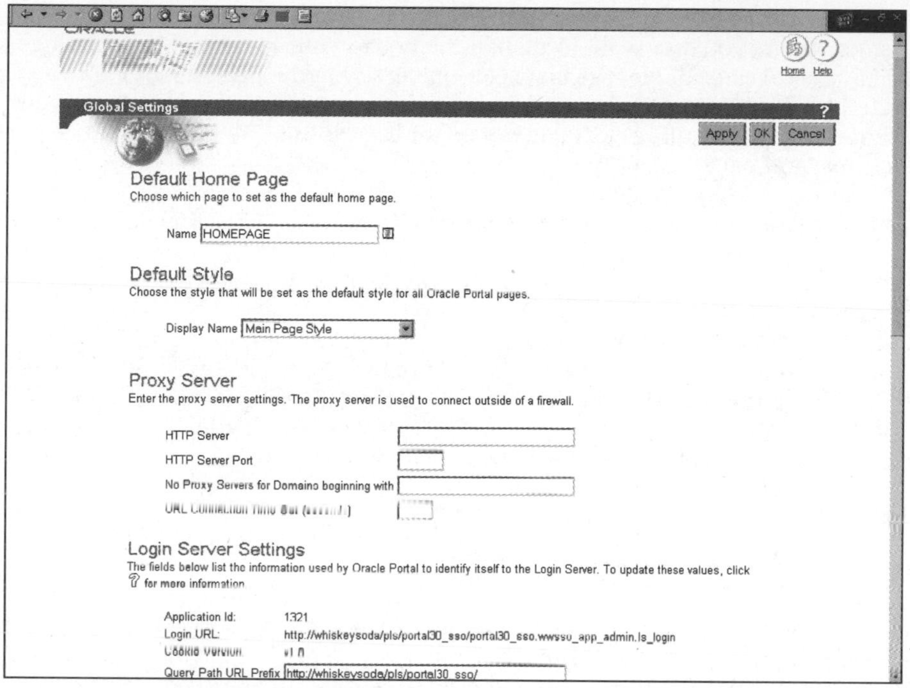

Figure 23-11: Proxy Server settings

Component deployment

Portal supports four types of deployment interfaces: static HTML pages, Portal Pages, Portal components, and Portal Content Areas. When you deploy your applications, you will likely find yourself using all of these options to get the structure you are looking for. Underneath the covers, you will almost always use Portal components to display content to your users, but you can vary the manner in which the components are packaged.

One common mechanism for deploying your components is to link to them from static HTML pages. This is especially true if you already have an existing intranet or Internet application in place. You may be replacing some of your static pages with dynamic content built with Portal. In such cases, you may replace links in your static pages with *new* links to Portal components as these components become available. Static Portal pages permit you more freedom in handcrafting the HTML code, which may be necessary to create the particular look and feel you are trying to achieve. In fact, many corporate sites use lots of images and image maps on their master pages for just this reason. The pages in your Portal application can use templates that emulate or complement the look of these static HTML pages.

Portal supports a Menu Wizard, and you can deploy your applications using these menus. Again, you may want to embed the link to your menu into an existing static HTML page. For example, the main Net University home page might feature an animated GIF that invites users to click through to see a list of upcoming campus events. Behind the GIF, a Portal menu might list various categories such as sports, lectures, and parties.

You may also elect to deploy your content to users through specialized portal pages. Portal pages can act as pointers to other content on your portal site, and they can also be deployed as the "front" interface for your portal.

Portal components can also be delivered through Content Areas. In Chapter 22, you were introduced to the basic concepts of Content Areas, including how to create them. Content Areas offer a formal structure for deploying interactive Web sites, and Portal components can be plugged directly into this structure. In the next section, we'll look at using Direct Access URLs to point to these components.

Using Direct Access URLs

Oracle Portal provides a special technique that allows you to reference individual portal components by using URLs. This allows you (and your portal users) to access content within the portal directly via simple URL paths. Direct Access URLs let you share URLs or relative URLs with other users outside of the portal environment. Table 23-2 lists the six basic types of Direct Access URLs.

Table 23-2 Direct Access URLs	
Object	**URL Path**
Pages	`http://<host:port>/pls/<DAD>/url/`*`page/<pagename>`*
Folders	`http://<host:port>/pls/<DAD>/url/`*`folder/<foldername>`*
Category	`http://<host:port>/pls/<DAD>/url/`*`category/`* *`<cagegoryname>`*
Perspective	`http://<host:port>/pls/<DAD>/url/`*`perspective/`* *`<perspectivename>`*
Document	`http://<host:port>/pls/<DAD>/url/`*`docs/<docname>`*
Component Item	`http://<host:port>/pls/<DAD>/`*`<owner>`*`.` `component.show`

The URL Path takes a familiar format. The first part of the URL (http://
<host:port>) is the hostname and the port that the Apache Listener is listening
on. You must substitute your hostname and port number for the placeholder as
shown in the string. The next portion of the URL is the virtual directory that points
to the PL/SQL gateway — in most cases this will be the literal string /pls/. The
virtual directory definition is stored in the plsql.conf file, which appears in the
/modplsql/cfg subdirectory of the Oracle Apache Listener directory. The plsql.
conf file includes a set of directives that define the virtual directory as follows:

```
<Location /pls>
  SetHandler pls_handler
  Order deny,allow
  Allow from all
</Location>
```

The Apache Listener uses the <location> directive to map URLs to specific handlers. It operates in a similar fashion to the <directory> directive, but it is used to
map handlers rather than directories or files. The location directive shown previously causes URLs that include the /pls string to be redirected to the Mod_PLSQL
gateway. You will not normally need to change this literal value. The next entry in
the Direct Access URL is the Database Access Descriptor (DAD) entry. By default,
you can use the PORTAL30 DAD, or any other DAD entry that you create for your
portal site. The remaining portion of the Direct Access URL will vary according to
the type of URL that you are attempting to connect to.

Pages

Portal pages are one of the most common types of objects that you will deploy to
users. They can be deployed directly as URLs or you can embed them as a link
within existing HTML pages.

1. Use the portal navigator to locate the NETU_MAIN portal page that you create
   in Chapter 7.

2. Open a new browser session and enter the following URL:

   http://whiskeysoda:80/pls/portal30/url/page/netu_main/

Remember to substitute your host name and port number for whiskeysoda:80 in
the preceding string. (You may need to substitute for the string portal30 if you
used a different installation account for Oracle Portal as well.)

Oracle Portal will display a panel similar to the one shown in Figure 23-12.

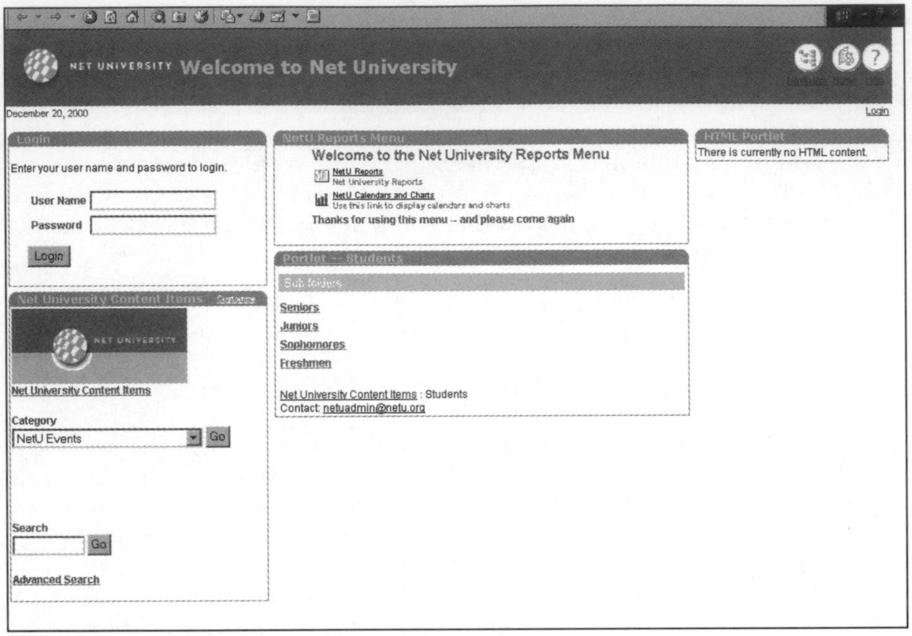

Figure 23-12: NetU Main Page — unauthenticated

Portal automatically displays the Login portlet, and any of the customized portal areas will appear blank as shown in Figure 23-12. Since you opened a new browser session, the user has not yet been logged into the Portal site. The NETU_MAIN page has been set so that it can be displayed to the public, so Portal displays the page to the "unauthenticated" user — but the customizations do not appear. (Portal does not allow unauthenticated users to customize portal pages.)

   3. Use the Login portlet in the upper-left corner of the page to log in to the site as the Portal Administrator and display the page as shown in Figure 23-13.

Once the user has been authenticated to Oracle Portal, the fully customized version of the portal page appears.

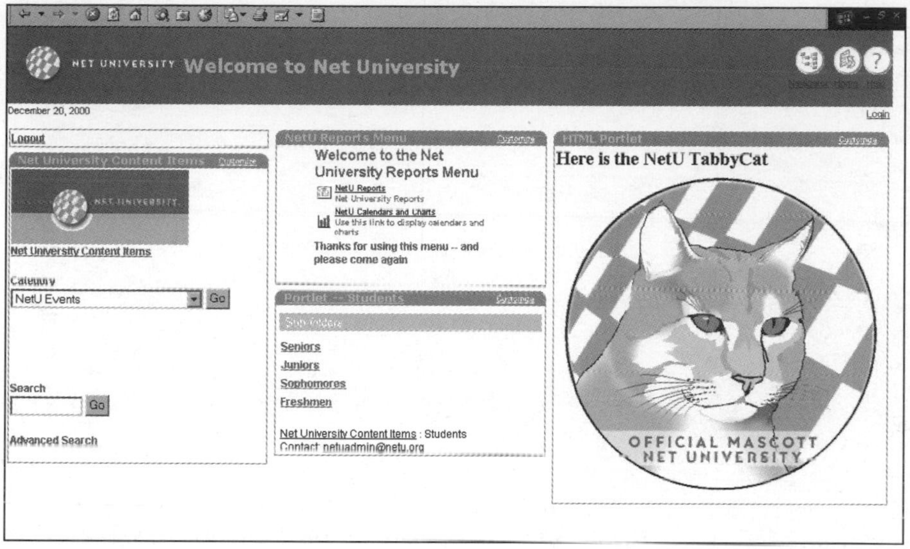

Figure 23-13: Authenticated NetU main page

Folders

Content Areas are one of the most common objects that you will deploy as individual URLs. If you already have existing intranet sites built with third-party Web servers you will find that Content Areas are ideal as embedded links. Content Areas employ a complete structure all their own, including both a folder area and a Navigation Bar. Thus, they are complete portals in their own right.

 Note
> The examples in this section and the next assume that you have completed Chapter 22 — Using Content Areas.

1. Enter the following URL in the *same* authenticated browser session that you used to view the NETU_MAIN page:

   ```
   http://whiskeysoda/pls/portal30/url/folder/netucontent
   ```

   Remember to substitute your host name and port number for `whiskeysoda:80` in the preceding string. (You may need to substitute for the string `portal30` if you used a different installation account for Oracle Portal as well.)

2. Choose the Edit Folder Link in the upper-right corner of the generated page to display the panel as shown in Figure 23-14.

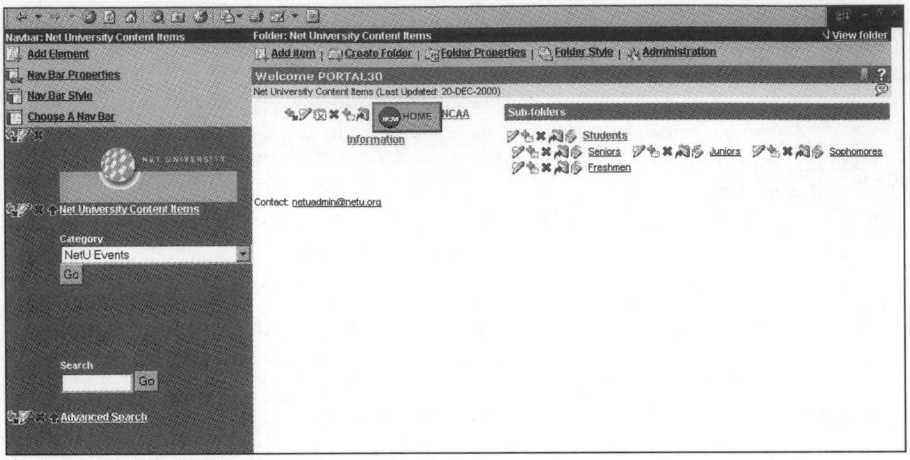

Figure 23-14: Net University Content Items

Oracle Portal displays the complete edit menu for the Content Area, even though you did not log in explicitly to the NETUCONTENT area. You already logged onto the portal through the Login portlet in the preceding section. Portal has marked your browser session as authenticated by means of a cookie. Thus, when you input the Direct Access URL for the NETUCONTENT folder you have full access to the update capabilities of the site.

3. Assuming that you created the `mydad` DAD in the previous section, enter the following direct URL in the same browser session:

```
http://whiskeysoda/pls/mydad/url/folder/netucontent
```

Remember to substitute your host name and port number for `whiskeysoda:80` in the original string. (You may need to substitute for the string `portal30` if you used a different installation account for Oracle Portal as well.)

4. Choose the Edit Folder link in the upper-right corner of the generated page to display the panel as shown in Figure 23-15.

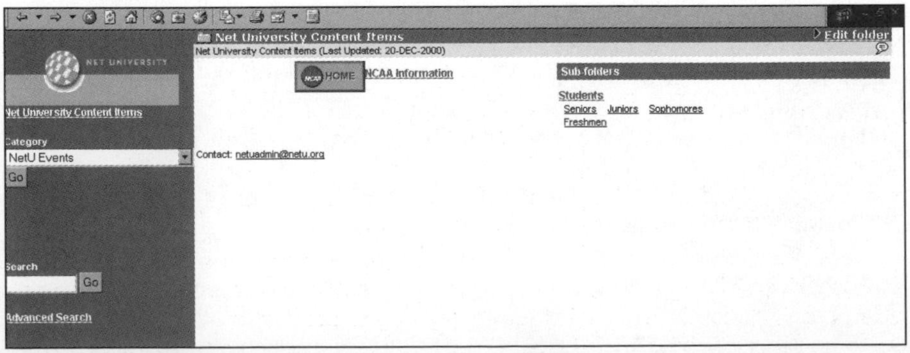

Figure 23-15: Net University Content Items — mydad

This time you are unable to edit the Content Area. Although you have already logged into the site—you did so as the `portal30` DAD. Oracle Portal considers the `mydad` entry to be a different logon. You will also notice that we have no way of logging onto the site when it is deployed in this fashion. (If we had added the Login link to the Navigation Bar—and discussed in Chapter 22—this would not have been a problem.)

You can navigate directly to subfolders using this technique as well. All you to do is to list the hierarchy of folders as part of the URL:

```
http://whiskeysoda/pls/portal30/url/folder/netucontent/seniors
http://whiskeysoda/pls/portal30/url/folder/netucontent/juniors
```

Categories and perspectives

You can also navigate directly to both categories and perspectives inside of Content Areas through Direct Access URLs.

1. Enter the following direct URL into an authenticated browser session:

```
http://whiskeysoda/pls/portal30/url/category/academics
```

Remember to substitute your host name and port number for `whiskeysoda:80` in the preceding string. (You may need to substitute for the string `portal30` if you used a different installation account for Oracle Portal as well.)

Caution

Folder, Category, and Perspective Direct Access URLs require the use of the internal name for the item. Although the display name for ACADEMICS is "Academic Information," we are required to use the internal name for the category—and this same rule applies to folders and perspectives as well.

2. Enter the following direct URL into an authenticated browser session:

```
http://whiskeysoda/pls/portal30/url/perspective/hot
```

Remember to substitute your host name and port number for `whiskeysoda:80` in the preceding string. (You may need to substitute for the string `portal30` if you used a different installation account for Oracle Portal as well.)

As with the Folders Direct Access URL, categories and perspectives will appear in the context of the overall Content Area. Individual documents, however, will display differently, as shown in the next section.

Documents

Content Areas provide a unique mechanism for storing and managing documents and other content items. However, you will often need to display these items outside of the Content Area. For example, we might choose to store the course catalog for Net University inside of the NetU portal. We may also want to include the course catalog as a link inside of the monthly e-mail burst that we send out to prospective students. Portal provides the direct access document URL for exactly this purpose.

Cross-Reference   This next example assumes that you uploaded some content into Seniors folder.

1. Navigate to the Seniors folders in the NETUCONTENT Content Area and copy the link associated with the NetU Course Catalog item as shown in Figure 23-16.

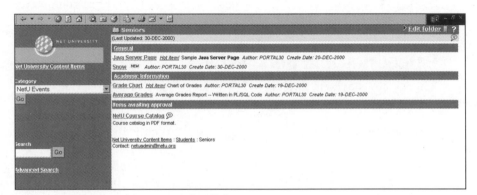

Figure 23-16: NetU Course Catalog link

2. Paste the link into a text editor so that you can view the text.

The text of the link will look similar to the following URL:

```
http://whiskeysoda/pls/portal30/docs/304.PDF
```

When you originally uploaded the PDF document it was called netu_courses.pdf, but Oracle Portal has associated this content item by its generated primary key. In most cases, the Direct Access URL will look similar to the one shown above.

Tip   In theory, the Direct Access URL should use the same format for all documents, but certain types of content (such as JPEG images) do not use the same format consistently. We recommend that you use the Copy Shortcut option in your browser to be sure that you get the correct URL format for a given content item.

You can paste this shortcut into an e-mail message as a Direct Access URL. Remember, however, if the item is not a *public* item, the user might not be able to view it.

Components

Component items can also be accessed directly via URLs, but you must be extra cautious with these objects. Components (forms, reports, charts, etc.) are always connected to database records and granting public access to them should be done with extra care. When you create a component, Oracle Portal generates a stored procedure inside of the application schema that owns it. In our examples throughout the book, we have been using the NETCOLLEGE application, which is owned by the NETU schema. Each form or report that is created is owned by the NETU account. The format of the generated procedure for each component is always the same:

```
<owner>.<name>.show
<owner>.<show>.show_parms
```

The first format displays the component and the second format displays the customization form (if it exists). An example report, called course_catalog, that is part of the NETCOLLEGE application would have the following generated procedures:

```
netu.course_catalog.show
netu.course_catalog.show_parms
```

These procedures can be accessed as direct URLs simply by prefixing them with the standard Portal URL information:

```
http://whiskeysoda/pls/portal30/netu.course_catalog.show
http://whiskeysoda/pls/portal30/netu.course_catalog.show_parms
```

If they are marked as public components, then the user need not even log on to the portal in order to view them. If they are *secure* components, then Portal will prompt the user with the login form. This particular technique can be very useful for embedding links to components within existing web pages or e-mail bursts.

Summary

Portal sites are easy to build, but they lack some of the formal processes for delivery you may be used to in more structured development environments. Portal sites by their very nature are more dynamic than their client/server brethren. They are often designed and implemented quickly to leverage a window of opportunity. The designers of Oracle Portal built the product in such as way as to enable you to deploy your applications quickly and easily.

Despite this fact, you can still apply a more formal framework for deploying your Portal applications. You also have the flexibility to deploy these applications using your existing Web infrastructure. In the next chapter, you will see how you can use Content Areas as frameworks for delivering your Portal content.

✦   ✦   ✦

Content Areas – Part II

✦ ✦ ✦ ✦

In This Chapter

Reviewing Content
Areas

Applying and
Securing Content
Areas

Adding Basic Content
to Your Site

Adding Content with
Advanced
Components to the
Site

Using Other Accounts
to Add Content

Considering Some
Advanced Topics

✦ ✦ ✦ ✦

Chapter 22 introduced you to the Content Area capabilities of Oracle9iAS Portal, and you created and customized your portal with Content Areas. The Content Area editors and the Content Area administration tools are only half of the solution, however, as most of the power of Content Areas lies in the hands of your portal users. Through Content Areas, you can create a framework for your portal, but the real value comes from the content that gets loaded into the Content Areas on your portal.

Typical collaborative portal sites suffer from several problems. The information is often disorganized and hard to find, which causes users to stop working with the portal. Even when the site is organized, the information may appear to be disorganized if individual users have made use of their own styles and techniques for storing content. If you try to provide a universal client-side framework that contributors must use to upload content, the information is often stale by the time it actually gets posted to the site.

Reviewing the Content Area Concept

Content Areas are the answer to all of these problems. They provide the framework for organizing and searching for content; and they provide built-in templates for making content appear in a uniform fashion. Contributors *do not* have to format the information in any way in order to take advantage of the display templates, and this helps them submit content to your portal in a more timely fashion.

A Web site built with Content Areas is ideal if the site is going to be a collaboration of efforts. You can divide Web applications into categories such as e-commerce, online catalog, and stock trading. Portal developers can easily add pages to your portal, and portal users can customize these pages with portlets. However, portals that involve collaboration among a community of users need the additional flexibility that Content Areas provide.

Content Areas provide a framework for organizing your content, searching for items, and displaying information using a consistent look and feel. The basic framework of Content Areas enforces a built-in consistency. The left side of an application serves as the navigation panel, and the body of the page on the right side contains content organized into categories. But if you are building a merchandising portal site, you might not want to use this format as the look and feel for your site. Instead, you might create a series of flashy portal pages for the top part of your site and then link these pages to Portal components for displaying and ordering items. However, you can still include Content Areas directly within these portal pages — even if you are not deploying the entire Content Area framework (for example, Navigation Bars) to your portal pages.

For instance, suppose you are selling a sophisticated piece of equipment such as a computer or a camera. Once you have sold the product to a consumer, you might want to point that consumer to a section of your portal site where they can exchange information with other users. This type of collaboration is exactly where Content Areas are most effective, because they come equipped with all the pieces you need to build a collaboration framework.

In order to understand how you can use Content Areas for portal applications, think of the example of a store. First, you decide what type of things you want to sell — shoes, clothes, food, furniture, and so on. Next, you find a location and build the store. Then, you decide on a color scheme, the layout for your store, and the store logo. Finally, you have to fill the store with merchandise so your customers have something to purchase. The merchandise serves two purposes: it draws people into your store and it provides your profit.

Within Portal, Content Areas are your store and the layout, color scheme, and images are the brand for your store. The folders, categories, and perspectives define the type of merchandise you have in the store, and the items uploaded into the site become the merchandise. A store is a type of framework — it is ideal for displaying merchandise and enabling people to select items and buy them. Stores are very flexible objects; they can be laid out in many different ways, they can be used to sell a variety of goods, and they can be built with a wide range of color schemes. You can use a store to sell many things, yet all stores share the same basic characteristics. Portal sites that incorporate content with Content Areas are much like the store: They can be used for a wide variety of tasks, but they all share the same basic format. Content Areas are ideal for building portal applications that consist of information organized for the purpose of collaboration. Portal developers use portlets to create custom content for portal users — but portal users themselves can use Content Areas to create custom portal content. In this chapter, you will go through the process of releasing your NETUCONTENT Content Areas to your portal users.

Applying and Securing Content Areas

Several factors can affect the design of your Content Area, but the most basic issue you will deal with is whether to make your site an anonymous portal site. Anonymous portal applications do not require that the user supply an individual user name and password in order to connect to the site. (In effect, the users connect to the site as PORTAL30_PUBLIC.) Anonymous portals need not be made available to the public, and they can be hidden behind a firewall or within an intranet. The alternative is to make your Content Areas application an *authenticated* portal application in which the users must log on to the site before they are allowed to view (or edit) content. This is not necessarily an either/or decision. You might choose to make the overall Content Area section of your portal an anonymous Web portal, but you can still require logons for accessing certain components of the portal.

Creating user accounts for Content Areas

User accounts that are created for use with Oracle Portal work with Content Areas as well, but Portal provides you with some specialized group information for Content Areas.

In order to complete the examples in this section you will need to have installed several portal-user accounts as outlined in Chapter 2.

1. Log on to Portal as a Portal Administrator.

2. Navigate to the Administration Panel and use the Create New Groups link to display the panel shown in Figure 24-1.

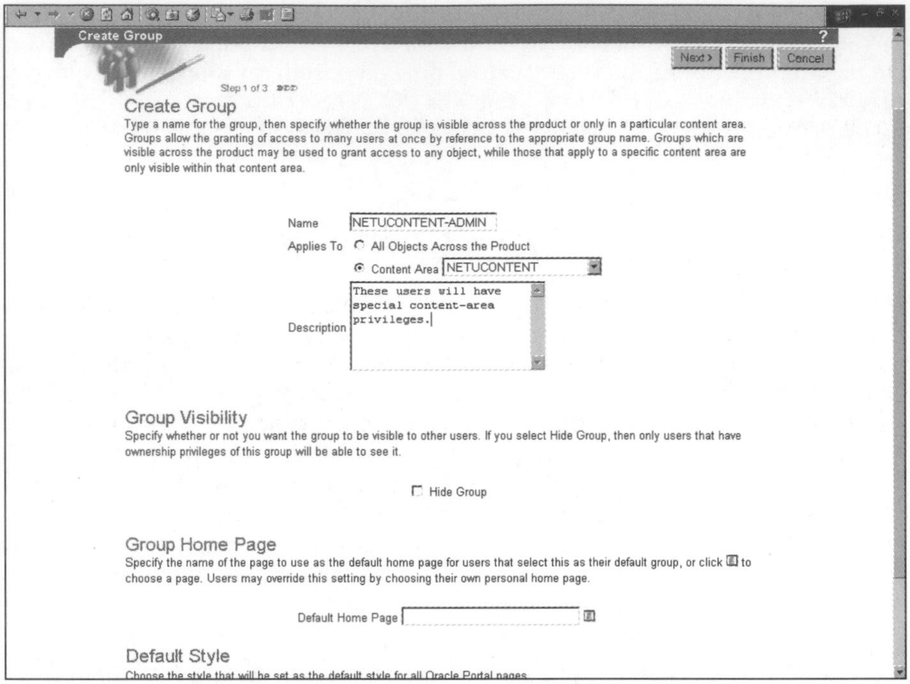

Figure 24-1: Creating Content Area groups

Oracle Portal provides some special consideration for Content Areas. Portal developers are primarily responsible for adding content to portal sites in the form of pages and portlets. Portal users can certainly customize portal pages (adding portlets to pages and customizing URLs) — but they generally do not design them from scratch. It's a different story when it comes to Content Areas, which have been designed specifically for end users of portal sites. In order to provide as much flexibility as possible for Content Areas, Oracle Portal allows administrators to create specialized group accounts for them. While you may not want to provide advanced privileges for portal users across the entire portal site, you will often want to give certain users additional capabilities within Content Areas. For example, you may elect to give certain students (such as Student Government members) the ability to manage content within the Net University Content Items area.

3. Enter the name **NETUCONTENT-ADMIN** as the name of your new group.

4. Use the Applies To radio button to select the Content Area option and then locate the NETUCONTENT Content Area (which you created in Chapter 22).

5. Enter a description and then use the Next button to display the panel as shown in Figure 24-2.

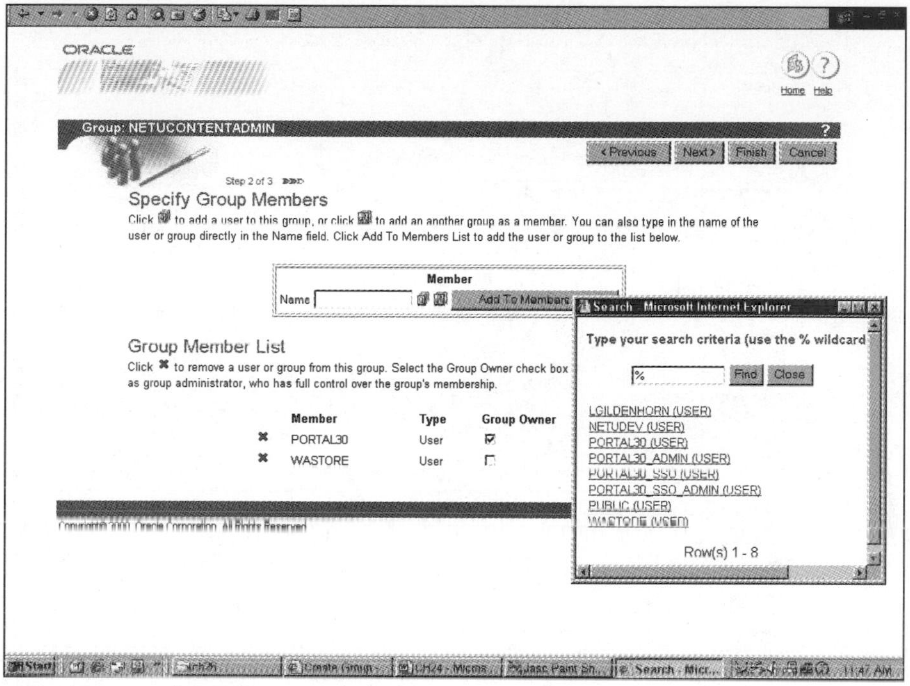

Figure 24-2: Adding Group Members

Once you have created the group, the next step in the process is to add members to the new group. The top part of the panel allows you to search for portal users with the familiar pop-up form. Once you have located a user, the Add To Members List button adds them to the Group Member List in the bottom part of the panel.

6. Locate the user WASTORE and add him to the Group Member List. Press the Next button to display the form as shown in Figure 24-3.

Although you are planning on working with a specific Content Area, Oracle Portal displays the complete list of Object Privileges that are available within the Portal environment.

Cross-Reference We'll take a more detailed look at this panel in Chapter 26. You do not need a complete understanding of security to work with the examples in this chapter. In fact, you will probably find it easier to understand Portal's security framework by first working with Content Areas.

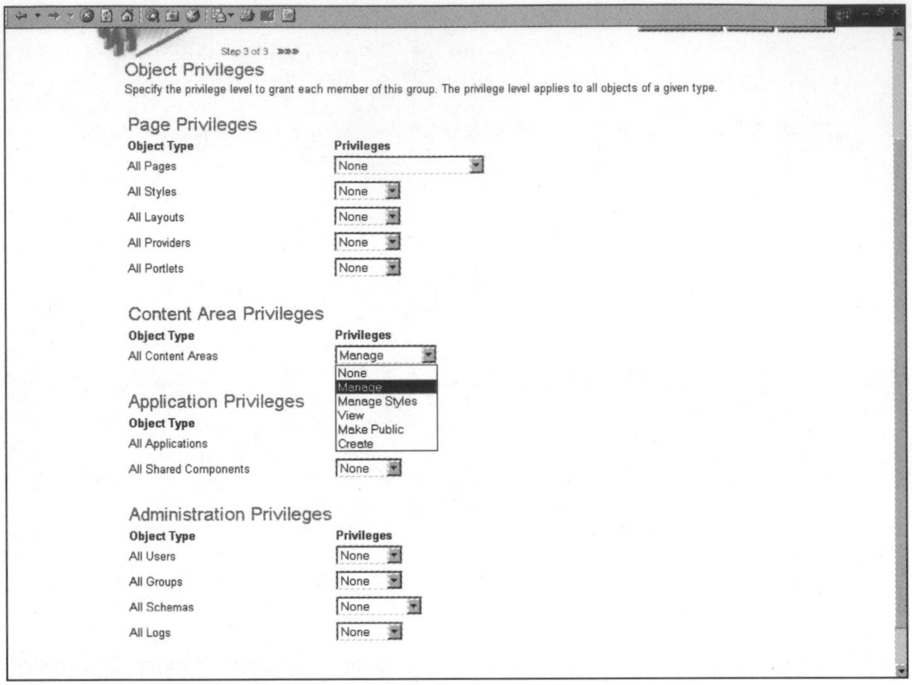

Figure 24-3: Object Privileges

There are six privileges available to users and groups within Content Areas:

✦ None

✦ Manage

✦ Manage Styles

✦ View

✦ Make Public

✦ Create

Set the Content Area Privileges to None when you create a user or a group that will have access to other areas of the Portal—but not to Content Areas. When you create a Content Area and Folders within the Content Area, you have the choice as to whether to make them Public. If you enable public access to a Content Area, then all portal users will be able to see the Content Area by default. On the other hand you can grant access to private Content Areas by giving users or groups the View privilege. In order for a group to have permission to upload items into a Content Area you will need to give them Create privileges. Users and groups with the Create privilege can add content—but it will not be visible to other portal users by default. Only groups with the Make Public privilege can approve content for public display.

The two most important privileges that you can grant are the Manage Styles and Manage privileges. Groups with the Manage Styles privilege can edit and apply visual styles to folders within the Content Area. You should be very selective about granting this privilege to users as this gives them the freedom to make wholesale look-and-feel changes to your folders. Managers have the same level of authority over your Content Areas as the Content Area administrators—they are, in fact, administrators for a section of your portal.

> 7. Select the Make Public privilege for the NETUCONTENT-ADMIN group and press the Finish button to create the group.

Adding users and groups to folders

Once you have created users and groups, you can deploy these accounts to the folders that make up your Content Areas site. Folder permissions are stored inside the folder object itself and you can set security options from the Folder Editor.

> 1. Edit the NETUCONTENT Content Area and navigate to the Folder Panel as shown in Figure 24-4.

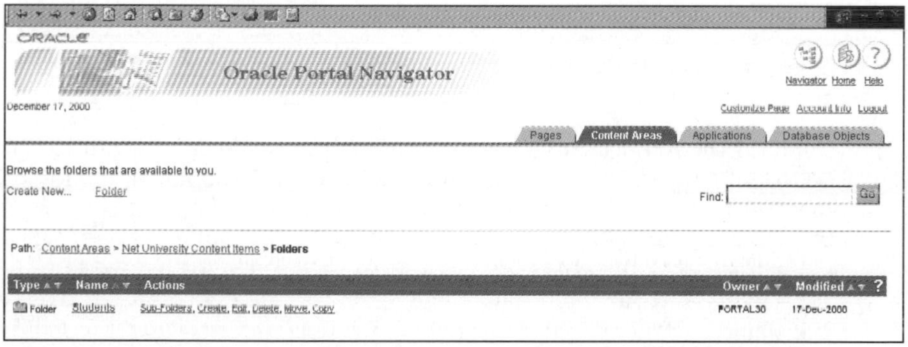

Figure 24-4: Students Folder

> 2. Select the Edit icon for the Students folder and press the Access tab on the page that appears to display the panel in Figure 24-5.

In Chapter 22, you created the basic hierarchy of folders that comprise the Net University Content Items area. Once you have created your users and groups, you can assign permissions for these users within the folders and subfolders.

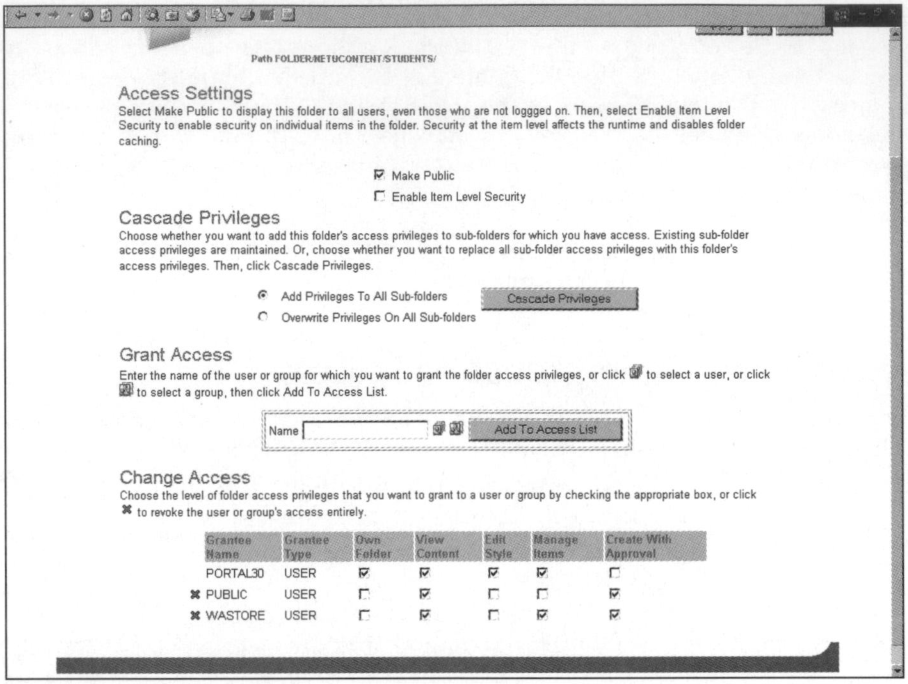

Figure 24-5: Folder Manager — Students folder

The first section of the folder panel, as depicted in Figure 24-5, should be familiar to you from Chapter 22. This panel controls the overall display of the folder and the base permissions. The critical item from a security standpoint is the Make Public check box. By default, your folders are not made available to the public. If you enable this check box, the public is able to view the items loaded into the folder. This would make the folder into an anonymous folder, as opposed to an authenticated folder. There will be cases where you might have some folders in your application set as public (anonymous) folders, while others require that the user log on to the site in order to view the contents.

> **Note** You can manually add groups and users to the permissions for the Content Area site by using the Grant Access and Change Access sections on this panel. They are almost identical to the settings on the three panels as shown in Figures 24-1 to 24-3 with one exception. The privilege Manage is referred to as Own Folder and the privilege Make Public is called Manage Items.

3. Locate the WASTORE user and add him to the Change Access list. Grant WASTORE the Manage Items privilege.

4. Press the OK button to save your changes.

Adding Content to Your Site

Chapter 22 introduced you to the basic components of a Content Areas application: the Navigation Bar, the banner area, the Content Area, folders, categories, and perspectives. These objects form the building blocks for all Content Areas applications.

Your site will typically start with a theme, which is the basic purpose of the site. For the fictional Net University Content Items area, the Content Area application is an information center for the university. The folders in this application form the basic categories for the items contained on the site. Within Net University are three main constituents — Alumni, Students, and Faculty. The Students group is further subdivided into Freshmen, Sophomores, Juniors, and Seniors. Each folder has a number of categories that correspond to an area of interest within the folder: events, academics, and athletics.

Although this is an oversimplification of what you might need for a real university, it does provide a basic organization that you can use as an example. In the real world, each of these categories could be a Web site or Content Areas application of its own. Many large colleges and universities have entire Web sites just for their sports teams. There is no reason why you could not use this same technique with Content Areas. You could just as easily create a Content Areas application dedicated entirely to Net University's sports teams and then build a folder for each team: Mens Basketball, Womens Basketball, Mens Football, and so on. The folders might then consist of the schedule, players, game results, and press coverage.

There is no hard-and-fast rule about what level you should use to organize your Content Areas application — it depends upon the level of detail your content is likely to take. The entity that drives the level of detail for your site is the content. The items stored or referenced within your Content Areas site are your content. Content items can take a variety of formats, as shown in the following list:

✦ Text items

✦ Files

✦ Images

✦ URLs

✦ Application components

✦ PL/SQL calls

✦ Java applications

✦ Zip files

✦ Folder links

Every content item loaded into a Content Areas application has a number of common attributes. Each item can be stored within a folder as part of a given category and each item has a title and a description. In addition, you can assign each item to a number of perspectives and index it by designated keywords. You will see these attributes in action later in this section.

The most basic of all content items is the Text item, which is nothing more than a block of HTML text. Text is the perfect choice for short messages where the content is nothing more than a message. Portal permits you to embed HTML tags in the text itself, so the item can display with fancy HTML rendering if you wish.

The next in the list is the File content item, which is a binary file added as content to the site. You still provide a title and a description for the item, but the link itself points to a binary file downloaded to the browser. The file is stored inside the Oracle database as a LONGRAW column. When the link is accessed at run time, Content Areas passes the file to the browser with the appropriate file extension and MIME type. For example, if you store an Adobe Portable Display Format (PDF) file in your site, Content Areas sends the file back to the site as PDF MIME type when the file is accessed. The browser deals with the file according to the current settings for that MIME type. Content Areas does not attempt to manage the MIME settings for the file, and it does not alter the attributes of the file when it is stored in the database.

The Image format is used to upload a graphic image (along with an optional client-side image map file). For example, you could upload a map of the Net University campus along with an image map of URLs to activate when a user clicks a given location.

If you need to reference another Web site from within your Content Areas application, you can use the URL content item to provide the link. With the URL content item, you can specify a complete URL string as the link for the content item. When the user activates the link in the content item, he or she is transferred to the location specified by the URL.

You can also use this format to connect to Application Component objects. This content item type is the means by which you link to Portal components from within Content Areas. However, the Portal content item type suffers from one critical problem. All Portal components that you plan to call using the Portal component type must be public components.

If you have created your own PL/SQL procedures, you can add these items as content objects. Chapter 21 provides details on building your own PL/SQL procedures, which are most often used as part of the Oracle Application Server. These procedures can be called directly from Content Areas folders as content items. PL/SQL procedures represent the ultimate in flexibility because they can output their own streams of HTML code.

The Oracle Application Server also supports Java technology as well as Oracle Portal. You can create Java Server Pages applications, load them into Java Archive Files, and upload the JAR files into Portal for display within Content Areas. You can create JSPs with Oracle's JDeveloper or with your favorite text editor.

Oracle Portal provides the Zip file item type as a means to upload entire Web sites or groups of files into a folder. Zip files are automatically associated with Portal's bulk load facility.

The last type of content item is a Folder link, which is used to link an item in one folder with a related item in another folder. Typically, you use the Folder link to make note of a major content item in one folder in a secondary folder. For example, say the Net University football team wins a game against their biggest rival. You might post a content item in the Students folder that describes this victory. By using a Folder link, you could also cross-reference this entry in the Alumni folder as well. This saves you from having to duplicate the entire article in multiple folders.

1. Navigate to the Students root folder.
2. Select the Edit button in the upper-right corner of the page to display the page as shown in Figure 24-6.

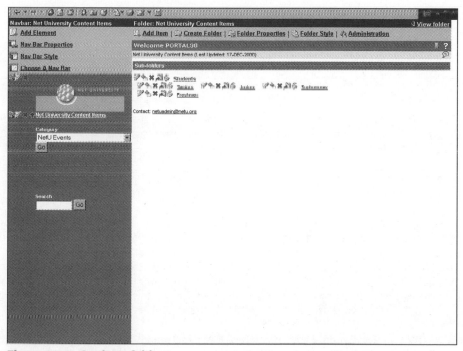

Figure 24-6: Students folder

Adding an item to a folder is accomplished by using a wizard interface that guides you through the process. Normally you start the process by navigating to the folder that you wish to add the content to, and then selecting the Edit button. If the Edit button does not appear in the upper-right corner of the folder page, you do not have permission to add content to this folder. In this particular case, you are positioned in the root folder for the site. You are going to start by adding the Net University mascot as the first entry into the root folder.

3. Press the Add Item link at the top of the page to start the Content Wizard as shown in Figure 24-7.

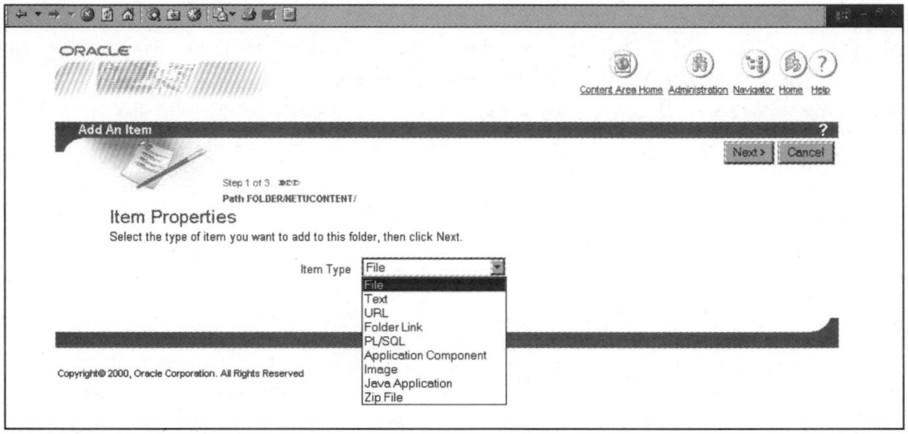

Figure 24-7: Item Types

The first selection you must make in the wizard is the item type, using the drop-down list box. The list of items matches the content types discussed at the beginning of this section.

4. Select the URL item type from the combo box and press the Next button to continue.

There are four possible display regions for content items that are detailed in the upper panel on the second page of the wizard. Regular Items are the most common, and they appear inside folders and categories. QuickPick items are intended to be links to common functions or other sites, and they appear at the top of your pages. You will most often create a QuickPick item as a hotlink to a popular menu choice or external URL site. For example, a QuickPick item for the Net University site might be a link to NCAA athletics site, or to the Amazon.com college textbook area.

Cross-Reference The regions that appear at the top of this page match the list of regions that you worked with in Chapter 22. The Content Wizard will display the various regions on this wizard according to the layout that you have chosen for the folder in which you are adding items. If you followed the examples in Chapter 22 the display of the regions should match the layout as shown in Figure 24-8.

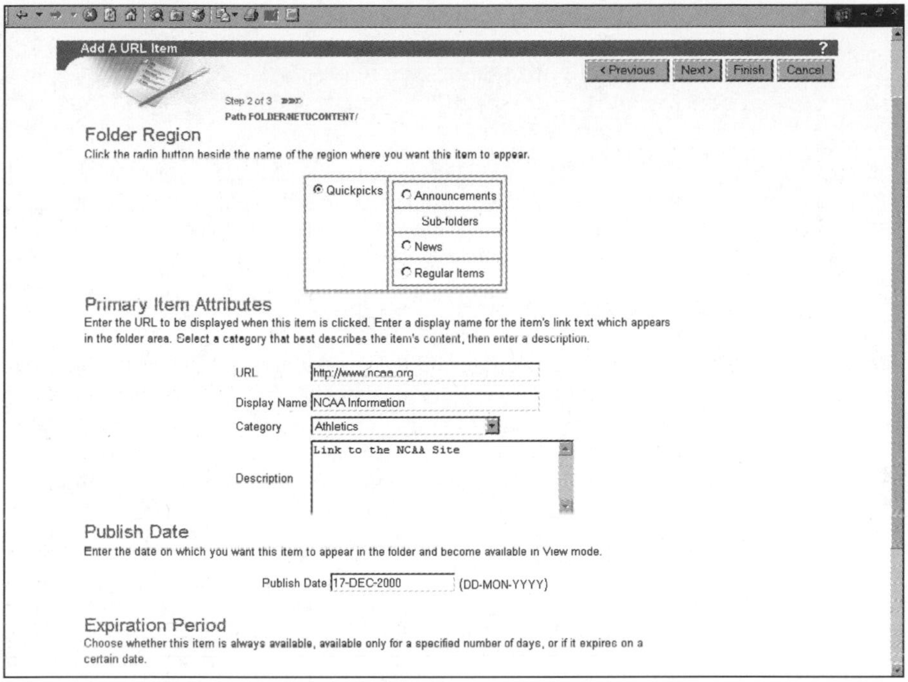

Figure 24-8: Region layout

Announcements are positioned just to the right of the QuickPick items (with the region layout that we have chosen), and they are intended to serve as special content items with a limited life span. They share the same format as the Regular item type, but they are displayed in a different region within each folder.

News items are the last type of content, and they are handled differently than other content items. Generally, News items have a limited life span and appear in a special category within each folder. For example, suppose that a limited number of tickets to the sold-out Net University football game have suddenly become available. You can use a News item to announce the availability of these tickets in the Events category of the Students folder and include a link to a page where the user can purchase the tickets.

5. The link from the Students folder will connect to the NCAA's Web Site, so choose the QuickPick radio button.

The primary attributes section of the panel deals with the attributes of the content item and will vary by the type of item that you select. However, a number of common fields appear in every panel regardless of the item type, as shown in Table 24-1.

Table 24-1
Common Required Settings and Values

Item	Description
Title (or name)	The title of the item is the string of text that displays as the first part of the item. It also serves as the link to the item itself. You can enter simple text, or you can include HTML formatting tags inside of the title string, such as \<B> or \<I>. Image maps are the only item type that does not support titles, because the image itself is the title and the description.
Description	The description field is the extended text that appears below the item to fully explain the associated content item. Content Areas automatically wrap the text for you, but as with the title string, you can embed HTML tags within the text to control the formatting yourself. Image maps do not have descriptions because the image itself serves as the description.
Category	Categories match the category settings that are created as part of the site. Categories are only available for Regular items, and QuickPicks, Announcements, and News items all appear in their own separate display areas as described previously.
Expiration	The Expiration combo box contains a range of days an item remains valid or a specific expiration date. The dates range from 1 day to 120 days in various increments, or you can set an item to be permanent, in which case it never expires. Expired items are not physically deleted until the system administrator executes the purge function.
Publish Date	Items can be preloaded into the Content Area for display at some point in the future. For example, NetU might post the Examination Scheduled on the last day of the semester. If the schedule is ready in advance the administrator could post it into the appropriate folder with the Publish Date set to the last day of the semester.

The remaining items on the Required Settings and Values panel vary according to the item type that you select. Table 24-2 lists the remaining fields that can be displayed on the second panel and the items to which they are connected.

Table 24-2
Extended Item Type Fields

Item	Description	Item Associated
URL	Fully qualified URL string that points to a Web address. Any valid URL string is allowed, including URLs with parameters. You can also call Portal components as URL strings.	URL
Filename	Filenames are the operating system files with extensions, which are subsequently loaded into the database. Content Areas maintain the file extension along with the file so that the MIME type can be passed along to the browser when the file is downloaded to the client.	File
Text	Block of text and HTML tags that are similar in format to the description string described previously.	Text item
Image	Image file in GIF or JPEG format that displays as the content item. The image is uploaded into the database when the content item is created.	Image map
Image Map	Block of image map HTML text associated with the image file. The image map code must follow the format for a client-side image map file.	Image map
Image Map Name	Logical name for the image map associated with the image map code and displayed as the title.	Image map
Folder	A folder is an internal link to another folder in the Content Areas site. You cannot explicitly enter a folder link, but Content Areas displays a panel that enables you to select a folder.	Folder
Portal Component	Combo box of Portal components that have been made accessible to the public role.	List of Portal Components
PL/SQL Code	Custom PL/SQL code that includes calls to HTF/HTP procedures and functions. Chapter 21 contains a detailed discussion of these procedures.	PL/SQL call
JAR	Java Archive File with Java Server Pages.	Java Archive (JAR file)
Zip file	Zip Archive file with HTML page and images.	Web files (HTML/Images stored in Zip Archive)

6. The item you are entering is a URL item type, as shown in Figure 24-8. Enter the URL `http://www.ncaa.org`.

7. Enter a title and description and set the expiration date for the item to Never Expires.

8. Assign this new item to the Athletics category.

9. Press the Next button to display the Secondary Item Attributes panel as shown in Figure 24-9.

Three items appear on the Secondary Items panel regardless of the type of item you create. The first item is the name of an image file that will be used as the image icon associated with the item when it is displayed in the site. This image file can be either a GIF or JPEG format file and serves the same purpose as an icon does on your desktop. The next item on the panel is the Basic Search Keywords text box, which stores keywords you want to be associated with the item. Search fields are not case sensitive and you can enter multiple keywords separated by commas. Both the basic search function and the advanced search function use these strings. The third field on the panel is the author text field and it will be filled in with the USERID used to enter the new item.

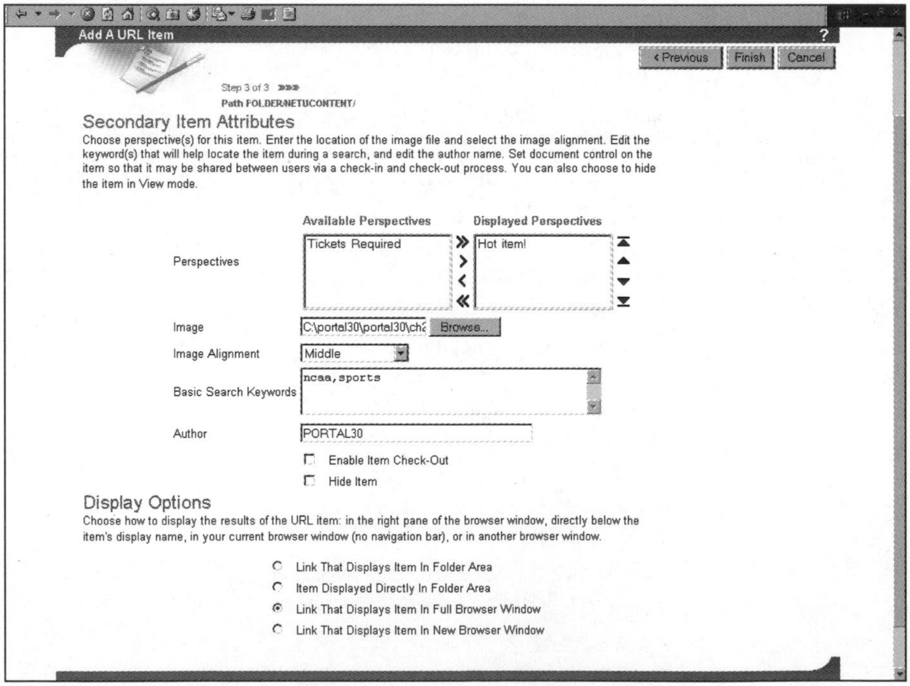

Figure 24-9: Secondary Items Attributes for a Content Area Item

Refer to Chapter 22 for a more detailed discussion of perspectives and categories.

If you have created perspectives for your site, a list of perspectives appears in a pair of list boxes on this panel. You can use the arrows to move perspectives from the Available to the Displayed list. Once you associate perspective records with an item, your end users are able to select records by their associated perspective values. The next block of fields are check boxes that control how the item displays when it is run, and the number of options varies with the item type.

You can choose to display the item within the folder area, which will cause Portal to display the item within the current folder area (retaining the Navigation Bar if it exists). Alternatively, you can elect to display the item directly in the folder area — in which case it will automatically appear when the folder appears.

The specific type of display options varies with the Item Type. For example, Images and Image Maps automatically use the "Item Displayed Directly in Folder Area" display option.

The remaining display options set the content to appear in a full browser window (in your current browser instance) or in a completely new browser window.

The final items on the panel are a pair of check boxes that indicates whether the item can be checked out for edit or hidden from view. (Only users with the Create or the Manage privilege for the current folder can edit content.) The site itself must have the Enable Item Checkout setting enabled for this check box to have any meaning. You can find this setting within the Site link on the main administration panel. You will typically use this setting to enable users to edit text items or download files and edit them while still keeping a placeholder for the item. If you choose to hide an item it will disappear in view mode — but privileged users will still be able to edit the item.

10. Select the NCAA.GIF image for the image field and enter any keywords that you like.

11. Click the Finish button to save your new entry as shown in Figure 24-10.

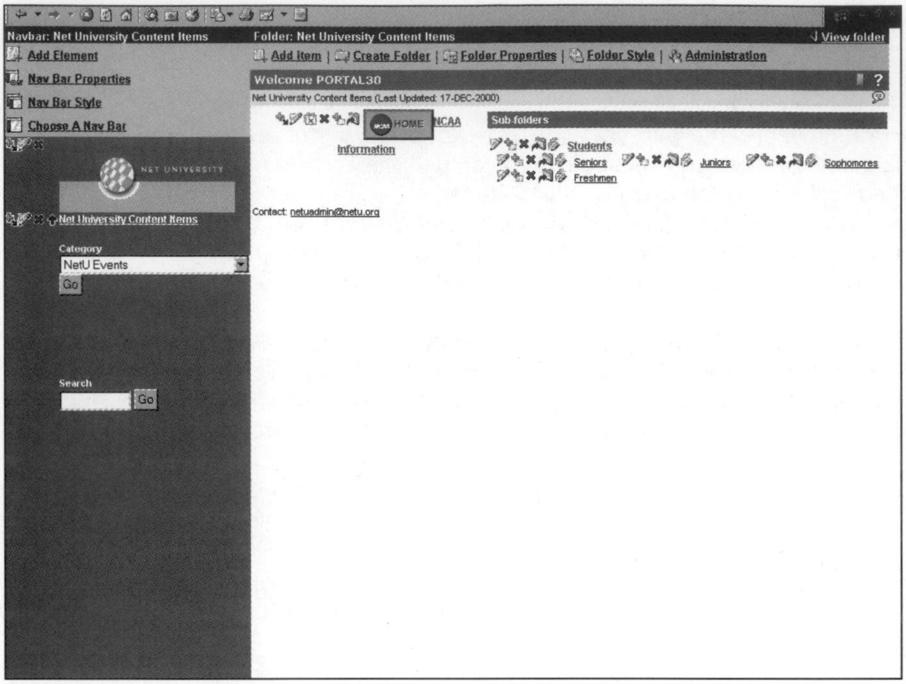

Figure 24-10: NCAA link

All of the changes that you might wish to make are available from the two menu bars that appear at the top of the folder region and the Navbar region. Content Area Administrators will see the entire list of customizing menu items:

- ✦ Add Element
- ✦ Navbar Properties
- ✦ Navbar Style
- ✦ Choose a Navbar
- ✦ Add Item
- ✦ Create Folder
- ✦ Folder Properties
- ✦ Folder Style
- ✦ Administration

The first four menu items provide links for modifying the Navigation Bar. The last five choices point to folder management functions. In both cases, these menu links are cross-linked to the very same design-time panels that you worked with in Chapter 22. Only folder administrators will have access to these menu choices.

Adding Content with Advanced Components to the Site

Documents, images, text, URLs, and Folder links all follow a similar workflow when they are uploaded into folders. Portal, however, provides some advanced item types in the form of Application components, PL/SQL, and Java applications.

Application components

The Content Area treats Application components as a special type of content and the Add-Item Wizard provides a specific entry solely for these components. When you choose the Portal item type, the wizard displays a list box of available components you can select from to use as the content item. You need to be aware of several critical restrictions with this interface, however.

Content Areas only display those components that have been set to *published as a portlet*.

Chapter 28 provides a detailed description of portlets. Oracle Portal automatically provides the "portlet" interface for all of its internal builders (reports, forms, charts, etc.).

The Add-Item Wizard displays only the SHOW procedure for your components, so you cannot pass parameters to portlet-enabled components that will restrict their output when they are run. The solution is to build your own URL and pass parameters to it.

1. Use SQL*Plus to load the Portal component ch24_cht_grades.sql script in the Chapter 24 directory of the Examples folder on the accompanying CD-ROM. This will create this example report.

2. Navigate to the Seniors Folder and use the Edit button to set the folder to edit mode. Use the Add Item button to start the Add-Item Wizard as shown in Figure 24-11.

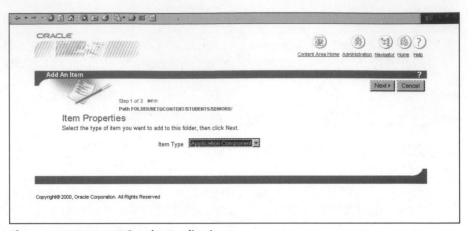

Figure 24-11: Item Wizard—Applications

3. Select the Application Component Item Type and use the Next button to continue.

The Add-Item Wizard loads a list of available application components into the Application Components combo box automatically. However, only those components that have been marked as "portlets" will appear.

> **Note** This is actually a two-part process; first you need to make sure that your application is marked as a "portlet provider." Then you must mark each individual component that you want exposed to the portal as a "portlet." In Chapter 2 you created the NETCOLLEGE application and marked it as a portlet provider. You can make individual components into portlets on the Access tab within each component manager. The ch24_cht_grades chart is already marked as such when you import it.

If you have marked other components as portlets in previous chapters, then they will appear in the combo box on this panel. As with any of the other item types, you can provide a title (which becomes the link to the component) and a detailed description. You can also provide a category for this component.

4. Select the ch24_cht_grades application component from the combo box. Enter a title and description and select the Academics category as shown in Figure 24-12.

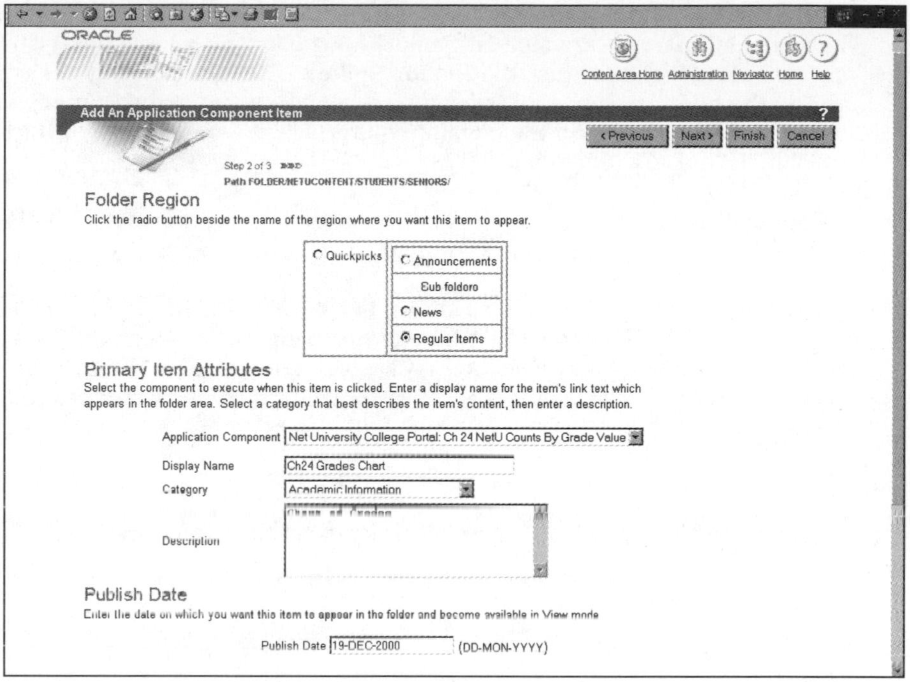

Figure 24-12: Application Component required parameters

5. Use the Next button to continue.

6. Items can appear within the region itself or they appear in a separate browser window. The sample chart is small enough to display in the folder region itself, so select the "Link That Displays Item In Folder Area" display option. Use the Finish button to save the new entry.

7. Test the entry using the link to display the panel as shown in Figure 24-13.

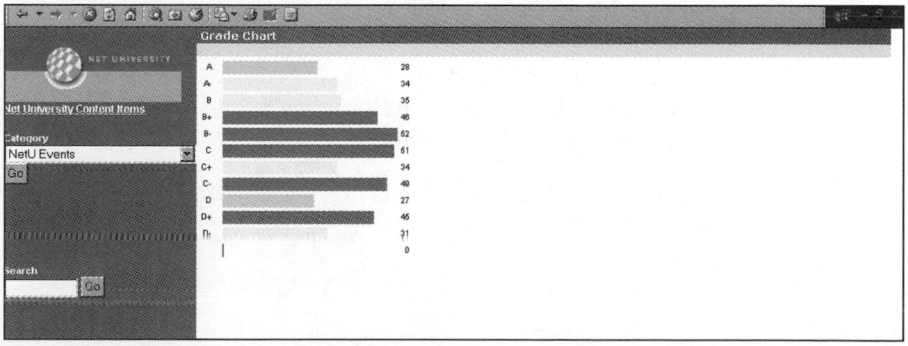

Figure 24-13: Grade Chart in folder region

Portal displays the resulting chart within the folder region itself. The sample chart has a default parameter value of "Senior" for the my_classcode BIND variable and so it displays the grade distribution for Seniors. The chart displays as a portlet within the folder region, so it takes on the color scheme of the Content Area. If you were to run this report in the developer interface, it would display with the PUBLIC.TEMPLATE_6 template.

8. Use the Category combo box in the Navigation Bar and select the Academic Information (press the "Go" button to start the search).

Portal displays a folder region as shown in Figure 24-14. You will notice that Portal automatically displays the folder banner for "Seniors," because this is the folder in which the category entry was found. Categories search across content in all of the folders that the portal user has access to within a selected Content Area. The folder banner helps the user figure out which folder the content is stored in.

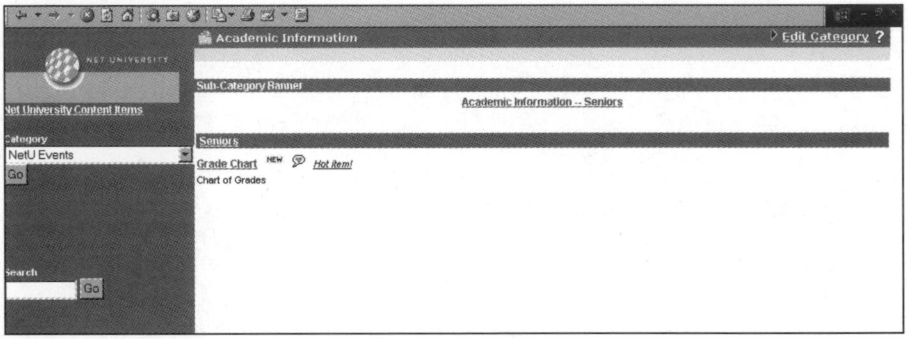

Figure 24-14: Category search

Application components with parameters

Ideally, you would put a link to the ch24_cht_grades chart in each of the four Student subfolders using a different classcode value. For each link, you would pass the my_classcode parameter so that this chart would show the grade distribution for each class. Unfortunately, Content Areas do not allow you to do this, because it cannot accept parameters or call the SHOW_PARMS procedure that would prompt the user for the parameter value at run time. The solution to this problem is to use the URL item type and call the component directly.

The following string shows the format of a relative URL that calls the Ch24_cht_grades chart and passes the value of "Junior" as the parameter value.

```
/pls/Portal30/netu.ch24_cht_grades.show?p_arg_names=my_classcod
e&p_arg_values=Junior
```

Oracle Portal will derive the server and port number from the page or component that calls the URL. Alternatively, you could embed the entire URL as shown here:

```
http://whiskeysoda.enter.net:2000/pls/Portal30/netu.ch24_cht_
grades.show?p_arg_names=my_classcode&p_arg_values=Junior
```

However, since the server name is embedded into the string, this will make it more difficult to move this Content Area to a different machine and/or port number in the future.

1. Navigate to the Juniors subfolder and add a new URL Item.

2. Navigate to the Primary Item Attributes panel as shown in Figure 24-15.

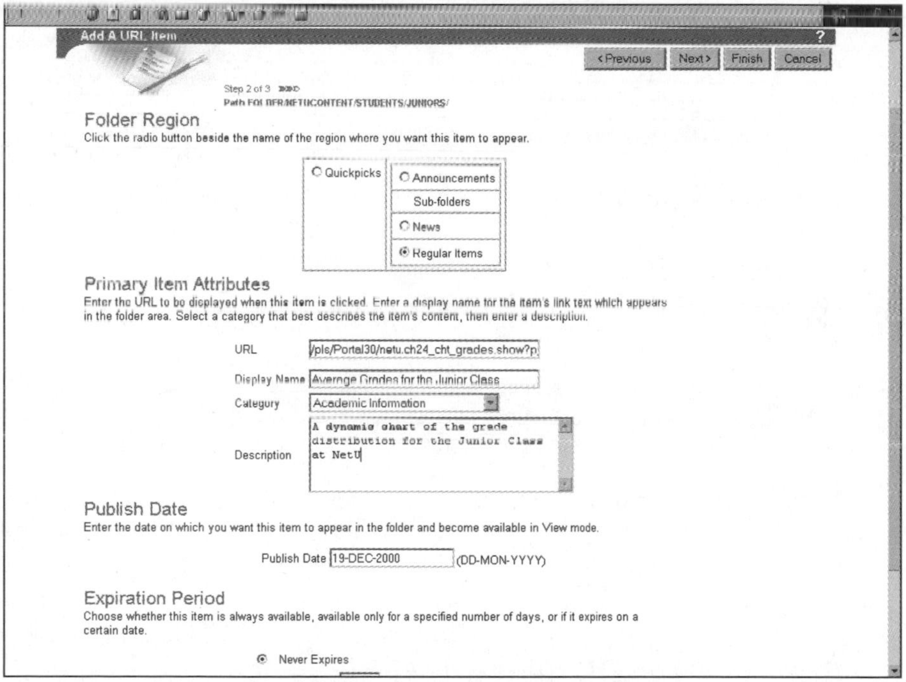

Figure 24-15: Primary Item Attributes panel for URLs with components

3. Enter the following URL into the URL field:

```
/pls/Portal30/netu.ch24_cht_grades.show?p_arg_names=my_
classcode&p_arg_values=Junior
```

4. Add a Display Name and Description for the new item, and select the Academic Information category.

5. Choose the Open Item in Full Browser window option.

6. Save the new item and then use the item link to display the panel as shown in Figure 24-16.

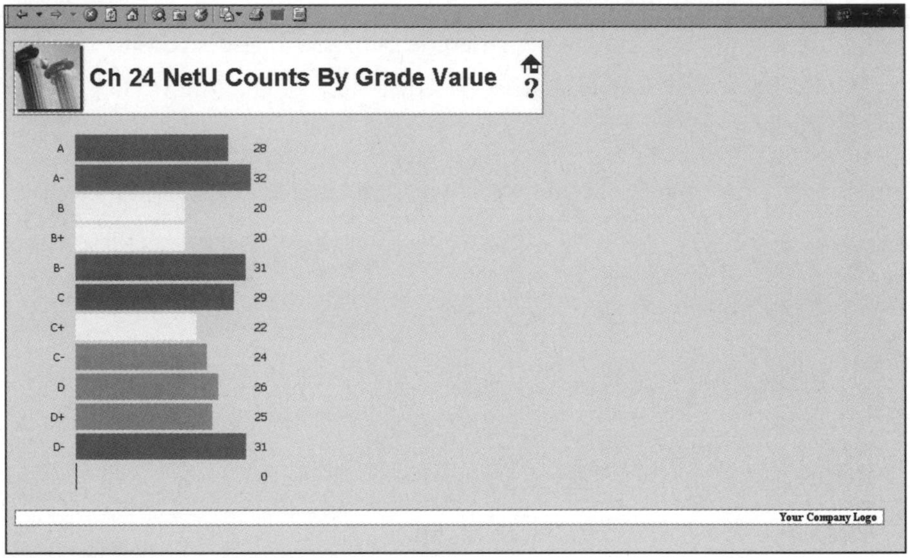

Figure 24-16: NetU Counts by Grade chart

Notice that the chart opens in a full browser and that it displays with the public template and not as a portlet. Portal only formats application components as portlets when they appear as a link/item within the folder area. (Portal implements Content Areas as portlets.)

Calling PL/SQL procedures

Chapter 28 details the process of creating portlets with PL/SQL code, but you can also use PL/SQL directly with Content Areas. As discussed in Chapter 21, Oracle provides a series of HTP procedures that can be embedded directly into PL/SQL code. Consider the code shown in Listing 24-1.

Listing 24-1: **PL/SQL-based Grade Report**

```
declare
v_avg_grades number(5,2);
v_classcode varchar2(12);
begin
htp.print('<HTML>');
htp.print('<HEAD>');
htp.print('</HEAD>');
htp.print('<BODY>');
htp.print('<H1>Average Student Grades</H1>');
htp.print('<table width="100%" border="1">');
htp.print('<tr>');
select u.classcode, avg(t.numeric_grade) into v_classcode,
v_avg_grades from netu.ugrads_and_transcripts u, netu.grades t
where u.grade=t.letter_grade and classcode='Senior' group by
u.classcode;
htp.print('<TD>'||v_classcode||'</TD>');
htp.print('<TD>'||to_char(v_avg_grades)||'</TD>');
htp.print('</TR>');
htp.print('<tr>');
select u.classcode, avg(t.numeric_grade) into v_classcode,
v_avg_grades from netu.ugrads_and_transcripts u, netu.grades t
where u.grade=t.letter_grade and classcode='Junior' group by
u.classcode;
htp.print('<TD>'||v_classcode||'</TD>');
htp.print('<TD>'||to_char(v_avg_grades)||'</TD>');
htp.print('</TR>');
htp.print('<tr>');
select u.classcode, avg(t.numeric_grade) into v_classcode,
v_avg_grades from netu.ugrads_and_transcripts u, netu.grades t
where u.grade=t.letter_grade and classcode='Sophomore' group by
u.classcode;
htp.print('<TD>'||v_classcode||'</TD>');
htp.print('<TD>'||to_char(v_avg_grades)||'</TD>');
htp.print('</TR>');
htp.print('<tr>');
htp.print('<TD>Freshmen</TD>');
htp.print('<TD>N/A</TD>');
htp.print('</TR>');
htp.print('</TABLE>');
htp.print('</BODY>');
htp.print('</HTML>');
end;
```

The AVG_GRADES procedure makes three separate queries against a view (alternatively you could have used a cursor). The results of the queries are loaded into variables and then HTP procedures format the results into a table. Portal allows you to call this procedure directly from a folder.

1. Navigate to the Seniors folder and create a new PL/SQL Item.

2. Advance to the primary panel as shown in Figure 24-17.

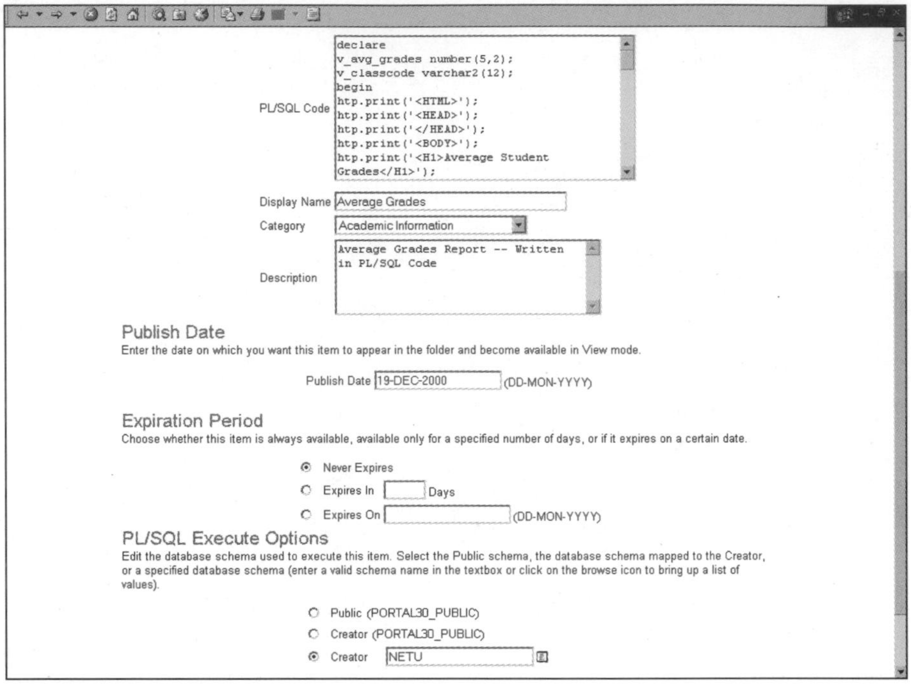

Figure 24-17: Custom PL/SQL code

You can post PL/SQL code directly into the PL/SQL code panel. All of the usual ground rules for PL/SQL apply, and you will have to declare variables for temporary storage and format the output yourself.

> **Cross-Reference** Chapter 21 provides a more detailed description of PL/SQL coding. You are free to use any of the techniques described in that chapter in the PL/SQL code window on the panel as shown in Figure 24-17.

3. Post the code as shown in Listing 24-1 into the PL/SQL Code panel. (You will find the code on the CD-ROM in the examples/ch24 subfolder.)

Oracle Portal does not automatically associate the code in the procedure with the underlying objects that the code references. For example, the default behavior on this panel is to run the code as the PORTAL30_PUBLIC. This user may not have permission to access the UGRADS_AND_TRANSCRIPTS and GRADES tables. You can either grant specific permissions to the public account, or you can use the text box at the bottom of the panel to set the code to run as a specified user.

4. Click the Creator radio button next to the text box with the find icon and use the Find icon to locate the NETU user as the creator for the PL/SQL code.

5. Save your changes and run the new link to display the panel as shown in Figure 24-18.

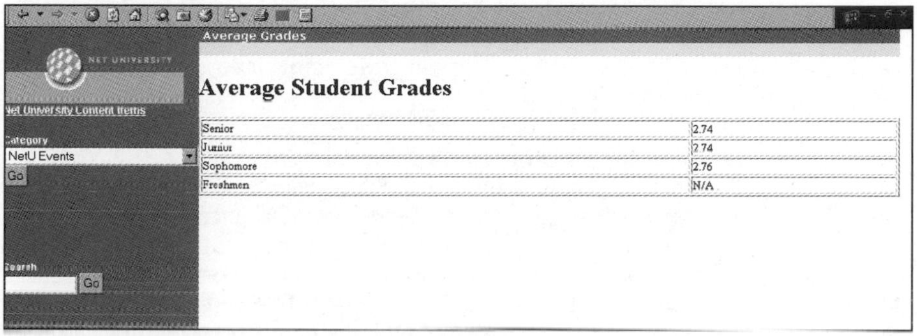

Figure 24-18: Average Student Grades—PL/SQL

The report as shown in Figure 24-18 lacks some of the amenities that you would find with the other Portal Component builders (forms, reports, calendars, charts, hierarchies and Dynamic Pages). You can add features such as background colors, fonts and even images—but you are forced to add this code by hand into the body of the procedure.

Java code

While PL/SQL has traditionally been the lingua franca of the database, Oracle has made great strides in adding support for Java to the database and to the application server. Although you can hand-code Java Servlets to run with the Oracle Application Server, you can also run these procedures within Content Areas. Portal provides the "Java" item type that accepts Java Server Pages-based content items. Listing 24-2 shows a very simple JSP object.

Listing 24-2: **NetU Java Server Page**

```
<HTML>
<HEAD><TITLE>A JSP Portal Page</TITLE></HEAD>
<BODY>
<H1>
<%
out.println("Your first JSP Page with Oracle Portal");
%>
</H1>
</BODY>
</HTML>
```

Java Server Pages are HTML pages that have Java Servlet code embedded within them. The application server layer (the database in this case) reads the Java code and executes it before the page is passed along to the browser. JSP code is embedded between the <% and %> directives as shown in Listing 24-2. JSPs support some very advanced options such as using Java Database Connectivity (JDBC) drivers and SQL to extract data from databases and call out to external applications. Essentially, there is nothing that you do with JSPs that you cannot also do with PL/SQL code (and Java Stored Procedures). However, developers that are new to Oracle may find it easier to write 3GL portal code using Java Server Pages, rather than trying to master PL/SQL code.

The example code directory for this chapter has two JSP objects, the NETU1.JSP source file and the NETU.JAR file, which contains the "archive" version of the JSP code. The Java platform allows you to combine code and external elements (such as images) into binary storage files called JARs. In order to upload JSPs into Oracle Portal, you must store the JSP source inside of a JAR. The code depicted in Listing 24-2 is the simplest type of JSP that you can create. It is nothing more than a standard HTML "Hello World" page with a single line of Java Servlet code. The code prints a line of text. The Servlet engine in the database will run this code and output the text into the body of the HTML page.

Note   Java Servlet Pages are a very advanced topic. If you plan on working with JSPs extensively we would recommend that you invest in a good JSP manual. Oracle also makes a world-class development platform for JSPs and Servlets with their JDeveloper product.

1. Locate the NETU.JAR Java archive, or create your own using the NETU1.JSP Java Server Page.

2. Start the Add Item Wizard in the Seniors folder and select the Java Application Item Type.

3. Navigate to the Primary Attributes panel as shown in Figure 24-19.

There are three new elements that you need to enter when you upload a JSP page — the JAR File, the Initial Page Name, and the Application Type. As mentioned in the preceding paragraph, you must store your Java code within a Java Archive in order to run the code within a Content Area. While this is not usually necessary with JSPs, it is a requirement for Portal. At the moment Portal only allows for JSPs, but in the future you will be able to run Servlets and even Enterprise Java Beans from within Portal. Thus, it makes sense to enforce the use of JARs; because this is a requirement for these other advanced Java program types. The Initial Page Name is the name of the JSP page within the JAR — and you must supply the full name, including the .JSP extension. The Application Type defaults to "Java Server Pages," but this may change in the future.

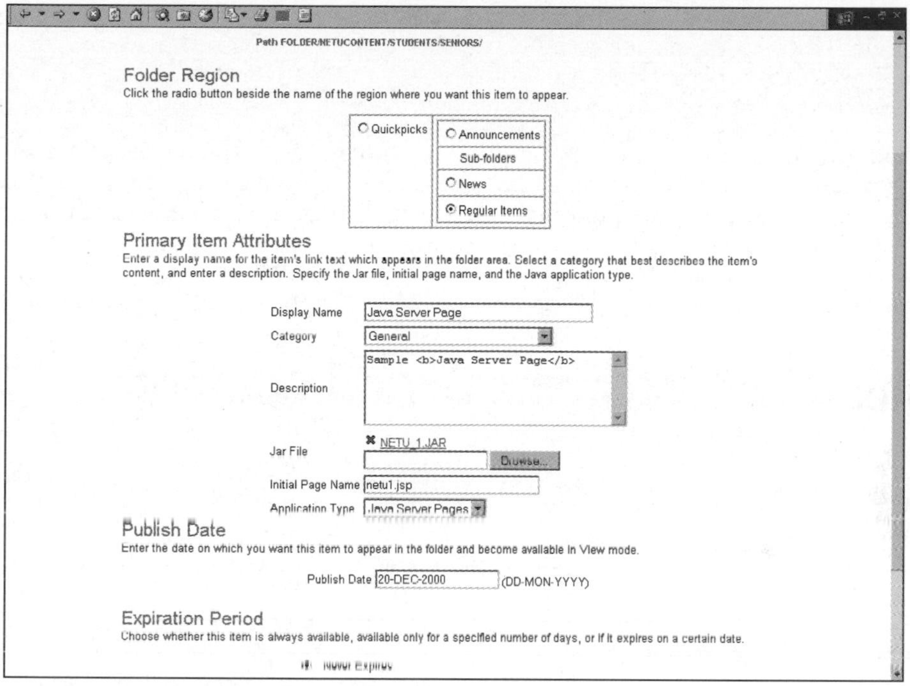

Figure 24-19: Adding a JSP page to a Content Area

4. Enter a Display Name, Category, and Description as shown in Figure 24-19.

5. Load the following Java components:

```
JAR File—netu.jar
Initial Page Name—netu1.jsp
Application Type—Java Server Pages
```

6. Navigate to the secondary attributes panel and save your new item. Run the link for this item to produce the page as shown in Figure 24-20.

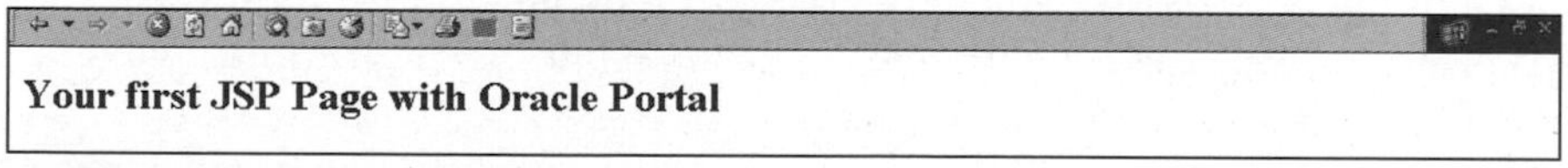

Your first JSP Page with Oracle Portal

Figure 24-20: Java Server Page output

The output as shown in Figure 24-20 is nothing more than an HTML page. In fact, the source for the HTML page is about as simple as you will get:

```
<HTML>
<HEAD><TITLE>A JSP Portal Page</TITLE></HEAD>
<BODY>
<H1>
```

```
Your first JSP Page with Oracle Portal
</H1>
</BODY>
</HTML>
```

You will also notice that the JSP appears as a full browser window. Portal does not provide any of the advanced display options for JSPs. This is due to the fact that JSPs are not implemented internally as portlets. If you wish your Java Server Pages to fit into the overall color scheme of your portal site, you will need to manually insert the proper colors, fonts, and images into the HTML page.

Using Other Accounts to Add Content

As you will recall from earlier discussions in this chapter, there are two additional classes of users that can access your Content Area folders — content approvers and viewers. Portal users with the View privilege in a Content Area will be able to see the items within folders — but they will not be presented with the Edit menu. Folder administrators and content approvers are able to manage and modify content using the edit icons that appear next to folder regions and items as shown in Figure 24-10. Each item has an associated set of edit icons that allow privileged users to make content changes to folders.

- ✦ **Edit:** Edit items (change categories, display names, etc.)
- ✦ **Add:** Add new items
- ✦ **Delete:** Delete existing items
- ✦ **Expire:** Cause an item to expire (which makes it non-viewable)
- ✦ **Approve:** Approve a new item for general display
- ✦ **Copy:** Copy an item from one folder to another
- ✦ **Move:** Move an item from one folder to another

Users that have been granted the "Create with Approval" privilege will be able to add new items — just like you did as the Portal Administrator. However, they will not appear to other users until they are approved by a user with the Manage Content privilege.

You created some additional managerial accounts and end-user accounts in the first part of this chapter, and you can use these accounts to add content to your site (if you have the proper permission).

1. Open another browser window and log on as **lgildenhorn**.

2. Navigate to the Students folder and press the Edit Folder link as shown in Figure 24-21.

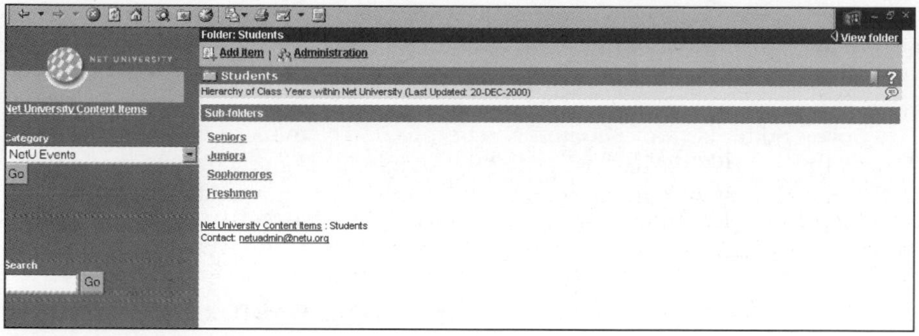

Figure 24-21: Students Folder edit mode—LGildenhorn

Caution
If the Add item link does not appear, or you do not see the subfolders, you need to use the portal administrator account to Make Public the Students folder and to Cascade this privilege to the subfolders.

The first thing that you will notice is that LGildenhorn is not permitted to make any changes to content—the only thing that she can do is add new items.

3. Open the Seniors folder.

4. Choose the Add Item link and add the following new item to the Students folder:

```
File
Regular Item
File: netu_courses.pdf
Display Name: NetU Course Catalog
Category: Academics
```

5. Set your own description for this item. The net result of adding this item appears on the page as shown in Figure 24-22.

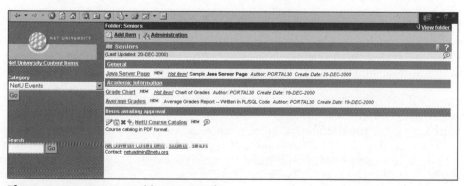

Figure 24-22: Items awaiting approval

Lori Gildenhorn's new item appears in a special category called "Items awaiting approval." Lori is permitted to add content to the site (Create with Approval), but she is not allowed to approve content.

The portal administrator account has permission to manage elements in the student folder, and items that are added to the folder are immediately made available to the site. The remaining undergraduate student accounts do not have this same level of permission. However, the WASTORE account that you created earlier in this chapter does have permission to approve items.

1. Log off the site and then log back on using the **WASTORE** account.

2. Navigate to the Seniors Folder and press the Edit Folder link to display the panel as shown in Figure 24-23.

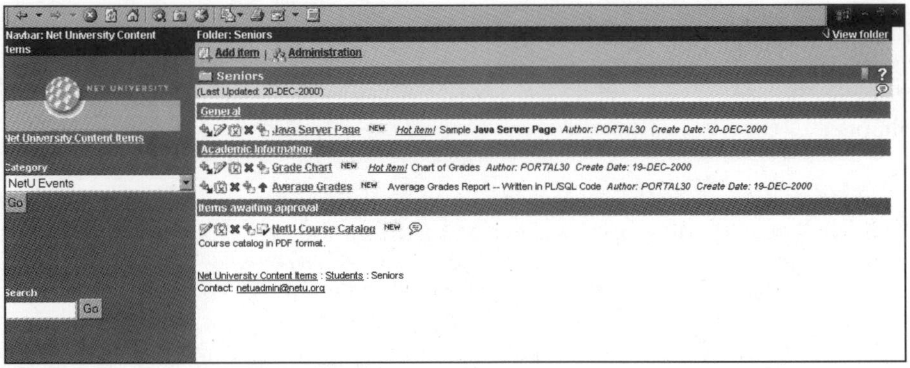

Figure 24-23: WASTORE's view of the Folder

Once you connect to the site as a privileged user, you only see the new item when you actually open up the Students folder. Content Areas automatically create a special internal category inside each folder that serves as the Approval folder. When you open any folder using a privileged account, you see this folder appear as shown in Figure 24-23.

Content Areas display a new icon next to the pending item called the "Approve" function. This function does not display a dialog panel, but rather serves as a one-button menu for marking the pending item as approved. You do not have a chance to confirm your choice, and the entry becomes final as soon as you use the Approve function. If you accidentally approve an item and want to revoke the approval, you have a limited number of choices. However, Portal displays a second icon next to the item that is called the "Property Sheet" (the little callout image). When you press this image, you will get a snapshot view of the major elements of the item as shown in Figure 24-24.

Figure 24-24: Property Sheet

The Property Sheet gives a fast heads-up overview of the object, including the author, type, perspectives, and display option. This gives the content approver the chance to give the item a quick once over before approving or rejecting it.

Note You will notice that the WASTORE account has full permission to approve items, but it cannot modify the structure of the site, or the style of the site. This is the difference between "managing content" and "owning" the site. You can feel comfortable in delegating authority to power users for item approval in folders and subfolders without giving them the keys to the kingdom.

Considering Some Advanced Topics

The best way to gain experience with your Content Areas site is to add items to the site and connect as a different class of user to test out your security scheme. You will find that Content Areas are easy to work with and do not require a steep learning curve from the user perspective. However, certain aspects of your Content Areas site require a little bit more explanation.

✦ Edit the properties of the NETUCONTENT Content Area and use the Items tab to display the panel as shown in Figure 24-25.

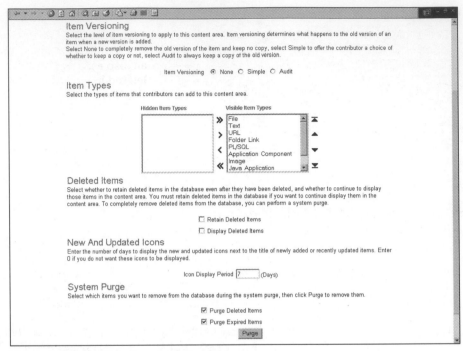

Figure 24-25: Setting item types for folders

Item management

Oracle Portal provides you with some advanced control over the items that you add to the site. These options give you fine-grained control over the lifespan of content and the type of items that your users are permitted to load onto the site.

Item versioning

By default, Portal does not enforce version control over content items (as it does over component items within the component building tools). You can use the Simple radio button to give content contributors the option of saving old versions. Alternatively, you can set the Audit radio button to enforce version control. Portal administrators then become responsible for removing outdated versions.

Item types

Although Portal supports a wide range of item types, you can restrict the item types that your content contributors have access to. The arrow keys allow you to move objects from the Visible Item Types list to the Hidden Item Types list. Hidden items will not appear in the combo box when content contributors run the Add-Item Wizard.

Deleted items

There are two types of deleted items: *expired* items and those items that have been explicitly *deleted*. You can choose to save deleted items until the next system purge by checking the Retain Deleted Items check box. You can also elect to continue to display deleted items to viewers by using the Display Deleted Items check box. (Deleted items will only be shown to administrators and folder managers.)

New and updated icons

Oracle Portal marks new content items (and updated items) with special icons on the display bar. By default, Portal displays these icons for seven days, but you can change this interval using the Icon Display Period text box.

System purge

You will have to manually delete content from Portal if you have elected to retain deleted items. Simply mark the type of deleted item that you want removed using the two check boxes and then use the Purge key to delete these item.

Advanced searching

Content Areas provides the Basic Search capability on the Navigation Bar by default. A user can enter a string into the Search text box on the Navigation Bar, and Content Areas searches the title, description, and keywords of all items for matching values. Users can surround words with the % wild card character to search for substrings. As your site grows, this can make the task of searching more difficult, as more and more items match the same set of keywords and phrases.

Content Areas provide a second search panel called the Advanced Search panel, which you can enable for a folder on the Navigation Bar Editor.

 Cross-Reference   Chapter 22 discusses the process for modifying the Navigation Bar on a folder-by-folder basis.

The Advanced Search panel shown in Figure 24-26 enables users to perform Boolean searches using a combination of "and" and "or."

Although you can add links to perspectives and categories on the Navigation panel, you can save space on the Navigation Bar by deploying them on the Advanced Search panel instead. The top portion of the panel enables the user to enter a combination of phrases and keywords. The bottom portion of the panel enables the user to search in specified folders, categories, and perspectives. You can even search for items that have been entered by a certain individual, or within a certain period of time.

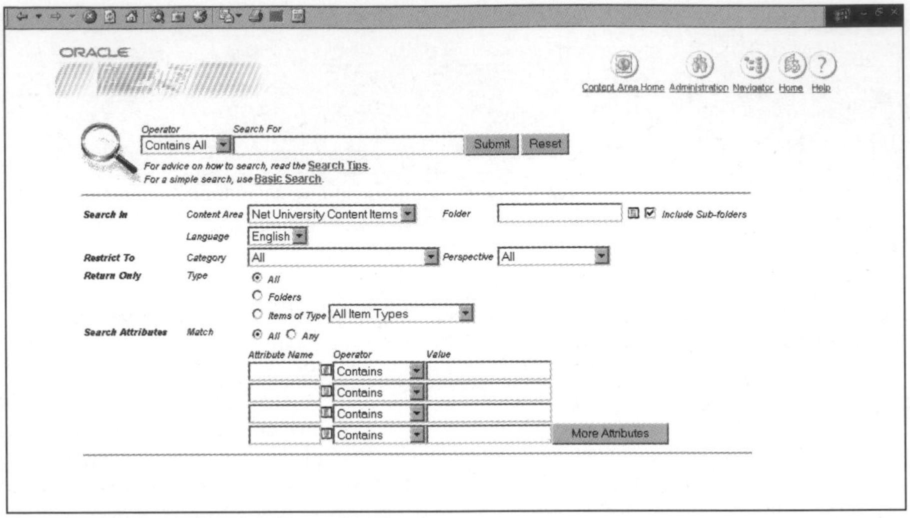

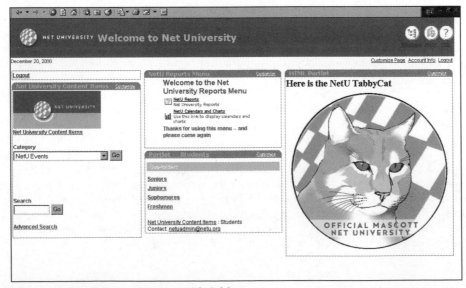

Figure 24-26: Advanced Search panel

Content Areas on portal pages

Content Areas can be deployed directly onto portal pages. Figure 24-27 shows the Students Folder hierarchy after it has been deployed onto the NETU_MAIN portal page.

Figure 24-27: NetU main page with folders

Portal displays the Student region as a portlet, and the subfolders appear as links within the portlet area (just as they do within Content Areas). Portal will display the output of the links as Content Areas and not as portlets. If you wish to have the folder links appear as portal pages then you will have to manually create portal pages for each folder.

Chapter 29 discusses a number of advanced topics for Content Areas including portal pages, custom attributes, and custom item types.

Summary

Adding content to Content Areas sites is an evolutionary process, and each site you build will evolve differently. The layout of your folders and the mix of items and formats that you implement are driven largely by the users of the site. Content Areas solve one part of the problem by providing a consistent framework. However, the larger problem with most sites is one of content.

No matter how visually stimulating your portal is, you will fail to keep users coming back if you cannot deliver the content they want in a timely fashion. By eliminating the complexity of formatting content for the portal using Content Areas, you make it easier for *users* to contribute content, and this helps keep your portal site fresh and interesting. In the next chapter, we'll take a look at managing an Oracle9*i*AS Portal.

✦   ✦   ✦

Administering Oracle9*i*AS Portal

In This Part

Chapter 25
Administering
Oracle9*i*AS Portal
Components

Chapter 26
Oracle9*i*AS Portal
Security

Chapter 27
Monitoring
Oracle9*i*AS Portal
Performance

Administering Oracle9*i*AS Portal Components

✦   ✦   ✦   ✦

In This Chapter

Using Version Control

Managing
Components

Managing
Applications

Exporting and
Importing Information

Administering
Oracle9*i*AS Portal

✦   ✦   ✦   ✦

By now, you've had quite a bit of experience creating
Oracle9*i*AS Portal components. If you have been following along with the examples in this book, you have created
reports, forms, charts, dynamic HTML pages, and menus to
bind them all together.

You have also started to see how an Oracle9*i*AS Portal system
can encompass many different components, and you may
have started to worry about how to manage all of them. This
chapter focuses on the specific tools and utilities you can use
to manage your Oracle9*i*AS Portal components, from changing
the name or copying a component to using the built-in version
control for Oracle9*i*AS Portal components and exporting and
importing existing Oracle9*i*AS Portal components. You will
also learn about the management options for your complete
application, and receive a high-level overview of some of the
administrative options available for the entire Oracle9*i*AS
Portal environment.

Using Oracle9*i*AS Portal Version Control

If you have created any Oracle9*i*AS Portal components, and
you have edited the components once you initially created
them, you have already experienced the built-in version control feature of Oracle9*i*AS Portal.

Every time you edit a component, Oracle9*i*AS Portal stores the new parameters for the component in a new version of the component. When you have finished your changes, Oracle9*i*AS Portal assigns a status to the new version of the component. Typically, you generate your component when you finish changing its parameters and, typically, the component compiles successfully. These two actions result in a new version of the component being added to your Oracle9*i*AS Portal system. The next time you bring up the Manage Component page for the component in Oracle9*i*AS Portal, you see one more listing under the heading of Version(s).

You would see the last listing having a higher version number and a status of PRODUCTION, with VALID package, while the previous version is now marked with a status of ARCHIVE. If you did not generate the component, or if the component was not generated successfully, you would still see a new version of the component, but it would have a different status associated with it.

This automatic versioning gives you an increased level of security when you are changing Oracle9*i*AS Portal components. No matter how much you change a particular version of a component, the previous version is always available to you, safe and sound. The only problem is that the previous version is identified by a (somewhat) cryptic version number. At this time, you cannot add descriptive information to a version number, so you have to use your own methods to track which version number has which features.

Cross-Reference We suggest a method to track versions later in this chapter in the sidebar called "Version Control."

Tip It is so easy to restore previous versions that you can always restore a version of a component and see what it contained. If it was not the version you were looking for, you could either bring the previous version back or look for another version of the component.

But all the earlier versions of a component are still there, waiting for you to bring them back to life.

It is easy to restore a previous version of a component. For this set of examples, you will be using a specially edited version of a component, although you could take the same steps for any component that you have already edited at least once.

1. Go to the Navigator and click on the name of any component that you have previously edited, which will bring up the Manage Component page.

2. Click on a previous version of the component — any one marked as ARCHIVE, which will bring up the page shown in Figure 25-1.

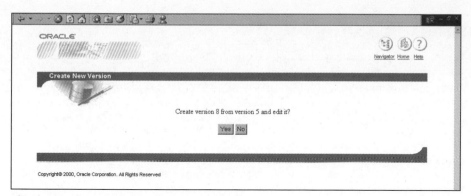

Figure 25-1: Restoring a previous version

You are asked whether you want to make a copy of the selected archive version of the component and make it into the newest version of the component, which will be identified with the next highest version number. If you respond by clicking the Yes button, you are immediately taken to the Edit page for the new version of the component.

3. Click the Yes button in the Create New Version page.

The new version of the component is not created until you have clicked the Finish button on the Edit page for the new component. If you leave the Edit page for the new component by clicking the Cancel button, Oracle9*i*AS Portal does not create a new version of the component. This makes sense. If you leave the Edit page by clicking the Cancel button, no new version of the component is generated, so the existing version of the component is identical to the previous version and therefore serves no purpose.

4. Make a change to the header of the report in the Add Text panel of the Edit page.

5. Click the Finish button.

The new version of the report should be listed on the Manage Component page when the generation of the new version is completed.

It is important to understand how versions work within Oracle9*i*AS Portal, because most of the management functions you will learn about later in this chapter only work on the current version of a component. The next section introduces you to the basic management capabilities for Oracle9*i*AS Portal components.

Managing Components

If you have been reading this book from the beginning, you are already quite familiar with some parts of the Manage Component page. In fact, the Manage Component page is the final page delivered to you when you are creating user interface components.

There are three tabs on the Manage Components page — Develop, Manage, and Access. Up until this point, you may not have even noticed the Manage and Access tabs, since you never had to use them. In this chapter, we will take a complete tour of the choices available to you on these other tabs, as well as the choices on the Develop tab that we have not yet explicitly discussed.

New Feature Most of the administrative functions discussed in this section also existed in WebDB, but many of them are found in different places in the Manage Components area.

The Develop tab

The links at the bottom of the Manage tab of the Manage Components page are the most commonly used feature of this page. You have already used the first four of these links extensively — Edit, Run, Run As Portlet, and Customize. There are three more links at the bottom of this page, discussed in the next sections.

The Add to Favorites link

You have seen the Favorites portlet on the OP home page for a while — this portlet was specifically introduced to you in Chapter 3. The Add to Favorites link simply adds a link for the current component to the my Links portlet on the home page. Clicking on the link will always take you to the Manage Components page for the component.

The link in the my Links portlet is placed in a group called Components.

The About link

The About menu choice, as shown in Figure 25-2, gives you some basic information about the current versions of a component and a complete listing of the values of all the parameters that you have assigned for the creation of a component.

There is an enormous amount of information presented on the About page. This data is essentially a recap of all the information stored in the Oracle9*i*AS Portal data tables about the component. All of the values you entered through the pages of the creation wizard are listed, with the prefix P_ preceding a descriptive name.

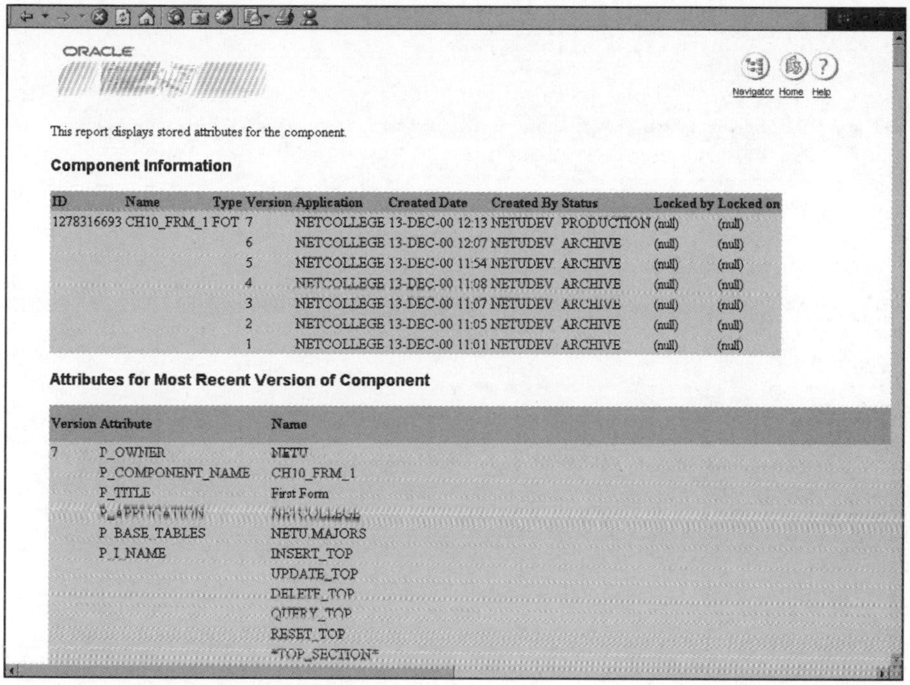

Figure 25-2: The About menu choice page

When you look at the values returned on the About page, you are able to see inside Oracle9*i*AS Portal. It's helpful to get to know the type of parameters used for a particular component, because many of them can be passed to your component if you are calling the PL/SQL package from a link, from another PL/SQL package, or directly from a browser. You will learn about these last two options later in this chapter.

🗑 The Delete link

The Delete option performs the same task that the Drop option did in WebDB — it gives you the ability to get rid of any or all of the versions of a component.

When you click the Delete menu choice, Oracle9*i*AS Portal delivers the Drop Component page, as shown in Figure 25-3.

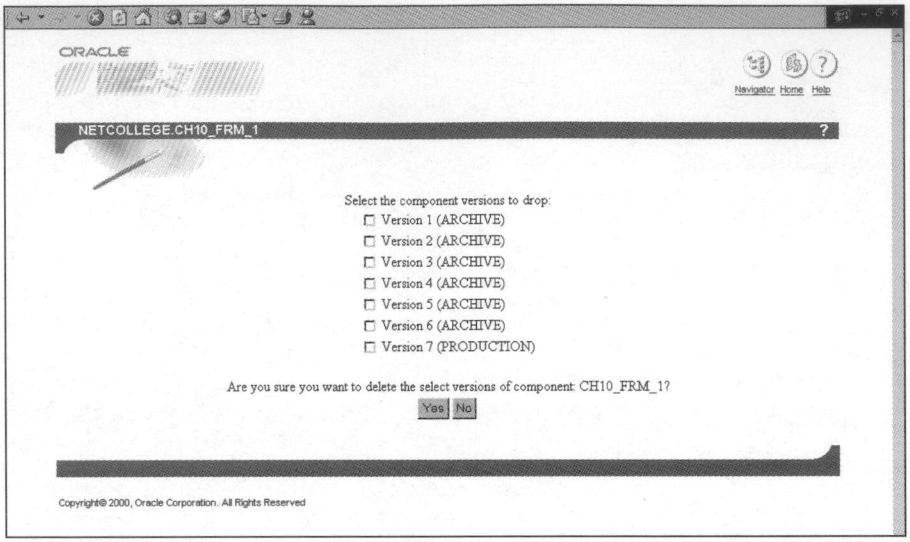

Figure 25-3: The Drop Component page

Oracle9*i*AS Portal gives you the opportunity to drop each individual version of a component. By default, none of the versions are selected for deletion by having the check box at the beginning of their name checked. Unless you want to delete a component completely, you should be careful to uncheck at least one of the boxes.

As you can probably guess at this point, dropping a version means that Oracle9*i*AS Portal deletes the rows in its internal tables that contain the parameters used to generate that version of the component. If you drop all the versions of a component, any generated PL/SQL packages are also dropped.

The Package Spec and Package Body links

In addition to the links at the bottom of the page, there are three hot links in the main body of the page.

As you probably already know, an Oracle9*i*AS Portal component is implemented as a PL/SQL package. The two hot links to the right of the PL/SQL source title show you the actual text of the PL/SQL package specification and the body of the package.

It is somewhat interesting to look at this source code, but unless you are quite familiar with PL/SQL (and have the patience to follow the code through), you may not be able to get a lot from these links.

Version Maintenance

In an iterative development environment, it is very easy to end up with a lot of versions for a component. In fact, because it is so easy to change an Oracle9*i*AS Portal component, it is almost inevitable that you end up with many versions of a given component. The built-in versioning feature of Oracle9*i*AS Portal is great from the standpoint of always being able to cancel out changes by returning to a previous version, but it is less than ideal for identifying which version is which, because the only identifier is a version number.

You can avoid version overload in one of two ways. The first is to be fairly ruthless about cleaning up versions during the development and release process. While your component is in developmental flux, you can just keep modifying the component and creating more versions. But as soon as you attain a steady state, you have to remember to go back to the Manage Component page and drop all the interim versions. This reduces the number of versions you have for a particular component, but you still have multiple versions of a component with "holes" in the version numbering scheme, as shown in the following figure.

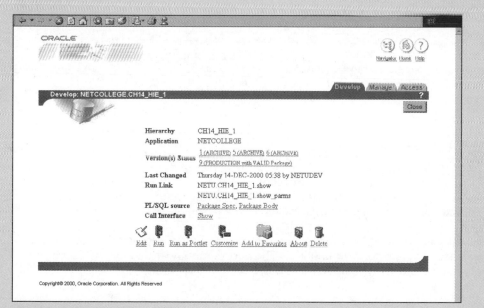

Version number holes

The second method is to make a fresh copy (which you will learn about later in this chapter) of each new version of a component that you want to keep. You can give each copy a more descriptive name, as shown in the following figure, which can help to administer the different versions of a component.

Continued

Continued

This page displays the results of the search string. Click links in the Name column to perform the default action of the Object. To perform actions, click on the appropriate action link.To sort a column, click the up or down arrow.

Find: [　　　　　　] [Go] [Close]

Type ▲ ▼	Name ▲ ▼	Actions	Owner ▲ ▼	Modified ▲ ▼ ?
Hierarchies	CH14_HIE_1	Manage, Run, Edit, Delete, Grant Access	NETCOLLEGE	14-Dec-2000
Hierarchies	CH14_HIE_1V1	Manage, Run, Edit, Delete, Grant Access	NETCOLLEGE	14-Dec-2000
Hierarchies	CH14_HIE_1V2	Manage, Run, Edit, Delete, Grant Access	NETCOLLEGE	14-Dec-2000
Hierarchies	CH14_HIE_1V3	Manage, Run, Edit, Delete, Grant Access	NETCOLLEGE	14-Dec-2000

Different versions of a component as different components

In either case, it is good practice to add some type of version indicator to your component, either in the header or footer of the component or, if your users object to seeing the version number on a page, as a hidden field. Having version numbers is not that useful if you have no way of knowing which version is being run at any particular time.

The Call Interface link

The Call Interface link provides a list of the parameters called for a component, an illustration of calling the procedure for the component from another stored procedure, and a sample URL that describes how to call the procedure at run time. The default values are also shown for each of the parameters.

When you create links, you will find that you are given a list of parameters that can be passed values for a component. The information returned for the Call Interface choice, as shown in Figure 25-4, can help you to understand the best way to build your links.

The syntax for the URL call can also help you understand how to integrate your Oracle9*i*AS Portal components in with standard HTML pages in a site.

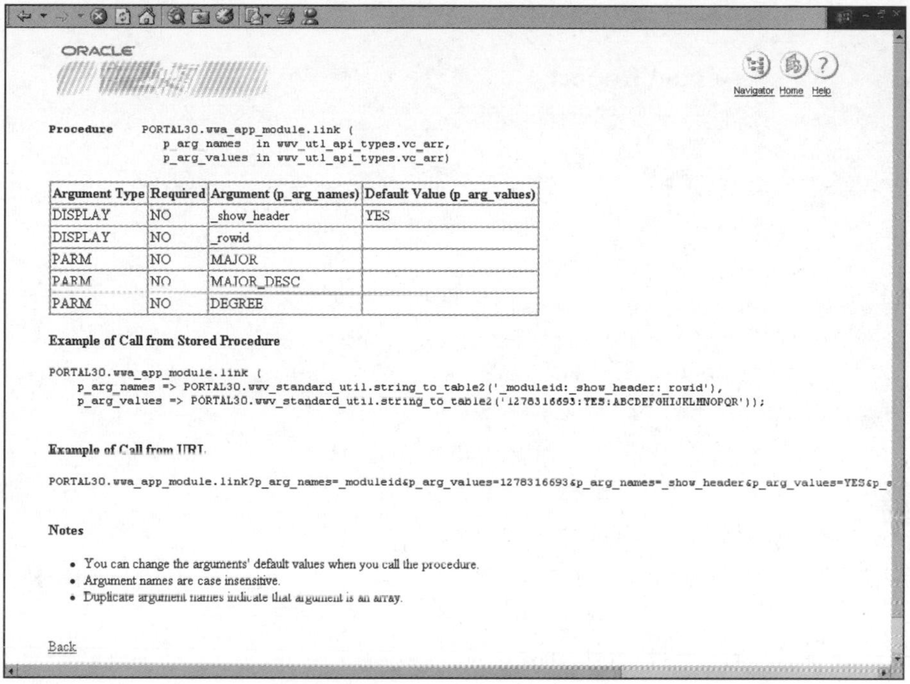

Figure 25-4: The returned Call Interface page for a form

The Manage tab

The Manage tab of the Manage Components page has either one or two hot links at the top of the page and five icons at the bottom of the page.

Show SQL Query Info link

Oracle9*i*AS Portal components that retrieve data from the database use SQL statements to get that data. For query components, such as reports, charts, and hierarchies, you can select the Show SQL Query Info choice.

When this choice is selected, the component will include the actual SQL string used to query the database at the top of the component, as shown in Figure 25-5.

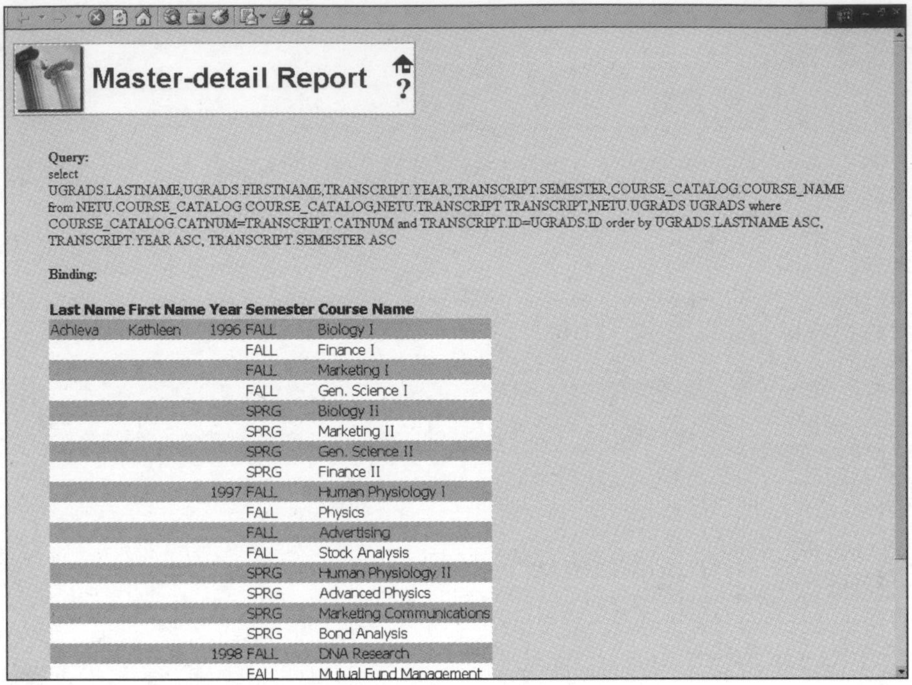

Figure 25-5: Showing a SQL string for a component

Once you have turned this option on for a component, the menu choice will change to read Hide SQL Query Info.

Show Lock on This Component link

Throughout this book, we have generally assumed that you will be the only user working on a particular component at a particular time. But because your Oracle database has the capability to have many users at the same time, Oracle9*i*AS Portal also enables you to have many different developers simultaneously. However, just as no two users can write to the same row of data at the same time, no two Oracle9*i*AS Portal developers can modify the same component at the same time. Although the component locks are not actual locks on the underlying rows in the Oracle9*i*AS Portal host database, the logical locking imposed by Oracle9*i*AS Portal serves the same purpose as the database locks implemented by the Oracle database.

When one developer is working on a component, the component is locked. You may occasionally see a status description for a version in the Manage Component page such as "PRODUCTION locked by *username*," where the *username* identifies the database user who is actively modifying the parameters for a component. You can use this choice to get further information about the lock that is being held on this component.

When the component is locked, you are unable to edit or perform any administrative tasks on the component. You may, however, be able to run the package generated by the component, because this package is independent of the data rows that have been locked by another developer.

Copy link

The Copy choice allows you to create a copy of a component. When you click the Copy menu choice, Oracle9*i*AS Portal delivers the Copy Component page, as shown in Figure 25-6.

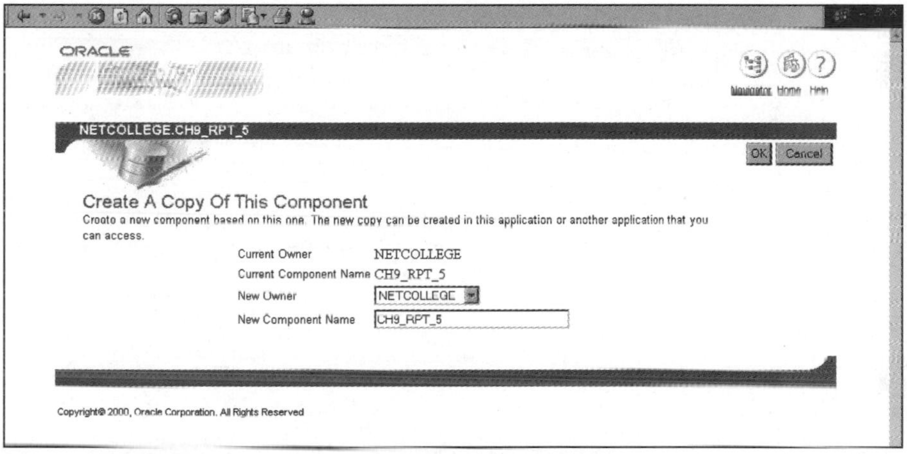

Figure 25-6: The Create A Copy Of This Component page

This page enables you to create a copy of the current version of a component under another name or to another application. The copied version of the component is given a version number of 1, because it is a new component. You can use this capability to copy a component to another application.

You can also use this page to create explicit versions of a component with meaningful names, as described in the "Version Maintenance" sidebar above. When you take this approach to versioning, every released version of a component has a version number of 1, so it's easy to identify whether a component is actively part of the development process.

✒ Rename

When you click the Rename menu choice, Oracle9*i*AS Portal brings up the Provide A New Name For This Component page, as shown in Figure 25-7.

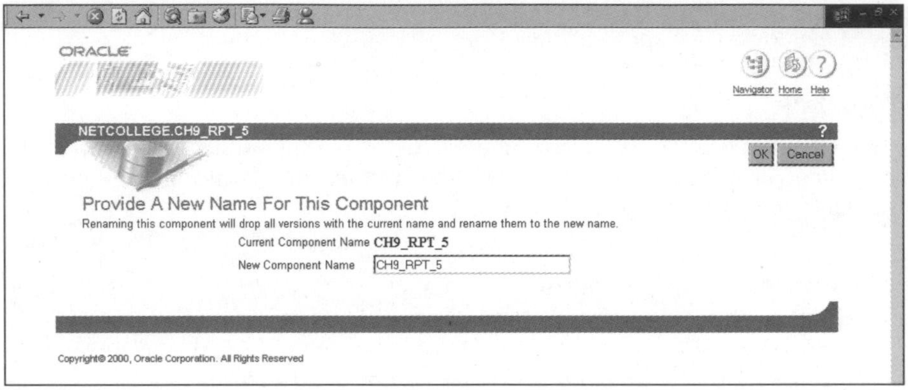

Figure 25-7: The Provide A New Name For This Component page

The Rename process is different from the Copy process in two ways. First, renaming a component maintains all the existing versions of the component, not just the current one. Second, the new name for the component is applied directly to the component, so it has the effect of deleting the current name of the component by overwriting it.

♀ Generate

You should be familiar with the Generate process by now. You generate the PL/SQL package that is your run-time component when you click the OK button at the end of an Oracle9*i*AS Portal wizard process or when you click the Finish button at the end of an editing session. Because these are typically the last things you do in your development process, why would you ever want to use the Generate choice?

Typically, you won't ever need to use it, but there may be occasions where you import the data in the Oracle9*i*AS Portal tables, but not the packages created from that data. In this situation, it may be faster for you to use the Generate choice rather than entering the Edit mode for a particular component.

When you use Oracle9*i*AS Portal to export your components, the SQL script that is created includes a call to the Generate procedure, so the script automatically generates the component.

If you select the Generate choice for an existing component and return to the Manage Component page, you will see that there is no new version number for the component — even though you may have heard the whirring of a disk drive that might have led you to believe that Oracle9*i*AS Portal was creating a new package.

Oracle9*i*AS Portal did create a new PL/SQL package, but because it had the exact same characteristics of the current version, there was no need to change the version number.

Keep in mind that a version is defined by a new set of parameters in the Oracle9*i*AS Portal database, not a new copy of the resulting package, so calling the Generate process has no effect on the version number of the component.

Monitor

The Monitor choice takes you to a page that shows you any events that have been logged for this particular component. Chapter 27 covers monitoring in detail, so it will not be discussed here.

Export

Exporting and importing the different portions of your Oracle9*i*AS Portal environment is a many-faceted topic, so we will be covering it in its own section, aptly called "Exporting and Importing Information," later in this chapter.

The Access tab

The Access tab of the Manage Component, as shown in Figure 25-8, is where you can indicate how you want a particular component to be accessed.

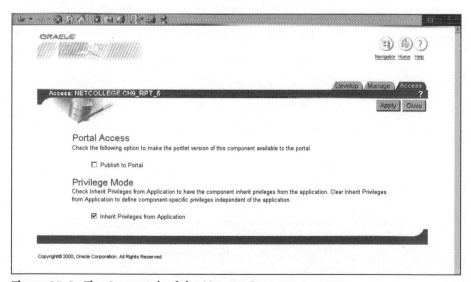

Figure 25-8: The Access tab of the Manage Component page

There can be up to two areas on this page. The top area is labeled Portal Access and contains a check box. If you check the box, this component will be accessible as a portlet. This entire section will only appear if you have specified that the application that the component belongs to is a portlet provider, which is described in the next section. If the application has not been specified as a portlet provider, this entire section will not be on the page.

The second section on the page is labeled Privilege Mode. By default, this section will contain a single, checked check box labeled Inherit Privileges from Application. Usually, you will define the access privileges at the application level, so leaving this default choice is good enough.

If you want to define a different set of security privileges for this particular component, you can uncheck this check box and click on the Apply button. This action will change this part of the page to look like Figure 25-9.

When you initially decide to define a different set of access rights for a component, the access rights shown are the same as those that apply to the application. You can change them in this new part of the page.

The entire topic of access rights and security is covered in depth in Chapter 26, so we will not go into greater detail in this chapter.

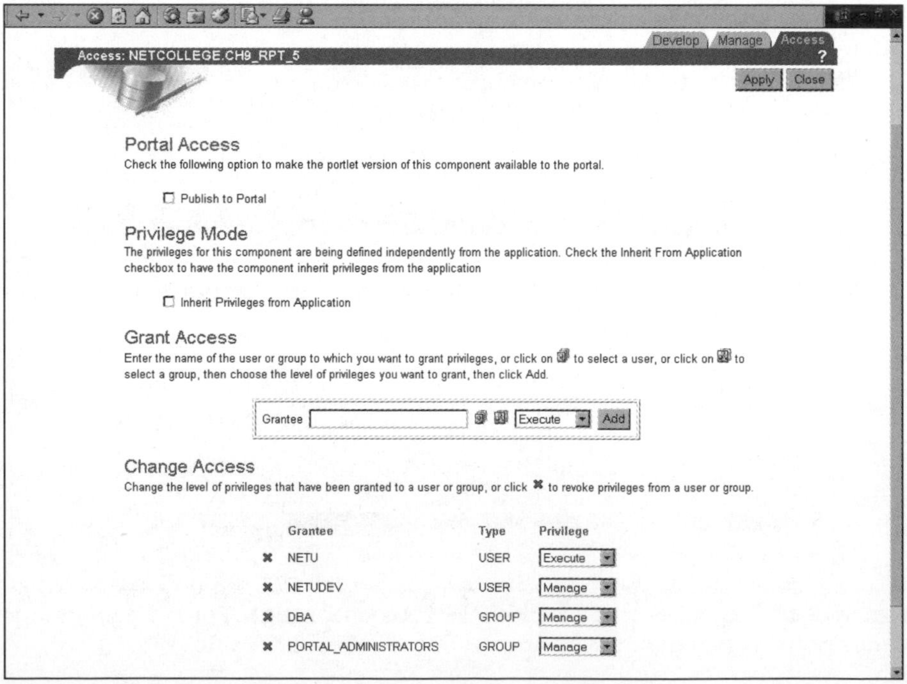

Figure 25-9: Defining separate access rights for a component

Managing Applications

You have always had the ability to manage components in the product now known as Oracle9*i*AS Portal. But the concept of the application is new to Oracle9*i*AS Portal, and so the ability to manage applications is also new.

You use the Navigator to access an application for management.

1. Go to the Navigator and click on the Applications tab.

2. If you are not at the top (application) level, click on the Application link in the Path at the top of the page.

3. Click on the Manage action link to bring up the page shown in Figure 25-10.

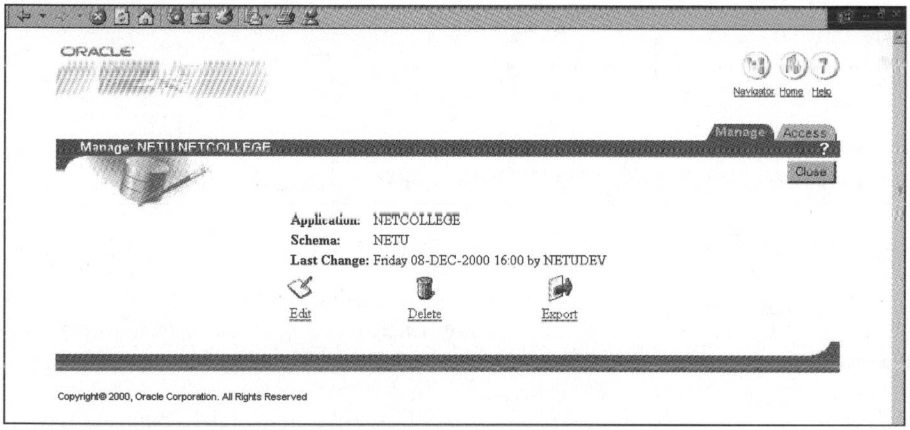

Figure 25-10: Managing an application—the Manage tab

The tab shown initially on this page is the Manage tab. You have three choices available to you on this tab:

✎ You can edit the Name or the Display Name of the application. You cannot, however, change the application schema where the application is stored.

🗑 You can delete the application. This action will delete the application and all of the objects that are part of the application. Of course, Oracle9*i*AS Portal will prompt you for a confirmation before it actually takes this drastic action.

📤 You can export the application. Exporting an application exports the actual application and all of the objects associated with the application. For more information about exporting an application, please refer to the next section.

4. Click on the Access tab in the Manage Applications page to bring up the page shown in Figure 25-11.

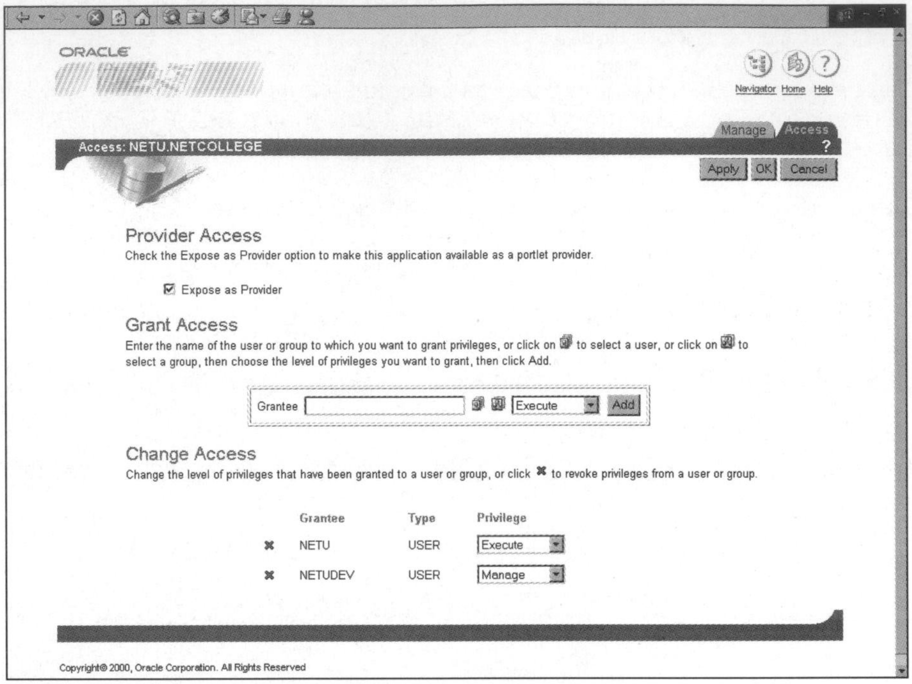

Figure 25-11: Managing an application — the Access tab

There are two basic types of access that you can grant for an application. You can allow an application to be exposed as a portlet provider. When an application is exposed as a portlet provider, you have the option to expose any of the components or Content Areas included in the application as a portlet. You will still have to explicitly expose an application component or Content Area as a portlet, as explained previously, but if you do not expose the application itself as a portlet provider, you cannot expose the components as portlets.

The other type of access you can grant is the right to use the application in a particular way. This topic of security is covered in depth in the next chapter.

Exporting and Importing Components and Applications

In the previous release of this book, we devoted a fair amount of space to the different potential ways you could export and import your WebDB systems. The reason for all of this earlier discussion was that these capabilities of WebDB were not really that complete.

In Oracle9*i*AS Portal, the introduction of the concept of the application, as well as an overall honing of the architecture of the product, have led to exporting and importing that are, in most ways, cleaner than the earlier processes. However, there are a number of different considerations involved in moving your systems to another machine.

There are two basic ways you can export information from your Oracle9*i*AS Portal server—through the use of export scripts, which are run from the command prompt of the server, or through the use of an internal Oracle9*i*AS Portal process.

All import processes are done using SQL*Plus, the standard interactive SQL utility that comes with every version of the Oracle database.

There are seven types of information that you should consider when you think about transferring your work to another Oracle9*i*AS Portal system. The process you will need to use for each of these types is described in the rest of this section. These processes are listed in the order in which you do them if you were planning on migrating an entire Oracle9*i*AS Portal system to another machine. Of course, you do not have to do all of these processes every time you want to move an object to another server, but you must do them in the listed order to ensure a smooth migration.

Caution
In the last version of this book, we stated that, since WebDB was simply composed of PL/SQL packages, you could use the standard Oracle import and export routines to move components and systems around. With this release, Oracle9*i*AS Portal is integrated with a host of other components, so we no longer advocate using anything other than the recommended processes to do export and imports.

Single sign-on accounts

The first step in moving to a new machine is to make sure that this machine has a complete complement of Oracle9*i*AS Portal users. Your first step is to export the single sign-on accounts for these users.

You export the single sign-on accounts with the ssoexp script. You must be in the admin\plsql\wwu directory of the Oracle9*i*AS Portal home to run the command. If your home for Oracle9*i*AS Portal was named Oportal on the D drive, the script would be run from the D:\Oportal\portal30\admin\plsql\wwu directory. The script will create a dump file, with a .dmp extension, which is then moved to the target machine.

Note
This script, and all other scripts mentioned in this section, come in two forms—with a command extension of .cmd for the Windows NT/2000 platform, and with a command extension of .csh for UNIX environments.

You import the single sign-on accounts with the ssoimp script. If you are importing these accounts to a machine that already has some user accounts, you can include a parameter to indicate whether the import process should skip any new accounts with the same names as existing accounts. You could also specify that the process should simply create a list of duplicate accounts, rather than importing any accounts. You would then use this list to determine exactly how to handle the accounts and run the script again.

> **Note**   The .dmp file includes all of the user names from the single sign-on server on the original machine. You cannot edit this file, as much of the information in it is in binary form. If you only want to migrate some of the users to a new machine, you will have to do this through the standard Login Server definition mechanism.

Another parameter in the import process gives you the option to associate all user accounts with the PUBLIC schema on the new machine, or to try to associate an account with the database schema it was linked to on the original database.

For more details on the specific parameters used with these scripts, and all the other scripts discussed in this section, please refer to the Oracle9*i*AS Portal documentation.

Security data for users and groups

Once the user accounts have been moved, you can move the actual security information that assigns privileges to these accounts.

The process for this export and import is exactly like the process described for single sign-on users. The export and import command scripts are called `secexp` and `secimp`, respectively, and you can specify the same actions with regard to duplicate user names and database schemas. However, you have to log into SQL*Plus in order to run these scripts.

If a group already exists on the target machine, the users in the imported group will be added to the users in the existing group.

Pages

The next step in a migration process is to move the pages in your Oracle9*i*AS Portal system. A page is actually a sophisticated object, so the export process for the page may take up to 15 minutes.

You use the `pageexp` and `pageimp` scripts to move a page definition, and you will have to call these scripts from SQL*Plus. You can include the security information associated with a page by including the `security` parameter in the command. If you have just done the security import processes discussed previously, there is no need to include this extra information in the export.

At the time of this writing, there is no way to export more than one page at a time.

Applications

Your new site is now ready to accept your Oracle9*i*AS Portal applications. You can move a complete application, or any of the components that make up the application.

You can export an application directly from the Oracle9*i*AS Portal environment.

1. Go to the Applications section of the Navigator. If you are not at the highest level in this section, click on the Applications link in the path links at the top of the Navigator page.

2. Click on the Manage action link.

3. Click on the Export icon, as described in the previous section.

This action will cause Oracle9*i*AS Portal to create an export script file containing all the objects in the application and the application itself. When the file has been created, you will be presented with a page similar to the one shown in Figure 25-12.

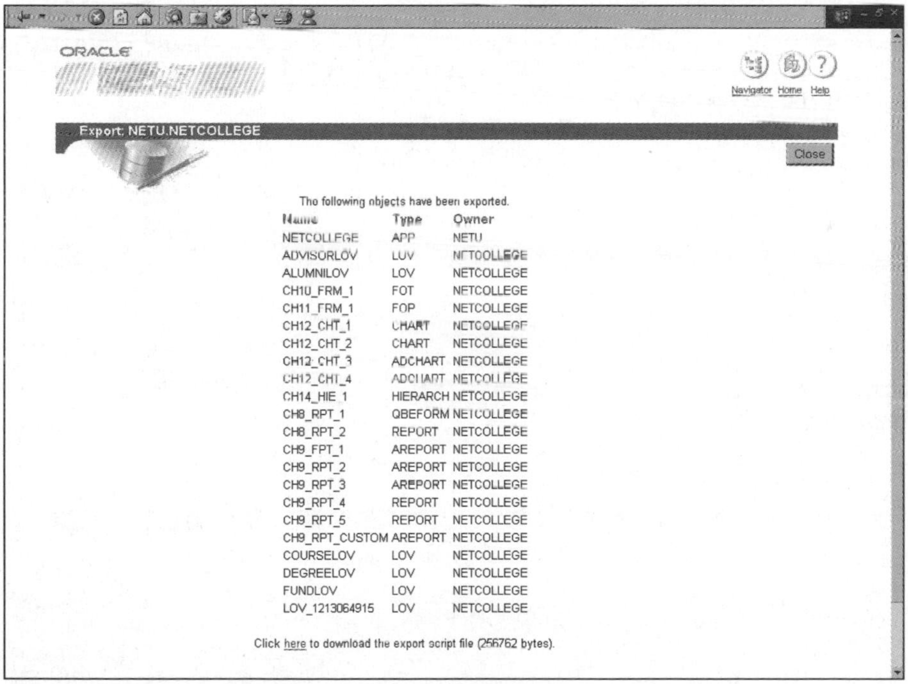

Figure 25-12: The results of exporting an application

The output of the export script is stored in a temporary file, so at the bottom of the page you are presented with a link that will allow you to immediately download the export file.

> **Caution** You must have defined a location for temporary files in order to export an application. The next section explains where to define this location.

To import a complete application, you use the `appimp` script from SQL*Plus.

You can also export individual components through the Manage tab of the Manage Components page.

Shared components

As its name implies, a shared component can be used by more than one application, so you have to export and import shared components through a separate process.

You export shared components directly from the Oracle9*i*AS Portal environment.

1. Go to the Applications section of the Navigator. If you are not at the highest level in this section, click on the Applications link in the path links at the top of the Navigator page.

2. Click on the name Shared Components in the list of applications, which will bring up the page shown in Figure 25-13.

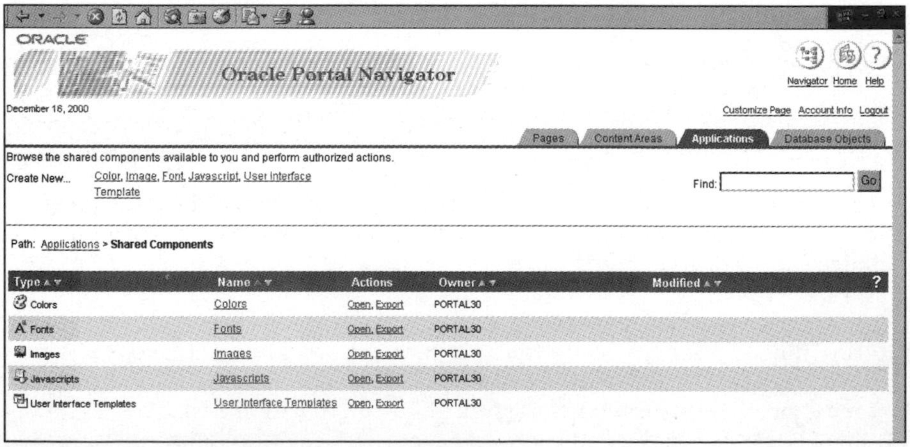

Figure 25-13: Managing shared components

You can see that you have the option of exporting each type of shared component. The results of the export are the same as the export process for an application — you are presented with a page listing the components that have been exported and given the option to download the export file.

If you have created your own shared components, you can export these components individually. Oracle9*i*AS Portal does not give you the option of exporting the standard shared components that come with the product, on the assumption that these have already been installed with the product.

Data

Of course, you still need to be able to export the data structures and data that your Oracle9*i*AS Portal system manipulates. You can do this with the standard export and import utilities that come with your Oracle database. If you are not familiar with these utilities, please refer to the Oracle documentation.

You can export the database schema that contains the components of your application. Remember, these components are merely PL/SQL packages — in fact, they may live in the same schema that holds your data. If you do export and import this schema, the PL/SQL packages will come along with it. But all of the information used to create and track these packages is stored in the schema used by Oracle9*i*AS Portal, so you will not be able to see these imported components in the new environment or edit them.

Note   In practice, you should export the data and the shared components before exporting the application.

You may be thinking that exporting and importing these schemas is a good way to create a read-only deployment. This practice will not work, because security is defined by the Oracle9*i*AS Portal environment, not simply by database security.

Content Areas

The last type of information to migrate are the Content Areas. You use command scripts called `contexp` and `contimp` to export and import Content Areas.

You can specify the same options for this process that you did for the page objects — how to handle duplicate names, database schemas, and whether to include security information.

You have an additional option with regard to shared objects with duplicate names. You can indicate that any content object that is being imported and is shared with another Content Area be treated as if it were a new object with a new unique name. Any references to the new object are correspondingly modified. This feature is helpful, since Content Areas usually continually grow with more information, and duplicate names are more likely to be encountered.

You don't have to explicitly move your system to simply add another machine that can service the customers of your Oracle9*i*AS Portal site. Oracle9*i*AS Portal gives you the ability to define remote nodes that can transparently cooperate with your main Oracle9*i*AS Portal server. This capability is discussed further in the final section in this chapter on node options.

Administering the Oracle9iAS Portal Environment

There is one more area that we will look at in this chapter — your ability to manage the overall Oracle9iAS Portal environment. Many of the issues involved in this form of administration are covered in other places in this book, and some of them are beyond the scope of this book. Nonetheless, we will spend some time going over the choices offered to you on the Administration tab of the Oracle9iAS Portal home page.

1. Make sure you are logged onto Oracle9iAS Portal as the NETUDEV user, because the NETU user does not have the security privileges to administer the Oracle9iAS Portal environment.

2. Return to the Oracle9iAS Portal home page and click on the Administration tab; this will bring up the page shown in Figure 25-14.

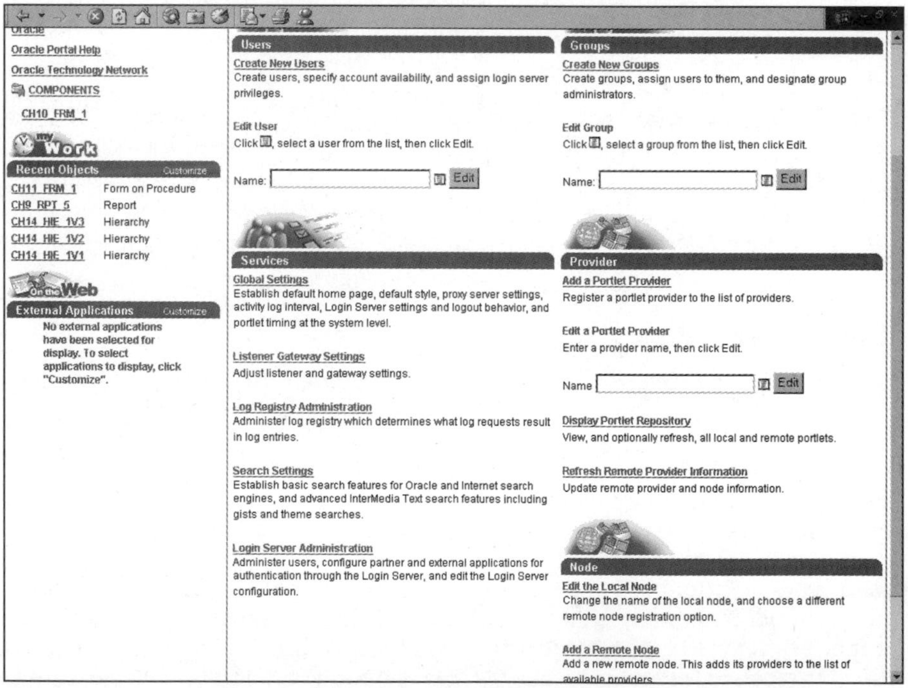

Figure 25-14: The Administration tab on the Oracle9iAS Portal home page

There are five portlets exposed on this tab:

   ✦ **Users**

   ✦ **Groups**

✦ **Services**

✦ **Provider**

✦ **Node**

The Users and Groups portlets were briefly discussed very early in this book, in Chapter 2, when you created the users for this book. These areas are also discussed in more depth in the following chapter on security, so we will not touch on them here.

Services portlet

The Services portlet contains a menu with five choices, which are each described in the following sections.

Global Settings page

The Global Settings page handles a grab bag of configuration information that applies to the overall operations of your Oracle9*i*AS Portal environment. The Global Settings page, as shown in Figure 25-15, includes the following sections:

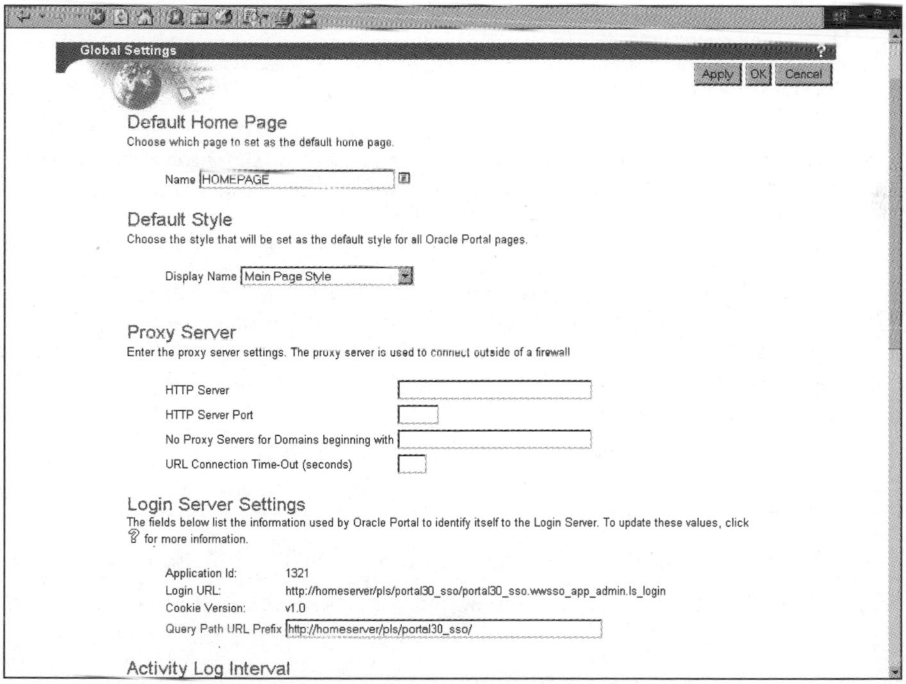

Figure 25-15: The Global Settings page

✦ **Default Home Page:** This page is the default for the home page for the Oracle9*i*AS Portal environment. Of course, individual users can set their own choices for their default page.

✦ **Default Style:** This style is the default style for all pages created for Oracle9*i*AS Portal.

✦ **Proxy Server:** If you are using a proxy server to connect from the Oracle9*i*AS Portal server to the Internet, you can specify the correct settings in this area.

✦ **Login Server Settings:** This section contains information about the settings for the Login Server. The only one of these settings you can change on this page is the query path to the schema, which contains the Login Server.

✦ **Activity Log Interval:** You can specify the type of logging that is to be done with the Log Registry Administration page, but this setting controls how many days a specific log will run before Oracle9*i*AS Portal begins a new log file. You can only view the log information from one log at a time.

Logging is discussed in much more detail in Chapter 27 on monitoring.

✦ **Portlet Timing:** You can have each portlet display the amount of time it took to create the portlet content. You enable this option for all portlets in this section of the Global Settings.

✦ **Temporary Directory:** The temporary directory is where Oracle9*i*AS Portal stores temporary files that it uses, such as the files created when you export objects.

✦ **Cookie Domain:** The cookie domain is used in the session cookie that tracks individual users. If you are running it with multiple Oracle9*i*AS Portal servers, you can set the same cookie domain for each of the servers to ensure that session information spans all of the servers.

✦ **Logout Behavior:** When users log out, they can log out of the application only or the application and the single sign-on. If you choose to specify that users only log out of the application, if they should come back to the Oracle9*i*AS Portal environment, they will maintain the same sign-on identity, as long as they have not rebooted their client machine.

✦ **Beta Features:** This section has check boxes that allow you to use parts of the Oracle9*i*AS Portal product that are included in the install but are officially in beta. At the time of this writing, the only listing here is for image charts.

✦ **Version Information:** This section indicates the current version of Oracle9*i*AS Portal.

Listener Gateway Settings page

The Listener Gateway Settings page let you set up the database access descriptor (DAD) settings and the global settings for the gateway, which were both described in Chapter 2. This option also lets you set some basic parameters to control the operation of both the PL/SQL cache (for components and other types of generated content) and the session cookie cache, which holds the cookies that identify a particular user.

Log Registry Administration page

This page lets you define and manipulate log registry records. You must create a log registry record in order to log events. The log registry record defines the area and the type of interactions you wish to log.

> **Cross-Reference** Chapter 27, which covers monitoring in Oracle9*i*AS Portal, discusses the use of logs in detail.

Search Settings page

This page lets you control how many results are returned on a single page from an Oracle9*i*AS Portal search, and which external search engine you want to specify to search the Internet, when a user requests it.

You can also enable the capabilities of *inter*Media, the Oracle database option that gives you a lot of flexibility in working with text and other types of large objects. *inter*Media lets your users do things like search for a particular theme within text and other very cool stuff. If you are interested in using *inter*Media, please refer to the *inter*Media documentation for more explanation.

Login Server Administration page

The Login Server Administration page controls the process of authenticating Oracle9*i*AS Portal users. The main menu for this area is shown in Figure 25-16.

As you can see, the top two choices allow you to work with the users who are defined within the Login Server and to configure the actions of the Login Server itself, such as how frequently it should expire passwords.

The last two menu choices have to do with integrating other applications with the Login Server. The Login Server is designed to offer single-sign-on capabilities, which means that a user can simply log in to the Login Server once and have all other authentication taken care of for them.

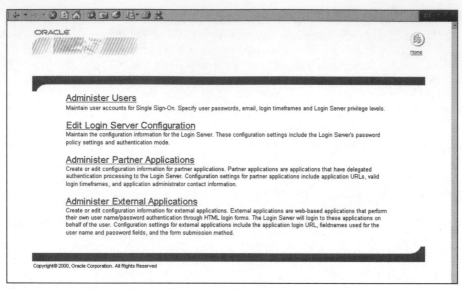

Figure 25-16: Choices for Login Server Administration

There are two ways that applications can take advantage of the Login Server. A partner application is an application that has agreed to let the Login Server take care of authentication for them. An external application maintains its own method of authentication, but the Login Server knows how to interact with that application, so the user does not have to log in to the external application again. As you saw in Chapter 4, you can store your user name and password for an external application in the Login Server and go directly into the applications with a single link. You can add your own external applications through this menu choice, but you will have to be very familiar with how the target application handles authentication.

Provider portlet

The Provider portlet gives you the option to create or edit information about portlet providers. One of the best ways to understand these options is to see how the application you have created and specified as a portlet provider is registered.

1. Click on the lookup window to the left of the text box under Edit a Portlet Provider. Select the Net University application you have been working on.

2. Click on the Edit button to bring up the page shown in Figure 25-17.

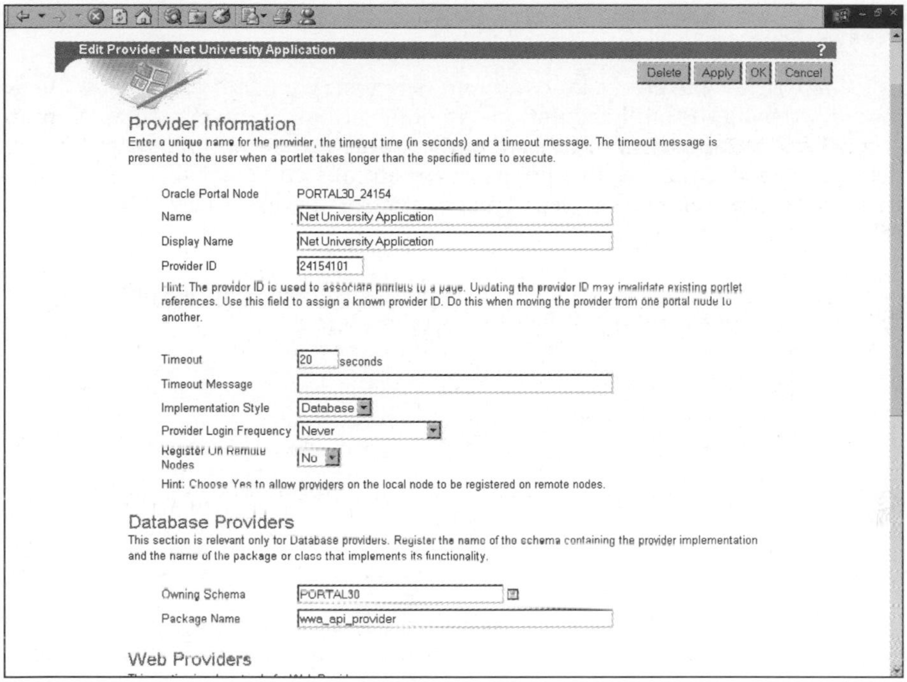

Figure 25-17: Portlet provider options

As you can see, each provider has its own unique provider ID. You can also specify that the application is to be registered on remote nodes, which will copy the registration information for the provider to remote nodes, as described in the Node portlet.

Node portlet

The Node portlet lets you describe other nodes to your local node. You have the ability to use multiple Oracle Portlet servers over multiple nodes — a distributed architecture for deployment. At this time, the use of Oracle9iAS Portal in a distributed configuration is too new to have been widely tested in production. We suggest you refer to the Oracle Technology Network (OTN) for more information if you are interested in this type of deployment scenario. You can access OTN through the main page at oracle.com.

Summary

This chapter has covered a lot of ground very fast. We could probably write a short book discussing the implementation and implications of the management of the Oracle9*i*AS Portal environment (and maybe someday we will). For now, this chapter has provided an overview of administrative options and covered in depth some of the more important ones, such as version control and exporting Oracle9*i*AS Portal objects.

The next chapter will dive into one of the topics we just touched on — using security and privileges in your Oracle9*i*AS Portal system.

✦   ✦   ✦

Oracle9*i*AS Portal Security

Portal applications are no different from other browser-based applications or even classic client/server or terminal-based applications when it comes to the need for security. Regardless of how you decide to deploy data to your users, you need to protect unauthorized access to the information in your databases. Portal has been designed to build off your existing investment in Oracle database security by leveraging the security mechanisms provided by the Oracle database. The database offers a very comprehensive set of security features that enables you to protect your data right at the source. In addition to the standard Oracle security features, the designers of Portal have provided some additional capabilities that help you deal with the stateless nature of the Internet. The resulting combination is a strong set of features that enable you to protect the data in your database from unauthorized access.

Understanding Oracle Database Security

Oracle's database security is based on the concept of *user names* and *passwords*. Every Oracle database user is required to provide a user name and password to connect to a database, just like they are required to provide a user name and password to connect to the network. Oracle users are defined by the user name they are given for accessing the database. Each user name is given an associated password that must be provided whenever the user attempts to connect to the database. The user keeps their password confidential, while the user name is generally visible to other users of the database.

In This Chapter

Understanding Oracle Database Security

Creating Privileged Accounts with Portal

Creating Groups and Group Privileges

Creating Privileges on Individual Objects

Setting Database Privileges

Using the Login Server

Oracle installations are organized around *instances*, which are equivalent to databases. Oracle uses instances to separate logical installations of the Oracle database. You will often find that development of an application occurs in one instance, but the production version of the application is run in a separate instance. This has the effect of protecting the production data from errors that occur during development. Later in this book, you will see that the same strategy can be used with Portal applications. User names are defined within Oracle instances and are specific to the instance under which they were created.

Oracle makes use of the user name to identify the user to the system and to organize the content within the database. Database objects, such as tables, are owned by the user name that creates them. In this way, it is relatively easy to locate all of the objects associated with a particular user. For example, when you installed Portal, you provided the installation program with a user name for Portal (PORTAL30). Oracle used that user name to store all of the tables and procedures for Portal that were created as part of the installation. This technique makes it easy both to secure access to these objects and to move them or back them up as a group.

Objects that one user creates are not normally accessible to other users unless specific access to these objects has been provided by use of the GRANT command. Specific object permissions are authorized by granting access to them. You can grant users access to objects and you can grant privileges to users. For example, when a new user is created, Oracle grants the CONNECT privilege to that user for the database layer. This enables the user to connect to the database using the designated user name and password.

If you have lots of objects and lots of users, it can become overly time-consuming to assign grants. Oracle simplifies the process by providing support for roles. Oracle roles are abstract users, and you can grant privileges to roles just like you can grant privileges to users. For example, if you have a group of users who will all use the same set of applications, accounting applications for example, you can create an accounting role to service them. By granting privileges to the role and then granting the role to the users, you can simplify the process of setting up the accounting group. Any change to the role is cascaded to the users automatically.

Oracle has made the security system available to you directly through SQL, and you can use SQL*Plus to completely manage users and roles. To make the process easier, Oracle also provides the Enterprise Manager tool and DBA Studio, which both offer a graphical client/server interface for managing users and security.

The designers of Portal have provided access to a subset of the security features that are available directly with SQL*Plus or Enterprise Manager. If you are familiar with all of the various Oracle security features, you will see that certain options are not provided within the Portal interface. With the release of Portal 3.0, Oracle has adopted a two-tier mechanism for managing security within the portal site. Content objects (pages, Content Areas, components) are still stored inside of Oracle database accounts — but Oracle's Login Server manages all access to the database.

You can create users, grant access to database objects, and define roles directly through the Portal interface. Portal itself is built from packages and tables in the database, and it comes with its own set of privileges and roles, which are used when you create new developers.

There are five classes of portal users as defined by the various portal roles:

✦ Portal developers

✦ Portal administrators

✦ Portlet publishers

✦ Database administrators (DBAs)

✦ Portal users

Portal developers are the programmers who create your Portal applications, which are then deployed to portal users. Portal developers work with the component development tools and page building tools. Outside of the DBA, the portal administrators have the highest level of privileges in Oracle9*i*AS Portal. They can view and modify anything in Oracle Portal, (even folders, pages, and applications that are marked as private). However, only DBAs can use the Database Explorer. When you installed Oracle Portal, a portal administrator account called PORTAL30_ADMIN was automatically created. This administrator account can create other portal administrators, as required.

> **Note** The default administration account is based upon the installation schema that you used when installing Portal. The default schema is named PORTAL30, but you are free to change this value during the installation process. The portal administration account uses the default schema name with the _ADMIN suffix as its name. Throughout the remainder of this chapter, we use the PORTAL30 schema as the default installation schema for the examples and explanations.

There are several tasks that a DBA may perform that an Oracle Portal administrator cannot. These include creating schemas, roles, tables, and all other database objects, as well as mapping portal user accounts onto database user accounts. DBAs are the most privileged users. Portal users are on the other end of the scale — they are the end users that will access your Portal site. There are also likely to be at least several classes of end users. For example, within the Net University system there are Students, Faculty, and Alumni. You will give each of these different types of users access to different objects and allow them different groups of privileges. For example, there is no need to give Students access to Alumni information, nor would you allow Students to have update access to transcript records. Portal *privileges* give you the tools to limit access to your data to properly authorized users.

> **Note** Although Oracle uses the same DBA moniker for portal DBAs and database DBAs, the two are not synonymous. A portal user who has been granted DBA access within Oracle Portal will not have DBA access outside of the portal environment.

In most cases you will begin adding Portal developer accounts to your portal as the starting point for your security scheme.

Creating Privileged Accounts with Portal

1. Log onto the Portal Site as the default Portal Administrator (PORTAL30_ADMIN).
2. Select the Administer link from the Portal home page to display the security menu shown in Figure 26-1.

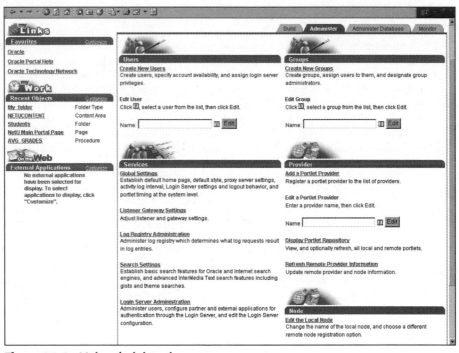

Figure 26-1: Main administration page

The Portal security user interface is composed of the following three major functions:

✦ Users

✦ Groups

✦ Services

Caution

If you are logged on to Portal as a nonprivileged user, you will not be able to see the Administer panel. Be sure to connect to Portal as the Portal installation account in order to gain access to the security subsystem and to complete the examples in this chapter.

In order to add a new portal developer account you must first create a new user account. From the User Manager page, you can add new users to the system and provide them with access to the Portal developer privileges.

3. Select the Create New Users link from the Users area of the administer page to go to the Create User panel shown in Figure 26-2.

The Create User panel enables you to define the information necessary to add a new user (USERID) to the system. The key item is the User Name field. The User Name field is restricted to 30 alphanumeric characters and it must begin with a letter. You are not allowed to use any embedded punctuation other than the underscore (_) character and the dollar sign ($). The User Name field permits you to enter both upper- and lowercase characters, but Portal converts all USERIDs to uppercase when the value is stored. Thus, the USERIDs "smith" and "SMITH" are considered identical.

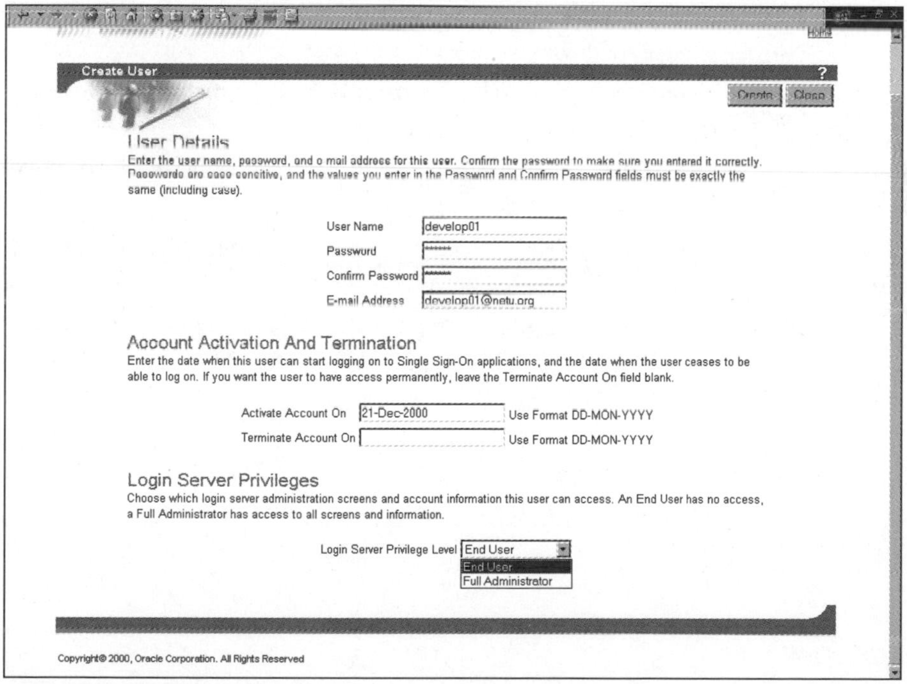

Figure 26-2: Create User

Directly below the User Name field is the Password field, which provides the password to be associated with the user name. The password is implemented as a password-style HTML form text field. The characters you enter into this field are masked by the asterisk character (*) at display time. Passwords follow the same length and character restrictions as user names, and you must reenter the password into the Confirm Password field to ensure that you have entered the password correctly. You can also enter an e-mail address for the new user account.

As the portal administrator, you can set accounts to activate and terminate on specified dates. You must enter these date strings in the standard Oracle North American NLS_DATE format — DD-MON-YYYY.

Previous releases of Oracle Portal relied upon database security for access and authentication. With the release of 3.0, Oracle Portal uses the Oracle Login Server for authentication and authorization. Portal's user accounts are stored as records within the Login Server. Portal automatically forwards authentication requests from the portal layer over to the Login Server. By default, the user accounts that you create will be *End User* accounts (even if they are portal developers or portal administrators). If you elect to grant the *Full Administrator* privileges on the Login Server, then the new account will be permitted to make changes to other user accounts using the Login Server administration panels. Login Administrators can:

✦ Create and edit any Single Sign-On user account (including non-Portal accounts).

✦ Configure the Login Server (including establish password restrictions and logout behavior).

✦ Administer third-party partner applications (applications that have delegated authentication processing to the Login Server).

✦ Administer external applications (other Web-based applications that perform their own user name/password authentication).

 Cross-Reference We'll talk more about the Login Server in the "Using the Login Server" section of this chapter. For the time being, just bear in mind that the Login Server is responsible for managing Portal user accounts.

4. Enter the name develop01 as the new user name, and set the password for this new account to oracle.

5. Set the Login Server Privilege Level to End User.

6. Press the Create button to save the new account.

By default, Portal will display a fresh copy of the "Create User" panel, allowing you to create another account. The DEVELOP01 link appears at the top of the panel so that you can modify the account that you just created.

7. Use the DEVELOP01 link to modify the developer account as shown in Figure 26-3.

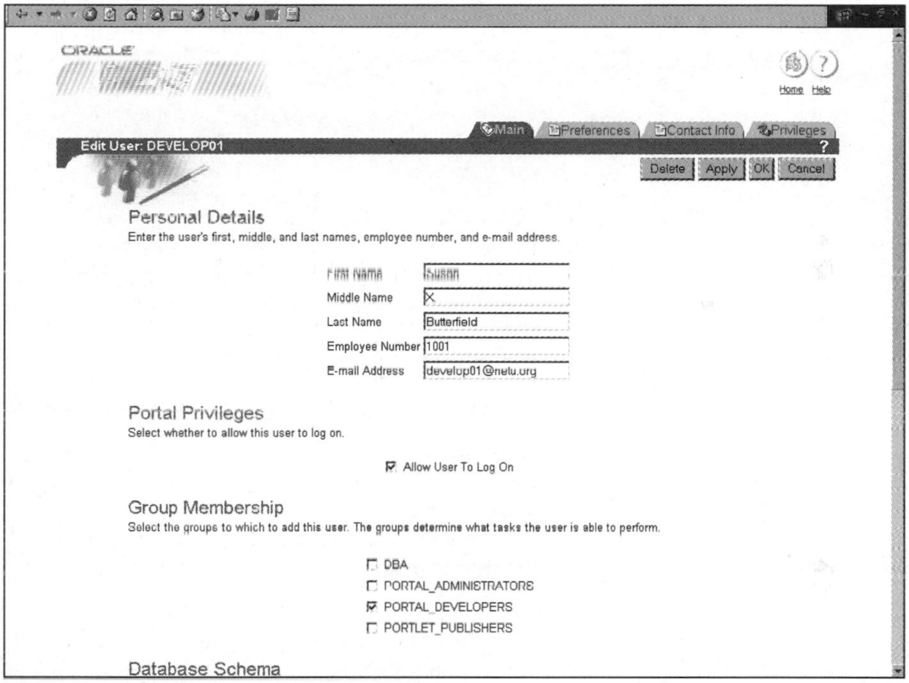

Figure 26-3: Edit User — Develop01

Personal details about the new user account are input into the panel at the top of the form. You are permitted to add the user's (actual) name, employee number information, and the user's e-mail address on this panel. If you wish to add additional profile data such as telephone numbers and postal address information, you can do so on the Contact Info tab.

The first security decision that you need to make is whether this user has permission to log on to the portal site. By default, new user accounts are granted the logon privilege. Users that are not authenticated against the Login Server are considered public users. Oracle Portal allows you to create accounts and then, via the Allow User to Log On check box, to prohibit their ability to log on to the site. This is a useful feature for temporarily disabling certain accounts without having to remove the account entirely or to change the user's password out from under them.

The main body of user account permissions falls under the Group Membership heading. There are four types of privileges that are conferred on user accounts through predefined *groups* as listed in Table 26-1.

Table 26-1 Built-in Group Privileges	
Group	**Privileges**
DBA	Select this check box to grant database administrator privileges to the user. However, the user will only be granted these privileges within the Portal environment—they will not have access to them within external programs (such as SQL*Plus).
PORTAL_ADMINISTRATORS	Select this check box to grant the user portal administrator privileges. Portal administrators have the authority to make changes to all aspects of a portal site including private pages.
PORTAL_DEVELOPERS	Select this check box to grant the user privileges to build applications with Oracle Portal. Portal developers have access to the component development tools. Their access to underlying data, however, is limited by the application schemas in which they are working.
PORTLET_PUBLISHERS	Select this check box to grant the user privileges to make Oracle Portal objects (folders, categories, application components, and pages) available as portlets. Users with these privileges will see the Publish As Portlet check box when they create or edit objects. Portal developers can create components, but they cannot deploy them as portlets without this privilege.

8. Check the PORTAL_DEVELOPERS check box for the DEVELOP01 account. Figure 26-4 shows the remaining fields on the main Edit User panel.

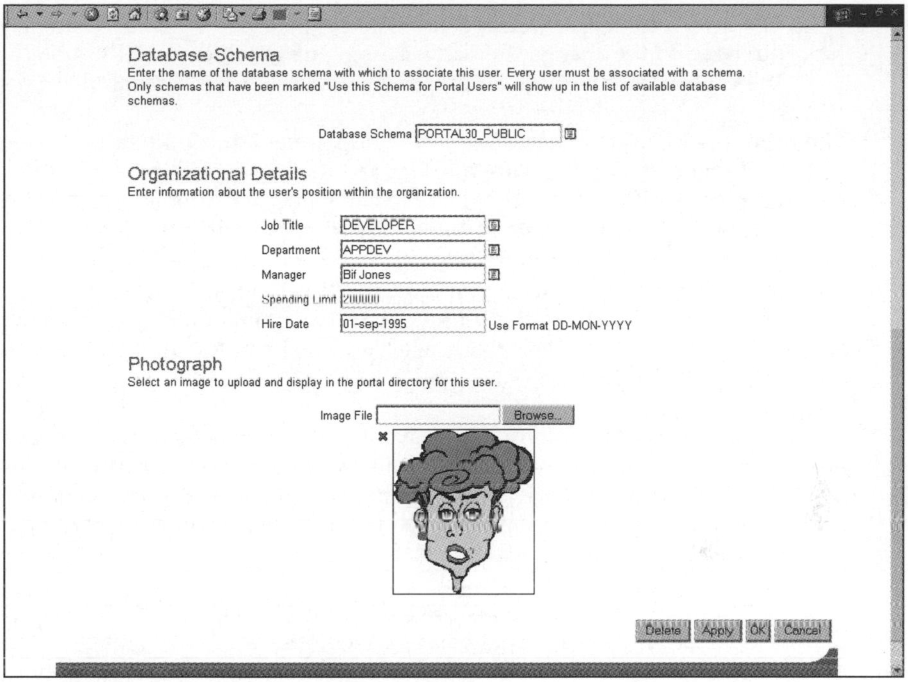

Figure 26-4: Edit User — Database Schema

Each Portal account is mapped to a physical Oracle database schema (a database user account). Portal accounts do not have direct access to the Oracle database. If you were to attempt to log on to the database through SQL*Plus with the DEVELOP01 account it would not work. Portal accounts are lightweight database users as defined to the Login Server. *Lightweight* users are Oracle user accounts that are valid within Oracle Portal (and the Login Server), but do not exist in the Oracle database. At the moment, the accounts that you define within the portal interface will only work with Oracle Portal.

Note
The Login Server is a complicated piece of software in its own right. It can be mapped to Lightweight Directory Access Protocol (LDAP) servers and work with user accounts that have been configured completely outside of the Oracle environment. This topic is outside the scope of this book, and we encourage you to use the OTN site for more information on the Login Server.

Your portal users essentially piggyback on standard Oracle Schemas when they connect to the database. By default, all portal users connect through the POR-TAL30_PUBLIC database schema.

Cross-Reference Chapter 23 contains a detailed discussion of database schemas. Generally, you will not need to the change the database schema to which portal users are mapped. The exception to this rule is component applications as discussed in Chapter 23.

The organizational details permit you to add some additional information about your portal users. The Job Title and Department fields are free-form fields. Once you enter a value for a user in each field the value will appear in the pop-up window for all other users. You will want to be careful about adding values to these fields — as you can fill the look-up windows with lots of clutter. The Manager field looks just like the Job Title and Department fields, but it is mapped to the portal user tables. If you enter a value for this field, it must match an existing Portal User Record. The Spending Limit and Hire Date fields are also free-form text and they are not validated against the database.

Tip Additional contact information can be stored for the user on the Contact Info panel. Most of this data is fairly elemental, but it does appear in the portal user directory. End users have permission to enter contact information for themselves — so it is not necessary to enter all of this extra information when you are creating new accounts.

The final element on this panel is the user photograph. Use the Browse button to upload a GIF or JPEG image that will be associated with this user.

9. Add a job title and department for DEVELOP01. Set the manager of this user to be the NETUDEV account.

10. Use one of the Student photos (u1001.gif — 1075.gif) as the photo for DEVELOP01.

11. Press the OK button to save your changes.

12. Create a second account called PADMIN01 and grant this account the PORTAL_ADMINISTRATORS role (Use the Create New Users link from the Users area of the administer page.)

13. Create a third account called DBA01 and grant this account the DBA group role.

Testing the default developer account settings

The default settings for new accounts provide for the minimal amount of Portal authority within the defined roles that have been granted to the accounts. Portal's strategy is to limit the capabilities of an account unless you explicitly request that additional privileges be assigned to the account.

1. Open a new browser session and navigate to your portal site and log on as DEVELOP01 to display the main panel as shown in Figure 26-5.

2. Navigate around in the various tools on the Build panel.

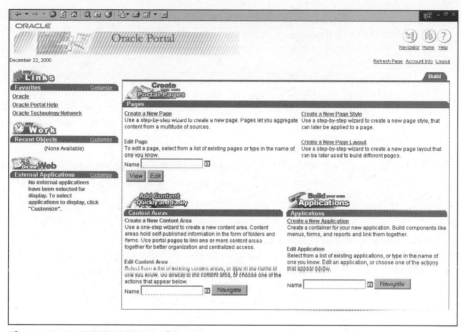

Figure 26-5: DEVELOP01 main page

The DEVELOP01 account has full access to the range of tools on the Build panel — but no access to any of the administration tools. If you were to navigate around in the three main builder sections — pages, Content Areas and applications — you would find that the DEVELOP01 has access to the following basic functions:

✦ Create a new page

✦ Create a new application within a SCHEMA

✦ Run and/or export application components

✦ Add content to a Content Area with PUBLIC folders

When you connect as the develop01 user, you will notice that the range of options at your disposal is limited. You are no longer able to create new accounts, assign roles, change listener settings, or grant access to database tables. Portal reads the capabilities of the account that you used to log on to the portal when it executes the procedure that builds the generated page for you. Because the account you created lacks certain privileges, Portal removes these privileges from the display. All of the "missing" functions are off limits to the DEVELOP01 account. For example, this account does not have access to any of the administration or database administration tools. Despite being a PORTAL_DEVELOPER, DEVELOP01 cannot even modify applications because it does not have specific grants against these existing applications.

3. Log off of the DEVELOP01 account and log back on using the PADMIN01 account to display the panel as shown in Figure 26-6.

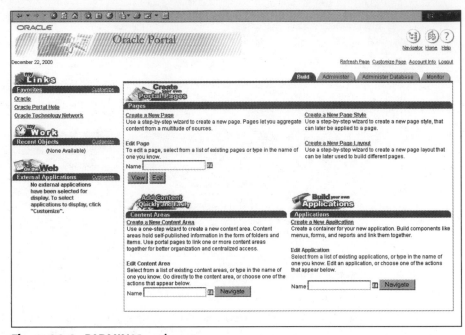

Figure 26-6: PADMIN01 main page

The PADMIN01 account has been granted the PORTAL_ADMINISTRATOR privilege, so this user has access to the full complement of the component development tools and the portal administration tools. This user can modify applications, components, and pages. They can even create new users and groups. However, PADMIN01 lacks two key capabilities:

✦ No access to database administration (or database objects)

✦ No access to the Login Server

Database administration requires the DBA privilege, so Portal does not display any data on either the Administer Database or the Database Objects panels within the Database Navigator.

4. Log off of the PADMIN01 account and log back on using the DBA01 account to display the panel shown in Figure 26-7.

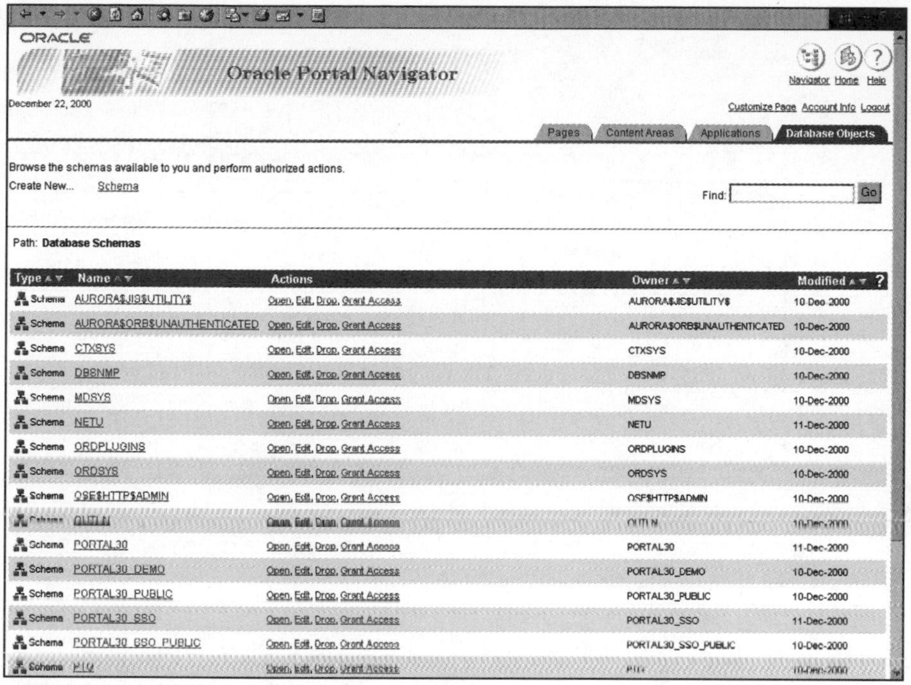

Figure 26-7: DBA—Database Objects Panel

The DBA01 account has full privileges on the portal site. This user can even modify database objects within the Navigator as shown in Figure 26-7. In effect, the DBA01 account is a real database DBA account. As with any of the other portal accounts, these privileges only apply within the portal environment. The DBA01 account would not even be able to log on to the database with Oracle's other administrative interfaces such as Enterprise Manager and SQL*Plus.

Note   This will undoubtedly change in the future as Oracle extends all of its products to leverage the Single Sign-on capabilities of the Login Server.

The DBA01 account can essentially handle every task with the exception of Login Server Administration. (We'll talk more about the Login Server panels later in this chapter.)

5. Use the Account Info link to display the panel shown in Figure 26-8.

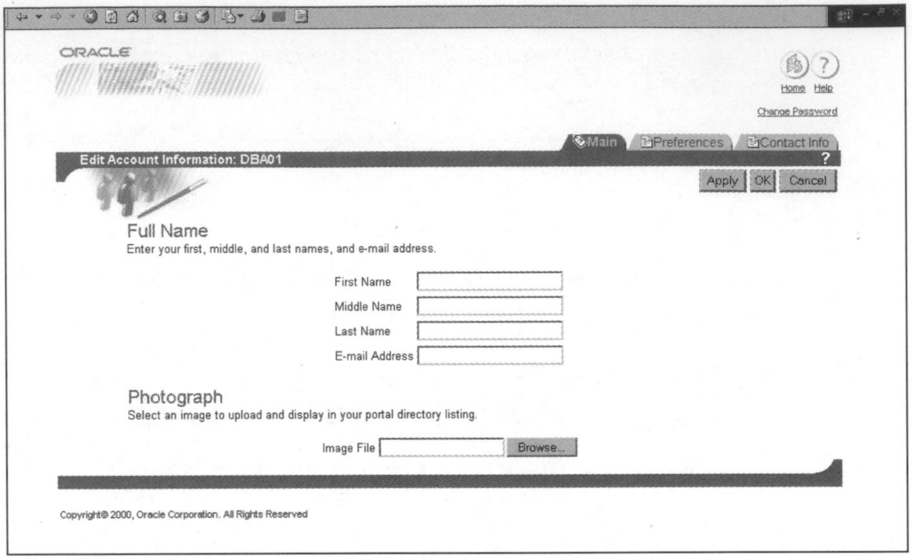

Figure 26-8: Edit Account Information

This panel displays the connection information for the account you are using to connect to the database from within Portal. From this panel the user can modify their contact information or make changes to their preferences. This is also the place that users can go to change their passwords. The Change Password link in the upper-right corner of the page links to a form that permits the user to change his/her password.

6. Log off of DBA01 and log back on as PORTAL30.

Modifying account privilege settings

7. Edit the DEVELOP01 user and use the Privileges tab to display the panel shown in Figure 26-9.

After you create a new account, or when you choose to modify an existing account, Portal displays the additional information shown in Figure 26-9.

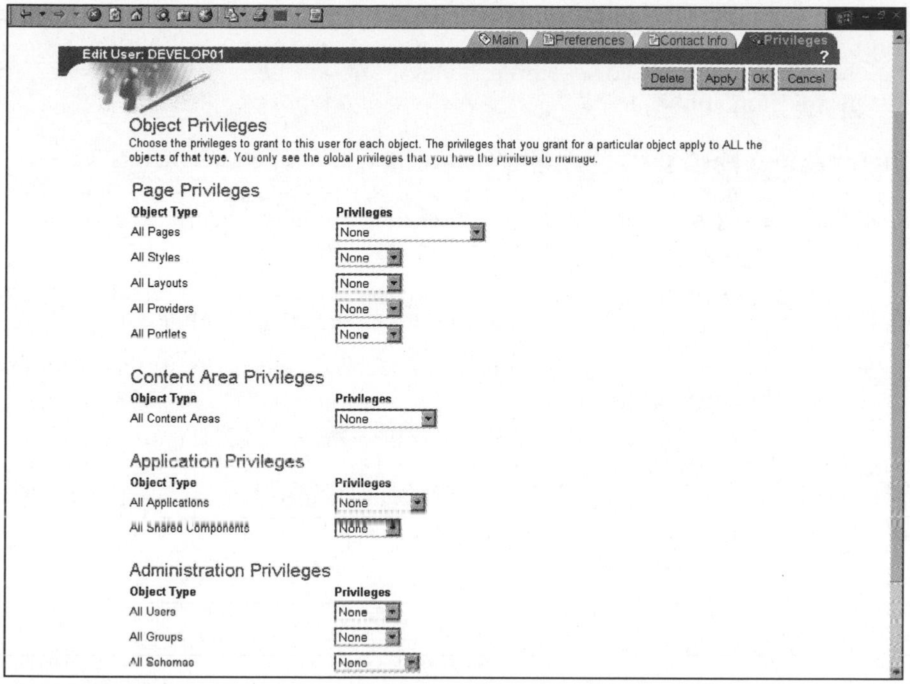

Figure 26-9: Object Privileges panel

There are four types of object privileges that can be granted to a user on a global basis:

✦ Page

✦ Content Area

✦ Application

✦ Administration

In previous chapters on the component building tools, you have worked with the Access panels to set security settings for individual objects. Every major object within the portal site, such as pages, reports, forms, charts, calendars, hierarchies and folders, can have individual permissions and grants associated with them. In order to simplify the process of granting lots of privileges to individual users, Portal provides the Object Privileges panel. Through this form, you can grant portal accounts *super-user* privileges for all four of the major functional areas of Oracle Portal.

For each of the categories shown on this panel there is one key concept to bear in mind. When you grant a user permissions for a given category, it applies to *all* of the objects of that type. For example, if you grant edit permissions on pages, the edit permission applies to *all pages across the entire portal*.

There are four basic principles to understanding the functions on this panel:

✦ Each privilege in the list includes all other privileges below it (in display order). If a user can *manage*, they can also view, publish, and create.

✦ The Manage privilege not only allows a user to manage objects of a given type, but also to grant global privileges on the object type to other users and groups.

✦ Users must be expressly granted the CREATE privilege in order to build new objects of a given type.

✦ By default, users do not have any privileges for any object.

The capabilities that are granted by individual privilege groups are listed in Tables 26-2 through 26-5.

Table 26-2 Page Privileges	
Page Object Subtypes	*Privileges*
Pages	Manage — Make any change to any page.
	Edit Contents — Add/delete tabs and portlets from any page public or private.
	Manage Style — Apply a new style to any page and create/delete page styles.
	Customization (Full) — Change the private version of a page (hide, show, or add portlets).
	Customization (Add-only) — Change the private version of a page by adding portlets. (User can also delete private portlets).
	View — Display any page in Oracle Portal.
	Create — Create a new page.
Styles, Layouts, Providers, Portlets	Manage — Edit, create and delete styles, layouts, and the portlet repository. Create or delete portlets.
	Create — Build a new style or layout.
	Publish — Register portlet providers or publish any object as a portlet.
	View — Display styles or layouts.

Table 26-3
Content Area Privileges

Object	Privileges
Content Areas	Manage — Perform any task that the content administrator can perform. (Chapter 22 provides some additional details on Content Areas). Essentially, this privilege grants the holder *owner* status for a Content Area.
	Manage Styles — Create, edit, and delete folder styles, apply new styles to folders.
	View — View any folder within a Content Area.
	Make Public — Mark any Content Area viewable by *public* users.
	Create — Create any Content Area object (folders, navigation bars, styles).

Table 26-4
Application and Shared Components Privileges

Application and Subtypes	Privileges
Applications	Manage — Create, edit, and delete any component. Export applications and components and assign privileges to applications and application components.
	Edit Contents — Edit or export applications and application components. (No permission to modify applications or to assign application privileges.)
	View Source — View the package specification for a component and run the component. No modification or privilege permissions.
	Customize — Run any component. Run any component with parameters for BIND variables.
	Run — Run any application or component. (May not run the customize forms.)
	Create — Create a new application. Application owners are automatically granted *manage* privileges for applications that they create.
Shared Components	Manage — Edit, create, and delete all shared components.
	Create — Create new *shared components* (which can then be modified or deleted). User may also view any other shared component.

	Table 26-5
	Administration Privileges
Administration Objects	**Privileges**
All Users	Manage — Edit any aspect of any user account (with the exception of password modification).
	Create — Create new user accounts within Portal.
All Groups	Manage — Modify any setting for any group (and create new groups).
	Create — Create new groups.
All Schemas	Manage — Create, edit, drop, and grant privileges for any database schema. Modify data within tables, compile procedures, create new tables, indexes, and views.
	Modify Data — Create new schemas, modify objects within user's own schemas. Insert, Update, Delete, and Select on any table/view in any schema. Compile and execute procedures in any schema.
	Insert Data — Create new schemas, modify objects within user's own schemas. Select/Insert on any table/view in any schema.
	View Data — Create new schemas, modify objects within user's own schemas. Select on any table/view in any schema.
	Create — Create new schemas, modify objects within user's own schemas.
All Logs	Manage — Edit/purge activity logs. Can also grant this privilege to other users.
	Edit — Edit/purge activity logs.
	View — View any logs (and log reports).

It becomes a simple process to a grant a complex set of privileges to any given user by selecting items from the combo boxes as shown in Figure 26-9. You will notice that the DEVELOP01 account lacks any privileges whatsoever — (all of the combo boxes are set to the value None). At this point, you might be wondering how the DEVELOP01 account was able to view the NETCOLLEGE application at all without any privileges. The answer is portal groups and group privileges.

   8. Press the Cancel button and return to the main Administer panel.

Creating Groups and Group Privileges

You have already been exposed to Portal's groups earlier on in this chapter. The Group Membership check boxes as shown in Figure 26-3 are based upon Portal's group technology. DBA, PORTAL_DEVELOPER, and PORTAL_ADMINISTRATOR are special groups that are predefined during the installation of Oracle Portal.

1. Make sure that you are logged onto Portal as the Portal administrator.

2. Navigate to the Administer panel and enter the string **PORTAL_DEVELOPERS** into the text box under the Edit Group heading. Click the Edit button to edit the PORTAL_DEVELOPERS group.

3. Use the Privileges tab to display the panel as shown in Figure 26-10.

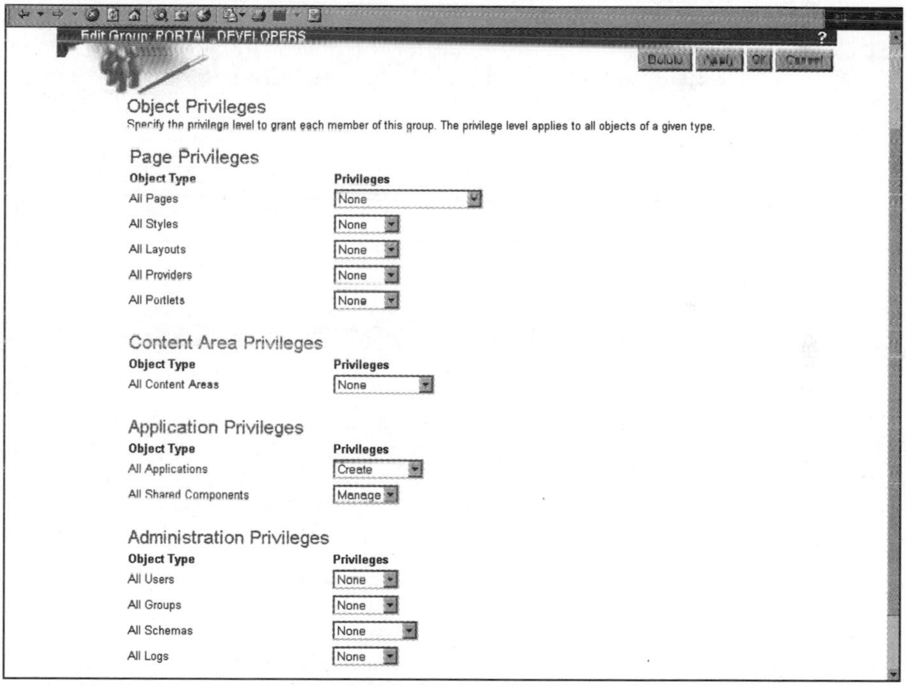

Figure 26-10: Portal Developer Group Privileges

Based upon the values that are shown in Figure 26-10 you will see that the group PORTAL_DEVELOPERS has been granted two privileges:

✦ All Applications — Create

✦ All Shared Components — Manage

Table 26-4 shows you how to decipher these two privileges. First, members of the PORTAL_DEVELOPERS group can create new applications and manage any application that they create. Second, they have full permissions to modify any of the Shared Components such as fonts, colors, templates, and JavaScripts. All of the remaining combo boxes are set to None, indicating that PORTAL_DEVELOPERS have not been granted any additional privileges. When you logged onto Portal as DEVELOP01 you saw this exact behavior. DEVELOP01 was able to view the NETCOLLEGE application that you created with the `NETUDEV` account—but it was not able to modify any of the content within the application.

If you wanted your PORTAL_DEVELOPERS to be able to modify any application component you could simply change the All Applications combo box to the value Edit Contents directly on the panel that is shown in Figure 26-10. Once you make this change, every Portal account that has been assigned to the PORTAL_DEVELOPERS group will gain this new privilege. This may not be exactly the behavior that you want. Before you make a change to this built-in group, you will probably want to check to see which of your users has been assigned to this group.

4. Use the Members tab at the top of the panel to display the page as shown in Figure 26-11.

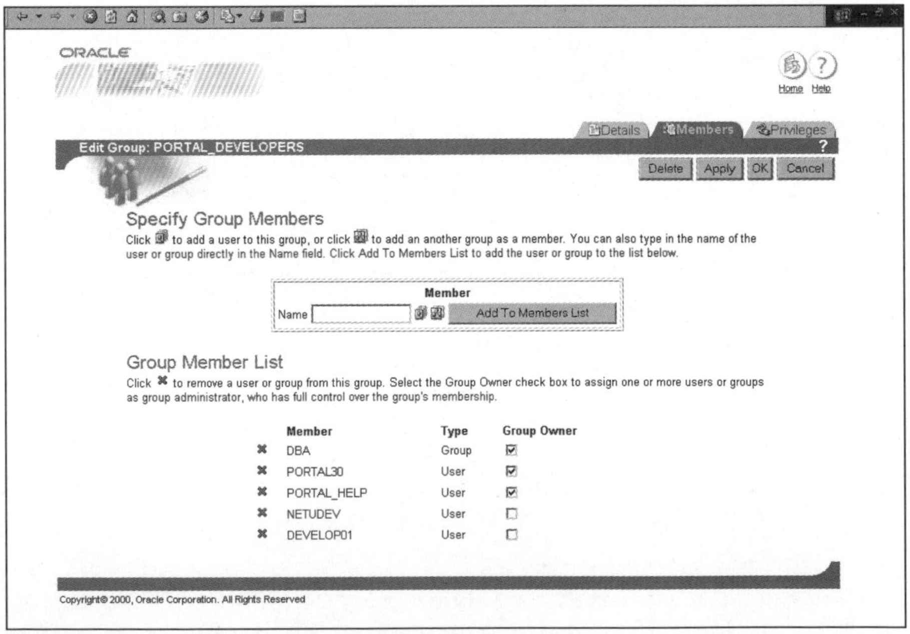

Figure 26-11: PORTAL_DEVELOPERS—Group Members

The users that are listed at the bottom of the panel as shown in Figure 26-11 are those users that have been assign to the PORTAL_DEVELOPERS group. You will notice that this list is composed of both individual user accounts and other groups.

✦ Groups can be composed of subgroups.

✦ Users can belong to several groups simultaneously.

From this panel, we can see the effects of changing the privileges of the PORTAL_ DEVELOPERS group. Each of the four users and the DBA group will be automatically granted the new privileges once they are assigned to the PORTAL_DEVELOPERS group. Although you are free to make changes to Portal's built-in groups, it is not a good idea to do so. Oracle may modify the capabilities of Portal's built-in groups in future releases, and these changes may conflict with your modifications. However, it is a simple matter to create a new group and assign your PORTAL_DEVELOPERS as members of that group.

5. Return to the main Administer panel.

Creating groups and assigning privileges

Although Portal comes equipped with several predefined groups it is a simple matter to create your own groups.

6. Use the Create New Groups link to display the panel shown in Figure 26-12.

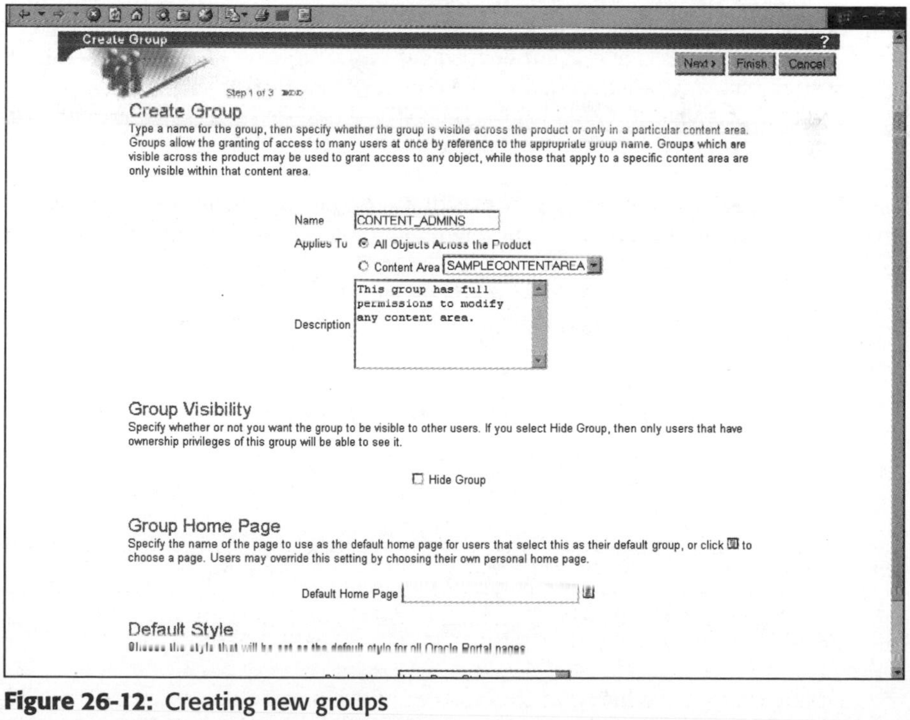

Figure 26-12: Creating new groups

The first step in creating a group is to name the group. You will notice that the built-in Portal groups all have descriptive names such as DBAS and PORTAL_DEVELOPERS. It is a good idea to give your custom groups a name that reflects the group's role or its block of privileges. Our group is going to be a super-user class that will have full permissions to modify any aspect of any Content Area. Since this group will be able to modify any Content Area — we'll give this new group the name CONTENT_ADMINS.

> **7.** Enter the name **CONTENT_ADMINS** for the new group.

The privilege set that you define can either apply to the entire portal area, or you can restrict its scope to individual Content Areas. We used this same panel in Chapter 22 in order to set some permissions for the NETUCONTENT Content Area. This time we want the privilege set so it applies across the board.

> **8.** Choose the All Objects Across the Product radio button. Enter a description for this group.

Sometimes you will not want other administrators to know that a particular group exists. For example, you may be in the process of creating the group over a period of days. During the modification process, you would not want other administrators to begin deploying this group to user accounts. Portal provides the Hide Group check box to prevent the group name from appearing in any of the search pop-ups for exactly this purpose. The privileges that we are planning to grant to the CONTENT_ADMINS group are relatively straightforward. However, we could create a very customized and complicated set of permissions and assign them to a group. In such cases we might wish to design a custom Portal Page as the default home page for this group. (This is an especially useful feature if you are mixing and matching lots of individual privilege settings.)

Note Certain panels, such as those that control the activity logs, appear only in the administration panels. You might grant a group of users the privilege to view and modify the logs without giving the group access to the rest of the Administration functions. In such a case, you might elect to construct a new home page and place the log portlets on this page so that this group could access the appropriate log functions.

> **9.** Use the Next button to display the panel shown in Figure 26-13.

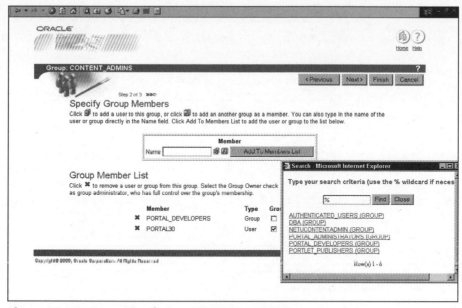

Figure 26-13: Group Members — CONTENT_ADMINS

Before you can assign any privileges to the new group, you are given the chance to add members to the new group. Portal provides two separate look-up functions on this panel. The first function (next to the Name text box) searches for individual portal users and the second function searches for other groups as shown in the overlay in Figure 26-13.

10. Search for the PORTAL_DEVELOPERS group and add it to the Group Member List as shown in Figure 26-13. Press the Next button to display the panel shown in Figure 26-14.

The panel shown in Figure 26-14 should be familiar to you from the preceding section. The privileges that you can assign to the group are identical to the privileges that you can grant to individual users. In our example case, we want to create a group that will be able to manage *any* aspect of *any* Content Area. The privilege setting that we need to grant is the Manage privilege in the All Content Areas section.

11. Select the Manage privilege for the All Content Areas combo box as shown in Figure 26-14.

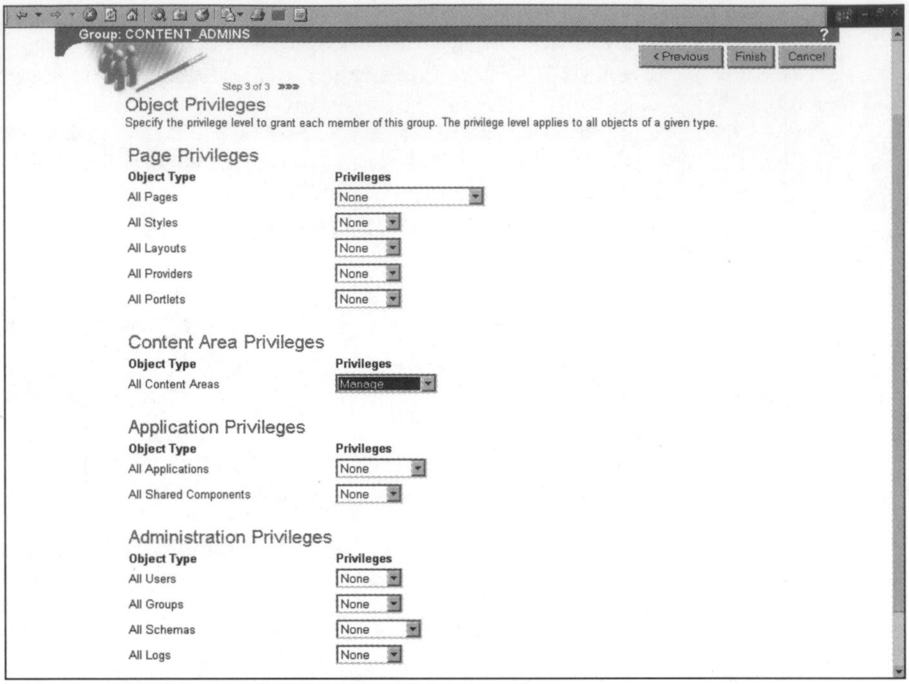

Figure 26-14: Defining privileges for Content Areas

12. Press the Finish button to save the new group.

13. Log on to Portal in a new browser session as the DEVELOP01 user.

14. Navigate to the NETUCONTENT Content Area Students folder and use the Edit Folder link to display the panel shown in Figure 26-15.

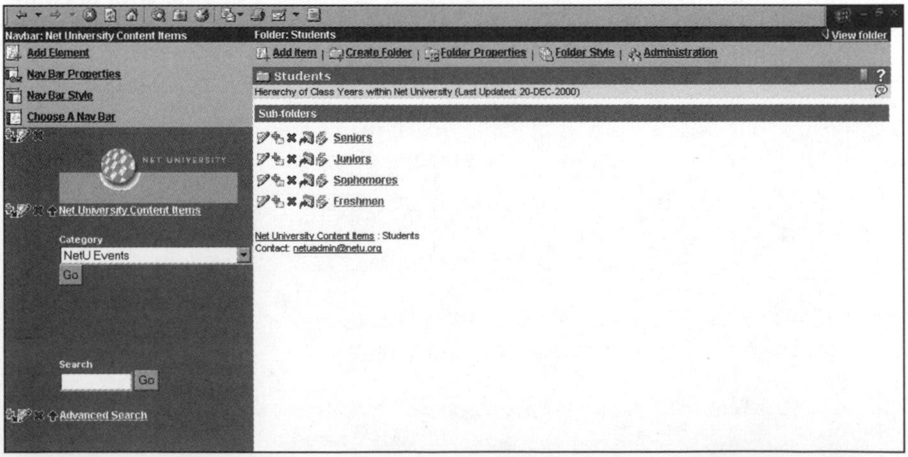

Figure 26-15: Students folder in Edit mode — DEVELOP01 Account

The DEVELOP01 account now has full access to all of the elements of the NETU-CONTENT Content Area. Even though you created this Content Area with the NETUDEV account, the Manage privilege applies to all Content Areas — not just those that are owned by the DEVELOP01 account.

> **Note**   We deployed the application privileges to the CONTENT_ADMINS group, but we added the PORTAL_DEVELOPERS group to the list of members of CONTENT_ADMINS. Thus, the privileges flowed through to the DEVELOP01 account from this hierarchy of groups.

The privileges that you deploy to users and groups from the Administer panel are particularly powerful as they apply to *groups* of objects. You can, however, limit access privileges directly to individual objects — as you'll see in this next section.

Creating Privileges on Individual Objects

Security configurations for end-user accounts generally require more individualized settings, because you do not give them free reign to access all of the data in your database. Oracle Portal makes the overall security process easier because you can restrict access to the database completely and only allow users to view data using specified application components.

All Portal users must have an account, even if you designate the public account as the default account. You can assign each account in turn to any number of groups. As discussed in the previous section, Portal comes equipped with some built-in groups, but you are free to add your own groups for the applications you create. For example, in the Net University system, you would likely set up four different groups for UGRADS, ALUMNI, FACULTY, and ADMINISTRATION. As the application grows, you may need to add specialized roles for subgroups within each major role. The ADMINISTRATION department might be further broken down into ACCOUNTING, LEGAL, and HUMAN RESOURCES, for example. A single user account can be part of multiple groups. Groups are a superior technique for assigning privileges to users (as compared to granting privileges directly to individual accounts). For example, the NETU system has 1,000 Alumni users. If you were to assign object privileges for each and every individual, you would have a full-time job just setting up security.

A better solution is to create a group and assign object privileges to a group. When new objects are created, you can then provide access to them by assigning permissions to the group rather than to the individual user accounts.

The object privileges that you grant to portal users will generally be based on Content Areas, applications, or components.

> **Cross-Reference**   Content Area privileges are discussed in detail in Chapter 24.

1. Open the Portal Navigator to the Applications panel as shown in Figure 26-16.

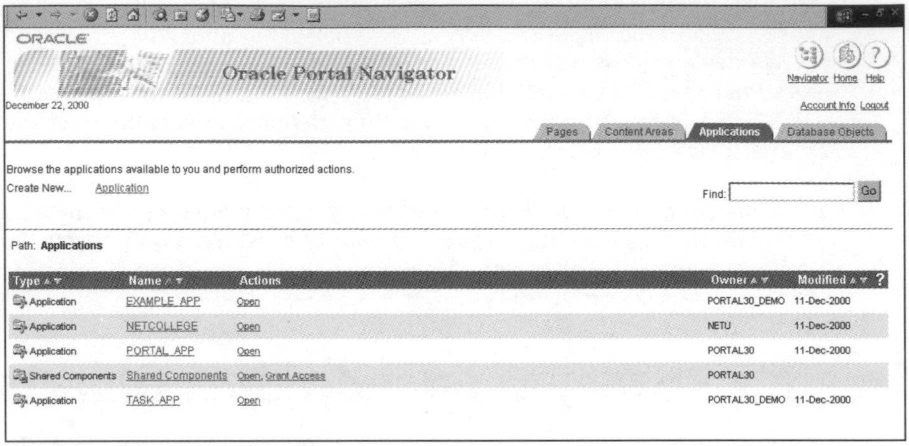

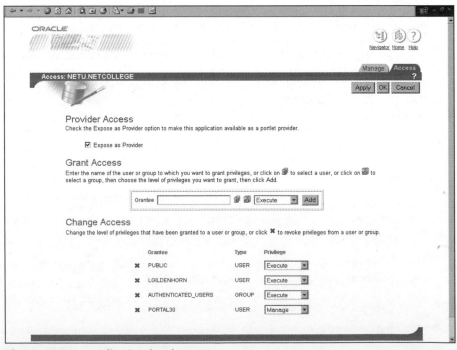

Figure 26-16: Portal Navigator — Applications

2. Click on the Grant Access link for the NETCOLLEGE application to display the panel as shown in Figure 26-17.

Figure 26-17: Application-level Access

Portal provides the same access panel for the NETCOLLEGE application as it does for group membership. The pop-up windows can be used to search for both individual users as well as groups of users. Figure 26-17 shows that several user accounts, including the public user, have Execute authority on this application. The privileges that are available on this form match those listed in Table 26-4. However, when we granted those application-level privileges in the earlier part of this chapter, we granted them for all applications. Since we have selected a *specific* application from the Portal Navigator, the privileges that we grant here *only* apply to the application (NETCOLLEGE) listed on the current panel.

Applications are treated as special objects within the portal environment. They act as container applications for the objects that are defined within them. You have the option of specifying individual permissions on each object within an application (form, report, menu, chart, calendar, etc.) Alternatively, you can allow these individual application objects to inherit their privileges from the application in which they are managed.

3. Choose the Cancel button to return to the Navigator

4. Open the NETCOLLEGE application and select any form or report that you have built within the application. Use the Grant Access link to open the Access panel for that object to display the panel as shown in Figure 26-18.

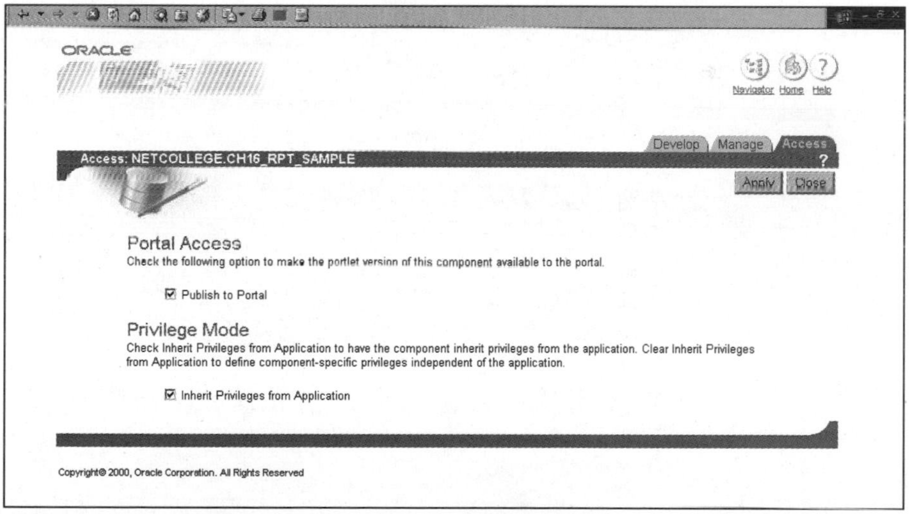

Figure 26-18: Default Object-level Access privileges

There are two option settings on the Access panel for individual component objects. If you wish to make the object available as a portlet, then you can enable the Publish to Portal check box.

Note To publish the component as a portlet, you must have the Publish Portlet privilege and you must make the application that owns the component available via the Expose as Provider check box on the Access Application panel as shown in Figure 26-17.

The default option for any component is to defer all privileges to the container application. When you create new components, the Access panel will initially appear with the Inherit Privileges from Application check box selected. This default option makes the most sense. For the most part, you will want to control the privileges for a group of components at the application level. Instead of having to manage security on dozens of forms, reports, and charts on an individual basis, you can control security centrally at the application level. However, this will not always be the best option. For example, you might deploy an application that has some sensitive forms or reports built into it. In the case of Net University, we might create a GRADES report that displays the grades of all of the students. While we might make this report available to the FACULTY group, we would not want to make it available to the STUDENTS group.

The solution to this problem is to set individual privileges on the report.

5. Uncheck the Inherit Privileges from Application check box on the form/report and press the Apply button to display the panel as shown in Figure 26-19.

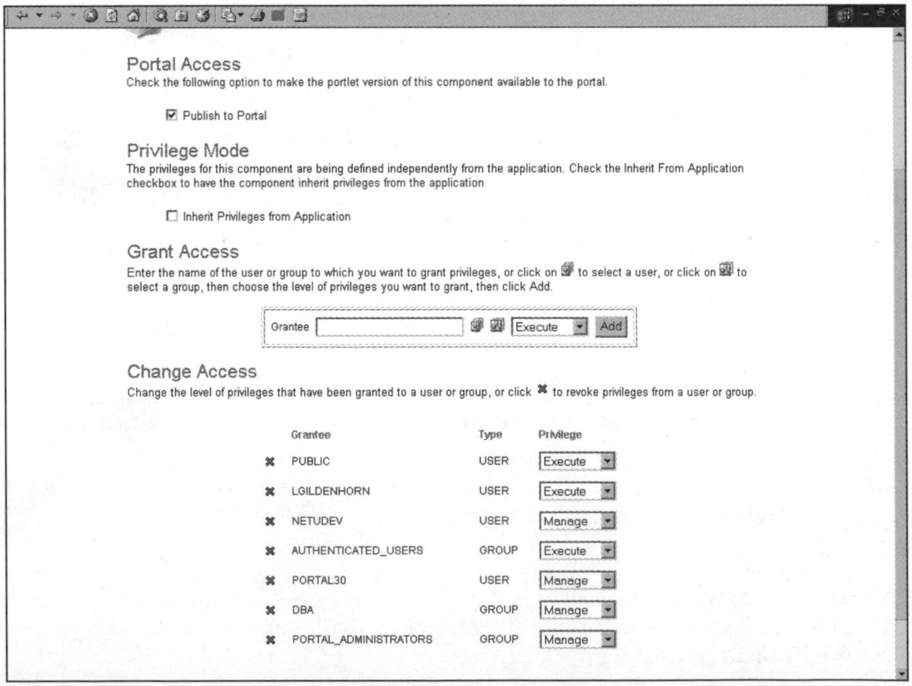

Figure 26-19: Setting privileges for individual components

Security Tables

Portal uses the WWSEC% tables in the PORTAL30 schema to store security settings for applications and components. You can create your own reports against these tables if you wish to view all of the privileges for groups of forms/reports on one long report instead of searching for them within each component builder and access panel.

Portal displays the familiar Grant Access section that you can use to search for users and groups to be added as privileged users. However, the default behavior of this panel is slightly different that you might expect. Portal will automatically populate this panel with the users and groups that have been granted access to this component at the *application level*. In the panel shown in Figure 26-19 the user LGILDENHORN has been granted access to the NETCOLLEGE application — and by default she is given access to this report as well. She can be removed from this report on an individual basis by using the delete icon next to her name.

Setting Schema Privileges

When you attach users to a group, you are combining users into categories that can then be managed as a group. In some cases, groups themselves confer privileges to users directly, such as when you assign the DBA group to a user. In other cases, the setting of the group merely creates the logical grouping, without granting any specific privileges. For example, you can create groups and not assign any privileges to them.

It is one thing for a group to be given access to an application or component. However, the schema that *owns* the application also needs to be given access to the underlying database objects (i.e., tables and views).

1. Make sure that you are logged on as the Portal administrator.
2. Navigate to the Administer Database panel as shown in Figure 26-20.

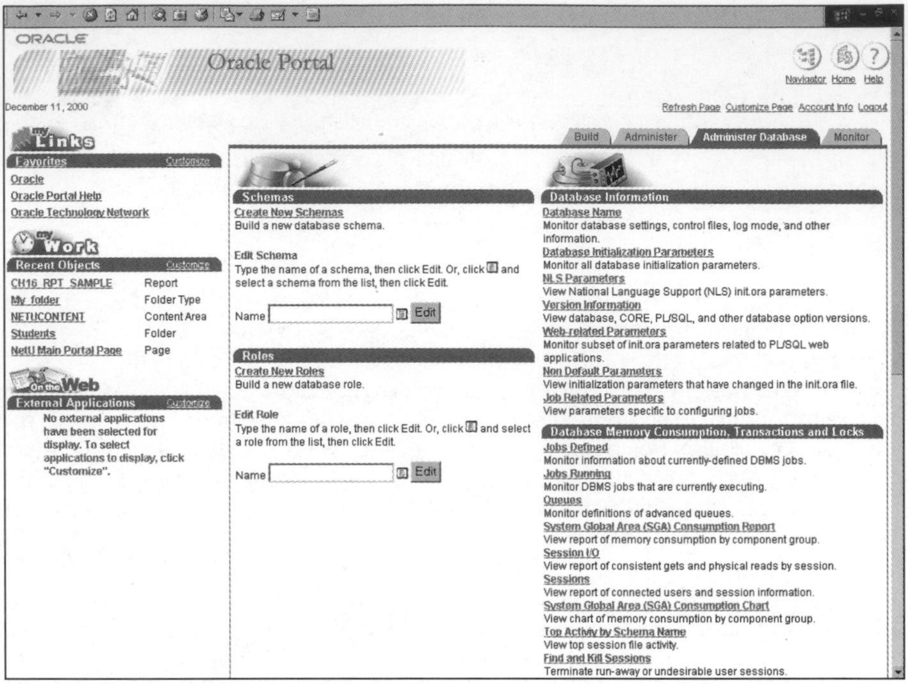

Figure 26-20: Administer Database

Physical database schemas act as the containers for applications. Although the source code for your applications is stored in the PORTAL30 schema—the generated database packages are stored in the application schema, which owns your application. The simplest way to understand this is to create a new schema (just like you did in Chapter 2).

3. Use the Create New Schemas link to display the panel as shown in Figure 26-21.

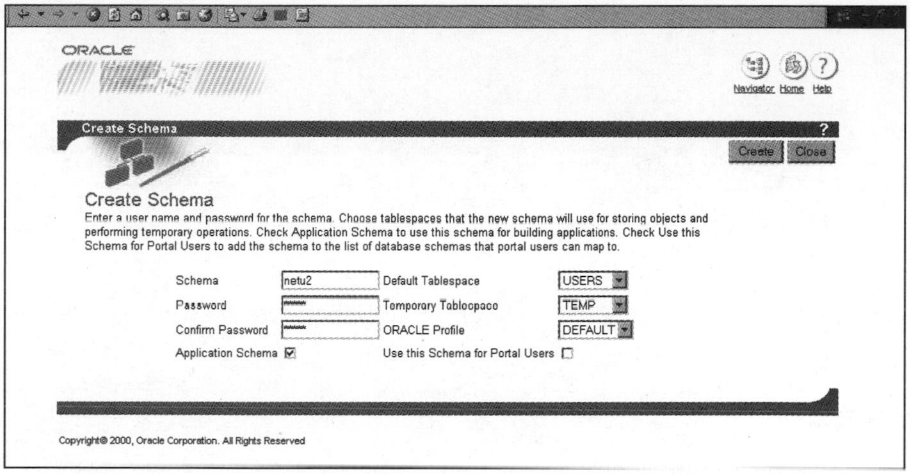

Figure 26-21: Create Schema panel

Up until this point, the user accounts that you have created have all been *lightweight* users. Schemas on the other hand are full-fledged Oracle database user accounts. Once you create a schema, it can be used to manage applications. You must provide a schema name and password for the new schema, just like a regular portal account. Schema names must start with a letter and can include the dollar sign ($) and the underscore (_) characters, but not the space character. By default, the new schema cannot be used as a portal application schema. However, once the Application Schema check box is checked — developers with appropriate application access privileges will be able to create components within this schema. Because the new schema is a full-fledged database account, you must also specify a tablespace and temporary tablespace for it.

4. Enter the name **netu2** as the name for the new schema and enter a password of your own choosing.

5. Accept the default tablespace values.

6. Check the Application Schema check box.

7. Click the Create button to create the new account.

8. Edit the new account and navigate to the Grants panel as shown in Figure 26-22.

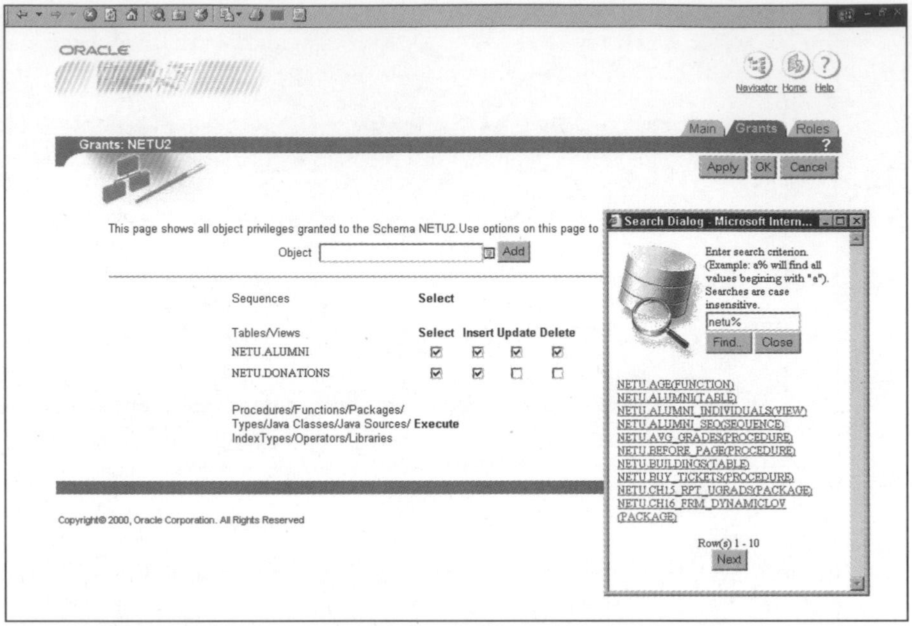

Figure 26-22: Schema Grants panel

Once you have created the schema it is ready to be used as a container account for Portal Applications and Components. By default, the new schema has access to any of the tables and views that are created within the schema itself. However, it does not necessarily have access to any tables in other schemas within the Oracle instance. For example, when you installed the Net University sample database you created it inside of the NETU account. If you want developers to be able to build forms and reports in the NETU2 schema against tables in the NETU account, you will need to grant the NETU2 account some additional privileges. These privileges can come in two forms — object privileges and roles. Object privileges are database-specific privileges that are granted against physical database objects such as tables or views. These privileges match the basic database privileges:

- ✦ Select
- ✦ Insert
- ✦ Update
- ✦ Delete
- ✦ Execute

Figure 26-22 shows that two specific grants have been made to the NETU2 account. NETU2 has full access (SELECT, INSERT, UPDATE, DELETE) to the NETU.ALUMNI table and limited access (SELECT, INSERT) to the NETU.DONATIONS table. Thus, Portal Developers can build portal applications (forms, reports, etc.) in the NETU2 account that will be able to access the ALUMNI and DONATIONS tables. The Grants panel works in a similar fashion to the Privileges panels that we discussed in the earlier parts of this chapter. The Find button displays a searchable list of database objects (as shown in the overlay in Figure 26-22).

Note

In order to create new schemas you must be logged onto Portal with the DBA privilege. Portal DBAs access the database with Oracle Database DBA privileges, so the list of objects that appear in the search panel will be extensive.

You also have the option to assign specific database roles to the new schema.

9. Click on the Roles tab to display the panel as shown in Figure 26-23.

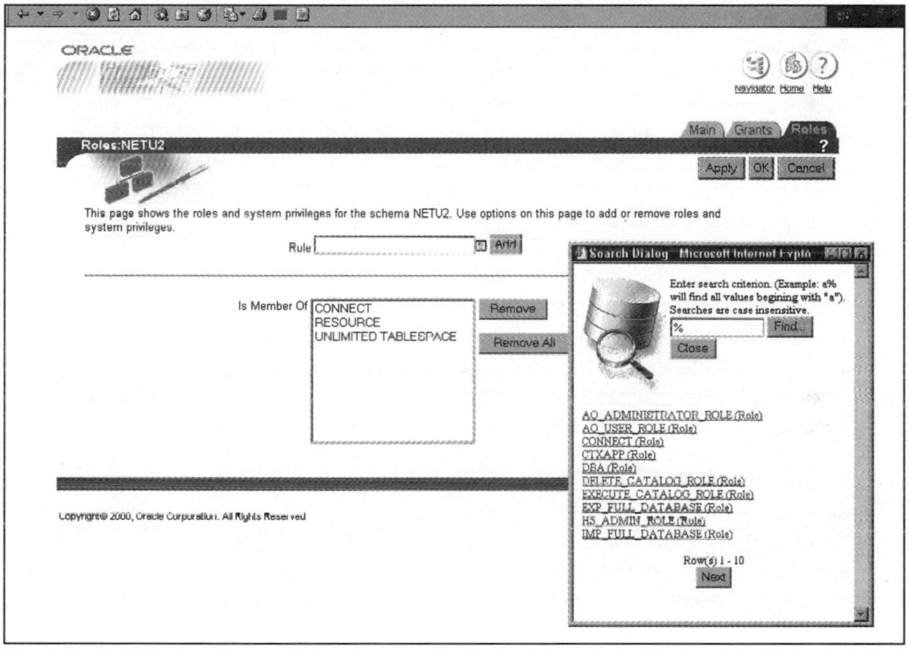

Figure 26-23: Database Roles

Because the new schema is a full-fledged Oracle database account, you also have the option of selecting from a list of database roles and assigning them to the schema. Database roles are similar to Portal Groups, but they apply to *database* USERIDs. For example, you could allow the NETU2 account to read any table in the database through the "Select Any Table" privilege using the Role combo box.

Schemas provide a powerful option for consolidating your security settings within the Portal environment. Normally, you will follow a consistent four-step process when you create a new application schema:

1. First, you create a new schema within Oracle Portal.

2. Next, you grant the new schema the specific database privileges to access tables and views in any of your other database schemas.

3. Third, you create a new application in the portal schema and create your components within this application (i.e., forms, reports, charts, calendars, menus, etc.)

4. Last, you assign application privileges and user privileges to your application components.

Using the Login Server

There is one final area of concern as far as security goes within the Oracle Portal environment — the Login Server. The Login Server manages the physical connections to the database and controls the authentication of individual users. The Login Server runs as a separate instance from the Portal Server as shown in Figure 26-24. When a portal user requests a page from the Portal Server, the portal engine checks for the presence of an application session cookie. If the user has not been authenticated already, the portal server forwards the request to the Login Server, which then prompts the user for a portal user name and password.

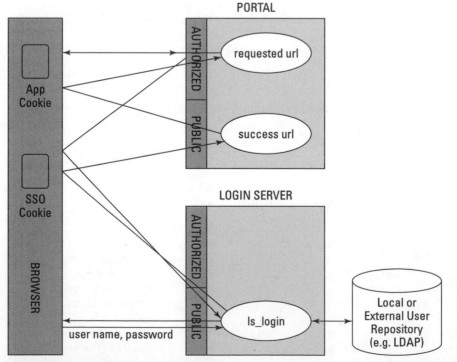

Figure 26-24: Login Server processing

From within the Oracle Portal environment you have access to certain functions of the Login Server.

1. Connect to Oracle Portal as the default Portal Administrator account — **PORTAL30**.

2. Navigate to the Administer panel.

3. Use the Login Server Administration link to display the panel as shown in Figure 26-25.

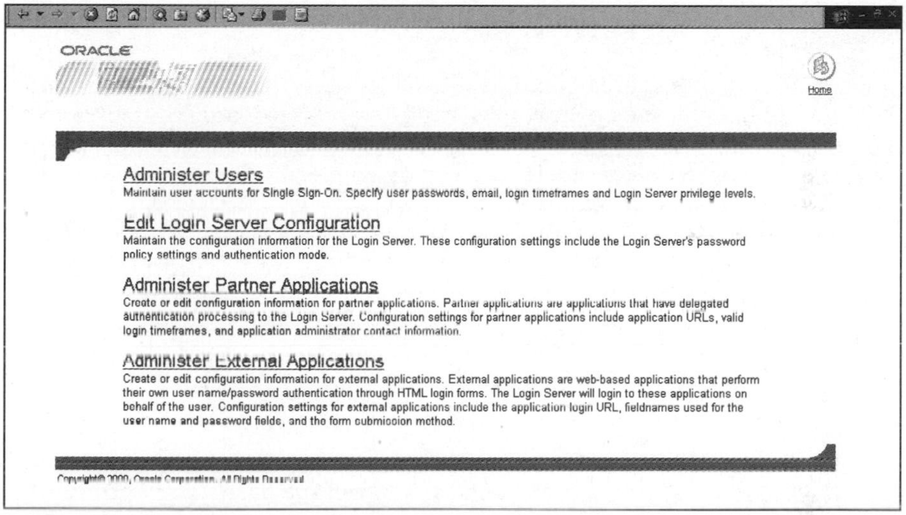

Figure 26-25: Main Login Server panel

Only Portal accounts that have been granted the Full Administrator privilege for the Login Server can view the panel as shown in Figure 26-25. The first two links on this current panel are the most commonly used Login Server panels.

4. Use the Edit Login Server Configuration link to display the panel as shown in Figure 26-26.

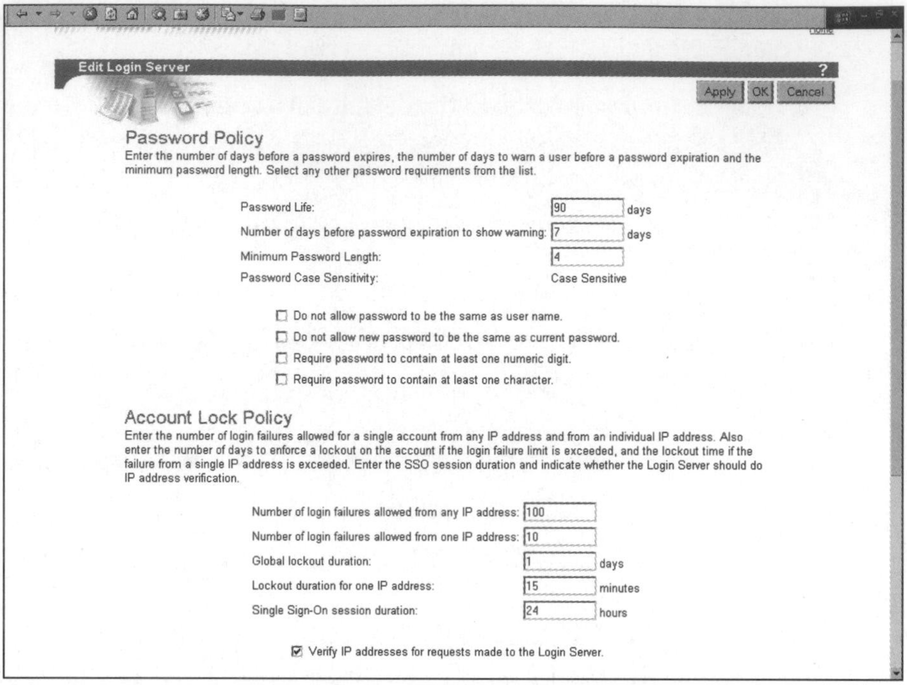

Figure 26-26: Configuration options

The top section of the Edit Login Server panel is the Password Policy section. Through this setting you can control some of the basic password properties such as the minimum length and the password's life. In order to prevent security breaches administrators will often want to set some advanced policies for passwords. For example, passwords that contain a mix of numbers and letters are harder to guess that simple string passwords. Security administrators can further protect their portal site by setting some Account Lockout Policies. Hackers will often try to breach the security of a site by repeatedly using the same user name with different passwords. Unfortunately, this is a common occurrence for Internet-based portal sites. Administrators can tighten security by setting lockout periods. For example, by default, when a user enters an invalid password ten times they will be locked out of the Login Server for 24 hours.

5. Press the OK button to return to the previous panel.

6. Click the Administer Users link and then edit the DEVELOP01 account.

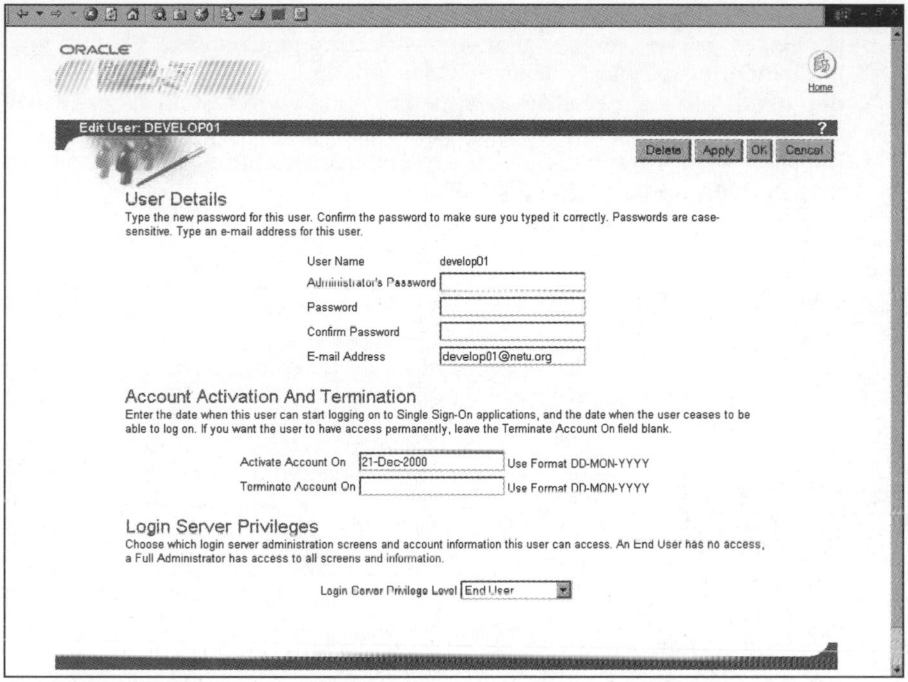

Figure 26-27: Edit User—DEVELOP01

The Edit User panel that is shown in Figure 26-27 controls the user settings and account activation for portal accounts. It matches the panel that is shown in Figure 26-2 with one exception—the Administrator's Password. Portal users that have access to this panel can change the password for *any* user account. When you change a user account you must reenter your administrator's password on this panel. This prevents a user from changing another user's password by walking up to an unattended Login Server browser session.

Cross-Reference The Login Server has some additional options for connecting to third-party applications as discussed in Chapter 23.

Summary

Portal's security mechanisms are built directly from the standards already in place within the Oracle database. If you are familiar with using Oracle USERIDs, passwords, grants, and roles at the database level, then you should have no problem applying that experience within the Portal environment. Novice developers will find that creating new accounts through the Portal interface makes it easier to learn the idiosyncrasies of the Oracle security mechanisms.

With Portal, user security is divided evenly between Portal privileges and schema privileges. We recommend that you work through Chapter 23 before you begin implementing a security scheme. Once you understand how Portal applications are deployed, you will be better equipped to build your system security using the principles you learned within this chapter. Once you have implemented security settings for your portal, the next task on the list is to monitor its performance. In the next chapter we'll be taking a look at Oracle Portal's monitoring tools and reports.

✦   ✦   ✦

Monitoring Oracle9*i*AS Portal Performance

◆   ◆   ◆   ◆

In This Chapter

Using Portal's
Component
Monitoring Utilities

Monitoring Concepts

Monitoring Database
Objects

Using Component
Monitors

Changing the Activity
Log Settings

Using Site Builder
Monitoring Tools

Interpreting Site
Builder Statistics

◆   ◆   ◆   ◆

One of the keys to a successful enterprise portal application is good performance. The biggest factor contributing to slow performance of portal applications is typically the speed at which users are connecting to your site.

If your applications make use of lots of large image files and users are typically connecting to your sites using 28.8 modems, they are likely to have a less successful experience using your applications. As higher-bandwidth Internet connections become available to users on a cost-effective basis, you can expect this to change. Intranet applications often do not suffer from this same problem, because these users are more likely to be connected to the Web server by a network backbone that offers much higher performance. However, even with a speedy connection, a Web site can often become slow if the server machine is straining under a heavy load of users.

Note   With the number of cable-modem installations and DSL modems on the rise, the average speed at which end users connect to an Internet Portal site is getting better all the time. Typically, intranet and extranet users are connecting at Ethernet backbone speeds, but good performance is still critical for these users as well.

There are many reasons for poor performance, including poor or excessive memory usage, lack of disk space, or even excessive use loads. Sometimes the problem is not with the entire Web infrastructure and server at all, but rather with poorly designed or enormously popular individual components. Even in cases where your applications are performing fast enough, you may find that your site is cluttered with unpopular items. Unpopular items are those objects that users are not choosing to access on your portal site. If you are spending time and resources to build components, it is important to know if the end users of your application are actually using them.

Although you may feel that your site is well designed and easy to use, your users may not feel the same way. Measuring usage patterns can help you to identify these conditions within your sites and to correct them. The key to avoiding performance problems is to understand exactly what is going on with your portal server and applications and take both corrective and preventive action. Portal provides a suite of reports, charts, and utilities to help you monitor and manage your Portal components and Portal sites.

Using Portal Monitoring Tools

There are two main tasks in monitoring a portal application. First, you need to keep track of the activity and identify bottlenecks and problem areas at the database level. Second, you need to be able to perform the same tasks on objects at the portal level.

Note	Ideally, you want to be able to *fix* most database and portal performance problems directly through the browser interface as well, but this is not always possible with Oracle9*i*AS Portal. The focus of Oracle Portal's monitoring tools is performance analysis — not database maintenance.

Portal supports both types of monitoring through two classes of tools for Portal Web sites and components as part of the monitoring subsystem. The database administration utilities are primarily concerned with managing the Oracle database upon which Oracle Portal is built. Portal provides three classes of database administration tools — all of which are aimed at the database administrator more than the portal developer. Portal also provides a set of portal-based monitoring tools that monitor your portal at the portal application level. We'll look at both types of tools in the following sections.

Portal's monitoring utilities are only available to Portal Administrators, DBAs, and Portal Developers. These utilities can be found on the Monitor tab on the main Oracle Portal Developer's page as shown in Figure 27-1.

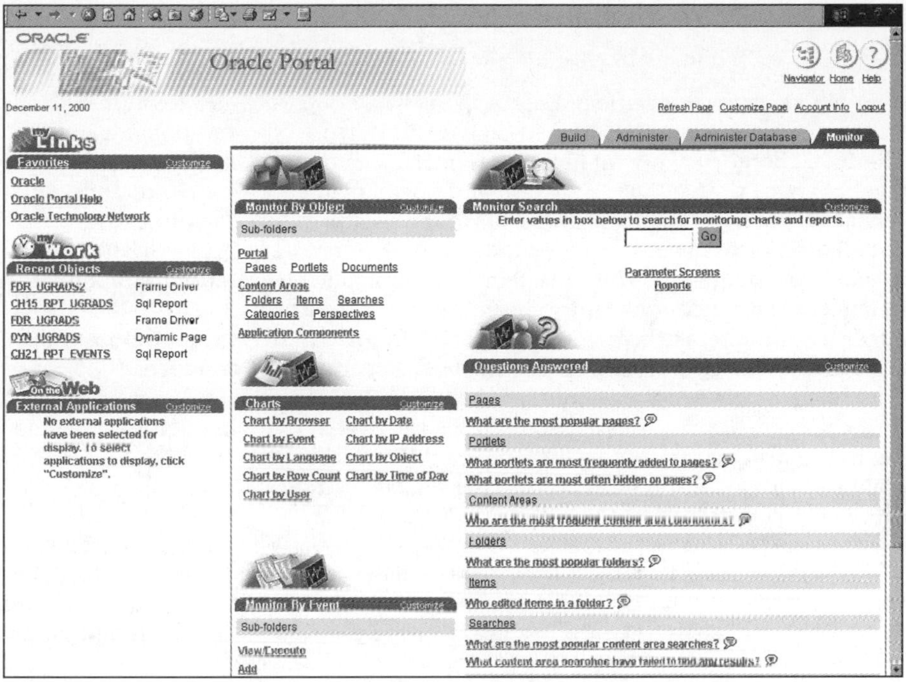

Figure 27-1: Main Monitor tab

Portal provides four classes of monitoring views:

✦ Object Based

✦ Charts

✦ Questions Answered

✦ Event Based

The Object-based monitoring tools are focused on the core objects that are part of your Portal. Objects are the basic elements of a portal site and all of the custom objects that you create including pages, Content Areas, and components such as reports and forms are all considered objects. Object-based monitoring tools are focused on the data within your portal. From a who-what-where-when point of view, *object monitors* are the *what*. *Chart monitors,* on the other hand, are focused on the *who-where-and-when*. Chart monitors will help to you to track the users of your site and the browsers that they are using to access your site. To make things even easier the developers of Oracle Portal have organized the most common types of tracking requests into *questions*. Questions are English-language style tracking reports that answer common portal performance questions such as:

✦ What are the most popular pages?

✦ Who edited items in a folder?

✦ What objects have been deleted?

The final category of portal monitor reports includes *events*. Events are the low-level changes that are made to data and portal elements—add, edit, and delete. Portal logs activity to a pair of database tables stored inside your Portal installation—`wwlog_activity_log1$` and `wwlog_activity_log2$`. These activity logs are designed to roll back and forth much like the standard Oracle redo logs. Portal continues to write information into the first activity log until it reaches the maximum number of days you have specified for that log. Once this saturation point is reached, Portal begins writing to the second log and leaves the first log in a dormant state. When the second anniversary date is reached, Portal stops writing to the second activity log. It also empties the first activity log before it begins writing to the first activity log again. This enables you to copy the contents of the dormant log into a backup table for further analysis later.

Caution   Oracle Portal does not maintain a *rolling* log interval. When the switch date arrives, Portal switches from the current log file to the secondary log file—and it automatically changes the log view to point to the new activity log. If you were to run a chart or report against the log just after the switch interval, the output would be very sparse, since the new log file would be relatively empty.

If you have the proper privileges, these activity logs can be accessed just like any other Oracle table. However, you may find that the data in the activity log tables are somewhat cryptic. The developers of Oracle Portal have simplified this process by providing a series of prebuilt portal views that organize and categorize the data in the activity log tables. These views are not mutually exclusive, and the same log records will often appear in multiple views. Table 27-1 displays the list of these views and their associated purpose.

Table 27-1
Activity Log Views

View Name	Description
WWLOG_ALL_CATEGORY_LOGS	Access and update activity to categories within Content Areas.
WWLOG_ALL_COMPONENT_LOGS	Access to components such as reports, forms, charts, calendars, hierarchies, menus, and Dynamic Pages.
WWLOG_ALL_DELETE_LOGS	Delete activity to records, components, and items in the portal.

View Name	Description
WWLOG_ALL_DOCUMENT_LOGS	Access and update activity of documents into the Content Areas of the portal site.
WWLOG_ALL_FOLDER_LOGS	Activity in folders within Content Areas. Content Areas are essentially file servers and folders are subdirectories within the Content Areas.
WWLOG_ALL_GROUP_LOGS	Activity organized by groups of users.
WWLOG_ALL_ITEM_LOGS	Document activity organized by the document item type.
WWLOG_ALL_OBJECT_LOGS	Access to components such as reports, forms, charts, calendars, hierarchies, menus, and Dynamic Pages and other essential portal objects such as portal pages.
WWLOG_ALL_PAGE_LOGS	Activity to custom-user pages and top-level portal pages.
WWLOG_ALL_PERSPECTIVE_LOGS	Document activity organized by perspective keywords.
WWLOG_ALL_PORTLET_LOGS	Activity within portal pages organized by portlet components.
WWLOG_ALL_SEARCH_LOGS	Successful and unsuccessful searches.
WWLOG_ALL_USER_LOGS	Activity to the portal site organized by user.
WWLOG_EVENT	Activity to the portal site organized by events (add, edit, and delete).
WWLOG_PORTAL_ADMIN_LOGS	Core portal administration logs, including changes to the base portal configuration.
WWLOG_USER_LOGS	Custom user logs.

Oracle Portal records a certain amount of activity in the activity logs based upon settings that are made when you install Oracle Portal. In order to track the custom objects and pages that are part of your Portal, you can provide your logging preferences to Oracle Portal through the Log registry.

Working with the Log registry

You will remember that a standard part of all of the component development tools is a check box option that indicates whether Portal should log activity on that object. When you select this option for any component, Oracle Portal automatically makes a call to the logging system whenever the component is accessed. However, the Portal logging system will only record an entry in the logging tables if there is a matching log-registry entry for that class of object.

Note   Activity logs can grow very rapidly, especially if your portal developers elect to record access to each and every component that they create. The Log registry allows portal administrators to exert some control and restraint over the logging process at a central level. By default, Oracle Portal logs access to all portal objects and all components (provided that application developers have marked components with the "log activity" check box).

The Log Registry Administration utility is part of the services portlet on the Administer tab as shown in Figure 27-2.

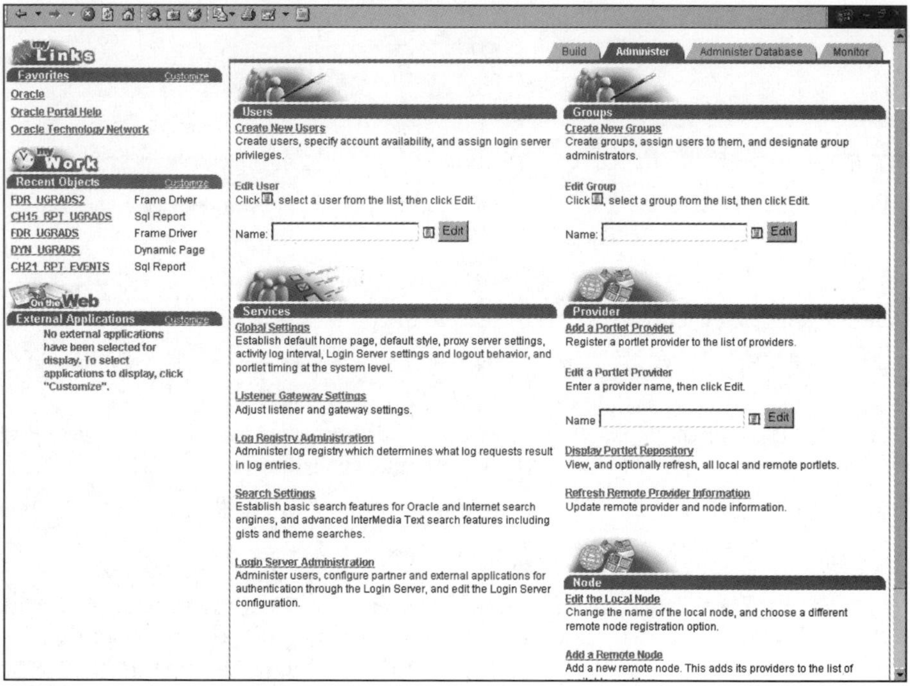

Figure 27-2: Services portlet

1. Click on the Log Registry Administration link to display the panel as shown in Figure 27-3.

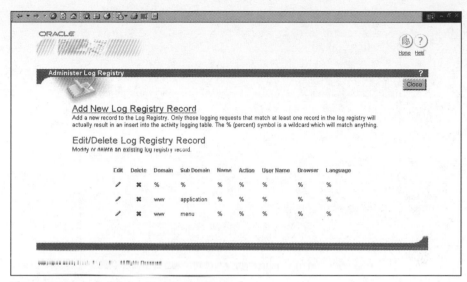

Figure 27-3: Administer Log Registry panel

The sample activity Log registry that is shown in Figure 27-3 is already loaded with several registry records — but your registry will initially have a single registry record that is filled with wild cards (%). This master record indicates that Oracle Portal should log all activity for all components. The main menu links for the registry permit you to either add log records or delete existing log records. Each log record will display its own link that will permit you to modify the attributes of the registry record as necessary.

2. Click on the Add New Log Registry Record link to display the panel as shown in Figure 27-4.

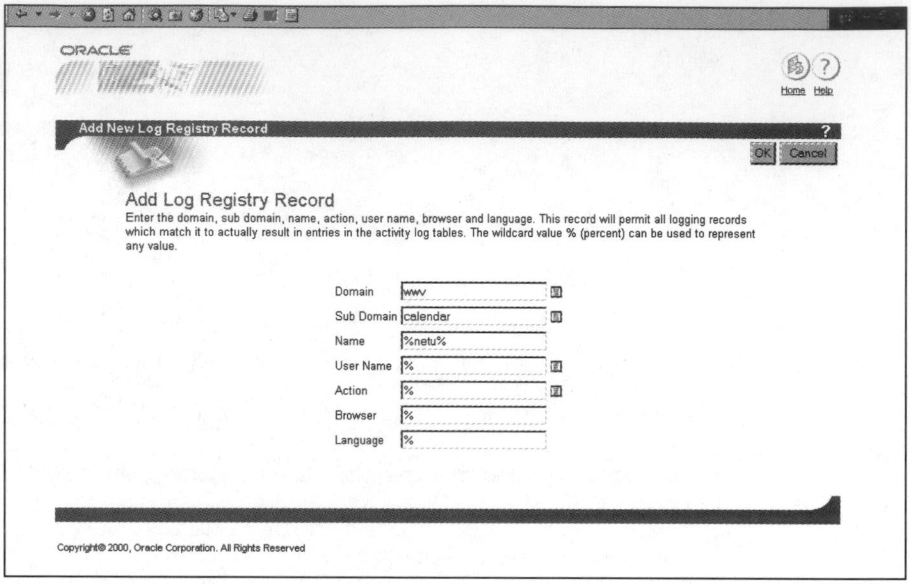

Figure 27-4: Add New Log Registry Record panel

The Log registry utilizes a very simple interface that is composed of seven entry fields:

- ✦ Domain
- ✦ Sub Domain
- ✦ Name
- ✦ User Name
- ✦ Action
- ✦ Browser
- ✦ Language

Oracle Portal has three types of domains, applications (wwv), Content Areas (wws), and portals (wwc). Portals represent the highest level in the domain food chain. If you select the portal entry as your domain value, the logging system will consider any and all activity as valid elements for logging.

3. Use the pop-up search button on the Domain field to locate the entry for application (wwv) as shown in Figure 27-4.

Once you have selected a domain, you can then select a subdomain. Subdomains are the basic building blocks for your portal and they map to the various component objects that have been discussed in the previous chapters of the book.

✦ Application: Application

✦ Application: Calendar

✦ Application: Chart

✦ Application: Dynamic Page

✦ Application: Form

✦ Application: Frame Driver

✦ Application: Hierarchy

✦ Application: Link

✦ Application: List of Values

✦ Application: Menu

✦ Application: Report

✦ Application: component

✦ Content Area: Category

✦ Content Area: Folder

✦ Content Area: Item

✦ Content Area: Perspective

✦ Content Area: Search

✦ Portal: Document

✦ Portal: Page

✦ Portal: Portlet

4. Use the pop-up search button to locate the entry for Application:Calendar as shown in Figure 27-4.

By selecting a subdomain you are essentially providing a filter for the logging system. When you select the entry for calendar you are telling the portal logging system to record activity for any *calendar* object that is used within your portal. Should you wish to log access to *specific* calendar objects, you would then add a string entry for the name field as shown in Figure 27-4.

Note

Even though Oracle Portal automatically groups components according to applications, it still makes sense to include some type of logical application code within the name for your component objects. For example, by including the string netu in the name string for all of your calendar objects within the NETCOLLEGE application you would easily be able to add a Log registry entry that finds all calendars within NETCOLLEGE.

All of the fields in the Log registry record support the use of wild cards, and you are also free to intermix strings and wild card characters as shown in Figure 27-4 (%netu%). By default, Portal will log activity for all users, but you can elect to record activity for individual users by selecting a user name value for the User Name field. The Action field allows you to filter log records based on certain operations such as edit, delete, or customize. This is a very advanced option, however, and we would recommend that you start by logging all event actions.

You will use the last two options, Browser and Language, less often than the other entries. Portal uses these values to filter records based on the browser version and the language code. For example, if you believe that your portal site is having performance or display problems with a specific *version* of a browser, you might elect to clear out all of the other log entries temporarily and record log records specifically for the problem browser type.

   5. Use the OK button to save your log record and return to the panel as shown in Figure 27-5.

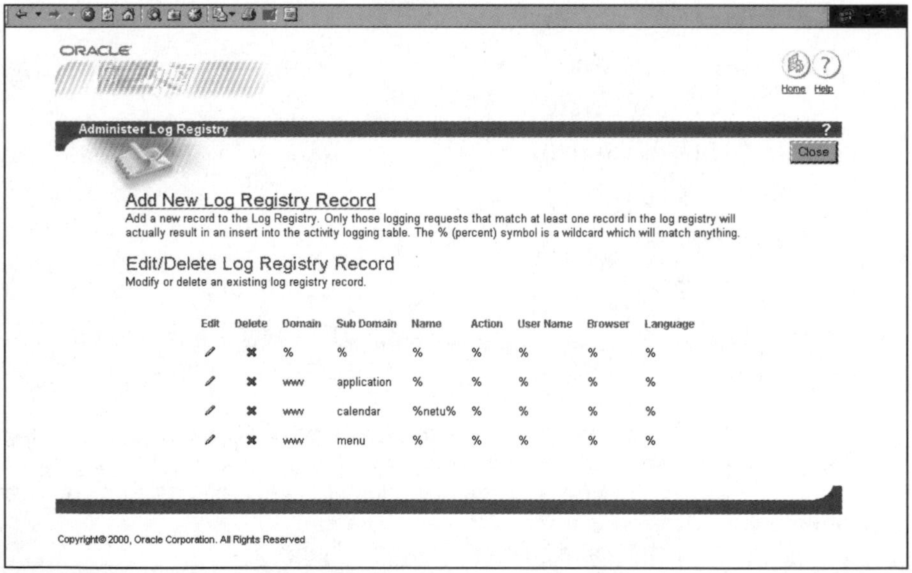

Figure 27-5: Modified Log registry

After adding a new log record, your registry will look like the page shown in Figure 27-5. The first record in the list is a wild card record, which is added by Oracle Portal automatically when the portal is installed. Since the registry includes a complete wild card record, Portal will log all activity for all objects. The record that you just added to log activity for calendar objects with the name %netu% is essentially redundant, since Portal will log calendars as part of the wild card record. In order to enforce the specific rule that you just entered you will have to delete the wild card rule.

Caution

Bear in mind that once you delete the default wild card rule Oracle Portal will only log entries that match the remaining registry records. Initially, we recommend that you stick with the default logging options for Portal until you get more experience working with the monitoring tools.

The ability to add individual logging records adds enormous flexibility and power to the logging system. You can clear out the activity logs and then enter custom registry options to profile certain aspects of your site's performance and activity.

6. Exit the Log registry and return to the Monitor tab.

Object monitoring tools

The object monitoring tools provide the most basic form of activity profiling. Objects are the core content items in your portal site and they are subdivided into a familiar list of categories as shown in Table 27-2.

Table 27-2
Object-Based Monitoring Tools

Class	Object Type	Description
Portal	Pages	Pages are the core objects in the Portal System. (The main monitor interface is itself a portal page.)
	Portlets	Portlet components that are loaded into portal pages.
	Documents	Any uploaded files including core Portal system objects such as portal images (GIFs and JPEGs).
Content Areas	Folders	Content that is uploaded by portal administrators and end users is organized into folders — much like subdirectories on a file server.
	Items	Items are the documents, presentations, Zip files, and other content documents that are uploaded into Content Areas.
	Searches	Users can search for components and documents within folders. Portal stores each successful and unsuccessful search.
	Categories	Uploaded document items are organized into categories.
	Perspectives	Uploaded document items in Content Areas can be indexed by perspective keywords.
Application Components	Reports, Forms, Charts, Calendars, Hierarchies, Dynamic Pages	Custom-built components which are deployed into applications, Content Areas, and pages.

Objects are the actual components that make up the bulk of your Web site. They are typically the starting point for any analysis. The pages, Content Areas, and components themselves are the core functions that are used by Portal to create the HTML pages that appear in your browser. As you no doubt recall from working with the component builders in the earlier sections of this book, each Portal report, form, calendar, chart, hierarchy, Dynamic Page, frame, and shared component is implemented as a database procedure, which can be tracked by the activity logs.

7. Use the Monitor by Object Link on the Monitor panel to display the panel shown in Figure 27-6.

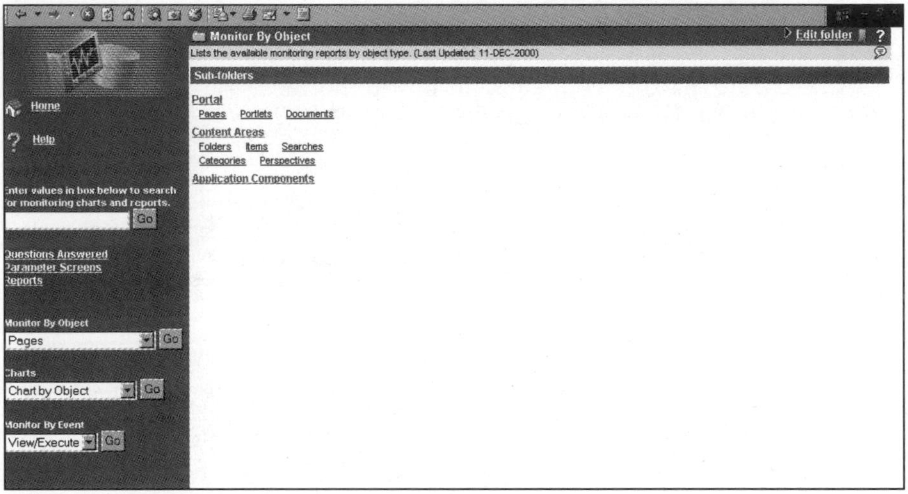

Figure 27-6: Monitor by Object panel

Oracle Portal uses a Content Area in which to store the various object monitoring reports and charts. Once you select a particular monitor group, you will no longer see the standard portal page interface that is used by the component development tools. (This may change with future releases of Oracle Portal.) All four of the monitor groups appear as links in the Navigation Bar that is shown on the left side of the panel. The right panel contains a folder for the monitor objects and subfolders for each of the object groups that are listed in Table 27-2.

8. Select the Pages item in the Monitor By Object combo box and then press the Go button to display the panel as shown in Figure 27-7.

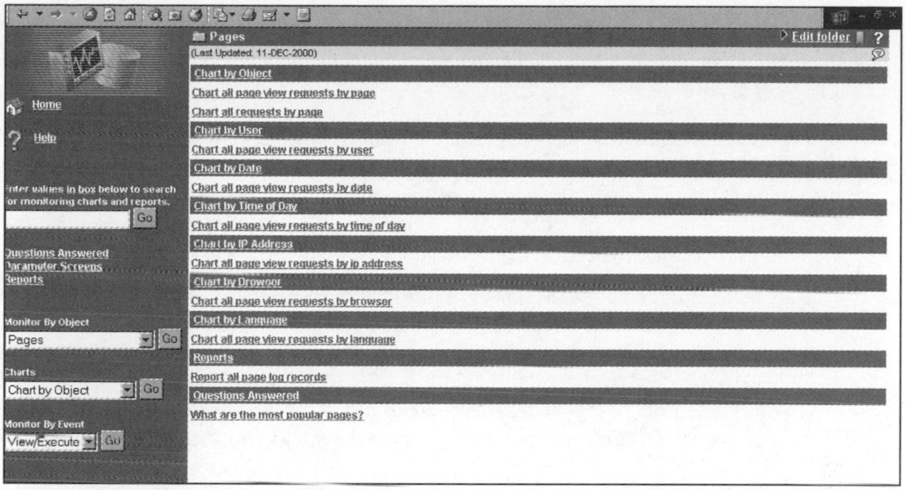

Figure 27-7: Monitoring pages

The specific reports and charts that appear in the Content Area for the different object types will vary slightly by the object type. However, in most cases you are able to view reports for each object by the report types that are listed in the Table 27-3.

Table 27-3
Object Report Types

Report Type	Description
Chart by Object	Displays the number of requests for a given page, report, form, etc.
Chart by User	Displays the number of requests for the selected object type charted by the user that requested the object.
Chart by Date	Displays requests for the object charted by the date of the access. (Portal automatically strips the time value off of the date fields for this report.)
Chart by Time of Day	Displays the number of requests for an object charted by the hour of the day in which the access was made. (This chart is useful in tracking the types of activity that end users undertake at different points in the day—such as first thing in the morning).
Chart by IP Address	Displays the number of requests for an object charted by the IP address of the client browser. Although this can be somewhat misleading if your users do not have fixed IP addresses, it is still useful as a means of tracking access by IP zones.

Continued

Table 27-3 *(continued)*

Report Type	Description
Chart by Browser Type	Displays the number of requests for an object charted by the specific version of the browser that was used to access the object. This report allows you to see which browser your users are using to access your portal — and which O/S platform they are using to run the browser.
Chart by Language	Displays the number of requests for an object charted by the Oracle Portal language code of the object.
Reports	Displays all of the log records for an object in a Portal Report.
What are the most popular objects?	Displays a chart of the most frequently requested objects of the selected object type — such as the most popular pages, reports, forms, etc.

Most of the monitoring reports are constructed using Portal's built-in charting capability and you will find that the user interface is the same for all of the various object reports.

9. Click on the "Chart all page view requests by browser" link to view the panel as shown in Figure 27-8.

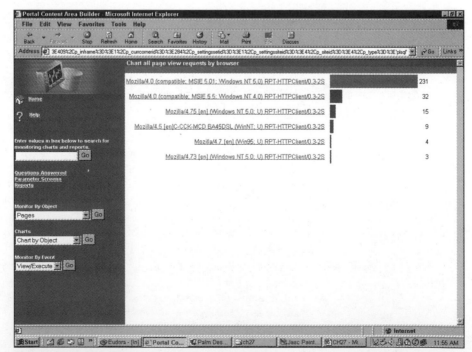

Figure 27-8: Charting page requests by browser

More of the Same

Portal also displays the contents of the Charts combo box in its own region of the main monitoring page, as shown in Figure 27-1. In fact, all of the options on the main monitor page can be found on the Navigation Bar.

The left side of the chart shows the various versions of the browser that have been used to access pages on the portal site. The bar charts to the right show the total number of page hits for each of the various browsers. All of the object-based charts within a particular object area work in a similar fashion. The title of the chart tells you what Portal is measuring, and the folder area determines which type of object you are restricting the chart values on. Thus, the chart shown in Figure 27-8 measures page requests by the version and operating system of the browser from which the requests were made. Our chart shows that the vast majority of the page requests have come from Internet Explorer 5.01 running on Windows 2000 (NT 5.0), but there is several other browser versions represented as well.

Note Under default conditions, the Portal log files automatically roll over every 14 days. Therefore, the information that is displayed in any given report or chart will reflect a maximum of 14 days worth of data. You can change the interval setting for log files using the Administration panels as discussed in Chapter 26.

Each of the object-based charts provides a similar set of options and reports, with some objects, such as items, offering some additional viewing options. For convenience purposes, Portal provides a Charts combo box on the Navigation Bar.

The Charts combo box provides access to the same set of charts and reports as the Monitor by Object combo box. While the Monitor by Object combo box organizes the charts by object, the Charts combo box organizes the reports by item such as browser, user, and date/time.

Note In fact, the two combo boxes are actually nothing more than Oracle Portal Perspectives. Portal stores the charts and reports as items with a Content Area and then marks each of them with several perspective headings. When you select a value from either combo box, you are effectively searching the Content Area for items that have the associated perspective value.

Using parameters

You can also filter the entries that are used in the selection of data by viewing the object reports using parameter entry screens.

10. Use the Parameter Screens link in the Navigation Bar to display the panel as shown in Figure 27-9.

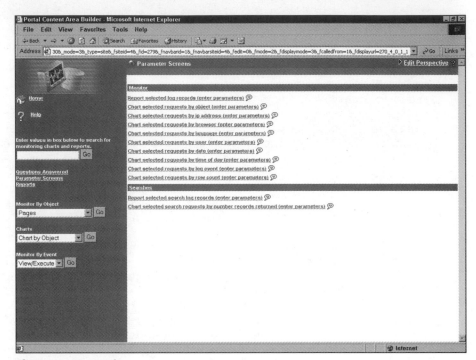

Figure 27-9: Monitor parameter screens

All of the charts that Portal provides as monitoring tools are built using the Chart Builder Component. Each of the charts provides a customization or parameter link just like any chart that you build with the Chart Wizard. Portal provides the Parameter Screens link as a perspective, which exposes the folders and items as listed in Figure 27-9. You will recognize the keywords in all of the descriptions as they match the default charts that were discussed in the preceding section. The critical difference between the two sets of charts is that the parameterized versions allow you to filter the content of the charts.

11. Select the "Chart selected requests by browser (enter parameters)" link to display the panel as shown in Figure 27-10.

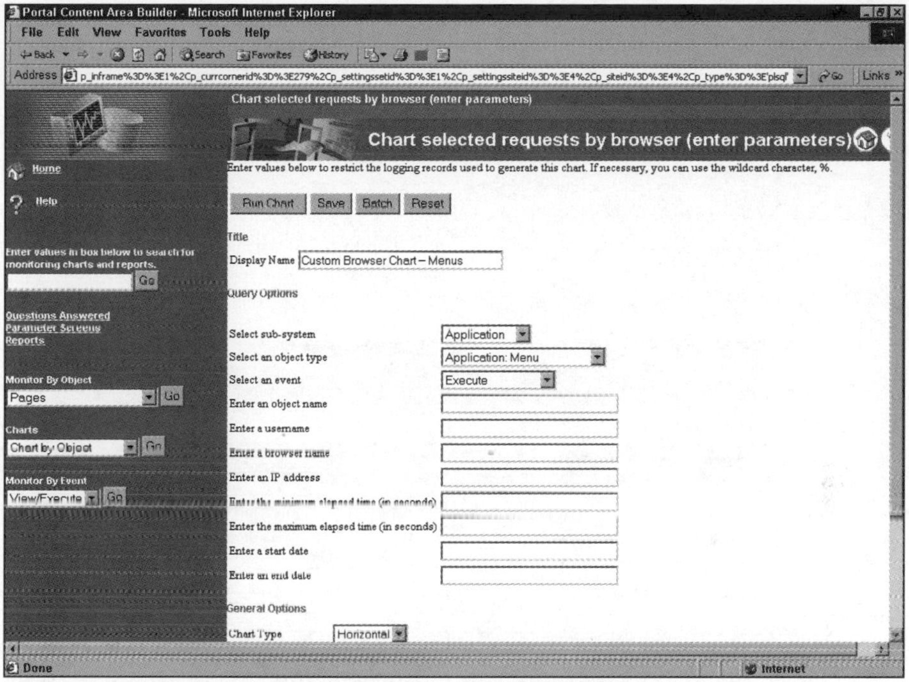

Figure 27-10: Chart all requests by browser with parameters

All of the fields that you see listed on the panel in Figure 27-10 are parameter fields within the various object monitor charts. Normally, Portal provides wild cards for these parameter fields so that all of the log records are referenced as part of the chart. When you elect to use the parameter forms however, you have control over the formatting of the chart and the filtering of the data.

12. Change the Display Name field to **Custom Browser Chart—Menus**.

The first three parameter fields on the form match the Log registry values that Portal itself uses to filter out log records. The subsystem allows you to select the entire portal, individual Content Areas, or applications. The object type field allows you to limit the scope of your chart to a specific type of component such as a report, form, or menu. Finally, you can limit the search to specific Portal events, such as an insert or delete operation. In plain English, these parameters allow you to create custom searches such as:

✦ What time of day do users most often delete items?

✦ Which browsers are being used to view portal pages?

✦ Are my end users customizing their pages?

Cross-Reference   A more complete discussion of these parameter options can be found in the pre-ceding Log registry section, entitled "Working with the Log registry."

13. Select the following values as search parameters:

```
Sub-system—Application
Object type - Application:Menu
Event—Execute
```

14. Use the Run Chart button to display the chart as shown in Figure 27-11.

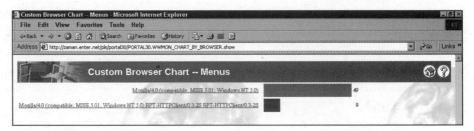

Figure 27-11: Customized chart

The version of the chart that you see in Figure 27-11 is the same chart as that shown in Figure 27-7. You will notice that some of the data that was displayed in Figure 27-7 no longer appears in the chart shown in Figure 27-11. In the first figure, the chart included log records for all objects, while the parameterized version limits the selection to menu objects. This restriction has eliminated some of the log records, causing fewer versions of the browser entries to appear in the chart.

15. Click on either of the browser links that appear the chart.

Portal links the detailed records for the chart as a report object behind the chart links as shown in Figure 27-12.

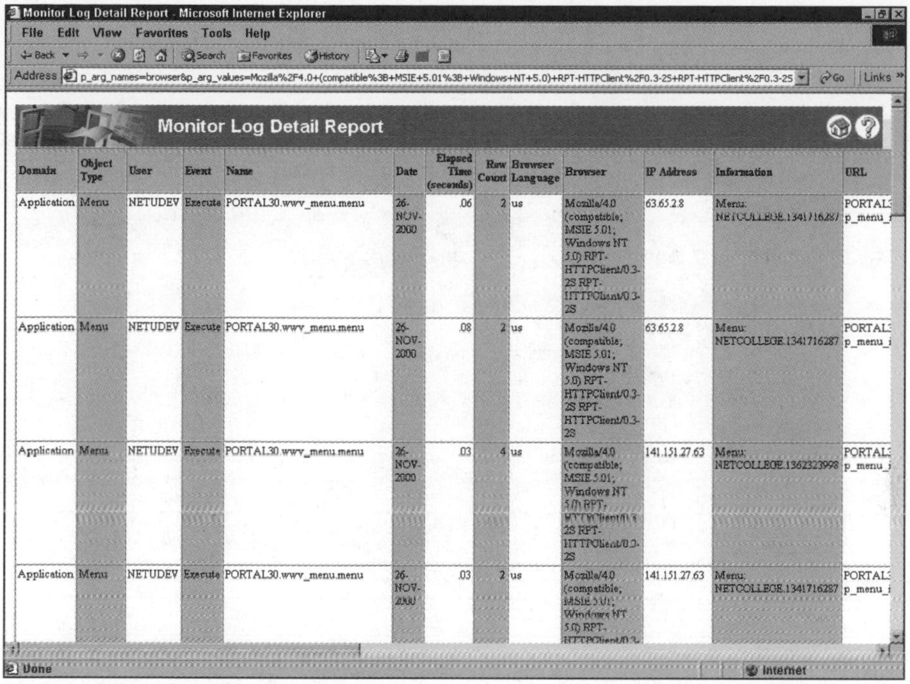

Figure 27-12: Monitor Log Detail Report

Each chart acts as a click-through object. The chart shows the summary data that you selected, and the detailed report *underneath* the chart shows the actual log records. The combination of the parameter forms and the click-through processing provides you with the necessary tools to look for trends within your portal site.

With charts and reports you can quickly search for trends, but Portal makes your job easier by preconfiguring a number of common trend reports into a category that is called "Questions Answered."

16. Return to the main monitor page by using the Monitor tab from the main portal page as shown in Figure 27-1.

Answers to common questions – customizing the interface

The developers of Oracle Portal have packaged together a number of preconfigured charts and reports into a questions-and-answers format. These charts and reports are nothing more than standard object charts with prefilled parameters and English-sounding descriptions.

1. Click on the link "What are the most popular pages?" to display the chart shown in Figure 27-13.

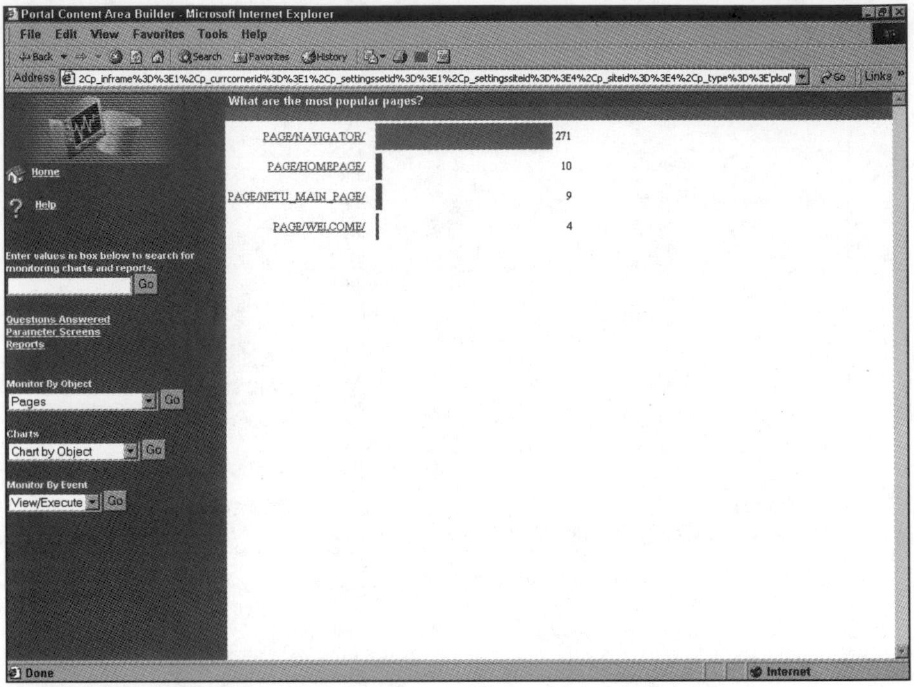

Figure 27-13: Popular page chart

The popular pages chart is nothing more than a regular object-monitor chart that graphs the most commonly referenced portal pages. The chart shows you which of your portal pages are most frequently visited. What makes this chart particularly clever is the title — it is instantly clear what the chart is intended to convey.

Tip   In fact, you can actually drill through the page names on the face of the chart to see the actual page that is referenced by the link. Thus, there is no need to try and figure out which pages the cryptic bar titles are meant to point to.

Because Portal uses its own framework to display the monitor charts and reports you are free to extend them to suite your own needs. If you wish, you can use the chart and report component builders to write custom reports against the WWLOG_ACTIVITY_LOG view (or any of the other views for that matter). One of the simplest customizations that you can make is to provide links to some of the existing reports and charts.

2. Use the Questions Answered link to display the Questions Answered Content Area.

3. Use the Edit Category link to place the Content Area into edit mode as shown in Figure 27-14.

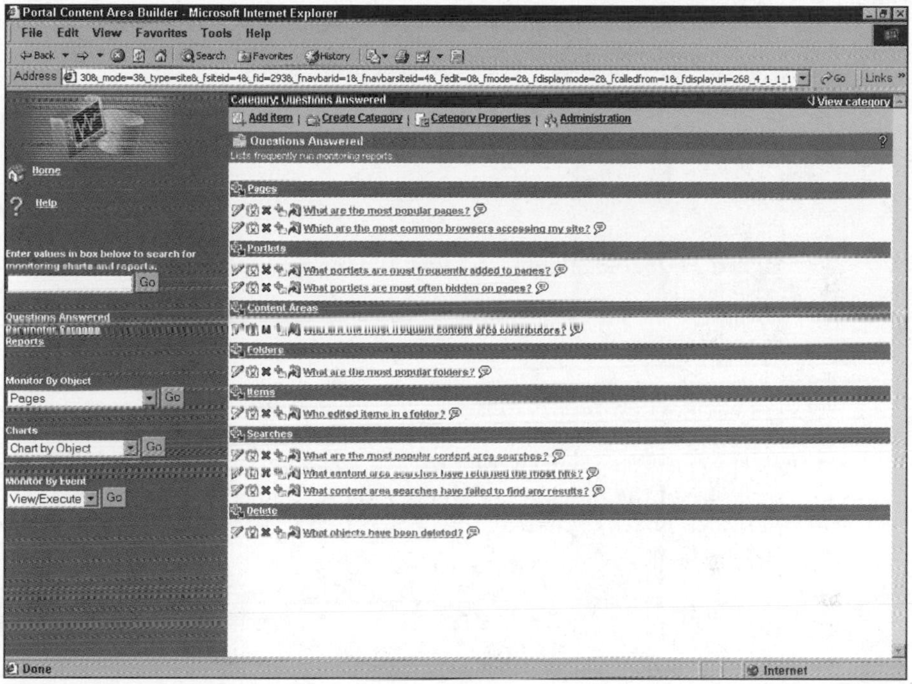

Figure 27-14: Questions Answered Content Area in edit mode

Note

In order to complete the following example you must be logged onto Portal as a Portal Administrator.

Once you have entered edit mode for the Content Area, you are able to add new entries to any of the categories and subfolders.

4. Click on the green plus sign in the banner for the Pages area to display the content wizard as shown in Figure 27-15.

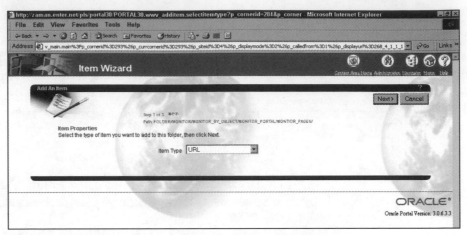

Figure 27-15: Adding new content to the pages subfolder

5. Select URL as the item type and use the Next button to continue.

We are adding a new report to the Pages area of the Questions Answered folder. If we had built our own custom report from scratch, we would use the custom URL for the report at this point in the process. However, we can just as easily make a reference to one of the preexisting object monitor reports. The link text below is the URL that Portal uses to display the browser chart — which was referenced in the previous section:

```
/pls/portal30/PORTAL30.WWMON_CHART_BY_BROWSER.show
```

The link text uses a relative URL format so it will run in the context of the main portal DAD entry (portal30).

6. Enter the following parameters into the Add a URL Item panel of the content wizard as shown in Figure 27-16.

```
Folder Region—Regular Items
URL—/pls/portal30/PORTAL30.WWMON_CHART_BY_BROWSER.show
Display Name—Which are the most common browsers accessing my
portal?
```

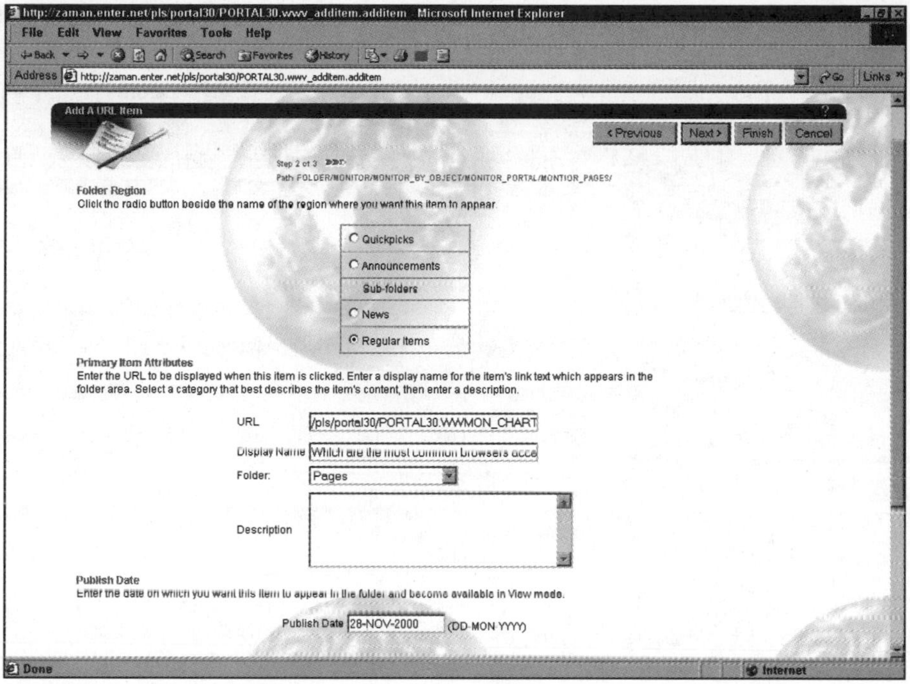

Figure 27-16: Item attribute panel

7. Press the Next button to continue, and then press the Finish button to save the new item entry.

When you return to the Content Area, as shown in Figure 27-17, you will notice that the new entry that you have made appears in the pages area as a Questions Answered item—just like the other entries. Oracle Portal automatically associates a number of perspectives with the new item in the Pages Content Area. In effect, you have just extended the Questions Answered Content Area with your own custom content.

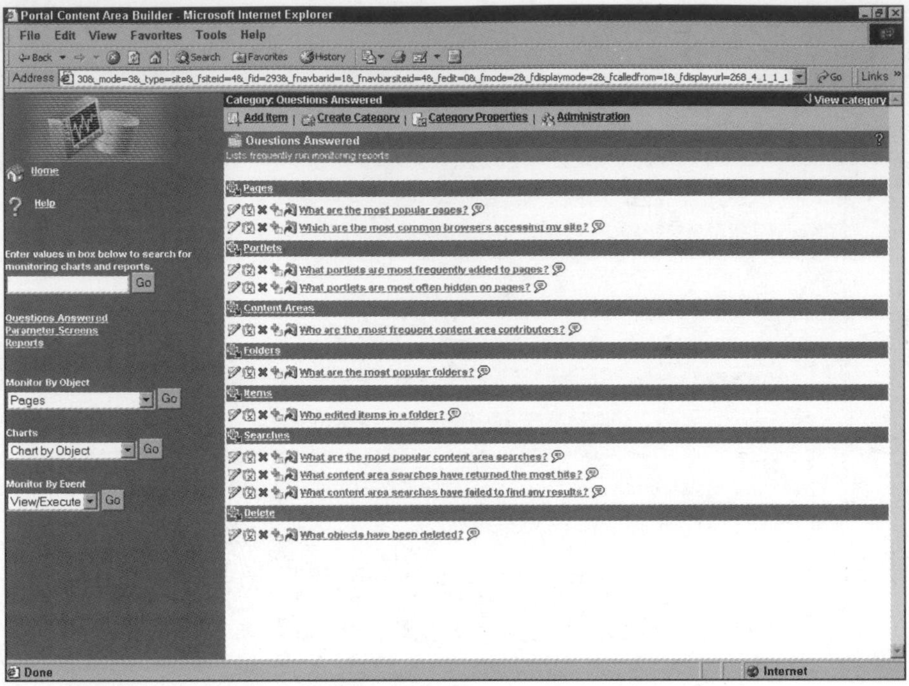

Figure 27-17: Modified Questions Answered panel

As you gain more experience working with the object charts and monitors, you may elect to use the chart and report wizards to create your own custom questions and answers based upon the various log file views. You may also elect to remove some of the preexisting Questions Answered reports if they do not meet your monitoring needs.

Monitoring Database Objects

There are two aspects to monitoring the performance of your Portal applications. In the preceding section, we introduced you to the various monitoring capabilities of the user objects through the Object monitoring tools. The run-time components are only half of the battle, however; you must also monitor activity at the database level in order to ensure that your site is performing up to expectations.

It is important to remember that part of the value proposition with Portal comes from storing both your code and your data inside the Oracle database. While you are no doubt familiar with the increased reliability and scalability that comes from this strategy, it also means that you must be careful to monitor the performance of your database and the Oracle server.

Note

In order to proceed with the following examples you will need to be logged on as a Portal Administrator. (You will also need DBA privileges for certain tasks.)

1. Navigate to the Administer Database panel from the main panel as shown in Figure 27-18.

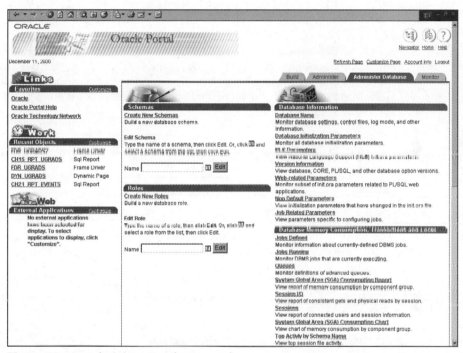

Figure 27-18: Administer Database panel

The database administration panel is divided into three basic sections.

✦ Database Information

✦ Database Memory Consumption, Transactions, and Locks

✦ Database Storage

If you are familiar with the database administrator tasks for the Oracle database, then you will note that these same items are accessible through the Oracle Enterprise Manager. Ideally, you will have the services of a professional Oracle DBA at your disposal before you deploy your Portal site into production. An experienced Oracle database administrator will likely have their own techniques and strategies for managing the database, and they are free to make use of these preexisting tools and techniques. There is nothing exceptional about Portal applications as far as the Oracle database is concerned. In fact, integration with the database is one of the strengths of the product.

Portal provides the database-monitoring tools to *supplement* the facilities of the Oracle Enterprise Manager. The Portal site administrator can use the database monitoring tools to complement the capabilities of the database administrator.

Caution   We would recommend that you have at least one database administrator available who is familiar with the care and feeding of the Oracle server before releasing a Portal application into production. It is not necessary for you to have access to a full-time database administrator, but the Oracle server and database should be professionally installed and configured before you embark on any serious application deployment with Portal.

Database information section

The first section in the database administration panel is the Database Information area. This section provides you with basic information about the Oracle server to which your Portal is connected.

All of the items in this section refer to the basic settings of the Oracle server. The information is delivered as Portal reports. None of these reports accept any parameters, because each link directly calls up a set of results. You cannot change any of the system parameters from these reports. The data these reports display give you the basic configuration of the database. From this panel, you can determine the version of the Oracle server and all of the associated information about the Oracle instance in which Portal is running. You are also permitted to view the initialization parameters set for the server from this interface.

Typically, you use the reports in this panel to verify that the server is properly configured. Portal provides this set of reports so you do not have to leave the Portal environment in order to verify these system settings.

Figure 27-19 displays the Database Initialization Parameters form, which is typical of the types of reports that are found in the Database Information section of the Administer database panel.

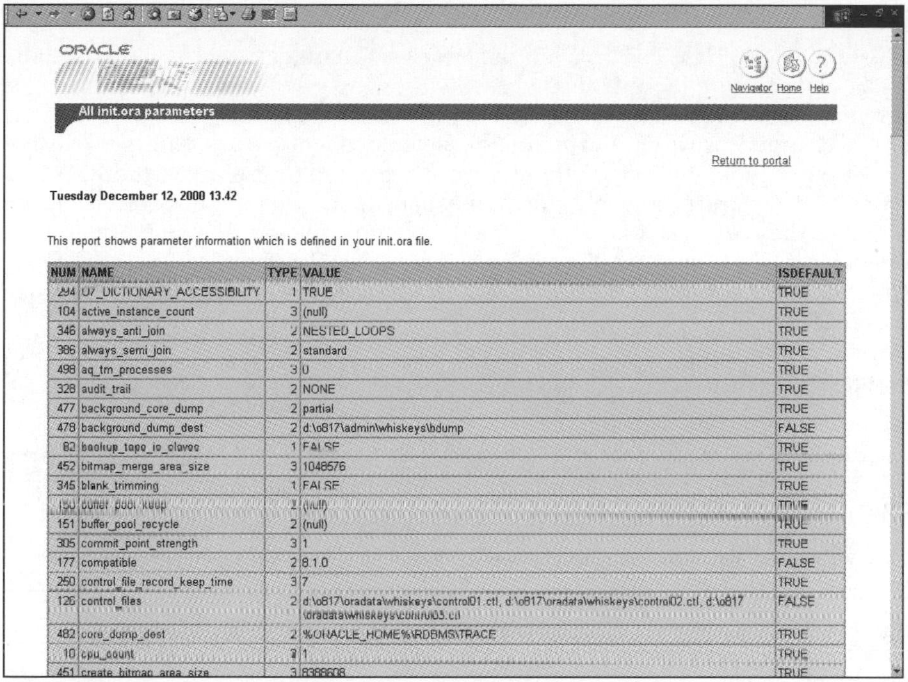

NUM	NAME	TYPE	VALUE	ISDEFAULT
294	O7_DICTIONARY_ACCESSIBILITY	1	TRUE	TRUE
104	active_instance_count	3	(null)	TRUE
346	always_anti_join	2	NESTED_LOOPS	TRUE
386	always_semi_join	2	standard	TRUE
498	aq_tm_processes	3	0	TRUE
328	audit_trail	2	NONE	TRUE
477	background_core_dump	2	partial	TRUE
478	background_dump_dest	2	d:\o817\admin\whiskeys\bdump	FALSE
82	backup_tape_io_slaves	1	FALSE	TRUE
452	bitmap_merge_area_size	3	1048576	TRUE
345	blank_trimming	1	FALSE	TRUE
150	buffer_pool_keep	2	(null)	TRUE
151	buffer_pool_recycle	2	(null)	TRUE
305	commit_point_strength	3	1	TRUE
177	compatible	2	8.1.0	FALSE
250	control_file_record_keep_time	3	7	TRUE
126	control_files	2	d:\o817\oradata\whiskeys\control01.ctl, d:\o817\oradata\whiskeys\control02.ctl, d:\o817\oradata\whiskeys\control03.ctl	FALSE
482	core_dump_dest	2	%ORACLE_HOME%\RDBMS\TRACE	TRUE
10	cpu_count	3	1	TRUE
451	create_bitmap_area_size	3	8388608	TRUE

Figure 27-19: Database Initialization Parameters report

A portal administrator would use the data in the Database Information reports when communicating configuration information to Oracle Support or to a database administrator. Portal does not allow you to change any of the parameters or settings in these reports. The real value of having them available within the portal interface is to allow administrators easy access to configuration information. This interface was not meant to replace utilities such as SQL*DBA or Oracle Enterprise Manager.

Database Memory Consumption, Transactions, and Locks section

The reports in this section of the Administer Database panel are more detailed than those in the preceding section. These reports are provided for database administrators and experienced Portal administrators. Performance problems with your Portal can often be uncovered by looking at the core transaction processing facilities of the database — such as memory, transaction statistics, and locks. Oracle Portal provides an interface to these lower-level configuration options so that experienced administrators can view this data directly from the portal, even if they are connecting from a remote location. Most of the information that is displayed in these reports is too detailed for a typical application developer, but an Oracle DBA will know exactly how to use this information.

Locks

The Oracle database controls multiuser access to objects by the use of database locks. Records are locked on an individual row-by-row basis in the database, which prevents multiple users from updating the same data at the same time. Because database updates within Portal do not typically occur across multiple HTML pages, they do not typically lock multiple rows at the same time. Furthermore, Portal defaults to *optimistic* locking, which only causes records to be locked at the exact moment they are updated. This limits the window of time in which updates from one user might block updates from a second user. However, users accessing the same data from outside of Portal using other applications may open and hold locks on records that block Portal users. You can use the lock reports within the Database Monitor to review the current status of locks within the current Oracle instance, as shown in Figure 27-20.

ORACLE

Report of Locks

Return to portal

Tuesday December 12, 2000 13.44

This report shows all locks.

ADDRESS OF LOCK STATE OBJECT	ADDRESS OF LOCK	SID	ORACLE USERNAME	OSUSER	TYPE OF LOCK	ID1	ID2	LOCK MODE HELD	LOCK MODE REQUESTED	CTIME	BLOCKING
028793FC	0287940C	2		SYSTEM	MR	6	0	4-share	4	0	No
0287943C	0287944C	2		SYSTEM	MR	5	0	4-share	4	0	No
0287947C	0287948C	2		SYSTEM	MR	4	0	4-share	4	0	No
028794BC	028794CC	2		SYSTEM	MR	3	0	4-share	4	0	No
028794FC	0287950C	2		SYSTEM	MR	2	0	4-share	4	0	No
0287953C	0287954C	2		SYSTEM	MR	1	0	4-share	4	0	No
028795BC	028795CC	2		SYSTEM	MR	7	0	4-share	4	0	No
028795FC	0287960C	3		SYSTEM	RT	1	0	6-exclusive	6	0	No
0287967C	0287968C	5		SYSTEM	TS	3	16777314	3-row exclusive	3	65478	No

Figure 27-20: Report of Locks

Note Within the development environment, Portal manages locks on components using *logical* locks as opposed to *physical* locks. These logical locks can be managed through the Utilities menu choice, but they do not appear in the lock reports. Physical locks are held by the database, whereas logical locks are changes to database fields that mark the record as "locked". Logical locks can persist across transactions (and sessions).

Redo logs and rollback segments

Oracle ensures that your data and transactions are reliable by the use of redo logs and rollback segments. Updates to the database are saved into redo logs, which can then be processed back against the database in the event of a system failure. The combination of database backups and redo logs ensures that your changes are not lost when your system fails. Portal provides the Redo Logs link to enable you to review the status of the redo logs for the current system.

When you write data to the database, Oracle copies the transaction information to a section of the database called a *rollback segment*. If an application needs to abort a particular transaction, Oracle uses the information contained in the rollback segments to restore the database to its original state. This is standard behavior for the database, and it is a requirement for supporting the transactional capabilities of SQL. In situations where you have lots of simultaneous updates to the database, the rollback segments can become a bottleneck. Portal provides several Rollback Segments links on the database administration page that enable you to check the status of the rollback segments.

| Note | You are not permitted to make any changes to either the redo logs or the rollback segments inside Portal. If you detect a problem in this area of the database, you need to have access to the Enterprise Manager in order to make the necessary adjustments. |

Sessions and memory structures

A large factor in determining the performance of your Oracle applications is the memory usage and allocation. The Oracle memory cache is called the System Global Area (SGA), and it contains the data cache and shared memory structures of the database. Through the Sessions and Memory Structures link on the Database Objects menu, you can monitor the status of the SGA from within Portal. Much of the data shown in these reports and charts are of no interest unless you have experience working as an Oracle database administrator. However, you can run the reports and share the output with Oracle support or your local database administrator if you are having performance problems with your Portal application. An Oracle DBA is able to determine that the SGA needs to be adjusted or tuned from the data in these reports.

Within the Sessions and Memory Structures section, there are two tools for monitoring individual user sessions inside the Oracle database. The Sessions link produces a report that shows the activity within the database on a user-by-user basis. The Sessions report contains a massive amount of detail about the users connected to Oracle, and it includes both Portal users as well as users connected to Oracle using other tools and applications.

| Caution | Portal makes use of a feature known as *connection pooling,* which enables multiple end users to share the same connection to the database. Portal makes at least one connection to the database for each DAD entry connected to Oracle. However, multiple end users may be accessing Oracle through the same connection within Portal. The Sessions report provides no indication of when several users are connection pooling through the same physical connection. |

In extreme cases, you may find that you need to isolate a USERID and terminate its connection to Oracle. Portal provides the Find and Kill Session(s) link to enable you to identify such processes.

1. Navigate to the Database Administration panel and click the Find and Kill Sessions link to display the panel as shown in Figure 27-21.

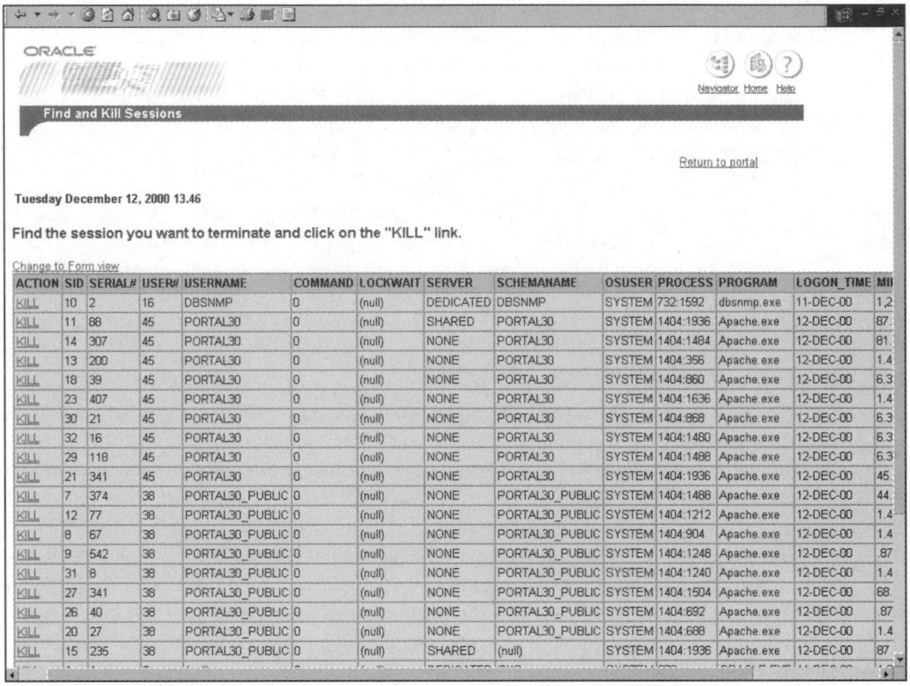

Figure 27-21: Find and Kill Sessions panel

This panel can display in two formats: as a form view or as a table view (as shown in Figure 27-21). The form view shows a single session at a time but you can scroll through all of the sessions. The table view shows all of the sessions as a series of entries in an HTML table similar to the standard Portal report format. Portal displays less information on this panel than the in the Sessions report because the goal of this panel is to enable you to find sessions and terminate them.

Portal displays all of the sessions connected to Oracle both inside and outside Portal. The Oracle database is composed of a number of system processes and all of them are connected to the database server and are listed in the report as shown in Figure 27-21. At the top of a report is a link next to the ACTION field called KILL. Clicking this link terminates the associated session. You do not have access to this option unless your Portal account has the DBA role assigned to it.

Caution Terminating user sessions should not be undertaken lightly. Killing a core Oracle session can cause the server to become unstable. We recommend that you get an Oracle DBA involved before you start terminating sessions. In situations where an end-user session is out of control, the ability to terminate the individual session is a powerful tool. However, if you are not familiar with the core Oracle server processes, you can inadvertently cause the server itself to shut down.

Portal provides this facility to enable you to rid the system of stray processes directly from the browser interface. Because Portal enables you to make use of any PL/SQL procedure, it is possible to create long-running update routines that may cause performance problems. You can use the Find and Kill Sessions report to identify the problem user session, and then terminate it with the KILL link.

Database objects and storage tools

System performance is affected by three factors: processing power, memory, and disk storage. In the preceding sections of this chapter, we introduced you to the various tools Portal provides for monitoring the performance of applications and your server in areas of processing speed and memory utilization. Portal provides an additional set of reports and charts under the Database Objects menu for monitoring disk space allocation and utilization. These particular charts and reports are useful to you even if you are not an experienced Oracle DBA. They are easy to read and provide you with a simple mechanism for ensuring that you are keeping track of the amount of space your applications are using and of how quickly your database tables and objects are growing.

Two classes of reports and charts are in this category: Objects and Storage. The Objects menu is focused on analyzing storage space usage by USERID and object type, while the Storage menu is geared toward reviewing the total amount of disk space available to you.

Oracle stores all objects into allocation units called *tablespaces,* and each tablespace is itself mapped onto one or more operating system files. The Database Storage section provides you with a series of charts and reports that display the status of the various tablespaces within the Portal database instance.

The starting point of your analysis will typically be the Chart of Tablespace Utilization link, which displays a set of charts showing the space utilization of the various tablespaces within your Portal environment. From these charts, you can determine whether you are running short of space in your tablespaces. Each of the charts has an associated report, and you can use the Report of Tablespace Utilization (in the Database Storage section of the Administer database panel) as shown in Figure 27-22 to review the status of your tablespaces in a report format.

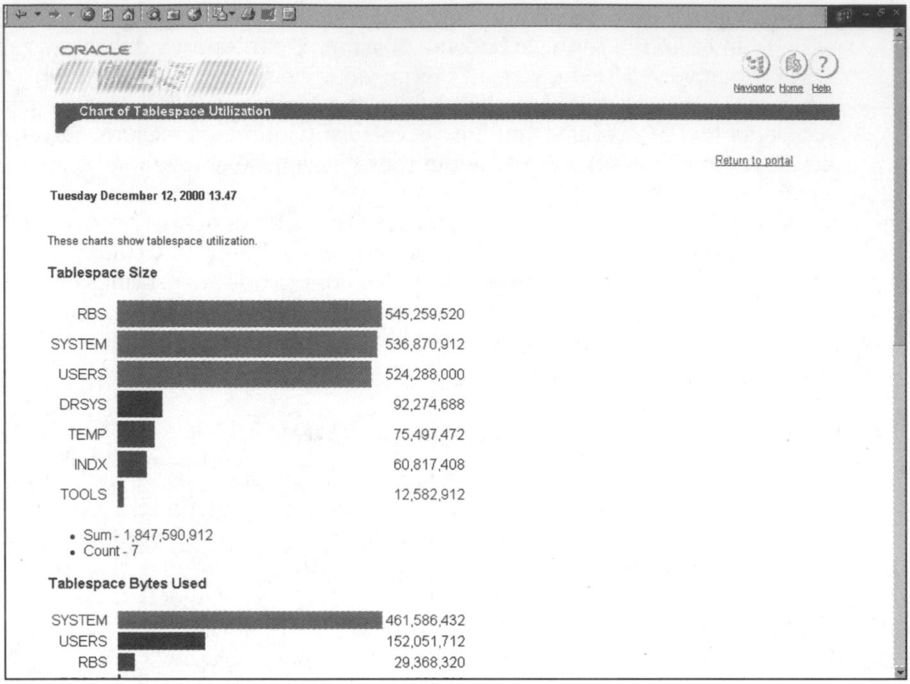

Figure 27-22: Chart of Tablespace Utilization

Once you have looked at the status of your tablespaces, you can use the Datafiles and Chart File Size links (in the Database Storage section of the Administer database panel) to examine the physical operating system files to which your tablespaces are mapped. If necessary, you can even look at the physical reads and writes to the operating system files. At the very least, you can use the data in these reports to take a snapshot of your application's use of disk space and spot trends over time. If you notice large jumps in the amount of space utilization over short periods of time, you may need to involve a professional Oracle DBA to help you determine the best course of action. Oracle provides the ability to limit database storage for users according to a quota system, and the final link on this page displays the quota limits for your users.

Note   The tablespace owner of each Oracle object is charged for all storage used by that object. Thus, when end users insert records into tables, the *owner* of the table is charged for the disk space usage of the new record. All of the examples and data for the sample applications in this book are stored in the NETU schema — and this is the USERID that is charged for the storage of all of the objects that you build.

Once you notice that a particular tablespace is filling up, you can use the additional links to review the detailed space usage for a selected tablespace.

There are two charts you can use to show the Oracle objects and USERIDs that are consuming the most disk space. The best use of these charts is tracking the use of space and the size of objects over time. By executing these charts on a weekly basis and comparing the results from week to week, you can spot trends in space utilization. Large changes in the size of objects over short periods are worth investigating.

You can also use these trends as a tool for planning purposes. For example, if your largest tables are consuming 25 percent of your total space and they are growing at 10 percent per week, you can plan ahead and acquire additional disk space before it is needed.

This particular panel area also provides a unique analysis tool in the form of the Recently Created Objects link. While all of the other links within the monitoring system are menus, reports, or charts, this particular menu choice points to a Portal calendar object. The calendar itself is built dynamically by Portal according to the dates on which all of the objects within your database were created. You can drill down on any individual date and view all of the objects that were created by any single Oracle USERID on that particular day. This can be a very powerful tool for investigating the history of the objects in your database. For example, you can determine the development patterns of your programmers by viewing the calendar across the development cycle for a particular application.

One additional report on this page displays the installation status of the Oracle HTP database packages. These packages are used by the database to render HTML pages, and they are used by Portal and the Oracle9iAS as well. The report link on this page shows you the status of the installation of these packages.

Changing the Activity Log Settings

You can set the interval for the log switching within the administration subsystem.

✦ Navigate to the main administration page (Figure 27-2) and select the Global Settings link to display the page shown in Figure 27-23.

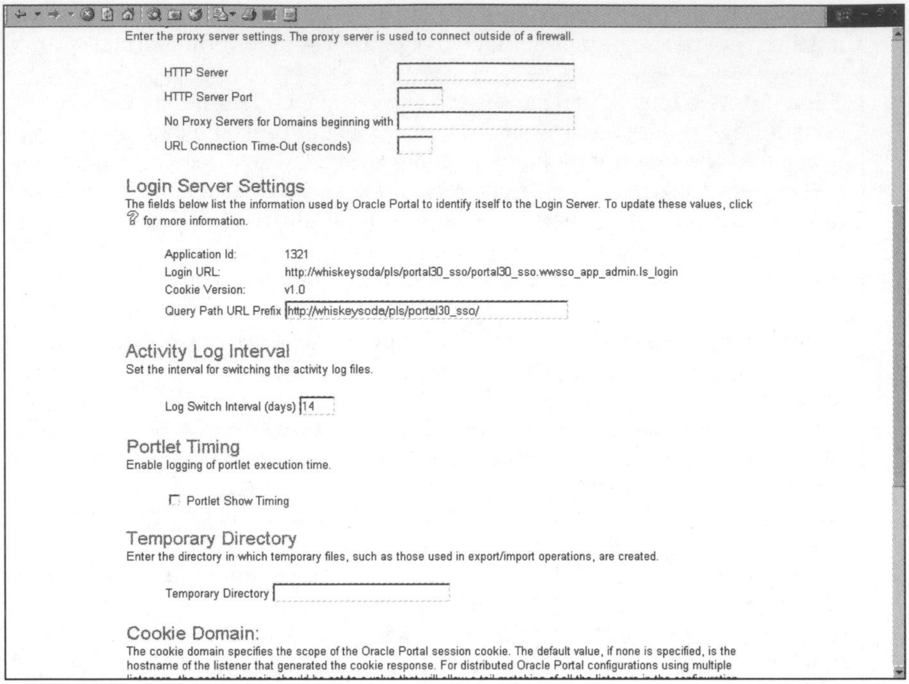

Figure 27-23: Set activity log attributes

The only attribute you have control over for the activity logs is the number of days that Portal waits between switching physical activity logs. The change is transparent to you, because Portal monitoring reports work the same regardless of which log is currently being used for processing. The default behavior is to switch to a new log every two weeks, but you may wish to switch logs more frequently if your Web site generates a lot of activity. Changing the interval is as simple as entering a new value and saving the change using the Apply button.

Tip   If you are interested in looking for long-term trends, you are free to export the data in the inactive log file to a backup table and create your own reports and charts against this backup table. This enables you to store and analyze the raw log data over a much longer period of time. (You will remember that Portal overwrites the data within the log files when it reaches the Log Switch Interval.)

Summary

Many things can have a positive or negative impact on your site, but two of the more important items are the performance of the site and the popularity of the items within the site. Sites that suffer from performance problems are rarely popular with users regardless of the cool items and applications contained within them. It is hard for users to be productive and happy when their response times are poor.

In this chapter, you worked with a set of tools that can help you to judge the performance of your site and keep your applications moving along swiftly. Even in cases where the performance is solid, however, users complain if they are forced to navigate through reams of data just to find the items they are looking for. Portal's monitoring tools enable you to determine the popularity of each item in your site and to profile the users accessing these items.

By reviewing this data carefully, you can determine whether users are having trouble finding the data they need, or whether certain items are just not useful. You can use this information to realign your site and weed out the less popular items to make your site concise and easy to use. In the next chapter we'll take a look at writing custom portlets for use with Oracle Portal.

✦   ✦   ✦

Advanced Techniques

P A R T

In This Part

Chapter 28
Creating Your Own
Portlet and Provider

Chapter 29
Advanced Tips and
Techniques

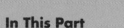

Creating Your Own Portlet and Provider

In This Chapter

Using the Portal Development Kit

Using Portal Services

Creating a Portlet with PL/SQL

Creating a Database Provider with PL/SQL

Registering Your Provider

Using Your Portlet

Customizing Your Portlet

Calling a Built-in Portlet

Creating a Web Portlet and Provider with Java Server Pages

At this point, you have become reasonably well versed in using Oracle9*i*AS Portal to create applications, components, Content Areas, and portal pages. Oracle9*i*AS Portal gives you the ability to create and integrate many types of content into a portal.

But what if you want to integrate information from a source that is not readily accessible through any of the means available in Oracle9*i*AS Portal? You have another option — to create your own portlet that can then be integrated into the Oracle9*i*AS Portal environment.

Using the Portal Development Kit

We have always believed that being able to extend a product to achieve a desired end result is a good thing, as opposed to having to shape your design and development efforts to fit into the limitations of the product. Oracle9*i*AS Portal gives you that ability with the Portlet Development Kit, or PDK.

The PDK is essentially a documentation set that explains the Application Programming Interface, or API, that you will need to use to create and use a portlet. To create a portlet with the PDK, you will have to create both the portlet provider, which will act as the interface between the portlet and the Oracle9*i*AS Portal environment, and the portlet itself, which will supply the information that will be seen in the portal page. Once you have created these components, though, you will be able to use the portlet in any Oracle9*i*AS Portal application, so the effort in creating a customized portlet can pay off for a long time.

Make no mistake, using the PDK will involve a level of coding that is far beyond what you have experienced up until now. We will be creating the code for the portlet and the portlet provider using PL/SQL, the internal language that is standard in the Oracle database. You could also create these components in Java, and the PDK contains examples of how to do this.

Our goal in this chapter is to help you to understand the scope of the task of creating a portlet, not to exercise all of the capabilities available to you in the PDK. To fully explain and examine the PDK would take another book the size of this one. Hopefully, the examples explained in the rest of this chapter will give you a feeling for what it takes to create your own portlets.

Before we jump into the process of coding a portlet and portlet provider, we should begin by explaining a few of the basic concepts and categories of portlets.

Categories of portlets

By now, you should be very familiar with the concept of portlets. You used portlets way back in Chapter 7 to create your own portal page. In fact, there are two types of portlets:

+ **Database portlets:** A database portlet is a portlet that you explicitly write to be run inside of an Oracle database. Consequently, you would create a database portlet with either PL/SQL or Java stored procedures. A database provider and its portlets communicate via internal procedure calls. All the built-in portlets, or portlets that are created from components or Content Areas, are database portlets.

+ **Web portlets:** A Web portlet is a portlet that you explicitly write to be run outside of the Oracle database. A Web portlet can be written in any Web language, such as Java Server Pages, Perl, or C — or even, for that matter, with Microsoft's Active Server Pages technology. A Web provider communicates with Oracle9iAS Portal using standard HTTP calls.

Why would you use one of these types of portlets instead of another? You would use a built-in portlet whenever you can, since Oracle9iAS Portal provides wizards for building these types of portlets, which makes them easy to implement.

You would use a database portlet whenever you are going to write your own portlet and you anticipate that it will access the database frequently. Both PL/SQL and Java stored procedures can be used to easily access data in your Oracle database, so you might as well take advantage of this integration when it makes sense. If you are an experienced Oracle developer, you might find it easier to create database portlets with stored procedures than to use another development environment.

You would use a Web portlet if you were more familiar with standard Web development tools, like Java Server Pages. You would also create a Web portlet if you wanted to integrate external applications into a portal framework, because it is probably easier to access these Web-based applications with a standard Web development environment.

You could also use a Web portlet to access routines implemented in the database. From a scalability and performance standpoint, this approach can sometimes work better.

Note   Later in this chapter you will learn how to create portlets with Dynamic Services, which are wizard-driven interfaces used to creating portlets that use information from other Web pages.

Both database portlets and Web portlets can use an array of services that are offered to portal developers by the Oracle9*i*AS Portal framework.

Using Portlet Services

In Chapter 6, you learned about the basic flow between the time a user requests a portal page and the time the page is delivered back to that user. The Portal Server plays a key role in this series of actions. The Portal Server also provides a set of services that portlet writers can use in building their portlets.

There are seven sets of services provided by the portal framework:

✦ **End-user personalization is used to store personalized information for each user that will shape the actions of their version of the portlet.** The end-user personalization services work just like the Customization pages used in the built-in portlets.

✦ **Session storage is used to store information for the duration of a user's session with Oracle9*i*AS Portal.** This type of information can be used by many different portlets, since it will exist beyond the scope of a single portlet.

✦ **Context provides connection information about the user, such as you can see within the Oracle9*i*AS Portal environment.**

✦ **Security allows you to validate a user's credentials within your own portlet.**

✦ **NLS gives you a framework for supporting multiple languages — the National Language Setting.** This service does not perform translations, but it allows you to include multiple translations in a single portlet and manipulate them, depending on the NLS setting of a particular user.

✦ **Logging gives you the ability to log various events within your portlet.**

✦ **Error handling, as the name implies, handles errors in your portlets.** Using this service provides for a consistent display of error messages in your portlet.

The Dynamic PDK

As mentioned several times in the text, we have included some routines and relevant pieces of code from the Portal Development Kit as part of the materials for this chapter. The version of the PDK that we are using was released in December of 2000.

You can get the latest and greatest version of the PDK from Oracle Technology Network (OTN), which you can sign up for at no cost. (You can get to OTN through the main Oracle Web page, www.oracle.com.) We strongly recommend that you do, because the PDK may be updated as frequently as once a month.

We also hand out this overall caveat—there may be changes in the PDK or its contents that make the examples in this chapter either less than optimal, or even invalid. We don't foresee a change that would actually make the code that you write for these samples invalid, because that would invalidate many other portlets, but there very well could be enhanced tools and support as part of future releases of the PDK. If either of these things happens, we will post a message about the changes on our Web site.

Each of these services can be accessed through an Application Program Interface, or API. You will be using some of these services as you create your own portals in the remainder of this chapter.

At this point, you have enough of an understanding of the portlet architecture to jump in and begin building your own portlets. You will start by creating a very simple portlet with PL/SQL, the language that has been a part of the Oracle database for years.

Creating a Portlet with PL/SQL

In this section, we will walk you through the creation of a very simple portlet with PL/SQL. Rather than create the entire PL/SQL package required for the portlet, you can copy a sample portlet that comes with the PDK as a starting point and simply modify portions of the code to create a new portlet.

There are a number of steps you have to take in order to create your first portlet.

Exposing the Oracle9*i*AS Portal APIs

The first step you must take to create a portlet is to expose the underlying API calls that your portlet will use. There is a simple script that lets you accomplish this goal.

1. Log on to SQL*Plus with the user name and password for the schema that contains your Oracle9*i*AS Portal packages. For a default installation, you should use the portal30 user name and password.

2. Run the script `provsyns.sql`, which is in the folder for the materials for this chapter on the CD-ROM included with this book, with the following command:

`@provsyns.sql provider_schema`

where `provsyns.sql` includes the pathname for the file and the `provider_schema` is the name of the schema where you will be installing your portlet. For the purposes of this example, we will be assuming that you will install your portlet in the `NETU` schema that you have been using to store the rest of your application.

Running this script creates a series of synonyms for the PL/SQL packages your portlet will call. These PL/SQL packages are, in effect, the API for Oracle9iAS Portal.

Note
For the rest of the next few sections, we will be dealing with PL/SQL code. A detailed explanation of the structure and syntax of PL/SQL is beyond the scope of this chapter and book. If you are unfamiliar with this language and want to learn more about it, we can recommend the excellent series of PL/SQL books by Steven Feuerstein, published by O'Reilly and Associates.

Caution
You could look into the PL/SQL packages to see exactly what they were doing, but we do not recommend this practice. The purpose of using an API is to guarantee an interface to an application. This guarantee allows the developers to modify the underlying implementation of those calls, while still not damaging any portlets that use the calls. If you muck around with the underlying implementations, these guarantees are null and void.

Also, the Oracle9iAS Portal team recommends that you create your portlets outside of the schema in which you installed Oracle9iAS Portal. There is a possibility that the calls that your portlet makes to the PL/SQL packages could inadvertently access internal, unreleased versions of the calls, which could lead to trouble down the road.

3. Rather than have you enter all the code necessary to create a portlet (and, in the next section, a portlet provider), we have provided shell packages that you will modify to create your portlet. We have "borrowed" these packages from the PDK itself. The shells for creating the portlet package specification and body are named CH28_1_PORTLET.PKS and CH28_1_PORTLET.PKB, respectively, and are found in the Chapter 28 directory on the book's CD-ROM.

4. Open the CH28_1_PORTLET.PKS in your favorite PL/SQL code editor.

On the CD-ROM
The CD-ROM for this book includes a nifty PL/SQL code editor, PL/SQL Developer.

The .PKS file is the PL/SQL specification for the package. The specification, as its name implies, describes the procedures that will be implemented in the PL/SQL package. You will not want to modify the substance of the specification, but you will want to change the name of the package.

5. Change the text at the top of the file, which currently reads

```
CREATE OR REPLACE
package HELLOWORLD_PORTLET
is
```

to

```
CREATE OR REPLACE
package CH28_1_PORTLET
is
```

6. Change the text at the end of the file from

```
end HELLOWORLD_PORTLET;
/
```

to

```
end CH28_1_PORTLET;
/
```

7. Save the changes to the file.

8. Open the file CH28_1_PORTLET.PKB in your favorite PL/SQL editor.

9. Change the package name at the beginning and end of the file to CH28_1_PORTLET, just as you did for the .PKS specification file.

10. At the top of the file, you have to identify the provider for the portlet, which we will create later in this chapter, and the portlet itself. Change the values in the existing code to the following code, which has the new values shown in bold:

```
function get_portlet_info
    (
        p_provider_id in integer
       ,p_language in varchar2
    )
    return wwpro_api_provider.portlet_record
    is
        l_portlet        wwpro_api_provider.portlet_record;
    begin
        l_portlet.id := ch28_provider.PORTLET_CH28_1;
        l_portlet.provider_id := p_provider_id;
        l_portlet.title := 'Chapter 28—First Portlet';
        l_portlet.name := 'PORTLET_CH28_1';
        l_portlet.description :=
            'This portlet is my first sample portlet';
```

You can see that the portlet ID is not the same name as you assigned to the portlet itself. The portlet ID and the portlet name are both used by the portlet to identify itself to the portlet provider, which you will create later in this chapter.

You should also note that you have changed the name of the provider shown as the first part of the `l_portlet.id` variable, which now points to the `ch28_provider` that you will be creating in the next section.

11. Use the find function of your editor to find the start of the show procedure, which starts with the text `procedure show`. The beginning of this procedure is where you will declare any additional variables you need in the procedure, so add the code shown in bold to specify a couple more variables that you will need in this portlet:

```
procedure show
    (
    p_portlet_record
wwpro_api_provider.portlet_runtime_record
    )
    is
        l_portlet        wwpro_api_provider.portlet_record;
        l_text_holder    VARCHAR2(20000);
        l_text           VARCHAR2(20000);
        l_date_holder    DATE;
    begin
```

You will be using the `l_text_holder` variable to assemble the text strings that you will then format to be included as a part of the display of your portlet. The `l_date_holder` variable is used to hold a date value. The `l_text` variable will be used to hold the same text as it is formatted by an Oracle9*i*AS Portal procedure for inclusion in the portlet, as you will see in the next step.

Note Make these two variables large, since you will be using them to receive a complete built-in portlet later in this chapter.

12. Find the following text in the file:

```
htp.p(wwui_api_portlet.portlet_text(
                p_string    =>  'Hello World - Mode Show'.
                p_level     =>  1
                ));
```

This code marks the beginning of the part of the SHOW procedure where you will add PL/SQL code to actually show the information you want in the portlet.

13. Add the following code in bold to the code in the package body:

```
htp.p(wwui_api_portlet.portlet_text(
                p_string    =>  'Hello World - Mode Show'
                ,p_level    =>  1
                ));
l_text_holder := <br> 'Welcome,' ||
INITCAP(wwctx_api.get_user || '!';
l_text := wwui_api_portlet.portlet_text(
p_string    =>  l_text_holder.
p_level     =>  1  );
htp.p(l_text);
htp.para;
```

The SHOW Procedure

The SHOW procedure is where the most visible work of the portlet takes place. As the name implies, this procedure is called when the Parallel Servlet that is used to assemble the page calls the portlet. The SHOW procedure can be called with one of seven modes that are used for different types of displays:

✦ **MODE_SHOW** displays the portlet as part of a shared page of portlets.

✦ **MODE_ABOUT** displays information about the portlet.

✦ **MODE_EDIT** calls a customization page for the portlet.

✦ **MODE_HELP** calls a help page for the portlet.

✦ **MODE_EDIT_DEFAULTS** calls a page that can be used to edit the default values for the customization of the page.

✦ **MODE_SHOW_DETAILS** displays the portlet in full-page mode. (This mode is the same as the standard full-page mode for components, while the MODE_SHOW is used when you click on the Run As Portlet menu choice on the Manage Component page.)

✦ **MODE_PREVIEW** calls a version of the portlet that is displayed when a user is adding the portlet to a page.

For this part of the chapter, you are modifying the code in the SHOW_MODE portion of the procedure, after the borders and header have been drawn. Later, you will create the page that will be used for the MODE_EDIT mode.

The first line of code assigns a value to the variable that will hold the text string targeted for your portlet. You are concatenating some standard, constant text — the welcome message and the trailing exclamation mark (because you are pretty dang excited about this new portlet thingy), and a value that is returned from one of the API calls to the Oracle9*i*AS Portal server. The `wwctx_api.get_user` call will return the name of the current user. This call is a part of the context service mentioned earlier in this chapter.

There are two other features in this line of code. First of all, you have inserted a specific HTML tag, the <BR>, or break, tag, at the beginning of the line, to ensure proper spacing. Secondly, you have used a PL/SQL function, the INITCAP function, to convert the user name from all capitals to the more attractive form of having the first letter of the name as a capital letter and the rest of the string in lowercase.

The next call reformats the string assembled in the `l_text_holder` variable to the `l_text` variable. The call used for this reformatting is `wwui_api_portlet.portlet_text`, another Oracle9*i*AS Portal API call. Remember that your portlet is part of a larger portal page, which in turn resides in the browser of a particular user. There are stylistic conventions that are used by Oracle9*i*AS Portal for displaying all the text in the browser in a consistent manner. Oracle9*i*AS Portal uses Cascading Style Sheets (CSS), an Internet standard, to format the text for a portlet so that it has a uniform look and feel. By simply leaving the reformatting to Oracle9*i*AS Portal, you can guarantee that your portlet will adopt whatever look and feel has been specified by anyone who uses it.

The last two lines of code simply use a PL/SQL procedure to write the text in HTML format, and then to add a paragraph tag (<P>) to the end of the code. These lines of code use procedures from the `htp` package, which contains calls for creating HTML code and tags from PL/SQL.

You could stop here, since you have created a portlet that will display something. But remember that the reason you might choose to use PL/SQL is because it is nicely integrated with the database, so let's add a few more lines of code

14. Add the following code in bold to the code in the package body:

```
htp.p(wwui_api_portlet.portlet_text(
                p_string    =>  'Hello World - Mode Show',
                p_level     =>  1
                ));
l_text_holder := 'Welcome,' || wwctx_api.get_user || '!';
l_text := wwui_api_portlet.portlet_text(
p_string    =>  l_text_holder,
p_level     =>  1  );
htp.p(l_text);
htp.para;
SELECT SYSDATE INTO l_date_holder FROM DUAL;

l_text_holder := '<br> The current date is ' ||

TO_CHAR(l_date_holder, 'Month DD, YYYY') || '.'
l_text := wwui_api_portlet.portlet_text(
p_string    =>  l_text_holder,
p_level     =>  1  );
htp.p(l_text);
htp.para;
```

The last four lines of this code are the same as the previous section of code, and they perform the same function of formatting the information and including it for display in the portal. The first line of code is a standard SQL statement that is used to retrieve the current date from the server into the date variable you declared earlier in this section. The second line of code simply creates a text string that will be formatted to match the portlet, with the date formatted to match the specification in the second part of the TO_CHAR function. Because you are using PL/SQL code, you can use the same TO_CHAR function that you would use in a standard SQL statement.

15. Save the changes to the package body file. You will wait until you have created and compiled the code for the portlet provider to compile this code.

There you have it — you have successfully created your first custom coded portlet. It really wasn't that difficult. There is a lot more that you can (and should) do with portlets, some of which we will get to later in the chapter. But for now, your next step is to create a provider for your portlet.

Creating a Database Provider with PL/SQL

As you learned back in Chapter 6, a portlet does not stand alone. A portlet provider is used as the intermediary between your Oracle9iAS Portal environment and the portlet itself. To complete the creation of your first custom portlet, you will have to create a database portlet provider for the portlet.

For this task, just as for the previous portlet creation, you will edit the code for an existing portlet provider. The code for the provider was taken from some sample code included in the PDK, and the files for the package spec and body are named CH28_PROVIDER.PKS and CH28_PROVIDER.PKB, respectively.

On the CD-ROM   These files are in the Chapter 28 directory on the CD-ROM included with this book. Also included in this file are completed versions of these files, if you would prefer to simply use them to install, under the names of CH28_PROVIDER_DONE.PKS and CH28_PROVIDER_DONE.PKB.

1. Open the CH28_PROVIDER.PKS file in your favorite PL/SQL editor.

2. Change the name of the package specification to `CH28_PROVIDER` at the start and end of the file, as you did for the portlet code.

3. At the very top of the package spec, you can see a line of code that reads

   ```
   PORTLET_HELLOWORLD constant integer := 1;
   ```

   You should change this line of code to point to your new portlet, so that it reads

   ```
   PORTLET_CH28_1 constant integer := 1;
   ```

   to reflect the name of the portlet you created in the previous section.

4. Save the changes you have made to the CH28_PROVIDER.PKS file and close the file.

5. Open the CH28_PROVIDER.PKB file.

6. Change the package body name to `CH28_PROVIDER` at the top and bottom of the file, as you did with the other files.

You will have to change many procedures in the package body for the provider. All of these changes involve changing a couple of values so that your provider can properly communicate with your portlet. Since both of these are PL/SQL packages, you can use simple names to point from the provider to the portlet.

7. The first procedure body you will have to modify in this file is the `get_port-let` procedure. This procedure calls the portlets associated with this provider to get information about them. Find this procedure in the text and you will see a block of code that looks like this:

```
if (p_portlet_id = PORTLET_HELLOWORLD) then
          return helloworld_portlet.get_portlet_info(
               p_provider_id  => p_provider_id,
               p_language     => p_language
               );
```

Change this piece of code by replacing the sections in bold:

```
if (p_portlet_id = portlet_ch28_1) then
          return ch28_1_portlet.get_portlet_info(
               p_provider_id  => p_provider_id,
               p_language     => p_language
               );
```

8. The next procedure in the package body is the `get_portlet_list`, which returns a list of the portlets available for this provider. Find the block of code shown here:

```
if (helloworld_portlet.is_runnable(
          p_provider_id     =>  p_provider_id,
          p_reference_path  =>  null)
     ) then
          l_cnt := l_cnt + 1;
          l_portlet_list(l_cnt) := get_portlet(
               p_provider_id  => p_provider_id,
               p_portlet_id   => PORTLET_HELLOWORLD,
               p_language     => p_language
               );

     end if;
```

Now change the reference to `helloworld_portlet` to `ch28_1_portlet` and the `p_portlet_id` value from `PORTLET_HELLOWORLD` to `PORTLET_CH28_1`.

9. The next procedure in the package body is the `is_runnable` procedure called in the previous step. This procedure is used to determine if the portlet should be made available through the portlet provider. Change the code in the first part of this procedure, replacing the existing values of `helloworld_portlet` and `PORTLET_HELLOWORLD` with the values in bold, so that the code reads

```
if (p_portlet_instance.portlet_id = PORTLET_CH28_1) then
          return ch28_1_portlet.is_runnable(
p_provider_id =>
   p_portlet_instance.provider_id,
               p_reference_path  =>
   p_portlet_instance.reference_path
               );
```

You might include code in this procedure that would impose restrictions on the display of the portlet in the portlet list, such as a security restriction based on the identity of the user.

10. The next procedure in the package body is the `register_portlet` procedure, which takes care of the task of registering the portlet properly. At this point, you should start to understand that you will have to change the bold sections of the code shown next:

```
if (p_portlet_instance.portlet_id = PORTLET_CH28_1) then
        ch28_1_portlet.register(p_portlet_instance);
```

11. If the provider registers the portlet, it also has to deregister the portlet, which is the next procedure in the package. You should change the bold values in the code here:

```
if (p_portlet_instance.portlet_id = PORTLET_CH28_1) then
        CH28_1_portlet.deregister(p_portlet_instance);
```

12. The `show_portlet` and `copy_portlet` procedures, which come next, have code that requires the same changes as the last two procedures. The `show_portlet` procedure calls the corresponding function in the portlet, with one of the modes mentioned in the sidebar. The `copy_portlet` procedure copies the customization and default settings for a portlet when the page containing the portlet is copied.

13. The final procedure in the package body, and the final procedure that you will have to change is the `describe_portlet_parameters` procedure. This procedure is an internal call used by the Oracle9*i*AS Portal environment to get the parameters associated with the portlet. You should modify the code to include the bold values shown here:

```
if (p_portlet_id = PORTLET_CH28_1) then
        return ch28_1_portlet.describe_parameters(
            p_provider_id     => p_provider_id
            ,p_language        => p_language
            );
```

Note

Were you beginning to think that you could have simply performed a global search and replace for the terms PORTLET_HELLOWORLD and HELLOWORLD_PORTLET in the file? You would be right — all you really did was replace references to the HELLOWORLD portlet with the corresponding references to the CH28_1_PORTLET. But we chose to have you go through the code to get some understanding of the different procedures and functions that make up the package.

14. You have completed making all the housekeeping changes to link your provider with your portlet. Save your new version of the provider file.

15. Once again, start SQL*Plus and log in as the owner of the schema that will own the portlet, as you did for the portlet code itself.

16. Enter the command `@CH28_PROVIDER.PKS` at the SQL*Plus prompt, preceding the file name with a path name if necessary. The code should compile without errors.

> **Note**
>
> If you are getting errors in your code, you can either track them down, which would be good for your learning process, or simply use completed versions of the code that we have included on the CD-ROM. We have included a clean version of the package spec and body in the Chapter 28 directory with the names CH28_1_PORTLET_DONE.PKS and CH28_1_PORTLET_DONE.PKB, respectively for the portlet and CH28_PROVIDER_DONE.PKS and CH28_PROVIDER_DONE.PKB, for the provider.

17. Enter the command `@CH28_PROVIDER.PKB` at the SQL*Plus prompt, preceding the file name with a path name if necessary. The code should compile without errors.

18. You can now compile the portlet code you created earlier. Enter the code `@CH28_1_PORTLET.PKS` at the SQL*Plus prompt, preceding the file name with a path name if necessary. The code should compile without errors.

19. Enter the code `@CH28_1_PORTLET.PKB` at the SQL*Plus prompt, preceding the file name with a path name if necessary. The code should also compile without errors.

20. Exit SQL*Plus.

You have successfully created your very own portlet and portlet provider. In order to be able to use them successfully, you have to make the Oracle9iAS Portal environment aware of their existence, which you will do in the next section.

Registering Your Provider

You have to register your portlet provider with Oracle9iAS Portal, so that the Portal Server knows to include your new provider in the list of providers used in the Add Portlet page.

1. Log on to Oracle9iAS Portal as the `NETUDEV` user, since you will need to have administrative privileges.

2. Click on the Administration tab in the main portlet region.

3. Click on the Add A Portlet Provider link in the Provider section of the page, which will bring up the page shown in Figure 28-1.

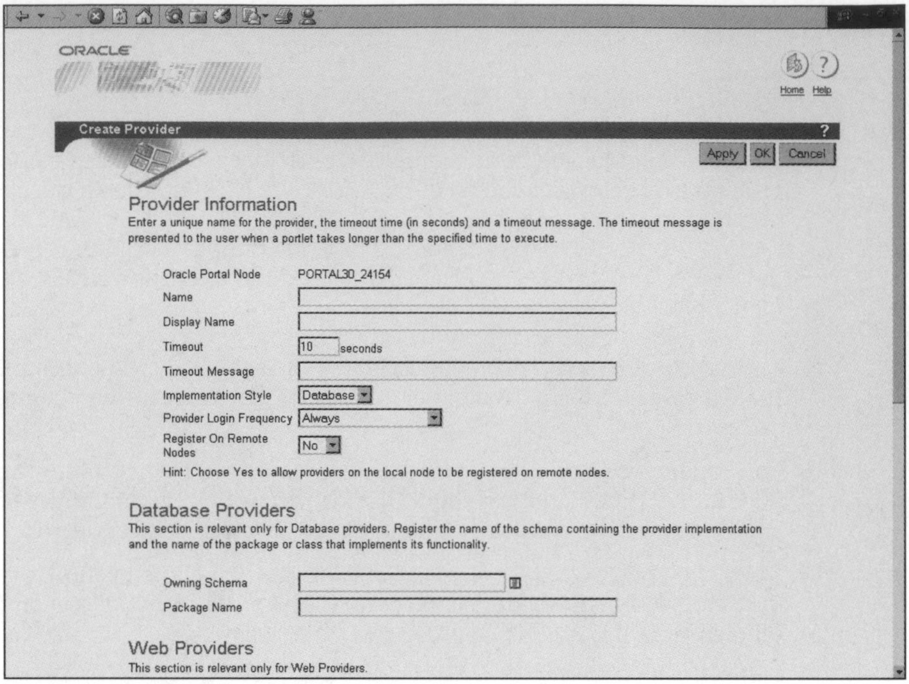

Figure 28-1: Adding a portlet provider

4. In the upper portion of the page, enter **Chapter28** as the Name and **Chapter 28** as the Display Name.

5. The Timeout value represents the number of seconds that the Parallel Page Engine will wait for a response from this provider. Enter **100** for this value, although in the real world you might not want a user waiting this long for a portal page to come back.

6. Enter **Application Provider timed out** as the Timeout Message.

7. Leave Database selected as the Implementation Style.

8. Change the value for the Provider Login Frequency by selecting Never. If a user comes to this portlet without logging in, the welcome message may be a bit impersonal, but for the purposes of this exercise, you don't have to require a log in.

9. Leave the value for the Register On Remote Nodes set to No.

10. Go to the next section of the page, labeled Database Providers. Enter **NETU** as the Owning Schema name, and **CH28_PROVIDER** as the Package Name.

11. Click on the OK button.

You are ready to rock with your very own personally created portlet.

Using Your Portlet

At this point, the beauty of the Oracle9iAS Portal environment will start to come through. You have done some mildly intensive coding work to set up all the links between your new provider and your new portlet, but you will see the value of that work in the seamless integration of your new portlet into the overall Oracle9iAS Portal world.

1. Go to the Navigator in the Oracle9iAS Portal environment and click on the Pages tab.

2. Click on the Top-Level Pages folder and click on the Edit link for the page you created in Chapter 7 (and have modified along the way), the Net University Home Page.

3. Click on the Add Portlet Icon in the region on the far left.

4. When the Add Portlet page comes up in a new browser window, scroll down to the bottom of the left frame. There it is, as shown in Figure 28-2 — your brand new provider and its own portlet!

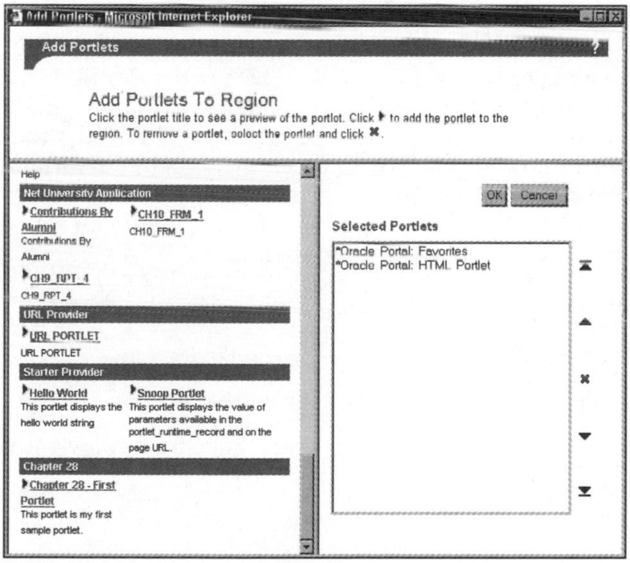

Figure 28-2: Your new provider and portlet

5. Click on the portlet shown for the Chapter 28 provider. When the portlet shows up in the window, you will see that the preview of the portlet, as shown in Figure 28-3, doesn't look exactly right.

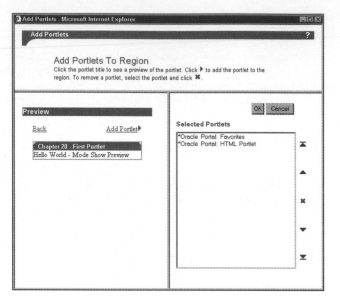

Figure 28-3: The lack of a preview of your new portlet

The reason for that is simple—we never bothered to change the MODE_PREVIEW code, so the preview code for the old HELLOWORLD portlet is still showing. As mentioned in the sidebar earlier in this chapter, the preview shown in this page is described with code that you write for the MODE_SHOW_PREVIEW mode of the SHOW procedure. We didn't want to take up more of this chapter with detailed coding in order to display a preview of the portlet. However, you would definitely want to spend the time and effort to include a preview of a portlet if you were planning on making the portlet available to other developers.

6. Click on the Add portlet link to add the new portlet to the region.

7. Click on the OK button to return to the Customize Page page.

8. Click on the Close button to close the Customize Page page.

9. Click on the name of the Net University Home Page in the Navigator to see the new version of the page, as shown in Figure 28-4.

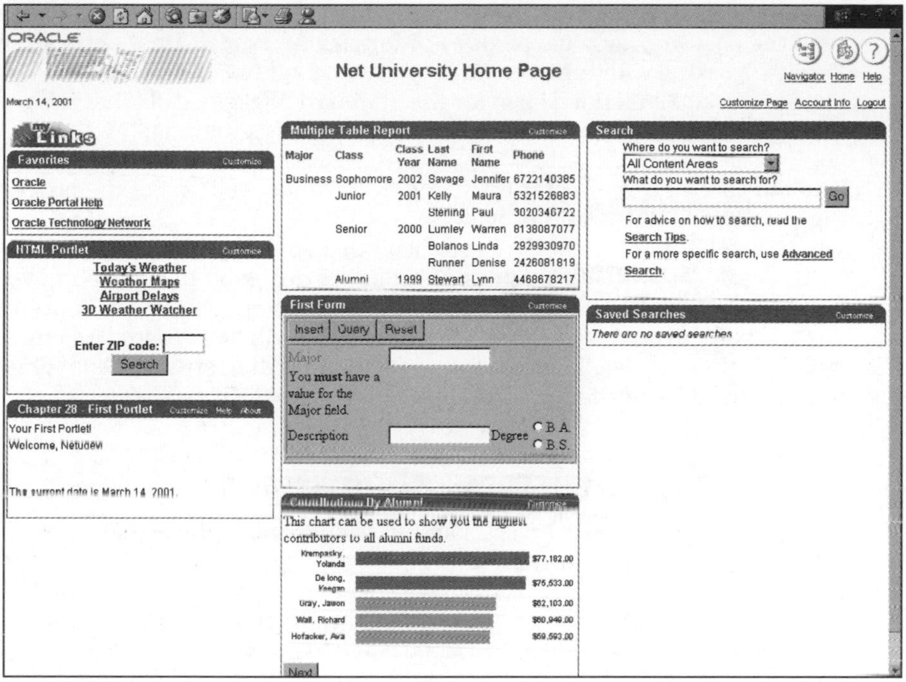

Figure 28-4: The new version of the Net University home page, with your new portlet

There it is, nicely molded into your environment. At this point, the labor you put into creating the portlet hopefully seems like a small price to pay to add functionality with the same look and feel as the rest of your environment — regardless of how that environment was designed for you or any of the users of your page.

In the next section, you will take the next step — enabling your new portlet for user customization.

Customizing Your Portlet

You have already experienced one of the cool things about creating your own portlets — they come out having the same look and feel as the other portlets on a page. But remember that the Oracle9*i*AS Portal environment includes a complete personalization system, which allows individual users to customize the look and feel of their own pages and portlets.

There are several steps that you need to implement in your portlet in order to support the customization capabilities of Oracle9*i*AS Portal. Most of these steps involve working with the specific API calls and syntax, both for the APIs used to support Oracle9*i*AS Portal and for the standard package calls that are used to created and build HTML within the database provider environment.

The purpose of this chapter is to provide a high-level fly-by of the process of creating your own portlets and providers. Step-by-step explanations of all the code you would need to implement the customization capability is beyond the scope of this limited goal. As with other bibles, this book is designed to give you guidance, not hands on instructions for every part of your development work. Consequently, this section will introduce you to the steps that you will have to implement, rather than describe them in detail. For more information on the actual code involved, we refer you to the latest version of the Portal Development Kit.

Creating user customization stores

The first step for allowing user customization of your portlet is to create a place to store the user personalization values.

Oracle9*i*AS Portal includes a complete storage system for personalization values. You can use the `wwwpre_api_name` package to create new storage areas for personalization values.

The process of creating a new storage area involves two steps. The first step is to create a path to a storage area. The path name is represented as a hierarchy, separated by dots, and typically takes the form

```
ORACLE.PORTAL.my_pers
```

where `ORACLE` and `PORTAL` are predefined steps in the hierarchy and the `my_pers` variable represents one or more levels in the hierarchy.

Once you have defined a path, you can add one or more value specifiers to that location. You use another call in the `wwwpre_api_name` package to add a value specifier to a path destination.

Each value location can actually hold at least three versions of the value:

✦ **A user-level version,** which is specific to each individual user

✦ **A group-level version,** which applies to all users in a group

✦ **A system-level version,** which can include one or more values that apply to different system levels

These different versions of the value correspond to different levels of default values in the system. For instance, the group-level value is a default value for a personalization parameter that can be set as the default for a group.

You use the wwwpre_api_value package to get and set the values for a personalization value. Each of these calls requests a value at a specific level, which refers back to the levels mentioned in the previous paragraphs. If there are no values for the preference at the requested level, the value from the next higher level is automatically assigned as a default.

Once you decide what sort of values you want to use in your customization page, your first step will be to define a path for the preference value store and individual preference values to hold the customizations. You should also define values for the higher levels of the preference value to establish defaults for the preferences. You would make the API calls to create the preference stores in the register procedure of your portlet, and corresponding calls to destroy the preference stores in the deregister procedure of the portlet.

Note You do not have to use the Oracle9iAS Portal personalization store for personalization values. You could use any code or storage area that you want to handle this task. But Oracle9iAS Portal's personalization stores associated with a user preference are automatically exported and imported with a component that accesses that preference; if you use your own code or storage area, you will have to handle this task manually.

Creating a customization form

Your next step is to create a customization form that will be called when the user clicks on the Customize link in the banner of your portlet. The code that creates this customization form will go in the SHOW procedure for the portlet, under the MODE_EDIT test, since the customization form is called by using this parameter value for the SHOW procedure.

You have probably already noticed that the customization forms that are automatically created for components in Oracle9iAS Portal have a set of four buttons at the top of the page: Apply, Revert to Defaults, OK, and Cancel. For consistency, you should have the same buttons at the top of your customization page.

Cross-Reference The actions of these buttons are described in the first chapter on Reports, Chapter 8.

The next step in creating the customization form is to add the text and data fields necessary to display and accept the user preference values you have just created. You will use procedures and functions from the same http package you used in creating the code for your portlet earlier in this chapter.

The last step in creating your customization form is to add the code that will initialize and store the user preference values. When you initialize the user preference values in your code, remember to search up the levels for the user preference — first looking at the user level for a value, then at the group and system levels. As soon as you find a value, you can stop your search. You use procedures from the `wwwpre_api_value` package to both retrieve and store the user preferences in your customization page.

Enabling customization

The last step in adding customization to your portlet is to let Oracle9*i*AS Portal know that you want to allow this functionality in your portlet.

Enabling customization for a portlet at this point is a simple matter of ensuring that the link to the customization page shows up on the portlet. In your portlet, there is a procedure called `get_portlet_info`, which returns various information about the portlet to the portlet provider. One of the values returned is called `has_show_edit_defaults`. You will have to make sure that you explicitly set this value to `true` in order to enable the display of the customization link.

You also have to specifically enable the display of the Customize link in the header of your portlet. You draw the header with the `wwui_api_portlet.draw_ portlet_header` procedure. One of the parameters passed to this package is the `p_has_edit` flag, which must be set to `true` in order to include the Customize link in the header.

Both of these changes have been automatically included in the sample code for a portlet. As the PDK adds tools to help you generate portlets, this code may be generated for you.

Hopefully, this section has given you a bit of a feel for the code you will have to implement in order to allow user personalization of your portlet. It seems like quite a bit of coding, and it is. But keep in mind that once you add this code, you will open up the whole world of user customization for your own custom portlet, which can in turn expand the range and scope of functionality and flexibility.

Your authors would not be surprised if future editions of the PDK include tools and wizards for automating the creation of custom portlets. There may even be a generator of some type in the current version of the PDK as you are reading this page.

Later in this chapter, we will look at a custom portlet that will allow you to make any URL into a portlet page — one that is included with the code for this book.

Calling a Built-in Portlet

In the previous sections, you learned how to build your own portlet and provider. The portlet you built was relatively simple — of necessity, since the purpose of those sections was to introduce you to the basics of building portlets.

The complexity of the portlet you have just built pales in comparison to the built-in portlets you have been creating in the earlier chapters of this book. But the PL/SQL packages created by the Oracle9*i*AS Portal wizards have the same structure as the portlets you have built.

Because of this, it is relatively easy to add the content generated for a built-in portlet to your own custom portlet. Essentially, all you have to do is to have the SHOW procedure of your portlet call the SHOW procedure of the built-in portlet whose content you want to include. At the same time, you can leverage the built-in package's EDIT_MODE capabilities in the same way from your portlet.

1. Open the code you wrote for the package body of your own custom portlet, which we suggested you named CH28_1_PORTLET.PKB.

On the CD-ROM A version of the completed version of this portlet is in the Chapter 28 directory of the examples included on the CD-ROM that comes with this book, under the name CH28_1_PORTLET_V2_DONE.PKB. If you simply want to use this version, make sure you rename the code to CH28_1_PORTLET.PKB before you compile it in step 7.

2. Add the code in bold that follows to the code you wrote for the SHOW procedure.

```
htp.p(wwui_api_portlet.portlet_text(
                p_string   => 'Hello World - Mode Show',
                p_level    => 1
                ));
l_text_holder := 'Welcome,' || wwctx_api.get_user || '!';
l_text := wwui_api_portlet.portlet_text(
p_string   => l_text_holder,
p_level    => 1 );
htp.p(l_text);
htp.para;
NETU.CH12_CHT_1.show (p_arg_names =>
PORTAL30.wwv_standard_util.string_to_table2(
'_show_header:_max_rows:_portal_max_rows'),
p_arg_values =>
PORTAL30.wwv_standard_util.string_to_table2(
'NO.25.25'));
SELECT SYSDATE INTO l_date_holder FROM DUAL;
```

```
l_text_holder := '<br> The current date is ' ||
TO_CHAR(l_date_holder, 'Month DD, YYYY') || '.'
l_text := wwui_api_portlet.portlet_text(
p_string     => l_text_holder,
p_level      => 1  );
htp.p(l_text);
htp.para;
```

This code looks a trifle complex, but you can probably follow the basic flow. The code calls the SHOW procedure in the CH12_CHT_1 package—the chart package from Chapter 12. The SHOW procedure take two arguments—an array called p_arg_names and an array called p_arg_values. As you might guess, these arrays are related—the p_arg_names array gives the name of a parameter to pass to the procedure, and the corresponding value in the p_arg_values array gives the value for the matching parameter name.

You can be forgiven if you feel a might confused about this code just plopped down here in the chapter—but only for a moment. The reason for our lack of forgiveness is that this code is easily available. If you remember from Chapter 25, the Manage Component page had a link to the Call Interface for the Show procedure. You can simply go to that page and copy the code.

The only difference between the code on that page and the code shown here is in the first value in the p_arg_values array. The standard call sets the value for this show_header parameter to YES, which would cause the header for the component to be displayed. Because you are embedding this component into your own portlet, you will change it to NO.

3. Save the new version of the package body.

4. Start SQL*Plus and log in as the owner of the schema that contains your application—NETU by default.

5. Enter the command @CH28_!_PORTLET.PKB at the SQL*Plus prompt, preceding the file name with a path name if necessary. The code should compile without errors.

6. Return to the Oracle9iAS Portal environment and use the Navigator to select the Net University Home Page.

7. Click on the Close button to return to the Navigator, and click on the name of the Net University Home Page to display the new version of the page, as shown in Figure 28-5.

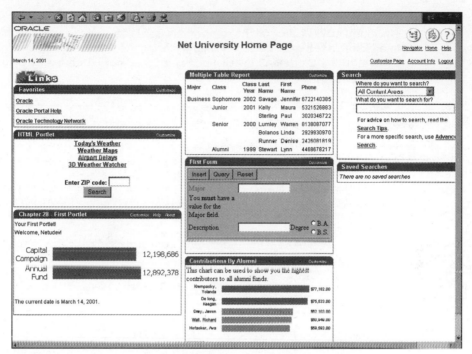

Figure 28-5: Using a custom portlet to modify a built-in portlet

Nifty, isn't it? Keep in mind that this is just the tip of the iceberg. There is almost no limit to the type of functionality you could add to a built-in portlet by "fronting" it with your own custom portlet. But, as always in this chapter, we will refer you to the latest version of the PDK for examples and instructions that are more complete.

Creating a Web Provider and Portlet with Java Server Pages

As mentioned at the beginning of this chapter, you can create database portlets or Web portlets. In this section, we will walk you through the process of using Java Server Pages, a scripting language built on top of Java, to create a simple Web portlet and provider.

1. Your first step is to install the Java classes necessary to provide the appropriate services for your portlets and providers to use. Follow the instructions in the most current version of the PDK to install the JPDK samples.

Note Installing the JPDK is not a difficult task, but if you are not familiar with the Java environment, explaining all the steps of this task is beyond the scope of this book. In addition, the current instructions for installing the JPDK require the addition of patches to the Oracle9*i*AS installation, which may not be necessary by the time you read this book.

2. Open a text editor to create a Java Server Page (JSP) for your first portlet.

3. Enter the following code:

```
<%@page import = "oracle.portal.provider.v1.*,
          oracle.portal.provider.v1.http.*" %>
<%PortletRenderRequest portletRequest =
  (PortletRenderRequest)
  request.getAttribute(HttpProvider.PORTLET_RENDER_REQUEST);
%>

Welcome <%= portletRequest.getUser().getName() %> to my
  first JSP portlet!
```

On the CD-ROM This JSP portlet is included in the Chapter 28 folder under the name of JSPportlet.jsp.

The first line of code imports the JSP code that contains all of the objects and services that you will need to create your portlet. In essence, this statement exposes the underlying API in the same way that running the `provsyns.sql` command did for the schema you built your database provider and portlets in.

The next line of code creates an object called `portletRequest`. This object is a member of the `PortletRenderRequest` class, which is like a portlet factory that contains all the functionality you will need to create your portlet.

The last line of code combines standard HTML and a JSP function. The JSP function asks the `portletRequest` object to get the name of the current user.

4. Create a directory for your new portlet and the provider you will be creating next. This directory should be under the default JSP directory you created when you installed the JPDK. For the purposes of this exercise, we will assume that the complete path for this directory is c:\iAS\Apache\Apache\ htdocs\JSPportlet.

5. Save the file you just created with the name of **JSPportlet.jsp** in the directory you just created.

As you can see, the structure of creating a portlet with JSP code is quite different from using PL/SQL with a database provider. Likewise, creating a Web provider is quite different.

6. Open a text editor again. Enter the following code, or simply cut and paste the code included on the CD-ROM in the Chapter 28 folder under the name of JSPProvider.xml.

```
<provider
class="oracle.portal.provider.v1.http.DefaultProvider"
session="true">
<portlet
class="oracle.portal.provider.v1.http.DefaultPortlet"
version="1" >
<id>1</id>
<name>MyFirstPortletJSP</name>
<title>My First Portlet - JSP</title>
<description>This is my first portlet implemented in
JSP.</description>
<timeout>5</timeout>
<timeoutMsg>My First Portlet timed out</timeoutMsg>
<showEdit>false</showEdit>
<showEditDefault>false</showEditDefault>
<showPreview>false</showPreview>
<showDetails>false</showDetails>
<hasHelp>false</hasHelp>
            <hasAbout>false</hasAbout>
<acceptContentTypes>
<item>text/html</item>
      </acceptContentTypes>
<portletRenderer
class="oracle.portal.provider.v1.http.PageRenderer" >
<appPath>/JSPportlet</appPath>
<appRoot>C:\iAS\Apache\Apache\htdocs\JSPPortlet
</appRoot>
<showPage>JSPPortlet.jsp</showPage>
</portletRenderer>
</portlet>
</provider>
```

This information is essentially the same information you assigned in your database provider, except that this time you are using XML to specify the values. XML is a markup language that is used to exchange data.

There is a difference between creating this XML file for a Web provider and creating the database provider, as you did earlier in this chapter. Oracle9iAS Portal comes with a generic Web provider, so all the provider.xml file does is pass parameters to this generic provider. You are not actually creating your own provider.

Note Yes, we have provided a correct version of this file on the CD-ROM, under the name of provider.xml. However, keep in mind that the appRoot in this file is correct for our home server. You will have to change the value to match your directory structure.

7. Save the text file as **provider.xml**. You should put this file into the same directory that you placed your JSP code, in this case c:\iAS\Apache\Apache\htdocs\JSPportlet.

You now have to change the configuration of the Oracle HTTP Server so that it recognizes the existence of your new provider. You accomplish this by editing a file called zone.properties.

8. Stop the Oracle HTTP Server.

9. Open the zone.properties file in a text editor. This file should be in the \Apache\Jserv\servlets directory under the home of your HTTP server.

10. Under the Servlet Aliases section, add the following line:

```
servlet.JSPportlet.code=
oracle.portal.provider.v1.http.HttpProvider
```

This line of code will tell the HTTP server to use the correct provider class for your new provider.

11. Under the Aliased Servlet Init Parameters section, add the following line of code:

```
servlet.jspportlet.initArgs=provider_root=
C:\myportletjsp,sessiontimeout=1800000
```

which provides the correct initialization parameters for the portlet.

12. Restart the Oracle HTTP Server.

Remember that a Web provider runs outside of the Oracle9iAS Portal environment. Because of this, you can check the operation of your portlet directly by calling its URL.

13. Enter the following URL in your browsers' address window:

```
http://host.domain:port/servlet/JSPPortlet
```

where host, domain and port are replaced by the hostname, domain name, and port of your Oracle HTTP Server. This address should bring up a test portlet in the browser window, as shown in Figure 28-6. The test page is returned directly from the Apache adapter. When you register your provider in Oracle9iAS Portal, you will be able to access the actual JSP page.

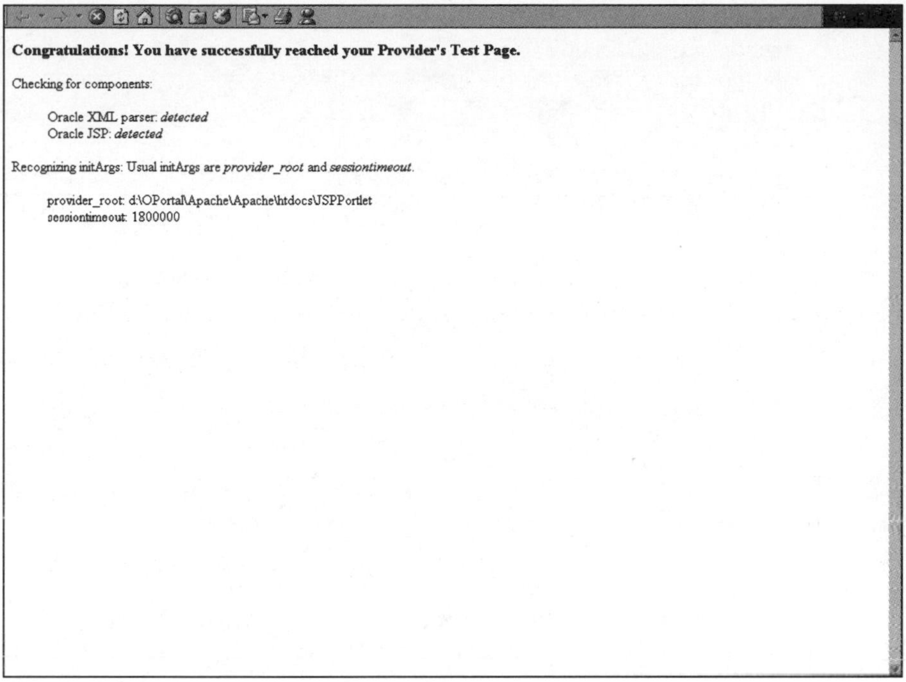

Figure 28-6: Ensuring that your Web portlet is available

14. Return to the Oracle9*i*AS PortalOracle9*i*AS Portal home page and click on the Administration tab.

15. Click on the Add a Portlet Provider link.

16. Enter the relevant information about the new provider. You should give the provider a descriptive name, like **My First Web Provider,** and be sure to select Web as the Implementation style.

17. Scroll down to the Web Providers section of the page, as shown in Figure 28-7.

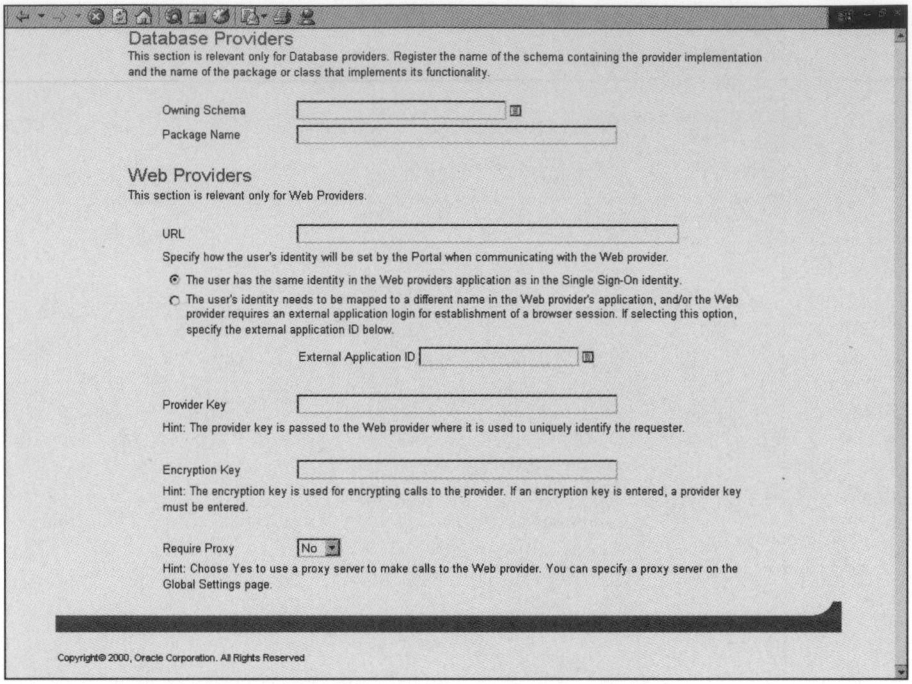

Figure 28-7: The Web Providers section of adding a provider

18. Enter the URL you used in step 13 as the URL for the Web provider. This is the only parameter value you will have to enter in this section.

19. Click on the OK button.

20. Go to the Navigator and click on the Edit link for the Net University Home Page.

21. To make room on the page for your new portlet, delete the CH28_1_PORTLET at the bottom-left region. Add the new portlet to the bottom of the left region, following the same steps as you did for the database portlet earlier in this chapter.

22. Click on the Close button to return to the Navigator, and click on the name of the Net University Home Page to bring up the new version of the home page, as shown in Figure 28-8.

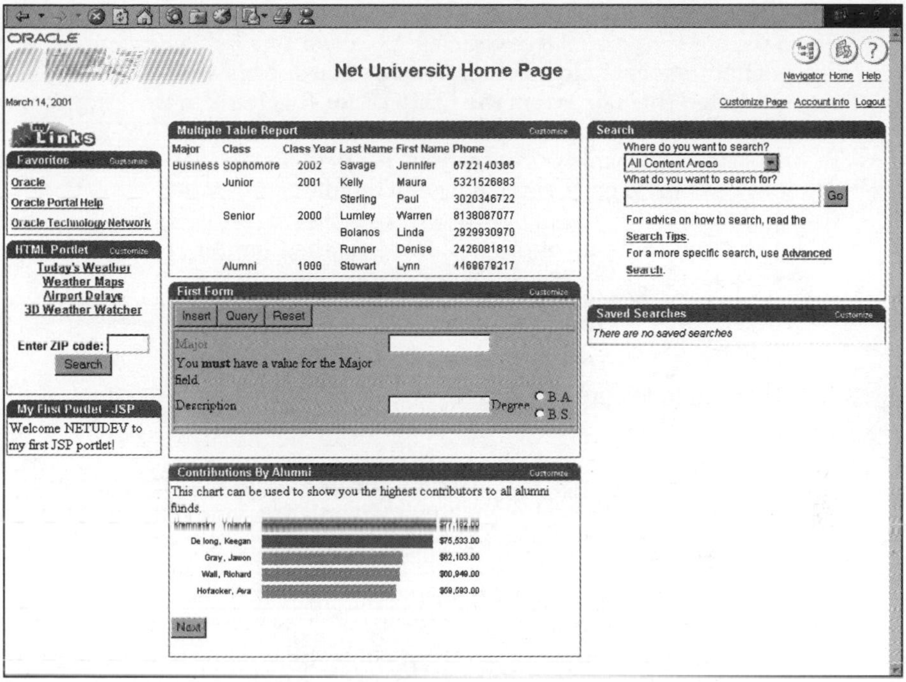

Figure 28-8: Your portal page with your first Web portlet

We have led you on a whirlwind tour of the process of creating and using a Web provider. We hope that you have gotten a basic feeling for the steps you will have to take to create a Web provider and the differences between creating a Web provider and a database provider.

For the last topic in this chapter, we will look at one of the third-party portlets that comes with the PDK — the URL portlet.

Using the URL Portlet

You have been building your own portlets in this chapter. You can also go to Oracle Technology Network to see a listing of the publicly available third party portlets. There are also some third-party portlets included in the Portal Development Kit that provide some nice functionality, such as portlets that you can use to access information from the Excite portlet.

One of the cool portlets included in the PDK is called the URL portlet. (The URL is also a part of version 3.0.8 of Oracle9*i*AS Portal.) As its name implies, you can use this portlet to access any information you can specify with a URL in a portlet. We have included this portlet on the CD-ROM for this book in the Chapter 28 directory.

To understand how this portlet works, it's best just to leap right in, install it, and add it to the portal page you have been building.

1. Copy the contents of the URL folder in the Chapter 28 folder on the CD-ROM that accompanies this book to your server.

2. Start SQL*Plus from the directory where you placed the files from the URL folder.

3. Run the following command:

```
urlinst -w portal30 -wp portal30 -s netu -p netu
```

which assumes that you installed the Oracle9*i*AS Portal software in the default schema (portal30) with a matching password, and you have used the NETU schema (with a password of NETU) for your application.

This process will install the URL portlet and provider.

4. Go to the Administer tab in the main region of the Oracle9*i*AS Portal home page and click on the Add A Portlet Provider link, as described earlier in this chapter.

5. Add the new portlet provider as you did earlier. The package name for the provider is url_provider.

6. Go to the Navigator and select the Net University Home Page for editing.

7. Once again, delete the JSP portlet you added in the previous section. Add the new URL portlet to the bottom of the center region of the home page. You can see the new provider at the bottom of the list of providers in the Add Portlets page.

8. Click on the Close button to return to the Navigator.

9. Click on the name of the Net University Home Page to bring up the new version of your portal page, which should look like Figure 28-9.

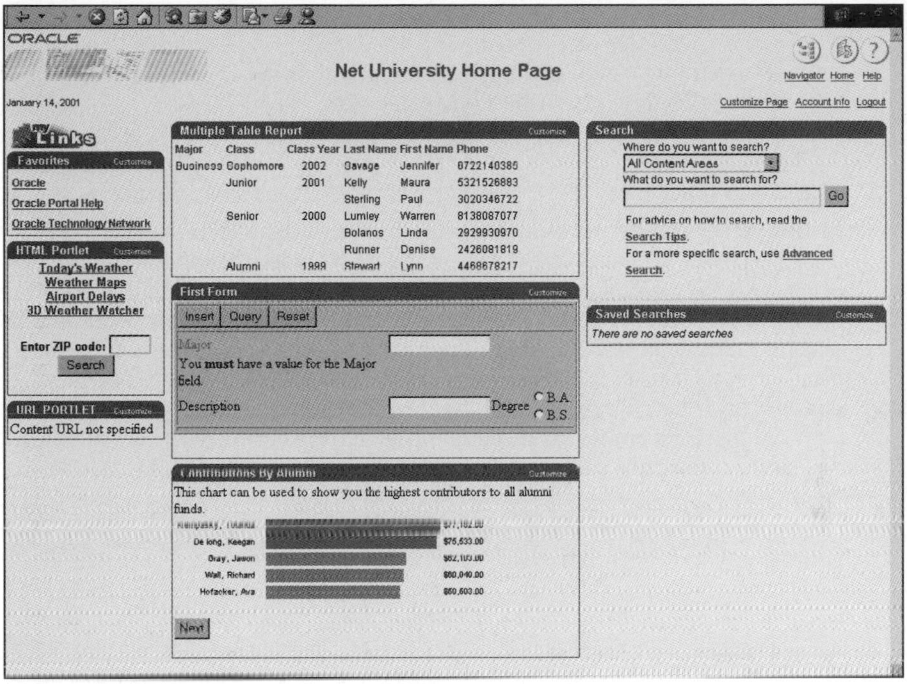

Figure 28-9: The URL portlet in your portal page

As you can see, the new portlet doesn't seem to offer much at this time. The reason for this is simple—you have not added a URL for display.

10. Click on the Customize link for the URL portlet, which will bring up the page shown in Figure 28-10.

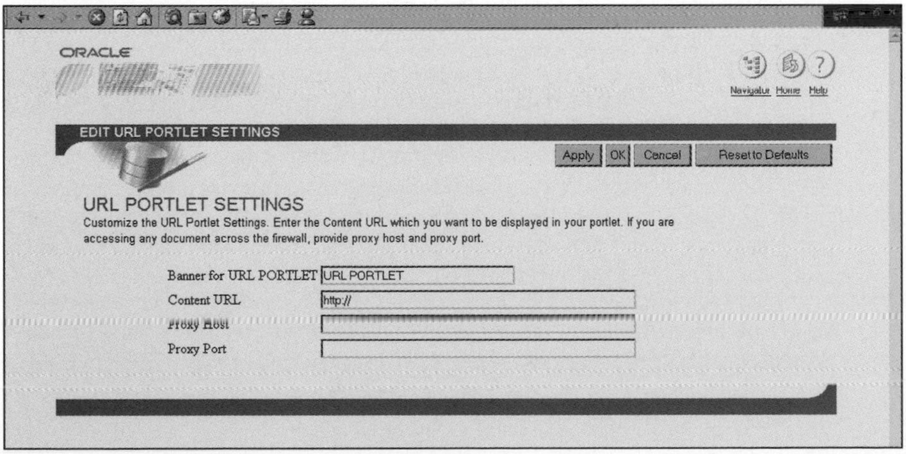

Figure 28-10: The URL Portlet Settings page

11. Enter a URL for a page you want to display as a portlet. Keep in mind that this page should be appropriate for portlet display, in that is can be easily shown in a reduced area, and legal for portlet display, in that is does not contain frames or any other unsupported code.

12. Click on the OK button to redisplay your portal page with the populated URL portlet.

Although this portlet provides some quick and dirty functionality, it is rather untamed. All you are doing is supplying a URL and hoping for the best. Since you don't own the URL, the contents of that location could change at any time. At the least, these changes could alter the aesthetic value of your own portal page. At the worst, changes in the URL could include code that is not supported in a portlet display, such as frames. Or, even worse, the Web site that includes that portlet could change, and the URL might no longer exist. Once you roll out the URL portlet, the first person to stumble across any of these developing problems will probably be one of your users — so you will get a call.

Because of these dangerous areas, you should not view the URL portlet as a be-all-end-all solution for integrating other pages into your portal environment.

Summary

In ways more than mere numbering, this has been the penultimate chapter of this book. You have taken a dive deep into the internals of the APIs that are used to create portlets and portlet providers, and come out standing. In this chapter, you got your hands dirty creating both a database portlet and a Web portlet.

There is a whole lot more to creating portlets, as we have mentioned a few times in this chapter. And, as we have also hammered home, the key resource for creating your own portlets and providers is the all-important Portal Development Kit, or PDK. You can get the latest versions of the PDK as a member of OTN, which can be found off of the main page www.oracle.com. The Portal Development Kit can be found in the Internet Tools area, under the Oracle9iAS Portal section. (At the time of this writing, the URL for this page is http://otn.oracle.com/products/iportal/, but we know these things can change by the time you read this book.)

The intention of the Oracle9iAS Portal development team is to update the materials in the PDK monthly, so you should definitely visit this area on a regular basis. As we mentioned earlier, we expect to see some very nice enhancements in the PDK by the time this book is published, so we strongly encourage you to download the most current version of the PDK and to revisit OTN regularly to get the latest version.

We have given you just a taste of the complete functionality that you can add to your own portlets through the use of the portlet services. The next, and final, chapter of this book will explore a few more advanced techniques you can use with Oracle9iAS Portal.

✦   ✦   ✦

Advanced Tips and Techniques

Despite all of the power that comes with Oracle9*i*AS Portal there are still certain things that are not easy to do with the product at first glance. However, one of the most important characteristics of Oracle Portal is its extensibility. Portal builds off the power of the Oracle9*i* database and it leverages programming skills that you already have within your organization. In this chapter we'll be taking a look at some advanced tips and techniques that you can use to build more complex applications with Portal.

◆   ◆   ◆   ◆

In This Chapter

Learning Tips and
Tricks in PL/SQL

Working with
Cookies

Adding Custom
Attributes and Types

◆   ◆   ◆   ◆

Learning Tips and Tricks in PL/SQL

Oracle Portal uses PL/SQL code to generate the forms and reports that appear in your browser window. Because PL/SQL code runs inside of the database you would naturally assume that it has complete access to the database — and it does. In order to gain access to the full power of PL/SQL within your Oracle Portal applications, however, you will have to work a little more closely with PL/SQL and with JavaScript. PL/SQL code runs solely in the database and JavaScript code (as far as Portal is concerned) runs solely inside of your browser. Thus, there is a fundamental disconnect when it comes to working with the two languages. However, in order to customize your forms and reports you will often want to take advantage of the data in your database. The only way to work with this data interactively inside of the browser is to use PL/SQL code to pass values to JavaScript. In this section we'll work with PL/SQL routines to send data to your JavaScript functions.

Passing generated default values to forms

Oracle Portal can automatically generate default values for fields on a form, but these generated defaults are simple values. You can, however, use PL/SQL to automatically generate more complex default values for form fields. It's a simple matter to use PL/SQL code to populate some JavaScript scripts.

1. Use the script ch29_example1_tbl.sql to load the sample table into the NETU account.

2. Use the script js_default_value.sql to load the sample PL/SQL procedure into the NETU account.

3. Load the form ch29_default_value.sql into the NETCOLLEGE application using the PORTAL30 account.

4. Log on to Portal using a developer account.

5. Edit the form ch29_default_value and select the CURRENT_DATE field as shown in Figure 29-1.

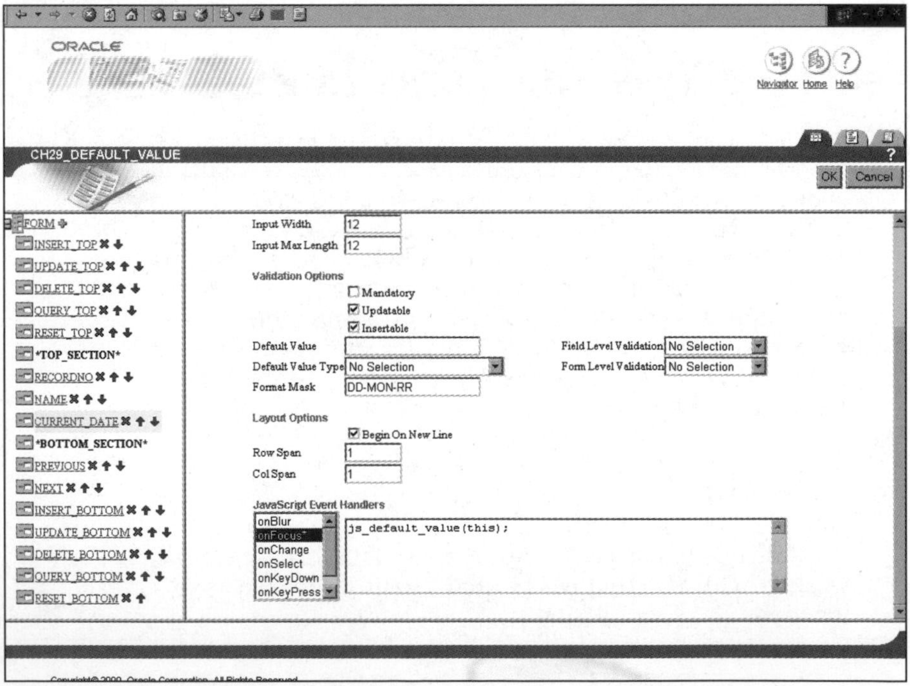

Figure 29-1: Current Date field

Back in Chapter 19 we worked with JavaScript events. You will notice that the CURRENT_DATE field has a JavaScript attached to its `onFocus` event. Whenever the field gains focus, Portal will call the `js_default_value` function.

6. Navigate to the Additional PL/SQL code panel using the tabs at the top of the page to display the panel shown in Figure 29-2.

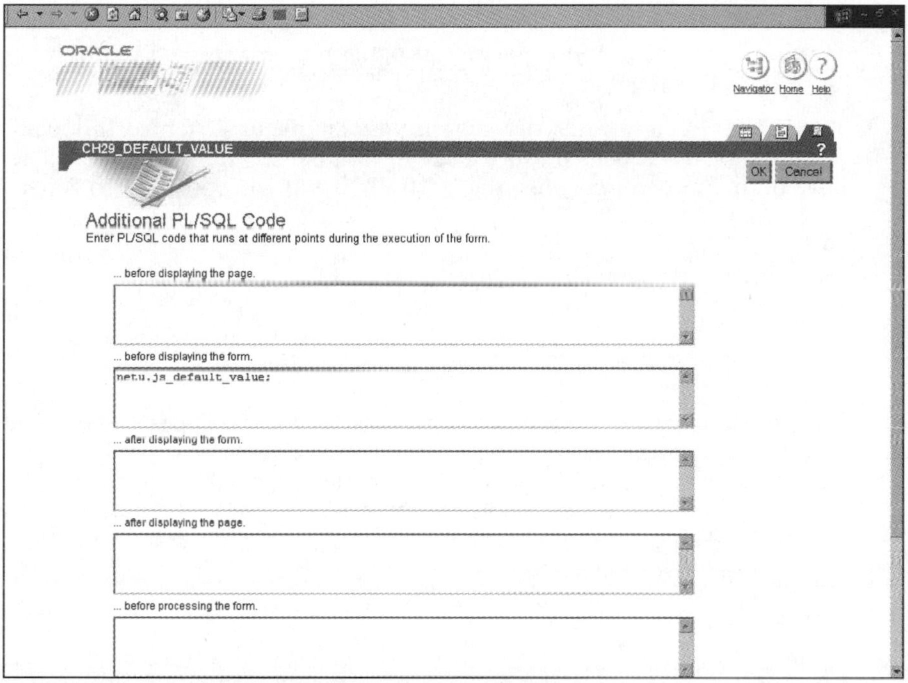

Figure 29-2: Advanced PL/SQL Panel – Default Value

The PL/SQL code panel has a single line of code loaded into it as shown in Figure 29-2. This line of code is a call to a PL/SQL procedure, which you loaded into the NETU account. The source of this procedure is shown in Listing 29-1.

Listing 29-1: **PL/SQL procedure to generate js_default_value function**

```
create or replace procedure js_default_value as
js_current_date varchar2(20);
begin
htp.print('<SCRIPT LANGUAGE="JavaScript1.1">');
htp.print('<!--');
```

Continued

Listing 29-1 *(continued)*

```
htp.print('function js_default_value(theElement){');
select to_char(sysdate) into js_current_date from dual;
htp.print('theElement.value ="'||js_current_date||'"');
htp.print('}');
htp.print('//-->');
htp.print('</SCRIPT>');
end;
```

The js_default_value procedure is very simple in structure. It does not take any parameters, but it does declare a single variable js_current_date. The next three lines of the procedure all use the HTP.PRINT built-in procedure to generate three lines of HTML output:

✦ The script open tag

✦ The script comment character

✦ The js_default_value function declaration

The next line of code is an SQL statement. This simple SELECT statement returns the current date as a string to the declared variable js_current_date. Once the date value is stored inside a variable, it is a simple matter to pass the value of the variable into the form field by use of the theElement.value = line of code. Since this script runs inside the server, the result of the PRINT statement will be a fixed string in the following format:

```
theElement.value = "05-JAN-01"
```

The final three PRINT statements close the function and then close out the SCRIPT tags. The call to the PL/SQL function is made before the form itself is generated, so this JavaScript will appear in the HTML page ahead of the form fields. The generated JavaScript function will look like the one shown in Listing 29-2.

Listing 29-2: Generated HTML code

```
<SCRIPT LANGUAGE="JavaScript1.1">
<!--
function js_default_value(theElement){
theElement.value ="05-JAN-01"
}
//-->
</SCRIPT>
```

Using PL/SQL Code to Load JavaScript

Up until this point we have always used Portal templates to load JavaScript into form objects. You can, however, use PL/SQL code to insert the relevant JavaScript into your forms. Oracle executes the PL/SQL code before the HTML page gets generated, so any HTP output automatically appears in the form. This is a superior technique for inserting JavaScript into forms because the JavaScript code can be fully dynamic. If we had used templates to insert the JavaScript function into our example form we would not have been able to fetch the current date from the server.

This is a very simple block of JavaScript code, one that is attached to the CURRENT_DATE field by means of JavaScript events. Run the form and navigate to the CURRENT_DATE field as shown in Figure 29-3.

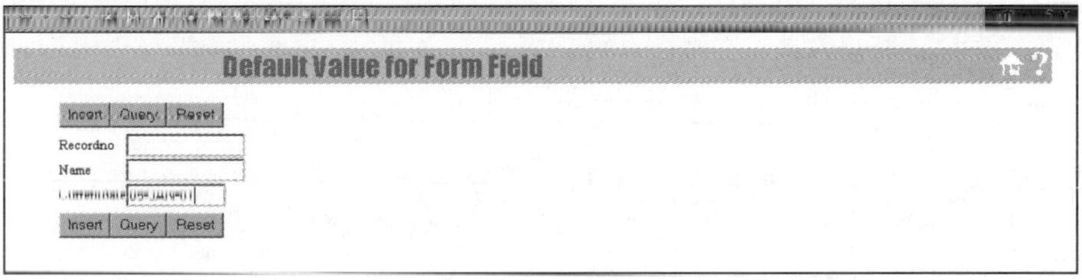

Figure 29-3: Current Date field with a default value

You will notice that Portal automatically populates the CURRENT_DATE field with the current date as it was generated from the database. The name of the CURRENT_DATE field is passed to the `js_default_value` function by means of the `theElement` parameter. The JavaScript function simply loads the current date (in string format) into the data field. This same technique can be used to leverage some advanced features of the database, such as triggers and sequences.

Generating primary keys using sequences and/or triggers

One of the more common tasks that you will need to run with PL/SQL code is the generation of primary keys. In order to avoid a round-trip from the browser to the server you will often wish to preload HTML pages with keys — or simply to generate the key values dynamically when records are stored into the database. Both tasks are easy to accomplish with some simple PL/SQL blocks. The starting point for generating keys is a sequence number as shown in Listing 29-3.

Listing 29-3: **Sequence script — CH29_SEQ.SQL**

```
CREATE SEQUENCE ch29_seq
 INCREMENT BY 1
 START WITH 1
 NOCYCLE
 NOCACHE
 ORDER;
```

1. Load the ch29_seq.sql script into the NETU account.

2. Load the JavaScript PL/SQL procedure js_sequence.sql into the NETU account.

3. Import the form object ch29_sequence.sql into the NETCOLLEGE application using the PORTAL30 account.

Once a sequence has been created, you can use the sequence as part of an SQL statement. Listing 29-4 shows a sample SELECT statement embedded into PL/SQL package, which generates a JavaScript function.

Listing 29-4: **JavaScript sequence — PL/SQL**

```
create or replace procedure js_sequence as
js_recordno number(4);
begin
htp.print('<SCRIPT LANGUAGE="JavaScript1.1">');
htp.print('<!--');
htp.print('function js_sequence(theElement){');
select ch29_seq.nextval into js_recordno from dual;
htp.print('theElement.value ='||to_char(js_recordno)||'');
htp.print('}');
htp.print('//-->');
htp.print('</SCRIPT>');
end;
```

When Oracle Portal executes this PL/SQL block as part of a form object it generates the HTML shown in Listing 29-5.

Listing 29-5: **JavaScript sequence — HTML**

```
<SCRIPT LANGUAGE="JavaScript1.1">
<!--
function js_sequence(theElement){
```

```
theElement.value =6
}
//-->
</SCRIPT>
```

The value that is assigned to the `theElement` field is determined by the ch29_seq sequence. Each time that the PL/SQL block executes, it will select the next available sequence number.

4. Run the ch29_seqence form and navigate to the RECORDNO field as shown in Figure 29-4.

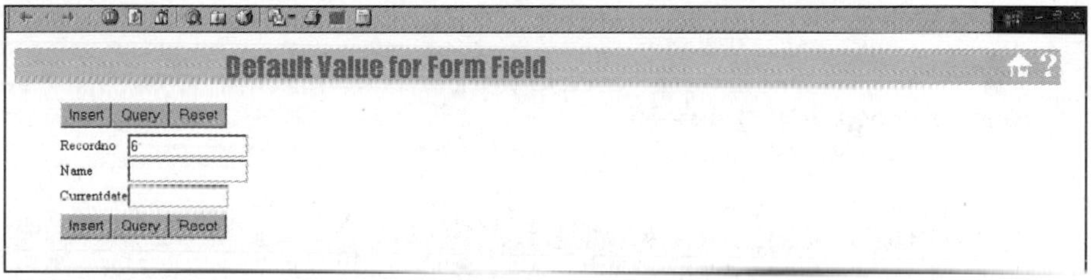

Figure 29-4: Ch29_sequence Form

The JavaScript function that we are using to call the sequence is very straightforward. Each time that the RECORDNO field gains focus the function will insert the sequence number into the RECORDNO field. The function will load the *same* number into the RECORDNO field no matter how many times you set the focus to it. Portal only executes the PL/SQL block when the form is loaded, so the sequence number will not change as long as the form is displayed.

5. Add a value for the Name field and then press the Insert button on the form to store the new record and display the panel shown in Figure 29-5.

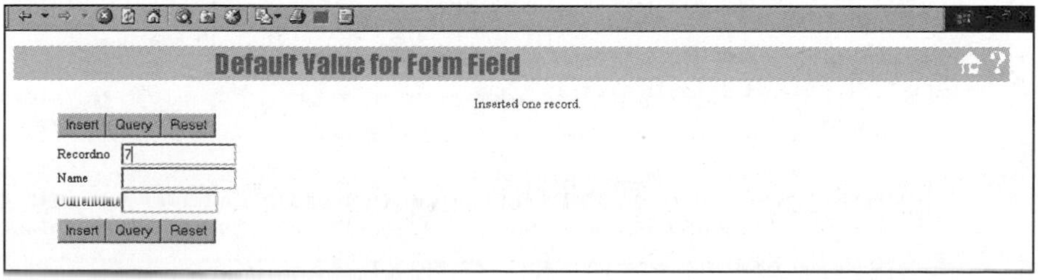

Figure 29-5: Inserted RECORDNO

Portal automatically redisplays the form when you insert, update, or delete a record on the form. Thus, the PL/SQL sequence block is automatically reexecuted to generate a new sequence number as shown in Figure 29-5. We have used the same default value technique as shown in the preceding example to insert the sequence number code into the form. Although the code itself is simple, you can easily extend the code to handle more complex key-generation algorithms. For example, we could use the sequence number as part of an alphanumeric key value:

```
select 'A'||to_char(ch29_seq.nextval) from dual;
```

Tip   In fact, you can make use of any block of PL/SQL commands to generate the sequence number, including `if...else` blocks, `for` loops, and any data access command.

One of the potential problems with this solution is that a user can run the form without actually inserting a record. This can create holes in the sequences, since the sequence value is generated when the form is run — not when the record is inserted into the database. You can work around this problem by using a database trigger shown in Listing 29-6.

Listing 29-6: **Sequence trigger**

```
create or replace trigger create_recordno
before insert on ch29_example1
for each row
begin
        if :new.recordno is null then
          select ch29_seq.nextval into :new.recordno from dual;
    end if;
end;
```

Triggers are associated with tables. The CREATE_RECORDNO trigger is associated with the ch29_example1 table and it is automatically called each time a record is inserted into the table. The SELECT statement is embedded in the body of the trigger, so it will only be executed when a record is actually inserted into the database. This ensures that the sequence number is not generated unless it is actually needed. This technique has the added attraction of allowing you to remove the RECORDNO field from the form — because the value need not appear on the screen.

Tip   This is a particularly powerful technique when used with *data-less keys*. Data-less keys are primary keys that do not contain any useful data other than the key value itself. For example, you could use an employee's social security number as the primary key for employee records. However, if you do not have the social security number at hand when you create the record, it will be impossible to add the employee to the system. So, instead of using the social security number as the primary (i.e., unique) key for the employee table, simply use a generated key value. Since the key has no *visible* value, you can easily leave it off your HTML form and generate the value in the database using a trigger.

Working with Cookies

Oracle Portal does not provide any built-in tools for navigating users from one form to another in a sequence. You can, however, *build* your own wizard-style interface by using the *redirect* feature of the Form object as shown in Figure 29-6.

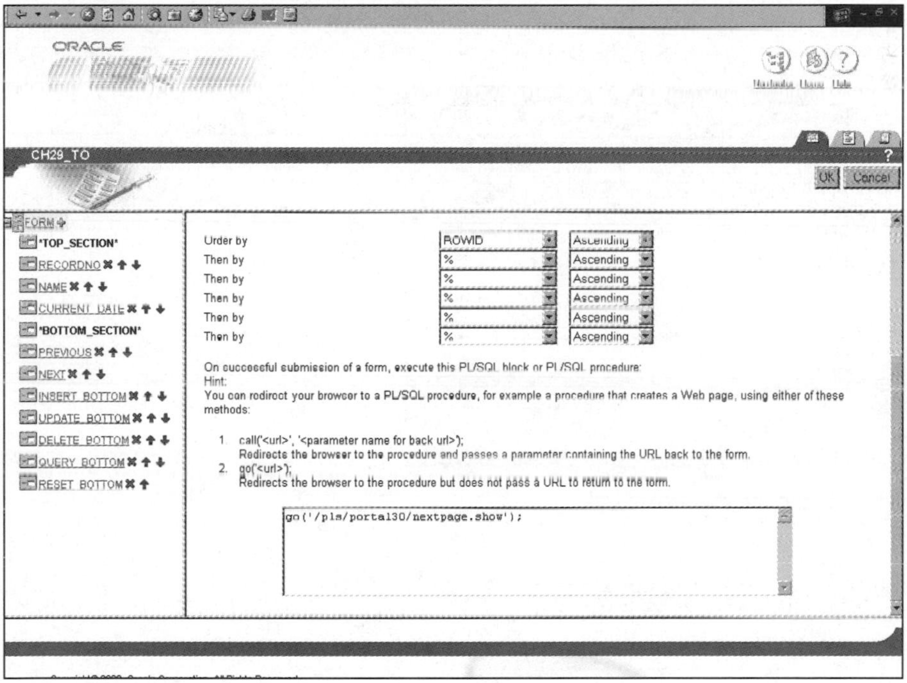

Figure 29-6: Form redirect

This technique requires you to actually store intermediate data into the database. There is no built-in method for passing data from the first form to a second form using redirects. You may find the need to pass data from one form to another within the browser. For example, you might wish to build a client-side shopping cart that remains with a user during a browser session. In order to store data within the user's browser session you will need to work with cookies. In our example case, we may want to input the RECORDNO for a record on one screen, and then complete the data-entry for the remaining fields on a second form.

Cookies are small data records that are stored within a user's browser. The browser can even store these records persistently across browser sessions. Oracle Portal itself makes use of cookies to store *security checks*. When the Logon Server authenticates your session it stores a cookie record to note the fact that you have been authenticated. (The cookie does not include any password information — and it is only valid for the current browser session.)

On the CD-ROM

You might find it useful to view browser cookies as you work with them. We have included a copy of Kookaburra Software's Cookie Pal on the CD-ROM. Cookie Pal allows you to manage cookies interactively. The examples in this section make use of Cookie Pal — but you can still work with these examples without it.

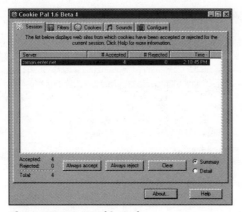

Figure 29-7: Cookie Pal

Figure 29-7 shows the cookie settings for the ZAMAN server for an Oracle Portal session. Since Portal requires the use of cookies, you might as well leverage them within a Portal application.

1. Load the form object ch29_from.sql into the NETCOLLEGE application using the PORTAL30 account.

2. Load the form object ch29_to.sql into the NETCOLLEGE application using the PORTAL30 account.

3. Locate the Cookie Pal setup program in the Cookie Pal directory on the CD-ROM and install Cookie Pal. (This step is optional.)

Working with cookies can be a complex process, so we've made the examples overly simple so that it will be easier to follow the logic. The two forms that you loaded are built against the same ch29_example1 table and they use the same fields. The first form is the CH29_FROM form, which calls the CH29_TO form and passes a value between the two forms by use of a cookie.

4. Run the CH29_FROM form as shown in Figure 29-8.

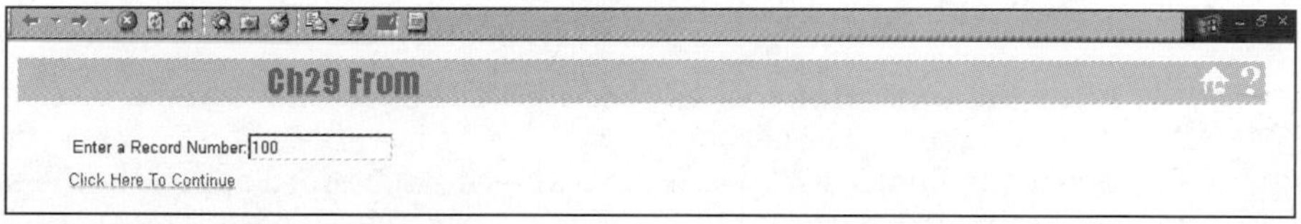

Figure 29-8: CH29_FROM form

The CH29_FROM form is very simple, consisting of a single data entry field and an HTML anchor link. When you enter a value into the text field the form will store the value as a cookie in the browser.

5. Enter a value for the Record Number and then tab out of the field to display the dialog box shown in Figure 29-9.

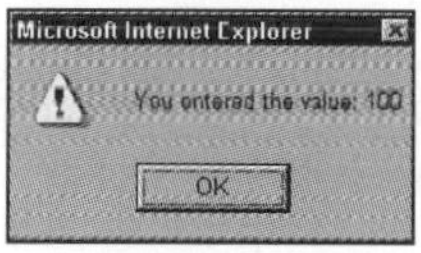

Figure 29-9: Value dialog box

The form object fires a block of JavaScript code when you exit the RECORDNO field. This same JavaScript function displays a dialog box that verifies the value that you entered into the field.

Note

It is not necessary to use dialog boxes to make these examples work, but it does make it easier to follow the code. While we have used dialog boxes in the samples, you do not need to follow this practice in your own production code.

6. Press the OK button to acknowledge the dialog box to display the panel as shown in Figure 29-10.

Figure 29-10: Cookie dialog box

Figure 29-10 shows a second dialog box that displays the value as it is stored by a second block of JavaScript code. This new JavaScript function processes the value and stores it within a session cookie that is called c_recordno.

7. Press the OK button to acknowledge this second dialog box.

If you are using Cookie Pal, you will see the cookie record appear in the session panel as shown in Figure 29-11.

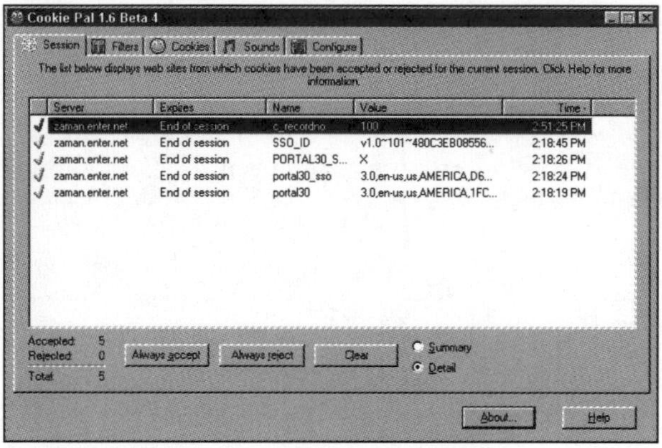

Figure 29-11: C_recordno Session Cookie

In the example case, we have set a single, scalar value of 100 into the c_recordno cookie. However, we could just as easily have stored multiple values with embedded string delimiters such as these:

```
sue,jones,100,accounting
sue          jones          100    ACCT
sue/jones/100/acct
```

In most cases, you will want to use as few cookies as possible. If you need to pass multiple values, it makes sense to store them in a single field if at all possible. The downside to this approach is that you have to *parse* the cookie strings on the receiving form.

8. Use the Click here to continue link to display the second form shown in Figure 29-12.

Figure 29-12: CH29_TO dialog box

The linked form executes a block of JavaScript code as soon as the form is launched. The JavaScript code extracts the cookie value and then displays the value of the cookie using a dialog box as shown Figure 29-12.

9. Press the OK button to acknowledge the dialog box and display the panel as shown in Figure 29-13.

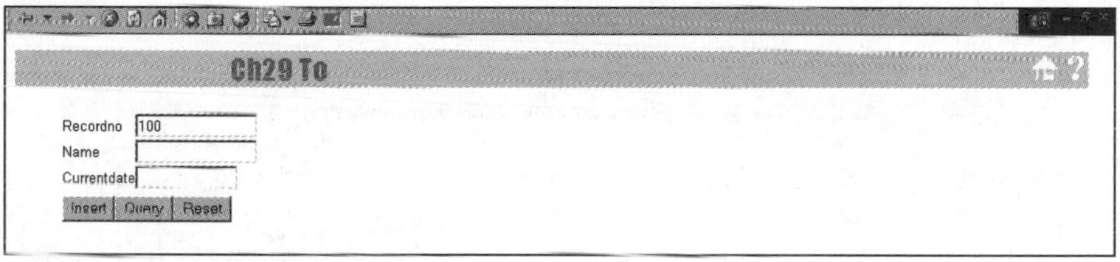

Figure 29-13: CH29_TO form

The value from the cookie appears in the RECORDNO field as shown in Figure 29-13. Once again, the dialog box is superfluous to the solution, but it allows you to see that the cookie value was moved from the first form to the second form. The final step in the process is to move the value from the cookie into the receiving form. This task is accomplished by means of a simple *anonymous* JavaScript.

Cookie source code

Oracle has changed the internals of Oracle Portal with this new release. Thus, the way in which you work both with cookies and forms has changed significantly from previous releases.

1. Navigate back to the Portal Navigator.

2. Edit the CH29_FROM form and select the RECORDNO field as shown in Figure 29-14.

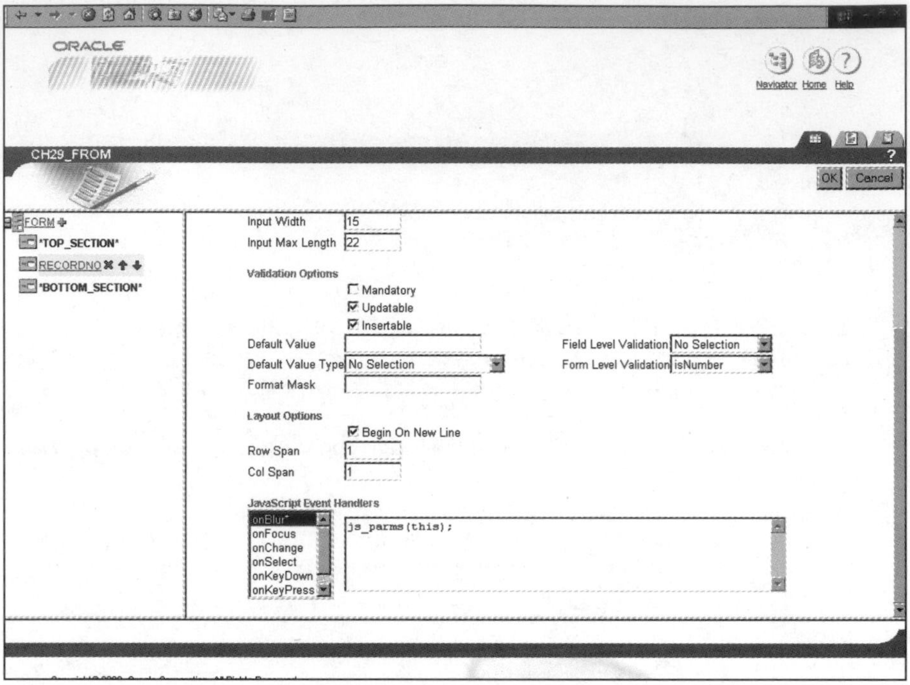

Figure 29-14: RECORDNO field on CH29_FROM form

In order to capture the contents of the RECORDNO field we have attached a JavaScript function called `js_parms` to the `onBlur` event.

Cross-Reference   JavaScript coding and JavaScript events are discussed in detail in Chapter 19.

3. Navigate to the Additional PL/SQL Code panel as shown in Figure 29-15.

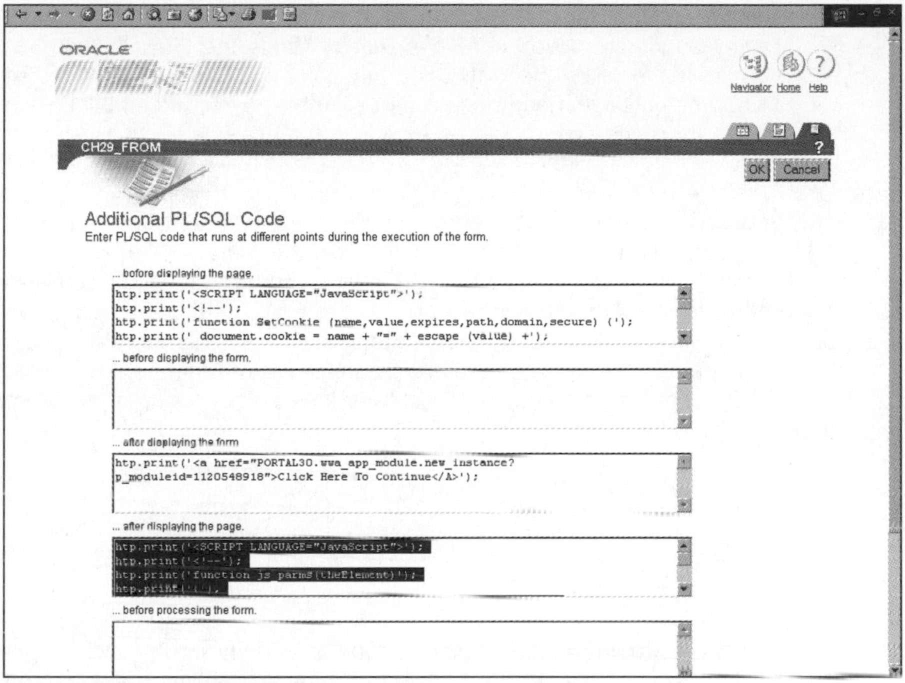

Figure 29-15: Additional PL/SQL Code—CH29_FROM

The first block of script code as shown in Listing 29-7 is the SetCookie function. This is the block of JavaScript code that actually stores the cookie value. We have encapsulated this function inside of HTP.PRINT PL/SQL code calls so that it can be embedded within a portal page.

Listing 29-7: **SetCookie code — before displaying the page**

```
htp.print('<SCRIPT LANGUAGE="JavaScript">');
htp.print('<!--');
htp.print('function SetCookie
(name,value,expires,path,domain,secure) {');
htp.print(' document.cookie = name + "=" + escape (value) +');
htp.print(' ((expires) ? "; expires=" + expires.toGMTString() :
"") +');
htp.print(' ((path) ? "; path=" + path : "") +');
htp.print(' ((domain) ? "; domain=" + domain : "") +');
htp.print(' ((secure) ? "; secure" : "");');
htp.print('alert("Setting the Cookie [c_recordno] with the
value:"|value)');
htp.print('}');
htp.print('//-->');
htp.print('</SCRIPT>');
```

> **Tip**
>
> The `SetCookie` function and the `GetCookie` function are discussed in detail in Danny Goodman's *JavaScript Bible* (Hungry Minds, Inc; ISBN: 0-7645-3342-8). The authors highly recommend that you buy a copy of this excellent reference to the JavaScript language. Goodman's cookie examples are based on Bill Dortch's generic cookie functions—which can be found on Bill's Web site `http://www.hidaho.com`.

This generic cookie function accepts six parameters. The first two parameters are the name/value pair. Cookies are actually stored within the browser in a very proprietary and compact format. The `SetCookie` and `GetCookie` functions simplify the parsing process by allowing you to work directly with name/value pairs. Although the cookie will be stored as a long string, the name/value pairs are a handy mechanism for locating and manipulating individual cookie records. Technically speaking, you can get or set cookies simply by using a document assignment:

```
document.cookie="name=value
[;expires=time-value]
[;path=pathvalue]
[;domain=domain-name]
[; secure]"
```

However, if you do not format the cookie string *exactly* right, it will not work. The `SetCookie` and `GetCookie` functions handle the formatting for you to ensure that it is done correctly.

The name/value pair is the only required value for cookies. The remaining parameters modify the name/value pair in some fashion. The EXPIRES parameter sets the expiration date for the cookie. If this value is NULL, the cookie record expires when the user exits the browser session. You can set a non-NULL value into this field in order to make the cookie persist across sessions. For example, you might want to store a "shopping cart" of cookies across sessions. When the user returns to the browser at some time in the future, your application could then redisplay the contents of the shopping cart using cookies.

> **Caution**
>
> We generally recommend against using cookies for persistent shopping cart applications. Cookies are only stored on the browser of the local machine. If the user reconnects to your portal from a different machine—the contents of the shopping cart will be NULL. It is far better to store the shopping cart in the database.

Expiration dates must be stored in GMT format and the `SetCookie` function automatically handles this for you. If you want to set an expiration date that is greater than the current session, all that you need to do is pass a numeric time value to the `SetCookie` function as follows:

```
var v_expire = new Date()
var v_oneweek = v_expire.getTime() + (7*24*60*60*1000)
v_expire.setTime(v_oneweek)
SetCookie("c_recordno",100,v_expire)
```

The Path and Domain settings enable you to save cookies in duplicate paths or along specific server domains. You can use them in tandem with the SECURE parameter to prevent applications from other servers from reading your cookie entries. For the purposes of our example code, these parameters have been left blank. In its simplest form, you can use this function to store a session-cookie called my_cookie with a value of oreo using the following JavaScript call:

```
SetCookie("my_cookie","oreo")
```

The source for the SetCookie code is placed in the "... before displaying the page." PL/SQL code window. By inserting this function at the top of the HTML output page, we are ensuring that this function will be available to all of the other code blocks.

The second block of code as shown in Listing 29-8 appears in the "... after display-ing the page." PL/SQL code window. This is the function that is called by the onBlur event on the RECORDNO field, so it can safely appear at the end of the page (because it will only be called after the page is rendered).

Listing 29-8: **JS_PARMS — after displaying the page**

```
htp.print('<SCRIPT LANGUAGE="JavaScript">');
htp.print('<!--');
htp.print('function js_parms(theElement)');
htp.print('{');
htp.print('alert("You entered the value: "+theElement.value)');
htp.print('SetCookie("c_recordno",theElement.value)');
htp.print('}');
htp.print('//-->');
htp.print('</SCRIPT>');
```

Once again, we have encapsulated this script within HTP.PRINT commands. This function is very simple. It accepts a single parameter, which is intended to be a pointer to the field from which it is called. The value that is stored in the field is dis-played in a dialog box using the alert JavaScript function. The last line of the script calls the SetCookie function and passes it the cookie named c_recordno with a value that is the value as entered into the field on the form.

The last block of code as shown in Listing 29-9 has nothing to do with cookies per se. This block of code inserts an HTML anchor below the fields on the form. This anchor is linked to an Oracle Portal function call with single a parameter.

Listing 29-9: **Anchor link — after displaying the form**

```
htp.print('<a
href="PORTAL30.wwa_app_module.new_instance?p_moduleid=112054891
8">Click Here To Continue</A>');
```

This string is in the format that you would use to call an Oracle Portal data entry form directly:

```
PORTAL30.wwa_app_module.new_instance?p_moduleid=1120548918
```

The number that is shown in bold is the internal object ID of the form object. The element that precedes the module number is the procedure call, which is composed of three parts. The first part is the form owner (PORTAL30), followed by the PL/SQL module name (wwa_app_module.new_instance) and the parameter name that is passed to the module (p_moduleid).

Tip You can find this internal number (shown in bold in the code) on the Manage panel of the Form Wizard.

This function creates a very simple link on the page that points to the CH29_TO form. When the user clicks on the link, Oracle Portal displays the second form.

4. Exit the CH29_FROM form.

5. Edit the CH29_TO form and navigate to the Additional PL/SQL code panel as shown in Figure 29-16.

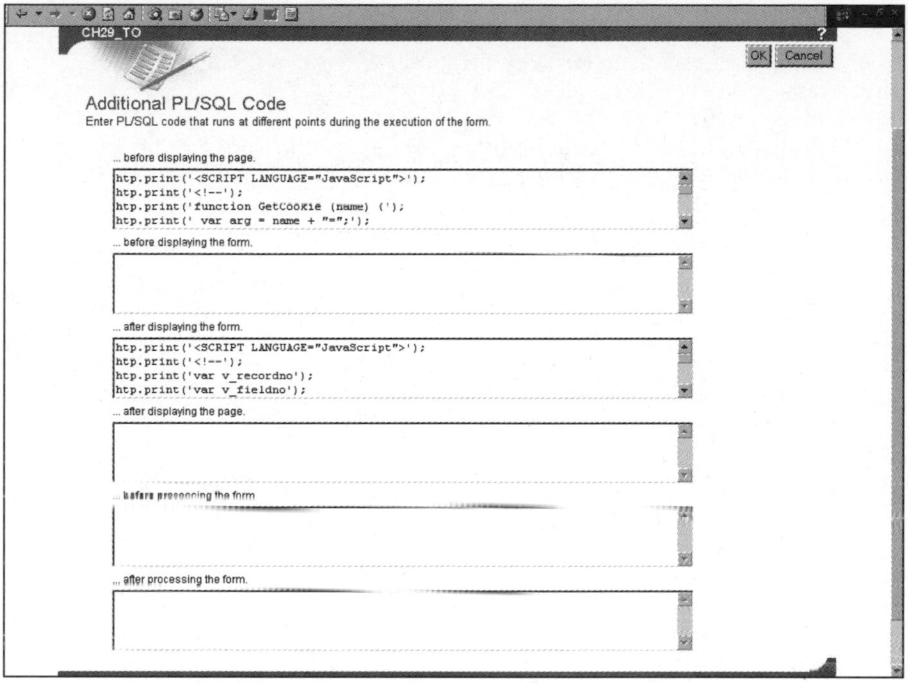

Figure 29-16: CH29_TO Additional PL/SQL code

The first block of code as shown in Listing 29-10 is the GetCookie code. The two functions in this block handle the parsing of cookies, just like the SetCookie function *sets* the value for a cookie.

The first function locates the cookie by name, and the second function extracts the value from the cookie. As with the previous examples, this JavaScript code is wrapped inside of HTP.PRINT calls so that it can appear within the PL/SQL code sections of the page.

Listing 29-10: **GetCookie script**

```
htp.print('<SCRIPT LANGUAGE="JavaScript">');
htp.print('<!--');
htp.print('function GetCookie (name) {');
htp.print(' var arg = name + "=";');
htp.print(' var alen = arg.length;');
htp.print(' var clen = document.cookie.length;');
htp.print(' var i = 0;');
```

Continued

Listing 29-10 *(continued)*

```
htp.print(' while (i < clen) {');
htp.print(' var j = i + alen;');
htp.print(' if (document.cookie.substring(i, j) == arg)');
htp.print(' return getCookieVal (j);');
htp.print(' i = document.cookie.indexOf(" ", i) + 1;');
htp.print(' if (i == 0) break; ');
htp.print(' }');
htp.print(' return null;');
htp.print('}');
htp.print('//-->');
htp.print('</SCRIPT>');

htp.print('<SCRIPT LANGUAGE="JavaScript">');
htp.print('<!--');
htp.print('function getCookieVal (offset) {');
htp.print(' var endstr = document.cookie.indexOf (";",
offset);');
htp.print(' if (endstr == -1)');
htp.print(' endstr = document.cookie.length;');
htp.print(' return unescape(document.cookie.substring(offset,
endstr));');
htp.print('}');
htp.print('//-->');
htp.print('</SCRIPT>');
```

The critical JavaScript logic appears in the "… after displaying the form." block as shown in Listing 29-11. Oracle Portal displays data using form fields, and the "after" block ensures that the JavaScript code will not execute until the form object has been created. You will notice that this JavaScript code lacks the customary *function* reserved word and the curly braces. By leaving the function qualifier off this block of JavaScript code we are creating an *anonymous* block of JavaScript. The browser will automatically execute this block of JavaScript as part of rendering the page.

Listing 29-11: Anonymous JavaScript Block

```
htp.print('<SCRIPT LANGUAGE="JavaScript">');
htp.print('<!--');
htp.print('var v_recordno');
htp.print('var v_fieldno');
htp.print('var form = document.forms[0]');
htp.print('v_recordno = GetCookie("c_recordno")');
htp.print('alert("Found c_recordno cookie with the value:
"+v_recordno)');
```

```
htp.print('for (i = 0; i <form.elements.length; i++){');
htp.print('v_fieldno = form.elements[i].name');
htp.print('if (v_fieldno.indexOf("RECORDNO")!=-1) {');
htp.print('form.elements[i].value = v_recordno');
htp.print('}');
htp.print('}');
htp.print('//-->');
htp.print('</SCRIPT>');
```

Because we are creating this code after the form object itself is created, the browser will create the form and then execute this code immediately. This allows the browser to extract the value of the cookie and then load the value into a field on the form without waiting for the user to trigger a JavaScript event. While the previous blocks of code are relatively easy to follow, this anonymous JavaScript is slightly more complicated. The first three lines of code declare local variables — one for the cookie value, one for the field into which the cookie value is to be loaded, and one for the form object.

```
var v_recordno
var v_fieldno
var form = document.forms[0]
```

The next line of code calls the `GetCookie` function and passes the literal name of the cookie to be located. The resulting value is stored in a local variable. The `alert` function displays the value of the cookie — and allows you to verify that the JavaScript function was executed. (Normally you will not include the `alert` call in your production code.)

```
v_recordno = GetCookie("c_recordno")
alert("Found c_recordno cookie with the value: "+v_recordno)
```

The final block of code is the most complex. The `form` variable has been set to the current page, so the `for` loop can be used to step through each form element on the page. With each step of the loop we set the `v_fieldno` variable to the name of the current form object. We then search the name for the RECORDNO string, which is the field into which the cookie value should be loaded.

```
for (i = 0; i <form.elements.length; i++){
v_fieldno = form.elements[i].name')
if (v_fieldno.indexOf("RECORDNO")!=-1) {
form.elements[i].value = v_recordno
}
}
```

If you find a match in the name of the field, then you set the value of the field
`form.elements[i].value` to the value that you extracted from the cookie
`v_recordno`.

Although it looks complex, it becomes a trivial matter to pass values from one form
to another by means of cookies.

Caution   Oracle Portal uses very long names for each of the fields on a form, and the name
is almost *never* the same between executions of the form. That means that every
time that the form is run, the actual name of the field will be different! However,
the *actual name* of the field as it is known to the database will always appear
within the generated field name. So, we can use the `indexOf` JavaScript function
to find the name within the name.

Adding Custom Attributes and Types

Chapters 22 and 24 introduced you to Oracle Portal's Content Areas. Content Areas
provide you with the tools that allow your portal's end users to add their own content to the portal site. You can build your own components, such as forms, reports,
and calendars — and end users can add content using these objects as well. The
advantage of building your own components is that they are more *structured*. Since
you control the look and feel, you can control the manner in which users add data
to the site. The obvious disadvantage is that you have to build these components
yourself.

Content Areas have many built-in components such as URLs, Files, and Text items.
However, when end users use these components they are only able to enter values
and content using the built-in set of attributes. For example, you might want users
to be able to add their own news stories as text to your site. For each news story
that the user enters, you might want to require the user to enter a value that indicates the importance or relevance of the story. The Text item might seem perfect
for this requirement. However, Portal's Content Area Text items do not have any
built-in capability to prompt for an "importance" parameter. As first glance, you
might think that you will need to handcraft a text component to solve this problem.

Think again. Oracle Portal allows you to build your own attributes and assign these
attributes to your folders and content items. In this section we'll take a look at creating custom attributes and using them with folders and items.

**Cross-
Reference**   In order to complete the examples in this section, you will need to have completed the exercises in Chapters 22 and 24.

1. Load the script lov_importance.sql into the NETCOLLEGE application using
   the PORTAL30 account.

2. Use the Oracle Portal Navigator and navigate to the Net University Content
   Items area as shown in Figure 29-17.

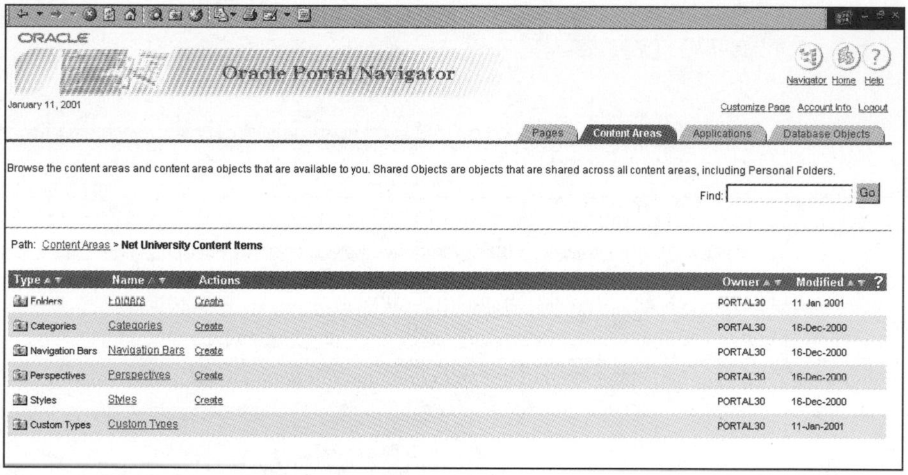

Figure 29-17: Oracle Navigator—Content Areas

3. The last link within the Content Area is the Custom Types. Click on this link to display the panel shown in Figure 29-18.

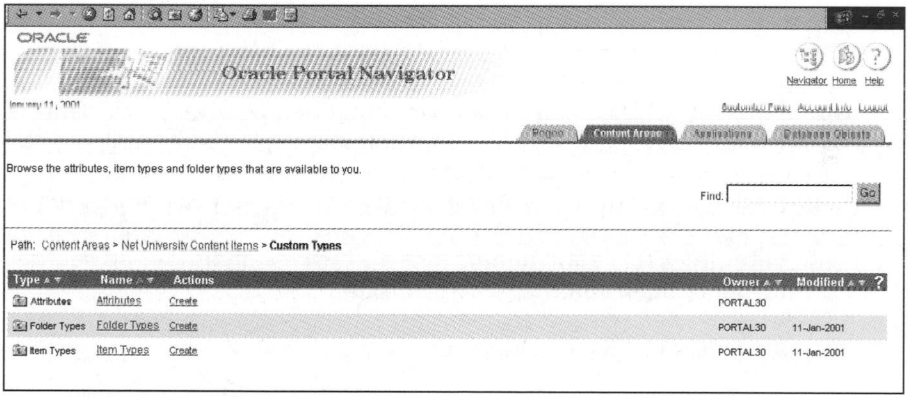

Figure 29-18: Custom Types

There are three custom types—attributes, folders, and items. When you upload content items into Content Areas, Oracle Portal automatically assigns values to the built-in attributes. For example, each item that is uploaded has a Create date and an Author—these values are two of the attributes for this content item. As discussed in Chapter 24, each of the content types has a common set of attributes. You are not limited, however, to using these prebuilt attributes. Oracle Portal allows you to add your own custom attributes.

4. Click on the Create button next to the Attributes line to display the panel shown in Figure 29-19.

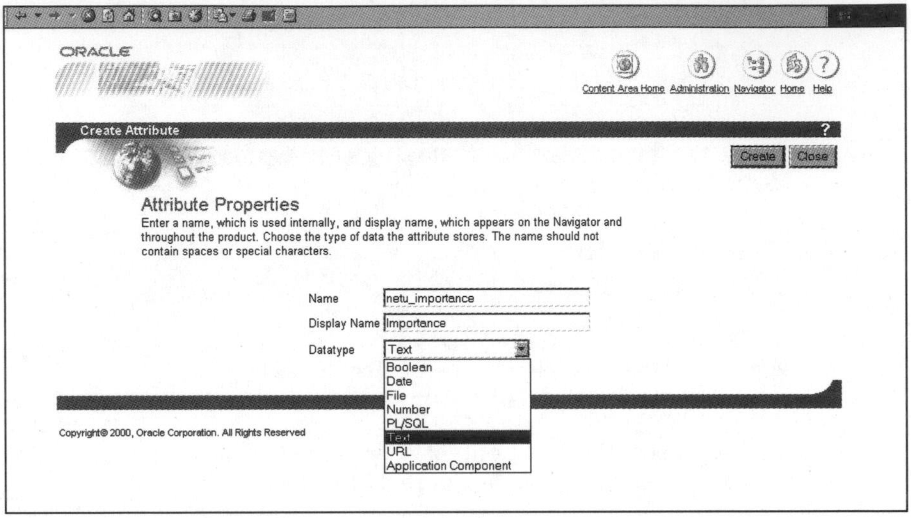

Figure 29-19: Create Attribute

There are three elements to a given attribute, the name, the display name, and the data type. The name and display name follow the same rules as any other object within Content Areas (such as categories and perspectives). The name is used as the internal reference for the attribute and the display name appears on forms and pages as seen by the end user. In our example case, we are adding a new attribute that will determine the level of importance of items that are added to the site.

5. Enter the name **netu_importance** for the new attribute and set the display name to **Importance** as shown in Figure 29-19.

Each attribute is built from a base data type:

✦ Boolean: TRUE/FALSE

✦ Date: dd-mon-yyyy

✦ File: Stores an uploaded file (HTML Page etc.)

✦ Number: Numeric value (855, 1001, etc.)

✦ PL/SQL: PL/SQL code (`htp.print('Some text');`)

✦ Text: Text value (`'Fred'`, `'Sue'`, `...`)

✦ URL: Web URL (`http://www.someserver.com/index.html`)

✦ Application Component: (NETUCOLLEGE:CH20_MENU)

In our example case we want to store a text value as an attribute. We can define multiple levels of importance and assign a text string for each value.

6. Choose the Text data type and press the Create button to store the new attribute.

7. Press the Importance link at the top of the generated page to display the panel shown in Figure 29-20.

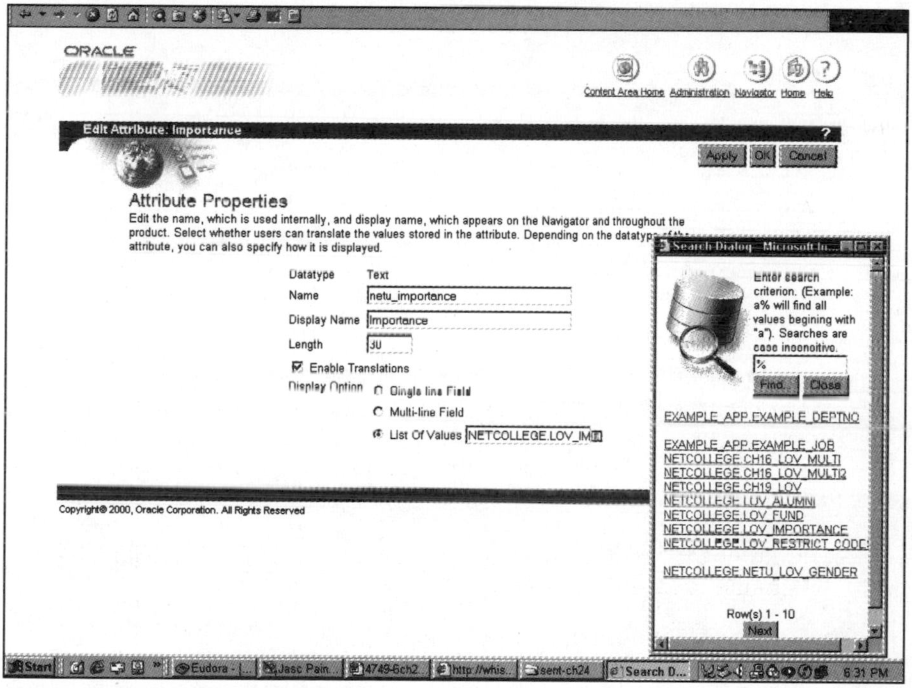

Figure 29-20: Attribute Properties

Each data type has an associated set of properties that you can edit. The text item, for example, allows you to set a length value, and it allows you to associate the text item with a list-of-values object. The pop-up overlay shows a LOVs that you can choose from, including the LOV_IMPORTANCE LOV object that you loaded into the system earlier in this chapter.

8. Locate the LOV_IMPORTANCE object and associate it with the Importance attribute as shown in Figure 29-20.

9. Use the OK button to save your changes.

Now that you have created a new attribute, it is a simple matter to create a new item type and deploy the attribute to this new item.

10. Navigate back to the Custom Types panel and click on the Create link next to the Item Types row to display the panel shown in Figure 29-21.

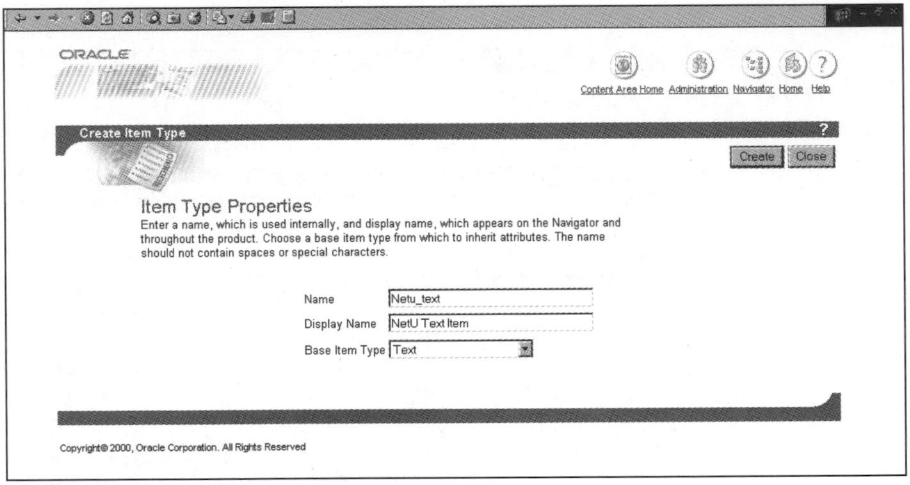

Figure 29-21: Create Item Type

It will come as no surprise to you that item types have three elements — a name, a display name, and a base item type. The name and display name work just like they do with the custom attributes. The base item type is the Content Item type on which this new item is to be based. For example, if you wanted to create a new URL link, then you would select the base item type of URL. In our example case, we are creating a new text item, so select Text from the Base Item Type combo box.

11. Press the Create button and then use the NetU Text Item link to display the panel as shown in Figure 29-22.

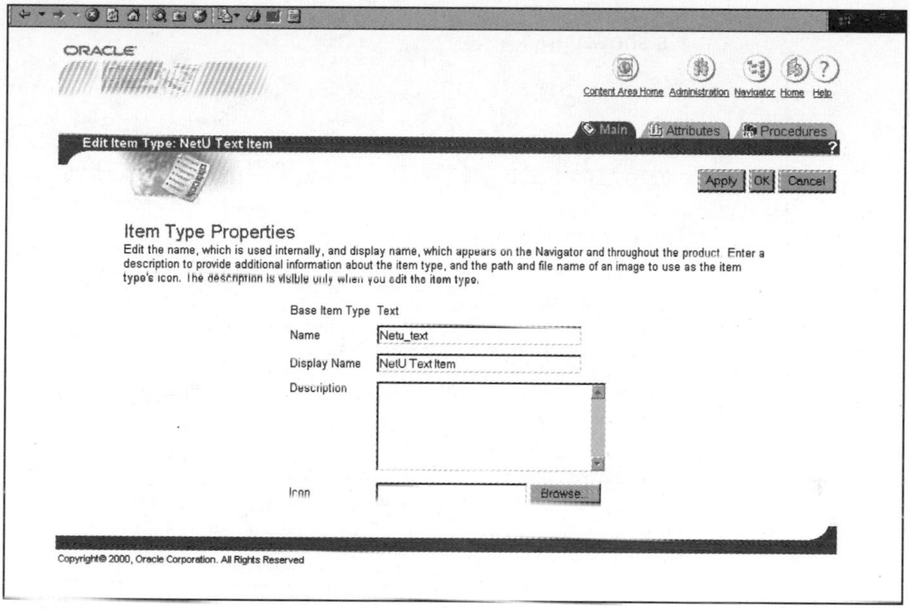

Figure 29-22: Edit Item Type: NetU Text Item

You are free to add a description for the new item, or you can add icon that will be associated with this custom item type.

12. Navigate to the Attributes panel as shown in Figure 29-23.

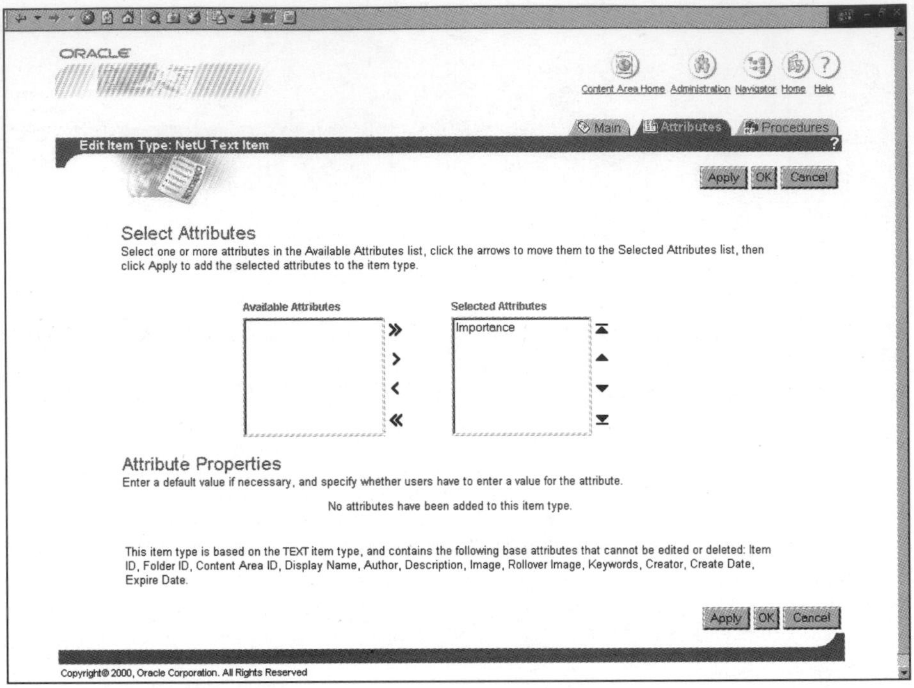

Figure 29-23: NetU Text Item — custom attributes

The Attributes panel contains the custom attribute Importance that you created earlier in this section. The arrow keys permit you to move any available attribute to the Selected Attributes list.

13. Use the single arrow key (>) to move the Importance attribute to the Selected Attributes list and then press the OK button to save the change.

14. Navigate to the Seniors folder in the Content Area and press the Edit folder link.

15. Use the Add item link to add a new item to any category and display the panel as shown in Figure 29-24.

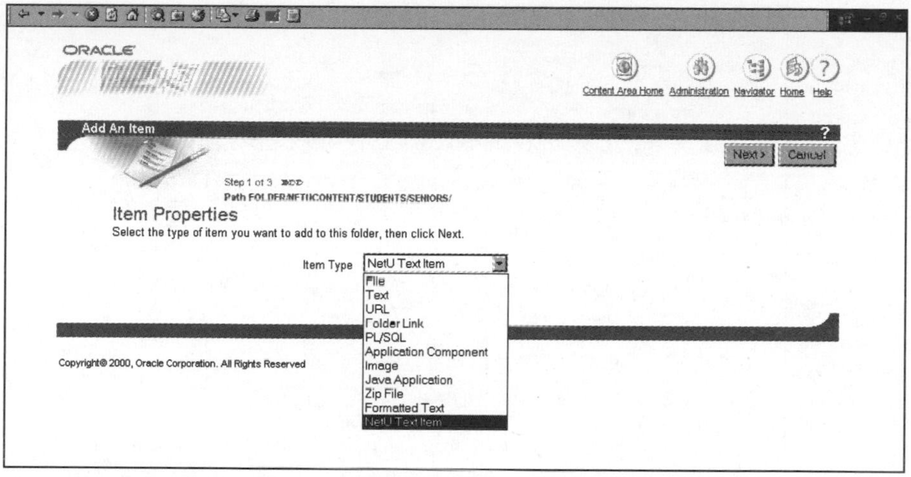

Figure 29-24: Adding a NetU Text Item

Your new text item appears automatically in the list of item types as shown in Figure 29-24. Because we created the custom item type in the NETUCONTENT Content Area, the NETU_TEXT_ITEM item type will only appear within this one Content Area.

Tip   You can create custom item types in the Shared Components area if you want them to appear in all Content Areas.

16. Choose the NETU_TEXT_ITEM type and navigate to the Primary Items panel. Add a title and description for the Text item and then navigate to the secondary items panel as shown in Figure 29-25.

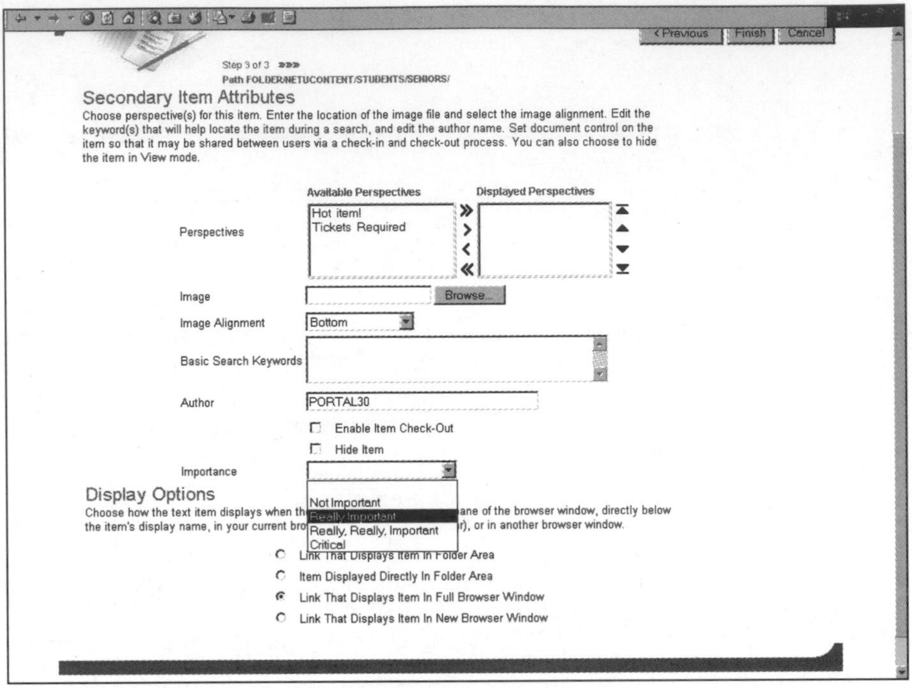

Figure 29-25: Secondary Items — "importance attribute"

You will notice that the custom attribute appears as part of the secondary items — and it automatically displays with the LOV_IMPORTANCE LOV object. Oracle Portal has associated the attribute with the new item type, and you can now automatically enter "importance" values for this item. Furthermore, the end users of your portal can search for items based upon this new attribute as shown in Figure 29-26.

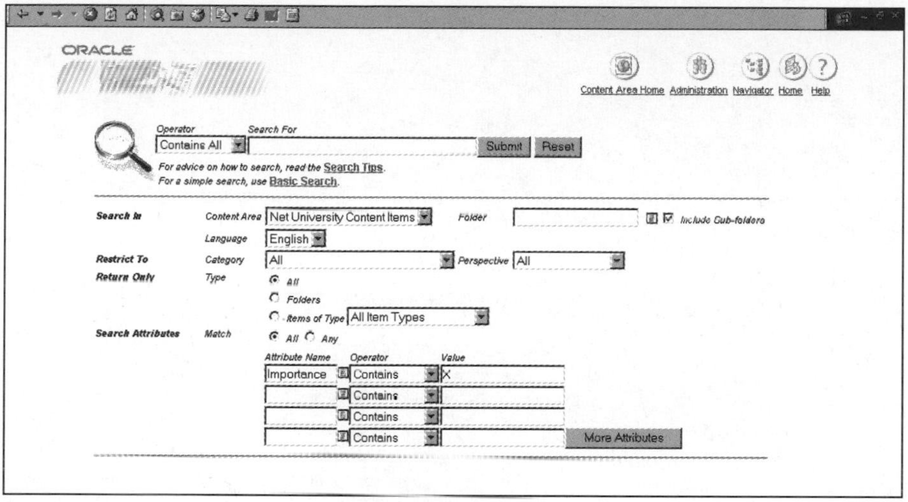

Figure 29-28: Searching on custom attributes

Summary

The advanced topics in this chapter covered a range of complex topics. Loading default values from the database and using cookies to control form navigation represent the most complex tasks that a portal developer might encounter — with the possible exception of Portlet development. At the other end of the spectrum is the ability to define custom attributes and items. You can add custom items and attributes as easy as adding items to your portal. This, however, is not the end of the road. Should you wish to delve deeper into Oracle Portal you can even create your own base types by writing PL/SQL procedures — but that's probably a topic for another book.

✦   ✦   ✦

What's On the CD-ROM

◆ ◆ ◆ ◆

**This CD-ROM
Contains the
Following Items:**

The Net University
Sample Database
Packaged as a Self-
Extracting ZIP File

A Directory of Scripts
and Files for Each
Chapter

A Trial Copy of
Kookaburra
Software's Cookie Pal

A Trial Copy of All
Around Automations
PL/SQL Developer

A Trial Copy of DJJ
Holdings SWiSH

The Entire Book in
Adobe PDF Format

A Free Copy of
Adobe Acrobat
Reader

Microsoft Internet
Explorer

◆ ◆ ◆ ◆

Net University Sample Database

The CD-ROM contains a self-extracting ZIP file of the Net University sample database. The sample database is composed of a series of PL/SQL scripts and image (GIF) files that are used to install and load the Net University model. Chapter 2 provides instructions on installing this database.

Directory of Sample Scripts

The CD-ROM contains a directory hierarchy labeled "Examples" that contains subdirectories for each chapter in which you are required to create or modify a component object. The files in these directories are stored in one of the following formats:

- ◆ PL/SQL Script (SQL or TXT)
- ◆ GIF Images
- ◆ JPEG Images
- ◆ HTML
- ◆ Adobe PDF

The PL/SQL Script format is the most common format, as this is the format Portal uses for importing and exporting component objects. Each component (form, chart, report, and so on) is packaged into a single PL/SQL script file that can be loaded into the database through SQL*Plus.

Graphic images that are used within the exercises (and viewed in the browser) are stored in either GIF or JPEG format, with the vast majority being stored in the lower resolution GIF format. The same image file is often used for exercises in multiple chapters, but a copy of the image is stored in each chapter folder to make them easier to work with.

Certain advanced examples make use of extended HTML code, and these examples are stored in HTML format on the CD-ROM. There is also a single file in Adobe PDF format that is used to simulate the loading of a large report file into Site Builder. (The electronic copy of *Oracle9iAS Portal Bible* is also stored in PDF format.) A free copy of the Adobe PDF viewer can be found on Adobe's Web site (`http://www.adobe.com`) Table A-1 lists all the book's example files by chapter number and filename.

<table>
<tr><th colspan="3">Table A-1
Example Files</th></tr>
<tr><th>Chapter</th><th>Filename</th><th>Description</th></tr>
<tr><td>1</td><td>N/A</td><td>No example files for this chapter</td></tr>
<tr><td>2</td><td>NA</td><td>No example files for this chapter</td></tr>
<tr><td>3</td><td>N/A</td><td>No example files for this chapter</td></tr>
<tr><td>4</td><td>N/A</td><td>No example files for this chapter</td></tr>
<tr><td>5</td><td>N/A</td><td>No example files for this chapter</td></tr>
<tr><td>6</td><td>N/A</td><td>No example files for this chapter</td></tr>
<tr><td>7</td><td>excitenews.txt</td><td>Sample HTML page in text format</td></tr>
<tr><td>8</td><td>ch8_rpt_1.sql</td><td>Student BIO report</td></tr>
<tr><td>8</td><td>ch8_rpt_2.sql</td><td>Students sorted by major report</td></tr>
<tr><td>9</td><td>ch9_rpt_1.sql</td><td>SQL-based student report</td></tr>
<tr><td>9</td><td>ch9_rpt_2.sql</td><td>Aggregate SQL report</td></tr>
<tr><td>9</td><td>ch9_rpt_3.sql</td><td>Student majors/average grade report</td></tr>
<tr><td>9</td><td>ch9_rpt_4.sql</td><td>Multitable majors/class years report</td></tr>
<tr><td>9</td><td>ch9_rpt_5.sql</td><td>Master/detail student report</td></tr>
<tr><td>9</td><td>custom_rep.txt</td><td>Text for custom report</td></tr>
<tr><td>10</td><td>degreelov.sql</td><td>NetU degree list-of-values (B.A./B.S.)</td></tr>
<tr><td>10</td><td>ch10_frm_1.sql</td><td>First form: Student majors</td></tr>
</table>

Chapter	Filename	Description
11	fundlov.sql	Donation Campaign Funds — LOV
11	alumnilov.sql	Alumni Firstname/Lastname — LOV
11	restrictlov.sql	Donation Restriction Codes — LOV
11	courselov.sql	Course Catalog — LOV
11	ch11_frm_1.sql	Donations form based on a stored procedure
11	netu_add_donation.sql	Stored procedure that adds records to the donations table
12	ch12_sql1.txt	SQL source code
12	ch12_sql2.txt	SQL source code
12	ch12_cht_1.sql	Total donations by fund chart
12	ch12_cht_2.sql	Donations to funds by restriction codes chart
12	ch12_cht_3.sql	Donations to funds by restriction codes with restriction names chart
12	ch12_cht_4.sql	Donations by alumni name chart
13	Map_*.gif	22 GIF files of the NETU campus
13	rpt_cal_event.sql	Detail report of a NETU event
13	rpt_cal_sched.sql	List report of NETU events
13	netu_cal_event.sql	Completed calendar object for events
14	advisorlov.sql	List of student advisors — LOV
14	studentlov.sql	List of students — LOV
14	ch14_hie_1.sql	Hierarchy component
15	u1*.gif	75 GIF files — class photos
15	netu_logo.jpg	NETU site logo
15	ch15_dynamic.htm	Simple HTML page
15	ch15_rpt_ugrads.sql	Completed UGRADS report with class photos
16	ch16_frm_dynamiclov.sql	Dynamic list-of-values source form
16	ch16_frm_ugrads.sql	UGRADS data entry form
16	ch16_lov_multi.sql	Destination LOV for multivalue list box example
16	ch16_lov_multi2.sql	Source LOV for class year codes and values
16	ch16_rpt_lov.sql	UGRADS report with LOV for query
17	ch17_mnu_help.htm	Static HTML file used as help text

Continued

Table A-1 *(continued)*

Chapter	Filename	Description
17	netu_about.htm	HTML "About" page for NETU Web site
17	netu_home.htm	Static HTML home page for NETU
17	netu_logo.jpg	JPEG image, NETU logo
17	netu_tabbycat.jpg	Net University mascot
17	ch17_cht_grades.sql	Chart of student grades
17	ch17_mnu_linked.sql	Linked menu object
17	ch17_rpt_courses.sql	Course catalog report
17	ch17_rpt_ugrads.sql	UGRADS student report
18	4749-6 fg1805.tif	Screenshot from the book of Web-safe colors
18	ch18_rpt_catalog	Course catalog report
18	ch18_tohex.htm	HTML page that converts RGB colors into HEX values
18	ch18_unstructured.htm	HTML code for unstructured template
18	netu_bg.gif	Background GIF image
18	netu_campus.gif	GIF logo for NETU
18	netu_help.gif	GIF image file for help link
18	netu_home.gif	GIF image file for home link
18	netu_internal_use.gif	Background GIF image for internal use only documents
18	netu_logo.gif	Alternative logo in GIF format
18	netu_tabbycat.gif	NETU mascot in GIF format
18	netu_heading.swf	Macromedia Flash file
18	netu_logo_animated.gif	Animated GIF file (alternative logo)
19	ch19_crossfield.sql	Template that includes JavaScript code for crossfield validations
19	ch19_frm_donations.sql	Data entry form
19	ch19_js_loop.sql	Simple JavaScript that loops through all fields on a form
19	ch19_frm_javascript.sql	Sample form that displays all JavaScript events

Chapter	Filename	Description
19	ch19_table.sql	Script that creates a simple table for JavaScript event examples
19	lov_restrict_codes.sql	LOV object for ch19_frm_donations
19	lov_fund.sql	LOV object for ch19_frm_donations
19	lov_alumni.sql	LOV object for ch19_frm_donations
19	netu_js_range_1_to_50000.js	JavaScript source
19	netu_js_makenull.js	JavaScript source
19	netu_js_currentyear.js	JavaScript source
19	listing-19-1.txt	"Show value" JS function source
19	listing-19-2.txt	"Hello World" JS function source
19	listing-19-3.txt	Alternative netu_js_makenull source
19	listing-19-4.txt	Alternative netu_js_range_1_to_5000 source
19	listing-19-5.txt	Alternative netu_js_currentyear source
19	listing-19-6.txt	JavaScript embedded into HTML source page
19	listing-19-7.txt	JavaScript loop code
20	ch20_cht_gender.sql	Chart of students by gender
20	ch20_rpt_classes.sql	Report student totals by class year
20	ch20_rpt_students.sql	List of students report
20	ch20_frm_students.sql	Data entry form for student records
20	view_netu_class_totals.sql	SQL script to create view for report examples
20	lnk_cht_gender.sql	Completed link script
20	lnk_frm_students.sql	Completed link script
20	lnk_rpt_classes.sql	Completed link script
21	ch21_plsql_show_ticket_form.sql	PL/SQL script of embedded HTML
21	ch21_plsql_buy_tickets.sql	SQL source for netu.buy_tickets PL/SQL procedure
21	ch21_rpt_classes.sql	Report of total students by class year
21	ch21_rpt_events.sql	Report of scheduled NETU events
22	netu_banner.jpg	NETU banner JPEG
22	netu_hg.jpg	NETU banner JPEG

Continued

Table A-1 *(continued)*

Chapter	Filename	Description
22	netu_logo.jpg	NETU logo JPEG
23	N/A	No example files for this chapter
24	netu_courses.pdf	Course catalog report in Adobe PDF format
24	netu.jar	Java JAR file
24	netu1.jsp	Sample Java server page
24	np1.htm	Static HTML page with link
24	np2.htm	Static HTML page (connects from link)
24	banner_spacer.gif	Spacer file in GIF format
24	ncaa.gif	NCAA logo in GIF format (used as link)
24	netu_imagemap.gif	Image file for use with associated image map
24	netu_logo1.gif	Alternative NETU logo file
24	netu_tabbycat.gif	Alternative NETU mascot image
24	netu_mascot.gif	NETU mascot image
24	ch24_cht_grades.sql	Chart of student grades
24	listing-24-1.sql	Source code in PL/SQL format for generated HTML
24	np.zip	Winzip archive file with two HTML pages and an image
25	N/A	No example files for this chapter
26	N/A	No example files for this chapter
27	N/A	No example files for this chapter
28	PROVIDER.XML	XML descriptor document
28	provsyns.sql	Macro to include synonyms for PDK packages
28	ch28_1_portlet.pks	Package specification for starter package for portlet
28	ch28_1_portlet.pkb	Package body specification for starter package for portlet
28	ch28_provider.pks	Package specification for starter package for provider
28	ch28_provider.pkb	Package body specification for starter package for provider

Chapter	Filename	Description
28	ch28_1_portlet_done.pks	Package specification for completed portlet
28	ch28_1_portlet_done.pkb	Package body specification for completed portlet
28	ch28_provider_done.pks	Package specification for completed provider
28	ch28_provider_done.pkb	Package body specification for completed provider
28	ch28_portlet_v2_done.pkb	Package body specification for second version of completed portlet
28	JSPportlet.jsp	Code for Java server page portlet
28	JSPProvider.xml	XML for Java server page provider
28	readme.html	Description of URL portlet and materials
28	urldisp.sql	Part of URL portlet
28	urlportl.pks	Part of URL portlet
28	urlportl.pkb	Part of URL portlet
28	urlprovd.pks	Part of URL portlet
28	urlprovd.pkb	Part of URL portlet
28	nlsurl.sql	Part of URL portlet
28	synurl.sql	Part of URL portlet
28	urlinstl.cmd	Part of URL portlet
28	gurlsys.sql	Part of URL portlet
28	gurlpkg.sql	Part of URL portlet
29	call_form.sql	Code fragment for PL/SQL Block
29	ch29_default_value.sql	Form component
29	ch29_example1_tbl.sql	Create table script for default value example.
29	ch29_seq.sql	Create sequence script
29	ch29_sequence.sql	Form component
29	js_default_value.sql	PL/SQL script for JavaScript default value function
29	listing_29_1.sql	PL/SQL script for JavaScript default value function
29	listing_29_2.txt	Text output of PL/SQL default value procedure

Continued

Chapter	Filename	Description
Table A-1 *(continued)*		
29	listing_29_4.sql	PL/SQL script for JavaScript sequence number function
29	listing_29_5.txt	HTML output in text format of sequence function
29	listing_29_6.sql	Trigger PL/SQL code block for inserting primary key values
29	listing_29_7.txt	PL/SQL code fragment for form
29	listing_29_8.txt	PL/SQL code fragment to set cookie value
29	listing_29_10.txt	Getcookie functions in PL/SQL code format
29	listing_29_11.txt	Anonymous block of JavaScript code
29	lov_importance.sql	LOV component script

Note Image files are either copied to a file system directory or loaded into Content Areas. They cannot be installed with a single install script, but the relevant chapters show you how to move them to the proper locations.

Other Installation Information

Additional installation information can be found in the README.TXT files in each of the subdirectories on the CD-ROM. There are three third-party tools that we have found useful when working with Oracle Portal.

Utilities

PL/SQL Developer by Allround Automations (Trial Version)

This editor makes it easy to code, debug, and test Oracle PL/SQL code, and we have found it to be an invaluable tool for working with the PL/SQL Language. One of the foundations of the Oracle database, and, by extension, Oracle Portal, is the PL/SQL language. Oracle provides a number of tools for writing and debugging PL/SQL, but most programmers have found these default utilities to be of minimal value. For more information about PL/SQL Developer, check out Allround Automations' Web site at http://www.allroundautomations.nl/plsqldev.html.

Cookie Pal by Kookaburra Software (Trial Version)

Cookie Pal is an interactive environment for managing browser cookies with Internet Explorer and Netscape Navigator. Oracle Portal makes extensive use of "cookies" for session management and authentication. The default cookie tools within most Web browsers make it difficult for programmers to view and manage cookies during the development process. For this reason we have included a trial copy of Kookaburra Software's Cookie Pal. For more information about Cookie Pal, check out Kookaburra Software's Web site at http://www.kburra.com/.

SWiSH by DJJ Holdings Pty Ltd (Trial Version)

SWiSH creates Flash-compatible graphics through an easy-to-use interface. Many popular Web sites make use of Macromedia's Flash product. Flash allows you to build complex, interactive graphics that make your Web sites and portals more spectacular from a visual perspective. However, Flash can be a complicated product to work with. For more information about SWiSH, check out DJJ Holdings Pty Ltd's Web site at http://www.swishzone.com/.

On the Web

Check the site http://www.oracleportalbible.com for updates, new samples, and more information on Portal.

✦   ✦   ✦

Loading Portal Examples

◆ ◆ ◆ ◆

In This Appendix

Loading Examples

Setting Your Working Directory

Loading a Component Using SQL*Plus

◆ ◆ ◆ ◆

Loading Examples into the System

You should install the PL/SQL script files using SQL*Plus, which is Portal's standard import/export utility. The first step for any installation is to set SQL*Plus' working directory to the directory where the source files are located.

Note   The source files take up less than 1MB of disk space, and we recommend that you copy the entire examples directory tree to a local hard drive before you attempt to install any of the components.

Set your working directory

The process of setting the working directory for SQL*Plus varies by platform. We recommend that you use the command line version of the SQL*Plus utility when you load in any of the Portal examples. (It is much easier to set your working directory with the command line version of SQL*Plus.)

The critical setting is the working directory. You need to point this setting to the directory where the script files are located. For example, assume that you have copied the examples directory to your local hard drive C:\. The result is a series of subdirectories much like the following list:

```
c:\examples\ch1
c:\examples\ch6
...
c:\examples\ch29
```

In order to load an individual component into the database, set your working directory to the full directory path where the component is stored on your hard drive. For example, to load the first component for Chapter 5, ch5_rep_1.sql, set your working directory to the path c:\portal30\examples\ch5.

Note Experienced SQL*Plus users will note that you can specify a complete path for SQL scripts inside SQL*Plus, making it unnecessary to set the working directory as described.

Connect to SQL*Plus and load a single component

You must load Portal components into the system using the PORTAL account (PORTAL30). The Portal import utility makes use of certain tables not made public to other Oracle accounts, forcing you to use the Portal account in order to load components into the system. Because the Portal account is equipped with DBA privileges, you may not be permitted access to this account. In such cases, you need to involve your systems administrator in order to gain access to the Portal account (or have them load the components into Portal for you). Once you have connected to SQL*Plus, the process of loading in a component is a quick and easy one.

Note Certain chapters contain instances where scripts need to be run inside the Net University account. In such cases, hands-on instructions within these chapters explicitly list this requirement.

1. Copy the \portal30\examples directory tree from the CD-ROM to your hard drive.

2. Open a command window and set your default directory to the location into which you copied the Appendix B code files (portal30\examples\appb, as shown in Figure B-1).

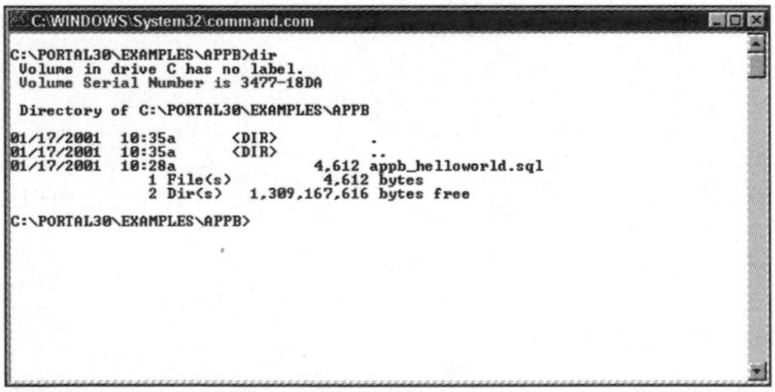

Figure B-1: Command window

3. Start SQL*Plus and log on to the PORTAL30 account as shown in Figure B-2.

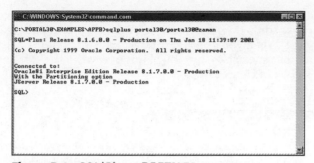

Figure B-2: SQL*Plus — PORTAL30 account

Oracle9iAS Portal packages components into SQL scripts, which are loaded into the database by SQL*Plus. SQL*Plus can load script files into the database by means of the @ character and a command string. The command string is nothing more than the name of the SQL script proceeded by the @ command character. For example, to load the first report in Chapter 9, you would enter the following command:

```
@ch9_rpt_1.sql
```

Once you enter the command string, SQL*Plus reads the script and begins loading the component into the system. As the script is processed, you will see a series of messages and prompts on the screen. SQL*Plus displays a final message at the end of the script to let you know that the component has been loaded and that the resulting procedure has been generated.

We have included a test procedure that you can use to verify that the import process is working on your portal site.

Caution   In order to load the test component into the system, you must complete all of the installation tasks as outlined in Chapter 2.

4. Install the test procedure by entering the following SQL*Plus command as shown in Figure B-3. (You should already have set your default to the working directory for this code in step 2.)

```
@appb_helloworld.sql
```

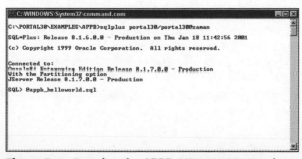

Figure B-3: Running the APPB_HELLOWORLD script

The installation script will prompt you for various parameters as it goes along. The first parameter that it asks for is the import mode. You can CREATE the component or CHECK the component. When you specify CHECK mode, the import script will verify whether the component exists — but it will not overwrite the existing version of the component as shown in Figure B-4.

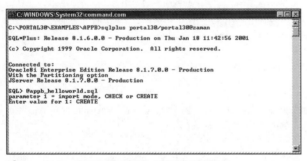

Figure B-4: CHECK mode

5. Specify **CREATE** mode to install the new component as shown in Figure B-5.

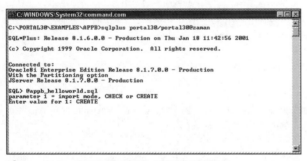

Figure B-5: CREATE APPB_HELLOWORLD

The next parameter for the import script is the name of the PORTAL30 schema. Under most conditions this will be the value PORTAL30. You can, however, specify a different schema during the *installation* of Oracle Portal, and the value that you input here must match the portal schema name. The import utility stores the source code for a component in the portal schema, but the production object (i.e., the PL/SQL procedure) is stored in the application account.

6. Enter the name of your **PORTAL30** schema as shown in Figure B-6.

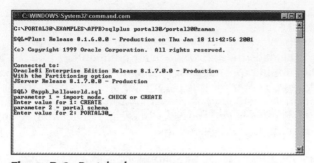

Figure B-6: Portal schema name

The next two parameters are the user name and password that you want Oracle to use to connect to the database. Technically speaking, you are already connected to the database when you run the script — but you can specify another account as the login account for the script. In most cases you should use the PORTAL30 account user name and password as shown in Figures B-7 and B-8.

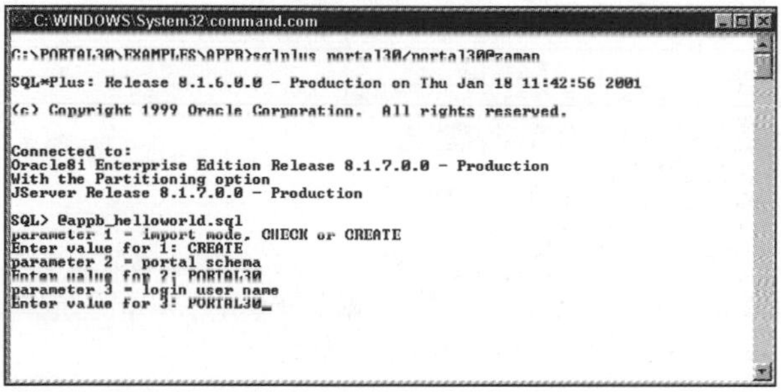

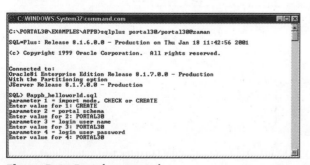

Figure B-7: Portal user name

Figure B-8: Portal password

7. Enter the portal user name and password for the PORTAL30 account as shown in Figures B-7 and B-8.

As just mentioned, Oracle loads the source code for components into the POR-TAL30 schema, but the production code is stored in an application schema. The name of the schema that you enter for this parameter should match the schema owner for the application into which you are loading the component. In this example, we use the NETU schema and the NETCOLLEGE application. A single schema (NETU) can "own" multiple applications.

8. Enter NETU as the owner of the component as shown in Figure B-9.

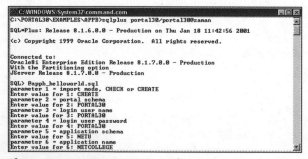

```
C:\WINDOWS\System32\command.com
C:\PORTAL30\EXAMPLES\APPB>sqlplus portal30/portal30@zaman

SQL*Plus: Release 8.1.6.0.0 - Production on Thu Jan 18 11:42:56 2001

(c) Copyright 1999 Oracle Corporation.  All rights reserved.


Connected to:
Oracle8i Enterprise Edition Release 8.1.7.0.0 - Production
With the Partitioning option
JServer Release 8.1.7.0.0 - Production

SQL> @appb_helloworld.sql
parameter 1 = import mode, CHECK or CREATE
Enter value for 1: CREATE
parameter 2 = portal schema
Enter value for 2: PORTAL30
parameter 3 = login user name
Enter value for 3: PORTAL30
parameter 4 = login user password
Enter value for 4: PORTAL30
parameter 5 = application schema
Enter value for 5: NETU_
```

Figure B-9: NETU account parameter

Each application schema can own several applications — but we are using a one-to-one relationship for the examples in this book. All components should be loaded into the NETCOLLEGE application as shown in Figure B-10.

```
C:\WINDOWS\System32\command.com
C:\PORTAL30\EXAMPLES\APPB>sqlplus portal30/portal30@zaman

SQL*Plus: Release 8.1.6.0.0 - Production on Thu Jan 18 11:42:56 2001

(c) Copyright 1999 Oracle Corporation.  All rights reserved.


Connected to:
Oracle8i Enterprise Edition Release 8.1.7.0.0 - Production
With the Partitioning option
JServer Release 8.1.7.0.0 - Production

SQL> @appb_helloworld.sql
parameter 1 = import mode, CHECK or CREATE
Enter value for 1: CREATE
parameter 2 = portal schema
Enter value for 2: PORTAL30
parameter 3 = login user name
Enter value for 3: PORTAL30
parameter 4 = login user password
Enter value for 4: PORTAL30
parameter 5 = application schema
Enter value for 5: NETU
parameter 6 = application name
Enter value for 6: NETCOLLEGE
```

Figure B-10: NETCOLLEGE Application Name

9. Enter **NETCOLLEGE** as the application name.

Oracle automatically makes a record of the import process via a log file. You have the option of specifying a log file name for the import operation. This log file is stored in the working directory of your current session.

10. Enter **appb_helloworld.log** as the log file name as shown in Figure B-11.

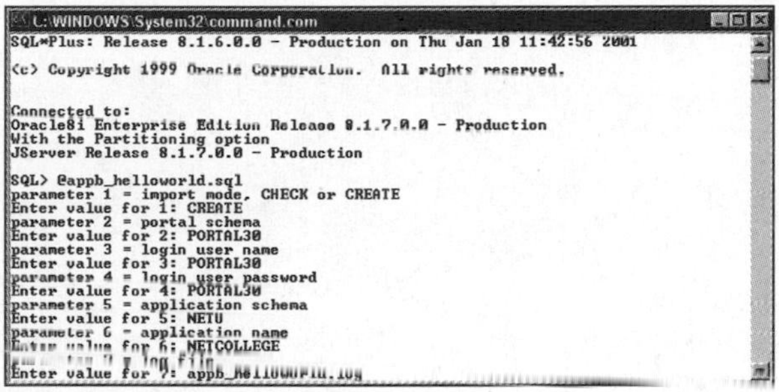

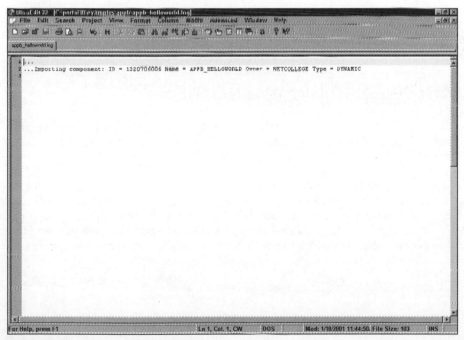

Figure B-11: Log file name

Under normal conditions, the log file will not have much information stored inside of it. If you encounter errors, however, these will be displayed in vivid detail within the log file, as shown in Figure B-12.

Figure B-12: Default log file output

The import script will run unattended after you enter the required parameters, and it will disconnect from the database and exit SQL*Plus after the import operation is complete. Once you have imported a component it will become available within the portal application immediately. In our example case, the APPB_HELLOWORLD component is stored in the NETCOLLEGE application as shown in Figure B-13.

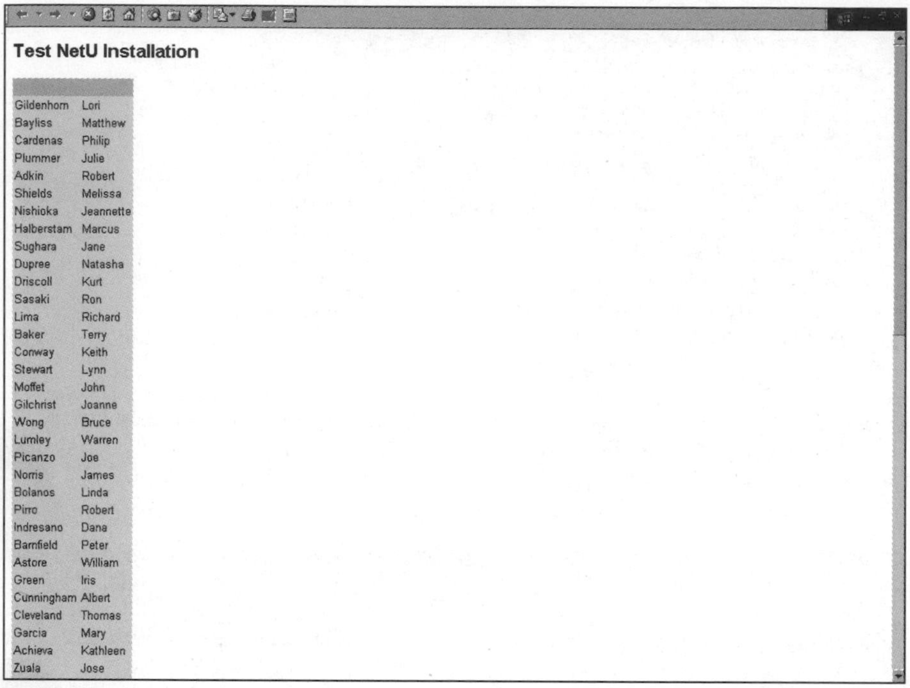

Test NetU Installation

Gildenhorn	Lori
Bayliss	Matthew
Cardenas	Philip
Plummer	Julie
Adkin	Robert
Shields	Melissa
Nishioka	Jeannette
Halberstam	Marcus
Sughara	Jane
Dupree	Natasha
Driscoll	Kurt
Sasaki	Ron
Lima	Richard
Baker	Terry
Conway	Keith
Stewart	Lynn
Moffet	John
Gilchrist	Joanne
Wong	Bruce
Lumley	Warren
Picanzo	Joe
Norris	James
Bolanos	Linda
Pirro	Robert
Indresano	Dana
Barnfield	Peter
Astore	William
Green	Iris
Cunningham	Albert
Cleveland	Thomas
Garcia	Mary
Achieva	Kathleen
Zuala	Jose

Figure B-13: Hello World!

All of the PORTAL components that are provided with this book can be imported by using this same format. Simply set your working directory to the chapter subdirectory within the examples folder and run the import.

Note   In some cases the examples require you to add new components to the NETU account. These scripts create tables, views, or other objects that are specific to the Net University sample database. When you import these components, you should log on to the NETU account — not the PORTAL30 account. You will not need to supply any of the parameters in such cases. Simply log on to the NETU account with SQL*Plus and run the script using the @ command string.

Index

Symbols

#BASE# substitution tag, 389
#BODY# keyword, User Interface Templates, 508
#FRAMELINK# keyword, User Interface Templates, 508
#HEADING# keyword, User Interface Templates, 508
#IMAGE_PREFIX# keyword, User Interface Templates, 508
#TITLE# keyword, User Interface Templates, 508
% (percent sign) wildcard for Find, 89
_ (underscore) wildcard for Find, 89
_break_cols parameter, Link Wizard, 566
_font_size parameter, Link Wizard, 566
_format_out parameter, Link Wizard, 566
_max_rows parameter, Link Wizard, 566
_orderby_col parameter, Link Wizard, 566
_orderby_ord parameter, Link Wizard, 566
_show_header parameter, Link Wizard, 566
_title parameter, Link Wizard, 567

A

About link, Manage Components, 732–733
abstract users (roles) for database security, 758, 759–760, 789
access control from portals and portlets, 132
access levels for portal pages, Page Wizard, 156, 157–159
access settings, Folder Wizard, 626–627
Access tab, Manage Components, 741–742, 743–744
accessing objects with Database Objects tab of Navigator, 100–103
Account Info
    home page, 61
    Navigator, 80
Account Lockout Policies, 792
Actions column
    Database Objects tab of Navigator, 96–100
    Navigator, 81
Activity Log Interval, 752
activity logs, monitoring performance, 790–790, 827–828
Add Favorite Group, home page, 63–64
Add Portlets page, 150–155. See also building portal page; creating own portlet and provider; Page Wizard; portals and portlets; reports as portlets

Add Column icon, 153–154
Add Portlet link, 151
available portlets, 151
Back Portlet link, 151
charts as portlets, 325–328
deleting portlets, 152
Edit Default links, 153
folder icon (move to another region), 152
forms as portlets, 278–279
hiding portlets, 152
moving portlets, 152, 153
red X icon (delete), 152
regions, 153–155, 159–160
Selected Portlets box, 151
upward-pointing arrow icon (move in display region), 153
Add to Favorites link, Manage Components, 732
Add-Item Wizard, Content Areas, 707–710
adding
    code to templates, JavaScript, 549–551
    colors, Color Wizard, 485–488
    content to site, 697–718
    database access code, PL/SQL, 602–605
    elements to Navigation Bar, 644–645, 646
    fonts, 490–492
    HTML code, Dynamic Pages Wizard, 387–390
    items, folder Wizard, 624
    items, Form Wizard, 256–257
    items, Menu Builder Wizard, 460, 461–466
    items to folders, Content Areas, 700–706
    SQL code, Dynamic Pages Wizard, 390–393
    templates, User Interface Templates, 502–506
    users and groups to folders, Content Areas, 695–696
Additional PL/SQL Code
    Dynamic Pages Wizard, 386
    PL/SQL logic integration, 598–602, 602–605
add_months() function, 331
Administer Database, NetU Database, 48–49
administration, 729–756. See also Manage Components; monitoring performance; security
    Activity Log Interval, 752
    Administration tab, 750–755
    application management, 743–744
    ARCHIVE status, 730
    Beta Features, 752

Continued

administration *(continued)*
    Cookie Domain, 752
    Default Home Page, 752
    Default Style, 752
    Global Settings, 751–752
    Listener Gateway Settings, 753
    Log Registry Administration, 753, 799–805
    Login Server Administration, 753–754
    Login Server Settings, 752
    Logout Behavior, 752
    managing applications, 743–744
    NETUDEV user, 750
    Node portlet, 755
    portal environment, 750–755
    Portlet Timing, 752
    PRODUCTION status, 730
    Provider portlet, 754–755
    Proxy Server, 752
    restoring previous versions, 730–731
    Search Settings, 753
    Services portlet, 751–754
    Temporary Directory, 752
    version control, 197, 729–731, 735–736
    Version Information, 752
Administrative icon, Navigation Bar, 644
Administrators
    Content Areas, 621, 718–721
    privileged account, 762, 764, 774
    security, 759
Advanced Options, portals and portlets, 134–135
Advanced Search, Content Areas, 723–724
ADVISORLOV choice, Hierarchy Wizard, 376
"After Page" text box, PL/SQL, 602
aggregate functions
    Chart Wizard, 305, 309
    SQL Query Link for reports, 222–226
alert() method, 529
Align Column Parameter, running reports, 201
Align of Column Formatting, Query-By-Example
    (QBE) Report Wizard, 180
ALUMNI table, NetU Database, 45
AM format mask element, 333
animated image files, 499
anonymous
    JavaScript block, 884–886
    PL/SQL blocks, 602
    portals, Content Areas, 691
Apache Listener
    configuration, setup.exe, 23
    deployment, 659–660, 661, 662–663

    portal installation, 37
    post-installation check, 38–39
    Uniform Resource Locators (URLs), 23, 37, 38–39,
        453, 454
Apache server disabling, 18, 19
appimp script, 748
Application combo box, Query-By-Example (QBE)
    Report Wizard, 175
Application components, Content Areas, 698,
    707–712
application creation for NetU Database, 47–50
application data, deployment, 662
Application Image Alt Text entry field, User Interface
    Templates, 505
application "owner," LOV Wizard, 417
Application Schema, deployment, 672–675, 676
applications. *See also* Content Area Create Wizard;
    Content Areas; data validation;
    deployment; Link Wizard; Lists-of-Values
    (LOVs); Menu Builder Wizard; PL/SQL
    logic integration; Shared Components
    exporting and importing, 747–748
    management, 743–744
    overview, 6, 14
    privileges, 773, 783–785
Applications tab, Navigator, 80, 85–88
Apply button, home page, 66
Approve icon, Content Areas, 720
archive kits extraction, setup.exe, 20
ARCHIVE status, 197, 348, 730
arrow images, 496
arrows on wizard panel, 75
ASCII formatting, Query-By-Example (QBE)
    Report Wizard, 185
attaching scripts to forms, JavaScript, 545–547
attributes of items, Style Manager, 637–638
authenticated portals, Content Areas, 691
authenticated (private) components, Database
    Access Descriptors (DADs), 671
authentication
    post-installation check, 43–44
    privileged accounts, 762
Authentication Mode, Database Access Descriptors
    (DADs), 666
author text field, Content Areas, 704
authorization, 762
automatic portlet generation, 137
automatic substitution for missing fonts,
    488, 489–490
Available Attributes list box, Style Manager, 638
available portlets, 151

AVG function
    Chart Wizard, 305
    SQL Query Link for reports (on CD-ROM),
        224–226
Axis combo box, Chart Wizard, 308

B

Back button, 55
background
    Form Wizard, 260
    Image And Banner Height Settings,
        Page Wizard, 149
    images, 496, 498
    Navigation Bar, 643
    Query-By-Example (QBE) Report Wizard, 183
    Style Manager, 633
    User Interface Templates, 503
banner
    area, home page, 58
    greeting, Page Wizard, 148–149
    icon for Navigator, 79
    links, Page Wizard, 149–150
    logo settings, Page Wizard, 149
    properties, home page, 61
    setting, Style Manager, 630–632
Bar Height combo box, Chart Wizard, 309
Bar Image text box, Chart Wizard, 309
Bar Width combo box, Chart Wizard, 309
base-level objects and containers, Navigator, 84–85
#BASE# substitution tag, 389
Basic Search Keywords text box, Content Areas, 704
batch reporting, 192, 249, 343
"Before Footer" text box, PL/SQL, 602
"Before Header" text box, PL/SQL, 601
"Before Page" text box, PL/SQL, 600–601
begin/end keywords, PL/SQL, 602, 604
Beta Features, 752
BIND variables
    Calendar Wizard, 337, 342, 357
    Dynamic Pages Wizard, 384, 395–397
    Frame Driver Wizard, 403, 405, 406, 407
    linking from frame drivers, 405, 406, 407
    Lists-of-Values (LOVs), 440–444
Blank item type, Form Wizard, 264, 267, 520
blue arrows icon (move), 257, 463
#BODY# keyword, User Interface Templates, 500
bookmarks, 55
Boolean datatype, JavaScript, 524
border
    Calendar Wizard, 342
    Form Wizard, 260
    Frame Driver Wizard, 402

Query-By-Example (QBE) Report Wizard, 186
brand recognition from consistency, 477
Break columns, Report Wizard, 215
break command, 527
Break conditions, Report Wizard, 213
Break Down option, Hierarchy Wizard, 367, 368
Break Options
    Query-By-Example (QBE) Report Wizard, 189, 190
    running reports, 205–206
_break_cols parameter, Link Wizard, 566
breaks, multiple tables in a report, 237–238
browser preferences, fonts, 488, 489, 491, 493
"browser-safe" palette, 482, 483
browsing (querying) data, 110–115. See also
        Database Objects tab of Navigator
    Column Information, 111
    Column Selection Criteria, 111
    Count Rows Only option, 113
    Display Results In Table with Borders option, 113
    Maximum Rows, 112–113
    Output Format, 112
    Query Button, 114–115
    Query Options, 113–114
    Query Rows action, 97, 110–115
    Replace ASCII new lines option, 114
    Reset button, 115
    Row Order Options, 112
    Show Horizontal Rule (HR) Between Rows
        option, 114
    Show Null As, 113
    Show Paging Buttons option, 114, 115
    Show SQL option, 113
    Show Total Row Count option, 113
    upper() function, 115
    WHERE clause, 112
Build tab, 54, 73–74
building portal page, 143–170. See also Add Portlets
        page; Page Wizard; portals and portlets;
        reports as portlets
    Close button, 162, 164, 167
    "Customize for" label, 164–167
    Customize link, 159–160, 161
    default page, 169
    Edit Region icon, 159–160
    HTML portlet, working with, 161–164
    JavaScript, adding to HTML portlet (on CD-ROM),
        162–163
    Make Default action, 169
    Make Top-Level action, 168–169
    My Pages, 83, 168–169

                                                    Continued

building portal page *(continued)*
    personalizing portal page, 161–169
    Preview button, 162, 163
    promoting a page, 167–169
    top-level pages, 168–169
    user, making changes as, 161–169
building portal sites. *See* Content Area Create
        Wizard; Content Areas; deployment
BUILDINGS table, NetU Database, 45
built-in portlet, calling, 853–855
Button item type, Form Wizard, 264, 267, 520
Button Location combo box, Frame Driver
        Wizard, 403
Button Name field, Frame Driver Wizard, 403
button options
    Calendar Wizard, 343–344
    Form Wizard, 261–262
    Hierarchy Wizard, 369
    Query-By-Example (QBE) Report Wizard, 192
Buy_tickets code example, PL/SQL, 605–608

C

caching
    option, setting, 54
    portals and portlets, 138–141
Calendar Wizard, 334–360. *See also* dates; Link
        Wizard; linking from calendar cells
    ARCHIVE status, 348
    Batch button, 343
    BIND variables, 337, 342, 357
    border combo box, 342
    Button options, 343–344
    category field, 351
    Cell Font Color Option, 341
    Cell Font Face option, 341
    Cell Font Size option, 341
    FROM clause, 337
    Common Options, 338–339
    concatenating strings, 350–352
    Customization Entry Form Display Options,
        339, 342–344, 357
    date field, 336
    date link, 337
    Day Font Color option, 341
    Day Font Face option, 341
    Default Value field, 358
    Display Options, 338–342
    EDIT status, 347
    editing, 350–352
    event_date field, 350

eventid field, 351
Expire After (Minutes) field, 338
Finish button, 346
Footer Text, 345
Full Page Options, 338, 339–340
Header Text, 345
Heading Background Color option, 342
Help Text, 345
Link Icon, 339
Log Activity check box, 340
Look and Feel Options, 340–342
Maximum Months Per Page option, 340, 343
Month Font Color/Face/Size option, 341
name link, 336–337
ORDER BY clause, 338
overview, 9–10
Page Width parameter, 340, 341
parameters, adding, 357–359
PL/SQL code, 346, 347
Portlet Options, 338, 342
PRODUCTION status, 347
Reset button, 343
running calendar, 343, 347–350
SELECT keyword, 336
Show Monday-Friday Only option, 338, 343
Show Query Conditions check box, 340
Show Timing option, 340
sorting data, 349–350
SQL Query, 336–338
string concatenation, 350–352
Table Background Color option, 342
target frame, 337
Template combo box, 345, 346
Text Options, 344–347
Title text, 345
WHERE clause, 337, 357
Call Interface label, running reports, 196
Call Interface link, Manage Components, 736–737
calling built-in portlet, 853–855
calling reports directly, 247–248
Cancel button
    home page, 66
    wizard panel, 76
Cascade Delete Detail Rows, master-detail forms, 291
cascading changes
    Color Wizard, 488
    Folder Wizard, security settings, 627, 629
Case Sensitive Column Parameter, running reports,
    201, 203
case/label statement, 526

categories
    Content Areas, 618, 648–649, 702
    Direct Access URLs, 680, 685
    Folder Wizard, 625, 648–659
    monitoring, 805
category field, Calendar Wizard, 351
CD-ROM, 897–905. *See also* installation and
        configuration
    Cookie Pal by Kookaburra Software, 874, 905
    directory of sample scripts and files for each
        chapter, 897–904
    Net University sample database, 898
    PL/SQL Developer by Allround Automations,
        106, 602, 612–613, 837, 904
    Swish by DJJ Holdings Pty Ltd, 905
    Web site for Oracle9*i*AS Portal, 45, 905
Cell Font Color option, Calendar Wizard, 341
Cell Font Face option, Calendar Wizard, 341
Cell Font Size option, Calendar Wizard, 341
cell highlighting feature, Query-By-Example (QBE)
        Report Wizard, 182
cell in HTML table, Form Wizard, 258–259
CH28_PROVIDER_PKS (on CD-ROM), 842, 853
Change Access option, Folder Wizard, 627, 696
changing working directory of SQL*Plus, 45–46
character and date fields, converting between, 332
character criteria, running reports, 202–204
charAt() method, 530
Chart by Browser Type report, 808
Chart by Date report, 807
Chart by IP Address report, 807
Chart by Language report, 808
Chart by Object report, 807
Chart by Time of Day report, 807
Chart by User report, 807
chart monitors, 797
Chart Name and Application, SQL Query Link for
        charts, 316
Chart Wizard, 301–315. *See also* Link Wizard; PL/SQL
        logic integration; Query-By-Example (QBE)
        Report Wizard; Report Wizard; SQL Query
        Link for charts; SQL Query Link for reports
    aggregate functions, 305, 309
    Axis combo box, 308
    Bar Height combo box, 309
    Bar Image text box, 309
    Bar Width combo box, 309
    Chart Name and Application, 302
    Chart Scale combo box, 309
    chart types, 308
    Column Conditions, 306

    Common Options, 307–308
    complex chart creation, 313–315
    Customization Entry Form Display Options, 310
    data entry elements, 304–306
    describing the chart, 303–306
    Display Options, 306–310
    Finish button, 310
    Formatting Options, 310
    Full Page Options, 307, 308–309
    Group Function combo box, 305
    Label combo box, 304
    Link object, 304
    monitoring reports, 807–813
    NULL value, 308, 314
    Order By combo box, 307
    overview, 9
    parameter page for a chart, 311, 312
    Portlet Options, 307
    running chart, 311–313
    Summary Options list box, 309, 311–312
    Table or View Columns, 303–306, 313–314
    Template combo box, 310
    Value field, 304
    Value Format Mask, 309
charts as portlets, 325–328
check box format, LOV Wizard, 418, 422, 433
CHECK constraints, creating database objects,
        124–125
check constraints, data validation, 555–556
CheckBox item type, Form Wizard, 264, 267, 520
children levels, Hierarchy Wizard, 364, 366
CLASSES table, NetU Database, 44
client-side validation, 513. *See also* JavaScript for
        client-side validation
Close button
    portal page, 162, 164, 167
    running reports, 202, 205
code table, Lists-of-Values (LOVs), 412
code types allowed, Dynamic Pages Wizard, 382–383
Color of Formatting Conditions, Query-By-Example
        (QBE) Report Wizard, 183
color reduction problems and images, 494
Color Wizard, 479–488. *See also* Shared Components;
        User Interface Templates
    adding colors, 485–488
    "browser-safe" palette, 482, 483
    cascading changes, 488
    Color Definition, 485–488
    color name field, 484, 485, 486
    Color Palette for Windows, 482

Continued

Color Wizard *(continued)*
   color usage, 486
   color value field, 484, 485, 486
   consistency factors, 486
   converting color numbers (on CD-ROM), 486–487
   format string, 484, 485
   hexadecimal (HEX) values for colors, 485, 486, 487
   Lynda Weinman's browser-safe color palette, 483
   rendering of colors, 482
   screen resolutions, 480–481, 482
   Super Video Graphics Adapter (SVGA), 479
   System colors, 484
   ToHex button, 487
   ToNum button, 487
   User colors, 484
   video color settings, 481–483
   video display, 479–481
   Video Graphics Adapter (VGA), 479
Column Conditions
   Chart Wizard, 306
   Hierarchy Wizard, 365
   Report Wizard, 209–210
column criteria, running reports, 200–202
Column Formatting, Query-By-Example (QBE) Report Wizard, 179–180
Column Heading, Query-By-Example (QBE) Report Wizard, 179
Column Parameter, running reports, 200
Column Selection Criteria, 111
column-oriented frame, 402
columns, entering for database, 122–123
columns and their meanings, Navigator, 81–82
Columns Formatting, Report Wizard, 211
combo box format, LOV Wizard, 418, 420, 433
ComboBox item type, Form Wizard, 264, 267–268, 520
comment information in JavaScript scripts, 522
comments, adding to database, 127
Common Options
   Calendar Wizard, 338–339
   Chart Wizard, 307–308
   Form Wizard, 266–267
   Hierarchy Wizard, 365, 366–367
   Query-By-Example (QBE) Report Wizard, 184–186
compatibility, JavaScript, 517–518
Compile action, Database Objects tab of Navigator, 97, 98, 99, 106–107
Component Call Interface, Link Wizard, 581–582
component information, running reports, 196
component items, Direct Access URLs, 680, 687

component procedure name, linking from frame drivers, 405
components. *See also* Calendar Wizard; Chart Wizard; Dynamic Pages Wizard; Form Wizard; Frame Driver Wizard; Hierarchy Wizard; Query-By-Example (QBE) Report Wizard; Report Wizard; SQL Query Link for reports
   deployment, 679–680
   monitoring, 805
   overview, 6, 7–14
   storage, NetU Database, 47–50
concatenating strings
   Calendar Wizard, 350–352
   Frame Driver Wizard, 400
confirm() method, 529
Connect Information string, portal installation, 33
CONNECT privilege, 758
Connection Pool Parameters, Database Access Descriptors (DADs), 666
connection pooling, database object monitoring, 823
consistency. *See* Shared Components
constraints, data validation, 555–557
Contact Info, privileged accounts, 766
Container folders, Folder Wizard, 622
containers and base-level objects, Navigator, 84–85
content approvers, Content Areas, 718
Content Area Create Wizard, 617–655. *See also* Content Areas; Folder Wizard; Navigation Bar; Style Manager
   administrator, 621
   categories, 618, 648–649
   content, 618
   Create Category, 648–649
   Create Perspective, 650–651
   Custom Labels and Icons, 652–653
   customizing, 621–629
   Data Access Descriptor setting, 652–653
   default Language, 620
   disk storage quota setting, 652
   display name, 620
   editing, 621
   folder properties setting, 652
   folders, 618
   items, 618, 622
   logo setting, 652–653
   name, 620
   perspectives, 618, 650–651
   primary key, 620
   properties, 650–654
   quota setting, 652

Content Area Map, Navigation Bar, 644
Content Areas, 689–725. *See also* Content Area Create
        Wizard; custom attributes and types;
        deployment; folders, adding items to
    Add-Item Wizard, 707–710
    adding content to site, 697–718
    adding users and groups to folders, 695–696
    administrators, 621, 718–721
    Advanced Search, 723–724
    advantages of, 689–691
    anonymous portals, 691
    Application components, 698, 707–712
    Approve icon, 720
    authenticated portals, 691
    categories, 618, 648–649, 702
    content approvers, 718
    Create New Groups, 691–695
    Create privilege, 694
    Create with Approval privilege, 718
    custom attributes and types, 886–895
    deleted items, 723
    Display Deleted Items check box, 723
    expired items, 723
    exporting and importing, 749
    File content item, 698
    Folder links, 699
    folders, adding users and groups to, 695–696
    help system, home page, 60
    Hidden Item Types, 722
    Icon Display Period text box, 723
    images, 698
    item management, 722–723
    Java applications, 699
    Java Server Pages (JSPs), 715–718
    Make Public privilege, 694, 696
    Manage Content privilege, 718
    Manage privilege, 695
    Manage Styles privilege, 695
    monitoring, 805
    Navigation Bar, 706–707
    new content item icon, 723
    None privilege, 694
    Object Privileges, 693–694
    overview, 6, 7, 14–15
    perspectives, 618, 650–651, 705
    PL/SQL procedures (on CD-ROM), 698, 712–715
    portal pages, Content Areas on, 724–725
    privileges, 693–694, 773
    Property Sheet icon, 720–721
    Purge Key, 723
    Retain Deleted Items check box, 723

    searching, 723–724
    security, 691–696, 718–721
    storing images using, 495
    theme for site, 697
    user accounts for, 691–695, 718–721
    versioning of items, 722
    view privilege, 694
    viewers (users), 718
    Visible Item Types, 722
Content Areas tab, Navigator, 80, 84–85
content creation versus standards enforcement,
        478–479
contents, Content Area Create Wizard, 618
contexp script, 749
context of tabs preservation, Navigator, 82
contimp script, 749
contracting list, Form Wizard, 256
control structures, JavaScript, 525–528
converting
    character and date fields, 332
    color numbers (on CD-ROM), Color Wizard,
        486–487
Cookie Domain, 752
Cookie Pal (Kookaburra Software) (on CD-ROM),
        874, 905
cookies, 873–886
    anonymous JavaScript block, 884–886
    GetCookie() function, 880, 883–884
    PL/SQL Web Toolkits, 586, 595, 596–598, 601
    redirect feature of Form, 873–877
    security checks, 874
    SetCookie() function, 879–883
    source code, 877–886
Copy link, Manage Components, 739
copying file to hard drive, NetU Database, 44
COUNT function
    Chart Wizard, 305
    SQL Query Link for reports (on CD-ROM),
        222–224
Count Rows Only option, 113
COURSE_CATALOG table, NetU Database, 45
Create a New Application, NetU Database, 49–50
Create a New Page link, Page Wizard, 143
Create Favorite, home page, 64–65
Create New Groups, Content Areas, 691–695
Create New Users, NetU Database, 50–51
Create New ... label, Navigator, 84
Create privilege, 694, 772, 773, 774
Create User, privileged accounts, 761–766
Create with Approval privilege, 628, 629, 718

creating database objects, 121–127. *See also*
Database Objects tab of Navigator
CHECK constraints, 124–125
columns, entering, 122–123
comments, adding, 127
Finish button, 127
FOREIGN KEY constraints, 125–126
naming tables, 122
Retrieve Keys button, 126
schema selection, 122
storage parameters specification, 126–127
table creation, 122–127
UNIQUE constraints, 123–124
creating own portlet and provider, 833–864
built-in portlet, calling, 853–855
calling built-in portlet, 853–855
CH28_PROVIDER_PKS (on CD-ROM), 842, 853
customizing portlet, 849–852
database portlets, 834
enabling customization, 852
exposing Oracle9*i*AS Portal APIs, 836–842
get_portlet_info package, 852
Java Server Pages (JSPs) for Web portlet and
provider, 855–861
p_arg_names, 854
p_arg_values, 854
PL/SQL Developer (on CD-ROM), 106, 602,
612–613, 837, 904
PL/SQL for creating database provider, 842–845
PL/SQL for creating portlet, 836–842
Portal Development Kit (PDK), 15, 137, 833–835
Portlet Server for, 835–836
provsyns.sql script (on CD-ROM), 837
registering your provider, 845–846
SHOW procedure, 839, 840, 853, 854
URL portlet, using (on CD-ROM), 861–864
user customization stores, 850–851
using portlet, 847–849
Web portlet and provider with Java Server Pages
(JSPs), 855–861
Web portlets, 834, 835
wwwpre_api_name package, 850–851, 852
creating portal components, 15–16
cross-field validation, 516, 551–554
cross-record validation, 555–557
custom attributes and types, Content Areas, 886–895
Custom Labels and Icons, Content Area Create
Wizard, 652–653
Custom Layout
Report Wizard, 210
SQL Query Link for reports (on CD-ROM),
227–230

customization
Content Area Create Wizard, 621–629
Dynamic Pages Wizard, 387–393
environment, 55
home page, 61
information views, portals and portlets, 136
Navigator, 80
portals and portlets, 133–135
portlet, 849–852
Customization (Add-Only) privilege,
Page Wizard, 157
Customization Entry Form Display Options
Calendar Wizard, 339, 342–344, 357
Chart Wizard, 310
Dynamic Pages Wizard, 385, 396–397
Hierarchy Wizard, 369
multiple tables in a report, 238–239, 241
SQL Query Link for charts, 319, 321–322
SQL Query Link for reports, 220, 230–234
Customization Form Display Options
linking from frame drivers, 406
Lists-of-Values (LOVs), 423–426
Query-By-Example (QBE) Report Wizard, 191–192
Report Wizard, 212
Customization (Full) privilege, Page Wizard, 157
Customization privilege, 772, 773
"Customize for" label, portal page, 164–167
Customize link, Report Wizard, 212–213
Customize Page, running reports, 199–207
Customize Page link, portal page, 159–160

D

DADs. *See* Database Access Descriptors
data, exporting and importing, 749
Data Access Definition, portal installation, 36
Data Access Descriptor
Content Area Create Wizard, 652–653
Uniform Resource Locators (URLs), 454
data entry box of help system, home page, 58, 59
data entry elements, Chart Wizard, 304–306
data field in HTML table, Form Wizard, 258
Data Field options, Form Wizard, 262–271.
See also Form Wizard
Blank item type, 264, 267, 520
Button item type, 264, 267, 520
CheckBox item type, 264, 267, 520
ComboBox item type, 264, 267–268, 520
Common Options, 266–267
default value, 268, 269
Field level validation option, 270
File Upload item types, 264
Font Color option, 267

Font Face option, 267
Font Size option, 267
Form level validation option, 270
Hidden item type, 265, 268–269
Horizontal Rule item type, 265, 269
Image item type, 265, 269
Input height option, 267
Input max length options, 269
Input option, 269
Input width option, 267
Insertable check box, 270
Item Type button options, 262, 264–271
Label Only item type, 265, 269
Label option, 266
Layout button option, 262
layout options, 267
Link option, 267
Lists-of Values (LOVs) option, 268
Mandatory check box, 269
Password item type, 265, 269–270, 521
Popup item type, 266, 270, 521
RadioGroup item type, 266, 270, 521
TextArea item type, 266, 271, 521
TextBox item type, 266, 271, 521
Updatable check box, 269
data integrity, multiple tables in a report, 236
data interaction. See interacting with data
data table, Lists-of-Values (LOVs), 112
data validation, 513–558. See also JavaScript for
            client-side validation
    check constraints, 555–556
    client-side validation, 513
    constraints, 555–557
    cross-field validation, 516, 551–554
    datatype validation, 515
    exact match validation, 514–515
    foreign key constraints, 555
    foreign key validation, 515
    NULL/Not NULL validation, 514
    pattern matching validation, 515–516
    primary key constraints, 555
    range validation, 515
    referential integrity validation, 292, 515
    server-side validation, 513, 515, 516, 557–558
    triggers, 558
data values, format limitation, stored procedure
            forms, 286
database
    access code, adding to PL/SQL blocks, 602–605
    browsing images, 497
    compatibility news, 18
    connection information, portal installation, 32–33
    entry purpose of forms, 252
    initialization parameters changes, 18, 19
    monitoring, 820–821
    object images, 497
    portlets, creating own portlet and provider, 834
    security, 757–760
Database Access Descriptors (DADs), 663–672.
            See also deployment
    Authentication Mode, 666
    Connection Pool Parameters, 666
    Default Home Page, 666, 667, 670
    Descriptor Name, 665, 667–668
    Document Access Path, 666, 667, 671, 672
    Document Access Procedure, 666, 667, 671, 672
    Document Table, 666, 667, 671–672
    extensions, LONGRAW, 666, 667
    Listener Gateway Settings, 663
    LONGRAW extensions, 666, 667
    Oracle Connect String, 665, 667, 668
    Oracle Password, 665, 667, 668
    Oracle User Name, 665, 667, 668
    Path Alias, 667
    Path Alias Procedure, 667
    portal installation, 33
    post-installation check, 40, 42
    private (authenticated) components, 671
    public (unauthenticated) components, 671
    security, 671
    Session Cookie Name, 666
    Session State, 666
    setup.cxe, 24
    URL path and, 681
database administrators (DBAs), 759, 764
database object monitoring, 818–827.
            See also monitoring performance
    connection pooling, 823
    Database Information, 820–821
    disk space allocation and utilization, 825–827
    Find and Kill Session, 824–825
    locks, 822
    memory consumption, 821
    memory structures, 823
    objects, 825, 827
    optimistic locking, 822
    Oracle Enterprise Manager and, 820
    Oracle Server, 820–821
    redo logs, 822–823
    rollback segments, 823

Continued

database object monitoring (continued)
　　sessions, 823–825
　　storage, 825–827
　　System Global Area (SGA), 823
　　tablespaces, 825–827
　　terminating user sessions, 824–825
　　transactions, 821
Database Objects tab of Navigator, 93–128. See also
　　　　browsing (querying) data; creating
　　　　database objects; interacting with data
　　accessing objects with, 100–103
　　Actions column, 96–100
　　Compile action, 97, 98, 99, 106–107
　　Drop action, 96
　　Edit action, 96, 98, 99, 105–106
　　Execute action, 98, 99
　　Export action, 97, 98, 99
　　function object, 94, 99
　　Get Next Value action, 99, 109
　　Grant Access action, 97, 98, 99, 102–103, 108–109
　　indexes, working with, 94, 98, 104–105
　　Modified column, 96
　　Modify Rows action, 97
　　Name column, 96
　　NETUDEV user, 101
　　NEW_CLASS_YEAR procedure, 105–108
　　objects in database, 93–95
　　Oracle9iAS Portal owner, 101–103
　　Owner column, 96
　　package object, 94, 98
　　PL/SQL Developer (on CD-ROM), 106, 602,
　　　　612–613, 837, 904
　　procedures, working with, 94, 98, 105–108
　　Query Rows action, 97
　　recompiling procedures, 106–107
　　Rename action, 97, 98, 99
　　schema, granting access to, 101–103
　　security privileges, 96, 101–102
　　sequences, working with, 95, 99, 109
　　Show Properties action, 96, 98, 99
　　sorting entries, 96
　　synonym object, 95, 99
　　tables, working with, 94, 97, 108–109
　　trigger object, 95, 99
　　Type column, 96
　　view object, 94, 97
　　working with, 104–110
data-less keys, PL/SQL, 872–873
data_schema, deployment, 676
Datatype Column Parameter, running reports, 201
datatype validation, 515

datatypes supported by JavaScript, 523–525
date check code example (on CD-ROM), JavaScript,
　　　　543–544
date field, Calendar Wizard, 336
date link, Calendar Wizard, 337
date methods, JavaScript, 531–532
Date Settings, Page Wizard, 148–149
date_link, linking from calendar cells, 353, 357
dates, 330–334. See also Calendar Wizard
　　add_months() function, 331
　　converting between character and date
　　　　fields, 332
　　formatting dates, 332–334
　　greatest() function, 331
　　last_day() function, 331
　　least() function, 331
　　mathematical functions for, 330–332
　　max() function, 331
　　min() function, 331
　　months_between() function, 331
　　newtime() function, 331
　　next_day() function, 331
　　punctuation in dates, 333
　　round() function, 332
　　to_char() function, 332, 333, 334
　　to_date function, 332, 333, 334
　　trunc() function, 332
　　WHERE clause and, 334
Day Font Color/Face options, 341
DAY format mask element, 333
DBA privileges, NetU Database, 46
DBAs. See database administrators
DD format mask element, 333
DeAugustine, Anna, 512
debugging, PL/SQL, 612–613
declaration of variables, JavaScript, 523–525
declarative development environment, 15–16, 75
default account (privileged) settings, testing,
　　　　766–770
default format
　　LOV Wizard, 418–419
　　Query-By-Example (QBE) Report Wizard, 185
default forms, 273
Default Home Page
　　administration, 752
　　Database Access Descriptors (DADs),
　　　　666, 667, 670
default language, Content Area Create Wizard, 620
default Navigation Bar, 640
default page, portal page, 169
Default Style, 752

default value
  Calendar Wizard, 358
  Form Wizard, 268, 269
  Hierarchy Wizard, 369
  passing to forms, PL/SQL, 866–869
defaults saving, running reports, 206–207
defining report, 174–178
deleted items, Content Areas, 723
DELETE_TOP button, master-detail forms, 291
deleting
  Form Wizard, 257
  Manage Components, 733–734
  master-detail forms, 298
  Navigation Bar elements, 644
  portlets, 152
  rows, 119
deployment, 657–687. See also Content Areas;
      Database Access Descriptors (DADs);
      Direct Access URLS
  Apache HTTP Server/Listener, 659–660, 661,
      662–663
  application data, 662
  Application Schema, 672–675, 676
  component deployment, 679–680
  data_schema, 676
  development and, 658, 661–662, 675, 678
  external images, 660
  fonts, 493–494
  HTP/HTF packages and utilities, 659
  logical packaging, 675–680
  Mod_PLSQL gateway, 659–660
  Oracle database, 658–659
  Oracle9i Application Server, 659
  Portal Repository, 662
  portal_schema, 676, 677
  portlets, 660
  procedures, 659
  proxy servers, 678–679
  schemas, 660, 672–675
  server configuration, 678–679
  staging areas, 677–678
  static LOV object to another component,
      422–426
  tables and data, 660
  templates into components, User Interface
      Templates, 511–512
  USERID, 672–674
  Web server (existing) replacing listener, 662–663
derived columns, Lists-of-Values (LOVs), 437–438
description
  Content Areas, 702
  Folder Wizard, 625
  Page Wizard, 144

description table, Lists-of-Values (LOVs), 412
Descriptor Name, Database Access Descriptors
      (DADs), 665, 667–668
design considerations and Dynamic Pages
      Wizard, 387
designing portal page, 136
detail table, Lists-of-Values (LOVs), 412
DETAIL_ACTIONS, master-detail forms, 293, 294,
      297, 299
Develop tab, Manage Components, 732–737
developer account creation, NetU Database, 50–52
developer advantages from portals and portlets, 132
development and deployment, 658, 661–662, 675, 678
Direct Access URLs, 680–687. See also deployment;
      Uniform Resource Locators (URLs)
  categories, 680, 685
  component items, 680, 687
  Database Access Descriptors (DADs) of URL
      path, 681
  documents, 680, 685–686
  folders, 680, 683–685
  hostname of URL path, 681
  pages, 680, 681–683
  perspectives, 680, 685
  virtual directory of URL path, 681
disk space. See also storage
  quota setting, Content Area Create Wizard, 652
  utilization, database object monitoring, 825–827
  verification before installation, 18, 19
Display As, Query-By-Example (QBE) Report
      Wizard, 180
Display Attributes list box, Style Manager, 638
Display button option, Form Wizard, 262
Display Deleted Items check box, Content Areas, 723
display (friendly) value, LOV Wizard, 419, 420
display name
  Content Area Create Wizard, 620
  Folder Wizard, 625
  Hierarchy Wizard, 369
  Page Wizard, 144
  Query-By-Example (QBE) Report Wizard, 194
Display Options
  Calendar Wizard, 338–342
  Chart Wizard, 306–310
  Content Areas, 705
  Dynamic Pages Wizard, 384–385
  Frame Driver Wizard, 402–403
  Hierarchy Wizard, 365–369
  Menu Builder Wizard, 467–470
  Page Wizard, 144, 145

                                        Continued

Display Options *(continued)*
    Query-By-Example (QBE) Report Wizard, 183–190
    Report Wizard, 212
    SQL Query Link for charts, 318–319
    SQL Query Link for reports, 220
display order value, LOV Wizard, 419
Display Results in Table with Borders option, 113
display_column, LOV Wizard, 429
do...while loop, 528
Document Access Path, Database Access
        Descriptors (DADs), 666, 667, 671, 672
document object model, JavaScript, 517–518,
        554, 555
document structure procedures, HTML packages,
        587–593
Document Table, Database Access Descriptors
        (DADs), 666, 667, 671–672
documents, Direct Access URLs, 680, 685–686
documents monitoring, 805
DONATIONS table, NetU Database, 45
Dortch, Bill, 880
Down button, Hierarchy Wizard, 371–372, 373–374
downloading Oracle9*i*AS, 17–18
Draw Lines Between Rows, Query-By-Example (QBE)
        Report Wizard, 188
drilling down/up
    Hierarchy Wizard, 367, 371–374
    links, 560, 564
driving frame, 399, 400, 403
Drop action, Database Objects tab of Navigator, 96
Drop Component, Manage Components, 733–734
DY format mask element, 333
dynamic links, 570–576
dynamic Lists-of-Values (LOVs) objects, 416, 426–433
Dynamic Pages Wizard, 380–397. *See also* Shared
        Components
    #BASE# substitution tag, 389
    adding HTML code, 387–390
    adding SQL code, 390–393
    Additional PL/SQL Code, 386
    BIND variables, 384, 395–397
    code types allowed, 382–383
    Customization Entry Form Display Options,
        385, 396–397
    customizing code code, 387–393
    design considerations, 387
    Display Options, 384–385
    Dynamic Page Content, 381–388
    Dynamic Page Name, 380–381
    Dynamic Pages as portlets, 390, 397
    editing code, 387–390

Finish button, 386
formatting functions, 387
Full Page Display Options, 384
HTML code, 379, 380, 387–390, 393–395
image files (on CD-ROM), 394
images, adding, 389
importing code into, 388, 389
links, adding, 389
Log Activity check box, 384
mixing HTML and SQL, 379, 380, 393–395
overview, 11
parameter setting, 395–397
PL/SQL Code Segments panel, 383
running, 397
SQL code, 379, 380, 383, 388, 390–395
SQL code mixed with HTML, 379, 380
template functionality, 385, 388, 389, 397
text in Dynamic Page Content, 381–383
text with HTML tags, 382
usage statistics, 384
validation of HTML code, 382, 389
dynamic query lists, Lists-of-Values (LOVs), 438
dynamic strings in Uniform Resource Locators
        (URLs), 454–455

E

ECMAScript, 518. *See also* JavaScript
Edit Contents privilege, 157, 772, 773
Edit Default link
    Add Portlets page, 153
    Page Wizard, 148–149
Edit Favorites Portlet Settings, home page, 62–63, 66
Edit Login Server, security, 791–792
Edit privilege, 774
Edit Region icon, 159–160
EDIT status, 196, 347
edit style permission, Folder Wizard, 628
Edit User, security, 793
editing
    Calendar Wizard, 350–352
    charts, SQL Query Link for charts, 320–322
    code, Dynamic Pages Wizard, 387–390
    Content Area Create Wizard, 621
    Database Objects tab of Navigator, 96, 98, 99,
        105–106
    folders, Folder Wizard, 624–625
    fonts, 492–493
    forms, 276–277
    hierarchies, 374–375
    JavaScript, 537
    link properties, 573–574, 578–579

master-detail forms, 296–297

Menu Builder Wizard, 460–462

Navigation Bar, 640–641, 644–646

privileged accounts, 770–774

Report Wizard, 214–216

Style Manager, 630

user accounts, NetU Database, 52

Elements tab, Navigation Bar, 644–647

Embed *inter*Media rich content, Query-By-Example
(QBE) Report Wizard, 185

embedding code, JavaScript, 549–551

Enable delete link, Query-By-Example (QBE)
Report Wizard, 185

Enable Item Checkout setting, Content Areas, 705

Enable Item level Security check box, Folder
Wizard, 626

Enable update link, Query-By-Example (QBE)
Report Wizard, 185

enabling customization, creating own portlet and
provider, 852

End User accounts, 762

enhancing hierarchies, 374–378

environment, 53–77. *See also* home page

arrows on wizard panel, 75

Back button, 55

bookmarks, 55

Build tab, 54, 73–74

caching option, setting, 54

Cancel button on wizard panel, 76

customizing, 55

declarative development environment, 15–16, 75

favorites list, 55, 62–68

Finish button on wizard panel, 76

Forward button, 55

Help icon on wizard panel, 75

Internet Explorer (Microsoft), 53, 54

logging in, 57

navigation features, 55

Navigator (Netscape), 53, 55

NETU, 73

NETUDEV user, 73–74

Next button on wizard panel, 75–76

portal_DAD, 55–56

portno, 55

Previous button on wizard panel, 75–76

security, 73–74

servername, 55

start page, 56

URL for Oracle9*i*AS Portal environment, 55

Windows NT and, 56, 482

wizards, 6, 16, 74–76

error loop caution, JavaScript, 546

error prevention
Form Wizard, 274–278

Hierarchy Wizard, 374–375

error statements, SQL Query Link for reports, 219

event handlers, Form Wizard, 267

event monitoring, 798–799

event_date field, Calendar Wizard, 350

eventid field, Calendar Wizard, 351

events, JavaScript, 519, 547–551

EVENTS table, NetU Database, 45

exact match validation, 514–515

Excel formatting, Query-By-Example (QBE)
Report Wizard, 185

Execute action, Database Objects tab of
Navigator, 98, 99

existing stored procedures, 284

Exit button, portal installation, 37

expanding list, Form Wizard, 266

Expiration setting, Content Areas, 702

Expire After field
Calendar Wizard, 338

Hierarchy Wizard, 367

Menu Builder Wizard, 469

Query-By-Example (QBE) Report Wizard, 186

expired items, Content Areas, 723

expiry-based (time-based) caching, portals and
portlets, 139–140, 141

exporting and importing, 744–749
applications, 747–748

code into Dynamic Pages Wizard, 388, 389

Content Areas, 749

data, 749

Database Objects tab of Navigator, 97, 98, 99

JavaScript, 537

master-detail forms (on CD-ROM), 292

pages, 746

security data for users and groups, 746

single sing-on accounts, 745–746

SQL Query Link for charts (on CD-ROM), 322

SQL*Plus for importing, 745

stored procedure forms (on CD-ROM), 286

Expose Page To Everyone, Page Wizard, 156

exposing Oracle9*i*AS Portal APIs, 836–842

expressions, JavaScript, 524–525

extending functionality of reports, SQL Query Link
for reports, 222–226

extensions, LONGRAW, 666, 667

external component links, 564

external images, deployment, 660

extracting archive kits, setup.exe, 20

F

favorites functionality, 55, 62–68

Feuerstein, Steven, 837

Field level validation option, Form Wizard, 270

field types and events, JavaScript, 520–521

field-level events, JavaScript, 519–520

File content item, Content Areas, 698

file installation, setup.exe, 23

File item type, Content Areas, 703

file locations, setup.exe, 21

file name, images, 496, 499

FILE protocol, Uniform Resource Locators (URLs), 446

file samples for each chapter (on CD-ROM), 898–904

File Transfer Protocol (FTP), Uniform Resource Locators (URLs), 446

File Upload item types, Form Wizard, 264

filtering reports, 809–813

Find and Kill Session, database object monitoring, 824–825

Find field, Navigator, 80

Find mechanism, Navigator, 88–90

Find Menu Options button, Menu Builder Wizard, 468, 469

Finish button on wizard panel, 76

fixed width fonts, 488, 489, 493

focus() method, 529

folder icon (move to another region), Add Portlets page, 152

Folder item type, Content Areas, 703

Folder Layout Tab, Style Manager, 634–639

Folder links, Content Areas, 699

folder properties setting, Content Area Create Wizard, 652

Folder Wizard, 622–629, 647–651. *See also* Content Area Create Wizard; Style Manager

    access settings, 626–627

    adding items, 624

    cascading security settings, 627, 629

    categories, 625, 648–659

    Change Access option, 627, 696

    Container folders, 622

    Create with Approval privilege, 628, 629

    description, 625

    display name, 625

    edit style permission, 628

    editing folders, 624–625

    Enable Item level Security check box, 626

    Folder Properties, 623

    Grant Access option, 627, 696

    groups permissions, 629

    individual permissions, 629

    Manage Items privilege, 628

    name, 625

    Own permission, 628

    permission settings, 627–629

    perspectives, 650–651

    PL/SQL folders, 622

    public folders, 626, 627

    Publish as Portal, 625

    required items, 625–626

    Search folders, 622, 623

    security, 626–629, 695–696

    subfolders, 624–625

    URL folders, 622, 623

    Use Page Style check box, 625

    View privilege, 628

folders

    adding users and groups to, 695–696

    Content Area Create Wizard, 618

    Direct Access URLs, 680, 683–685

    monitoring, 805

folders, adding items to, 700–706. *See also* Content Areas

    author text field, 704

    Basic Search Keywords text box, 704

    categories, 618, 648–649, 702

    Description setting, 702

    Display Options, 705

    Enable Item Checkout setting, 705

    Expiration setting, 702

    File item type, 703

    Folder item type, 703

    image file, 704

    Image Map item type, 703

    Java Archive (JAR) File, 703

    news and announcement items, 701

    perspectives, 618, 650–651, 705

    PL/SQL Code item type, 703

    Portal Component item type, 703

    QuickPick items, 700

    Regular Items, 700

    Required Settings and Values, 702–703

    Secondary Items, 704

    Text item type, 698, 703

    Title setting, 702

    URL item type, 703, 710–712

    Zip file type, 699, 703

Font Color

    Form Wizard, 267

    Query-By-Example (QBE) Report Wizard, 187

Font Face

    Form Wizard, 267

    Menu Builder Wizard, 461

Font Size
    Form Wizard, 267
    Menu Builder Wizard, 461
    Query-By-Example (QBE) Report Wizard, 186
fonts, 488–494. *See also* Shared Components;
        User Interface Templates
    adding fonts, 490–492
    automatic substitution for missing fonts,
        488, 489–490
    browser preferences, 488, 489, 491, 493
    Create Font Definition, 491–492
    deploying, 493–494
    editing, 492–493
    fixed width fonts, 488, 489, 493
    font name, 491
    font value, 491
    PostScript, 490
    standard fonts preinstalled, 493
    System fonts, 490
    TrueType, 490
    User fonts, 490
    variable width (proportional) fonts, 488, 489, 493
    View link, 491–492
_font_size parameter, Link Wizard, 566
footer
    Calendar Wizard, 345
    Menu Builder Wizard, 458, 459
    Query-By-Example (QBE) Report Wizard, 194
for loop, 527
foreign key constraints, data validation, 555
FOREIGN KEY constraints, database, 125–126
foreign key validation, 515
form creation with HTP procedural code example,
        PL/SQL, 608–611
Form Elements, JavaScript, 518–521
Form Layout
    master-detail forms, 290
    Report Wizard, 210
    SQL Query Link for reports, 220, 221
Form Name and Application, stored procedure
        forms, 284
Form Object, JavaScript, 518
form procedures, HTML packages, 593–595, 601
Form Text, stored procedure forms, 287
Form Wizard, 251–279. *See also* Data Field options,
        Form Wizard; data validation; Link Wizard;
        master-detail forms; PL/SQL logic
        integration, stored procedure forms
    adding new items, 256–257
    areas of form, 257–258
    Background option, 260

blue arrows icon (move), 257
Border option, 260
Bottom Section of form, 257, 258
button options, 261–262
cell in HTML table, 258–259
contracting list, 256
data field in HTML table, 258
database entry purpose of forms, 252
default forms, 273
Delete button, 257
dialog box, 276
Display button option, 262
editing forms, 276–277
error prevention, 274–278
event handlers, 267
expanding list, 256
finishing form, 271–272
Form Layout, 254
Formatting and Validation Options,
    254–255, 258–271
form-creation concepts, 256–259
forms as portlets, 278–279
forms defined, 251
green cross icon (add), 256–257
HTML tables, 258–259
Insert button, 257
layout of form, 258–259
Log Activity check box, 260
Middle Section of form, 258
minus sign icon (contract list), 256
moving fields, 257
navigating Formatting and Validation Options,
    256–257
overview, 8
PL/SQL and, 261, 262, 271–272
plus sign (expand list), 256
Query button, 257, 272–275, 277–278
red X icon (delete), 257
report versus forms, 252
Reset button, 257, 273, 275
row in HTML table, 258
running form, 272–278
sorting, 260
Table or View, 254
Template combo box, 271
Top Section of form, 257
updating forms, 273–274
user error prevention, 274–278
view-based forms, 253
Format Mask, Query-By-Example (QBE) Report
    Wizard, 180

Format Mask Column Parameter, running reports, 201
format string, Color Wizard, 484, 485
_format_out parameter, Link Wizard, 566
Formatting and Validation Options
   Detail Row, master-detail forms, 292–294
   Form Wizard, 254–255, 258–271
   JavaScript, 545–546
   Master Row, master-detail forms, 291–292
   stored procedure forms, 285–287
Formatting Conditions
   Query-By-Example (QBE) Report Wizard, 181–183
   Report Wizard, 211–212
   SQL Query Link for reports, 220
formatting values and limiting rows, SQL Query Link for charts, 323–325
forms. *See also* Form Wizard
   attaching JavaScripts to, 545–547
   passing default values to, PL/SQL, 866–869
   portlets, forms as, 278–279
Forward button, 55
Frame Driver Wizard, 397–408. *See also* linking from frame drivers
   BIND variables, 403, 405, 406, 407
   border between frames, 402
   Button Location combo box, 403
   Button Name field, 403
   column-oriented frame, 402
   concatenating strings, 400
   Display Options, 402–403
   driving frame, 399, 400, 403
   HTML tables versus frames, 398
   HTML/Text result frame, 400
   layout of frame set, 402
   List-of-Values (LOVs) Type field, 400
   Name string literal, 400
   NULL values, 401
   overview, 11–12
   parameter setting, 404–408
   PL/SQL result (target) frame, 400, 403
   result (target) frame, 399, 400, 401, 402–403
   row-oriented frame, 402
   running, 403–404
   SQL code linked into HTML framed page, 379
   SQL Query, 398–402, 403
   string concatenation, 400
   Template list box, 403
   Text Options, 403
   URL result frame, 400
#FRAMELINK# keyword, User Interface Templates, 508

framework services, portals and portlets, 136
frequently used information, portals and portlets, 138–141
FROM clause, Calendar Wizard, 337
FTP. *See* File Transfer Protocol
Full Page Options
   Calendar Wizard, 338, 339–340
   Chart Wizard, 307, 308–309
   Dynamic Pages Wizard, 384
   Hierarchy Wizard, 365
   Query-By-Example (QBE) Report Wizard, 186–188
function object, Database Objects tab of Navigator, 94, 99

G
gateway check, post-installation, 39–42
Generate process, Manage Components, 740–741
generating primary keys using sequences/triggers, PL/SQL, 869–873
Get Next Value action, Database Objects tab of Navigator, 99, 109
GetCookie() function, 880, 883–884
getDate() method, 531
getDay() method, 531
GetHours() method, 531
GetMinutes() method, 531
GetMonth() method, 531
get_portlet_info package, 852
GetSeconds() method, 531
GetTime() method, 531
GetYear() method, 531
GIF. *See* Graphics Interchange Format
global caching, portals and portlets, 140
Global Settings, 751–752
global variables, JavaScript, 552–553, 554
Goodman, Danny, 880
GOPHER protocol, Uniform Resource Locators (URLs), 446
GRADES table, NetU Database, 45
Grant Access
   Database Objects tab of Navigator, 97, 98, 99, 102–103, 108–109
   Folder Wizard, 627, 696
GRANT command, security, 758
Grantee field, Page Wizard, 157
Grants (Schema), security, 788–789
Graphics Interchange Format (GIF), 494
greatest() function, 331
green cross icon (add), 256–257, 460, 461–466, 644–645, 646
Greenwald, Rick, 127

GROUP BY clause
    region setting, Style Manager, 639
    SQL Query Link for charts, 323
    SQL Query Link for reports, 225
Group Function combo box, Chart Wizard, 305
Group Membership, NetU Database, 52
Group privileges, 764, 774, 775–781
grouping portlets, Page Wizard, 156
groups permissions, Folder Wizard, 629

H

header
    Calendar Wizard, 342, 345
    Menu Builder Wizard, 458, 459
    Query-By-Example (QBE) Report Wizard, 194
    User Interface Templates, 504
heading icon images, 497, 498
#HEADING# keyword, User Interface Templates, 508
Help icon on wizard panel, 75
Help Image, User Interface Templates, 505
Help Link field, Menu Builder Wizard, 457–458
help system, home page, 58–60
Help Text
    Calendar Wizard, 345
    master-detail forms, 296–297
    Query-By-Example (QBE) Report Wizard, 194
hexadecimal (HEX) values for colors, 485, 486, 487
HH format mask element, 333
HH24 format mask element, 333
hidden codes, Lists-of-Values (LOVs), 415
Hidden item type
    Content Areas, 722
    Form Wizard, 265, 268–269
hiding portlets, 152
hierarchy navigation using Path, Navigator, 80
hierarchy of favorites, home page, 66–68
Hierarchy Wizard, 361–378. *See also* Link Wizard
    ADVISORLOV choice, 376
    Break Down option, 367, 368
    button options, 369
    children, levels of, 364, 366
    Column Conditions, 365
    Common Options, 365, 366–367
    Customization Entry Form Display Options, 369
    default values, 369
    Display Name check box, 369
    Display Options, 365–369
    Down button, 371–372, 373–374
    drilling down/up indicators, 367, 371–374
    editing hierarchies, 374–375

    enhancing hierarchies, 374–378
    error prevention, 374–375
    Expire After field, 367
    Finish button, 369
    Full Page Options, 365
    hierarchies as portlets, 378
    hierarchies defined, 361
    Hierarchy Name and Application, 363
    hierarchy type, 367, 369
    HTML table option, 367
    Lists-of-Values (LOVs), 364, 375–377
    Log Activity check box, 368
    many-to-many relationship, 362–363
    master-detail (one-to-many) relationships,
        362, 363
    Max Children field, 366, 369
    Maximum Child Levels combo box, 366, 369, 374
    middle of hierarchy, starting in, 377
    navigating through a hierarchy, 370–374
    overview, 10
    Parent Key Column, 364
    parents, levels of, 364, 366
    parts explosion example, 362
    Portlet Options, 365
    Primary Key Column, 364
    ranking groups of data, 361
    recursive relationship, 361
    Show Parent Level check box, 369
    SQL script loading (on CD-ROM), 376
    Start with Column combo box, 364
    Start with Value, 369, 374, 375–377
    Table or View Column, 363–365
    three-level hierarchy, 372–373
    two-level hierarchy, 371–372
    Up button, 372
    user error prevention, 374–375
    Value Type combo box, 367
Home Link, User Interface Templates, 505
home page, 57–73. *See also* building portal page;
        environment
    Account Info, 61
    Add Favorite Group, 63–64
    Apply button, 66
    banner area, 58
    banner properties, 61
    Cancel button, 66
    Content Areas of help system, 60
    Create Favorite, 64–65
    customization, 61

Continued

home page *(continued)*
    data entry box of help system, 58, 59
    Edit Favorites Portlet Settings, 62–63, 66
    favorites functionality, 55, 62–68
    help system, 58–60
    hierarchy of favorites, 66–68
    links in help system, 58, 59, 60
    logging in, 57
    Logout, 61
    my Links portlet, 61–68
    my Work portlet, 68–69
    Navigate Favorites, 63, 66
    navigation bar of help system, 58, 59
    On The Web portlet, 69–73
    refreshing, 61, 138–141
    Reset to Defaults button, 66
    sign-on access to applications, 69–73
home page check, post-installation, 38–42
Horizontal Rule item type, Form Wizard, 265, 269
hostname of URL path, 681
HR_LINE, master-detail forms, 293, 294
HTF. *See* hypertext function
HTML. *See* Dynamic Pages Wizard; Frame Driver
        Wizard
HTML code, Dynamic Pages Wizard, 379, 380,
        387–390, 393–395
HTML formatting, Query-By-Example (QBE) Report
        Wizard, 185
HTML in Uniform Resource Locators (URLs), 445
HTML link type, Link Wizard, 563, 564
HTML packages, 585–595. *See also* PL/SQL logic
        integration; PL/SQL Web Toolkits
    document structure procedures, 587–593
    form procedures, 593–595, 601
    HTML tags and, 585, 586
    hypertext function (HTF) package, 585–586, 659
    hypertext procedure (HTP) package, 585–586, 659
    printing and formatting procedures, 587
    search engines and meta tags, 588–589
    `strong` command, 586
HTML page "all-or-none" limitations and portals and
        portlets, 133
HTML portlet, working with, 161–164
HTML table
    Form Wizard, 258–259
    frames versus, 398
    Hierarchy Wizard, 367
    SQL Query Link for reports (on CD-ROM),
        227–230
HTML tags and HTML packages, 585, 586

HTML/Text result frame, 400
HTP. *See* hypertext procedure
`htp.anchor` procedure, 590
`htp.bodyClose` procedure, 588
`htp.bodyOpen` procedure, 588
`htp.br` procedure, 587
`htp.comment` procedure, 590
`htp.emphasis` procedure, 587
`htp.fontClose` procedure, 591
`htp.fontOpen` procedure, 591
`htp.formCheckbox` procedure, 594
`htp.formClose` procedure, 593, 594
`htp.formHidden` procedure, 594
`htp.formOpen` procedure, 593, 594
`htp.formPassword` procedure, 594
`htp.formSubmit` procedure, 594
`htp.formText` procedure, 594
`htp.headClose` procedure, 588
`htp.header` procedure, 591
`htp.headOpen` procedure, 588
`htp.htmlClose` procedure, 588
`htp.htmlOpen` procedure, 588
`htp.img` procedure, 592
`htp.italic` procedure, 587
`htp.keyboard` procedure, 587
`htp.line` procedure, 587
`htp.mailto` procedure, 592
`htp.meta` procedure, 588–589
`htp.preClose` procedure, 592–593
`htp.preOpen` procedure, 592–593
`htp.print` procedure, 587
`htp.strong` procedure, 587
`htp.teletype` procedure, 587
`htp.title` procedure, 588
HTTP. *See* Hypertext Transport Protocol
HTTPS protocol, Uniform Resource
        Locators (URLs), 446
hypertext function (HTF) package, 585–586, 659
hypertext procedure (HTP) package, 585–586, 659
Hypertext Transport Protocol (HTTP), Uniform
        Resource Locators (URLs), 445, 446

I

ICANN. *See* Internet Corporation for Assigned
        Names and Numbers
Icon Display Period text box, Content Areas, 723
Icon Height region setting, Style Manager, 639
icon images, 497
Icon Width region setting, Style Manager, 639
`if-else` statement, 525–526

image file
    Content Areas, 704
    Dynamic Pages Wizard (on CD-ROM), 394
Image item type, Form Wizard, 265, 269
Image Map item type, Content Areas, 703
#IMAGE_PREFIX# keyword, User Interface
        Templates, 508
images, 494–500. *See also* Content Areas; Shared
        Components; User Interface Templates
    adding images, 498–500
    animated image files, 499
    arrow images, 496
    background images, 496, 498
    color reduction problems, 494
    Content Areas, 698
    Content Areas for storing, 495
    Create Image Definition, 499–500
    database browsing images, 497
    database object images, 497
    Dynamic Pages Wizard and, 389
    file name, 496, 499
    Graphics Interchange Format (GIF), 494
    heading icon images, 497, 498
    icon images, 497
    image name, 496, 499
    Image type (indicator), 496–498
    Joint Photographic Expedition
            Graphics (JPEG), 494
    logical image categories, 495
    logo images, 497, 498
    miscellaneous images, 497, 498
    public template art images, 497
    storage of, 494–495
    System images, 496
    template images, 497
    User images, 496
    User Interface Templates, 503, 504–505
    View link, 500
    wizard images, 497
importing code into Dynamic Pages Wizard, 388, 389
importing objects. *See also* exporting and importing
    master-detail forms (on CD-ROM), 292
    SQL Query Link for charts (on CD-ROM), 322
    stored procedure forms (on CD-ROM), 286
"in" clause, LOV Wizard, 437
indexes, Database Objects tab of Navigator, 94, 98,
        104–105
IndexOf() method, 530
individual permissions, Folder Wizard, 629
information access from portals and portlets, 132

Inherit Privileges
    Menu Builder Wizard, 468
    security, 783–784
init.ora file, 19
Input height option, Form Wizard, 267
Input max length options, Form Wizard, 269
Input option, Form Wizard, 269
Input width option, Form Wizard, 267
Insert
    Data privilege, 774
    New Rows button, 117
    Rows button, 119–120
Insert button
    Form Wizard, 257
    master-detail forms, 297
    Query-By-Example (QBE) Report Wizard, 192
    stored procedure forms, 288
Insertable check box, Form Wizard, 270
INSERT_TOP button, master-detail forms, 291
Install button, setup.exe, 25–26
installation and configuration, 17–52. *See also* NetU
        Database creation and use; network
        installation and configuration; portal
        installation and configuration; setup.exe
        program
    Apache server disabling, 18, 19
    database compatibility news, 18
    database initialization parameters changes, 18, 19
    disk space verification, 18, 19
    downloading Oracle9*i*AS, 17–18
    init.ora file, 19
    installation types, setup.exe, 21–22
    java_pool_size parameter, 19
    large_pool_size parameter, 19
    Oracle 8.1.6/8.1.7 databases, 18, 19
    Oracle9*i* Portal, obtaining copy of, 17–18
    sample data, NetU Database, 45–47
    SYS account password, 19
instance name, portal installation, 33
instances of databases, security, 758
integrity rules caution for data, 120–121
interacting with data, 116–121. *See also* browsing
        (querying) data; creating database
        objects; Database Objects tab of Navigator
    deleting rows, 119
    Insert New Rows button, 117
    Insert Rows button, 119–120
    integrity rules caution, 120–121
    Modify Rows action, 97, 116–121

Continued

interacting with data *(continued)*
> Query button, 117–118, 119
> Update button, 118–119
> writing data caution, 120–121

*inter*Media searching and indexing technology, 453

Internet changes and Oracle9*i*AS Portal, 3

Internet Corporation for Assigned Names and
> Numbers (ICANN), 447

Internet Explorer (Microsoft), 53, 54, 517, 536

iSuites, setup.exe, 21

item management, Content Areas, 722–723

Item Type button options, Form Wizard, 262, 264–271

items
> Content Area Create Wizard, 618, 622
> monitoring, 805
> Style Manager, 630, 632–633

J

JAR. *See* Java Archive File

Java applications, Content Areas, 699

Java Archive (JAR) File, Content Areas, 703

Java language, 516–517

Java Server Pages (JSPs)
> Content Areas, 715–718
> Web portlet and provider, 855–861

`java_pool_size` parameter, 19

JavaScript, 516–521. *See also* JavaScript for client-
> side validation; JavaScript functions
> adding to HTML portlet (on CD-ROM), 162–163
> comment information in scripts, 522
> compatibility, 517–518
> Document object, 518
> document object model, 517–518, 554, 555
> events, 519, 547–551
> field types and events, 520–521
> field-level events, 519–520
> Form Elements, 518–521
> Form Object, 518
> global variables, 552–553, 554
> Lists-of-Values (LOVs) events, 519
> `onBlur` event, 520, 521, 538–540
> `onChange` event, 520, 521
> `onClick` event, 520, 521, 538–540
> `onFocus` event, 520, 521
> `onKeyDown` event, 520, 521
> `onKeyPress` event, 520, 521
> `onKeyUp` event, 520, 521
> `onMouseDown` event, 520, 521
> `onMouseUp` event, 520, 521
> `onSelect` event, 520, 521
> Oracle9*i*AS Portal and, 16
> script population, PL/SQL, 867–869

scripts, 519, 521–530
> VBScript versus, 517, 533
> Window object, 518

JavaScript Bible (Goodman), 880

JavaScript for client-side validation, 532–557. *See
> also* data validation; JavaScript; JavaScript
> functions; Shared Components
> adding code to templates, 549–551
> attaching scripts to forms, 545–547
> complicated script building, 540–545
> Create JavaScript, 533–536
> cross-field validations, 551–554
> cross-record validations, 555–557
> date check code example (on CD-ROM), 543–544
> editing, 537
> embedding code, 549–551
> error loop caution, 546
> events, using other, 547–551
> exporting, 537
> Formatting and Validation Options, 545–546
> forms, attaching scripts to, 545–547
> global variables, 552–553, 554
> language field, 534
> Lists-of-Values (LOVs) for, 532
> missing data code example (on CD-ROM),
> 542–543
> name field, 533–534
> NULL data code example (on CD-ROM), 542–543
> parameter value name, 535
> range check code example (on CD-ROM), 542–543
> running, 536–540
> script code field, 534–535
> templates, adding code to, 549–551
> testing in Oracle9*i*AS, 537–540
> testing with browsers, 536–537
> `theElement`, 535, 540
> `this` keyword, 540
> unstructured templates for embedding JavaScript
> code, 549–551

JavaScript functions, 522–532. *See also* JavaScript for
> client-side validation; JavaScript
> Boolean datatype, 524
> `break` command, 527
> `case/label` statement, 526
> control structures, 525–528
> datatypes supported, 523–525
> date methods, 531–532
> declaration of variables, 523–525
> `do...while` loop, 528
> expressions, 524–525
> `for` loop, 527
> `if-else` statement, 525–526

method calls, 523
NULL keyword, 525
number datatype, 524
operators supported, 524–525
parameter list, 523
string datatype, 524
switch statement, 526–527
variables in functions, 523–525
while loop, 528
Join Conditions
master-detail forms, 290
multiple tables in a report, 236–237, 241
join query, Lists-of-Values (LOVs), 413
join table, Lists-of-Values (LOVs), 412
Joint Photographic Expedition Graphics (JPEG), 494
JPEG. *See* Joint Photographic Expedition Graphics
js_default_value() function, 867–868
JSPs. *See* Java Server Pages
justification, Navigation Bar, 640

K

keywords for unstructured User Interface Templates,
507–508

L

Label combo box, Chart Wizard, 304
Label Only item type, Form Wizard, 265, 269
Label option, Form Wizard, 266
label style, Navigation Bar, 643
language field, JavaScript, 534
large_pool_size parameter, 19
last_day() function, 331
Layout button option, Form Wizard, 262
layout of form
Form Wizard, 258–259, 267
stored procedure forms, 285
layout of frame set, Frame Driver Wizard, 402
Layout Template, Page Wizard, 146
Layouts privileges, 772
least() function, 331
levels of caching, portals and portlets, 140–141
lightweight users, 765, 787
LIKE comparison, Menu Builder Wizard, 459
like condition use, SQL Query Link for reports, 233
limiting rows, SQL Query Link for charts, 323–325
Link, Query-By-Example (QBE) Report Wizard, 181
Link Icon, Calendar Wizard, 339
Link object, Chart Wizard, 304
Link option, Form Wizard, 267
link style, Navigation Bar, 643

Link Wizard, 559–583. *See also* linking from calendar
cells; linking from frame drivers; PL/SQL
logic integration
_break_cols parameter, 566
Component Call Interface, 581–582
drilling down/up with links, 560, 564
dynamic links, 570–576
editing link properties, 573–574, 578–579
external component links, 564
_font_size parameter, 566
_format_out parameter, 566
HTML link type, 563, 564
Link Target Inputs, 565–567, 571–575
linking from existing component, 560–570
_max_rows parameter, 566
_orderby_col parameter, 566
_orderby_ord parameter, 566
overview, 14
parameter arrays, 580–583
parameters, 565–567
parameters, passing, 572–575
p_arg_names, 568, 580, 581, 583
p_arg_values, 568, 580, 582, 583
passing column parameters, 572–575
Portal Component Customization Form link type,
563, 564
Portal Component link type, 563, 564
query parameters, 581–582
running, 567–570
SHOW procedure, 564, 570
_show_header parameter, 566
SHOW_PARAMETER procedure, 564
source link, 563
system parameters, 565, 566–567
target link, 563
Target Type and Name, 562–565
testing, 567–570
_title parameter, 566
updating data with links, 576–579
user parameters, 565, 581
linking capabilities, Uniform Resource Locators
(URLs), 448–452, 463–466
linking from calendar cells, 352–357. *See also*
Calendar Wizard; Link Wizard
date_link, 353, 357
menu for navigating to other content, 354
name_link, 353, 357
nested linking, 356–357
package name, 354

Continued

linking from calendar cells *(continued)*
    parameter value, 354
    P_ARG_NAMES, 354
    P_ARG_VALUES, 354
    procedure parameter, 354
    underlining text (links), 355
    visual image of big picture, 354
    WWW_USER_UTILITIES, 354
linking from frame drivers, 404–408. *See also*
        Frame Driver Wizard; Link Wizard
    BIND variables, 405, 406, 407
    component procedure name, 405
    Customization Form Display Options, 406
    parameters list, 405
    P_ARG_NAMES, 405
    P_ARG_VALUES, 405
    values list, 405
    WWW_USER_UTILITIES, 405
linking root menus, 467. *See also* Menu Builder
        Wizard; Uniform Resource Locators
        (URLs)
links
    Dynamic Pages Wizard and, 389
    help system, home page, 58, 59, 60
    Menu Builder Wizard, 463–466
listener currently in use warning, 29
Listener Gateway Settings, 663, 753
listeners, network installation, 28–30
Lists-of-Values (LOVs), 411–444. *See also* LOV Wizard
    BIND variables, 440–444
    code table, 412
    Customization Form Display Options, 423–426
    data table, 412
    defining, 411–415
    deploying static LOV object to another
        component, 422–426
    derived columns, 437–438
    description table, 412
    detail table, 412
    dynamic LOV objects, 426–433
    dynamic query lists, 438
    events, JavaScript, 519
    Form Wizard, 268
    Frame Driver Wizard, 400
    hidden codes, 415
    Hierarchy Wizard, 364, 375–377
    JavaScript, 519, 532
    join query, 413
    join table, 412
    multiselect LOVs, 434–437
    multivalue tables, 438–439

    overview, 13
    query Lists-of-Values (LOV) object, 415–416
    Query-By-Example (QBE) Report Wizard, 181
    sample report (on CD-ROM), 423
    source table, 412
    static LOV objects, 416–426
    `substr()` function, 414
    SYNONYMS, 413
    update Lists-of-Values (LOV) object, 415–416
    updating records with dynamic LOV objects,
        431–433
Lists-of-Values (LOVs), importing (on CD-ROM)
    master-detail forms, 292
    SQL Query Link for charts, 322
    stored procedure forms, 286
LiveScript. *See* JavaScript
loading Portal examples, 907–914
    connecting to SQL*Plus and loading single
        component, 908–914
    working directory, setting, 907–908
locking, Manage Components, 738–739
locks, database object monitoring, 822
Log Activity
    Calendar Wizard, 340
    Dynamic Pages Wizard, 384
    Form Wizard, 260
    Hierarchy Wizard, 368
    Menu Builder Wizard, 468
    Query-By-Example (QBE) Report Wizard, 188
Log On Prompt, Navigation Bar, 644
Log Registry, 753, 799–805
loggin on, post-installation check, 43–44
logging in, home page, 57
logical image categories, 495
logical packaging for deployment, 675–680
Login Server
    Administration, 753–754
    privileged account, 762, 765, 790–793
    Settings, 752
logo images, 497, 498
logo setting, Content Area Create Wizard, 652–653
Logout, home page, 61
Logout, Navigator, 80
Logout Behavior, 752
logs privileges, 774
LONGRAW extensions, 666, 667
Look and Feel Options, Calendar Wizard, 340–342
LOV Wizard, 416–420, 426–431. *See also*
        Lists-of-Values (LOVs)
    application "owner," 417
    check box format, 418, 422, 433

combo box format, 418, 420, 433
Default Format combo box, 418–419
display (friendly) value, 419, 420
display order value, 419
display_column, 429
dynamic LOV objects, 416, 426–433
"in" clause, 437
multiple select format, 418, 422
multiselect LOVs, 434–437
naming LOV object, 418
NULL values, 419
ORDER BY clause, 429
pop-up format, 418, 420–421, 433
radio group format, 418, 421, 433
return value, 419, 420
running, 419
SQL SELECT statement, 428–430
static LOV objects, 416–420
table_name, 429
testing, 419
value_column, 429
LOVs. *See* Lists-of-Values

M

MAILTO protocol, Uniform Resource Locators
    (URLs), 446
Main Banner, Style Manager, 631
MAJOR_REQS table, NetU Database, 44, 45
MAJORS table, NetU Database, 44
Make Default action, 169
Make Public privilege, 694, 696, 773
Make Top-Level action, 168–169
Manage Components, 732–742. *See also*
    administration; exporting and importing
    About link, 732–733
    Access tab, 741–742, 743–744
    Add to Favorites link, 732
    Call Interface link, 736–737
    Copy link, 739
    Delete link, 733–734
    Develop tab, 732–737
    Drop Component, 733–734
    Generate process, 740–741
    locking, 738–739
    Manage tab, 737–741
    Monitor, 741
    Navigator, 87–88
    Package Spec/Body link, 734
    Portal Access, 742
    Privilege Mode, 742
    Rename process, 740

    running reports, 196–207
    Show Lock on This Component link, 738–739
    Show SQL Query Info link, 737–738
Manage Content privilege, Content Areas, 718
Manage Items privilege, Folder Wizard, 628
Manage privilege, 157, 158, 695, 772, 773, 774
Manage Style privilege, 157, 695, 772, 773
Manage tab, Manage Components, 737–741
management of portals and portlets, 136
managing applications, 743–744
Mandatory check box, Form Wizard, 269
many-to-many relationships, 362–363
MASTER_ACTIONS, 292, 293, 294
master-detail forms, 288–299. *See also* Form Wizard
    Cascade Delete Detail Rows, 291
    defined, 253, 288–289
    Delete button, 298
    DELETE_TOP button, 291
    DETAIL_ACTIONS, 293, 294, 297, 299
    editing form, 296–297
    Form Layout, 290
    Formatting and Validation Options for
        Detail Row, 292–294
    Formatting and Validation Options for
        Master Row, 291–292
    help text, adding, 296–297
    HR_LINE, 293, 294
    importing objects (on CD-ROM), 292
    Insert button, 297
    INSERT_TOP button, 291
    Join Conditions, 290
    Lists-of-Values (LOVs), importing
        (on CD-ROM), 292
    master-detail (one-to-many) relationships,
        234, 240–242, 362, 363
    MASTER_ACTIONS, 292, 293, 294
    Number of Detail Rows option, 293
    orphans, avoiding, 292
    Query button, 295, 297, 298
    referential integrity, 292
    running form, 294–299
    Tables or Views, 289–290
    UPDATE_TOP button, 291
mathematical functions for dates, 330–332
Max Children field, Hierarchy Wizard, 366, 369
MAX function, Chart Wizard, 305
max() function, dates, 331
Maximum Child Levels combo box, Hierarchy
        Wizard, 366, 369, 374
Maximum Months Per Page option, Calendar Wizard,
        340, 343

Maximum Rows, browsing data, 112–113
Maximum Rows Per Page, Query-By-Example (QBE)
  Report Wizard, 188
_max_rows parameter, Link Wizard, 566
Members tab, security, 776
memory monitoring
  consumption, 821
  structures, 823
Menu Builder Wizard, 456–475. *See also* Link Wizard;
    Shared Components; Uniform Resource
    Locators (URLs)
  adding items, 460, 461–466
  blue arrows icon (move), 463
  Display Options, 467–470
  editing, 460–462
  Expire After field, 469
  Find Menu Options button, 468, 469
  Finish button, 458
  Font Face combo box, 461
  Font Size combo box, 461
  footer, 458, 459
  green cross icon (add), 460, 461–466
  header, 458, 459
  Help Link field, 457–458
  Inherit Privileges from Application check box, 468
  LIKE comparison, 459
  linking root menus, 467
  links, 463–466
  Log Activity check box, 468
  menu body, 459
  Menu Items and Submenus, 457–460
  menus as portlets, 457, 470–475
  moving items, 463
  Name and Application, 456
  name field, 457
  overview, 12–13
  relative links, 450, 458, 464
  search function, 459, 463
  Show Frame check box, 468
  Show Timing check box, 468
  Sub Levels combo box, 467–468
  submenus, 461–462
  template field, 457, 459
menu for navigating to other content, linking from
    calendar cells, 354
menus as portlets, 457, 470–475
meta-data
  Page Wizard, 145
  portals and portlets, 139, 140, 141
method calls, JavaScript, 523
MI format mask element, 333

middle of hierarchy, starting in, 377
MIN function, Chart Wizard, 305
min() function, dates, 331
Minimum Banner Height field, Page Wizard, 149
minus sign icon (contract list), Form Wizard, 256
miscellaneous images, 497, 498
missing data code example (on CD-ROM), JavaScript,
    542–543
mistakes correction, setup.exe, 25
mixing HTML and SQL, Dynamic Pages Wizard,
    379, 380, 393–395
MM format mask element, 333
Modified column
  Database Objects tab of Navigator, 96
  Navigator, 81
Modify Data privilege, 774
Modify Rows action, 97, 116–121
Mod_PLSQL gateway
  deployment, 659–660
  post-installation check, 39, 41
MON format mask element, 333
Monitor, Manage Components, 741
monitoring performance, 795–829. *See also* database
    object monitoring
  activity logs, 798–799, 827–828
  chart monitors, 797
  event monitoring, 798–799
  Log Registry, 753, 799–805
  Object-based monitoring tools, 797
  overview, 7
  Questions Answered, 797–798, 813–818
  reasons for, 795–796
monitoring reports, Chart Wizard, 807–813
Month Font Color option, Calendar Wizard, 341
Month Font Face option, Calendar Wizard, 341
Month Font Size option, Calendar Wizard, 341
MONTH format mask element, 333
months_between() function, 331
moving
  fields, Form Wizard, 257
  items, Menu Builder Wizard, 463
  portlets, 152, 153
multiple select format, LOV Wizard, 418, 422
multiple table charts, SQL Query Link for charts,
    316–325
multiple tables in a report, 234–242. *See also*
    Hierarchy Wizard; Menu Builder Wizard;
    Report Wizard; SQL Query Link for reports
  breaks, 237–238
  Customization Entry Form Display Options,
    238–239, 241

data integrity, 236
Join Conditions, 236–237, 241
master-detail (one-to-many) relationship,
        234, 240–242, 362, 363
normalization, 234
parameter setting, 238
primary key-foreign key relationship, 236
referential relationship, 234, 235–240, 241
sorting, 237, 241–242
suppressing redundant values, 238
Tables and Views, 235–236
multiselect Lists-of-Values (LOVs), 434–437
multivalue tables, Lists-of-Values (LOVs), 438–439
my Links portlet, home page, 61–68
My Pages, 83, 168–169
my Work portlet, home page, 68–69

N

Name and Application, Menu Builder Wizard, 456
name changes of Oracle9iAS Portal, 131–132
Name column
        Database Objects tab of Navigator, 96
        Navigator, 81
name field
        Content Area Create Wizard, 620
        Folder Wizard, 625
        JavaScript, 533–534
        Menu Builder Wizard, 457
        Page Wizard, 144
name link, Calendar Wizard, 336–337
Name string literal, Frame Driver Wizard, 400
Named Pipes (NMP) Protocol, 28
name_link, linking from calendar cells, 353, 357
naming conventions, Query-By-Example (QBE)
        Report Wizard, 175
naming methods, network installation, 30
naming tables, database, 122
Navigate Favorites, home page, 63, 66
navigating
        ease from consistency, 477
        features, 55
        Formatting and Validation Options, Form Wizard,
                256–257
        hierarchy, 370–374
        hierarchy using Path, Navigator, 80
Navigation Bar, 640–647. See also Style Manager
        adding elements, 644–645, 646
        Administrative icon, 644
        background, 643
        Content Area Map, 644
        Content Areas, 706–707

default, 640
deleting elements, 644
editing, 640–641, 644–646
Elements tab, 644–647
green cross icon (add), 644–645, 646
justification, 640
label style, 643
link style, 643
Log On Prompt, 644
portal access, 641–644
properties, 640
public access, 641
red X icon (delete), 644
Search field, 644
Search Field Width, 643
style, Style Manager, 630
Style Properties, 642–644
text style, 643
width, 643, 644
navigation bar of help system, home page, 58, 59
Navigator, 79–91. See also building portal page;
                Content Areas; Database Objects tab of
                Navigator; Shared Components
        % (percent sign) wildcard for Find, 89
        _ (underscore) wildcard for Find, 89
        Account Info, 80
        Actions column, 81
        Applications tab, Part iii, Part iv, 80, 85–88
        banner, icon for, 79
        base-level objects and containers, 84–85
        columns and their meanings, 81–82
        containers and base-level objects, 84–85
        Content Areas tab, 80, 84–85
        context of tabs, preserving, 82
        Create New ... label, 84
        customization, 80
        Database Objects tab, 80, 93–128
        Find field, 80
        Find mechanism, 88–90
        hierarchy navigation using Path, 80
        Logout, 80
        Manage Component action, 87–88
        Modified column, 81
        My Pages, 83, 168–169
        Name column, 81
        navigation of hierarchy using Path, 80
        overview, 6
        Owner column, 81
        Page Layouts, 83

Continued

Navigator *(continued)*
  Page Styles, 83
  Pages tab, 80, 82–84
  Path for navigating hierarchy, 80
  security privileges and appearance of, 82
  Shared Objects Content Area, 85
  sorting entries, 82
  tabs and their meanings, 80–82
  Top-Level Pages, 80–81, 83
  Type column, 81
  User Pages, 83
  wildcards for Find, 89
Navigator (Netscape), 53, 55, 517, 536
nested linking, linking from calendar cells, 356–357
Net 8 Configuration Assistant, 26–31
Net Service Name, network installation, 30–31
Net University sample database (on CD-ROM), 898
NETCOLLEGE application creation, 47–50
Netscape Communications Corporation, 516
NETU, 73
NetU Database creation and use, 44–52. *See also*
      installation and configuration
  Administer Database, 48–49
  ALUMNI table, 45
  application creation for, 47–50
  BUILDINGS table, 45
  changing working directory of SQL*Plus, 45–46
  CLASSES table, 44
  components storage, 47–50
  copying file to hard drive, 44
  COURSE_CATALOG table, 45
  Create a New Application, 49–50
  Create New Users, 50–51
  DBA privileges, 46
  developer account creation, 50–52
  DONATIONS table, 45
  editing user accounts, 52
  EVENTS table, 45
  existing tablespace for, 46
  GRADES table, 45
  Group Membership, 52
  installing sample data, 45–47
  MAJOR_REQS table, 44, 45
  MAJORS table, 44
  NETCOLLEGE application creation, 47–50
  NETUDEV account creation, 50–52
  netuniversity#.exe ZIP file, 44
  PLEDGES table, 45
  privileged developer account creation, 50–52

  RESTRICT_CODES table, 45
  REVISION_HISTORY table, 45
  schemas and applications, 47
  SIZE keyword, 46
  SQL*Plus and, 44, 45, 745, 908–914
  STATES table, 44
  tablespace for, 46
  temporary tablespace specification, 46
  TICKETS table, 45
  TRANSCRIPT table, 45
  UGRADS table, 44, 45
NETU user, 157–158
NETUDEV account creation, 50–52
NETUDEV user, 73–74, 101, 134, 143, 750
netuniversity#.exe ZIP file, 44
network installation and configuration, 26–31. *See
      also* installation and configuration
  listener currently in use warning, 29
  listeners, 28–30
  Named Pipes (NMP) Protocol, 28
  naming methods, 30
  Net 8 Configuration Assistant, 26–31
  Net Service Name, 30–31
  Oracle database communication, 26–31
  port number for listener, 29
  TNSNAMES, 29, 30
  Transmission Control Protocol (TCP), 28
new content item icon, Content Areas, 723
NEW_CLASS_YEAR procedure, Database Objects tab
      of Navigator, 105–108
news and announcement items, 634–635, 701
newtime() function, 331
Next button on wizard panel, 75–76
next_day() function, 331
NMP. *See* Named Pipes Protocol
NNTP protocol, Uniform Resource Locators
      (URLs), 446
Node portlet, 755
None privilege, Content Areas, 694
normalization, multiple tables in a report, 234
NULL data code example (on CD-ROM), JavaScript,
      542–543
NULL keyword, JavaScript, 525
NULL/Not NULL validation, 514
NULL value
  Chart Wizard, 308, 314
  Frame Driver Wizard, 401
  LOV Wizard, 419
number datatype, JavaScript, 524

`number()` method, 530

Number of Columns/Rows region setting, Style Manager, 639

Number of Detail Rows option, master-detail forms, 293

O

object-based monitoring tools, 805–813. *See also* monitoring performance
    categories monitoring, 805
    components monitoring, 805
    Content Areas monitoring, 805
    defined, 797
    documents monitoring, 805
    filtering reports, 809–813
    folders monitoring, 805
    items monitoring, 805
    pages monitoring, 805
    parameters for filters, 809–813
    perspectives monitoring, 805
    Popular Objects report, 808
    portlets monitoring, 805
    reports, 807–808
    searches monitoring, 805

object name in Uniform Resource Locators (URLs), 454–455

Object Privileges, 693–694, 771–774, 781–785, 788

objects, database object monitoring, 825, 827

objects in database, 93–95

On The Web portlet, home page, 69–73

`onBlur` event, JavaScript, 520, 521, 538–540

`onChange` event, JavaScript, 520, 521

`onClick` event, JavaScript, 520, 521, 538–540

`onFocus` event, JavaScript, 520, 521

`onKeyDown` event, JavaScript, 520, 521

`onKeyPress` event, JavaScript, 520, 521

`onKeyUp` event, JavaScript, 520, 521

`onMouseDown` event, JavaScript, 520, 521

`onMouseUp` event, JavaScript, 520, 521

`onSelect` event, JavaScript, 520, 521

operators supported by JavaScript, 524–525

optimistic locking, database object monitoring, 822

Oracle Connect String
    Database Access Descriptors (DADs), 665, 667, 668
    post-installation check, 40–42

Oracle database. *See also* Database Objects tab of Navigator
    8.1.6/8.1.7 versions, 18, 19
    communication, network installation, 20–31
    deployment, 658–659

Oracle Enterprise Manager and database object monitoring, 820

Oracle Essentials (Greenwald, Stackowiak, and Stern), 127

Oracle HTTP Server Only option, setup.exe, 22

Oracle Password, Database Access Descriptors (DADs), 665, 667, 668

Oracle Portal Configuration Assistant, 31–38

Oracle Server, database object monitoring, 820–821

Oracle Technology Network (OTN), 15, 17, 137, 836

Oracle User Name, Database Access Descriptors (DADs), 665, 667, 668

Oracle Web Application Server. *See* Oracle9*i*AS

Oracle8*i* database for Oracle9*i*AS Portal, 5

Oracle9*i*AS Portal, 3–16. *See also* administration; applications; components; Database Objects tab of Navigator; environment; installation and configuration; Navigator; portals and portlets

ORDER BY clause
    Calendar Wizard, 338
    Chart Wizard, 307
    LOV Wizard, 429
    Report Wizard, 213, 215
    running reports, 204–205
    SQL Query Link for reports, 220

`_orderby_col` parameter, Link Wizard, 566

`_orderby_ord` parameter, Link Wizard, 566

organizational details and privileged accounts, 766

orphans, master-detail forms, 292

OTN. *See* Oracle Technology Network

Output Format, browsing data, 112

OWA_COOKIE, 586, 595, 596–598, 601

OWA_IMAGE, 595

OWA_INIT, 595

OWA_PARMS, 596

OWA_PATTERN, 595

OWA_SEC, 596

OWA_TEXT, 596

OWA_UTIL, 596

Own permission, Folder Wizard, 628

"owner" application, LOV Wizard, 417

Owner column
    Database Objects tab of Navigator, 96
    Navigator, 81

owner name in Uniform Resource Locators (URLs), 454

OWS_OPT_LOCK, 595

P

package name, linking from calendar cells, 354
package object, Database Objects tab of Navigator, 94, 98
Package Spec/Body link, Manage Components, 734
packaging of Oracle9iAS Portal, 5
page caching
    Page Wizard, 144, 145
    portals and portlets, 140–141
Page Layouts, Navigator, 83
Page privileges, 772
Page Properties, Page Wizard, 144
Page Styles, Navigator, 83
Page Width, Calendar Wizard, 340, 341
Page Wizard, 143–150. *See also* Add Portlets page;
        building portal page; portals and portlets;
        Shared Components
    access levels for portal pages, 156, 157–159
    Background Image And Banner Height
        Settings, 149
    Banner Greeting, 148–149
    Banner Links, 149–150
    Banner Logo Settings, 149
    Create A New Page link, 143
    Customization (Add-Only) privilege, 157
    Customization (Full) privilege, 157
    Date Settings, 148–149
    Description field, 144
    Display Name field, 144
    Display Options, 144, 145
    Edit Contents privilege, 157
    Edit Default link, 148–149
    Expose Page To Everyone, 156
    Finish button, 158
    Grantee field, 157
    grouping portlets, 156
    Layout Template, 146
    Manage privilege, 157, 158
    Manage Style privilege, 157
    meta-data, 145
    Minimum Banner Height field, 149
    Name field, 144
    NETU user, 157–158
    NETUDEV user, 143
    Page Caching, 144, 145
    Page Properties, 144
    privilege levels for portal pages, 157–159
    Publish As Portlet wizard, 156
    Secondary Links, 150
    Style combo box, 147
    View-Only privilege, 157

pageexp script, 746
pageimp script, 746
pages. *See also* Page Wizard
    Direct Access URLs, 680, 681–683
    exporting and importing, 746
    monitoring, 805
    overview, 6, 7
Pages tab, Navigator, 80, 82–84
parameter arrays, Link Wizard, 580–584
parameter list, JavaScript, 523
parameter page for a chart, 311, 312
parameter setting
    Calendar Wizard, 357–359
    Dynamic Pages Wizard, 395–397
    Frame Driver Wizard, 404–408
    Link Wizard, 565–567, 572–575
    multiple tables in a report, 238
    running reports, 199–207
    SQL Query Link for reports, 230–234
    stored procedure forms, 285–286
parameter value, linking from calendar cells, 354
parameter value name, JavaScript, 535
parameters for filters, object-based monitoring, 809–813
parameters list, linking from frame drivers, 405
Parent Key Column, Hierarchy Wizard, 364
parents levels, Hierarchy Wizard, 364, 366
P_ARG_NAMES
    linking from calendar cells, 354
    linking from frame drivers, 405
p_arg_names
    creating own portlet and provider, 854
    Link Wizard, 568, 580, 581, 583
P_ARG_VALUES
    linking from calendar cells, 354
    linking from frame drivers, 405
p_arg_values
    creating own portlet and provider, 854
    Link Wizard, 568, 580, 582, 583
passing column parameters, Link Wizard, 572–575
passing default values to forms, PL/SQL, 866–869
password. *See also* security
    database security, 757
    field, privileged accounts, 762
    item type, Form Wizard, 265, 269–270, 521
    policy, 792
Path Alias, Database Access Descriptors (DADs), 667
Path for navigating hierarchy, Navigator, 80
path of Uniform Resource Locators (URLs), 448, 452
pattern matching validation, 515–516
PDK. *See* Portal Development Kit

percent sign (%) wildcard for Find, 89
performance monitoring. *See* monitoring
            performance
permission settings, Folder Wizard, 627–629
personal details and privileged accounts, 763
personalizing portal page, 161–169
perspectives
    Content Areas, 618, 650–651, 705
    Direct Access URLs, 680, 685
    Folder Wizard, 650–651
    monitoring, 805
photographs and privileged accounts, 766
physical directory, Uniform Resource Locators
            (URLs), 452, 453
PL/SQL. *See also* PL/SQL logic integration; PL/SQL
            tips and tricks; PL/SQL Web Toolkits; SQL
            code
    Calendar Wizard, 346, 347
    Content Areas, 703
    database provider creation using, 842–845
    Dynamic Pages Wizard, 383
    folders, Folder Wizard, 622
    Form Wizard and, 261, 262, 271–272
    Oracle9iAS Portal and, 16
    package, running reports, 196
    portlet creation using, 836–842
    result (target) frame, 400
    warning, portal installation, 35
PL/SQL Developer (on CD-ROM), 106, 602, 612–613,
            837, 904
PL/SQL logic integration, 585–614. *See also* HTML
            packages; PL/SQL Web Toolkits
    adding database access code, 602–605
    Additional PL/SQL Code, 598–602, 602–605
    "After Page" text box, 602
    anonymous PL/SQL blocks, 602
    "Before Footer" text box, 602
    "Before Header" text box, 601
    "Before Page" text box, 600–601
    begin/end keywords, 602, 604
    Buy_tickets code example, 605–608
    database access code, adding to PL/SQL blocks,
            602–605
    debugging, 612–613
    form creation with HTP procedural code
            example, 608–611
    PL/SQL Developer (on CD-ROM), 106, 602,
            612–613, 837, 904
    Show Errors command, 612

PL/SQL procedures
    Content Areas (on CD-ROM), 698, 712–715
    Query-By-Example (QBE) Report Wizard, 195
    stored procedure forms, 282, 284
PL/SQL tips and tricks, 865–873
    data-less keys, 872–873
    default values, passing to forms, 866–869
    forms, passing default values to, 866–869
    generating primary keys using
            sequences/triggers, 869–873
    JavaScript script population, 867–869
    js_default_value() function, 867–868
    passing default values to forms, 866–869
    primary key generation using sequences/triggers,
            869–873
PL/SQL Web Toolkits, 595–598. *See also* HTML
            packages
    OWA_COOKIE, 586, 595, 596–598, 601
    OWA_IMAGE, 595
    OWA_INIT, 595
    OWA_PARMS, 596
    OWA_PATTERN, 595
    OWA_SEC, 596
    OWA_TEXT, 596
    OWA_UTIL, 596
    OWS_OPT_LOCK, 595
PLEDGES table, NetU Database, 45
plus sign (expand list), Form Wizard, 256
pop-up format, LOV Wizard, 418, 420–421, 433
Popular Objects report, 808
Popup item type, Form Wizard, 266, 270, 521
port# field, portal installation, 33
port number for listener, 29
port, of Uniform Resource Locators (URLs), 447
portal access
    Manage Components, 742
    Navigation Bar, 641–644
portal application program interface (API), 136
Portal Component Customization Form link type,
            Link Wizard, 563, 564
Portal Component item type, Content Areas, 703
Portal Component link type, Link Wizard, 563, 564
portal developers, privileged account, 759, 760, 764
Portal Development Kit (PDK), 15, 137, 833–835
portal environment, 53–77, 750–755
portal installation and configuration, 31–38. *See also*
            installation and configuration
    Apache Listener, 37
    Connect Information string, 33
    Data Access Definition, 36

Continued

portal installation and configuration *(continued)*
    Database Access Descriptors (DADs), 33
    database connection information, 32–33
    Exit button, 37
    Finish button, 36
    instance name, 33
    Oracle Portal Configuration Assistant, 31–38
    PL/SQL warning, 35
    port# field, 33
    PORTAL30 user, 35, 36, 40, 42, 135
    progress messages, 36
    rebooting system after installation, 38
    remote database, 33, 38
    schemas created, 33–34
    server field, 33
    Single Sign-On Server, 33, 34
    SYS password, 33
    System tablespace, 35
    Tablespace Options, 34–35
    TNSNAMES.ORA file, 33
    USERS tablespace, 35
Portal Repository, deployment, 662
portal sites. *See* Content Area Create Wizard;
            Content Areas; deployment
Portal-to-Go product, 24–25
PORTAL30, 35, 36, 40, 42, 135
"portal30" default value, setup.exe, 23
PORTAL_ADMINISTRATORS group, 135
portal_DAD, 55–56
portals and portlets, 131–142. *See also* Add Portlets
            page; building portal page; Content Areas;
            creating own portlet and provider;
            deployment; Page Wizard; portal
            installation and configuration
    access control from, 132
    Advanced Options, 134–135
    automatic portlet generation, 137
    caching, 138–141
    customization, 133–135
    customizing information views, 136
    deployment, 660
    designing portal page, 136
    designing with Oracle9*i*AS Portal, 3–4
    developer advantages from, 132
    framework services, 136
    frequently used information, 138–141
    global caching, 140
    HTML page "all-or-none" limitations and, 133
    information access from, 132

    levels of caching, 140–141
    management of, 136
    meta-data, 139, 140, 141
    monitoring, 805
    NETUDEV user, 134
    page caching, 140–141
    portal application program interface (API), 136
    portal definition, 132
    Portal Development Kit (PDK), 15, 137, 833–835
    portal pages, Content Areas on, 724–725
    PORTAL30 user, 35, 36, 40, 42, 135
    PORTAL_ADMINISTRATORS group, 135
    portlet caching, 140–141
    portlet definition, 133–135
    portlet providers, 137, 138
    portlets defined, 7
    productivity increase from, 132
    proxy calls, 136
    "real-time" page caching, 141
    Refresh Page link, 141, 150
    runtime implementation of, 137–138
    security implemented by, 137
    server-based capabilities for Web clients
            from, 132
    static page caching, 141
    supporting portlets in Oracle9*i*AS Portal, 136–137
    time-based (expiry-based) caching, 139–140, 141
    user identification by, 137
    users, 759, 760
    validation-based caching, 139, 140
portal_schema, deployment, 676, 677
portlet caching, 140–141
Portlet Options
    Calendar Wizard, 338, 342
    Chart Wizard, 307
    Hierarchy Wizard, 365
    Query-By-Example (QBE) Report Wizard, 188–189
portlet providers, 137, 138
portlet publishers, privileged account, 759, 764
Portlet Server for creating own portlet and provider,
            835–836
Portlet Timing, 752
portlets
    charts as portlets, 325–328
    Dynamic Pages as portlets, 390, 397
    forms as portlets, 278–279
    hierarchies as portlets, 378
    menus as portlets, 457, 470–475
portlets privileges, 772

portno, 55
post-installation checks, 38–44. *See also* installation
        and configuration
    Apache Listener check, 38–39
    authentication, 43–44
    Database Access Descriptor Settings (DADS),
        40, 42
    gateway check, 39–42
    home page check, 38–42
    loggin on, 43–44
    Mod_PLSQL gateway check, 39, 41
    Oracle Connect String field, 40–42
    PORTAL30, 40, 42
    proxy log on failure, 39–40
    TNSNAMES entry check, 40
    TNSNAMES.ORA file, 41–42
PostScript font, 490
previewing
    portal page, 162, 163
    Query-By-Example (QBE) Report Wizard, 193–194
    User Interface Templates, 505–506, 510
Previous button on wizard panel, 75–76
primary key
    constraints, data validation, 555
    Content Area Create Wizard, 620
    generation using sequences/triggers, PL/SQL,
        869–873
    Hierarchy Wizard, 364
primary key-foreign key relationship, multiple tables
        in a report, 236
printing and formatting procedures, HTML
        packages, 587
private (authenticated) components, Database
        Access Descriptors (DADs), 671
privilege levels for portal pages, Page Wizard,
        157–159
Privilege Mode, Manage Components, 742
privileged accounts, 760–774. *See also* security
    Administrators, 762, 764, 774
    applications privileges, 773
    authentication, 762
    authorization, 762
    Contact Info, 766
    Content Areas privileges, 773
    Create privilege, 694, 772, 773, 774
    Create User, 761–766
    Customization privilege, 772, 773
    database administrators (DBAs), 759, 764
    default account settings, testing, 766–770
    Edit Contents privilege, 157, 772, 773

    Edit privilege, 774
    editing, 770–774
    End User accounts, 762
    Group privileges, 764, 774, 775–781
    Insert Data privilege, 774
    Layouts privileges, 772
    lightweight users, 765, 787
    Login Server, 762, 765, 790–793
    logs privileges, 774
    Make Public privilege, 694, 696, 773
    Manage privilege, 157, 158, 695, 772, 773, 774
    Manage Style privilege, 157, 695, 772, 773
    Modify Data privilege, 774
    Object Privileges, 693–694, 771–774, 781–785, 788
    organizational details, 766
    Page privileges, 772
    Password field, 762
    personal details, 763
    photographs, 766
    portal developers, 759, 760, 764
    portlet publishers, 759, 764
    portlets privileges, 772
    providers privileges, 772
    public users, 764
    Run privilege, 773
    schemas and users, 765, 774
    Shared Components privileges, 773
    Styles privileges, 772
    super-user privileges, 771
    testing default account settings, 766–770
    User Name field, 761
    View privilege, 628, 694, 772, 773, 774
privileged developer account creation, NetU
        Database, 50–52
privileges, Content Areas, 693–694, 773
procedure parameter, linking from calendar
        cells, 354
procedures, Database Objects tab of Navigator,
        94, 98, 105–108
procedures, deployment, 659
PRODUCTION status, 196, 347, 730
productivity increase from portals and portlets, 132
progress messages, portal installation, 36
promoting a page, 167–169
Prompt field, SQL Query Link for reports, 231
prompt method, 529
properties
    Content Area Create Wizard, 650–654
    Navigation Bar, 640
Property Sheet icon, Content Areas, 720–721

proportional (variable width) fonts, 488, 489, 493
`protocol` values for Uniform Resource Locators (URLs), 446
Provider portlet, 754–755
providers privileges, 772
`provsyns.sql` script (on CD-ROM), 837
proxy calls, portals and portlets, 136
proxy log on failure, post-installation check, 39–40
Proxy Server, 678–679, 752
public
    access, Navigation Bar, 641
    components, Database Access Descriptors (DADs), 671
    folders, Folder Wizard, 626, 627
    template art images, 497
    users, 764
Publish as Portal, Folder Wizard, 625
Publish As Portlet, Page Wizard, 156
punctuation in dates, 333
Purge Key, Content Areas, 723

Q

QBE. *See* Query-By-Example Report Wizard
QBE Report and Customization Form Text, 193–195
QBE Report Name and Application, 175–176
Query button
    data, 117–118, 119
    Form Wizard, 257, 272–275, 277–278
    master-detail forms, 295, 297, 298
    Query-By-Example (QBE) Report Wizard, 192
Query-By-Example (QBE) Report Wizard, 175–195.
        See also PL/SQL logic integration; Report Wizard; running reports; Shared Components
    Align of Column Formatting, 180
    Application combo box, 175
    ASCII formatting, 185
    Background Color, 183
    Batch button, 192
    Border Size, 186
    Break Options, 189, 190
    button options, 192
    cell highlighting feature, 182
    Color of Formatting Conditions, 183
    Column Formatting, 179–180
    Column Heading, 179
    Common Options, 184–186
    Customization Form Display Options, 191–192
    Default Format, 185
    defining a report, 174–178
    Display As, 180

Display Name, 194
Display Options, 183–190
Draw Lines Between Rows, 188
Embed *inter*Media rich content, 185
Enable delete/update link, 185
Excel formatting, 185
Expire After, 186
Finish button, 195
Font Color, 187
Font Size, 186
Footer Text, 194
Format Mask of, 180
Formatting Conditions, 181–183
Full Page Options, 186–188
Header Text, 194
Help Text, 194
HTML formatting, 185
Insert button, 192
Link, 181
Lists-of-Values (LOVs), 181
Log Activity check box, 188
Maximum Rows Per Page, 188
naming conventions, 175
PL/SQL procedure creation, 195
Portlet Options, 188–189
Preview Template button, 193–194
QBE Report and Customization Form Text, 193–195
QBE Report Name and Application, 175–176
Query button, 192
Reset button, 192
Row Order Options, 189–190, 204
Search dialog box, 176–177
Selected Columns list box, 178
Sequence, 183
shaping your report, 179–190
Show NULL Values as, 185
Show Timing, 188
Show Total Row Count, 184
Size, 181
Sum, 180
Table or View, 176
Table or View Columns, 177–178
Table Row Color(s), 187
templates, 192–195
text addition, 192–195, 194–195
Type, 180
Type Face, 183, 186
user shaping of report, 190–192
Width Type, 181

query code (on CD-ROM), SQL Query Link for charts, 323

query Lists-of-Values (LOV) object, 415–416

Query Options line, SQL Query Link for reports, 232–234

query parameters, Link Wizard, 581–582

Query Rows action, 97, 110–115

Query Wizard versus SQL Query Link for reports, 221–222. *See also* Chart Wizard; Report Wizard

querying data. *See* browsing (querying) data

Questions Answered, monitoring performance, 797–798, 813–818

Quick Picks, Style Manager, 634

QuickPick items, Content Areas, 700

quota setting, Content Area Create Wizard, 652

R

radio group format, LOV Wizard, 418, 421, 433

RadioGroup item type, Form Wizard, 266, 270, 521

range check code example (on CD-ROM), JavaScript, 542–543

range validation, 515

ranking groups of data, Hierarchy Wizard, 361

"real-time" page caching, portals and portlets, 141

rebooting system
    portal installation, 38
    setup.exe, 22

recompiling procedures, Database Objects tab of Navigator, 106–107

recursive relationship, Hierarchy Wizard, 361

red X icon (delete), 152, 257, 644

redirect feature of Form and cookies, 873–877

redo logs, database object monitoring, 822–823

referential integrity, 292, 515

referential relationship, multiple tables in a report, 234, 235–240, 241

Refresh Page link, portals and portlets, 141, 150

refreshing home page, 61, 138–141

region properties, Style Manager, 636–639

regions, Add Portlets page, 153–155, 159–160

registering your provider, 845–846

Regular Items
    Content Areas, 700
    Style Manager, 635

relative links
    Menu Builder Wizard, 150, 158, 161
    Uniform Resource Locators (URLs), 450, 458, 464

remote database, portal installation, 33, 38

Rename process
    Database Objects tab of Navigator, 97, 98, 99
    Manage Components, 740

rendering of colors, 482

Replace ASCII new lines option, 114

Report and Customization Form Text, Report Wizard, 212

Report Browser, running reports, 197–198

Report Layout Page, Report Wizard, 210

report versus forms, 252

Report Wizard, 207–216. *See also* Chart Wizard; Link Wizard; multiple tables in a report; PL/SQL logic integration; Query-By-Example (QBE) Report Wizard; reports as portlets; running reports; SQL Query Link for reports
    Break columns, 215
    Break conditions, 213
    Column Conditions, 209–210
    Columns Formatting, 211
    Custom Layout, 210
    Customization Form Display Options, 212
    Customize link, 212–213
    defining reports, 174
    Display Options, 212
    editing, 214–216
    Finish button, 212
    Form Layout, 210
    Formatting Conditions, 211–212
    ORDER BY clause, 213, 215
    overview, 7–8
    Report and Customization Form Text, 212
    report browser, 212–213
    Report Layout Page, 210
    Run Report button, 213
    sorting, 213, 215
    SQL statements for reports versus, 221–222
    Table or View Columns, 209
    Tables and Views, 208
    Tabular Layout, 210

reports, object-based monitoring, 807–808

reports as portlets, 243–247. *See also* Add Portlets page
    default values, 246
    design considerations, 244–245
    editing, 246–247
    Publish to Portal, 243

Required Settings and Values, Content Areas, 702–703
Reset button
    Calendar Wizard, 343
    Form Wizard, 257, 273, 275
    Query-By-Example (QBE) Report Wizard, 192
Reset to Defaults button, home page, 66
restoring previous versions, 730–731
RESTRICT_CODES table, NetU Database, 45
result (target) frame, Frame Driver Wizard, 399, 400, 401, 402–403
Retain Deleted Items check box, Content Areas, 723
Retrieve Keys button, database, 126
return value, LOV Wizard, 419, 420
reusing SQL statements, SQL Query Link for reports, 221
REVISION_HISTORY table, NetU Database, 45
roles (abstract users) for database security, 758, 759–760, 789
rollback segments, database object monitoring, 823
round() function, 332
row in HTML table, Form Wizard, 258
Row Order Options
    browsing data, 112
    Query-By-Example (QBE) Report Wizard, 189–190, 204
row-oriented frame, 402
rows. See Database Objects tab of Navigator
RRYY format mask element, 333
Run privilege, 773
running reports, 196–207. See also Query-By-Example (QBE) Report Wizard; Report Wizard; SQL Query Link for reports
    Align Column Parameter, 201
    ARCHIVE status, 197
    batch reporting, 192, 249, 343
    Break Options, 205–206
    Call Interface label, 196
    calling reports directly, 247–248
    Case Sensitive Column Parameter, 201, 203
    character criteria, 202–204
    Close button, 202, 205
    column criteria, 200–202
    Column Parameter, 200
    component information, 196
    Customize Page, 199–207
    Datatype Column Parameter, 201
    defaults, saving, 206–207
    EDIT status, 196
    Format Mask Column Parameter, 201
    Help icon, 198
    Manage Component, 196–207
    ORDER BY clause, 204–205
    parameter setting, 199–207
    PL/SQL package, 196
    PRODUCTION status, 196
    Report Browser, 197–198
    Run link, 197
    saving defaults, 206–207
    Show Column Parameter, 200
    show procedure, 247–248
    show_params procedure, 247–248
    sorting reports, 199–205
    Value Column Parameter, 201
    version control, 197
runtime implementation of portals and portlets, 137–138

S

sample scripts and files for each chapter (on CD-ROM), 898–904
schema(s)
    deployment, 660, 672–675
    granting access with Database Objects tab of Navigator, 101–103
    NetU Database, 47
    portal installation, schemas created, 33–34
    privileges, 785–790
    selection, 122
    users, privileged accounts, 765, 774
screen resolutions and Color Wizard, 480–481, 482
script code field, JavaScript, 534–535
script samples for each chapter (on CD-ROM), 898–904
ScriptBuilder (NetObject), 537
scripts, JavaScript, 519, 521–530
search engines
    meta tags (HTML packages) and, 588–589
    Uniform Resource Locators (URLs) and, 453–454
Search folders, Folder Wizard, 622, 623
Search Settings, 753
searches monitoring, 805
searching
    Content Areas, 723–724
    Menu Builder Wizard, 459, 463
    Navigation Bar, 643, 644
    Query-By-Example (QBE) Report Wizard, 176–177
secexp script, 746
secimp script, 746
Secondary Items, Content Areas, 704

Secondary Links, Page Wizard, 150
security, 757–794. *See also* administration; privileged
         accounts
    Account Lockout Policies, 792
    administrators, 759
    applications privileges, 783–785
    CONNECT privilege, 758
    Content Areas, 691–696, 718–721
    cookies, 874
    data for users and groups, exporting and
             importing, 746
    Database Access Descriptors (DADs), 671
    database administrators (DBAs), 759, 764
    database security, 757–760
    Edit Login Server, 791–792
    Edit User, 793
    environment, 73–74
    Folder Wizard, 626–629, 695–696
    GRANT command, 758
    Grants (Schema), 788–789
    groups and group privileges, 764, 774, 775–781
    Inherit Privileges, 783–784
    instances of databases, 758
    lightweight users, 765, 787
    Login Server, 762, 765, 790–793
    Members tab, 776
    object privileges, 693–694, 771–774, 781–785, 788
    Password Policy, 792
    passwords for database security, 757
    portal developers, 759, 760
    portal users, 759
    portals and portlets for implementing, 137
    portlet publishers, 759, 764
    roles (abstract users) for database security,
             758, 759–760, 789
    schema privileges, 785–790
    user names for database security, 757, 758
    WWSEC% tables, 785
security privileges
    Database Objects tab of Navigator, 96, 101–102
    Navigator appearance and, 82
SELECT keyword, Calendar Wizard, 336
select() method, 530
SELECT statement, SQL Query Link for charts, 318
Selected Columns list box, Query-By-Example (QBE)
         Report Wizard, 178
Sequence, Query-By-Example (QBE) Report
         Wizard, 183
sequences, Database Objects tab of Navigator,
         95, 99, 109

server-based capabilities for Web clients from
         portals and portlets, 132
server configuration, deployment, 678–679
server field, portal installation, 33
server-side validation, 513, 515, 516, 557–558
servername
    environment, 55
    Uniform Resource Locators (URLs), 446–447, 448
Services portlet, 751–754
Session Cookie Name, Database Access Descriptors
         (DADs), 666
Session State, Database Access Descriptors
         (DADs), 666
sessions, database object monitoring, 823–825
set() methods, 531
SetCookie() function, 879–883
setup.exe program, 20–26. *See also* Installation and
         configuration
    Apache Listener configuration, 23
    archive kits extraction, 20
    Database Access Descriptor Panel, 24
    extracting archive kits, 20
    file installation, 23
    file locations, 21
    Install button, 25–26
    installation types, 21–22
    iSuites, 21
    mistakes, correcting, 25
    Oracle HTTP Server Only option, 22
    "portal30" default value, 23
    Portal-to-Go product, 24–25
    Previous button, 25
    rebooting system, 22
    system reboot, 22
    TNS Connect String field, 24
    TNSNAMES, 23
SGA. *See* System Global Area
shaping your report, Query-By-Example (QBE)
         Report Wizard, 179–190
Shared Components, 477–512. *See also* Color Wizard;
         fonts; images; JavaScript for client-side
         validation; User Interface Templates
    brand recognition from, 477
    content creation versus standards enforcement,
             478–479
    exporting and importing, 748–749
    navigation ease from, 477
    privileges, 773
    standards enforcement versus content creation,
             478–479

Shared Objects Content Area, Navigator, 85
Show Column Parameter, running reports, 200
Show Errors command, PL/SQL, 612
Show Frame check box, Menu Builder Wizard, 468
Show Horizontal Rule (HR) Between Rows
        option, 114
Show Lock on This Component link, Manage
        Components, 738–739
Show Monday-Friday Only option, Calendar Wizard,
        338, 343
Show Null As, browsing data, 113
Show NULL Values as, Query-By-Example (QBE)
        Report Wizard, 185
Show Paging Buttons option, 114, 115
Show Parent Level check box, Hierarchy Wizard, 369
SHOW procedure
        creating own portlet and provider, 839, 840,
                853, 854
        Link Wizard, 564, 570
        running reports, 247–248
Show Properties action, Database Objects tab of
        Navigator, 96, 98, 99
Show Query Conditions check box, Calendar
        Wizard, 340
Show SQL option, browsing data, 113
Show SQL Query Info link, Manage Components,
        737–738
Show Timing
        Calendar Wizard, 340
        Menu Builder Wizard, 468
        Query-By-Example (QBE) Report Wizard, 188
Show Total Row Count
        browsing data, 113
        Query-By-Example (QBE) Report Wizard, 184
_show_header parameter, Link Wizard, 566
SHOW_PARAMETER procedure, Link Wizard, 564
show_params procedure, running reports, 247–248
sign-on access to applications, home page, 69–73
Single Sign-On Server, portal installation, 33, 34
single sing-on accounts, 745–746
Size, Query-By-Example (QBE) Report Wizard, 181
SIZE keyword, NetU Database, 46
sorting
        Calendar Wizard, 349–350
        Database Objects tab of Navigator, 96
        Form Wizard, 260
        multiple tables in a report, 237, 241–242
        Navigator, 82
        region setting, Style Manager, 639
        Report Wizard, 213, 215
        reports, 199–205

source link, Link Wizard, 563
source table, Lists-of-Values (LOVs), 412
SQL code. See also PL/SQL
        Dynamic Pages Wizard, 379, 380, 383, 388,
                390–395
        linked into HTML framed page, 379
        mixed with HTML, Dynamic Pages Wizard,
                379, 380
        script loading (on CD-ROM), Hierarchy Wizard,
                376
        SELECT statement, LOV Wizard, 428–430
        statements for reports versus Report Wizard,
                221–222
        stored procedure forms, 281–282
SQL*Plus, 44, 45, 745, 908–914
SQL Query
        Calendar Wizard, 336–338
        Frame Driver Wizard, 398–402, 403
SQL Query Link for charts, 316–325. See also Chart
                Wizard; Link Wizard
        Chart Name and Application, 316
        charts as portlets, 325–328
        Customization Entry Form Display Options,
                319, 321–322
        Display Options, 318–319
        editing charts, 320–322
        Finish button, 319
        formatting values and limiting rows, 323–325
        GROUP BY clause, 323
        importing objects (on CD-ROM), 322
        limiting rows, 323–325
        Lists-of-Values (LOVs), importing
                (on CD-ROM), 322
        multiple table charts, 316–325
        query code (on CD-ROM), 323
        running charts, 319
        SELECT statement, 318
        SQL Query page, 317–318
        SQL statement sample (on CD-ROM), 318
        Template combo box, 319
        the_data column, 318
        the_link column, 318
        the_name column, 318
SQL Query Link for reports, 217–234. See also Link
                Wizard; multiple tables in a report; Report
                Wizard
        aggregate functions, 222–226
        AVG aggregate function (on CD-ROM), 224–226
        COUNT aggregate function (on CD-ROM), 222–224
        Custom Layout option (on CD-ROM), 227–230

Customization Entry Form Display Options, 220, 230–234
Display Options, 220
error statements, 219
extending functionality of reports, 222–226
Finish button, 220
Form Layout option, 220, 221
Formatting Conditions, 220
GROUP BY clause, 225
HTML table (on CD-ROM), 227–230
like condition use, 233
ORDER BY clause, 220
parameter setting, 230–234
Prompt field, 231
Query Options line, 232–234
Query Wizard for reports versus, 221–222
reusing SQL statements, 221
SQL familiarity for, 221
validating entries, 234
Value Required field, 231–232
SS format mask element, 333
ssoexp script, 745
ssoimp script, 745
Stackowlak, Robert, 127
staging areas, deployment, 677–678
standard fonts preinstalled, 493
standards enforcement versus content creation, 478–479
start page, 56
Start with Column combo box, Hierarchy Wizard, 364
Start with Value, Hierarchy Wizard, 369, 374, 375–377
STATES table, NetU Database, 44
static HTML page, Uniform Resource Locators (URLs), 448–452
static Lists-of-Values (LOVs) objects, 416–426
static page caching, portals and portlets, 141
STDDEV function, 305
Stern, Jonathan, 127
storage. See also disk space
    database object monitoring, 825–827
    images, 494–495
    parameters specification, database, 126–127
stored procedure forms, 281–288. See also Form Wizard
    data values, format limitation, 286
    defined, 253
    existing stored procedures, 284
    Finish button, 287
    Form Name and Application, 284
    Form Text, 287
    Formatting and Validation, 285–287

importing objects (on CD-ROM), 286
Insert button, 288
layout of form, 285
Lists-of-Values (LOVs), importing (on CD-ROM), 286
parameter setting, 285–286
PL/SQL procedures, 282, 284
running form, 287–288
Structured Query Language (SQL), 281–282
Template combo box, 287
string concatenation
    Calendar Wizard, 350–352
    Frame Driver Wizard, 400
string datatype, JavaScript, 524
string() method, 530
strong command, 586
structured User Interface Templates, 502–506
Style combo box, Page Wizard, 147
Style Manager, 629–647. See also Content Area Create Wizard; Folder Wizard; Navigation Bar
    attributes of items, 637–638
    Available Attributes list box, 638
    backgrounds, 633
    banner setting, 630–632
    Display Attributes list box, 638
    editing styles, 630
    Folder Layout Tab, 634–639
    Folder Layouts, 635–636
    Group By region setting, 639
    Icon Height region setting, 639
    Icon Width region setting, 639
    items style, 630, 632–633
    Main Banner, 631
    Navigation Bar style, 630
    news and announcement items, 634–635
    Number of Columns/Rows region setting, 639
    overview, 6
    Quick Picks, 634
    region properties, 636–639
    Regular Items, 635
    Sort By region setting, 639
    Style Properties, 631
    Sub Banner, 631
    subfolders, 635
Style Properties, Navigation Bar, 642–644
Styles privileges, 772
Sub Banner, Style Manager, 631
Sub Levels, Menu Builder Wizard, 467–468
subfolders, 624–625, 635
submenus, Menu Builder Wizard, 461–462

substr() function, 414
Sum, Query-By-Example (QBE) Report Wizard, 180
SUM function, 305
Summary Options list box, Chart Wizard,
    309, 311–312
Sun/AOL/Netscape Alliance, 528
super-user privileges, 771
Super Video Graphics Adapter (SVGA), 479
suppressing redundant values, multiple tables
    in a report, 238
SVGA. See Super Video Graphics Adapter
SWiSH (DJJ Holdings Pty Ltd) (on CD-ROM), 905
SWiSH (SWiSHzone), 510
switch statement, 526–527
synonym object, Database Objects tab of Navigator,
    95, 99
SYNONYMS, Lists-of-Values (LOVs), 413
SYS password, 19, 33
system
    colors, 484
    fonts, 490
    images, 496
    parameters, Link Wizard, 565, 566–567
    reboot, setup.exe, 22
    tablespace, portal installation, 35
    templates, 502
System Global Area (SGA), database object
    monitoring, 823

T
Table Background Color option, Calendar
    Wizard, 342
table-based forms. See Form Wizard
table creation, database, 122–127
Table or View
    Form Wizard, 254
    master-detail forms, 289–290
    multiple tables in a report, 235–236
    Query-By-Example (QBE) Report Wizard, 176
    Report Wizard, 208
Table or View Columns
    Chart Wizard, 303–306, 313–314
    Hierarchy Wizard, 363–365
    Query-By-Example (QBE) Report Wizard, 177–178
    Report Wizard, 209
Table Row Color(s), Query-By-Example (QBE)
    Report Wizard, 187
table_name, LOV Wizard, 429
tables, Database Objects tab of Navigator,
    94, 97, 108–109

tables and data, deployment, 660
tablespace for NetU Database, 46
Tablespace Options, portal installation, 34–35
tablespaces, database object monitoring, 825–827
tabs and their meanings of Navigator, 80–82
Tabular Layout, Report Wizard, 210
target frame, Calendar Wizard, 337
target link, Link Wizard, 563
target (result) frame, Frame Driver Wizard,
    399, 400, 401, 402–403
Target Type and Name, Link Wizard, 562–565
TCP. See Transmission Control Protocol
TELNET protocol, Uniform Resource Locators
    (URLs), 446
Template Header Properties, User Interface
    Templates, 504
template images, 497
templates. See also User Interface Templates
    adding JavaScript to, 549–551
    Calendar Wizard, 345, 346
    Chart Wizard, 310
    Dynamic Pages Wizard, 385, 388, 389, 397
    Form Wizard, 271
    Frame Driver Wizard, 403
    Menu Builder Wizard, 457, 459
    overview, 6
    Query-By-Example (QBE) Report Wizard, 192–195
    SQL Query Link for charts, 319
    stored procedure forms, 287
Temporary Directory, 752
temporary tablespace specification, NetU
    Database, 46
terminating user sessions, database object
    monitoring, 824–825
testing
    default account (privileged) settings, 766–770
    JavaScript in Oracle9iAS, 537–540
    JavaScript with browsers, 536–537
    Link Wizard, 567–570
    LOV Wizard, 419
text
    addition, Query-By-Example (QBE) Report
        Wizard, 192–195, 194–195
    Dynamic Page Content, 381–383
    Navigation Bar, 643
    with HTML tags, Dynamic Pages Wizard, 382
Text item type, Content Areas, 698, 703
Text Options
    Calendar Wizard, 344–347
    Frame Driver Wizard, 403

TextArea item type, Form Wizard, 266, 271, 521
TextBox item type, Form Wizard, 266, 271, 521
the_data column, SQL Query Link for charts, 318
theElement, 535, 540
the_link column, SQL Query Link for charts, 318
the_name column, SQL Query Link for charts, 318
theme for site, Content Areas, 697
this keyword, 540
three-level hierarchy, 372–373
TICKETS table, NetU Database, 45
time-based (expiry-based) caching, portals and
        portlets, 139–140, 141
title font color/face/size, User Interface
        Templates, 504
#TITLE# keyword, User Interface Templates, 508
_title parameter, Link Wizard, 566
Title setting, Content Areas, 702
Title text, Calendar Wizard, 345
TNS Connect String field, setup.exe, 24
TNSNAMES
        entry check, post-installation, 40
        network installation, 29, 30
        setup.exe, 23
TNSNAMES.ORA file, 33, 41–42
to_char() function, 332, 333, 334
to_date function, 332, 333, 334
ToHex button, Color Wizard, 487
ToNum button, Color Wizard, 487
tools, Oracle9iAS Portal, 6
top-level pages, 80–81, 83, 168–169
transactions, database object monitoring, 821
TRANSCRIPT table, NetU Database, 45
Transmission Control Protocol (TCP), 28
trigger object, Database Objects tab of Navigator,
        95, 99
triggers, data validation, 558
TrueType font, 490
trunc() function, 332
two-level hierarchy, 371–372
Type, Query-By-Example (QBE) Report Wizard, 180
Type column
        Database Objects tab of Navigator, 96
        Navigator, 81
Type Face, Query-By-Example (QBE) Report Wizard,
        183, 186

U

UGRADS table, NetU Database, 44, 45
unauthenticated (public) components, Database
        Access Descriptors (DADs), 671

underlining text (links), 355
underscore (_) wildcard for Find, 89
Uniform Resource Locators (URLs), 445–455. See
        also Direct Access URLs; Link Wizard;
        Menu Builder Wizard
        Apache Listener, 23, 37, 38–39, 453, 454
        Data Access Descriptor in, 454
        dynamic strings in, 454–455
        FILE protocol, 446
        File Transfer Protocol (FTP), 446
        folders, Folder Wizard, 622, 623
        GOPHER protocol, 446
        Home Link, User Interface Templates, 505
        HTML, 445
        HTTPS protocol, 446
        Hypertext Transport Protocol (HTTP), 445, 446
        interMedia searching and indexing
                technology, 453
        item type, Content Areas, 703, 710–712
        linking capabilities, 448–452, 463–466
        MAILTO protocol, 446
        NNTP protocol, 446
        object name in, 454–455
        Oracle9iAS Portal environment, 55
        owner name in, 454
        path of, 448, 452
        physical directory, 452, 453
        port of, 447
        portlet, using (on CD-ROM), 861–864
        protocol values for, 446
        relative links, 450, 458, 464
        result frame, 400
        search engines and, 453–454
        servername of, 446–447, 448
        static HTML page, 448–452
        TELNET protocol, 446
        virtual directory, 452–455
UNIQUE constraints, database, 123–124
unstructured templates for embedding JavaScript
        code, 549–551
unstructured User Interface Templates, 502, 506–510
Up button, Hierarchy Wizard, 372
Updatable check box, Form Wizard, 269
UPDATE_TOP button, master-detail forms, 291
updating
        data, 118–119
        data with links, Link Wizard, 576–579
        forms, 273–274
        Lists-of-Values (LOV) object, 415–416
        records with dynamic LOV objects, 431–433

upper( ) function, 115
upward-pointing arrow icon (move in display region), add Portlets page, 153
URLs. *See* Uniform Resource Locators
usage statistics, Dynamic Pages Wizard, 384
Use Page Style check box, Folder Wizard, 625
user, making changes as, 161–169
user accounts. *See* privileged accounts
user accounts for Content Areas, 691–695, 718–721
User colors, 484
user customization stores, 850–851
user error prevention
　　Form Wizard, 274–278
　　Hierarchy Wizard, 374–375
User fonts, 490
user identification by portals and portlets, 137
User images, 496
User Interface Templates, 501–512. *See also* Color Wizard; fonts; images; Shared Components; templates
　　adding templates, 502–506
　　Application Image, 505
　　Application Image Alt Text entry field, 505
　　background color, 503
　　deploying templates into components, 511–512
　　heading background color, 504
　　Help Image, 505
　　Home Link, 505
　　images, 503, 504–505
　　keywords for unstructured templates, 507–508
　　previewing, 505–506, 510
　　structured templates, 502–506
　　System templates, 502
　　Template Header Properties, 504
　　Template Name, 503
　　Template Title, 504
　　title font color, 504
　　title font face, 504
　　title font size, 504
　　unstructured templates, 502, 506–510
　　URL of Home Link, 505
　　User templates, 502
User Name field, privileged accounts, 761
user names for database security, 757, 758
User Pages, Navigator, 83
user parameters, Link Wizard, 565, 581
user shaping of report, Query-By-Example (QBE) Report Wizard, 190–192
USERID, deployment, 672–674
USERS tablespace, portal installation, 35

V

validating entries, SQL Query Link for reports, 234
validation of HTML code, Dynamic Pages Wizard, 382, 389
validation-based caching, portals and portlets, 139, 140
Value Column Parameter, running reports, 201
Value field, Chart Wizard, 304
Value Format Mask, Chart Wizard, 309
Value Required field, SQL Query Link for reports, 231–232
Value Type combo box, Hierarchy Wizard, 367
value_column, LOV Wizard, 429
values list, linking from frame drivers, 405
variable width (proportional) fonts, 488, 489, 493
variables in JavaScript functions, 523–525
VARIANCE function, 305
VBScript versus JavaScript, 517, 533
version control, 197, 729–731, 735–736
Version Information, 752
versioning of items, Content Areas, 722
VGA. *See* Video Graphics Adapter
video color settings, 481–483
video display and colors, 479–481
Video Graphics Adapter (VGA), 479
view object, Database Objects tab of Navigator, 94, 97
View privilege, 628, 694, 772, 773, 774
view-based forms, 253
View-Only privilege, Page Wizard, 157
viewers (users), Content Areas, 718
viewing
　　fonts, 491–492
　　images, 500
virtual directory
　　Uniform Resource Locators (URLs), 452–455
　　URL path, Direct Access URLs, 681
Visible Item Type, Content Areas, 722
visual image of big picture, linking from calendar cells, 354

W

Web portlet and provider with Java Server Pages (JSPs), 855–861
Web portlets, 834, 835
Web server (existing) replacing listener, 662–663
Web site for Oracle9*i*AS Portal, 45, 905
WebDB, 3–4. *See also* Oracle9*i*AS Portal
Weinman, Lynda, 483

WHERE clause
    browsing data, 112
    Calendar Wizard, 337, 357
    dates and, 334
while loop, 528
width of Navigation Bar, 643, 644
Width Type, Query-By-Example (QBE) Report
        Wizard, 181
wildcards for Find, 89
Window object, JavaScript, 518
Windows (Microsoft) and environment, 56, 482
wizard images, 497
wizards, 6, 16, 74–76
writing data caution, 120–121
WWLOG_ALL_CATEGORY_LOGS, 798
WWLOG_ALL_COMPONENT_LOGS, 798
WWLOG_ALL_DELETE_LOGS, 798
WWLOG_ALL_DOCUMENT_LOGS, 799
WWLOG_ALL_FOLDER_LOGS, 799
WWLOG_ALL_GROUP_LOGS, 799
WWLOG_ALL_ITEM_LOGS, 799

WWLOG_ALL_OBJECT_LOGS, 799
WWLOG_ALL_PAGE_LOGS, 799
WWLOG_ALL_PERSPECTIVE_LOGS, 799
WWLOG_ALL_PORTLET_LOGS, 799
WWLOG_ALL_SEARCH_LOGS, 799
WWLOG_ALL_USER_LOGS, 799
WWLOG_EVENT, 799
WWLOG_PORTAL_ADMIN_LOGS, 799
WWLOG_USER_LOGS, 799
WWSEC% tables, 785
wwwpre_api_name package, 850–851, 852
WWW_USER_UTILITIES, 354, 405

Y

YEA format mask element, 333
YY format mask element, 333
YYYY format mask element, 333

Z

Zip file type, Content Areas, 699, 703

Hungry Minds, Inc. End-User License Agreement

READ THIS. You should carefully read these terms and conditions before opening the software packet(s) included with this book ("Book"). This is a license agreement ("Agreement") between you and Hungry Minds, Inc. ("HMI"). By opening the accompanying software packet(s), you acknowledge that you have read and accept the following terms and conditions. If you do not agree and do not want to be bound by such terms and conditions, promptly return the Book and the unopened software packet(s) to the place you obtained them for a full refund.

1. **License Grant.** HMI grants to you (either an individual or entity) a nonexclusive license to use one copy of the enclosed software program(s) (collectively, the "Software") solely for your own personal or business purposes on a single computer (whether a standard computer or a workstation component of a multi-user network). The Software is in use on a computer when it is loaded into temporary memory (RAM) or installed into permanent memory (hard disk, CD-ROM, or other storage device). HMI reserves all rights not expressly granted herein.

2. **Ownership.** HMI is the owner of all right, title, and interest, including copyright, in and to the compilation of the Software recorded on the disk(s) or CD-ROM ("Software Media"). Copyright to the individual programs recorded on the Software Media is owned by the author or other authorized copyright owner of each program. Ownership of the Software and all proprietary rights relating thereto remain with HMI and its licensers.

3. **Restrictions On Use and Transfer.**

    (a) You may only (i) make one copy of the Software for backup or archival purposes, or (ii) transfer the Software to a single hard disk, provided that you keep the original for backup or archival purposes. You may not (i) rent or lease the Software, (ii) copy or reproduce the Software through a LAN or other network system or through any computer subscriber system or bulletin-board system, or (iii) modify, adapt, or create derivative works based on the Software.

    (b) You may not reverse engineer, decompile, or disassemble the Software. You may transfer the Software and user documentation on a permanent basis, provided that the transferee agrees to accept the terms and conditions of this Agreement and you retain no copies. If the Software is an update or has been updated, any transfer must include the most recent update and all prior versions.

4. **Restrictions on Use of Individual Programs.** You must follow the individual requirements and restrictions detailed for each individual program in Appendix A of this Book. These limitations are also contained in the individual license agreements recorded on the Software Media. These limitations may include a requirement that after using the program for a specified period of time, the user must pay a registration fee or discontinue use. By opening the Software packet(s), you will be agreeing to abide by the licenses and restrictions for these individual programs that are detailed in Appendix A and on the Software Media. None of the material on this Software Media or listed in this Book may ever be redistributed, in original or modified form, for commercial purposes.

5. Limited Warranty.

(a) HMI warrants that the Software and Software Media are free from defects in materials and workmanship under normal use for a period of sixty (60) days from the date of purchase of this Book. If HMI receives notification within the warranty period of defects in materials or workmanship, HMI will replace the defective Software Media.

(b) **HMI AND THE AUTHOR OF THE BOOK DISCLAIM ALL OTHER WARRANTIES, EXPRESS OR IMPLIED, INCLUDING WITHOUT LIMITATION IMPLIED WARRANTIES OF MERCHANTABILITY AND FITNESS FOR A PARTICULAR PURPOSE, WITH RESPECT TO THE SOFTWARE, THE PROGRAMS, THE SOURCE CODE CONTAINED THEREIN, AND/OR THE TECHNIQUES DESCRIBED IN THIS BOOK. HMI DOES NOT WARRANT THAT THE FUNCTIONS CONTAINED IN THE SOFTWARE WILL MEET YOUR REQUIREMENTS OR THAT THE OPERATION OF THE SOFTWARE WILL BE ERROR FREE.**

(c) This limited warranty gives you specific legal rights, and you may have other rights that vary from jurisdiction to jurisdiction.

6. Remedies.

(a) HMI's entire liability and your exclusive remedy for defects in materials and workmanship shall be limited to replacement of the Software Media, which may be returned to HMI with a copy of your receipt at the following address: Software Media Fulfillment Department, Attn.: *Oracle9iAS*™ *Portal Bible*, Hungry Minds, Inc., 10475 Crosspoint Blvd., Indianapolis, IN 46256, or call 1-800-762-2974. Please allow four to six weeks for delivery. This Limited Warranty is void if failure of the Software Media has resulted from accident, abuse, or misapplication. Any replacement Software Media will be warranted for the remainder of the original warranty period or thirty (30) days, whichever is longer.

(b) In no event shall HMI or the author be liable for any damages whatsoever (including without limitation damages for loss of business profits, business interruption, loss of business information, or any other pecuniary loss) arising from the use of or inability to use the Book or the Software, even if HMI has been advised of the possibility of such damages.

(c) Because some jurisdictions do not allow the exclusion or limitation of liability for consequential or incidental damages, the above limitation or exclusion may not apply to you.

7. U.S. Government Restricted Rights.
Use, duplication, or disclosure of the Software for or on behalf of the United States of America, its agencies and/or instrumentalities (the "U.S. Government") is subject to restrictions as stated in paragraph (c)(1)(ii) of the Rights in Technical Data and Computer Software clause of DFARS 252.227-7013, or subparagraphs (c) (1) and (2) of the Commercial Computer Software - Restricted Rights clause at FAR 52.227-19, and in similar clauses in the NASA FAR supplement, as applicable.

8. General.
This Agreement constitutes the entire understanding of the parties and revokes and supersedes all prior agreements, oral or written, between them and may not be modified or amended except in a writing signed by both parties hereto that specifically refers to this Agreement. This Agreement shall take precedence over any other documents that may be in conflict herewith. If any one or more provisions contained in this Agreement are held by any court or tribunal to be invalid, illegal, or otherwise unenforceable, each and every other provision shall remain in full force and effect.

CD-ROM Installation Instructions

To install the CD-ROM, insert the disk into the CD-ROM drive on your computer. You can access the contents of the CD-ROM through Windows Explorer, or by opening My Computer on the desktop. All the files on the CD can be accessed as local file system files; there is no SETUP.EXE program. Installation of third-party utility programs is detailed in README.TXT files in each relevant subdirectory. Installation of code and program examples is detailed in Appendix B.

The CD-ROM provides a trial copy of several utility programs (PL/SQL Developer and Cookie Pal) along with the various sample component objects and images that are referenced in the examples. Appendix A provides a complete list of the contents of the CD-ROM, and you will find a README.TXT file on the CD that explains any late-breaking changes to the content on the CD-ROM.